Frommer's

W9-AAR-908

Europe

2004

Here's what the critics say about Frommer's:

"Amazingly easy to use. Very portable, very complete."
—*Booklist*

"Detailed, accurate, and easy-to-read information for all price ranges."
—*Glamour Magazine*

"Hotel information is close to encyclopedic."
—*Des Moines Sunday Register*

"Frommer's Guides have a way of giving you a real feel for a place."
—*Knight Ridder Newspapers*

WILEY

Wiley Publishing, Inc.

Published by:

Wiley Publishing, Inc.

111 River St.

Hoboken, NJ 07030

ISBN 0-7645-3902-7
ISSN 1091-9511

Editors: Alexis Lipsitz Flippin, *with* Elizabeth Albertson, John Vorwald, and Kathleen Warnock
Production Editor: Heather Wilcox
Cartographer: Roberta Stockwell
Photo Editor: Richard Fox
Production by Wiley Indianapolis Composition Services

Front cover photo: Leaning Tower of Pisa with La Fontana dei Putti in foreground, Pisa, Italy
Back cover photo: El Alcázar, Segovia, Spain

For information on our other products and services or to obtain technical support, please contact our Customer Care Department within the U.S. at 800-762-2974, outside the U.S. at 317-572-3993 or fax 317-572-4002.

Wiley also publishes its books in a variety of electronic formats. Some content that appears in print may not be available in electronic formats.

Manufactured in the United States of America

5   4   3

Contents

7 Germany 383

by Darwin Porter & Danforth Prince

8 Greece 465

by Sherry Marker

9 Hungary 548

by Joseph S. Lieber & Christina Shea

10 Ireland 579

by Suzanne Rowan Kelleher

List of Maps

About the Authors

Darwin Porter, a native of North Carolina, was assigned to write the very first edition of a Frommer's guide devoted solely to one European country. Since then, he has written many bestselling Frommer's guides to all the major European destinations. In 1982, he was joined in his research efforts by **Danforth Prince,** formerly of the Paris bureau of the *New York Times,* who has traveled and written extensively about Europe.

Suzanne Rowan Kelleher is a freelance travel writer and the former Europe Editor of *Travel Holiday* magazine. She has traveled extensively in Ireland, is married to an Irishman, and currently lives in County Dublin. She is the author of *Frommer's Ireland* and a co-author of *Frommer's Europe from $70 a Day.*

All four of **Joseph S. Lieber**'s grandparents emigrated from Eastern Europe at the turn of the 20th century, settling in New York City, where he was born and raised. Mr. Lieber lived in Hungary for several years in the early 1990s. He presently practices law in Boston and is the co-author of *Frommer's Budapest & the Best of Hungary* and *Frommer's Europe from $70 a Day.* **Christina Shea** served as a Peace Corps volunteer in Hungary and subsequently directed Peace Corps language-training programs in Lithuania and Kyrghyzstan. She's the author of the novel *Moira's Crossing* (St. Martin's) and a co-author of *Frommer's Budapest & the Best of Hungary* and *Frommer's Europe from $70 a Day.*

Herbert Bailey Livesey is a native New Yorker. After an early career as a university administrator, he decided to devote himself to writing full-time. He's the author or co-author of 10 travel guides (including *Frommer's New England, Frommer's Canada,* and *Frommer's Montréal & Québec City*), a novel about deep-sea sportfishing, and several books on education and sociology. His articles have appeared in *Travel & Leisure, Food & Wine,* and *Playboy.*

George McDonald has lived and worked in both Amsterdam and Brussels as deputy editor of the KLM in-flight magazine and as editor-in-chief of the Sabena in-flight magazine. Now a freelance journalist and travel writer, he has written extensively on both the Netherlands and Belgium for magazines and guidebooks. He's the author of *Frommer's Amsterdam* and *Frommer's Belgium, Holland & Luxembourg,* and a co-author of *Frommer's Europe from $70 a Day*

Sherry Marker's love of Greece began when she majored in classical Greek at Harvard. She has studied at the American School of Classical Studies in Athens and studied ancient history at the University of California at Berkeley. Author or co-author of a number of guides to Greece (such as *Frommer's Greece* and *Frommer's Greek Islands*), she has published articles in the *New York Times, Travel & Leisure,* and *Hampshire Life.* She's also the co-author of *Frommer's Europe from $70 a Day* and has written books on a variety of subjects, including a history of London for young adults.

Hana Mastrini is a native of the western Czech spa town of Karlovy Vary who became a veteran of the "Velvet Revolution" as a student in Prague in 1989. She began contributing to Frommer's guides while helping her husband, John, better understand his new home in the Czech Republic.

An Invitation to the Reader

In researching this book, we discovered many wonderful places—hotels, restaurants, shops, and more. We're sure you'll find others. Please tell us about them, so we can share the information with your fellow travelers in upcoming editions. If you were disappointed with a recommendation, we'd love to know that, too. Please write to:

Frommer's Europe 2004
Wiley Publishing, Inc. • 111 River St. • Hoboken, NJ 07030

An Additional Note

Please be advised that travel information is subject to change at any time—and this is especially true of prices. We therefore suggest that you write or call ahead for confirmation when making your travel plans. The authors, editors, and publisher cannot be held responsible for the experiences of readers while traveling. Your safety is important to us, however, so we encourage you to stay alert and be aware of your surroundings. Keep a close eye on cameras, purses, and wallets, all favorite targets of thieves and pickpockets.

Other Great Guides for Your Trip:

Frommer's Europe from $70 a Day
Frommer's Gay & Lesbian Europe
Europe For Dummies
Hanging Out in Europe
Frommer's Road Atlas Europe

Frommer's Star Ratings, Icons & Abbreviations

Every hotel, restaurant, and attraction listing in this guide has been ranked for quality, value, service, amenities, and special features using a **star-rating system**. In country, state, and regional guides, we also rate towns and regions to help you narrow down your choices and budget your time accordingly. Hotels and restaurants are rated on a scale of zero (recommended) to three stars (exceptional). Attractions, shopping, nightlife, towns, and regions are rated according to the following scale: zero stars (recommended), one star (highly recommended), two stars (very highly recommended), and three stars (must-see).

In addition to the star-rating system, we also use **seven feature icons** that point you to the great deals, in-the-know advice, and unique experiences that separate travelers from tourists. Throughout the book, look for:

Finds	Special finds—those places only insiders know about
Fun Fact	Fun facts—details that make travelers more informed and their trips more fun
Kids	Best bets for kids and advice for the whole family
Moments	Special moments—those experiences that memories are made of
Overrated	Places or experiences not worth your time or money
Tips	Insider tips—great ways to save time and money
Value	Great values—where to get the best deals

The following **abbreviations** are used for credit cards:

AE	American Express	DISC	Discover	V	Visa
DC	Diners Club	MC	MasterCard		

Frommers.com

Now that you have the guidebook to a great trip, visit our website at **www.frommers.com** for travel information on more than 3,000 destinations. With features updated regularly, we give you instant access to the most current trip-planning information available. At Frommers.com, you'll also find the best prices on airfares, accommodations, and car rentals—and you can even book travel online through our travel booking partners. At Frommers.com, you'll also find the following:

- Online updates to our most popular guidebooks
- Vacation sweepstakes and contest giveaways
- Newsletter highlighting the hottest travel trends
- Online travel message boards with featured travel discussions

What's New in Europe

Here are some of the latest developments in Europe.

AUSTRIA Vienna The big news in middle Europe is the opening of the **MuseumsQuartier Complex,** Vienna's major statement for the new millennium. It's been compared to combining the Guggenheim and New York's Museum of Modern Art, with a few more institutions tossed in as well.

BELGIUM Bruges Bruges celebrated its 2002 reign as a European Capital of Culture by opening the doors of the **Concertgebouw,** a brand-new principal venue for classical music, opera, and ballet. It remains to be seen how this ultra-modern facility will go down in a city where medieval Gothic architecture is as Bruggean as *appelgebaak* (apple pie). The initial signs are that it'll do just fine.

DENMARK Copenhagen More and more passengers to the Danish capital are riding the Metro, which was expanded in 2002 and now provides an alternative to the traditional tram.

ENGLAND London Former fading beauty **Claridge's,** Brook Street, W1 (℅ **020/7629-8860**), has reclaimed its front-ranking position following a $75-million rebirth. London's best chef, Gordon Ramsay, rattles his pots and pans here.

The first major crossing over the Thames in a century, the wobbly **Millennium Bridge** is once again open. The bridge closed after its opening at the millennium, as it was feared unsafe. After the installation of 100 dampers and shock absorbers, the 315m- (1,050-ft.-) long span welcomes thousands of foot passengers every day.

FRANCE Paris Ever since First Lady Laura Bush dropped into **Ze Kitchen Galerie,** 4 rue des Grands-Augustins, 6e (℅ **01-44-32-00-32**), this new restaurant has been on the culinary map. The First Lady made a wise choice: Its French and international dishes are sublime.

The French Riviera Acclaimed as the world's greatest chef, Alain Ducasse has invaded St-Tropez with **Spoon Byblos,** in the Hotel Byblos, avenue Paul-Signac (℅ **04-94-56-68-00**). Mediterranean produce is fashioned into some of the resort's most palate-pleasing temptations.

GERMANY Munich The Bavarian capital's newest museum, **Pinakothek der Moderne,** has opened at Barerstrasse 40 (℅ **089/23805-118**), displaying the largest collection of fine and applied arts in Germany. It's a stunning collection, Munich's version of London's fabled Tate Gallery.

GREECE Athens Greeks are gearing up to welcome visitors from around the world to the 2004 Summer Olympics, to be held August 13 to 29 in and around Athens, the first home of the Olympic Games. At press time, the monuments of the Acropolis were undergoing extensive renovation. The Temple of Nike had been entirely dismantled, and the Propylaia and Parthenon were encased in scaffolding; all should be spiffed up and open in time for the Olympics. The National Archaeological Museum also closed for renovations in 2002 and is slated to reopen in May 2004.

IRELAND Dublin The newest addition to Dublin's public transportation network is the sleek light-rail tram known as LUAS, due for completion at the end of 2003 and the answer, many hope, to Dublin's congestion problems. Traveling at a maximum speed of 70 kilometers per hour (45mph) and departing every 5 minutes in peak hours, LUAS brings the city's transportation into the 21st century.

ITALY Rome Once hailed as Rome's grandest and best restaurant, Sans Souci faded into history like the Italian lira. Now the good news: The staff has reincarnated the restaurant. It's called Antico Bottaro, Passegiata di Ripetta 15 (© 06-3236763), and its classic Franco/Italian cuisine is better than ever.

NETHERLANDS Amsterdam There's bad news for visitors who come to Amsterdam to admire some of the best of both Dutch and world art. The nation's premier cultural collection, the Rijksmuseum, Stadhouderskade 42 (© 020/670-7047), is closed for renovation for 5 long years beginning in late 2003. As a consolation, one wing remains open to display important paintings by the 17th-century Dutch Masters. At the opposite end of Museumplein, the modern-art Stedelijk Museum, Paulus Potterstraat 13 (© 020/573-2737), closed its doors completely for renovation and new construction for more than 2 years beginning at the start of 2003. Plans are in place to put some of the museum's collection on view at other city venues.

NORWAY Oslo The first high-speed train between Oslo and Stockholm has reduced travel time to 4 hours and 50 minutes between these two once remotely linked Scandinavian capitals. Depending on the day, there are two to three trains daily in each direction. This high-speed train now competes directly with air travel.

PORTUGAL Lisbon One of Lisbon's newest hotels, rated five stars by the Portuguese government and associated with some of the most glamorous hotels of the Algarve and Madeira, the Dom Pedro, Avenida Engenheiro, Duarte Pacheco (© 21-389-6600), is set within the central Amoreiras district, across from one of the city's biggest shopping centers. Rooms are lavishly furnished, with video games, work desks, sitting areas, and double-glazed windows.

SCOTLAND Edinburgh The latest of the city's attractions is the Real Mary King's Close, Writers' Court, off the Royal Mile (© 0870/243-0160). Beneath the City Chambers a warren of hidden streets has been dug out and opened to the public, revealing a place where people lived and worked for centuries.

SPAIN Madrid Grand dining is to be had at Santceloni, in the Hesperia Madrid hotel, Paseo de la Castellana 57 (© 91-210-8840), currently the rage among serious Madrid foodies. Santi Santamaria, ranked among the top three chefs in Spain, made his fame in a restaurant outside Barcelona but today also dazzles Madrileños with his succulent Mediterranean cuisine.

SWEDEN Stockholm The Swedish capital's newest hotel is one of its most daring. Nothing evokes life in the far north more than the Nordic Hotel (© 800/337-4685), a resort complex whose decor was inspired by both the watery calm of the Nordic

Sea and by the "post-minimalist luminescence" of the northern lights.

SWITZERLAND   Bern   In Switzerland's capital, the landmark government-rated five-star hotel, **Bellevue Palace,** Kochergasse 3–5 (© **031/320-45-45**), has reopened to critical acclaim. The finest restoration touches were completed in 2003, and this Belle Epoque beauty is better than ever, once again the most lavish and ornately decorated luxury choice in Bern.

Planning Your Trip to Europe

by Darwin Porter & Danforth Prince

The mainland of Europe may not be one United States of Europe yet, but you can now spend the same bill along Rome's Via Veneto as you can along Paris's Champs-Elysées. The euro, the new currency of the Continent, made its debut on January 1, 2002, as 12 nations, including Italy, France, and Germany, adopted a single currency. The change has virtually made these nations kissin' cousins.

Historically, this is the first time a monetary confederation, with the euro as the single currency of that union, has preceded a political union. Historian Nicholas Kilby has pronounced the switch "very much a leap into the darkness."

Like the dream of the invading Huns centuries ago, the euro has taken the Continent by storm, conquering the French franc, the Spanish peseta, the Greek drachma, the German mark, and the Italian lira. On its lonely island, Britain still clings to its pound, and the krone remains the coin of the realm in such countries as Denmark and Sweden.

Of course, you don't visit Europe to fret over economies. The rich culture and histories in each of its myriad countries and regions have always been the lure, and they remain so today. From the splendor of a walled hill town rising above the verdant Tuscan landscape to the majestic snowcapped peaks of the Alps, from the sound of flamenco in a Madrid *tablaos* (flamenco nightclub) to the blasting of a brass band in Munich's Hofbraühaus—one Europe it may be on the map (and now in the bank books), but on the ground, it's still a Europe of countless facets and proud, distinct, diverse heritages. There's no other place where you can experience such enormous cultural changes by driving from one mountain valley to the next, where in just a few miles you're likely to encounter not only a different language but also different food, architecture, and culture.

Europe has seen some of the greatest intellectual and artistic developments the world has ever known, and the landscape is dense with museums, cathedrals, palaces, and monuments serving as repositories for much of this past glory. But the good news is that the Continent is still in a dynamic creative mode; artistic and cultural ferment are very much part of the present, and Europe helps set the trends in fashion, industrial design, cinema, technology, music, literature, and science. The dynamic environment is all about life, innovation, entertainment, and food, which exist side by side with the artistic and cultural grandeur of the past.

Europe is also about people. Europeans have seen the best and the worst of times, and a better-educated, more sophisticated younger generation is waiting to welcome you. They're as diverse and fascinating as the lands they come from, and throughout this book we've noted places not only where you'll meet other visitors, but where you'll have a chance to meet and chat with the locals, enriching your experience immeasurably.

Irresistible and intriguing, the ever-changing Europe at the beginning of the new millennium offers you more excitement, experiences, and memories than ever. In compiling this book, we've tried to open the door to Europe's famous cities (their art and architecture, restaurants and theater, hotels and history) and guide you to all the experiences no one would want to miss on even a cursory visit. So though this guide has to point out the highlights, we've also tossed in offbeat destinations and adventurous suggestions leading to surprises and delights around every corner.

This introductory chapter is designed to equip you with what you need to know before you go—the advance-planning tools for an enjoyable and successful trip.

1 Visitor Information

TOURIST OFFICES

Start with the **European tourist offices** in your own country; for a complete list, see below. If you aren't sure which countries you want to visit, send for an information-packed free booklet called *Planning Your Trip to Europe,* revised annually by the 31-nation **European Travel Commission,** 1 Rockefeller Plaza, Suite 214, New York, NY 10020 (© **212/218-1200;** www.visiteurope.com). Or check out *Europe For Dummies,* available at most bookstores.

AUSTRIAN NATIONAL TOURIST OFFICE

www.anto.com or www.Austria-tourism.com; info@oewnyc.com

IN THE U.S. P.O. Box 1142, 500 Fifth Ave., New York, NY 10110 (© **212/944-6880;** fax 212/730-4568).

IN CANADA 2 Bloor St. W., Suite 3330, Toronto, ON M4W 1A8 (© **416/967-3381;** fax 416/967-4101).

IN THE U.K. 14 Cork St., London W1X 1PF (© **020/7629-0461;** fax 020/7499-6038).

IN AUSTRALIA 36 Carrington St., 1st Floor, Sydney, NSW 2000 (© **02/9299-3621;** fax 02/9299-3808).

BELGIAN TOURIST OFFICE

www.visitbelgium.com; info@visitbelgium.com

IN THE U.S. 780 Third Ave., New York, NY 10017 (© **212/758-8130;** fax 212/355-7675).

IN CANADA P.O. Box 760 NDG, Montreal, PQ H4A 382 (© **514/457-2888;** fax 514/489-8965).

IN THE U.K. 217 Marsh Wall, London E14 9FJ (© **020/7531 0391;** fax 020/7531-0393).

BRITISH TOURIST AUTHORITY

www.visitbritain.com or www.travelbritain.org; travelinfo@bta.org.uk

IN THE U.S. 551 Fifth Ave., Suite 701, New York, NY 10176-0799 (© **800/462-2748** or 212/986-2266; fax 212/986-1188).

IN CANADA 5915 Airport Rd., Mississaugua, ON L4V 1TI (© **888/VISITUK;** fax 905/405-1835).

IN AUSTRALIA Level 16, Gateway, 1 Macquarie Place, Sydney, NSW 2000 (© **02/9377-4400;** fax 02/9377-4499).

IN NEW ZEALAND Fay Richwhite Blvd., 17th Floor, 151 Queen St., Auckland 1 (© **09/303-1446;** fax 09/377-6965).

CZECH TOURIST AUTHORITY

www.czechcenter.com or www.czech.cz; travel czech@pop.net

IN THE U.S. 1109 Madison Ave., New York, NY 10028 (© **212/288-0830;** fax 212/288-0971).

IN CANADA c/o Czech Airlines, 401 Bay St. Suite 1510, Toronto, ON M5H 2Y4 (© **416/363-9928;** fax 416/363-0239; ctacanada@iprimus.ca).

Europe

Number, Please: Calling Europe

To make a phone call **from the United States to Europe,** dial the international access code, **011,** then the **country code** for the country you're calling, then the **city code** for the city you're calling, and then the regular phone number. For an operator-assisted call, dial **01,** then the country code, then the city code, and then the regular phone number; an operator then comes on the line.

The following are the codes for the countries and major cities in this guide. These are the codes you use to call from overseas or from another European country. If you're calling from within the country or within the city, see "Telephone" in the "Fast Facts" section for each city.

European phone systems are undergoing a prolonged change. **Italy, France, Spain, Monaco, Copenhagen, and now Portugal no longer use separate city codes.** The code is now built into all phone numbers, and you must always dial the initial zero or nine (which was previously—and still is in most other countries—added before a city code only when dialing from another city within the country). Also, be aware of these two recent changes: The city codes for London (171 and 181) have been replaced by a new single code, 20, which is then followed by an eight-digit number beginning with either 7 or 8; and the city code for Lisbon has changed from 1 to 21.

Austria	3	Denmark	45
Innsbruck	12	England	44
Salzburg	62	Bath	1225
Vienna	1	London	20
Belgium	32	Oxford	1865
Bruges	50	Stratford-upon-Avon	1789
Brussels	2	France	33
Ghent	9	Germany	49
Czech Republic	420	Berlin	30
Prague	2	Munich	89

IN THE U.K.   95 Great Portland St., London W1W 7NY (© 020/7291-9925; fax 020/7436-8300).

FRENCH GOVERNMENT TOURIST OFFICE
www.franceguide.com; info@francetourism.com

IN THE U.S.   444 Madison Ave., 16th Floor, New York, NY 10022 (© 212/838-7800; fax 212/838-7855); 676 N. Michigan Ave., Suite 3360, Chicago, IL 60611 (© 312/751-7800; fax 312/337-6339); 9454 Wilshire Blvd., Suite 715, Beverly Hills, CA 90212 (© 310/271-6665; fax 310/276-2835). To request information at any of these offices, call the **France on Call hot line** at © 900/990-0040 (50¢ per min.).

IN CANADA   Maison de la France/French Government Tourist Office, 1981 av. McGill College, Suite 490, Montreal, PQ H3A 2W9 (© 514/876-9881; fax 514/845-4868); 30 St. Patrick St., Suite 700, Toronto, ON M5T 3A3 (© 416/491-7622; fax 416/979-7587).

Greece	30	Norway	47
Athens	1	Oslo	22
Delphi	265	Portugal	351
Hungary	36	Scotland	44
Budapest	1	Edinburgh	131
Ireland	353	Spain	34
Dublin	1	Sweden	46
Italy	39	Stockholm	8
Monaco	377	Switzerland	41
Netherlands	31	Bern	31
Amsterdam	20	Geneva	22

The easiest and cheapest way to call home from abroad is with a calling card. On the road, you just dial a local access code (almost always free) and then punch in the number you're calling as well as the calling-card number. If you're in a non–touch-tone country, just wait for an English-speaking operator to put your call through. The "Telephone" entry in the "Fast Facts" for each city gives the AT&T, MCI, and Sprint access codes for that country (your calling card will probably come with a wallet-size list of local access numbers). You can also call any one of those companies' numbers to make a collect call as well; just dial it and wait for the operator.

When it comes to dialing direct, calling from the United States to Europe is much cheaper than the other way around, so whenever possible, have friends and family call you at your hotel rather than you call ing them. To dial direct back to the **United States** and **Canada** from Europe, the international access code is often, but not always, **00**; the country code is **1**, and then you punch in the area code and number. For **Australia** and **New Zealand**, the access code is also **00**; the country codes are **61** and **64**, respectively.

IN THE U.K. Maison de la France/ French Government Tourist Office, 178 Piccadilly, London, W1J 9AL (© **0906/824-4122;** fax 020/7493-6592).

IN AUSTRALIA French Tourist Bureau, 25 Bligh St., Sydney, NSW 2000 (© **02/9231-5244;** fax 02/9221-8682).

GERMAN NATIONAL TOURIST OFFICE
www.visits-to-germany.com; gntony@aol.com or germanto@idirect.com

IN THE U.S. 122 E. 42nd St., 52nd Floor, New York, NY 10168-0072 (© **800/637-1171** or 212/661-7200; fax 212/661-7174).

IN CANADA P.O. Box 65162, Toronto, ON M4K 3Z2 (© **877/ 315-6237;** fax 416/968-1986).

IN THE U.K. P.O. Box 2695, London W1A 3TN (© **020/7317-0908** or 020/7495-6129).

IN AUSTRALIA P.O. Box A980, Sydney, NSW 1235 (© **02/9267-8148;** fax 02/9267-9035).

GREEK NATIONAL TOURIST ORGANIZATION

www.gnto.gr; ento@greektourism.com

IN THE U.S.   645 Fifth Ave., Suite 903, New York, NY 10022 (© 212/421-5777; fax 212/826-6490).

IN CANADA   91 Scollard St., Toronto, ON 1G4 3K8 (© 416/968-2220; fax 416/968-6533).

IN THE U.K.   4 Conduit St., London W1S 2DJ (© 020/7734-5997; fax 020/7287-1369).

IN AUSTRALIA   51–57 Pitt St., Sydney, NWS 2000 (© 02/9241-1663; fax 02/9235-2174).

HUNGARIAN NATIONAL TOURIST OFFICE

www.hungarytourism.hu or www.gotohungary.com; info@gotohungary.com

IN THE U.S. & CANADA   150 E. 58th St., 33rd Floor, New York, NY 10155 (© 212/355-0240; fax 212/207-4103).

IN THE U.K.   c/o Embassy of the Republic of Hungary, Trade Commission, 46 Eaton Place, London, SW1X 8AL (© 020/7823-1032; fax 020/7823-1459).

IRISH TOURIST BOARD

www.ireland.travel.ie or www.irelandvacations.com; info@irishtouristboard.com

IN THE U.S.   345 Park Ave., New York, NY 10154 (© 800/223-6470 or 212/418-0800; fax 212/371-9052).

IN THE U.K.   British Visitors Centre, 1 Regents St., London SW1Y 4XT (walk-in only).

IN AUSTRALIA   36 Carrington St., 5th Floor, Sydney, NSW 2000 (© 02/9299-6177; fax 02/9299-6323).

ITALIAN GOVERNMENT TOURIST BOARD

www.enit.it or www.italiantourism.com; enitny@bway.net, 739145@icam.net, or enitlond@globalnet.co.uk

IN THE U.S.   630 Fifth Ave., Suite 1565, New York, NY 10111 (© 212/245-4822; fax 212/586-9249); 500 N. Michigan Ave., Suite 2240, Chicago, IL 60611 (© 312/644-0996; fax 312/644-3019); 12400 Wilshire Blvd., Suite 550, Los Angeles, CA 90025 (© 310/820-1898; fax 310/820-6357).

IN CANADA   175 Bloor St. E., South Tower, Suite 907, Toronto, ON M4W 3R8 (© 416/925-4882; fax 416/925-4799).

IN THE U.K.   1 Princes St., London W1R 8AY (© 020/7408-1254; fax 020/7493-6695).

MONACO GOVERNMENT TOURIST OFFICE

www.monaco-tourism.com or www.monaco.mc; Monaco@Monaco.co.uk

IN THE U.S. & CANADA   565 Fifth Ave., New York, NY 10017 (© 800/753-9696 or 212/286-3330; fax 212/286-9890).

IN THE U.K.   3–8 Chelsea Garden Market, Chelsea Harbour, London, SW10 0XF (© 0500/006-114 or 020/7352-9962; fax 020/7352-2103).

NETHERLANDS BOARD OF TOURISM

www.holland.com; info@goholland.com

IN THE U.S.   355 Lexington Ave., 19th Floor, New York, NY 10017 (© 888/464-6552 or 212/370-7360; fax 212/370-9507).

IN CANADA   25 Adelaide St. E., Suite 710, Toronto, ON M5C 1Y2 (© 888/464-6552; fax 416/363-1470).

IN THE U.K.   Imperial House, 7th Floor, 15–19 Kingsway, London, WC2B 6UN (© 020/7539-7950; fax 020/7539-7953).

PORTUGUESE NATIONAL TOURIST OFFICE

www.portugal.org or www.portugalinsite.pt; icelond@aol.com

IN THE U.S.   590 Fifth Ave., 4th Floor, New York, NY 10036 (© 212/354-4403; fax 212/764-6137).

IN CANADA   60 Bloor St. W., Suite 1005, Toronto, ON M4W 3B8 (© 416/921-7376; fax 416/921-1353).

IN THE U.K.   22–25A Sackville St., 2nd and 4th Floors, London W1X 1DE (© 0891/600-370 or 020/7494-1875; fax 020/7494-1868).

SCANDINAVIAN TOURIST BOARDS (DENMARK, NORWAY & SWEDEN)
www.goscandinavia.com, www.visitdenmark.com, www.visitnorway.com, or www.visit-sweden.com; usa@nortra.no, info@gosweden.org, dtb.london@dt.dk, or greatbritain@nortra.no

IN THE U.S. & CANADA   P.O. Box 4649, Grand Central Station, New York, NY 10163-4649 (© 212/885-9700; fax 212/885-9710).

IN THE U.K.   Danish Tourist Board, 55 Sloane St., London SW1X 9SY (© 020/7259-5959; fax 020/7259-5955); Norwegian Tourist Board, 5 Regent St., London, SW1Y 4LR (© 020/7839-6255; fax 020/7839-6014); Swedish Travel & Tourism Council, 11 Montagu Place, London W1H 2AL (© 020/7724-5868; fax 020/7724-5872).

SWITZERLAND TOURISM
www.switzerlandtourism.com; stnewyork@switzerlandtourism.com or info.uk@switzerland tourism.ch

IN THE U.S.   608 Fifth Ave., New York, NY 10020 (© 800/794-7795, 877/794-8037, or 212/757-5944; fax 212/262-6116).

IN THE U.K.   Swiss Centre, 1 New Coventry St., London, W1V 8EE (© 020/7734-1921; fax 020/7437-4577).

TOURIST OFFICE OF SPAIN
www.okspain.org; oetny@here-i.com

IN THE U.S.   666 Fifth Ave., 35th Floor, New York, NY 10103 (© 212/265-8822; fax 212/265-8864); 845 N. Michigan Ave., Suite 915E, Chicago, IL 60611 (© 312/642-1992; fax 312/642-9817); 8383 Wilshire Blvd., Suite 956, Los Angeles, CA 90211 (© 323/658-7188; fax 323/658-1061); 1221 Brickell Ave., Suite 1850, Miami, FL 33131 (© 305/358-1992; fax 305/358-8223).

IN CANADA   2 Bloor St. W., 34th Floor, Toronto, ON M5S 1M9 (© 416/961-3131; fax 416/961-1992).

IN THE U.K.   22–23 Manchester Sq., London W1M 5AP (© 020/7486-8077; fax 020/7486-8034).

TRAVEL AGENTS
Travel agents can save you plenty of time and money by hunting down the best airfare for your route and arranging for rail passes and rental cars. For now, most travel agents still charge you nothing for their services—they're paid through commissions from the airlines and other agencies they book for you. However, a number of airlines have begun cutting commissions, and increasingly, agents are finding they have to charge you a fee to hold the bottom line (or else unscrupulous agents will offer you only the travel options that bag them the juiciest commissions). Shop around and ask hard questions.

If you decide to use a travel agent, make sure the agent is a member of the **American Society of Travel Agents (ASTA)**, 1101 King St., Alexandria, VA 22314 (© 703/739-8739; www.astanet.com). If you send them a self-addressed stamped envelope, ASTA will mail you the booklet *Avoiding Travel Problems* for free.

2 Entry Requirements & Customs

PASSPORTS

If you don't already have one, you can download a passport application from the websites listed below. Countries covered in this guide do *not* require visas for U.S. or Canadian citizens for stays less than 90 days. Though a valid U.S. state driver's license usually suffices, it's wise to carry an **International Driving Permit** ($12), which you can obtain from any AAA branch if you bring two passport-size photos.

U.S. CITIZENS If you're applying for a first-time passport, you need to do it in person at a U.S. passport office; a federal, state, or probate court; or a major post office (though not all post offices accept applications; call the number below to find the ones that do). You need to present a certified birth certificate as proof of citizenship, and it's wise to bring along your driver's license, state or military ID, and social security card as well. You also need two identical passport-size photos (2 in. by 2 in.), taken at any corner photo shop (not one of the strip photos, however, from a photo-vending machine).

For people over 15, a passport is valid for 10 years and costs $60; for those 15 and under, it's valid for 5 years and costs $40. If you're over 15 and have a valid passport that was issued within the past 12 years, you can renew it by mail for $40. Allow plenty of time before your trip to apply; processing normally takes 3 weeks but can take

longer during busy periods (especially spring). For general information, call the **National Passport Agency** (© 202/647-0518). To find your regional passport office, either check the U.S. State Department website (http://travel.state.gov) or call the **National Passport Information Center** (© 900/225-5674); the fee is 35¢ per minute for automated information and $1.05 per minute for operator-assisted calls.

CANADIAN CITIZENS Canadian passports are valid for 5 years and cost $60. Children under 16 may be included on a parent's passport but need their own to travel unaccompanied by the parent. Applications, which must be accompanied by two identical passport-size photographs and proof of Canadian citizenship, are available at passport offices throughout Canada, at post offices, or from the central **Passport Office, Department of Foreign Affairs and International Trade,** Ottawa, ON K1A 0G3 (© 800/567-6868; www.dfait-maeci.gc.ca). Processing takes 5 to 10 days if you apply in person, or about 3 weeks by mail.

U.K. CITIZENS As a member of the European Union, you need only an identity card, not a passport, to travel to other EU countries. However, if you already possess a passport, it's always useful to carry it. To pick up an application for a regular 10-year passport (the Visitor's Passport has

---

Tips Savvy Travel Safeguards

Safeguard your passport in an inconspicuous, inaccessible place like a money belt. If you lose it, visit the nearest consulate of your native country as soon as possible for a replacement. Before leaving home, make two photocopy collages of your important documents: the first page of your passport (the page with the photo and identifying info), driver's license, and other ID. Leave one copy at home with a family member or friend and carry the other with you (separate from the originals!).

been abolished), visit your nearest passport office, major post office, or travel agency. You can also contact the **United Kingdom Passport Service** at (℃ **0870/521-0410** or search its website at www.ukpa.gov.uk. Passports are £33 for adults and £19 for children under 16.

IRISH CITIZENS You can apply for a 10-year passport, costing €57 at the **Passport Office,** Setanta Centre, Molesworth Street, Dublin 2 (℃ **01/ 671-1633;** www.irlgov.ie/iveagh). Those under age 18 and over 65 must apply for a 3-year passport costing €12. You can also apply at 1A South Mall, Cork (℃ **021/272-525**); or over the counter at most main post offices.

AUSTRALIAN CITIZENS Apply at your local post office or passport office or search the government website at **www.passports.gov.au.** Passports cost A$144 for adults and A$72 for those under 18. The **Australia State Passport Office** can be reached at (℃ **02/131232;** travelers must schedule an interview to submit your passport application materials.

NEW ZEALAND CITIZENS You can pick up a passport application at any travel agency or Link Centre. For more info, contact the **Passport Office,** Department of Internal Affairs, 47 Boulcott House, Wellington (℃ **0800/225-050;** www.passports. govt.nz). Passports are NZ$71 for adults and NZ$36 for those under 16.

CUSTOMS

U.S. CITIZENS Returning **U.S. citizens** who have been away for at least 48 hours are allowed to bring back, once every 30 days, $800 worth of merchandise duty-free. You'll be charged a flat rate of 10% duty on the next $1,000 worth of purchases. Be sure to have your receipts handy. On mailed gifts, the duty-free limit is $200. You cannot bring fresh foodstuffs into the United States; some

tinned foods, however, are allowed. For more information, contact the **U.S. Customs Service,** 1300 Pennsylvania Ave. NW, Washington, DC 20229 (℃ **202/354-1000**) and request the free pamphlet *Know Before You Go.* It's also available on the Web at **www.customs.gov.** (Click on "Traveler Information," then on "Know Before You Go.")

U.K. CITIZENS If you are **returning from a European Community (EC) country,** you will go through a separate Customs Exit (called the "Blue Exit") especially for EC travelers. In essence, there is no limit on what you can bring back from an EC country, as long as the items are for personal use (this includes gifts), and you have already paid the necessary duty and tax. However, Customs law sets out guidance levels. If you bring in more than these levels, you may be asked to prove that the goods are for your own use. Guidance levels on goods bought into the EC for your own use are 800 cigarettes, 200 cigars, 1 kilogram of smoking tobacco, 10 liters of spirits, 90 liters of wine (of this not more than 60 liters can be sparkling wine), and 110 liters of beer. For more information, contact **HM Customs & Excise,** National Advice Service, Dorset House, Stamford St., London SE1 9PY (℃ **020/7928-3344;** or consult their website at www. hmce.gov.uk).

U.K. citizens returning from a non-EC country have a Customs allowance of 200 cigarettes; 50 cigars; 250 grams of smoking tobacco; 2 liters of still table wine; 1 liter of spirits or strong liqueurs (over 22% volume); 2 liters of fortified wine, sparkling wine or other liqueurs; 60cc (ml) of perfume; 250cc (ml) of toilet water; and £145 worth of all other goods, including gifts and souvenirs. People under 17 cannot have the tobacco or alcohol allowance. For more information, contact **HM Customs & Excise** (see above).

CANADIAN CITIZENS For a clear summary of **Canadian** rules, write for the booklet *I Declare*, issued by the **Canada Customs and Revenue Agency** (© 800/461-9999 in Canada, or 204/983-3500; www.ccraadrc.gc.ca). Canada allows its citizens a C$750 exemption, and you're allowed to bring back duty-free one carton of cigarettes, 1 can of tobacco, 40 imperial ounces of liquor, and 50 cigars. In addition, you're allowed to mail gifts to Canada valued at less than C$60 a day, provided they're unsolicited and don't contain alcohol or tobacco (write on the package "Unsolicited gift, under $60 value"). All valuables should be declared on the Y-38 form before departure from Canada, including serial numbers of valuables you already own, such as expensive foreign cameras. *Note:* The $750 exemption can only be used once a year and only after an absence of 7 days.

AUSTRALIAN CITIZENS The duty-free allowance in **Australia** is A$400 or, for those under 18, A$200. Upon returning to Australia, citizens can bring in 250 cigarettes or 250 grams of loose tobacco, and 1,125ml of alcohol. If you're returning with valuable goods you already own, such as foreign-made cameras, you should file Form B263. A helpful brochure, available from Australian consulates or Customs offices, is *Know Before You Go*. For more information, contact **Australian Customs Services,** 477 Pitt St., GPO Box 8, Sydney NSW 2000 (© **02/6275-6666** in Australia; 202/797-3189 in the U.S.), or go to **www.customs.gov.au.**

NEW ZEALAND CITIZENS The duty-free allowance for **New Zealand** is NZ$700. Citizens over 17 can bring in 200 cigarettes, or 50 cigars, or 250 grams of tobacco (or a mixture of all three if their combined weight doesn't exceed 250g); plus 4.5 liters of wine and beer, or 1.125 liters of liquor. New Zealand currency does not carry import or export restrictions. Fill out a certificate of export, listing the valuables you are taking out of the country; that way, you can bring them back without paying duty. Most questions are answered in a free pamphlet available at New Zealand consulates and Customs offices: *New Zealand Customs Guide for Travellers, Notice no. 4.* For more information, contact **New Zealand Customs,** 17–21 Whitmore St., P.O. Box 2218, Wellington, NZ (© **09/359-6655**).

3 Money

Traveler's checks, while still the safest way to carry money, are going the way of the dinosaur. The aggressive evolution of international computerized banking and ATM networks has led to the triumph of plastic in Europe— even if cold cash is still the most trusted currency. Odds are you can saunter up to an ATM in the dinkiest Bavarian village with your bank card or PIN-enabled Visa and get some local cash out of it. Never rely on credit cards and ATMs alone, however. Though most hotels and many restaurants around Europe accept plastic, smaller towns and cheaper places are still wary, and occasionally the phone lines and computer networks used to verify your card can go down and render your plastic useless. Always carry some local currency and some traveler's checks for insurance.

Although currency conversions in this guide were accurate at press time, European exchange rates fluctuate. For up-to-date rates, look in the business pages or travel section of any major U.S. newspaper, check online at

The World's Greatest Financial Merger: The Euro

On March 1, 2002, the euro officially replaced the legacy currencies as legal tender in the "euro zone," including the countries of Austria, Belgium, Finland, France, Germany, Greece, Ireland, Italy, Luxembourg, the Netherlands, Portugal, and Spain. Britain, Denmark, and Sweden do not fall under the euro umbrella, even though they are members of the EU. The Czech Republic, Hungary, Norway, and Switzerland are not part of the EU.

Euros come in note denominations of 5, 10, 20, 50, 100, 200, and 500, and coin denominations of 1- and 2-euros and 1, 2, 5, 10, 20, and 50 cents. Coins have a common face on one side. The opposite face has a design chosen by the issuing country.

Note: Since the euro's inception, the U.S. dollar and the euro have traded almost on par (i.e., $1 approximately equals 1€); therefore, all prices in this book are given in euros when providing rates for hotel, restaurant, and attractions listings and transportation and touring costs. But as this book went to press, 1€ was worth approximately $1.15 and gaining in strength, so your dollars might not go as far as you'd expect. For up-to-the-minute exchange rates between the euro and the dollar, check the currency converter website **www.xe.com/ucc**.

the **Universal Currency Converter** (www.xe.com), or call **Thomas Cook** (see "Traveler's Checks," below).

It's more expensive to purchase foreign currency in your own country than once you've reached your destination. But it's a good idea to arrive in Europe with a bit of the local currency—at least enough to get you from the airport to your hotel, so you can avoid the bad rates you get at airport exchanges. Bring along about $30 to $50 in the local currencies— usually euros—of every European city you'll be visiting (call around to the major branches of local banks in your hometown to find the best rate).

While traveling, either withdraw local currency from an ATM (see below) or convert your cash or traveler's checks at a bank whenever possible—banks invariably give better rates than tourist offices, hotels, travel agencies, or exchange booths. You lose money every time you make a transaction, so it's often better to convert

large sums at once (especially in flat-fee transactions). The rates for converting traveler's checks are usually better than those for cash, but you get the best rates by withdrawing money from an ATM with your bank or credit card.

ATMS

PLUS, Cirrus, and other networks work on many ATMs in Europe, giving you local currency and drawing it directly from your checking account. This is the fastest, easiest, and least expensive way to change money. You take advantage of the bank's bulk exchange rate (better than anything you'll get on your own exchanging cash or traveler's checks) and, unless your home bank charges you for using a nonproprietary ATM, you won't have to pay a commission. Make sure the PINs on your bank and credit cards will work in Europe; you usually need a four-digit code (six digits often won't work). Keep in mind you're usually able to access only your checking account, not savings, from ATMs abroad.

Both the **Cirrus** (© 800/424-7787; www.mastercard.com) and the **PLUS** (© 800/843-7587; www.visa.com) networks have ATM locators listing the banks in each country that accept your card; alternately, you can just search out any machine with your network's symbol on it. Europe is getting to be like America—with a bank on virtually every corner—and most banks are globally networked. You'll get the best exchange rate if you withdraw money from an ATM, but keep in mind that many banks impose a fee every time a card is used at an ATM in a different city or bank. On top of this, the bank from which you withdraw cash may charge its own fee.

You can also get a cash advance through Visa or MasterCard (contact the issuing bank to enable this feature and get a PIN), but note that the credit-card company will begin charging you interest immediately, and many have begun assessing a fee every time. American Express card cash advances are usually available only from Amex offices, which you'll find in every European city.

CREDIT CARDS

Most middle-bracket and virtually all first-class and deluxe hotels, restaurants, and shops in Europe accept major credit cards—American Express, Diners Club, MasterCard, and Visa (not Discover). Some budget establishments accept plastic; others don't. The most widely accepted cards these days are Visa and MasterCard, but it pays to carry American Express, too. Note that you can now often choose to charge credit-card purchases at the price in euros or in the local currency; since most European currencies are now locked together, the dollar amount always comes out the same, but it could help you comparison-shop. If you do choose to stick with plastic,

keep in mind that your credit card company will likely charge a commission (1% or 2%) on every foreign purchase you make.

TRAVELER'S CHECKS

Most large banks sell traveler's checks, charging fees of 1% to 2% of the value of the checks. AAA (American Automobile Association) members can buy American Express checks commission-free. Traveler's checks are great travel insurance because if you lose them—and have kept a list of their numbers (and a record of which ones were cashed) in a safe place separate from the checks themselves—you can get them replaced at no charge. Hotels and shops usually accept them, but you get a lousy exchange rate. Use traveler's checks for exchanges for local currency at banks or American Express offices. Personal checks are next to useless in Europe.

American Express (© 800/221-7282; www.americanexpress.com) is one of the largest issuers of traveler's checks, and theirs are the most commonly accepted. They also sell checks to holders of certain types of American Express cards at no commission. **Thomas Cook** (© 800/223-7373 in the U.S. and Canada, or 020/7530-7080 collect from other parts of the world; www.thomascook.com) issues MasterCard traveler's checks. **Citicorp** (© 800/645-6556; www.citibank.com) and many other banks issue checks under their own name or under MasterCard or Visa. Get checks issued in dollar amounts (as opposed to, say, French francs), as they're more widely accepted abroad.

WIRE SERVICES

MoneyGram, 7401 W. Mansfield Ave., Englewood, CO 80155 (© 800/926-9400; www.moneygram.com), allows friends back home to wire you money in an emergency in less than 10 minutes. Senders should call to learn the address of the closest outlet that handles MoneyGrams. Cash, credit card, or the occasional personal check (with ID) are acceptable forms of payment. The fee is $19 for the first $500, with a sliding scale for larger sums. The service includes a short telex message and a 3-minute phone call from sender to recipient. The beneficiary must present a photo ID at the outlet where the money is received.

VALUE-ADDED TAX (VAT)

All European countries charge a **value-added tax (VAT)** of 15% to 25% on goods and services—it's like a sales tax that's already included in the price. Rates vary from country to country (as does the name—it's called the IVA in Italy and Spain, the TVA in France, and so on), though the goal in EU countries is to arrive at a uniform rate of about 15%. Citizens of non-EU countries can, as they leave the country, get back most of the tax on purchases (not services) if you spend above a designated amount (usually $80–$200) in a single store.

Regulations vary from country to country, so inquire at the tourist office when you arrive to find out the procedure; ask what percentage of the tax is refunded, and if the refund is given to you at the airport or mailed to you later. Look for a TAX FREE SHOPPING FOR TOURISTS sign posted in participating stores. Ask the storekeeper for the necessary forms, and, if possible, keep the purchases in their original packages. Save all your receipts and VAT forms from each EU country to process all of them at the **"Tax Refund"** desk in the airport of the last country you visit before flying home (allow an extra 30 min. or so at the airport to process forms).

To avoid VAT refund hassles, ask for a Global Refund form ("Shopping Checque") at a store where you make a purchase. When leaving an EU country, have it stamped by customs, after which you take it to the Global Refund counter at more than 700 airports and boarder crossings in Europe. Your money is refunded on the spot. For information, contact **Global Refund** (✆ **800/566-9828**).

4 When to Go

Europe is a continent for all seasons, offering everything from a bikini beach party on the Riviera in summer to the finest skiing in the world in the Alps in winter.

Europe has a continental climate with distinct seasons, but there are great variations in temperature from one part to another. Northern Norway is plunged into Arctic darkness in winter, but in sunny Sicily the climate is usually temperate—though snow can fall even on the Greek Islands in winter, and winter nights are cold anywhere. Europe is north of most of the United States, but along the Mediterranean they see weather patterns more along the lines of the U.S. southern states. In general, however, seasonal changes are less extreme than in most of the United States.

The **high season** lasts from mid-May to mid-September, with the most tourists hitting the Continent from mid-June to August. In general, this is the most expensive time to travel, except in Austria and Switzerland, where prices are actually higher in winter during the ski season. And since Scandinavian hotels depend on business clients instead of tourists, lower prices can often be found in the fleeting summer, when business clients vacation and a smaller number of tourists take over.

You'll find smaller crowds, relatively fair weather, and often lower prices at hotels in the **shoulder seasons,** from

What Time Is It, Anyway?

Based on U.S. Eastern Standard Time, Britain, Ireland, and Portugal are 5 hours ahead of New York City; Greece is 7 hours ahead of New York. The rest of the countries in this book are 6 hours ahead of New York. For instance, when it's noon in New York, it's 5pm in London and Lisbon; 6pm in Paris, Copenhagen, and Amsterdam; and 7pm in Athens. The European countries now observe daylight savings time. The time change doesn't usually occur on the same day or during the same month as in the United States.

If you plan to travel to Ireland or Continental Europe from Britain, keep in mind that the time will be the same in Ireland and Portugal, 2 hours later in Greece, and 1 hour later in the other countries in this guide.

Easter to mid-May and mid-September to mid-October. **Off season** (except at ski resorts) is from November to Easter, with the exception of December 25 to January 6. Much of Europe, Italy especially, takes August off, and from August 15 to August 30 is vacation time for many locals, so expect the cities to be devoid of natives but the beaches packed.

WEATHER

BRITAIN & IRELAND Everyone knows it rains a lot in Britain and Ireland. Winters are rainier than summers; August and from September to mid-October are the sunniest months. Summer daytime temperatures average from the low 60s Fahrenheit (10s Celsius) to the mid-60s (20s Celsius), dropping to the 40s (5s Celsius) on winter nights. Ireland, whose shores are bathed by the Gulf Stream, has a milder climate and the most changeable weather—a dark rainy morning can quickly turn into a sunny afternoon, and vice versa. The Scottish Lowlands have a climate similar to England's, but the Highlands are much colder, with storms and snow in winter.

CENTRAL EUROPE In Vienna and along the Danube Valley the climate is moderate. Summer daytime temperatures average in the low 70s Fahrenheit (20s Celsius), falling at night to the low 50s (10s Celsius). Winter temperatures are in the 30s Fahrenheit (below 0 Celsius) and 40s (10s Celsius) during the day. In Budapest, temperatures can reach 80°F (25°C) in August and dip to 30°F (0°C) in January. Winter is damp and chilly, spring is mild, and May and June are usually wet. The best weather is in the late summer through October. In Prague and Bohemia, summer months have an average temperature of 65°F (18°C) but are the rainiest, while January and February are usually sunny and clear, with temperatures around freezing.

FRANCE & GERMANY The weather in Paris is approximately the same as in the U.S. mid-Atlantic states, but like most of Europe, there's less extreme variation. In summer, the temperature rarely goes above the mid-70s Fahrenheit (mid-20s Celsius). Summers are fair and can be hot along the Riviera. Winters tend to be mild, in the 40s Fahrenheit (10s Celsius), though it's warmer along the Riviera. Germany's climate ranges from the moderate summers and chilly, damp winters in the north to the mild summers and very cold, sunny winters of the alpine south.

NORTHERN EUROPE In the Netherlands, the weather is never extreme at any time of year. Summer temperatures average around 67°F (20°C) and the winter average is about 40°F (5°C). The climate is rainy, with the driest months from February to May. From Mid-April to mid-May, the tulip fields burst into color. The climate of northern Germany is very similar. Belgium's climate is moderate, varying from 73°F (23°C) in July and August to 40°F (5°C) in December and January. It does rain a lot, but the weather is at its finest in July and August.

SCANDINAVIA Summer temperatures above the Arctic Circle average around the mid-50s Fahrenheit (mid-10s Celsius), dropping to around 14°F (−10°C) during the dark winters. In the south, summer temperatures average around 70°F (22°C), dropping to the 20s Fahrenheit (below 0s Celsius) in winter. Fjords and even the ocean are often warm enough for summer swimming, but rain is frequent. The sun shines 24 hours in midsummer above the Arctic Circle, where winter brings semi-permanent twilight. Denmark's climate is relatively mild by comparison. It has moderate summer temperatures and winters that can be damp and foggy, with temperatures just above the mid-30s Fahrenheit (0s Celsius).

SOUTHERN EUROPE Summers are hot in Italy, Spain, and Greece, with temperatures around the high 80s Fahrenheit (30s Celsius) or even higher in some parts of Spain. Along the Italian Riviera, summer and winter temperatures are mild, and except in the alpine regions, Italian winter temperatures rarely drop below freezing. The area around Madrid is dry and arid, and summers in Spain are coolest along the Atlantic coast, with mild

temperatures year-round on the Costa del Sol. Seaside Portugal is very rainy but has temperatures of 50°F to 75°F (10°C–25°C) year-round. In Greece there's sunshine all year, and winters are usually mild, with temperatures around 50°F to 54°F (10°C–12°C). Hot summer temperatures are often helped by cool breezes. The best seasons to visit Greece are from mid-April to June and mid-September to late October, when the wildflowers bloom and the tourists go home.

SWITZERLAND & THE ALPS The alpine climate is shared by Bavaria in southern Germany and the Austrian Tyrol and Italian Dolomites—winters are cold and bright, and spring comes late, with snow flurries well into April. Summers are mild and sunny, though the alpine regions can experience dramatic changes in weather any time of year.

EUROPE CALENDAR OF EVENTS

January
Epiphany celebrations, Italy, nationwide. All cities, towns, and villages in Italy stage Roman Catholic Epiphany observances. One of the most festive celebrations is the Epiphany Fair at Rome's Piazza Navona. January 6, 2004.

February
Carnevale, Venice, Italy. At this riotous time, theatrical presentations and masked balls take place throughout Venice and on the islands in the lagoon. The balls are by invitation only (except the Doge's Ball), but the street events and fireworks are open to everyone. Contact the **Venice Tourist Office,** San Marco, Giardinetti Reali, Palazzo Selva, 30124 Venezia (✆ **041/529-8711**). The week before Ash Wednesday, the start of Lent.

February Basler Fasnacht, Basel, Switzerland. Called "the wildest of carnivals," with a parade of "cliques" (clubs and associations). Call ℂ 061/268-68-68 or visit www.fasnacht.ch for more information. First Monday after Ash Wednesday.

March

Holmenkollen Ski Festival, Oslo, Norway. This is one of Europe's largest ski festivals, with World Cup Nordic skiing and biathlons and international ski-jumping competitions, all held at Holmenkollen Ski Jump on the outskirts of Oslo. To participate or request more information, contact **Skiforeningen,** Kongeveien 5, Holmenkollen, N-0390 Oslo 3 (ℂ 22-92-32-00; www.skiforeningen.no). March 6 to 9.

St. Patrick's Dublin Festival, Dublin, Ireland. This massive 4-day fest is open, free, and accessible to all. Street theater, carnival acts, music, fireworks, and more culminate in Ireland's grandest parade. Call ℂ 01/676-3205 or go to www.stpatricksday.ie. March 15 to 18.

Budapest Spring Festival, Budapest, Hungary. For 2 weeks, performances of everything from opera to ballet, from classical music to drama, are held in all the major halls and theaters of Budapest. Simultaneously, temporary exhibitions open in many of Budapest's museums. Tickets are available at 1053 Budapest, Egyetem tér 5 (ℂ 36/1-486-3311; www.festivalcity.hu) and at the individual venues. Mid- to late March.

April

Semana Santa (Holy Week), Seville, Spain. Although many of the country's smaller towns stage similar celebrations, the festivities in Seville are by far the most elaborate. From Palm Sunday to Easter

Sunday, processions with hooded penitents move to the piercing wail of the *saeta,* a love song to the Virgin or Christ. Call the **Seville Office of Tourism** for details (ℂ 95-422-1404). Usually the last week of March.

Holy Week observances, Italy, nationwide. Processions and age-old ceremonies—some from pagan days, some from the Middle Ages—are staged. The most notable procession is led by the pope, passing the Colosseum and the Roman Forum up to Palatine Hill; a torch-lit parade caps the observance. 4 days before Easter Sunday; sometimes at the end of March but often in April.

Pasqua (Easter Sunday), Rome, Italy. In an event broadcast around the world, the pope gives his blessing from the balcony of St. Peter's.

Feria de Sevilla (Seville Fair), Seville, Spain. This is the most celebrated week of revelry in all of Spain, with all-night flamenco dancing, entertainment booths, bullfights, flower-decked coaches, and dancing in the streets. Reserve your hotel early. Contact the **Seville Office of Tourism** (ℂ 95-422-1404). Second week after Easter.

May

Brighton Festival, Brighton, England. The country's largest arts festival features some 400 cultural events. Contact the **Brighton Tourist Information Centre,** 10 Bartholomew Sq., Brighton BN1 1JS (www.visitbrighton.com). Most of May.

Prague Spring Music Festival, Prague, Czech Republic. This world-famous 3-week series of classical music and dance performances brings some of the world's best talent to Prague. For details, call ℂ 420/25732 0468 or go to www.festival.cz. May 12 to June 3, 2004.

Festival International du Film (Cannes Film Festival), Cannes, France. Movie madness transforms this city into a media circus. Reserve early and make a deposit. Admission to the films is by invitation only. There are box-office tickets for the other films, which play 24 hours. Contact the **Festival International du Film (FIF)**, 99 bd. Des Malesherbes, 75008 Paris (✆ **01-53-59-61-00**). Two weeks before the festival, the event's administration moves to the Palais des Festivals, esplanade Georges-Pompidou, 06400 Cannes. May 12 to 23, 2004.

International Music Festival, Vienna, Austria. This traditional highlight of Vienna's concert calendar features top-class international orchestras, conductors, and classical greats. The venue and booking address is **Wiener Musikverein**, Lothringer-Strasse 20, A-1030 Vienna (✆ **01/242-002**). Early May through first 3 weeks of June.

Fiesta de San Isidro, Madrid, Spain. Madrileños run wild with a 10-day celebration honoring their city's patron saint. Food fairs, street parades, parties, dances, bullfights, and other events mark the occasion. Expect crowds and traffic. For details, contact the **Oficina Municipal de Información y Turismo** (✆ **91-588-1636**). May 13 to 20.

Bath International Music Festival, Bath, England. One of Europe's most prestigious international festivals of music and the arts features as many as 1,000 performers at various venues. Contact the **Bath Festivals Trust**, 5 Broad St., Bath, Somerset BA1 5LJ (✆ **01225/462231**). Late May to early June.

Bergen Festspill (Bergen International Festival), Bergen, Norway. This world-class music event features artists from Norway and around the world. Many styles of music are presented, but classical music—especially the work of Grieg—is emphasized. This is one of the largest annual musical events in Scandinavia. For information, contact the **Bergen International Festival**, Slottsgaten 1, 4055, Dregen N-5835 Bergen (✆ **55-21-06-30**). May 21 to June 1.

Maggio Musicale Fiorentino (Musical May Florentine), Florence, Italy. Italy's oldest and most prestigious music festival emphasizes music from the 14th century to the 20th century but also presents ballet and opera. For schedules and tickets, contact the **Maggio Musicale Fiorentino/Teatro Comunale**, Corso Italia 12, 50123 Firenze (✆ **055-27-791** or 055-211-158). Late April to beginning of July.

June

Hellenic Festival (Athens, Lycobettus & Epidaurus festivals), Greece. The three festivals are now organized under the umbrella term of Hellenic Festival. The Athens Festival features superb productions of ancient drama, opera, modern dance, ballet, and more in the Odeum of Herodes Atticus, on the southwest side of the Acropolis. The Lycabettus Festival presents performances at the amphitheater on Mount Lycovitos. The Epidaurus Festival presents classic Greek drama in its famous amphitheater. For details, call (✆ **210/322-1459** or go to www.hellenicfestival.gr. June to early October.

Festival di Spoleto, Spoleto, Italy. Dating from 1958, this festival was the artistic creation of maestro and world-class composer Gian Carlo Menotti, who still presides over the event. International performers convene for 3 weeks of dance, drama, opera, concerts, and art exhibits in this Umbrian hill town.

The main focus is music composed from 1300 to 1799. For tickets and details, contact the **Spoleto Festival,** Piazza Duomo 8, 06049 Spoleto (© **0743/45028;** www.spoleto festival.it). June 27 to July 13, 2004.

Roskilde Festival, Roskilde, Denmark. Europe's biggest rock festival has been going strong for more than 30 years, now bringing about 90,000 revelers each year to the central Zealand town. Besides major rock concerts, scheduled activities include theater and film presentations. For details, call © **46-36-66-13;** or check www. roskilde-festivaldk. June 26 to 29.

July

Tour de France, France. Europe's most hotly contested bicycle race pits crews of wind-tunnel-tested athletes along an itinerary that detours deep into the Massif Central and ranges across the Alps. The race is decided at a finish line drawn across the Champs-Elysées. Call © **01-41-33-15-00.** Month of July.

Karlovy Vary International Film Festival, Karlovy Vary, Czech Republic. This annual 10-day event predates Communism and has regained its "A" rating from the international body governing film festivals, which puts it in the same league as Cannes and Venice but without the star-drawing power of the more glittery stops. For more information, call © **420/221-41-1-011** or check www.iffkv.cz. July 4 to 12.

Montreux International Jazz Festival, Montreux, Switzerland. More than jazz, this festival features everything from reggae bands to African tribal chanters. Monster dance-fests also break out nightly. The 2½-week festival concludes with a 12-hour marathon of world music. For more information, write

to the **Montreux Jazz Festival,** Case Postale Box 97, CH-1820 Montreux, or call © **021/963-82-82.** Beginning of July.

Bastille Day, France, nationwide. Celebrating the birth of modern-day France, the nation's festivities reach their peak in Paris with street fairs, pageants, fireworks, and feasts. In Paris, the day begins with a parade down the Champs-Elysées and ends with fireworks at Montmartre. July 14, 2004.

Around Gotland Race, Sandhamn, Sweden. The biggest and most exciting open-water Scandinavian sailing race starts and finishes at Sandhamn in the Stockholm archipelago. About 450 boats, mainly from Nordic countries, take part. Call the **Stockholm Tourist Center** (© **08/789-24-00)** for information. Two days in mid-July.

Salzburg Festival, Salzburg, Austria. Since the 1920s, this has been one of the premier cultural events of Europe, sparkling with opera, chamber music, plays, concerts, appearances by world-class artists, and many other cultural presentations. Always count on stagings of Mozart operas. For tickets, write several months in advance to the **Salzburg Festival,** Postfach 140, A-5010 Salzburg (© **0662/8045).** July 26 to August 31, 2003.

Il Palio, Siena, Italy. Palio fever grips this Tuscan hill town for a wild and exciting horse race from the Middle Ages. Pageantry, costumes, and the celebrations of the victorious *contrada* (sort of a neighborhood social club) mark the spectacle. For details, contact the **Azienda di Promozione Turistica,** Piazza del Campo 56, 53100 Siena (© **0577-280551).** July 2 to August 16, 2004.

The Proms, London, England. A night at "The Proms"—the annual

Henry Wood promenade concerts at Royal Albert Hall—attracts music aficionados from around the world. Staged almost daily (except for a few Sun), these traditional concerts were launched in 1895 and are the principal summer engagements for the BBC Symphony Orchestra. Cheering and clapping, Union Jacks on parade, banners, and balloons—it's great summer fun. Call © 020/7589-8212, or go to www.bbc.co.uk/proms. Mid-July to mid-September.

Richard Wagner Festival, Bayreuth Festspielhaus, Germany. One of Europe's two or three major opera events, this festival takes place in the composer's Festspielhaus in Bayreuth, the capital of upper Franconia. *Note:* Opera tickets often must be booked years in advance. Contact **Festival Administration,** Bayreuther Festspiele, Am Festspiele, Kartenbüro Postfach 100262, D-95445 Bayreuth (© 0921/7-87-80; www.festspiele.de). Late July to late August.

Festival d'Avignon, Avignon, France. This world-class festival has a reputation for exposing new talent to critical acclaim. The focus is usually on avant-garde works in theater, dance, and music. Much of the music is presented within the 14th-century courtyard of the Palais de l'Ancien Archeveché (the Old Archbishop's Palace). Make hotel reservations early. For information, call © 04-90-27-66-50 or fax 04-90-27-66-83. Last 3 weeks of July.

August

Edinburgh International Festival, Edinburgh, Scotland. Scotland's best-known festival is held for 3 weeks. Called an "arts bonanza," it draws major talent from around the world, with more than a thousand shows presented and a million tickets sold. Book, jazz, and film festivals

are also staged at this time. Contact the **Edinburgh International Festival,** The Hub, Castle Hill, Edinburgh EH1 2NE (© 0131/473-2001; www.eif.co.uk). Three weeks in August.

Fire Festival Regatta, Silkeborg, Denmark. Denmark's oldest and biggest festival features nightly cruises on the lakes, with thousands of candles illuminating the shores. The fireworks display on the last night is the largest and most spectacular in northern Europe. Popular Danish artists provide entertainment at a large fun fair. Contact the **Turistbureau,** Godthåbsuej 4, DK-8600 Silkeborg (© 86-82-19-11). Early August.

Festas da Senhora da Agopnia, Viana do Castelo, north of Porto, Portugal. The most spectacular festival in the north honors "Our Lady of Suffering." A replica of the Virgin is carried through the streets over carpets of flowers. Float-filled parades mark the 3-day and-a-night event as a time of revelry. A blaze of fireworks ends the festival. Call the **tourist office** (© 258/82-2620) for exact dates, which vary from year to year. Mid-August.

St. Stephen's Day, Hungary. This is Hungary's national day. The country's patron saint is celebrated with cultural events and a dramatic display of fireworks over the Danube at 9pm. Hungarians also ceremoniously welcome the first new bread from the crop of July wheat. August 20.

September

Highland Games & Gathering, Braemar, Scotland. The queen and many members of the royal family often show up for this annual event, with its massed bands, piping and dancing competitions, and performances of great strength by a tribe of gigantic men. Contact the **tourist office** in Braemar, The Mews, Mar Road, Braemar, Aberdeenshire, AB35 5YP (✆ **01339/755-377**). First Saturday in September.

Oktoberfest, Munich, Germany. Germany's most famous festival happens mainly in September, not October. Millions show up, and hotels are packed. Most activities are at Theresienwiese, where local breweries sponsor gigantic tents that can hold up to 6,000 beer drinkers. Always reserve hotel rooms well in advance. Contact the **Munich Tourist Office** (✆ **089/2-33-03-00;** www.muenchentourist.de). Mid-September to the first Sunday in October.

October
Autumn Wine Growers' Festival, Lugano, Switzerland. A parade and other festivities mark harvest time. Little girls throw flowers from blossom-covered floats, and oxen pull festooned wagons in a colorful procession. For information call

✆ **091/921-46-64.** Three days in early October.

November
All Saints' Day, Spain, nationwide. This public holiday is reverently celebrated, as relatives and friends lay flowers on the graves of the dead. November 1.

December
La Scala Opera Season, Teatro alla Scala, Milan. At the most famous opera house of them all, the season opens on December 7, the feast day of Milan's patron St. Ambrogio, and runs into July. Even though opening-night tickets are close to impossible to get, it's worth a try; call ✆ **02/7200-3744** for information or 02/86-0775 for reservations.

Nobel Peace Prize Ceremony, Oslo, Norway. This major event on the Oslo calendar attracts world attention. It's held at Oslo City Hall on December 10. Attendance is by invitation only. For details, contact the **Nobel Institute,** Drammensveien 19, N-0255 Oslo 2 (✆ **22-44-36-80;** www.nobel.se).

5 Active & Other Special-Interest Vacations

CYCLING
Cycling tours are a great way to see Europe at your own pace. Some of the best are conducted by the **Cyclists' Tourist Club,** Cotterell House, 69 Meadrow, Godalming, Surrey, England GU7 3H5 (✆ **01483/417-217;** www.ctc.org.uk). **Holland Bicycling Tours, Inc.,** P.O. Box 6086, Huntington Beach, CA 92615 (✆ **800/852-3258;** fax 714/593-1710; www.hollandbicyclingtours.com), leads 8-day bicycle tours throughout Europe. **Experience Plus Specialty Tours,** 415 Mason Ct., Fort Collins, CO 80524 (✆ **800/685-4565;** fax 970/493-0377; www.experienceplus.com), runs bike tours across Europe. **Ciclismo Classico,** 30 Marathon St.,

Arlington, MA 02474 (✆ **800/866-7314** or 781/646-3377; fax 781/641-1512; www.ciclismoclassico.com), is an excellent outfit running tours of Italy. Florence-based **I Bike Italy, Inc.** ®, P.O. Box 64-3824, Vero Beach, FL (✆ **561/388-0783;** www.ibikeitaly.com), offers guided single-day rides in the Tuscan countryside.

HIKING
Wilderness Travel, 1102 9th St., Berkeley, CA 94710 (✆ **800/368-2794** or 510/558-2488; fax 510/558-2489; www.wildernesstravel.com), specializes in walking tours, treks, and inn-to-inn hiking tours of Europe, as well as less strenuous walking tours. **Sherpa Expeditions,** 131A Heston Rd., Hounslow, Middlesex, England

TW5 ORF (© 020/8577-2717; www.sherpaexpeditions.com), offers both self-guided and group treks through off-the-beaten-track regions; it's represented in the United States by **Himalayan Travel,** 8 Berkshire Place, Danbury, CT 06901 (© **800/225-2380** or 203/743-2349; fax 203/797-8077; www.himalayantravelinc.com). Two somewhat upscale walking tour companies are **Butterfield & Robinson,** 70 Bond St., Suite 300, Toronto, ON M5B 1X3 (© **800/678-1147** or 416/864-1354; fax 416/864-0541; www.butterfield.com); and **Country Walkers,** P.O. Box 180, Waterbury, VT 05676-0180 (© **800/464-9255** or 800/244-1387; fax 802/244-5661; www.countrywalkers.com).

Most European countries have associations geared toward aiding hikers and walkers. In England it's the **Ramblers' Association,** 87–90 Albert Embankment; London SE1 7TW, 2nd Floor, Camelford House (© **020/7339-8500;** www.ramblers.org.uk). In Italy, contact the **Club Alpino Italiano,** 6 Via Silvo Pellico, Milan 20121 (© **02/8646-3516;** www.caimilano.it). For Austria, try the **Osterreichischer Alpenverein (Austrian Alpine Club),** Wilhelm-Greil-Strasse 15, A-6010 Innsbruck (© **0512/595470;** fax 0512/575528; www.alpenverein.at). In Norway, it's the **Norwegian Mountain Touring Association,** Dennorske Touristforening, Storgata 3, Box 7 Sentrum 0101 Oslo (© **22-82-28-00;** fax 22-82-28-01; www.turistforeningen.no).

HORSEBACK RIDING

One of the best companies is **Equitour,** P.O. Box 807, Dubois, WY 82513 (© **800/545-0019** or 307/455-3363; fax 307/455-2354; www.ridingtours.com), which offers 5- to 7-day rides through many of Europe's most popular areas, such as Tuscany and the Loire Valley.

EDUCATIONAL TRAVEL

The best (and one of the most expensive) of the escorted tour operators is **IST Cultural Tours** (© **800/833-2111;** www.ist-tours.com), whose tours are first class all the way and accompanied by a certified expert in whatever field the trip focuses on. If you missed out on study abroad in college, the brainy **Smithsonian Journeys** (© **877/EDU-TOUR** or 202/357-4700; fax 202/633-9250; www.smithsonianjourneys.org) may be just the ticket, albeit a pricey one. Study leaders are often world-renowned experts in their field. Journeys are carefully crafted and go to some of the most compelling places in Europe, avoiding tourist traps. Also contact your alma mater or local university to see if it offers summer tours open to the public and guided by a professor specialist.

The **National Registration Center for Studies Abroad (NRCSA),** 823 N2 St., Milwaukee, WI 53203 (© **414/278-0631;** fax 414/224-3466; www.nrcsa.com); and the **American Institute for Foreign Study (AIFS),** River Plaza, 9 W. Broad St., Stamford, CT 06902 (© **800/727-2437** or 203/399-5000; fax 203/399-5590; www.aifs.com), can both help you arrange study programs and summer programs abroad.

The biggest organization dealing with higher education in Europe is the **Institute of International Education,** with headquarters at 809 United Nations Plaza, New York, NY 10017-3500 (© **800/445-0443** or 212/883-8200; www.iie.org). A few of its booklets are free, but for $47, plus $6 postage, you can buy the more definitive *Short Term Study Abroad.* To order publications, check out the IIE's online bookstore at www.iie.org; call © **800/445-0443** or 301/617-7804; fax 301/206-9789; or write to the Institute of International Education,

P.O. Box 371, Annapolis Junction, MD 20701-0371.

A clearinghouse for information on European-based language schools is **Lingua Service Worldwide,** 75 Prospect St., Suite 4, Huntington, NY 11743 (© **800/394-LEARN** or 631/ 424-0777; fax 631/271-3441; www. linguaserviceworldwide.com).

CULINARY SCHOOLS

Cuisine International, P.O. Box 25228, Dallas, TX 75225 (© **214/ 373-1161;** fax 214/373-1162; www. cuisineinternational.com), brings together some of the top independent cooking schools and teachers based in various European countries so you can book your weeklong culinary dream vacation.

Apicius, Via Guelfa 85, 50129 Florence, Italy (© **055/2658135**), is the finest cooking school in Florence, an expert on Tuscan culinary arts. Its monthly programs are taught by local chefs and food experts, with an emphasis on wine appreciation. From May to October, the **International Cooking School of Italian Food and Wine,** 201 E. 28th St., Suite 15B, New York, NY 10016-8538 (© **212/ 779-1921;** fax 212/779-3248; www. marybethclark.com), offers courses in Bologna, the "gastronomic capital of Italy." **Le Cordon Bleu,** 8 rue Léon-Delhomme, 75015 Paris (© **800/ 457-2433** in the U.S., or 01-53-68-22-50; www.cordonbleu.edu), was established in 1895 as a means of spreading the tenets of French cuisine to the world at large. It offers many programs outside its flagship Paris school.

6 Health & Insurance

HEALTH

In most of Europe the tap water is generally safe to drink (except on trains and wherever it's marked as nondrinking water), the milk pasteurized, and health services good. You will, however, be eating foods and spices your body isn't used to, so you might want to bring along Pepto-Bismol or Imodium tablets in case indigestion or diarrhea strikes.

If you worry about getting sick away from home, you may want to consider **medical travel insurance** (see below). In most cases, however, your existing health plan will provide all the coverage you need. Be sure to carry your ID card in your wallet.

If you suffer from a chronic illness, consult your doctor before your departure. For conditions like epilepsy, diabetes, or heart problems, wear a **Medic Alert Identification Tag** (© **800/825-3785;** www.medic alert.org), which will immediately alert doctors to your condition and give them access to your records through Medic Alert's 24-hour hot line.

Contact the **International Association for Medical Assistance to Travelers (IAMAT;** © **716/754-4883;** www.iamat.org) for tips on travel and health concerns in the countries you're visiting, and for lists of local, English-speaking doctors. The United States **Centers for Disease Control and Prevention** (© **800/311-3435** or 404/639-3534; www.cdc.gov) provides up-to-date information on necessary vaccines and health hazards by region or country (their booklet, *Health Information for International Travel,* is $25 by mail; on the Internet, it's free). Any foreign consulate can provide a list of area doctors who speak English. If you get sick, consider asking your hotel concierge to recommend a local doctor—even his or her own.

Most health insurance policies cover you if you get sick away from home—but check, particularly if you're insured by an HMO. With the

> **_Tips_ A Packing Tip**
>
> Pack prescription medications in your carry-on luggage. Carry written prescriptions in generic (not brand-name) form, and dispense all prescription medications from their original labeled vials. This helps foreign pharmacists fill them and Customs officials approve them. If you wear contact lenses, pack an extra pair in case you lose one.

exception of certain HMOs and Medicare/Medicaid, your medical insurance should cover medical treatment—even hospital care—overseas. Many European hospitals are partially socialized, and you'll usually be taken care of speedily, often at no charge for simple ailments. However, most out-of-country hospitals make you pay your bills up front, and send you a refund after you've returned home and filed the necessary paperwork. Members of **Blue Cross/Blue Shield** can now use their cards at selected hospitals in most major cities worldwide (℃ **800/810-BLUE** or www.blue cares.com for a list of hospitals).

INSURANCE

Check your existing insurance policies before you buy travel insurance to cover trip cancellation, lost luggage, medical expenses, or car rental insurance. You're likely to have partial or complete coverage. But if you need some, ask your travel agent about a comprehensive package. The cost of travel insurance varies widely, depending on the cost and length of your trip, your age and overall health, and the type of trip you're taking. More dangerous activities may be excluded from basic policies.

And keep in mind that in the aftermath of the September 11, 2001, terrorist attacks, a number of airlines, cruise lines, and tour operators are no longer covered by insurers. **_The bottom line:_** Always, always check the fine print before you sign on; more and more policies have built-in exclusions and restrictions that may leave

you out in the cold if something does go awry.

For information, contact one of the following popular insurers:

- **Access America** (℃ **866/807-3982;** www.accessamerica.com)
- **Travel Guard International** (℃ **800/826-4919;** www.travel guard.com)
- **Travel Insured International** (℃ **800/243-3174;** www.travel insured.com)
- **Travelex Insurance Services** (℃ **888/457-4602;** www.travelex-insurance.com)

Some credit cards (American Express and certain gold and platinum Visas and MasterCards, for example) offer automatic flight insurance against death or dismemberment in case of an airplane crash if you charged the cost of your ticket.

If you require additional insurance, try one of the following companies:

- **MEDEX International,** 8501 LaSalle Rd., Suite 200, Towson, MD 21286 (℃ **888/MEDEX-00** or 410/453-6300; fax 410/453-6301; www.medexassist.com)
- **Travel Assistance International** (℃ **800/821-2828;** www.travel assistance.com), 9200 Keystone Crossing, Suite 300, Indianapolis, IN 46240 (for general information on services, call the company's Worldwide Assistance Services, Inc., at ℃ **800/777-8710**).

Lost-Luggage Insurance On international flights (including U.S. portions of international trips), baggage is limited to approximately $9.05 per pound, up to approximately $635 per checked bag. If you plan to check items more valuable than the standard liability, you may purchase "excess valuation" coverage from the airline, up to $5,000. Lost luggage may also be covered by your homeowner's or renter's policy. Many platinum and gold credit cards cover you as well. If you choose to purchase additional lost-luggage insurance, be sure not to buy more than you need. Buy in advance from the insurer or a trusted agent (prices will be much higher at the airport).

For information on **car renter's insurance,** see "Getting Around," later in this chapter.

7 Tips for Travelers with Special Needs

FOR TRAVELERS WITH DISABILITIES

Europe won't win any medals for accessibility for travelers with disabilities, but in the past few years its big cities have made an effort to accommodate travelers with disabilities.

AGENCIES/OPERATORS

- **Flying Wheels Travel** (© 507/451-5002; fax 507/451-1685; www.flyingwheelstravel.com) offers escorted tours and cruises that emphasize sports and private tours in minivans with lifts.
- **Accessible Journeys** (© 800/TINGLES or 610/521-0339; www.disabilitytravel.com) caters specifically to slow walkers and wheelchair travelers and their families and friends.

ORGANIZATIONS

- **The Moss Rehab Hospital** (© 215/456-5882; www.mossresourcenet.org) provides friendly, helpful phone assistance through its **Travel Information Service.**
- **The Society for Accessible Travel and Hospitality** (© 212/447-7284; fax 212-725-8253; www.sath.org) offers a wealth of travel resources for all types of disabilities and informed recommendations on destinations, access guides, travel agents, tour operators, vehicle rentals, and companion services. Annual membership costs $45 for adults; $30 for seniors and students.

- **The American Foundation for the Blind** (© 800/232-5463 or 212/502-7600; www.afb.org) provides information on traveling with Seeing Eye dogs.

PUBLICATIONS

- **Twin Peaks Press** (© 360/694-2462) publishes travel-related books for travelers with special needs.
- *Open World Magazine,* published by the Society for Accessible Travel and Hospitality (see above), is full of good resources and information. A year's subscription is $18 ($35 outside the U.S.).

For U.K. Citizens The **Royal Association for Disability and Rehabilitation (RADAR),** Unit 12, 250 City Rd., London EC1V 8AF (© 020/7250-3222; fax 020/7250-0212; www.radar.org.uk) publishes three holiday "fact packs." The first provides general info, including planning and booking a holiday, insurance, finances, and useful organizations and holiday providers; the second outlines transportation and rental equipment options; and the third deals with specialized accommodations. Another good service is the **Holiday Care Service,** Imperial Building, 2nd Floor, Victoria Road, Horley, Surrey RH6 7PZ (© 01293/774-535; fax 01293/784-647), a national charity that advises on accessible accommodations for seniors and persons with disabilities. Annual membership is £35.

FOR FAMILIES

Europeans expect to see families traveling together. It's a multigenerational continent, and you'll sometimes see the whole clan traveling around. And Europeans tend to love kids. You'll often find that a child guarantees you an even warmer reception at hotels and restaurants.

At **restaurants,** ask waiters for a half portion to fit junior's appetite. If you're traveling with small children, three- and four-star hotels may be your best bet—**babysitters** are on call so you can take the occasional romantic dinner, and such hotels have a better general ability to help you access the city and its services. But even cheaper hotels can usually find you a sitter. Traveling with a pint-size person usually means pint-size rates. An **extra cot** in the room won't cost more than 30% extra (if anything), and most museums and sights offer **reduced or free admission** for children under a certain age (which can range from 6–18). And kids almost always get discounts on plane and train tickets.

AGENCIES/OPERATORS

Familyhostel (② 800/733-9753 or 603/862-1147; www.learn.unh.edu/familyhostel) takes the whole family on moderately priced domestic and international learning vacations. All trip details are handled by the program staff, and lectures, field trips, and sightseeing are guided by a team of academics. The trips are for kids ages 8 to 15 accompanied by their parents and/or grandparents.

FOR GAYS & LESBIANS

Much of Europe has grown to accept same-sex couples over the past few decades, and in most countries homosexual sex acts are legal. To be on the safe side, do a bit of research and test the waters for acceptability in any one city or area. As you might expect, smaller towns tend to be less accepting than cities. Gay centers include London,

Paris, Amsterdam, Berlin, Milan, and the Greek Islands (Mykonos). For coverage of the gay scene in Europe's top destinations, consider purchasing a copy of *Frommer's Gay & Lesbian Europe.*

The **International Gay & Lesbian Travel Association** (IGLTA; ② 800/448-8550 or 954/776-2626; fax 954/776-3303; www.iglta.com) links travelers with gay-friendly hoteliers, tour operators, and airline and cruise-line representatives. It offers monthly newsletters, marketing mailings, and a membership directory that's updated once a year. Membership is $300 yearly, plus a $100 administration fee for new members.

AGENCIES/OPERATORS

- **Above and Beyond Tours** (② 800/397-2681 or 760/325-0702; www.abovebeyondtours. com) offers gay and lesbian tours worldwide and is the exclusive gay and lesbian tour operator for United Airlines.
- **Now, Voyager** (② 800/255-6951; www.nowvoyager.com) is a San Francisco–based gay-owned and -operated travel service.

PUBLICATIONS

- *Out and About* (② 800/929-2268 or 415/644-8044; www.out andabout.com) offers guidebooks and a newsletter 10 times a year packed with solid information on the global gay and lesbian scene.

FOR SENIORS

Don't be shy about asking for discounts, but always carry some kind of ID, such as a driver's license, showing your date of birth. Also mention that you're a senior when you first make your travel reservations. Many hotels offer seniors discounts, and in most cities, people over age 60 qualify for reduced admission to theaters, museums, and other attractions as well as discounted fares on public transportation.

Members of **AARP** (formerly known as the American Association of Retired Persons), 601 E St. NW, Washington, DC 20049 (ⓒ **800/ 424-3410** or 202/434-2277; www. aarp.org), get discounts on hotels, airfares, and car rentals. AARP offers members a wide range of benefits, including *AARP The Magazine* and a monthly newsletter. Anyone over 50 can join.

Though these specialty books are U.S.–focused, they do provide general advice and contacts for savvy travelers: *The 50+ Traveler's Guidebook* (St. Martin's Press), *The Seasoned Traveler* (Country Roads Press), and *Unbelievably Good Deals and Great Adventures That You Absolutely Can't Get Unless You're Over 50* (Contemporary Books). Also check out your newsstand for the quarterly magazine *Travel 50 & Beyond.*

AGENCIES/OPERATORS

- **Elderhostel** (ⓒ **877/426-8056;** www.elderhostel.org) arranges study programs for those ages 55 and over (and a spouse or companion of any age) in the U.S. and in more than 80 countries around the world. Most courses last 5 to 7 days in the U.S. (2–4 weeks abroad), and many include airfare, accommodations in university dormitories or modest inns, meals, and tuition.

FOR STUDENTS

If you're planning to travel outside the U.S., you'd be wise to arm yourself with an **international student I.D. card,** which offers substantial savings on rail passes, plane tickets, and entrance fees. It also provides you with basic health and life insurance and a 24-hour help line. The card is available for $22 from **STA Travel** (ⓒ **800/781-4040;** www.statravel. com), the biggest student travel agency in the world. If you're no longer a student but are still under 26, you can get an **International Youth Travel Card (IYTC)** for the same price from the same people, which entitles you to insurance and some discounts (but not on museum admissions).

In Canada, **Travel CUTS** (ⓒ **800/ 667-2887** or 416/614-2887; www. travelcuts.com) offers similar services.

PUBLICATIONS

The Hanging Out Guides (www. frommers.com/hangingout), published by Frommer's, is the top student travel series for today's students, covering everything from adrenaline sports to the hottest club and music scenes.

8 Planning Your Trip Online

SURFING FOR AIRFARES

The "big three" online travel agencies, **Expedia.com, Travelocity.com,** and **Orbitz.com,** sell most of the air tickets bought on the Internet. (Canadian travelers should try expedia.ca and Travelocity.ca; U.K. residents can go for expedia.co.uk and opodo.co.uk.) Each has different business deals with the airlines and may offer different fares on the same flights, so it's wise to shop around. Expedia and Travelocity will also send you **e-mail notification** when a cheap fare becomes available to your favorite destination. Of the smaller travel agency websites, **Side-Step** (www.sidestep.com) has gotten the best reviews from Frommer's authors. It's a browser add-on that purports to "search 140 sites at once," but in reality only beats competitors' fares as often as other sites do.

Also remember to check **airline websites,** especially those for low-fare carriers such as Southwest, JetBlue, AirTran, WestJet, or Ryanair, whose fares are often misreported or simply missing from travel agency websites. Even with major airlines, you can often shave a few bucks from a fare by

> **Tips** **Vigilance Overseas: Leave the 10-Gallon Hat at Home**
>
> American citizens around the globe face increased fears they may be targeted for more terrorist attacks. American embassies, companies, museums, and schools, even the American Library in Paris, are on increased alert. Government officials have announced that the threat to U.S. institutions "is particularly high and seems likely to remain so." Terrorist experts recommend that U.S. citizens traveling abroad forego such traditional garb as cowboy boots or draping symbols of the American flag on their backs or luggage. The American Express in Rome has been so cautious as to install metal detectors in its offices.
>
> The U.S. State Department continues to monitor information about potential threats to Americans overseas, and issues data on the Web at **http://travel.state.gov**. Citizens planning to travel abroad should consult the State Department's announcements, travel warnings, and consular information sheets, all available at this website.
>
> In addition to the Internet, U.S. travelers may hear recorded information by calling the department in Washington at **202/647-5225**.

booking directly through the airline and avoiding a travel agency's transaction fee. But you'll get these discounts only by **booking online:** Most airlines now offer online only fares that even their phone agents know nothing about. For the websites of airlines that fly to and from your destination, go to "Getting There," below.

Great **last-minute deals** are available through free weekly e-mail services provided directly by the airlines. Most of these are announced on Tuesday or Wednesday and must be purchased online. Most are only valid for travel that weekend, but some (such as Southwest's) can be booked weeks or months in advance. Sign up for weekly e-mail alerts at airline websites or check mega-sites that compile comprehensive lists of last-minute specials, such as **Smarter Living** (http://smarterliving.com). For last-minute trips, **site59.com** in the U.S. and **lastminute.com** in Europe often have better deals than the major-label sites.

If you're willing to give up some control over your flight details, use an opaque fare service like **Priceline** (www.priceline.com; www.priceline.co.uk for Europeans) or **Hotwire** (www.hotwire.com). Both offer rock-bottom prices in exchange for travel on a "mystery airline" at a mysterious time of day, often with a mysterious change of planes en route. The mystery airlines are all major, well-known carriers—and the possibility of being sent from Philadelphia to Chicago via Tampa is remote; the airlines' routing computers have gotten a lot better than they used to be. But your chances of getting a 6am or 11pm flight are pretty high. Hotwire tells you flight prices before you buy; Priceline usually has better deals than Hotwire, but you have to play their "name our price" game. If you're new at this, the helpful folks at **BiddingForTravel** (www.biddingfortravel.com) do a good job of demystifying Priceline's prices. Priceline and Hotwire are great for flights between the U.S. and Europe. But for flights to other parts of the world, consolidators will almost always beat their fares.

> **_Tips_ Europe Online**
>
> For country- and city-specific websites, see **"Visitor Information"** sections within each chapter. Also, check individual listings for hotel, restaurant, and attraction websites.

For much more about airfares and savvy air-travel tips and advice, pick up a copy of *Frommer's Fly Safe, Fly Smart* (Wiley Publishing, Inc.).

SURFING FOR HOTELS

Shopping online for hotels is much easier in the U.S., Canada, and certain parts of Europe than it is in the rest of the world. Also, many smaller hotels and B&Bs—especially outside the U.S.—don't show up on websites at all. Of the "big three" sites, **Expedia** may be the best choice, thanks to its long list of special deals. **Travelocity** runs a close second. Hotel specialist sites **hotels.com** and **hoteldiscounts.com** are also reliable. An excellent free program, **TravelAxe** (www.travelaxe.net), can help you search multiple hotel sites at once, even ones you may never have heard of.

SURFING FOR RENTAL CARS

For booking rental cars online, the best deals are usually found at rental-car company websites, although all the major online travel agencies also offer rental-car reservations services. Priceline and Hotwire work well for rental cars, too; the only "mystery" is which major rental company you get, and for most travelers the difference between Hertz, Avis, and Budget is negligible.

ONLINE TRAVELER'S TOOLBOX

Veteran travelers usually carry some essential items to make their trips easier.

Following is a selection of online tools to bookmark and use.

- **Visa ATM Locator** (www.visa. com), for locations of PLUS ATMs worldwide, or **MasterCard ATM Locator** (www.mastercard. com), for locations of Cirrus ATMs worldwide.
- **Foreign Languages for Travelers** (www.travlang.com). Learn basic terms in more than 70 languages and click on any underlined phrase to hear what it sounds like. *Note:* Free audio software and speakers are required.
- **Intellicast** (www.intellicast.com) and **Weather.com** (www.weather. com). Weather forecasts for all 50 states and for cities around the world.
- **Mapquest** (www.mapquest.com). This best of the mapping sites lets you choose a specific address or destination and, in seconds, it will return a map and detailed directions.
- **Universal Currency Converter** (www.xe.com). See what your dollar or pound is worth in more than 100 other countries.
- **Travel Warnings** (www.travel. state.gov). Reports on places where health concerns or unrest might threaten U.S. travelers. It also lists the locations of U.S. embassies around the world.

---

9 Getting There

FLYING FROM NORTH AMERICA

Most major airlines charge competitive fares to European cities, but price

wars break out regularly and fares can change overnight. Tickets tend to be cheaper if you fly midweek or off season. **High season** on most routes is

Frommers.com: The Complete Travel Resource

For an excellent travel-planning resource, we highly recommend **Frommers. com** (www.frommers.com). We're a little biased, of course, but we guarantee that you'll find the travel tips, reviews, monthly vacation giveaways, and online-booking capabilities thoroughly indispensable. Among the special features are our popular **Message Boards,** where Frommer's readers post queries and share advice (sometimes even our authors show up to answer questions); **Frommers.com Newsletter,** for the latest travel bargains and insider travel secrets; and **Frommer's Destinations Section,** where you'll get expert travel tips, hotel and dining recommendations, and advice on the sights to see for more than 3,000 destinations around the globe. When your research is done, the **Online Reservations System** (www.frommers.com/book_a_trip) takes you to Frommer's preferred online partners for booking your vacation at affordable prices.

usually from June to mid-September—the most expensive and most crowded time to travel. **Shoulder season** is from April to May, mid-September to October, and December 15 to 24. **Low season** —with the cheapest fares—is from November to December 14 and December 25 to March.

MAJOR NORTH AMERICAN AIRLINES North American carriers with frequent service and flights to Europe are **Air Canada** (© **888/247-2262** U.S.; 800/268-7240 Canada; www.aircanada.ca), **American Airlines** (© **800/433-7300;** www.aa.com), **Continental Airlines** (© **800/525-0280;** www.continental. com), **Delta Airlines** (© **800/221-1212;** www.delta.com), **Northwest Airlines** (© **800/225-2525;** www.nwa.com), and **US Airways** (© **800/428-4322;** www.usairways. com).

For the latest on airline websites, check **www.itn.com**.

EUROPEAN NATIONAL AIRLINES Not only will the national carriers of European countries offer the greatest number of direct flights from the United States (and can easily book you through to cities beyond the major hubs), but since their entire U.S. market is to fly you to their home country, they often run more competitive deals

than most North American carriers. Major national and country-affiliated European airlines include the following:

Austria: Austrian Airlines. *In the U.S. and Canada:* 800/843-0002. *In the U.K.:* 20/7766-0300. *In Australia:* 800/642-438. www.aua. com.

Belgium: Sabena. *In the U.S. and Canada:* 800/955-2000. *In the U.K.:* 0845/601-0933. www. sabena.com.

Czech Republic: CSA Czech Airlines. *In the U.S.:* 212/765 6545. *In Canada:* 416/363-3174. *In the U.K.:* 020/7255-1898. *In Australia:* 02/9247-7706. www.csa.cz.

France: Air France. *In the U.S.:* 800/237-2747. *In Canada:* 514/847-1106. *In the U.K.:* 0845/0845-111. *In Australia:* 02/9244-2100. *In New Zealand:* 064/9308-3352. www.airfrance.com.

Germany: Lufthansa. *In the U.S.:* 800/645-3880. *In Canada:* 800/563-5954. *In the U.K.:* 0845/773-7747. *In Australia:* 1300-655-727. *In New Zealand:* 09/303-1529. www.lufthansa-usa.com.

Greece: Olympic Airways. *In the U.S.:* 800/223-1226, or 718/269-2200 in New York State. *In Canada:* 514/878-3891 (Montreal) or 416/914-7137 (Toronto). *In the U.K.:* 0870/606-0460. *In Australia:* 02/9251-1040. www. olympic-airways.gr.com.

Hungary: Malev Hungarian Airlines. *In the U.S.:* 800/223-6884 outside New York, 212/566-9944 within New York. *In Canada:* 416/944-0093. *In the U.K.:* 020/7439-0577. *In Australia:* 02/9244-2111. *In New Zealand:* 09/379-4455. www.hungarianairlines.com.

Ireland: Aer Lingus. *In the U.S.:* 866/IRISH-FLY. *In the U.K.:* 020/8899-4747. *In Australia:* 02/9244-2123. *In New Zealand:* 09/308-3351. www.aerlingus.com.

Italy: Alitalia. *In the U.S. and Canada:* 800/223-5730. *In the U.K.:* 020/8745-8200. *In Australia:* 02/9247-1307. www.alitalia.com.

The Netherlands: KLM Royal Dutch Airlines. *In the U.S. and Canada:* 800/374-7747. *In the U.K.:* 0878/507-4074. www.klm.com.

Portugal: TAP Air Portugal. *In the U.S.:* 800/221-7370. *In the U.K.:* 0845/601-0932.   www.tap-air portugal.pt.

Scandinavia (Denmark, Norway, Sweden): SAS Scandinavian Airlines. *In the U.S.:* 800/221-2350. *In the U.K.:* 0845/600-7767. *In Australia:* 612/9283-9111. www. scandinavian.net.

Spain: Iberia. *In the U.S. and Canada:* 800/772-4642. *In the U.K.:* 0845/601-2854. www.iberia.com.

Switzerland: Swiss International Airlines. *In the U.S.:* 800/221-4750. *In Canada:* 800/267-9477. *In the U.K.:* 0845/601-0956. www.swiss air.com.

United Kingdom: (1) British Airways. *In the U.S. and Canada:* 800/247-9297. *In the U.K.:* 0845/773-3377. *In Australia:* 02/8904-8800. www.britishairways.com. (2) Virgin Atlantic Airways. *In the U.S. and Canada:* 800/862-8621.

In the U.K.: 01293/747-747. *In Australia:* 02/9244-2747. www. fly.virgin.com.

PACKAGE TOURS Package tours aren't the same thing as escorted tours. They're simply a way of buying your airfare and accommodations at the same time and getting an excellent rate on both. Your trip is your own. In many cases, a package including airfare, hotel, and transportation to and from the airport costs less than the hotel alone if you booked it yourself. The downside is that many stick you in large international-style hotels (which in Europe are often outside the historic city center). You do get a good rate for that sort of hotel, but with a little more work (and the hotel reviews in this book), you can easily find on your own a midrange pension or friendly B&B for the same price or less and right in the heart of the action.

All major airlines flying to Europe sell vacation packages (see phone numbers and websites, above). The best place to start looking for independent packagers is the travel section of your local Sunday newspaper and national travel magazines. **Online Vacation Mall** (© **800/839-9851;** www.onlinevacationmall.com) allows you to search for and book packages offered by a number of tour operators and airlines. **Central Holidays** (© **800/935-5000;** www.central holidays.com) is one of the best and most reputable package-tour operators. **Liberty Travel** (© **888/271-1584;** www.libertytravel.com) is one of the biggest packagers in the Northeast and usually boasts a full-page ad in Sunday papers. **Kemwel Holiday Auto** (© **800/678-0678;** www. kemwel.com) is a reputable option, too.

FLY/DRIVE TOURS Fly/drive vacations, which combine airfare and car rental, are increasing in popularity and are a lot cheaper than booking

(Tips) Flying for Less: Tips for Getting the Best Airfares

Passengers sharing the same airplane cabin rarely pay the same fare. Travelers who need to purchase tickets at the last minute, change their itinerary at a moment's notice, or fly one-way often get stuck paying the premium rate. Here are some ways to keep your airfare costs down.

- Passengers who can book their ticket **long in advance,** who can **stay over Saturday night,** or who **fly midweek** or at **less-trafficked hours** will pay a fraction of the full fare. If your schedule is flexible, say so, and ask if you can secure a cheaper fare by changing your plans.
- You can also save on airfares by keeping an eye out in local newspapers for **promotional specials** or **fare wars,** when airlines lower prices on their most popular routes. You rarely see fare wars offered for peak travel times, but if you can travel in the off-months, you may snag a bargain.
- **Search the Internet** for cheap fares. See "Planning Your Trip Online," earlier in this chapter.
- **Consolidators,** also known as bucket shops, are great sources for international tickets. Start by looking in Sunday newspaper travel sections; U.S. travelers should focus on the *New York Times, Los Angeles Times,* and *Miami Herald.* For less-developed destinations, small travel agents who cater to immigrant communities in large cities often have the best deals. *Beware:* Bucket shop tickets are usually nonrefundable or rigged with stiff cancellation penalties, often as high as 50% to 75% of the ticket price, and some put you on charter airlines with questionable safety records. Several reliable consolidators are worldwide and available on the Net. **STA Travel** is now the world's leader in student travel, thanks to their purchase of Council Travel. It also offers good fares for travelers of all ages. **Flights.com** (© 800/TRAV-800; www.flights.com) started in Europe and has excellent fares worldwide, but particularly to that continent. It also has "local" websites in 12 countries. **FlyCheap** (© 800/FLY-CHEAP;** www.1800flycheap.com) is owned by package-holiday megalith MyTravel and so has especially good access to fares for sunny destinations. **Air Tickets Direct** (© 800/778-3447; www.airticketsdirect.com) is based in Montreal and leverages the currently weak Canadian dollar for low fares; it'll also book trips to places that U.S. travel agents won't touch, such as Cuba.
- For many more tips about air travel, including a rundown of the major frequent-flier credit cards, pick up a copy of *Frommer's Fly Safe, Fly Smart* (Wiley Publishing, Inc.).

both airfare and car rental independently. They're available mainly through major European airlines (see above).

ESCORTED GROUP TOURS

With a good escorted group tour, you'll know ahead of time what your trip will cost, and you won't have to worry about transportation, luggage, hotel reservations, communicating in foreign languages, and other basics—an experienced guide will take care of all that and lead you through all the sightseeing. The downside of a guided tour is that you trade much of the freedom and personal free time independent travel grants you and often see only the canned postcard-ready side of Europe through the tinted windows of a giant bus. You get to *see* Europe, but rarely do you get the chance to really *know* it. Consult a good travel agent for the latest offerings and advice.

The two largest tour operators conducting escorted tours of Europe are **Globus/Cosmos** (© **800/338-7092;** www.globusandcosmos.com) and **Trafalgar** (www.trafalgartours.com). Both companies have first-class tours that run about $100 a day and budget tours for about $75 a day. The differences are mainly in hotel location and the number of activities. There's little difference in the companies' services, so choose your tour based on the itinerary and preferred date of departure. Brochures are available at travel agencies, and all tours must be booked through travel agents.

GETTING TO THE CONTINENT FROM THE UNITED KINGDOM

BY TRAIN Many rail passes and discounts are available in the United Kingdom for travel in continental Europe. One of the most complete overviews is available from **Rail Europe Special Services Department,** 10 Leake St., London SE1 7NN (© 0870/584-8848). This organization is particularly well versed in information about discount travel as it applies to persons under 26, full-time or part-time students, and seniors.

The most prevalent option for younger travelers, the **EuroYouth passes,** are available only to travelers under 26 and entitle the pass holder to unlimited second-class rail travel in 26 European countries.

BY CHUNNEL The Eurostar train shuttles between London and both Paris and Brussels; the trip time is less than 3 hours (compared to 10 hr. on the traditional train-ferry-train route). **Rail Europe** (© **800/361-RAIL** or 800/848-7245; www.raileurope.com) sells tickets on the Eurostar between London and Paris or Brussels (both $279 one-way).

For Eurostar reservations, call © **800/EUROSTAR** in the U.S. (www.eurostar.com), 0870/530-0003 in London, 08-36-35-35-39 in Paris. Eurostar trains arrive at/depart from Waterloo Station in London, Gare du Nord in Paris, and Central Station in Brussels.

BY FERRY & HOVERCRAFT

Brittany Ferries (© 08703/665-333; www.brittanyferries.com) is the largest British ferry/drive outfit, sailing from the southern coast of England to five destinations in Spain and France. From Portsmouth, sailings reach St-Malo and Caen; from Poole, Cherbourg. From Plymouth, sailings go to Santander in Spain. **P&O Ferries** (© 0870/520-2020; www.poferries. com) operates car and passenger ferries between Portsmouth and Cherbourg (three departures a day; 5–7 hr.); between Portsmouth and Le Havre, France (three a day; 5 hr.); and between Dover and Calais, France (25 sailings a day; 1¼ hr.).

Unless you're interested in a leisurely sea voyage, passengers without cars might be better off using the quicker, and slightly cheaper, **Hoverspeed** (© 0870/5240-241; www.hoverspeed. com). Hoverspeeds make the 35-minute crossing between Calais and Dover 7 to 15 times per day, with the more curtailed schedule in winter. Prices are £26 ($42) adults on foot or £13 ($21) children; vehicle fares are £122 to £134 ($195–$214). Prices are one-way.

BY CAR Many car-rental companies won't let you rent a car in Britain and take it to the Continent, so always check ahead. There are many "drive-on/drive-off" car-ferry services across the Channel; see "By Ferry & Hovercraft," above. There are also Chunnel trains that run a drive-on/drive-off service every 15 minutes (once an hour at night) for the 35-minute ride between Ashford and Calais.

BY COACH   Though travel by coach is considerably slower and less comfortable than travel by train, if you're on a budget you might opt for one of Eurolines's regular departures from London's Victoria Coach Station to destinations throughout Europe. Contact **Eurolines** at 52 Grosvenor Gardens, Victoria, London SW1W OAU (*©* **020/7730-8235;** www. eurolines.co.uk).

10 Getting Around

BY TRAIN

In Europe, the shortest—and cheapest—distance between two points is lined with rail tracks. European trains are less expensive than those in the United States, far more advanced in many ways, and certainly more extensive. Modern high-speed trains (130 mph) make the rails faster than the plane for short journeys, and overnight trains get you where you're going without wasting valuable daylight hours—and you save money on lodging to boot.

SOME TRAIN NOTES   Many European high-speed trains, including the popular EC (EuroCity), IC (Inter-City), and EN (EuroNight), require you to pay a **supplement** in addition to the regular ticket fare. It's included when you buy tickets but not in any rail pass, so check at the ticket window before boarding; otherwise, the conductor will sell you the supplement on the train—along with a fine. **Seat reservations** ($20–$50 or more, when a meal is included) are required on some high-speed runs—any marked with an R on a printed train schedule. You can usually reserve a seat within a few hours of departure, but be on the safe side and book your seat a few days in advance. You need to reserve any sleeping couchette or sleeping berth, too.

With two exceptions, there's no need to buy individual train tickets or make seat reservations **before you leave the United States.** However, on the high-speed Artesia run (Paris–Turin and Milan) you must buy a supplement, on which you can get a substantial discount if you have a rail pass, but only if you buy the supplement in the United States along with the pass. It's also wise to reserve a seat on the Eurostar, as England's frequent "bank holidays" (long weekends) book the train solid with Londoners taking a short vacation to Paris.

The difference between **first class** and **second class** on European trains is minor—a matter of 1 or 2 inches of extra padding and maybe a bit more elbow room. European **train stations** are usually as clean and efficient as the trains, if a bit chaotic at times. In stations you'll find posters showing the track number and timetables for regularly scheduled runs (departures are often on the yellow poster). Many stations also have tourist offices and hotel reservations desks, banks with ATMs, and newsstands where you can buy phone cards, bus and metro tickets, maps, and local English-language event magazines.

You can get many more details about train travel in Europe and automated schedule information by fax by contacting **Rail Europe** (*©* **800/848-7245;** fax 800/432-1329; www. raileurope.com). If you plan on doing a lot of train travel, consider buying the *Thomas Cook European Timetable* ($28 from travel specialty stores; or order it at © **800/ FORSYTH;** www.forsyth.com). Each country's national railway website, which includes schedules and fare information, occasionally in English, is listed at **Mercurio (http://mercurio. iet.unipi.it).**

RAIL PASSES The greatest value in European travel has always been the **rail pass,** a single ticket allowing you unlimited travel (or travel on a certain number of days) within a set time period. If you plan on going all over Europe by train, buying a rail pass will end up being much less expensive than buying individual tickets. Plus, a rail pass gives you the freedom to hop on a train whenever you feel like it, and there's no waiting in ticket lines. For more focused trips, you might want to look into national or regional passes or just buy individual tickets as you go.

Passes Available in the United States The granddaddy of passes is the **Eurailpass,** covering 17 countries (most of western Europe except Britain). It has been joined by the **Europass,** covering 5 to 12 countries (depending on which version you buy); this pass is mainly for travelers who are going to stay in the heart of western Europe.

Rail passes are available in either **consecutive-day** or **flexipass** versions (in which you have, say, 2 months in which to use 10 days of train travel). Consecutive-day passes are best for those taking the train frequently (every few days), covering a lot of ground, and making many short train hops. Flexipasses are for folks who want to range far and wide but plan on taking their time over a long trip and intend to stay in each city for a

while. If you're under 26, you can opt to buy a regular first-class pass or a second-class youth pass; if you're 26 or over, you're stuck with buying a first-class pass. Passes for kids 4 to 11 are half price, and kids under 4 travel free.

It's best to buy these passes in the United States (they're available from some major European train stations but are up to 10% more expensive). You can get them from most travel agents, but the biggest supplier is **Rail Europe** (© **800/848-7245;** www. raileurope.com), which also sells most national passes, except for a few minor British ones. The company also publishes a free annual brochure, "Europe on Track," outlining a traveler's various pass and rail options.

The rates below are for 2003; they rise each year, usually after press time, so we can't include rates for 2004 here.

Eurailpass: Consecutive-day Eurailpass at $588 for 15 days, $762 for 21 days, $946 for 1 month, $1,338 for 2 months, or 1,606 for 3 months.

Eurail Flexipass: Good for 2 months of travel at $694 for 10 days (consecutive or not) or $914 for 15 days.

Eurail Saverpass: Good for two to five people traveling together at $498 per person for 15 days, $648 for 21 days, $804 for 1 month, $1,138 for 2 months, or $1,408 for 3 months.

Eurail Saver Flexipass: Good for two to five people traveling together at $592 per person for 10 days within 2 months, or $778 per person for 15 days within 2 months.

Countries Honoring Train Passes

Eurail Countries: Austria, Belgium, Denmark, Finland, France, Germany, Greece, Hungary, Ireland, Italy, Luxembourg, the Netherlands, Norway, Portugal, Spain, Sweden, Switzerland.

ⓘ *Tips* **Train Trip Tips**

To make your train travels as pleasant as possible, remember a few general rules:

- **Hold on to your train ticket** after it's been marked or punched by the conductor. Some European railroad systems require that you present your ticket when you leave the station platform at your destination.
- While you sleep—or even nap—**be sure your valuables are in a safe place;** You might temporarily attach a small bell to each bag to warn you if someone attempts to take it. If you've left bags on a rack in the front or back of the car, consider securing them with a small bicycle chain and lock to deter thieves, who consider trains happy hunting grounds.
- Few European trains have drinking fountains, and the dining car may be closed just when you're at your thirstiest, so **take along a bottle of mineral water.** As you'll soon discover, the experienced European traveler comes loaded with hampers of food and drink and munches away throughout the trip.
- If you want to leave bags in a train station locker, **don't let anyone help you store them in it.** A favorite trick among thieves is feigned helpfulness, then pocketing the key to your locker while passing you the key to an empty one.

Eurail Youthpass: Second class pass for travelers under 26 at $414 for 15 days, $534 for 21 days, $664 for 1 month, $938 for 2 months, or $1,160 for 3 months.

Eurail Youth Flexipass: Only for travelers under 26 at $488 for 10 days of travel within 2 months or $642 for 15 days within 2 months.

Eurail Selectpass: Travelers can select three countries linked by rail or ferry out of the 17 countries covered by Eurailpass. Passes are available for 5, 6, 8, or 10 days within a 2-month period; prices vary, beginning at $356 for a 5-day pass, $542 for a 10-day pass.

EurailDrive Pass: Mixes train travel and rental cars (through Hertz or Avis) for less money than it would cost to do them separately (and one of the only ways to get around the high daily car-rental rates in Europe when you rent for less than a week). You get 4 rail days and 2 car days within a 2-month period. Prices (per person for one adult/two adults) vary with the class of the car: $452/$409 economy class, $481/$423 compact, and $496/$431 midsize. You can add up to 5 extra rail and/or car days. Extra rail days are $45 each; car days are $49 each for economy class, $64 compact, and $75 midsize. You have to reserve the first car day a week before leaving the United States but can make other reservations as you go (always subject to availability). If there are more than two adults, the extra passengers get the car portion free but must buy the 4-day rail pass for $365.

Eurail Selectpass Drive: This is a fine way to visit three to five

European countries with great flexibility. You're granted 3 days of unlimited train travel and 2 days of car rental with unlimited mileage from Avis or Hertz. You have 2 months to complete your travel, all of which is first class on the rail. Prices depend on your choice of car. Typical prices range from $291 to $331 per person based on two passengers traveling together.

There are also **national rail passes** of various kinds and **regional passes** like ScanRail (Scandinavia), BritRail (Great Britain), and the European East Pass (Austria, Czech Republic, Slovakia, Hungary, Poland). Some national passes you have to buy in the United States, some you can get on either side of the Atlantic, and still others you must buy in Europe. Remember: Seniors, students, and youths can usually get discounts on European trains—in some countries just by asking, in others by buying a discount card good for a year or for some other period of time. Rail Europe or your travel agent can fill you in on all the details.

If you plan on traveling in Great Britain, then **BritRail** (© 877/ **677-1066;** fax 877/477-1066; www. britrail.com), which specializes in rail passes for use in Great Britain, is your best bet.

Passes Available in the United Kingdom Many rail passes are available in the United Kingdom for travel in Britain and Europe.

The **InterRail Card** is the most popular rail ticket for anyone who has lived in Europe at least 6 months and is 26 or under (an over-26 version exists but offers discounts in fewer countries). It costs around £169 ($270) and is valid for 12 days, or £209 ($334) for 22 days; it entitles you to unlimited second-class travel in 28 European countries. It also gives you a 34% discount on rail travel in Britain and Northern Ireland, plus an up-to-50% discount on the rail portion of travel from London to various Continental ports, plus special rates on Eurostar trains. You'll also get a reduction (30%–50%) on most sailings to Europe and a variety of other shipping services around the Mediterranean and Scandinavia. If you're not planning to travel in 28 countries, you can buy a lower-price card for more limited travel.

For help in determining the best option for your trip and to buy tickets, stop in London at the **International Rail Centre,** in Victoria Station (© **0870/5848848**).

BY CAR

Many rental companies grant discounts if you **reserve in advance** (usually 48 hr.) from your home country. Weekly rentals are almost always less expensive than day rentals. Three or more people traveling together can usually get around cheaper by car than by train (even with rail passes).

When you reserve a car, be sure to ask if the price includes the EU value-added tax (VAT), personal accident insurance (PAI), collision-damage waiver (CDW), and any other insurance options. If not, ask what these extras cost, because at the end of your rental, they can make a big difference in your bottom line. The CDW and other insurance might be covered by your credit card if you use the card to pay for the rental; check with the card issuer to be sure.

If your credit card doesn't cover the CDW (and it probably won't in Ireland), **Travel Guard International** 1145 Clark St., Stevens Point, WI 54481 (© **800/826-1300** or 715/ 345-0505; www.travelguard.com), offers it for $7 per day. Avis and Hertz, among other companies, require that you purchase a theft-protection policy in Italy.

The Rules of the Road: Driving in Europe

- First off, know that European drivers tend to be more aggressive than their American counterparts.
- Drive on the right except in England, Scotland, and Ireland, where you drive on the left. And *do not drive* in the left lane on a four-lane highway; it is truly only for passing.
- If someone comes up from behind and flashes his lights at you, it's a signal for you to slow down and drive more on the shoulder so he can pass you more easily (2-lane roads here routinely become 3 cars wide).
- Except for the German autobahn, most highways do indeed have speed limits of around 100 to 135 kilometers per hour (60–80 mph).
- Remember that everything's measured in kilometers here (mileage and speed limits). For a rough conversion, 1 kilometer = 0.6 miles.
- Be aware that although gas may look reasonably priced, the price is per liter, and 3.8 liters = 1 gallon—so multiply by four to estimate the equivalent per-gallon price.
- Never leave anything of value in the car overnight, and don't leave anything visible any time you leave the car (this goes double in Italy, triple in Naples).

The main car-rental companies are **Avis** (© 800/331-1212; www.avis.com), **Budget** (© 800/472-3325; https://rent.drivebudget.com/Home.jsp), **SIXT** (known as Dollar in the U.S.; © 800/800-6000; www.e-sixt.com), **Hertz** (© 800/654-3131; www.hertz.com), and **National** (© 800/227-7368; www.nationalcar.com). U.S.-based companies specializing in European rentals are **Auto Europe** (© 800/223-5555; www.autoeurope.com), **Europe by Car** (© 800/223-1516, or 212/581-3040 in New York; www.europebycar.com), and **Kemwel Holiday Auto** (© 800/678-0678; www.kemwel.com). Europe by Car, Kemwel, and **Renault Eurodrive** (© 800/221-1052; www.renaultusa.com) also offer a low-cost alternative to renting for longer than 15 days: **short-term leases** in which you technically buy a fresh-from-the-factory car and then sell it back when you return it. All insurance is included, from liability and theft to personal injury and CDW, with no deductible. And unlike at many rental agencies, who won't rent to anyone under 25, the minimum age for a lease is 18.

The **AAA** supplies good maps to its members. **Michelin maps** (© 800/423-0485 or 864/458-5619; www.michelin.com) are made for the tourist. The maps rate cities as "uninteresting" (as a tourist destination); "interesting"; "worth a detour"; or "worth an entire journey." They also highlight particularly scenic stretches of road in green, and have symbols pointing out scenic overlooks, ruins, and other sights along the way.

BY PLANE

Though trains remain the cheapest and easiest way to get around in Europe, air transport options have improved drastically in the past few years. Intense competition with rail and ferry companies has slowly forced airfares into the bargain basement.

British Airways (© **800/AIRWAYS** in the U.S., or 0345/222111 in the U.K.; www.britishairways.com) and other scheduled airlines fly regularly from London to Paris for only £107 ($171) round-trip, depending on the season. Lower fares usually apply to midweek flights and carry advance-purchase requirements of 2 weeks or so.

The biggest airline news in Europe is the rise of the **no-frills airline** modeled on American upstarts like Southwest. By keeping their overheads down through electronic ticketing, forgoing meal service, and flying from less popular airports, these airlines are able to offer low fares. Most round-trip tickets are $67 to $170. This means now you can save lots of time, and even money, over long train hauls, especially from, say, London to Venice or from central Europe out to peripheral countries like Greece and Spain. Budget airlines include **EasyJet** (© **0870/6-000-000** in England; www.easyjet.com) and British Airway's subsidiary **Go** (© **1279/666-388**) in England; **Ryanair** (© **0870/ 333-1231** in England; www.ryanair. com) in Ireland; and **Virgin Express** (© **020/7744-0004;** www.virgin-express.com), an offshoot of Virgin Air, in Belgium. Be aware, though, that the names might change because these small airlines are often economically vulnerable and can fail or merge with a big airline. Still, as quickly as one disappears, another will take off.

Lower airfares are also available throughout Europe on **charter flights** rather than regularly scheduled ones. Look in local newspapers to find out about them. Consolidators cluster in cities like London and Athens.

Flying across Europe on regularly scheduled airlines can destroy a budget and be super-expensive. Whenever possible, book your total flight on one ticket before leaving. For example, if you're flying from New York to Rome, but also plan to visit Palermo, Florence, and Turin, have the total trip written up on one ticket. Don't arrive in Rome and book separate legs of the journey, which costs far more when it's done piecemeal.

Sometimes national carriers offer remarkable deals to non-European residents, which cuts the cost of flying within Europe. A good example is **Alitalia's** "Europlus." First, you have to book a transatlantic flight, perhaps from New York to Rome. After that, and for only $315, you can buy a package of three flight coupons entitling you to fly on any three flights anywhere in Europe served by Alitalia (not just Italy). You can also purchase unlimited additional tickets, one-way, for another $100 per ticket.

Another fine deal is offered in London by **Go Fly** (© **0870/607-6543** in London; www.go-fly.com), a subsidiary of British Airways. Go Fly offers 40% off standard round-trip airfares. There is a 2-night minimum stay. Sample round-trip air fares from London are as follows: Edinburgh £43 ($69), Madrid £93 ($149), and Zurich £109 ($174).

American citizens can contact **Europe by Air** (© **888/387-2479;** www.europebyair.com) for their Europe flight pass serving 30 countries, 30 airlines, and 150 European cities. It costs only $99 to travel one-way between these cities.

Because discount passes are always changing on air routes within Europe, it's best to check in with **Air Travel Advisory Bureau** in London (© **020/ 7636-5000;** www.atab.co.uk). This bureau offers a free service directory to the public for suppliers of discount airfares from all major U.K. airports.

BY BUS

Bus transportation is readily available throughout Europe; it sometimes is less expensive than train travel and covers a more extensive area but can be slower and much less comfortable.

European buses, like the trains, outshine their American counterparts, but they're perhaps best used only to pick up where the extensive train network leaves off. One major bus company serves all the countries of western Europe (no service to Greece): **Eurolines** in London (© **0870/514-3219;** www.eurolines.com), whose staff can check schedules, make reservations, and quote prices.

11 Tips on Accommodations

Traditional European hotels tend to be simpler than American ones and emphasize cleanliness and friendliness over amenities. For example, even in the cheapest American chain motel, free cable is as standard as indoor plumbing. In Europe, however, few hotels below the moderate level even have in-room TVs.

Unless otherwise noted, all hotel rooms in this book have **private en-suite bathrooms.** However, the standard European hotel bathroom might not look like what you're used to. For example, the European concept of a shower is to stick a nozzle in the bathroom wall and a drain in the floor. Shower curtains are optional. In some cramped private bathrooms, you'll have to relocate the toilet paper outside the bathroom before turning on the shower and drenching the whole room. Another interesting fixture is the "half tub," in which there's only room to sit, rather than lie down. The half tub usually sports a shower nozzle that has nowhere to hang—so your knees get very clean and the floor gets very wet. Hot water may be available only once a day and not on demand—this is especially true with shared bathrooms. Heating water is costly, and many smaller hotels do it only once daily, in the morning.

GETTING THE BEST ROOM AT THE BEST RATE

The **rack rate** is the maximum rate that a hotel charges for a room. Hardly anybody pays this price, however. To lower the cost of your room:

- **Ask about special rates or other discounts.** Always ask whether a room less expensive than the first one quoted is available, or whether any special rates apply to you. You may qualify for corporate, student, military, senior, or other discounts. Mention membership in AAA, AARP, frequent-flier programs, or trade unions, which may entitle you to special deals as well. Find out the hotel policy on children—do kids stay free in the room or is there a special rate?

- **Dial direct.** When booking a room in a chain hotel, you'll often get a better deal by calling the individual hotel's reservation desk than the chain's main number.

- **Book online.** Many hotel websites offer Internet-only discounts.

Tips Home Exchanges

Intervac U.S., 30 Coate San Fernanco, Tiburon, CA 94159 (© **800/756-HOME** or 415/435-3497; www.intervacus.com), is part of the largest worldwide home-exchange network, with a special emphasis on Europe. It publishes four catalogs a year, listing homes in more than 36 countries. Members contact each other directly. Depending on your type of membership, fees begin at $65.

> **_Tips_ A Traveler's Tip**
>
> If you call a hotel from home to reserve a room, *always follow up with a confirmation fax.* Not only is it what most hotels prefer, but it is also printed proof you've booked a room. Keep the language simple—state your name, number of people, what kind of room (like "double with bathroom and one bed" or "double with bathroom and two beds"), how many nights you'd like to stay, and the starting date for the first night. Remember that Europeans abbreviate dates day/month/year, not month/day/year.

- **Look into group or long-stay discounts.** If you come as part of a large group, you should be able to negotiate a bargain rate, since the hotel can then guarantee occupancy in a number of rooms. Likewise, if you're planning a long stay (at least 5 days), you might qualify for a discount. As a general rule, expect 1 night free after a 7-night stay.

- **Investigate reservations services.** These outfits usually work as consolidators, buying up or reserving rooms in bulk, and then dealing them out to customers at a profit. You can get 10% to 50% off; but remember, these discounts apply to inflated rack rates that savvy travelers rarely end up paying. You may get a decent rate, but always call the hotel as well to see if you can do better. Among the more reputable reservations services, offering both telephone and online bookings, are: **Accommodations Express** (✆ **800/950-4685;** www.accommodationsexpress.com); **Hotels.Com** (✆ **800/715-7666;** www.hotels.com or www.180096 HOTEL.com); and **Quikbook** (✆ **800/789-9887;** includes fax

on demand service; www.quikbook.com). Online, try booking your hotel through **Frommers.com** (www.frommers.com). **Microsoft Expedia** (www.expedia.com) features a "Travel Agent" that will also direct you to affordable lodgings.

HOTEL BOOKING SERVICES

When you arrive in town, you'll find that a desk in the train station or at the tourist office (or both) acts as a central hotel reservations service for the city. Tell them your price range, where you'd like to be in the city, and sometimes even the style of hotel, and they'll use a computer database to find you a room in town.

The advantages of booking services are that they do all the room-finding work for you—for a nominal fee—and always speak English, while individual hoteliers may not. When every hotel in town seems to be booked up (during a convention or festival or just in high season), they can often find space for you at inns not listed in guidebooks or other main sources. On the downside, hotels in many countries often charge higher rates to people booking through such a service.

1

Austria

by Darwin Porter & Danforth Prince

Austria stands at the crossroads of Europe, as it did in the heyday of the Austro-Hungarian Empire. Its capital, Vienna, stranded during the postwar years on the edge of western Europe, is taking its place again as an important international city.

The country offers a lot to do, from exploring historic castles and palaces to skiing on some of the world's finest alpine slopes.

1 Vienna ★★★

Vienna still retains much of the glory and grandeur of the empire's heady days. Museum treasures from all over Europe, baroque palaces through which Maria Theresa and her brood wandered, Johann Strauss's lively music, Gustav Klimt's paintings, the concert halls, the unparalleled opera—it's all still here, as if the empire were still flourishing.

Tourism is growing as thousands arrive every year to view Vienna's great art and architecture, to feast on lavish Viennese pastries, to explore the Vienna Woods, to sail down the Danube, to attend Vienna's balls, operas, and festivals, and to listen to the "music that never stops."

Visitors today face a newer and brighter Vienna, a city with more joie de vivre and punch than it's had since before the war. There's also a downside: Prices are on the rise—they haven't reached the height of the Ferris wheel at the Prater, but they're climbing there.

ESSENTIALS

GETTING THERE   By Plane   Vienna International Airport (VIE; ⓒ 01/ 70070; http://english.viennaairport.com) is about 19km (12 miles) southeast of the city center. There's regular bus service between the airport and the **City Air Terminal,** adjacent to the Vienna Hilton and directly across from the **Wien Mitte/Landstrasse** rail station, where you can easily connect with subway and tram lines. Buses run every 20 minutes from 6:30am to 11:30pm, and hourly from midnight to 5am. The trip takes about 25 minutes and costs 5€ per person. Tickets are sold on the bus and must be purchased with Austrian money. There's also bus service between the airport and two railroad stations, the Westbahnhof and the Südbahnhof, leaving every 30 minutes to an hour. Fares are also 5€.

There's also local train service, Schnellbahn (S-Bahn), between the airport and the Wien Nord and Wien Mitte rail stations. Trains run hourly from 4:30am to 9:30pm and leave from the basement of the airport. Trip time is 40 to 45 minutes, and the fare is 3€.

The official **Vienna Tourist Information Office** in the arrival hall of the airport is open daily: October through May from 9am to 10pm and June through September from 8:30am to 9pm.

By Train   Vienna has four principal rail stations, with frequent connections from all Austrian cities and towns and from all major European cities. For train information for all stations, call 𝄢 **05/1717.**

Westbahnhof (West Railway Station), on Europaplatz, is for trains arriving from western Austria, France, Germany, Switzerland, and some eastern European countries. It has frequent links to major Austrian cities such as Salzburg, which is a 3-hour train ride from Vienna. The Westbahnhof connects with local trains, the U3 and U6 underground lines, and several tram and bus routes.

Südbahnhof (South Railway Station), on Südtirolerplatz, has train service to southern and eastern Austria, Italy, Hungary, Slovenia, and Croatia. It is linked with local rail service and tram and bus routes.

Both of these stations house useful travel agencies (**Österreichisches Verkehrsbüro**) that provide tourist information and help with hotel reservations. In the Westbahnhof the agency is in the upper hall and at the Südbahnhof, in the lower hall.

Other stations in Vienna include **Franz-Josef Bahnhof,** on Franz-Josef-Platz, used mainly by local trains, although connections are made here to Prague and Berlin. You can take the D-tram line to the city's Ringstrasse from here. **Wien Mitte,** at Landstrasser Hauptstrasse 1, is also a terminus for local trains, plus a depot for trains to the Czech Republic and to Vienna International Airport.

By Bus   The **City Bus Terminal** is at the Wien Mitte rail station, Landstrasser Hauptstrasse 1. This is the arrival depot for Post buses and Bundesbuses from points all over the country, and also the arrival point for private buses from various European cities. The terminal has lockers, currency-exchange kiosks, and a ticket counter open daily from 6:15am to 6pm. For bus information, call 𝄢 **05/1717** daily from 6:15am to 6pm.

By Car   You can reach Vienna from all directions via major highways (*Autobahnen*) or by secondary highways. The main artery from the west is Autobahn

    ## Native Behavior

Get accustomed to hearing *Grüss Gott* (God bless you) when Austrians greet you and *Auf Wiedersehen* when they leave. These greetings are practiced by everybody from your hotel manager to the shoeshine man.

Although no one will kick you off the premises, it is a local custom to dress up for a night at the opera or ballet. You can show up in a jogging suit or jeans but you might feel out of place.

Austria is perhaps the most formal of the countries reviewed in this guide. Yes, some gents nostalgic for the old Austro-Hungarian Empire still bow and click their heels when introduced to a lady. Prepare to shake hands on both meeting and parting. The Austrians are great sticklers for titles, however minor or honorific, including *Doktor* or *Professor.*

If you've never hung out in coffeehouses before, making it your second living room, Austria is a wonderful introduction to this custom. The Viennese especially can sit for hour after hour over a single cup of coffee reading magazines and newspapers or else watching the world parade by.

A1, coming in from Munich 468km (291 miles), Salzburg 336km (209 miles), and Linz 187km (116 miles). Autobahn A2 arrives from the south, from Graz 200km (124 miles) and Klagenfurt 309km (192 miles). Autobahn A4 comes in from the east, connecting with Route E58, which runs to Bratislava and Prague. Autobahn A22 takes traffic from the northwest, and Route E10 connects to the cities and towns of southeastern Austria and Hungary.

VISITOR INFORMATION **Tourist Office** The official **Wien Tourist-Information,** Albertinaplatz 7 (© **01/211-14-481;** www.info.wien.at), is open daily from 9am to 7pm. You can make room reservations here.

Websites Besides Wien Tourist-Information **(www.info.wien.at),** go to the Austrian National Tourist Office **(www.austria-tourism.at/us)** for current information on culture and events.

CITY LAYOUT Vienna has evolved into one of the largest metropolises of central Europe, with a surface area covering 415 sq. km (160 sq. miles). It's divided into 23 districts *(Bezirke),* each identified by a Roman numeral.

The size and shape of the **First District,** known as the **Innere Stadt (Inner City),** roughly corresponds to the original borders of the medieval city. Other than the Cathedral of St. Stephan, very few Gothic or medieval buildings remain—many were reconstructed in the baroque or neoclassical style, whereas others are modern replacements of buildings bombed during World War II. As Austria's commercial and cultural nerve center, the central district contains dozens of streets devoted exclusively to pedestrian traffic. The most famous of these is **Kärntnerstrasse,** which bypasses the Vienna State Opera House during its southward trajectory toward the province of Carinthia (Kärnten).

Ringstrasse is a circular boulevard about 4km (2½ miles) long whose construction between 1859 and 1888 was one of the most ambitious (and controversial) examples of urban restoration in the history of central Europe. The boulevard surrounds the Inner City. Confusingly, the name of this boulevard changes many times during its encirclement of the Inner City. Names that apply to it carry the suffix *-ring:* for example, Opernring, Schottenring, Burgring, Dr.-Karl-Lueger-Ring, Stubenring, Parkring, Schubertring, and Kärntner Ring.

Vienna

ACCOMMODATIONS

Drei Kronen **4**
Grand Hotel Wien **19**
Hotel Astoria **16**
Hotel Bristol **20**
Hotel Das Triest **25**
Hotel Imperial **21**
Hotel Kaiserin Elisabeth **23**
Hotel Kärntnerhof **29**

Hotel König Von Ungarn **28**
Hotel Royal **24**
Hotel Sacher Wien **17**

Vienna ✷
● Salzburg
AUSTRIA

✝ Church
✉ Post Office
ⓘ Information
⋯⋯ Railway
⚋ ⚋ Ⓤ U-Bahn

Surrounding Ringstrasse and the Inner City, in a more or less clockwise direction, are the inner suburban districts (2–9), which contain many hotels and restaurants popular for their close proximity to the city center. The outer districts (10–23) form another concentric ring of suburbs, comprising a variety of neighborhoods from industrial parks to rural villages.

Northeast of the Inner City, beyond the Danube Canal, is the **2nd District,** home to the famous amusement park, the Prater. East of the center, in the **3rd District,** you'll find the art treasures and baroque setting of the Belvedere Palace. West of the center is Schönbrunn Palace.

GETTING AROUND   By Public Transportation   Wiener Verkehrsbetriebe (Vienna Transport), with its network of facilities covering hundreds of miles, can take you where you want to go—by U-Bahn (subway), tram (streetcar), or bus. **Informationdienst der Wiener Verkehrsbetriebe (Vienna Public Transport Information Center)** has five locations: Opernpassage (an underground passageway adjacent to the Wiener Staatsoper), Karlsplatz, Stephansplatz (near Vienna's cathedral), Westbahnhof, and Praterstern. For information about any of these outlets, call © **01/790-9105.**

Vienna maintains a uniform fare that applies to all forms of public transport. A ticket for the bus, subway, or tram will cost 1.50€ if you buy it in advance at a Tabac-Trafiks (a store or kiosk selling tobacco products and newspapers) or 2€ if you buy it on board. Smart Viennese buy their tickets in advance, usually in blocks of at least five at a time, from any of the city's thousands of Tabac-Trafiks or at any of the public transport centers noted above. No matter what vehicle you decide to ride within Vienna, remember that once a ticket has been stamped (validated) by either a machine or a railway attendant, it's valid for one trip in one direction, anywhere in the city, including transfers.

By U-Bahn (Subway)   The U-Bahn consists of five lines labeled as U1, U2, U3, U4, and U6 (there is no U5). Karlsplatz, in the heart of the Inner City, is the most important underground station for visitors, as the U1, U2, and U4 converge here. The U2 traces part of the Ring, the U4 goes to Schönbrunn, and the U1 stops in Stephansplatz. The U3 also stops in Stephansplatz and connects with the Westbahnhof. The U-Bahn runs daily from 6am to midnight.

Value **The Vienna Card**

The **Vienna Card** gives you access to all public modes of transportation (subway, bus, and tram) within Vienna—as well as discounts in city museums, shops, and restaurants—for a single discounted price. A 24-hour network pass costs 5€ and is good for a full day of public transport. A 72-hour network pass sells for 12€. There's also a green ticket, priced at 24€, that contains eight individual partitions. Each of these, when stamped, is good for 1 day of unlimited travel. An individual can opt to reserve all eight of the partitions for his or her own use, thereby gaining 8 days of cost-effective travel on the city's transport system. Or the partitions can be subdivided among a group of several riders, allowing—for example—two persons 4 days each of unlimited rides. Vienna Cards are easy to find throughout the capital, or you can buy one outside Vienna by calling © **01/7984-40028** with a credit card.

By Bus Buses traverse Vienna in all directions and operate Monday through Saturday from 6am to 10pm and Sunday from 6am to 8pm. Bus nos. 1A, 2A, and 3A will get you around the Inner City. Convenient night buses are available on weekends and holidays starting at 12:15am. They go from Schwedensplatz to the outer suburbs (including Grinzing). Normal tickets are not valid on these late "N" buses. Instead, you pay a special fare of 1.50€ on board.

By Tram Riding the red-and-white trams *(Strassenbahn)* is not only a practical way to get around, it's a great way to see the city. Tram stops are well marked and lines are labeled as numbers or letters. Lines 1 and 2 will bring you to all the major sights on the Ringstrasse. Line D skirts the outer Ring and goes to the Süd-bahnhof, whereas line 18 goes between the Westbanhof and the Südbahnhof.

By Taxi Taxi stands are marked by signs, or you can call for a radio cab by phoning ② **31300**, 60160, 81400, 91011, or 40100. Fares are indicated on an officially calibrated taximeter. The basic fare is 4€, plus 1.10€ per kilometer.

There's an extra charge of 1€ for luggage carried in the trunk. For rides after 11pm, and for trips on Sunday and holidays, there's a surcharge of 1€. There is an additional charge of 2€ if the taxi is ordered by phone.

By Car   Major car-rental companies operating in Vienna include **Avis,** Opernring 3–5 (**℃ 800/654-3001** in the U.S., or 01/700-732-700 in Vienna; U-Bahn: Karlsplatz); **Budget Rent-a-Car,** Hilton Air Terminal (**℃ 800/472-3325** in the U.S., or 01/714-6565 in Vienna; U-Bahn: Landstrasse/Wien Mitte); and **Hertz,** in the Marriott Hotel, Parkring 12A (**℃ 01/512-8677**).

By Bicycle   Vienna has more than 250km (155 miles) of marked bicycle paths within the city limits. In the summer, many Viennese leave their cars in the garage and ride bikes. You can take bicycles on specially marked U-Bahn cars for free, but only Monday through Friday from 9am to 3pm and 6:30pm to midnight. On weekends in July and August bicycles are carried free from 9am to midnight.

Rental stores abound at the Prater and along the banks of the Danube Canal, which is the favorite bike route for most Viennese. One of the best of the many sites specializing in bike rentals is **Pedalpower,** Ausstellungsstrasse 3 (**℃ 01/729-7234**), which is open May through October from 9am to 8pm. The Vienna Tourist Board can also supply a list of rental shops and more information about bike paths. Bike rentals begin at about 27€ per day.

 ***FAST FACTS:* Vienna**

American Express   The office at Kärntnerstrasse 21–23 (℃ 01/51540-770), near Stock-im-Eisenplatz, is open Monday through Friday from 9am to 5:30pm and Saturday from 9am to noon.

Business Hours   Most shops are open Monday through Friday from 9am to 6pm and Saturday from 9am to noon, 12:30pm, or 1pm, depending on the store. On the first Saturday of every month, shops customarily remain open until 4:30 or 5pm. The tradition is called *langer Samstag.*

City Code   The telephone city code for Vienna is **01.** It is only used when you're calling from outside Vienna.

Currency Exchange   During off-hours you can exchange money at *bureaux de change* (exchange bureaus) throughout the Inner City (there's one at the intersection of Kohlmarkt and the Graben), as well as at travel agencies, train stations, and the airport. There's also a 24-hour exchange service at the post office (Hauptpostamt) at Fleischmarkt 19.

Dentists/Doctors   For dental problems, call ℃ **01/512-2078.** A list of physicians can be found in the telephone directory under *Arzte.* If you have a medical emergency at night, call ℃ **141** daily from 7pm to 7am.

Drugstores   Called *Apotheke,* they're open Monday through Friday from 8am to noon and 2 to 6pm and Saturday from 8am to noon. Each Apotheke posts in its window a list of shops that take turns staying open at night and on Sunday.

Embassies/Consulates   The embassy of the **United States** is at Boltzmanngasse 16, A-1090 Vienna (℃ **01/31339;** U-Bahn: Stadtpark). The consular section, Gartenbaupromenade 2–4, A-1010 Vienna (© **01/31339**), handles lost passports, tourist emergencies, and other matters. Both are open Monday through Friday from 8:30am to noon and 1 to 4pm.

The embassy of **Canada,** Laurenzerberg 2 (© **01/531-380**), is open Monday through Friday from 8:30am to 12:30pm and 1:30 to 3:30pm. The embassy of the **United Kingdom,** Jauresgasse 12 (© **01/71613-0**), is open Monday through Friday from 9am to 1pm and 2 to 4pm. The embassy of **Australia,** Mattiellistrasse 2–4 (© **01/50674**), is open Monday through Thursday from 8:30am to 1pm and 2 to 5:30pm, Friday from 8:30am to 1:15pm. The embassy of **New Zealand,** Springsiedelgasse 28 (© **01/318-8505**), is open Monday through Friday from 8:30am to 5pm, but it's best to call to see if it's actually open. The embassy of **Ireland,** at Hilton Center, Landstrasser Hauptstrasse 2 (© **01/715-4246**), is open Monday though Friday from 9 to 11:30am and 1:30 to 4pm.

Emergencies Call © **122** to report a fire, © **133** for the police, or © **144** for an ambulance.

Internet Access **Café Stein,** Währingerstrasse 6 (© **01/319-72-41**), offers Internet access at the rate of 3€ every half hour and is open daily from 5 to 11pm.

Police The emergency number is © **133.**

Post Office Post offices in Vienna can be found in the heart of every district. Addresses for these can be found in the telephone directory under "Post." Post offices are generally open for mail services Monday through Friday from 8am to noon and 2 to 6pm. The central post office (Hauptpostamt), Barbaragasse 2 (© **01/515090**), and most general post offices are open 24 hours a day, 7 days a week.

Safety In recent years, Vienna has been plagued by purse-snatchers. Small foreign children often approach sympathetic adults and ask for money. As the adult goes for his wallet or her purse, full-grown thieves rush in and grab the money, fleeing with it. Unaccompanied women should hold onto their purses tightly, and never open them in public.

Telephone The **country code** for Austria is **43.** The **city code** for Vienna is **1;** use this code when you're calling from outside Austria. If you're within Austria, use **01** before the local number (01 is included in all telephone numbers in this chapter, so it is not necessary to add any other numbers when calling these telephone numbers within Austria).

Hotels add huge surcharges to long-distance calls; go to the post office instead. Consider purchasing a **phone card** at any post office. **International direct dial** numbers include **AT&T** (© **022-90-30-11**); **MCI** (© **022-90-30-12**); and **Sprint** (© **0800-20-02-36**).

Tipping A service charge of 10% to 15% is included on hotel and restaurant bills, but it's a good policy to leave something extra for waiters and 1.85€ per day for your hotel maid. Railroad station, airport, and hotel porters get 1.45€ per piece of luggage, plus a .75€ tip. Tip your hairdresser 10% of the bill, and give the shampoo person a 1.45€ gratuity. Toilet attendants are usually given .35€, and coat-check attendants expect .50€ to 1.10€.

WHERE TO STAY
INNERE STADT (INNER CITY)
Very Expensive

Grand Hotel Wien ☆☆☆   Some of the most discerning hotel guests in Europe, often music lovers, prefer this seven-story deluxe hotel to the more traditional and famous Imperial or Bristol. Only a block from the Staatsoper, it's a honey. You enter a world of beveled mirrors, crystal chandeliers, and a grand staircase. The spacious accommodations are posh, with all the modern extras such as heated floors, phones in the marble bathrooms, and even "anti-fog" mirrors. The more expensive units have more elaborate furnishings and decoration, including delicate stuccowork.

Kärnter Ring 9, A-1010 Vienna. ✆ **01/515-800.** Fax 01/515-13-13. http://grandhotelwien.com. 205 units. 370€–450€ double; from 660€ suite. AE, DC, MC, V. U-Bahn: Karlsplatz. **Amenities:** 3 restaurants; 2 bars; fitness center; boutiques; salon; room service; massage; babysitting; laundry/dry cleaning service. *In room:* A/C, TV, minibar, coffeemaker, hair dryer, safe.

Hotel Bristol ☆☆☆   This six-story landmark is a superb choice—only the Imperial is grander. When it was constructed in 1894 across the street from the State Opera, it was the ultimate in luxury style, but it's been updated to give guests the benefit of black-tiled bathrooms equipped with tub/shower combos and modern conveniences. Rooms are sumptuously appointed. The club floor offers luxurious comfort, enhanced by period furnishings. Corkscrew columns of rare marble grace the Korso, Bristol's restaurant, which is one of the best in Vienna.

Kärntner Ring 1, A-1015 Vienna. ✆ **888/625-5144** in the U.S., or 01/515-160. Fax 01/515-16-550. www.westin.com/bristol. 146 units. 208€–345€ double; from 590€ suite. AE, DC, MC, V. Parking 28€. U-Bahn: Karlsplatz. Tram: 1 or 2. **Amenities:** 2 restaurants; bar; fitness center; sauna; room service; babysitting; laundry/dry cleaning service. *In room:* A/C, TV, minibar, hair dryer, safe.

Hotel Imperial ☆☆☆   This hotel is Vienna's grandest and the most "imperial" looking in Austria, 2 blocks from the State Opera and 1 block from the Musikverein. The hotel was built in 1869 as a private residence and was converted into a private hotel in 1873. Everything is outlined against a background of polished marble, crystal chandeliers, Gobelin tapestries, and fine rugs. Some of the royal suites are palatial, but all rooms are soundproof and generally spacious, with deluxe full bathrooms. The Hotel Imperial Restaurant is a fabled turn-of-the-20th-century restaurant.

Kärntner Ring 16, A-1015 Vienna. ✆ **800/325-3589** in the U.S., or 01/501100. Fax 01/5011-0410. www.luxurycollection.com/imperial. 138 units. 510€–625€ double; from 880€ suite. AE, DC, MC, V. Parking 30€. U-Bahn: Karlsplatz. **Amenities:** 2 restaurants; bar; health club; sauna; room service; massage; babysitting; laundry/dry cleaning service. *In room:* A/C, TV, hair dryer, safe.

Hotel Sacher Wien ☆☆☆   Much of the glory of the Hapsburgs is still evoked by the public rooms here, although the hotel is no longer the grandest in Vienna, having lost out to the Bristol or Imperial. The red velvet, crystal chandeliers, and brocaded curtains are reminiscent of Old Vienna. The hotel is popular with groups, however, and the heavy traffic is taking a toll. The reception desk is fairly flexible about making arrangements for salons or apartments, or joining two rooms together. Rooms near the top are small with cramped bathrooms, but most accommodations are generous in size and often have sitting areas and midsize marble bathrooms with shower-tub combinations.

Philharmonikerstrasse 4, A-1010 Vienna. ✆ **01/514560.** Fax 01/512-56-810. www.sacher.com. 112 units. 294€–633€ double; from 989€ suite. AE, DC, MC, V. Parking 29€. U-Bahn: Karlsplatz. Tram: 1, 2, 62, 65, D, or J. Bus: 4A. **Amenities:** 2 restaurants; bar; fitness center; room service; massage; babysitting; laundry/dry cleaning service. *In room:* A/C, TV, minibar, hair dryer, safe.

EXPENSIVE

Hotel Astoria ⭐ This landmark is for nostalgia buffs who want to recall the grand life of the closing days of the Austro-Hungarian Empire. A first-class hotel, the Astoria has a desirable location on the shopping mall close to St. Stephan's Cathedral and the State Opera. Decorated in a slightly frayed late-19th-century style, the hotel offers well-appointed and traditionally decorated rooms. The interior rooms tend to be too dark, and singles are just too cramped. It was most recently renovated in 1996, but the old style has been respected. Bathrooms are luxurious with dual basins, shower-tub combos, and heated racks.

Kärntnerstrasse 32–34, A-1015 Vienna. ℂ **01/515770.** Fax 01/515-7782. www.austria-trend.at. 118 units. 190€–212€ double; 292€ suite. Rates include breakfast. AE, DC, MC, V. Parking 22€. U-Bahn: Stephansplatz. **Amenities:** Restaurant; bar; room service; babysitting; laundry/dry cleaning service. *In room:* TV, minibar, hair dryer, safe.

Hotel Das Triest ⭐⭐ *Finds* Sir Terence Conran, the famous English architect and designer, has created the interior decoration for this contemporary hotel in the center of Vienna, a 5-minute walk from St. Stephan's Cathedral. Conran has done for Das Triest what Philippe Starck did for New York's Paramount Hotel—created a stylish address in the heart of one of the world's most important cities. An emerging favorite with artists and musicians, this hip hotel has such grace notes as a courtyard garden. Its old cross-vaulted rooms, which give the structure a distinctive flair, have been transformed into lounges and suites. Guest rooms are midsize to spacious, tastefully furnished, and comfortable. The white-tiled bathrooms have heated racks, shower-tub combinations, deluxe toiletries, and vanity mirrors. In the afternoon some guests gather for tea in front of the cozy fireplace.

Wiedner Hauptstrasse 12, A-1040 Vienna. ℂ **01/589-18.** Fax 01/589-18-18. www.nethotels.com/das_triest. 73 units. 245€ double; from 299€ suite. Rates include buffet breakfast. AE, DC, MC, V. Parking 21€. U-Bahn: Stephansplatz. **Amenities:** Restaurant; bar; fitness center; sauna; salon; room service; massage; babysitting; laundry/dry cleaning service. *In room:* A/C, TV, minibar, hair dryer, safe.

Hotel König Von Ungarn ⭐ In a choice site on a narrow street near the cathedral, this hotel has been in the business for more than 4 centuries and is Vienna's oldest continuously operated accommodation. It's an evocative, intimate, and cozy retreat in an early-17th-century building, once a pied-à-terre for Hungarian noble families visiting the Austrian capital. Everywhere you look you'll find low-key luxury, tradition, and modern convenience. Mozart reportedly lived here in 1791. Guest rooms have been newly remodeled with Biedermeier accents and traditional furnishings. Most bathrooms are generous in size and have dual basins, shower-tub combinations, and tiled walls. The professional staff is highly efficient, keeping the hotel spotless. The hotel restaurant is one of Vienna's finest.

Schulerstrasse 10, A-1010 Vienna. ℂ **01/515840.** Fax 01/515848. www.kvu.at. 33 units. 182€ double; 210€–290€ apt. Rates include breakfast. AE, DC, MC, V. U-Bahn: Stephansplatz. **Amenities:** Restaurant; bar; room service; babysitting; laundry/dry cleaning service. *In room:* A/C, TV, minibar, hair dryer, safe.

Moderate

Hotel Kaiserin Elisabeth ⭐ This yellow-stoned hotel is conveniently located near the cathedral. The interior is decorated with Oriental rugs on well-maintained marble and wood floors. The small, quiet rooms have been considerably updated since Wolfgang Mozart, Richard Wagner, Franz Liszt, and Edvard Grieg stayed here, and their musical descendents continue to patronize the place. Polished wood, clean linen, and perhaps another Oriental rug grace each guest room. Bathrooms are a bit cramped, but they are tiled and equipped with shower-tub combinations and vanity mirrors.

Weihburggasse 3, A-1010 Vienna. © **01/515260.** Fax 01/515267. kaiserin@ins.at. 63 units. 193€ double; 215€ suite. Rates include buffet breakfast. AE, DC, MC, V. Parking 25€. U-Bahn: Stephansplatz. **Amenities:** Restaurant; bar; room service; laundry/dry cleaning service. *In room:* A/C, TV, minibar, hair dryer, safe.

Hotel Royal 🌟🌟   The lobby of this hotel less than a block from St. Stephan's contains the piano where Wagner composed *Die Meistersinger von Nürnberg.* Each good-size room is furnished differently, in a style influenced by 19th-century Italy, with some good reproductions of antiques and an occasional original. The entire facility was built in 1960 and reconstructed in 1982. Try for a room with a balcony and a view of the cathedral. Corner rooms with spacious foyers are also desirable, although those facing the street tend to be noisy. Most bathrooms have both tub and shower.

Singerstrasse 3, A-1010 Vienna. © **01/515680.** Fax 01/513-9696. 81 units. 127€–167€ double; 211€ suite. Rates include breakfast. AE, DC, MC, V. U-Bahn: Stephansplatz. **Amenities:** Restaurant; bar; room service; laundry/dry cleaning. *In room:* TV, minibar, hair dryer.

Inexpensive

Drei Kronen 🌟   The celebrated architect Ignaz Drapala designed this splendid Art Nouveau building in a charming section of Vienna close to the famous Naschmarkt. The hotel enjoys one of Vienna's best locations, close to such monuments as the Vienna State Opera and St. Stephan's Cathedral. The midsize to spacious guest rooms are fresh and bright, with comfortable furnishings along with immaculate bathrooms with shower. Some of the rooms are large enough to contain three beds.

Schleifmuehlgasse 25, A-1040 Vienna. © **01/587-3289.** Fax 01/710-1920. http://vienna.nethotels.com/ nethotels/deutsch/hotels/drei_kronen/default.htm. 41 units. 72€–101€ double; 91€ triple. Rates include breakfast buffet. AE, DC, MC, V. Parking 13€. U-Bahn: Karlsplatz. **Amenities:** Breakfast room; lounge; babysitting. *In room:* TV, safe in some.

Hotel Kärntnerhof 🌟 *(Kids*   A 4-minute walk from the cathedral, the Kärntnerhof advertises itself as a family-oriented hotel. The decor of the public areas is tastefully arranged around Oriental rugs, well-upholstered chairs and couches with cabriole legs, and an occasional 19th-century portrait. The midsize rooms are more up-to-date, usually with the original parquet floors and striped or patterned wallpaper set off by curtains. The small private bathrooms glisten with tile walls and floors; about half of them contain shower-tub combinations.

Grashofgasse 4, A-1011 Vienna. © **01/512-1923.** Fax 01/5132-22833. www.karntnerhof.com. 44 units. 105€–143€ double; 180€–225€ suite. Rates include buffet breakfast. AE, DC, MC, V. Parking 16€. U-Bahn: Stephansplatz. **Amenities:** Breakfast room; lounge; room service; laundry/dry cleaning service. *In room:* TV.

Hotel Pension Suzanne 🌟 *(Kids*   Only a 45-second walk from the opera house, this is a real discovery. Once you get past its postwar facade, the interior warms considerably, brightly decorated in a comfortable, traditional style, with antique beds, plush chairs, and the original molded ceilings. Rooms are midsize and exceedingly well maintained, either facing the busy street or else a courtyard. Families often stay here because some accommodations contain three beds. A number of guest rooms are like small apartments with kitchenettes. Each unit comes with a private bathroom with a shower-tub combination.

Walfischgasse 4. © **01/513-25-07.** Fax 01/513-25-00. www.pension-suzanne.at. 26 units. 83€–108€ double; 105€ double with kitchenette; 99€–139€ triple. Rates include continental breakfast. AE, DC, MC, V. U-Bahn: Karlsplatz. **Amenities:** Breakfast room; lounge; babysitting. *In room:* TV, hair dryer.

WHERE TO DINE
INNERE STADT (INNER CITY)
Very Expensive

Drei Husaren ✸✸✸ VIENNESE/INTERNATIONAL   Just off Kärntner-strasse, this enduring favorite—a Viennese landmark since 1935—serves an inventive and classic Viennese cuisine. To the music of Gypsy melodies, you'll dine on such stellar dishes as freshwater salmon with pike soufflé, mussel soup, breast of guinea fowl, an array of sole dishes, and longtime favorites like *Tafelspitz* (boiled beef). The chef specializes in veal, including his deliciously flavored *Kalbsbrücken Metternich*. The place is justifiably celebrated for its repertoire of more than 35 hors d'oeuvres, which are rolled around the dining room on four separate carts.

Weihburggasse 4. ✆ 01/512-1092. Reservations required. Main courses 16€–32€; *menu dégustation* (6 courses) 62€; 4-course fixed-price business lunch 32€. AE, DC, MC, V. Daily noon–3pm and 6pm–1am. U-Bahn: Stephansplatz.

König von Ungarn (King of Hungary) ✸ VIENNESE/INTERNATIONAL   This beautifully decorated restaurant is inside the famous hotel of the same name. Food is well prepared but traditional—not at all experimental. You dine under a vaulted ceiling in an atmosphere of crystal, chandeliers, antiques, and marble columns. If you're in doubt about what to order, try the *Tafelspitz*, a savory boiled-beef specialty elegantly dispensed from a cart. Other seasonal choices include a ragout of seafood with fresh mushrooms, tournedos of beef with a mustard-and-horseradish sauce, and appetizers like scampi in caviar sauce. The service is superb.

Schulerstrasse 10. ✆ 01/512-5319. Reservations required. Main courses 14€–18€; fixed-price menu 34€ lunch, 39€ dinner. AE, DC, MC, V. Mon–Fri noon–2:30pm and 6–10:30pm. U-Bahn: Stephansplatz. Bus: 1A.

Korso bei der Oper ✸✸✸ VIENNESE/INTERNATIONAL   This chic and glittering choice is decorated with tasteful paneling, sparkling chandeliers, and, flanking either side of a baronial fireplace, two of the most breathtaking baroque columns in Vienna. The kitchen concocts an alluring mixture of traditional and modern cuisine for discriminating palates. Your meal may feature filet of char with a sorrel sauce, saddle of veal with cèpe mushrooms and homemade noodles, or the inevitable *Tafelspitz* (boiled beef). The rack of lamb is excellent, as are the medallions of beef with a shallot-infused butter sauce and Roquefort-flavored noodles. The wine list is extensive.

In the Hotel Bristol, Kärntneering 1. ✆ 01/5151-6546. Reservations required. Main courses 23€–36€; fixed-price menu 38€ lunch, 72€ dinner. AE, DC, MC, V. Sun–Fri noon–2pm; daily 7–11pm. U-Bahn: Karlsplatz. Tram: 1 or 2.

Mörwald ✸✸✸ VIENNESE   In the Hotel Ambassador, this is the most stylish and one of the best restaurants in Vienna. Bankers, diplomats, and what one local food critic called "Helmut Lang–clad hipsters" show up here to see and be seen, but also to enjoy the delectable modern Viennese cuisine of Christian Domschitz. He's shown a genius for giving classic Viennese dishes a modern twist. Prepared with élan and precision, some of his best dishes include saddle of suckling pig with white cabbage dumplings, veal meatloaf with puréed spring onions, and a spicy brook char, one of the better fish offerings. You might start with his velvety smooth foie gras in Kirschwasser. For dessert, we recommend the diced semolina pancakes.

In the Hotel Ambassador, Kärntner Strasse 22. ✆ 01/961-61-0. www.ambassador.at. Reservations required. Main courses 21€–27€. Mon–Sat noon–3pm and 6:30–11pm. AE, DC, MC, V. U-Bahn: Stephansplatz.

Sacher Hotel Restaurant ✿ AUSTRIAN/INTERNATIONAL This is a long-enduring favorite for pre- or post-opera dining. It seems like all celebrities who come to Vienna eventually are seen either in the Red Bar, with its adjacent dining room, where live piano music is presented every evening from 7pm to midnight, or in the brown-and-white Anna Sacher Room, the site of many a high-powered meal. There's no better place in Vienna to sample the restaurant's most famous dish, *Tafelspitz,* the Viennese boiled-beef platter that's fit for an emperor. The chef serves it with a savory, herb-flavored sauce. Other delectable dishes include fish terrine and veal steak with morels. For dessert, the Sacher torte enjoys world renown. It's primarily a chocolate sponge cake that's sliced in half and filled with apricot jam. This most famous of pastries in Vienna was supposedly created in 1832 by Franz Sacher when he served as Prince Metternich's apprentice.

Philharmonikerstrasse 4. ⓒ **01/514560.** Reservations required. Main courses 18€–29€. AE, DC, MC, V. Daily noon–3pm and 6–11:30pm. U-Bahn: Karlsplatz.

Expensive

Dö & Co ✿ CONTINENTAL/INTERNATIONAL Stylish, upscale, and rather expensive, this restaurant is owned by one of Austria's most esoteric food stores. Its location is on the seventh floor of the aggressively ultra-modern Haas Haus, which stands in jarring proximity to Vienna's cathedral. Menu items change with the season, but considering the rarefied nature of the organization presenting it, each is appropriately rare, and unusual. Examples include Uruguayan beef; Austrian venison; grilled baby turbot from the coast of Norway; deep-fried monkfish; and carpaccio "Parmigiana," as well as traditional Austrian specialties. There's also a repertoire of Thai dishes, including crispy pork salad, red curried chicken, and sweet-and-sour red snapper. And there's a "wok buffet," wherein you assemble the ingredients for your meal on a plate, then deliver it to a uniformed chef who will quick-sear it for you with whatever sauces you want.

In the Haas Haus, Stephansplatz 4. ⓒ **01/512-26-66.** Reservations recommended. Main courses 8€–14€. V. Daily noon–3pm and 6pm–midnight. U-Bahn: Stephansplatz.

Plachutta ✿ VIENNESE Few restaurants have built such a culinary shrine around one dish: *Tafelspitz,* the boiled beef dish that was the favorite of Emperor Franz Josef throughout his prolonged reign. Whichever of the 10 versions you order, it will invariably come with sauces and garnishes that perk up what sounds like a dull dish into a delectable culinary traipse through the tastes of yesteryear. The differences between the versions are a function of the cut of beef you request as part of your meal. Regardless of the cut you specify, your meal will be accompanied with hash brown potatoes, chives, and an appealing mixture of horseradish and chopped apples.

Wollzeile 10. ⓒ **01/512-1577.** Reservations recommended. Main courses 13€–25€. DC, MC, V. Daily 11:30am–11:15pm. U-Bahn: Stubentor.

Wiener Rathauskeller ✿✿ VIENNESE/INTERNATIONAL City halls throughout the Teutonic world have traditionally maintained restaurants in their basements, and Vienna is no exception. In half a dozen richly atmospheric dining rooms, with high vaulted ceilings and stained-glass windows, you can enjoy good and reasonably priced food. The chef's specialty is a *Rathauskellerplatte* for two, consisting of various cuts of meat, including a veal schnitzel, lamb cutlets, and pork medallions. Beginning at 8pm, live musicians ramble through the world of operetta, waltz, and *Schrammel* (traditional Viennese music), as you dine.

Rathausplatz 1. ⓒ **01/4051-2190.** Reservations required. Main courses 13€–19€; Vienna music evening with dinner (Tues–Sat 8pm) 36€. AE, DC, MC, V. Mon–Sat 11:30am–3pm and 6–11pm. U-Bahn: Rathaus.

Coffeehouses & Cafes

The windows of the much-venerated **Café Demel,** Kohlmarkt 14 (© **01/533-5516;** U-Bahn: Stephansplatz), are filled with fanciful spun-sugar creations of characters from folk legends. You can definitely expect to see St. Nicholas at Christmastime. Inside is a splendidly baroque Viennese landmark with black marble tables, cream-colored embellished plaster walls, and crystal chandeliers covered with white milk-glass globes. Dozens of pastries are offered every day, including cream-filled horns *(Gugelhupfs)*. If you want to be traditional, ask for a Demel-Coffee, which is filtered coffee served with milk, cream, or whipped cream. It's open daily from 10am to 7pm.

Café Dommayer, Dommayergasse 1 (© **01/877-220811;** U-Bahn: Schönbrunn), boasts a reputation for courtliness that goes back to 1787. In 1844, Johann Strauss, Jr., made his musical debut here, and beginning in 1924, the site became known as *the* place in Vienna for tea dancing. During clement weather, a garden with seats for 300 opens in back. The rest of the year, the venue is restricted to a high-ceilinged black-and-white old-world room. Every Saturday from 2 to 4pm, a pianist and violinist perform; and every third Saturday, an all-woman orchestra plays mostly Strauss. It's open daily from 7am to midnight.

One of the Ring's great cafes, **Café Landtmann,** Dr.-Karl-Lueger-Ring 4 (© **01/532-0621;** tram: 1, 2, or D), dates from the 1880s. Overlooking the Burgtheater, it has traditionally drawn a mix of politicians, journalists, and actors, and was Freud's favorite. The original chandeliers and the pre-war chairs have been refurbished. We highly suggest spending an hour or so here, whether perusing the newspapers, sipping on coffee, or planning the day's itinerary. The cafe is open daily from 7:30am to midnight (lunch is served 11:30am–3pm and dinner 5–11pm).

MODERATE

Griechenbeisl AUSTRIAN   This local favorite opened in 1450 and is still one of Vienna's leading restaurants. It has a labyrinthine collection of dining areas on three floors, all with low vaulted ceilings, smoky paneling, and wrought-iron chandeliers. As you go in, be sure to see the so-called inner sanctum, with signatures of such former patrons as Mozart, Beethoven, and Mark Twain. The food is hearty, ample, and solidly bourgeois. Menu items include deer stew, both Hungarian and Viennese goulash, sauerkraut garni, Wiener schnitzel, and venison steak—in other words, all those favorite recipes from Grandmother's kitchen. As an added treat, the restaurant features nighttime accordion and zither music.

Fleischmarkt 11. © **01/533-1941.** Reservations required. Main courses 14€–22€; fixed-price menu 23€–40€. AE, DC, MC, V. Daily 11am–1am (last orders at 11:30pm). Tram: N, 1, 2, or 21.

Inexpensive

Augustinerkeller AUSTRIAN   The beer and wine flow at this Viennese legend. Augustinerkeller, in the basement of the part of the Hofburg complex that shelters the Albertina Collection, has served wine, beer, and food since 1857, although the vaulted ceilings and sense of timelessness evoke an establishment even older than that. It attracts a lively group of patrons from all walks of life, and sometimes they get boisterous, especially when the *Schrammel* music goes late into the night. It's one of the best values for wine tasting in Vienna. Aside from the wine and beer, the establishment serves simple food, including roast chicken on a spit, schnitzel, and *Tafelspitz.*

Augustinerstrasse 1. ℂ 01/533-1026. Main courses 8€–15€. AE, DC, MC, V. Daily 11am–midnight. U-Bahn: Stephansplatz.

Buffet Trzésniewski ✿ SANDWICHES   Everyone in Vienna knows about this place, from the most hurried office workers to the city's elite hostesses. Its current incarnation is unlike any buffet you may have seen, with six or seven cramped tables and a rapidly moving queue of clients who jostle for space next to the glass countertops. You'll indicate to the waitress the kind of sandwich you want, and if you can't read German signs, just point. Most people come here for the delicious finger sandwiches, which include 18 combinations of cream cheese, egg, onion, salami, mushrooms, herring, green and red peppers, tomatoes, lobster, and many more items. If you order a drink, the cashier will give you a rubber token, which you'll present to the person at the far end of the counter.

Dorotheergasse 1. ℂ 01/512-3291. Reservations not accepted. Sandwiches .80€. No credit cards. Mon–Fri 9:30am–7:30pm; Sat 9am–5pm. U-Bahn: Stephansplatz.

Café Leopold ✿ INTERNATIONAL   Critics have defined this restaurant as a postmodern version, in architectural form, of the Viennese Expressionist paintings (including many by Egon Schiele) that are exhibited within the museum that contains it. During the day, the place functions as a conventional cafe and restaurant, serving a postmodern blend of *mitteleuropäische* (central European) and Asian food. Three nights a week, however, from around 10pm till at least 2am, any hints of kitsch and coziness are banished as soon as a DJ begins cranking out dance tunes for a hard-drinking denizens-of-the-night crowd.

In the Leopold Museum, Museumsplatz 1. ℂ 01/523-67-32. Reservations not necessary. Main courses 4.50€–11€. 2-course set-price menu 8.50€. AE, DC, MC, V. Daily 9am–2am. U-Bahn: Volkstheater or Babenbergstrasse/MuseumsQuartier.

Café Restaurant Halle INTERNATIONAL   Set within the Kunsthalle, this is the direct competitor of the also-recommended Café Leopold. Larger, and with a more sophisticated menu than the Café Leopold's, it's a postmodern, airy, big-windowed quartet of wood-trimmed, cream-colored rooms. The menu will always contain a half-dozen meal-size salads, many garnished with strips of steak, chicken, or shrimp; two daily homemade soups; and a rotating series of platters.

In the Kunsthalle Wien, Museumsplatz 1, in the MuseumsQuartier. ℂ 01/523-7001. Reservations not necessary. Main courses 6€–15€. MC, V. U-Bahn: MuseumsQuartier.

Gulaschmuseum ✿ AUSTRIAN/HUNGARIAN   If you thought that *Gulasch* (goulash) was available in only one form, think again. This restaurant celebrates at least 15 varieties of it, each of them an authentic survivor of the culinary traditions of Hungary, and each redolent with the taste of that country's most distinctive spice, paprika. You can order versions of goulash based on roast beef, veal, pork, and fried chicken livers. Vegetarians rejoice: Versions made with potatoes, beans, or mushrooms are also available. Boiled potatoes and rough-textured brown or black bread will usually accompany your choice. An excellent beginning is a dish so firmly associated with Hungary that it's been referred to as the Magyar national crepe, *Hortobágyi Palatschinken,* stuffed with minced beef and paprika-flavored cream sauce.

Schulerstrasse 20. ☏ **01/512-1017.** Reservations recommended. Main courses 6€–12€. MC, V. Mon–Fri 9am–midnight; Sat–Sun 10am–midnight. U-Bahn: Wollzeile or Stephansplatz.

Hansen ✮ MEDITERRANEAN/INTERNATIONAL   Part of the charm of this intriguing and stylish restaurant involves trekking through masses of plants and elaborate garden ornaments on your way to your dining table. Choose from a small but savory menu that changes every week. Excellent examples include a spicy bean salad with strips of chicken breast served in a summer broth; risotto with cheese and sour cherries; and poached *Saibling* (something akin to trout from the cold-water streams of the Austrian Alps) with a potato and celery purée and watercress.

In the cellar of the Börsegebäude (Vienna Stock Exchange), Wipplingerstrasse 34 at the Schottenring. ☏ **01/532-05-42.** Reservations recommended. Main courses 8€–17€. AE, DC, MC, V. Mon–Fri 9am–8pm (last order); Sat 9am–3pm (last order). U-Bahn: Schottenring.

Palmenhaus AUSTRIAN   Architectural grace and marvelous food combine for a happy marriage here. Many architectural critics consider the Jugendstil glass canopy of this greenhouse the most beautiful in Austria. A sophisticated menu changes monthly, and might include perfectly prepared fresh Austrian goat cheese with stewed peppers and zucchini salad; young herring with sour cream, horseradish, and deep-fried beignets stuffed with apples and cabbage; or breast of chicken layered with goose liver. If you've already eaten, no one will mind if you drop in just for a drink and one of the voluptuous pastries.

In the Burggarten. ☏ **01/533-1033.** Reservations recommended for dinner. Main courses 4€–15€; pastries 3€–3.80€. AE, DC, MC. V. Daily 10am–2am. U-Bahn: Opera.

Restaurant Salzamt ✮ AUSTRIAN   This is the best restaurant in the neighborhood. It evokes a turn-of-the-20th-century Viennese bistro, replete with Weiner Werkstatte–inspired chairs and lighting fixtures, cream-colored walls, and dark tables and banquettes. Sit within its vaulted interior or—if weather permits—move out to any of the tables on the square, overlooking Vienna's oldest church, St. Ruprecht. Well-prepared items include a terrine of broccoli and artichoke hearts; light-textured pastas; filets of pork with a Gorgonzola-enriched cream sauce; roast beef with wild lettuce salad; several kinds of goulash; and fresh fish. One of the most noteworthy of these is fried filets of *Saibling,* a fish native to the cold-water streams of western Austria, served with lemon or tartar sauce.

Ruprechtsplatz 1. ☏ **01/533-5332.** Reservations recommended. Main courses 8.50€–17€. V. Mon–Fri 11am–2am; Sat–Sun 3pm–2am. U-Bahn: Schwedenplatz.

Zwölf-Apostelkeller VIENNESE   For those seeking a taste of old Vienna, this is the place. Sections of this old wine tavern's walls predate 1561. Rows of wooden tables stand under vaulted ceilings, with lighting provided partially by streetlights set into the masonry floor. This place is popular with students, partly because of its low prices and because of its proximity to St. Stephan's. In addition to beer and wine, the establishment serves hearty Austrian fare. Specialties include roast pork with dumplings, Hungarian goulash soup, a limited number of vegetarian dishes, and a *Schlachtplatte* (hot black pudding, liverwurst, pork, and pork sausage with a hot bacon-and-cabbage salad).

Sonnenfelsgasse 3. ☏ **01/512-6777.** Main courses 5.30€–10€. AE, DC, MC, V. Daily 4pm–midnight. Closed July. Tram: 1, 2, 21, D, or N. Bus: 1A. U-Bahn: Stephansplatz.

IN LANDSTRASSE

Steirereck ✴✴✴ VIENNESE/AUSTRIAN *Steirereck* means "corner of Styria," which is exactly what Heinz and Margarethe Reitbauer have created in the rustic decor of this intimate restaurant. On the Danube Canal, between Central Station and the Prater, it has been acclaimed by some Viennese as the best restaurant in the city. The Reitbauers offer both traditional Viennese dishes and "new Austrian" selections. You might begin with a caviar-semolina dumpling, roasted turbot with fennel (served as an appetizer), or the most elegant and expensive item of all, goose-liver Steirereck. The menu is wisely limited and well prepared, changing daily depending on the fresh produce available at the market. The restaurant is popular with after-theater diners. The large wine cellar holds some 35,000 bottles.

Rasumofskygasse 2. ② 01/713-3168. Reservations required. Main courses 22€–28€. 3-course fixed-price lunch 31€; 5-course fixed-price dinner 69€. AE, DC, MC, V. Mon–Fri 10:30am–2pm and 7pm–midnight. Closed holidays. Tram: N. Bus: 4.

SEEING THE SIGHTS OF VIENNA

The Inner City (Innere Stadt) is the tangle of streets from which Vienna grew in the Middle Ages. Much of your exploration will be confined to this area, encircled by the boulevards of "The Ring" and the Danube Canal. The main street of the Inner City is **Kärntnerstrasse,** most of which is a pedestrian mall. The heart of Vienna is **Stephansplatz,** the square on which St. Stephan's Cathedral sits.

SIGHTSEEING SUGGESTIONS FOR FIRST-TIME VISITORS

If You Have 1 Day Begin at **St. Stephan's Cathedral,** and from there branch out for a tour of the enveloping Inner City. But first, climb the tower of the cathedral for a panoramic view of the city (you can also take an elevator to the top). Stroll down **Kärntnerstrasse,** the main shopping artery, and enjoy the 11am ritual of coffee in a grand cafe, such as the **Café Imperial.** In the afternoon, visit **Schönbrunn,** seat of the Hapsburg dynasty. Have dinner in a typical Viennese wine tavern.

If You Have 2 Days On the second day, explore other major attractions of Vienna, including the

Hofburg, the Imperial Crypts, and the **Kunsthistorisches Museum.** In the evening, attend an opera performance or some other musical event.

If You Have 3 Days On your third day, try to attend a performance of either the **Spanish Riding School** (Tues–Sat) or the **Vienna Boys' Choir** (singing at Sun Mass). Explore the **Belvedere Palace** and its art galleries; visit the art complex at MuseumsQuartier; stroll through the **Naschmarkt,** the city's major open-air market; and cap the day with a visit to one or more of Vienna's cabarets, wine bars, or beer cellars.

EXPLORING THE HOFBURG PALACE COMPLEX ✴✴✴

The winter palace of the Hapsburgs, known for its vast, impressive courtyards, the Hofburg sits in the heart of Vienna. To reach it (you can hardly miss it), head up Kohlmarkt to Michaelerplatz 1, Burgring (② 01/587-5554). You can take the U-Bahn to Stephansplatz, Herrengasse, or Mariahilferstrasse, or else tram 1, 2, D, or J to Burgring.

This complex of imperial edifices, the first of which was constructed in 1279, grew and grew as the empire did, so that today the Hofburg Palace is virtually a city within a city. The palace, which has withstood three major sieges and a great fire, is called simply *die Burg,* or "the palace," by Viennese. Of its more than 2,600 rooms, fewer than two dozen are open to the public.

Schatzkammer (Imperial Treasury) ★★★   This is the greatest treasury in the world. It's divided into two sections: the Imperial Profane and the Sacerdotal Treasuries. One part displays the crown jewels and an assortment of imperial riches; the other exhibits ecclesiastical treasures. The most outstanding exhibit is the imperial crown, dating from 962. It's so big that, even though padded, it probably slipped down over the ears of many a Hapsburg at his coronation. Studded with emeralds, sapphires, diamonds, and rubies, this 1,000-year-old symbol of sovereignty is a priceless treasure. Also on display is the imperial crown worn by the Hapsburg rulers from 1804 to the end of the empire. You'll see the saber of Charlemagne and the holy lance. Among great Schatzkammer prizes is the Burgundian Treasure seized in the 15th century, rich in vestments, oil paintings, gems, and robes.

Hofburg, Schweizerhof. © **01/533-7931.** Admission 7€ adults; 5€ children, seniors, and students; free for children under 6. Wed–Mon 10am–6pm.

Kaiserappartements (Imperial Apartments) ★★   The Hofburg complex includes the Kaiserappartements, where the emperors and their wives and children lived, on the first floor. To reach these apartments, enter via the rotunda of Michaelerplatz. The apartments are richly decorated with tapestries, many from Aubusson. The Imperial Silver and Porcelain Collection provides an insight into Hapsburg court etiquette. Most of these pieces are from the 18th and 19th centuries. Leopoldinischer Trakt (Leopold's Apartments) dates from the 17th century. These Imperial Apartments are more closely associated with Franz Josef than with any other emperor.

Michaeler Platz 1 (inside the Ring, about a 7-min. walk from Stephansplatz; entrance via the Kasertor in the Inneren Burghof). © **01/533-7570.** Admission 7.50€ adults, 5.90€ students under 25, 3.90€ children 6–15, free for children 5 and under. Daily 9am–4:30pm. U-Bahn: U-1 or U-3 to Stephansplatz. Tram: 1, 2, 3, or J to Burgring.

Die Burgkapelle (Home of the Vienna Boys' Choir)   Construction of this Gothic chapel began in 1447 during the reign of Emperor Frederick III, but the building was subsequently massively renovated. From 1449, it was the private chapel of the royal family. Today the Burgkapelle is the home of the

---

Moments The Vienna Boys' Choir

In 1498, the emperor Maximilian I decreed that 12 boys should be included among the official court musicians. Over the next 500 years, this group evolved into the world-renowned Vienna Boys' Choir *(Wiener Sängerknaben).* They perform in Vienna at various venues, including the Staatsoper, the Volksoper, and Schönbrunn Palace. The choir also performs at Sunday and Christmas Masses with the Hofmusikkapelle (Court Musicians) at the Burgkapelle (see review for details). The choir's boarding school is at Augartenpalais, Obere Augartenstrasse. For more information on where they are performing and how to get tickets, go to the choir's website (www.wsk.at).

Hofmusikkapelle (Court Musicians) 𝕬𝕬, an ensemble consisting of the Vienna Boys' Choir and members of the Vienna State Opera chorus and orchestra, which performs works by classical and modern composers. Written applications for reserved seats should be sent at least 8 weeks in advance. Use a credit card; do not send cash or checks. For reservations, write to Verwaltung der Hofmusikkapelle, Hofburg, A-1010 Vienna. If you fail to reserve in advance, you may be lucky enough to secure tickets from a block sold at the Burgkapelle box office every Friday from 11am to 1pm or 3 to 5pm, plus Sunday from 8:15 to 8:45am. The line starts forming at least half an hour before that. If you're willing to settle for standing room, it's free.

Hofburg (entrance on Schweizerhof). ℂ 01/533-9927. Mass: Seats and concerts 5€–29€; standing room free. Masses (performances) held only Jan–June and mid-Sept to Dec, Sun and holidays 9:15am. Concerts May–June and Sept–Oct Fri 4pm.

Neue Hofburg   The last addition to the Hofburg complex was the Neue Hofburg (New Château). Construction started in 1881 and continued until work was halted in 1913. The palace was the residence of Archduke Franz Ferdinand, the nephew and heir apparent of Franz Josef, whose assassination at Sarajevo set off the chain of events that led to World War I. The **arms and armor collection** 𝕬𝕬 is second only to that of the Metropolitan Museum of Art in New York. It's in the **Hofjagd and Rüstkammer,** on the second floor of the New Château. On display are crossbows, swords, helmets, pistols, and armor. Another section, the **Musikinstrumentensammlung** 𝕬 (ℂ 01/52524), is devoted to musical instruments, mainly 17th- and 18th-century. In the **Ephesos-Museum (Museum of Ephesian Sculpture),** with an entrance behind the Prince Eugene monument, you'll see high-quality finds from Ephesus in Turkey and the Greek island of Samothrace. Here the prize exhibit is the Parthian monument, the most important relief frieze from Roman times ever found in Asia Minor. It was erected to celebrate Rome's victory in the Parthian wars (A.D. 161–65).

Heldenplatz. ℂ 01/525-24-484. Admission for each museum 8€ adults, 6.50€ children. Wed–Mon 10am–6pm.

Albertina 𝕬   One of the greatest graphics collections in the world—scheduled to reopen in 2003—is housed within the Hofburg. The museum, named for a son-in-law of Maria Theresa, traces the development of graphic arts since the 14th century. The most outstanding treasure is the Dürer collection. Unfortunately, what you'll usually see are copies—the originals are shown only on special occasions. Be sure to view Dürer's *Praying Hands,* which has been reproduced throughout the world. The 20,000-some drawings and more than 250,000 original etchings and prints include work by such artists as Poussin, Fragonard, Rubens, Rembrandt, Michelangelo, and Leonardo da Vinci. Exhibitions of both ancient and modern drawings and prints are always changing.

Albertinaplatz. ℂ 01/53483. www.albertina.at. Admission 9€ adults, 7€ students, free for children under 6. Tues–Sun 10am–5pm.

Augustinerkirche   This church was constructed in the 14th century as part of the Hofburg complex to serve as the parish church of the imperial court. In the latter part of the 18th century it was stripped of its baroque embellishments and returned to the original Gothic features. The Chapel of St. George, dating from 1337, is entered from the right aisle. The **Tomb of Maria Christina** 𝕬, the favorite daughter of Maria Theresa, is housed in the main nave near the rear entrance, but there's no body in it. (The princess was actually buried in the

Imperial Crypt.) This richly ornamented empty tomb is one of Canova's masterpieces. The royal weddings of Maria Theresa and François of Lorraine (1736), Marie Antoinette and Louis XVI of France (1770), Marie-Louise of Austria to Napoléon (1810, but by proxy—he didn't show up), and Franz Josef and Elizabeth of Bavaria (1854) were all held in the church. The most convenient, and dramatic, time to visit is Sunday at 11am, when a High Mass is celebrated with choir, soloists, and orchestra.

Augustinerstrasse 3. © 01/533-70-99. Daily 6:30am–6pm. Free admission. U-Bahn: Stephansplatz.

Spanische Reitschule (Spanish Riding School) ✪ The Spanish Riding School is in the crystal-chandeliered white ballroom in an 18th-century building of the Hofburg complex. We always marvel at the skill and beauty of the sleek Lipizzaner stallions as their adept trainers put them through their paces in a show that hasn't changed in 4 centuries. These are the world's most famous, classically styled equine performers. Reservations for performances must be made in advance, as early as possible. Order your tickets for the Sunday and Wednesday shows by writing to Spanische Reitschule, Hofburg, A-1010 Vienna (fax 01/533-903-240), or through a travel agency in Vienna. (Tickets for Sat shows can be ordered only through a travel agency.) Tickets for training sessions with no advance reservations can be purchased at the entrance.

Michaelerplatz 1, Hofburg. © 01/533-9032. www.lipizzaner.at. Regular performances 33€–145€ seats, 25€ standing room. Classical art of riding with music 22€ adults, free for children 3–6 with an adult; children under age 3 not admitted. Training session 12€ adults, 5€ children. Regular shows Mar–June and Sept to mid-Dec, most Sun at 11am and some Fri at 6pm. Classical dressage with music performances Apr–June and Sept, most Sat at 10am. Training sessions Mar–June, first 2 weeks in Sept, and mid-Oct to mid-Dec, Tues–Sat 10am–noon.

Lipizzaner Museum The latest attraction at the Hofburg is this museum near the stables of the famous white stallions. The exhibition begins with the historic inception of the Spanish Riding School in the 16th century and extends to the stallions' near destruction in the closing weeks of World War II. Exhibits such as paintings, historic engravings, drawings, photographs, uniforms, and bridles, plus video and film presentations, bring to life the history of the Spanish Riding School, offering an insight into the breeding and training of these champion horses. Visitors to the museum are able to see through a window into the stallions' stables while they are being fed and saddled.

Reitschulgasse 2, Stallburg. © 01/533-7811. www.lipizzaner.at. Admission 9€ adults, 6.50€ children. Daily 9am–6pm. U-Bahn: Stephansplatz.

EXPLORING THE MUSEUMSQUARTIER COMPLEX ✪✪✪

The big cultural news of Vienna, perhaps of Europe, is the long-awaited premiere of this giant modern art complex. Art critics claimed that the assemblage of art installed in former Hapsburg stables has tipped the city's cultural center of gravity from Hapsburgian pomp into the new millennium. This massive complex, one of the 10 largest cultural complexes in the world, is like the result of combining the Guggenheim Museum with New York's Museum of Modern Art and tossing in the Brooklyn Academy of Music, a children's museum, an architecture and design center, theaters, art galleries, video workshops, and much more. There's even an ecology center, architecture museum, and, yes, a tobacco museum. For more information, go the MuseumsQuartier website at **www.mqw.at**.

Kunsthalle Wien ✪ Cutting-edge contemporary and classic modern art are showcased here. Exhibits focus on specific subjects and seek to establish a link between modern art and current trends. You'll find works by everyone from Picasso and Juan Miró to Jackson Pollock and Paul Klee, from Wassily Kandinsky to Andy Warhol and, surprise, Yoko Ono. From expressionism to cubism to abstractionism, exhibits reveal the major movements in contemporary art since the mid–20th century. There are five floors that can be explored in 1 to 2 hours, depending on what interests you.

Museumsplatz 1. ℂ 01/521-89-0. Admission 8€ adults; 5€ seniors, students, and children. Daily 10am–7pm (Thurs to 10pm).

Leopold Museum 🌟🌟   This extensive collection of Austrian art includes the world's largest treasure trove of the works of Egon Schiele (1890–1918), who was once forgotten in art history but now takes his place alongside van Gogh and Modigliani in the ranks of great doomed artists. Dying before he was 28, his collection of art at the Leopold includes more than 2,500 drawings and watercolors and 330 oil canvases. Other Austrian modernist masterpieces include paintings by Oskar Kokoschka, the great Gustav Klimt, Anton Romaki, and Richard Gerstl. Major statements in Arts and Crafts from the late 19th and 20th centuries include works by Josef Hoffmann, Kolo Moser, Adolf Loos, and Franz Hagenauer.

Museumsplatz 1. ℂ 01/525-70. Admission 9€ adults, 6€ students and children over 7. Mon and Wed–Thurs 11am–7pm; Fri 11am–9pm; Sat–Sun 10am–7pm. Closed Tues.

MUMOK (Museum of Modern Art Ludwig Foundation) 🌟   This gallery presents one of the most outstanding collections of contemporary art in Central Europe. It comprises mainly works from American Pop Art mixed with concurrent Continental movements such as the Hyperrealism of the 1960s and '70s. The museum features five exhibition levels (three of them aboveground and two underground). So that it will be easier to cross and compare a single art movement such as cubism or surrealism, paintings "in the same family" are grouped together. Expect to encounter works by all the fabled names such as Robert Indiana, Jasper Johns, Roy Lichtenstein, Robert Rauschenberg, George Segal, and, of course, Andy Warhol.

Museumsplatz 1. ℂ 01/525-00. Admission 8€ adults, 2€ children. Daily 9am–6pm.

OTHER TOP ATTRACTIONS IN THE INNER CITY

Domkirche St. Stephan (St. Stephan's Cathedral) 🌟🌟🌟   The cathedral was founded in the 12th century in what was the town's center. Stephansdom was virtually destroyed in a 1258 fire, and in the early 14th century the ruins of the Romanesque basilica gave way to a Gothic building. It suffered terribly in the Turkish siege of 1683 and from the Russian bombardments of 1945. Reopened in 1948, the cathedral is today one of the greatest Gothic structures in Europe, rich in woodcarvings, altars, sculptures, and paintings. The chief treasure of the cathedral is the carved, wooden **Wiener Neustadt altarpiece** 🌟🌟 that dates from 1447. Richly painted and gilded, the altar was discovered in the Virgin's Choir. In the Apostles' Choir look for the curious **Tomb of Emperor Frederick III** 🌟🌟. Made of a pinkish Salzburg marble, the carved 17th-century tomb depicts hideous little hobgoblins trying to enter and wake the emperor from his eternal sleep. The steeple, rising some 135m (450 ft.), has come to symbolize the very spirit of Vienna. You can climb the 343-step South Tower, which dominates the Viennese skyline and offers a view of the Vienna Woods. Called Alter Steffl (Old Steve), the tower with its needlelike spire was built between 1350 and 1433. The North Tower (Nordturm), reached by elevator, was never finished, but was crowned in the Renaissance style in 1579. From here you get a panoramic sweep of the city and the Danube.

Stephansplatz 1. ☏ **01/515-52563**. Cathedral, free admission; tour of catacombs 3€ adults, 1€ children under 15. Guided tour of cathedral 3€ adults, 1€ children under 15. North Tower 3.50€ adults, 1€ children under 15; South Tower 3.50€ adults, 1€ students, 1€ children under 15. Evening tours, including tour of the roof, 10€ adults, 3.50€ children under 15. Cathedral daily 6am–10pm except times of service. Tour of catacombs Mon–Sat 10, 11, and 11:30am, 12:30, 1:30, 2, 2:30, 3:30, 4, and 4:30pm; Sun 2, 2:30, 3, 3:30, 4, and 4:30pm. Guided tour of cathedral Mon–Sat 10:30am and 3pm; Sun at 3pm. Special evening tour Sat 7pm (June–Sept). North Tower Oct–Mar daily 8:30am–5pm; Apr–Sept daily 9am–6pm. South Tower daily 9am–5:30pm. Bus: 1A, 2A, or 3A. U-Bahn: Stephansplatz.

Gemäldegalerie der Akademie der Bildenden Kunste (Gallery of Painting and Fine Arts) ℛ

Visit this painting gallery to see the *Last Judgment* by the incomparable Hieronymus Bosch. In this work, the artist conjured up all the demons of the nether regions for a terrifying view of the suffering and sins of humankind. There are many 15th-century Dutch and Flemish paintings and several works by Lucas Cranach the Elder. The academy is noted for its 17th-century art by van Dyck, Rembrandt, Botticelli, and a host of others. Rubens is represented here by more than a dozen oil sketches. You can see Rembrandt's *Portrait of a Woman* and scrutinize Guardi's scenes of 18th-century Venice.

Schillerplatz 3. ☏ **01/58816**. Admission 3.50€ adults, 1.45€ students and children. Tues–Sun 10am–4pm. U-Bahn: Karlsplatz.

Haus der Musik ℛ

Mozart is long gone, but Vienna finally got around to opening a full-scale museum devoted to music. This hands-on museum is high-tech. You can take to the podium and conduct the Vienna Philharmonic. Wandering the halls and niches of this museum, you can encounter nostalgic reminders of the great composers who have lived in Vienna, not only Mozart but Beethoven, Schubert, Brahms, and others. In the rooms you can listen to your favorite renditions of their works and explore their memorabilia. A memorial, *Exodus,* pays tribute to the Viennese musicians driven into exile or murdered by the Nazis. At the Musicantino Restaurant on the top floor you can enjoy a panoramic view of the city and some good food. On the ground floor is a coffeehouse.

Sellerstätte 30. ☏ 01/516-48-51. Admission 8.05€ adults, 5.85€ students and seniors, 4€ children. Daily 10am–10pm.

Kunsthistorisches Museum (Museum of Art History) ℛℛℛ

Across from the Hofburg, this huge building houses the fabulous art collections gathered by the Hapsburgs. A highlight is the fine collection of ancient Egyptian and Greek art. The museum also has works by many of the greatest European masters, such as Velázquez, Titian, Brueghel the Elder, van Dyck, Ruben, Rembrandt, and Dürer.

Maria-Theresien-Platz, Burgring 5. ☏ **01/525-24-405**. Admission 9€ adults, 6.50€ students and seniors, free for children under 6. Daily 10am–6pm, Thurs until 9pm. U-Bahn: Mariahilferstrasse. Tram: 52, 58, D, or J.

ATTRACTIONS OUTSIDE THE INNER CITY

Schönbrunn Palace ℛℛℛ

A Hapsburg palace of 1,441 rooms, Schönbrunn was designed and built between 1696 and 1712 in a grand baroque style meant to surpass that of Versailles. When Maria Theresa became empress in 1740, she changed the original plans, and the Schönbrunn we see today, with its delicate rococo touches, is her conception. It was the imperial summer palace during Maria Theresa's 40-year reign, the scene of great ceremonial balls, lavish banquets, and the fabulous receptions during the Congress of Vienna in 1815. The State Apartments are the most stunning. Much of the interior ornamentation is in 23½-karat gold, and many porcelain tile stoves are in evidence. Of the 40 rooms that you can visit, particularly fascinating is the "Room of Millions" decorated with Indian and Persian miniatures, the grandest rococo salon in the world. Also on the grounds at Schönbrunn is the **Schlosstheater** (© **01/876-4272**), which still has summer performances.

Schönbrunner Schlossstrasse. © **01/8113**. www.schoenbrunn.at. Admission 9.80€ adults, 5€ children 6–15, free for children under 6. Apartments Apr–Oct daily 8:30am–5pm; Nov–Mar daily 9am–4:30pm. U-Bahn: Schönbrunn.

Österreichische Galerie Belvedere ✹✹   The Belvedere Palace was built as a summer home for Prince Eugene of Savoy and consists of two palatial buildings. The pond reflects the sky and palace buildings, which are made up of a series of interlocking cubes, and the interior is dominated by two great, flowing staircases. The Unteres Belvedere (Lower Belvedere), with its entrance at Rennweg 6A, was constructed from 1714 to 1716 and contains the Gold Salon, one of the palace's most beautiful rooms. It also houses the Barockmuseum (Museum of Baroque Art). The original sculptures from the Neuermarkt fountain, the work of Georg Raphael Donner, are displayed here. The Oberes Belvedere (Upper Belvedere) was started in 1721 and completed in 1723. It contains the Gallery of 19th- and 20th-Century Art, with an outstanding collection of the works of Gustav Klimt, including his extraordinary *Judith*. The Museum of Medieval Austrian Art is in the Orangery.

Prinz-Eugen-Strasse 27. © **01/79557**. www.belvedere.at. Admission 7.50€ adults, free for children 11 and under. Tues–Sun 10am–6pm. Tram: D to Schloss Belvedere.

ORGANIZED TOURS

Wiener Rundfahrten (Vienna Sightseeing Tours), Stelzhamergasse 25 (© **01/7124-6830**; www.viennasightseeingtours.com; U-Bahn: Landstrasse Wien Mitte), offers some of the best organized tours of Vienna and its surroundings. Tours depart from a signposted area in front of the State Opera (U-Bahn: Karlsplatz) and include running commentary in both German and English.

CITY TOURS   A **"Historical City Tour,"** which includes visits to Schönbrunn and Belvedere palaces, leaves the Staatsoper daily at 9:45am and 10:30am (U-Bahn: Karlsplatz). It lasts about 3 hours and costs 32€ adults and 15€ children. It's ideal for visitors who are pressed for time and yet want to be shown the major (and most frequently photographed) monuments of Vienna. It takes you past the historic buildings of Ringstrasse—the State Opera, Hofburg Palace, museums, Parliament, City Hall, the Burgtheater, the University, and the Votive Church—into the heart of Vienna.

Another tour, **"Following Sisi's Footsteps,"** is the same as the "Historical City Tour" except that you also watch the Lipizzaner horses being trained at the Spanish Riding School. These tours leave at 9:45am Tuesday through Saturday. They cost 32€ adults and 15€ children, with the entrance fee to the Spanish Riding School (12€) to be paid separately.

TOURS OUTSIDE THE CITY   "Vienna Woods—Mayerling," another popular excursion, lasting about 4 hours, leaves from the Staatsoper and takes you to the towns of Perchtoldsdorf and Modling, and also to the Abbey of Heiligenkreuz, a center of Christian culture since medieval times. The tour also takes you for a short walk through Baden, the spa that was once a favorite summer resort of the aristocracy. Tours cost 39€ adults and 15€ children.

THE SHOPPING SCENE

Vienna is known for the excellent quality of its works, including petit point, hand-painted porcelain, work by goldsmiths and silversmiths, handmade dolls, ceramics, enamel jewelry, wrought-iron articles, and leather goods. Also popular is loden, a boiled and rolled wool fabric made into overcoats, suits, and hats, as well as knitted sweaters. Popular destinations can be found on **Kärntnerstrasse,** between the Staatsoper and Stock-im-Eisen-Platz; the **Graben,** between Stock-im-Eisen-Platz and Kohlmarkt; **Kohlmarkt,** between the Graben and Michaelplatz; and **Rotensturmstrasse,** between Stephansplatz and Kai. You can also shop on **Mariahilferstrasse,** between Babenbergerstrasse and Schönbrunn, one of the longest streets in Vienna; **Favoritenstrasse,** between Südtiroler Platz and Reumannplatz; and **Landstrasser Hauptstrasse.**

The **Naschmarkt** is a vegetable-and-fruit market with a lively scene every day. It's at Linke and Rechte Wienzeile, south of the opera district.

Albin Denk, Graben 13 (℗ **01/512-4439;** U-Bahn: Stephansplatz), is the oldest continuously operating porcelain store in Vienna, in business since 1702. You'll see thousands of objects from Meissen, Dresden, and other regions.

Opened in 1830 by the Plankl family, **Loden Plankl,** Michaelerplatz 6 (℗ **01/533-8032;** U-Bahn: Stephansplatz), is the oldest and most reputable outlet in Vienna for traditional Austrian clothing. You'll find Austrian loden coats, shoes, trousers, dirndls, jackets, lederhosen, and suits for men, women, and children. The building, opposite the Hofburg, dates from the 17th century. The three-floor **Ö. W. (Österreichische Werkstatten),** Kärntnerstrasse 6 (℗ **01/512-2418;** U-Bahn: Stephansplatz), sells hundreds of handmade art objects from Austria. Some 200 leading artists and craftspeople throughout the country organized this cooperative to showcase their wares. It's easy to find, only half a minute's walk from St. Stephan's Cathedral.

VIENNA AFTER DARK

The best source of information about what's happening on the cultural scene is **Wien Monatsprogramm,** distributed free at tourist information offices and at many hotel reception desks. **Die Presse,** the Viennese daily, publishes a special magazine in its Thursday edition outlining the major cultural events for the coming week. It's in German but might still be helpful.

THE PERFORMING ARTS

OPERA & CLASSICAL MUSIC   Music is at the heart of cultural life in Vienna. This has been true for a couple of centuries or so, and the city continues to lure composers, musicians, and music lovers.

The **Wiener Staatsoper (State Opera),** Opernring 2 (℗ **01/5144-42250;** www.wiener-staatsoper.at; U-Bahn: Karlsplatz), is one of the three most important opera houses in the world. With the Vienna Philharmonic in the pit, some of the leading opera stars of the world perform here. In their day, Richard Strauss and Gustav Mahler worked as directors. Daily performances are given September through June. Tickets range from 10€ to 178€. Tours are offered two to five times daily, for 4.50€ per person; times are posted on a board outside the entrance.

Count yourself fortunate if you get to hear a concert at **Musikverein,** Dumbastrasse 3 (℗ **01/505-8190;** www.musikverein-wien.at; U-Bahn: Karlsplatz). The Golden Hall is regarded as one of the four acoustically best concert halls in the world. Some 600 concerts per season (Sept–June) are presented here. Only 10 to 12 of these are played by the Vienna Philharmonic, and these are subscription concerts, so they're always sold out long in advance. Standing room is

Wine Tasting in the *Heurigen*

Heurigen are Viennese wine taverns, celebrated in operettas, films, and song. They are found on the outskirts of Vienna, principally in Grinzing (the most popular district) and in Sievering, Neustift, Nussdorf, or Heiligenstadt. **Grinzing** (tram: 38) lies at the edge of the Vienna Woods, a 15-minute drive northwest of the center.

Only 20 minutes from Vienna, **Weingut Wolff**, Rathstrasse 50, Neustift (© 01/440-3727; tram: 41), is one of the most endurable and beloved of Heurigen. Although aficionados claim the best are "deep in the countryside" of Lower Austria, this one comes closest on the borderline of Vienna to offering an authentic experience. In summer, you're welcomed to a flower-decked garden set against a backdrop of ancient vineyards. You can really fill up your platter here, with some of the best wursts (sausages) and roast meats (especially the delectable pork), as well as fresh salads. Find a table under a cluster of grapes and sample the fruity young wines, especially the chardonnay, Sylvaner, and Gruner Veltliner. The tavern is open daily from 11am to 1am with main courses ranging from 5.80€ to 11€.

Altes Presshaus, Cobenzigasse 15 (© 01/320-0203), was established in 1527, the oldest continuously operating Heurige in Grinzing, with an authentic cellar you might ask to visit. The place has an authentic, smoke-stained character with wood paneling and antique furniture. The garden terrace blossoms throughout the summer. Try such Heurigen-inspired fare as smoked pork shoulder, roast pork shank, sauerkraut, potatoes, and dumplings. Meals cost 10€ to 17€; drinks begin at 3€. It's open daily from 4pm to midnight; closed January and February.

available at almost any performance, but you must line up hours before the show. Tickets are 3€ for standing room; up to 120€ for seats. The box office is open Monday through Friday from 9am to 7:30pm; Saturday from 9am to 5pm.

Vienna is the home of four major symphony orchestras, including the world-acclaimed Vienna Symphony and the Vienna Philharmonic. In addition to the ÖRF Symphony Orchestra and the Niederöster-reichische Tonkünstler, there are literally dozens of others, ranging from smaller orchestras to chamber orchestras. The orchestras sometimes perform at the **Konzerthaus,** Lothringerstrasse 20 (© **01/242-002;** www.konzerthaus.at; U-Bahn: Stadt-Park), a major concert hall with three auditoriums, and also the venue for chamber music and other programs.

THEATER   For performances in English, head to **Vienna's English Theatre,** Josefsgasse 12 (© **01/402-12600;** www.englishtheatre.at; U-Bahn: Rathaus). The **Burgtheater (National Theater),** Dr.-Karl-Lueger-Ring 2 (© **01/5144-4145;** www.burgtheater.at; tram: 1, 2, D, or J to Burgtheater), produces classical and modern plays. Even if you don't understand German, you might want to attend a performance here, especially if a familiar Shakespeare play is being staged. This is one of Europe's premier repertory theaters. Tickets are 9€ to 178€ for seats, 2€ to 3.50€ for standing room.

NIGHTCLUBS, CABARETS & BARS

The noteworthy architect Adolf Loos designed the very dark, sometimes myste-rious **Loos American Bar,** Kärntnerdurchgang 10 (© **01/512-3283;** U-Bahn: Stephansplatz), in 1908. Today it welcomes singles, couples who tend to be bilingual and very hip, and all manner of clients from the arts and media scenes of Vienna. The mixologist's specialties include six kinds of martinis, plus five kinds of Manhattans. It's open Sunday through Wednesday from noon to 4am, and Thursday through Saturday from noon to 5am.

The most famous jazz pub in Austria, **Jazzland,** Franz-Josefs-Kai 29 (© **01/ 533-2575;** U-Bahn: Schwedenplatz), is noted for the quality of its U.S.- and cen-tral European–based performers. It's in a deep, 200-year-old cellar, of the type the Viennese used to store staples during the city's many sieges. Amid exposed brick walls and dim lighting, you can order drinks or dinner. The place is open nightly from 7pm to 1am. Music begins at 9pm, and three sets are performed.

The ancient bricks and scarred wooden tables of **Esterházykeller,** Haarhof 1 (© **01/533-3483;** U-Bahn: Stephansplatz), are permeated with the aroma of spilled beer. This is one of the most authentic beer cellars in all of Austria. Grip the railing firmly and begin your descent into this tavern, where a fun-loving crowd gathers nightly. The place is open Monday through Friday from 11am to 11pm and Saturday and Sunday from 4 to 11pm.

The late-night set flocks to **Franco's Club,** Johannesgasse 27 (© **01/512-8282;** U-Bahn: Stadpark), an elegant Italian dinner and dance restaurant/bar combined. Live entertainment from a five-member dance band is provided, beginning around 8:30pm, and a roster of available singles is almost guaranteed for anyone looking for a dance partner. Most Thursdays through Saturdays after 11pm, Franco Andolfo, a well-known Italy-born singer (he's been referred to as "the Frank Sinatra of *Mitteleuropa*"), will sing, tell jokes, and entertain. The complex is open Tuesday through Saturday from 3pm till 4am, with the restau-rant open from 3pm until midnight, but frankly, the joint doesn't start to get interesting until around 9pm.

Alfi's Goldener Spiegel, Linke Wienzeile 46 (entrance on Stiegengasse; © **01/586-6608;** U-Bahn: Kettenbrückengasse), is the most enduring gay restaurant in Vienna and also its most popular gay bar, attracting mostly male clients to its position near Vienna's Naschmarkt. The place is very cruisy. The bar is open Wednesday through Monday from 7pm to 2am.

Frauencafé, Langegasse 11 (© **01/406-37-54;** U-Bahn: Lerchenfelder-strasse), is exactly what a translation of its name would imply: a politically con-scious cafe for lesbians and (to a lesser degree) heterosexual women who appreciate the company of other women. Established in 1977 in cramped quar-ters in a century-old building, it's filled with magazines, newspapers, modern paintings, and a clientele of Austrian and foreign women.

2 Salzburg ★★★

A baroque city on the banks of the Salzach River, set against a mountain back-drop, Salzburg is the beautiful capital of the state of Salzburg. The city and the river were named after its early residents who earned their living in the salt mines. In this "heart of the heart of Europe," Mozart was born in 1756, and the composer's association with the city beefs up tourism.

The **Old Town** lies on the left bank of the river, where a monastery and bish-opric were founded in 700. From that start, Salzburg grew in power and prestige, becoming an archbishopric in 798. In the heyday of the prince-archbishops, the city became known as the "German Rome." Responsible for much of its architectural grandeur are those masters of the baroque, Fischer von Erlach and Lukas von Hildebrandt.

"The City of Mozart," "Silent Night," and *The Sound of Music*—Salzburg lives essentially off its rich past. It is a front-ranking cultural mecca for classical music year-round. The city is the setting for the Salzburg Festival, a world-renowned annual event that attracts music lovers, especially Mozart fans, from all over the globe. Salzburg's natural setting among alpine peaks on both banks of the Salzach River gives it the backdrop perpetuating its romantic image.

As one of Europe's greatest tourist capitals, most of Salzburg's day-to-day life spins around promoting its music and its other connections. Although *The Sound of Music* was filmed in 1964, this Julie Andrews blockbuster has become a cult attraction and is definitely alive and well in Salzburg. Ironically, Austria was the only country in the world where the musical failed when it first opened. It played for only a single week in Vienna, closing after audiences dwindled.

Salzburg is only a short distance from the Austrian–German frontier, so it's convenient for exploring many of the attractions of Bavaria (see chapter 7). Situated on the northern slopes of the Alps, the city lies at the intersection of traditional European trade routes and is well served by air, Autobahn, and rail.

ESSENTIALS

GETTING THERE   By Plane   The **Salzburg Airport–W.A. Mozart,** Innsbrucker Bundesstrasse 95 (© **0662/8580;** www.salzburg-airport.com), lies 3km (2 miles) southwest of the city center. It has regularly scheduled air service to all Austrian airports, as well as to Frankfurt, Amsterdam, Brussels, Berlin, Dresden, Düsseldorf, Hamburg, London, Paris, and Zurich. Major airlines serving the Salzburg airport are Austrian Airlines (© **0662/85-45-11**), Air France (© **01/50-2222-403**), Lufthansa (© **081010/258-080**), and Tyrolean (© **0662/85-45-33**).

Bus no. 77 runs between the airport and Salzburg's main rail station. Departures are frequent, and the 20-minute trip costs 2.80€ one-way. By taxi it's only about 15 minutes, but you'll pay at least 10€ to 15€.

By Train   Salzburg's main rail station, the **Salzburg Hauptbahnhof,** Südtirol-erplatz (© **05/1717**), is on the major rail lines of Europe, with frequent arrivals from all the main cities of Austria and from European cities such as Munich. Between 5:05am and 8:05pm, trains arrive every 30 minutes from Vienna (trip time: 3½ hr.); a one-way fare is 32€. There are eight daily trains from Innsbruck (2 hr.); a one-way fare is 25€. Trains also arrive every 30 minutes from Munich (2½ hr.), with a one-way ticket costing 22€.

From the train station, buses depart to various parts of the city, including the Altstadt. Or you can walk to the Altstadt in about 20 minutes. Taxis are also available. The rail station has a currency exchange and storage lockers.

By Car   Salzburg is 334km (209 miles) southwest of Vienna and 152km (95 miles) east of Munich. It's reached from all directions by good roads, including Autobahn A8 from the west (Munich), A1 from the east (Vienna), and A10 from the south. Route 20 comes into Salzburg from points north and west, and Route 159 serves towns and cities from the southeast.

VISITOR INFORMATION   Tourist Offices   The **Salzburg Information Office,** Mozartplatz 5 (© **0662/88987-330;** www.salzburginfo.at; bus: 5, 6, or 51), is open July through September daily from 9am to 8pm and off season Monday through Saturday from 9am to 6pm. The office makes hotel reservations for a 7.2% deposit (which will be credited to your hotel bill), plus a 2.20€

Salzburg

ATTRACTIONS ●

Dom (Salzburg Cathedral) **19**
Festspielhaus (Festival Theater) **13**
Glockenspiel (Carillon) **20**
Hohensalzburg Fortress **16**
Mirabell-Garten (Mirabell Gardens) **6**
Mönchsberg **15**
Mozart Geburtshaus (Mozart Birthplace) **25**
Mozart Wolnhaus (Mozart Residence) **8**
Mozarteum **7**
Museum Carolino Augusteum **10**
Petersfriedhof (St. Peter's Cemetery) **17**
Residenz State Rooms **18**
Schloss Mirabell (Mirabell Palace) **3**
Stiftskirche St. Peter **17**

ACCOMMODATIONS ■

Altstadthotel Weisse Taube **21**
Altstadthotel Wolf-Dietrich **4**
Altstadt SAS Radisson **23**
Goldener Hirsch **11**
Hotel Am Nussdorferhof **14**
Hotel Auersperg **2**
Hotel Blaue Gans **12**
Hotel Elefant **24**
Hotel Gastein **22**
Pension Bergland **5**
Sacher Salzburg Osterreichischer Hof **9**
Salzburg Sheraton Hotel **1**

booking fee. There's also a **tourist information office** on Platform 2A of the Hauptbahnhof, Südtirolerplatz (✆ **0662/88987-340**).

CITY LAYOUT   Most of what visitors come to see lies on the left bank of the Salzach River in the **Altstadt (Old Town)**. If you're driving, you must leave your car in the modern part of town—the right bank of the Salzach—and enter the Old Town on foot, as most of it is for pedestrians only.

The heart of the inner city is **Residenzplatz,** which has the largest and finest baroque fountain this side of the Alps. On the western side of the square stands the **Residenz,** palace of the prince-archbishops, and on the southern side of the square is the **Salzburg Cathedral** (or Dom). To the west of the Dom lies **Domplatz,** linked by archways dating from 1658. Squares to the north and south appear totally enclosed. On the southern side of Max-Reinhardt-Platz and Hofstallgasse, edging toward **Mönchsberg,** stands the **Festspielhaus (Festival Theater),** built on the foundations of the 17th-century court stables.

GETTING AROUND   By Bus/Tram   The city buses and trams provide quick, comfortable service through the city center from the Nonntal parking lot to Sigsmundsplatz, the city-center parking lot. The one-ride fare is 1.45€ adults, .85€ children 6 to 15; those 5 and under travel free. Note that buses stop running at 11pm.

By Taxi   You'll find taxi stands scattered at key points all over the city center and in the suburbs. The Salzburg Funktaxi–Vereinigung (radio taxis) office is at Rainerstrasse 2 (✆ **0662/8111** to order a taxi in advance). Fares start at 2.90€.

By Car   Driving a car in Salzburg isn't recommended. However, you'll probably want a car for touring the areas outside the city (such as Land Salzburg), as using public transportation can be time consuming. Arrangements for car rentals are always best if made in advance. Try **Avis** (✆ **0662/877278**) or **Hertz** (✆ **0662/876674**), both at Ferdinand-Porsche-Strasse 7 and open Monday through Friday from 8:30am to 6pm and Saturday from 8am to 1pm.

By Horse-Drawn Cab   You rent a horse-drawn cab (called a *Fiaker* in German) at Residenzplatz. Four people usually pay 22€ for 20 minutes, 45€ for 50 minutes. But all fares are subject to negotiation.

(*Value* **The Salzburg Card**

The **Salzburg Card** not only lets you use **unlimited public transportation,** but it acts as an admission ticket to the city's most important **cultural sights.** With the card you can visit Mozart's birthplace, the Hohensalzburg fortress, the Residenz gallery, the world-famous water fountain gardens at Hellbrunn, the Baroque Museum in the Mirabell Gardens, and the gala rooms in the Archbishop's Residence. The card is also good for sights outside of town, including the Hellbrunn Zoo, the open-air museum in Grossingmain, the salt mines of the Dürnberg, and the gondola trip at Untersberg. The card, approximately the size of a credit card, comes with a brochure with maps and sightseeing hints.

Cards are valid for 24, 48, and 72 hours and cost 19€, 27€, and 33€, respectively. Children up to 15 years of age receive a 50% discount. You can buy the pass from Salzburg travel agencies, hotels, tobacconists, and municipal offices.

By Bicycle   City officials have developed a network of bicycle paths, which are indicated on city maps. May through September, you can rent bicycles at **Top-bike,** at the Staatsbrücke or Main Bridge (© **0662/6764-76-7259**), daily from 9am to 7pm. Rentals cost about 13€ per day, with a 10% discount for Salzburg Cardholders.

 ## FAST FACTS: Salzburg

American Express The office at Mozartplatz 5–7, adjacent to Residenz-platz (© **0662/8080**; bus: 5 or 6), is open Monday through Friday from 9am to 5:30pm and Saturday from 9am to noon.

Business Hours Most shops and stores are open Monday through Friday from 9am to 6pm and Saturday usually from 9am to noon. Some of the smaller shops shut down at noon for a lunch break. Salzburg observes *langer Samstag,* which means that most stores stay open until 5pm on selected Saturdays. Banks are open Monday through Friday from 8am to noon and 2 to 4:30pm.

Currency Exchange You can exchange money at the Hauptbahnhof on Südtirolerplatz daily from 7am to 10pm, and at the airport daily from 9am to 4pm.

Dentists For an English-speaking dentist, call **Dentistenkammer,** Faber-strasse 2 (© **0662/87-34-66**).

Doctors If you suddenly fall ill, your best source of information for find-ing a doctor is the reception desk of your hotel. If you want a compre-hensive list of doctors and their respective specialties, which you can acquire in Salzburg or even before your arrival, contact **Ärztekammer für Salzburg,** Bergstrasse 14, A-5020 Salzburg (© **0662/87-13-27**). And if your troubles flare up over a weekend, the **Medical Emergency Center of the Austrian Red Cross** maintains a hot line (© **141**), which you can use to describe your problem. A staff member there will either ask you to visit their headquarters at Karl Renner Strasse 7, or send a medical expert to wherever you're staying. This service is available from 5pm on Friday to 8am on Monday, and on public holidays.

Drugstores (Apotheke) Larger pharmacies, especially those in the city cen-ter, tend to remain open without a break Monday through Friday from 8am to 6pm and Saturday from 8am to noon. For night service, and service on Saturday afternoon and Sunday, pharmacies display a sign giving the address of the nearest pharmacy that has agreed to remain open over the weekend or throughout the night. A pharmacy that's particularly conven-ient to Salzburg's commercial center is **Elisabeth-Apotheke,** Elisabethstrasse 1 (© **0662/87-14-84**), north of Rainerstrasse toward the train station.

Embassies/Consulates The consular agency of the **United States,** at Alter Markt 1 (© **0662/84-87-76**), is open Monday through Thursday from 9am to noon to assist U.S. citizens with emergencies. The consulate of **Great Britain,** at Alter Markt 4 (© **0662/84-81-33**), is open Monday through Fri-day from 9am to noon.

Emergencies Call © **133** for police, © **122** to report a fire, and © **144** for an ambulance.

Internet Access The most convenient cafe with Internet capability is the **Internet Café**, Mozartplatz (© **0662/84-48-22;** bus: 5 or 6), across from the tourist office. It's open daily from 9am to 11pm and charges 9€ per hour of Internet access.

Post Office The main post office is at Residenzplatz 9 (© **0662/844-1210;** bus: 5 or 6). The post office at the main railway station is open daily from 7am to 10pm.

Telephone The **country code** for Austria is **43**. The **city code** for Salzburg is **662;** use this code when you're calling from outside Austria. If you're within Austria, use **0662**.

WHERE TO STAY
ON THE LEFT BANK (ALTSTADT)
Very Expensive

Altstadt SAS Radisson 🏵🏵 This is not your typical Radisson property—in fact, it's a radical departure for the chain in style and charm. Dating from 1377, it's a luxuriously and elegantly converted Altstadt hostelry. Its closest rival in town is the old-world Goldener Hirsch, to which it comes in second. The old and new are blended in perfect harmony here, and the historic facade conceals top-rate comforts and amenities. In a structure of this size, rooms naturally vary greatly in size, but all have a certain charm and sparkle and are exceedingly comfortable with some of the city's best beds, plus luxurious bathrooms with showers.

Rudolfskai 28/Judengasse 15, A-5020 Salzburg. © 800/333-3333 in the U.S., or 0662/848-571. Fax 0662/ 848-571-6. www.austria-trend.at. 62 units. 215€–495€ double; 470€–610€ suite. Rates include buffet breakfast. AE, DC, MC, V. Parking 25€. Bus: 5, 6, or 55. **Amenities:** Restaurant; bar; room service; baby-sitting; laundry/dry cleaning service. *In room:* TV, minibar, hair dryer, safe.

Goldener Hirsch 🏵🏵🏵 The award for the finest hotel in Salzburg goes to this place, steeped in legend and with a history dating from 1407. The hotel is built on a small scale yet it absolutely reeks of aristocratic elegance, which is enhanced by the superb staff. Near Mozart's birthplace, the hotel is composed of four medieval town houses, three of which are joined together in a labyrinth of rustic hallways and staircases. The fourth, called "The Coppersmith's House," is across the street and contains 17 charming, spacious rooms. All rooms in the complex are beautifully furnished and maintained, with luxurious full-size bathrooms.

Getreidegasse 37, A-5020 Salzburg. © 800/325-3535 in the U.S., or 0662/8084. Fax 0662/8485-178-45. www.goldenerhirsch.com. 69 units. 331€–650€ double; 593€–1,090€ suite. Higher rates at festival time (the 1st week of Apr and mid-July to Aug). AE, DC, MC, V. You can double-park in front of the Getreidegasse entrance or at the Karajanplatz entrance, and a staff member will take your vehicle to the hotel's garage for 28€. Bus: 55. **Amenities:** 2 restaurants; bar; room service; babysitting; laundry/dry cleaning service. *In room:* TV, minibar, hair dryer, safe.

Moderate

Altstadthotel Weisse Taube This hotel is in the pedestrian area of the Old Town a few steps from Mozartplatz, but you can drive up to it to unload baggage. Constructed in 1365, the Weisse Taube has been owned by the Haubner family since 1904. Rooms are, for the most part, renovated and comfortably streamlined, with traditional furnishings, frequently renewed beds, and small but efficiently laid-out bathrooms with shower-tub combinations. The whole place is kept up with spotless housekeeping.

Kaigasse 9, A-5020 Salzburg. © **0662/84-24-04.** Fax 0662/84-17-83. www.weissetaube.at. 31 units. 93€–125€ double. Rates include breakfast. AE, DC, MC, V. Garage 9€. Bus: 5, 51, or 55. **Amenities:** Breakfast room; bar; lounge. *In room:* TV, minibar, hair dryer, safe.

Hotel Am Nussdorferhof   The only drawback to this hotel is its location in a quiet residential suburb—a 20-minute walk south of Salzburg's historic core. If that isn't a problem for you, it might make a safe and happy refuge for you during your time in Salzburg. Its congenial owners, Herbert and Ilse Kronegger, know the cultural and geographical features of their city in intricate detail and are eager to help newcomers with the city's logistics. About half the guest rooms are outfitted in old-fashioned Teutonic patterns, with touches of wood and alpine references. The other half are conservatively international, with bland 1970s-era furnishings and enough modern comforts to ensure a pleasant overnight stay. Bathrooms are trimmed in tile and in most cases come with shower-tub combinations. On-site are a bar and a cozy Italian restaurant (La Fontana), with a menu that features well-prepared versions of pizza, pasta, and (usually) tried-and-true northern Italian cuisine.

Moosstrasse 36, A-5020 Salzburg. © **0662/824838.** Fax 0662/824-8389. www.nussdorferhof.at. 30 units. High season 130€ double; winter 98€–115€ double. Rates include breakfast and parking. AE, DC, MC, V. Bus: 15, 16. **Amenities:** Restaurant; bar; room service; babysitting. *In room:* TV, hair dryer.

Hotel Blaue Gans   Only a short walk from the much more expensive Goldener Hirsch, the much-renovated "Blue Goose" has been functioning as an inn for more than 400 years. The building that houses the inn is probably 700 years old, but the rooms were renovated extensively between 1998 and 2000. All have good beds with firm mattresses and full bathrooms. Those facing the courtyard are quieter and much more desirable. Room nos. 332 and 336 are the most spacious.

Getreidegasse 43, A-5020 Salzburg. © **0662/84-13-17.** Fax 0662/84-13-179. www.blauegans.at. 38 units. 129€–179€ double. Rates include buffet breakfast. AE, DC, MC, V. Parking 14€. Bus: 1 or 2. **Amenities:** Restaurant; bar; babysitting; laundry/dry cleaning service. *In room:* TV, minibar, hair dryer, safe.

Hotel Elefant   Near the Old Town Rathaus, in a quiet alley off Getreidegasse, is this well-established, family-run hotel. It, too, is in one of Salzburg's most ancient buildings—more than 700 years old. The well-furnished and high-ceilinged rooms have small bathrooms with shower-tub combinations. Inside the hotel are two restaurants serving Austrian and international cuisine: the vaulted Bürgerstüberl, where high wooden banquettes separate the tables, and the historic Ratsherrnkeller, known as the wine cellar of Salzburg in the 17th century.

Sigmund-Haffner-Gasse 4, A-5020 Salzburg. © **0662/84-33-97.** Fax 0662/84-01-0928. www.elefant.at. 31 units. 122€–176€ double. Rates include buffet breakfast. AE, DC, MC, V. Parking 7.30€. Bus: 1, 2, 5, 6, or 51. **Amenities:** 2 restaurants; bar; room service; babysitting; laundry/dry cleaning service. *In room:* TV, minibar, hair dryer, safe.

ON THE RIGHT BANK
Expensive
Sacher Salzburg Osterreichischer Hof ✸✸✸   Only the Goldener Hirsch rivals this charmer. Built as the Hotel d'Autriche in 1866, this hotel has survived the ravages of war and has been renovated countless times. A new era began when the Gürtler family, owners of the Hotel Sacher in Vienna, took over in 1988, turning the hotel into a jewel amid the villas on the riverbank. The cheerful rooms are well furnished, quite spacious, and individually decorated; each has a luxurious bathroom equipped with a tub/shower combo. Try to reserve one overlooking the river. The cafe serves Austria's most fabled pastry, the original Sacher torte.

Schwarzstrasse 5–7, A-5020 Salzburg. © **800/223-6800** in the U.S. and Canada, or 0662/889-77. Fax 0662/889-77-551. www.sacher.com. 127 units. 205€–800€ double; 555€–1,890€ suite. Rates include buffet breakfast. AE, DC, MC, V. Parking 25€. Bus: 1, 5, 6, 29, or 51. **Amenities:** 2 restaurants; 2 bars; cafe; lounge; fitness center; sauna; room service; laundry/dry cleaning service. *In room:* TV, minibar, hair dryer, safe.

Salzburg Sheraton Hotel 🏵🏵 One of the crown jewels of the Sheraton chain, this government-rated five-star seven-story hotel opened in 1984 in a desirable location about a 10-minute walk from Mozartplatz. The Austrian architect who designed this place took great pains to incorporate it into its 19th-century neighborhood. Rooms have thick wall-to-wall carpeting and contain beds with built-in headboards. Bathrooms have make-up mirrors and hair dryers. The exclusive junior, queen, and presidential suites are filled with elegant Biedermeier furniture. Half the rooms overlook the Mirabell Gardens.

Auerspergstrasse 4, A-5020 Salzburg. © **800/325-3535** in the U.S., or 0662/88-99-90. Fax 0662/88-17-76. www.sheraton.at. 184 units. 130€–287€ double; 321€–535€ suite. AE, DC, MC, V. Parking 12€. Bus: 1. **Amenities:** 2 restaurants; bar; pool; sauna; room service; babysitting; laundry/dry cleaning service. *In room:* TV, minibar, hair dryer, safe.

Moderate

Hotel Auersperg 🏵 With its own sunny gardens, this traditional family-run hotel consists of two buildings: a main structure and a less expensive and less desirable annex. There's an old-fashioned look of charm wherever you go, from the reception hall with its molded ceilings to the antique-filled drawing room to the convivial and informal library bar. The warm, cozy, and large guest rooms are especially inviting, with excellent beds and well-equipped bathrooms with tubs and showers.

Auerspergstrasse 61, A-5027 Salzburg. © **0662/889-44-0.** Fax 0662/88-944-55. www.auersperg.at. 51 units. 129€–176€ double; 173€–227€ suite. Rates include breakfast. AE, DC, MC, V. Free parking. Bus: 15 from the train station. **Amenities:** Breakfast room; bar; fitness center; sauna; laundry/dry cleaning. *In room:* TV, minibar, hair dryer, safe.

Inexpensive

Altstadthotel Wolf-Dietrich 🏵 Two 19th-century town houses were joined together to make this select little hotel. The lobby and ground-floor reception area have a friendly and elegant atmosphere and bright, classical furnishings. The smallish rooms are appealing and comfortably furnished, with excellent beds and tiny bathrooms with shower-tub combinations. The ground-floor cafe, Weiner Kaffeehaus, is reminiscent of the extravagant coffeehouses built in the former century in Vienna, Budapest, and Prague.

Wolf-Dietrich-Strasse 7, A-5020 Salzburg. © **0662/87-12-75.** Fax 0662/88-23-20. www.salzburg-hotel.at. 27 units. 109€–179€ double. Rates include breakfast. AE, DC, MC, V. Parking 11€. Closed Feb to Mar 15. Bus: 1, 2, 5, 6, or 51. **Amenities:** 2 restaurants; bar, cafe; pool; sauna; solarium; room service; babysitting; laundry/dry cleaning service. *In room:* TV, minibar, hair dryer.

Hotel Gastein 🏵 This prosperous-looking Teutonic villa lies amid calm green scenery on the bank of the Salzach River. Only a few minutes from the center of the town's oldest boroughs, the house offers true Salzburg atmosphere. You'll feel like you're staying in an upper-class private home. During the annual music festival the place is filled with musicians, who love the spacious flowering garden for breakfast or afternoon tea. The large guest rooms have furniture crafted by well-known Salzburg artists, firm beds, and private balconies. Bathrooms, though often small, are exceedingly well maintained and equipped with shower-tub combinations.

Ignaz-Rieder-Kai 25, A-5020 Salzburg. © 0662/62-25-65. Fax 0662/62-25-659. www.hotel-gastein.at. 16 units. 105€–156€ double; 156€–248€ suite. Rates include breakfast. AE, DC, MC, V. Free parking. Bus: 49. **Amenities:** Breakfast room; lounge. *In room:* TV, minibar.

Pension Bergland ⭐ *Finds* Cozy, personalized, and substantial, this guest-house sits in a quiet residential neighborhood. It welcomes visitors in a "music room" where there's a bar serving beer, wine, and coffee, and a collection of gui-tars and lutes displayed on the walls. Guest rooms are comfortable, minimalist, and modern looking, with larger-than-expected bathrooms containing shower-tub combinations and, in many cases, a piece of furniture handmade by mem-bers of the Kuhn family, your hosts. The pension will rent you a bike and dispense information about where to ride.

15 Rupertsgasse, A-5020 Salzburg. © 0662/872318. Fax 0662/872318-8. www.berglandhotel.at. 18 units. 80€ double. Rates include buffet breakfast. AE, DC, MC, V. Closed Nov. Free parking. Bus: 29. **Amenities:** Breakfast room; lounge. *In room:* TV, hair dryer.

WHERE TO DINE

Two special desserts you'll want to sample while here are the famous *Salzburger Nockerln,* a light mixture of stiff egg whites, as well as the elaborate confection known as the *Mozart-Kugeln,* with bittersweet chocolate, hazelnut nougat, and marzipan. You'll also want to taste the beer in one of the numerous Salzburg breweries.

ON THE LEFT BANK (OLD TOWN)
Very Expensive

Goldener Hirsch ⭐⭐⭐ AUSTRIAN/VIENNESE The best restaurant in Salzburg's best hotel attracts the brightest luminaries of the international music and business community. The venue is chic, top-notch, impeccable, and charm-ing, richly sought after during peak season. It's staffed with a superb team of chefs and waiters who preside over an atmosphere of elegant simplicity. The food is so tasty and beautifully served that the kitchen ranks among the top two or three in Salzburg. Specialties include saddle of farm-raised venison with red cab-bage; king prawns in an okra-curry ragout served with perfumed Thai rice; and tenderloin of beef and veal on morel cream sauce with cream potatoes. In sea-son, expect a dish devoted to game, such as venison or roast duckling.

Getreidegasse 37. © 0662/80-84-0. Reservations required. Main courses 20€–26€. 3-course fixed-price lunch or dinner 36€; 5-course fixed-price dinner 52€. AE, MC, V. Daily noon–2:30pm and 6:30–9:30pm. Bus: 55.

Purzelbaum ⭐ AUSTRIAN/FRENCH In a residential neighborhood, this restaurant is near a duck pond at the bottom of a steep incline leading up to Salzburg Castle. During the Salzburg Festival you're likely to see the most dedi-cated music lovers in Europe hanging out here. Menu items change according to the whim of the chef and include such well-prepared dishes as turbot-and-olive casserole; lamb in white wine sauce with beans and polenta; and the house specialty, scampi Grüstl, composed of fresh shrimp with sliced potatoes baked with herbs in a casserole.

Zugallistrasse 7. © 0662/84-88-43. Reservations required. Main courses 20€–28€; 4-course fixed-price menu 45€. AE, DC, MC, V. Mon–Sat noon–2pm and 6–11pm. Also open Sun in Aug. Closed July 1–14. Bus: 55.

Moderate
Herzl Tavern ⭐⭐ *Value* AUSTRIAN/VIENNESE With an entrance on the landmark Karajanplatz, Herzl Tavern lies next door to the glamorous Goldener

Cafe Society

Café-Restaurant Glockenspiel, Mozartplatz 2 (© 0662/84-14-03-0; bus: 55), is the city's most popular cafe, with about 100 tables with armchairs out front. You might want to spend an afternoon here, particularly when there's live chamber music. Upon entering, you can't miss a glass case filled with every caloric delight west of Vienna. For dinner, you can sit on the balcony and look over Salzburg's famous buildings while enjoying regional and international specialties. Many people, however, come just for the drinks and pastries. Try the Maria Theresia, which contains orange liqueur. In summer, the cafe is open daily from 9am to midnight (food served to 11pm); the rest of the year, daily from 9am to 8pm (food served to 6pm). It's closed the second and third weeks of November and January.

Established in 1705, **Café Tomaselli** ⋩, Alter Markt 9 (© 0662/84-44-88; bus: 5, 6, or 55), opens onto one of the most charming cobblestone squares of the Altstadt. Aside from the summer chairs placed outdoors, you'll find a high-ceilinged room with many tables. It's a great place to just sit and talk. Another, more formal room to the right of the entrance with oil portraits of well-known 19th-century Salzburgers attracts a haute bourgeois crowd. A waiter will show you a pastry tray filled with 40 different kinds of cakes, which you're free to order or wave away. Other menu items include omelets, wursts, ice cream, and a wide range of drinks. Of course, the pastries and ice cream are all homemade. The cafe is open Monday through Saturday from 7am to midnight and Sunday from 8am to 9pm.

Hirsch, of which it's a part. Good value attracts both visitors and locals to its pair of cozy rooms, one paneled and timbered. Waitresses in dirndls serve appetizing entrees, which are likely to include roast pork with dumplings, various grills, game stew (in season), and, for the heartiest eaters, a farmer's plate of boiled pork, roast pork, grilled sausages, dumplings, and sauerkraut.

Karajanplatz 7. © 0662/808-4889. Reservations recommended. Main courses 10€–15€; fixed-price menu 12€. AE, DC, MC, V. Daily 11:30am–11pm. Bus: 55.

Stiftskeller St. Peter (Peterskeller) ⋩ AUSTRIAN/VIENNESE Legend has it that Mephistopheles met with Faust in this tavern, which isn't that farfetched, considering it was established by Benedictine monks in A.D. 803. In fact, it's the oldest restaurant in Europe and is housed in the abbey of the church that supposedly brought Christianity to Austria. Aside from a collection of baroque banquet rooms, there's an inner courtyard with rock-cut vaults, a handful of dignified wood-paneled rooms, and a brick-vaulted cellar. In addition to wine from the abbey's own vineyards, the tavern serves good home-style Austrian cooking, including roast pork in gravy with sauerkraut and bread dumplings, and loin of lamb with asparagus. Vegetarian dishes, such as semolina dumplings on noodles in a parsley sauce, are also featured. They are especially known here for their desserts. Try the apple strudel or sweet curd strudel with vanilla sauce or ice cream, and, most definitely, the famed *Salzburger Nockerln.*

St.-Peter-Bezirk 1–4. ℂ **0662/84-12-680.** Reservations recommended. Main courses 14€–15€; fixed-price menus 18€–46€. AE, MC, V. Daily 11:30am–2:30pm and 6–10pm. Closed Sept 24. Bus: 29.

Zum Eulenspiegel ⚜ AUSTRIAN/VIENNESE   Opposite Mozart's birthplace, this restaurant sits at one end of a quiet cobblestone square in the Old Town. Inside, guests have a choice of five rooms on three different levels, all rustically but elegantly decorated. A small and rustic bar area on the ground floor is a pleasant place for pre-dinner drinks. Traditional Austrian cuisine is meticulously adhered to here. The menu features such classic dishes as *Tafelspitz* (boiled beef), the famous Wiener schnitzel, braised trout with dill-flavored potatoes, pork cutlets with fresh herbs, filet of pork with warm cabbage salad and bacon, and *Salzburger Nockerln* or peaches with hot fudge and vanilla ice cream for dessert.

Hagenauerplatz 2. ℂ **0662/84-31-80.** Reservations required. Main courses 12€–20€. AE, MC, V. Mon–Sat 11am–2pm and 6–10:30pm. Closed Feb 1–Mar 15. Tram: 2. Bus: 2.

Inexpensive

Festungsrestaurant ⚜ (Kids) SALZBURG/AUSTRIAN   Come here and you'll be dining at the former stronghold of the prince-archbishops of Salzburg. The restaurants and gardens are actually in the castle, perched on a huge rock 122m (400 ft.) above the Old Town and the Salzach. The restaurant commands a panoramic view of the city and the surrounding countryside. From Easter to October classical concerts are held nightly in the *Fürstenzimmer,* often featuring the work of Mozart. The kitchen offers local specialties such as a Salzburger *Bierfleisch* (goulash) and Salzburger schnitzel, along with many other dishes. This is good old-fashioned Austrian cooking. In winter, when the restaurant is closed, the *Burgtaverne* inside the castle serves food and drink.

Hohensalzburg, Mönchsberg 34. ℂ **0662/84-17-80.** Reservations required July–Aug. Main courses 7.50€–14€. MC, V. Apr–Oct, daily 10am–9pm; Dec–Mar, daily 10am–5pm. Closed Nov. Funicular from the Old Town

Krimpelstätter SALZBURGER/AUSTRIAN   This is an enduring Salzburg favorite dating from 1548. In summer, the beer garden, full of roses and trellises, attracts up to 300 visitors at a time. If you want a snack, a beer, or a glass of wine, head for the paneled door marked *Gastezimmer* in the entry corridor. If you're looking for a more formal, less visited area, three cozy antique dining rooms sit atop a flight of narrow stone steps. You'll find tasty and high-quality Land Salzburg regional cuisine featuring wild game dishes. Start with the cream of goose soup or homemade chamois sausage. Traditional main courses include roast pork with dumplings, and fried sausages with sauerkraut and potatoes. Spinach dumplings are topped with a cheese sauce, and marinated beef stew comes with noodles in butter.

Müllner Hauptstrasse 31. ℂ **0662/43-22-74.** Reservations recommended. Main courses 5.60€–14€. No credit cards. Tues–Sat 11am–2pm and 6pm–midnight (also Mon May–Sept). Closed 3 weeks in Jan. Bus: 49 or 95.

Sternbräu AUSTRIAN   This place seems big enough to have fed half the Austro-Hungarian army, with a series of rooms that follow one after the other in varying degrees of formality. The Hofbräustübl is a rustic fantasy. You can also eat in the chestnut tree–shaded beer garden, usually packed on a summer's night, or under the weathered arcades of an inner courtyard. Daily specials include typical Austrian dishes such as Wiener and chicken schnitzels, trout recipes, cold marinated herring, Hungarian goulash, hearty regional soups, and lots of other *gutbürgerlich* selections. You come here for hearty portions—not for refined cuisine.

Griesgasse 23. © 0662/84-21-40. No reservations. Main courses 5.50€–15€; fixed-price menu 11€–15€. AE, MC, V. Daily 10am–11:30pm. Bus: 2, 5, 12, 49, or 51.

ON THE RIGHT BANK

Expensive

Restaurant Bristol CONTINENTAL   This is the dining counterpart to the upscale restaurant in Salzburg's other top-notch hotel, the Goldener Hirsch. In this case, the venue is a stately, baronial-looking area outfitted in tones of pale orange and accented with large-scale oil paintings. A well-trained staff organizes meals, the best of which include scampi with arugula salad and tomatoes; carpaccio of beef or (in season) venison; Arctic char served with homemade noodles, saffron sauce, and goose liver; roasted lamb served with a gratin of polenta and spinach; and all-vegetarian casseroles.

In the Hotel Bristol, Makartplatz 4. © 0662/873-5577. Reservations recommended. Main courses 18€–25€. AE, DC, MC, V. Mon–Sat 11am–2pm and 6–10pm. Bus: 1, 5, 29, or 51.

Inexpensive

BIO Wirtshaus Hirschenwirt ⊛ *(Finds* AUSTRIAN   This is a hotel dining room, but a hotel dining room with a difference: All of the ingredients used in its cuisine derive from organically grown ingredients, raised in Austria without chemical fertilizers or insecticides. The setting is a quartet of cozy and traditional-looking dining rooms. Menu items change with the season, but might include a creamy pumpkin soup, carpaccio of Austrian beef, *Tafelspitz* (boiled beef), several versions of Wiener schnitzel, and about five different vegetarian dishes, the best of which is small spaetzle in a cheese-flavored onion sauce.

In the Hotel zum Hirschen, St. Julien Strasse 23. © 0662/88-13-35. Reservations recommended. Main courses 7.90€–17€. AE, DC, MC, V. Mon–Sat 12:30–3pm and 6–10pm. Tram: 3 or 6.

Hotel Stadtkrug Restaurant AUSTRIAN/INTERNATIONAL   Across the river from the Altstadt, on the site of a 14th-century farm, this restaurant occupies a structure rebuilt from an older core in 1458. In the 1960s, a modern hotel was added in back. In an antique and artfully rustic setting, you can enjoy hearty, traditional Austrian cuisine, such as cream of potato soup "Old Vienna" style; braised beef with burgundy sauce; or glazed cutlet of pork with caraway seeds, deep-fried potatoes, and French beans with bacon. A dessert specialty is a honey parfait with raspberry sauce.

Linzer Gasse 20. © 0662/87-35-45. Reservations recommended. Main courses 18€–25€. AE, DC, MC, V. Wed–Mon noon–2pm and 6–11pm. Bus: 27 or 29.

Zum Fidelen Affen AUSTRIAN   On the eastern edge of the river near the Staatsbrücke, this is the closest thing in Salzburg to a loud, animated, and jovial pub with food service. It's in one of the city's oldest buildings, dating from 1407. Management's policy is to allow only three reserved tables on any particular evening; the remainder are given to whoever happens to show up. It's best to give your name to the maître d'hôtel, then wait at the bar. Menu items are simple, inexpensive, and based on regional culinary traditions. A house specialty is a gratin of green (spinach) noodles in cream sauce with strips of ham. Also popular are Wiener schnitzels, ham goulash with dumplings, casseroles of seasonal meats and mushrooms, and at least three different kinds of main-course dumplings flavored with meats, cheeses, herbs, and various sauces.

Priesterhausgasse 8. © 0662/877-361. No reservations. Main courses 8€–13€. DC, MC, V. Mon–Sat 5–11:30pm.

SEEING THE SIGHTS IN THE CITY OF MOZART

The Old Town lies between the left bank of the Salzach River and the ridge known as the **Mönchsberg**, which rises to a height of 500m (1,650 ft.) and is the site of Salzburg's gambling casino. The main street of the Altstadt is **Getreidegasse**, a narrow little thoroughfare lined with five- and six-story burghers' buildings. Most of the houses along the street are from the 17th and 18th centuries. Mozart was born at no. 9 (see below). Many lacy-looking wrought-iron signs are displayed, and a lot of the houses have carved windows.

You might begin your tour at **Mozartplatz**, with its outdoor cafes. From here you can walk to the even more expansive Residenzplatz, where torchlight dancing is staged every year, along with outdoor performances.

SIGHTSEEING SUGGESTIONS FOR FIRST-TIME VISITORS

If You Have 1 Day Start slowly with a cup of coffee at the **Café-Restaurant Glockenspiel** on Mozartplatz. Then, from the Altstadt, take the funicular to the **Hohensalzburg Fortress** for a tour. After lunch in an old tavern, visit **Mozart's birthplace** on Getreidegasse, and stroll along the narrow street, most typical in the city. Later, visit the **Residenz.**

If You Have 2 Days In the morning of your second day, explore the Dom and the **cemetery of St.** Peter's, and take a walking tour in the afternoon through the **Altstadt.**

If You Have 3 Days On day 3, visit the many attractions of Salzburg you've missed so far: the **Mönchsberg**, the **Mozart Wohnhaus**, and the **Museum Carolino Augusteum** in the morning. In the afternoon, see the **Mirabell Gardens** and **Mirabell Palace** and at least look at the famous **Festspielhaus (Festival Hall)**, dating from 1607; tours are sometimes possible.

THE TOP ATTRACTIONS

Residenz State Rooms/Residenzgalerie Salzburg ☆☆ This opulent palace, just north of Domplatz in the pedestrian zone, was the seat of the Salzburg prince-archbishops after they no longer needed the protection of the gloomy Hohensalzburg Fortress of Mönchsberg. The Residenz dates from 1120, but work on its series of palaces, which comprised the ecclesiastical complex of the ruling church princes, began in the late 1500s and continued until about 1796. The 17th-century Residenz fountain is one of the largest and most impressive baroque fountains north of the Alps. The child prodigy Mozart often played in the Conference Room for guests. More than a dozen state rooms, each richly decorated, are open to the public via guided tour. On the second floor you can visit the **Residenzgalerie Salzburg** (✆ **0662/84-04-51**, ext. 24), an art gallery containing European paintings from the 16th century to the 19th century.

Residenzplatz 1. ✆ **0662/80-42-26-90** or 0662/84-04-51. Admission to Residenz State Rooms, 5€ adults, 4€ students 16–18 and seniors, 2€ children 6–15, free for children 5 and under. Combined ticket to state rooms and gallery, 7.25€. Residenzgalerie, 4.70€ adults, 3.60€ students 16–18 and seniors, 1.80€ children 6–16. Jan–Apr and Nov Mon–Fri 10am–5pm; May–Oct and Dec daily 10am–4:30pm. Bus: 5 or 6.

Glockenspiel (Carillon) The celebrated glockenspiel with its 35 bells stands across from the Residenz. You can hear this 18th-century carillon at 7am, 11am, and 6pm. At press time, actual visitation of the interior was not allowed. The ideal way to hear the chimes is from one of the cafes lining the edges of the Mozartplatz while sipping your favorite coffee or drink.

Mozartplatz 1. © 0662/80-42-27-84. Bus: 1.

Dom (Salzburg Cathedral) ☆ Located where Residenzplatz flows into Domplatz, this cathedral is world renowned for its 4,000-pipe organ. Hailed by some critics as the "most perfect" northern Renaissance building, the cathedral has a marble facade and twin symmetrical towers. The mighty bronze doors were created in 1959. The themes are Faith, Hope, and Love. The interior has a rich baroque style with elaborate frescoes, the most important of which, along with the altarpieces, were designed by Mascagni of Florence. In the crypt, traces of the old Romanesque cathedral have been unearthed.

The treasure of the cathedral and the "arts and wonders" the archbishops collected in the 17th century are displayed in the **Dom Museum** entered through the cathedral. The **cathedral excavations** around the corner (left of the Dom entrance), show the ruins of the original foundation.

South side of Residenzplatz. © 0662/84-41-89. Free admission to cathedral; excavations, 1.80€ adults, .70€ children 6–15, free for children 5 and under; museum, 4.50€ adults, 1.50€ children. Cathedral daily 8am–7pm (to 6pm in winter); excavations, Easter to mid-Oct, Wed–Sun 9am–5pm (closed mid-Oct to Easter); museum Wed–Sun 9am–5pm, Sun 1–6pm. Closed Nov–Apr. Bus: 1, 3, or 5.

Stiftskirche St. Peter ☆☆ Founded in A.D. 696 by St. Rupert, whose tomb is here, this is the church of St. Peter's Abbey and Benedictine Monastery. Once a Romanesque basilica with three aisles, it was completely overhauled in the 17th and 18th centuries in elegant baroque style. The west door dates from 1240. The church is richly adorned with art treasures that include altar paintings by Kremser Schmidt.

St.-Peter-Bezirk. © 0662/844-578. Free admission. Daily 9am–6pm. Bus: 5, 6, or 55.

Petersfriedhof (St. Peter's Cemetery) ☆☆ This cemetery lies at the stone wall that merges into the Mönchsberg. Many of the aristocratic families of Salzburg lie buried here, as do many other noted persons, including Nannerl Mozart, sister of Wolfgang Amadeus(4 years older than her better-known brother, Nannerl was also an exceptionally gifted musician). You can see the Romanesque Chapel of the Holy Cross and St. Margaret's Chapel, dating from the 15th century. You can also take a self-guided tour through the early Christian catacombs in the rock above the church cemetery.

St.-Peter-Bezirk. © 0662/84-45-78-0. Free admission to cemetery. Catacombs 1€ adults, .60€ children. May–Sept daily 10:30am–5pm; Oct–Apr daily 10:30am–3:30pm. Bus: 1.

Hohensalzburg Fortress ☆☆ *Kids* The stronghold of the ruling prince-archbishops before they moved "downtown" to the Residenz, this fortress towers 120m (400 ft.) above the Salzach River on a rocky dolomite ledge. The massive fortress crowns the Festungsberg and literally dominates Salzburg. Work on Hohensalzburg began in 1077 and wasn't finished until 1681. This is the largest completely preserved castle in central Europe. The elegant state apartments, once the courts of the prince-archbishops, are on display. The **Burgmuseum** contains a collection of medieval art. Plans and prints tracing the growth of Salzburg are on exhibit, as well as instruments of torture and many Gothic artifacts. The **Rainermuseum** has displays of arms and armor. The beautiful late-Gothic **St. George's Chapel** (1501) is adorned with marble reliefs of the apostles. If you're athletic you can reach the fortress on foot from Kapitelplatz by way of Festungsgasse or from the Mönchsberg via the Schartentor.

Visit Hohensalzburg even if you're not interested in the fortress, just for the view from the terrace. From the Reck watchtower you get a panoramic sweep of the Alps. The Kuenberg bastion has a fine view of Salzburg's domes and towers.

You can see the fortress grounds on your own or take a tour of the interior. Conducted 40- to 50-minute tours go through the fortress daily, but hours and departure times depend on the season: November through March, from 10am to 4:30pm; April through June, from 9:30am to 5pm; July through August, from 9am to 6pm; and September through October, from 9:30am to 5pm. The conducted tour of the fortress and the Rainier Museum costs 3€ adults, 1.50€ children 6 to 15, free for children under 6.

Mönchsberg 34. ✆ 0662/84-24-30-11. Admission (excluding guided tour but including museum) 7.10€ adults, 4€ children 6–19, free for children 5 and under. Family ticket 8.70€. Fortress and museums, Oct–Mar daily 9:30am–5pm; Apr–Sept daily 9am–6pm.

MORE ATTRACTIONS

Mozart Geburtshaus (Mozart's Birthplace) ⚐
The house where Wolfgang Amadeus Mozart was born on January 27, 1756, contains exhibition rooms and the apartment of the Mozart family. The main treasures are the valuable paintings (such as the well-known *Mozart and the Piano*, by Joseph Lange) and the violin Mozart used as a child; his concert violin; and his viola, fortepiano, and clavichord.

Getreidegasse 9. ✆ 0662/84-43-13. Admission 5.50€ adults, 4.50€ students, 1.50€ children. Daily 9am–5pm.

Mozart Wohnhaus (Mozart Residence) ⚐
In 1773, the Mozart family vacated the cramped quarters of Mozart's birthplace, and the young Mozart lived here with his family until 1780. In the rooms of the former Mozart family apartments, a museum documents the history of the house and the life and work of Wolfgang Amadeus. The original house was destroyed by bombing in 1944, was rebuilt, and reopened on the eve of Mozart's birthday in 1996. A mechanized audio tour in six languages with relevant musical samples accompanies the visitor through the rooms of the museum.

Makartplatz 8. ✆ 0662/84-43-13. Admission 5.50€ adults, 4.45€ students, 1.50€ children 15 and under. June–Sept daily 9am–5pm; Oct–May daily 10am–5pm. Bus: 1 or 5.

Schloss Mirabell (Mirabell Palace) ⚐
This palace and its gardens were built as a luxurious private residence called Altenau. Prince-Archbishop Wolf Dietrich had it constructed in 1606 for his mistress and the mother of his children, Salome Alt. Not much remains of the original grand structure. Lukas von Hildebrandt rebuilt the *Schloss* in the first quarter of the 18th century, and it was modified after a great fire in 1818. The palace, which is a smaller version of the Tuileries in Paris, today serves as the official residence of the mayor of Salzburg. The ceremonial marble *Barockstiege-Englesstiege,* "angel staircase" with sculptured cherubs, carved by Raphael Donner in 1726, leads to the Marmorsaal, a marble and gold hall used for concerts and weddings.

Rainerstrasse. ✆ 0662/8072-0. Free admission. Staircase: daily 8am–6pm. Marmorsaal: Mon, Wed, and Thurs 8am–4pm; Tues and Fri 9am–4pm. Bus: 1, 5, 6, or 51.

Museum Carolino Augusteum
Several collections are brought together under one roof in this museum reflecting Salzburg's cultural history. The archaeological collection contains the well-known Dürnberg beaked pitcher, as well as Roman mosaics. Some 15th-century Salzburg art is on view, and there are many

paintings from the Romantic period, as well as works by Hans Makart, born in Salzburg in 1840.

Museumsplatz 1. (℃ **0662/6208-08-111.** Admission 3.20€ adults, 2€ seniors over 60, 1€ children 6–19, free for children 5 and under. Daily 9am–5pm. Bus: 1, 49, or 95.

Mönchsberg ⭑⭑   This heavily forested ridge extends for some 2km (1½ miles) above the Altstadt and has fortifications dating from the 15th century. A panoramic view of Salzburg is possible from Mönchsberg Terrace just in front of the Grand Café Winkler.

West of the Hohensalzburg Fortress. (℃ **0662/448-06-285.** The elevators leave daily 9am–11pm; round-trip fare is 2.40€ adults, 1.25€ children 6–15, free for children 5 and under.

Mirabell-Garten (Mirabell Gardens) ⭑   Laid out by Fischer von Erlach on the right bank of the river off Makartplatz, these baroque gardens are studded with statuary and reflecting pools, making them a virtual open-air museum. Be sure to visit the bastion with fantastic marble baroque dwarfs and other figures, by the Pegasus Fountains in the lavish garden west of Schloss Mirabell. You'll also find a natural theater. In summer, free brass band concerts are held Wednesday at 8:30pm and Sunday at 10:30am. From the gardens, you have an excellent view of the Hohensalzburg Fortress.

Admission free. Daily 7am–8pm. Bus: 1, 5, 6, or 51.

ORGANIZED TOURS

The best organized tours are offered by **Salzburg Panorama Tours,** Mirabellplatz (℃ **0662/88-32-11-0;** www.panoramatours.at), which is the Gray Line company for Salzburg.

The original *"Sound of Music* Tour" combines the Salzburg city tour with an excursion to the lake district and other places where the 1965 film with Julie Andrews was shot. The English-speaking guide shows you not only the highlights from the film, but also historical and architectural landmarks in Salzburg and parts of the Salzkammergut countryside. The 4½-hour tour departs daily at 2pm and costs 33€.

You must take your passport along for any of the three trips into **Bavaria** in Germany. One of these—called the **"Eagle's Nest Tour"**—takes visitors to Berchtesgaden and on to Obersalzburg, where Hitler and his inner circle had a vacation retreat. The 4½-hour tour departs daily at 9am, May 15 through October 20, and costs 45€. **"The City & Country Highlights"** tour takes in historic castles and the surrounding Land Salzburg landscape. This 5-hour tour departs daily at 1pm, and costs 45€. Coffee and pastry at the Castle Fuschl are an added treat.

You can book these tours at the bus terminal at Mirabellplatz/St. Andrä Kirche (℃ **0662/87-40-29**). Tour prices are the same for all ages

THE SHOPPING SCENE

Good buys in Salzburg include souvenirs of Salzburg state, dirndls, lederhosen, petit point, and all types of sports gear. **Getreidegasse** is a main shopping thoroughfare, but you'll also find some intriguing little shops on **Residenzplatz.**

Opened in 1871, **Drechslerei Lackner,** Badergasse 2 (℃ **0662/84-23-85;** bus: 68 or 81), offers both antique and modern country wood furniture. Among the new items are chests, chessboards, angels, cupboards, crèches, candlesticks, and, most definitely, chairs. **Musikhaus Pühringer,** Getreildegasse 13 (℃ **0662/ 84-32-67;** bus: 5, 6, or 55), established in 1910, sells all kinds of classical musical instruments, especially those popular in central Europe, as well as a large selection of electronic instruments (including synthesizers and amplifiers). You'll find classical and folk-music CDs and tapes, plus many classical recordings, especially those by Mozart.

Salzburger Heimatwerk, Am Residenzplatz 9 (© **0662/84-41-10;** bus: 5, 6, or 55), is one of the best places in town to buy local Austrian handcrafts and original regional clothing.

Wiener Porzellanmanufaktur Augarten Gesellschaft, Alter Markt 11 (© **0662/84-07-14;** bus: 68 or 81), might very well tempt you to begin a porcelain collection. The origins of this world-class manufacturer go back 275 years. Today, its product is legendary and its patterns, such as *Wiener Rose, Maria Theresia,* and the highly distinctive *Biedermeier,* are well known. The company also produces such historical pieces as the black-and-white demitasse set created by architect/designer Josef Hoffman.

SALZBURG AFTER DARK
THE PERFORMING ARTS

It's said there's a musical event—often a Mozart concert—staged virtually every night in Salzburg. To find the venue, visit the **Salzburg tourist office,** Mozartplatz 5 (© **0662/88987-330**). Here you'll be given a free copy of *Offizieller Wochenspiegel,* a monthly pamphlet listing all major and many minor local cultural events. The annual Mozart Week is in January.

The major ticket agency affiliated with the city of Salzburg is located adjacent to Salzburg's main tourist office, at Mozartplatz 5. The **Salzburger Ticket Office** (© **0662/84-03-10**) is open Monday through Friday from 9am to 6pm (to 7pm in midsummer) and Saturday from 9am to noon.

If you don't want to pay a ticket agent's commission, you can go directly to the box office of a theater or concert hall. However, many of the best seats may have already been sold, especially those at the Salzburg Festival.

CONCERTS & OTHER ENTERTAINMENT

The rich collection of concerts that combine every summer to form the Salzburg Festival's program are presented in several different concert halls scattered throughout Salzburg. The largest is the **Festspielhaus,** Hofstallgasse 1 (© **0662/ 8045;** bus: 1, 5, or 6). Within the Festspielhaus complex you'll find the **Felsenreitschule,** an outdoor auditorium with a makeshift roof. Originally built in 1800 as a riding rink, it's famous as the site where scenes from *The Sound of Music* were filmed. Tickets cost from 8€ to 200€ (the higher cost for the best seats at the Salzburg Festival); average but good seats run 35€ to 80€. Instead of going directly to the Festspielhaus, you can purchase tickets in advance at the box office at Waagplatz 1A (© **0662/84-53-46**), close to the tourist office, Monday through Friday from 9:30am to 4:30pm.

On the right back of the Salzach River, near the Mirabell Gardens, is the **Mozarteum,** Schwarzstrasse 26 and Mirabellplatz 1 (© **0662/87-31-54;** bus: 1, 5, 6, or 51), the major music and concert hall of Salzburg. All the big orchestra

---

Tips Getting Tickets to the Salzburg Festival

One of the premier music attractions of Europe, the Salzburg Festival celebrated its 83rd season in 2003. Details on the festival are available by contacting **Salzburg Festival,** Hofstallgasse 1, A-5020 Salzburg, Austria (© **0662/8045-579;** www.salzburgfestival.at).

concerts, as well as organ recitals and chamber-music evenings, are offered here. It's also a music school, and you can ask about free events staged by the students. The box office is open Monday through Thursday from 9am to 2pm and Friday from 9am to 4pm. Performances are at 11am or 7:30pm. Tickets cost 8€ to 185€; the best seats run from 90€ to 185€.

Besides the venues above, you can attend a concert in dramatic surroundings in the Fürstenzimmer (Prince's Chamber) of the **Hohensalzburg Fortress.** You're likely to hear heavy doses of Mozart and, to a lesser degree, works by Schubert, Brahms, and Beethoven. From mid-May to mid-October, performances are likely to be held at 8 or 8:30pm every night of the week. The rest of the year, they're presented most (but not all) nights, with occasional weeklong breaks, usually at 7:30pm. The box office for the events is at Adlgasser Weg 22 ((②) **0662/82-58-58**). To reach the fortress, take the funicular from Festungsgasse.

BEER GARDENS

Regardless of the season, you'll have one of your most enjoyable and authentic evenings in Salzburg at **Augustiner Bräustübl,** Augustinergasse 4 ((②) **0662/43-12-46; bus: 27**). This Bierstube and Biergarten has been dispensing oceans of beer since it was established in 1622. Depending on the weather, the city's beer-drinking fraternity gathers either within the cavernous interior, where three separate rooms each hold up to 400 people, or in the chestnut-shaded courtyard. You'll find about a dozen kiosks, where you can buy takeout portions of wursts, sandwiches, and pretzels. Farther on, choose a thick stoneware mug from the racks and carry it to the beer tap, paying the cashier as you go. A full liter begins at 4€; a half liter costs 2€ depending on the type of beer. The place is open Monday through Friday from 3 to 11pm and Saturday and Sunday from 2:30 to 11pm.

Immediately below the Hohensalzburg Fortress and established in the early 1800s, part of the **Stiegelkeller,** Festungsgasse 10 ((②) **0662/84-26-81; bus: 5, 6, or 55**), is carved into the rocks of Mönchsberg. To get here, you'll have to negotiate a steep cobblestone street that drops off on one side to reveal a panoramic view of Salzburg. The cavernous interior is open only in summer, when you can join hundreds of others in drinking beer and eating sausages, schnitzels, and other *Bierkeller* food.

Sound of Music **dinner shows,** featuring music from the film, are presented in the Stiegelkeller May through September, daily from 7:30 to 10pm. A three-course meal and show cost 40€. Or you can arrive at 8:15pm to see the show and just have *Apfelstrudel* and coffee for 25€. On the first Sunday of the month, a *Fruhschoppen*—a traditional Salzburger music fest—is presented from 10:30pm to midnight. No ticket is necessary—you pay for what you eat and drink. Likewise, no ticket is necessary to attend another musical evening, a *Happing,* staged May through September, every Thursday from 6 to 8pm.

No one in Salzburg is really sure whether to classify **Salzburger Altstadtkeller,** Rudolfskai 27 ((②) **0662/849688**), as a restaurant, an inn, a pub, or a nightclub, since it combines so gracefully elements of all of them. The result is fun and convivial. The setting is a medieval cellar beneath the Altstadt Radisson Hotel, immediately adjacent to the banks of the river. Don't come here expecting fine dining: What you'll get is a short list of Austrian-style platters, and a reverberating roster of musical acts that include swing, Latino, jazz, and blues. Every Thursday, the acts get more nostalgic and folkloric, as the stage is turned over to bands specializing in Austrian or Bavarian "evergreen" music.

Music plays from around 9:15pm to 1am, with guests then lingering over their drinks for at least another hour. There's no cover charge, but a half-liter mug of beer costs 3.10€. Main courses cost from 8€ to 12€. Service is Tuesday through Sunday from 7pm to 2:30am.

3 Innsbruck ⋆ & Tyrol

Land of ice and mountains, dark forests and alpine meadows full of spring wild-flowers, summer holidays and winter sports—that's Tyrol. Those intrepid tourists, the British, discovered its vacation delights and made it a fashionable destination in the last century. Tyrol is now the most frequented winter playground in Austria, and in summer, the extensive network of mountain paths lures visitors.

Skiers flock here in winter for a ski season that runs from mid-December to the end of March. Many prefer its ski slopes to those of Switzerland. It's been a long time since the eyes of the world focused on Innsbruck at the Winter Olympics in 1964 and 1976, but the legacy lives on in the ski conditions and facilities on some of the world's choicest slopes.

INNSBRUCK

Innsbruck has a particularly lovely medieval town center, and town planners have protected this historic Altstadt. Visitors can take countless excursions in the environs; at Innsbruck's doorstep lie some of the most beautiful drives in Europe. Just take your pick: Head in any direction, up any valley, and you'll be treated to mountains and alpine beauty almost unmatched anywhere else, including Switzerland.

ESSENTIALS

GETTING THERE   By Plane   Innsbruck's airport, **Flughafen Innsbruck-Kranebitten,** Fürstenweg 180 (© **0512/22525;** www.Innsbruck-airport.com), is 3km (2 miles) west of the city. It offers regularly scheduled air service from the major airports of Austria and of Europe's major cities.

By Train   Innsbruck is connected with all parts of Europe by international railway links. Trains arrive at the main railway station, the **Hauptbahnhof,** Südtiroler Platz (© **05/1717** for all rail information). There are at least five daily trains from Munich (trip time: 3 hr.) and eight daily trains from Salzburg (1 hr.).

By Car   If you're **driving** down from Salzburg in the northeast, take Autobahn A8 west, which joins Autobahn A93 (later it becomes the A12), heading south-west to Innsbruck. This latter Autobahn (A93/A12) is the main artery from Munich. From the south, you can take the Brenner toll motorway.

VISITOR INFORMATION   The **tourist office,** Burggraben 3 (© **0512/56-20-00;** www.innsbruck-tourismus.com), is open Monday through Saturday from 8am to 6pm and Sunday from 9am to 6pm. It will supply you with a wealth of information, as well as a list of inexpensive private rooms for rent in Innsbruck. The office can also book bus or walking tours of the city.

CITY LAYOUT   This historic city is divided by the Inn River into left- and right-bank districts. Two major bridges cross the Inn, the **Universittssbrücke** and the **Alte Innsbrücke (Old Inn Bridge).** Many of the attractions, including the Hofkirche and the Goldenes Dachl, are on the right bank. If you arrive at the Hauptbahnhof, take Salurner Strasse and Brixener Strasse to Maria-Theresien-Strasse, which will put you into the very heart of Innsbruck.

The **Altstadt** is bounded on the north by the Inn River and on the south by Burggraben and Marktgrabben. The main street of this historic district is **Herzog-Friedrich-Strasse,** which becomes **Maria-Theresien-Strasse,** the axis of the postmedieval new part of town. The Altstadt becomes a pedestrian zone after 10:30am (wear good shoes on the cobblestone streets).

GETTING AROUND   A network of three **tram** and 25 **bus lines** covers all of Innsbruck and its close environs, and buses and trams use the same tickets. Single tickets in the central area cost 1.50€, and a booklet of four tickets goes for 3.20€. The tram is called either *Strassenbahn* or *Trambahn.* On the left bank of the Inn River, the main tram and bus arteries are Museumstrasse and Mariahilfstrasse. On the right bank, trams and buses aren't routed into the pedestrian zone but to their main stop in Marktgraben. For information about various routes, call the **Innsbrucker Verkehrsbetriebe** (© 0512/530-7102). Most tickets can be purchased at the Innsbruck tourist office, tobacco shops, and automated vending machines. A *Tageskarte* **(day pass)** is available only from the tourist information office, tobacco shops, and cafes.

Austria Postal Service buses (one of two different bus networks maintained by the Austria government) leave from the Autobushof (Central Bus Station), adjacent to the Hauptbahnhof on Sterzinger Strasse. Here buses head for all parts of Tyrol. The station is open Monday through Friday from 7:30am to 6pm and Saturday from 7am to 1pm. For information about bus schedules, call © 0512/58-51-55.

Taxi stands are scattered at strategic points throughout the city, or you can call a radio car (© 0512/5311). For a nostalgic ride, you can hire a horse-drawn carriage *(Fiaker)* from a spot adjacent to the **Tiroler Landestheater,** Rennweg.

If neither the tram nor the carriage options appeal to you, consider renting a **bike** at the Hauptbahnhof. Rentals cost 20€ per day. You can return these bikes to any rail station in Austria if you don't plan to return to Innsbruck. Rentals are available April through early November only. For more information, call **Sport Neuner** (© 0512/561-501).

Although you can make a better deal renting a car before you leave North America, it's possible to rent cars in Innsbruck. You might try **Avis,** Salurner Strasse 15 (© 0512/57-17-54); or **Hertz,** Südtirolerplatz 1 (© 0512/58-29-51), across from the Hauptbahnhof. Although paperwork and billing errors are harder to resolve whenever you rent from a non-U.S.-based car-rental outfit, you might also check the rates at a local car outfitter, **Ajax,** Amrasserstrasse 6 (© 0512/583-232).

 FAST FACTS: Innsbruck

Currency Exchange Banks are usually open Monday through Thursday from 7:45 am to 12:30pm and 2:30 to 4pm; and Friday from 7:45am to 3pm. There are also exchange facilities at Innsbruck's tourist office (see above). The automated currency exchange facilities at the Hauptbahnhof are available 24 hours a day.

Dentists/Doctors Check with the tourist office for a list of private English-speaking dentists and doctors; or contact the **University Clinic,** Anichstrasse 35 (© 0512/504).

Drugstores In the heart of Innsbruck, **St.-Anna Apotheke**, Maria-Theresien-Strasse 4 (℃ **0512/58-58-47**), is open Monday through Friday from 8am to 12:30pm and 2:30 to 6pm, and Saturday from 8am to noon. The pharmacy posts addresses of other pharmacies open on weekends or at night.

Emergencies In case of trouble, call ℃ **133** for the police, ℃ **122** for a fire, or ℃ **144** for an ambulance.

Internet Access You can check e-mail or access the Internet for a fee of 11€ an hour at the **Picasso Internet Café**, Maria-Theresien-Strasse 16 (℃ **0512/58-48-48**; tram: 3). It's open Monday through Friday from 9am to 1am, Saturday from 3pm to 1am, and Sunday from 5pm to 1am.

Post Office The **Hauptpostamt (Central Post Office)**, Maximilianstrasse 2 (℃ **0512/5000**), is open daily from 8am to 9pm. The post office at the **Hauptbahnhof**, Bruneckstrasse 1–3 (℃ **0512/5000**), is open Monday through Saturday from 6:30am to 9pm.

Telephone The **country code** for Austria is **43**. The **city code** for Innsbruck is **512**; use this code when you're calling from outside Austria. If you're within Austria, use **0512**.

WHERE TO STAY
Very Expensive

Hotel Europa Tyrol 🌟🌟   The town's finest and most elegant hotel stands opposite the rail station, inviting you inside its formal lobby. The spacious rooms and suites are handsomely furnished, with all the modern conveniences and Tyrolean or Biedermeier-style decorations. Each tasteful unit offers a bathroom equipped with a tub/shower combo. The restaurant, **Europastüberl** (p. 92), is the finest in Tyrol.

Südtirolerplatz 2, A-6020 Innsbruck. ℃ **800/223-5652** in the U.S. and Canada, or 0512/5931. Fax 0512/58-78 00. www.europatyrol.com. 122 units. 152€–240€ double; 268€–374€ suite. Rates include breakfast. AE, DC, MC, V. Parking 11€. **Amenities:** Restaurant; bar; sauna; solarium; room service; babysitting; laundry/dry cleaning service. *In room:* TV, minibar, hair dryer, safe.

Expensive

Romantik Hotel-Restaurant Schwarzer Adler 🌟🌟   This is it for those who like authentic Austrian charm. The hotel's owners, the Ultsch family, have furnished the charming interior with hand-painted regional furniture, antiques, and lots of homey clutter, making for a cozy and inviting ambience. The midsize rooms are virtually one of a kind, each with its special character. Beds are exceedingly comfortable, with some of the thickest mattresses in town and well-stuffed duvets. Bathrooms have dual basins and tub/shower combos with powerful showerheads. We prefer the older accommodations, which are more spacious and have more Tyrolean character.

Kaiserjägerstrasse 2, A-6020 Innsbruck. ℃ **0512/58-71-09.** Fax 0512/56-16-97. www.deradler.com. 39 units. 141€–202€ double; 255€–470€ suite. Additional person 46€. Rates include breakfast. AE, DC, MC, V. Parking 9€. Tram: 1 or 3. **Amenities:** Restaurant; bar; fitness center; health spa; room service; massage; laundry/dry cleaning service. *In room:* A/C, TV, minibar, hair dryer, safe.

Moderate

Hotel Central   One of the most unusual hotels in Innsbruck, Hotel Central was originally built in the 1860s, but from its very modern exterior you might not realize it. The comfortable rooms have an Art Deco design that evokes an almost Japanese simplicity. Most rooms are quite spacious with excellent beds. Bathrooms are small, with shower units. In total contrast to the simplicity of the rest of the hotel, the ground floor contains a grand Viennese cafe with marble columns, sculpted ceilings, and large gilt-and-crystal chandeliers.

Gilmstrasse 5, A-6020 Innsbruck. ℭ **0512/59-20.** Fax 0512/58-03-10. www.central.co.at/central. 85 units. 122€–144€ double. Rates include breakfast. Additional person 21€ extra. AE, DC, MC, V. Parking 12€. Tram: 1 or 3. **Amenities:** Restaurant; bar; fitness center; sauna; room service; laundry/dry cleaning service. *In room:* TV, minibar, hair dryer.

Hotel Goldener Adler 🏰🏰   Even the phone booth near the reception desk of this 600-year-old family-run hotel is outfitted in antique style. Famous guests have included Goethe, Mozart, and the violinist Paganini, who cut his name into the windowpane of his room. Rooms are handsomely furnished, and vary in size and decor. Some have decorative Tyrolean architectural features such as beamed ceilings. Others are furnished in a more modern style. The bathroom's size depends on your room assignment; bathrooms can be everything from spacious combination models to cramped rooms with shower stalls.

Herzog-Friedrich-Strasse 6, A-6020 Innsbruck. ℭ **0512/57-11-11.** Fax 0512/58-44-09. www.goldeneradler. com. 35 units. 128€–168€ double; from 198€ suite. Rates include breakfast. AE, DC, MC, V. Parking 11€. Tram: 1 or 3. **Amenities:** 5 restaurants; bar; room service; babysitting; laundry/dry cleaning service. *In room:* TV, minibar, hair dryer, safe.

Inexpensive

City-Hotel Goldene Krone *(Value*   Near the Triumphal Arch on Innsbruck's main street, this baroque house is one of the best budget bets. All rooms are modern, comfortable, well maintained, and, for the most part, spacious with plenty of light. The duvet-covered beds are comfortable, and bathrooms are small but spotless, with shower stalls. The hotel offers a Viennese-inspired coffeehouse/restaurant, the Art Gallery-Café.

Maria-Theresien-Strasse 46, A-6020. Innsbruck. ℭ **0512/58-61-60.** Fax 0512/580-18-96. www.city-crown hotel-innsbruck.com. 37 units. 74€–103€ double; 108€–139€ suite. Rates include breakfast. AE, MC, V. Parking 7.50€. Tram: 1. Bus: A, H, K, or N. **Amenities:** Restaurant; cafe; lounge; babysitting. *In room:* TV.

Gasthof-Hotel Weisses Kreuz 🏰 *(Value*   This atmospheric inn, located in the center of Innsbruck, has not changed much during its lifetime. Rooms are cozy and atmospheric, either small or medium size, with comfortable furnishings. Some have private bathrooms with neatly kept shower units. Hallway bathrooms are adequate and well maintained. In 1769, 13-year-old Wolfgang Mozart and his father, Leopold, stayed here.

Herzog-Friedrich-Strasse 31, A-6020 Innsbruck. ℭ **0512/594790.** Fax 0512/59-47-990. www.weisseskreuz.at. 40 units (31 with bathroom). 63€–66€ double without bathroom; 83€–95€ double with bathroom. Rates include breakfast. AE, MC, V. Parking 9€. Tram: 3. **Amenities:** 2 restaurants; bar; room service. *In room:* TV.

WHERE TO DINE
Expensive

Europastüberl 🏰🏰 AUSTRIAN/INTERNATIONAL   This distinguished restaurant, with a delightful Tyrolean ambience, is in a hotel that's the finest address in Innsbruck. The chef succeeds beautifully in fashioning creative takes on traditional regional cooking. Diners can choose from both warm and cold appetizers, ranging from iced anglerfish with Chinese tree morels to a small ragout of crayfish in a spicy biscuit with kohlrabi. Some dishes are served only for two people, such as Bresse guinea hen roasted and presented with an herb sauce. Fresh Tyrolean trout almost always appears on the menu, or you may prefer the

Innsbruck

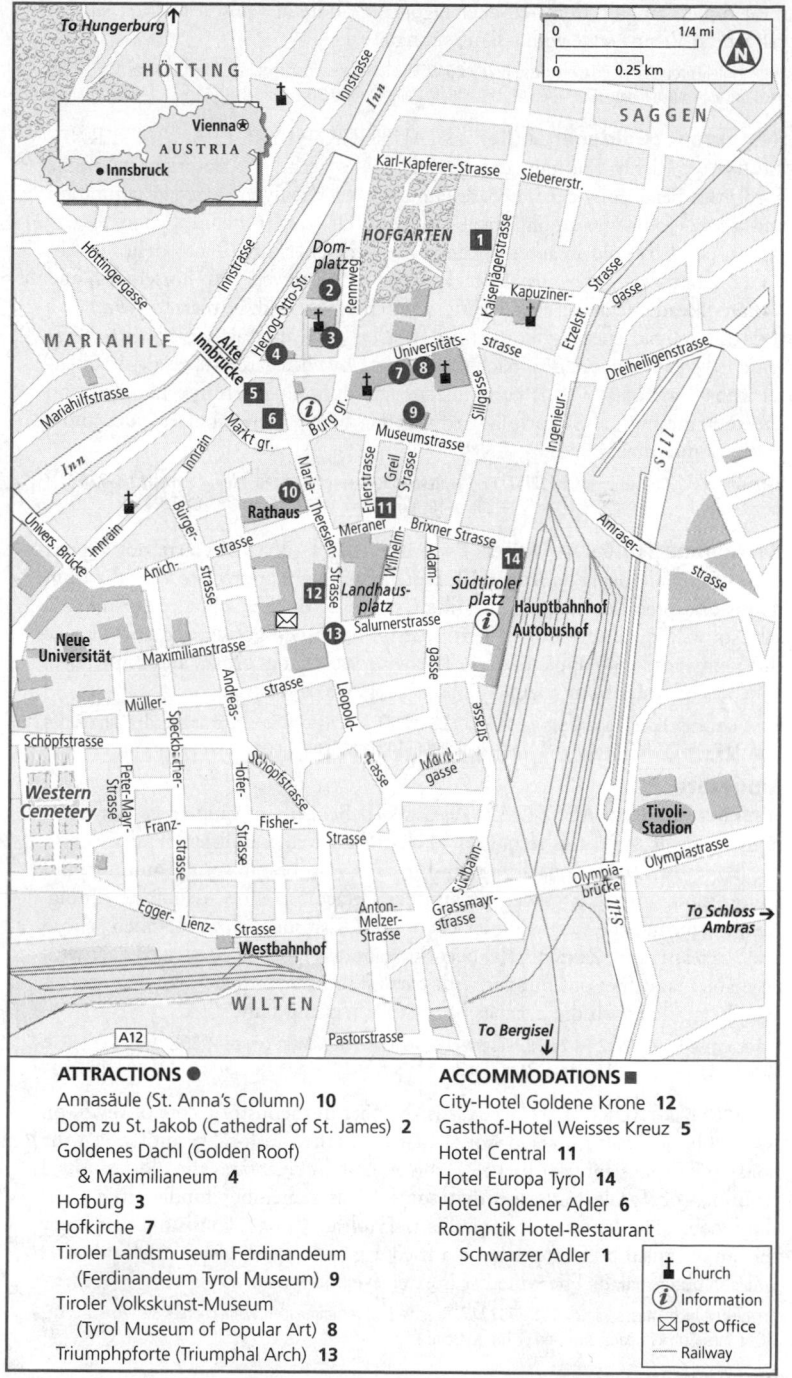

To Hungerburg ↑

HÖTTING

Vienna ✱
AUSTRIA
• Innsbruck

0   1/4 mi
0   0.25 km

SAGGEN

Karl-Kapferer-Strasse   Siebererstr.

HOFGARTEN   **1**

Dom-
platz   **2**

MARIAHILF

Kapuziner-

4   **3**

Universitäts-   **7** **8**

5

ⓘ   **9**

6   Museumstrasse

Rathaus   **10**

11   Brixner Strasse

Meraner

14

12   Landhaus-   Südtiroler
platz   platz   Hauptbahnhof
ⓘ   Autobushof

Neue   **13**   Salurnerstrasse
Universität

Maximilianstrasse

Western
Cemetery

Tivoli-
Stadion

To Schloss →
Ambras

Westbahnhof

WILTEN

A12   Pastorstrasse   To Bergisel ↓

ATTRACTIONS ●

Annasäule (St. Anna's Column) **10**
Dom zu St. Jakob (Cathedral of St. James) **2**
Goldenes Dachl (Golden Roof)
  & Maximilianeum **4**
Hofburg **3**
Hofkirche **7**
Tiroler Landsmuseum Ferdinandeum
  (Ferdinandeum Tyrol Museum) **9**
Tiroler Volkskunst-Museum
  (Tyrol Museum of Popular Art) **8**
Triumphpforte (Triumphal Arch) **13**

ACCOMMODATIONS ■

City-Hotel Goldene Krone **12**
Gasthof-Hotel Weisses Kreuz **5**
Hotel Central **11**
Hotel Europa Tyrol **14**
Hotel Goldener Adler **6**
Romantik Hotel-Restaurant
  Schwarzer Adler **1**

✝ Church
ⓘ Information
✉ Post Office
── Railway

meat dishes, ranging from red deer ragout to saddle of venison to fried jelly of calf's head Vienna-style with a lamb's tongue salad.

In the Hotel Europa Tyrol, Brixnerstrasse 6. ℂ 0512/5931. Reservations required. Main courses 10€–25€; fixed-price 4-course menu 36€–40€. AE, DC, MC, V. Daily 11am–2:30pm and 6:30–11pm.

Restaurant Goldener Adler ⊛ AUSTRIAN/TYROLEAN/INTERNA-TIONAL   Richly Teutonic and steeped in the decorative traditions of alpine Tyrol, this beautifully decorated restaurant has a deeply entrenched reputation and a loyal following among local residents. The menu includes good, hearty fare inspired by cold-weather outdoor life—the chefs aren't into delicate subtleties. Examples of the cuisine are Tyrolean bacon served with horseradish and farmer's bread; cream of cheese soup with croutons; and Tyroler *Zopfebraten,* a flavorful age-old specialty consisting of strips of veal steak served with herb-enriched cream sauce and spinach dumplings. A well-regarded specialty is a platter known as *Adler Tres.* It contains spinach dumplings, stuffed noodles, and cheese dumplings, all flavorfully tied together with a brown butter sauce and a gratin of mountain cheese.

Herzog-Friedrich-Strasse 6. ℂ 0512/57-11-11. Reservations recommended. Main courses 12€–22€; set menus 12€–18€. AE, DC, MC, V. Daily 11:30am–10:30pm. Tram: 1 or 3.

Restaurant Schwarzer Adler ⊛⊛ AUSTRIAN   Even if you're not a guest at the richly atmospheric Romantik Hotel, you might appreciate a meal within its historic premises. Among the finest examples of the elaborate cuisine is a salad of wild quail served with lentils, strips of braised goose liver, and a sauce that's enhanced with apple liqueur. The wine list is long, broad, and impressive, with lots of wines from relatively obscure regions of Austria.

In the Romantik Hotel, Kaiserjägerstrasse 2. ℂ 0512/587-109. Reservations recommended. Main courses 17€–22€. AE, DC, MC, V. Mon–Sat 11am–2pm and 6–10:30pm. Tram: 1 or 3.

Moderate

Hirschen-Stuben AUSTRIAN/ITALIAN   Beneath a vaulted ceiling in a house built in 1631, this restaurant is charming, well established, and welcoming. By its own admission, the establishment is at its best in spring, autumn, and winter, since it lacks a garden or outdoor terrace for alfresco summer dining. Menu items include steaming platters of pasta, fish soup, trout meunière, sliced veal in cream sauce Zurich style, beef Stroganoff, pepper steak, stewed deer with vegetables, and filet of flounder with parsley and potatoes. The kitchen staff is equally familiar with the cuisines of both Austria and Italy.

Kiebachgasse 5. ℂ 0512/58-29-79. Reservations recommended. Main courses 8.80€–19€. DC, MC, V. Mon–Sat 11am–2pm and 6–11pm. Tram: 1 or 3.

Jörgele *(Value* AUSTRIAN/TYROLEAN   Set in the historic core of town, on two floors of a half-timbered house first mentioned in local records as a wine house (Weinhaus Jörgele) in 1580, this restaurant celebrates the old-fashioned traditions of Tyrolean cuisine that some locals remember fondly from their childhoods. The best example of this is Tyrolean *Gröstel,* consisting of a spicy version of boiled beef capped with a fried egg and served with roasted potatoes and a cabbage salad. The wine list is extensive and worldly.

Herzog-Friedrich-Strasse 13. ℂ 0512/582217. Reservations recommended. Main courses 8€–26€. AE, DC, MC, V. Tues–Sun 11:30am–2pm and 6–10pm. Tram: 1, 3.

Inexpensive

Restaurant Ottoburg ⊛ AUSTRIAN/INTERNATIONAL   This historic restaurant, established around 1745, occupies a 13th-century building that some historians say is the oldest in Innsbruck. Inside, four intimate and atmospheric dining rooms—with a decor that is best described as "19th-century neo-Gothic"—lie scattered over two different floors. Hearty dishes include venison stew, "grandmother's mixed grill," and fried trout. In summer, a beer garden operates in the rear, open daily from 10:30am to 11:30pm. During the lifetime of this edition, management will change, and there may be some alterations in policies and cuisine.

Herzog-Friedrich-Strasse 1. © 0512/58-43-38. Reservations recommended. Main courses 7.25€–22€. AE, DC, MC, V. Tues–Sun 11am–3pm and 5:30pm–midnight. Tram: 1 or 3.

Weisses Rössl AUSTRIAN/TYROLEAN   You'll enter this time-honored place through a stone archway set on one of the Old Town's most famous streets. At the end of a flight of stairs, marked with a very old crucifix, you'll find a trio of dining rooms with red-tile floors and a history of welcoming guests since 1590. At first glance, the menu appears simple, listing such dishes as a Tyroler *Grüstl* (a kind of hash composed of sautéed onions, sliced beef, alpine herbs, and potatoes cooked and served in a frying pan), *Saftgoulash* with polenta, several kinds of schnitzels, and a grilled platter *(Alt Insprugg)* for two diners.

Kiebachgasse 8. © 0512/58-30-57. Reservations recommended. Main courses 9€–16€. AE, MC, V. Mon–Sat 11:30am–2pm and 6–10pm. Closed 2 weeks after Easter and 2 weeks in Nov. Tram: 1 or 3.

EXPLORING THE TOWN

The Altstadt and the surrounding alpine countryside are Innsbruck's main attractions. Often it's fascinating just to watch the passersby, who are occasionally attired in Tyrolean regional dress.

Maria-Theresien-Strasse, which cuts through the heart of the city from north to south, is the main street and a good place to begin exploring the city. Many 17th- and 18th-century houses line this wide street. On the south end of the street, there's a **Triumphpforte (Triumphal Arch),** modeled after those in Rome. Maria Theresa ordered it built in 1765 to honor her son's marriage and to commemorate the death of her beloved husband, Emperor Franz I. From this arch southward the street is called Leopoldstrasse.

Going north from the arch along Maria-Theresien-Strasse, you'll see **Annasäule (St. Anna's Column)** in front of the 19th-century Rathaus (town hall). The column was erected in 1706 to celebrate the withdrawal in 1703 of invading Bavarian armies during the War of the Spanish Succession. Not far north of the Annasäule, the wide street narrows and becomes **Herzog-Friedrich-Strasse,** running through the heart of the medieval quarter. This street is arcaded and flanked by a number of well-maintained burghers' houses with their jumble of turrets and gables; look for the multitude of dormer windows and oriels.

Goldenes Dachl (Golden Roof) & Maximilianeum   "The Golden Roof," Innsbruck's greatest tourist attraction and its most characteristic landmark, is a three-story balcony on a house in the Altstadt; the late-Gothic oriels are capped with 2,657 gold-plated tiles. It was constructed for Emperor Maximilian I in the beginning of the 16th century to serve as a royal box where he could sit in luxury and enjoy tournaments in the square below.

There's a small museum, the **Maximilianeum,** on the second floor of the municipal building attached to the Goldenes Dachl. Inside are exhibits celebrating the life and accomplishments of the Innsbruck-based Hapsburg emperor, Maximilian I, who bridged the gap between the Middle Ages and the German Renaissance.

You can also visit the **Stadtturm (City Tower)**, Herzog-Friedrich-Strasse 21 (℃ **0512/561-5003**). Formerly a prison cell, the tower dates from the mid-1400s and stands adjacent to the Rathaus. Its top affords a panoramic view of the city rooftops and the mountains beyond. It's open daily from 10am to 5pm (to 8pm July and Aug). Admission is 2.50€ adults and 1.25€ children 17 and under.

Herzog-Friedrich-Strasse 15. ℃ 0512/581-111. Admission to the Maximilianeum 3.60€ adults, 2.70€ seniors and students, 1.40€ children 17 and under. No charge for views of the Goldenes Dachl, and no restrictions as to when it can be viewed. Maximilianeum summer daily 10am–6pm; winter Tues–Sun 10am–12:30pm and 2–5pm. Tram: 1 or 3.

Swarovski Kristallwelten (Crystal Worlds) ★★★ *Kids*   Designed by the Viennese multimedia artist, Andrew Heller, this attraction some 15km (9 miles) from Innsbruck is dedicated to the vision of Daniel Swarovski, founder of the world's leading producer of full crystal. Since it opened in 1995, millions of visitors have descended on the site, and you can easily spend 2 hours here.

After entering the giant head with its glittering eyes and waterfall, you'll immediately see a long wall of crystal with 12 tons of the finest cut stones in the world. In other chambers you can wander into the "Planet of the Crystals," with a 3-D light show. Crystalline works of art on display were designed by everybody from Andy Warhol to Salvador Dalí. In the Crystal Dome you get an idea of what it's like being inside a giant crystal, and in the Crystal Theater a fairy-tale world of color, mystery, and graceful movement unfolds.

Kristallweltenstrasse 1. ℃ 05224/51080. www.kristallwelten.com. Admission 5.45€; free for children under 12. Daily 9am–6pm. Take the Wattens motorway exit (A 12) and follow signs to Kristallwelten, or take the Wattens bus from the Busbahnhof, next to the Hauptbahnhof.

Hofburg ★   The 15th-century imperial palace of Emperor Maximilian I, flanked by a set of domed towers, was rebuilt in the baroque style (with rococo detailing) during the 18th century on orders of Maria Theresa. It's a fine example of baroque secular architecture, with four wings and a two-story *Riesensaal* (Giant's Hall), painted in white and gold and filled with portraits of the Hapsburgs. Also of compelling interest are the State Rooms, the chapel, and a scattering of private apartments. You can wander at will through the rooms, but if you want to participate in a guided tour, management conducts two a day, at 11am and 2pm, in a multilingual format that includes English. Each tour lasts 30 to 45 minutes and costs 2€.

Rennweg 1. ℃ 0512/58-71-86. Admission 5.45€ adults, 2.54€ students, 1.10€ children under 12. Daily 9am–4:30pm. Tram: 1 or 3.

Hofkirche   The most important treasure in the Hofkirche is the cenotaph of Maximilian I, a great example of German Renaissance style. It has 28 bronze 16th-century statues of Maximilian's real and legendary ancestors surrounding the kneeling emperor.

Universitätsstrasse 2. ℃ 0512/58-43-02. Admission 4.35€ adults, 1.45€ students or children, free for children 5 and under. Mon–Sat 9am–5pm. Tram: 1 or 3.

Dom zu St. Jakob (Cathedral of St. James)   Designed and rebuilt from 1717 to 1724 by Johann Jakob Herkommer, the Dom has a lavishly embellished baroque interior. A chief treasure is Lucas Cranach the Elder's *Maria Hilf (St. Mary of Succor)* on the main altar.

Domplatz 6. ℃ 0512/58-39-02. Free admission. Winter daily 6:30am–6pm; summer daily 7am–7pm. Closed Fri noon–3pm. Tram: 1 or 3.

Tiroler Landesmuseum Ferdinandeum (Ferdinandeum Tyrol Museum) ⋆
This celebrated gallery of Flemish and Dutch masters also traces the development
of popular art in Tyrol, with highlights from the Gothic period. You'll see the original bas-reliefs used in designing the Goldenes Dachl.

Museumstrasse 15. ℂ 0512/59-489. Admission 4.50€ adults, 3€ students, 1.50€ children. May–Sept daily
10am–5pm, Thurs 10am–5pm and 7–9pm; Oct–Apr Tues–Sat 10am–noon and 2–5pm, Sun 10am–1pm. Tram:
1 or 3.

Tiroler Volkskunst-Museum (Tyrol Museum of Popular Art) ⋆⋆   This
popular art museum is in the Neues Stift (New Abbey) adjoining the Hofkirche
on its eastern side. It contains one of the largest and most impressive collections
of Tyrolean artifacts, ranging from handcrafts, furniture, Christmas cribs, and
national costumes to religious and secular popular art. You'll also find a collection of models of typical Tyrolean houses.

Universitätsstrasse 2. ℂ 0512/58-43-02. Admission 4.35€ adults, 1.45€ children and students. Mon–Sat
9am–5:30pm; Sun 9am–noon. Tram: 1 or 3.

ENJOYING THE GREAT OUTDOORS

Five sunny, snow-covered, avalanche-free **ski areas** around the Tyrol are served
by five cableways, 44 chairlifts, and ski hoists. The area is also known for bob-
sled and toboggan runs and ice-skating rinks.

In summer you can play tennis at a number of courts, and golf on either a 9-
or an 18-hole course; or you can go horseback riding, mountaineering, gliding,
swimming, hiking, or shooting.

The **Hofgarten,** a public park containing lakes and many shade trees, lies north
of Rennweg. Concerts are often presented in the garden during the summer.

THE SHOPPING SCENE

You'll find a large selection of Tyrolean specialties and all sorts of skiing and
mountain-climbing equipment for sale in Innsbruck. Stroll around **Maria-
Theresien-Strasse, Herzog-Friedrich-Strasse,** and **Museumstrasse,** ducking in
and making discoveries of your own. Here are some suggestions.

Lodenbaur, Brixner Strasse 4 (ℂ 0512/58-09-11), is devoted to regional
Tyrolean dress, most of which is made in Austria. There's a full array for men,
women, and children. **Tiroler Heimatwerk,** Meraner Strasse 2 (ℂ **0512/58-23-
20**), is one of the best stores in Innsbruck for handcrafted sculpture and pewter,
carved chests, furniture and lace. Do-it-yourselfers can buy regionally inspired
fabrics and dress patterns, and whip up a dirndl (or whatever).

Using old molds discovered in abandoned Tyrolean factories, **Zinnreproduk-
tionen U,** Kiebachgasse 8 (ℂ 0512/58-92-24), offers fine reproductions of century-old regional pewter at reasonable prices. The owner also reproduces rare
pewter objects acquired from auctions throughout Europe. Look for a copy of
the 18th-century pewter barometer emblazoned with representations of the sun
and the four winds.

INNSBRUCK AFTER DARK

THE PERFORMING ARTS   The major venue for the performing arts is the
150-year-old **Landestheater,** Rennweg 2 (ℂ **0512/52-074**). The box office is
open daily from 9:30am to 7pm, and performances usually begin at 7:30 or
8pm. Ticket prices are 7€ to 36€ for most operas or operettas, 7€ to 40€ for
theater seats. It's also the showcase for musicals and light operetta. For tickets,
call ℂ **0512/53-56-30.** Concerts are presented in the Hofgarten in summer.

BARS, CLUBS & FOLK MUSIC   In summer, the outdoor bar at **Club Filou,** Stiftsgasse 12 (© **0512/58-02-56**), blossoms with ivy-covered trellises and parasols. Inside you'll find an intimate hangout filled with Victorian settees and pop art. In a separate, very old room is the disco. The cafe is open daily from 6pm to 4am; the disco daily from 8pm to 2am. Food is available until 3am.

If you're looking for the biggest and the best in Innsbruck, head for the **Hofgartencafé,** Rennweg 6 (© **0512/58-88-71**), where a lively crowd of young people, mostly in their twenties and thirties, grace the largest beer garden in town. With three massive outdoor bars and a modern indoor decor, this hot spot is the place to be seen. You'll find live music here during the summer. It's open in summer daily from 10am to 2am. In winter, hours are Tuesday through Thursday from 6pm to 2am and Friday and Saturday from 6pm to 4 am.

Young people hang out at **Treibhaus,** Angerzellgasse 8 (© **0512/58-68-74**), a combination cafe, bar, and social club. Within its battered walls, you can attend a changing roster of art exhibitions, cabaret shows, and protest rallies, Monday through Saturday from 10am to 1am, with live music presented at erratic intervals. Cover for live performances is 10€ to 17€.

Throughout the Christmas season, Easter, and the high season, from 6 to 11pm, you can visit the **Goethe Stube,** in the Restaurant Goldener Adler, Herzog-Friedrich-Strasse 6 (© **0512/57-11-11;** tram: 1 or 3), to hear authentic Tyrolean melodies, including the zither and "jodlers." There's a one-drink minimum.

ST. ANTON AM ARLBERG 𝄞𝄞𝄞

A modern resort has grown out of this old village on the Arlberg Pass, 99km (62 miles) west of Innsbruck. At St. Anton (1,288m/4,225 ft.), Hannes Schneider developed modern skiing techniques and began teaching tourists how to ski in 1907. Before his death in 1955, Schneider saw his ski school rated as the world's finest. Today the school is still one of the world's largest and best, with about 300 instructors (most of whom speak English). St. Anton am Arlberg in winter is popular with the wealthy and occasional royalty—a more conservative segment of the rich and famous than you'll see at other posh ski resorts.

There's so much emphasis on skiing here that few seem to talk of the summertime attractions. In warm weather, St. Anton is tranquil and bucolic, surrounded by meadowland. A riot of wildflowers blooming in the fields announces the beginning of spring.

ESSENTIALS

GETTING THERE   By Train   Because of St. Anton's good rail connections to eastern and western Austria, most visitors arrive by train. St. Anton is an express stop on the main lines crossing the Arlberg Pass between Innsbruck and Bregenz. About one train per hour arrives in St. Anton from both directions. Trip time from Innsbruck is 75 to 85 minutes; from Bregenz, around 85 minutes. For rail information, call © **05/1717.**

By Car   Motorists should take Route 171 west from Innsbruck.

VISITOR INFORMATION   The **tourist office** in the **Arlberghaus** in the town center (© **05446/22-690;** www.stantonamarlberg.com) is open Monday through Friday from 8am to noon and 2 to 6pm, Saturday from 9am to noon, and Sunday from 10am to noon.

WHERE TO STAY

Hotel Schwarzer Adler 𝄞𝄞   Owned and operated by the Tschol family since 1885, this is our preferred stopover at the resort. The beautiful building in the center of St. Anton was constructed as an inn in 1570 and became known for its hospitality to pilgrims crossing the treacherous Arlberg Pass. The 400-year-old frescoes on the exterior were discovered during a restoration. The interior is rustic yet elegant, with blazing fireplaces, painted Tyrolean baroque armoires, and Oriental rugs. There are handsomely furnished and well-equipped guest rooms in the main hotel, plus 13 slightly less-well-furnished (but less expensive) rooms in the annex, which is across the street above the Café Aquila. Nearly all bathrooms have big bathtubs, although a few singles offer only showers.

A-6580 St. Anton am Arlberg. (©) 800/528-1234 in the U.S., or 05446/22-440. Fax 05446/22-44-62. www. tiscover.com/adler.stanton. 50 units. Winter 131€–297€ double; summer 112€–176€ double. Rates include half board. AE, DC, MC, V. Closed May–June and Sept to Dec 5. **Amenities:** Restaurant (see below); bar; pool; fitness center; sauna; room service; massage; babysitting; laundry/dry cleaning service. *In room:* TV, hair dryer, safe.

WHERE TO DINE

Raffl-Stube ⭐ AUSTRIAN   This restaurant didn't exist until 1982, when members of the Raffl family enclosed a corner of their lobby. The place contains only eight tables, and in the peak of the season, reservations are imperative, especially if you're not staying here. Overflow diners are offered a seat in a spacious but less special dining room across the hall. Quality ingredients are always used, and the kitchen prepares such tempting specialties as roast goose liver with salad, cream of parsley soup with sautéed quail eggs, filet of salmon with wild rice, trout "as you like it," and roast filet of pork, along with the ever-popular fondue bourguignon.

In the Hotel St. Antoner Hof, St. Anton am Arlberg. (©) 05446/29-10. Reservations required. Main courses 14€–28€; fixed-price menu 35€–52€. AE, DC, MC, V. Daily 11:30am–2pm and 6–10:30pm. Closed mid-Oct to mid-Dec and mid-Apr to mid-June.

MORE DINING   If you're not able to secure a reservation at Raffl Stube, don't despair. You can get classic Austrian dishes at the historic **Hotel Alte Post Restaurant,** A-6580 St. Anton am Arlberg (© 05446/25530); and at the first-rate **Hotel Kertess Restaurant,** A-6580 St. Anton am Arlberg (© 05446/2005), located high on a slope in the suburb of Oberdorf. For superb international cuisine, head to the medieval **Hotel Schwarzer Adler Restaurant,** A-6580 St. Anton am Arlberg (© 05446/22440).

HITTING THE SLOPES IN ST. ANTON

The snow in this area is perfect for skiers, and the total lack of trees on the slopes makes the situation ideal. The ski fields of St. Anton stretch over some 16 sq. km (6 sq. miles). Beginners stick to the slopes down below, and more experienced skiers head to the runs from the **Galzig** and **Valluga** peaks. A cableway will take you to Galzig (2,092m/6,860 ft.), where there's a self-service restaurant. You go from here to Vallugagrat (2,649m/8,685 ft.). The peak of the Valluga (2,812m/9,220 ft.), which commands a panoramic view, is also reached by cableway.

Other major ski areas include the **Gampen/Kapall,** an advanced-intermediate network of slopes, whose lifts start just behind St. Anton's railway station; and the **Rendl,** a relatively new labyrinth of runs to the south of St. Anton that offers many novice and intermediate slopes.

You'll find many other cold-weather pursuits in St. Anton, including ski jumping, mountain tours, curling, skating, tobogganing, and sleigh rides, plus après-ski relaxing.

THE KITZBÜHEL ALPS ✯✯✯

Hard-core skiers and the rich and famous are attracted to this ski region. The Kitzbühel Alps are covered with such a dense network of lifts that they now form the largest skiing complex in the country, with a series of superlative runs. The action centers on the town of Kitzbühel, but there are many satellite resorts that are much less expensive, including St. Johann in Tyrol. Kitzbühel is, in a sense, a neighbor of Munich, which lies 130km (81 miles) to the northeast: Most visitors to the Kitzbühel Alps use Munich's international airport.

ESSENTIALS

ARRIVING   By Train   Two and three **trains** per hour (many express) arrive in Kitzbühel from Innsbruck (trip time: 60 min.) and Salzburg (2½ hr.).

By Bus   The most useful of these bus lines runs every 30 to 60 minutes between Kitzbühel and St. Johann in Tyrol (25 min.). In addition, about half a dozen buses travel every day from Salzburg's main railway station to Kitzbühel (2¼ hr.). For regional bus information, call ✆ 05356/627-15.

By Car   Kitzbühel is 449km (279 miles) southwest of Vienna and 100km (62 miles) east of Innsbruck. If you're driving from Innsbruck, take Autobahn A12 east to the junction with Route 312 heading to Ellmau. After bypassing Ellmau, continue east to the junction with Route 342, which you take south to Kitzbühel.

VISITOR INFORMATION   The **tourist office,** Hinterstadt 18 (✆ **05356/ 621-55;** www.kitzbuhel.com), is open Monday through Friday from 8:30am to 6pm, Saturday from 8:30am to noon and 4 to 6pm, and Sunday from 10am to noon and 4 to 6pm.

WHERE TO STAY

Hotel Bruggerhof ✯ *(Finds*   About a mile west of the town center, near the Schwarzsee, is this countryside chalet with a sun terrace. Originally built as a farmhouse in the 1920s, it later gained local fame as a restaurant. The interior has massive ceiling beams and a corner fireplace. Rooms are comfortable and cozy and decorated in an alpine style. All have a well-lived-in look, although housekeeping is attentive. Firm beds are most inviting. Bathrooms, which contain shower-tub combinations, can be a bit cramped.

Reitherstrasse 24, A-6370 Kitzbühel. ✆ **05356/628-06.** Fax 05356/64-47-930. www.bruggerhof.camping.at. 25 units. Winter 150€–240€ double; summer 106€–140€ double. Rates include half board. AE, DC, MC, V. Closed Apr and Oct 15–Dec 15. **Amenities:** Restaurant; bar; pool; 2 tennis courts; fitness center; Jacuzzi; sauna; solarium; minigolf; room service; babysitting; laundry/dry cleaning service. *In room:* TV, minibar, hair dryer, safe.

Hotel Zur Tenne ✯   This hotel combines Tyrolean *Gemütlichkeit* with urban style and panache, and the staff shows genuine concern for its clientele. The hotel was created in the 1950s by joining a trio of 700-year-old houses. Rooms are as glamorous as anything in Kitzbühel: wood trim, comfortable beds, eiderdowns, and copies of Tyrolean antiques. Many have working fireplaces and canopied beds for a romantic touch. Bathrooms are generally large, with vanity mirrors and shower-tub combinations. In addition to intimate lounges, niches, and nooks, the hotel sports the most luxurious health complex in town, complete with a tropical fountain, two hot tubs, and a hot-and-cold foot bath.

Vorderstadt 8–10, A-6370 Kitzbühel. ✆ **05356/64-44-40.** Fax 05356/648-03-56. www.zurtenne.at. 50 units. Winter 276€ double, 345€ suite for 3; summer 138€–212€ double, 278€ suite for 3. Rates include breakfast. Half board 28€ per person extra in winter, 23€ in summer. AE, DC, MC, V. Free parking outdoors; 11€

in covered garage nearby. **Amenities:** 2 restaurants; bar; lounge; fitness center; 2 Jacuzzis; sauna; room service; massage; babysitting; laundry/dry cleaning service. *In room:* TV, minibar, hair dryer, safe.

WHERE TO DINE

The Dining Rooms in the Schloss Lebenberg ⭐ AUSTRIAN/INTERNA-
TIONAL   Although the Schloss Lebenberg hotel offers comfortable rooms, we actually prefer it for its well-managed restaurant and its sense of history. Originally built in 1548, it was transformed in 1885 into Kitzbühel's first family-run hotel. Always-reliable specialties include cream of tomato soup with gin, Tyrolean-style calf's liver, Wiener schnitzel, roulade of beef, and many desserts, which often feature mountain berries.

Lebenbergstrasse 17. ℂ **05356/690-10.** Reservations required. Main courses 11€–19€. AE, DC, MC, V. Daily noon–2pm and 6–9:30pm.

Restaurant Goldener Greif ⭐⭐ TYROLEAN   The setting is cozy and
warm, and the cuisine is some of the resort's best. The dining room features vaulted ceilings, intricate paneling, ornamental ceramic stoves, 19th-century paintings, and, in some cases, views out over the base of some of Kitzbühel's busy cable cars. Menu items are savory and designed to satisfy appetites heightened by the bracing alpine climate. You might order veal steak with fresh vegetables, pepper steak Madagascar, or venison. Many kinds of grilled steaks are regularly featured. A "Vienna pot" is one of the chef's specials, and fresh Tyrolean trout is offered daily. All the meat, sausages, and smoked meat come from the restaurant's own butcher.

Hinterstadt 24. ℂ **05356/643-11.** Reservations recommended. Main courses 7€–30€. Fixed-price menus 18€–23€. AE, DC, MC, V. Daily 10am–2pm and 7–10pm. Closed mid-Apr to late May and mid-Oct to mid-Dec.

SEEING THE SIGHTS IN TOWN

The town has two main streets, both pedestrian walkways. **Vorderstadt** and **Hinterstadt.** Along these streets Kitzbühel has preserved its traditional architectural style. You'll see three-story stone houses with oriels and scrollwork around the doors and windows, heavy overhanging eaves, and Gothic gables.

The **Pfarrkirche (Parish Church)** was built from 1435 to 1506 and renovated in the baroque style during the 18th century. The lower part of the **Liebfrauenkirche (Church of Our Lady)** dates from the 13th century, the upper part from 1570. Between these two churches stands the **Ölbergkapelle (Ölberg Chapel)** with a 1450 "lantern of the dead" and frescoes from the latter part of the 16th century.

In the **Heimatmuseum,** Hinterstadt 34 (ℂ **05356/645-88**), you'll see artifacts from prehistoric European mining eras and the north alpine Bronze Age, a winter-sports section with trophies of Kitzbüheler skiing greats, and exhibits detailing the town's history. The museum is open year-round Monday through Saturday from 10am to 1pm. Admission is 4€ adults, 2€ persons under 18.

HITTING THE SLOPES & OTHER OUTDOOR ACTIVITIES

SKIING   In winter the emphasis in Kitzbühel, 702m (2,300 ft.) above sea level, is on skiing, and facilities are offered for everyone from novices to experts. The ski season starts just before Christmas and lasts until late March. With more than 62 lifts, gondolas (cable cars), and mountain railroads on five different mountains, Kitzbühel has two main ski areas, the **Hahnenkamm** (renovated in 1995) and the **Kitzbüheler Horn** ⭐⭐. Cable cars (Hahnenkammbahn) are within easy walking distance, even for those in ski boots.

The linking of the lift systems on the Hahnenkamm has created the celebrated **Kitzbühel Ski Circus** ⭐⭐⭐, which makes it possible to ski downhill for more than 80km (50 miles), with runs that suit every stage of proficiency. Numerous championship ski events are held here; the World Cup event each January pits the skills of top-flight skiers against the toughest, fastest downhill course in the world, a stretch of the Hahnenkamm especially designed for maximum speed. Its name, *Die Streif,* is both feared and respected among skiers.

OTHER WINTER ACTIVITIES There's also curling, ski-bobbing, ski jumping, ice-skating, tobogganing, hiking on cleared trails, and hang gliding, as well as indoor activities like tennis, bowling, and swimming. The children's ski school, **Schi-schule Rote Teufel,** Museumkeller, Hinterstadt (© 05356/635-00), provides training for the very young skier. And don't forget the après-ski, with bars, nightclubs, and dance clubs rocking from teatime until the wee hours.

SUMMER ACTIVITIES Kitzbühel has summer pastimes, too, such as walking tours, visits to the **Wild Life Park at Aurach** (about 3km/2 miles from Kitzbühel), tennis, horseback riding, golf, squash, brass-band concerts in the town center, cycling, and swimming. For the last, there's an indoor swimming pool, but we recommend going to the **Schwarzsee (Black Lake).** This *See,* about a 15-minute walk northwest of the center of town, is an alpine lake with a peat bottom that keeps the water relatively murky. Covering an area of 6.4 hectares (16 acres), with a depth that doesn't exceed about 8m (25 ft.), it's the site of beaches and **Seiwald Boosverleih,** Schwartzsee (© 05356/623-81), an outfit that rents rowboats and putt-putt electric-driven engines in case you want to fish or sunbathe from a boat.

One of the region's most exotic collection of alpine flora is clustered into the jagged and rocky confines of the **Alpine Flower Garden Kitzbühel,** where various species of gentian, gorse, heather, and lichens are found on the sunny slopes of the Kitzbüheler Horn. Set at a height of around 1,830m (6,000 ft.) above sea level, the garden—which is owned and maintained by Kitzbühel as an incentive to midsummer tourism—is open from late May to early September, daily from 8:30am to 5:30pm, and is most impressive in June, July, and August. Admission is free. Many visitors see the garden by taking the Seilbahn Kitzbüheler cable car to its uppermost station and then descending on foot via the garden's labyrinth of footpaths to the gondola's middle station. (You can also climb upward within the garden, reversing the order of the gondola stations, although that would require a lot more effort.) The **Seilbahn Kitzbüheler cable car** (© 05356/69-51), 14€ round-trip, departs from Kitzbühel at half-hour intervals daily throughout the summer and winter. In spring and autumn, it operates Saturday and Sunday only.

2

Belgium

by George McDonald

Modest little Belgium has never been known to boast of its charms, yet its variety of language, culture, history, and cuisine would do credit to a country many times its size. Belgium's diversity stems from its location at the cultural crossroads of Europe. The boundary between the Continent's Germanic north and Latin south cuts clear across the nation's middle, leaving Belgium divided into two major ethnic regions: Dutch-speaking Flanders and French-speaking Wallonia.

Although international attention is focused on Brussels as the "capital of Europe," there's another Belgium of Gothic cathedrals, medieval castles, cobblestone streets, and tranquil canals waiting in the wings. In a country the size of Maryland, the timeless beauty of Bruges and Ghent are accessible, even to the most hurried visitor.

1 Brussels

A city with a notable history, Brussels is carving out a bright future. The "capital of Europe" has begun to act like Europe's Washington, D.C.—a focus of economic and political power, where decisions are made that affect the lives of people around the world. Headquarters of the European Union (EU), Brussels both symbolizes the Continent's vision of unity and is a bastion of officialdom, a breeding ground for the regulations that govern and often exasperate the rest of Europe.

Bruxellois have ambivalent feelings about their city's transformation into a power center. At first, the waves of Eurocrats brought a new cosmopolitan air to a somewhat provincial city, but as old neighborhoods were leveled to make way for office towers, people wondered whether Brussels was losing its soul. After all, this city doesn't only mean politics and business. It inspired surrealism and Art Nouveau, worships comic strips, prides itself on handmade lace and chocolate, and serves each one of its craft beers in its own unique glass.

Fortunately, not all of Brussels's individuality has been lost in this transition, and though the urban landscape has suffered from wanton "development," the city's spirit survives in traditional cafes, bars, bistros, and restaurants. Whether elegantly Art Nouveau or eccentrically festooned with posters, curios, and knickknacks, such centuries-old establishments provide a warm, convivial ambience that is peculiarly Belgian.

ESSENTIALS

GETTING THERE   By Plane   Brussels National Airport (© **0900/70-000** for flight information; www.brusselsairport.be) is 14km (9 miles) northeast of the city. In the arrival hall are currency-exchange offices, a tourist information office, ATMs, bars, restaurants, and shops.

A **train** connects the airport with Brussels's three major train stations (see below) every 20 minutes daily from 5:30am to 11:30pm; a one-way ride is

2.50€ second class and 3.75€ first class; trip time to Gare Centrale is 25 minutes. The **Airport Line bus,** no. 12, departs from the airport every 25 to 30 minutes to the Parc de Bruxelles (stop: Ducale) in the city center, with stops on the way, and costs 2.50€; **De Lijn bus** BZ connects the airport hourly with the Gare du Nord train station for the same price. A **taxi** from the airport to the city center costs around 35€.

By Train   High-speed Eurostar trains from London; Thalys from Paris, Amsterdam, and Cologne; and TGV from France (not Paris) arrive at Gare du Midi, rue de France, south of the city center. Other international trains arrive at Gare du Midi; Gare Centrale, Carrefour de l'Europe, downtown, a few blocks from the Grand-Place; and Gare du Nord, rue du Progrès, north of the city center. For international information, call ℂ **0900/10-366;** for Belgium call ℂ **02/555-25-25;** or go to **www.sncb.be** for both. All three stations are served by Métro, tram, and bus, and have taxi ranks outside.

Warning: Muggers, attracted by rich pickings from international travelers, haunt the environs of Gare du Midi, which are in the middle of a years-long redevelopment. Pickpockets and bag-snatchers work the interior. The police seem unable to control the problem. To avoid this threat, do not travel to or leave the station on foot—take a taxi or public transportation. Inside, keep a close eye on your possessions.

By Bus Eurolines (ℂ **02/203-07-07;** www.eurolines.com) coaches from London, Paris, Amsterdam, and other cities arrive at the bus station adjoining Gare du Nord train station.

By Car   Major expressways to Brussels are E19 from Amsterdam and Paris, and E40 from Ostend and Cologne. Avoid if possible the "hell on wheels" R0 Brussels ring road. Then, do yourself a favor: Leave the car at a parking garage.

VISITOR INFORMATION   On the ground floor of the Hôtel de Ville (Town Hall), **Tourist Information Brussels (TIB),** Grand-Place, 1000 Bruxelles (ℂ **02/513-89-40;** fax 02/514-45-38; www.tib.be; Métro: Gare Centrale), answers questions and sells the *Brussels Guide and Map* for 2€. TIB can reserve you a room for free and reserve concert/theater tickets for 1€. In addition, it sells tickets for public transportation and organizes guided walking tours. The office is open April through December, daily from 9am to 6pm; January through March, Monday through Saturday from 9am to 6pm.

The **Belgian Tourist Information Center,** rue du Marché-aux-Herbes 63, 1000 Bruxelles (ℂ **02/504-03-90;** fax 02/504-02-70; www.opt.be and www. toervl.be; Métro: Gare Centrale), a block from the Grand-Place, covers the entire country, including Brussels. It stocks a variety of brochures and reserves hotel rooms in Brussels and elsewhere in Belgium (you pay a deposit based on the room rate). This is the place to come before planning side trips. The office is open June to September, Monday through Saturday from 9am to 7pm, Sunday from 9am to 6pm; October to March, Monday through Saturday from 9am to 6pm; April, May, and October Sunday 9am to 6pm and to 5pm November to March.

For English-speaking visitors, the most useful publication is the weekly magazine *The Bulletin,* published on Thursdays and filled with local news, articles, information on special events and shopping, and useful addresses.

Websites   A good starting point for exploring Brussels and the Wallonia and Flanders regions of Belgium on the Web are the official tourist office websites **www.visitbelgium.com**, **www.opt.be**, and **www.toervl.be.** You might also want to check out the independent **www.trabel.com**. A new website in English that covers Belgian news, weather, tourism, and more is **www.xpats.com**. A good website for hotel research, where you can compare prices and see pictures of the rooms, is **www.hotels-belgium.com**.

CITY LAYOUT The city center's small, cobbled streets are clustered around the magnificent **Grand-Place.** Two of the most traveled lanes nearby are restaurant-lined **rue des Bouchers** and **petite rue des Bouchers,** part of an area known as the **Ilôt Sacré (Sacred Islet).** A block from the Grand-Place is the classical colonnaded Bourse (Stock Exchange). A few blocks north, on **place de la Monnaie,** is the Monnaie opera house and ballet theater, named after the coin mint that once stood here. Brussels's busiest shopping street, pedestrianized **rue Neuve,** starts from place de la Monnaie and runs north for several blocks.

The Upper Town is spread along an escarpment southeast of the center, where you find the second great square, **place du Grand-Sablon,** the Royal Fine Arts Museums, and the Royal Palace. If you head southwest and cross the broad **boulevard de Waterloo,** where you find the most exclusive designer stores, you come to **place Louise.** From here, Brussels's most fashionable thoroughfare, **avenue Louise,** runs south all the way to a large wooded park called the **Bois de la Cambre.** Both main streets are flanked by attractive residential side streets.

Between the Palais de Justice and Gare du Midi, the unpretentious working-class **Marolles** area has cozy cafes, drinking-man's bars, and inexpensive restaurants; its denizens even speak their own dialect.

East of this zone, the **Ixelles** district, near the Free University, has many casual, inexpensive restaurants, bars, and cafes. North of Ixelles, the modern European Union district surrounds **place Schuman.**

Brussels

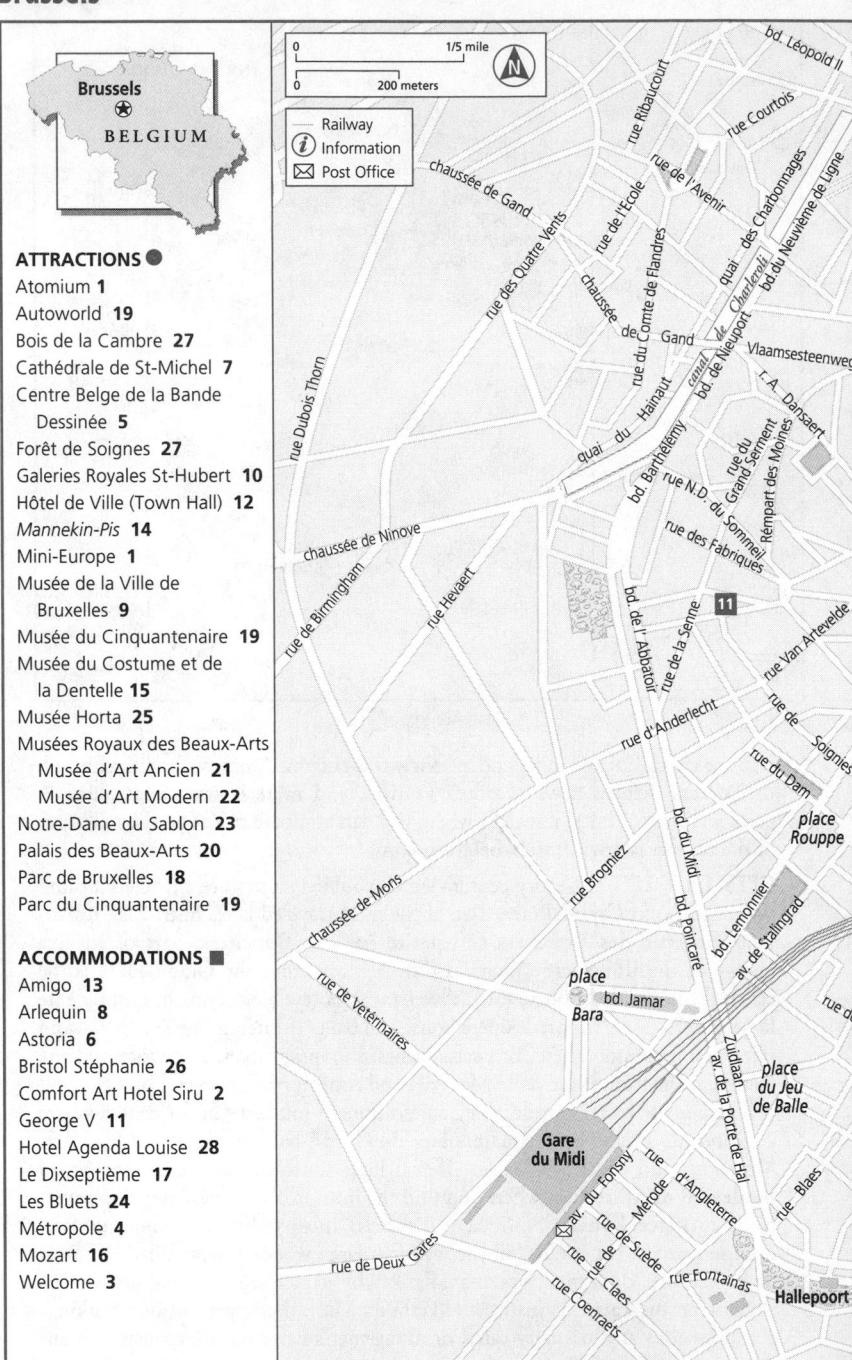

ATTRACTIONS ●

Atomium **1**
Autoworld **19**
Bois de la Cambre **27**
Cathédrale de St-Michel **7**
Centre Belge de la Bande
 Dessinée **5**
Forêt de Soignes **27**
Galeries Royales St-Hubert **10**
Hôtel de Ville (Town Hall) **12**
Mannekin-Pis **14**
Mini-Europe **1**
Musée de la Ville de
 Bruxelles **9**
Musée du Cinquantenaire **19**
Musée du Costume et de
 la Dentelle **15**
Musée Horta **25**
Musées Royaux des Beaux-Arts
 Musée d'Art Ancien **21**
 Musée d'Art Modern **22**
Notre-Dame du Sablon **23**
Palais des Beaux-Arts **20**
Parc de Bruxelles **18**
Parc du Cinquantenaire **19**

ACCOMMODATIONS ■

Amigo **13**
Arlequin **8**
Astoria **6**
Bristol Stéphanie **26**
Comfort Art Hotel Siru **2**
George V **11**
Hotel Agenda Louise **28**
Le Dixseptième **17**
Les Bluets **24**
Métropole **4**
Mozart **16**
Welcome **3**

> ## Tips Rules of the Road
>
> Elsewhere in this chapter, I describe the behavior of Brussels's car driv-
> ers as "piggish," a moderate term employed because finding the per-
> tinent adjective would tax even the considerable powers of the English
> language as an instrument of personal abuse.
>
> Part of the blame attaches to the *priorité de droite* traffic rule,
> whereby in some cases (but not always), traffic from the right has the
> right of way, even if it is coming from a minor road onto a more impor-
> tant one. You can imagine how this plays at multiple-road intersec-
> tions, particularly since Belgians will relinquish their *priorité* under no
> known circumstances, cost what it might. For proof of this, just look at
> the number of autos with crumpled *left* sides.
>
> Their hoggish behavior is extended to pedestrians, too. Don't expect
> cars to stop for you just because you're crossing at a black-and-white
> "pedestrian crossing." It's only recently that drivers have been obliged
> legally to stop at these, and most of them haven't got the message yet.

In this bilingual city, called *Bruxelles* in French and *Brussel* in Dutch, street names and places are in both languages. Grand-Place is *Grote Markt* in Dutch; Gare Centrale is *Centraal Station;* Théatre Royal de la Monnaie is *Koninklijke Munttheater.* For convenience and to save space, I use only the French names in this chapter.

GETTING AROUND   By Métro, Tram & Bus   Public transportation begins at around 6am and the regular service ends around midnight. After that, there are infrequent night buses. The Métro (subway) network is good for get-ting to major destinations around and on the edge of town. Métro stations are indicated by signs showing a large white M on a blue background. Trams (street-cars) and buses are yellow; stop them by extending your arm as they approach. Stops are marked with red-and-white signs.

A single ride (a *direct*) costs 1.50€. You can also buy a 1-day pass for 3.60€, a 5-ride card for 6.25€, and a 10-ride card for 9.25€. Insert your ticket into the orange machines on buses and trams and at Métro platforms. Your ticket must be inserted each time you enter a new vehicle, but you can transfer from Métro to tram to bus for up to 1 hour.

Free pocket maps of the public transportation network are available from the tourist office, the main Métro stations, and the **STIB** public transportation company, Galerie de la Toison d'Or 20 (© **02/515-20-00;** www.stib.irisnet.be; Métro: Louise). Maps of the network are posted at all Métro stations and on many bus and tram shelters.

By Taxi   The fare starts at 2.40€ during the day and at 4.25€ between 10pm and 6am, increasing by .95€ per kilometer inside the city (tariff 1) and 1.90€ per kilometer outside (tariff 2)—make sure the meter is set to the correct tariff. Taxis cannot be hailed on the street, but there are stands at prominent locations around town. Call **Taxis Bleus** (© **02/268-00-00**), **Taxis Oranges** (© **02/349-43-43**), or **Taxis Verts** (© **02/349-49-49**).

By Rental Car   Driving in Brussels is akin to life during the Stone Age—nasty and brutish, the only difference being that it's rarely short. If you must drive, all the top international firms rent here: **Avis,** rue Américaine 145 (© **02/720-09-44;** tram: 91 or 92); **Budget,** av. Louise 327 (© **02/646-51-30;** Métro: Louise); **Europcar,** rue du Page 29 (© **02/348-92-12;** tram: 81 or 82); and **Hertz,** bd. Maurice-Lemmonier 8 (© **02/726-49-50;** Métro: Anneessens). All of these firms also have desks at the airport. Rates begin at around 45€ for a small car with unlimited mileage. The smallest car at **ABC Rent a Car,** rue d'Anderlecht 133 (© **02/513-19-54;** tram: 18), is 43€ a day, unlimited mileage and tax included.

Remember: You get the best deal if you arrange the rental before leaving home.

By Bike Brussels's piggish drivers and biased road laws combine to make this a poor option. If you want to rent a bike anyway, try **Pro Vélo,** rue de Londres 13–15 (© **02/502-73-55;** Métro: Porte de Namur). July and August, it's open daily from 9am to 6pm; September through June, hours are Monday through Friday from 9am to 6pm. Rental is 7.50€ for a half day, 13€ for a full day, and 20€ for a weekend. They also organize bike tours with commentary in English.

By Foot There's no better way to explore the historic core of the town than walking, especially around Grand-Place. You'll also enjoy strolling uptown around place du Grand-Sablon. Beyond these areas, you'll want to use transportation.

 FAST FACTS: Brussels

American Express The office at bd. du Souverain 100, 1000 Bruxelles (© 02/676-21-11; Métro: Horrmann-Debroux), is open Monday through Friday from 9am to 1pm and 2 to 5pm. Call ahead before visiting, as the office is out in the suburbs.

Babysitters Many hotels can provide reliable babysitting service. A student babysitting roster is maintained by ULB Service, "Jobs," av. P. Héger 22, 1000 Bruxelles (© 02/650-21-71).

Business Hours Banks are open Monday through Friday from 9am to 1pm and 2 to 4:30 or 5pm. Open hours for **offices** are Monday through Friday from 9 or 10am to 4 or 5pm. Most **stores** are open Monday through Saturday from 9 or 10am to 6 or 7pm; some stay open on Friday to 8 or 9pm.

Currency Belgium uses the euro (€).

Currency Exchange Banks give the best rates, and currency exchange offices in train stations come close. Hotels and *bureaux de change* (currency-exchange offices), open regular hours plus evenings and weekends, charge a low commission (or none at all) but give a low rate. If you carry American Express traveler's checks, change them at **American Express** (see above), where there's no commission charge. **Thomas Cook,** Grand-Place 4 (© 02/513-28-45; Métro: Gare Centrale), also has fair rates.

Always know *exactly* how much you are going to get in your hand before agreeing to the transaction. You'll find many **ATMs** around town, identified by "Bancontact" and "Mister Cash" logos.

Dentists/Doctors For emergency dental care, you can reach a local dental referral service at © 02/426-10-26 or 02/428-58-58. For emergency medical service in the Greater Brussels area (around the clock), dial © 02/513-02-02.

Drugstores A pharmacy is called a *pharmacie* in French and an *apotheek* in Dutch. Regular pharmacy hours are Monday through Saturday from 9am to 6pm (some close earlier on Sat). Try the centrally located **Grande**

Pharmacie de Brouckère, Passage du Nord 10–12 (✆ **02/218-05-07;** Métro: De Brouckère). All pharmacies have details of nearby all-night and Sunday pharmacies posted on the door.

Embassies The embassy of the **United States,** bd. du Régent 25–27 (✆ **02/ 508-21-11;** Métro: Arts-Loi), is open Monday through Friday from 9am to noon for visas and 1:30 to 4:30pm for assistance. The embassy of **Canada,** av. de Tervuren 2 (✆ **02/741-06-11;** Métro: Mérode), is open Monday, Wednesday, and Friday from 9am to noon and 2 to 4pm; Tuesday and Thursday from 9am to noon. The embassy of the **United Kingdom,** rue Arlon 85 (✆ **02/287-62-11;** Métro: Maalbeek), is open Monday through Friday from 9:30am to noon. The embassy of **Ireland,** rue Froissart 89 (✆ **02/230-53-37;** Métro: Schuman), is open Monday through Friday from 10am to 12:30pm. The embassy of **Australia,** rue Guimard 6–8 (✆ **02/286-05-00;** Métro: Arts-Loi), is open Monday through Friday from 9am to 12:30pm and 2 to 4pm. The embassy of **New Zealand,** Square de Meeûs 1 (✆ **02/512-10-40;** Métro: Trone), is open Monday through Friday from 9am to 1pm and 2 to 3:30pm. The embassy of **South Africa,** rue de la Loi 26 (✆ **02/285-44-00;** Métro: Arts-Loi), is open Monday through Friday from 9 to 11:30am.

Emergencies For police assistance, call ✆ **101.** For an ambulance or the fire department, call ✆ **100.**

Holidays Holidays are January 1 (New Year's Day), Easter Monday, May 1 (Labor Day), Ascension, Pentecost Monday, July 21 (Independence Day), August 15 (Assumption), November 1 (All Saints), November 11 (Armistice Day), and December 25 (Christmas). The dates of three holidays change each year; in 2003, these were Easter Monday, April 21; Ascension, May 29; Pentecost Monday, June 9.

Hospital The **Cliniques Universitaires St-Luc,** av. Hippocrate 10 (✆ **02/764-11-11;** Métro: Alma), has an emergency department.

Internet Access In the city center, the large Internet center **easyInternet-café,** place de Brouckère 9–13 (✆ **02/211-08-20;** www.easyeverything. com; Métro: De Brouckère), is open daily from 8am to 11pm; access begins at 2.50€ per hour.

Mail Most **post offices** are open Monday through Friday from 9am to 5pm. The office at Centre Monnaie, place de la Monnaie (✆ **02/226-21-11;** Métro: De Brouckère), is open Monday through Friday from 9am to 5pm, Saturday from 9:30am to 3pm. The office at Gare du Midi, av. Fonsny 1E/F (✆ **02/538-33-98;** Métro: Gare du Midi), is open 24 hours.

　　Postage for a postcard or letter to the U.S., Canada, Australia, New Zealand, or South Africa is .85€; to the U.K. or Ireland .45€.

Safety Brussels is generally safe, but crimes, including violent crimes, were up 20% (from a low base) over a 5-year period to 2000. There is a growing trend of pickpocketing, theft from and of cars, and muggings in places such as Métro station foot tunnels. Don't overestimate the risk, but take sensible precautions, particularly in obvious circumstances such as on crowded Métro trains and when taking cash from an ATM at night.

Taxes There's a value-added tax (TVA) of 6% on hotel bills and 21.5% on restaurant bills and all goods. If you spend over 125€ in some stores, and you are not a resident of the European Union, you can get a tax refund when you leave the EU. For more information, see "The Shopping Scene," later in this chapter.

Telephone Belgium's **country code** is 32. Brussels's **city code** is 2; use the **32-2** code when calling from the United States or any other country outside Belgium. In Belgium, use the **area code 02**. You need to dial the **02** area code both from inside Brussels and from elsewhere in Belgium.

A local phone call from a pay phone costs .25€ per minute at peak time (Mon–Fri 8am–7pm) and .25€ per 2 minutes at off-peak time. An international call, per minute, to the U.S., Canada, the U.K., or Ireland costs .35€; to Australia or New Zealand 1€; to South Africa 2€. You can use most pay phones in booths all around town with a plastic Belgacom **telecard,** selling for 5€, 13€, and 25€ at post offices, train ticket counters, and newsstands. Some pay phones take coins of .05€, .10€, .20€, .50€, and 1€. On both card and coin phones, watch the digital reading, which tracks your decreasing deposit so you know when to add another card or more coins. For information inside the country, call ℂ **1207** or **1307;** for international information in English, call ℂ **1405.**

To charge a call to your calling card, dial **AT&T** (ℂ **0800/100-10**); **MCI** (ℂ **0800/100-12**); **Sprint** (ℂ **0800/100-14**); **Canada Direct** (ℂ **0800/100-19**); or **British Telecom** (ℂ **0800/100-24**).

Tipping The prices on most restaurant menus already include a service charge of 16%, so it's unnecessary to tip. However, if the service is good, it's usual to show appreciation with a tip. Service is included in your hotel bill as well. For taxi drivers, you can round up the fare if you like, but you need not add a tip unless you have received an extra service such as help with luggage.

Toilets Be sure to *pay the person* who sits at the entrance to a *toilette*. He or she has a saucer in which you put your money. If you don't, you might have a visitor in the inner sanctum while you're transacting your business. Even if you have paid, in busy places the attendant may have forgotten your face by the time you emerge and will then pursue you out of the toilet and along the street. It's tiresome, but toilet use is usually only about .10€

WHERE TO STAY

The business of Brussels is business (and politics), a fact reflected in the cost and nature of available accommodations. Hotels in the upper price range have a wealth of facilities for business travelers and offer efficient, though often impersonal, service. Some of the city's family hotels in old town houses are small and fill up quickly, but they often have lots of homespun charm at fairly reasonable prices. At every level, hotels fill up during the week and empty out on weekends and during July and August. In off-peak periods, rates can drop as much as 50% from those quoted below; be sure to ask for lower rates and be certain that you're quoted the complete rates, which include 6% value added tax (TVA), 10% city tax, and 16% service charge.

The TIB office in the Grand-Place and the Belgian Tourist Information Center at rue du Marché-aux-Herbes 63 (see "Visitor Information," earlier) make same-day reservations, if you go in person, for a small fee (deducted by the hotel from its room rate). TIB publishes an annual *Hotel Guide* with listings by price range, and can provide complete information, including space availability, on hostels. **Belgian Tourist Reservations,** bd. Anspach 111, 1000 Bruxelles (☎ **02/513-74-84;** fax 02/513-92-77; Métro: Bourse), reserves hotel rooms throughout Belgium and can often give substantial discounts.

The **Sheraton Brussels Airport** hotel, Brussels National Airport (facing Departures), Zaventem 1930 (☎ **800/325-3535** in the U.S. and Canada, or 02/725-10-00; fax 02/710-80-80; www.sheraton.com), couldn't be more convenient to the airport without being on the runway. And you have all the comfort you would expect of a top-flight Sheraton. Doubles cost 375€ to 395€ a night.

AROUND THE GRAND-PLACE
Very Expensive
Amigo 𝄖𝄖   In Brussels slang, an "amigo" is a prison, and indeed a prison once stood here, in a highly convenient location (both then and now) across the street from the Town Hall. But any resemblance to the former accommodations is purely nominal. Under new ownership, the Amigo has gone from being a worthy but somewhat dull lodging to one of the city's finest. The hotel's Spanish Renaissance architecture, stately corridors, and flagstone lobby are right at home in this ancient neighborhood. The rooms are quite spacious and traditionally elegant, but with touches of modern Flemish design to brighten things up—and motifs from the classic comic, *Tintin,* in the bathrooms to add an element of whimsy. Ask for a room with a view of the Town Hall's fantastic Gothic spire.

Rue de l'Amigo 1–3 (off the Grand-Place), 1000 Bruxelles. ☎ 02/547-47-47. Fax 02/513-52-77. www.rocco fortehotels.com. 177 units. 420€–540€ double; from 790€ suite. AE, DC, MC, V. Valet parking 15€. Métro: Bourse. **Amenities:** Restaurant; bar; lounge; health club; concierge; 24-hr. business center; 24-hr. room service; babysitting; laundry service; same-day dry cleaning; nonsmoking rooms; executive rooms. *In room:* A/C, TV w/pay movies, dataport, minibar, hair dryer, safe.

Expensive
Hotel Métropole 𝄖𝄖   Even if you're not staying here, the hotel is worth a visit on its own account. An ornate, marble-and-gilt interior distinguishes this late-19th-century hotel several blocks from the Grand-Place. Soaring ceilings, potted palms, and lavishly decorated public rooms add to the Belle Epoque allure. Spacious rooms have classic furnishings and some modern luxuries, including heated towel racks, hair dryers, and trouser presses. An elegant French restaurant, **L'Alban Chambon,** caters to the sophisticated diner, and the Belle Epoque **Café Métropole** to the sophisticated cafe hound.

⌒Tips Booking in a B&B

An alternative to hotels is a bed-and-breakfast. Brussels has two B&B organizations: **Bed & Brussels,** rue Kindermans 9, 1050 Bruxelles (☎ **02/644-07-37;** fax 02/644-01-14; www.bnb-brussels.be); and **Windrose,** av. Brugman 11, 1060 Bruxelles (☎ **02/534-71-91;** fax 02/534-50-70; nadine@wep-edu.be). Both have a database of several hundred rooms, from the simple to the grand, and based on your requirements will provide you with several options. You can choose on the website and book online at the former and book by e-mail at the latter. The booking fee is 13€ per reservation; rates run from 28€ for a single without bathroom to 80€ for a deluxe double with bathroom, including breakfast.

Place de Brouckère 31 (close to Centre Monnaie), 1000 Bruxelles. ✆ **02/217-23-00**. Fax 02/218-02-20. www. metropolehotel.be. 410 units. 315€–415€ double; from 450€ suite. Rates include buffet or continental breakfast. AE, DC, MC, V. Parking 13€. Métro: De Brouckère. **Amenities:** Restaurant; lounge; sidewalk cafe; health club & spa; concierge; 24-hr. room service; laundry service; dry cleaning. *In room:* TV w/pay movies, minibar, coffeemaker, hair dryer, safe.

Moderate

Arlequin 🔍   You can't get closer to the heart of the city than this, with the restaurant-lined rue des Bouchers right outside the hotel's back entrance. Then there's the fine views from some rooms of the Town Hall spire in the neighboring Grand-Place (spectacular when lit at night) and of the Old City's rooftops and narrow medieval streets from the top-floor breakfast room. The guest rooms themselves are not quite as spectacular as the views, but all have modern, comfortable furnishings, and most have plenty of natural light.

Rue de la Fourche 17–19 (off rue des Bouchers), 1000 Bruxelles. ✆ **02/514-16-15**. Fax 02/514-22-02. www. arlequin.be. 92 units. 80€–115€ double. Rates include buffet breakfast. AE, DC, MC, V. No parking. Métro: Bourse. **Amenities:** Limited room service; laundry service; dry cleaning. *In room:* TV w/pay movies, hair dryer.

Le Dixseptième 🔍🔍   This graceful 17th-century house, once the official residence of the Spanish ambassador, stands close to the Grand-Place in a neighborhood of restored dwellings. Guest rooms have wood paneling and marble chimneys, and are as big as the suites in many hotels; some have balconies. All are in 18th-century style and are named after Belgian painters from Brueghel to Magritte. Two beautiful lounges are decorated with carved wooden medallions and 18th-century paintings.

Rue de la Madeleine 25 (off place de l'Albertine), 1000 Bruxelles. ✆ **02/502-57-44**. Fax 02/502-64-24. www.ledixseptieme.be. 24 units. 180€–360€ double. Rates include buffet breakfast. AE, DC, MC, V. Limited street parking. Métro: Gare Centrale. **Amenities:** Lounge; laundry service; dry cleaning. *In room:* A/C, TV, minibar, hair dryer, safe.

Inexpensive

Mozart   Go up a flight from the busy, cheap-eats street level, and guess which famous composer's music wafts through the lobby? Salmon-colored walls, plants, and old paintings create a warm, intimate ambience that's carried over into the guest rooms. Although furnishings are blandly modern, colorful fabrics and exposed beams lend each room a rustic originality. Several are duplexes with a sitting room underneath the loft bedroom. Top-floor rooms have a great view.

Rue du Marché-aux-Fromages 15A (close to Grand-Place), 1000 Bruxelles. ✆ **02/502-66-61**. Fax 02/502-77-58. www.hotel-mozart.be. 47 units. 90€ double. AE, DC, MC, V. No parking. Métro: Gare Centrale. **Amenities:** Lounge. *In room:* TV.

AROUND THE FISH MARKET
Moderate

Welcome 🔍🔍   The Welcome is a little gem of a hotel—the smallest in the old city center—at the Fish Market. Think of it as a country *auberge* right in the heart of town. Rooms are furnished and styled on individual themes, like Provence, Tibet, and Laura Ashley, all to a high standard. Guests get a discount in the fancy attached seafood restaurant, La Truite d'Argent. Book ahead for the hotel because regular guests are fiercely loyal and it's often full—admittedly not a difficult feat.

Rue du Peuplier 1 (at the Marché-aux-Poissons), 1000 Bruxelles. ✆ **02/219-95-46**. Fax 02/217-18-87. www. hotelwelcome.com. 8 units. 70€–120€ double; 150€ suite. DC, MC, V. Free parking. Métro: Ste-Catherine. **Amenities:** Restaurant; lounge; free airport shuttle. *In room:* A/C, TV, minibar.

Inexpensive

George V ✸   This agreeable little hotel is tucked away in a corner of the city center that looks more down at the heels than it really is and is currently being reborn as a trendy shopping-and-eating area. Situated in a town house from 1859 within easy walking distance of the Grand-Place, the George provides a free shuttle bus to this square and the main museums, and to Gare du Midi. The rooms are plain but clean and have new furnishings, but some of the fittings are in clear need of replacement.

Rue 't Kint 23 (off place du Jardin-aux-Fleurs), 1000 Bruxelles. ✆ **02/513-50-93**. Fax 02/513-44-93. www.george5.com. 16 units. 60€–65€ double. Rates include continental breakfast. AE, MC, V. Parking 6.50€. Métro: Bourse. **Amenities:** Restaurant; bar; 24-hr. room service. *In room:* TV.

THE UPPER CITY
Expensive

Astoria ✸✸   This fine luxury hotel has an ideal location for exploring both the old Brussels of the city center and the newer Upper Town. You're transported to a more elegant age the moment you walk into the Belle Epoque foyer, where the sumptuous surroundings feature Corinthian columns, antique furnishings, and textured marble. Guest rooms, which are somewhat smaller than in other hotels of this category, are attractively and comfortably furnished, though not extravagantly so, in a style that's in keeping with the hotel's character. You can dine at the beautiful French restaurant, Le Palais Royal, and have a drink in the ornate Pullman Bar, which is based on the restaurant car of the legendary Orient Express train.

Rue Royale 103 (close to Colonne du Congrès), 1000 Bruxelles. ✆ **800/SOFITEL** in the U.S. and Canada, or 02/227-05-05. Fax 02/219-30-46. www.sofitel.com. 118 units. 350€ double; from 450€ suite. AE, DC, MC, V. Parking 18€. Métro: Botanique. **Amenities:** Restaurant (French); lounge; health club & spa; concierge; 24-hr. room service; laundry service; dry cleaning. *In room:* A/C, TV w/pay movies, minibar, coffeemaker, hair dryer, safe.

AROUND AVENUE LOUISE
Expensive

Bristol Stephanie ✸✸   From its lobby fittings to furnishings in the kitchenette suites, every feature of this sleek Norwegian-owned hotel, set on one of the city's toniest shopping streets, is streamlined, functional, and representative of the best in Nordic design. Some rooms have four-poster beds and "anti-allergy" hardwood floors; all are furnished to a high level of modern style and comfort (though the standard rooms could use a little more Nordic drawer space). The rooms are quite large, but should you need more space, it's worth the extra 40€ or so to upgrade to a far larger executive room. Try to get a room in the main building; the security in the back building is good, but nothing beats a 24-hour doorman. Restaurant Le Chalet d'Odin has a refined French menu.

Av. Louise 91–93, 1050 Bruxelles. ✆ **02/543-33-11**. Fax 02/538-03-07. www.bristol.be. 142 units. 350€–390€ double; from 600€ suite. AE, DC, MC, V. Parking 20€. Métro: Louise. **Amenities:** Restaurant; lounge; bar; heated indoor pool; exercise room; Jacuzzi; sauna; concierge; business center; 24-hr. room service; babysitting; laundry service; dry cleaning; nonsmoking rooms; executive rooms. *In room:* A/C, TV w/pay movies, minibar, coffeemaker, hair dryer, iron, safe.

Moderate

Hotel Agenda Louise ✸   This exquisite little hotel has modern rooms decorated with light-colored wood furniture and gold and orange curtains and fittings. All have coffeemakers and come with complete kitchens. Ask for a room that overlooks the inner courtyard for the best view.

Rue de Florence 6 (off av. Louise), 1000 Bruxelles. ℂ **02/539-00-31.** Fax 02/539-00-63. www.hotel-agenda. com. 37 units. 116€ double. Rates include buffet breakfast. AE, DC, MC, V. Parking 6€. Métro: Louise. **Amenities:** Lounge; same-day dry cleaning; nonsmoking rooms. *In room:* TV, minibar, coffeemaker, hair dryer.

Inexpensive

Les Bluets ✮✮   If you're searching for classic European charm or are a fan of American B&Bs, you'll enjoy it here. The town house from 1864 is more comfortable country residence than hotel. You feel as though you're staying with friends when you breakfast in the antiques-filled dining room or in the sunroom. A sweeping stairway (no elevator) leads up to the rooms, several of which have 4m (14-ft.) ceilings and ornate moldings; all have antiques and knick-knacks. This is one of the city's few nonsmoking hotels.

Rue Berckmans 124 (off av. Louise), 1060 Bruxelles. ℂ **02/534-39-83.** Fax 02/543-09-70. www.belge.net/ bluets. 10 units. 53€–81€ double. Rates include continental breakfast. MC, V. Limited street parking. Métro: Hôtel des Monnaies. *In room:* TV.

AROUND GARE DU NORD
Moderate

Comfort Art Hotel Siru ✮✮   This is a fascinating midsize hotel in an area that was formerly decrepit—it used to be a red-light district and still has some peep-show joints and offbeat appliances shops—but that has been going upmarket fast since a slew of fancy office blocks were built nearby. What sets the Siru apart is that the owner of this art-gallery-cum-hotel in a redeveloped business district persuaded 130 Belgian artists, including some of the country's biggest names, to "decorate" each of the coolly modern, well-equipped rooms and the corridors with a work on travel. Given the unpredictable nature of reactions to modern art, some clients apparently reserve the same room time after time; others ask for a room change in the middle of the night. It is not easily forgotten.

Place Rogier 1 (opposite Gare du Nord), 1210 Bruxelles. ℂ **800/228-3323** in the U.S. and Canada, or 02/ 203-35-80. Fax 02/203-33-03. www.comforthotelsiru.com. 101 units. 90€–180€ double. Rates include buffet breakfast. AE, DC, MC, V. Parking 15€. Métro: Rogier. **Amenities:** Restaurant; babysitting; laundry service; same-day dry cleaning; nonsmoking rooms; executive rooms. *In room:* TV w/pay movies, dataport, minibar, hair dryer, safe.

WHERE TO DINE

Food is a passion in Brussels. The city's French- and Dutch-speaking residents may have their differences, but they both value a good meal. This gastronomic obsession has generated 2,000 restaurants in all categories, so you can always find somewhere to eat well at a reasonable price. Indeed, you'll find it hard to eat badly in Brussels. Note that your check will include a 21.5% value-added tax (TVA) and usually a 16% service charge.

Among the sturdy regional dishes you find on menus around town are: *waterzooï,* fish or chicken stew with a parsley-and-cream sauce; *stoemp,* a puree of vegetables and potatoes with sausage, steak, or chops; *paling in 't groen,* eel in a grass-green sauce; *ballekes,* spicy meatballs; *hochepot,* stew; *lapin à la gueuze,* rabbit with a Brussels beer sauce; and *carbonnades à la flamande,* beef stew with a beer sauce. A selection of the country's 300 craft cheeses is a good way to finish off.

While most of the city's favorite dishes are based on local products, the famous *moules* (mussels)—prepared in countless ingenious variations and served in tureens—come from Zeeland in neighboring Holland.

Belgian beer is the perfect accompaniment to all of these. The country is renowned for its 400 brands of beer produced by hundreds of small breweries. Belgian chefs use beer in their sauces the way French chefs use wine. Beef,

---

Tips On Your Guard in the Ilôt Sacré

A few restaurants (not reviewed here) in this colorful restaurant district off the Grand-Place take advantage of tourists. If you don't want to get fleeced, be sure to ask the price of everything *before* you order it. Most visitors leave the Ilôt Sacré with no more serious complaint than an expanded waistline, but a little caution is in order.

---

chicken, and fish are often bathed in a savory sauce based on the local *gueuze, faro,* and *kriek* brews.

The main restaurant areas center around the Grand-Place and the Marché-aux-Poissons (Fish Market) in the city center; and in trendy Ixelles and St-Gilles south of the city center. The city has few vegetarian restaurants, though many others have a vegetarian section on their menu with at least a few nonmeat items. If you are a nonsmoker you're mostly out of luck—get ready to consume a garnish of secondhand smoke with your meal.

Don't fret if the service is slow: People take their time dining out here, and just sitting in a good restaurant is part of the pleasure.

AROUND THE GRAND-PLACE
Very Expensive

Comme Chez Soi ★★★ CLASSIC FRENCH   A visit to the revered, Art Nouveau "Just Like Home," which sports the maximum three Michelin stars, will surely be the culinary highlight of your trip to Brussels. Although the food is a long way from what most people actually eat at home, the welcome from master chef Pierre Wynants is warm, and his standards are high enough for the most rigorous taste buds. Ask for a table in the kitchen, where you can watch the master at work. The sautéed lobster with truffles and chanterelles or the roast saddle of lamb are memorable main courses; for dessert, try the soufflé of preserved oranges in Mandarine Napoléon liqueur. Book as far ahead as possible. Getting a table at short notice is more likely at lunchtime, which is generally a shade less busy than the evenings.

Place Rouppe 23 (at av. de Stalingrad). © 02/512-29-21. Reservations required. Main courses 31€–94€; fixed-price menus 56€–124€. AE, DC, MC, V. Tues–Sat noon–1:30pm and 7–9:30pm. Métro: Anneessens.

La Maison du Cygne ★★ CLASSIC FRENCH   This grande dame of Brussels's internationally recognized restaurants overlooks the Grand-Place from the former guild house of the Butchers Guild—where Karl Marx worked on *The Communist Manifesto* during a 3-year sojourn in Brussels. The service, though a tad stuffy, is as elegant as the polished walnut walls, bronze wall sconces, and green velvet. The menu has haute cuisine Belgian and French classics, such as *waterzooï de homard* (a souplike lobster stew), veal sautéed with fresh wild mushrooms, and *tournedos* (filet steak) with green peppercorns. There are fine chicken and fish dishes, and specialties such as *huîtres au champagne* (oysters in champagne) and *goujonette de sole mousseline* (sole mousse). Because of its location, the restaurant is usually crowded at lunchtime, but dinner reservations are likely to be available.

Grand-Place 9 (entrance at rue Charles Buls 2). © 02/511-82-44. Reservations recommend. Main courses 24€–40€; *menu du jour* 58€. AE, DC, MC, V. Mon–Fri noon–2:15pm; Mon–Sat 7pm–midnight. Métro: Gare Centrale.

Expensive

De l'Ogenblik ★★ FRENCH/BELGIAN   In the elegant surrounds of the Galeries Royales St-Hubert, this restaurant supplies good taste in a Parisian bistro–style setting that's popular with off-duty actors and audiences from the nearby Gallery theater, among others. It often gets busy, but the ambience in the split-level, wood-and-brass-outfitted dining room, with a sand-strewn floor, is convivial, though a little too tightly packed when it's full. Look for garlicky meat and seafood menu dishes, and expect to pay a smidgen more for atmosphere than might be strictly justified by results on the plate. In the former category, if you like duck, try the *magret du canard mulard aux deux poivres, gratin dauphinois* (filet of duck with peppers and potatoes gratin). A good seafood choice is the *ragoût de coquilles St-Jacques et gambas, sauce diable* (scallop and prawn stew in a "devil"—spicy—sauce).

Galerie des Princes 1 (in the Galeries Royales St-Hubert). ✆ **02/511-61-51.** Main courses 22€–28€; *plat du jour* 11€. AE, DC, MC, V. Mon–Thurs noon–2:30pm and 7pm–midnight; Fri–Sat noon–2:30pm and 7pm–12:30am. Métro: De Brouckère.

Moderate

Brasserie de la Roue d'Or ★★ TRADITIONAL BELGIAN   This welcoming Art Nouveau brasserie, with lots of dark wood, mirrors, a high frescoed ceiling, Magritte images on the walls, and marble-topped tables, has a loyal local following. An extensive menu, ranging from grilled meats to a good selection of salmon and other seafood, as well as old Belgian favorites like *stoemp* (a purée of vegetables and potatoes with sausage, steak, or chops), caters to just about any appetite, and the beer, wine, and spirits list is equally long. Jeff De Gelas, the colorful owner (he also owns 't Kelderke; see below), is known locally as the "King of Stoemp."

Rue des Chapeliers 26 (off the Grand-Place). ✆ **02/514-25-54.** Main courses 12€–22€; fixed-price menus 44€–53€. AE, DC, MC, V. Daily noon–12:30am. Métro: Gare Centrale.

Falstaff Gourmand ★ *Value* BELGIAN/FRENCH   The Falstaff cafe across from the Bourse (see "Brussels After Dark," later in this chapter) is widely renowned as a classic Art Nouveau cafe. Around the corner, its former sister establishment—now operating on its own hook—has a different but equally notable style. Service is attentive, prompt, and friendly. First-class Belgian and French menu dishes include one of the best deals in Brussels: a three-course *menu gourmand,* which includes an aperitif, a glass of wine with a starter, and a small pitcher of wine with the main course.

Rue des Pierres 38 (near the Bourse). ✆ **02/512-17-61.** Main courses 13€–20€; *menu gourmand* 28€. AE, DC, MC, V. Tues–Sat 11:30am–3pm and 7–11pm; Sun 7–11pm. Métro: Bourse.

Inexpensive

L'Auberge des Chapeliers ★★ *Value* TRADITIONAL BELGIAN   In a 17th-century building that was once the headquarters of the hat makers' guild, L'Auberge des Chapeliers preserves its historic charm. Behind a beautiful brick facade, the first two floors are graced with timber beams and paneling and are connected by a narrow wooden staircase. Popular with locals who live and work in the area, as well as with tourists fortunate enough to find it, the place can be crowded at the height of lunch hour, so it's a good idea to come just before noon or just after 2pm. The food is typical hearty Belgian fare, with an accent on mussels in season and dishes cooked in beer. The prices are modest, considering the location.

Rue des Chapeliers 1–3 (off Grand-Place). ℂ **02/513-73-38.** Reservations recommended on weekends. Main courses 8.50€–18€; set-price menus 15€–21€. AE, DC, MC, V. Mon–Thurs noon–2pm and 6–11pm; Fri noon–2pm and 6pm–midnight; Sat noon–3pm and 6pm–midnight; Sun noon–3pm and 6–11pm. Métro: Gare Centrale.

't Kelderke ★★ TRADITIONAL BELGIAN   Despite being on the square that is the focus of tourism in Brussels, this is far from being a tourist trap. As many Bruxellois as tourists throng the long wooden tables in a 17th-century, brick-arched cellar, and all are welcomed with time-honored respect, even if that may be perceived as being a little rough and ready. Memorable traditional Belgian fare, with little in the way of frills, is served from an open kitchen. This is a great place to try local specialties such as *bloedpens* (blood sausage) a la Bruxelloise, *stoemp* (mashed potatoes and vegetables) with *boudin* (sausage)—owner Jef De Gelas is renowned locally as the "King of Stoemp"—*carbonnades à la flamande* (Flemish beef stew), *lapin à la gueuze* (rabbit in Brussels beer), and big, steaming pans piled high with Zeeland mussels.

Grand-Place 15. ℂ **02/513-73-44.** Main courses 9.50€–19€; *plat du jour* 7.50€. AE, DC, MC, V. Daily noon–2am. Métro: Gare Centrale.

AROUND AVENUE LOUISE
Expensive
La Quincaillerie ★★ MODERN FRENCH/OYSTER BAR   In the Ixelles district, where fine restaurants are as common as streetlights, this spot stands out, even though it may be a little too aware of its own modish good looks and a shade pricey. The setting is a traditional former hardware store from 1903, with a giant train station clock, wood paneling, and masses of wooden drawers, designed by students of Art Nouveau master Victor Horta. It's busy enough to get the waitstaff harassed and absent-minded, yet they're always friendly. Seafood dishes predominate on the menu. Specialties include *escalope du saumon rôti au gros sel* (salmon in roasted rock salt) and *canette laquée au miel et citron vert* (baby duck with a crust of honey and lime). You don't need to look much further than a crisp Sancerre as the ideal wine accompaniment to most dishes.

Rue du Page 45 (at rue Américaine). ℂ **02/533-98-33.** www.quincaillerie.be. Main courses 16€–24€; fixed-price menus 13€–25€. AE, DC, MC, V. Mon–Fri noon–2:30pm and 7pm–midnight; Sat–Sun 7pm–midnight. Tram: 81, 82, 91, or 92 to chaussée de Charleroi.

Le Joueur de Flûte ★★ MODERN FRENCH/BELGIAN   Dining in this tiny Marolles restaurant is nothing if not straightforward. There is only one menu, with a couple of variations for the main course. Don't let that, or the fact it serves only 16 diners each evening, put you off. Owner and chef Philippe Van Cappelen, who is no stranger to critical acclaim, now likes to keep things simple. He changes the decor to suit the changing seasons and cooks whatever he feels like cooking—it's all but guaranteed to be delicious.

Rue de l'Epée 26 (adjacent to the Palais de Justice). ℂ **02/513-43-11.** Reservations required. Fixed-price menu 33€. MC, V. Mon–Fri 8–10pm. Métro: Louise.

Moderate
L'Amadeus ★★ MODERN BELGIAN   The postmodern chic of this restaurant/wine bar/oyster bar in a former sculptor's studio with garden-courtyard terrace makes a refreshing change from traditional Belgian style. Its candlelit interior is so dim you would think they're hiding something, but the cooking is nothing to be ashamed of. The menu includes such vegetarian treats as lasagna and ricotta-and-spinach tortellini; for meat eaters, there's caramelized spare ribs and several salmon dishes. All are accompanied by delicious homemade nut

bread. The Sunday brunch is an all-you-can-eat affair that includes smoked fish, cheese, eggs, bread, cereal, juice, and coffee.

Rue Veydt 13 (off chaussée de Charleroi). ℂ **02/538-34-27.** Main courses 15€–23€; *plat du jour* Mon–Fri 9.50€; Sun brunch 18€. AE, DC, MC, V. Tues–Fri and Sun noon–2:30pm and 7pm–1am; Mon and Sat 7pm–1am. Tram: 91, 92.

Inexpensive
Shanti ℞ VEGETARIAN/SEAFOOD An exotic look keeps faith with Shanti's multicultural menus: Lots of greenery and flowers create a garden-like feel, and crystal lamps, mirrors, and old paintings adorn the walls. Try "Neptune's pleasure," crab with avocado and seaweed, as a starter. For a main course, shrimp masala with mixed vegetables and coriander is excellent, as is eggplant with ricotta in a tomato-and-basil sauce.

Av. Adolphe Buyl 68. ℂ **02/649-40-96.** Main courses 7.50€–12€; fixed-price menus 22€–25€. AE, DC, MC, V. Tues–Sat noon–2pm and 7–10pm. Tram: 92 or 93.

SEEING THE SIGHTS
Brussels has such a variety of things to see and do that it can sometimes be overwhelming. There are more than 75 museums dedicated to just about every special interest under the sun, in addition to impressive public buildings, leafy parks, and interesting squares. History is just around every corner. Fortunately, numerous sidewalk cafes offer respite for weary feet, and there's good public transportation to those attractions beyond walking distance of the compact, heart-shaped city center, which contains many of Brussels's most popular attractions.

SIGHTSEEING SUGGESTIONS FOR FIRST-TIME VISITORS

If You Have 1 Day Beginning in the **Grand-Place,** visit the 15th-century Hôtel de Ville and the Musée de la Ville de Bruxelles, and view the decorated facades of the square's elegant guild houses. Squeeze in a pilgrimage to the nearby *Manneken-Pis* statue before returning to the Grand-Place for lunch at the convivial restaurant 't Kelderke. Shop (or window-shop), at the elegant 19th-century **Galeries Royales St-Hubert,** on the way to the **Cathédrale de St-Michel.** End with the adventures of comic-book heroes at the **Centre Belge de la Bande-Dessinée.** After a dinner that should include mussels, in season, spend the evening checking out one or more of the city's famed cafes.

If You Have 2 Days View Belgian art masterpieces by Brueghel and Rubens at the **Musée d'Art Ancien,** and by Magritte and Delvaux at the **Musée d'Art Moderne** next door. After lunch, take a look at the neoclassical harmony of **place Royale,** the elegant **Palais Royal,** and the adjacent **Parc de Bruxelles.** Buy a bag of chocolates at Wittamer on **place du Grand-Sablon,** then browse the antiques stores around the square. Stroll through the 15th-century church of **Notre-Dame au Sablon** before heading over to tranquil **place du Petit-Sablon** for a rest.

If You Have 3 Days Get up early and stop by the **Vieux Marché** flea market on place du Jeu de Balle in the Marolles district. Then, head out to **Bruparck,** an attractions park on the city's northern edge that includes Mini-Europe and the Océade water leisure center. Nearby are the giant spheres of the **Atomium** and a panoramic view of the city from its viewing deck. Return to earth by having dinner in one of the guild hall restaurants, like La Maison du Cygne, that overlook the Grand-Place.

If You Have 4 or 5 Days On day 4, compare the old and the new by spending the morning in the city's most ancient quarter, around place Ste-Catherine, and the afternoon at the ultra-modern European District.

On day 5, head out of town to critique Napoléon's grasp of military strategy at the battlefield of **Waterloo,** south of Brussels. If military history isn't your thing, explore instead Brussels's Art Nouveau architectural heritage by visiting the **Musée Horta,** and by strolling the side streets off avenue Louise and around square Ambiorix.

TOP MONUMENTS & MUSEUMS

Ornamental gables, medieval banners, gilded facades, sunlight flashing off gold-filigreed rooftop sculptures, a general impression of harmony and timelessness—there's a lot to take in all at once when you first enter the historic **Grand-Place** ✸✸✸ (Métro: Gare Centrale). The city's central square has always been the very heart of Brussels. Characterized by French playwright Jean Cocteau as "a splendid stage," it's the city's theater of life. Some call it the world's most beautiful square.

The Grand-Place has been the center of the city's commercial life and public celebrations since the 12th century. Most of it was destroyed in 1695 by the army of France's Louis XIV and then rebuilt over the next few years. Thanks to the town's close monitoring of later alterations, each building preserves its baroque splendor. Important guilds owned most of these buildings, and each competed to outdo the others with highly ornate facades of gold leaf and statuary, often with emblems of their guilds. Some now house cafes and restaurants. The illuminated square is even more beautiful at night than during the day.

Top honors go to the Gothic **Hôtel de Ville** and the neo-Gothic **Maison du Roi.** You'll also want to admire no. 9, **Le Cygne,** former headquarters of the butchers' guild and now a tony restaurant, **Le Cygne;** no. 10, **L'Arbre d'Or,** headquarters of the brewers' guild and location of the Brewing Museum; and nos. 13 to 19, an ensemble of seven mansions known as the **Maison des Ducs de Brabant,** adorned with busts of 19 dukes.

Two blocks south of the Grand-Place, at the intersection of rue de l'Etuve and rue du Chêne, is the ***Manneken-Pis*** ✸ (Métro: Bourse). A small bronze statue of a urinating child, Brussels's favorite character gleefully does what a little boy's gotta do, generally ogled by a throng of admirers. Children especially enjoy his bravura performance. No one knows when this child first came into being, but it's clear he dates from quite a few centuries ago—the 8th century, according to one legend. Thieves have made off with the tyke several times in history. One criminal who stole and shattered the statue in 1817 was sentenced to a life of hard labor. The pieces were used to recast another version and that one has been removed for safekeeping. King Louis XV of France began the tradition of presenting colorful costumes to "Little Julian," which he wears on special occasions (during Christmas season he dons a Santa suit, complete with white beard), to make amends for Frenchmen having kidnapped the statue in 1747. The vast wardrobe is housed in the Musée de la Ville de Bruxelles in the Grand-Place (see below).

Hôtel de Ville (Town Hall) ✸✸   The facade of the dazzling Town Hall, from 1402, shows off Gothic intricacy at its best, complete with dozens of arched windows and sculptures—some of these, like the drunken monks, a sleeping

Moor and his harem, and St. Michael slaying a female devil, displaying a sense of humor. A 66m (215-ft.) tower sprouts from the middle, yet it's not placed directly in the center. A colorful but untrue legend has it that when the architect realized his "error," he jumped from the summit of the tower.

The building is still the seat of the civic government, and its wedding room is a popular place to tie the knot. You can visit the interior on 40-minute tours, which start in a room full of paintings of the past foreign rulers of Brussels, who have included the Spanish, Austrians, French, and Dutch. In the spectacular Gothic Hall, open for visits when the city's aldermen are not in session—and surrounded by mirrors, presumably so each party can see what underhanded maneuvers the others are up to—you can see baroque decoration. In other chambers are 16th- to 18th-century tapestries. One of these depicts the Spanish duke of Alba, whose cruel features reflect the brutal oppression he and his Council of Blood imposed on the Low Countries; others show scenes from the life of Clovis, first king of the Franks.

Grand-Place. © 02/279-43-55. Admission (for guided tours only) 2.50€ adults, 2€ children 5–15, free for children under 5. Apr–Sept Tues 11:30am and 3:15pm, Wed 3:15pm, Sun 12:15pm; Oct–Mar Tues 11:30am and 3:15pm, Wed 3:15pm. Métro: Gare Centrale.

Musée de la Ville de Bruxelles (Museum of the City of Brussels) ⓐ★
The 19th-century neo-Gothic Maison du Roi (King's House)—though no king ever lived here—displays a mixed collection associated with the art and history of Brussels. On the ground floor you can admire detailed tapestries from the 16th and 17th centuries, and porcelain, silver, and stone statuary. After climbing a beautiful wooden staircase, you can trace the history of Brussels in old maps, prints, photos, and models. Among the most fascinating exhibits are old paintings and scaled reconstructions of the historic city center, particularly those showing the riverside ambience along the now-vanished River Senne. On the third floor are more than 500 costumes that have been given to *Manneken-Pis* (see above), including an Elvis costume.

Grand-Place. © 02/279-43-50. Admission 2.50€ adults, 2€ children 5–15, free for children 4 and under. Mon–Thurs 10am–12:30pm and 1:30–5pm (4pm Oct–Mar); Sat–Sun 10am–1pm. Closed Jan 1, May 1, Nov 1, Dec 25. Métro: Gare Centrale.

Musées Royaux des Beaux-Arts ⓐ★ⓐ★ⓐ★   This multi-building complex combines the **Musée d'Art Ancien** and the **Musée d'Art Moderne** under one roof, connected by a passage. The collection shows off works, most of them Belgian, from the 14th century to the 20th century, starting in the historical section with Hans Memling's portraits from the late 15th century, which are marked by sharp lifelike details, works by Hieronymus Bosch, and Lucas Cranach's *Adam and Eve*. You should particularly seek out the subsequent rooms featuring Pieter Brueghel, including his *Adoration of the Magi*. Don't miss his unusual *Fall of the Rebel Angels*, with grotesque faces and beasts. But don't fear—many of Brueghel's paintings, like those depicting Flemish village life, are of a less fiery nature. Later artists represented include Rubens, Van Dyck, Frans Hals, and Rembrandt.

Next door, in a circular building connected to the main entrance, the modern art section has an emphasis on underground works—if only because the museum's eight floors are all below ground level. The overwhelming collection includes works by van Gogh, Matisse, Dalí, Tanguy, Ernst, Chagall, Miró, and local boys Magritte, Delvaux, De Braekeleer, and Permeke.

Rue de la Régence 3 (at place Royale). © 02/508-32-11. Admission 3.75€ adults, 2.50€ students/seniors/people with disabilities, 1.25€ children 12–18, free for children under 12. Museum of Historical Art

Value **Passport to Brussels**
One of the best discounts is the **Brussels Tourist Leisure Pass,** available at Tourist Information Brussels for 8€. It includes a restaurant guide; two 1-day public transportation passes and a transit map; and discounted admission to several top attractions such as the Atomium, Mini-Europe, Belgian Comic Strip Centre, Horta Museum, and Autoworld.

Tues–Sun 10am–noon and 1–5pm; Museum of Modern Art Tues–Sun 10am–1pm and 2–5pm. Closed Jan 1, May 1, Nov 1 and 11, Dec 25. Métro: Parc.

PARC DU CINQUANTENAIRE

Designed to celebrate the half centenary of Belgium's 1830 independence, the Cinquantenaire Park was a work in progress from the 1870s until well into the 20th century. Extensive gardens have at their heart a triumphal arch topped by a bronze four-horse chariot sculpture, representing *Brabant Raising the National Flag,* flanked by several fine museums.

Autoworld *(Kids*   Even if you're not a car fanatic, you'll find this display of 500 historic cars set in the hangarlike Palais Mondial fascinating. The collection starts with early motorized tricycles from 1899 and moves on to a 1911 Model T Ford, a 1924 Renault, a 1938 Cadillac that was the official White House car for FDR and Truman, a 1956 Cadillac used by Eisenhower and then by Kennedy during his June 1963 visit to Berlin, and more. Parc du Cinquantenaire. (C) 02/736-41-65. Admission 5€ adults, 3.75€ students/seniors/people with disabilities, 2€ children 6–13, free for children 5 and under. Apr–Sept daily 10am–6pm; Oct–Mar daily 10am–5pm. Métro: Mérode.

Musée du Cinquantenaire 🔍   This vast museum shows off an eclectic collection of antiques, decorative arts (tapestries, porcelain, silver, and sculptures), and archaeology. Some highlights are an Assyrian relief from the 9th century B.C., a Greek vase from the 6th century B.C., a tabletop model of imperial Rome in the 4th century A.D., the A.D. 1145 reliquary of Pope Alexander, some exceptional tapestries, and colossal statues from Easter Island. Parc du Cinquantenaire. (C) 02/741-72-11. Admission 3.75€ adults, 2.50€ students/seniors, 1.25€ children 12–18, free for children 11 and under; free for everyone 1st Wed afternoon of the month (except during special exhibits). Tues–Fri 9:30am–5pm; Sat–Sun and public holidays 10am–5pm. Métro: Mérode.

BRUPARCK

Built on the site of the 1958 Brussels World's Fair, this attractions park (Métro: Heysel) is home to the **Atomium** and **Mini-Europe** (see below); **The Village,** a collection of restaurants and cafes, including a restaurant in a 1930s railway car of the legendary Orient Express; **Océade,** an indoor/outdoor watersports pavilion with water slides, pools, and saunas; a **planetarium;** and **Kinepolis,** a 26-screen movie multiplex. Ask for cheaper combination tickets if you plan to visit more than one Bruparck attraction.

Atomium 🔍🔍   As the Eiffel Tower is the symbol of Paris, the Atomium is the symbol of Brussels and, like Paris's landmark, it was built for a world's fair, the 1958 Brussels World's Fair. Rising 102m (335 ft.) like a giant plaything of the gods that's fallen to earth, the Atomium is an iron crystal molecule magnified 165 billion times. Its metal-clad spheres, representing individual atoms, are connected by enclosed escalators and elevators. Within is an exhibit on human life and medical research. However, it's the topmost atom that attracts most people: a restaurant/observation deck that provides a sweeping panorama of the metropolitan area.

Bd. du Centenaire, Heysel. (C) **02/474-89-77.** www.atomium.be. Admission 5.50€ adults, 4€ children 12 and under, free for children under 1.2m (4 ft.). Apr–Aug daily 9am–8pm; Sept–Mar daily 10am–6pm (Panorama to 9:30pm). Métro: Heysel.

Mini-Europe *Kids* Because Brussels is the "capital of Europe," it's fitting that the city is home to a miniature rendering of all the Continent's most notable architectural sights. Even a few natural wonders and technological developments are represented. Built on a scale of ⅟₂₅ of the originals, Big Ben, the Leaning Tower of Pisa, the Seville bullring, the Channel Tunnel, the Brandenburg Gate, and more, exhibit remarkable detail. Although children like Mini-Europe the best, adults certainly find it fun.

Bruparck, Heysel. (C) **02/478-05-50.** Admission 11€ adults, 8.50€ children 12 and under, free for children under 1.2m (4 ft.). Apr–June and Sept 9:30am–6pm; 1st 2 weeks of July and last 2 weeks of Aug 9:30am–8pm; mid-July to mid-Aug 9:30am–midnight; Oct–Jan 10am–6pm. Closed Feb–Mar. Métro: Heysel.

MORE MUSEUMS & ATTRACTIONS

Centre Belge de la Bande Dessinée *Kids* As you'll soon find out, Belgians are crazy for cartoons. The unique Belgian Center for Comic-Strip Art, called the "CéBéBéDé" for short, focuses on Belgium's own popular cartoon characters, like Lucky Luke, Thorgal, and, of course, Tintin, complete with redand-white-checkered moon rocket, yet it doesn't neglect the likes of Superman, Batman, and the Green Lantern. The building, the Maisons des Waucquez, designed by Art Nouveau architect Victor Horta, is an attraction in itself.

Rue des Sables 20 (off bd. de Berlaimont). (C) **02/219-19-80.** Admission 6.25€ adults, 5€ students/seniors, 2.50€ children 11 and under. Tues–Sun 10am–6pm. Métro: Gare Centrale.

Musée du Costume et de la Dentelle Honoring a once-vital industry— 10,000 Bruxellois made lace in the 18th century—that now operates in a reduced but still notable fashion, this museum shows off particularly fine costumes and lace from 1599 to the present, and mounts frequently changing exhibitions.

Rue de la Violette 6 (near Grand-Place). (C) **02/512-77-09.** Admission 2.50€ adults, 2€ children 6–16, free for children 5 and under. Mon–Tues and Thurs–Fri 10am–12:30pm and 1:30–5pm (until 4pm Oct–Mar); Sat–Sun 2–4:30pm. Closed Jan 1, May 1, Nov 1 and 11, Dec 25. Métro: Gare Centrale.

Musée Horta *Finds* Brussels owes much of its rich Art Nouveau heritage to Victor Horta (1861–1947), a resident architect who led the development of the style. His home and adjoining studio in St-Gilles, restored to their original condition, showcase his use of flowing, sinuous shapes and colors, in both interior decoration and architecture.

Rue Américaine 25 (off chaussée de Charleroi). (C) **02/543-04-90.** Admission 3.75€ on weekdays; 5€ on weekends. Tues–Sun 2–5:30pm. Tram: 81, 82, 91, or 92.

CHURCHES

Cathédrale de St-Michel Victor Hugo considered this magnificent church to be the "purest flowering of the Gothic style." Begun in 1226, it was officially consecrated as a cathedral only in 1961. The 16th-century Habsburg Emperor Charles V donated the superb stained-glass windows. Apart from these, the spare interior decoration focuses attention on its soaring columns and arches. The bright exterior stonework makes a fine sight. On Sunday at 10am, the Eucharist is celebrated with a Gregorian choir. In July, August, and September, polyphonic Masses are sung by local and international choirs at 10am. From

August to October, chamber music and organ concerts are occasionally performed on weekdays at 8pm. In spring and autumn at 12:30pm, Mass is sung accompanied by instrumental soloists and readings by actors (in French).

Parvis Ste-Gudule (set back off bd. de l'Impératrice 2 blocks west of Gare Centrale). ℭ **02/217-83-45**. Cathedral, free admission; crypt, 1€. Apr–Sept daily 7am–7pm; Oct–Mar daily 7am–6pm. Métro: Gare Centrale.

Notre-Dame au Sablon This late-Gothic 15th-century to 16th-century structure is noted for its four-fold gallery with brightly colored stained-glass windows, illuminated from the inside at night, in striking contrast with the gray-white Gothic arches and walls. Also worth seeing are the two baroque chapels, which are decorated with funeral symbols in white marble.

Rue de la Régence 3B (at place du Grand-Sablon). ℭ **02/511-57-41**. Free admission. Daily 9am–6pm. Tram: 92, 93, or 94.

OTHER HISTORIC SQUARES

Considered classier than the Grand-Place (see above) by the locals, though busy traffic diminishes your enjoyment of its cafe-terraces, **place du Grand-Sablon** ✹✹ (tram: 92, 93, or 94) is lined with gabled mansions. This is antiques territory, and many of those mansions house antiques stores or private art galleries, with pricey merchandise on display. On Saturday and Sunday an excellent antiques market sets up its stalls in front of Notre-Dame au Sablon Church (see above).

Across rue de la Régence, the Grand-Sablon's little cousin, **place du Petit-Sablon** ✹ (tram: 92, 93, or 94), has a small sculptured garden with a fountain and pool at its center. This magical little retreat from the city bustle is surrounded by wrought-iron railings, atop which stand 48 small statues of medieval guildsmen.

Meeting-point of rue de la Régence and rue Royale (streets on which stand many of the city's premier attractions), **place Royale** ✹ (tram: 92, 93, or 94) is graced by an equestrian statue of Duke Godefroid de Bouillon, leader of the First Crusade. Also in place Royale is the neoclassical St-Jacques-sur-Coudenberg Church.

PARKS & GARDENS

The most attractive park in town is the **Parc de Bruxelles** ✹✹ (Métro: Parc), extending in front of the Palais Royal. Once the property of the dukes of Brabant, this well-designed park with geometrically divided paths running through it—which form the outline of Masonic symbols—became public in 1776. The many benches make it a fine place to stop for a picnic. It's also historic: The first shots in Belgium's 1830 war of independence were fired here. In 2001, the park was restored as closely as possible to its 18th-century look. The refurbished 1840s bandstand hosts regular summer concerts.

The big public park called the **Bois de la Cambre** ✹ begins at the top of avenue Louise in the southern section of Brussels (tram: 23, 90, 93, or 94). This is the city's lung, and it gets busy on sunny weekends. Its centerpiece is a small lake with an island in its center that you can reach via an electrically operated pontoon. Some busy roads run through the park and traffic moves fast on them, so be careful with children at these points.

Continuing south from the Bois, the **Forêt de Soignes** ✹ is no longer a park with playing areas and regularly mown grass, but a forest stretching almost to Waterloo; this is great for getting away from it all, particularly in the fall, when the colors are dazzling.

ORGANIZED TOURS

De Boeck, rue de la Colline 8, off Grand-Place (© **02/513-77-44;** Métro: Gare Centrale), operates a guided 3-hour "Brussels City Tour" by coach for 20€ adults, 18€ students and seniors, and 10€ children. You can book tours at most hotels, and arrangements can be made for hotel pickup.

From June 15 to September 15, **Chatterbus,** rue des Thuyas 12 (© **02/673-18-35),** operates a 3-hour tour daily at 10am from the Galeries Royales St-Hubert (Métro: Gare Centrale), a mall next to rue du Marché-aux-Herbes 90, a few steps off the Grand-Place. A walking tour covers the historic center, followed by a bus ride through areas the average visitor never sees. You hear about life in Brussels and get a real feel for the city. The price is 8.75€. You don't need a reservation for this fascinating experience—just be there by 10am.

ARAU, bd. Adolphe-Max 55 (© **02/219-33-45;** Métro: De Brouckère), organizes tours that help you discover not only Brussels's countless treasures but also problems the city faces. It runs 3-hour themed coach tours: "Grand-Place and Its Surroundings," "Brussels 1900—Art Nouveau," "Brussels 1930—Art Deco," "Surprising Parks and Squares," and "Alternative Brussels." You are advised to book ahead. Tours are 15€ and take place on Saturday mornings from March to November; private group tours can be arranged year-round.

THE SHOPPING SCENE

Lace is the overwhelming favorite purchase, followed by crystal, jewelry, antiques, and pewter. Chocolate, beer, and other foods are more economical. And in souvenir stores you find replicas of *Manneken-Pis,* so you can bring the little guy home with you.

Don't look for many bargains. As a general rule, Upper Town around avenue Louise and Porte de Namur is more expensive than Lower Town around rue Neuve. You can enjoy a stroll along modern shopping promenades, the busiest of which is the pedestrians only rue Neuve, starting at place de la Monnaie and running north to place Rogier; it's home to boutiques; big department stores like Inno, H&M, and Marks & Spencer; and several malls.

The trendiest boutiques are on rue Antoine-Dansaert, across from the Bourse. An interesting street for window-shopping, rue des Eperonniers, near the Grand-Place, hosts many small stores selling antiques, toys, old books, and clothing.

Watch for the TAX-FREE SHOPPING sign in some store windows. These stores provide visitors who are not resident in the European Union the form they need for recovering the whopping 21.5% value-added tax (TVA) when they leave the EU. At the airport, show the Customs official your purchase and receipt and he or she will stamp the form. You mail this form back to the Belgian Tax Bureau (the address is on the form) or bring it directly to the Best Change office at the airport, which charges a small commission but gives you an on-the-spot refund.

STORES & OUTDOOR MARKETS

The **Galeries Royales St-Hubert** (Métro: Gare Centrale) is an airy arcade hosting expensive boutiques, cafes with outdoor terraces, and buskers playing classical music. Opened in 1847, architect Pierre Cluysenaer's Italian neo-Renaissance gallery has a touch of class and is well worth a stroll through, even if you have no intention of shopping. The elegant gallery is near the Grand-Place, between rue du Marché-aux-Herbes and rue de l'Ecuyer, and is split by rue des Bouchers.

In a former guild house, **Maison Antoine,** Grand-Place 26 (© **02/512-48-59;** Métro: Gare Centrale), is one of the best places in town to buy lace. The quality is superb, the service is friendly, and the prices aren't unreasonable.

Tips   Hot Chocs

If you have a sweet tooth, you'll feel you're in heaven when you see Brussels's famous chocolate stores, filled with sumptuous soft-centered pralines, from around 12€ a kilogram (2¼ lb.). You find some of the best confections at **Chocolatier Mary,** rue Royale 73 (✆ **02/217-45-00;** Métro: Parc), supplier to the royal court; **Neuhaus,** Galerie de la Reine 25 (✆ **02/502-59-14;** Métro: Gare Centrale); **Wittamer,** place du Grand-Sablon 12 (✆ **02/512-37-42;** tram: 92, 93, or 94); and **Léonidas,** bd. Anspach 46 (✆ **02/218-03-63;** Métro: Bourse).

Brussels has several outdoor markets, where half the fun is finding an alluring item and the other half is bargaining down the price. The city's favorite *marché aux puces* (flea market) is the **Vieux Marché** (**Old Market;** Métro: Porte de Hal), on place du Jeu de Balle, a large cobblestone square in the Marolles district, open daily from 7am to 2pm. Every Sunday from 7am to 2pm, hundreds of merchants assemble their wares in a **street market** outside Gare du Midi (Métro: Gare du Midi), and because many of the merchants are of Arab origin, the scene resembles a *casbah.* You can find many excellent food bargains, making it a perfect place to gather provisions for a few days. You can also find household items and odds and ends at low cost. Hold onto your wallet because the market attracts pickpockets.

BRUSSELS AFTER DARK

Although the city isn't as noted for its nightlife as some other European capitals, it has a full array of things to do. And if the range is smaller than in bigger cities such as London and Paris, the quality is not. A listing of upcoming events—opera, classical music, dance, theater, live music, film, and other events—is in the *What's On* guide in the weekly English-language magazine *The Bulletin.*

You can order tickets for performing-arts venues from the **Central Booking Office** (✆ **0800/21-221**), open Monday through Friday from 9am to 7pm, Saturday from 10am to 7pm. The tourist office in the Town Hall on the Grand-Place (see "Visitor Information," earlier in this chapter) sells concert and theater tickets.

THE PERFORMING ARTS

An opera house in the grand style, the **Théâtre Royal de la Monnaie** 𝒜𝒜, place de la Monnaie (✆ **02/229-12-11;** Métro: Brouckère), is home to the Opéra Royal de la Monnaie, which has been called the best in the French-speaking world, and to the Orchestre Symphonique de la Monnaie. The resident modern dance company, Anne Theresa de Keersmaeker's Group Rosas, is noted for its original moves. The box office is open Tuesday through Saturday from 11am to 6pm. Tickets run 7.50€ to 88€; for students 25 and under, they're 5€ and available 5 minutes before a show.

The **Palais des Beaux-Arts,** rue Royale 10 (✆ **02/507-84-66;** Métro: Parc), is home to the Belgian National Orchestra. The box office is open Monday through Saturday from 11am to 6pm, with tickets running 10€ to 75€. The **Cirque Royal,** rue de l'Enseignement 81 (✆ **02/218-20-15;** Métro: Parc), formerly a real circus, now hosts music, opera, and ballet. The box office is open Tuesday through Saturday from 11am to 6pm, with tickets for 7.50€ to 63€.

CABARET

A bit of a laugh, the transvestite cabaret **Chez Flo,** rue au Beurre 25 (© **02/513-31-52;** Métro: Bourse), is outrageous and comfortable at the same time. Dinner and floor show are 38€ to 75€; the highest price includes a half-bottle of champagne a head. The show begins at 8pm. Brussels isn't Paris when it comes to putting on Moulin Rouge–type shows, but **Show Point,** place Stéphanie 14 (© **02/511-53-64;** Métro: Louise), adopts a similar approach. From 10pm until dawn, showgirls, scantily clad or wearing fanciful costumes, strut their stuff in a variety of fetching choreographies. Drinks cost 25€. There's no cover. Hours are Monday through Saturday from 10pm to 5am; the show begins at 12:30am.

CAFES & BARS

The city's many watering holes run the gamut from Art Nouveau palaces to plain and convivial. You should linger a few hours in one, preferably savoring one of the incredible variety of beers for which Belgium is famous.

It's always satisfying to sit at a sidewalk cafe on the Grand-Place and drink in the beauty of the floodlit golden buildings ringing the square. Drinks on a Grand-Place terrace are more expensive than those in ordinary cafes, but once you've ordered one you can nurse it for hours—or until the waiter's patience wears out and he grabs the glass from you, empty or not.

The city's oldest cafe, in a 1690 building, **Le Roy d'Espagne,** Grand-Place 1 (© **02/513-08-07;** Métro: Gare Centrale), accommodates patrons in several areas. In addition to the outdoor tables, you can drink in a room preserving a 17th-century Flemish interior—a masterpiece of wooden architecture with a wooden walkway, wooden beams above, and a fireplace covered by a black metal hood. The fourth-floor view of the Grand-Place is spectacular. It's open daily from 10am to 1am.

Although its name means "Sudden Death," you'll likely survive **A la Mort Subito,** rue Montagne-aux-Herbes-Potagères 7 (© **02/513-13-18;** Métro: Gare Centrale), a 1911 cafe with stained-glass mirrors, old photographs, paintings, and prints. A good place to enjoy an afternoon coffee or an evening beer, it's open daily from 10am to 1am. A block from the Grand-Place, in a 1642 house, **A l'Image de Notre-Dame,** rue du Marché-aux-Herbes 6–8 (© **02/219-42-49;** Métro: Gare Centrale), is often filled with people of all ages enjoying reasonably priced beer amid wooden ceiling beams and old wooden tables. It's open daily from noon to midnight.

Shock reverberated through the city in 1999, when the legendary Art Nouveau tavern **Falstaff,** rue Henri-Maus 17–25 (© **02/511-98-77;** Métro:

(Moments Puppet Theater

As crazy as the Belgians are about cartoons, it should come as no surprise that a popular venue is a traditional Brussels marionette theater: **Théâtre Toone VII,** impasse Schuddeveld, petite rue des Bouchers 6 or 21 (© **02/511-71-37;** Métro: Gare Centrale). In a tiny theater in an old cafe of the same name, puppet master José Géal presents adaptations of classic tales like *Faust* and *The Three Musketeers.* Some performances are in English, others are in French, Dutch, German, or the local dialect, Bruxellois, with plots and characters so familiar that even if you don't understand a word, you'll be able to follow the action. Performances are held Tuesday through Saturday at 8:30pm, with tickets at 10€.

Bourse), went bankrupt. It has reopened, and you can still enjoy a drink in this stunning setting—though its cool image has suffered. It's open daily from 8am to around 3am (4am on weekends). Across the way, at **Le Cirio,** rue de la Bourse 18 (© **02/512-13-95;** Métro: Bourse), you sip your drink in quiet, refined surroundings that make the exercise seem worthwhile. It's open daily from 10am to 1am.

In a 17th-century building, **Le Fleur en Papier Dore,** rue des Alexiens 53, off place de la Chapelle (© **02/511-16-59;** Métro: Bourse), calls itself a "temple of surrealism" because Magritte used to relax here. Despite the grandmotherly decor, the cafe attracts a wide assortment of arty types. On Friday and Saturday from 9 or 10pm, an accordion player pumps out some tunes, and there are occasional poetry readings upstairs. The cafe is open daily from 11am to 11pm.

Gargoyles, devils, and other assorted creatures from the darker recesses of the human mind—the decor at **Halloween,** rue des Grands-Carmes 10 (© **02/514-12-56;** www.resto-halloween.be; Métro: Bourse)—are enough to give you the creeps. The decor helps create a memorable ambience in a bar patronized mostly by the young and the hip. It's open Tuesday to Sunday from 7pm to 1am.

In an early-1900s town house on the edge of the city center, **De Ultieme Hallucinatie,** rue Royale 316 (© **02/217-06-14;** Métro: Botanique), has rocky walls and plants along one side, a long marble-top bar along the other, and a small outdoor cafe area in back. You can choose from beers and wines (a wide selection), coffee, and a few snacks. Downstairs, a futuristic dance club has abstract outer-space art. The bar is open Monday through Friday from 11am to 3am, Saturday and Sunday from 4pm to 3am.

A DAY TRIP TO WATERLOO 🏛🏛

Europe's Gettysburg, the battle that ended Napoléon's empire was fought on rolling farmland near **Waterloo,** just outside Brussels. On June 18, 1815, 72,000 British, Dutch, Belgian, and German troops, aided before the day's end by around 40,000 Prussians, defeated the mighty Napoléon Bonaparte and his 76,000 French, leaving 40,000 dead and wounded on the field. Napoléon survived, but his attempt to rebuild his empire was crushed; he was exiled to the island of St. Helena, where he died 6 years later.

From Brussels, bus W leaves for Waterloo on the half hour and on the hour from a small terminal on avenue de Stalingrad, at place Rouppe (Métro: Anneessens). The 18km (11-mile) ride takes 50 minutes and costs 2.50€. The

---

⸤Tips Belgian Brews Pack a Punch

Be warned: Belgian beers are stronger than their American counterparts—alcohol content can be as high as 12%. Try a rich, dark Trappist ale brewed by monks from Chimay, Orval, Rochefort, Sint-Benedictus, Westmalle, and Westvleteren monasteries. Brussels is well known for its lambic beers, which use naturally occurring yeast for fermentation, are often flavored with fruit, and come in bottles with champagne-type corks. Unlike any other beer, they're more akin to a sweet sparkling wine. *Gueuze,* a blend of young and aged lambic beers, is one of the least sweet. If you prefer something sweeter, try raspberry-flavored *framboise* or cherry-flavored *kriek. Faro* is a low-alcohol beer, sometimes sweetened or lightly spiced.

bus stops at both the Wellington Museum in Waterloo itself and at the battle-field visitor center, south of the village (see below). By **car** from Brussels, take the ring road (R0) to Exit 27 for Waterloo, and N5 south to the battlefield.

The battlefield remains much as it was on that terrible day. Before touring it, you should study a 360-degree **panoramic mural** and see a short audiovisual presentation of the battle, including scenes from Sergei Bondarchuk's epic movie *Waterloo,* at the **Centre du Visiteur,** route du Lion 252–254, Braine L'Alleud (© **02/385-19-12**). To survey the battlefield, climb the nearby **Butte du Lion,** a conical hill surmounted by a bronze lion, behind the center. These three sites are open daily: April through September from 9:30am to 6:30pm; October from 9:30am to 5:30pm; November through February from 10:30am to 4pm; and March from 10am to 5pm. The combined ticket costs 9.65€ adults, 7.90€ stu-dents/seniors, 6.15€ children 6 to 12, free for children 5 and under.

You can fill in details of the battle at the **Musée Wellington,** chaussée de Bruxelles 147, Waterloo (© **02/354-78-06**), a former inn that was Wellington's headquarters and where he wrote his victory dispatch. It's open daily, April through September from 9:30am to 6:30pm; October through March from 10:30am to 5pm. Admission is 2.50€ adults, 2€ students/seniors, 1€ children 6 to 12, and free for children 5 and under.

2 Bruges & Ghent

Both Flemish cities are showcases of medieval art and architecture. Some of the northern Renaissance's most outstanding paintings hang in their museums and churches. Yet each has a distinctive character that makes visiting them comple-mentary. Walking around the almost perfectly preserved city of Bruges is like taking a step back in time. Ghent is austere but more authentic. You can easily visit both in day trips from Brussels, but for a more thorough inspection you'll want to stay overnight.

BRUGES (BRUGGE) ✲✲✲

From its 13th-century origins as a cloth-manufacturing town to its current incarnation as a tourism mecca, Bruges seems to have changed little. As in a fairy tale, swans glide down the winding canals and the stone houses look like they're made of gingerbread. Even though glass-fronted stores have taken over the ground floors of ancient buildings, and the swans scatter before tour boats chug-ging along the canals, Bruges has made the transition from medieval to modern with remarkable grace. The town seems revitalized rather than crushed by the tremendous influx of tourists.

ESSENTIALS

GETTING THERE   By Train   Bruges is 55 minutes from Brussels, and trains depart every hour. Bruges is well connected to Ghent, Antwerp, and the North Sea ferry ports of Ostend and Zeebrugge. Bruges station (look out for BRUGGE, the town's Dutch name, on the destination boards) is on Stationsplein (© **050/38-23-82** for train information), 1.5km (1 mile) from the city center. To get to the center, take a 20-minute walk or a short bus ride—choose any bus labeled CENTRUM and get out at the Markt.

By Bus   Eurolines (© **02/203-07-07;** www.eurolines.com) coaches from London, Paris, Amsterdam, and other cities arrive at the bus station adjoining Bruges train station.

By Car   If you're driving from Brussels or Ghent, take E40 (A10). Drop off your car at a parking lot or garage (see "Getting Around," below). The network of one-way streets in the center makes driving a trial.

By Plane   Brussels National Airport is the main airport for Bruges. There is a small airport at Ostend (Oostende) just 24km (15 miles) from Bruges at the Belgian coast, but it handles mostly charter and air-taxi flights.

VISITOR INFORMATION   Toerisme Brugge, Burg 11, 8000 Brugge (© **050/44-86-86;** fax 050/44-86-00; www.brugge.be), provides brochures outlining walking, coach, canal, and horse-drawn cab tours, and detailed info on many attractions; they can also make hotel reservations. The office is open April through September, Monday through Friday from 9:30am to 6:30pm, Saturday and Sunday from 10am to noon and 2 to 6:30pm; October through March, Monday through Friday from 9:30am to 5pm, and Saturday and Sunday from 9:30am to 1pm and 2 to 5:30pm.

CITY LAYOUT   Narrow streets fan out from two central squares, the **Markt** and the **Burg.** A network of canals threads its way to every section of the small city, and the center is almost encircled by a canal that opens at its southern end to become a swan-filled lake, the **Minnewater**—this translates as Lake of Love, though the name actually comes from the Dutch *Innen Water,* meaning Inner Harbor—bordered by the Begijnhof and a fine park.

GETTING AROUND   Street names and traffic boards are in Dutch; some transportation information is in English, which in any case is widely spoken, so you should have no problem getting directions.

By Bus   De Lijn city buses (© **059/56-53-53**) depart the bus station beside the train station, and from the big square called 't Zand, west of the Markt. Several bus routes pass through the Markt.

By Car   Movement by car through the old center has been tightly restricted. Leave your car in your hotel's parking garage, if it has one. You can use one of the large, prominently signposted underground parking garages around the center—these get expensive for long stays—or the inexpensive parking lot at the train station, from where you can take a bus or walk into the heart of the city.

By Taxi   There's a taxi rank outside the train station (© **050/38-46-60**), and another at the Markt (© **050/33-44-44**).

By Bicycle   Biking is a terrific way to get around town. You can rent a bike from the train station (© **050/38-58-71**) for 8.15€ a day or for 6.25€ with a train ticket, plus a deposit. Some hotels and stores rent bikes.

WHERE TO STAY

Bruges's hotels fill up fast. Don't arrive without a reservation, particularly in summer. If you do, the tourist office has a reservation service; you can book in advance there and at tourist offices throughout the country. Accommodations are less heavily booked on weekdays than on weekends.

Expensive

Die Swaene 🐦🐦🐦   This small hotel on the beautiful city-center Groenerei canal has been called one of the most romantic in Europe, thanks in part to the care lavished on it by the Hessels family. The comfortable rooms are elegantly and individually furnished, and the lounge, from 1779, was once the Guild Hall of the Tailors. The in-house restaurant, where the specialty is seafood, has won good reviews from guests and critics alike.

Bruges

ATTRACTIONS ●

Basiliek van het Heilig Bloed **10**
Begijnhof **17**
Belfort and Hallen **9**
Burg **4**
Groeninge Museum **13**
Gruuthuse Museum **14**
Heilige-Bloedbasiliek **8**
Kantcentrum (Lace Center) **1**
Landhuis van het Brugse Vrije
   (Palace of the Liberty of Bruges) **11**
Markt **3**
Onze-Lieve-Vrouwekerk **15**
Stadhuis (Town Hall) **7**

ACCOMMODATIONS ■

Die Swaene **5**
Duc de Bourgogne **6**
Egmond **18**
Lucca **2**
Rembrandt-Rubens **16**
Romantik Pandhotel **12**

✝ Church
ⓘ Information
✉ Post Office
─── Railway

Steenhouwersdijk 1, 8000 Brugge. ℂ **050/34-27-98.** Fax 050/33-66-74. www.dieswaene-hotel.com. 32 units. 170€–245€ double; 320€–420€ suite. Rates include buffet breakfast. AE, DC, V. Parking 10€. **Amenities:** Restaurant; lounge; bar; heated indoor pool; exercise room; sauna; concierge; limited room service; babysitting; laundry service; secretarial services. *In room:* A/C (some units), TV, minibar, hair dryer.

Romantik Pandhotel ★★
Close to the Markt, this lovely 18th-century mansion surrounded by plane trees is an oasis of tranquility. Although it provides modern conveniences, its exquisite, old-fashioned furnishings lend special grace to comfortable rooms. Guests praise Mrs. Chris Vanhaecke-Dewaele for her hospitality and attention to detail. You can use an Internet-connected computer in the lobby to send and receive e-mail.

Pandreitje 16, 8000 Brugge. ℂ **050/34-06-66.** Fax 050/34-05-56. www.pandhotel.com. 24 units. 150€–195€ double; 215€–320€ suite. Rates include full breakfast. AE, DC, MC, V. Limited street parking. **Amenities:** Bar; concierge; 24-hr. room service; in-room massage; babysitting; laundry service; dry cleaning; nonsmoking rooms. *In room:* A/C, TV, dataport, minibar, hair dryer.

Moderate
Duc de Bourgogne ★
This elegant, small hotel in a 17th-century canal-side building has quite large, luxuriously furnished rooms, with antiques scattered throughout. A ground-floor restaurant overlooks the canal, which is illuminated at night.

Huidenvettersplein 12, 8000 Brugge. ℂ **050/33-20-38.** Fax 050/34-40-37. www.duc.bourgogne.be. 10 units. 110€–150€ double. Rates include continental breakfast. AE, DC, MC, V. Limited street parking. **Amenities:** Restaurant; lounge; limited room service, babysitting, laundry service; dry cleaning. *In room:* TV, hair dryer, safe.

Egmond ★★
In a rambling mansion next to Minnewater Park, the Egmond has just eight rooms, but the lucky few who stay here will find ample space, plenty of family ambience, abundant local color, and lots of peace and tranquility. All guest rooms have recently been redecorated and are furnished in an individual style with views of the garden and Minnewater Park. Every afternoon, free coffee and tea are served in the new garden terrace or in the lounge, which has an 18th-century fireplace. At the "honesty bar" you can help yourself to a drink and leave the payment.

Minnewater 15, 8000 Brugge. ℂ **050/34-14-45.** Fax 050/34-29-40. www.egmond.be. 8 units. 112€–120€ double. Rates include buffet breakfast. No credit cards. Free parking. *In room:* A/C (some units),TV, dataport, hair dryer, safe.

Inexpensive
Lucca ★★ (Value
Built in the 14th century by a wealthy merchant from Lucca, Italy, the high ceilings and wide halls of this mansion convey a sense of luxury. Guest rooms are in excellent condition and sport pine furnishings. Units with bathrooms also have TVs. Breakfast is served in a cozy medieval cellar.

Naaldenstraat 30, 8000 Brugge. ℂ **050/34-20-67.** Fax 050/33-34-64. www.hotellucca.be. 17 units, 14 with bathroom. 50€ double without bathroom; 78€ double with bathroom. Rates include continental breakfast. AE, DC, MC, V. Limited street parking. *In room:* TV (some units).

Rembrandt-Rubens
You won't get much more in the way of genuine Bruges atmosphere, nor much less in the way of facilities, than in this marvelously atmospheric old hotel, right in the heart of romantic Bruges. The welcome is warm and the antique surroundings memorable, so maybe you won't miss the TV and the phone. This hotel's style suits Bruges perfectly and adds a warmth that coldly efficient modern rooms can't equal.

Walplein 38, 8000 Brugge. ℂ **050/33-64-39.** 15 units (11 with bathroom). 50€–65€ double. Rates include breakfast. No credit cards. Free parking. *In room:* No phone.

WHERE TO DINE

Bruges isn't short of restaurants. You'll be tripping over the places all the time in the city center. Most are okay, but some have become too complacent about the tourists who are their main market. The restaurants reviewed here aim to make dining in Bruges a memory you'll savor back home.

Expensive

De Karmeliet 金金 BELGIAN/FRENCH In 1996, chef Geert Van Hecke became the first Flemish chef to be awarded three Michelin stars. He has described his award-winning menu as "international cuisine made with local products" that aims to merge French quality with Flemish quantity. The result is outstanding, and the decor is as elegant as the cuisine deserves.

Langestraat 19. ℭ 050/33-82-59. Reservations required. Main courses 20€–35€; fixed-price menus 68€–83€. AE, DC, V. Tues–Sat noon–2pm and 7–9:30pm; Sun 7–9:30pm except June–Sept.

't Pandreitje 金金 FRENCH/BELGIAN This restaurant is one of the nicest spots in town. It's in the shade of the medieval Market Hall's bell tower, just off the Rozenhoedkaai, one of the most beautiful canalsides in Bruges. The interior of this Renaissance-era private home has been turned into an elegant Louis XVI setting for a menu of classic dishes. The four-course a la carte meal is superb, and the fixed-price menu is excellent. Try the sea bass served with fennel, parsley sauce, and sautéed potatoes, or the salad of Dublin Bay prawns with artichokes and a truffle vinaigrette.

Pandreitje 6. ℭ 050/33-11-90. www.pandreitje.be. Reservations required. Main courses 30€–140€; fixed-price menus 50€–80€. AE, DC, MC, V. Mon–Tues and Thurs–Sat noon–2pm and 7–9:30pm.

Moderate

De Stove 金金 FLEMISH/SEAFOOD This small, family-owned restaurant combines a rustic atmosphere with a more modern style than is the norm in Bruges. The seafood specialties are well worth a try, particularly the Flemish fish stew with *fruits de mer*.

Kleine Sint-Amandsstraat 4. ℭ 050/33-78-35. Main courses 17€–30€; fixed-price menus 40€–56€. AE, MC, V. Fri–Tues noon–1:45pm and 6:30–9:30pm.

Kasteel Minnewater 金金 FRENCH/BELGIAN Old paintings on the walls, chandeliers, and fine table linens complement this château/restaurant's location close to the Begijnhof, with a garden terrace on the Minnewater (Lake of Love). It exudes an unstuffy charm, and though its prices are edging up, it still provides a good deal considering the setting. Specialties include sole Ostendaise, North Sea shrimp, and lamb cutlet with potatoes gratiné.

Minnewater 4 (near the Begijnhof). ℭ 050/33-42-54. Main courses 11€–25€; Markt-menu 26€. V. Summer: daily 11am–11pm (food at lunch and dinner times only); winter: Mon–Fri noon–2:30pm and 6:30–11pm, Sat–Sun 11am–11pm (food at lunch and dinner times only).

Inexpensive

Brasserie Erasmus 金 FLEMISH Small but popular, this is a great stop after viewing the cathedral and nearby museums. It serves a large variety of dishes, including a very good *waterzooï* with fish and rabbit in a beer sauce, and has around 150 different brands of beer.

Wollestraat 35. ℭ 050/33-57-81. Main courses 15€–25€; fixed-price menus 20€–30€. MC, V. Tues–Sun noon–4pm (summer also Mon) and 6–11pm.

Lotus 金 VEGETARIAN Even nonvegetarians will likely enjoy the delicious lunch here. There are just two menu options—but you can choose from small,

medium, or large servings—each with a hearty assortment of imaginatively prepared vegetables, served in a tranquil but cheery Scandinavian-style dining
room.

Wapenmakersstraat 5. ☏ **050/33-10-78.** Fixed-price lunch menus 7.50€–9€. No credit cards. Mon–Sat
11:45am–2pm.

EXPLORING HISTORIC BRUGES

Walking is by far the best way to see Bruges, since the town center is traffic-free
(but wear good walking shoes, as those charming cobblestones can be hard
going). Begin at the **Markt** ✸✸, where a sculpture group in the center depicts
two Flemish heroes, butcher Jan Breydel and weaver Pieter de Coninck, who led
a bloody 1302 uprising against pro-French merchants and nobles who dominated the guilds, then went on to an against-all-odds victory over French knights
later the same year at the Battle of the Golden Spurs. The large neo-Gothic
Provinciaal Hof, which was constructed in 1887, houses the government of
West Flanders province.

An array of beautiful buildings, which adds up to a trip through the history
of Bruges architecture, stands in the **Burg** ✸✸✸, a square just steps away from
the Markt, where during the 9th century Count Baldwin "Iron Arm" of Flanders built a castle at a tiny riverside settlement that would grow into Bruges.

One of the most tranquil spots in Bruges is the **Begijnhof** ✸✸, Wijngaard-
straat (☏ **050/33-00-11**). Begijns were religious women, similar to nuns, who
accepted vows of chastity and obedience but drew the line at poverty. Today, the
begijns are no more, and the Begijnhof is occupied by Benedictine nuns who try
to keep the begijn traditions alive. Little whitewashed houses surrounding a lawn
with trees make a marvelous place of escape. Admission to one of the begijn's
houses that has been set up as a museum is 1.50€ adults and 1€ children. March
through November, it's open daily from 10am to noon and 1:45 to 5pm (weekends to 5:30pm Apr–Sept); December through February, it's open Monday, Tuesday, and Friday from 11am to noon and Wednesday and Thursday from 2 to
4pm. The Begijnhof itself is permanently open and admission is free.

Belfort en Hallen (Belfry and Market Halls) ✸✸   The 13th-century to
16th-century belfry's octagonal tower soars 84m (272 ft.) and has a magnificent
47-bell carillon. If you have enough energy, climb the 366 steps to the summit
for a panoramic view of the old town. Much of the city's cloth trade and other
commerce was conducted in the Hallen in centuries past. Local art dealers now
use it for exhibits.

Markt. ☏ **050/44-87-11.** Admission 2.50€ adults, 1.25€ children 5–18, free for children under 4. Daily
9:30am–5pm.

Groeninge Museum ✸✸✸   This is one of Belgium's leading traditional
museums of fine arts, with a collection that covers Low Countries painting from
the 15th century to the 20th century. The Flemish Primitives Gallery has 30
works—which seem far from primitive—by such painters as Jan van Eyck (portrait of his wife, Margerita van Eyck), Rogier van der Weyden, Hieronymus
Bosch *(The Last Judgment),* and Hans Memling. Works by Magritte and Delvaux are also on display.

Dijver 12. ☏ **050/44-87-11.** Admission 6.25€ adults, 3.75€ children 5–18, free for children under 5.
Wed–Mon 9:30am–5pm.

Gruuthuse Museum ✸   In a courtyard next to the Groeninge Museum is the
ornate mansion where Flemish nobleman Lodewijk van Gruuthuse lived in the

1400s. It contains thousands of antiques and antiquities, including paintings, sculptures, tapestries, lace, weapons, glassware, and richly carved furniture.

Dijver 17 (in a courtyard next to the Groeninge Museum). ℂ 050/44-87-11. Admission 3.25€ adults, 1.75€ children 5–18, free for children under 5, 6.25€ families with children under 18. Wed–Mon 9:30am–5pm.

Basiliek van het Heilig Bloed (Basilica of the Holy Blood) ★★
Since 1149, this richly decorated Romanesque basilica next to the Town Hall has been the repository of a fragment of cloth stained with what's said to be Christ's holy blood, brought to Bruges after the Second Crusade by the count of Flanders. The relic is in the basilica museum inside a rock-crystal vial that's kept in a magnificent gold-and-silver reliquary and is exposed frequently for the faithful to kiss. Every Ascension Day, in the Procession of the Holy Blood, the bishop carries the relic through the streets, accompanied by costumed residents acting out biblical scenes.

Burg 10. ℂ 050/33-67-92. Basilica, free admission; museum, 1€ adults, .50€ children. Apr–Sept daily 9:30am–noon and 2–6pm; Oct–Mar daily 10am–noon and 2–4pm (closed Wed afternoon).

Kantcentrum (Lace Center) ★
Bruges lace is famous the world over, and there's no lack of stores to tempt you with the opportunity to take some home. The Lace Center, in the 15th-century Jerusalem Almshouse founded by the Adornes family of Genoese merchants, is where the ancient art of lace-making is passed on to the next generation. You get a firsthand look at craftspeople making items for future sale in all the town's lace stores (handmade lace is the best, but it's more expensive than machine-made).

Peperstraat 3A. ℂ 050/33-00-72. Admission 1.50€ adults, 1€ children 5–18, free for children 4 and under. Mon–Fri 10am–noon and 2–6pm; Sat 10am–5pm.

Onze-Lieve-Vrouwekerk (Church of Our Lady) ★★
It took 2 centuries (the 13th to the 15th) to build the magnificent Church of Our Lady, and you can see its soaring spire, 122m (396 ft.) high, from a wide area around Bruges. Among its many art treasures are a marvelous marble *Madonna and Child* ★★★ by Michelangelo (one of his few works outside Italy); the *Crucifixion,* a painting by Anthony Van Dyck; and inside the church sanctuary the impressive side-by-side bronze **tomb sculptures** ★ of Charles the Bold of Burgundy (d. 1477), and his daughter Mary of Burgundy (d. 1482).

Onze-Lieve-Vrouwekerkhof Zuid. ℂ 050/34-53-14. Church and *Madonna and Child* altar, free admission; sanctuary of Charles and Mary and museum, 2.50€ adults, 1.50€ children. Mon–Fri 9am–12:30pm and 1:30–5pm; Sat 9am–12:30pm and 1:30–4pm; Sun 1:30–4pm.

Landhuis van het Brugse Vrije (Palace of the Liberty of Bruges) ★
Dating mostly from 1722 to 1727, when it replaced a 16th-century building as the seat of the Liberty of Bruges—the Liberty being the district around Bruges in the Middle Ages—the palace later became a courthouse and now houses the city council's administration. Inside, at no. 11A, is the **Renaissancezaal Brugse Vrije (Renaissance Hall of the Liberty of Bruges)** ★★, the Liberty's council chamber, which has been restored to its original 16th-century condition.

Burg 11A. ℂ 050/44-87-11. Courtyard, free admission; Renaissance Hall, 1.50€ adults, .50€ children. Daily 9:30am–5pm.

Stadhuis (Town Hall) ★★
This beautiful Gothic building, from the late 1300s, is Belgium's oldest. Don't miss the upstairs **Gotische Zaal (Gothic Room)** ★★, with ornate, oak-carved vaulted ceiling and murals depicting biblical scenes and highlights of the town's history.

Burg 12. ℂ 050/44-87-11. Admission 1.50€ adults, .50€ children. Daily 9:30am–5pm.

BOAT TRIPS & OTHER ORGANIZED TOURS

You really should try to take a **boat trip** ☆☆☆ on the canals. The open-top tour boats operate year-round from five departure points, all marked with an anchor icon on maps available at the tourist office. March through November, the boats operate daily from 10am to 6pm; December through February, they operate Saturday, Sunday, and school holidays from 10am to 6pm (except if the canals are frozen). A half-hour cruise is 4.75€ for adults, 2.40€ for adult-accompanied children ages 4 to 11, and free for children 3 and under.

Minivan tours by **Sightseeing Line** (© 050/35-50-24) last 50 minutes and depart hourly every day from the Markt; the first tour leaves at 10am. The last tour leaves at 7pm July through September, at 6pm March through June and October through November, and at 4pm December through February. Fares are 9.50€ adults, 6.25€ children ages 6 to 12, free for children 5 and under.

Another lovely way to tour Bruges is by **horse-drawn carriage.** From March to November, carriages are stationed in the Burg (Wed in the Markt); a 30-minute ride costs 25€, and 13€ for each extra 15 minutes. Horse-drawn trams are cheaper but no less romantic: **Den Oekden Peerdentram** (© 050/34-41-82) has 30-minute tours from 't Zand, at 5€ adults, 2.50€ children ages 4 to 11, free for children 3 and under. **Firmin's Paardentram** (© 050/33-61-36) has 45-minute tours from the Markt, at 8.75€ adults, 4.40€ children ages 4 to 11, free for children 3 and under.

If you'd like a qualified guide to accompany you, the tourist office can provide one for 38€ for the first 2 hours, 19€ for each additional hour. In July and August, join a daily guided **walking tour** at 3pm from the tourist office for 3.75€, free for children under 14.

You can ride through Bruges, and get out of town into the West Flanders countryside, on a bicycle tour with **Quasimodo Back Road Bikes** (© 050/37-04-70). Call ahead to book; meeting and departure point is the Burg. Tours run from 16€, 14€ for those ages 26 and under.

BRUGES AFTER DARK

For information, pick up a copy of the free monthly *Events@Brugge* brochure from the tourist office.

THE PERFORMING ARTS   In 2002, Bruges welcomed the opening of the ultramodern **Concertgebouw** ('t Zand 34; © 050/37-69-99; www.concert gebouw.be), a brand-new principal venue for classical music, opera, and ballet.

Step back in time to medieval Bruges, at *Brugge Anno 1468*, Vlamingstraat 84–86 (© 050/34-75-72), in a former Jesuit church. Players re-create the wedding of Duke Charles the Bold of Burgundy to Margaret of York while the audience piles into a period banquet. Performances are 53€ to 68€, and take place April through October, Thursday through Saturday from 7:30 to 10pm; November through March, Saturday from 7:30 to 10pm.

GHENT (GENT) ☆☆

The old town, at the confluence of the Scheldt and Leie rivers, has been spruced up, and Ghent has never looked so good. Although this former seat of the powerful counts of Flanders is larger and more citified than Bruges, it has enough cobblestone streets, meandering canals, and antique Flemish architecture to make it nearly as magical as its more famous sister.

Ghent

0   1/5 mile
0   200 meters

ATTRACTIONS ●

Belfort and Lakenhalle **9**
Graslei guild houses **6**
Gravensteen (Castle of the Counts) **2**
Museum voor Schone Kunsten **12**
Museum voor Volkskunde **3**
Sint-Baafskathedraal **10**
Stadhuis (Town Hall) **8**
Vrijdagmarkt **4**

ACCOMMODATIONS ■

Eden **11**
Erasmus **5**
Gravensteen **1**
Novotel Gent Centrum **7**

†   Church
ⓘ   Information
✉   Post Office

ESSENTIALS

GETTING THERE By Train Ghent is 32 minutes from Brussels, and trains depart every half hour or so. The main train station, **Gent Sint-Pieters,** Maria Hendrikaplein (© **09/222-44-44**), is 1.5km (1 mile) south of the city center. Take tram no. 1, 10, 11, or 12 to the center.

By Bus The **bus station** (© **09/210-94-91**) adjoins Sint-Pieters train station.

By Car Take E40 from Brussels and Bruges, and E17 from Antwerp.

VISITOR INFORMATION The Ghent **Tourist Office (Dienst Toerisme)** is at Predikherenlei 2, 9000 Gent (© **09/225-36-41;** fax 09/225-62-88; www. gent.be); it's open Monday through Friday from 8:30am to noon and 1 to 4:30pm. More convenient for personal visits is the **Inquiry Desk (Infokantoor)** in the cellar of the Belfry, Botermarkt 17A, 9000 Gent (© **09/266-52-32;** fax 09/224-15-55); it's open April through October daily from 9:30am to 6:30pm, November through March daily from 9:30am to 4:30pm.

GETTING AROUND Ghent has an excellent tram and bus system (© **09/ 210-94-91**), with many lines converging at Korenmarkt and Sint-Pieters train station. Walking is the best way to see the city center and experience its effortless combination of history and modernity at a human pace. Beyond the center, use public transportation. For a taxi, call **V-Tax** (© **09/222-22-22**).

WHERE TO STAY

The tourist office (see above) makes hotel reservations for a returnable deposit. Ghent has fewer hotels than you might expect, and those in the city center are often full at peak times, so try to book ahead.

Expensive

Novotel Gent Centrum ⟨★★⟩ Designed to fit, more or less, into its ancient surroundings, this modern hotel has an enviable position near the Town Hall, within easy reach of all the city's top sights. The rooms are furnished in a bright, efficient style. The facilities are all you'd expect from a top hotel and include sunny public rooms and a garden terrace.

Goudenleeuwplein 5, 9000 Gent. © **800/221-4542** or 09/224-22-30. Fax 09/224-32-95. www.novotel.com. 117 units. 130€ double; 175€ suite. AE, DC, MC, V. Parking 7.50€. **Amenities:** Restaurant; bar; heated indoor pool; health club; sauna; 24-hr. room service. *In room:* A/C, TV w/pay movies, minibar, hair dryer.

Moderate

Erasmus ⟨★★⟩ Each room is different in this converted 16th-century house, and all are plush, furnished with antiques and knickknacks. Rooms have high oak-beam ceilings, and bathrooms are modern. Some rooms have leaded-glass windows, some overlook a carefully manicured inner garden, and some have elaborate marble fireplaces. Breakfast is served in an impressive room that would have pleased the counts of Flanders.

Poel 25, 9000 Gent. © **09/224-21-95.** Fax 09/233-42-41. 11 units. 88€–105€ double. Rates include buffet breakfast. AE, MC, V. Limited street parking. **Amenities:** Bar. *In room:* TV, coffeemaker, hair dryer.

Gravensteen ⟨★★⟩ You enter this lovely mansion, built in 1865 as the home of a Ghent textile baron, through the old carriageway (made up of ornamented pillars and an impressive wall niche occupied by a marble statue), which sets the tone for what you find inside. The elegant, high-ceilinged parlor is a sophisticated blend of pastels, gracious modern furnishings, and antiques, with a small bar tucked into one corner. The rooms are attractive and comfortably furnished.

Jan Breydelstraat 35 (a short walk from Graslei and the Castle of the Counts), 9000 Gent. ℭ **09/225-11-50.** Fax 09/225-18-50. www.gravensteen.be. 46 units. 120€–150€ double; 180€ suite. AE, DC, MC, V. Parking 4€. **Amenities:** Bar; laundry service. *In room:* TV, minibar, hair dryer.

Inexpensive

Eden ✿ Not far from the city center, this is a nice hotel in its price range. The decor is pleasantly modern, and each room has a tapestry on the wall. Although most bathrooms are small, each has at least a toilet and shower, and some rooms have full bathrooms.

Zuidstationstraat 24, 9000 Gent. ℭ **09/223-51-51.** Fax 09/233-34-57. 28 units. 63€–83€ double. Rates include buffet breakfast. MC, V. Free parking. *In room:* TV.

WHERE TO DINE

Ghent restaurants keep Flemish culinary traditions alive and well, and prices are generally well below those in Brussels.

Expensive

Jan Breydel ✿✿ SEAFOOD/FLEMISH High honors go to this exquisite restaurant on a quaint street near the Castle of the Counts. Its interior is a garden delight of greenery, white napery, and light woods. Proprietors Louis and Pat Hellebaut see to it that dishes issued from their kitchen are as light as the setting, with delicate sauces and seasonings enhancing fresh ingredients. Seafood and regional specialties like the traditional Ghent fish stew, *waterzooï,* are all superb.

Jan Breydelstraat 10 (opposite Museum voor Sierkunst en Vormgeving). ℭ **09/225-62-87.** Main courses 18€–32€; fixed-price menus 32€–50€. AE, DC, MC, V. Tues–Sat noon–2pm and 7–10pm; Mon 7–10pm.

Moderate

Bistro-Grill Crypte ✿ FLEMISH Housed in what is allegedly Belgium's oldest crypt, dating back to the 12th century, this restaurant radiates an authentic Flemish atmosphere and serves superbly prepared food to match. The favorite dish is roast goose—every second table orders it. Other dishes range from T-bone steak to grilled pike.

Korenlei 24. ℭ **09/233-06-95.** Main courses 9.50€–12€; fixed-price menus 17€–38€. AE, MC, V. Thurs–Tues 11am–3pm and 6pm–midnight.

Brasserie Pakhuis ✿✿ FLEMISH/CONTINENTAL In a town where the Middle Ages are *big,* this place is almost modern and certainly hip. In fact, Pakhuis (which means "warehouse" in Dutch) may be a little too conscious of its own sense of style. The oyster and seafood platters are notable, and you won't go wrong with meat-based offerings like baked ham in a mustard sauce, or Flemish favorites like *waterzooï* and *garnaalkroketten* (shrimp croquettes).

Schuurkenstraat 4 (off Veldstraat). ℭ **09/223-55-55.** Main courses 9.60€–19€; fixed-price menus 19€–27€. AE, DC, MC, V. Mon–Sat 11:30am–midnight.

Inexpensive

't Buikske Vol ✿✿ BELGIAN/FRENCH This is one of the city's gems, thanks to chef Peter Vyncke's insistence on the best ingredients, served in a cozy, intimate atmosphere. In recent times he has done even better, delivering the same quality at lower prices. The restaurant isn't open much, but when it is, it's busy.

Kraanlei 17. ℭ **09/225-18-80.** Reservations recommended on weekends. Main courses 14€–25€; fixed-price menus 26€–46€. AE, MC, V. Mon–Tues and Thurs–Fri noon–2pm and 7–10pm; Sat 7–10pm.

EXPLORING HISTORIC GHENT

The city's historic monuments have a solemn, forbidding look. In the case of the Castle of the Counts of Flanders, this was intentional because Ghent's citizens were often in revolt against their overlord.

A row of gabled **guild houses** ★★ built along **Graslei** between the 1200s and 1600s, when the waterway was Ghent's harbor, forms an ensemble of colored facades reflected in the Leie River. This is the ideal spot to snap a picture that captures the essence of Ghent. To view them as a whole, cross the bridge over the Leie to Korenlei, and stroll along the bank. These buildings were once the headquarters of the craftsmen, tradespeople, and merchants who formed the city's commercial core.

The **Vrijdagmarkt,** a popular meeting spot today, was a rallying point in times past. A statue of Jacob Van Arteveld pays tribute to this local rebel hero of the 1300s. The square is now a shopping and dining area and hosts a lively street market every Friday. A short distance away, smaller **Kanonplein** is guarded by a big cannon of the 1400s, called *Dulle Griet* (Mad Meg).

Belfort en Lakenhalle (Belfry and Cloth Hall) ★★   These form a glorious medieval ensemble. From the 14th-century Belfry, great bells have rung out Ghent's civic pride down through the centuries, and a 54-bell carillon does so today. You can get high in the belfry with a guide and the aid of an elevator. The Cloth Hall of 1425 was the gathering place of medieval wool and cloth merchants.

Sint-Baafsplein. ✆ **09/223-99-22.** Admission 2.50€ adults, .75€ children ages 7–16, free for children 6 and under. Tours Tues–Sun hourly 2:10–5:10pm.

Gravensteen ★★   Formidable and forbidding, the Castle of the Counts was designed by the counts of Flanders to send a clear message to rebellion-inclined Gentenaars: Don't get any ideas. Surrounded by the waters of the Leie River, the castle begun by Count Philip of Alsace, fresh from the Crusades in 1180, has walls 2m (6 ft.) thick, and battlements and turrets. If these failed to intimidate the populace, the counts could turn to a well-equipped torture chamber; some of its accouterments are on display in a small museum.

Sint-Veereplein. ✆ **09/225-93-06.** Admission 5€ adults, 1.25€ students/seniors and ages 12–26, free for children 11 and under. Apr–Sept daily 9am–6pm; Oct–Mar daily 9am–5pm.

Museum voor Schone Kunsten ★   The Museum of Fine Arts, in a park close to Sint-Pieters train station, is home to old and new masterpieces, including works by Van der Weyden, Brueghel, Rubens, Van Dyck, and Bosch, along with moderns like James Ensor and Constant Permeke.

Citadel Park. ✆ **09/222-17-03.** Admission 2.50€ adults, 1.25€ children ages 12–18, free for children 11 and under. Tues–Sun 9:30am–5pm.

Sint-Baafskathedraal ★★★   The 14th-century St. Bavo's Cathedral's plain Gothic exterior belies a splendid baroque interior and some priceless art. A 24-panel altarpiece, *The Adoration of the Mystic Lamb,* completed by Jan van Eyck in 1432, is St. Bavo's showpiece. Other treasures include Rubens's *The Conversion of St. Bavo* (1624), in the Rubens Chapel off the semicircular ambulatory behind the high altar.

Sint-Baafsplein. ✆ **09/225-16-26.** Free admission to cathedral; *Mystic Lamb* chapel and crypt 2.50€ adults (includes audio guide in English), 1.75€ children ages 6–12, free for children 5 and under. Apr–Oct cathedral daily 8:30am–6pm; *Mystic Lamb* chapel and crypt Mon–Sat 10:30am–noon and 2:30–6pm, Sun 2–5pm. Nov–Mar cathedral daily 8:30am–5pm; *Mystic Lamb* chapel and crypt Mon–Sat 10:30am–noon and 2–4pm, Sun 2–5pm.

Stadhuis ⭒⭒ The Town Hall's several styles—Renaissance on one side and Gothic on another—reflect the changing tastes of a construction period that ran from 1518 until the 18th century. In the **Pacificatiezaal** (Pacification Room), the Pacification of Ghent, a declaration of 1567, declared the intention of the Low Countries to repudiate Spanish rule and permit religious freedom.

Botermarkt and Hoogpoort. ℂ 09/223-99-22. Admission 2.50€ adults, .75€ children. Guided tours May–Oct Mon–Thurs 2pm from tourist office in belfry "Raadskelder."

BOAT TRIPS & OTHER ORGANIZED TOURS

A **boat trip** ⭒ on the canals (ℂ 09/223-88-53) is a good way to see the city's highlights. From April to October, both open-top and covered tour boats operate daily from 10am to 7pm from Graslei and Korenlei. A half-hour cruise is 5.75€ for adults, 3€ for children 11 and under.

If you'd like a qualified guide to accompany you, the tourist office can provide one for 38€ for the first 2 hours, 15€ for each additional hour. In July and August, join a daily guided **walking tour** at 3pm from the tourist office for 3.75€; free for children under 14.

Easter to October, tours by **horse-drawn carriage** leave from Sint-Baafsplein and Korenlei daily from 10am to 7pm. A half-hour ride is 20€.

GHENT AFTER DARK

The last week of July witnesses the annual **Gentse Feesten (Ghent Festivities),** a time of music, dancing, and generally riotous fun and games throughout the city.

THE PERFORMING ARTS Opera is performed at the 19th-century **Vlaamse Opera,** Schouwburgstraat 3 (ℂ 09/225-24-25).

BARS & TAVERNS You should have a memorable evening in any one of Ghent's atmospheric cafes. **De Witte Leeuw,** Graslei 6 (ℂ 09/233-37-33), has a 17th-century setting and more than 300 varieties of beer. At **Dulle Griet,** Vrijdagmarkt 50 (ℂ 09/224-24-55), you'll be asked to deposit one of your shoes before being given a potent Kwak beer in a too-collectible glass with a wood frame that allows the glass to stand up. The town's former Toll House, the smallest building on Graslei, is now a nice little tavern called **Het Tolhuisje,** Graslei 10 (ℂ 09/224-30-90)

Het Waterhuis aan de Bierkant, Groentenmarkt 9 (ℂ 09/225-06-80), has more than 100 different Belgian beers, including locally made Stopken. A couple of doors along, **'t Dreupelkot,** Groentenmarkt 12 (ℂ 09/224-21-20), specializes in deadly little glasses of *jenever* (a stiff spirit similar to gin), of which it has a hundred varieties. Across the tramlines, the tiny **'t Galgenhuisje,** Groentenmarkt 5 (ℂ 09/233-42-51), is popular with students.

3

The Czech Republic

by Hana Mastrini

The Czech Republic, comprising the ancient kingdoms of Bohemia, Moravia, and Silesia, is the westernmost of the former Soviet satellite countries and probably the best place to explore what used to be the other side of the Iron Curtain. If you have time to visit only one eastern European city, it should be Prague—widely regarded as one of the most beautiful cities in Europe, if not the world. The quirky and compact heart of Bohemia is a jumble of architecture. Gothic bestrides baroque, Renaissance adjoins cubist, with a splash of socialist realism and postmodern kitsch thrown in for good measure. On the hills and plains fronting the River Vltava you will glimpse the triumphs and tragedies of the past 10 centuries spiked with the peculiarity of the post-Communist reconstruction.

Nearly 15 years after 1989's bloodless "Velvet Revolution" over Communism, and over a decade after the peaceful split with the Slovak part of the former Czechoslovakia, the European Union will put the Czechs at the head of its new intake of states in May 2004.

But Prague isn't the Czech Republic's only draw. Visitors are flocking to west Bohemia after some of the world's best-known spas were restored to their Victorian-era splendor, while castles abound in the countryside.

1 Prague ✶✶✶

Exactly 80 years after native-son Franz Kafka's death, Prague's mix of the melancholy and the magnificent, the shadows and the fog of everyday life, set against some of Europe's most spectacular architecture, still confounds all who live or visit here. Its tightly wound brick paths have felt the hooves of kings' horses, the jackboots of Hitler's armies, the heaving tracks of Soviet tanks, and the shuffle of students in passive revolt. The 6-centuries-old Charles Bridge is today jammed with visitors and venture capitalists looking for memories or profits from a once-captive city now enjoying yet another renaissance.

Fate tested the city once again in August 2002 when record floodwaters from the River Vltava engulfed much of Lesser Town and part of Old Town, putting many restaurants and attractions near the riverfront out of business for months. By early 2003, however, most of the damaged streets, buildings, and underground stations had been repaired or were on their way to rebirth. Praguers have shrugged off the latest disaster with a familiar *"ach jo"* ("oh well"), and life has quickly returned to the main haunts, even though visitor numbers have been down since the floods—the product of an overreaction to the pictures of devastation beamed around the world during the crisis. So for the better-informed traveler who knows that Prague is open for business (like those of you reading this book), you get to enjoy the eclectic energy of this city with a little more room to breathe. ***Note:*** While most owners and operators vowed to reopen by the start of the high season in 2003, you should e-mail or call ahead to confirm their status before your trip.

ESSENTIALS

GETTING THERE   **By Plane**   Newly rebuilt **Ruzyně Airport** (☏ 220 111 111) is 19km (12 miles) west of the city center. You'll find a bank for changing money (usually open daily 7am–11pm), telephones, and several car-rental offices.

Plenty of taxis line up in front of the airport. CEDAZ (☏ 220 114 296) operates an airport shuttle bus to náměstí Republiky in central Prague. It leaves the airport daily every 30 minutes from 6am to 9pm and stops near the Náměstí Republiky Metro station (trip time: 30 min.). Returning, the bus leaves every 30 minutes from 5:30am to 9:30pm. The shuttle costs 90Kč ($3). You can also take city bus no. 119 to the Dejvická Metro station (Line A) for 12Kč (40¢).

By Train   Of the two central rail stations, **Hlavní nádraží,** Wilsonova třída 80, Praha 1 (☏ 224 614 030), is the grander and more popular; however, it's also seedier. The basement holds a 24-hour luggage-storage counter charging 30Kč ($1) per bag over 15 kilograms (33 lb.) per day (counted from midnight). The nearby lockers aren't secure and should be avoided. On the second floor is the train information office (marked by a lowercase "i"), open daily from 6am to 10pm. From the main train station it's a 5-minute stroll to the "top" end of Wenceslas Square or a 15-minute walk to Old Town Square. Metro Line C connects the station to the rest of the city. Metro trains depart from the lower level, and city-center no-transfer tickets, costing 8Kč (25¢), are available at the newsstand near the Metro entrance. Taxis line up outside the station day and night.

Tips Getting a Fair Fare

Most of Prague's taxi drivers will take advantage of you; getting an honestly metered ride from the airport is close to impossible. The fare from the airport to Wenceslas Square should be no more than about 700Kč ($23).

Prague

Prague Castle

HRADČANSKÁ Ⓜ

Milady Horákové

See inset above

Mariánské hradby   CHOTKOVY SADY

Jelení   Chotkov

HRADČANY

Keplerova   Nový Svět   U Brusnice   U Kasáren   **Prague Castle**

2   MALOSTRANSKÁ Ⓜ

Loretánské nám.   **4**   **12**

1   Loretánská   **11**   Nerudova   MALÁ STRANA

Úvoz   **13**

3   LOBKOVICKÁ ZAHRADA

STRAHOVSKÁ ZAHRADA   SEMINÁŘSKÁ ZAHRADA

Strahovská   **14**

Karmelitská   Malostr. nábřeží

Olympijská   Petřín Tower   PETŘÍNSKÉ SADY

Spartakiádní Stadion   Funicular   STŘELECKÝ OSTROV

Chaloupeckého   Újezd

Jezdecká

KINSKÉHO ZAHRADA

⊛ **Prague**
CZECH REPUBLIC

Peškové   Janáčkovo nábřeží

Holečkova   V botanice   Na Df..

Zborovská

Kartouzská

Plzeňská   Dušková   **15**   Ⓜ ANDĚL

Mozartova   Radlická   Svornosti

Ostrovského   SMÍCHOV

Nádraží Holešovice, Partyzánská at Vrbenského, Praha 7 (© **224 224 200**), usually serves trains from Berlin and other points north. Although it isn't as centrally located as the main station, its more manageable size and position at the end of Metro Line C make it almost as convenient.

VISITOR INFORMATION   Those arriving by train at either of the two primary stations can get information from **AVE Ltd.** (© **224 223 226** or 224 223 521; fax 257 312 984; www.avetravel.cz), an accommodations agency that also distributes printed information. The two train station AVE offices are open daily from 6am to 10pm.

The city's **Cultural and Information Center,** on the ground floor of the remodeled Obecní dům (Municipal House), nám. Republiky 5, Praha 1 (© **222 002 100;** fax 222 002 636; Metro: Náměstí Republiky), is a new attempt at visitor-friendly relations, offering advice, tickets, souvenirs, refreshments, and restrooms. It's open daily from 9am to 5pm.

Websites   The city's own information service, PIS, has regularly updated cultural information in English and acts as a gateway to tourism websites at **www.pis.cz** or **www.prague-info.cz**. For visa and other consular information, the Foreign Ministry site is **www.czech.cz**. For the latest local news updates, try the *Prague Post* at **www.praguepost.cz**. Tom's Travel has developed a number of websites, including **www.travel.cz** for general Czech tourist information and accommodations.

The well-designed **www.czechsite.com** offers tips on local transport, attractions, museums, galleries, and restaurants. You can book your lodging and a rental car and also find an online message board. The extensive **www.czechtourism.com** roundup of links to other websites was pulled together by a Net veteran who awards a Czech flag icon to sites he considers especially worthy. The well-organized **www.hotelsczech.com** shows hotels by the number of stars bestowed by the government. Click on a hotel to find prices by date and photos of the buildings and rooms. Reservations aren't instant—after you fill out the form, an agent is supposed to get back to you within 48 hours.

CITY LAYOUT   The River Vltava bisects Prague. **Staré Město (Old Town)** and **Nové Město (New Town)** are on the east (right) side of the river, while the **Hradčany (Castle District)** and **Malá Strana (Lesser Town)** are on the west (left) bank.

Bridges and squares are the most prominent landmarks. **Charles Bridge,** the oldest and most famous of those spanning the Vltava, is at the epicenter and connects Old Town with Lesser Town and the Castle District. Several important streets radiate from Old Town Square, including fashionable Pařížská to the northwest, historic Celetná to the east, and Melantrichova, connecting to

---

Tips **Reading Maps**

When reading maps or searching for addresses, keep in mind that *ulice* (abbreviated ul.) means "street," *třída* means "avenue," *náměstí* (abbreviated nám.) is a "square" or "plaza," a *most* is a "bridge," and *nábřeží* is a "quay." In Czech, none of these terms are capitalized. In addresses, street numbers follow the street name (like Václavské nám. 25). Each address is followed by a district number, such as Praha 1 (Praha is "Prague" in Czech).

Wenceslas Square (Václavské nám.) to the southeast. On the west side of Charles Bridge is Mostecká, a 3-block-long connection to Malostranské náměstí, Malá Strana's main square. Hradčany, the Castle District, is just northwest of the square, while a second hill, Petřín, is just southwest.

GETTING AROUND   By Metro, Bus & Tram   Prague's public transport network is a vast—and usually efficient—system of subways, trams, and buses. You can ride a maximum of four stations on the Metro or 15 minutes on a tram or bus, without transfers, for 8Kč (25¢); children 5 and under ride free. This is usually enough for trips in the historic districts. Rides of more than four stops on the Metro, or longer tram or bus rides, with unlimited transfers for up to 1 hour after your ticket is validated, cost 12Kč (40¢). You can buy tickets from coin-operated orange machines in Metro stations or at most newsstands marked TABÁK or TRAFIKA. Hold on to your ticket (which you must validate at the orange or yellow stamp clocks in each tram or bus when you get on board or at the entrance to the Metro) during your ride—you'll need it to prove you've paid if a ticket collector asks.

If you're caught without a valid ticket, you have to pay a 400Kč ($13) fine to a ticket controller on the spot. Make sure he or she shows you a very official-looking badge. ***Warning:*** Oversize luggage (larger than carry-on size) requires a single trip ticket for each piece. You may be fined 50Kč ($1.65) for not having tickets for your luggage.

A 1-day pass good for unlimited rides costs 70Kč ($2.35); a 3-day pass 200Kč ($6.65); a 7-day pass 250Kč ($8.35); and a 15-day pass 280Kč ($9.35). If you're staying for more than 2 weeks, buy a monthly pass for 420Kč ($14). You can buy the day passes at the "DP" windows at any Metro station, but the photo-ID monthly pass is available only at the **Dopravní podnik** (transport department) office on Na bojišti 5, near the I. P. Pavlova Metro station (© **296 191 111**).

Metro trains operate daily from 5am to midnight and run every 3 to 8 minutes. The most convenient stations are Můstek, at the foot of Václavské náměstí (Wenceslas Sq.); Staroměstská, for Old Town Square and Charles Bridge; and Malostranská, serving Malá Strana and the Castle District.

The electric tram lines run practically everywhere. You never have to hail trams; they make every stop. The most popular, no. 22 (the "tourist tram" or "pickpocket express") and no. 23, run past top sights like the National Theater and Prague Castle. Regular bus and tram service stops at midnight, after which selected routes run reduced schedules, usually only once per hour. If you miss a night connection, expect a long wait for the next.

By Funicular   The cog railway makes the scenic run up and down Petřín Hill every 15 minutes or so from 9:15am to 8:45pm, with an intermediate stop at the Nebozízek Restaurant in the middle of the hill overlooking the city. It requires the same 12Kč (40¢) ticket as other public transport. The funicular departs from a small house in the park just above the middle of Újezd in Malá Strana.

By Taxi   Avoid taxis! If you must, hail one in the streets or in front of train stations, large hotels, and popular attractions, but be forewarned that many drivers simply gouge tourists. The best fare you can hope for is 17Kč (55¢) per kilometer, but twice or three times that isn't rare. The rates are usually posted on the dashboard, making it too late to haggle once you're in and on your way. Negotiate a price and have it written down before getting in. Better yet, go on foot or by public transport. Somewhat reputable companies with English-speaking dispatchers are **AAA Taxi** (© **140 14** or 222 333 222); **SEDOP** (© **271 726 666**); and the unfortunately named **ProfiTaxi** (© **140 35**). Get a receipt (and send it to the mayor).

By Car   Driving in Prague is not worth the money or effort. The roads are frustrating and slow, and parking is minimal and expensive. If you want to rent a car to explore the environs, try **Europcar,** Pařížská 28, Praha 1 (© **224 811 290;** www.europcar.cz; Metro: Staroměstská), or at Ruzyně Airport (the latter open daily from 8am to 8pm). Also, there's **Hertz,** at Karlovo nám. 28, Praha 2 (© **220 102 424;** www.hertz.com; Metro: Karlovo Náměstí); at Ruzyně Airport; or at Hotel Diplomat, Praha 6 (Metro: Dejvická). **Budget** is at Ruzyně Airport (© **220 113 253**) and in the Hotel Inter-Continental, nám. Curieových, Praha 1 (© **224 889 995;** www.budget.cz; Metro: Staroměstská).

Local Czech car-rental companies sometimes offer lower rates than the big international firms. Try **Secco Car,** Přístavní 39, Praha 7 (© **220 800 647;** www.seccocar.cz; Metro: Nádraží Holešovice, then tram 12 or 25).

 FAST FACTS: Prague

American Express For travel arrangements, traveler's checks, currency exchange, and other member services, visit the office at Václavské nám. 56 (Wenceslas Sq.), Praha 1 (© **222 800 237;** fax 222 211 131; Metro:

Muzeum), open daily from 9am to 7pm. To report lost or stolen cards, call ℂ **222 800 222.**

Business Hours Most **banks** are open Monday through Friday from 8am to 6pm. Pubs are usually open daily from 11am to midnight. Most restaurants open for lunch from noon to 3pm and for dinner from 6 to 11pm; only a few stay open later.

Currency The basic unit of currency is the koruna (plural: koruny) or crown, abbreviated Kč. Each koruna is divided into 100 haléřů or hellers. At this writing, $1 = approximately 30Kč; or 1Kč = 3¢. £1 = 45Kč; or 1Kč = £0.02.

Currency Exchange Banks generally offer the best exchange rates. Don't hesitate to use a credit or debit card to withdraw cash for the best rates. **Komerční banka** has three convenient Praha 1 locations with ATMs: Na Příkopě 33, Národní 32, and Václavské nám. 42 (ℂ **222 432 111** central switchboard for all branches; Metro: Můstek). The exchange offices are open Monday through Friday from 8am to 5pm, but the ATMs are accessible 24 hours.

Doctors/Dentists If you need a doctor or dentist and your condition isn't life threatening, you can visit the **Polyclinic at Národní,** Národní 9, Praha 1 (ℂ **222 075 120;** Metro: Můstek), during walk-in hours, from 8am to 5pm. For the emergencies operator, dial ℂ **140 533.** Dr. Stránský is an Ivy League–trained straight-talking physician. For emergency medical aid, call the **Foreigners' Medical Clinic,** Na Homolce Hospital, Roentgenova 2, Praha 5 (ℂ **257 272 146** or 257 272 191 after hours; Metro: Anděl, then bus no. 167).

Drugstores The most central pharmacy (*lékárna*) is at Václavské nám. 8, Praha 1 (ℂ **224 227 532;** Metro: Můstek), open Monday through Friday from 8am to 6pm. The nearest emergency (24-hr.) pharmacy is at Palackého 5, Praha 1 (ℂ **224 946 982;** Metro Můstek). If you're in Praha 2, there's an emergency pharmacy on Belgická 37 (ℂ **222 519 731;** Metro: Náměstí Míru).

Embassies The embassy of the **United States** is at Tržiště 15, Praha 1 (ℂ **257 530 663**). The embassy of **Canada** is at Mickiewiczova 6, Praha 6 (ℂ **272 101 811**). The embassy of the **United Kingdom** is at Thunovská 14, Praha 1 (ℂ **257 402 111**). The honorary consul of **Australia** is at Klimentská 10, Praha 1 (ℂ **251 018 350**). The embassy of **Ireland** is at Tržiště 13, Praha 1 (ℂ **257 530 061**). The honorary consul of **New Zealand** is at Dykova 19, Praha 10 (ℂ **222 514 672**).

Emergencies You can reach Prague's **police** and **fire** services by calling ℂ **158** from any phone. For an **ambulance,** call ℂ **155.**

Hospitals Particularly welcoming to foreigners is **Nemocnice Na Homolce,** Roentgenova 2, Praha 5 (ℂ **257 272 146** or 257 272 191 after hours; Metro: Anděl, then bus no. 167). The English-speaking doctors can also make house calls.

Internet Access The best of the cybercafes is **The Globe,** Pštrossova 6, Praha 1 (ℂ **224 934 203;** www.globebookstore.cz). It's a cafe, bookstore, and Internet access in one. You can browse the Internet for 15 Kč (50¢) for the first 15 minutes and 1Kč for each additional 15 minutes. Its new location here is open daily from 10am till midnight.

Telephone The **country code** for the Czech Republic is **420.** In 2002 the Czech telephone network underwent a massive overhaul and, virtually overnight, all telephone numbers changed. In all cases, the **city codes** are now connected to the local number in front so that the entire number that must be dialed locally has nine digits. All numbers in this edition have been revised, but be aware that with such a project there will be some confusion and inconvenience for locals and visitors alike. To check the particular phone number, go to **www.zlatestranky.cz.** For directory assistance in English and for information on services and rates calling abroad, dial ✆ **1181.**

There are two kinds of pay phones. One accepts coins and the other operates only with a phone card, available from post offices and news agents in denominations ranging from 50Kč to 500Kč ($1.65–$17). The minimum cost of a local call is 4Kč (12¢). Coin-op phones, if they work, have displays telling you the minimum price for your call. They don't make change, so don't load more than you have to. You can add more coins as the display gets near zero. The more efficient phone card telephones deduct the price of your call from the card. If you're calling home, get a phone card with plenty of points, as calls run about 20Kč (65¢) per minute to the United States and 15Kč (30p) to the United Kingdom. Hotels usually add their own surcharge, sometimes as hefty as 100% to 200%, which may surprise you when you're presented with the bill. Ask before placing any call from a hotel. Charging to your phone credit card from a public telephone is often the most economical way to call home.

A fast, convenient way to call home from Europe is via services that bypass the foreign operator and automatically link you to an operator with your long-distance carrier in your home country. The access number in the Czech Republic for **AT&T USA Direct** is ✆ **00 420 00101,** for **MCI Call USA** ✆ **00 420 00112,** and for **Sprint Global One** ✆ **00 420 87187.** Canadians can connect with **Canada Direct** at ✆ **00 420 00151,** and Brits with **BT Direct** at ✆ **00 420 04401.** From a pay phone in the Czech Republic, your local phone card will be debited only for a local call.

Tipping At most restaurants and pubs, locals just round the bill up to the nearest few koruny. When you're given good service at tablecloth places, a 10% tip is proper. Washroom and cloakroom attendants usually demand a couple of koruny, and porters in airports and rail stations usually receive 20Kč (65¢) per bag. Taxi drivers should get about 10%, unless they've already ripped you off.

WHERE TO STAY

Prague's full-service hotels have had to tighten efficiency in the face of heavier international competition, but due to low supply, room rates still top those of many similar or better-quality hotels in western Europe. Pensions with limited services are cheaper than hotels, but compared with similar western European B&Bs, they're pricey. The best budget lodgings are rooms in private homes or apartments.

Expect to pay between 1,000Kč and 2,000Kč ($33–$66) for a single, and between 1,500Kč and 6,000Kč ($50–$200) for an apartment for two. All kinds of private housing are offered by several local agencies. The leader now is Prague-based **E-TRAVEL.CZ** (formerly known as Tom's Travel), which offers all types of accommodation at their main website, or you can tap their large pictured database of apartments at www.apartments.cz. The office is near the National Theater at Ostrovní 7, Praha 1 (© **224 990 990;** fax 224 990 999; www.travel.cz; Metro: Národní třída). Another good agency, especially for those arriving late by train or air, is **AVE Travel Ltd.** (© **224 223 226;** fax 224 223 463; www.avetravel.cz). It has outlets at the airport (7am–10pm); at the main train station, Hlavní nádraží (6am–11pm); and at the north train station, nádraží Holešovice (7am–9pm).

STARÉ MĚSTO (OLD TOWN) & JOSEFOV
Very Expensive

Four Seasons Hotel 🏆🏆🏆 Prague's most prestigious new residence opened at the dawn of the 21st century. Guests can choose from rooms in the neo-Renaissance house with its towering ceilings, or in the neoclassical wing with suites offering some of the best views of the bridge and the castle. For an unbelievable splurge, you can book the Presidential Suite in the baroque wing. Its rate of $1,800 to $3,500 per night depends on the season, but no prince or potentate could have a view from his own bed as precious as this view. The Allegro Restaurant offers Prague's poshest meal.

Veleslavinova 2a, Praha 1. © 221 427 000. Fax 221 426 666. www.fourseasons.com. 162 units. From 8,400Kč ($280) double; from 19,500Kč ($650) suite. Rates exclude taxes and breakfast. AE, DC, MC, V. Metro: Staroměstská. **Amenities:** Restaurant; bar and grill; health club; concierge; business service; 24-hr. room service; laundry; dry cleaning overnight. *In room:* A/C, TV/VCR, CD player, dataport, minibar, hair dryer, safe.

Hotel Inter-Continental Prague 🏆 The upper suites have hosted luminaries such as Michael Jackson, Madeleine Albright, and, so legend has it, terrorist Carlos the Jackal. The standard rooms aren't very large but are comfortable, with decent but not exceptional furniture and computer ports. A riverside window might give you a glimpse of the castle or the metronome at the top of Letná Park across the river.

Nám. Curieových 43/5, Praha 1. © 224 881 111. Fax 224 810 071. www.interconti.com. 364 units. From 6,600Kč ($220) double; from 10,500Kč ($350) suite. Rates include buffet breakfast. AE, DC, MC, V. Metro:

Native Behavior

The Czechs are the quintessential live-and-let-live people. Simple pleasures are the most important, the main one being the requisite evenings in the local *hospoda* (pub) inhaling liters of the national liquid gold.

Still, for people who spend a disproportionate number of hours in beer joints, Czechs remain proud of their erudite traditions. The highly educated populace has a vast interest in literature, film, theater, and, of course, serious music.

Most Czechs are easygoing with strangers and happy to give advice, and many will even invite complete strangers to their weekend cottages to see how real Bohemians live.

Staroměstská. **Amenities:** Restaurant; cafe; indoor swimming pool; fitness center; concierge; car-rental desk; business service; salon; 24-hr. room service; massage; laundry. *In room:* A/C, TV, minibar, hair dryer.

Hotel Paříž ⚛   At the edge of náměstí Republiky and across from the Municipal House, the Paříž provides a rare glimpse back into the gilded First Republic. Each light fixture, etching, and curve at this Art Nouveau landmark recalls the days when Prague was one of the world's richest cities. For a glimpse of the hotel's atmosphere, rent the film *Mission Impossible;* you can see Tom Cruise plotting his revenge from within one of the fine suites. The rooms are some of the most comfortable in Prague, with modern updates of Art Deco accents.

U Obecního domu 1, Praha 1. ✆ **222 195 195.** Fax 224 225 475. www.hotel-pariz.cz. 94 units. 9,000Kč ($300) double; from 12,300Kč ($410) suite. Rates include breakfast. AE, DC, MC, V. Metro: Náměstí Republiky. **Amenities:** Restaurant; cafe; exercise room; sauna; concierge; car-rental desk; business service; 24-hr. room service; massage; babysitting; laundry; dry cleaning. *In room:* A/C, TV, minibar, hair dryer, safe.

Expensive

Hotel Ungelt ⚛ *(Value* *(Kids*   The Ungelt offers airy, spacious suites. Each contains a living room, a full kitchen, and a bathroom. Beds are standard-issue. One of our friends and his family raved about the location and spaciousness, especially with two small boys in tow.

Štupartská 1, Praha 1. ✆ **224 828 686.** Fax 224 828 181. www.ungelt.cz. 10 units. 6,330Kč ($211) 1-bedroom suite for 2; 9,070Kč ($302) 2-bedroom suite for 3 or 4. Rates include breakfast. AE, MC, V. Metro: Staroměstská or Náměstí Republiky. **Amenities:** Bar; tour desk; car-rental desk; business service; laundry. *In room:* TV, kitchen, minibar, fridge, coffeemaker, hair dryer, iron.

Moderate

Betlem Club ⚛ *(Value*   This small hotel offers a great location on a cobblestone square across from where Protestant firebrand Jan Hus once preached. Rooms are bland but comfortable and fairly priced. One great advantage is that if you come by car, the Betlem lets you park in front of the hotel, a rarity in this parking-deficient city.

Betlémské nám. 9, Praha 1. ✆ **222 221 575.** Fax 222 220 580. www.betlemclub.cz. 22 units. 3,900Kč ($130) double; 4,500Kč ($150) suite. Rates include breakfast. MC, V. Metro: Národní třída. **Amenities:** Babysitting; laundry; safe. *In room:* TV, minibar, hair dryer.

Inexpensive

Hotel Cloister Inn *(Value*   Between Old Town Square and the National Theater, the Cloister Inn occupies a building that the secret police converted into holding cells. It sounds ominous, but it offers sparse, clean accommodations at an unbeatable price for the location. Proprietor Jiří Tlaskal has taken over management from the secret police and the Sisters of Mercy (the nuns, not the rock group). He has refurbished the hotel side with comfortable Scandinavian furniture.

Bartolomějská 9, Praha 1. ✆ **224 211 020.** Fax 224 210 800. www.cloister-inn.cz. 73 units with en suite showers. 4,200Kč ($140) double. Rates include breakfast. AE, MC, V. Metro: Národní Třída. **Amenities:** Concierge; tour desk. *In room:* TV, hair dryer, safe.

NOVÉ MĚSTO (NEW TOWN)
Very Expensive

Palace Hotel ⚛   Now surpassed in overall comfort only by the Savoy in Hradčany, the Palace is a top, upscale, central-city offering, a block from Wenceslas Square, although if given the choice, the Paříž has far more character. Rooms are some of the largest and most modern luxury accommodations in Prague. Two rooms for travelers with disabilities are available.

Panská 12, Praha 1. ✆ **224 093 111.** Fax 224 221 240. www.palacehotel.cz. 124 units. 6,000Kč ($200) double; from 9,630Kč ($321) suite. Rates include breakfast. AE, DC, MC, V. Metro: Můstek. **Amenities:** 2 restaurants;

2 lounges; concierge; tour desk; car-rental desk; courtesy limo; business service; 24-hr. room service; babysitting; laundry. *In room:* A/C, TV, VCR, minibar, hair dryer, safe.

Expensive

Hotel Esplanade 🛧   Located on a side street at the top of the square, the Esplanade began life as a bank and the offices of an Italian insurance company. Rooms are bright and airy, some with standard beds, others with French Provincial headboards, and still others with extravagant canopies. Number 101 is over-the-top with antique wooden chairs, intricate inlaid tables, and a fascinating embossed wall covering. You might be put off by the main train station across the street, but an honest-looking doorman says the hotel is safe. Just the same, be advised not to stroll alone in the neighborhood at night.

Washingtonova 19, Praha 1. ⓒ **224 501 172.** Fax 224 229 306. www.esplanade.cz. 74 units. 4,500Kč ($150) double; from 7,230Kč ($241) suite. Rates include breakfast. AE, MC, V. Metro: Muzeum. **Amenities:** Restaurant; cafe; bar; sauna; concierge; tour desk; room service; massage; babysitting; laundry; dry cleaning; executive level rooms. *In room:* TV, minibar, dataport, safe, hair dryer.

Prague Marriott Hotel 🛧🛧 *(Kids)*   The Marriott provides just what you would expect: a high-standard space with tasteful, homogenized furniture and all of the phones, faxes, dataports, and services demanded by the virtual salesperson. As well as being newer and slightly better appointed, the Marriott is about 10 paces closer to the Czech central bank than its sister, the Hotel Renaissance, right off náměstí Republiky and around the corner from the headquarters of the largest merchant bank, Komerční banka. This proximity, while not on the attractive end of Old Town, could pay off if you've overslept on that last day of closing the next big post-Communist deal. The massive fitness center, "The World Class Health Academy," is better equipped than the Inter-Continental's. The hotel also wants to attract families and as such offers Sunday family brunches in the Brasserie Praha, where kids are welcome and are offered PC games to play.

V Celnici 8, Praha 1. ⓒ **222 888 888.** Fax 222 888 889. www.marriott.com. 328 units. 6,900Kč ($230) double; 8,400Kč ($280) executive level double; from 10,800Kč ($360) suite. Rates for suites and executive rooms include breakfast. AE, DC, MC, V. Metro: Náměstí Republiky. **Amenities:** Restaurant; cafe; bar; fitness center with indoor swimming pool; sauna; whirlpool; gym; therapy rooms; concierge; fully equipped business center; salon; 24-hr. room service; laundry; dry cleaning. *In room:* A/C, TV, minibar, dataport, hair dryer, safe.

Moderate

Andante 🛧 *(Value)*   A new addition to this guide as the best value choice near Wenceslas Square, the understated Andante is tucked away on a dark side street, about 2 blocks off the top of the square. Despite its less-than-appealing neighborhood, this is the most comfortable property in the $100-to-$125 range. It lacks the character of the old Hotel Evropa (see below) but also the neglect. A close friend of mine, a young businesswoman, said she enjoyed the stay at the Andante, but she felt safer having her boyfriend with her.

Ve Smečkách 4, Praha 1. ⓒ **222 210 021.** Fax 222 210 591. www.andante.cz. 32 units. 3,450Kč ($115) double; 4,560Kč ($152) suite. Rates, which fluctuate based on the latest crown rate against the dollar because of the crown's volatility, include breakfast. AE, MC, V. Metro: Muzeum. **Amenities:** Restaurant; bar; tour desk; business service; limited room service. *In room:* TV, minibar; hair dryer, iron available at reception.

Inexpensive

Hotel Evropa   The statue-studded exterior is still one of the most striking landmarks on Wenceslas Square, but unlike other early-20th-century gems, it hasn't been polished and so continues to get duller. Rooms are aging and most don't have bathrooms; some are just plain shabby. The best choice is a room facing the square with a balcony, but all are falling into various levels of disrepair. Still, this is an affordable chance to stay at one of Wenceslas Square's once-grand addresses.

Václavské nám. 25, Praha 1. © 224 228 117. Fax 224 224 544. 90 units, 23 with bathroom. 2,600Kč ($86) double without bathroom, 3,990Kč ($133) double with bathroom; from 4,700Kč ($156) suite. Rates include continental breakfast. AE, MC, V. Metro: Můstek. **Amenities:** Restaurant; cafe.

MALÁ STRANA (LESSER TOWN)

I used to recommend the **Hotel Dům U červeného lva,** Nerudova 41 (© 257 533 832), as the top pick near the castle, but with ever more tourists walking up Nerudova, the noise has become prohibitive in summer, according to a few Frommer's regulars. Try this place during the colder months when your windows will remain closed.

Expensive

U Krále Karla ⚔ This Castle Hill property does so much to drive home its Renaissance roots, King Charles's heirs should be getting royalties. Replete with period-print open-beamed ceilings and stained-glass windows, the atmosphere is almost Disneyesque in its pretense, but it's somehow appropriate for this location at the foot of Prague Castle. This is a fun, comfortable choice, with heavy period furniture and colorful angelic accents everywhere.

Nerudova-Úvoz 4, Praha 1. © 257 532 869. Fax 257 533 591. www.romantichotels.cz. 19 units. 6,900Kč ($230) double; 7,900Kč ($263) suite. Rates include breakfast. AE, MC, V. Tram: 22 or 23 to Malostranské nám. **Amenities:** Restaurant; cafe; bar; solarium; bike or scooter rental; concierge; tour desk; car-rental desk; courtesy limo; limited room service; babysitting; laundry. *In room:* TV, kitchenette, minibar, hair dryer, iron, safe.

Moderate

Hotel Kampa The Kampa has a choice location on a quiet winding alley off the park, giving you quick access to Malá Strana and Charles Bridge. The rooms smack of Communist chintz, but they're comfortable if you don't expect first-class surroundings. The best rooms boast a park view, so request one when booking or checking in.

Všehrdova 16, Praha 1. © 257 320 508. Fax 257 320 262. www.euroagentur.cz or www.worldlandmarks. com. 84 units. 5,800Kč ($193) double. Rates include breakfast. AE, MC, V. Metro: Malostranská, then tram 12, 22, or 23 to Hellichova. **Amenities:** Restaurant; bar; room service; laundry service; dry cleaning. *In room:* TV, minibar, hair dryer, safe.

HRADČANY

Very Expensive

Hotel Savoy ⚔⚔ Prague's finest hotel, opened in 1994, belongs to the company that manages the more venerable Palace on Wenceslas Square. Behind the massive Foreign Ministry and Černín Palace, and a few blocks from the castle, it welcomes you with a tastefully modern lobby. Rooms are richly decorated. Beds are consistently huge, a rejection of the central-European twin-beds-shoved-together look. The pleasant staff provides an attention to detail that's a cut above the service at most hotels in town. The Savoy's Hradčany Restaurant is also one of the finest dining rooms in town (see "Where to Dine," below).

Keplerova 6, Praha 1. © 224 302 430. Fax 224 302 128. www.hotel-savoy.cz. 61 units. From 9,600Kč ($320) double; from 12,600Kč ($420) suite. Rates include breakfast. AE, DC, MC, V. Tram: 22 or 23. **Amenities:** Restaurant; bar; fitness center with sauna; Jacuzzi; concierge; tour desk; car-rental desk; business service; salon; laundry; nonsmoking rooms. *In room:* A/C, TV/VCR w/pay movies, fax, dataport, minibar, hair dryer, safe.

Expensive

Romantik Hotel U raka ⚔⚔ Hidden among the stucco houses and cobblestone streets of a pristine medieval neighborhood on the far side of Prague

Castle is this most pleasant surprise. In a ravine below the Foreign Ministry gardens, the old-world farmhouse has been lovingly reconstructed. This is the quietest getaway you could imagine in tightly packed Prague. The rustic rooms have heavy wooden furniture, open-beam ceilings, and exposed brick. The much-sought-after suite has a fireplace and adjoins a private garden, making it a favorite for honeymooners.

Černínská 10, Praha 1. ℂ **220 511 100.** Fax 220 510 511. 6 units. 5,580Kč ($186) double; 6,390Kč ($213) suite. Rates include breakfast. AE, MC, V. Tram: 22 or 23. **Amenities:** Concierge; laundry. *In room:* A/C, TV, minibar, hair dryer.

ELSEWHERE IN PRAGUE
Very Expensive

Hilton Prague *(Overrated* The Hilton was built in a galleria style seemingly out of place in Prague, and its rooms are relatively cushy and functional, somewhat like those in a better-than-average U.S. motel. The location of this modern mammoth just outside the central city isn't ideal, but the hotel has an overpriced Mercedes ready to take you where you want, and the service is pure Hilton.

Pobřežní 1, Praha 8. ℂ **224 841 111.** Fax 224 842 378. www.hilton.com. 788 units. 6,900Kč ($230) double; from 9,450Kč ($315) suite. Breakfast not included. AE, DISC, MC, V. Metro: Florenc. **Amenities:** Restaurant; indoor pool; putting greens; tennis club; health club; sauna; concierge; tour desk; car-rental desk; courtesy limo; business center; 24-hr. room service; massage; laundry; dry cleaning; casino. *In room:* A/C, TV, fax and dataport (executive rooms only), kitchen with coffeemaker (suites only), minibar, hair dryer.

WHERE TO DINE

The true Czech dining experience can be summed up in three native words: *vepřo, knedlo, zelo*—pork, dumplings, cabbage. If that's what you want, try most any *hostinec* (Czech pub). Most offer a hearty *guláš* or pork dish with dumplings and cabbage for about 80Kč to 150Kč ($2.65–$5). After you wash it down with Czech beer, you won't care about the taste—or your arteries.

At most restaurants, menu prices include VAT. Tipping has become more commonplace in restaurants where the staff is obviously trying harder; rounding up the bill to about 10% or more is usually adequate.

STARÉ MĚSTO (OLD TOWN) & JOSEFOV
Expensive

Bellevue *★★* INTERNATIONAL In short, when in Prague, go to the Bellevue (a great castle view), just a few dozen steps from Charles Bridge on the Old Town side of the river. The intelligent menu boasts choice beef, nouvelle sauces, well-dressed fish and game, delicate pastas, and gorgeous desserts. Poached Norwegian salmon glistens in a light herb sauce, and prawns dance on a piquant garlic glaze. Several wild game options stand out, like fallow deer with oysters and mushrooms. The consistent food and presentation and the pleasant and perfectly timed service make dinner at the Bellevue an evening to remember.

Smetanovo nábřeží 18, Praha 1. ℂ **222 221 438.** Reservations recommended. Main courses 490Kč–790Kč ($16–$26); fixed-price menus 1,250Kč–2,190Kč ($42–$73). AE, DC, MC, V. Mon–Sat noon–3pm and 5:30–11pm; Sun 11am–3:30pm (jazz brunch) and 7–11pm (jazz dinner). Metro: Staroměstská.

Tips Snack Alert

Beware: Some restaurants gouge customers by charging exorbitant amounts for nuts or other seemingly free pre-meal snacks left on your table. Ask before you eat.

V zátiší 🌟🌟 INTERNATIONAL   V zátiší ("still life") has a casual elegance, like the living room of a beachfront Mediterranean villa with cushy, upholstered, wrought-iron chairs and plenty of artfully arranged flora. Here, you'll find several fish and game choices, and a scampi that never disappoints. The dessert selections often echo those at the Bellevue, which is run by the same restaurant group.

Liliová 1, Praha 1. ⓒ 222 221 155. Reservations recommended. Main courses 275Kč–775Kč ($9–$26); fixed-price menus 700Kč–1,275Kč ($23–$42). AE, DC, MC, V. Mon–Sat noon–3pm and 5:30–11pm. Metro: Národní Třída.

Moderate

Kogo 🌟🌟 *Value* ITALIAN   This ristorante-pizzeria has become very trendy and popular. Fresh and well-prepared specialties are served by an above-average waitstaff in a pleasant atmosphere. The wide selection of salads, pizza, pasta, and main dishes makes you browse through the menu for a while. Beyond the standard and tasty pasta roster, the *vitello al forno a legna* (roasted veal) should be your choice for 250Kč ($8.30); or try a rare and (for Prague) tasty seafood dish, *cozze al vino bianco e aglio* (mussels in white wine and garlic), for 290Kč ($9.60).

A second Kogo restaurant is located at Na Příkopě 22, Praha 1 (ⓒ 221 451 259; Metro: Můstek).

Havelská 27, Praha 1. ⓒ 224 214 543. Reservations recommended. Main courses 130Kč–400Kč ($4.30–$13). AE, MC, V. Daily 11am–11pm. Metro: Můstek.

La Provence FRENCH   A French country wine cellar meets urban kitsch. The din of the crowd allows you to discuss private matters without too much eavesdropping. La Provence offers a wide array of French Provençal dishes, as well as tangy Italian pastas and the spiciest scampi in Prague. Salads, from Caesar to niçoise, are large and fresh and come with fresh French bread and garlic butter. Weekends often attract drag queens from the Banana Cafe upstairs for a funky lip-synch floor show.

Štupartská 9, Praha 1. ⓒ 257 535 050. Reservations recommended. Main courses 170Kč–650Kč ($5.60–$21). AE, MC, V. Daily 11am–2am. Metro: Náměstí Republiky.

Inexpensive

Creperie Café Gallery Restaurant FRENCH   This more convenient and affordable faux French eatery rests at the foot of Charles Bridge on the Old Town side. Occupying a wing of the St. Francis church complex, the Creperie maintains its links to the Knights of Malta, and does well in approximating the feel of a cozy farmhouse with old wooden chairs and hand-stitched pillows thrown on sturdy benches. The savory galettes are filled with spinach, tangy niva cheese, or chicken, and provide a sufficient light lunch in the middle of a heavy day of trudging. The sweet crepes with chocolate, fruit compote, or whipped cream are good for an afternoon break or dessert following an evening stroll across the bridge. The dining room is split into halves, so try to get a table on the right side of the foyer where the bar is, or you may be forgotten by the waitstaff, who congregate around the tavern.

Křížovnické nám. 3, Praha 1. ⓒ 221 108 240. Crepes and galettes 75Kč–129Kč ($2.50–$4.30). AE, MC, V. Daily 10am–midnight. Metro: Staroměstská.

Pivnice Radegast CZECH   The raucous Radegast dishes up Prague's best pub *gulᚹ* (goulash) in a single narrow vaulted hall, where the namesake Moravian brew seems to never stop flowing from its taps. Around the corner from a bunch of popular bars, the Radegast attracts a good mix of visitors and locals and a young, upwardly mobile crowd.

Templová 2, Praha 1. ℂ **222 328 069.** Main courses 60Kč–240Kč ($2–$8). AE, MC, V. Daily 11am–midnight. Metro: Můstek or Náměstí Republiky.

Pizzeria Rugantino 🜲 *Kids* PIZZA   The wood-fired stoves and handmade dough result in a crisp, delicate crust—a perfect platform for a multitude of cheeses, vegetables, and meats. The Diabolo with fresh garlic bits and very hot chiles goes nicely with a cool iceberg salad and a pull of Krušovice beer. The constant buzz, the nonsmoking area, and heavy childproof wooden tables make this place a family favorite.

Dušní 4, Praha 1. ℂ **222 318 172.** Individual pizzas 100Kč–300Kč ($3.35–$10). No credit cards. Mon–Sat 11am–11pm; Sun 5–11pm. Metro: Staroměstská.

U medvídků 🜲🜲 CZECH   Bright and noisy, the House at the Little Bears serves a better-than-average *vepřo, knedlo,* and *zelo* (pork, dumplings, and cabbage), made with a two-color cabbage. The pub, on the right after you enter, is much cheaper and livelier than the bar to the left. It's a hangout for locals, German tour groups, and foreign journalists in search of the original Czech Budweiser beer, Budvar. In high season, an oompah band plays in the beer wagon.

Na Perštýně 7, Praha 1. ℂ **224 211 916.** Main courses 90Kč–250Kč ($3–$8.35). AE, MC, V. Daily 11am–11pm. Metro: Národní Třída.

NOVÉ MĚSTO (NEW TOWN)
Moderate

Restaurant U Čížků 🜲 *Value* CZECH   One of the city's first private restaurants, this cozy cellar-cum-hunting-lodge on Charles Square can be recognized by the long line of German tour buses outside. The fare is purely Czech, and the massive portions of game, smoked pork, and other meats are guaranteed to stay with you for a while. The traditional *Staročeský talíř* (local pork meat, dumplings, and cabbage) is about as authentically Czech as it gets. The still excellent value earns this pioneer a star.

Karlovo nám. 34, Praha 2. ℂ **222 232 257.** Reservations recommended. Main courses 170Kč–320Kč ($5.60–$11). AE, MC, V. Daily noon–10pm. Metro: Karlovo Náměstí.

Inexpensive

Café-Restaurant Louvre CZECH/INTERNATIONAL   This big, breezy upstairs hall, the artsy restaurant formerly known as Gany's, is great for a coffee, an inexpensive pre-theater meal, or an upscale game of pool. A fabulous Art Nouveau interior with huge original chandeliers buzzes with local coffee talk, the shopping crowd, business lunches, and students. Starters include smoked salmon, battered and fried asparagus, and ham au gratin with vegetables. Main dishes range from trout with horseradish to beans with garlic sauce. Avoid the always-overcooked pastas and stick to the basic meats and fish. In the snazzy billiards parlor in back, drinks and light meals can be served.

Národní třída 20, Praha 1. ℂ **224 930 949.** Reservations not accepted. Main courses 100Kč–300Kč ($3.35–$10). AE, DC, MC, V. Daily 8am–11:30pm. Metro: Národní Třída.

Jarmark 🜲 *Value* CZECH   This is Bohemia's answer to those endless cafeteria lines your parents dragged you through, except this one serves a really tasty variety of meats, sides, and salads, and, of course, beer. And this one is not all-you-can-eat for one price despite its convenient come-and-shove-it-in system. Everyone gets a ticket upon entering, which is validated at each stop you make among the rows of steaming hot tables, veggie carts, and drink dispensers.

Vodičkova 30, Dům "U Nováků." ℂ **224 233 733.** Reservations not accepted. Main courses 70Kč–150Kč ($2.30–$5). No credit cards. Daily 11am–10pm; Mon–Fri breakfast 8am–10am. Metro: Můstek.

Moments Kavárna Society

Cafe life is back in a big way in Prague, now that the Slavia and the Municipal House Kavárna have returned. From dissident blues to high society, these are the places where nonpub Praguers spend their afternoons and evenings, sipping coffee and smoking cigarettes while reading, writing, or talking with friends.

Kavárna Slavia 𝕣, Národní at Smetanovo nábřeží 2, Praha 1 (✆ **224 218 493;** Metro: Národní Třída), reopened in 1997, after a half-decade sleep. The restored crisp Art Deco room recalls the Slavia's 100 years as the meeting place for the city's cultural and intellectual crowd. You'll still find a relatively affordable menu of light fare served with the riverfront views of Prague Castle and the National Theater. The cafe is open daily from 8am to midnight.

The quaint **Café Milena,** Staroměstské nám. 22, Praha 1 (✆ **221 632 602;** Metro: Staroměstská), is managed by the Franz Kafka Society and named for Milena Jesenská, one of the writer's lovers. The draw is a great view of the Orloj, the astronomical clock with the hourly parade of saints on the side of Old Town Square's city hall. It's open daily from 10am to 8pm. American Express, MasterCard, and Visa are accepted.

Of all the beautifully restored spaces in the Municipal House, **Kavárna Obecní dům** 𝕣, nám. Republiky 5, Praha 1 (✆ **222 002 763;** Metro: Náměstí Republiky), might be the most spectacular room. Lofty ceilings, marble accents and tables, an altarlike mantle, huge windows, and period chandeliers provide the awesome setting for coffees, teas, and other drinks, along with pastries and light sandwiches. The cafe is open daily from 7:30am to 11pm, and accepts American Express, MasterCard, and Visa.

In the neighborhood behind the National Theater is **Angel Café** 𝕣, Opatovická 3, Praha 1 (✆ **224 930 019;** Metro: Národní Třída). This cafe best reflects the light-and-bright 1990s restaurant movement captured by Pret A Manger in Britain. Unlike the cash-and-carry Pret, you can sit comfortably in the relaxing Angel atmosphere and linger over tasty sandwiches served with quality cheeses, spreads, and vegetables on fresh bread. French pastries highlight the breakfast lineup along with properly stiff espressos. Who needs Starbucks?

A New Age alternative to the clatter of the kavárnas is **Dahab** 𝕣𝕣, Dlouhá 33, Praha 1 (✆ **224 827 375;** Metro: Náměstí Republiky). This tearoom was founded by Prague's king of tea, Luboš Rychvalský, who introduced the city to Eastern and Arabic tea cultures soon after the 1989 revolution. Here you can choose from about 20 sorts of tea and more than 10 kinds of coffee. Arabic soups, hummus, tahini, couscous, pita, and tempting sweets are on the menu.

MALÁ STRANA
Expensive
Ostroff 𝕣𝕣𝕣 *Finds* ITALIAN   *Note:* This venue was damaged during the floods in August 2002, but was expected to be repaired and operating by the

2003 season. Nowhere else in Prague is Italian as intricately prepared as at Ostroff, on a river island across from the National Theater. Begin with a flaky vegetable flan laden with goat cheese, a wafer-thin sea bass carpaccio, or oysters on the half shell. Follow it with a plate of tagliatelle in a white bean sauce or a fine minestrone soup. Meat and fresh seafood top the entrees, including a tender grilled rack of lamb or entrecôte with rosemary. The daily three-course lunch special is a great value. Before or after your meal, you can have a cocktail at the riverside bar, where a stunning view of the gold-domed National Theater casts a romantic nighttime glow on the Ostroff and your partner.

Střelecký ostrov 336, Praha 1. (*) 224 934 576. www.ostroff.cz. Reservations recommended. Main courses 500Kč–700Kč ($17–$23). AE, MC, V. Mon–Fri noon–2pm; Mon–Sat 7–10:30pm. Tram 6, 9, 22, or 23 to Národní divadlo, then walk midway across the bridge (most Legií), down the stairs to the island below (Střå elecký ostrov).

U Malířů *(*) FRENCH   The owners of U Malířů have given in to the pressure of competition and now offer a more affordable chance to sample the finer attributes of a Parisian kitchen. Surrounded by Romantic-age murals and gorgeously appointed tables in three intimate dining rooms, you're faced with some tough choices. Creamy scallops ragout swim in light vanilla sauce, pikeperch comes with truffles, rack of lamb is glazed in tarragon, and an exotic set of quail chicks bathe in Armagnac. If you want a truly old-world evening of elegant romance and French specialties, U Malířů is finally getting to be worth it.

Maltézské nám. 11, Praha 1. (*) 257 530 000. Reservations recommended. Main courses 520Kč–1,490Kč ($17–$49). Set-price menus 1,190Kč ($39), 1,490Kč ($49), and 2,500Kč ($83). AE, DC, MC, V. Daily 7pm–2am. Metro: Malostranská.

Moderate
U modré kachničky CZECH/WILD GAME   The "Blue Duckling," on a narrow Malá Strana street, tries (and often succeeds at) turning traditional Czech food into Bohemian cuisine, but sometimes its results fall short. The menu is loaded with wild game and quirky spins on Czech village favorites. Try the Malá Strana Templar's Sword, a skewered sampling of several domesticated and wild meats.

Nebovidská 6, Praha 1. (*) 257 320 308. Reservations recommended. Main courses 300Kč–500Kč ($10–$17). AE, MC, V. Daily noon–4pm and 6:30–11:30pm. Metro: Malostranská.

Inexpensive
Bohemia Bagel *(Value)* BAGELS/SANDWICHES   Bohemia Bagel emerged in 1997 at the base of Petřín Hill as the answer to the lazy-morning bagel-less blues. The roster of golden-brown, hand-rolled, stone-baked bagels is stellar. Plain, cinnamon raisin, garlic, or onion provide a sturdy but tender frame for Scandinavian lox and cream cheese or jalapeño-cheddar cheese (on which you can dollop Tex-Mex chili for the Sloppy Bagel). The cushioned wooden booths in an earthy contemporary setting are comfortable.

Újezd 16, Praha 1. (*) 257 310 694. Bagels and sandwiches 25Kč–145Kč (85¢–$4.85). No credit cards. Mon–Fri 7am–midnight; Sat–Sun 8am–midnight. Tram: 6, 9, 12, 22, or 23 to Újezd.

HRADČANY
Expensive
Hradčany Restaurant *(*) INTERNATIONAL   Matching the crisp English setting of the Savoy Hotel in which it resides, the Hradčany is the most elegant choice this side of the castle. The menu lists a variety of beef, pork, and seafood, including succulent poached salmon and lean sliced veal in herb cream sauce. There are also surprises, such as herb-stuffed tortellini and prawns in avocado

mousse. The service sets the standard for Prague, and the new lunch sitting is sure to attract a solid crowd to this jewel beyond the castle gates.

In the Hotel Savoy, Keplerova 8, Praha 1. ⓒ **224 302 150.** Reservations recommended. Main courses 590Kč–790Kč ($20–$26). AE, MC, V. Daily noon–11pm. Tram: 22 or 23, 2 stops past Prague Castle.

Inexpensive

Saté Indonesian Restaurant INDONESIAN   A lunchtime savior near the castle, the Saté has made quite a business out of serving simple Indonesian dishes at simple prices. The unassuming Saté storefront on the same side as the Swedish embassy doesn't scream out to you, so look closely. The pork satay comes in a peanut sauce along with a hearty noodle *mie goreng.* The casual atmosphere eagerly welcomes foot-dragging visitors in search of a bite and a rest.

Pohořelec 3, Praha 1. ⓒ **220 514 552.** Main courses 80Kč–200Kč ($2.65–$6.65). No credit cards. Daily 11am–10pm. Tram: 22 or 23.

IN VINOHRADY
Moderate

Ponte *(Value* INTERNATIONAL   My favorite choice above Wenceslas Square in Vinohrady, Ponte is especially great for shunning the cold of an autumn or winter evening near the roaring fire in the brick cellar dining room. As its name suggests, this place is a bridge between Italian cuisine and other Continental foods. Ponte is also one of the best values in a full-service restaurant in Prague. Beyond the penne and pesto, you can start with black bean soup with bacon and fresh tomato, or tangy spinach salad with chunks of niva cheese. There are several vegetarian and low-calorie, chicken-based selections. Jazz combos play on most nights from a small stage in the corner.

Anglická 15, Praha 2. ⓒ **224 221 665.** Reservations recommended. Main courses 350Kč–500Kč ($12–$17). AE, MC, V. Daily noon–11pm. Metro: I. P. Pavlova or Náměstí Míru.

Inexpensive

Radost FX *&* VEGETARIAN   In vogue and vegetarian, Radost is a clubhouse for hip New Bohemians. The veggie burger is well seasoned and substantial on a grain bun, and the soups, like lentil and onion, are light and full of flavor. The dining area is a dark rec room of upholstered armchairs, chaise lounges, couches from the 1960s, and coffee tables from which you eat.

Bělehradská 120, Praha 2. ⓒ **224 254 776.** Main courses 100Kč–250Kč ($3.35–$8.35). MC, V. Daily 10am–5am. Metro: I. P. Pavlova.

SEEING THE SIGHTS

In Prague, you'll get the most enjoyment from a slow, aimless wander through the city's heart. Except for the busy main streets, where you may have to dodge traffic, Prague is ideal for walking—really the only way to explore the city. Most of the city's oldest areas are walking zones, with motor traffic restricted. If you have the time and energy, absorb the grand architecture of Prague Castle and the Old Town skyline (best from Charles Bridge) at sunrise and then at sunset. You'll see two completely different cities.

SIGHTSEEING SUGGESTIONS FOR FIRST-TIME VISITORS

If You Have 1 Day If you have only 1 day, do what visiting kings and potentates do on a short visit:

Walk the **Royal Route** from the top of the Hradčany hill (tram nos. 22 or 23 or a taxi are suggested for the ride up unless you're very fit). Tour **Prague Castle,** and then stroll across Charles Bridge on the way to the winding alleys of **Staré Město (Old Town).**

If You Have 2 Days On day 2, explore the varied sights of **Staré Město (Old Town), Malá Strana (Lesser Town),** and **Josefov (the Jewish Quarter).** Wander and browse through numerous shops and galleries offering the finest Bohemian crystal, porcelain, and modern artwork, as well as top boutiques, cafes, and restaurants.

If You Have 3 Days On day 3, visit the **National Art Gallery** at Šternberk Palace and the **Strahov Monastery** with its ornate libraries. Include the **Loreto Palace,** with its peculiar artwork.

If You Have 4 or 5 Days Beyond day 3, tour one of the many other museums or galleries. For a great respite from the crowded city, visit the old southern citadel over the Vltava, **Vyšehrad,** where you get a completely different view of the city you've just explored.

PRAGUE CASTLE & CHARLES BRIDGE

Dating from the 14th century, **Karlův most (Charles Bridge)** 𝒜𝒜𝒜, Prague's most celebrated structure, links Prague Castle to Staré Město. For most of its 600 years, the 518m (1,700-ft.) span has been a pedestrian promenade, although for centuries walkers had to share the concourse with horse-drawn vehicles and trolleys. Today, the bridge is filled with hordes walking among folksy artists and street musicians.

The best times to stroll across the bridge are in early morning and around sunset, when the crowds have thinned and the shadows are more mysterious. You'll be crisscrossing the bridge throughout your stay.

Pražský Hrad (Prague Castle) 𝒜𝒜𝒜 *(Moments* The huge hilltop complex known collectively as Pražský Hrad encompasses dozens of towers, churches, courtyards, and monuments. A visit could easily take an entire day or more. Still, you can see the top sights—St. Vitus Cathedral, the Royal Palace, St. George's Basilica, the Powder Tower, plus Golden Lane—in the space of a morning or an afternoon.

Chrám sv. Víta (St. Vitus Cathedral) 𝒜, constructed in A.D. 926 as the court church of the Premyslid princes, was named for a wealthy 4th-century Sicilian martyr and has long been the center of Prague's religious and political life. The key part of its Gothic construction took place in the 14th century. In the 18th and 19th centuries, subsequent baroque and neo-Gothic additions were made. In 1997, Pope John Paul II visited Prague to honor the 1,000th anniversary of the death of 10th-century Slavic evangelist St. Vojtěch.

Královský palác (the Royal Palace) 𝒜, in the third courtyard of the castle grounds, served as the residence of kings between the 10th and the 17th centuries. Vaulted Vladislav Hall, the interior's centerpiece, was used for coronations and is still used for inauguration of the Czech presidents and for special occasions. The adjacent Diet was where the king met with advisers and where the supreme court was held. You'll find a good selection of guidebooks, maps, and related information at the entrance.

Kostel sv. Jiří (St. George's Basilica), adjacent to the Royal Palace, is Prague's oldest Romanesque structure, dating from the 10th century. It was also Bohemia's first convent, which now houses a museum of historic Czech art.

Zlatá ulička (Golden Lane) is a picturesque, fairy-tale street of tiny 16th-century servants' houses built into the castle fortifications. The houses now contain shops, galleries, and refreshment bars. In 1917, Franz Kafka lived briefly at no. 22.

Prašná věž, aka Mihulka **(the Powder Tower)** forms part of the northern bastion of the castle complex just off the Golden Lane. Originally a gunpowder storehouse and a cannon tower, it was turned into a laboratory for the 17th-century alchemists serving the court of Emperor Rudolf II.

Tickets are sold at the **Prague Castle Information Center** (© **224 373 368**), in the second courtyard after you pass through the main gate from Hradčanské náměstí. The center also arranges tours in various languages and sells tickets for individual concerts and exhibits.

Hradčanské nám., Hradčany, Praha 1. © **224 373 368.** Fax 224 310 896. www.hrad.cz. Grounds free. Combination ticket to 5 main attractions (St. Vitus Cathedral, Royal Palace, St. George's Basilica, Powder Tower, Golden Lane): without guide, 220Kč ($7.30) adults, 110Kč ($3.65) students; with English-speaking guide, 300Kč ($10) adults, 190Kč ($6.30) students. Guided tours for group of 5 and more. (guided tours only Tues–Sun 9am–4pm). V. Ticket valid 1 day. Castle daily 9am–5pm (to 4pm Nov–Mar). Metro: Malostranská, then tram 22 or 23, up the hill 2 stops.

THE JEWISH MUSEUM

The Jewish Museum manages all the Jewish landmarks in Josefov, which forms the northwest quarter of Old Town. The museum offers English-language guided package tours as part of a comprehensive admission price. The package includes the Ceremonial Hall, Old Jewish Cemetery, Pinkas Synagogue, Klaus Synagogue, Maisel Synagogue, and Spanish Synagogue.

Maisel Synagogue Maisel Synagogue is used as the exhibition space for the Jewish Museum. Most of Prague's ancient Judaica was destroyed by the Nazis during World War II. Ironically, those same Germans constructed an "exotic museum of an extinct race," thus salvaging thousands of objects, such as the valued Torah covers, books, and silver now displayed here.

Maiselova 10 (between Široká and Jáchymova 3), Praha 1. © **222 317 191.** Fax 222 317 181. www.jewish museum.cz. Admission to the 6 museum sites listed above is 290Kč ($9.65) adults, 200Kč ($6.65) students. Apr–Oct open daily except Sat and Jewish holidays 9am–6pm; Nov–Mar daily 9am–4:30pm. Metro: Staroměstská.

Staronová synagoga (Old-New Synagogue) ⊛ First called the New Synagogue to distinguish it from an even older one that no longer exists, the Old-New Synagogue, built around 1270, is Europe's oldest Jewish house of worship. Jews have prayed here continuously for more than 700 years, carrying on even after a massive 1389 pogrom in Josefov that killed more than 3,000 Jews. Worship was interrupted only between 1941 and 1945, during the Nazi occupation. The synagogue is also one of Prague's largest Gothic buildings, with vaulted ceilings and Renaissance-era columns.

Červená 3. © **222 317 191.** Admission 200Kč ($6.65) adults, 140Kč ($4.65) students. Sun–Thurs 9am–6pm; Fri 9am–5pm. Metro: Staroměstská.

Starý židovský hřbitov (Old Jewish Cemetery) ⊛ Dating from the mid–15th century, this is one of Europe's oldest Jewish burial grounds, 1 block from the Old-New Synagogue. Because the local government of the time didn't allow Jews to bury their dead elsewhere, graves were dug deep enough to hold 12 bodies vertically, with each tombstone placed in front of the last. The result is one of the world's most crowded cemeteries: a 1-block area filled with more than 20,000 graves. Among the most famous persons buried here are the celebrated Rabbi Loew (died 1609), who created the legendary Golem (a clay "monster" to protect Prague's Jews). The adjoining Ceremonial Hall at the end of the path is worth a look for the heart-wrenching drawings by children held at the Terezín concentration camp during World War II (see "Day Trips from Prague," later in this chapter, for more on Terezín).

U Starého hřbitova 3A. © **222 317 191.** Fax 222 317 181. www.jewishmuseum.cz. Admission to all Jewish Museum sites, except Old-New Synagogue, 290Kč ($9.65) adults, 200Kč ($6.65) students. Sun–Fri 9am–6pm. Metro: Staroměstská.

THE NATIONAL GALLERY

The national collection of fine art is grouped for display in the series of venues known collectively as the **Národní Galerie** (**National Gallery;** www.ngprague. cz). Remember, this term refers to several locations, not just one gallery.

The most extensive collection of classic European works spanning the 14th to 18th centuries is found at the Archbishop's Palace complex in the **Šternberský palác** across from the main gate to Prague Castle. **Veletržní Palace** houses most of the 20th-century art collection, and now also shows the important national revival works from Czech artists of the 19th century. While much of the national collection is shown at **Kinský Palace** on Old Town Square, Gothic pieces may be seen at **St. George's Convent** at Prague Castle, and 19th-century Czech painters and sculptors are shown at **St. Agnes Convent** near the river in Old Town.

Šternberk palác (Šternberský Palace) ✻   The jewel in the National Gallery crown (also known casually as the European Art Museum), the gallery at Šternberský Palace, adjacent to the main gate of Prague Castle, displays a wide menu of European art throughout the ages. It features 5 centuries of everything from Orthodox icons to Renaissance oils by Dutch masters. Pieces by Rembrandt, El Greco, Goya, and Van Dyck are mixed among numerous pieces by Austrian imperial-court painters.

Hradčanské nám. 15, Praha 1. © **220 514 634.** Admission 100Kč ($3.35) adults, 50Kč ($1.65) students and children. Tues–Sun 10am–6pm. Metro: Malostranská or Hradčanská. Tram: 22 or 23.

Klášter sv. Anežky české (St. Agnes Convent)   This complex of early Gothic buildings and churches dates from the 13th century. The convent, tucked in a corner of Staré Město, is scheduled to feature 19th century Czech painters and sculptors.

U milosrdný ch 17, Praha 1. © **224 810 628.** Admission 100Kč ($3.35) adults, 50Kč ($1.65) children. Tues–Sun 10am–6pm. Metro: Staroměstská.

Klášter sv. Jiří na Pražském hradě (St. George's Convent at Prague Castle)   Dedicated to displaying traditional Czech art, the castle convent is especially packed with Gothic and baroque Bohemian iconography as well as portraits of patron saints. The most famous among the unique collection of Czech Gothic panel paintings are those by "the Master of the Hohenfurth Altarpiece" and the Master Theodoricus.

Jiřské nám. 33. © **257 531 644.** Admission 50Kč ($1.65) adults, 20Kč (65¢) students. Tues–Sun 10am–6pm. Metro: Malostranská or Hradčanská. Tram: 22 or 23.

Palác Kinských (Kinský Palace) ✻ *Finds*   This rococo palace houses graphic works from the National Gallery collection, including pieces by Georges Braque, André Derain, and other modern masters. Pablo Picasso's 1907 *Self-Portrait* is here and has virtually been adopted as the National Gallery's logo.

Staroměstské nám. 12, Praha 1. © **224 810 758.** Admission 100Kč ($3.35) adults, 50Kč ($1.65) students. Tues–Sun 10am–6pm. Metro: Line A to Staroměstská.

National Gallery The 1925 constructivist Veletržní Palace, built for trade fairs, holds the bulk of the National Gallery's collection of 20th-century works by Czech and other European artists. Three atrium-lit concourses provide a comfortable setting for some catchy and kitschy Czech sculpture and multimedia works. Alas, the best cubist works from Braque and Picasso, Rodin bronzes, and many other primarily French pieces have been relegated to the second floor. Other displays are devoted to peculiar works by Czech artists that demonstrate how creativity flowed even under the weight of the Iron Curtain.

Veletržní at Dukelských hrdinů 47, Praha 7. ℭ **224 301 111.** Admission to all 3 floors 200Kč ($6.65) adults, 100Kč ($3.35) students; to 2 floors 150Kč ($5) adults, 70Kč ($2.35) students; to 1 floor 100Kč ($3.35) adults, 50Kč ($1.65) students. Free admission 1st Wed of each month. Tues–Sun 10am–6pm. Metro: Vltavská. Tram: 5,12 or 17 to Veletržní stop.

FAMOUS SQUARES

The most celebrated square, **Staroměstské náměstí (Old Town Square),** is surrounded by baroque buildings and packed with colorful craftspeople, cafes, and entertainers. In ancient days, the site was a major crossroads on central European merchant routes. At its center stands a memorial to Jan Hus, the 15th-century martyr who crusaded against Prague's German-dominated religious and political establishment and the persecution of Czech nationalists. Unveiled in 1915, on the 500th anniversary of Hus's execution, the Art Nouveau monument's most compelling features are the asymmetry of the composition and the fluidity of the figures.

The **Orloj (Astronomical Clock)** at Staroměstská radnice (Old Town Hall) performs a glockenspiel spectacle daily on the hour from 8am to 8pm. Originally constructed in 1410, the clock has long been an important symbol of Prague.

Václavské náměstí (Wenceslas Sq.), a former horse market, has thrice been the focal point of riots and revolutions—in 1918, 1968, and 1989.

MORE ATTRACTIONS

Bertramka (W. A. Mozart Museum) Mozart loved Prague, and when he visited he often stayed with the family that owned this villa, the Dušeks. Now a museum, the villa contains displays that include his written work and harpsichord. There's also a lock of Mozart's hair, encased in a cube of glass. Much of the Bertramka villa was destroyed by fire in the 1870s, but Mozart's rooms, where he finished composing *Don Giovanni,* miraculously remained untouched.

Mozartova 169, Praha 5. ℭ **257 318 461.** Admission 90Kč ($3) adults, 70Kč ($2.35) students. Daily 9:30am–6pm. Metro: Anděl, then tram 4, 6, 7, 9, 10, 14, or 16.

Stavovské divadlo (Estates' Theater) ⑂ The theater was completed in 1783 by the wealthy Count F. A. Nostitz. There are no daily tours, but tickets for performances—and the chance to sit in one of the elegant private boxes—are

---

Fun Fact **Mozart in Prague**

Mozart staged the premier of *Don Giovanni* at the Estates' Theater in 1787 because he felt the conservative patrons in Vienna didn't appreciate him or his passionate and often shocking work. "Praguers understand me," Mozart was quoted as saying. Czech director Miloš Forman returned to his native country to film his Oscar-winning *Amadeus,* shooting the scenes of Mozart in Prague with perfect authenticity at the Estates'.

usually available. Tour events are occasionally scheduled, and you can arrange individual tours by calling the city heritage group of Pražská informační služba (PIS; ✆ 224 901 487; www.pis.cz).

Ovocný trh 1, Praha 1. ✆ 224 901 448. Metro: Můstek.

Strahovský klášter a knihovna (Strahov Monastery and Library) ⚜

The second-oldest monastery in Prague, Strahov was founded high above Malá Strana in 1143 by Vladislav II. It's still home to Premonstratensian monks, a scholarly order closely related to the Jesuits, and their dormitories and refectory are off-limits. What draws visitors are the monastery's ornate libraries, holding more than 125,000 volumes.

Strahovské nádvoří 1, Praha 1. ✆ 220 516 695. Admission 30Kč ($1) adults, 15Kč (50¢) students. Tues–Sun 9am–noon and 1–5pm. Metro: Malostranská, then tram 22 or 23.

Chrám sv. Mikuláše (Cathedral of St. Nicholas)

This church is critically regarded as one of the best examples of the high baroque north of the Alps. K. I. Dienzenhofer's 1711 design was augmented by his son Kryštof's 80m (260-ft.) dome, which has dominated the Malá Strana skyline since its completion in 1752. Prague's smog has played havoc with the building's exterior, but its gilded interior is stunning. Gold-capped marble-veneered columns frame altars packed with statuary and frescoes.

Malostranské nám., Praha 1. ✆ 257 534 215. Free admission. Daily 9am–5pm; concerts are usually held at 5pm. Metro: Malostranská, then tram 12, 22, or 23 one stop to Malostranské nám.

PARKS & GARDENS

From **Vyšehrad**, Soběslavova 1 (✆ **224 920 735;** tram 3 from Karlovo náměstí to Výtoň south of New Town), legend has it that Princess Libuše looked out over the Vltava valley toward the present-day Prague Castle and predicted the founding of a great state and capital city. Vyšehrad was the seat of the first Czech kings of the Premyslid dynasty before the dawn of this millennium. Today, within the confines of the citadel, lush lawns and gardens are crisscrossed by dozens of paths leading to historic buildings and cemeteries. From here you'll see one of the city's most panoramic views.

Královská zahrada (The Royal Garden) at Prague Castle, once the site of the sovereigns' vineyards, was founded in 1534. Dotted with lemon trees and surrounded by 16th-, 17th-, and 18th-century buildings, the garden is laid out with abundant shrubbery and fountains. Enter from U Prašného mostu (the street north of the castle complex).

In Hradčany, the castle's **Zahrada na Valech (Garden on the Ramparts),** below the castle with a gorgeous city panorama, was reopened in spring 1995 after being thoroughly refurbished. The park is open Tuesday through Sunday from 9am to 5pm. Part of the excitement of **Wallenstein Valdštejnská zahrada (Waldstein Gardens)** is its location, behind a 9m (30-ft.) wall on the back streets of Malá Strana. Inside, elegant, leafy gravel paths, dotted by classical bronze statues and gurgling fountains, fan out in every direction. Recently refurbished sections include the Ledeburská, the Small and Great Pálffyovská, the Kolowratská, and the Small Furstenberská gardens. All of the gardens are open Tuesday through Sunday from 9am to 6pm (most of them are closed during winter months).

THE SHOPPING SCENE

Czech porcelain, glass, and cheap but well-constructed clothing draw hordes of day-trippers from Germany. Private retailers have been allowed to operate here

---

Value **A Special Group Tour**

If you're traveling in a large group and want a unique sightseeing experience, why not rent your own classic trolley? With enough people, it really is affordable, thanks to the **Historic Tram Tour** (Elektrické dráhy DP), Patočkova 4, Praha 6 (© **233 343 349;** fax 296 124 901).

If you send a fax with details 1 day ahead, the city transport department can arrange a private tour using one of the century-old wooden trams that once traveled on regular lines through Prague. Up to 24 people can fit in one car, which sports wood-planked floors, cast-iron conductor's levers, and the "ching-ching" of a proper tram bell. A tour costs 3,255Kč ($109) per hour. Up to 60 people can fit into a double car for 4,368Kč ($146) per hour. You can order a cold smorgasbord with coffee, beer, champagne, a waiter to serve you, and an accordion player. You can choose the route the tram takes—the no. 22 route is the best.

---

only since late 1989, but many top international retailers have already arrived. Shops lining the main route from Old Town Square to Charles Bridge are also great for browsing. For clothing, porcelain, jewelry, garnets, and glass, stroll around Wenceslas Square and Na Příkopě, connecting Wenceslas Square with náměstí Republiky.

For glass and crystal, try **Moser,** at Na Příkopě 12, Praha 1 (© **224 228 686;** Metro: Můstek), or at Malé nám. 11, Praha 1 (© **221 611 520;** Metro: Můstek). The Moser family began selling Bohemia's finest crystal in central Prague in 1857, drawing customers from around the world. The store at Na Příkopě is open Monday through Friday from 9am to 8pm, Saturday and Sunday from 10am to 6pm; the Malé náměstí store is open Monday through Friday from 10am to 7pm, Saturday and Sunday from 10am to 6pm.

Celetná Crystal, Celetná 15, Praha 1 (© **224 811 376;** Metro: Náměstí Republiky), has a wide selection of world-renowned Czech crystal, china, arts and crafts, and jewelry displayed in a spacious three-floor showroom right in the heart of Prague. At **Cristallino,** Celetná 12, Praha 1 (© **224 223 027;** Metro: Náměstí Republiky), you'll find a good selection of stemware and vases in traditional designs. The shop's central location belies its excellent prices.

Havelskýtrh (Havel's Market), Havelská ulice, Praha 1 (Metro: Můstek), is on a short street running perpendicular to Melantrichova, the main route connecting Staroměstské náměstí with Václavské náměstí. This open-air market (named well before a Havel became president in 1989) features dozens of private vendors selling seasonal homegrown fruits and vegetables. Other goods, including flowers and cheese, are also for sale. Since this place is designed primarily for locals, the prices are exceedingly low by western European standards. The market is open Monday through Friday from 7am to 6pm.

PRAGUE AFTER DARK

Prague's nightlife has changed completely since the Velvet Revolution—for the better if you plan to go clubbing, for the worse if you hope to sample the city's classical offerings. Still, seeing *Don Giovanni* in the Estates' Theater, where Mozart first premiered it, is worth the admission. Ticket prices, while low by western European standards, have become prohibitively high for the average

Czech. However, you'll find the exact reverse in the rock and jazz scene. Dozens of clubs have opened, and world-class bands are finally adding Prague to their European tours.

Turn to the *Prague Post* (www.praguepost.cz) for listings of cultural events and nightlife around the city; it's available at most newsstands in Old Town and Malá Strana.

Once in Prague, you can buy tickets at theater box offices or from any one of dozens of agencies throughout the city center. Large, centrally located agencies (take the Metro to Můstek for all) are **Prague Tourist Center,** Rytířská 12, Praha 1 (© **224 212 209**), open daily from 9am to 8pm; **Bohemia Ticket International,** Na Příkopě 16, Praha 1 (© **224 215 031**); and **Čedok,** Na Příkopě 18, Praha 1 (© **224 197 640**).

THE PERFORMING ARTS

Although there's plenty of music year-round, the symphonies and orchestras all come to life during the **Prague Spring Music Festival,** a 3-week series of concerts featuring the country's top performers, as well as noted guest conductors, soloists, and visiting symphony orchestras. The festival runs from May 12 to June 2. Tickets for concerts are 250Kč to 2,000Kč ($8.35–$66).

The **Czech Philharmonic** and **Prague Symphony** orchestras usually perform at the **Rudolfinum,** náměstí Jana Palacha, Praha 1 (© **227 059 352;** Metro: Staroměstská). The Czech Philharmonic is the traditional voice of the country's national pride, often playing works by Dvořák and Smetana; the Prague Symphony phony ventures into more eclectic territory. Tickets are 100Kč to 600Kč ($3.35–$20). Ticket orders and purchases can be made in advance (and you are advised to book well in advance) through the agency **TICKETPRO,** Salvátorská 10, 110 00 Praha 1, Czech Republic (© **296 329 999;** fax 296 328 888; www.ticketpro.cz). All major credit cards are accepted.

Any remaining tickets are sold at the venues of the performances, which have various opening hours, but usually few seats remain within a month of the festival.

In a city full of spectacularly beautiful theaters, the massive pale-green **Stavovské divadlo (Estates' Theater),** Ovocny trh 1, Praha 1 (© **224 215 001;** Metro: Můstek), is one of the most awesome. Built in 1783 and site of the premiere of Mozart's *Don Giovanni* (conducted by the composer), the theater now hosts many of the classic productions of European opera and drama. Simultaneous English translation, transmitted via headphone, is available for most plays. Tickets cost 200Kč to 1,000Kč ($6.65–$33).

Lavishly constructed in the late-Renaissance style of northern Italy, the goldcrowned **Národní divadlo (National Theater),** Národní třída 2, Praha 1 (© **224 901 448;** Metro: Národní Třída), overlooking the Vltava River, is one of Prague's most recognizable landmarks. Completed in 1881, the theater was built to nurture the Czech National Revival—a grassroots movement to replace the dominant German culture with that of native Czechs. Today, classic productions are staged here in a larger setting than at the Estates' Theater, but with about the same ticket prices.

The **National Theater Ballet** performs at the National Theater. The troupe has seen most of its top talent go west since 1989, but it still puts on a good show. Some critics complained that Prague's top company had been performing virtually the same dances for many years, and that they were in serious need of refocusing. Choreographer Libor Vaculík responded with humorous and quirky stagings of off-the-wall ballets such as *Some Like It Hot* and *Psycho.* Tickets cost 200Kč to 600Kč ($6.65–$20).

Laterna Magika, Národní třída 4, Praha 1 (© **224 931 482;** Metro: Národní Třída), is a performance-art show in the new wing of the National Theater. The multimedia show, which combines live theater with film and dance, was once considered on the radical edge. The shows are not for those easily offended by nudity. Tickets are 400Kč ($13).

THE CLUB & MUSIC SCENE

Prague's club and music scene is limited but lively. Local acts still have a garage-band sound but are adding more sophisticated numbers to their gigs. Many venerable jazz groups who toiled in the cellar clubs are finding a new audience in visitors who stumble upon their smoky underground venues. It is no longer a huge shock to see well-known western European bands playing sets in Prague.

JAZZ CLUBS Upscale by Czech standards, **AghaRTA Jazz Centrum,** Krakovská 5, Praha 1 (© **222 211 275;** Metro: Muzeum), regularly features some of the best music in town, from standard acoustic trios to Dixieland, funk, and fusion. Hot Line, the house band led by AghaRTA part-owner and drummer extraordinaire Michal Hejna, regularly takes the stage with its keyboard-and-sax Crusaders-like sound. Bands usually begin at 9pm. The club is open Monday through Friday from 5pm to 1am and Saturday and Sunday from 7pm to 1am. Cover is 100Kč ($3.35). **Reduta Jazz Club,** Národní třída 20, Praha 1 (© **224 933 487;** Metro: Národní Třída), is a smoky subterranean room that looks exactly like a jazz cellar should. An adventurous booking policy, which even included a saxophone gig with a U.S. president in 1994, means that different bands play almost every night. Music usually starts around 9pm. Hours are from 9pm to midnight; cover is usually 100Kč ($3.35).

PUBS & BARS

You'll experience true Czech entertainment in only one kind of place—a smoky local pub serving some of the world's best beer. Remember to put a cardboard coaster in front of you to show you want a mug, and never wave for service, as the typically surly waiter will just ignore you.

Originally a brewery dating from 1459, **U Fleků,** Křemencova 11, Praha 2 (© **224 934 019;** Metro: Národní Třída), is Prague's most famous beer hall, and one of the only pubs that still brews its own beer. This huge place has a myriad of timber-lined rooms and a large, loud courtyard where an oompah band performs. Tourists come here by the busload, so U Fleků is avoided by disparaging locals who don't like its German atmosphere anyway. The pub's special dark beer is excellent, however, and not available anywhere else. It's open daily from 9am to 11pm.

One of the most famous Czech pubs, **U Zlatého tygra,** Husova 17, Praha 1 (© **222 221 111;** Metro: Staroměstská or Můstek), was a favorite watering hole of former president Václav Havel and the late writer Bohumil Hrabal. Particularly smoky, and not especially tourist friendly, "At the Golden Tiger" is a one-stop education in Czech culture. Václav Havel and Bill Clinton joined Hrabal for a traditional Czech pub evening here during Clinton's 1994 visit to Prague. It's open daily from 3 to 11pm.

DAY TRIPS FROM PRAGUE

KARLŠTEJN CASTLE By far the most popular day trip from Prague, this medieval castle, 30km (18 miles) southwest of Prague, which has been restored to its original state, was built by Charles IV in the 14th century to safeguard the crown jewels of the Holy Roman Empire. As you approach, little can prepare you for your first view: a spectacular castle perched high on a hill, surrounded by lush forests and vineyards. The Holy Rood Chapel is famous for the more than 2,000 precious and semiprecious inlaid gems that adorn its walls, and the Chapel of St. Catherine was King Karel IV's private oratory. Both the Audience Hall and the Imperial Bedroom are impressive, despite being stripped of their original furnishings. To see the Holy Rood Chapel you need to make a reservation (© 274 008 154; fax 274 008 152; www.spusc.cz or www.hradkarlstejn.cz).

Admission for a short tour is 200Kč ($6.65) adults and 100Kč ($3.35) students; the longer tour with the Holy Rood Chapel is 300Kč ($10) adults, 100Kč ($5) students. The castle is open Tuesday through Sunday: May, June, and September from 9am to noon and 12:30 to 5pm; July and August from 9am to noon and 12:30 to 6pm; April and October from 9am to noon and 1 to 4pm; November, December, and March from 9am to noon and 1 to 3pm; closed January and February.

Getting There   The best way to get to Karlštejn is by **train** (there's no bus service). Most trains leave from Prague's Smíchov Station (Metro: Smíchovské Nádraží) hourly throughout the day (trip time: 30 min.). One-way second-class fare is 40Kč ($1.35). You can also **drive:** Leave Prague on Highway 4 southwest in the direction of Strakonice and take the Karlštejn cutoff, following the signs (and traffic!).

TEREZÍN (THERESIENSTADT)   *Note:* This site was damaged during the floods in August 2002, but it was expected to be operating (at least partially) by the 2003 season. The name Terezín (Theresienstadt in German) occupies a unique place in the atrocious history of Nazism. This former Austro-Hungarian imperial fortress, turned into a concentration camp, 50km (30 miles) northwest of Prague, witnessed no gas chambers, mass machine-gun executions, or medical testing; it was used instead as a transit camp. About 140,000 people passed though Terezín's gates; many died here, and more than half ended up at the death camps of Auschwitz and Treblinka.

Terezín stands as a memorial to the dead and a monument to human depravity. Once inside the **Major Fortress,** you'll immediately be struck by its drab, plain streets. Just off the main square lies the **Museum of the Ghetto,** chronicling the rise of Nazism and life in the camp. English pamphlets describing the exhibits are provided. Admission is 140Kč ($4.65) adults and 110Kč ($3.65) children. A ticket to enter both the **Minor Fortress** and the **Museum of the Ghetto** is 160Kč ($5.35) adults and 120Kč ($4) children. The Minor Fortress is open daily October through March from 8am to 4:30pm and April through September from 8am to 6pm. The Museum of the Ghetto is open daily October through March from 9am to 5:30pm and April through September from 9am to 6pm. The Minor Fortress is about a 10-minute walk from the Major Fortress over the Ohře River. Just in front of the fortress's main entrance is the **Národní hřbitov (National Cemetery),** where the bodies exhumed from the mass graves were buried. As you enter the main gate, the sign above it, ARBEIT MACHT FREI (Work Sets One Free), sets a gloomy tone. You can walk through the prison barracks, execution grounds, workshops, and isolation cells. For more information or reservations for the guided tour, phone © **416 782 225,** fax 416 782 300, or visit www.pamatnik-terezin.cz.

Getting There   Terezín is a 45-minute **drive** from Prague, on the main highway north towards Berlin via Dresden. Six **buses** leave daily from Florenc Bus Station (trip time: 1 hr.). The Prague-based **AHARON travel** (© **235 353 589;** www.aharontravel.cz) organizes a 6-hour tour with guides that includes lunch, a documentary, and transportation, well worth 1,300Kč ($43). The bus leaves daily (except Sat and Jewish holidays) at 10am from Maiselova 15, from April to September only.

2 West Bohemia & the Spas

The Czech Republic is composed of two regions: Bohemia and Moravia. The larger of the two, Bohemia, occupying the central and western areas of the country, has for centuries been caught between a rock (Germany) and a hard place (Austria). Bohemia was almost always at the center of regional conflicts, both secular and religious. But the area also flourished, as witnessed by the wealth of castles that dot the countryside and the spa towns that were once the playgrounds of the rich and famous.

Although Bohemia is historically undivided, there are clear-cut distinctions in the region's geography that make going from town to town easier if you "cut" Bohemia into sections. This section focuses on west Bohemia, home to the country's spa towns. It's also one of the few regions in the Czech Republic where a full-blown tourist infrastructure is already in place. Its main towns—Karlovy Vary (Carlsbad), Mariánské Lázně (Marienbad), and, to a lesser extent, Plzeň and Cheb—offer a wide array of accommodations, restaurants, and services. All are constantly being reconstructed and restored.

A relatively inexpensive network of trains and buses covers the region. West Bohemia is generally rougher terrain, so only serious cyclists should consider touring the area on two wheels. For those with a car, the highways can range from top-notch, such as the Prague–Plzeň motorway, to an asphalt horror ride such as the Prague–Karlovy Vary route. Roads generally are much slower than in western Europe, so leave yourself plenty of time. Gas stations are constantly springing up, so stops for food and fuel are rarely hard to come by. *Note:* If you drive the D-5 (Prague–Plzeň) and D-1 (Prague–Brno) highways, your car must display the country's highway sticker. These stickers, which you can buy at most gas stations and border crossings, cost 100Kč ($3.35) for 10 days, 200Kč ($6.65) for 1 month, and 800Kč ($26) for 1 year; they save you from being hassled by the police.

Most towns are distant enough that you should drive from one to another. However, if you'd rather stay in one place and make day trips, we recommend staying in Karlovy Vary. The **Kur-Info,** Vřídelní kolonáda, 360 01 Karlovy Vary (© **353 229 312;** fax 353 224 667; www.karlovyvary.cz/ruzne/kurinfo.htm), can provide information on bus trips to Mariánské Lázně and other regional sights.

KARLOVY VARY (CARLSBAD)

The discovery of Karlovy Vary (Carlsbad), 120km (75 miles) west of Prague, by Charles IV reads something like a 14th-century episode of *The Beverly Hillbillies.* According to local lore, the king was out huntin' for food when up from the ground came a-bubblin' water (though discovered by his dogs, not an errant gunshot). Knowing a good thing when he saw it, Charles immediately set to work building a small castle, naming the town that evolved around it Karlovy Vary

(Charles's Boiling Place). The first spa buildings were built in 1522, and before long, notables like Albrecht of Wallenstein, Russian Czar Peter the Great, and later Bach, Beethoven, Freud, Goethe, and Marx, all came to take the waters.

After World War II, East Bloc travelers (following in the footsteps of Marx, no doubt) discovered the town, and Karlovy Vary became a destination for the proletariat. On doctors' orders, most workers enjoyed regular stays of 2 or 3 weeks, letting the mineral waters ranging from 110°F to 162°F (44°C–72°C) from the town's 12 spas heal their tired and broken bodies. Even now, most spa guests are there by doctor's prescription.

Most of the 40-plus years of Communist neglect have been erased by a barrage of renovators bent on restoring the spa's former glory. Gone is the statue of Yuri Gagarin, the Russian cosmonaut. Gone are almost all the crumbling building facades that used to line both sides of the river. In their places now stand restored buildings, cherubs, caryatids, and more.

Nearly 100,000 people travel annually to the spa resort to sip, bathe, and frolic. Most enjoy the "13th spring," actually a local figure of speech denoting a hearty herb-and-mineral liqueur called Becherovka that is favored over the non-alcoholic versions available at the 12 previous springs. Czechs will tell you that all have medicinal benefits.

ESSENTIALS

GETTING THERE   By Train   At all costs, avoid the train from Prague (trip time: over 4 hr.). If you're arriving from another direction, Karlovy Vary's main train station is connected to the town center by bus no. 11.

By Bus   Frequent express buses make the trip from Prague's Florenc station, platform 21 or 22, to Karlovy Vary (trip time: 2½ hr.); tickets cost 55Kč ($1.65). Take a 10-minute walk or local bus no. 4 into Karlovy Vary's center. Note that you must have a ticket to board local transport. You can buy tickets for 8Kč (25¢) at the main station stop or, if you have no change, the kiosk across the street sells tickets during regular business hours.

By Car   The drive from Prague isn't difficult but can be at times a little hair-raising (trip time: 2 hr.). Take Highway E-48 from the western end of the city and follow it straight through to Karlovy Vary. This two-lane highway widens in a few spots to let cars pass slow-moving vehicles on hills.

VISITOR INFORMATION   **Kur-Info,** inside the Vřídelní kolonáda (© **353 229 312**), is open April through October, Monday through Friday from 7am to 5pm, Saturday and Sunday from 9am to 3pm; November through March it's open Monday through Friday from 7am to 4pm. It provides accommodation services, arranges guided tours and spa treatments, and sells tickets for some events. Pick up the *Cultural Calendar,* a comprehensive collection of events with a small map of the town center.

There are also two privately run **Info-Centrum** booths: one in the train station and the other in a parking lot at the base of Jana Palacha ulice. Both give

---

⎛Tips Warning to Drivers

Be warned that Highway E-48 from Prague to Karlovy Vary is a popular route for reckless drivers heading to and from the capital. Please take extra care when driving.

away free maps and a brochure of current cultural listings and events called *Promenáda*. Info-Centrum also books accommodations in private rooms and sells tours. For more information about this spa town, visit **www.spas.cz/ karlovyvary**.

SPECIAL EVENTS   The **International Film Festival Karlovy Vary** is one of the few places to see and be seen. Each summer (1st 2 weeks of July), film stars and celebrities take part in one of Europe's biggest film festivals. Six venues screen more than 200 films during the 14-day festival. Go to www.iffkv.cz for more information.

Karlovy Vary plays host to several other events, including a **jazz festival** and **beer Olympiad** in May, the **Dvořák singing contest** in June, the **Summer Music Festival** in August, and the **Dvořák Autumn Music Festival** in September and October.

For more information on any of the festivals, contact **Kur-Info** (© **353 229 312**).

WHERE TO STAY

Private rooms used to be the best places to stay in Karlovy Vary for both quality and price, but this is changing as more and more hotels renovate and raise standards—as well as prices. Private accommodations can still provide better value, but it takes a little extra work. If you want to arrange a room, try the Kur-Info (see "Visitor Information," above). Expect to pay about 500Kč to 1,000Kč ($17–$33) for a single and 750Kč to 1,200Kč ($25–$40) for a double.

Some of the town's major spa hotels accommodate only those who are paying for complete treatment, unless their occupancy rates are particularly low. The hotels I've listed below accept guests for stays of any length.

Grandhotel Pupp ✵✵✵   Well known as one of Karlovy Vary's best hotels, the Pupp, built in 1701, is also one of Europe's oldest. While the hotel's public areas ooze with splendor and charm, guest rooms aren't as consistently enchanting. The best tend to be on the upper floors facing the town center. The Grand Restaurant serves up as grand a dining room as you'll find, with the food to match (see "Where to Dine," below).

Mírové nám. 2, 360 91, Karlovy Vary. © **353 109 631**. Fax 353 226 638. www.pupp.cz. 112 units. 6,600Kč ($220) double deluxe; from 8,400Kč ($280) suite. Breakfast not included (extra 390Kč/$13). The crown rate for the room fluctuates, based on the latest crown rate against the dollar on the day the payment is made because of the crown's volatility. The dollar rate remains constant for those paying in dollars or by credit card. A daily exchange rate is used for those who want to pay in crowns by cash. AE, DC, MC, V. **Amenities:** 2 restaurants; cafe; 3 bars; golf; Roman spa with sauna; Jacuzzi; concierge; car-rental desk; salon; room service; massage; laundry; dry cleaning; casino. *In room:* A/C (partly), TV w/pay movies, minibar, hair dryer, safe.

Hotel Dvořák   Now part of the Vienna International hotel/resort chain, the Dvořák has improved immensely, especially in terms of service. If the Pupp has the history and elegance, the Dvořák has the facilities. However, the rooms, for all their creature comforts, lack the old-world charm found at the Pupp.

Nová Louka 11, 360 21, Karlovy Vary. © **353 102 111**. Fax 353 102 119. www.hotel-dvorak.cz. 79 units. 2,490Kč ($83) double; 3,451Kč ($115) suite. A daily exchange rate is used for those who want to pay in crowns by cash. Breakfast is included. AE, DC, MC, V. **Amenities:** Restaurant; cafe; bar; indoor pool; fitness center; spa treatment with health packages; sauna. *In room:* A/C, TV w/pay movies, minibar, hair dryer.

Hotel Embassy ✵✵   This family-run hotel manages to evoke the turn of the last century with elegantly decorated rooms. Although smaller than those at the Pupp, they're impeccably furnished and overlook the river. The restaurant

(Moments) Spa Cures & Treatments

Most visitors to Karlovy Vary come specifically to get a spa treatment, a therapy that lasts 1 to 3 weeks. After consulting with a spa physician, guests are given a regimen of activities that may include mineral baths, massages, waxings, mudpacks, electrotherapy, and pure oxygen inhalation. After spending the morning at a spa or sanatorium, guests are then usually directed to walk the paths of the town's surrounding forest.

The common denominator of all the cures is an ample daily dose of hot mineral water, which bubbles up from 12 springs. This water definitely has a distinct odor and taste. You'll see people chugging it down, but it doesn't necessarily taste very good. Some thermal springs actually taste and smell like rotten eggs. You might want to take a small sip at first.

You'll also notice that almost everyone in town seems to be carrying "the cup," basically a mug with a built-in straw that runs through the handle. Young and old alike parade through town with their mugs, filling and refilling them at each new thermal water tap. You can buy these mugs everywhere for as little as 100Kč ($3.35) or as much as 500Kč ($16); they make a quirky souvenir. *Warning:* None of the mugs can make the hot springs taste any better!

The minimum spa treatment lasts 1 week and must be arranged in advance. A package traditionally includes room, full board, and complete therapy regimen; the cost varies from about $40 to $100 per person per day, depending on the season and facilities. Rates are highest from May to September and lowest from November to February. For information and reservations in Prague, contact **Čedok**, Na Příkopě 18, Praha 1 (🕐 **224 197 777**; www.cedok.cz). Many hotels also offer spa and health treatments, so ask when you book your room. Most will happily arrange a treatment if they don't provide it directly.

Visitors to Karlovy Vary for just a day or two can experience the waters on an "outpatient" basis. The **Sanatorium Baths III-VESO**, Mlýnské nábřeží 7 (🕐 **353 223 473**), welcomes day-trippers with mineral baths, massages, saunas, and a cold pool. It's open for spa treatments Monday through Friday from 7am to 2pm. The swimming pool and sauna are open Monday through Friday from 3 to 6pm, Saturday from 1 to 5pm.

downstairs is where a lot of movers and shakers at the Karlovy Vary film festival get away from the glitz and get down to business.

Nová Louka 21, 360 01, Karlovy Vary. 🕐 353 221 161. Fax 353 223 146. www.embassy.cz. 20 units. 2,980Kč ($99) double; 3,290Kč ($109) double deluxe; 3,830Kč ($127) suite. Rates include breakfast. AE, V. Free parking. **Amenities:** Restaurant; tour desk. *In room:* TV, minibar, hair dryer, safe.

Parkhotel Pupp 🍙   This is how the other half live at the Pupp. At four stars, this wing of the Grandhotel Pupp is housed within the same complex as its five-star cousin, but it's a world apart in terms of frills—and price. Still, rooms are large and all the same facilities are available. The views are just less spectacular.

Mírové nám. 2, 360 91, Karlovy Vary. ⓒ 353 109 111. Fax 353 224 032. www.pupp.cz. 205 units. 3,450Kč ($115) double; 4,650Kč ($155) suite. Breakfast $8 extra. AE, DC, MC, V. **Amenities:** Restaurant; cafe; bar; golf; fitness center; spa; concierge; car-rental desk; salon; room service; laundry; casino. *In room:* TV, minibar, hair dryer.

WHERE TO DINE

Embassy CZECH/CONTINENTAL   On the ground floor of the hotel of the same name, the Embassy restaurant has a pub on one side and an intimate dining room on the other. On a cold day the pub works wonders with a hearty goulash soup. But dining is the Embassy's hidden treasure. What the meals lack in flair, they more than make up for in sophistication. Salmon with a delicate dill sauce or beef with a surprisingly light mushroom sauce are two of the choices that set this restaurant apart.

Nová Louka 21. ⓒ 353 221 161. Reservations recommended. Main courses 145Kč–895Kč ($4.80–$30). AE, V. Daily 10:30am–11pm.

Grand Restaurant CONTINENTAL   It's no surprise that the Grandhotel Pupp has the nicest dining room in town, an elegant affair with tall ceilings, huge mirrors, and glistening chandeliers. A large menu gives way to larger portions of salmon, chicken, veal, pork, turkey, and beef in a variety of heavy and heavier sauces. Even the trout with mushrooms is smothered in butter sauce.

In the Grandhotel Pupp, Mírové nám. 2. ⓒ 353 109 646. Reservations recommended. Main courses 240Kč–1,350Kč ($8–$45). AE, V. Daily noon–3pm and 6–10pm.

Hospoda U Švejka CZECH   This addition to the pub scene plays on the tried-and-true Good Soldier Švejk tourist theme. Luckily, once inside, you find a refreshingly nonsmoky though thoroughly Czech atmosphere. Locals and tourists alike rub elbows while throwing back some fine lager and standard pub favorites such as goulash and beef tenderloin in cream sauce.

Stará Louka 10. ⓒ 353 232 276. Main courses 99Kč–269Kč ($3.30–$8.95); beer 20Kč (65¢). MC, V. Daily 11am–11pm.

Promenáda ⚜ CZECH/CONTINENTAL   This intimate spot may not be as elegant as the Grand, but for Karlovy Vary residents it has become one of the favored places to dine. Across from the Vřídelní kolonáda, the Promenáda serves the best food around, offering a wide selection in generous portions. The daily menu usually includes well-prepared wild game, but the mixed grill for two or the chateaubriand, both flambéed at the table, are the chef's best dishes.

Tržiště 31. ⓒ 353 225 648. Reservations highly recommended. Main courses 210Kč–599Kč ($7–$20). AE, V. Daily noon–11pm.

EXPLORING KARLOVY VARY

The town's slow pace and pedestrian promenades, lined with Art Nouveau buildings, turn strolling into an art form. Nighttime walks take on an even more mystical feel as the sewers, river, and many major cracks in the roads emit steam from the hot springs underneath.

If you're traveling here by train or bus, a good place to start is the **Hotel Thermal** at the north end of the old town's center. The 1970s glass, steel, and concrete Thermal, between the town's eastern hills and the Ohře River, sticks out like a sore Communist thumb amid the 19th-century architecture. Nonetheless, you'll find three important places here: its outdoor pool (the only one centrally located); its upper terrace, boasting a spectacular view; and its cinema, Karlovy Vary's largest, which holds many of the film festival's premier events. Look at it, and then turn and walk away. Try not to picture it again.

As you enter the heart of the town on the river's west side, you'll see the renovated ornate white wrought-iron **Sadová kolonáda** adorning the beautifully manicured park **Dvořákovy sady.** Continue following the river, and about 100m (330 ft.) later you'll encounter the **Mlýnská kolonáda,** a long, covered walkway housing several Karlovy Vary springs, which you can sample 24 hours a day. Each spring has a plaque beside it telling which mineral elements are present and the temperature of the water. Bring your own cup or buy one just about anywhere to sip the waters, since most are too hot to drink from your hands.

When you hit the river's bend, the majestic **Church of St. Mary Magdalene** sits perched atop a hill, overlooking the **Vřídlo,** the hottest spring in town. Built in 1736, the church is the work of Kilian Ignac Dientzenhofer, who also created two of Prague's more notable churches—both named St. Nicholas. Housing Vřídlo, which blasts water some 15m (50 ft.) into the air, is the glass building where the statue of Soviet astronaut Gagarin once stood. (Gagarin's statue has since made a safe landing at the Karlovy Vary airport.) Now called the **Vřídelní kolonáda,** the structure, built in 1974, houses several hot springs you can sample for free. The building also holds the Kur-Info information center and several kiosks selling postcards, stone roses, and drinking cups.

Heading away from the Vřídelní kolonáda are Stará and Nová Louka streets, which line either side of the river. Along **Stará (Old) Louka** you'll find several fine cafes and glass and crystal shops. **Nová (New) Louka** is lined with hotels and the historic **Town's Theater,** just newly reconstructed.

Both streets lead to the **Grandhotel Pupp.** After a massive reconstruction, the Pupp is once again the crown jewel of the town. Gone are the effects of nearly 50 years of Communism (it was temporarily called the Grand Hotel Moskva); once again, splendor radiates from its restored facade. Regardless of capitalism or Communism, the Pupp remains what it always was: the grande dame of hotels in the area, a place that once catered to nobility from all over central Europe. The Pupp still houses one of the town's finest restaurants, the Grand, and its grounds are a favorite with the hiking crowd. The reconstruction has also brought with it a plethora of designer shops catering to those who just don't know what to wear.

If you still have the energy, atop the hill behind the Pupp stands the **Diana Lookout Tower.** Footpaths leading through the forests eventually spit you out at the base of the tower, as if to say, "Ha, the trip is only half over." The five-story climb tests your stamina, but the view of the town is more than worth it. For those who aren't up to the climb just to get to the tower, a cable car runs to the tower every 15 minutes or so.

THE SHOPPING SCENE

Crystal and porcelain are Karlovy Vary's other claims to fame. Dozens of shops throughout town sell everything from plates to chandeliers.

Ludvík Moser founded his first glassware shop in 1857 and soon became one of the country's foremost names in glass. Now his name can be found in almost every store along the river. Many of the stores will pack and ship your purchases, either back to Prague or all the way home. We recommend comparison shopping, as prices for similar items can sometimes vary greatly.

ČESKÝ KRUMLOV

If you have time for only one day trip, consider making it Český Krumlov, 155km (96 miles) south of Prague. One of Bohemia's prettiest towns, Krumlov is a living gallery of elegant Renaissance-era buildings housing charming cafes, pubs, restaurants, shops, and galleries. In 1992, UNESCO named Český Krumlov a World Heritage Site for its historic importance and physical beauty.

Bustling since medieval times, the town, after centuries of embellishment, is exquisitely beautiful. In 1302, the Rožmberk family inherited the castle and used it as their main residence for nearly 300 years. Looking out from the Lazebnický bridge, with the waters of the Vltava below snaking past the castle's gray stone, you'll feel that time has stopped. At night, with the castle alight, the view becomes even more dramatic.

Few deigned to change the appearance of Český Krumlov over the years, not even the Schwarzenbergs, who usually had an unrestrained flair for opulence. At the turn of the 19th century, several house facades in the town's outer section were built, as were inner courtyards. Thankfully, economic stagnation in the area during Communism meant little money for "development," so no glass-and-steel edifices, like the Hotel Thermal in Karlovy Vary, jut out to spoil the architectural beauty. Instead, a medieval impression reigns supreme, now augmented by the many festivals and renovations that keep the town's spirit alive.

Note: At press time, the city was still dealing with the serious damage caused by floods in August 2002. Most of its venues along the river should be cleaned up by the time you visit, but you should double-check before you travel there. The town has a very good website with the latest news on flood repairs: **www.ckrumlov.cz.**

ESSENTIALS

GETTING THERE   By Train   The only way to reach Český Krumlov by train from Prague is via České Budějovice, a slow ride that deposits you at a station relatively far from the town center (trip time: 3 hr. 50min.); the fare is 224Kč ($7.45).

By Bus   The 3-hour bus ride from Prague costs 120Kč ($4). The bus station in Český Krumlov is a 15-minute walk from the town's main square.

By Car   From Prague, it's a 2½-hour drive along E-55.

VISITOR INFORMATION   On the main square, the **Infocentrum,** nám. Svornosti 2, 381 01 Český Krumlov (©/fax **380 704 621;** www.ckrumlov.cz), offers a complete array of services, from booking accommodations to reserving tickets for events, as well as a phone and fax service. It's open daily from 9am to 6pm.

SPECIAL EVENTS   After being banned during Communism, the **Slavnost pětilisté růže (Festival of the Five-Petaled Rose)** has made a triumphant comeback. It's held each year on the summer solstice. Residents of Český Krumlov dress up in Renaissance costumes and parade through the streets.

Tips Traveler's Tip

Consider yourself warned: Word has spread about Český Krumlov. Summer season can be unbearable, as thousands of visitors blanket its medieval streets. If possible, try to visit in the off season—we suggest autumn to take advantage of the colorful surrounding hills—when the crowds recede, the prices decrease, and the town's charm can really shine. Who knows? You might even hear some Czech!

Afterward, the streets become a stage with plays; chess games with people dressed as pieces; music; and even duels "to the death."

Český Krumlov also plays host to a 2-week **International Music Festival** every August, attracting performers from all over the world. Performances are held in nine spectacular venues. For information or ticket reservations, contact the Infocentrum's ticket hot line (© **380 704 621**).

WHERE TO STAY

Hotels are sprouting up or are getting a "new" old look; PENSION and ZIMMER FREI signs line Horní and Rooseveltova streets and offer some of the best values in town. For a comprehensive list of area hotels and help with bookings, call or write the Infocentrum listed above.

Expensive

Hotel Růže (Rose Hotel) ✪   Once a Jesuit seminary, this stunning Italian Renaissance building has been turned into a well-appointed hotel. Comfortable in a big-city kind of way, it's packed with amenities and is one of the top places to stay in Český Krumlov. This well-reconstructed hotel will allow you to enjoy all the conveniences of our age in a historical setting.

Horní 153, 381 01 Český Krumlov. ✆ **380 772 100.** Fax 380 713 146. www.hotelruze.cz. 71 units. 5,200Kč ($173) double; 6,600Kč ($220) suite. Rates include breakfast. AE, MC, V. **Amenities:** Restaurant; bar; Internet cafe; indoor pool; fitness center; sauna; bike rental; rafting; concierge; tour desk; courtesy minibus; salon; limited room service; massage; laundry. *In room:* TV, minibar, hair dryer.

Inexpensive

Hotel Konvice *(Value* If you can get a room with a view out the back, take it immediately. Rooms themselves are small but clean and comfortable, with nice parquet floors and well-appointed bathrooms. As you look over the river and the castle on the opposite bank, you'll wonder why anyone would stay at the Růže just a few doors up.

Horní ul. 144, 381 01 Český Krumlov. ✆ **380 711 611.** Fax 380 711 327. 10 units. 1,600Kč ($53) double; 1,700Kč–2,600Kč ($56–$86) suite. Rates include breakfast. No credit cards. **Amenities:** Restaurant. *In room:* TV.

Pension Anna *☆* Along "pension alley," this is a comfortable and rustic choice. What makes this a favorite is the friendly management and the homey feeling you get as you walk up to your room. Forget hotels—this is the kind of place where you can really relax. The owners even let you buy drinks and snacks at the bar downstairs and take them to your room. Suites, with four beds and a living room, are great for families and groups.

Rooseveltova 41, 381 01 Český Krumlov. ✆ **380 711 692.** 6 units. 1,500Kč ($50) double; 2,100 ($70) suite. Rates include breakfast. No credit cards. **Amenities:** Restaurant-bar with billiard table. *In room:* TV.

Pension Na louži Smack-dab in the heart of the Inner Town, the small Na louži, built in 1459 and decorated with early-20th-century wooden furniture, is full of charm. The only drawback is beds with footboards that can be a little short for tall people. Don't worry about the noise—the pub downstairs is not open late!

Kájovská 66, 381 01 Český Krumlov. ✆/fax **380 711 280.** 7 units. 1,100Kč ($36) double; 1,350Kč ($45) triple. Rates include breakfast. No credit cards. **Amenities:** Czech pub.

Pension Ve Věži (In the Tower) *☆☆* A private pension in a renovated medieval tower just a 5-minute walk from the castle, Ve Věži is one of the most magnificent places to stay in town. It's not the rooms themselves that are so grand—none have a bathroom and all are sparsely decorated—it's the wonderful ancient ambience. Advance reservations are always recommended.

Pivovarská 28, 381 01 Český Krumlov. ✆ **380 711 742.** 4 units, none with bathroom. May–Sept 1,550Kč ($52) double; 1,950Kč ($65) quad. Oct–Apr 800Kč ($26) double; 1,250Kč ($42) quad. Rates include breakfast. No credit cards. *In room:* Minibar.

WHERE TO DINE

Hospoda Na louži *(Value* CZECH   The large wooden tables encourage you to get to know your neighbors in this Inner Town pub, located in a 15th-century house. The atmosphere is fun and the food above average. If no table is available, stand and have a drink; the seating turnover is pretty fast, and the staff is accommodating. In summer, the terrace seats only six, so dash over if a seat becomes empty.

Kájovská 66. ✆ **380 711 280.** Main courses 49Kč–129Kč ($1.65–$4.30). No credit cards. Daily 10am–10pm.

Restaurant Eggenberg CZECH   Located in the former cooling room of the local Eggenberg Brewery, this is one of the few big beer halls in town, with some of the freshest draft anywhere. Traditional meat-and-dumplings Czech food is augmented by vegetarian dishes.

Latrán 27. (✆ **380 711 917.** Main courses 80Kč–195Kč ($2.65–$6.50). MC, V. Daily 10am–11pm.

Restaurant Na Ostrově (On the Island) CZECH   In the shadow of the castle and, as the name implies, on an island, this restaurant is best on a sunny day when the terrace overflows with flowers, hearty Czech food with plenty of chicken and fish dishes, and lots of beer. The staff is very friendly and very slow—usually only two waiters work a shift. This is a great place to relax and enjoy the view.

Na Ostrově 171. (✆ **380 711 326.** Main courses 60Kč–245Kč ($2–$8). No credit cards. Daily 11am–11pm.

Rybářská bašta Jakuba Krčína ⍟ CZECH   One of the town's most celebrated restaurants, this place specializes in freshwater fish from surrounding lakes. Trout, perch, pike, and eel are sautéed, grilled, baked, and fried in a variety of herbs and spices. Venison, rabbit, and other game are also available, along with the requisite roast beef and pork cutlet.

Kájovská 54. (✆ **380 712 692.** Reservations recommended. Main courses 90Kč–310Kč ($3–$10). AE, MC, V. Daily 7am–11pm.

EXPLORING ČESKÝ KRUMLOV

Bring a good pair of walking shoes and be prepared to wear them out. Český Krumlov not only lends itself to hours of strolling, but its hills and alleyways demand it. No cars, thank goodness, are allowed in the historic town, and the cobblestones keep most other vehicles at bay. The town is split into two parts—the Inner Town and Latrán, which houses the castle. They're best tackled separately, so you won't have to crisscross the bridges.

Begin at the **Okresní Muzeum (Regional Museum;** (✆ **380 711 674)** at the top of Horní ulice. Once a Jesuit seminary, the three-story museum now contains artifacts and displays relating to Český Krumlov's 1,000-year history. The highlight of this mass of folk art, clothing, furniture, and statues is a giant model of the town that offers a bird's-eye view of the buildings. Admission is 35Kč ($1.15), and the museum is open Tuesday through Sunday from 10am to 12:30pm and 1 to 6pm.

Across the street is the **Hotel Růže (Hotel Rose),** which was once a Jesuit student house. Built in the late 16th century, the hotel and the prelature next to it show the development of architecture; Gothic, Renaissance, and rococo influences are all present. If you're not staying at the hotel, don't be afraid to walk around and even ask questions at the reception desk.

Continue down the street to the impressive late Gothic **St. Vitus Cathedral.** Be sure to climb the church tower, which offers one of the most spectacular views of both the Inner Town and the castle across the river.

As you continue down the street, you'll come to **náměstí Svornosti.** For such an impressive town, the main square is a little disappointing, with few buildings of any character. The **Radnice (Town Hall),** at nám. Svornosti 1, is one of the few exceptions. Its Gothic arcades and Renaissance vault inside are exceptionally beautiful in this otherwise run-down area. From the square, streets fan out in all directions. Take some time just to wander through them. You might want to grab a light snack before crossing the bridge.

As you cross the bridge and head toward the castle, you'll see immediately to your right the former **hospital and church of St. Jošt.** Founded at the beginning of the 14th century, it has since been turned into apartments. Feel free to snoop around, but don't enter the building.

One of Český Krumlov's most famous residents was Austrian-born 20th-century artist Egon Schiele. He was a bit of an eccentric who, on more than one occasion, raised the ire of the town's residents (many were distraught with his use of their young women as his nude models); his stay was cut short when residents' patience ran out. But the town readopted the artist in 1993, setting up the **Egon Schiele Foundation** and the **Egon Schiele Centrum** in Inner Town, Široká 70–72, 381 01, Český Krumlov (© **380 704 011;** fax 380 711 191). Back across the river from the castle, it documents his life and work, housing a permanent selection of his paintings as well as exhibitions of other 20th-century artists. Admission depends on the exhibitions being displayed. The center is open daily from 10am to 6pm.

For a different perspective on what the town looks like, take the stairs from the **Městské divadlo (Town Theater)** on Horní ulice down to the riverfront and rent a boat from **Maleček boat rentals** at Rooseveltova 28 (© **380 712 508;** www.malecek.cz); rental is 400Kč ($13) per half hour. Always willing to lend his advice, the affable Pepa Maleček will tell you what to watch out for and where the best fishing is (no matter how many times you say that you don't want to fish!).

SEEING THE ČESKÝ KRUMLOV CHÂTEAU ⚑

Reputedly the second-largest castle in Bohemia (after Prague Castle), the **Český Krumlov Château** was constructed in the 13th century as part of a private estate. Throughout the ages, it has passed to a variety of private owners, including the Rožmberk family, Bohemia's largest landholders, and the Schwarzenbergs, the Bohemian equivalent of *Dynasty*'s Carrington family.

From the entrance, by the bear moat, you'll begin the long climb up to the castle. Greeting you is a round 12th-century tower—painstakingly renovated—with its Renaissance balcony. You'll pass over the moat, now occupied by two brown bears. Beyond it is the **Dolní Hrad (Lower Castle)** and then the **Horní Hrad (Upper Castle).**

Perched high atop a rocky hill, the château is open from April to October only, exclusively by guided tour. Visits begin in the rococo **Chapel of St. George,** continue through the portrait-packed **Renaissance Hall,** and end with the **Royal Family Apartments,** outfitted with ornate furnishings that include Flemish wall tapestries and European paintings. Tours last 1 hour and depart frequently. Most are in Czech or German, however. If you want an English-language tour, arrange it ahead of time (© **380 704 721;** fax 380 704 710; www. castle.ckrumlov.cz).

The guided tour costs 140Kč ($4.60) adults and 70Kč ($2.30) students. The castle hours are from Tuesday to Sunday: June through August from 9am to noon and 1 to 6pm; April, May, September, and October from 9am to noon and 1 to 5pm. The last entrance is 1 hour before closing.

Once past the main castle building, you can see one of the more stunning views of Český Krumlov from **Most Na Plášti,** a walkway that doubles as a belvedere over the Inner Town. Even farther up the hill lie the castle's riding school and gardens.

Most visitors don't realize that beyond this part of the castle, you can have one of the Czech Republic's finest dining experiences at **Krčma Markéta** ⚑, Latrán 67 (© **380 711 453**). To get there, walk all the way up the hill through the castle, past the Upper Castle and past the Castle Theater. Walk through the raised walk-way and into the Zámecká zahrada (Castle Garden), where you'll eventually find this Renaissance pub. Going inside is like leaving this century. There's no need for plates here, as meals are served on wooden blocks. Drinks come in pewter mugs. Although owners have come and gone, the atmosphere and good times are still the same. There's no menu—just go up to the spit and see what's roasting; usually there's a wide variety of meat, including succulent pork cutlets, rabbit, chickens, and pork knees, a Czech delicacy. The waiter/cook will bring bread and a slab of spiced pork fat (considered a good base for drinking), but don't worry—refusing to eat it won't raise anyone's ire. Instead, wait until the entree comes. Yes, that obligatory smattering of cabbage is all the vegetables you're going to get. Vegetar-ians need not apply. Krčma Markéta is open daily from 6 to 11pm. Reservations are recommended. Main courses cost from 75Kč to 155Kč ($2.50–$5.10). No credit cards are accepted.

MARIÁNSKÉ LÁZNĚ (MARIENBAD)

When Thomas Alva Edison visited Mariánské Lázně in the late 1800s, he pro-claimed, "There is no more beautiful spa in all the world." The town is 47km (29 miles) southwest of Karlovy Vary and 160km (100 miles) west of Prague.

While this spa town stands in the shadow of the Czech Republic's most famous spa town, Karlovy Vary, it wasn't always that way. First mentioned in 1528, the town's mineral waters gained prominence at the end of the 18th cen-tury and the beginning of the 19th. Nestled among forested hills and packed with romantic and elegant pastel hotels and spa houses, the town, commonly known by its German name, Marienbad, has played host to such luminaries as Goethe (where his love for Ulrika von Levetzow took root); Mark Twain; com-posers Chopin, Strauss, and Wagner; and Freud and Kafka. England's Edward VII found the spa resort so enchanting he visited nine times and even commis-sioned the building of the country's first golf club.

ESSENTIALS

GETTING THERE   By Train   The express train from Prague costs 224Kč ($7.45; trip time: 2 hr. 55 min.). Eight trains run to Mariánské Lázně from Prague every 2 to 3 hours beginning at 6am, with the last train leaving Prague just after 9:45pm. Mariánské Lázně train station, Nádražní nám. 292, is south of the town center; take bus no. 5 into town.

By Bus   The 3-hour bus trip from Prague costs 120Kč ($4). The Mariánské Lázně bus station is adjacent to the train station on Nádražní náměstí; take bus no. 5 into town. Three buses run daily between Prague and Mariánské Lázně.

By Car   Driving from Prague, take E-50 through Plzeň to Stříbro—about 22km (14 miles) past Plzeň—and head northwest on Highway 21. The clearly marked route can take up to 2 hours. From Karlovy Vary, the trip is about 80km (50 miles). Take Highway 20 south and then turn right onto Highway 24 in the town of Bečov.

VISITOR INFORMATION   Along the main strip lies **Infocentrum**, Hlavní 47, 353 01, Mariánské Lázně (© **354 622 474**). In addition to dispensing advice, the staff sells maps and concert tickets and can arrange accommodations in hotels and private homes. It's open daily from 9am to noon and 12:30 to 6pm.

SPECIAL EVENTS   Mariánské Lázně honors one of its frequent visitors, Chopin, with a yearly festival devoted to the Polish composer and his works.

The **Chopin Festival** usually runs for 8 to 10 days near the end of August. Tickets range from 70Kč to 1,500Kč ($2.35–$50).

Each June, the town also plays host to a **classical music festival** featuring many of the Czech Republic's finest musicians, as well as those from around the world. For more information or ticket reservations for either event, contact Infocentrum (see "Visitor Information," above).

Patriotic Americans can show up on **July 4th** for a little down-home fun, including a parade and other flag-waving special events commemorating the town's liberation by U.S. soldiers in World War II.

WHERE TO STAY

The main strip along **Hlavní třída** is lined with hotels, many with rooms facing the colonnade. If you feel comfortable about doing this, I suggest walking the street and shopping around for a room; most hotels charge from 2,000Kč to 3,500Kč ($66–$116) for a double from May to September. Off-season prices can fall by as much as half.

For private accommodations, try **Palackého ulice,** running south of the main spa area.

Hotel Koliba ⚜   Away from the main strip but still only a 7-minute walk from the colonnade, the Koliba is a rustic hunting lodge set in the hills on Dusíkova, the road leading to the golf course and Karlovy Vary. Rooms are very comfortable. The hotel offers a wide array of spa and health treatments, which cost extra. A small hill directly outside the hotel, serviced by two ski lifts, is perfect for teaching the children how to ski or for a romantic cross-country skiing weekend. The restaurant is a good choice for lunch or dinner (see "Where to Dine," below).

Dusíkova 592, 353 01 Mariánské Lázně. ☎ 354 625 169. Fax: 354 626 310. 10 units. 1,295Kč–1,591Kč ($43–$53) double. AE, MC, V. **Amenities:** Restaurant; spa. *In room:* TV, minibar.

Hotel Palace ⚜⚜   The 1920s Palace is a beautiful Art Nouveau hotel just 90m (300 ft.) from the colonnade. Rooms are not tremendously spacious, but they're comfortable and tastefully, almost regally, decorated with early-20th-century furniture and lavish curtains and chandeliers.

Hlavní třída 67, 353 01 Mariánské Lázně. ☎ 354 685 200. Fax 354 624 262. 45 units. 2,331Kč–3,885Kč ($78–$129) double; 3,034Kč–5,550 ($101–$185) suite. AE, DC, MC, V. **Amenities:** Restaurant; cafe; wine room; snack bar; Jacuzzi; sauna; salon. *In room:* TV, minibar, hair dryer.

Hotel Villa Butterfly   The Butterfly has upgraded its rather ordinary rooms into 94 first-rate spacious living quarters. Oddly enough, the renovations have had a reverse effect on the hotel's prices, now a good 15% lower. An English-speaking staff and a good selection of foreign-language newspapers at the reception are added bonuses, as is one of the better cups of coffee in town at the ground floor cafe.

Hlavní třída 72, 353 01 Mariánské Lázně. ☎ 354 654 111. Fax 354 654 200. www.marienbad.cz. 94 units. 3,780Kč ($126) double; 5,950Kč ($198) suite; 7,910Kč ($263) apt. Rates include breakfast. AE, DC, MC, V. **Amenities:** Restaurant; cafe; bar; fitness center; tour guide; room service; babysitting. *In room:* TV, minibar, hair dryer.

Hotel Zvon   Next to the Palace, in a prime spot directly across from the colonnade, the Zvon lacks a bit of the panache that its smaller neighbor has, but it still ranks as one of the town's nicer hotels. Ask for a room facing the kolonáda. Not only is the view spectacular, but rooms on this side tend to be larger and brighter.

Hlavní třída 68, 353 01 Mariánské Lázně. ℭ **354 622 015.** Fax 354 623 245. 79 units. 1,720Kč–4,720Kč ($57–$157) double; 2,370Kč–8,460Kč ($79–$282) suite. AE, DC, MC, V. **Amenities:** Cafe restaurant; bar; whisky club; spa. *In room:* TV, minibar.

Parkhotel Golf   One of the more luxurious hotels, the Golf isn't actually in town but across from the golf course about 3km (2 miles) down the road leading to Karlovy Vary. This hotel is busy, so reservations are recommended. The English-speaking staff delivers on its pledge to cater to every wish. Rooms are bright and spacious—but sparsely decorated and far from luxurious. Not surprisingly, the staff can help arrange a quick 18 holes across the street. The hotel has also recently opened its own spa center. In the winter, the golf course is used freely by cross-country skiers.

Zádub 580, 353 01 Mariánské Lázně. ℭ **354 622 651.** Fax 354 622 655. 28 units. 2,479Kč–3,922Kč ($82–$130) double; 4,699Kč–6,068Kč ($156–$202) suite. Rates include breakfast. AE, DC, MC, V. **Amenities:** Restaurant; cafe; indoor pool; golf; spa. *In room:* TV, minibar.

WHERE TO DINE

Churchill Club Restaurant CZECH   A lively bar atmosphere makes the Churchill one of the few fun places to be after dark. Don't let the name fool you—the food is traditional Czech with few surprises, which is both good and bad. A large selection of beers also sets the Churchill apart from other places along the main strip.

Hlavní třída 121. ℭ **354 622 705.** Main courses 150Kč–400Kč ($5–$13). AE, MC, V. Daily 11am–11pm.

Hotel Koliba Restaurant CZECH   Like the hotel it occupies, the Koliba restaurant is a shrine to the outdoors. The rustic dining room, centered on an open fire grill, boasts a hearty rustic atmosphere that goes perfectly with the restaurant's strength: wild game. Check the daily menu to see what's new, or choose from the wide assortment of specialties *na roštu* (from the grill), including wild boar and venison. The second room off the dining area makes for a great lunch stop, especially on a cold winter day when the fireplace is roaring.

Dusíkova 592. ℭ **354 625 169.** Reservations recommended. Main courses 85Kč–385Kč ($2.80–$13). No credit cards. Daily 11am–11pm.

Restaurant Fontaine CZECH/INTERNATIONAL   The restaurant has undergone a major transformation for the better. The dining room is large but remains quiet, albeit a little too well lit. Bow-tied waiters serve traditional Bohemian specialties, like succulent roast duck, boiled trout, and chateaubriand, as well as some inventive variations such as shark.

In the Villa Butterfly, Hlavní třída 72. ℭ **354 626 201.** Main courses 120Kč–390Kč ($4–$13). AE, DC, MC, V. Daily 6–11pm.

TAKING THE WATERS AT MARIÁNSKÉ LÁZNĚ

When walking through the town, it's almost impossible to miss the **Lázeňská kolonáda,** just off Skalníkovy sady. From Hlavní třída, walk east on Vrchlického ulice. Recently restored to its former glory, the eye-catching cast-iron and glass colonnade is adorned with ceiling frescoes and Corinthian columns. Built in 1889, it connects a half-dozen major springs in the town center; this is the focal point of those partaking in the ritual. Bring a cup to fill or, if you want to fit in with the thousands of guests who are serious about their spa water, buy one of the porcelain mugs with a built-in straw that are offered just about everywhere. Do keep in mind that the waters are used to treat internal disorders, so the minerals may act to cleanse the body thoroughly. You can wander the colonnade any time; water is distributed daily from 6am to noon and 4 to 6pm.

For a relaxing mineral bubble bath or massage, make reservations through the **Spa Information Service,** Masarykova 22, 353 29, Mariánské Lázně (© **354 655 555;** fax 354 655 500; www.marienbad.cz). Also ask your hotel about spa treatments and massages they offer or can arrange. Treatments cost from 300Kč ($10).

MORE TO SEE & DO

There's not much town history, since Mariánské Lázně officially came into existence only in 1808, but engaging brevity is what makes the two-story **Městské Muzeum (City Museum),** Goethovo nám. 11 (© **354 622 740**), recommendable. Chronologically arranged displays include photos and documents of famous visitors. Goethe slept in the upstairs rooms in 1823, when he was 74 years old. If you ask nicely, the museum guards will play an English-language tape that describes the contents of each of the rooms. You can also request to see the museum's English-language film about the town. Admission is 20Kč (65¢), and the museum is open Wednesday through Sunday from 9am to noon and 1 to 4pm (July–Sept till 5pm).

You can also take a walk in the woods. The surrounding **Slavkovský les (Slavkov Forest)** has about 70km (45 miles) of marked footpaths and trails through the area's gentle hills.

The **Mariánské Lázně Golf Club** (© **354 624 300;** www.golfml.cz), a 6,195m (6,775-yard), par-72 championship course, lies on the edge of town. The club takes pay-as-you-play golfers, and a fully equipped pro shop rents clubs. Greens fees are 1,300Kč ($43) on weekdays or 1,500Kč ($50) weekends, and club rental is 500Kč ($17).

ČESKÉ BUDĚJOVICE

This fortress town was born in 1265, when Otakar II decided that the intersection point of the Vltava and Malše rivers would be the perfect site to protect the approaches to southern Bohemia. Although Otakar was killed at the Battle of the Moravian Field in 1278, and the town was subsequently ravaged by the rival Vítkovic family, the construction of České Budějovice continued, eventually taking the shape originally envisaged.

Today, České Budějovice, hometown of the original Budweiser brand beer, is more a bastion for the beer drinker than a protector of Bohemia. But its slow pace, relaxed atmosphere, and interesting architecture make it a worthy stop, especially as a base for exploring southern Bohemia or for those heading on to Austria.

ESSENTIALS

GETTING THERE   By Train   Daily express trains from Prague make the trip to České Budějovice in about 2½ hours. The fare is 204Kč ($7).

By Bus   Several express buses run from Prague's Anděl station, Na Knížecí, Praha 5, each day (trip time: 2 hr. 20 min.), at a cost of 118Kč ($3.95).

By Car   Leave Prague to the south via the main D-1 expressway and take the cutoff for Highway E-55, which runs straight to České Budějovice (trip time: 1½ hr.).

VISITOR INFORMATION   Tourist Infocentrum, nám. Přemysla Otakara II 2 (©/fax **386 359 480**), provides maps and guidebooks and finds lodging.

SPECIAL EVENTS   Each August, České Budějovice hosts the largest **International Agricultural Show,** the country's massive "state fair."

WHERE TO STAY

Several agencies can locate reasonably priced private rooms. Expect to pay about 500Kč ($17) per person, in cash. Tourist Infocentrum (see "Visitor Information," above) can point you toward a wide selection of conveniently located rooms and pensions.

Grandhotel Zvon   Location is everything for the city's most elegant hotel, which occupies several historic buildings on the main square. Upper-floor rooms have been renovated and tend to be more expensive, especially those with a view of the square—they're not only brighter, they're larger and nicer, too. Others are relatively plain and functional. Try to avoid the smaller rooms, usually reserved for tour groups. There's no elevator, but if you don't mind the climb, stay on the fourth floor. One of the biggest changes here in recent years has been the staff, which seems to be learning that guests like respect and quality treatment.

Nám. Přemysla Otakara II 28, 370 42 České Budějovice. ⓒ 387 311 384. Fax 387 311 385. www.hotel-zvon.cz. 75 units. 1,600Kč–3,080Kč ($53–$102) double; 2,420Kč–4,030Kč ($80–$134) suite. AE, DC, MC, V. **Amenities:** 4 restaurants; bar; tour desk. *In room:* TV, minibar.

Hotel Malý Pivovar (Small Brewery) ⟨⟨   Around the corner from the Zvon (see above), a renovated 16th-century microbrewery combines the charms of a B&B with the amenities of a modern hotel. Rooms are bright and cheery, with antique-style wooden furniture. Exposed wooden ceiling beams lend a farmhouse feel. The hotel is definitely worth consideration if being only 30m (100 ft.) from the square isn't a problem.

Ulice Karla IV 8–10, 370 01 České Budějovice. ⓒ 386 360 471. Fax 386 360 474. budvar.hotel@cbu.pvtnet.cz. 29 units. 1,890Kč–2,450Kč ($63–$82) double; 1,690Kč–2,750Kč ($56–$92) suite. Rates include breakfast. AE, MC, V. **Amenities:** 2 restaurants; cafe; bar; brewery tours. *In room:* TV, minibar.

WHERE TO DINE

Masné Krámy (Meat Shops) ⟨ CZECH   If you've pledged not to go to any "tourist traps," you might make an exception for this one housed in a historic building. Just northwest of náměstí Přemysla Otakara II, labyrinthine Masné Krámy occupies a series of drinking rooms on either side of a long hall, and is a must for any serious pubgoer. The inexpensive and filling food is pure Bohemia, including several pork, duck, and trout dishes. Come for the boisterous atmosphere, or for what's possibly the best goulash in the Czech Republic.

Krajinská 29. ⓒ 387 318 609. Main courses 85Kč–180Kč ($2.85–$6). No credit cards. Daily 10am–11pm.

U paní Emy *Value* CZECH/INTERNATIONAL   Usually crowded, U paní Emy has good menu selections, with reasonable prices for both food and beverages. The chicken and fish dishes are the most popular. The pan-fried trout tastes very light, not oily as most Czech restaurants tend to make it. A wine bar here stays open to the wee hours.

Široká 25. ⓒ 387 312 846. Main courses 69Kč–200Kč ($2.30–$6.65). No credit cards. Daily 10am–3am.

EXPLORING THE TOWN

You can comfortably see České Budějovice in a day. At its center is one of central Europe's largest squares, the cobblestone **náměstí Přemysla Otakara II.** The square contains the ornate **Fountain of Sampson,** an 18th-century water well that was once the town's principal water supply, plus a mishmash of baroque and Renaissance buildings. On the southwest corner is the **town hall,** an elegant baroque structure built by Martinelli between 1727 and 1730. On top of the town hall, the larger-than-life statues by Dietrich represent the civic virtues: justice, bravery, wisdom, and diligence.

One block northwest of the square is the **Černá věž (Black Tower),** visible from almost every point in the city. Its 360 steps are worth the climb to get a bird's-eye view in all directions. The most famous symbol of České Budějovice, the 70m (232-ft.) 16th-century tower was built as a belfry for the adjacent **St. Nicholas Church.** This 13th-century church, one of the town's most important sights, was a bastion of Roman Catholicism during the 15th-century Hussite rebellion. You shouldn't miss the flamboyant white-and-cream 17th-century baroque interior.

TOURING A BEER SHRINE

On the town's northern edge sits a shrine for those who pray to the gods of the amber nectar. This is where it all began, where **Budějovický Budvar,** the original brewer of Budweiser brand beer, has its one and only factory. Established in 1895, Budvar draws on more than 700 years of Bohemian brewing tradition to produce one of the world's best beers. Contact Budvar n.p., Karolíny Světlé 4, České Budějovice (© **387 705 341;** www.budvar.cz).

Trolley bus nos. 2, 4, 6, and 8 stop by the brewery. The trolley ride to the brewery costs 8Kč (25¢). You can also hop a cab from the town square for about 100Kč to 150Kč ($3.35–$5).

Tours can be arranged by phoning ahead, but only for groups. If you're traveling alone or with only one or two other people, ask a hotel concierge at one of the bigger hotels (we suggest the Zvon) if he or she can put you in with an already scheduled group. Failing that, you might want to take a chance and head up to the brewery where, if a group has arrived, another person or two won't be noticed.

PLZEŇ (PILSEN)

Some 400 years ago, a group of men formed Plzeň's first beer-drinking guild, and today, beer is probably the only reason you'll want to stop at this industrial town 90km (55 miles) southwest of Prague. Alas, the town's prosperity and architecture were ravaged during World War II, leaving few buildings untouched. The main square, náměstí Republiky, is worth a look, but after that, there's not much to see.

ESSENTIALS

GETTING THERE   By Train   It's more comfortable to take the train from Prague to Plzeň (trip time: 1½ hr.) than to take the bus. Trains between the two cities are plentiful and fit most every schedule. Fare costs 140Kč ($4.65). To get from the Plzeň train station to town, walk out the main entrance, take Americká Street across the river, and turn right onto Jungmannova, which leads to the main square.

By Bus   The bus from Prague costs 60Kč ($2) but tends to be cramped (trip time: 1½ hr.). If you do take the bus, head back into town along Husova to get to the square.

By Car   A highway makes the drive between Prague and Plzeň one of the few worry-free trips a motorist can make in the country. Go west from Prague on D-5 (trip time: 45 min.).

VISITOR INFORMATION   The **City Information Center Plzeň,** nám. Republiky 41, 301 16 Plzeň (© **377 032 750;** fax 377 032 752), is packed with literature to answer travelers' questions. A helpful, multilingual staff will also point you in the right direction. It's open Monday through Friday from 10am to 5pm, Saturday and Sunday from 10am to 3:30pm.

SPECIAL EVENTS   If you're an American or speak English, being in Plzeň in May is quite an experience. On May 8, Gen. George S. Patton was forced to halt his advance after liberating the area, in accordance with an Allied agreement. The Russians were then allowed to liberate Prague. Forty years of Communist oppression, however, means that the town now celebrates May 8, or **Liberation Day,** with a vengeance. Although the celebrations have cooled some from the heady days just after the Velvet Revolution of 1989, you'll still be feted and praised into the wee hours, as the city's people give thanks to the forces that ended Nazi occupation.

Anxious to capitalize on its beer heritage and always happy to celebrate, Plzeň has started its own Oktoberfest, called **Pivní slavnosti.**

WHERE TO STAY

For private rooms that are usually outside the town center but a little cheaper, try **Čedok** at Prešovská 10 (© **377 222 609;** fax 377 223 703), open Monday through Friday from 9am to noon and 1 to 5pm (to 6pm in summer) and Saturday from 9am to noon. Expect to pay about 500Kč to 1,000Kč ($17–$33) for a double.

Hotel Central   This rather sterile building is across from St. Bartholomew's Church and has generously given itself a four-star rating. The surly staff notwithstanding, it is clean and quiet for such a central location. Rooms are very plain, but beds are surprisingly comfortable. With few choices around, you could do worse than the Central.

Nám. Republiky 33, 305 28 Plzeň. © 377 226 757. Fax 377 226 064. 50 units. 2,390Kč ($80) double. AE, MC, V. **Amenities:** 2 restaurants; exercise room; sauna. In room: TV.

Interhotel Continental ♣   About a block from the old town square, the modern Continental is considered by locals to be one of the best in town, but keep in mind that there's not much to choose from in the first place. Rooms are spacious and comfortable.

Zbrojnická 8, 305 34 Plzeň. © 377 236 479. Fax 377 221 746. 55 units (10 with shared shower/bathroom, 20 with private shower only, 25 with private bathroom). 850Kč ($28) double with shared bathroom; 1,590Kč ($53) double with shared bathroom and private shower; 2,150Kč ($72) double with bathroom; 3,700Kč ($123) deluxe double. AE, MC, V. **Amenities:** Restaurant; cafe; nightclub. In room: TV.

WHERE TO DINE

Měšťanská Beseda CZECH/CONTINENTAL   The high ceilings and wall murals add a touch of elegance to this large restaurant frequented by the theater crowd. The prices are reasonable for the center, but the meals are unimaginative. It's a great place to stop for a late-evening coffee and some strudel or a nightcap.

Kopeckého sady 13. © 377 236 667. Main courses 39Kč–149Kč ($1.30–$4.95). MC, V. Sun–Thurs 10am–11pm; Fri–Sat 10am–midnight.

Pilsner Urquell—Original Restaurant CZECH   This isn't a visitor-oriented pub; in the same building that houses the brewery's management, the pub has remained true to its beer suppliers by cooking hearty basic Czech meals, although it has become a little pricey.

U Prazdroje 7 (just outside the brewery gates). ℂ **377 235 608.** Main courses 65Kč–220Kč ($2.15–$7.35). AE, MC, V. Mon–Sat 10am–10pm.

Restaurace Na Spilce (At the Fermenting Cellar) *Value* CZECH The Na Spilce looks like a 600-seat tourist trap, but the food is quite good and reasonably priced. The standard *řízky* (schnitzels), goulash, and *svíčková na smetaně* (pork tenderloin in cream sauce) are hearty and complement the beer that flows from the brewery. If you've got a big appetite or just can't decide, try the *Plzeňá ská bašta*, with ample servings of roasted pork, smoked pork, sausage, sauerkraut, and two kinds of dumplings.

U Prazdroje 7 (just inside the brewery gates). ℂ **377 062 754.** Main courses 32Kč–195Kč ($1.05–$6.50). AE, MC, V. Mon–Thurs and Sat 11am–10pm; Fri 11am–11pm; Sun 11am–9pm.

EXPLORING PLZEŇ

Founded in 1295 by Přemysl King Václav II, Plzeň was, and remains, western Bohemia's administrative center. Václav's real gift to the town, however, was granting it brewing rights. As a result, more than 200 microbreweries popped up in almost every street-corner basement. Realizing the brews they were drinking had become mostly inferior by the late 1830s, rebellious beer drinkers started demanding quality from their brewers. "Give us what we want in Plzeň, good and cheap beer!" became the battle cry. By 1842, the brewers had combined their expertise to produce a superior brew through what became known as the Pilsner brewing method.

Plzeňský Prazdroj (Pilsner Breweries), at U Prazdroje 7, will interest anyone who wants to learn more about the brewing process. It's actually made up of several breweries, pumping out brands like Pilsner Urquell and Gambrinus, the most widely consumed beer in the Czech Republic. The 1-hour tour of the factory (which has barely changed since its creation) includes a 15-minute film and visits to the fermentation cellars and brewing rooms. The tour starts at 12:30pm daily (Apr–Sept), Monday through Friday from October to March; the tour is also offered at 2pm in July and August. It costs 120Kč ($4); the price includes a dozen beer-oriented postcards and a tasting of freshly brewed beer. (For details on other tours available, call ℂ **377 062 888** or e-mail visit@pilsner-urquell.com.)

If you didn't get your fill of beer facts at the brewery, the **Pivovarské Muzeum (Beer Museum;** ℂ **377 224 955)** is 1 block away on Veleslavínova 6. Inside this former 15th-century house, you'll learn everything there is to know about beer but were afraid to ask. In the first room, once a 19th-century pub, the guard winds up an old German polyphone music box from 1887 that plays the sweet though scratchy strains of Strauss's *Blue Danube.* Subsequent rooms display a wide collection of pub artifacts, brewing equipment, and mugs. Most displays have English captions, but ask for a more detailed museum description in English when you enter. Admission is 60Kč ($2), and hours are Tuesday through Sunday from 10am to 6pm (to 5pm in winter months).

Now full of more brewing knowledge than you might have wanted, proceed to the main square to see what's hopping (sorry, we couldn't resist). Dominating the center is the Gothic **Cathedral of St. Bartholomew,** boasting the tallest steeple in the Czech Republic at 100m (333 ft.). Inside the church, a beautiful marble Madonna graces the main altar.

You'll see an Italian flair to the first four floors of the 16th-century Town Hall and in the sgrafitto adorning its facade. Later on, more floors were added, as well as a tower, gables, and brass flags, creating the illusion that another building had just fallen on top of the original. In front of the Town Hall, a 1681 **memorial** commemorates victims of the plague.

Just west of the square on Sady pětatřicátníků lie the shattered dreams of the 2,000 or so Jews who once called Plzeň home. The **Great Synagogue,** the world's third largest, was built in the late 19th century. Sadly, its doors remain locked, although funds are being raised to support urgent repairs.

CHEB (EGER) & FRANTIŠKOVY LÁZNĚ (FRANZENSBAD)

As with Plzeň, few people who travel through **Cheb,** 170km (105 miles) west of Prague and 40km (25 miles) southwest of Karlovy Vary, actually stop and look around. From the outside, that's understandable, but it's too bad. The center of Cheb is one of the more architecturally interesting places in west Bohemia, and its history is fascinating as well.

A former stronghold for the Holy Roman Empire on its eastern flank, Eger, as it was then known, became part of Bohemia in 1322. Cheb stayed under Bohemian rule until it was handed to Germany as part of the 1938 Munich Pact. After World War II, it returned to Czech hands, when most of the area's native Germans, known as Sudeten Germans, were expelled for their open encouragement of the invading Nazis. This bilingual, bicultural heritage can be seen in the town's main square, which could easily sit on either side of the border if it weren't for the Czech writing on the windows. These days, the Germans have returned, but only for a few hours at a time, many for the town's thriving sex trade and cheap alcohol. Don't be surprised to see women around almost every corner looking to ply their trade. Still, Cheb is worth exploring for its mélange of architectural styles, the eerie Jewish quarter of Špalíček, and the enormous Romanesque Chebský Hrad (Cheb Castle).

Only about 20 minutes up the road from Cheb is the smallest of the three major west Bohemian spa towns, **Františkovy Lázně (Franzensbad).** Although it pales in comparison to Karlovy Vary and Mariánské Lázně, Františkovy Lázně has taken great strides in the past few years to try to erase the decline it experienced under Communism. There's not much to see save for the **Spa Museum,** which holds an interesting display of bathing artifacts, but it's a much quieter and cleaner place to spend the night than Cheb.

ESSENTIALS

GETTING THERE   By Train   Express trains from Prague usually stop in Cheb, as do several trains daily from Karlovy Vary. Cheb is on a main train route, so it's easy to catch many international connections here. The train ride costs 250Kč ($8.35); trip time is 3½ hours.

By Bus   Cheb is a long bus ride from Prague, and I suggest avoiding it if possible. It's more manageable to take the bus from Karlovy Vary to Cheb.

By Car   Cheb is located on E-48, one of the main highways leading to Germany. If you're driving from Prague, take the same route you would to Karlovy Vary, which eventually brings you to Cheb (trip time: 2½ hr.). To get to Františkovy Lázně from Cheb by car, take E-49 (trip time: 20 min.).

VISITOR INFORMATION   You'll find maps, guidebooks, lodging, and even a currency exchange (at a fairly steep price, so use it only if desperate) at the **Turistické Infocentrum Cheb,** nám. Krále Jiřího z Poděbrad 33 (© **354 422 705;** fax 354 434 385).

WHERE TO STAY

Hotel Hvězda   Overlooking the rather noisy main square, the Hvězda is a lone star in the Cheb hotel universe. Small but clean rooms make it bearable, and the staff tries to make your stay comfortable. If you can't stay in Františkovy Lázně and don't want to drive farther, this is really the only hotel we'd recommend in town.

Nám. Krále Jiřího z Poděbrad 4, 350 01 Cheb. ℭ **354 422 549.** Fax 354 422 546. 44 units. 1,000Kč ($33) double. AE, MC, V. **Amenities:** Restaurant. *In room:* TV.

Hotel Tři lilie   In 1808, Goethe stayed here, and he knew what he was doing. The Three Lilies is worth the extra money since it's the only luxury hotel in the area (Cheb needs a nice hotel like this). You can relax here; the spotless, spacious, well-appointed rooms block out any noise. The staff is very attentive and can arrange spa treatments, massages, and other health services.

Jiráskova 17, 351 01 Františkovy Lázně. ℭ **354 942 350.** Fax 354 942 970. 32 units. 3,250Kč ($108) double; 4,700Kč ($156) suite. AE, MC, V. **Amenities:** Restaurant; bar. *In room:* TV.

WHERE TO DINE

Restaurace Fortuna CZECH   If you need to have one last schnitzel before leaving, this is as good a place as any. The food is uniformly good but not great, with most Czech specialties accounted for. It's one of the only restaurants open late, and a terrace right on the main square lends to its appeal.

Nám. Krále Jiřího z Poděbrad 29. ℭ **354 422 110.** Main courses 79Kč–185Kč ($2.60–$6.15). No credit cards. Daily 10am–2am.

Staročeská Restaurace CZECH/CHINESE   This restaurant serves much the same fare as all the other restaurants on or around the square, but what caught my eye were the few Chinese meals offered. The *kuře kung-pao* (kung pao chicken) was a good spicy alternative to the sausages, meat, and dumplings most of the other diners were having.

Kamenná 1. No phone. Main courses 69Kč–190Kč ($2.30–$6.35). No credit cards. Daily 10am–10pm.

EXPLORING CHEB

The main square, **náměstí Krále Jiřího z Poděbrad,** attracts most of the attention, and is a good place to begin a tour of the old town. Although it has been overrun with touristy shops and cafes that serve mediocre German fare, the square still shines with Gothic burgher houses and the baroque **Stará radnice (old town hall).** At its south end, the **statue of Kašna Roland,** erected in 1591, is a former symbol of capital punishment, reminding people of the strength justice can wield. At the other end of the square stands the **Kašna Herkules,** a monument to the town's former power. Next to it is a cluster of 11 timber houses, called **Špalíček.** These houses used to be owned by Jews in the early 14th century, but a fervently anti-Semitic clergy in the area incited such hatred against them that they were forced into an alley now called ulička Zavražděných (Murder Victim's Lane), where they were unceremoniously slaughtered in 1350.

Across from Špalíček is the **Cheb Museum** (ℭ **354 422 246**), where another murder took place almost 300 years later in 1634—that of Albrecht von Wallenstein, a major player in the Thirty Years' War and hero of a dramatic trilogy by Schiller. On the upper level a display vividly depicts the assassination. The museum's first floor displays many 20th-century paintings from which you can trace the town's slow demise. Admission is 30Kč ($1), and it's open Tuesday through Sunday from 9am to 12:30pm and 1 to 5pm.

The old town of Cheb is also packed with several churches. The most interesting is **St. Nicholas,** around the corner from the museum. It's a hodgepodge of architectural styles: Romanesque tower windows, a Gothic portal, and a baroque interior.

TOURING CHEB CASTLE

An excellent example of Romanesque architecture is **Cheb Castle,** in the northeast part of the old town. Overlooking the Elbe River, the late-12th-century castle is one of central Europe's largest Romanesque structures.

The castle's main draws are its **chapel of Sts. Erhard and Ursala** and the **Černá věž (Black Tower).** The two-tiered early Gothic chapel has a somber first floor where the proletariat would congregate, while the emperor and his family enjoyed the much cheerier and brighter second floor with its Gothic windows. Alas, there are no tours of the castle, and the English text provided at the entrance does little to inform you. Admission is 50Kč ($1.65). It's open Tuesday to Sunday: June through August from 9am to noon and 1 to 6pm, May and September from 9am to noon and 1 to 5pm, and April and October from 9am to noon and 1 to 4pm.

Across the courtyard from the chapel stands the Černá věž (Black Tower). From its 18m (60-ft.) lookout, you can see the best views of the town. The tower seems dusty and smeared with pollution, but its color isn't from the emissions of the Škodas that drive through the streets. Rather, the tower is black because it's actually made from lava rocks taken from the nearby Komorní hůrka volcano (now dormant).

4

Denvmark

by Darwin Porter & Danforth Prince

In this chapter, we concentrate on Copenhagen, Denmark's capital, and have added a few important side trips you can take in a day or two. Copenhagen got its name from the word *københavn,* meaning "merchants' harbor." This city grew in size and importance because of its position on the *Øresund* (the Sound) between Denmark and Sweden, guarding the entrance to the Baltic. From its humble beginnings, Copenhagen has become the largest city in Scandinavia, home to 1.5 million people.

If you'd like to tie in a visit to Copenhagen with the châteaux country of Sweden, it's as easy as crossing a bridge: In 2000 Denmark was linked to Sweden by the 16km (10-mile) Øresund Bridge. The two cities of Copenhagen and Malmö, Sweden, are the hubs of the Øresund Region, northern Europe's largest domestic market, larger than Stockholm and equal in size to Berlin, Hamburg, and Amsterdam. The bridge is the longest combined rail-and-road bridge in the world.

1 Copenhagen

Copenhagen is a city with much charm, as reflected in its canals, narrow streets, and old houses. Its most famous resident was Hans Christian Andersen, whose memory still lives on. Another of Copenhagen's world-renowned inhabitants was Søren Kierkegaard, who used to take long morning strolls in the city, planning his next essay; his completed writings eventually earned him the title "father of existentialism."

But few modern Copenhageners are reading Kierkegaard today, and neither are they as melancholy as Hamlet. Most of them are out having too much fun. Copenhagen epitomizes the Nordic joie de vivre, and the city is filled with a lively atmosphere, good times (none better than at the Tivoli Gardens), sex shows, countless outdoor cafes, and all-night dance clubs. Of course, if you come in winter, the fierce realities of living above the 55th parallel set in. That's when Copenhageners retreat inside their smoky jazz clubs and beer taverns.

Modern Copenhagen still retains some of the characteristics of a village. If you forget the suburbs, you can cover most of the central belt on foot, which makes it a great tourist spot. It's almost as if the city were designed for pedestrians, as reflected by its **Strøget** (strolling street), Europe's longest and oldest walking street.

ESSENTIALS

GETTING THERE   By Plane   SAS (© 800/221-2350; www.scandinavian. net) is the major carrier to Copenhagen. **Finnair** (© 800/950-4768; www. finnair.com) offers flights through Helsinki from New York, Miami, and San Francisco. **Icelandair** (© 800/223-5500; www.icelandair.com) has service through Reykjavik from several North American cities.

You arrive at **Kastrup Airport** (℡ **70-10-30-30**), 12km (7¼ miles) from the center of Copenhagen. Since 1998, air rail trains have linked the airport with Copenhagen's Central Railway Station, in the center of the hotel zone, and the whole affair now takes a mere 11 minutes and costs 23DKK ($2.95). The Air Rail Terminal is underneath the airport's arrivals and departure halls, just a short escalator ride from the gates. You can also take an SAS bus to the city terminal; the fare is 23DKK ($2.95). A taxi to the city center costs around 128DKK ($17). Yet another option is a local bus, no. 250S, which leaves from the international arrivals terminal every 15 or 20 minutes for Town Hall Square in central Copenhagen and costs 23DKK ($2.95).

By Train   Trains from the Continent arrive at the **Hoved Banegård (Central Railroad Station),** in the very center of Copenhagen, near the Tivoli and the Rådhuspladsen. For **rail information,** call ℡ **33-14-17-01.** The station operates a luggage-checking service, but room bookings are available only at the tourist office (see "Visitor Information," below). You can also exchange money at the **Den Danske Bank** branch on-site, open daily from 7am to 8pm.

From the Central Railroad Station, you can connect with **S-tog,** the local subway, with trains leaving from platforms in the terminus itself. Ask at the information desk near Tracks 5 and 6 about which train you should board to reach your destination.

Copenhagen

Lille Triangel

GARNISONS KIRKEGÅRD

Dag Hammerskjölds Allé

Kristianiagade

Hovedvej

Ryesgade

HOLMENS KIRKEGÅRD

Østbanegade

Folke Bernadottes Allé

Østport Station

Oslo Plads

KASTELLET

Fredensbro

Øster Søgade

Øster Farimagsgade

Stockholmsgade

Forbindelsesvej

9

Sø

ØSTER ANLÆG

Store Kongensgade

Grønningen

†St. Alban's

7

Suensonsgade

Gernersgade

CHURCHILL PARK

8

Sølvgade

Øster Voldgade

Rigensgade

10

Øster Farimagsgade

Esplanaden

20

Sølvgade

Klerkegade

Adelgade

Borgergade

Bredgade

Toldbodgade

6

Rosenborg Palace

Kronprinsessegade

†

†

28

KONGENS HAVE

†

12

11 Amalienborg Palace

5

Gothersgade

Store Kongensgade

Bredgade

13

INDRE BY **26**

Pilestræde

Gothersgade

Skt. Annæ Plads

27

Købmagergade

14

Krystalgade

Kongens Nytorv

Nyhavn

15

University

†Vor Frue Kirke

25

Studiestræde

Østergade

Strøget

Inderhavnen

CHRISTI-ANIA

24

Vimmels- Amagertory kaffet

Nygade

Højbro Plads

Niels Juels

Holbergsgade

16

Vestergade

Frederiksberggade

Gl. Strand

Holmens Kanal

CHRISTIANSHAVN

Rådhus Plads

23

Christiansborg Palace

Børsen

Havnegade

17

21

H.C. Andersens Boulevard

22

Tøjhusgade

SLOTSHOLMEN

Knippelsbro

Strandgade

Overgaden oven Vandet

Prinsessegade

20

Vester Voldgade

18

Christians Brygge

Torvegade

Skt. Annæ Gade

†Vor Frelsers Kirke

19

Mitchellsgade

Hambrosgade

Langebro

Langebrogade

Prinsessegade

Christmas Møllers Plads

Sydhavnen

Thorshavnsgade

Stadsgraven

Amager Boulevard

Ved Stadsgraven

Amager Fælled Vej

To Airport

By Car If you're driving from Germany, a car-ferry will take you from Travemünde to Gedser in southern Denmark. From Gedser, get on E-55 north, an express highway that will deliver you to the southern outskirts of Copenhagen. If you're coming from Sweden and crossing at Helsingborg, you'll land on the Danish side at Helsingør. Take express highway E-55 south to the northern outskirts of Copenhagen. If you're coming from Malmö, Sweden, you can cross on the Øresund Bridge.

VISITOR INFORMATION Tourist Office The **Copenhagen Tourist Information Center,** Bernstorffsgade 1 (© **33-25-38-44;** see website below), across from Tivoli's main entrance, is open daily from 8am to 11pm in July and August; daily from 9am to 8pm in May, June, and early September; and Monday through Friday from 9am to 4:30pm September 16 through the end of April.

Websites The Copenhagen Tourist Information Center website (**www.visit copenhagen.dk**) takes a while to load but is worth the wait; you'll find all the basics on dining, lodging, and attractions. The **Danish Tourist Board (www. visitdenmark.com)** offers a wide-ranging website where you'll find late news and transportation tips; the accommodation choices range from castles and manor houses to farm holidays.

CITY LAYOUT The heart of **Old Copenhagen** is a maze of pedestrian streets, formed by Nørreport Station to the north, Town Hall Square (Rådhuspladsen) to the west, Kongens Nytorv to the east, and the Inderhavnen (Inner Harbor) to the south. One continuous route, **Strøget,** the world's longest pedestrian street, goes east from Town Hall Square to Kongens Nytorv and is made up of five streets: Frederiksberggade, Nygade, Vimmelskaftet, Amagertorv, and Østergade. Strøget is lined with shops, bars, restaurants, and sidewalk cafes in summer. **Pistolstraede,** a narrow street a 3-minute walk west of Kongens Nytorv, is a maze of galleries, restaurants, and boutiques, all housed in restored 18th-century buildings.

Fiolstræde (Violet St.), a dignified street with antiques shops and bookshops, cuts through the university (Latin Quarter). If you turn into Rosengaarden at the top of Fiolstræde, you'll come to **Kultorvet (Coal Sq.)** just before you reach Nørreport Station. Here you join the third main pedestrian street, **Købmagergade (Butcher St.),** which winds around and finally meets Strøget on Amagertorv.

At the end of Strøget you approach **Kongens Nytorv (King's Sq.),** the site of the Royal Theater and Magasin, the largest department store. This will put you at the beginning of **Nyhavn,** the former seamen's quarter that has been gentrified into an upmarket area of expensive restaurants, apartments, cafes, and boutiques. The government of Denmark is centered on the small island of **Slotsholmen,** connected to the center by eight bridges. Several museums, notably Christiansborg Castle, are found here.

The center of Copenhagen is **Rådhuspladsen (Town Hall Sq.).** From here it's a short walk to the Tivoli Gardens, the major attraction, and to the Central Railroad Station, the main railroad and subway terminus. The wide boulevard, **Vesterbrogade,** passes by Tivoli until it reaches the Central Railroad Station. Another major street is named after Denmark's most famous writer; **H. C. Andersens Boulevard** runs along Rådhuspladsen and the Tivoli Gardens.

GETTING AROUND A joint zone-fare system includes Copenhagen Transport buses and State Railway and S-tog trains in Copenhagen and North

⟨Value⟩ Traveling for Less

The **Copenhagen Card** entitles you to free and unlimited travel by bus and rail throughout the metropolitan area (including North Zealand), 25% to 50% discounts on crossings to and from Sweden, and free admission to many sights and museums. The card is available for 1, 2, or 3 days and costs 215DKK ($28), 375DKK ($49), and 495DKK ($65), respectively. Children 11 and under are given a 50% discount. For more information, contact the Copenhagen Tourist Information Center (see above).

Zealand, plus some private rail routes within a 40km (25-mile) radius of the capital, enabling you to transfer from train to bus and vice versa with the same ticket.

A *grundbillet* (basic ticket) for both buses and trains costs 19DKK ($2.40). You can buy 10 tickets for 90DKK ($12). Children under 12 ride for half fare; those under 5 travel free on local trains, and those under 7 free on buses. You can purchase a ticket allowing 24-hour bus and train travel through nearly half of Zealand for 70DKK ($9.15); half price for children 7 to 11; free for children under 7.

Students who have an **International Student Identity Card** (ISIC) are entitled to a number of travel breaks. You can buy a card in the United States at **STA Travel** (© **800/781-4040;** www.statravel.com).

For information about low-cost train and plane trips, go to **Waastels,** Skoubogade 6 (© **33-14-46-33**). Hours are Monday through Friday from 9am to 6pm and Saturday from 10am to 2pm. Waastels specializes in inexpensive travel by plane within Europe, and they also are the experts on special youth fares.

Eurailpasses and Nordturist Pass tickets are accepted on local trains.

By Bus   Copenhagen's well-maintained buses are the least expensive method of getting around. Most buses leave from Rådhuspladsen. A basic ticket allows 1 hour of travel and unlimited transfers within the zone where you started your trip. For information, call © **36-13-14-15.**

By S-tog (Subway)   The S-tog connects heartland Copenhagen with its suburbs. Use of the tickets is the same as on buses (above). You can transfer from a bus line to an S-train on the same ticket. Eurailpass holders generally ride free. For more information, call © **33-14-17-01** at any time.

By Metro   In 2001 Copenhagen launched its first Metro line, taking passengers from east to west across the city and vice versa. Operating around the clock, the Metro runs as far west as Vanløse and as far south as Vestamager. Nørreport is the transfer station to the S-tog system, the commuter rail link to the suburbs. Metro trains run every 2 minutes during rush hours and every 15 minutes at night. Fares are integrated into the existing zone system (see "By Bus," above).

By Car   It's best to park your car in any of the dozens of city parking lots, then retrieve it when you're ready to explore the capital's environs. Many parking lots are open 24 hours; a few others tend to close between 1 and 7am. Some close on Saturday afternoon and on Sunday during non-peak business hours when traffic is presumably lighter. Costs tend to range from 23DKK to 25DKK ($2.95–$3.30) per hour or 240DKK ($31) per 24 hours. Two of the most central parking lots are **Industriens Hus,** H. C. Andersens Blvd. 18 (© **33-91-21-75**), open Monday through Friday from 7am to 1:30am and Saturday and Sunday from 9am to 12:45am; and the more reasonable **Statoil,** Israels Plads (© **33-14-37-76**), open 24 hours.

By Taxi Watch for the FRI (free) sign or green light to hail a taxi. Be sure the taxis are metered. **Københavns Taxa** (© **35-35-35-35**) operates the largest fleet of cabs. *Note:* Tips are included in the meter price: 232DKK ($2.95) at the drop of the flag and 11DKK ($1.40) per kilometer thereafter, Monday through Friday from 6am to 6pm. From 6pm to 6am and all day and night on Saturday and Sunday, the cost is 15DKK ($1.95) per kilometer. Basic drop-of-the-flag costs remain the same, however. Many drivers speak English.

By Bicycle To reduce pollution from cars, Copenhageners ride bicycles. For 75DKK ($9.85) per day, you can rent a bike at **Københavns Cykler,** Reventlowsgade 11 (© **33-33-86-13**). Hours are Monday through Friday from 8:30am to 5:30pm, Saturday from 9am to 1pm, and Sunday from 10am to 1pm.

 FAST FACTS: Copenhagen

American Express American Express is represented throughout Denmark by **Neiman & Schultz,** Nørregade 7A (© 33-13-11-81), with a branch in Terminal 3 of the Copenhagen Airport. Fulfilling all the functions of American Express except foreign-exchange services, the main office is open Monday through Thursday from 8:30am to 4:30pm, and Friday from 8:30am to 4pm. The airport office remains open till 8:30pm Monday through Friday. On weekends, and overnight on weekdays, a recorded message, in English, will deliver the phone number of a 24-hour Amex service in Stockholm. This is useful for anyone who has lost a card or traveler's checks. As for foreign exchange, you'll find Neiman & Schultz offices scattered throughout Copenhagen, including a branch that's open 24 hours a day at the railway station.

Business Hours Most **banks** are open from Monday through Friday from 9:30am to 4pm (Thurs to 6pm). **Stores** are generally open Monday through Thursday from 9am to 6pm, Friday from 9am to 7 or 8pm, and Saturday from 9am to 2pm; most are closed Sunday.

Currency The Danish currency is the **krone (crown),** or DKK, made up of 100 øre. The rate of exchange used in this chapter is $1 = 7.64DKK, or 1DKK = 13 U.S. cents. At press time, £1 = 11DKK (or 1DKK = 9 pence). Note that in contrast to the fiscal policies of most of western Europe, Denmark opted not to convert its monetary system to the euro in January of 2001, despite its membership in the EU. Therefore, at least as of this writing, the euro is not the legal tender of Denmark.

Currency Exchange Banks are generally your best bet to exchange currency. When banks are closed, you can exchange money at **Forex** (© 33-11-29-05; S-tog: Central Station) in the Central Railroad Station, open daily from 8am to 9pm, or at the **Change Group** (© 33-93-04-55; bus 1, 6, or 9), Østergade 61, open Monday through Saturday from 8:30am to 10pm and Sunday from 9am to 8pm.

Dentists/Doctors For emergency dental treatment, go to **Tandlaegevagten,** Oslo Plads 14 (© 35-38-02-51; S-tog: Østerport), near Østerport Station and the U.S. Embassy. It's open Monday through Friday from 8am to 9:30pm and Saturday, Sunday, and holidays from 10am to noon. Be prepared to pay in cash. To reach a doctor, dial ✆ **33-93-63-00** Monday through Friday from 8am to 4pm or ✆ **38-88-60-41** after hours. The doctor's fee is payable in cash. Virtually every doctor speaks English.

Drugstores An *apotek* (pharmacy) open 24 hours a day in central Copenhagen is **Steno Apotek,** Vesterbrogade 6C (✆ **33-14-82-66;** bus: 6).

Embassies All embassies are in Copenhagen. The embassy of the **United States** is at Dag Hammärskjölds Allé 24, DK-2100 København (✆ 35-55-31-44). Other embassies are the **United Kingdom,** Kastelsvej 40, DK-2100 København (✆ 35-44-52-00); **Canada,** Kristen Berniskows Gade 1, DK-1105 København (✆ 33-48-32-00); **Australia,** Dampfaergeveg 26, DK-2100 København (✆ 70-26-36-76); and **Ireland,** Østbanegade 21, DK-2100 København (✆ 35-42-32-33).

Emergencies Dial ✆ **112** for the fire department, the police, or an ambulance; or to report a sea or air accident.

Internet Access To check your e-mail or to send messages, go to **Copenhagen Hovebibliotek,** Krystalgade 15 (✆ **33-73-60-60;** bus: 5, 14, or 16), open Monday through Friday from 10am to 7pm, Saturday from10am to 2pm. Access is free.

Post Office For information about the Copenhagen post office, call ✆ **33-41-56-00.** The main post office is at Tietgensgade 35–39, DK-1570 København (✆ **31-41-56-00;** S-tog: Central Station), open Monday through Friday from 8am to 6pm, Saturday from 10am to 1pm. The post office at the Central Railroad Station is open Monday through Friday from 8am to 10pm, Saturday from 9am to 4pm, and Sunday from 10am to 4pm.

Taxes The 25% VAT (value-added tax) on goods and services is known in Denmark as *moms* (pronounced "mumps"). Special tax-free exports are possible, and many stores will mail goods home to you, circumventing *moms.* If you want to take your purchases with you, look for shops displaying Danish tax-free shopping notices. Such shops offer tourists' tax refunds for personal export. This refund applies to purchases of at least 300DKK ($39) for U.S. and Canadian visitors. Your tax-free invoice must be stamped by Danish Customs when you leave the country. You can receive your refund at Copenhagen's Kastrup International Airport when you depart. If you go by land or sea, you can receive your refund by mail. Mail requests for refunds to Danish Tax-Free Shopping A/S, H. J. Holstvej 5A, DK-2605 Brøndby, Denmark. You'll be reimbursed by check, cash, or credit- or charge-card credit in the currency you want. Service and handling fees are deducted from the total, so actual refunds come to about 18%.

A 25% *moms* is included in hotel and restaurant bills, service charges, entrance fees, and repair bills for foreign-registered cars. No refunds are possible on these items.

Telephone The country code for Denmark is **45.** It should precede any call made to Denmark from another country.

Danish phones are fully automatic. Dial the eight-digit number; there are no city area codes. Don't insert any coins until your party answers. At public telephone booths, use two 50-øre coins or a 1-krone or 5-krone coin only. You can make more than one call on the same payment if your time hasn't run out. Remember that calling direct from your hotel room can be expensive. Emergency calls are free. You can reach a U.S. operator with an **AT&T** calling card by dialing ℭ **800/CALL-ATT.** For **MCI** dial ℭ **800/ 888-8000.**

Tipping Tips are seldom expected, but when they are, you should give only 1 or 2DKK. Porters charge fixed prices, and tipping is not customary for hairdressers or barbers. Service is built into the system, and hotels, restaurants, and even taxis include a 15% service charge in their rates. Because of the service charge, plus the 25% *moms,* you'll probably have to pay an additional 40% for some services!

Consider tipping only for special services—some Danes would feel insulted if you offered them a tip.

WHERE TO STAY
NEAR KONGENS NYTROV & NYHAVN
Very Expensive

Hotel d'Angleterre 𝕽𝕽𝕽 At the top of Nyhavn, this seven-story hotel, built in 1755 and extensively renovated in the 1980s, is the premier choice for Denmark (though it's a bit staid and stodgy). The rooms are beautifully furnished with art objects and the occasional antique. They vary in size, but each has a grand bed that has sheltered notables ranging from Hans Christian Andersen to Madonna. The bathrooms come with phones and scales.

Kongens Nytorv 34, DK-1050 København. ℭ 800/44-UTELL in the U.S., or 33-12-00-95. Fax 33-12-11-18. www.remmen.dk. 123 units. 2,470DKK–3,470DKK ($324–$455) double; from 4,470DKK ($586) suite. AE, DC, MC, V. Parking 180DKK ($24). Bus: 1, 6, or 9. **Amenities:** Restaurant; bar; pool; fitness center; sauna; room service; babysitting; laundry/dry cleaning. *In room:* A/C, TV, minibar, hair dryer, safe.

Phoenix Copenhagen 𝕽𝕽 More than any other hotel, this top-of-the-line lodging poses a challenge to the discreet grandeur of the nearby d'Angleterre. Opened in 1991, the Phoenix was a royal guesthouse, originally built in the 1700s to accommodate the aristocratic courtiers of Amalienborg Palace. The spacious rooms are tastefully elegant and decorated with discreet Louis XVI reproductions. The large beds sport fine linens, and the bathrooms are state-of-the-art. The very best units also have faxes, bathrobes, and phones in the bathrooms.

Bredgade 37, DK-1260 København. ℭ 33-95-95-00. Fax 33-33-98-33. 213 units. 1,990DKK–2,890DKK ($261–$379) double; from 3,500DKK ($459) suite. AE, DC, MC, V. Parking 113DKK ($15). Bus: 1, 6, 9, or 10. **Amenities:** Restaurant; bar; room service; babysitting; laundry/dry cleaning. *In room:* A/C, TV, minibar, hair dryer, safe.

Expensive

71 Nyhavn 𝕽𝕽 On the corner between Copenhagen harbor and Nyhavn Canal, this hotel is housed in a restored old warehouse from 1804, and was thoroughly renovated in 1997. Most of the rooms have a harbor and canal view. The rooms have a nautical decor, with exposed brick, dark woods, and crisscrossing timbers. Bathrooms are rather small; most have a stall shower. The best rooms are equipped with faxes and bathrobes, and computer plugs are available at the reception desk.

Nyhavn 71, DK-1051 København. ℭ 33-43-62-00. Fax 33-43-62-01. www.71nyhavnhotelcopenhagen.dk. 150 units. Mon–Thurs 1,650DKK–1,710DKK ($216–$224) double; 3,000DKK–5,000DKK ($393–$655) suite. Fri–Sun 1,290DKK–1,790DKK ($169–$234) double; 2,190DKK–3,800DKK ($287–$498) suite. Rates include breakfast. AE, DC, MC, V. Free parking. Bus: 550-S. **Amenities:** Restaurant; bar; room service; babysitting; laundry/dry cleaning. *In room:* A/C, TV, minibar, hair dryer, safe.

Moderate

Copenhagen Strand ✦   One of the city's newest hotels, opened in 2000, lies within a pair of former brick-and-timber factories. The savvy architects retained as many of the old-fashioned details as they could. The medium-size rooms are filled with comfortable, contemporary-looking furnishings. The hotel is rated three stars by the Danish government, but frankly, all that it lacks for elevation into four-star status is a full-fledged restaurant.

Havnegade 37, DK-1058 København K. ✆ **33-48-99-00.** Fax 33-48-99-01. www.copenhagenstrand.dk. 174 units. 1,613DKK ($211) double; 2,858DKK–3,270DKK ($374–$428) suite. AE, DC, MC, V. Parking 113DKK ($15). Tram: 1 or 6. **Amenities:** Bar; business center; room service; babysitting; laundry/dry cleaning. *In room:* TV, minibar, hair dryer.

NEAR RÅDHUSPLADSEN & TIVOLI
Expensive

Sofitel Copenhagen ✦   This successful overhaul of an older hotel near the rail station combines first-class comfort and antique furnishings. Opposite the Tivoli Gardens, the hotel was commissioned by King Frederik VIII in 1913 and has entertained its share of celebrities and royalty. Rooms vary greatly in size and resemble what you might find in an English country house—but with all the modern amenities. The antiques, double-glazed windows, and views from many rooms make this a good choice. Bathrooms are generous in size. The Library Bar is one of Copenhagen's most charming.

Bernstorffsgade 4, DK-1577 København. ✆ **800/223-5652** or 33-14-92-62. Fax 33-93-93-62. www.accor hotel.dk. 93 units. 1,943DKK ($255) double; 2,220DKK–6,450DKK ($291–$845) suite. AE, DC, MC, V. Parking 142DKK ($19). Bus: 1 or 6. **Amenities:** Restaurant; bar; fitness center; room service; babysitting; laundry/dry cleaning. *In room:* A/C, TV, minibar, hair dryer, safe.

Moderate

Ascot Hotel ✦ *Value*   On a side street, 180m (600 ft.) from the Tivoli and a 2-minute walk from Town Hall Square, sits one of Copenhagen's best small hotels. The Ascot was built in 1902 and enlarged and modernized in 1994. The furniture is standard but very comfortable, and a few of the units offer a kitchenette. The finest rooms open onto the street, though the rooms in the rear get better air circulation and more light. Bathrooms are large and tidily maintained.

Studiestræde 61, DK-1554 København. ✆ **33-12-60-00.** Fax 33-14-60-40. www.ascothotel.dk. 163 units. 1,280DKK ($168) double; 2,190DKK–2,560DKK ($287–$335) suite. Rates include buffet breakfast. Winter discounts available. AE, DC, MC, V. Free parking. Bus: 14 or 16. **Amenities:** Restaurant; bar; fitness center; room service; laundry/dry cleaning. *In room:* TV, hair dryer.

Hotel Kong Arthur ✦ *Value*   An orphanage when it was built in 1882, this hotel sits behind a private courtyard next to the tree-lined Peblinge Lake. It's a terrific value. It's been completely renovated into a contemporary hostelry, and a recent expansion offers more spacious rooms, including 20 for nonsmokers. Bathrooms are medium-size.

Nørre Søgade 11, DK-1370 København. ✆ **33-11-12-12.** Fax 33-32-61-30. www.kongarthur.dk. 107 units. 1,400DKK–1,600DKK ($183–$210) double; from 3,113DKK ($408) suite. Rates include buffet breakfast. AE, DC, MC, V. Free parking. Bus: 5, 7, or 16. **Amenities:** 3 restaurants; bar; sauna; room service; babysitting; laundry/dry cleaning. *In room:* TV, minibar, hair dryer, safe.

Inexpensive

Hotel Valberg   Simple but well kept, this five-story hotel is about a 10-minute walk from the Central Railroad Station. Renovated in the late 1980s, it's unpretentious and unassuming, with bright, acceptably decorated guest rooms. Each has a sink with hot and cold running water, but aside from six of the rooms, toilets and showers are in the central corridors. Breakfast is the only meal served.

Sønder Blvd. 53, DK-1720 København. € **33-25-25-19**. Fax 33-25-25-83. www.valberg.dk. 20 units, 6 with bathroom. 900DKK ($118) double with or without bathroom. Rates include breakfast. DC, DISC, MC, V. Bus: 10. **Amenities:** Lounge. *In room:* TV, hair dryer (in some).

Hotel Vestersøhus   One of the best features of this simple hotel is the view from about half the guest rooms (top two floors). They overlook a canal-shaped body of water, Skt. Jørgens Lake, which the Danes refer to as "the lakes." (The remainder of the rooms sits above the quiet, more prosaic backyard.) Set in the heart of town, behind a redbrick facade, the Vestersøhus was originally built around 1900 as an apartment house. Its simple rooms are small and comfortably—but not particularly imaginatively—furnished. Most units come with well-maintained bathrooms with shower-tub combinations. If you want to do your own cooking, know in advance that the 12 rooms with kitchenettes are usually booked far in advance by business travelers setting up long-term lodgings. Only breakfast is served, but it's included in the room price.

Vester Søgade 58, DK-1601 København. € **33-11-38-70**. Fax 33-11-00-90. www.vestersoehus.dk. 44 units, 36 with bathroom. 715DKK ($94) double without bathroom; 1,240DKK ($162) double with bathroom; 1,525DKK ($200) double with bathroom and kitchenette. AE, DC, MC, V. Bus: 29. **Amenities:** Bar; lounge; laundry/dry cleaning. *In room:* TV.

A GAY HOTEL

Hotel Jørgensen   No longer a book publishing house as it was in 1906, this hotel is the leading gay hotel of Denmark, and has been since it was founded in 1984. This establishment, located on a busy boulevard in central Copenhagen, obviously appeals to gay men and lesbians, but it also welcomes straight guests. The staff is most helpful. Prices are reasonable, and the rooms are conventional and well organized. The 13 dormitories, which accommodate 6 to 14 people each, are segregated by gender.

Rømersgade 11, DK-1362 København. € **33-13-81-86**. Fax 33-15-51-05. www.hoteljorgensen.dk. 24 units; 13 dormitory rooms (72 beds). 700DKK ($92) double; 120DKK ($16) per person in dormitory. Rates include breakfast. MC, V. Free parking. Bus: 14 or 16. **Amenities:** Lounge. *In room:* TV.

WHERE TO DINE

That national institution, the *smørrebrød* (open-faced sandwich), is introduced at lunch. Literally, this means "bread and butter," but the Danes stack this sandwich as if it were the Leaning Tower of Pisa—then they throw in a slice of curled cucumber and bits of parsley or perhaps sliced peaches or a mushroom for added color.

NEAR KONGENS NYTORV & NYHAVN
Very Expensive

Era Ora ♠♠♠ ITALIAN   This reminder of the "Golden Age" is on virtually everyone's list as the best Italian restaurant in Denmark, and is one of the consistently best restaurants of any kind within Copenhagen. Established in 1982 by Tuscan-born partners Alessandro and Elvio, it offers an antique-looking dining room. Enjoy a cuisine based on Tuscan and Umbrian models, with sophisticated variations inspired by Denmark's superb array of fresh seafood and produce. Traditional favorites include a platter of 10 types of antipasti. All pastas are freshly made every day. Depending on the season and the inspiration of the chef, main courses include succulent veal dishes, rack of venison with balsamic vinegar and chanterelles, and ultra-fresh fish.

Overgaden Neden Vandet 33B. ℂ 32-54-06-93. Reservations required. Fixed-price menus 540DKK–650DKK ($71–$85). AE, DC, MC, V. Mon–Sat 6pm–midnight. Bus: 2 or 8.

Godt ✫✫✫ INTERNATIONAL   This small-scale favorite is known to everyone in the neighborhood, including the queen of Denmark. Despite its fame, there's an appealing lack of pretentiousness here. Food is prepared fresh every day, based on ingredients that are the best at the market. The repertoire served here is splendid and the atmosphere so special it is worth reserving for your final night in Copenhagen. Examples might include crab and rascasse soup with leeks; fried Norwegian redfish with a purée of celery and watercress sauce; and roasted rack of hare with cranberries and chanterelles.

Gothersgade 38. ℂ 33-15-21-22. Reservations required. Fixed-price menus 445DKK–565DKK ($58–$74). Tues–Sat 6–10pm. Closed July and Dec 23–Jan 3. Bus: 6, 10, or 14.

Kommandanten ✫✫ INTERNATIONAL   Built in 1698 as the residence of the city's military commander, this deluxe restaurant is the epitome of Danish chic and charm. The menu offers a mouthwatering array of classical dishes mixed with innovative selections, a medley of strong yet subtle flavors. The finest seasonal ingredients are used, and the menu changes every 2 weeks. You might be offered the grilled catch of the day, breast of duck with port-wine sauce, grilled turbot with olive sauce, or gratiné of shellfish. The service is the best in Copenhagen.

Ny Adelgade 7. ℂ 33-12-09-90. Reservations required. Main courses 270DKK–320DKK ($35–$42); fixed-price menu 380DKK ($50). AE, DC, MC, V. Mon–Fri noon–2pm; Mon–Sat 6–10pm. Bus: 1 or 6.

Kong Hans Kaelder ✫✫✫ INTERNATIONAL   This vaulted Gothic cellar may be the best restaurant in Denmark. Its most serious competition comes from Kommandanten, which many discriminating palates hail as the best. On "the oldest corner of Copenhagen," the restaurant has been carefully restored and is now a Relais Gourmand. A typical three-course dinner would include smoked salmon from the restaurant's smokehouse, breast of duck with *bigarade* (sour orange) sauce, and plum ice cream with Armagnac. The a la carte menu is divided into "country cooking," including such items as *coq au vin* (chicken with wine) from Alsace and daube of beef; and *les spécialités*, featuring tournedos with foie gras sauce or fresh fish from the daily market, perhaps beginning with an essence and ballotine of quails with truffles.

Vingårdsstræde 6. ℂ 33-11-68-68. Reservations required. Main courses 195DKK–345DKK ($26–$45); fixed-price menus 605DKK–790DKK ($79–$103). AE, DC, DISC, MC, V. Mon–Sat 6pm–1am. Closed July 20–Aug 4, Dec 24–26. Bus: 1, 6, or 9.

Moderate

Café Lumskebugten ✫ *Finds* DANISH   This restaurant is a well-managed bastion of Danish charm, with an unpretentious elegance. Now-legendary matriarch Karen Marguerita Krog established it in 1854 as a rowdy tavern for sailors. A tastefully gentrified version of the original beef hash is still served. Two glistening-white dining rooms are decorated with antique ships' models, oil paintings, and pinewood floors. The food and service are excellent. Specialties include tartar of salmon with herbs, Danish fish cakes with mustard sauce and minced beet root, sugar-marinated salmon with mustard-cream sauce, and a symphony of fish with saffron sauce and new potatoes. A filling lunch platter of assorted house specialties is offered for 190DKK ($25).

Esplanaden 21. ℂ **33-15-60-29.** Reservations recommended. Main courses 178DKK–225DKK ($23–$29); 3-course fixed-price lunch 275DKK ($36); 4-course fixed-price dinner 540DKK ($71). AE, DC, MC, V. Mon–Fri 11am–10:30pm; Sat 5–10:30pm. Bus: 1, 6, or 9.

Inexpensive

Ida Davidsen 🄯 *Kids* SANDWICHES   This restaurant has flourished since 1888, when the forebears of its present owner, Ida Davidsen, established a sandwich shop. Today, five generations later, the matriarch and namesake is known as the "smørrebrød queen of Copenhagen." Her restaurant sells a greater variety of open-faced sandwiches (250 kinds) than any other in Denmark. The fare has even been featured at royal buffets at Amalienborg Castle. You select by pointing to your choice in a glass-fronted display case; a staff member carries it to your table. The vast selection includes salmon, lobster, smoked duck with braised cabbage and horseradish, liver paté, ham, and boiled egg. Two of them, perhaps with a slice of cheese, make a worthy lunch. If in doubt, a member of the service team, or perhaps Ida's charming husband, Adam Siesbye, will offer suggestions.

Store Kongensgade 70. ℂ **33-91-36-55.** Reservations recommended. Sandwiches 45DKK–250DKK ($5.90–$33). DC, MC, V. Mon–Fri 9am–4pm. Bus: 1, 6, or 9.

NEAR RÅDHUSPLADSEN & TIVOLI

Moderate

Copenhagen Corner *Kids* SCANDINAVIAN   In the very heart of Copenhagen, this restaurant opens onto Rådhuspladsen, around the corner from the Tivoli Gardens. It offers well-prepared, unpretentious, and reasonably priced meals. The menu features the Danes' favorite dishes, beginning with three kinds of herring or freshly peeled shrimp with dill and lemon. The fish is fresh and beautifully prepared, especially the steamed Norwegian salmon with a "lasagna" of potatoes, and baked halibut with artichokes. Meat and poultry courses, although not always equal to the fish, are tasty and tender, especially the veal liver Provençal.

H. C. Andersens Blvd. 1A. ℂ **33-91-45-45.** Reservations recommended. Main courses 98DKK–225DKK ($13–$29); 3-course fixed-price menu 295DKK ($39). AE, DC, MC, V. Daily 11:30am–11pm. Bus: 1, 6, or 8.

Søren K 🄯 INTERNATIONAL   Named after Denmark's most celebrated philosopher, this is an artfully minimalist dining room that's on the ground floor of the newest addition to the Royal Library. Opened in 1999, it has big-windowed views that stretch out over the sea. Menu items change frequently, but might include carpaccio of veal, foie gras, oyster soup, and main courses such as veal chops served with lobster sauce and a half-lobster, and venison roasted with nuts and seasonal berries and a marinade of green tomatoes. The restaurant virtually never cooks with butter, cream, or high-cholesterol cheeses, making a meal here a dietetic as well as a savory experience.

On the ground floor of the Royal Library's Black Diamond Wing, 1 Søren Kierkegaards Plads. ℂ **33-47-49-49.** Reservations recommended. Main courses 65DKK–125DKK ($8.50–$16) lunch, 195DKK–225DKK ($26–$29) dinner. 3-course fixed-price dinner 330DKK ($43). DC, MC, V. Mon–Sat noon–midnight. Bus: 8.

Inexpensive

Axelborg Bodega DANISH   Across from the Benneweis Circus and near Scala and the Tivoli, this 1912 cafe has outdoor tables where you can enjoy a brisk Scandinavian evening. Order the *dagens ret* (daily special). Typical Danish dishes are featured, including *frikadeller* (meatballs) and pork chops. A wide selection of club sandwiches is also available for 48DKK to 76DKK ($6.30–$9.95) each. Although the atmosphere is somewhat impersonal, this is a local favorite; diners enjoy recipes that seem drawn from grandma's kitchen.

Axeltorv 1. 🕿 **33-11-06-38.** Reservations recommended. Main courses 74DKK–135DKK ($9.70–$18). AE, DC, MC, V. Daily 11:30am–8:45pm; bar daily 10am–2am. Bus: 1 or 6.

Domhus Kælderen DANISH/INTERNATIONAL The good food at this bustling, old-fashioned emporium of Danish cuisine draws a mixed crowd from City Hall's courtrooms across the square as well as visiting foreigners. The half-cellar room holds memorabilia from its 50 years as a restaurant (before that, it was a butcher shop). Lunch tends to be more conservative and more Danish than dinner. It might include *frikadeller* (meatballs) and heaping platters of herring, cheeses, smoked meats and fish, and salads. Dinner could be pickled salmon; prime rib of beef with horseradish; and fine cuts of beef, served with béarnaise or pepper sauce. Also look for the catch of the day, prepared just about any way you like. You get no culinary surprises here, but you are rarely disappointed.

Nytorv 5. 🕿 **33-14-84-55.** Reservations recommended. Main courses 42DKK–128DKK ($5.50–$17) lunch, 98DKK–168DKK ($13–$22) dinner. Fixed-price menus 190DKK–225DKK ($25–$29). AE, DC, MC, V. Daily 11am–4pm and 5:30–10:30pm. Bus: 5.

NEAR ROSENBORG SLOT
Very Expensive
Skt. Gertruds Kloster 🛱 INTERNATIONAL Near Nørreport Station and south of Rosenborg Castle, this is the most romantic restaurant in town. There's no electricity in the labyrinth of 14th-century underground vaults, and the 1,500 flickering candles, open grill, iron sconces, and rough-hewn furniture create an elegant medieval ambience. The food is equally impressive. Try the fresh homemade foie gras with black truffles; lobster served in turbot bouillon; scallops sautéed with herbs in sauterne; venison with green asparagus and truffle sauce; or fish and shellfish terrine studded with chunks of lobster and salmon.

Hauser Plads 32. 🕿 **33-14-66-30.** Reservations required. Main courses 248DKK–295DKK ($32–$39); fixed-price menus 425DKK–690DKK ($56–$90); children's menu 95DKK ($12). AE, DC, MC, V. Daily 5–11pm. Closed Dec 25–Jan 1. Bus: 4E, 7E, 14, or 16.

AT GRÅBRØDRETORV
Moderate
Bøf & Ost DANISH/FRENCH "Beef & Cheese" is housed in a 1728 building, and its cellars come from a medieval monastery. In summer, a pleasant outdoor terrace overlooks Gray Friars Square. Specialties include lobster soup, fresh Danish bay strips, a cheese plate with six selections, and some of the best grilled tenderloin in town. One local diner confided: "The food is not worthy of God's own table, but it's so good I come here once a week."

Gråbrødretorv 13. 🕿 **33-11-99-11.** Reservations required. Main courses 149DKK–189DKK ($20–$25); fixed-price lunch 118DKK ($15). DC, MC, V. Mon–Sat 11:30am–10:30pm. Closed Jan 1, Dec 24–25. Bus: 5.

Peder Oxe's Restaurant/Vinkælder Wine Bar DANISH The building dates from the 1700s, but the crowd is young, fun, and value conscious. The salad bar is 20DKK ($2.60) when accompanied by a main course. It's so tempting that many prefer to enjoy it alone for 56DKK ($7.35) per person. Dishes include lobster soup, Danish bay shrimp, fresh asparagus, open-faced sandwiches, hamburgers, and fresh fish. The bill of fare, although standard, is well prepared.

Gråbrødretorv 11. 🕿 **33-11-00-77.** Reservations recommended. Main courses 79DKK–189DKK ($10–$25); fixed-price lunches 108DKK–118DKK ($14–$15). DC, MC, V. Daily 11:30am–midnight. Bus: 5.

Inexpensive
Pasta Basta *Value* ITALIAN/INTERNATIONAL This restaurant's main attraction is an enormous buffet (sometimes called the "Pasta Basta Table")

loaded with cold antipasti and salads. With more than nine selections, it's one of the best deals in town at 69DKK ($9.05). The restaurant is divided into half a dozen cozy dining rooms decorated in the style of ancient Pompeii, with faded frescoes patterned after originals from Italy. It's on a historic cobblestone street off the main shopping street, Strøget. Menu choices include at least 15 kinds of pasta (all made fresh on the premises); a platter with three kinds of Danish caviar (whitefish, speckled trout, and vendace, served with chopped onions, lemon, toast, and butter); fresh mussels cooked in dry white wine with pasta and creamy saffron sauce; thinly sliced salmon with a cream-based sauce of salmon roe; and sliced Danish suckling lamb with fried spring onions and tarragon.

Valkendorfsgade 22. ⓒ **33-11-21-31.** Reservations recommended. Main courses 64DKK–150DKK ($8.40–$20). DC, MC, V. Sun–Thurs 11:30am–3am; Fri–Sat 11:30am–5:30am. Bus: 5.

AT CHRISTIANSBORG
Very Expensive
Krogs Fiskerestaurant ☞ SEAFOOD   A short walk from Christiansborg Castle, the most famous restaurant in the district was built in 1789 as a fish shop. The canal-side plaza where fishers once moored their boats is now the site of the restaurant's outdoor dining terrace. The restaurant serves fresh seafood in a single large room decorated in antique style, with old oil paintings. The well-chosen menu includes lobster soup, bouillabaisse, oysters, mussels steamed in white wine, and poached salmon trout with saffron sauce. Each dish is impeccably prepared and flavorful. A selection of meat dishes is available, but the fish is better.

Gammel Strand 38. ⓒ **33-15-89-15.** Reservations required. Main courses 328DKK–585DKK ($43–$77); 4-course fixed-price menu 685DKK ($90); 5-course fixed-price menu 895DKK ($117). AE, DC, MC, V. Mon–Sat 11:30am–4pm and 5:30–10:30pm. Bus: 1, 2, 10, 16, or 29.

Expensive
Nouvelle ☞ DANISH   Nouvelle has been one of the capital's special restaurants since 1950. It's on the first floor of an 1870 house beside a canal. If you've won the lottery, the restaurant has a special caviar menu, with Sevruga and Beluga. Otherwise, you can explore the a la carte menu, which changes frequently but is likely to include goose-liver terrine with three kinds of glazed onions, or warm oysters and mussels gratiné. The superb fish dishes include North Sea turbot grilled or poached and served on a tomato, rosemary, and artichoke parfait. Lobster is served as a fricassee with green apples and curry hollandaise. Meat selections are likely to include grilled goose liver with glazed spring cabbage and curry, or lamb medallions with white truffles and new onions.

Gammel Strand 34. ⓒ **33-13-50-18.** Reservations required. Main courses 272DKK–330DKK ($36–$43); 3-course fixed-price lunch 475DKK ($62); 4-course fixed-price dinner 610DKK ($80). AE, DC, MC, V. Mon–Fri 11:30am–3pm and 6–10pm; Sat 7:30–9pm. Closed Dec 22–Jan 6. Bus: 28, 29, or 41.

Moderate
Den Gyldne Fortun ☞ DANISH/SEAFOOD   Popular at lunchtime, this restaurant opposite Christiansborg Castle lives up to its name, "golden fortune." Dating from 1796, it has been visited by Hans Christian Andersen, Jenny Lind, and Henry Wadsworth Longfellow. You climb green marble stairs to enter the formal restaurant, which resembles an English club. Amid crystal chandeliers, modern lithographs, and bubbling aquariums, you can order the kinds of dishes requested by members of Denmark's royal family after shopping expeditions on the nearby Strøget. Choices include a Scandinavian version of bouillabaisse

(served only in winter); fried filet of plaice in butter sauce; fried Danish lamb with red wine and tarragon sauce; oven-baked salmon with Noilly Prat (a vermouth) sauce; and halibut with red wine sauce and herbs. Dessert offerings include the restaurant's well-known sweet plate, with the day's freshest mousses and pastries, or a range of exotic sherbets that changes almost every week.

Ved Stranden 18. Ⓒ **33-12-20-11.** Reservations recommended. Main courses 178DKK–200DKK ($23–$26); 4-course fixed-price menu 398DKK ($52). AE, DC, MC, V. Mon–Sat 10am–11pm. Bus: 1, 6, or 10.

Inexpensive

Cafeen Nikolaj DANISH   This cafe, which evokes Greenwich Village in the 1950s, is on the site where Hans Tausen, a father of the Danish Reformation, delivered thundering sermons in the 16th century. Today no one is thundering now—they're ordering an array of typical Danish lunches, including a tasty variety of open-faced sandwiches and homemade soups. You can always count on various types of herring. Danish sliced ham on good homemade bread is a perennial favorite, and there is also a selection of Danish cheeses. The place makes no pretense of being more than it is: a simple cafe that prepares good-tasting food with fresh ingredients at fair prices.

Nikolaj Plads 12. Ⓒ **70-26-64-64.** Main courses 75DKK–225DKK ($9.85–$29). AE, DC, DISC, MC, V. Mon–Sat 11:30am–5pm. Bus: 2, 6, 10, 27, 28, or 29.

IN TIVOLI

Food prices inside Tivoli are about 30% higher than elsewhere. Try skipping dessert at a restaurant and picking up a less expensive treat at one of the many stands. Take bus no. 1, 6, 8, 16, 29, 30, 32, or 33 to reach the park and either of the following restaurants. *Note:* These restaurants are open only from May to mid-September.

Very Expensive

Divan II ★★ DANISH/FRENCH   This is the finest restaurant in Tivoli and certainly the most expensive. It was established in 1843, the same year as the gardens, and despite it name, it's older than its nearby competitor, the less formal Divan I. Service is almost unrelentingly impeccable in a garden setting where the cuisine is among the most sophisticated in the Danish capital. Stellar examples include fried filet of salmon served with a turbot bisque and tomato-and-basil concassé, and monkfish medallions sautéed with veal bacon and served with fricassee of morels. Dinners here are elaborate, memorable, and highly ritualized.

Vesterbrogade 3, Tivoli. Ⓒ **33-12-51-51.** Reservations recommended. Main courses 125DKK–365DKK ($16–$48); fixed-price lunch 395DKK ($52). AE, DC, MC, V. Daily noon–midnight.

Moderate

Færgekroen DANISH   In a cluster of trees at the edge of the lake, this restaurant resembles a pink half-timbered Danish cottage. In warm weather, try to sit on the outside terrace. The menu offers drinks, snacks, and full meals. Meals might include omelets, beef with horseradish, fried plaice with melted butter, pork chops with red cabbage, curried chicken, or fried meatballs. If you like honest and straightforward fare, without fancy trimmings, and don't like to spend a lot of money, this is the place for you. A pianist provides sing-along music every evening starting at 8pm.

Vesterbrogade 3, Tivoli. Ⓒ **33-12-94-12.** Main courses 85DKK–185DKK ($11–$24); fixed-price lunch 115DKK ($15). AE, DC, MC, V. Daily 11am–midnight (hot food until 9:45pm).

EXPLORING COPENHAGEN
SIGHTSEEING SUGGESTIONS FOR FIRST-TIME VISITORS

If You Have 1 Day Take a walking tour through the heart of the old city, which will give you time to recover from jet lag. Spend the late afternoon at **Christiansborg Palace** on Slotsholmen Island, where the queen of Denmark receives guests. Early in the evening, head to the Tivoli.

If You Have 2 Days On day 2, visit **Amalienborg Palace,** the queen's residence. Try to time your visit to witness the changing of the guard. Continue beyond the palace to *The Little Mermaid* **statue.** In the afternoon, see the **art treasures** of Ny Carlsberg Glyptotek. At night, seek out a local tavern.

If You Have 3 Days On the morning of the third day, journey to **Rosenborg Castle,** summer palace of King Christian IV, then wander through the park and gardens. Have lunch at one of the restaurants lining the canal at Nyhavn, the traditional seamen's quarter of Copenhagen. In the afternoon, go to **Rundetårn (Round Tower)** for a panoramic view of the city, and if time remains, stop in at the **National Museum** and **Denmark's Fight for Freedom Museum.**

If You Have 4 Days Head north to **Louisiana,** the modern-art museum, and continue on to Helsingør to visit **Kronborg Castle,** famously associated with Shakespeare's *Hamlet.* Return by train to Copenhagen in time for a stroll along the Strøget, Europe's longest walking street. For dinner, visit the village of Dragør.

If You Have 5 Days On the fifth day, visit **Frilandsmuseet,** at Lyngby, a half-hour train ride from Copenhagen. Have lunch at the park. Return to Copenhagen and take a walking tour along its canals. If time remains, tour the **Carlsberg brewery.** Pay a final visit to the Tivoli to cap your adventure in the Danish capital.

THE TIVOLI GARDENS

Tivoli Gardens *฿฿*   Since it opened in 1843, this 8-hectare (20-acre) garden and amusement park in the center of Copenhagen has been a resounding success, with its thousands of flowers, a merry-go-round of tiny Viking ships, games of chance and skill (pinball arcades, slot machines, shooting galleries), and a Ferris wheel of hot-air balloons and cabin seats. There's even a playground.

An Arabian-style fantasy palace, with towers and arches, houses more than two dozen restaurants in all price ranges, from a lakeside inn to a beer garden. Take a walk around the edge of the tiny lake, with its ducks, swans, and boats.

Tivoli's newest attraction, The Golden Tower, rises 19 stories high over the city's skyline, and is crowned with a golden cupola. Patrons are taken 57m (190 ft.) straight up to enjoy a panoramic view over Copenhagen before being dropped back to earth at a blazing speed that's even faster than a natural free fall. The tower is set in elaborate Asian-themed surroundings, with exotic plants and colored tiles.

A parade of the red-uniformed Tivoli Boys Guard takes place on weekends at 5:20 and 7:20pm, and their regimental band gives concerts Friday at 10pm on the open-air stage. The oldest building at Tivoli, the Chinese-style Pantomime Theater, with its peacock curtain, stages pantomimes in the evening.

Vesterbrogade 3. © **33-15-10-01.** Admission 55DKK ($7.20) adults, 30DKK ($3.95) children under 14; combination ticket including admission and all rides 100DKK ($13). May to mid-Sept daily 11am–midnight. Partial Christmastime opening from mid-Nov until Christmas Eve (reduced admission). Closed mid-Sept to Apr. Bus: 1, 16, or 29.

THE TOP MUSEUMS

Don't worry about not understanding the explanations in the museums; virtually all have write-ups in English.

Ny Carlsberg Glyptotek 🏛🏛🏛 The Glyptotek, behind the Tivoli, is one of Scandinavia's most important art museums. Founded by 19th-century art collector Carl Jacobsen, the museum holds modern art and antiquities. The modern section has both French and Danish art, mainly from the 19th century; sculpture, including works by Rodin; and works of the Impressionists and related artists, including van Gogh's *Landscape from St-Rémy.* Antiquities include Egyptian, Greek, Roman, and Etruscan works. The Egyptian collection is outstanding; the prize is a prehistoric rendering of a hippopotamus. A favorite of ours is the Etruscan art display. In 1996, the Ny Glyptotek added a French Masters' wing, where you'll find an extensive collection of masterpieces.

Dantes Plads 7. © **33-41-81-41.** Admission 30DKK ($3.95) adults, free for children; free for all Wed and Sun. Tues–Sun 10am–4pm. Bus: 1, 2, 5, 6, 8, or 10.

Statens Museum for Kunst (Royal Museum of Fine Arts) 🏛🏛 This well-stocked museum, one of the best in Scandinavia, houses painting and sculpture from the 13th century to the present. There are Dutch golden-age landscapes and marine paintings by Rubens, plus portraits by Frans Hals and Rembrandt. Eckersberg, Købke, and Hansen represent the Danish golden age. French 20th-century art includes 20 works by Matisse. In the Royal Print Room are 300,000 drawings, prints, lithographs, and other works by such artists as Dürer, Rembrandt, Matisse, and Picasso.

A major expansion in 1998 added a concert hall, a Children's Art Museum, and a glass wing designed for temporary exhibits.

 Copenhagen's *Little Mermaid*

The one statue *everybody* wants to see is the life-size bronze of **Den Lille Havfrue** 🏛, inspired by Hans Christian Andersen's "The Little Mermaid," one of the world's most famous fairy tales. The statue, unveiled in 1913, was sculpted by Edvard Eriksen and rests on rocks right off the shore. The mermaid has been attacked more than once, losing an arm in one misadventure, decapitated as recently as January 6, 1998.

All year, there's a 2½-hour **City and Harbor Tour** of Copenhagen that makes a significant stop at the *Little Mermaid* and costs 180DKK ($23) adults, 90DKK ($11) children. For more information, call Copenhagen Excursions at © **32-54-06-06.** In summer, a special "Mermaid Bus" leaves from Rådhuspladsen (Vester Voldgade) at 10:30am and then at half-hour intervals until 5:30pm. On the "Langelinie" bus there's a 20-minute stop at *The Little Mermaid.* If you want more time, take bus no. 1, 6, or 9.

Sølvgade 48–50. ℂ **33-74-84-94.** Admission 50DKK–60DKK ($6.55–$7.85) adults, 35DKK ($4.60) students, free for children under 16. Higher admission for special exhibitions only. Tues and Thurs–Sun 10am–5pm; Wed 10am–8pm. Bus: 10, 14, 43, or 184.

Den Hirschsprungske Samling (The Hirschsprung Collection)   This collection of 19th- and early-20th-century Danish art is in Ostre Anlaeg, a park in the city center. Tobacco merchant Heinrich Hirschsprung (1836–1908) created the collection, and it has been growing ever since. The emphasis is on the Danish golden age, with such artists as Eckersberg, Købke, and Lundbye, and on the Skagen painters, P. S. Krøyer, and Anna and Michael Ancher. Some furnishings from the artists' homes are exhibited.

Stockholmsgade 20. ℂ **35-42-03-36.** Admission 35DKK ($4.60) adults, free for children under 16. Wed–Mon 11am–4pm. Bus: 10, 14, 40, 42, or 43.

Nationalmuseet (National Museum) 🏛🏛🏛   A gigantic repository of anthropological artifacts, this museum features objects from prehistory, the Middle Ages, and the Renaissance in Denmark, including Viking stones, helmets, and fragments of battle gear. Especially interesting are the "lur" horn, a Bronze Age musical instrument among the oldest in Europe, and the world-famous Sun Chariot, an elegant Bronze Age piece of pagan art. The Royal Collection of Coins and Medals contains various coins from antiquity. There are also outstanding collections of Egyptian and Classical antiquities.

Ny Vestergade 10. ℂ **33-13-44-11.** Admission 40DKK ($5.25) adults, 30DKK ($3.95) students, free for children under 16. Tues–Sun 10am–4pm. Closed Dec 24, 25, and 31. Bus: 1, 2, 5, 6, 8, 10, or 41.

Frihedsmuseet (Museum of Danish Resistance, 1940–45)   The horrors of the Nazi occupation of Denmark live on here. On display are relics of torture and concentration camps, the equipment used by the Danish resistance for forbidden wireless communications and the production of illegal propaganda films, British propaganda leaflets, satirical caricatures of Hitler, information about both Danish Jews and Danish Nazis, and the paralyzing nationwide strikes. Also look for an armed car used for drive-by shootings of Danish Nazi informers and collaborators.

Churchillparken. ℂ **33-13-77-14.** Admission 30DKK ($3.95) adults, free for children under 16. May–Sept 15 Tues–Sat 10am–4pm, Sun 10am–5pm; Sept 16 to Apr Tues–Sat 11am–3pm, Sun 11am–4pm. Bus: 1, 6, or 9.

Frilandsmuseet (Open-Air Museum) 🏛   This reconstructed village in Lyngby, on the fringe of Copenhagen, captures Denmark's one-time rural character. The "museum" is nearly 36 hectares (90 acres); a 3.2km (2-mile) walk around the compound reveals a dozen authentic buildings—farmsteads, windmills, fishers' cottages. Exhibits include a half-timbered 18th-century farmstead from one of the tiny windswept Danish islands, a primitive longhouse from the remote Faroe Islands, thatched fishers' huts from Jutland, tower windmills, and a mid-19th-century potter's workshop.

Kongevejen 100. ℂ **33-13-44-11.** Admission 40DKK ($5.25) adults, free for children under 16. Easter–Sept Tues–Sun 10am–5pm; Oct 1–20 Tues–Sun 10am–4pm. Closed Oct 21–Easter. S-tog: Copenhagen Central Station to Sorgenfri (trains leave every 20 min.). Bus: 184 or 194.

Erotica Museum 🏛   This is the only museum in the world where you can learn about the sex lives of Freud, Marilyn Monroe, Hugh Hefner, Nietzsche, and Duke Ellington. Founded by Ole Ege, a well-known Danish photographer of nudes, it's within walking distance of the Tivoli and the Central Railroad Station. In addition to revealing a glimpse into the sex lives of the famous, it presents a

---

Tips Native Behavior

If you want to be taken for a real Copenhagener, rent a bike and pedal your way around the city, up and down its streets and along its canals. It's estimated that half the population does the same.

After all that exercise, do as the Danes do and order your fill of smørrebrød for lunch. Sold all over the city, these are open-faced sandwiches on which Danes are known to pile almost anything edible. Our favorite is a mound of baby shrimp, although mounds of roast beef topped with pickle is another tasty offering. And to top off the native experience, order aquavit (the famous snaps) with your lunch, though less reliable stomachs may opt instead for a Carlsberg or Tuborg beer.

Whatever you do, though, don't tell any Dane that you eat pancakes for breakfast. In Denmark, a pancake is strictly a dessert.

And finally, greet everyone you encounter with a *"God dag"* ("Good day"). If you do, you'll no doubt end up having one yourself.

---

survey of erotica around the world and through the ages. The exhibits range from Etruscan drawings and Chinese paintings to Greek vases depicting sexual activity.

Købmagergade 24. ✆ **33-12-03-11.** Admission 89DKK ($12). May–Sept daily 10am–11pm; Oct–Apr Mon–Fri 11am–8pm, Sat 10am–9pm, Sun 10am–8pm. S-tog: Nørreport. Those ages 16–18 must be accompanied by an adult. No one under 16 admitted.

Tøjhusmuseet (Royal Arsenal Museum) This museum features a fantastic display of weapons used for hunting and warfare. On the ground floor is the Canon Hall, the longest vaulted Renaissance hall in Europe, stocked with artillery equipment dating from 1500 up to the present day. Above the Canon Hall is the impressive Armory Hall, which houses one of the world's finest collections of small arms, colors, and armor.

Tøjhusgade 3. ✆ **33-11-60-37.** Admission 40DKK ($5.25) adults, 20DKK ($2.60) students and seniors, free for children under 15. Tues–Sun noon–4pm. Closed Jan 1; Dec 24, 25, and 31. Bus: 1, 2, 5, 6, 8, 10, 28, 29, 30, 32, 33, 34, or 35.

Amalienborg Palace 🎯🎯 These four 18th-century French-inspired rococo mansions are the home of the Danish royal family, a position they have held since 1794, when the original royal palace burned. Visitors flock to witness the changing of the guard at noon when the royal family is in residence. A swallow-tail flag at mast signifies that the queen is in Copenhagen. The Royal Life Guard in black bearskin busbies leaves Rosenborg Castle at 11:30am and marches to Amalienborg. After the event, the guard, still accompanied by the band, returns to Rosenborg Castle.

In 1994, some of the official and private rooms in Amalienborg were opened to the public for the first time. The rooms, reconstructed to reflect the period 1863 to 1947, belonged to members of the reigning royal family, the Glücksborgs, who ascended the throne in 1863. The highlight is the period devoted to the long reign (1863–1906) of King Christian IX and Queen Louise.

Christian VIII's Palace. ✆ **33-12-21-86.** Admission 40DKK ($5.25) adults, 25DKK ($3.30) students and seniors, 5DKK (65¢) children 5–12, free for children under 5. Jan–Apr and Oct–Dec 13 Tues–Sun 11am–4pm; May and Dec 26–30 daily 11am–4pm; June–Aug daily 10am–4pm; Sept daily 11am–4pm. Closed Dec 14–25. Bus: 1, 6, 9, or 10.

Christiansborg Palace ✐

This granite-and-copper palace on the Slotshol-men—a small island that has been the center of political power in Denmark for more than 800 years—houses the Danish parliament, the Supreme Court, the prime minister's offices, and the Royal Reception Rooms. A guide will lead you through richly decorated rooms, including the Throne Room, banqueting hall, and Queen's Library. Before entering, you'll be asked to put on soft overshoes to protect the floors. Under the palace, visit the well-preserved ruins of the 1167 castle of Bishop Absalon, founder of Copenhagen.

Christiansborg Slotsplads. ✆ 33-92-64-92. Royal Reception Rooms, 45DKK ($5.90) adults, 10DKK ($1.30) children; parliament, free; castle ruins, 20DKK ($2.60) adults, 5DKK (65¢) children. Reception rooms, guided tours May–Sept daily at 11am, 1pm, and 3pm; Oct–Apr Tues–Thurs and Sat–Sun at 3pm. Parliament, English-language tours daily 11am, 1pm, and 3pm year-round. Ruins, May–Sept daily 9:30am–3:30pm; Oct–Apr Tues–Thurs and Sat–Sun 9:30am–3:30pm.

Rosenborg Castle ✐✐✐

This redbrick Renaissance-style castle houses everything from narwhal-tusk and ivory coronation chairs to Frederik VII's baby shoes—all from the Danish royal family. Its biggest draws are the dazzling crown jewels and regalia in the basement Treasury, where a lavishly decorated corona-tion saddle from 1596 is also shown. Try to see the Knights Hall (room no. 21), with its coronation seat, three silver lions, and relics from the 1700s. Room no. 3 was used by founding father Christian IV, who died in this bedroom decorated with Asian lacquer art and a stucco ceiling.

Øster Voldgade 4A. ✆ 33-15-32-86. Admission 60DKK ($7.85) adults, 40DKK ($5.25) students and seniors, 10DKK ($1.30) children 5–12, free for children 4 and under. Palace and treasury (royal jewels), June–Aug daily 10am–4pm; May and Sept to mid-Oct daily 11am–3pm; mid-Oct to Apr Tues–Sun 11am–2pm. S-tog: Nørre-port. Bus: 5, 10, 14, 16, 31, 42, 43, 184, or 185.

CHURCHES & OTHER ATTRACTIONS

Frederikskirke

This 2-centuries-old church, with its green copper dome—one of the largest in the world—is a short walk from Amalienborg Palace. After an unsuccessful start during the neoclassical revival of the 1750s in Denmark, the church was finally completed in Roman baroque style in 1894. In many ways, it's more impressive than Copenhagen's cathedral.

Frederiksgade 4. ✆ 33-15-01-44. Free admission to church; dome, 20DKK ($2.60) adults, 10DKK ($1.30) children. Church, Mon–Thurs 10am–5pm; Fri–Sun noon–5pm. Dome, June–Sept 1 daily 1–3pm; Sept 2–May Sat–Sun 1–3pm. Bus: 1, 6, or 9.

Vor Frue Kirke (Copenhagen Cathedral)

This early-19th-century Greek Revival–style church, near Copenhagen University, features Bertel Thorvaldsen's white marble neoclassical works, including *Christ and the Apostles*. The funeral of H. C. Andersen took place here in 1875, and that of Søren Kierkegaard in 1855.

Nørregade. ✆ 33-14-41-28. Free admission. Mon–Fri 9am–5pm. Bus: 5.

Rådhus (Town Hall) and World Clock ✐

Built in 1905, the Town Hall has impressive statues of H. C. Andersen and Niels Bohr, the Nobel Prize–winning physicist. Jens Olsen's famous **World Clock** is open for viewing Monday through Friday from 10am to 4pm and Saturday at noon. The clockwork is so exact that the variation over 300 years is 0.4 seconds. Climb the tower for an impressive view.

Rådhuspladsen. ✆ 33-66-25-82. Rådhus, 30DKK ($3.95); clock, 10DKK ($1.30) adults, 5 DKK (65¢) children. Guided tour: Rådhus, Mon–Fri 3pm, Sat 10am; tower, Mon–Sat noon. Bus: 1, 6, or 8.

Rundetårn (Round Tower) ✸ This 17th-century public observatory, attached to a church, is visited by thousands who climb the spiral ramp (no steps) for a panoramic view of Copenhagen. The tower is one of the crowning architectural achievements of the Christian IV era. Peter the Great, in Denmark on a state visit, galloped up the ramp on horseback.

Købmagergade 52A. ⓒ 33-73-03-73. Admission 20DKK ($2.60) adults, 5DKK (65¢) children. Tower, June–Aug Mon–Sat 10am–8pm, Sun noon–8pm; Sept–May Mon–Sat 10am–5pm, Sun noon–5pm. Observatory Oct 15–Mar 20 Tues–Wed 7–10pm. Bus: 5, 7E, 14, 16, or 42.

Botanisk Have (Botanical Gardens) Planted from 1871 to 1874, the Botanical Gardens, across from Rosenborg Castle, are on a lake that was once part of the city's defensive moat. Special features include a cactus house and a palm house, all of which appear even more exotic in the far northern country of Denmark. An alpine garden contains mountain plants from all over the world.

Gothersgade 128. ⓒ 35-32-22-40. Free admission. May–Sept daily 8:30am–6pm; Oct–Apr Tues-Sun 8:30am–4pm. S-tog: Nørreport. Bus: 5, 7, 14, 16, 24, 40, or 43.

ORGANIZED TOURS

BUS & BOAT TOURS For orientation, try the 1½-hour **City Tour** (2½ hr. with a visit to a brewery) that covers major scenic highlights like *The Little Mermaid,* Rosenborg Castle, and Amalienborg Palace. On workdays, tours also visit the Carlsberg brewery. Tours depart daily at 1pm from May 30 to September 13 and cost 130DKK ($16) adults and 90DKK ($12) children.

The **City and Harbor Tour,** a 2½-hour trip by launch and bus, departs from Town Hall Square. The boat tours the city's main canals, passing *The Little Mermaid* and the Old Fish Market. It operates from May 30 to September 13. Tours cost 175DKK ($22) adults and 90DKK ($11) children under 12.

Shakespeare buffs will be interested in an afternoon excursion to the castles of North Zealand. The 7-hour English-language tour explores the area north of Copenhagen, including a visit to Kronborg (Hamlet's Castle); a brief trip to Fredensborg, the queen's residence; and a stopover at Frederiksborg Castle and the National Historical Museum. Tours depart from the Town Hall Square May 2 through October 16, Wednesday, Saturday, and Sunday at 10:15am. The cost is 335DKK ($44) adults, half price for children.

For more information about these tours, contact **Copenhagen Excursions** (ⓒ 32-54-06-06; www.cex.dk) or **Vikingbus** (ⓒ 31-57-26-00).

GUIDED WALKS THROUGH COPENHAGEN Staff members of the Copenhagen Tourist Information Office conduct 2-hour guided walking tours of the city Monday through Saturday at 10:30am, between May and September. The price is 80DKK ($10) for adults, 25DKK ($3.30) for children. For information, contact the **Copenhagen Tourist Information Center,** Bernstorffsgade 1 (ⓒ 33-25-38-44 or 32-97-14-40; www.woco.dk).

THE SHOPPING SCENE

Royal Copenhagen, Amagertorv 6 (ⓒ 33-13-71-81; www.royalcopenhagen. com; bus: 1, 2, 6, 8, 28, 29, or 41 for the retail outlet, 1 or 14 for the factory), was founded in 1775. Royal Copenhagen's trademark, three wavy blue lines, has come to symbolize quality in porcelain throughout the world.

In the Royal Copenhagen retail center, legendary **Georg Jensen,** Amagertorv 6 (ⓒ 33-11-40-80; www.georgjensen.com; bus: 1, 6, 8, 9, or 10), is known for its fine silver. For the connoisseur, there's no better address—this is the largest and best collection of Jensen hollowware in Europe. Jewelry in traditional and modern design is also featured. One department specializes in seconds produced by various porcelain and glassware manufacturers.

Customers refer to the two owners of **The Amber Specialist,** Frederiksberggade 28 (© **33-11-88-03;** bus: 28, 29, or 41), as "The Amber Twins." These blonde-haired ladies specialize in "the gold of the north." This stone—really petrified resin—originated in the large coniferous forests that covered Denmark some 35 million years ago.

The elegant **Magasin,** Kongens Nytorv 13 (© **33-11-44-33;** bus: 1, 6, 9, or 10), is the biggest department store in Scandinavia. It offers an assortment of Danish designer fashion, glass and porcelain, and souvenirs. Goods are shipped abroad tax-free.

COPENHAGEN AFTER DARK

In Copenhagen, a good night means a late night. On warm weekends hundreds of rowdy revelers crowd Strøget until sunrise, and jazz clubs, traditional beer houses, and wine cellars are routinely packed. The city has a more serious cultural side as well, exemplified by excellent theaters, operas, and ballets. **Half-price tickets** for some concerts and theater productions are available the day of the performance from the ticket kiosk opposite the Nørreport rail station, at Nørrevoldgade and Fiolstræde; it's open Monday through Friday from noon to 7pm and Saturday from noon to 3pm. On summer evenings there are outdoor concerts in Fælled Park near the entrance, near Frederik V's Vej; inquire about dates and times at the Copenhagen tourist office.

THE PERFORMING ARTS

Det Kongelige Teater (Royal Theater), Kongens Nytorv (© **33-69-69-69;** www.kgl-teater.dk; bus: 1, 6, 9, or 10), which dates from 1748, is home to the world-renowned **Royal Danish Ballet** and the **Royal Danish Opera.** Because the arts are state subsidized in Denmark, ticket prices are comparatively low, and some seats may be available at the box office the day before a performance. We recommend making reservations in advance. The season runs from August to May. Tickets are 60DKK to 615DKK ($7.85–$81), half price for seniors 67 and over and those under 26 (1 week before a show begins). The box office is open Monday through Saturday from 1 to 8pm; phone hours are Monday through Saturday from 1 to 7pm.

LIVE-MUSIC CLUBS

In the very heart of the city, **Den Røde Pimpernel (the Scarlet Pimpernel),** H. C. Andersens Blvd. 7 (© **33-12-20-32;** bus: 28 or 30), with its lively atmosphere, is a good place for people-watching and dancing. If you can stand the scrutiny, you'll be admitted only after being inspected through a peephole. The club is open Tuesday through Saturday from 9pm to 8am. There's a 50DKK ($6.55) cover Friday and Saturday.

Copenhagen JazzHouse, Niels Hammingsensgade 10 (© **33-15-26-00;** S-tog: Nørreport), plays host to more non-Danish jazz artists than just about any other jazz bar in town. Live music tends to begin around 8:30pm and usually finishes reasonably early. Around midnight on Thursday, Friday, and Saturday, the venue shifts from a live concert hall into a dance club. Cover is 70DKK to 360DKK ($9.15–$47); closed Monday.

Mojo Blues Bar, Løngangsstraede 21C (© **33-11-64-53;** bus: 2, 8, or 30), is a candlelit drinking spot that offers blues music, mostly performed by Scandinavian groups. It's open daily from 8pm to 5am. There's no cover from Sunday to Thursday, a cover of 50DKK ($6.55) Friday and Saturday.

BARS & CELLARS

Det Lille Apotek, Stor Kannikestraede 15 (© **33-12-56-06;** bus: 2, 5, 8, or 30), is a good spot for English-speaking foreign students to meet their Danish contemporaries. Though the menu varies, keep an eye out for the prawn cocktail and tenderloin. The main courses run about 88DKK to 128DKK ($12–$18) at dinner. It's open daily from 11am to midnight.

Frequented by celebrities and royalty, the **Library Bar,** in the Hotel Plaza, Bernstorffsgade 4 (© **33-14-15-19;** bus: 6), was rated by the late Malcolm Forbes as one of the top five bars in the world. In a setting of antique books and works of art, you can order everything from a cappuccino to a cocktail. It's open Monday through Saturday from 11:30am to 1am and Sunday from 11:30am to midnight.

Nyhavn 17, Nyhavn 17 (© **33-12-54-19;** bus: 1, 6, 27, or 29), is the last of the honky-tonks that used to make up the former sailors' quarter. This cafe is a short walk from the Kongens Nytorv and d'Angleterre hotels. In summer you can sit outside. On Tuesday to Saturday evenings there's free entertainment from a solo guitarist or guitar duet. The cafe is open Sunday through Thursday from 10am to 2am and Friday and Saturday until 3am. Built in 1670, **Hvids Vinstue,** Kongens Nytorv 19 (© **33-15-10-64;** bus: 1, 6, 9, or 10), is a wine cellar that's a dimly lit safe haven for an eclectic crowd, many patrons—both theatergoers and actors and dancers—drawn from the Royal Theater across the way. It's open daily from 10am to 1am, but closed Sunday in July and August.

A leading nightlife venue, popular with gay men and women, is **Sebastian Bar & Café,** Hyskenstraede 10 (© **33-32-22-79**), which operates a good restaurant serving an international cuisine and also has a cruisy bar. It's an all-around rendezvous point for many of the capital's gay men and women, also attracting a lot of foreign visitors looking for action. The bar and cafe is open daily from noon to 2am, the restaurant daily from 5 to 11pm.

DAY TRIPS FROM COPENHAGEN

DRAGØR *ßß*   Visit the past in this old seafaring town on the island of Amager, 5km (3 miles) south of Copenhagen's Kastrup Airport. It's filled with well-preserved, half-timbered, ocher-and-pink 18th-century cottages with steep red-tile or thatch roofs, many of them under the protection of the National Trust.

Dragør (pronounced *Drah-wer*) was a busy port on the herring-rich Baltic Sea in the early Middle Ages, but when fishing fell off, it became just another sleepy waterfront village. After 1520, Amager Island and its villages—Dragør and Store Magleby—were inhabited by the Dutch, who brought their own customs, Low-German language, and agricultural expertise, especially their love of bulb flowers. In Copenhagen, you still see wooden-shoed Amager islanders selling their hyacinths, tulips, daffodils, and lilies in the streets.

A rich trove of historic treasures is in the **Amager Museum,** Hovedgaden 4–12, Store Magleby (© **32-53-93-07;** bus: 30, 33, or 350S), outside Dragør. The exhibits reveal the affluence achieved by the Amager Dutch, with rich textiles, fine embroidery, and amenities like carved silver buckles and buttons. The interiors of a Dutch house are especially interesting. Admission is 20DKK ($2.60) adults, 10DKK ($1.30) children. The museum is open April through September Wednesday through Sunday from noon to 4pm; October through March, Wednesday and Sunday from noon to 4pm.

The exhibits at the harbor-front **Dragør Museum,** Havnepladsen 2–4 (© **32-53-41-06;** bus: 30, 33, or 350S), show how the Amager Dutch lived from prehistoric times to the 20th century. Farming, goose breeding, seafaring, fishing, ship piloting, and ship salvage are delineated through pictures and artifacts. Admission is 20DKK ($2.60) adults, 10DKK ($1.30) children. It's open May through September Tuesday through Sunday from noon to 4pm; closed October through April.

LOUISIANA   Established in 1958, the **Louisiana Museum of Modern Art** ⭐⭐⭐, Gl. Strandvej 13 (© **49-19-07-19;** www.louisiana.dk), is idyllically situated in a 19th-century mansion on the Danish Riviera, surrounded by a sculpture park opening directly onto the Øresund. Paintings and sculptures by modern masters, such as Giacometti and Henry Moore, as well as the best and most controversial works of modern art, are displayed. The museum's name came from the estate's first owner, Alexander Brun, who had three wives, each named Louise. Admission is 68DKK ($8.90) adults, 60DKK ($7.85) students, 20DKK ($2.60) children 4 to 16, and free for children under 4. It's open Thursday through Tuesday from 10am to 5pm, Wednesday from 10am to 10pm; closed December 24, 25, and 31.

Getting There   **Humlebaek,** the nearest town to Louisiana, may be reached by train from Copenhagen (København–Helsingør). Two trains an hour leave from the main station in Copenhagen (trip time: 40 min.). Once you're at Humlebaek, follow signs to the museum, a 15-minute walk.

HELSINGØR (ELSINORE) ⭐   Helsingør is visited chiefly for "Hamlet's Castle." Aside from its literary associations, the town has a certain charm: a quiet market square, medieval lanes, and old half-timbered and brick buildings, remains of its once-prosperous shipping industry. The **Tourist Office,** Havnepladsen 3 (© **49-21-13-33**), is open Monday through Friday from 9am to 5pm and Saturday from 10am to 1pm.

There's no evidence Shakespeare ever saw this sandstone-and-copper Dutch Renaissance-style castle, full of intriguing secret passages and casemates, but he made **Kronborg Slot** ⭐⭐⭐, Kronborg (© **49-21-30-78**), famous in *Hamlet.* According to 12th-century historian Saxo Grammaticus, though, if Hamlet had really existed, he would have lived centuries before Kronborg was erected (1574–85). Over the years, some famous productions of *Hamlet* have been staged here, the castle's bleak atmosphere providing a good foil to the drama.

During its history, the castle has been looted, bombarded, gutted by fire, and used as a barracks (1785–1922). The starkly furnished Great Hall is the largest in northern Europe. The church with its original oak furnishings and the royal chambers are also worth exploring. Admission to the castle is 40DKK ($5.25) adults, 15DKK ($1.95) children 6 to 14. May through September, it's open daily from 10:30am to 5pm; October and April, hours are Tuesday through Sunday from 11am to 4pm; November through March, it's open Tuesday through Sunday from 11am to 3pm (closed Christmas). The castle is 1km (½ mile) from the rail station.

Getting There   Once you reach Helsingør, 40km (25 miles) north of Copenhagen, you'll be deposited in the center of town and can cover all the major attractions on foot. There are frequent trains from Copenhagen, taking 50 minutes. Some 30 buses daily leave Copenhagen for the 1-hour trip to Helsingør.

England

by Darwin Porter & Danforth Prince

London is the most happening city in Europe—lively, fast paced, and teeming with action. London now touts its fascinating contradictions: It's both an overwhelming jumble of antiquity and a world leader in the latest music, fashion, and food (the cuisine is better than ever). As stimulating as the city is, however, you'll want to tear yourself away from it to visit legendary Stonehenge, Oxford University, and the classic city of Bath.

1 London

Samuel Johnson said, "When a man is tired of London, he is tired of life; for there's in London all that life can afford." We'll survey a segment of that life: ancient monuments, literary shrines, museums, walking tours, Parliament debates, royal castles, waxworks, palaces, cathedrals, and parks.

ESSENTIALS

GETTING THERE   By Plane   Heathrow Airport (© **0870/000-123**) is divided into four terminals, each relatively self-contained. The 24km (15-mile) trip from Heathrow to the center of London takes 35 to 40 minutes by the London subway, the **Underground (Tube);** the fare is £5.50 ($8.80). A **taxi** is likely to cost from £35 to £40 ($56–$64). For more information about Tube or bus connections, call © **020/72221234.**

The British Airport Authority now operates **Heathrow Express** (© **0845/ 600-1515** or 877/677-1066; www.heathrowexpress.com), a 160 kilometer-per-hour (100-mph) train service running every 15 minutes daily from 5:10am until 11:40pm between Heathrow and Paddington Station in the center of London. Trips cost £13 ($21) each way in economy class, rising to £21 ($34) in first class. Children under 15 go for free (when accompanied by an adult). You can save £1 ($1.60) by booking online or by phone. The trip takes 15 minutes each way between Paddington and Terminals 1, 2, and 3; 23 minutes to or from Terminal 4. The trains have special areas for wheelchairs. From Paddington, passengers can connect to other trains and the Underground, or you can hail a taxi. You can buy tickets on the train or at self-service machines at Heathrow Airport (also available from travel agents).

At Paddington, a bus link, **Hotel Express,** takes passengers to a number of hotels in central London. The cost is £3 ($4.80) for adults, £2 ($3.20) for children 5 to 15, free for children under 5. The service has revolutionized travel to and from the airport, much to the regret of London cabbies. Hotel Express buses are clearly designated outside the station, with frequent departures throughout the day.

By Train   Each of London's train stations is connected to the city's vast bus and Underground network, and each has phones, restaurants, pubs, luggage storage areas, and London Transport Information Centres.

If you're coming from France, the fastest way to get to London is by the **HoverSpeed** connection between Calais and Dover, where you can get a BritRail train into London. For one-stop travel, you can take the Chunnel train direct from Paris to Waterloo Station in London.

By Car   If you're taking a car across the Channel, you can quickly connect by motorway (superhighway) into London. London is encircled by a ring road. Determine which part of the city you wish to enter, and follow the signs. You should confine your driving in London to the *bare minimum;* before you arrive, call your hotel for advice on where to park. Be warned—parking is scarce and expensive. The most important tip for driving in England: *Remember to drive on the left.*

VISITOR INFORMATION   Tourist Offices   The **British Travel Centre,** Rex House, 4–12 Lower Regent St., London SW1 4PQ (Tube: Piccadilly Circus), caters to walk-in visitors who need information about all parts of Britain. Telephone service has been suspended; you must show up in person and often wait in a lengthy line. On the premises, you'll find a British Rail ticket office, travel and theater ticket agencies, a hotel-booking service, a bookshop, and a souvenir shop. The center is open Monday through Friday from 9am to 6:30pm, and Saturday and Sunday from 10am to 4pm, with extended hours on Saturday from June to September.

London Tourist Board's Tourist Information Centre, Victoria Station Forecourt, SW1 (walk-ins only; no phone; Tube: Victoria Station), can help you with almost anything. The center deals chiefly with accommodations in all price categories and can handle the whole spectrum of travelers' questions. It also arranges tour ticket sales and theater reservations, and offers a wide selection of books and souvenirs. From Easter to October, the center is open daily from 8am to 7pm; from November to Easter, it's open Monday through Saturday from 8am to 6pm and Sunday from 9am to 4pm.

The London Tourist Board also has tourist information centers at Heathrow Terminals 1, 2, and 3; on the Underground concourse at Liverpool Street Railway Station; the Arrivals Hall at the Waterloo International train terminal; and at 1 Regent St., Piccadilly Circus.

Websites   The British Tourist Authority's site expressly for U.S. travelers (**www.visitbritain.com**) lets you order brochures, provides trip-planning hints, and even allows e-mail questions for prompt answers. The outstanding Automobile Association site (**www.theaa.co.uk**) provides a route-planning service similar to its U.S. counterpart. It also lists lodgings, ranked by price and quality; many accept online bookings. The extensive London Theatre Guide (**www. officiallondontheatre.co.uk**) carries not only information on half-price tickets and what's on but also casting news, upcoming openings, and "last chance to see" shows. The official site from the British monarchy (**www.royal.gov.uk/ palaces/bp.htm**) offers history, images, and descriptions of the "working palace" and "visitors' palace."

CITY LAYOUT   For our purposes, London begins at **Chelsea,** on the north bank of the Thames, and stretches north through Kensington to **Hampstead,** then east and south to **Tower Bridge.** Within this area, you'll find all the hotels and restaurants and nearly all the sights that are usually of interest to visitors.

The logical, though not geographical, center of this area is **Trafalgar Square.** Stand here facing the steps of the imposing National Gallery; you're looking northwest. That's the direction of **Piccadilly Circus**—the real core of tourist

London—and the maze of streets that makes up **Soho.** Farther north runs **Oxford Street,** London's gift to moderately priced shopping, and still farther northwest lie Regent's Park and the zoo.

At your back (south) runs **Whitehall,** which houses or skirts nearly every British government building, including the official residence of the prime minister at **10 Downing Street.** A bit farther south stand the Houses of Parliament and Westminster Abbey. Flowing southwest from Trafalgar Square is the table-smooth **Mall,** flanked by parks and mansions and leading to Buckingham Palace, the queen's residence. Farther along in the same direction lie **Belgravia** and **Knightsbridge,** the city's plushest residential areas; and south of them are chic **Chelsea** and **King's Road** (an upscale boulevard for shopping).

Due west stretches the superb and high-priced shopping area bordered by **Regent Street** and **Piccadilly.** Farther west lie the equally elegant shops and even more elegant homes of **Mayfair.** Then comes **Park Lane,** with its deluxe hotels. Beyond is **Hyde Park,** the biggest park in central London and one of the largest in the world. **Charing Cross Road** runs north from Trafalgar Square, past **Leicester Square,** and intersects with **Shaftesbury Avenue.** This is London's Theaterland. A bit farther along, Charing Cross Road turns into a browser's paradise, lined with shops selling new and secondhand books. At last, it funnels into **St. Giles Circus.** Beyond is **Bloomsbury,** site of the University of London, the British Museum, and erstwhile stamping ground of the famed "Bloomsbury group," led by Virginia Woolf. Northeast lies **Covent Garden,** known for its Royal Opera House; today it's a major shopping, restaurant, and cafe district.

Follow **The Strand** eastward from Trafalgar Square and you'll come to **Fleet Street.** From the 19th century through most of the 20th century, this area was the most concentrated newspaper district in the world. **Temple Bar** stands where The Strand becomes Fleet Street, and only here do you enter the actual City of London, or "the City." Its focal point and shrine is the Bank of England on **Threadneedle Street,** with the Stock Exchange next door and the Royal Exchange across the street. In the midst of all the hustle and bustle rises **St. Paul's Cathedral,** Sir Christopher Wren's monument to beauty and tranquillity. At the far eastern fringe of the City looms the **Tower of London,** shrouded in legend, blood, and history and permanently besieged by battalions of visitors.

GETTING AROUND By Public Transportation The London Underground subway, known locally as "the Tube," and the city buses are operated by **London Transport** (✆ 020/7222-1234; www.londontransport.co.uk) on a system of six fare zones that radiate out in rings from the central Zone 1, which is where most visitors spend the majority of their time. It covers an area from Aldgate East and Tower Gateway in the east to Notting Hill in the west, and from Waterloo in the south to Baker Street, Euston, and King's Cross in the north. To travel beyond these boundaries, you need at least a two-zone ticket. Note that all one-way, round-trip, and 1-day-pass tickets are valid only on the day of purchase. **LT Information Centres** are at several major Tube stations: Euston, King's Cross, Oxford Circus, St. James's Park, Liverpool Street Station, and Piccadilly Circus, as well as the British Rail stations at Euston and Victoria and each terminal at Heathrow Airport. Most are open daily (some close Sun) from at least 9am to 5pm.

All stations in the **Underground** are clearly marked with a red circle and blue crossbar. Fares are based on zones. The flat fare for one trip within Zone 1 is £1.60 ($2.40). Trips from Zone 1 to destinations in the suburbs generally range from £1.90 to £3.60 ($2.85–$5). Be sure to keep your ticket, as it must be presented when you exit at your destination.

The **bus system** is almost as good as the Underground, and you'll have a better view of the city. As with the Underground, fares vary according to distance traveled. Generally, bus fares are 70p to £1 ($1.10–$1.60), slightly less than Tube fares. If you travel for two or three stops, the cost is £1.50 ($2.40). To find out about current routes, pick up a free bus map at any Underground station or at one of the LT Information Centres listed above.

A regular fare in Zone 1 in the center of London is £1 ($1.50) adults, 40p (60¢) children; a 1-day pass costs £2.40 ($3.60) adults, £1 ($1.50) children. It's also possible to purchase weekly passes for £7.50 ($11) adults or £4 ($6) children in Zone 1.

Note: See the inside back cover of this guide for a map of the London Underground.

By Taxi London cabs are among the most comfortable and best designed in the world. You can pick one up either by heading for a cab rank or by hailing one in the street (the taxi is available if the yellow taxi sign on the roof is lighted); once it has stopped for you, a taxi is obliged to take you anywhere you want within 9.5km (6 miles) of the pickup point, provided it's within the metropolitan area. To **call a cab,** phone ✆ **020/7272-0272** or 020/7253-5000.

Discount Passes for Public Transportation

If you plan to use public transportation a lot, investigate the range of fare discounts available. **Travelcards** offer unlimited use of buses, Underground, and British Rail services in Greater London for any period ranging from a day to a year. Travelcards are available from Underground ticket offices, Tourist Information Centres, main post offices in the London area, and some newsstands. You need to bring a passport-size photo to purchase a Travelcard; you can take a photo at any of the instant photo booths in London's train stations. Children under age 5 generally travel free on the Tube and buses.

The **1-Day Travelcard** allows you to go anywhere throughout Greater London. For travel anywhere within Zones 1 and 2, the cost is £5.10 ($8.15) for adults or £2 ($3.20) for children 5 to 15. The **Off-Peak 1-Day Travelcard,** which isn't valid until after 9:30am on weekdays (or on night buses), is even cheaper. For travel within Zones 1 and 2, the cost is £4.10 ($6.55) for adults and £2 ($3.20) for children 5 to 15.

Weekend Travelcards are valid for 1 weekend, plus Monday if it's a national holiday. They're not valid on night buses. Travel anywhere within Zones 1 and 2 all weekend costs £7.60 ($12) for adults, £3 ($4.80) for kids 5 to 15.

1-Week Travelcards cost adults £20 ($31) and children £8 ($13) for travel in Zones 1 and 2.

The 1-day **Family Travelcard** allows as many journeys as you want on the Tube, on buses (excluding night buses) displaying the London Transport bus sign, and even on the Docklands Light Railway or any rail service within the travel zones designated on your ticket. The family card is valid Monday through Friday after 9:30am and all day on weekends and public holidays. It's available for families as small as two (one adult and one child) and as large as six (two adults and four children). The cost is £3.40 ($5.45) per adult and 80p ($1.30) per child.

The meter starts at £3.80 ($6.10), with increments of 20p (30¢) thereafter, based on distance or time. Each additional passenger is charged 40p (65¢). Passengers pay 10p (15¢) for each piece of luggage in the driver's compartment and any other item more than .6m (2 ft.) long. Surcharges are imposed after 8pm and on weekends and public holidays. All these tariffs include VAT. Fares usually increase annually. It's recommended that you tip 10% to 15% of the fare.

If you call for a cab, the meter starts running when the taxi receives instructions from the dispatcher, so you could find that the meter already reads a few pounds more than the initial drop of £3.80 ($6.10) when you climb inside.

By Car Rent a car only if you plan to take excursions into the environs. Because of traffic and parking difficulties, it's virtually impossible to see London by car.

By Bicycle One of the most popular bike-rental shops is **On Your Bike,** 52–54 Tooley St., London Bridge, SE1 (© **020/7378-6669;** Tube: London Bridge), open Monday through Friday from 8am to 7pm, and Saturday from

9:30am to 5:30pm. The first-class mountain bikes, with high seats and low-slung handlebars, cost £12 ($19) per day, £25 ($40) per weekend, or £60 ($96) per week, and require a £200 ($320) deposit on a credit card.

 FAST FACTS: London

American Express The main office is at 30–31 Haymarket, SW1 (© 020/7484-9600; Tube: Piccadilly Circus). Full services are available Monday through Saturday from 9am to 6pm; foreign-exchange only is open Sunday from 10am to 5pm.

Business Hours Banks are usually open Monday through Friday from 9:30am to 3:30pm. **Pubs and bars** are open Monday through Saturday from 11am to 11pm and Sunday from noon to 10:30pm; some pubs close Sunday from 3 to 7pm. **Stores** are generally open daily from 9am to 5:30pm, to 7pm Wednesday or Thursday. Most central shops close Saturday around 1pm.

Currency The basic unit of currency is the **pound sterling** (£), which is divided into 100 pence (p). The rate of exchange used in this chapter was £1 = $1.60.

Dentists/Doctors For dental emergencies, call **Eastman Dental Hospital** (© 020/7915-1000; Tube: King's Cross). Some hotels have doctors on call. **Medical Express**, 117A Harley St., W1 (© 020/7499-1991; Tube: Regent's Park), is a private British clinic that's not part of the free British medical establishment. It's open Monday through Friday from 9:30am to 5:30pm and Saturday from 9:30am to 2:30pm.

Drugstores In Britain, they're called "chemists." Every police station in the country has a list of emergency chemists. Dial "0" (zero) and ask the operator for the local police, who will give you the name of the chemist nearest you.

Embassies The embassy of the **United States** is at 24 Grosvenor St., W1 (© 020/7499-9000; Tube: Bond St.). For passport and visa information, go to the U.S. Passport and Citizenship Unit, 55–56 Upper Brook St., London, W1 (© 020/7499-9000, ext. 2563 or 2564; Tube: Marble Arch), Monday through Friday from 8:30am to 11:30am and 2 to 4pm (Tues the office closes at noon). The high commission of **Canada**, MacDonald House, 38 Grosvenor St., W1 (© 020/7258-6600; Tube: Bond St.), is open Monday through Friday from 8 to 11am. The high commission of **Australia**, Australia House, Strand, WC2 (© 020/7379-4334; Tube: Charing Cross or Aldwych), is open Monday through Friday from 9:30am to 3:30pm. The high commission of **New Zealand**, New Zealand House, 80 Haymarket at Pall Mall, SW1 (© 020/7930-8422; Tube: Charing Cross or Piccadilly Circus), is open Monday through Friday from 10am to noon and 2 to 4pm. The embassy of **Ireland**, 17 Grosvenor Place, SW1 (© 020/7235-2171; Tube: Hyde Park Corner), is open Monday through Friday from 9:30am to 1pm and 2:15 to 5pm. The high commission of **South Africa**, South Africa House, 15 Whitehall, SW1 (© 020/7925-8900; Tube: Westminster), is open Monday through Friday from 10am to noon and 2 to 4pm.

Emergencies In London, for police, fire, or an ambulance, dial © **999**.

Hospitals Emergency care 24 hours a day, with the first treatment free under the National Health Service, is offered by **Royal Free Hospital,** Pond Street, NW10 (© **020/7794-0500;** Tube: Belsize Park); and by **University College Hospital,** Gower Street, WC1 (© **020/7387-9300;** Tube: Warren St.).

Internet Access You can send e-mails or check your messages at **Cyberia,** 39 Whitfield St. (© **020/7209-0984;** www.cyberiacafe.net).

Post Office The **Main Post Office,** 24-28 William IV St., WC2N 4DL (© **020/ 7484-9307;** Tube: Charing Cross), operates as three separate businesses: inland and international postal service and banking; philatelic postage stamp sales; and the post shop, selling greeting cards and stationery. All are open Monday through Saturday from 8:30am to 9pm.

Safety Stay in well-lit areas and out of questionable neighborhoods, especially at night. In Britain, most of the crime perpetrated against tourists is pickpocketing and mugging. These attacks usually occur in such cities as London, Birmingham, or Manchester. Most villages are safe.

Taxes To encourage energy conservation, the British government levies a 25% tax on gasoline (petrol). There is also a 17.5% national value-added tax (VAT) that is added to all hotel and restaurant bills and is included in the price of many items you purchase. This can be refunded if you shop at stores that participate in the Retail Export Scheme (signs are posted in the window). For information on getting your VAT refund, go to the "Money" section of the "Planning Your Trip to Europe" chapter.

A departure tax is included in the price of your ticket.

Telephone The country code for the United Kingdom is **44.** London's city code is **020.**

For directory assistance in London, dial **142;** for the rest of Britain, **192.**

There are three types of public pay phones: those taking only coins, those accepting only phone cards (called Cardphones), and those taking both phone cards and credit cards. At coin-operated phones, insert your coins before dialing. The minimum charge is 10p (15¢).

Phone cards are available in four values: £2 ($3.20), £4 ($6.40), £10 ($16), and £20 ($32)—and are reusable until the total value has expired. Cards can be purchased from newsstands and post offices.

To make an international call from Britain, dial the international access code **(00),** then the country code, then the area code, and finally the local number. Or call through one of the following long-distance access codes: **AT&T Direct Service** (© 0800/890011), **Canada Direct** (© 0800/890016), **Australia** (© 0800/890061), and **New Zealand** (© 0800/890064). Common country codes are: USA and Canada, **1;** Australia, **61;** New Zealand, **64;** and South Africa, **27.**

Tipping For cab drivers, add about 10% to 15% to the fare on the meter. If the driver loads or unloads your luggage, add something extra.

In hotels, porters receive 75p ($1.20) per bag, even if you have only one small suitcase. Hall porters are tipped only for special services. Maids receive £1 ($1.60) per day. In top-ranking hotels, the concierge will often submit a separate bill showing charges for newspapers and other items; if he or she has been particularly helpful, tip extra.

Hotels often add a service charge of 10% to 15% to bills. In smaller bed-and-breakfasts, the tip is not likely to be included. Therefore, tip those who perform special services, such as the waiter who serves you breakfast. If several people have served you in a bed-and-breakfast, you may ask that 10% to 15% be added to the bill and divided among the staff.

In both restaurants and nightclubs, a 15% service charge is added to the bill, which is distributed among all the help. To that, add another 3% to 5%, depending on the service. Waiters in deluxe restaurants and nightclubs are accustomed to the extra 5%. Sommeliers (wine stewards) get about £1 ($1.60) per bottle of wine served. Tipping in pubs isn't common, but in wine bars, the server usually gets about 75p ($1.20) per round of drinks.

WHERE TO STAY
MAYFAIR
Very Expensive

Raffles Brown's Hotel ✿✿✿   Almost every year a new hotel attempts to evoke an English country house ambience with Chippendale furniture and chintz, but this quintessential town house hotel always comes out on top. Created by a former manservant to Lord Byron, Brown's opened its doors in 1837, the same year Queen Victoria took the throne. Today Brown's occupies 14 historic houses off Berkeley Square. The guest rooms show stately, restrained taste—even the washbasins are tasteful antiques. Accommodations have such extras as voice mail, dual phone lines, and dataports, and bathrooms are equipped with robes, cosmetics, tubs, and showers. In keeping with the atmosphere of the rest of the hotel, the lounges pay homage to the past: They include the Roosevelt Room (TR honeymooned here in 1886), the Rudyard Kipling Room (the author was a frequent visitor), and the paneled St. George's Bar.

30 Albemarle St., London W1S 4BP. © 020/7493-6020. Fax 020/7493-9381. www.rafflesbrownshotel.com. 118 units. £225–£320 ($360–$512) double; from £540 ($864) suite. AE, DC, MC, V. Off-site parking £40 ($64). Tube: Green Park. **Amenities:** 3 restaurants; bar; health club; concierge; courtesy car; business center; 24-hr. room service; laundry service; same-day dry cleaning. *In room:* A/C, TV/VCR, dataport, minibar, hair dryer, safe.

Sheraton Park Lane Hotel ✿✿   Since 1924, this has been the most traditional of the Park Lane mansions. The hotel was sold in 1996 to the Sheraton Corporation, which continues to upgrade it but maintains its quintessential British style. Its Silver Entrance remains an Art Deco marvel that has been used as a backdrop in many films, including the classic BBC miniseries *Brideshead Revisited*. Overlooking Green Park, the hotel offers luxurious accommodations that are a good deal—well, at least for pricey Park Lane, where anything under $500 a night is a bargain. Many suites have marble fireplaces and original marble bathrooms. All rooms have double-glazed windows to block out noise.

Piccadilly, London W1J 7BX. © 800/325-3535 in the U.S. or 020/7499-6321. Fax 020/7499-1965. www. starwood.com/sheraton. 307 units. £270–£310 ($432–$496) double; from £429 ($686) suite. AE, DC, MC, V. Parking £35 ($56). Tube: Hyde Park Corner or Green Park. **Amenities:** Restaurant; afternoon tea in the fabled 1920s Palm Court; 2 bars; health club; concierge; business center; 24-hr. room service; laundry service; same-day dry cleaning. *In room:* A/C (in most rooms), TV w/pay movies, dataport, minibar, hair dryer, iron, safe.

Expensive

The Chesterfield Mayfair ✿✿   Just a short distance from Berkeley Square, the elegant Chesterfield serves up a traditional English atmosphere and offers a lot more bang for your buck than most hotels in pricey Mayfair. The hotel, once home to the earl of Chesterfield, still sports venerable features that evoke an air of nobility, including richly decorated public rooms featuring woods, antiques, fabrics, and marble. The secluded Library Lounge is a great place to relax, and the glassed-in conservatory is a good spot for tea. The sumptuously decorated restaurant is well regarded, as is the bar, where a pianist plays on most nights. The staff, from the reception clerks to the chambermaids, couldn't be nicer. The guest rooms are generally not huge, but they are dramatically decorated and make excellent use of space—there's a ton of closet and counter space—and feature such unusual amenities as complimentary bottled waters and jelly beans.

35 Charles St., London W1J 5EB. (C) **877/955-1515** in the U.S. and Canada, or 020/7491-2622. Fax 020/7491-4793. www.chesterfieldmayfair.com. 110 units. £190–£260 ($304–$416) double; £250–£595 ($400–$950) suite. Special packages available. AE, DC, MC, V. Tube: Green Park. **Amenities:** 2 restaurants; bar; concierge; business services; 24-hr. room service; babysitting; laundry service; same-day dry cleaning. *In room:* A/C, TV w/pay movies, dataport, coffeemaker, hair dryer, iron, safe.

ST. JAMES'S
Very Expensive

Dukes Hotel ★★★   Dukes provides elegance without ostentation. Since 1908, it has stood in a quiet courtyard off St. James's Street. It attracts the urbane guest who's looking for charm, style, and tradition. Each well-furnished room is decorated in the style of a particular period, ranging from Regency to Edwardian. The well-maintained bathrooms contain tub/shower combos.

35 St. James's Place, London SW1A 1NY. (C) **800/381-4702** in the U.S. or 020/7491-4840. Fax 020/7493-1264. www.dukeshotel.co.uk. 89 units. £225–£260 ($360–$416) double; from £350 ($560) suite. AE, DC, MC, V. Parking £54 ($86). Tube: Green Park. **Amenities:** Restaurant; bar; health club; spa; concierge; tour desk; business services; 24-hr. room service; babysitting; laundry service; same-day dry cleaning. *In room:* A/C, TV, dataport, minibar, hair dryer, safe.

SOHO
Expensive

Charlotte Street Hotel ★★   In North Soho, a short walk from the heartbeat of Soho Square, this town house has been luxuriously converted into a high-end hotel that is London chic at its finest, with everything from a Los Angeles–style juice bar to a private screening room. The latter has made it a hit with the movie, fashion, and media crowd, many of whom had never ventured to North Soho before. Midsize to spacious rooms have fresh modern English interiors. Bathrooms are state of the art, designed in solid granite and oak with twin basins, tubs, walk-in showers, even TVs. Guests relax in the elegant drawing room and library with a log-burning fireplace. The decor evokes memories of the fabled Bloomsbury set of Virginia Woolf.

15 Charlotte St., London W1P IRJ. (C) **800/553-6674** in the U.S., or 020/7806-2000. Fax 020/7806-2002. www.firmdale.com. 52 units. £210–£240 ($336–$384) double; from £595 ($952) suite. AE, DC, MC, V. Tube: Tottenham Court. **Amenities:** Restaurant and long pewter bar; exercise room; concierge; 24-hr. room service; laundry service; same-day dry cleaning. *In room:* A/C, TV/VCR, fax, dataport, minibar, hair dryer, safe.

BAKER STREET
Inexpensive

Wigmore Court *Value*   A convenient family hotel, this inn lies near the street made famous as the fictional address of Sherlock Holmes. It is close to Marble Arch, Oxford Street, and Madame Tussaud's. A somber Victorian structure, it has been tastefully converted into a fine B&B suitable only for serious stair climbers, as there is no elevator. There's traffic outside, so request a room in the rear if you're bothered by the noise. Rooms, many quite spacious, are comfortably

London Accommodations

Academy Hotel **23**
The Beaufort **9**
Boston Court Hotel **16**
The Byron Hotel **12**
Charlotte Street Hotel **21**
Chesterfield Mayfair **17**
Claverley Hotel **10**
Collin House **7**
Covent Garden Hotel **24**
Diplomat Hotel **8**
Dukes Hotel **19**
Edward Lear Hotel **15**
Fielding Hotel **25**

Goring Hotel **6**
James & Cartref House **4**
Miller's Residence **11**
Myhotel **22**
The Pavilion **13**
Philbeach Hotel **1**
Raffles Brown's Hotel **20**
Sheraton Park Lane **18**
The Sloane **2**
Tophams Belgravia **5**
Wigmore Court **14**
Willett Hotel **3**

furnished. Most contain double or twin beds. About half of the small bathrooms have tub/shower combos.

23 Gloucester Place, London W1H 3PB. ℂ 020/7935-0928. Fax 020/7487-4254. www.wigmore-court-hotel. co.uk. 18 units. £75 ($120) double; £90 ($144) triple. MC, V. Tube: Marble Arch. **Amenities:** Guest kitchen; coin-op washers and dryers. In room: TV, dataport, coffeemaker.

BLOOMSBURY
Expensive
Academy Hotel ☆   The Academy is in the heart of London's publishing district. Looking out your window, you'll see where members of the literary Bloomsbury Group used to pass by. Many original architectural grace notes were preserved when these three 1776 Georgian row houses were joined. The hotel was substantially upgraded in the 1990s, with a bathroom added to every guest room (whether there was space or not). With their overstuffed armchairs and half-canopied beds, rooms here evoke English country-house living, but that of the poorer relations. The beds, so they say, were built to "American specifications." True or not, they assure you of a restful night's sleep. *Warning:* If you have a problem with stairs, this may not be the place for you—there are no elevators rising to the four floors.

21 Gower St., London WC1E 6HG. ℂ 800/678-3096 in the U.S., or 020/7631-4115. Fax 020/7636-3442. www.etontownhouse.com. 49 units. £163–£200 ($261–$320) double; £225 ($360) suite. AE, DC, MC, V. Tube: Tottenham Court Rd., Goodge St., or Russell Sq. **Amenities:** Bar; 24-hr. room service; laundry service; same-day dry cleaning. In room: A/C, TV, hair dryer, safe.

Myhotel ☆ *Finds*   Creating shock waves among staid Bloomsbury hoteliers, Myhotel is a London row house on the outside with an Asian *moderne*-style interior. It is designed according to *feng shui* principles—the ancient Chinese art of placement that analyzes the flow of energy in a space. The rooms have mirrors, but they're positioned so you don't see yourself when you first wake up—*feng shui* rule no. 1 (probably a good rule, *feng shui* or no *feng shui*). Rooms are havens of comfort, taste, and tranquility. Excellent sleep-inducing beds are found in all units, along with a small bathroom with a shower stall. Tipping is discouraged, and each guest is assigned a personal assistant responsible for that guest's happiness. Aimed at today's young, hip traveler, Myhotel lies within a short walk of Covent Garden and the British Museum.

11–13 Bayley St., Bedford Sq., London WC1B 3HD. ℂ 020/7667-6000. Fax 020/7667-6001. www.myhotels. co.uk. 78 units. £190–£210 ($304–$336) double; from £360 ($576) suite. AE, DC, MC, V. Tube: Tottenham Court Rd. **Amenities:** Breakfast cafe; restaurant; bar; exercise room; spa; car at discounted rate; 24-hr. room service; massage; babysitting; laundry service; same-day dry cleaning. In room: A/C, TV w/pay movies, dataport, hair dryer, safe.

COVENT GARDEN
Very Expensive
Covent Garden Hotel ☆☆☆   This former hospital building lay neglected for years until it was reconfigured in 1996 by hot hoteliers Tim and Kit Kemp—whose flair for interior design is legendary—into one of London's most charming boutique hotels in one of the West End's hippest shopping neighborhoods. *Travel & Leisure* called this hotel one of the 25 hottest places to stay in the *world*. It remains so. The hotel has a welcoming lobby outfitted with elaborate inlaid furniture and elegant draperies, plus two charming restaurants. Upstairs, accessible via a dramatic stone staircase, soundproof bedrooms are furnished in English style with Asian fabrics and contain such luxurious amenities as two phone lines with voice mail, full marble bathrooms with double vanities, and deep soaking tubs.

10 Monmouth St., London WC2H 9HB. © **800/553-6674** in the U.S., or 020/7806-1000. Fax 020/7806-1100. www.firmdale.com. 58 units. £245–£295 ($392–$472) double; £350–£795 ($560–$1,272) suite. AE, MC, V. Tube: Covent Garden or Leicester Sq. **Amenities:** Restaurant; bar; small exercise room; concierge; tour desk; business services; 24-hr. room service; massage; babysitting; laundry service; same-day dry cleaning; video library. *In room:* A/C, TV/VCR, dataport, minibar, hair dryer, safe.

Moderate

Fielding Hotel ✿ *(Finds)*   One of London's more eccentric hotels, the Fielding is cramped, quirky, and quaint, and an enduring favorite. Luring media types, the hotel is named after novelist Henry Fielding of *Tom Jones* fame, who lived in Broad Court. It lies on a pedestrian street still lined with 19th-century gas lamps. The Royal Opera House is across the street; and the pubs, shops, and restaurants of lively Covent Garden are just beyond the front door. Rooms are small, but charmingly old-fashioned. Some units are "touched up" every year, though floors dip and sway, and the furnishings and fabrics, though clean, have known better times. But with a location like this, in the heart of London, the Fielding keeps guests coming back; in fact, many love the hotel's rickety charm.

4 Broad Ct., Bow St., London WC2B 5QZ. © 020/7836-8305. Fax 020/7497-0064. www.the-fielding-hotel. co.uk. 24 units. £100–£115 ($160–$184) double; £130 ($208) suite. AE, DC, MC, V. Tube: Covent Garden. **Amenities:** Bar. *In room:* TV, coffeemaker.

VICTORIA
Very Expensive

Goring Hotel ✿✿✿   For tradition and location, the Goring is our first choice in Westminster. Just behind Buckingham Palace, it lies within easy reach of the royal parks, Victoria Station, Westminster Abbey, and the Houses of Parliament. It also offers the finest personal service of all its nearby competitors. Built in 1910, this was the first hotel in the world to have central heating and a private bathroom in every room. Today's guest rooms still offer all the comforts, including luxurious refurbished bathrooms with extra-long tubs, red marble walls, dual pedestal basins, bidets, deluxe toiletries, and power showerheads. Rooms overlooking the garden are best. The charm of a traditional English country hotel is conjured in the paneled drawing room, where fires crackle in the ornate fireplaces on nippy evenings. The adjoining bar overlooks the rear gardens.

15 Beeston Place, Grosvenor Gardens, London SW1W 0JW. © 020/7396-9000. Fax 020/7834-4393. www. goringhotel.co.uk. 74 units. £235–£285 ($376–$456) double; from £365 ($584) suite. AE, DC, MC, V. Parking £21 ($34). Tube: Victoria. **Amenities:** Grand afternoon tea in the drawing room; classic restaurant; bar; free use of nearby health club; concierge; 24-hr. room service; babysitting; laundry service; same-day dry cleaning. *In room:* A/C, TV w/pay movies, dataport, hair dryer, safe.

Expensive

Tophams Belgravia ✿   Tophams came into being in 1937, when five small row houses were interconnected. With its flower-filled window boxes, the place has a bucolic flavor. All guest rooms are tastefully furnished, and the best are appointed with four-poster beds and private bathrooms equipped with shower-tub combinations. Not all rooms have private bathrooms. The restaurant offers traditional and modern English cooking for lunch and dinner. And the location is ideal, especially if you plan to cover a lot of ground by Tube or train: It's only a 3-minute walk to Victoria Station.

28 Ebury St., London SW1W 0LU. © 020/7730-8147. Fax 020/7823-5966. www.tophams.co.uk. 39 units, 34 with bathroom. £110 ($176) double without bathroom, £130–£170 ($208–$272) double with bathroom; £170 ($272) triple with bathroom. AE, DC, MC, V. Tube: Victoria. **Amenities:** Restaurant; bar; access to nearby health club; limited room service; babysitting; laundry service; same-day dry cleaning. *In room:* TV, dataport, coffeemaker, hair dryer, iron.

Inexpensive

Collin House ✦   This B&B emerges as a winner on a street lined with the finest Victoria Station–area B&Bs. Queen Victoria was halfway through her long reign when this house was constructed in 1830. Private, shower-only bathrooms have been discreetly installed, and everything works efficiently. For rooms without bathrooms, there are adequate hallway facilities, some of which are shared by only two rooms. Traffic in this area of London is heavy outside, and the front windows are not soundproof, so be warned if you're a light sleeper. Year after year, the owners continually make improvements, and all guest rooms are comfortably furnished and well maintained. A generous breakfast awaits you each morning in the basement of this nonsmoking facility.

104 Ebury St., London SW1W 9QD. ©/fax 020/7730-8031. www.collinhouse.co.uk. 12 units, 8 with bathroom (shower only). £70 ($112) double without bathroom, £85 ($136) double with bathroom; £98 ($157) triple without bathroom. Rates include English breakfast. No credit cards. Tube: Victoria. *In room:* TV in most, hair dryer available, safe, no phone.

James & Cartref House *Kids*   Hailed by many publications as one of the top 10 B&B choices in London, James House and Cartref House (across the street from each other) deserve their accolades. *Warning:* Whether or not you like this hotel will depend on your room assignment. Some accommodations are fine but several rooms (often when the other units are full) are hardly large enough to move around in. This is especially true of some third-floor units. Some "bathrooms" reminded us of those found on small ocean-going freighters. On the plus side, each room is individually designed, and those with bunk beds make nice family choices. The English breakfast is so generous that you might end up skipping lunch—and you're just a stone's throw from Buckingham Palace should the queen invite you over for tea.

108 and 129 Ebury St., London SW1W 9QD. James House © 020/7730-7338; Cartref House © 020/7730-6176. Fax 020/7730-7338. www.jamesandcartref.co.uk. 19 units, 12 with bathroom. £70 ($112) double without bathroom, £85 ($136) double with bathroom; £135 ($216) quad with bathroom. Rates include English breakfast. AE, MC, V. Tube: Victoria. *In room:* TV, dataport, coffeemaker, hair dryer, no phone.

KNIGHTSBRIDGE
Very Expensive

The Beaufort ✦✦   If you'd like to stay at one of London's finest boutique hotels, offering personal service in an elegant, tranquil town-house atmosphere just 200 yards from Harrods, head here. Owner Diana Wallis, a television producer, combined a pair of adjacent houses from the 1870s, ripped out the old decor, and created a stylish hotel that has the feeling of a private house. Each guest room is individually decorated in a modern color scheme and adorned with well-chosen paintings by London artists. Rooms come with earphone radios, flowers, and a selection of books. Included in the rates are a 24-hour free bar, continental breakfast, and light meals from room service, plus English cream teas each afternoon, and brandy, chocolates, and shortbread in each room. Junior suites include complimentary limo to or from the airport.

33 Beaufort Gardens, London SW3 1PP. © **888/668-8141** in the U.S. or Canada, or 020/7584-5252. Fax 020/7589-2834. www.thebeaufort.co.uk. 28 units. £195–£260 ($312–$416) double; £310 ($496) junior suite. Rates include continental breakfast, bar, light meals, and afternoon tea. AE, DC, MC, V. Tube: Knightsbridge. **Amenities:** Bar; access to nearby health club; 24-hr. room service; babysitting; laundry service; same-day dry cleaning. *In room:* A/C, TV, dataport, hair dryer, iron.

Expensive

Claverley Hotel ✦   Located on a quiet cul-de-sac, this tasteful hotel, one of the neighborhood's very best (and winner of the Spencer Trophy for the Best

Bed & Breakfast Hotel in Central London), is just a few blocks from Harrods. It's a small, cozy place accented with Georgian-era accessories. The lounge has the atmosphere of a country house. Most rooms have wall-to-wall carpeting and comfortably upholstered armchairs. Recently refurbished rooms have a marble bathrooms and "power showers."

13–14 Beaufort Gardens, London SW3 1PS. © **800/747-0398** in the U.S., or 020/7589-8541. Fax 020/7584-3410. www.claverleyhotel.co.uk. 29 units. £120–£140 ($192–$224) double; £170–£195 ($272–$312) junior suite. Rates include English breakfast. AE, DC, MC, V. Free parking on Sun; £21 ($34) during the week. Tube: Knightsbridge. **Amenities:** Same-day dry cleaning. *In room:* TV, dataport, hair dryer, safe.

BELGRAVIA
Expensive
Diplomat Hotel *(Finds)*   Part of the Diplomat's charm is that it is a small, reasonably priced hotel located in an otherwise prohibitively expensive neighborhood. Only minutes from Harrods Department Store, it was built in 1882 as a private residence by noted architect Thomas Cubbitt. It's very well appointed and was completely overhauled in 2002 and 2003. The registration desk is framed by the sweep of a partially gilded circular staircase. The staff is helpful, well mannered, and discreet. The high-ceilinged guest rooms are tastefully done in Victorian style. You get good—not grand—comfort here.

2 Chesham St., London SW1X 8DT. © 020/7235-1544. Fax 020/7259-6153. www.btinternet.com/~diplomat. hotel. 26 units. £125–£170 ($200–$272) double. Rates include English buffet breakfast. AE, DC, MC, V. Tube: Sloane Sq. or Knightsbridge. **Amenities:** Snack bar; nearby health club; business services; laundry service; same-day dry cleaning. *In room:* TV, dataport, coffeemaker, hair dryer, iron.

CHELSEA
Expensive
The Sloane *(★★)*   This "toff" (dandy) address, a redbrick Victorian-era town house that has been tastefully renovated in recent years, is located in Chelsea near Sloane Square. It combines valuable 19th-century antiques with modern comforts. Our favorite spot here is the rooftop terrace; with views opening onto Chelsea, it's ideal for a relaxing breakfast or drink. Guest rooms range from small to spacious, but all are opulently furnished with flouncy draperies, tasteful fabrics, and sumptuous beds. The deluxe bathrooms have chrome power-showers, wall-width mirrors (in most rooms), and luxurious toiletries.

29-34 Draycott Place, London SW3 2SH. © **800/324-9960** in the U.S., or 020/7581-5757. Fax 020/7584-1348. www.sloanehotel.com. 22 units. £195–£240 ($312–$384) double; £225 ($360) suite. AE, DC, MC, V. Tube: Sloane Sq. **Amenities:** Airport transportation (by prior arrangement); business services; 24-hr. room service; laundry service; same-day dry cleaning. *In room:* A/C, TV/VCR (plus pay movies), dataport, hair dryer, safe.

Moderate
Willett Hotel *(Value)*   On a tree-lined street leading off Sloane Square, this restored town house lies in the heart of Chelsea. It evokes the days when King Edward was on the throne; stained glass and chandeliers reflect the opulence of that age. Under a mansard roof with projecting bay windows, the hotel is just a 5-minute walk from the shopping mecca of King's Road and close to such stores as Peter Jones, Harrods, and Harvey Nichols. Individually decorated guest rooms come in a wide range of sizes. Some are first class, but a few of the standard twins are best left for Lilliputians.

32 Sloane Gardens, London SW1 8DJ. © **020/7824-8415**. Fax 020/7730-4830. www.eeh.co.uk. 19 units. £90–£155 ($144–$248) double. Rates include English or continental breakfast. AE, DC, MC, V. Tube: Sloane Sq. **Amenities:** Bar; concierge; 24-hr. room service; laundry service; same-day dry cleaning. *In room:* A/C in most, TV/VCR (plus pay movies), dataport, minibar in suites, coffeemaker, hair dryer, iron.

SOUTH KENSINGTON
Moderate
The Gallery *(* *Finds* This is the place to go if you want to stay in an exclusive little town house hotel but don't want to pay £300 ($475) a night for the privilege. Two splendid Georgian residences have been restored and converted into this remarkable and relatively unknown hotel. The location is ideal, near the Victoria and Albert Museum, Royal Albert Hall, Harrods, Knightsbridge, and King's Road. Guest rooms are decorated in Laura Ashley style, with half-canopied beds and marble-tiled bathrooms with brass fittings and tub-and-shower combos. The junior suites have private roof terraces, minibars, Jacuzzis, and air-conditioning. A team of butlers takes care of everything. The lounge, with its mahogany paneling and deep colors, has the ambience of a private club.

8–10 Queensberry Place, London SW7 2EA. © 020/7915-0000. Fax 020/7915-4400. www.eeh.co.uk. 36 units. £120–£145 ($192–$232) double; from £220 ($352) junior suite. Rates include buffet English breakfast. AE, DC, MC, V. Tube: South Kensington. **Amenities:** Bar; access to nearby health club; courtesy car; business center; babysitting; laundry service; same-day dry cleaning; 24-hr. butler service. *In room:* TV, dataport, coffeemaker, hair dryer, safe.

PADDINGTON
Moderate
The Pavilion *(Finds* Until the early 1990s, this was a rather ordinary-looking B&B. Then, a team of entrepreneurs with ties to the fashion industry took over and redecorated the rooms with sometimes-wacky themes. The result is a theatrical and often outrageous decor that's appreciated by the many fashion models and music-industry folks who regularly make this their temporary home in London. Rooms are, regrettably, rather small, but each has a distinctive style. Examples include a kitschy 1970s room ("Honky-Tonk Afro") and an Asian bordello–themed room ("Enter the Dragon").

34–36 Sussex Gardens, London W2 1UL. © 020/7262-0905. Fax 020/7262-1324. www.eol.net.mt/pavilion. 29 units. £100 ($160) double; £120 ($190) triple. Rates include continental breakfast. AE, DC, MC, V. Parking £5 ($8). Tube: Edgware Rd. **Amenities:** Same-day dry cleaning. *In room:* TV, dataport, coffeemaker.

MARYLEBONE
Inexpensive
Boston Court Hotel Upper Berkeley is a classic street of B&Bs. In days of yore, it was home to Elizabeth Montagu (1720–1800), the "queen of the bluestockings" (a pejorative term for the women's literary clubs that sprang up in the 18th c.). She defended Shakespeare against attacks by Voltaire, who was fond of saying such things as: "Shakespeare is a savage with sparks of genius which shine in a horrible night." Today, it's a good, safe retreat at an affordable price. The simply decorated hotel offers accommodations in a centrally located Victorian-era building within walking distance of Oxford Street shopping and Hyde Park. The small, basic rooms have been refurbished and redecorated with a no-nonsense decor. Guest rooms come with well-kept bathrooms with private showers.

26 Upper Berkeley St., Marble Arch, London W1H 7PF. © 020/7723-1445. Fax 020/7262-8823. www.boston courthotel.co.uk. 15 units (7 with shower only). £69 ($110) double with shower only; £75 ($120) double with bathroom; £85 ($136) triple with bathroom. Rates include continental breakfast. MC, V. Tube: Marble Arch. **Amenities:** Laundry service; same-day dry cleaning. *In room:* TV w/pay movies, fridge, coffeemaker, hair dryer.

Edward Lear Hotel This popular hotel, situated 1 block from Marble Arch, is made all the more desirable by the bouquets of fresh flowers in its public rooms. It occupies a pair of brick town houses dating from 1780. The western house was the London home of 19th-century artist and poet Edward Lear, famous for his nonsense verse, and his illustrated limericks adorn the walls of one of the sitting rooms. Steep stairs lead up to cozy rooms which range from spacious to broom-closet size. Things are a bit tattered here and there, but with this location and price level, few can complain, as this is an area of £400- ($640-) a-night mammoths. If you're looking for classiness, know that the bacon on your plate came from the same butcher used by the queen. One major drawback to the hotel: This is a very noisy part of town. Rear rooms are quieter. Bathrooms are tidy and well maintained, each with a shower and tub.

28–30 Seymour St., London W1H 5WD. © 020/7402-5401. Fax 020/7706-3766. www.edlear.com. 31 units, 12 with bathroom. £55–£66 ($88–$106) double without bathroom, £72–£89 ($115–$142) double with bathroom; £89–£105 ($142–$168) suite. Rates include English breakfast. MC, V. Tube: Marble Arch. *In room:* TV w/pay movies, dataport, coffeemaker.

BAYSWATER
Expensive
Miller's Residence ★ *Finds* Staying here is like spending a night in Charles Dickens's *Old Curiosity Shop*. Others say that the little hotel looks like a set of *La Traviata*. Miller's calls itself an 18th-century rooming house, and there's nothing quite like it in London. A roaring log fire blazes in the large book-lined drawing room in winter. The individually designed rooms are named after Romantic poets. They vary in shape and size, but all are luxuriously furnished with antiques, prints, and tasteful curios. Each guest room includes a small bathroom with a shower and tub. For guests who are staying longer than a week, Miller's offers sumptuous apartments with multiple bedrooms, a drawing room, and a kitchen.

111A Westbourne Grove, London W2 4UW. © 020/7243-1024. Fax 020/7243-1064. www.millersuk.com. 6 units. £150 ($240) double; £230 ($368) suite; from £1,600 ($2,580) per week apt. Rates include continental breakfast. AE, DISC, MC, V. Tube: Bayswater or Notting Hill Gate. **Amenities:** Limited business services; babysitting; laundry service; same-day dry cleaning. *In room:* TV/VCR, dataport.

Moderate
The Byron Hotel *Value* A mostly American clientele appreciates this family-run hotel, just north of Kensington Gardens, for its country-house atmosphere, its helpful staff (who spend extra time with guests to make their stay in London special), and the good value it offers. The interior was recently redesigned and refurbished, and the rooms are better than ever, with ample closets and tile bathrooms with good showers. An elevator services all floors, and breakfast is served in a bright and cheery room.

36–38 Queensborough Terrace, London W2 3SH. © 020/7243-0987. Fax 020/7792-1957. www.capricorn hotels.co.uk. 45 units. £120 ($192) double; £150–£180 ($240–$288) suite. Rates include English/continental breakfast. AE, DC, MC, V. Tube: Bayswater or Queensway. **Amenities:** 24-hr. room service; laundry service; same-day dry cleaning. *In room:* A/C, TV, dataport, coffeemaker, hair dryer, iron, safe.

A GAY HOTEL
Philbeach Hotel One of Europe's largest gay hotels, the Philbeach is a Victorian row house on a wide crescent behind the Earl's Court Exhibition Centre, open to both men and women. It offers standard budget-hotel rooms; the showers are tiny, but the shared bathrooms are clean. Room no. 8A, a double with a shower-only bathroom, has a balcony overlooking the small back garden.

30–31 Philbeach Gardens, London SW5 9EB. © 020/7373-1244. Fax 020/7244-0149. www.philbeach hotel.freeserve.co.uk. 40 units, 16 with bathroom. £35 ($56) single without bathroom, £65 ($104) single with bathroom; £70 ($112) double without bathroom, £90 ($144) double with bathroom. Rates include continental breakfast. AE, DC, MC, V. Tube: Earl's Court. **Amenities:** Restaurant; gay bar (Jimmies); laundry service; same-day dry cleaning. *In room:* TV.

WHERE TO DINE

All restaurants and cafes in Britain are required to display the prices of their food and drink in a place that the customer can see before entering the eating area. Charges for service and any minimum charge or cover must also be made clear. Most restaurants add a 10% to 15% service charge to your bill, but if nothing has been added, leave a 12% to 15% tip.

MAYFAIR
Very Expensive

Gordon Ramsay at Claridge's 🌟🌟🌟 EUROPEAN   Gordon Ramsay, the volatile and outspoken Scotsman who once played soccer for the Glasgow Rangers, is the hottest high-octane chef in London today. Ramsay now rules at the staid, traditional Claridge's hotel. The famed Art Deco dining room retains many of its original architectural features, but the cuisine is hardly the same. In "bad boy" Ramsay's own words, he got "rid of the dribble mats and the waltzing."

We were recently dazzled by the lunch set menu, which is relatively reasonably priced and which included roast monkfish tails served on a bed of lobster and crushed potatoes with a creamy coriander-laced lemon-grass sauce; and pot-roasted belly of pork with an eggplant caviar and baby spinach. A three-course dinner featured such delights as filet of sea bass wrapped in fresh basil leaves and served with a caviar sauce; and roast Scottish baby lobster cooked slowly in lime butter and served with tomato couscous. The desserts are among our favorite in London, including a bread and butter brioche pudding with clotted-cream ice cream.

Brook St., W1. ⓒ 020/7499-0099. Reservations required as far in advance as possible. Fixed-price meals £25 ($40) lunch; £50 ($80) dinner. AE, DC, MC, V. Mon–Sat noon–3pm and 5:45–11pm; Sun 6–10:30pm. Tube: Bond St.

Le Gavroche 🌟🌟🌟 FRENCH   Although challengers come and go, this *luxe* dining room remains the number-one choice in London for classical French cuisine, although not of the "essentially old-fashioned bourgeois repertoire" as some critics suggest. The service is faultless and the ambience is chic without being stuffy. Try some of the signatures: soufflé Suissesse, papillote of smoked salmon, or whole Bresse chicken with truffles and a Madeira cream sauce. Other menu options include an herb-seasoned cassoulet of snails with frog thighs, mousseline of lobster in champagne sauce, pavé of braised turbot with red Provençal wine and smoked bacon, and filet of red snapper with caviar and oyster-stuffed tortellini. Lighter, more modern dishes include red mullet with a cockle risotto, and poached lobster flavored with star anise.

43 Upper Brook St., W1. ⓒ 020/7408-0881. Fax 020/7491-4387. Reservations required as far in advance as possible. Main courses £24–£45 ($38–$72); fixed-price lunch £40 ($64); *menu exceptionnel* for entire table £80 ($128) per person. AE, MC, V. Mon–Fri noon–2pm and Mon–Sat 7–11pm. Tube: Marble Arch.

Expensive

L'Oranger 🌟 FRENCH   This bistro-cum-brasserie manages to elevate a Gallic brasserie into an artfully upscale dining experience for a clientele that has been described as "people who have made it." The set-price menus are likely to include foie gras poached in a red Pessac wine sauce; and pan-fried filet of sea bass with zucchini, tomatoes, basil, and a black-olive vinaigrette. Other delectable staples might be crispy cod filets with bouillabaisse sauce and new potatoes; or braised leg of rabbit in Madeira sauce with whole cloves of yellow garlic *en confit* and braised cabbage.

5 St. James's St., SW1A. ✆ **020/7839-3774.** Reservations recommended. Fixed-price meals £18–£23 ($29–$37) lunch; £45 ($72) dinner. AE, DC, MC, V. Mon–Fri noon–2pm; Mon–Sat 6:30–11pm. Tube: Green Park.

Petrus ✿✿ FRENCH   Clubby and not at all stuffy, this is the domain of Marcus Wareing, a former boxer from Lancashire. Here in a sleek, opulent setting, you get reasonably priced food that is prepared with a technical precision but also a touch of whimsy. It's best to order the chef's six-course tasting menu to appreciate his culinary ambitions. You're likely to be dazzled with everything from marinated foie gras to an apple and artichoke salad, from Bresse pigeon in a truffle confit to a Valhrona chocolate fondant. We've delighted in all the dishes sampled here, from the eggplant caviar to crisp roast sea bass paired with caramelized endive and plump oysters.

33 St. James's St., SW1. ✆ **020/7930-4272.** Reservations required. Fixed-price menu £26–£56 ($42–$90) for 3 courses; £60 ($96) for 6-course tasting menu. AE, DC, MC, V. Mon–Fri noon–2:30pm; Mon–Sat 6:45–10:45pm. Tube: Green Park.

PICCADILLY & LEICESTER SQUARE
Expensive

J. Sheekey ✿ SEAFOOD   British culinary tradition lives on in this restored fish joint, long a favorite of West End actors. The same jellied eels that delighted Laurence Olivier and Vivien Leigh are still here, along with an array of fresh oysters from the coasts of Ireland and Brittany, plus that Victorian favorite, fried whitebait. Sheekey's fish pie is still on the menu, as is a delightful Dover sole, even a Cornish fish stew that's quite savory. The old "mushy" vegetables still appear but the chefs get experimental and occasionally more daring and offer the likes of steamed organic sea beet. The double chocolate pudding soufflé is a delight. But look for something daring every now and then—perhaps fried plum ravioli with yogurt ice cream.

28–32 St. Martin's Court, WC2. ✆ **020/7240-2565.** Reservations recommended. Main courses £10–£31 ($16–$50). AE, DC, MC, V. Daily noon–3pm and 7:30pm–midnight. Tube: Charing Cross.

Moderate

Atlantic Bar & Grill ✿✿ MODERN BRITISH   A titanic restaurant in a former Art Deco ballroom off Piccadilly Circus, this cosmopolitan locale draws a trendy crowd to London's heart. Chef Steve Carter is doing much to recapture the restaurant's mid-1990s chic, with emphasis on organic and homegrown produce, seafood, and meats. Many dishes are quite complex and taste as good as they sound: swordfish dumplings with a salsa of plum tomatoes, fresh cilantro, sautéed shiitake, soy-infused ginger, and fresh wilted spinach; or the loin of yellowfin tuna served with a wild parsley-and-eggplant relish and a pesto made of roasted red bell peppers.

20 Glasshouse St., W1. ✆ **020/7734-4888.** Reservations required. Main courses £13–£22 ($20–$34); fixed-price 3-course lunch £16 ($26). AE, DC, MC, V. Mon–Fri noon–3pm; Mon–Sat 6pm–3am; Sun 6–10:30pm. Tube: Piccadilly Circus.

The Criterion Brasserie ✿ MODERN BRITISH/FRENCH   Designed by Thomas Verity in the 1870s, this palatial neo-Byzantine mirrored marble hall is a glamorous backdrop for superb cuisine, served under a golden ceiling with peacock-blue draperies, by a mainly French staff. The menu is wide ranging, offering everything from Paris brasserie food to "nouvelle-classical," a combination of classic French cooking techniques with some of the lighter, more experimental leanings of modern French cuisine. The food is excellent, but falls short of sublime. The roast skate wing with deep-fried snails is delectable, as is the roast saddle of lamb stuffed with mushrooms and spinach.

224 Piccadilly, W1. ✆ **020/7930-0488.** Main courses £14–£23 ($22–$36). Fixed-price 2-course lunch £15 ($24); fixed-price 3-course lunch £18 ($29). AE, MC, V. Daily noon–2:30pm and 5:30–11:30pm. Tube: Piccadilly Circus.

SOHO
Very Expensive

Spoon+ ✿ AMERICAN/INTERNATIONAL   Housed in Ian Schrager's hot new Sanderson Hotel, this is a branch of the Spoon restaurant in Paris where master chef Alain Ducasse cooks for *tout Paris*. It's Monsieur Ducasse's take on American fusion cuisine. And who can beat Spoon+ when it comes to dishing up the best bubble-gum ice cream in London? We don't mean to make a caricature of the food, but some items seemed designed to shock. This is the only place you can go in London to eat a French version of that American classic—macaroni and cheese. Of course, there's also lobster in banana leaves if you want to go native. Much of what is offered, though, is really good, especially the crab ceviche, and the iced tomato soup. Spoon+ chefs allow you to compose your own meal or at least pair ingredients—perhaps a beautiful sole with a crushed lemon confit, or do you prefer it with satay sauce? On our last visit we found the restaurant ridiculously overpriced, but reconsidered when the entertainment of the evening arrived. Our fellow diners turned out to be none other than Madonna and her groom, Guy Ritchie.

50 Berners St., W1. ✆ **020/7300-1400.** Reservations required. Main courses £17–£30 ($27–$48). AE, DC, MC, V. Daily noon–3pm and 6–11:30pm (till 10:30pm Sun). Tube: Leicester Sq. or Covent Garden.

Moderate

The Ivy ✿✿ MODERN BRITISH/INTERNATIONAL   Effervescent and sophisticated, The Ivy is the dining choice of visiting theatrical luminaries. It has been intimately associated with the theater district ever since it opened in 1911. With its ersatz 1930s look and tiny bar near the entrance, this place is fun and hums with the energy of London's glamour scene. The kitchen has a solid appreciation for fresh ingredients. Our favorite dishes include white asparagus with sea kale and truffle butter; seared scallops with spinach, sorrel, and bacon; and salmon fish cakes.

1–5 West St., WC2. ✆ **020/7836-4751.** Reservations required. Main courses £9–£35 ($14–$56); Sat–Sun fixed-price 3-course lunch £18 ($29). AE, DC, MC, V. Daily noon–3pm and 5:30pm–midnight (last order). Tube: Leicester Sq.

Mezzo EUROPEAN/ASIAN   This 750-seat, blockbuster Soho spot—the creation of Sir Terence Conran—is the biggest restaurant in London. The mammoth space is the former site of rock's legendary Marquee club. Mezzo is actually composed of several restaurants: **Mezzonine** upstairs, serving Thai/Asian cuisine with a European flair; swankier **Mezzo** downstairs, offering modern European cuisine in a 1930s Hollywood atmosphere; and **Mezzo Cafe,** where you can stop in for a simple sandwich and a drink.

The food is at its most ambitious downstairs at Mezzo, where 100 chefs work behind glass to feed up to 400 diners at a time. This is dinner-as-theater. Not surprisingly for a restaurant of this size, the cuisine tends to be uneven. We suggest the rotisserie rib of beef with red wine and creamed horseradish, or the roast cod, which is crisp-skinned and cooked to perfection. A live jazz band entertains after 10pm from Wednesday to Saturday.

100 Wardour St., W1. ℂ 020/7314-4000. Reservations recommended. Mezzo 3-course fixed-price dinner £17 ($26); Mezzonine 3-course dinner £15 ($23); Mezzo Cafe main courses £5–£10 ($8–$16). AE, DC, MC, V. Mezzo: Wed–Fri noon–3pm; Sun 12:30–3pm; Mon–Thurs 6pm–1am; Fri–Sat 6pm–3am; Sun 6–11pm. Mezzonine: Mon–Fri noon–3pm; Sat noon–4pm; Mon–Thurs 5:30pm–1am; Fri–Sat 5:30pm–3am. Mezzo Cafe: Mon–Sat 8am–11pm. Tube: Piccadilly Circus.

Rasa Samundra ⊛ *Value* INDIAN   Whereas most Indian restaurants in London specialize in the cuisine of the north, Rasa Samundra features the cooking of the southern state of Kerala, whose specialties are plucked from the sea. Try *malslam pattichathu* (king fish cooked in fresh spices, with green chile and coconut paste), *para konju nirachathu* (lobster cooked with black pepper, garlic, and Indian shallots and served with whole lemon and beet root curry), *masala dosa* (paper-thin rice and black graham pancake filled with potato and ginger masala), and *moru kachlathu* (green bananas and mangoes cooked in a yogurt sauce with turmeric and onions).

5 Charlotte St., W1. ℂ 020/7637-0222. Reservations required. Main courses £10–£30 ($15–$45). Fixed-price lunch £20 ($30); fixed-price dinner £30 ($45). AE, DC, MC, V. Daily noon–11pm. Tube: Tottenham Court Rd.

BLOOMSBURY
Moderate
Townhouse Brasserie ⊛ FRENCH/INTERNATIONAL   Near the British Museum, this old Georgian town house is one of the most up-and-coming restaurants in Bloomsbury. The ground floor is enhanced with contemporary art, and upstairs is a traditional old English dining room, except for an infusion of Peruvian art. The menu is a culinary tour de force, drawing inspiration from around the world. Launch your repast with the cream of leek soup or sweet potato soup with basil. Then it's on to a delectable charcoal-grilled duck breast with an Asian-style salad. Especially pleasing is a fresh seafood pasta flavored with chives, thick cream, and white wine. It's worth it to save up room for one of the tempting desserts, made fresh daily.

24 Coptic St., WC1. ℂ 020/7636-2731. Reservations recommended. Main courses £11–£18 ($18–$29). AE, DC, MC, V. Mon–Sat 11am–11pm; Sun 10am–6pm. Tube: Tottenham Court Rd. or Holborn.

Villandry ⊛ INTERNATIONAL/CONTINENTAL   Food lovers and gourmands flock to this combination food store, florist, delicatessen, and restaurant. The setting is an oversized Edwardian-style storefront north of Oxford Circus. Inside, ingredients change so frequently the menu is revamped and rewritten twice a day. You're likely to face such perfectly crafted dishes as breast of duck with fresh spinach and a gratin of baby onions; boiled haunch of pork with blood sausages, mashed potatoes, kale, and mustard sauce; filet of black codfish with prosciutto, radicchio, and creamed lentils; and pan-fried turbot with deep-fried celery, artichoke hearts, and hollandaise sauce.

170 Great Portland St., W1. ℂ 020/7631-3131. Reservations recommended. Main courses £16–£21 ($26–$34). AE, DC, MC, V. Restaurant: Mon–Sat noon–3pm and 6–10:30pm. Food store: Mon–Sat 8am–10pm; Sun 10am–4pm. Tube: Great Portland St.

Wagamama JAPANESE   This noodle joint, in a basement just off New Oxford Street, is noisy and overly crowded, and you'll have to wait in line for a table. The fast-serve, fast-out concept calls itself a "non-destination food station" and caters to some 1,200 customers a day. All dishes are built around ramen noodles with your choice of chicken, beef, or salmon served with gyoza, a light pancake filled with vegetables. Vegetarian dishes are available, but skip the so-called Korean-style dishes.

4 Streatham St., WC1. © 020/7323-9223. Reservations not accepted. Main courses £5.50–£11 ($8.80–$18). AE, MC, V. Mon–Sat noon–11pm; Sun 12:30–10pm. Tube: Tottenham Court Rd.

COVENT GARDEN & THE STRAND
Expensive

Rules *₲* TRADITIONAL BRITISH If you're looking for London's most quintessentially British restaurant, eat here. London's oldest restaurant was established in 1798 as an oyster bar; today, the antler-filled Edwardian dining rooms exude nostalgia. You can order such classic dishes as Irish or Scottish oysters, jugged hare, and mussels. Game dishes are offered from mid-August to February or March, including wild Scottish salmon; wild sea trout; wild Highland red deer; and game birds like grouse, snipe, partridge, pheasant, and woodcock. As a finale, the "great puddings" continue to impress.

35 Maiden Lane, WC2. © 020/7836-5314. Reservations recommended. Main courses £15–£20 ($24–$32). AE, DC, MC, V. Daily noon–11:30pm. Tube: Covent Garden.

Moderate

Porter's English Restaurant *₲₲* *Kids* TRADITIONAL BRITISH The seventh earl of Bradford serves "real English food at affordable prices" at this restaurant. He succeeds notably—and not just because Lady Bradford turned over her carefully guarded recipe for banana-and-ginger pudding. This comfortable, two-story restaurant is family-friendly, informal, and lively. Porter's specializes in classic English pies, including Old English fish pie; lamb and apricot pie; and ham, leek, and cheese pie. Bangers and mash is another popular dish. Main courses are so generous—and accompanied by vegetables and side dishes—that you hardly need to start with appetizers. A traditional English tea is served from 2:30 to 5:30pm for £4.75 ($7.60) per person.

17 Henrietta St., WC2. © 020/7836-6466. Reservations recommended. Main courses £8.95–£13 ($14–$21); fixed-price menu £20 ($32). AE, DC, MC, V. Mon–Sat noon–11:30pm; Sun noon–10:30pm. Tube: Covent Garden or Leicester Sq.

Inexpensive

Sarastro *₲* TURKISH/CYPRIOT The setting makes you feel like you're in a prop room of an opera house. This is a fun place, especially after a show in Theaterland. The restaurant takes its name from a character in Mozart's *The Magic Flute*. The cuisine celebrates the bounty of the Mediterranean, especially Turkey and Cyprus. Launch yourself with such delights as asparagus in red wine sauce or fresh grilled sardines. Market-fresh fish is usually the way to go, especially river trout or grilled halibut. A zesty favorite is lamb Anatolian style (that is, with eggplant and zucchini). We're also fond of the well-seasoned lamb meatballs. A good-tasting specialty is chicken Sarastro with walnuts and raisins.

126 Drury Lane, WC2. © 020/7836-0101. Reservations required. Main courses £8.50–£15 ($14–$24). Fixed-price menu £10–£20 ($16–$32); pre-theater menu £10 ($16). AE, DC, MC, V. Daily noon–midnight. Tube: Covent Garden.

FLEET STREET
Moderate

Ye Olde Cheshire Cheese TRADITIONAL BRITISH Dating from the 13th century, this is the most famous of the old city chophouses (restaurants) and pubs. It claims to be the spot where Samuel Johnson entertained admirers. Later, many of the ink-stained journalists and scandalmongers of Fleet Street made its four-story premises their "local." Within, you'll find six bars and two dining rooms. The house specialties include "Ye Famous Pudding"—steak, kidney,

(Moments) Where to Have a Cuppa Tea

The lounge at **Raffles Brown's Hotel,** 29–34 Albemarle St., W1 (② 020/ 7493-6020; Tube: Green Park), is decorated with English antiques, oil paintings, and floral chintz, much like an English country estate. Give your name to the concierge upon arrival (reservations aren't accepted); arrangements will be made for you to be seated on clusters of sofas and settees or at low tables. Served daily from 3 to 5:45pm, the regular afternoon tea (£25/$40) includes a choice of 12 teas, plus sandwiches, scones, and pastries. The teatime rituals at **Claridge's,** Brook Street, W1 (② 020/7629-8860; Tube: Bond St.), have managed to persevere through the years with as much pomp and circumstance as the empire itself. A portrait of Lady Claridge gazes beneficently from the paneled walls as a choice of 17 teas is served ever so politely. Reservations are recommended, and jackets are required for men. It's served Monday through Friday for £26 ($42); and on Saturday and Sunday for £35 ($56), including champagne.

A flood of visitors is somehow gracefully herded into the high-volume but nevertheless elegant **Georgian Restaurant,** on the fourth floor of Harrods, 87–135 Brompton Rd., SW1 (② 020/7255-6800; Tube: Knightsbridge), in a room so long its staff refers to its shape and size as the "Mississippi River." The list of teas available—at least 50—is sometimes so esoteric the experience might remind you of choosing among vintages in a sophisticated wine cellar. Served Monday through Saturday from 3:15 to 5:30pm (last order), high tea runs £19 ($30) per person; reservations are recommended. **The Orangery,** in the gardens just north of Kensington Palace, W8 (② 020/7376-0239; Tube: Kensington High St. or Queensway), occupies a long and narrow garden pavilion built in 1704 by Queen Anne as a site for her tea parties. Tea is still served (daily 10am–6pm) amid rows of potted orange trees basking in sunlight from soaring windows. Reservations are not accepted. A pot of tea costs £1.75 to £1.85 ($2.85–$3.10), and summer cakes and puddings run £2.95 to £3.95 ($4.70–$6.30).

mushrooms, and game—and Scottish roast beef with Yorkshire pudding and horseradish sauce.

Wine Office Court, 145 Fleet St., EC4. ② 020/7353-6170. Main courses £7.50–£10 ($12–$16). AE, DC, MC, V. Meals Mon–Fri noon–10pm; Sat noon–2:30pm and 6–10pm; Sun noon–2:30pm. Drinks and bar snacks daily 11:30am–11pm. Tube: St. Paul's or Blackfriars.

WESTMINSTER
Moderate
Tate Restaurant (★★ (Value MODERN BRITISH   Located in the Tate Britain gallery (see below), this restaurant is particularly attractive to wine fanciers. It offers what may be the best bargains for superior wines anywhere in Britain. Bordeaux and burgundies are in abundance, and the management keeps the markup between 40% and 65%, rather than the 100% to 200% added in most restaurants. In fact, the prices here are lower than they are in most wine shops. Wine

begins at £15 ($24) per bottle, or £3.85 ($6.15) per glass. Oenophiles frequently come for lunch. The restaurant offers an English menu that changes about every month. Dishes might include pheasant casserole, pan-fried skate with black butter and capers, and a selection of vegetarian dishes. One critic found the staff and diners as traditional "as a Gainsborough landscape." Access to the restaurant is through the museum's main entrance on Millbank.

Millbank, SW1. ⓒ 020/7887-8877. Reservations recommended. Main courses £11–£18 ($17–$29). Fixed-price lunch £17 ($27) 2 courses; £20 ($31) 3 courses. AE, DC, MC, V. Mon–Sat noon–3pm; Sun noon–4pm. Tube: Pimlico. Bus: 77 or 88.

KNIGHTSBRIDGE
Very Expensive
Zafferano ✿✿ ITALIAN   There's something honest and satisfying about this restaurant, where decor consists of little more than ocher-colored walls, immaculate linens, and a bevy of diligent staff members. A quick review of past clients includes Margaret Thatcher, Richard Gere, and Eric Clapton. The modernized interpretation of Italian cuisine features such dishes as ravioli of pheasant with black truffles, wild pigeon with garlic purée, sea bream with spinach and balsamic vinegar, and monkfish with almonds. Joan Collins claimed that the chefs produce culinary fireworks, but found the bright lighting far too harsh.

15 Lowndes St., SW1. ⓒ 020/7235-5800. Reservations required. Set menus £29–£35 ($46–$56). AE, MC, V. Daily noon–2:30pm and 7–11pm. Tube: Knightsbridge.

Expensive
English Garden ✿ TRADITIONAL BRITISH   This is a metropolitan restaurant par excellence. The decor in this historic town house is pretty and lighthearted: The Garden Room is whitewashed brick with a domed conservatory roof; vivid florals, rattan chairs, banks of plants, and candy-pink linens to complete the scene. Every component of the meal is carried out perfectly. Some of the dishes sound as if they were copied directly from an English cookbook of the Middle Ages—and are they ever good. For a main course, opt for such delights as roast baron of rabbit with oven-dried tomato, prunes, and olive oil mash; or saddle of venison with potted cabbage. Desserts, especially the rhubarb and cinnamon ice cream, and the candied orange tart with orange syrup, would've pleased Miss Marple. Only fixed-price menus are served.

10 Lincoln St., SW3. ⓒ 020/7584-7272. Reservations required. Fixed-price meals £24 ($38) lunch; £29 ($46) 3-course dinner. AE, DC, MC, V. Mon–Sat noon–3pm; Sun 12:30–2pm; daily 6:30–10:30pm. Tube: Sloane Sq.

KENSINGTON
Moderate
Joe's MODERN BRITISH   This is one of three London restaurants established by fashion designer Joseph Ettedgui. Thanks to its sense of glamour and fun, it's often filled at breakfast and lunch with well-known names from the British fashion, music, and entertainment industries. You can enjoy such dishes as tuna niçoise, salmon fish cakes, or Joe's rather juicy and tasty burger. It's all good, but unexciting. We found that making a meal of appetizers, as many of the models here do, is a great choice. Our favorite appetizers included a pea and mint soup; a caramelized red onion, tomato, and goat cheese tart; and a rocket salad served with shaved Parmesan. The atmosphere remains laid-back and unstuffy, just like trendsetters in South Ken prefer it. With a name like Joe's, what else could it be?

126 Draycott Ave., SW3. ⓒ 020/7225-2217. Reservations required. Main courses £10–£15 ($16–$24). AE, DC, MC, V. Mon–Sat 9:30am–6pm; Sun 9:30am–5pm. Tube: South Kensington.

Pasha MOROCCAN   Few ethnic restaurants equal the zest and stylishness of this re-created Marrakech palace. Within a duet of dining rooms outfitted with flickering candles, belly dancing music, and artifacts from the sub-Sahara, you'll enjoy regional and time-honored specialties. The best examples include a crispy lamb salad with pomegranate and mint; grilled sea bass with warm hummus and a parsley salad; chicken *merguez* (spicy sausage) with a coriander tagine; and charcoal-grilled skewered chicken with green chile salsa. And if you like couscous, you'll have at least three kinds from which to choose.

1 Gloucester Rd., SW7. ℂ 020/7589-7969. Reservations recommended. Main courses £9.75–£17 ($16–$27). AE, DC, MC, V. Mon–Sat noon–3pm and 6–11pm; Sun 5:30–10pm. Tube: Gloucester Rd.

SOUTH KENSINGTON
Expensive
Greens Restaurant & Oyster Bar SEAFOOD/TRADITIONAL BRITISH Critics say it's a triumph of tradition over taste, but as far as seafood in London goes, this is a tried-and-true favorite, thanks to an excellent menu with moderately priced dishes, a central location, and a charming staff. This place has a cluttered entrance leading to a crowded bar where you can sip fine wines and, from September to April, enjoy oysters. In the faux-Dickensian dining room, you can choose from a long menu of fresh seafood dishes, which changes monthly depending on what is in season. The standard menu ranges from fish cakes with leaf spinach to whole Scottish lobster. Desserts include bread-and-butter pudding. *Note:* London has two different Duke streets. Greens is on the one in St. James's.

36 Duke St., St. James's, SW1. ℂ 020/7930-4566. Reservations recommended. Main courses £12–£38 ($18–$61). AE, DC, MC, V. Restaurant daily 11:30am–3pm; Mon–Sat 5:30–11pm. Oyster Bar Mon–Sat 11:30am–3pm and 5:30–11pm; Sun noon–3pm and 5:30–9pm. Tube: Green Park.

CHELSEA
Inexpensive
Admiral Codrington ✪ *Finds* MODERN BRITISH/CONTINENTAL Once a lowly pub, this stylish bar and restaurant is all the rage nowadays. The old "Cod," as it is affectionately known, offers plush dining with a revitalized decor by Nina Campbell, and a glass roof that rolls back on sunny days. The bartenders still offer a traditional pint, but the sophisticated menu features such delectable fare as homemade tortellini of pumpkin and Parmesan cheese, or caramelized breast of duckling with sweet potato. A real palate pleaser is the monkfish spring roll with fresh herbs and thyme salsa. Stars of the menu are the grilled breast-of-chicken salad with bean sprouts, apple slices, and cashews; and the grilled tuna with a couscous salad and eggplant "caviar."

17 Mossop St., SW3. ℂ 020/7581-0005. Reservations recommended. Main courses £10–£15 ($16–$24). MC, V. Mon–Sat noon–11:30pm; Sun noon–11pm. Tube: South Kensington.

MARYLEBONE
Expensive
Orrey ✪✪ INTERNATIONAL/FRENCH   This is one of London's classic French restaurants. Sea bass from the shores of Montpellier, olive oil from Maussane-les-Alpilles, mushrooms from the fields of Calais, and poultry from Bresse—it all turns up on this highly refined menu, the creation of chef Chris Galvin, who is enjoying his first Michelin star. On the first floor of The Conran Shop in Marylebone, the restaurant changes its menu seasonally to take advantage of the best produce. Our favorites are tagine of pigeon with a saffron-flavored couscous; Barbary duck with foie gras; and seared scallops with pieces

of pork belly and cauliflower. A wild mushroom consommé arrives with a medley of such fungi as *pieds de bleu, pieds de mouton,* chanterelles, and *trompettes de morte,* all from French forests. Lazy summer evenings are to be enjoyed on a fourth-floor terrace, where you can drink and order light fare from the bar menu.

55 Marylebone High St., W1. © 020/7616-8000. Reservations required. Main courses £17–£30 ($27–$48). Fixed-price menu £24 ($38) 3 courses; £50 ($80) 5 courses. AE, DC, MC, V. Daily noon–3pm; Mon–Sun 7–11pm. Tube: Baker St. or Regency Park.

Moderate

Caldesi ITALIAN   Good food, reasonable prices, fresh ingredients, and authentic Tuscan family recipes attract a never-ending stream of diners to this eatery. The extensive menu includes a wide array of pasta, antipasti, fish, and meat dishes. Start with an excellent *insalata Caldesi,* made with tomatoes slow roasted in garlic and rosemary oil and served with mozzarella flown in from Tuscany. Pasta dishes include an especially flavor-filled homemade tortelloni stuffed with salmon and ricotta and served with a creamy spinach sauce. Monkfish and prawns are flavored with wild fennel and fresh basil, or you might sample the tender duck breast a l'orange, steeped in white wine, honey, thyme, and rosemary.

15–17 Marylebone Lane, W1. © 020/7935-9226. Reservations required. Main courses £8–£19 ($13–$30). AE, MC, V. Mon–Fri noon–2:30pm; Mon–Sat 6–11pm. Tube: Bond St.

NOTTING HILL GATE
Expensive

Pharmacy Restaurant and Bar ⑁ EUROPEAN   The theme of this medical-chic restaurant evokes all sorts of drug-related venues, from a harmless small-town pharmacy to a drug lord's secret stash of mind-altering pills. This ambiguity is appreciated by the arts-conscious crowd that flocks here, partly because they're interested in what Damien Hirst (*enfant terrible* of London's art world) has created, and partly because the place can be a lot of fun. A drink menu lists lots of highly palatable martinis as well as a somewhat icky concoction known as a Cough Syrup (cherry liqueur, honey, and vodka that's shaken, not stirred, over ice). Bottles of pills, bar stools with seats shaped like aspirins, and painted representations of fire, water, air, and earth decorate the bar area. Upstairs in the restaurant, the pharmaceutical theme is less pronounced but subtly omnipresent. Menu items include trendy but comforting food items such as carpaccio of whitefish, chargrilled lamb, pan-fried cod in red wine with Jerusalem artichokes and shallots, and roast saddle of hare in pear sauce.

150 Notting Hill Gate, W11. © 020/7221-2442. Reservations required Fri–Sat, strongly recommended other nights. Main courses £14–£20 ($22–$32). AE, DISC, MC, V. Daily noon–3pm and 7–10:30pm. Tube: Notting Hill Gate.

THE CITY
Expensive

Prism ⑁⑁ MODERN BRITISH/CONTINENTAL   In the financial district, called "The City," this restaurant attracts London's movers and shakers. In the former Bank of New York, Harvey Nichols—known for his chic department store in Knightsbridge—took this 1920s neo-Grecian hall and installed Mies van der Rohe chairs in chrome and lipstick-red leather. In such a setting, traditional English dishes from the north are given a light touch—try the tempura of Whitby cod or cream of Jerusalem artichoke soup with roasted scallops and truffle oil. For a first course, you might opt for a small seared calf's liver with a mushroom risotto, or else a salad composed of flecks of Parmesan cheese seasoning a

Savoy cabbage salad and Parma ham. Unusual for a restaurant, the staff will compose a set menu for each individual table.

147 Leadenhall St., EC3. © 020/7256-3888. Reservations required. Main courses £16–£25 ($26–$40). Set menus £25 ($40). AE, DC, DISC, MC, V. Mon–Fri noon–3pm and 6–10pm. Tube: Bank.

SEEING THE SIGHTS
LONDON ATTRACTIONS

London isn't a city to visit hurriedly. It is so vast, so stocked with treasures, that it would take a lifetime to explore it thoroughly. But even a quick visit will give you a chance to see what's creating the hottest buzz in shopping and nightlife as well as the city's time-tested treasures.

SIGHTSEEING SUGGESTIONS FOR FIRST-TIME VISITORS

If You Have 1 Day No first-time visitor should leave London without visiting **Westminster Abbey.** See **Big Ben** and the **Houses of Parliament,** then walk over to see the **Changing of the Guard** at Buckingham Palace if it's being held. Have dinner in **Covent Garden,** perhaps at Porter's English Restaurant. For your nightcap, head over to the **Red Lion,** 2 Duke of York St. (© **020/7930-2030**), in Mayfair, quite a Victorian pub.

If You Have 2 Days Devote a good part of your second day to exploring the **British Museum,** one of the world's largest and best museums. Spend the afternoon visiting the **Tower of London** and seeing the crown jewels (but expect slow-moving lines). Cap your day by boarding one of the London Launches to experience the city from the river. Go to one of London's landmark restaurants such as **Rules,** 35 Maiden Lane.

If You Have 3 Days In the morning of your third day, go to the **National Gallery** on Trafalgar Square. Then enjoy an afternoon at **Madame Tussaud's Waxworks.** Take some time to stroll through **St. James's** and try to catch a cultural performance at the South Bank Centre, site of the Royal Festival Hall, or a play or musical in the West End.

If You Have 4 Days In the morning of your fourth day, head for the **City,** the financial district. Tour **St. Paul's Cathedral.** Spend a few hours strolling the City and visit a few of its many attractions. In the late afternoon, head down **King's Road** in Chelsea to shop the many and varied boutiques.

If You Have 5 Days On your fifth day, explore the **Victoria and Albert Museum** in the morning, then head to the **Tate Restaurant** for lunch. Finally, see where history was made during the dark days of World War II in the **Cabinet War Rooms** at Clive Steps, where Churchill directed the British operations against the Nazis. In the evening, attend the theater.

THE TOP ATTRACTIONS

Note: One of Britain's greatest private art collections, the **Saatchi Gallery,** should have opened at County Hall by the time you read this. On London's South Bank, the new gallery stands right between the sites of the two Tate galleries: Tate Modern and Tate Britain. Devoted to modern, often very controversial and headline-grabbing art, the gallery focuses on the work of younger British

London Attractions

Church ✝
Information ⓘ
Tube stop ⊖
Note: not all Tube stations are featured on this map

0 — 1 mi
0 — 1 km

ISLINGTON
SHOREDITCH
King's Cross Station
KING'S CROSS ST. PANCRAS
ST. PANCRAS
Coram's Fields
FINSBURY
OLD ST.
CLERKENWELL
FARRINGDON
RUSSELL SQUARE
CHANCERY LANE
BARBICAN
The Barbican Centre
LIVERPOOL ST. STATION
Liverpool St. Station
6 British Museum
HOLBORN
ST. PAUL'S
MOORGATE
18
ALDGATE
COVENT GARDEN
Law Courts
St. Paul's Cathedral 17
Bank of England
THE CITY
Stock Exchange
THE EAST END →
COVENT GARDEN
Leicester Square
TEMPLE
BLACKFRIARS STATION
MANSION HOUSE
Cornhill
TOWER HILL
THE STRAND
LEICESTER SQUARE
Blackfriars Bridge
Upper Thames St.
CANNON ST. STATION
MONUMENT
Tower of London 19
rafalgar quare
EMBANKMENT
Waterloo Bridge
Millenium Bridge
Southwark Bridge
London Bridge
Tower Bridge
10 Whitehall
Hungerford Bridge
Globe Theatre
16 SOUTHWARK
LONDON BRIDGE
London Bridge Station
11 Downing Street
SOUTH BANK
Union St.
DOCKLANDS
2 WESTMINSTER
WATERLOO STATION
THE BOROUGH
14 13
Westminster Abbey
LAMBETH NORTH
BOROUGH
stminster Abbey
Lambeth Bridge
NEWINGTON
WEST-MINSTER
LAMBETH
ELEPHANT & CASTLE (BAKERLOO)
New Kent Rd.
ate llery
15
ELEPHANT & CASTLE
Vauxhall Bridge
WALWORTH
VAUXHALL
KENNINGTON
VAUXHALL
OVAL

Apsley House **4**
Big Ben **13**
British Museum **6**
Buckingham Palace **5**
Cabinet War Rooms **12**
Houses of Parliament **13**
Kensington Palace **2**
Madame Tussaud's **1**
Millennium Wheel London Eye **11**
Museum of London **18**

National Gallery **8**
National Portrait Gallery **7**
St. Martin-in-the-Fields Market **9**
St. Paul's Cathedral **17**
Tate Britain **15**
Tate Modern **16**
Tower of London **19**
Victoria & Albert Museum **3**
Westminster Abbey **14**
Whitehall **10**

artists, such as Damien Hirst. Ex-adman Charles Saatchi has amassed one of the largest independent collections of modern British and international art in the world.

Tower of London ✦✦✦ *(Kids)*   This ancient fortress continues to pack in visitors because of its macabre associations with legendary figures who were imprisoned and/or executed here (Sir Walter Raleigh, Anne Boleyn and her daughter Elizabeth, Lady Jane Grey). The finest structure is the White Tower. Here you can view the Royal Armouries collection of armor and weapons. Instruments of torture and execution are on view in Bowyer Tower. In summer, go early in the day to see the **Crown Jewels** because long lines often form. Uniformed Yeoman Warders (also known as "Beefeaters") give 1-hour tours at frequent intervals, starting at 9:30am from the Middle Tower near the main entrance. The tour includes the Chapel Royal of St. Peter ad Vincula (St. Peter in Chains). The last guided walk starts at about 3:30pm in summer, 2:30pm in winter.

Insider's tip: The secret of avoiding the Tower's notoriously long lines is to buy your ticket in a kiosk inside the Tube station before emerging above ground. Also, go early in the morning. Avoid Sunday between noon and 2pm if you can—crowds are at their worst then.

Tower Hill, EC3. ☎ 020/7709-0765. www.hrp.org.uk. Admission £12 ($18) adults, £8.75 ($14) students and seniors, £7.50 ($12) children, free for children under 5, £34 ($54) family of 5 (but no more than 2 adults). Mar–Oct Mon–Sat 9am–5pm, Sun 10am–5pm; Nov–Feb Tues–Sat 9am–4pm, Sun and Mon 10am–4pm. Tube: Tower Hill.

Westminster Abbey ✦✦✦   In 1065, the Saxon king, Edward the Confessor, founded a Benedictine abbey on this spot overlooking Parliament Square. The first king crowned in the abbey was Harold in 1066. The coronation tradition has continued to the present day, broken only twice (Edward V and Edward VIII). The abbey is the site of state occasions, including the September 1997 funeral of Diana, princess of Wales. The Gothic structure existing today owes more to Henry III's plans than to those of any other sovereign, although many architects, including Wren, have contributed to the abbey. Henry VII Chapel is one of the loveliest in Europe, with its fan vaulting, Knights of Bath banners, and Torrigiani-designed tomb of the king. You can also visit the most hallowed spot in the abbey, the shrine of Edward the Confessor (canonized in the 12th c.). In the saint's chapel is the Coronation Chair, made at the command of Edward I in 1300 to display the Stone of Scone. Another noted spot is the Poets' Corner, to the right of the entrance to the Royal Chapel, with monuments to Chaucer, Shakespeare, "O Rare Ben Johnson" (his name misspelled), Samuel Johnson, the Brontë sisters, Thackeray, Dickens, Tennyson, Kipling, even the American Longfellow.

On Sunday, the Royal Chapels are closed, but the rest of the church is open unless a service is being conducted. For times of services, phone the **Chapter Office** (☎ 020/7222-5152). The College Garden is open Tuesday through Thursday, April through September from 10am to 6pm and October through March from 10am to 4pm.

Broad Sanctuary, SW1. ☎ 020/7654-4900. www.westminster-abbey.org. Admission £6 ($9.60) adults; £3 ($4.80) for students, seniors, and children 11–18; free for children under 11; £12 ($19) family. Mon–Fri 9:30am–4:45pm; Sat 9am–2:45pm. Tube: Westminster or St. James's Park.

Houses of Parliament ✦✦   These Houses are the stronghold of Britain's democracy. Both Houses (Commons and Lords) are situated in the former royal Palace of Westminster, the king's residence until Henry VIII moved to Whitehall.

Tips Blair in the Hot Seat

The hottest ticket and most exciting time to visit the Houses of Parliament
is during **Prime Minister's Question Time,** Wednesday from 3 to 3:30pm,
which must seem like hours to Tony Blair, who is virtually in the hot seat.
But Blair holds his own admirably against any and all who try to embar-
rass him and his government.

The present Houses of Parliament were built in 1840, but the Commons chamber was bombed and destroyed by the Luftwaffe in 1941. The 98m (320-ft.)
tower houses Big Ben, the "symbol of London." Except for the Strangers' Galleries, the two Houses of Parliament are closed to tourists. To be admitted to the
Strangers' Galleries, join the public line outside the St. Stephen's entrance; often
there's a delay before the line is admitted.

Westminster Palace, Old Palace Yard, SW1. House of Commons ℂ 020/7219-4272. House of Lords ℂ 020/
7219-3107. www.parliament.uk. Both houses are open for tours: July 26–Aug Mon, Tues, Fri, and Sat
9:15am–4:30pm, Wed and Thurs 1:15–4:30pm, closed Sun; Sept 19–Oct 5 Mon, Fri, and Sat 9:15am–4:30pm,
Tues, Wed, and Thurs 1:15–4:30pm, closed Sun. Join the line at St. Stephen's entrance. Tube: Westminster.

British Museum 🏛🏛🏛 This fabled attraction shelters one of the world's
most comprehensive collections of art and artifacts. Even on a cursory first visit,
be sure to see the Asian collections (the finest assembly of Islamic pottery outside the Islamic world), the Chinese porcelain, the Indian sculpture, and the Prehistoric and Romano-British collections. The overall storehouse is divided into
collections of antiquities; prints and drawings; coins and medals; and ethnography. The Assyrian Transept on the ground floor displays the winged and human-
headed bulls and lions that once guarded the gateways to the kings' palaces.
From here, you can continue into the hall of Egyptian sculpture to see the
Rosetta Stone, whose discovery led to the deciphering of hieroglyphs. Also on
the ground floor are the Parthenon Sculptures, which used to be known as the
Elgin Marbles. The Anglo-Saxon burial ship *Sutton Hoo* discovered in Suffolk is,
in the words of an expert, "the richest treasure ever dug from English soil." The
Portland Vase, one of the most celebrated possessions of the museum, was found
in 1582 outside Rome.

The museum's inner courtyard, hidden for 150 years, has been transformed
into the Great Court, a 1-hectare (2-acre) square spanned by a spectacular glass
roof. The court houses a center for education, galleries, and more exhibition
space. Following the removal of the British Library to St. Pancras, the Reading
Room has been restored as a public reference library.

Great Russell St., WC1. ℂ 020/7323-8299 or 020/7636-1555. www.thebritishmuseum.ac.uk. Free admission. Sat–Wed 10am–5:30pm; Thurs–Fri 10am–8:30pm. Tube: Holborn, Tottenham Court Rd., Goodge St., or
Russell Sq.

Buckingham Palace 🏛🏛 This massively graceful building is the official residence of the queen. You can tell when Her Majesty is at home by the Royal
Standard flying over the palace. The staterooms and picture gallery are usually
open to the public for 8 weeks in August and September, when the royal family
is away on vacation. The tours include the Throne Room and the grand staircase. The queen's picture gallery has some world-class masterpieces rarely on
public view.

Buckingham Palace's most famous spectacle is the **Changing of the Guard.** The new guard, marching behind a band, comes from either the Wellington or Chelsea Barracks and takes over from the old guard in the forecourt of the palace. When this martial ceremony occurs is the subject of mass confusion— *when* it happens, it begins at 11:30am. In theory, that is supposed to be from mid-April to July and on alternate days the rest of the year. It can be canceled in bad weather and during major state events. Call ahead to see if this world-famous military ritual is likely to be staged during your visit.

At end of The Mall (on the road running from Trafalgar Sq.). ℭ **020/7389-1377** or 020/7321-2233. www. royal.gov.uk. Palace tours £12 ($19) adults, £10 ($16) seniors, £6 ($9.60) children under 17. Changing of the Guard free. Palace open for tours Aug 6–Sept 28 daily 9:30am–4:15pm. Changing of the Guard daily Apr–July at 11:30am, and every other day for the rest of the year at 11am. Tube: St. James's Park, Green Park, or Victoria.

Madame Tussaud's ⚘ *Kids*   In 1770, an exhibition of life-size wax figures was opened in Paris by Dr. Curtius. He was soon joined by his niece, Strasbourg-born Marie Tussaud, who learned the secret of making lifelike replicas of the famous and the infamous. During the French Revolution, the head of almost every distinguished victim of the guillotine was molded by Madame Tussaud or her uncle. An enlarged Grand Hall continues to house years of old favorites, as well as many of today's heads of state and political leaders. In the Chamber of Horrors, you can have the vicarious thrill of walking through a Victorian London street where special effects include the shadowy terror of Jack the Ripper. Planetarium shows begin at 10:20am daily and are presented every 40 minutes.

Marylebone Rd., NW1. ℭ **0870/400-3000.** www.madame-tussauds.com. Admission £15 ($24) adults, £12 ($19) seniors, £11 ($17) children ages 5–16, free for children under 5. Combination tickets including the new planetarium £17 ($27) adults, £14 ($22) seniors, £8 ($13) children under 16. Mon–Fri 10am–5:30pm; Sat–Sun 9:30am–5:30pm. Tube: Baker St.

Tate Britain ⚘⚘⚘   What's now known as Tate Britain was known as the Tate Gallery before the modern works in its collection were moved to a new building (see below). Fronting the Thames near Vauxhall bridge in Pimlico, the gallery houses the national collection of British art from the 16th century to the present. The works include some of the best of Gainsborough, Reynolds, Stubbs, Blake, Constable, and Hogarth (particularly his satirical *O the Roast beef of Old England,* known as *The Gate of Calais*). The illustrations of William Blake, the incomparable mystical poet, for such classic works as *The Book of Job, The Divine Comedy,* and *Paradise Lost* are here. The collection of works by J. M. W. Turner is its largest by a single artist; Turner himself willed most of the paintings and watercolors here to the nation. Also on display are the works of many major 19th- and 20th-century painters, including Paul Nash.

Millbank, SW1. ℭ 020/7887-8000. www.tate.org.uk. Free admission; special exhibitions £3–£8.50 ($4.80–$14). Daily 10am–5:50pm. Tube: Pimlico.

Tate Modern ⚘⚘⚘   In a transformed Bankside Power Station in Southwark, this museum draws some two million visitors a year to see the greatest collection of international 20th-century art in Britain. As such it is one of the three or four most important modern art galleries in the world. Tate Modern is viewer friendly with eye-level hangings. All the big painting stars are here, a whole galaxy ranging from Dalí to Matisse to Rothko to Warhol. The Modern is also a gallery of new and exciting art. Instead of exhibiting art chronologically and by school, the Tate Modern, in a radical break from tradition, takes a thematic approach. This allows displays to cut across movements. You can cross the newly reopened Millennium Bridge, a pedestrian-only walk from the steps of St. Paul's, over the Thames to the new gallery.

Bankside, SE1. ℂ 020/7887-8008. www.tate.org.uk. Free admission. Sun–Thurs 10am–6pm; Fri–Sat 10am–10pm. Tube: Southwark.

National Gallery ⋆⋆⋆ This museum houses a comprehensive collection of Western paintings, representing all the major schools from the 13th century to the early 20th century. Of the early Gothic works, the *Wilton Diptych* is the rarest treasure; it depicts Richard II being introduced to the Madonna and Child by John the Baptist and the Saxon king, Edward the Confessor. The 16th-century Venetian masters and the northern European painters are well represented.

North side of Trafalgar Sq., WC2. ℂ 020/7747-2885. www.nationalgallery.org.uk. Free admission. Thurs–Tues 10am–6pm; Wed 10am–9pm. Tube: Charing Cross, Embankment, Leicester Sq., or Piccadilly Circus.

St. Paul's Cathedral ⋆⋆⋆ It was during the Great Fire of 1666 that the old St. Paul's was destroyed, making way for a baroque structure designed by Sir Christopher Wren and built between 1675 and 1710. The dome of St. Paul's dominates the City's square mile. The cathedral houses few art treasures but has many monuments, including a memorial chapel to American service personnel who lost their lives in World War II. Encircling the dome is the Whispering Gallery, where vocal discretion is advised. Wren lies in the crypt, along with the duke of Wellington and Lord Nelson. Of course, this was where Prince Charles married Lady Diana Spencer in 1981.

St. Paul's Churchyard, EC4. ℂ 020/7236-4128. www.stpauls.co.uk. Cathedral and galleries £6 ($9.60) adults, £3 ($4.80) children 6–16. Guided tours £2.50 ($4) adults, £2 ($3.20) students and seniors, £1 ($1.60) children; recorded tours £3.50 ($5.60). Free for children 5 and under. Sightseeing Mon–Sat 8:30am–4pm; galleries Mon–Sat 9:30am–4pm. No sightseeing Sun (services only). Tube: St. Paul's.

Victoria & Albert Museum ⋆⋆⋆ On display here are fine and decorative arts, the world's greatest collection. Medieval holdings include many treasures, such as the Eltenberg Reliquary; the Early English Gloucester Candlestick; the Byzantine Veroli Casket, with its ivory panels based on Greek plays; and the Syon Cope, an English embroidery from the early 14th century. Islamic art includes the 16th-century Persian Ardabil carpet. The V&A has the largest collection of Renaissance sculpture outside Italy, including a Donatello marble relief. Raphael's cartoons for tapestries for the Sistine Chapel, owned by the queen, can also be seen here.

V&A has recently opened 15 new galleries—called the **British Galleries** ⋆⋆⋆—unfolding the story of British design from 1500 to 1900. From Chippendale to Morris, all of the top British designers are featured. Star exhibits range from the 5m (17-ft.) high Melville Bed (1697), with its red silk velvet hangings, to the wedding suite of James II and one of the most prized possessions, the "Great Bed of Ware," mentioned in Shakespeare's *Twelfth Night*.

Cromwell Rd., SW7. ℂ 020/7942-2000. www.vam.ac.uk. Free admission. Daily 10am–5:45pm (Wed until 10pm). Tube: South Kensington.

Kensington Palace ⋆ This mansion dates from 1605 but was redesigned by Sir Christopher Wren in 1689. Since the end of the 18th century, it has been home to various members of the royal family, and the State Apartments are open for tours. The palace was the London home of the late Princess Margaret and was once the home of Diana, princess of Wales, and her two sons. Newly restored, the State Apartments and Ceremonial Dress Collection display trompe l'oeil murals by William Kent and ceremonial robes belonging to Queen Mary and George V. Visitors are guided through a series of theme rooms, including a tailor shop stocked with materials used in court dress. Of the 30 rooms, 15, including the restored King's Gallery and the Cupola Room, where Queen Victoria was baptized, are permanently open to the public. In the northwestern corner of Kensington Gardens (see below) is the **Princess Diana Memorial Playground,** dedicated to the late princess in 2000.

The Broad Walk, Kensington Gardens, W8. ⓒ **020/8781-9792**. Admission £9 ($14) adults, £7 ($11) seniors and students, £6.50 ($10) children, £28 ($42) family. June–Sept daily 10am–5pm; off season daily 10am–4pm. Tube: Queensway or Bayswater on north side of gardens; High St. Kensington on south side.

Whitehall ✵   Whitehall extends south from Trafalgar Square to Parliament Square. Along it you'll find the Home Office, the Old Admiralty Building, and the Ministry of Defense. Visitors today can see the **Cabinet War Rooms** ✵, a bombproof bunker suite of rooms, just as they were left by Winston Churchill at the end of World War II. You can see the Map Room with its huge wall maps; the Atlantic map is a mass of pinholes (each hole represents at least one convoy). Next door is Churchill's bedroom-cum-office, which has two BBC microphones on the desk for his broadcasts of those famous speeches that stirred the nation.

Clive Steps at the end of King Charles St., SW1, off Whitehall near Big Ben. ⓒ **020/7930-6961**. Admission £5.80 ($9.30) adults, £4.20 ($6.70) seniors and students, free for children under 17. May–Sept daily 9:30am–6pm (last admission 5:15pm); Oct–April daily 10am–5:30pm. Closed Christmas holidays. Tube: Westminster or St. James's.

MUSEUMS

Apsley House ✵   This former town house of the duke of Wellington (1769–1852), who defeated Napoléon at the Battle of Waterloo and later became prime minister, was opened as a public museum in 1952. The building was designed by Robert Adam and constructed from 1771 to 1778.

149 Piccadilly, Hyde Park Corner, W1. ⓒ **020/7499-5676**. www.apsleyhouse.org.uk. Admission £4.50 ($7.20) adults, £3 ($4.80) seniors, free for children under 18. Tues–Sun 11am–5pm. Tube: Hyde Park Corner.

Museum of London ✵✵   In the Barbican near St. Paul's, the museum traces London's history from prehistoric times through relics, costumes, household effects, maps, and models. Anglo-Saxons, Vikings, Normans—they're all here, displayed on two floors around a central courtyard.

150 London Wall, EC2. ⓒ **020/7600-3699**. www.museumoflondon.org.uk. Free admission. Mon–Sat 10am–5:50pm; Sun noon–5:50pm. Tube: St. Paul's or Barbican.

National Portrait Gallery ✵✵   This museum was founded in 1856 to collect the likenesses of famous British men and women. Today the collection is the most comprehensive of its kind in the world and constitutes a unique record of those who created the history and culture of the nation. A few paintings will catch your eye, including Sir Joshua Reynolds's portrait of Samuel Johnson ("a man of most dreadful appearance"). You'll also see a portrait of William Shakespeare, which is claimed to be the most "authentic contemporary likeness" of its subject, and the portrait of the Brontë sisters, painted by their brother Branwell. The most recent additions to the gallery include portraits of British sports figures, a tribute to athletic icons from the *Chariots of Fire* athletes of the 1920s to the superstars of today.

In 2000, Queen Elizabeth opened the Ondaatje Wing of the gallery, granting the gallery more than 50% more exhibition space. The most intriguing part of the new space is the splendid Tudor Gallery, with portraits of Richard III and

Wheeling Around

The world's largest observation wheel, the **Millennium Wheel London Eye** ⚐, Millennium Jubilee Gard (ⓒ **0870/500-0600;** www.londoneye. com), opened in February 2000. The fourth-tallest structure in London, it offers panoramic views that extend for some 40km (25 miles) if the weather's clear. Passengers are carried in 32 "pods" that make a complete revolution every half hour. Along the way you see some of London's landmarks from a bird's-eye point of view. Some two million visitors are expected to ride the eye every year.

Tickets for the ride are £11 ($18) for adults, £10 ($16) for seniors, and £5.50 ($8.80) for children. In May and September, hours are Monday through Thursday from 9:30am to 8pm, Friday through Sunday from 9:30am to 9pm; in June, Monday through Thursday 9:30am to 9pm, Friday through Sunday from 9:30am to 10pm; in July and August, daily from 9:30am to 10pm; and from October to April, daily from 9:30am to 8pm. Tube: Embankment or Waterloo.

Henry II, his conqueror in the Battle of Bosworth in 1485, as well as a portrait of Shakespeare first acquired by the gallery in 1856.

St. Martin's Place, WC2. ⓒ 020/7306-0055. www.npg.org.uk. Free admission; fee charged for certain temporary exhibitions. Mon–Wed 10am–6pm; Thurs–Fri 10am–9pm; Sat–Sun 10am–6pm. Tube: Charing Cross or Leicester Sq.

LONDON'S PARKS

London's parklands easily rate as the greatest "green lung" system of any large city. One of the largest is **Hyde Park** ⚐. With the adjoining Kensington Gardens, it covers 257 hectares (636 acres) of central London with velvety lawn interspersed with ponds, flower beds, and trees. **Kensington Gardens** are home to the celebrated statue of Peter Pan (with the bronze rabbits that toddlers are always trying to kidnap) and to the **Princess Diana Memorial Playground.** East of Hyde Park, across Piccadilly, stretch **Green Park** ⚐ and **St. James's Park** ⚐, forming an almost unbroken chain of landscaped beauty. This is an ideal area for picnics. You'll find it hard to believe this was once a festering piece of swamp near the leper hospital. **Regent's Park,** north of Baker Street and Marylebone Road, was designed by the 18th-century genius John Nash to surround a palace that never materialized. The **open-air theater** and the **London Zoo** ⚐⚐ are in this most classically beautiful of London's parks.

In July 2000, a 11km (7-mile) **walk commemorating the life of Princess Diana** opened. The walk passes through four of London's royal parks—St. James's Park, Green Park, Hyde Park, and Kensington Gardens. A **memorial fountain** to Diana is expected to be in place next to the Serpentine in Hyde Park by the sixth anniversary of Diana's death in August 2003.

ORGANIZED TOURS

For the first-timer, the quickest and most economical way to bring the big city into focus is to take a bus tour. One of the most popular is **The Original London Sightseeing Tour,** which passes all the major sights in just about 1½ hours. The tour, which uses a traditional double-decker bus with live commentary by a guide, costs £15 ($24) for adults, £7.50 ($12) for children under 16, free for those under 5. The tour allows you to hop on or off the bus at any point in the tour at no extra charge. The tour plus admission to Madame Tussaud's is £30 ($48) for adults, £20 ($31) for children.

Departures are from convenient points within the city; you can choose your departure point when you buy your ticket. Tickets can be purchased on the bus or at a discount from any London Transport or London Tourist Board Information Centre. Most hotel concierges also sell tickets. For information or phone purchases, call ✆ **020/88771722.** It's also possible to book online at **www.the originaltour.com**.

Touring boats operate on the Thames year-round and can take you to various places within Greater London and beyond. Main embarkation points are Westminster Pier, Charing Cross Pier, and Tower Pier, a system that enables you, for instance, to take a "water taxi" from the Tower of London to Westminster Abbey, or a more leisurely cruise from Westminster to Hampton Court Palace or Kew Gardens. Several companies operate motor launches offering panoramic views en route. For information and reservations, contact the **Westminster-Greenwich Thames Passenger Boat Service,** Westminster Pier, Victoria Embankment, SW1 (✆ **020/7930-4097;** www.westminsterpier.co.uk).

The Original London Walks, 87 Messina Ave., P.O. Box 1708, London NW6 4LW (✆ **020/7624-3978;** http://london.walks.com), the oldest established walking-tour company in London, is run by an Anglo-American journalist/actor couple, David and Mary Tucker. Their hallmarks are variety, reliability, reasonably sized groups, and—above all—superb guides. The renowned crime historian Donald Rumbelow, the leading authority on Jack the Ripper and author of the classic guidebook *London Walks,* is a regular guide, as are several prominent actors (including classical actor Edward Petherbridge). Walks are regularly scheduled daily and cost £5 ($8) for adults, £4 ($6.40) for students and seniors; children under 15 go free. Call for a schedule; no reservations are needed.

THE SHOPPING SCENE
THE TOP SHOPPING STREETS & NEIGHBORHOODS
THE WEST END As a neighborhood, the West End includes Mayfair and is home to the core of London's big-name shopping. Most of the department stores, designer shops, and chain stores have their flagships in this area.

The key streets are **Oxford Street** for affordable shopping (Tube: Bond St.), and **Regent Street,** which intersects Oxford Street at Oxford Circus (Tube: Oxford Circus). **Marks & Spencer**'s Marble Arch store (on Oxford St.) is their flagship and worth shopping at for their high-quality goods. There's a grocery store in the basement and a home furnishings department upstairs. Regent Street has fancier shops—more upscale department stores (including the famed **Liberty of London**), chain stores **(Laura Ashley),** and specialty dealers—and leads all the way to Piccadilly.

In between the two, parallel to Regent Street, is **Bond Street.** Divided into New and Old, Bond Street (Tube: Bond St.) also connects Piccadilly with Oxford Street and is synonymous with the luxury trade. Bond Street has had a recent revival and is the hot address for international designers. **Burlington Arcade** (Tube: Piccadilly Circus), the famous glass-roofed, Regency-style passage leading off Piccadilly, is lined with intriguing shops and boutiques specializing in fashion, jewelry, Irish linen, cashmere, and more.

Just off Regent Street, **Carnaby Street** (Tube: Oxford Circus) might sound like a tired name from the Swinging '60s, but it's still alive and flourishing. The area includes surrounding streets as well: Newburg, Ganton, Marlborough Court, Lowndes Court, Marshall, Beak, Kingly, and Foubert's Place. Each of these streets has new and exciting shops along with trendy cafes and bars. New retailers are moving in all the time, including a concept by Levi's to sell its vintage clothing under the label "Red." You can expect the unexpected here, and innovative boutiques come and go virtually every week. The entire district is also a place to hang out at such bars as JUS Cafe, on Foubert's Place, the most fashionable juice bar in London.

For a total contrast, check out **Jermyn Street,** on the far side of Piccadilly, a tiny 2-block-long street devoted to high-end men's haberdashers and toiletries shops; many have been doing business for centuries. Several hold royal warrants, including **Turnbull & Asser,** where HRH Prince Charles has his pj's made.

The West End also includes the theater district, so there are two more shopping areas: the still-not-ready-for-prime-time **Soho,** where sex shops are slowly being turned into cutting-edge designer shops; and **Covent Garden,** which is a masterpiece unto itself. The original marketplace has taken over the surrounding neighborhood so that even though the streets run a little higgledy-piggledy and you can easily get lost, it's fun to just wander and shop. Covent Garden is especially mobbed on Sundays (Tube: Covent Garden).

KNIGHTSBRIDGE & CHELSEA   This is the second-most-famous retail district because it's the home of **Harrods,** 87–135 Brompton Rd., Knightsbridge (© **020/7730-1234;** www.harrods.com; Tube: Knightsbridge). Harrods is London's—indeed Europe's—top department store. The sheer range, variety, and quality of merchandise are dazzling; be sure not to miss the delicatessen and food halls. A small street nearby, Sloane Street, is chockablock with designer shops; and another street in the opposite direction, **Cheval Place,** is lined with designer resale shops.

Walk toward Museum Row and you'll soon find **Beauchamp Place** (pronounced *Bee*-cham). The street is only 1 block long, but it features the kinds of shops where young British aristos buy their clothing. Head out at the **Harvey Nichols** ("Harvey Nicks") end of Knightsbridge, away from Harrods, and shop your way through the designer stores on Sloane Street (**Hermès, Armani, Prada,** and the like), then walk past Sloane Square and you're in an altogether different neighborhood: Chelsea.

King's Road (Tube: Sloane Sq.), the main street of Chelsea, which starts at Sloane Square, will forever remain a symbol of London in the Swinging Sixties. More and more, King's Road is a lineup of markets and "multistores," large or small conglomerations of indoor stands, stalls, and booths within one building or enclosure. Chelsea doesn't begin and end with King's Road. If you choose to walk in the other direction from Harrods, you connect to a part of Chelsea called **Brompton Cross,** another hip and hot area for designer shops made popular when Michelin House was rehabbed by Sir Terence Conran for **The Conran Shop,** 81 Fulham Rd., SW 3 (© **020/7589-7401**).

Also, seek out **Walton Street,** a tiny little snake of a street running off Brompton Cross. About 2 blocks are devoted to fairy-tale shops where a *lady* buys aromatherapy, needlepoint, or costume jewelry, or meets with her interior designer. Finally, don't forget all those museums right there in the corner of the shopping streets. They have great gift shops.

KENSINGTON & NOTTING HILL   **Kensington High Street** (Tube: High St. Kensington) is the most recent hangout of the classier breed of teen, who has graduated from Carnaby Street and is ready for street chic. While there are a few staples of basic British fashion on this strip, most of the stores feature items that stretch, are very, very short, or are very, very tight.

From Kensington High Street, you can walk up **Kensington Church Street,** which, like Portobello Road, is one of the city's main shopping avenues for antiques. Kensington Church Street dead-ends into the Notting Hill Gate Tube station, which is where you would arrive for shopping in **Portobello Road.** The weekend market is 2 blocks beyond.

THE TOP MARKETS

THE WEST END   The most famous market in all of England, **Covent Garden Market** (© **020/7836-9136;** Tube: Covent Garden), offers several different markets daily from 9am to 5pm (we think it's most fun to come on Sun). **Apple Market** is the fun, bustling market in the courtyard, where traders sell, well, everything. Many of the items are what the English call collectible nostalgia; they include a wide array of glassware and ceramics, leather goods, toys, clothes, hats, and jewelry. Some of the merchandise is truly unusual. This becomes an antiques market on Monday. Meanwhile, out back is **Jubilee Market** (© **020/7836-2139**), which is also an antiques market on Monday. Every other day of the week, it's sort of a fancy hippie-ish market with cheap clothes and books. Out front are a few tents of cheap stuff, except again on Monday, when antiques dealers take over here, too.

St. Martin-in-the-Fields Market (Tube: Charing Cross) is good for teens and hipsters who don't want to trek all the way to Camden Market and can be satisfied with imports from India and South America, crafts, and local football souvenirs. It's near Trafalgar Square and Covent Garden; hours are Monday through Saturday from 11am to 5pm, Sunday from noon to 5pm.

NOTTING HILL   The area has become synonymous with the Julia Roberts and Hugh Grant movie, but Londoners already know that whatever you collect, you'll find it at the **Portobello Market** (Tube: Notting Hill Gate). It's mainly a Saturday happening from 6am to 5pm. You needn't be here at the crack of dawn; 9am is fine. You just want to beat the motor-coach crowd. Once known mainly for fruit and vegetables (still sold here throughout the week), Portobello in the past 4 decades has become synonymous with antiques. But don't take the stall holder's word for it that the fiddle he's holding is a genuine Stradivarius left to him in the will of his Italian great-uncle; it might just as well have been nicked from an East End pawnshop.

The market is divided into three major sections. The most crowded is the antiques section, running between Colville Road and Chepstow Villas to the south. (***Warning:*** There's a great concentration of pickpockets in this area.) The second section (and the oldest part) is the "fruit and veg" market, lying between Westway and Colville Road. In the third and final section, there's a flea market, where Londoners sell bric-a-brac and lots of secondhand goods they didn't really want in the first place. Looking around makes for interesting fun.

LONDON AFTER DARK

Weekly publications such as *Time Out* and *Where,* available at newsstands, give full entertainment listings and contain information on restaurants, nightclubs, and theaters. You'll also find listings in daily newspapers, notably *The Times* and *The Telegraph.*

THE PERFORMING ARTS

To see specific shows, especially hits, purchase your tickets in advance. The best method is to buy your tickets from the theater's box office, which you can do over the phone using a credit card. You'll pay the theater price and pick up the tickets the day of the show. You can also go to a reliable ticket agent (the greatest cluster is in Covent Garden), but you'll pay a fee, which varies depending on the show. You can also make theater reservations through ticket agents. In the case of hit shows, only brokers may be able to get you a seat, but you'll pay for the privilege. For tickets and information before you go, try **Global Tickets,** 234 West 44th St., Suite 1000, New York, NY 10036 (© **800/223-6108** or 212/398-1468; www.keithprowse.com). They also have offices in London at the **British Visitors Center,** 1 Regents St., W1 V1PJ (© **020/7014-8550**); and at the **Harrods** ticket desk, 87–135 Brompton Rd. (© **020/7589-9109**), located on the lower-ground floor opposite the British Airways desk. They'll mail tickets to your home, or fax you a confirmation and leave your tickets at the box office. Instant confirmations are available with special "overseas" rates for most shows. A booking and handling fee of up to 20% is added to the ticket price.

THEATER   Occupying a prime site on the South Bank of the River Thames is the flagship of British theater, the **Royal National Theatre,** South Bank, SE1 (© **020/7452-3000;** www.nt-online.org; Tube: Waterloo, Embankment, or Charing Cross). The National houses three theaters. Tickets are £10 to £38 ($16–$61).

   Barbican Theatre–Royal Shakespeare Company, Barbican Centre, Silk Street, Barbican, EC2 (© **020/7638-8891;** www.rsc.org.uk; Tube: Barbican, Moorgate, or Liverpool St.), is one of the world's finest theater companies. The core of the company's work remains the plays of William Shakespeare, but it also presents a wide-ranging program. There are three different productions each week in the Barbican Theatre, the main auditorium, and the Pit, a small studio space where much of the company's new writing is presented. Barbican Theatre tickets are £5 to £35 ($8–$56); the Pit, £7 to £11 ($23–$35).

   A recent addition to London's theater scene is the replica of Shakespeare's **Globe Theatre,** New Globe Walk, Bankside, SE1 (© **020/7902-1400;** www.shakespeares-globe.org; Tube: Mansion House). Performances are staged, on the theater's original site, as they were in Elizabethan times: without lighting, scenery, or such luxuries as cushioned seats or a roof over the audience. From May to September, the company intends to hold performances Tuesday through Saturday at 2 and 7pm. There will be a limited winter schedule. In any season, the schedule may be affected by weather, because this is an outdoor theater. Tickets are £5 ($8) for groundlings, £11 to £27 ($18–$43) for gallery seats.

   Sadler's Wells Theatre, Rosbery Avenue, EC1 (© **020/7863-8000;** www. sadlers-wells.com; Tube: Angel), is London's premier venue for dance. This new

---

Tips Fringe Benefits

Some of the best theater in London is performed on the "fringe"—at the dozens of so-called fringe theaters that usually attempt more adventurous productions than the established West End theaters; they're also dramatically lower in price and staged in more intimate surroundings. Check _Time Out_ for schedules and show times.

theater can change its interior shape, size, mood, and even color for almost any performance. The program for Sadler's for each year will be approximately 25 weeks of dance and 10 to 12 weeks of opera. The remaining time will offer a medley of visual theater. The box office is open Monday through Saturday from 10am to 8pm. Tickets are £9 to £45 ($14–$72).

CLASSICAL MUSIC & OPERA The **Royal Opera** and **Royal Ballet** are back at the newly restored **Royal Opera House,** Bow St., Covent Garden, WC2 (© **020/7304-4000** or 020/7212-9123; www.royalopera.org; Tube: Covent Garden). New additions include two annexes with shops and restaurants, and rehearsal rooms. Opera performances are usually sung in the original language with English subtitles; tickets are £10 to £155 ($16–$248). The Royal Ballet performs a repertory with a tilt toward the classics, including works by its earlier choreographer-director, Sir Frederick Ashton, and Sir Kenneth MacMillan; tickets are £44 to £77 ($71–$124).

London Coliseum, St. Martin's Lane, WC2 (© **020/7632-8300;** www.eno. org; Tube: Leicester Sq.), is London's largest and most splendid theater. **English National Opera** performs a wide range of works in English, from great classics to Gilbert and Sullivan to new and experimental works, staged with flair and imagination. Tickets are £6 to £61 ($9.60–$98). About 100 discount balcony tickets are sold on the day of performance.

Royal Albert Hall, Kensington Gore, SW7 (© **020/7589-8212;** www.royal alberthall.org.uk; Tube: South Kensington), is the annual setting for the BBC Henry Wood Promenade Concerts ("The Proms") from mid-July to mid-September. A British tradition since 1895, the programs are outstanding, often presenting newly commissioned works for the first time. Tickets are £15 to £50 ($24–$79).

Across Waterloo Bridge rises **Royal Festival Hall,** South Bank, SE1 (© **020/7960-4242;** Tube: Waterloo or Embankment). Here are three of the most comfortable and acoustically perfect concert halls in the world: Royal Festival Hall, Queen Elizabeth Hall, and the Purcell Room. Within their precincts, more than 1,200 performances a year are presented. Tickets are £6 to £55 ($9.60–$88).

THE CLUB & MUSIC SCENE

ROCK A long-established venue for rock 'n' roll, blues, and indie bands, **The Rock Garden,** 6–7 The Piazza, Covent Garden (© **020/7240-3961;** Tube: Covent Garden), maintains a bar and a stage in the cellar and a restaurant on the street level. The cellar area, known as The Venue, has hosted such bands as Dire Straits, The Police, and U2 before they became famous. It's open Monday through Thursday from 5pm to 3am; Friday and Saturday from 5pm to 4am; and Sunday from 5pm to 2am. Cover is £5 to £15 ($8–$24); diners enter free.

JAZZ & BLUES The reasonably priced **100 Club,** 100 Oxford St., W1 (© **020/7636-0933;** Tube: Tottenham Court Rd.), is a serious rival to the city's upscale jazz clubs. Its cavalcade of bands includes the best British jazz musicians, as well as many touring Americans. Rock, R&B, and blues are also presented. It's open Monday through Thursday from 7:30pm to 11:30pm; Friday from noon to 3pm and 8:30pm to 2am; Saturday from 7:30pm to 1am; and Sunday from 7:30 to 11:30pm. Cover is £10 to £12 ($16–$19); discounts available for club members.

Mention the word "jazz" in London and people immediately think of **Ronnie Scott's Club,** 47 Frith St., W1 (© **020/7439-0747;** Tube: Leicester Sq.), long the citadel of modern jazz in Europe, where the best English and American

Moments The Pub Crawl, London Style

Dropping into the local pub for a pint of real ale or bitter is the best way to soak up the character of the different villages that make up London. You'll hear the accents and slang and see first-hand how far removed upper-crust Kensington is from blue-collar Wapping. Catch the local gossip or football talk—and, of course, enjoy some of the finest ales, stouts, ciders, and malt whiskies in the world.

Central London is awash with wonderful historic pubs as rich and varied as the city itself. The **Cittie of Yorke,** 22 High Holborn, WC1 (© 020/7242-7670; Tube: Holborn or Chancery Lane), boasts the longest bar in Britain, rafters ascending to the heavens, and a long row of immense wine vats, all of which give it the air of a great medieval hall—appropriate since a pub has existed at this location since 1430. Samuel Smiths is on tap, and the bar offers novelties like chocolate-orange–flavored vodka.

Dickens once hung out in the **Lamb & Flag,** 33 Rose St., off Garrick Street, WC2 (© 020/7497-9504; Tube: Leicester Sq.), and the room itself is little changed from the days when he prowled this neighborhood. The pub has an amazing and somewhat scandalous history. John Dryden was almost killed by a band of thugs outside its doors in December 1679; the pub gained the nickname the "Bucket of Blood" during the Regency era (1811–20) because of the routine bare-knuckled prizefights that broke out. Tap beers include Courage Best, Courage Directors, Old Speckled Hen, John Smiths, and Wadworths 6X.

The **Nag's Head** (10 James St., WC2; © 020/7836-4678; Tube: Covent Garden) is one of London's most famous Edwardian pubs. In days of yore, patrons had to make their way through lorries of fruit and flowers to drink here. But when the market moved, 300 years of British tradition faded away. Today, the pub is patronized mainly by young people. The draft Guinness is very good. Lunch is typical pub grub: sandwiches, salads, pork cooked in cider, and garlic prawns. Snacks are available in the afternoon.

The snug little **Dog & Duck** (18 Bateman St., corner of Frith St., W1; © 020/7494-0697), a Soho landmark, is the most intimate pub in London. One former patron was author George Orwell, who came here to celebrate his sales of *Animal Farm* in the United States. A wide mixture of patrons of all ages and persuasions flock here, chatting amiably while ordering the delights of Tetley's LA or Timothy Taylor Landlord. If business warrants it, the cozy upstairs bar is opened.

groups are booked. Featured on almost every bill is an American band, often with a top-notch singer. In the Main Room, you can either stand at the bar to watch the show or sit at a table, where you can order dinner. The Downstairs Bar is more intimate. On weekends, the separate Upstairs Room has a disco called Club Latino. It's open Monday through Saturday from 8:30pm to 3am. Cover for nonmembers is £15 to £25 ($24–$40). For members it's £5 ($8); on Friday and Saturday £10 ($16).

DANCE CLUBS **Bar Rumba,** 326 Shaftesbury Ave., W1 (© 020/7287-2715; Tube: Piccadilly Circus), is a Latin bar and club that could be featured in a book on "Underground London" in spite of its location on Shaftesbury Avenue. It leans toward radical jazz fusion on some nights, funk on other occasions. It boasts two full bars and a different musical theme every night. Tuesday and Wednesday are the only nights you won't have to queue at the door. Monday's "That's How It Is" showcase features jazz, hip hop, and drum and bass; and Saturday's "Garage City" buzzes with house and garage. On weeknights you have to be 18 or older; on Saturday and Sunday nobody under 21 is allowed in. The club is open Monday through Thursday from 6pm to 3:30am; Friday from 6pm to 4am; Saturday from 7pm to 6am; and Sunday from 8pm to 1:30am. Cover is £3 to £12 ($4.80–$19).

   Equinox, Leicester Square, WC2 (© 020/7437-1446; Tube: Leicester Sq.), has nine bars, the largest dance floor in London, and a restaurant modeled along the lines of an American diner from the 1950s. Virtually every kind of dance music, save "rave," is featured here. It's open Monday through Thursday from 9pm to 3am and Friday and Saturday from 9pm to 4am. Cover is £5 to £12 ($9.60–$19); £3 ($4.50) students. **Hippodrome,** Leicester Square, WC2 (© 020/7437-4311; Tube: Leicester Sq.), is one of London's greatest discos, an enormous place where light and sound envelop you from all directions. Revolving speakers even descend from the roof to deafen you in patches, and you can watch yourself on closed-circuit video. It's open Monday through Friday from 9pm to 3am, Saturday from 9pm to 3:30am. Cover is £8 to £11 ($13–$18).

THE GAY & LESBIAN SCENE

The most reliable source of information on gay clubs and activities is the (always busy) 24-hour **Gay and Lesbian Switchboard** at © 020/7837-7324.

   Adjacent to one of Covent Garden's best-known traffic junctions, **The Box,** at Seven Dials, 32–34 Monmouth St., WC2 (© 020/7240-5828; Tube: Covent Garden or Leicester Sq.), is a Mediterranean-style bar. Gay men outnumber lesbians, though the venue is sophisticated and blasé about sexual definition. Year-round, the place defines itself as a "summer bar," throwing open its doors and windows to a cluster of outdoor tables that attracts a crowd at the slightest hint of warmth. It's open Monday through Saturday from 11:30am to 11pm and Sunday from noon to 10:30pm. No cover.

   First Out, 52 St. Giles High St., WC2 (© 020/7240-8042; Tube: Tottenham Court Rd.), prides itself on being the first (est. 1986) all-gay coffee shop in London. Set in a 19th-century building whose venerable wood panels have been painted all colors of the rainbow, it maintains two intimate floors (read: not particularly cruisy) where menu items are exclusively vegetarian. Don't expect raucousness; some clients have even brought their grandmothers here. First Out is open Monday through Saturday from 10am to 11pm and Sunday from 11am to 10:30pm.

THE BAR SCENE

At the **American Bar,** in The Savoy, The Strand, WC2 (© 020/7836-4343; Tube: Embankment or Covent Garden), still one of the most sophisticated gathering places in London, the bartender is known for such special concoctions as the "Savoy Affair" and the "Prince of Wales," as well as for pouring the best martini in town. The bar is open Monday through Saturday from 11am to 11pm; jazz piano music begins at 7pm.

Very much the place to be seen, the **Met Bar** (in the Metropolitan Hotel, 19 Old Park Lane, W1; ℂ **020/7447-1000;** Tube: Hyde Park Corner) has become the hottest bar in London. Mix with the elite of the fashion, TV, and music world. A lot of American celebrities have been seen here, sipping on a martini, from Demi Moore to Courteney Cox. Despite the caliber of the clientele, the bar has managed to maintain a relaxed and unpretentious atmosphere.

DAY TRIPS FROM LONDON

HAMPTON COURT PALACE ✮✮✮   On the north side of the Thames, 21km (13 miles) west of London in East Molesey, Surrey, this 16th-century palace of Cardinal Wolsey can teach us a lesson: Don't try to outdo your boss, particularly if he happens to be Henry VIII. The rich cardinal did just that. He eventually lost his fortune, power, and prestige—and he ended up giving his lavish palace to the Tudor monarch. Although the palace enjoyed prestige and pomp in Elizabethan days, it owes much of its present look to William and Mary—or rather to Sir Christopher Wren, who designed and built the Northern or Lion Gates. You can parade through the apartments today, filled as they are with porcelain, furniture, paintings, and tapestries. The Renaissance Gallery is graced with paintings by old masters on loan from Queen Elizabeth II.

Hampton Court (ℂ **0870/752-7777;** www.hrp.org.uk) is easily accessible. Frequent trains run from Waterloo Station (Network Southeast) to **Hampton Court Station** (ℂ **08457/484-950** or 01603/764776). **London Transport** (ℂ **020/7730-3466**) bus nos. 11, 131, 216, 267, and 461 make the trip from Victoria Coach Station on Buckingham Palace Road (just southwest of Victoria Station). If you're driving from London, take the A308 to the junction with the A309 on the north side of Kingston Bridge over the Thames.

Admission to Hampton Court is £11 ($18) adults, £8.25 ($13) students and seniors, £7.25 ($12) children 5 to 15, free for children under 5, £33 ($53) family. Gardens are open year-round daily from 7am to dusk (no later than 9pm); admission is free to all except Privy Garden (admission £3/$4.80 adults, £2/$3.20 children) without a palace ticket during summer months. Cloisters, courtyards, state apartments, the great kitchen, cellars, and Hampton Court exhibition are open March 30 through October 26, Monday from 10:15am to 6pm, Tuesday through Sunday from 9:30am to 6pm (last entry 5:15pm); October 27 through March 29, Monday from 10:15am to 4:30pm, Tuesday through Sunday from 9:30am to 6pm (last entry 5:15pm).

WINDSOR CASTLE ✮✮✮   When William the Conqueror ordered a castle built on this spot, he began a legend and a link with English sovereignty that has known many vicissitudes, the most recent being a 1992 fire. The state apartments display many works of art, porcelain, armor, furniture, three Verrio ceilings, and several 17th-century Gibbons carvings. Several works by Rubens adorn the King's Drawing Rooms. Of the apartments, the grand reception room, with its Gobelin tapestries, is the most spectacular.

Queen Mary's Doll's House is a palace in perfect miniature. It was given to Queen Mary in 1923 as a symbol of national goodwill. The house, designed by Sir Edwin Lutyens, was created on a scale of 1 to 12. It took 3 years to complete and involved the work of 1,500 tradespeople and artists.

St. George's Chapel is a gem of the Perpendicular style, sharing the distinction with Westminster Abbey as a pantheon of English monarchs (Victoria is a notable exception). The present St. George's was founded in the late 15th century by Edward IV on the site of the original Chapel of the Order of the Garter (from 1348).

Lying 34km (21 miles) west of London, Windsor Castle (© **020/7321-2233;** www.royalresidences.com) can be reached in 50 minutes by train from Paddington Station. Admission is £12 ($18) adults, £6 ($9.60) children 16 and under, £29 ($46) family of four. The castle at Castle Hill is open March through October daily from 9:45am to 5:15pm and November through February daily from 9:45am to 4pm.

2 Oxford & Stratford-upon-Avon

TOWN & GOWN: OXFORD 𝕽𝕽

Oxford is a city of business and commerce, home to several industries; it's much more of a real city than Cambridge. Oxford isn't entirely dominated by its university, although the college spires are the reason the hordes, including tour buses, flock here. The fast-flowing pedestrian traffic may cause you to think you've been transported back to London instead of delivered to not-so-sleepy Oxford.

At any time of the year, you can tour the colleges, many of which represent a peak in England's architectural kingdom, as well as a valley of Victorian contributions. The Oxford Tourist Information Centre (see below) offers guided walking tours daily year-round. Just don't mention the other place (Cambridge), and you shouldn't have any trouble. Comparisons between the two universities are inevitable of course, Oxford being better known for the arts and Cambridge more for the sciences.

The city predates the university—in fact, it was a Saxon town in the early part of the 10th century. By the 12th century, Oxford was already growing in reputation as a seat of learning, at the expense of Paris. The first colleges were founded in the 13th century. The story of Oxford is filled with local conflicts: The relationship between town and gown wasn't as peaceful as it is today, and riots often flared over the rights of the university versus the town. Nowadays, the young people of Oxford take out their aggressions in sporting competitions.

Ultimately, the test of a great university lies in the caliber of the people it turns out. Oxford can name-drop a mouthful: Roger Bacon, Sir Walter Raleigh, John Donne, Sir Christopher Wren, Samuel Johnson, William Penn, Lewis Carroll, Harold Macmillan, Graham Greene, T. E. Lawrence, just to name a select few.

ESSENTIALS

GETTING THERE   Oxford is 87km (54 miles) northwest from London.

By Train   Trains from London's Paddington Station depart hourly for Oxford (trip time: 1½ hr.). A cheap, same-day round-trip ticket costs £16 ($26); call © **08457/484950** or visit www.railtrack.co.uk for information.

By Bus   **Oxford Citylink** provides coach service from London's Victoria Station (© **08705/808080**) to the Oxford bus station. Coaches usually depart about every 30 minutes during the day (trip time: about 1¾ hr.). A same-day round-trip ticket costs £10 ($16) adults, £8 ($13) children.

By Car   Take M-40 west from London and follow the signs. Traffic and parking are a disaster in Oxford; you may want to use one of the four "Park and Ride" lots just outside the city.

VISITOR INFORMATION   The **Oxford Tourist Information Centre,** at 15–16 Broad St., Gloucester Green (© **01865/726871;** www.oxfordcity.co.uk), sells maps, brochures, and souvenirs, as well as the famous Oxford University T-shirt. It also provides hotel booking services for £2.50 ($3.75). Guided walking tours leave from the center daily (see below). It's open Monday through Saturday from 9:30am to 5pm and Sunday and bank holidays in summer from 10am to 3:30pm.

GETTING AROUND   Competition thrives in Oxford transportation, and the public benefits with swift, clean service by two companies. The **Oxford Bus Company,** 395 Cowley Rd. (© **01865/785400;** www.oxfordbus.co.uk), has green Park and Ride buses that leave from four parking lots in the city using the north–south or east–west routes. A round-trip ticket costs £1.70 ($2.70). Their blue CityLink buses travel to London, Heathrow, and Gatwick. The company's red CityLink buses cover 15 routes in all suburbs; a day pass allows unlimited travel for £2.70 ($4.30). Weekly and monthly passes are available. The competition, **Stagecoach of Oxfordshire,** Unit 4, Horsepath, Cowley (© **01865/ 772250;** www.stagecoach-oxford.co.uk), uses blue-and-cream minibuses and tricolored red, blue, and orange coaches. City buses leave from Queen Street in Oxford's city center. Stagecoach's Explorer Pass is a 1-day unlimited pass for travel in central and southeast England. Abington Road buses are marked WANTAGE and Iffley Road buses are labeled ROSE HILL.

WHERE TO STAY

Oxford Tourist Information Centre, Gloucester Green, opposite the bus station (© **01865/726871**), operates a year-round room-booking service for a fee of £3 ($4.80), plus a refundable deposit. The center has a list of accommodations, maps, and guidebooks.

Very Expensive

Old Parsonage Hotel 🏵🏵   This extensively renovated hotel, near St. Giles Church and Keble College, is so old it looks like an extension of one of the ancient colleges. Originally a 13th-century hospital, it was restored in the early 17th century. In the 20th century, a modern wing was added, and in 1991 it was completely renovated and made into a first-rate hotel. This intimate old hotel is filled with hidden charms such as tiny gardens in its courtyard and on its roof terrace. In this tranquil area of Oxford, you feel like you're living at one of the colleges yourself. The rooms are individually designed but not large, each opening onto the private gardens. All have bathrooms with shower-tub combinations.

1 Banbury Rd., Oxford OX2 6NN. © **01865/310210.** Fax 01865/311262. www.oxford-hotels-restaurants. co.uk. 30 units. £133–£168 ($213–$269) double; £193 ($309) suite. AE, DC, MC, V. Bus: 7. **Amenities:** Restaurant; bar; room service; laundry/dry-cleaning service. *In room:* TV, dataport, hair dryer, safe, trouser press.

The Randolph 🏵   Since 1864, the Randolph has overlooked St. Giles, the Ashmolean Museum, and the Cornmarket. The hotel is an example of how historic surroundings can be combined with modern conveniences to make for elegant accommodations. The lounges, though modernized, are cavernous enough for dozens of separate and intimate conversational groupings. The furnishings are traditional. Some rooms are quite large; others are a bit cramped. All units come equipped with well-maintained bathrooms containing shower-tub combinations. The double-glazing on the windows seems inadequate to keep out the noise of midtown traffic. In this price range, we'd opt first for the more stylish and intimate Old Parsonage.

Beaumont St., Oxford, Oxfordshire OX1 2LN. © **800/225-5843** in the U.S. and Canada, or 0870/4008200. Fax 01865/791678. www.macdonaldhotels.co.uk. 114 units. £120–£195 ($192–$312) double; from

£355–£600 ($568–$960) suite. AE, DC, MC, V. Parking £22 ($35). Bus: 7. **Amenities:** Restaurant; 2 bars; concierge; room service; babysitting; laundry/dry-cleaning service. *In room:* TV, dataport, coffeemaker, hair dryer, iron.

Expensive

Eastgate Hotel 🐾   The Eastgate, built on the site of a 1600s structure, stands within walking distance of Oxford College and the city center. Recently refurbished, it offers modern facilities while somewhat retaining the atmosphere of an English country house. The guest rooms are well worn but still cozy, and range in size from small to medium. The bathrooms have minimum space, but are equipped with shower-tub combinations.

23 Merton St., The High St., Oxford, Oxfordshire, OX1 4BE. ⓒ 0870/4008201. Fax 01865/791681. www. macdonaldhotels.co.uk. 64 units. £160 ($256) double; £180 ($288) suite. AE, DC, MC, V. Bus: 3, 4, 7, or 52. **Amenities:** Restaurant; bar; room service; babysitting; laundry/dry-cleaning service. *In room:* A/C, TV, coffeemaker, hair dryer, trouser press.

Old Bank Hotel 🐾🐾🐾   Located on Oxford's main street and surrounded by some of its oldest colleges and sights, the building dates to the 18th century and was once a bank. The first hotel created in the center of Oxford in 135 years, it opened late in 1999, immediately surpassing the traditional favorite, the Randolph, in style and luxuries. The guest rooms are comfortably and elegantly appointed, often opening onto views. Linen bedcovers trimmed in velvet and shantung silk give the accommodations added style. Each unit includes a well-kept bathroom with terra-cotta or marble tiles and a shower-tub combination.

92–94 High St., Oxford OX1 4BN. ⓒ 01865/799599. Fax 01865/799598. www.oxford-hotels-restaurants. co.uk. 42 units. £160–£235 ($256–$376) double; from £265–£320 ($424–$512) suite. AE, DC, MC, V. Bus: 7. **Amenities:** Restaurant; bar; concierge; room service; babysitting; laundry/dry-cleaning service. *In room:* A/C, TV, dataport, coffeemaker, hair dryer, CD player.

Moderate

The Oxford Hotel   This is a good choice if you have a car; the hotel is 3km (2 miles) north of the city center, and hidden from traffic at the junction of A40 and A34. It attracts a lot of business travelers, but also visitors. It's a good base for exploring not only Oxford but the Cotswolds, which are within easy reach. The M40 motorway is just a 13km (8-mile) drive away. Rooms are motel-like, with modern, contemporary furnishings that are comfortable and spacious, but as of this writing, the hotel is undergoing extensive refurbishing and upgrading.

Godstow Rd., Wolvercote Roundabout, Oxford, Oxfordshire OX2 8AL. ⓒ 01865/489988. Fax 01865/ 310259. www.paramount-hotels.co.uk. 168 units. £159–£179 ($254–$286) double. AE, DC, MC, V. Bus: 6. **Amenities:** Restaurant; bar; pool; 2 squash courts; spa; room service; laundry/dry-cleaning service. *In room:* A/C, TV, dataport, coffeemaker, hair dryer, trouser press, safe.

Inexpensive

Tilbury Lodge Private Hotel *Kids*   On a quiet country lane about 3km (2 miles) west of the center of Oxford, this small hotel is less than a mile from the railway station, where hotel staff will pick you up to save you the walk. Eddie and Eileen Trafford accommodate guests in their comfortable, well-furnished rooms. The most expensive room has a four-poster bed. Rooms vary in size, but most are cozy with adequate space. Bathrooms, although tiny, are well kept, usually with a shower stall. The guesthouse also has a Jacuzzi and welcomes children.

5 Tilbury Lane, Eynsham Rd., Botley, Oxford, Oxfordshire OX2 9NB. ⓒ 01865/862138. Fax 01865/863700. 9 units. £66–£75 ($106–$120) double. Rates include English breakfast. MC, V. Bus: 4A, 4B, or 100. **Amenities:** Jacuzzi. *In room:* TV, coffeemaker, hair dryer.

WHERE TO DINE
Very Expensive

Le Manoir aux Quat' Saisons ☆☆ FRENCH (MODERN)   Some 19km (12 miles) southeast of Oxford, Le Manoir aux Quat' Saisons offers the finest cuisine in the Midlands. The gray- and honey-colored stone manor house was originally built by a Norman nobleman in the early 1300s, and over the years has attracted many famous visitors. Today, the restaurant's connection with France has been masterfully revived by the Gallic owner and chef, Raymond Blanc. His reputation for comfort and cuisine attracts guests from as far away as London. You can enjoy such creative treats as roasted squab and foie gras ravioli with wild mushrooms; roasted grouse in a blackberry and red wine sauce; or a truly delicious roasted breast of Barbary hen duck with figs and fennel seeds and a pan-fried foie gras. Each dish is an exercise in studied perfection.

Accommodations are also available here. The gabled house was built in the 1500s and improved and enlarged in 1908. An outdoor swimming pool was added much later. Each very pricey room—rates are £265 to £855 ($424–$1,368) for a double—is decorated boudoir-style with luxurious beds and linens, ruffled canopies, and high-quality antique reproductions.

Church Rd., Great Milton, Oxford, Oxfordshire OX44 7PD. ☎ 800/845-4274 in the U.S., or 01844/278881. Fax 01844/278847. www.manoir.com. Reservations required. Main courses £26–£38 ($42–$61); lunch *menu du jour* £45 ($72); lunch or dinner *menu gourmand* £95 ($152). AE, DC, MC, V. Daily noon–2:30pm and 7–9:15pm. Take Exit 7 off M40 and head along A329 toward Wallingford; look for signs for Great American Milton Manor about 1.6km (1 mile) down the road.

Expensive

Cherwell Boathouse Restaurant ☆ FRENCH/MODERN ENGLISH   An Oxford landmark on the River Cherwell, this restaurant is owned by Anthony Verdin, assisted by a young crew. The cooks change the fixed-price menu every 2 weeks to take advantage of the availability of fresh vegetables, fish, and meat. The kitchen is often cited for its "sensible combinations" of ingredients, as reflected quite well by its cream of artichoke and celery soup for a starter, or its shellfish terrine with a velvety chive-flavored crème fraîche. The success of the main dishes is founded on savory treats such as a pink and juicy breast of pigeon matched with a salad of smoked bacon on which tantalizing dribbles of raspberry dressing have been dropped. The tender and flavorful pork is perfectly married to an apple and prune compote. In summer, the restaurant also serves meals on the terrace.

Bardwell Rd. ☎ 01865/552746. www.cherwellboathouse.co.uk. Reservations recommended. 3-course fixed-price meals: dinner from £22 ($34); Sun lunch £22 ($34); Mon–Fri lunch £20 ($31). AE, DC, MC, V. Mon–Sun noon–2:30pm and 6:30–10pm. Closed Dec 24–30. Bus: Banbury Road.

Restaurant Elizabeth ☆ FRENCH/CONTINENTAL   The restaurant was named after its original owner, a matriarch who founded this stone-sided house opposite Christ Church College in the 1930s. Today you're likely to find a well-trained staff from Spain, serving beautifully presented dishes in the French style. The larger of the two dining rooms displays reproductions of paintings by Goya and Velázquez and exudes a restrained dignity; the smaller room is devoted to *Alice in Wonderland* designs inspired by Lewis Carroll. Dishes are based on the use of fine produce prepared with skilled culinary technique, as exemplified by filet of salmon sautéed in butter and cooked with a white wine sauce, or the grilled filet steak in a Madeira-flavored mushroom sauce. Breast of chicken is cooked in butter and delectably served in a creamy sauce of cognac and white wine.

82 St. Aldate's St. ℂ **01865/242230**. Reservations recommended. Main courses £14–£33 ($22–$53); fixed-price lunch £16 ($26). AE, DC, MC, V. Tues–Sat 12:30–2:30pm and 6:30–11pm; Sun 7–10:30pm. Closed Good Friday and Christmas week. Bus: 7.

Moderate

Gee's Restaurant ℱ MEDITERRANEAN/INTERNATIONAL This restaurant, in a spacious Victorian glass conservatory, was converted from what for 80 years was the leading florist of Oxford. Its original features were retained by the owners, the Old Parsonage Hotel (see above), who have turned it into one of the most nostalgic and delightful places to dine in the city. Around since 1984, it has come more into fashion under a new chef. From students to professors, clients are mixed, but all enjoy a well-chosen list of offerings that ranges from succulent pastas to chargrilled steaks, from fresh fish to crisp salads. The grilled halibut steak with a lemon-and-thyme butter is predictable but nonetheless fine in every way. The confit of duck is a savory choice, enhanced by Savoy cabbage, smoked bacon, and herb-roasted potatoes. Count on a freshly made soup and Mediterranean-inspired salads with roast pepper, French beans, and olives. Always reliable is Scottish prime rib-eye steak with mushrooms and shoestring "chips."

61 Banbury Rd. ℂ **01865/553540**. Reservations recommended. Main courses £10–£19 ($16–$30). Fixed-price lunch £9.50 ($15). AE, MC, V. Daily noon–2:30pm and 6–11pm.

Inexpensive

Al-Salam ℱ *Value* LEBANESE Some Oxford students think this place offers the best food value in the city, and we tend to agree. You'll dine within one of three sand-colored dining rooms, each separated from the other with antique (and very solid) wooden doors. Ironically, the newest of the three rooms, added in 2002, looks as if it's the oldest, thanks to stone-built arches and a commitment to the kinds of raw materials (wood and masonry) that would have been available in Lebanon a century ago. The menu depends on what's available in the marketplace, and the chef's skill is reflected in such dishes as king prawns sautéed with a garlic and tomato sauce, or spicy lamb with a chili and onion sauce. Long lines can form at the door, especially on Friday and Saturday.

6 Park End St. ℂ **01865/245710**. Reservations recommended. Main courses £7–£12 ($11–$19). MC, V. Daily noon–midnight. Bus: 52.

WALKING AROUND THE COLLEGES

The best way to get a running commentary on the important sights is to take a 2-hour **walking tour** through the city and the major colleges. The tours leave daily from the Oxford Tourist Information Centre at 11am and 2pm. Tours costs £6.50 ($10) for adults and £3 ($4.80) for children; the tours do not include New College or Christ Church.

AN OVERVIEW For a bird's-eye view of the city and colleges, climb **Carfax Tower** ℱ, located in the center of the city. This structure is distinguished by its clock and figures that strike on the quarter hour. Carfax Tower is all that remains from St. Martin's Church, where William Shakespeare once stood as godfather for William Davenant, who also became a successful playwright. A church stood on this site from 1032 until 1896. The tower used to be higher, but after 1340 it was lowered, following complaints from the university to Edward III that townspeople threw stones and fired arrows at students during town-and-gown disputes. Admission is £1.50 ($2.40) for adults, £1 ($1.60) for children. The tower is open year-round, except from Christmas Eve to January 1. April through October, its hours are from 10am to 5pm daily. Off-season hours are

Monday through Saturday from 10am to 3:30pm. Children under 5 are not admitted. For information, call ℂ **01865/792653.**

CHRIST CHURCH 🌟🌟   Begun by Cardinal Wolsey as Cardinal College in 1525, Christ Church (ℂ **01865/276150;** www.chch.ox.ac.uk), known as the House, was founded by Henry VIII in 1546. Facing St. Aldate's Street, Christ Church has the largest quadrangle of any college in Oxford. Tom Tower houses Great Tom, an 18,000-pound bell. It rings at 9:05pm nightly, signaling the closing of the college gates. The 101 times it peals originally signified the number of students in residence at the time of the founding of the college.

The college chapel was constructed over a period of centuries, beginning in the 12th century. The cathedral's most distinguishing features are its Norman pillars and the vaulting of the choir, dating from the 15th century. In the center of the great quadrangle is a statue of Mercury mounted in the center of a fishpond. The college and cathedral can be visited daily from 9am to 5:30pm. The entrance fee is £3 ($4.50) adults and £2 ($3) children.

MAGDALEN COLLEGE 🌟🌟   Magdalen (pronounced *Maud*-lin) College, High Street (ℂ **01865/276000;** www.magd.ox.ac.uk), was founded in 1458 by William of Waynflete, bishop of Winchester and later chancellor of England. Its alumni range from Wolsey to Wilde. Opposite the botanic garden, the oldest in England, is the bell tower, where the choristers sing in Latin at dawn on May

---

 Calling on Churchill at Blenheim Palace

Just 13km (8 miles) northwest of Oxford stands the extravagantly baroque **Blenheim Palace** 🌟🌟🌟 (ℂ **01993/811325;** www.blenheim palace.com), England's answer to Versailles. Blenheim is the home of the 11th duke of Marlborough, a descendant of John Churchill, the first duke, who was an on-again, off-again favorite of Queen Anne's. In his day (1650–1722), the first duke became the supreme military figure in Europe. Fighting on the Danube near a village named Blenheim, Churchill defeated the forces of Louis XIV, and the lavish palace of Blenheim was built for the duke as a gift from the queen. It was designed by Sir John Vanbrugh; the landscaping was created by the famous 18th-century landscape gardener, Capability Brown. You may recognize Blenheim because it was used as the setting for Kenneth Branagh's *Hamlet.*

The palace is loaded with riches: antiques, porcelain, oil paintings, tapestries, and chinoiserie. North Americans know Blenheim as the birthplace of Sir Winston Churchill. His birth room is included in the palace tour, as is the Churchill exhibition, four rooms of letters, books, photographs, and other relics. Today the former prime minister lies buried in Bladon Churchyard, near the palace.

Blenheim Palace is open from November to mid-March daily from 9am to 5pm. Admission is £10 ($16) adults, £8 ($13) seniors/students, and £5 ($8) children 5 to 15; free for children 4 and under. If you're driving, take the A-44 from Oxford; otherwise, the no. 20 Gloucester Green bus (ℂ **01865/772250**) leaves Oxford about every 30 minutes during the day for the half-hour trip.

Day. The reflection of the 15th-century tower is cast in the waters of the Cherwell below. On a not-so-happy day, Charles I—with his days numbered—watched the oncoming Roundheads from this tower. Visit the 15th-century chapel, in spite of many of its latter-day trappings. Ask when the hall and other places of special interest are open. The grounds of Magdalen are the most extensive of any Oxford college; there's even a deer park. You can visit year-round from 1pm to dusk daily. Admission is £3 ($4.80).

MERTON COLLEGE 🎔🎔 Founded in 1264, Merton College, Merton Street (✆ **01865/276310;** wwwmerton.ox.ac.uk), is among the three oldest colleges at the university. It stands near Corpus Christi College on Merton Street, the sole survivor of Oxford's medieval cobbled streets. Its library, built between 1371 and 1379, is said to be the oldest college library in England. There was once a tradition of keeping some of its most valuable books chained. Now only one book is so secured, to illustrate that historical custom. One treasure of the library is an astrolabe (an astronomical instrument used for measuring the altitude of the sun and stars) thought to have belonged to Chaucer. You pay £1 ($1.60) to visit the ancient library, as well as the Max Beerbohm Room (the satirical English caricaturist who died in 1956). The library and college are open Monday through Friday from 2 to 4pm and Saturday from 10am to 4pm (closed for 1 week at Easter, 1 week at Christmas, and on winter weekends).

THE SHOPPING SCENE

In its way, **Alice's Shop,** 83 St. Aldate's (✆ **01865/723793**), might have played a more important role in English literature than any other shop in Britain. Set in a 15th-century building, it functioned as a general store (brooms, hardware, and so on) during the period that Lewis Carroll, at the time a professor of mathematics at Christ Church College, was composing *Alice in Wonderland.* As such, it is believed to have been the model for important settings in the book. Today, the place is a favorite stop of Lewis Carroll fans, who gobble up commemorative pencils, chess sets, party favors, bookmarks and, in rare cases, original editions of some of Carroll's works.

Bodleian Library Shop, Old School's Quadrangle, Radcliffe Square, Broad Street (✆ **01865/277216**), specializes in Oxford-derived souvenirs. There are more than 2,000 objects inventoried here, including books describing the history of the university and its various colleges, paperweights made of pewter and crystal, and Oxford banners and coffee mugs. **Castell & Son (The Varsity Shop),** 13 Broad St. (✆ **01865/244000**), is the best outlet for clothing emblazoned with the Oxford logo or heraldic symbol. Objects include both whimsical and dead-on-serious neckties, hats, T-shirts, sweatshirts, pens, bookmarks, beer and coffee mugs, and cuff links.

STRATFORD-UPON-AVON 🎔🎔

Stratford is virtually overrun by visitors in the summer months; the crowds dwindle in winter, allowing you at least to walk on the streets and seek out the places of genuine historic interest. Stratford is 146km (91 miles) northwest of London and 64km (40 miles) northwest of Oxford.

William Shakespeare, of course, was born here. Little is known about his early life, and many of the stories connected with Shakespeare's days in Stratford are largely fanciful, invented to amuse the vast number of literary fans who make the pilgrimage. David Garrick, the actor, really launched the shrine in 1769 when he organized the first of the Bard's commemorative birthday celebrations.

Stratford-upon-Avon

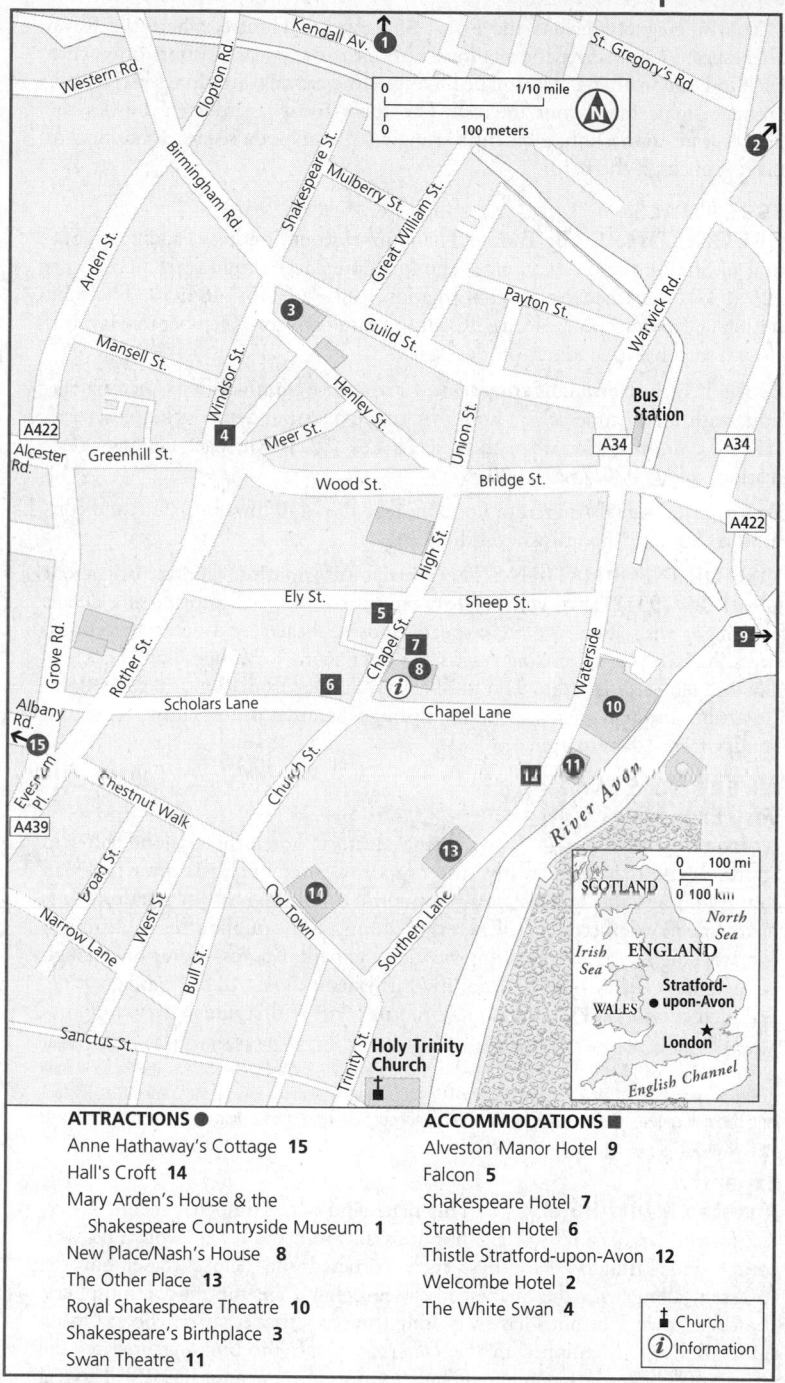

ATTRACTIONS ●

Anne Hathaway's Cottage **15**

Hall's Croft **14**

Mary Arden's House & the
  Shakespeare Countryside Museum **1**

New Place/Nash's House **8**

The Other Place **13**

Royal Shakespeare Theatre **10**

Shakespeare's Birthplace **3**

Swan Theatre **11**

ACCOMMODATIONS ■

Alveston Manor Hotel **9**

Falcon **5**

Shakespeare Hotel **7**

Stratheden Hotel **6**

Thistle Stratford-upon-Avon **12**

Welcombe Hotel **2**

The White Swan **4**

✝ Church
ⓘ Information

Tourist magnets include the Royal Shakespeare Theatre, where the Royal Shakespeare Company performs for 11 months each year. Visitors often rush back to London after a performance. Despite the crowds, Stratford's literary pilgrimage sights merit your interest. The town today aggressively hustles the Shakespeare connection, a bit suffocatingly so; everybody seems in business to make a buck off the Bard.

ESSENTIALS
GETTING THERE   By Train   The journey from London's Paddington Station to Stratford-upon-Avon takes about 2 hours and a round-trip ticket costs £23 ($37). For schedules and information, call ✆ **0845/7484950.** The train station at Stratford is on Alcester Road. On Sundays from October to May, it is closed, so you'll have to rely on the bus.

By Bus   Eight **National Express** buses a day leave from London's Victoria Station, with a trip time of 3¼ hours. A single-day round-trip ticket costs £13 ($21) except on Friday, when the price is £20 ($32). For schedules and information, call ✆ **020/7529-2000.**

By Car   If you're driving from London, take the M40 toward Oxford and continue to Stratford-upon-Avon on the A34.

VISITOR INFORMATION   The **Tourist Information Centre,** Bridgefoot (✆ **01789/293127;** www.shakespeare-country.co.uk), will provide any details you might wish about the Shakespeare houses, theater, and other attractions, and will assist you in booking rooms. It's open April 1 through October, Monday through Saturday from 9am to 6pm and Sunday from 10:30am to 4:30pm; November through March, Monday through Saturday from 9am to 5pm and Sunday from 10am to 4pm.

WHERE TO STAY
Very Expensive
Welcombe Hotel 😺😺😺   For a formal, historic hotel, there's none better in Stratford, and that includes Alveston Manor. One of England's great Jacobean country houses, this hotel is a 10-minute ride from the heart of Stratford. It is surrounded by 64 hectares (157 acres) of grounds. The public areas are heroic in size, with high windows providing views of the park. Rooms—some big enough for tennis matches—are luxuriously furnished; those in the garden wing, although comfortable, are small. Bathrooms come with a tub/shower combo.

Warwick Rd., Stratford-upon-Avon, Warwickshire CV37 ONR. ✆ 01789/295252. Fax 01789/414666. www. welcombe.co.uk. 64 units. £185–£275 ($296–$440) double; £275–£350 ($440–$560) suite. Rates include English breakfast. AE, DC, MC, V. Take A439 2km (1½ miles) northeast of the town center. **Amenities:** Restaurant; bar; golf course; tennis court; room service; laundry/dry-cleaning service. *In room:* TV, coffeemaker, hair dryer, iron.

Expensive
Alveston Manor Hotel 😺😺   This black-and-white timbered manor is perfect for theatergoers; it's just a 2-minute walk from the River Avon. The Welcombe and Ettington Park may have cornered the deluxe trade, but the Alveston, along with the Shakespeare (see below), are the most atmospheric choices in town. The hotel has everything from an Elizabethan gazebo to Queen Anne windows. Mentioned in the *Domesday Book,* the building predates the arrival of William the Conqueror. The 19 rooms in the manor house will appeal to those who appreciate old slanted floors, overhead beams, and antique furnishings; some have half-tester beds. Other accommodations—full of tour

groups—are in a 30-year-old motel-like wing. The lounges are in the manor; there's a view of the centuries-old tree at the top of the garden—said to have been the background for the first presentation of *A Midsummer Night's Dream.*

Clopton Bridge (off B4066), Stratford-upon-Avon, Warwickshire CV37 7HP. 🕾 **800/225-5843** in the U.S. and Canada, or 0845/7585593. Fax 01789/414095. www.heritage-hotels.co.uk. 114 units. £145–£160 ($232–$256) double; £230 ($368) suite. AE, DC, MC, V. **Amenities:** Restaurant; bar; room service; babysitting; laundry/dry-cleaning service. *In room:* TV, minibar, coffeemaker, hair dryer.

Shakespeare Hotel 🕿🕿   Filled with historical associations, the original core of this hotel, dating from the 1400s, has seen many additions in its long life. Quieter and plusher than the Falcon (see below), it is equaled in the central core of Stratford only by Alveston Manor. Residents relax in the post-and-timber–studded public rooms, within sight of fireplaces and playbills from 19th-century productions of Shakespeare's plays. Guest rooms are named in honor of noteworthy actors, Shakespeare's plays, or Shakespearean characters. The oldest are capped with hewn timbers, and all have modern comforts. Even the newer accommodations are at least 40 to 50 years old and have rose-and-thistle patterns carved into many of their exposed timbers.

Chapel St., Stratford-upon-Avon, Warwickshire CV37 6ER. 🕾 **800/225-5843** in the U.S. and Canada, or 0870/4008182 or 01789/294771. Fax 01789/415411. www.macdonaldhotels.co.uk. 74 units. £136–£162 ($218–$259) double; £216–£240 ($346–$384) suite. Children up to 16 stay free in parent's room. AE, DC, MC, V. **Amenities:** Restaurant; bar; room service; laundry service. *In room:* AC, TV, minibar, coffeemaker, hair dryer, iron.

Thistle Stratford-upon-Avon 🕿   Theatergoers flock here, because The Arden is across the street from the main entrance of the Royal Shakespeare and Swan theaters. The Thistle chain completely refurbished the interior after buying the hotel in 1993. Its redbrick main section dates from the Regency period, although over the years a handful of adjacent buildings were included and an uninspired modern extension added. Today, the interior has a lounge and bar; a dining room with bay windows; a covered garden terrace; and comfortable but narrow bedrooms. Most rooms are graced with a two- or four-poster bed. The small bathrooms are adequate and well maintained, each with a shower or tub.

44 Waterside, Stratford-upon-Avon, Warwickshire CV37 6BA. 🕾 **0870/3339146.** Fax 0870/3339246. www.stratford-upon-avon.co.uk/thistle.htm. 63 units. £73–£179 ($117–$286) double. AE, DC, MC, V. **Amenities:** Restaurant; bar; room service; babysitting; laundry/dry-cleaning service. *In room:* TV, coffeemaker, hair dryer, trouser press.

Moderate

Falcon   Located in the heart of Stratford, the Falcon blends the very old and the very new. The inn was licensed a quarter of a century after Shakespeare's death. A 1970s guest-room extension is connected to its rear by a glass passageway. The recently upgraded guest rooms in the mellowed part have oak beams, diamond leaded-glass windows, some antique furnishings, and good reproductions. Each room is comfortable and clean, but there is not enough soundproofing to drown out the BBC on your next-door neighbor's telly. Rooms in the newer section are also comfortable but more sterile in tone. Some of the bathrooms are rather unsightly, with brown linoleum floors and plastic tub enclosures. The comfortable lounges, also recently upgraded, are some of the finest in the Midlands.

Chapel St., Stratford-upon-Avon, Warwickshire CV37 6HA. 🕾 **01789/279953.** Fax 01789/414260. www.regalhotels.co.uk. 84 units. £80–£125 ($128–$200) double; from £140 ($224) suite. AE, DC, MC, V. **Amenities:** Restaurant; 2 bars; room service. *In room:* TV, coffeemaker, hair dryer.

The White Swan ⚜ This cozy, intimate hotel is one of the most atmospheric in Stratford and is, in fact, the oldest building here. In business for more than a century before Shakespeare appeared on the scene, it competes successfully with the Falcon in offering an ancient atmosphere. The gabled medieval front would present the Bard with no surprises, but the modern comforts inside would surely astonish him, even though many of the rooms have been preserved. Guest rooms are comfortable but generally lack style. Except for an occasional four-poster or half-canopy bed, most are twins or doubles.

Rother St., Stratford-upon-Avon, Warwickshire CV37 6NH. © 01789/297022. Fax 01789/268773. www. e-travelguide.info/whiteswan. 41 units. £88 ($141) double. Children up to 16 half price in parent's room. Rates include English breakfast. AE, DC, MC, V. **Amenities:** Restaurant; bar; limited room service. *In room:* TV, coffeemaker, hair dryer, trouser press.

Inexpensive

Stratheden Hotel A short walk north of the Royal Shakespeare Theatre, the Stratheden Hotel is tucked away in a desirable location. Built in 1673, and currently the oldest remaining brick building in the town center, it has a tiny rear garden and top-floor rooms with slanted, beamed ceilings. Under the ownership of the Wells family for the past quarter century, it has improved again in both decor and comfort with the addition of fresh paint, new curtains, and good beds. Most of the small bathrooms have shower stalls, although a few have bathtubs.

5 Chapel St., Stratford-upon-Avon, Warwickshire CV37 6EP. ©/fax 01789/297119. www.ukstay.com/ warwick/stratheden. 9 units. £66–£72 ($106–$115) double. Rates include full English breakfast. AE, MC, V. **Amenities:** Breakfast room. *In room:* TV.

WHERE TO DINE

Desports ⚜⚜ ECLECTIC/INTERNATIONAL At last Stratford has a restaurant worth writing home about. In the town center between the Shakespeare Centre and Market Place, Desports was installed in a 16th-century building. Extremely professional cooking, a vivid use of spices, imaginative menus, and reasonable prices attract a never-ending stream of visitors and locals alike. Is this the Stratford of yore, you ask, as you taste the aromatic pumpkin and Cerny cheese tagliatelle with almond pesto, tomato, and candied eggplant. Grilled vegetables in lemon oil with rosemary chickpeas and saffron couscous are followed by cashew nut and herb risotto with wilted rocket and shaved Parmesan. Even such English classics as pan-fried calves' liver, bacon, kidneys, and bubble and squeak (cabbage and potatoes) are given zest by an orange Dubonnet sauce.

13–14 Meer St. © 01789/269304. Main courses £12–£18 ($19–$29). Fixed-price lunch £20 ($32) 2 courses; £24 ($38) 3 courses. AE, DC, MC, V. Tues–Sat noon–2pm and 5:45–10:30pm.

The Quarto's Restaurant ⚜ FRENCH/ITALIAN/ENGLISH This restaurant enjoys the best location in town—in the theater itself, with glass walls providing an unobstructed view of swans on the Avon. You can purchase an intermission snack feast of smoked salmon and champagne, or dine by flickering candlelight after the performance. Many dishes, such as apple-and-parsnip soup, are definitely old English; others reflect a Continental touch, such as fried polenta with filets of pigeon and bacon. For your main course, you may select Dover sole, pheasant supreme, or roast loin of pork. Homemade crème brûlée is an old-time favorite. The theater lobby has a special phone for reservations.

In the Royal Shakespeare Theatre, Waterside. © 01789/403415. Reservations required. Matinee lunch £16 ($26); dinner £14–£20 ($22–$32). AE, MC, V. Thurs and Sat noon–2:30pm; Mon–Sat 5:30pm–midnight.

Thai Boathouse ⚜ THAI The only restaurant set on the Avon, this charming choice is reached by crossing Clopton Bridge toward Oxford and Banbury.

The second-floor dining room opens onto vistas of the river. This restaurant, originally established 4 decades ago in Bangkok, has brought spice and zest to Stratford's lazy restaurant scene. The decor comes from Thailand itself, with elephants, woodcarvings, and Buddhas. Seasonal specialties such as wild duck and pheasant are special features of the menu. Fresh produce, great skill in the kitchen, and exquisite presentations are the hallmarks of this restaurant. Sample a selection of authentic Thai appetizers before going on to such delectable main courses as fresh sea bass in lemon grass or lime leaves wrapped in banana leaf and grilled over charcoal, or a salmon stir-fried with curry sauce and coconut cream, enhanced by the use of Thai herbs. One of our favorites is their lamb in a yellow curry with potatoes, onions, and cashew nuts.

Swan's Nest Lane. (②) 01789/297733. Reservations recommended. Main courses £5.50–£12 ($8.80–$19). Fixed-price menus £21–£26 ($34–$42). MC, V. Sun–Fri noon–2:30pm and daily 5:30–10:30pm.

PUBS

The Black Swan ("The Dirty Duck") ⭐⭐ ENGLISH Affectionately known as The Dirty Duck, this has been a popular hangout for Stratford players since the 18th century. The wall is lined with autographed photos of its many famous patrons. The front lounge and bar crackle with intense conversation. Typical English grills, among other dishes, are featured in the Dirty Duck Grill Room, though no one has ever accused it of serving the best food in Stratford. You'll have a choice of a dozen appetizers, most of which would make a meal in themselves. In fair weather, you can have drinks in the front garden and watch the swans glide by on the Avon.

Waterside. (②) 01789/297312. Reservations required for dining. Main courses £8–£15 ($13–$24); bar snacks £5–£7.25 ($8–$12). AE, DC, MC, V (in the restaurant only). Daily 11am–11pm.

The Garrick Inn ENGLISH Near Harvard House, this black-and-white timbered Elizabethan pub has an unpretentious charm. The front bar is decorated with tapestry-covered settles, an old oak refectory table, and an open fireplace that attracts the locals. The back bar has a circular fireplace with a copper hood and mementos of the triumphs of the English stage. The specialty is homemade pies such as steak and kidney or chicken and mushroom.

25 High St. (②) 01789/292186. Main courses £6.25–£13 ($10–$20). MC, V. Meals daily noon–9pm. Pub Mon–Sat 11am–11pm; Sun noon–10:30pm.

THEATER

Royal Shakespeare Company has a major showcase at the Royal Shakespeare Theatre, Waterside, Stratford-upon-Avon CV37 6BB ((②) 01789/403403; www.rsc.org.uk), on the banks of the Avon. Plays, including on average five by Shakespeare each season, are staged at the 1,500-seat Royal Shakespeare and the 430-seat Swan Theatre as well as at 170-seat **The Other Place,** a smaller, more experimental venue.

You usually need **ticket reservations,** with two successive booking periods, each one opening about 2 months in advance. You can pick these up from a North American or English travel agent. A small number of tickets are always held for sale on the day of a performance, but it may be too late to get a good seat if you wait until you arrive in Stratford. Tickets can be booked through **Global Tickets** ((②) 800/223-6108 in North America or 207/014-8550 in London; or **Keith Prowse** ((②) 800/6698687 in North America or 870/8401111 in London. Both will add a service charge.

You can also call the **theater box office** directly ((②) 01789/403403) and charge your tickets. The box office is open Monday through Saturday from

9:30am to 8pm, although it closes at 6pm on days when there are no perform-ances. Seat prices range from £8 to £50 ($13–$80). You can make a credit-card reservation and pick up your tickets on the performance day, but you must can-cel at least 2 full weeks in advance to get a refund.

SHAKESPEARE PILGRIMAGE SIGHTS

Besides the attractions on the periphery of Stratford, there are many Elizabethan and Jacobean buildings in town, many of them administered by the Shakespeare Birthplace Trust. One combination ticket—costing £13 ($21) adults, £12 ($19) seniors and students, and £6 ($9.60) children—lets you visit the five most important sights: Shakespeare's Birthplace, Anne Hathaway's Cottage, Mary Arden's House & the Shakespeare Countryside Museum, Hall's Croft, and New Place/Nash's House. You can also buy a family ticket to all five sights (good for two adults and three children) for £29 ($46)—a good deal. You can buy tickets at any of the Trust properties.

Hall's Croft   It was here that Shakespeare's daughter Susanna probably lived with her husband, Dr. John Hall. Furnished in the style of a middle-class home of the time, Hall's Croft is an outstanding Tudor house with a beautiful walled garden. Dr. Hall was widely respected and built up a large medical practice in the area, and exhibits illustrating the theory and practice of medicine in Dr. Hall's time are on view. You're welcome to use the adjoining Hall's Croft Club, which serves morning coffee, lunch, and afternoon tea.

Old Town (near Holy Trinity Church). ℭ 01789/292107. Admission £3.50 ($5.60) adults, £1.70 ($2.70) chil-dren. Hours are Nov–Mar daily 11am–4pm; Apr–May daily 11am–5pm; June–Aug Mon–Sat 9:30am–5pm, Sun 10am–5pm; Sept–Oct daily 11am–5pm. Closed Dec 23–26. To reach Hall's Croft, walk west from High St., which becomes Chapel St. and Church St. At the intersection with Old Town, go left.

Shakespeare's Birthplace 𝄢   The son of a glover and whittawer (leather worker), the Bard was born here on St. George's Day (Apr 23) in 1564 and died 52 years later on the exact same date. Filled with Shakespeare memorabilia, including a portrait and furnishings of the writer's time, the Trust property is a half-timbered structure, dating from the first part of the 16th century. The house, bought by public donors in 1847, is preserved as a national shrine. You can visit the oak-beamed living room, the bedroom where Shakespeare was probably born, a fully equipped kitchen of the period (look for the "baby-min-der"), and a Shakespeare Museum, illustrating his life and times.

Henley St. (in the town center near the post office, close to Union St.). ℭ **01789/204016.** Admission £6.50 ($10) adults, £5.50 ($8.80) students and seniors, £2.50 ($4) children. For all 5 Shakespeare-related houses, £29 ($46) family (2 adults, 3 children). Hours are Nov–Mar Mon–Sat 10am–4pm, Sun 10:30am–4pm; Apr and May Mon–Sat 10am–4pm, Sun 10:30am–5pm; June–Aug Mon–Sat 9am–5pm, Sun 9:30am–5pm; and Sept and Oct Mon–Sat 10am–5pm, Sun 10:30am–5pm. Closed Dec 23–26.

Anne Hathaway's Cottage 𝄢   In the hamlet of Shottery, 1.6km (1 mile) from Stratford, is the thatched, wattle-and-daub cottage where Anne Hathaway lived before her marriage to Shakespeare. It's the most interesting of the Trust properties, and the most unchanged. The Hathaways were yeoman farmers, and the cottage provides a rare insight into the life of a family of Shakespeare's day. Many original furnishings, including the courting settle and utensils, are pre-served inside the house, which was occupied by descendants of Shakespeare's wife's family until 1892.

Cottage Lane, Shottery. ℭ **01789/292100.** Admission £5 ($8) adults, £4 ($6.40) children. For all 5 Shake-speare-related houses, £29 ($46) family (2 adults, 3 children). Hours are Nov–Mar daily 10am–4pm; Apr–May

A Visit to Warwick Castle

Perched on a rocky cliff above the Avon River in the town center, **Warwick Castle** ★★★ is a stately late-17th-century–style mansion surrounded by a magnificent 14th-century fortress. The first significant fortifications were built by Ethelfleda, daughter of Alfred the Great, in 914. Two years after the Norman Conquest in 1068, William the Conqueror ordered the construction of a "motte and bailey" castle. The mound is all that remains today of the Norman castle.

The Beauchamp family, earls of Warwick, is responsible for the appearance of the castle today, and much of the external structure remains unchanged from the mid–14th century. The staterooms and Great Hall house fine collections of paintings, furniture, arms, and armor. The armory, dungeon, torture chamber, ghost tower, clock tower, and Guy's tower create a vivid picture of the castle's turbulent past and its important role in the history of England.

Sir Walter Scott described Warwick Castle in 1828 as "that fairest monument of ancient and chivalrous splendor which yet remains uninjured by time." Visitors can also see the Victorian rose garden, a re-creation of an original design from 1868 by Robert Marnock. On Castle Hill, Warwick Castle (© **0870/442-2000;** www.warwick-castle.co.uk) is open April through September daily from 10am to 6pm (to 7pm in Aug); October through March daily from 10am to 5pm; closed Christmas Day. Admission is £13 ($20) adults, £7.50 ($12) children 4 to 16, £9 ($14) seniors, free for children 4 and under, and £32 ($51) family.

Trains run frequently between Stratford-upon-Avon and Warwick. Call © **0045/7404950** for schedules and information. One **Stagecoach** bus per hour departs Stratford-upon-Avon during the day. The trip takes 15 to 20 minutes. Call the Tourist Information Centre (© **01789/ 293127)** for schedules. Motorists should take the A46 from Stratford-upon-Avon.

Mon–Sat 9:30am–5pm, Sun 10am–5pm; June–Aug Mon–Sat 9am–5pm, Sun 9:30am–5pm; Sept–Oct Mon–Sat 9:30am–5pm, Sun 10am–5pm. Closed Dec 23–26. Take a bus from Bridge St. or walk via a marked pathway from Evesham Place in Stratford across the meadow to Shottery.

New Place/Nash's House   This is the site where Shakespeare retired in 1610, a prosperous man. He died 6 years later, at the age of 52. Regrettably, his former home was torn down, and only the site remains. You enter the gardens through Nash's House (Thomas Nash married a granddaughter of the poet). The house has 16th-century period rooms and an exhibition illustrating the history of Stratford. The delightful Knott Garden adjoins the site and represents the style of a fashionable Elizabethan garden. New Place has its own great garden, which once belonged to Shakespeare.

Chapel St. © **01789/204016.** Admission £3.50 ($5.60) adults, £3 ($4.80) seniors and students, £1.70 ($2.70) children. For all 5 Shakespeare-related houses, £29 ($46) family (2 adults, 3 children). Hours are Nov–Mar daily 11am–4pm; Apr and May daily 11am–5pm; June–Aug Mon–Sat 9:30am–5pm, Sun 10am–5pm; Sept and Oct daily 11am–5pm. Closed Dec 23–26. Walk west down High St.; Chapel St. is a continuation of High St.

Mary Arden's House & the Shakespeare Countryside Museum ✿ So what if millions of visitors have been tricked into thinking this timber-framed farmhouse with its old stone dovecote and various outbuildings was the girlhood home of Shakespeare's mother, Mary Arden? It's still one of the most intriguing sights outside Stratford, even if local historian, Dr. Nat Alcock, discovered in 2000 that the actual childhood home of Arden was the dull-looking brick-built farmhouse, Glebe Farm, next door. It was all the trick of an 18th-century tour guide, John Jordan, who decided Glebe Farm was too unimpressive to be the home of the Bard's mother, so he told tourists it was this farmstead instead. The so-called Mary Arden's House wasn't actually constructed until the late 16th century, a little late to be her home. Nonetheless, visit it anyway as it contains country furniture and domestic utensils. In the barns, stable, cow shed, and farmyard is an extensive collection of farming implements illustrating life and work in the local countryside from Shakespeare's time to the present.

Wilmcote. ✆ **01789/204016.** Admission £5.50 ($8.80) adults, £5 ($8) students and seniors, and £2.50 ($4) children. Hours are Nov–Mar Mon–Sat 10am–4pm, Sun 10:30am–4pm; Apr and May Mon–Sat 10am–5pm, Sun 10:30am–5pm; June–Aug Mon–Sat 9:30am–5pm, Sun 10am–5pm; Sept–Oct Mon–Sat 10am–5pm, Sun 10:30am–5pm. Closed Dec 23–26. Take A3400 (Birmingham) for 5.5km (3½ miles).

ORGANIZED TOURS

Besides the attractions on the periphery of Stratford, many Elizabethan and Jacobean buildings are in town, a number of them administered by the **Shakespeare Birthplace Trust** (✆ **01789/204016**). One ticket—costing £13 ($21) adults, £12 ($19) seniors and students, and £6 ($9.60) children—lets you visit the five most important sights. You can also buy a family ticket to all five sights (good for two adults and three children) for £29 ($46)—a good deal. Pick up the ticket if you're planning to do much sightseeing (obtainable at your first stopover at any one of the Trust properties).

Guided tours of Stratford-upon-Avon leave from near the **Guide Friday Tourism Centre,** Civic Hall, Rother Street (✆ **01789/294466**). In summer, open-top double-decker buses depart every 15 minutes daily from 10am to 6pm. You can take a 1-hour ride without stops, or you can get off at any or all of the town's five Shakespeare properties. Though the bus stops are clearly marked along the historic route, the most logical starting point is the sidewalk in front of the Pen & Parchment Pub, at the bottom of Bridge Street. Tour tickets are valid all day so you can hop on and off the buses as many times as you want. The tours cost £8.50 ($14) for adults, £7 ($11) for seniors or students, and £3 ($4.80) for children under 12. A family ticket sells for £18 ($29), and children under 5 go free.

THE SHOPPING SCENE

At the **National Trust Shop,** 45 Wood St. (✆ **01789/262197**), you'll find textbooks and guidebooks describing esoteric places in the environs of Stratford, descriptions of National Trust properties throughout England, stationery, books, china, pewter, and toiletries, each inscribed, embossed, or painted with logos that evoke some aspect of English tastes and traditions. Set in an antique house that lies across from Shakespeare's Birthplace, the **Shakespeare Bookshop,** 39 Henley St. (✆ **01789/292176**), is the region's premier source for textbooks and academic treatises on the Bard and his works. It specializes in books conceived for every level of expertise, from picture books for junior high school students to weighty tomes geared toward anyone pursuing a Ph.D. in literature.

3 Stonehenge & Bath

Many visitors with very limited time head for the West Country, where they explore its two major attractions: Stonehenge—the most important prehistoric monument in Britain—and Bath, England's most elegant city, famed for its architecture and its hot springs. If you have the time, you might also visit Salisbury Cathedral and the other prehistoric sites in the area, at Avebury and Old Sarum.

STONEHENGE ✶✶✶

At the junction of A-303 and A-344/A-360, 3km (2 miles) west of Amesbury and about 15km (9 miles) north of Salisbury, stands the renowned monument of Stonehenge, a stone circle believed to be approximately 5,000 years old. This circle of lintels and megalithic pillars is the most important prehistoric monument in Britain.

ESSENTIALS

GETTING THERE **By Car** To reach Stonehenge from London, head in the direction of Salisbury (see below), 145km (90 miles) to the southwest. Take the M-3 to the end of the run, continuing the rest of the way on A-30. Once at Salisbury, after stopping to view its cathedral (see below), head north on Castle Road. At the first roundabout (traffic circle), take the exit toward Amesbury (A-345) and Old Sarum. Continue along this route for 13km (8 miles) and then turn left onto A-303 in the direction of Exeter. Stonehenge is signposted, leading you up the A-344 to the right. In all, it's about 19km (12 miles) from Salisbury.

By Train or Bus A **Network Express** train departs hourly from Waterloo Station bound for Salisbury (trip time: 2 hr.). Call **08457/484950** or visit **www. railtrack.co.uk** for information. Buses also depart four or five times per day from Victoria Station heading for Salisbury (2½ hr.). Once at Salisbury, take a **Wilts & Dorset bus** (℗ **01722/336855** for schedules), which runs several vehicles daily, depending on demand, from Salisbury to Stonehenge. This company's buses depart from the train station at Salisbury, heading directly to Stonehenge (40 min.). Round-trip fare is £5.50 ($8.80) adults, £2.75 ($4.40) children under 14. Use Salisbury as a refueling stop.

EXPLORING STONEHENGE

Despite its familiarity, visitors cannot help but be impressed when they first see Stonehenge, an astonishing engineering feat. The boulders, the bluestones in particular, were moved many miles, possibly from as far away as southern Wales, to this site.

The widely held view of the 18th- and 19-century Romantics that Stonehenge was the work of the Druids is without foundation. The boulders, many

---

Finds Biking to Stonehenge

If you'd like to bike out to Stonehenge, go to **Hayball's Cycle Shop,** 26–30 Winchester St. (℗ **01722/411378**), which rents mountain bikes for £9 ($14) per day. For an extra £2.50 ($4), you can keep the bike overnight. A £25 ($40) deposit is required. A 7-day rental is £65 ($104). Hours are daily from 9am to 5pm.

weighing several tons, are believed to have predated the arrival in Britain of the Celtic Druidic cult. Recent excavations continue to bring new evidence to bear on the origin and purpose of the prehistoric circle; controversy has surrounded the site, especially since the publication of *Stonehenge Decoded* by Gerald S. Hawkins and John B. White, which maintains that Stonehenge was an astronomical observatory—that is, a Neolithic calendar capable of predicting eclipses.

The site is now surrounded by a fence to protect it from vandals and souvenir hunters. Your ticket permits you to go inside the fence, all the way up to a short rope barrier about 15m (50 ft.) from the stones. Spring 1996 saw the start of the full circular tour around Stonehenge; a modular walkway has been introduced to cross the archaeologically important area that runs between the Heel Stone and the main circle of stones. This lets you complete a full circuit of the stones, an excellent addition to the well-received audio tour.

Admission to Stonehenge (© **01980/623108**) is £4.40 ($7) adults, £3.30 ($4.95) students and seniors, and £2.20 ($3.30) children. It's open March 16 through May and September through October 15 daily from 9:30am to 6pm; June through August daily from 9am to 7pm; and October 16 through March 15 daily from 9:30am to 4pm.

AVEBURY 🕿🕿

Avebury, one of Europe's largest prehistoric sites, lies 32km (20 miles) north of Stonehenge on the Kennet River, 11km (7 miles) west of Marlborough. The small village actually lies within the vast stone circle. Unlike Stonehenge, you can walk around the 11-hectare (28-acre) site, winding in and out of the circle of more than 100 stones, some of which weigh up to 50 tons. The stones are made of sarsen, a sandstone found in Wiltshire. Inside this large circle are two smaller ones, each with about 30 stones standing upright. Native Neolithic tribes are believed to have built these circles.

GETTING THERE Avebury is on A-361 between Swindon and Devizes and 1.6km (1 mile) from the A-4 London–Bath road. The closest rail station is at Swindon, some 19km (12 miles) away, which is served by the main rail line from London to Bath. A limited bus service (no. 49) runs from Swindon to Devizes through Avebury.

You can also reach Avebury by bus from Salisbury by taking one of two buses (nos. 5 and 6) run by **Wilts & Dorset** (© **01722/336855**). The buses leave three times a day from Monday to Saturday and twice on Sunday (trip time: 1½ hr.).

AN ARCHAEOLOGICAL MUSEUM

The **Alexander Keiller Museum** (© **01672/539250**) houses one of Britain's most important archaeological collections. It began with material from excavations at Windmill Hill and Avebury, and now includes artifacts from other prehistoric digs at West Kennet, Long Barrow, Silbury Hill, West Kennet Avenue, and the Sanctuary. Admission is £4 ($6) adults, £2 ($3) children. The museum is open April through October, daily from 10am to 6pm; November through March, daily from 10am to 4pm.

SALISBURY 🕿🕿

Long before you enter Salisbury, the spire of the cathedral comes into view, just as John Constable painted it many times. Salisbury lies in the Avon River Valley, and is a fine place to stop for lunch and a look at the cathedral on your way to Stonehenge.

ESSENTIALS

GETTING THERE **By Train** **Network Express trains** depart for Salisbury hourly from Waterloo Station in London; the trip takes 1½ hours. Sprinter trains offer fast, efficient service every hour from Portsmouth, Bristol, and South Wales. Direct rail service is also available from Exeter, Plymouth, Brighton, and Reading. For information, call ✆ **0845/7484950** in the United Kingdom.

By Bus Three **National Express buses** per day run from London's Victoria Coach Station to Salisbury, Monday through Friday. On Saturday and Sunday, three buses depart daily. The trip takes 2½ hours. Call ✆ **020/7529-2000** for schedules and information.

By Car If you're driving from London, head west on the M3 to the end of the run, continuing the rest of the way on the A30.

VISITOR INFORMATION The **Tourist Information Centre** at Fish Row (✆ **01722/334956**) is open October through April, Monday through Saturday from 9:30am to 5pm; in May, Monday through Saturday from 9:30am to 5pm and Sunday from 10:30am to 4:30pm; June through September, Monday through Saturday from 9:30am to 6pm and Sunday from 10:30am to 4:30pm.

WHERE TO STAY

The Beadles 🌟🌟 *Finds* A traditional modern Georgian house with antique furnishings and a view of the cathedral, The Beadles offers unobstructed views of the beautiful Wiltshire countryside from its .4-hectare (1-acre) gardens. It's situated in a small, unspoiled English village, 13km (8 miles) from Salisbury, which offers excellent access to Stonehenge, Wilton House, the New Forest, and the rambling moors of Thomas Hardy country. Even the road to Winchester is an ancient Roman byway. Furnished tastefully, this nonsmoking household contains rooms with twins or doubles, each with a full private bathroom. Owners David and Anne Yuille-Baddeley delight in providing information on the area.

Middleton, Middle Winterslow, near Salisbury, Wiltshire SP5 1QS. ✆ **01980/862922.** Fax 01980/863565. www.guestaccom.co.uk/754.htm. 3 units. £60 ($96) double. Rates include English breakfast. MC, V. Turn off A30 at Pheasant Inn to Middle Winterslow. Enter the village, make the 1st right, turn right again, and it's the 1st right after TREVANO. **Amenities:** Dining room; tour services. *In room:* TV, coffeemaker, hair dryer, trouser press.

The Rose and Crown 🌟🌟🌟 This half-timbered, 13th-century gem stands with its feet almost in the River Avon; beyond the water, you can see the tall spire of the cathedral. Because of its tranquil location, it's our top choice. From here, you can easily walk over the arched stone bridge to the center of Salisbury in 10 minutes. Old trees shade the lawns and gardens between the inn and the river, and chairs are set out so that you can enjoy the view and count the swans. The inn has both a new and an old wing. The new wing is modern, but the old wing is more appealing, with sloping ceilings and antique fireplaces and furniture. Guest rooms in the new wing are more spacious and better designed than those in the main house. Bathrooms include a shower-and-tub combination.

Harnham Rd., Salisbury, Wiltshire SP2 8JQ. ✆ **01722/399955.** Fax 01722/339816. 28 units. £118 ($189) double. AE, DC, MC, V. Take A3094 2.5km (1½ miles) from the center of town. **Amenities:** Restaurant; 2 bars; room service; laundry/dry cleaning. *In room:* TV, coffeemaker, hair dryer, trouser press.

WHERE TO DINE

Harper's Restaurant ENGLISH/INTERNATIONAL The chef-owner of this place prides himself on specializing in "real food," homemade and wholesome. The pleasantly decorated restaurant is on the second floor of a redbrick building at the back end of Salisbury's largest parking lot, in the center of town. In the same all-purpose dining room, you can order from two different menus, one with affordable bistro-style platters, including beefsteak casserole with "herbey dumplings." A longer menu, listing items that take a bit more time to prepare, includes all-vegetarian pasta diavolo, or spareribs with french fries and rice.

6–7 Ox Row, Market Sq. ℂ 01722/333118. Reservations recommended. Main courses £6.50–£14 ($10–$22); 2-course fixed-price meal £7.20–£11 ($12–$18) at lunch and dinner. AE, DC, MC, V. Mon–Sat noon–2pm; daily 6–9:30pm (till 10pm on Sat). Closed Sun Oct–May.

Howard's House Hotel Restaurant ℱ INTERNATIONAL   If you'd like to dine in one of the loveliest places in the area, and enjoy a refined cuisine at the same time, leave Salisbury and head for this previously recommended hotel. It's a 14km (9-mile) drive to Teffort Evias but well worth the trip. The village itself is one of the most beautiful in Wiltshire. The elegantly appointed restaurant, with flower arrangements, showcases a finely honed cuisine prepared with first-class ingredients such as mallard duck or local pheasant. The menu changes daily but is likely to feature such delights as home-smoked filet of salmon in a saffron sauce with a side dish of steamed leeks. Desserts include white peach ice cream with an orange coulis, or chilled mango mousse with marinated strawberries.

Teffont Evias, near Salisbury. ℂ 01722/716392. Reservations required. Main courses £14–£20 ($22–$32). Fixed-price menu £24 ($38). AE, DC, MC, V. Daily 7:30–9pm; Sun noon–2pm. Leave Salisbury on the A36 until you reach a roundabout. Take the 1st left leading to the A30. On the A30, continue for 5km (3 miles) coming to the turnoff (B3089) for Barford Saint-Martin. Continue for 6.5km (4 miles) on this secondary road to the town of Teffont Evias, where the hotel is signposted.

Salisbury Haunch of Venison ENGLISH   Right in the heart of Salisbury, this creaky-timbered 1320 restaurant serves excellent dishes, especially English roasts and grills. Stick to what it's known for, and you'll rarely go wrong. Begin perhaps with tasty grilled venison sausages in a Dijon mustard sauce, then follow with the time-honored house specialty: roast haunch of venison with gin and juniper berries. Many other classic English dishes are served, such as a medley of fish and shellfish or else grilled Barnsley lamb chops with "bubble and squeak" (cabbage and potatoes).

1 Minster St. ℂ 01722/322024. Main courses £8.25–£14 ($13–$22); bar platters for lunches, light suppers, and snacks £5–£8 ($8–$13). MC, V. Daily noon–2pm; Mon–Sat 6–9pm. Pub Mon–Sat 11am–11pm; Sun noon–3pm and 7–10:30pm. Closed Christmas and Easter.

IN & AROUND SALISBURY

Salisbury Cathedral ℱℱℱ   You can search all of England, but you'll find no better example of early English or pointed style than Salisbury Cathedral. Construction began as early as 1220 and took 38 years to complete; this was rather fast since it was customary in those days for a cathedral building to require at least 3 centuries. The soaring spire was completed at the end of the 13th century. Despite an ill-conceived attempt at renovation in the 18th century, the architectural integrity of the cathedral has been retained.

The 13th-century octagonal chapter house (note the fine sculpture), which is especially attractive, possesses one of the four surviving original texts of the Magna Carta, along with treasures from the diocese of Salisbury and manuscripts and artifacts belonging to the cathedral. The cloisters enhance the beauty of the cathedral, and the exceptionally large close, with at least 75 buildings in its compound (some from the early 18th c., others earlier), sets off the cathedral most effectively.

© **01722/555120.** www.salisburycathedral.org.uk. Suggested donation £3.50 ($5.60) adults, £2.50 ($4) students and seniors, £2 ($3.20) children, £8 ($13) family. Jan–May and Sept–Dec, Mon–Sat 7:15am–6:15pm; June–Aug, Mon–Sat 7:15am–8:15pm. Year-round Sun 7:15am–6:15pm.

Old Sarum ✿   This relic from antiquity is believed to have been an Iron Age fortification. The earthworks were known to the Romans as *Sorbiodunum*. Much later, Saxons also used the fortification. The Normans built a cathedral and a castle here in what was then a Middle Ages walled town. Parts of the old cathedral were taken down to build the city of New Sarum (Salisbury).

3km (2 miles) north of Salisbury off A345 on Castle Rd. © **01722/335398.** Admission £2 ($3.20) adults, £1.50 ($2.40) seniors, £1 ($1.60) children. Daily year-round 10am–5pm. Bus nos. 3, 5, 6, 7, 8, and 9 run every 20 min. during the day from the Salisbury bus station.

Wilton House ✿✿   This home of the earls of Pembroke is in the town of Wilton. It dates from the 16th century but has undergone numerous alterations, most recently in Victoria's day, and is noted for its 17th-century staterooms, designed by celebrated architect Inigo Jones. Shakespeare's troupe is said to have entertained here, and Eisenhower and his advisers prepared here for the D-Day landings at Normandy, with only the Van Dyck paintings as silent witnesses.

The house is filled with beautifully maintained furnishings and world-class art, including paintings by Rubens, Brueghel, and Reynolds. You can visit a reconstructed Tudor kitchen and Victorian laundry plus "The Wareham Bears," a unique collection of some 200 miniature dressed teddy bears.

On the 8.4-hectare (21-acre) estate are giant cedars of Lebanon trees, the oldest of which were planted in 1630, as well as rose and water gardens, riverside and woodland walks, and a huge adventure playground for children.

5km (3 miles) west of Salisbury on A36. © **01722/746720.** www.wiltonhouse.com. Admission £9.25 ($15) adults, £7.50 ($12) seniors, £5 ($8) children 5–15, £22 ($35) family, free for children under 5. Price inclusive of grounds. Easter–Oct daily 10:30am–5:30pm (last entrance at 4:30pm).

BATH ✿✿✿

The city of Bath has had two lives. Originally, it was a Roman spa known as Aquae Sulis. The foreign legions founded their baths here (which may be visited today) to ease their rheumatism in the curative mineral springs. In 1702 Queen Anne made the trek from London, 185km (115 miles) west to the mineral springs of Bath, thereby launching a fad that was to make the city England's most celebrated spa.

The most famous personage connected with Bath's growing popularity was the 18th-century dandy Beau Nash. The master of ceremonies of Bath, Nash cut a striking figure. In all the plumage of a bird of paradise, he was carted around in a sedan chair, dispensing (at a price) trinkets to courtiers and aspirant gentlemen. This polished arbiter of taste and manners succeeded in making dueling déclassé.

The 18th-century architects John Wood the Elder and his son envisioned a proper backdrop for Nash's activities. They designed a city of honey-colored stone from the nearby hills, a feat so substantial and lasting that Bath today is the most harmoniously laid-out city in England. The city attracted leading political and literary figures, such as Dickens, Thackeray, Nelson, Pitt, and, most important, of course, Jane Austen. Canadians may already know that General Wolfe lived on Trim Street, and Australians may want to visit the house at 19 Bennett St. where their founding father, Admiral Phillip, lived.

Remarkable restoration and careful planning have ensured that Bath retains its handsome look today. It has somewhat of a museum appearance, with the attendant gift shops. Prices, stimulated by massive tourist invasion, tend to be high. But Bath remains one of the high points of the West Country.

ESSENTIALS

GETTING THERE   By Train   Trains leave London's Paddington Station bound for Bath once every half hour during the day. The trip takes about 1½ hours. For rail information, call ℂ **0845/7484950.**

By Bus   A **National Express** coach leaves London's Victoria Coach Station every 2 hours during the day. The trip takes 3½ hours. Coaches also leave Bristol bound for Bath and make the trip in 40 minutes. For schedules and information, call ℂ **020/7529-2000.**

By Car   Drive west on the M4 to the junction with the A4, on which you continue west to Bath.

VISITOR INFORMATION   The **Bath Tourist Information Centre,** at Abbey Chambers, Abbey Church Yard (ℂ **01225/477101;** www.bath.co.uk), opposite the Roman Baths, is open June through September, Monday through Saturday from 9:30am to 6pm, Sunday from 10am to 4pm; off season, Monday through Saturday from 9:30am to 5pm, Sunday from 10am to 4pm.

SPECIAL EVENTS   For 17 days in late May and early June the city is filled with more than 1,000 performers—orchestras, soloists, and artists from all over the world. The **Bath International Music Festival** focuses on classical music, jazz, new music, and opening-night celebrations with fireworks. There's also all the best in walks, tours, and talks, plus free street entertainment. For more information, contact the **Bath Festivals Box Office,** 2 Church St., Abbey Green, Bath BA1 1NL (ℂ **01225/463362**).

GETTING AROUND   One of the best ways to explore Bath is by bike. You can rent one from **Somerset Valley Bike Hire** (ℂ **01225/442442**), behind the train station. It's open daily from 9am to 5:30pm, charging £14 to £25 ($22–$38) per day, £50 ($80) per week, depending on the type of bike. Deposits are £300 ($480) or a credit card imprint.

WHERE TO STAY
Very Expensive

Bath Priory 🏵🏵🏵   Converted from one of Bath's Georgian houses in 1969, the Priory is situated on .8 hectares (2 acres) of formal and award-winning gardens with manicured lawns and flower beds. The hotel reopened in the spring of 1997, vastly refurbished and more inviting than ever. The rooms are furnished with antiques; our personal favorite is Clivia (all rooms are named after flowers or shrubs), a nicely appointed duplex in a circular turret. Rooms range from medium in size to spacious deluxe units, the latter with views, large sitting areas, and generous dressing areas. Each has a lovely old English bed, often a half-tester; bathrooms are beautifully kept and come with a set of deluxe toiletries.

Weston Rd., Bath, Somerset BA1 2XT. ℂ **01225/331922.** Fax 01225/448276. www.thebathpriory.co.uk. 28 units. £345 ($552) standard double; £315 ($504) deluxe room. Rates include English breakfast and dinner. AE, DC, MC, V. **Amenities:** Restaurant; bar; 2 pools; health club; Jacuzzi; sauna; concierge; room service; babysitting; laundry/dry cleaning; croquet lawn. *In room:* A/C, TV, hair dryer.

Bath Spa Hotel 🏵🏵🏵   This stunning restored 19th-century mansion is a 10-minute walk from the center of Bath. Behind a facade of Bath stone, it lies at the end of a tree-lined drive on 2.8 hectares (7 acres) of landscaped grounds, with a Victorian grotto and a Grecian temple. In its long history, it served many purposes (once as a hostel for nurses) before being returned to its original grandeur. The hotel uses log fireplaces, elaborate moldings, and oak paneling to create country house charm. The rooms are handsomely furnished, and most of

Bath Abbey 7
The Circus 2
Jane Austen Centre 3
North Parade 8
No. 1 Royal Crescent 1
Pulteney Bridge 5
**Pump Room and
  Roman Baths 6**
Queen Square 4

them are spacious. Most beds are doubles, and some even offer an old-fashioned four-poster. The marble bathrooms are among the city's finest, with long tubs, hand-held showers, and deluxe toiletries.

Sydney Rd. (east of the city, off A36), Bath, Somerset BA2 6JF. ⓒ **01225/444424.** Fax 01225/444006. www. bathspahotel.com. 102 units. Sun–Thurs £290 ($464) double; Fri–Sat £300 ($480) double. Daily £315–£355 ($504–$568) suite for 2. AE, DC, MC, V. **Amenities:** 2 restaurants; bar; pool; tennis court; health spa; children's nursery; room service; salon; laundry service; valet. *In room:* TV, minibar, coffeemaker, hair dryer, trouser press, safe.

The Queensberry Hotel ⚐   A gem of a hotel, this early Georgian-era town house has been beautifully restored by Stephen and Penny Ross. In our view, it is now among the finest places to stay in a city where the competition for restored town-house hotels is fierce. The marquis of Queensberry commissioned John Wood the Younger to build this house in 1772. Rooms—often spacious but usually medium in size—are delightful, each tastefully decorated with antique furniture and such thoughtful extras as fresh flowers. Bathrooms are well kept and equipped with good showers.

Russel St., Bath, Somerset BA1 2QF. © 800/323-5463 in the U.S., or 01225/447928. Fax 01225/446065. www.bathqueensberry.com. 29 units. £120–£225 ($192–$360) double. Rates include continental breakfast. MC, V. Free parking. **Amenities:** Restaurant; bar; room service; laundry/dry cleaning. *In room:* TV, hair dryer.

Royal Crescent Hotel 🌟🌟🌟 (Finds)

This special place stands proudly in the center of the famed Royal Crescent. Long regarded as Bath's premier hotel (before the arrival of the even better Bath Spa), it has attracted the rich and famous. The guest rooms, including the Jane Austen Suite, are lavishly furnished with such amenities as four-poster beds and marble tubs. Each room is individually designed and offers such comforts as bottled mineral water, fruit plates, and other special touches. Guest rooms, generally quite spacious, are elaborately decked out with thick wool carpeting, silk wall coverings, and antiques, each with a superb and rather sumptuous bed. Bathrooms are equally luxurious, with deluxe toiletries and robes.

15–16 Royal Crescent, Bath, Somerset BA1 2LS. © 888/295-4710 in the U.S., or 01225/823333. Fax 01225/ 339401. www.royalcrescent.co.uk. 45 units. £240–£340 ($384–$544) double; from £486 ($778) suite. AE, DC, MC, V. **Amenities:** Restaurant; bar; health club; Jacuzzi; steam room; concierge; car-rental desk; room service; babysitting; laundry/dry cleaning. *In room:* TV, minibar, hair dryer, safe.

Expensive

The Francis on the Square 🌟

An integral part of Queen Square, the Francis is an example of 18th-century taste and style, but we find it too commercial and touristy. Originally consisting of six private residences dating from 1729, the Francis was opened as a private hotel by Emily Francis in 1884 and has offered guests first-class service for more than 100 years. Many of the well-furnished and traditionally styled guest rooms overlook Queen Square, named in honor of George II's consort, Caroline. Rooms range in size from rather small to medium, with either twin or double beds. Accommodations in the older building have more charm, especially the upper floor. Bathrooms are small but equipped with heated towel racks, plus a combination tub and shower.

Queen Sq., Bath, Somerset BA1 2HH. © 888/892-0038 in the U.S. and Canada, or 0870/4008223. Fax 01225/319715. 95 units. £150 ($240) double; £210 ($336) suite. AE, DC, MC, V. **Amenities:** Restaurant; bar; room service; laundry/dry cleaning. *In room:* TV, hair dryer.

Moderate

Pratt's Hotel 🌟

Once the home of Sir Walter Scott, Pratt's dates from the heady days of Beau Nash. Functioning as a hotel since 1791, it has become part of the legend and lore of Bath. Several elegant terraced Georgian town houses were joined together to form this complex with a very traditional British atmosphere. Rooms are individually designed, and as is typical of a converted private home, they range from small to spacious (the larger ones are on the lower floors). Regardless of their dimensions, the rooms are furnished in a comfortable though utilitarian style, with small but efficiently organized shower-only bathrooms.

S. Parade, Bath, Somerset BA2 4AB. © 01225/460441. Fax 01225/448807. www.forestdale.com. 46 units. £125–£160 ($200–$256) double. Children under 15 sharing a room with 2 adults stay free. Rates include English breakfast. AE, DC, MC, V. Parking £10 ($16). **Amenities:** Restaurant; bar; room service; babysitting; laundry/dry cleaning. *In room:* TV, coffeemaker, hair dryer, trouser press.

Inexpensive

Apsley House Hotel 🌟🌟 (Finds)

This charming and stately building, just 1.5km (1 mile) west of the center of Bath, dates from 1830, during the reign of William IV. In 1994, new owners refurbished the hotel, filling it with country-house chintzes and a collection of antiques borrowed from the showrooms of an antiques store they own. (Some furniture in the hotel is for sale; inquire further about details.) Style and comfort are the keynote here, and all the relatively spacious guest rooms are inviting, appointed with plush beds.

141 Newbridge Hill, Bath, Somerset BA1 3PT. © **01225/336966.** Fax 01225/425462. www.apsley-house.co.uk. 9 units. £75–£140 ($120–$224) double; £120–£140 ($192–$224) suite. Rates include English breakfast. AE, MC, V. Take A4 to Upper Bristol Rd., fork right at the traffic signals into Newbridge Hill, and turn left at Apsley Rd. **Amenities:** Bar; room service; babysitting. *In room:* TV, coffeemaker, hair dryer.

Duke's Hotel   A short walk from the heart of Bath, this 1780 building is fresher than ever following a complete restoration in 2001. Many of the original Georgian features, including cornices and moldings, have been retained. Rooms, ranging from small to medium, are exceedingly comfortable. All of the bathrooms are small but efficiently arranged and sport shower-tub combinations and bathrobes. Guests can relax in a refined drawing room or patronize the cozy bar overlooking a garden. The entire setting has been called a "perfect *Masterpiece Theatre* take on Britain," with a fire burning in the grate. A traditional English menu is also offered.

53–54 Great Pulteney St., Bath, Somerset BA2 4DN. © **01225/787960.** Fax 01225/787961. www.dukes bath.co.uk. 18 units. £125–£145 ($200–$232) double; £195–£235 ($312–$376) family unit. Rates include continental breakfast. MC, V. Bus: 18. **Amenities:** Restaurant; bar; room service; babysitting; laundry; dry cleaning. *In room:* TV, hair dryer.

In Nearby Hinton Charterhouse

Homewood Park ✿✿   This small, family-run hotel, set on 4 hectares (10 acres) of grounds, dates back to the 18th century. Overlooking the Limpley Stoke Valley, it's a large Victorian house with grounds adjoining the 13th-century ruin of Hinton Priory. You can play croquet in the garden. Riding and golfing are available nearby, and beautiful walks in the Limpley Stoke Valley lure guests. Each of the small to midsize rooms is luxuriously decorated; most overlook the award-winning gardens and grounds or offer views of the valley. Each unit comes with a well-managed bathroom with a shower-tub combination.

Hinton Charterhouse, Bath, Somerset BA2 7TB. © **01225/723731.** Fax 01225/723820. www.homewood park.com. 19 units. £145–£265 ($232–$424) double; £265 ($424) suite. Rates include English breakfast. AE, DC, MC, V. Take A36 (Bath–Warminster Rd.) 9.5km (6 miles) south of Bath. **Amenities:** Restaurant; bar; pool; room service; babysitting; laundry; dry cleaning. *In room:* TV, hair dryer.

In Nearby Ston Easton

Ston-Easton Park ✿✿✿ *Finds*   This is one of the great country hotels of England. From the moment you pass a group of stone outbuildings and century-old beeches set on a 12-hectare (30-acre) park—up the road from Farrington Gurney—you know you've come to a very special place. The mansion was created in the mid-1700s from the shell of an Elizabethan house; in 1793, Sir Humphry Repton designed the landscape. In 1977, after many years of neglect, Peter and Christine Smedley acquired the property and poured money, love, and labor into its restoration. The tasteful rooms are filled with flowers and antiques, and feature spacious, sumptuous beds. A gardener's cottage was artfully upgraded from a utilitarian building to contain a pair of intensely decorated and very glamorous suites. In addition to the cottage suite, plus the "standard and deluxe" rooms of the main house, you'll find half a dozen "state rooms," four of which have four-poster beds, and all of which contain lavish but genteel decor. Bathrooms are equally luxurious, with deluxe toiletries and shower-tub combinations.

Ston Easton, Somerset BA3 4DF. © **01761/241631.** Fax 01761/241377. www.stoneaston.co.uk. 24 units, 1 cottage suite, 7 state rooms. £185–£345 ($296–$552) double; from £750 ($1,200) 3-room cottage suite; £345

($552) state room. AE, DC, MC, V. Lies 19km (12 miles) south of Bath; follow A39 south to the signposted turnoff to the hamlet of Ston Easton. **Amenities:** Restaurant; room service; babysitting; laundry/dry cleaning. *In room:* TV, hair dryer, safe.

In Nearby Hunstrete

Hunstrete House 🐦🐦   This fine Georgian house is situated on 37 hectares (92 acres) of private parkland. Six units in the Courtyard House are attached to the main structure and overlook a paved courtyard. Swallow Cottage, which adjoins the main house, has its own private sitting room, double bedroom, and bathroom. Units in the main house are decorated with antiques; all have sitting areas with armchairs and sofas. Awaiting you are little extras such as a decanter of sherry. The shower-only bathrooms are also luxurious and well maintained.

Hunstrete, Chelwood, near Bristol, Somerset BS38 4NS. ✆ **01761/490490.** Fax 01761/490732. www. hunstretehouse.co.uk. 25 units. £170 ($272) double; £195 ($312) superior double; £300–£360 ($480–$576) suite. Half board £350 ($560) double; £400 ($640) suite for 2. Rates include English breakfast. AE, DC, MC, V. Take A4 about 5.5km (3½ miles) west of Bath, then A368 another 5.5km (3½ miles) toward Weston-super-Mare. **Amenities:** 3 restaurants; bar; pool; room service; babysitting; laundry/dry-cleaning service. *In room:* TV, hair dryer.

WHERE TO DINE
Expensive

The Moody Goose 🐦🐦🐦 ENGLISH   In a highly competitive city, this "bird" serves the finest and most refined cuisine. In an elegant and landmarked Georgian terrace in the center of the city, the restaurant has two cozy dining rooms and a little bar. The kitchen has an absolute passion for fresh ingredients and food cooked to order, and the chefs believe in using produce grown as near home as possible, though the Angus beef comes in from Scotland, fresh fish from the coasts of Cornwall and Devon. Natural flavors are appreciated here and not smothered in sauces. Even the breads, ice creams, and petits fours are homemade.

Launch your repast with such temptations as pan-fried veal sweetbreads with a salad of pink grapefruit and walnuts, or a brown trout confit in puff pastry. For a main dish, be dazzled with whole roasted quail with braised chicory and roasted apple, roasted rump of lamb, or poached filet of halibut with fresh clams. We're especially fond of the desserts, particularly a fresh rhubarb cheesecake.

7A Kingsmead Sq. ✆ **01225/466688.** Reservations required. Fixed-price meals £18 ($28) lunch; £25 ($40) dinner. Main courses £18–£20 ($29–$31). AE, DC, MC, V. Mon–Sat noon–1:30pm and 6–9:30pm.

Moderate

Beaujolais *Kids* FRENCH   This is the best-known bistro in Bath, maintaining its regulars while attracting new admirers every year. Diners are drawn to the honest fare and good value. The house wines are modestly priced. Begin with grilled monkfish served with a creamy white sauce, and follow it with roast partridge or duck confit. Also served is a wide variety of vegetarian dishes, one of them a mushroom-and-spinach combination. One area of the restaurant is reserved for nonsmokers. Persons with disabilities will appreciate the wheelchair access, and parents can order special helpings for children.

5 Chapel Row, Queen Sq. ✆ **01225/423417.** Reservations recommended. 2- and 3-course lunches £13–£17 ($20–$27); dinner main courses £12–£18 ($19–$28). AE, MC, V. Mon–Sat noon–2:30pm, daily 6–10pm.

The Olive Tree MODERN ENGLISH/MEDITERRANEAN   Stephen and Penny Ross operate one of the most sophisticated little restaurants in Bath. Stephen uses the best local produce, with an emphasis on freshness. The menu is changed to reflect the season, with game and fish being the specialties. You might begin with grilled scallops with noodles and pine nuts, or Provençal fish soup with rouille and croutons. Proceed with roast squab pigeon, salsify purée, and crispy parsnip; or grilled Aberdeen Angus rump filet, creamed onions, and rosemary in a red-wine-and-peppercorn jus. Stephen is also known for his desserts, which are likely to include such treats as a hot chocolate soufflé or an apricot and almond tart.

In the Queensberry Hotel, Russel St. (C) 01225/447928. Reservations highly recommended. Main courses £17–£18 ($26–$29). 3-course fixed-price meals £16 ($25) lunch; £26 ($42) dinner. MC, V. Mon–Sat noon–2pm and 7–10pm; Sun 7–9:30pm.

Popjoy's Restaurant MODERN BRITISH/CONTINENTAL Two sprawling dining rooms on separate floors are in this Georgian home (ca. 1720) where Beau Nash and his mistress, Julianna Popjoy, once entertained friends and set the fashions of the day. Inventiveness and solid technique go into many of the dishes. The food is unpretentious and generally quite satisfying. The starters are always imaginative and good tasting, as exemplified by the guinea fowl and wood pigeon terrine with cranberry jam and brandy-soaked prunes. Equally excellent is the smoked-fish plate with oak-smoked salmon, tuna, trout, and egg with fresh horseradish served with a glass of iced Smirnoff Black Label. A certain exoticism appears in the oven-roasted Barbary duck breast with a wild bramble and cherry marmalade, or the stir-fried shiitake mushrooms, bok choy, zucchini, and roasted almonds on sun-dried tomato blinis with spicy sour cream and chickpeas.

Sawclose. (C) 01225/460494. www.popjoy.co.uk. Reservations recommended. Main courses £18–£22 ($28–$35); 3-course fixed-price lunch £16 ($25). AE, DC, MC, V. Mon–Sat noon–2pm and 6–11pm.

Inexpensive
The Moon and Sixpence INTERNATIONAL One of the leading restaurants and wine bars of Bath, The Moon and Sixpence occupies a stone structure east of Queen Square. The food may not be as good as that served at more acclaimed choices, including The Hole in the Wall, but the value is unbeatable. At lunch, a large cold buffet with a selection of hot dishes is featured in the wine bar section. In the upstairs restaurant overlooking the bar, full service is offered. Main courses may include filet of lamb with caramelized garlic or roast breast of duck with Chinese vegetables. Look for the daily specials on the Continental menu.

6A Broad St. (C) 01225/460962. Reservations recommended. Main courses £14–£15 ($22–$23). Fixed-price meals £7.50 ($12) lunch; £21–£25 ($33–$40) dinner. AE, MC, V. Daily noon–2:30pm; Mon–Thurs 5:30–10:30pm; Fri–Sat 5:30–11pm; Sun 6–10:30pm.

Woods *Value* MODERN ENGLISH/FRENCH/ASIAN Named after John Wood the Younger, architect of Bath's famous Assembly Room across the street, this restaurant is run by horse-racing enthusiast David Price and his French-born wife, Claude. A fixed-price menu is printed on paper, whereas the seasonal array of a la carte items is chalked onto a frequently changing blackboard. Good bets include the pear and parsnip soup or chicken cooked with mushrooms, red wine, and tarragon.

9–13 Alfred St. (C) 01225/314812. Reservations recommended. Main courses £9.50–£18 ($15–$29). Fixed-price meals £9.50 ($15) lunch; £25 ($40) dinner. MC, V. Mon–Sat noon–2:30pm and 6–10:30pm.

EXPLORING BATH
Stroll around to see some of the buildings, crescents, and squares in town. The **North Parade** (where Goldsmith lived) and the **South Parade** (where English novelist and diarist Frances Burney once resided) represent harmony, as well as the work of John Wood the Elder, who also designed beautiful **Queen Square,**

where both Jane Austen and Wordsworth once lived. Also of interest is **The Circus** 𝄞𝄞𝄞, built in 1754, as well as the shop-lined **Pulteney Bridge,** designed by Robert Adam and often compared to the Ponte Vecchio of Florence.

The younger John Wood designed the **Royal Crescent** 𝄞𝄞𝄞, an elegant half-moon row of town houses (copied by Astor architects for their colonnade in New York City in the 1830s). At **No. 1 Royal Crescent** (© **01225/428126**), the interior has been redecorated and furnished by the Bath Preservation Trust to look as it might have toward the end of the 18th century. The house is located at one end of Bath's most magnificent crescents, west of the Circus. Admission is £4 ($6.40) for adults and £3.50 ($5.60) for children, seniors, and students; a family ticket is £10 ($16). The house is open from mid-February to October, Tuesday through Sunday from 10:30am to 5pm, and in November, Tuesday through Sunday from 10:30am to 4pm (last admission 30 min. before closing); closed Good Friday.

The **Jane Austen Centre,** 40 Gay St. (© **01225/443000**), is located in a Georgian town house on an elegant street where Miss Austen once lived. Exhibits and a video convey a sense of life in Bath during the Regency period. The center is open Monday through Saturday from 10am to 5pm and Sunday from 10:30am to 5:30pm. Admission is £4.45 ($7.10) for adults, £3.65 ($5.85) students, and £2.45 ($3.90) children.

Bath Abbey 𝄞   Built on the site of a much larger Norman cathedral, the present-day abbey is a fine example of the late perpendicular style. When Queen Elizabeth I came to Bath in 1574, she ordered a national fund set up to restore the abbey. The interior and its many windows plainly illustrate why the abbey is called the "Lantern of the West." Note the superb fan vaulting, with its scalloped effect. Beau Nash was buried in the nave and is honored by a simple monument totally out of keeping with his flamboyant character. In 1994 the Bath Abbey Heritage Vaults opened on the south side of the abbey. This subterranean exhibition traces the history of Christianity at the abbey site since Saxon times.

Orange Grove. © 01225/422462. www.bathabbey.org. £2.50 ($4) donation requested. Admission to the Heritage Vaults £2.50 ($4) adults; £1.50 ($2.40) students, children, and seniors. Abbey Apr–Oct Mon–Sat 9am–6pm; Nov–Mar Mon–Sat 9am–4:30pm; year-round Sun 1–2:30pm and 4:30–5:30pm. The Heritage Vaults year-round Mon–Sat 10am–4pm.

Pump Room 𝄞 **and Roman Baths** 𝄞𝄞   Founded in A.D. 75 by the Romans, the baths were dedicated to the goddess Sulis Minerva; in their day they were an engineering feat. Today, still fed by Britain's most famous hot-spring water, they're among the finest Roman remains in the country. After centuries of decay, the original baths were rediscovered during Queen Victoria's reign. The site of the Temple of Sulis Minerva has been excavated and is now open to view. The museum displays many interesting objects from Victorian and recent digs (look for the head of Minerva). Coffee, lunch, and tea, usually with music from the Pump Room Trio, can be enjoyed in the 18th-century pump room, overlooking the hot springs. There's also a drinking fountain with hot mineral water that tastes horrible but is supposedly beneficial.

In the Bath Abbey churchyard. © 01225/477785. www.romanbaths.co.uk. Admission £8.50 ($14) adults, £4.50 ($7.20) children, £22 ($35) family. Apr–Sept daily 9am–6pm; Oct–Mar Mon–Sat 9am–5pm.

American Museum   Some 4km (2½ miles) from Bath is the first American museum established outside the United States. In a Greek Revival house (Claverton Manor), the museum sits on extensive grounds high above the Avon valley. Authentic exhibits of pioneer days have been shipped over from the

Two More Magnificent Houses: Longleat House & Stourhead

Between Bath and Salisbury, 6.5km (4 miles) southwest of Warminster and 7km (4½ miles) southeast of Frome on A-362, is **Longleat House** ☆☆☆, Warminster, Wiltshire (© **01985/844400;** www.longleat. co.uk), owned by the seventh marquess of Bath. The first view of this Elizabethan house, built in the early Renaissance style, is romantic enough, but the wealth of paintings and furnishings in its lofty rooms is dazzling. From the Elizabethan Great Hall to the library, state rooms, and grand staircase, the house is filled with fine tapestries and paintings. The library contains the finest private collection in the country. The Victorian kitchens are open, and various exhibitions are mounted in the stable yard.

Admission to Longleat House is £9 ($14) adults, £6 ($9.60) children. The house is open daily from 10am to 5:30pm. The park is open April through November 2, daily from 10am to 6pm (last cars admitted at 5pm or sunset).

After a visit to Longleat, you can drive 10km (6 miles) down B-3092 to Stourton, a village just off the highway 5km (3 miles) northwest of Mere (A-303). A Palladian house, **Stourhead** ☆☆☆ (© **01747/841152)** was built in the 18th century by the banking family of Hoare. The fabulous gardens, blending art and nature, became known as *le jardin anglais.* Set around an artificial lake, the grounds are decorated with temples, bridges, islands, and grottoes, as well as statuary. From March to October, admission to the gardens and house is £8.90 ($14) adults, £4.70 ($7) children; admission to the gardens or house alone is £5.10 ($8.15) adults, £2.90 ($4.65) children. Off season the admission is: gardens only, £3.95 ($6.30) adults, £1.90 ($3.05) children. The Stourhead house and gardens are open Friday through Tuesday from 9am to 7pm (or until dusk). Last admission is at 4:30pm.

States. On the grounds are a copy of Washington's flower garden at Mount Vernon and an American arboretum. A permanent exhibition in the New Gallery displays the Dallas Pratt Collection of Historical Maps.

Claverton Manor, Bathwick Hill. © **01225/460503.** www.americanmuseum.org. Admission £6 ($9.60) adults, £5.50 ($8.80) students and seniors, £3.50 ($5.60) children 5–16, free for ages 4 and under. Late Mar to Nov: Tues–Sun 2–5pm for the museum; Tues–Fri 1–6pm and Sat–Sun noon–6pm for the garden. Bus: 18.

ORGANIZED TOURS

Free 1¾-hour walking tours are conducted throughout the year by the **Mayor's Honorary Society** (© **01225/477786**). Tours depart from outside the Roman Baths Sunday through Friday at 10:30am and 2pm, Saturday at 10:30am; May through September, another tour is added on Tuesday, Friday, and Saturday at 7pm. To tour Bath by bus, you can choose among several tour companies. One of the best is **Patrick Driscoll,** Elmsleigh, Bathampton (© **01225/462010**), with tours that are more personalized than most.

River Avon boat cruises depart from a pier adjacent to the Pulteney Bridge (directly across the water from the Parade Gardens). Cruises last 50 minutes and are £5 ($7.50) for adults, £2.50 ($3.75) for children. They run from Easter to October via two boats maintained by **The Boating Station** (*©* **01225/ 466407**).

THE SHOPPING SCENE

Bath has the finest shopping possibilities outside of London. Here is a sampling to get you started. The four floors of merchandise at **Rossiter's,** 38–41 Broad St. (*©* **01225/462227**), might remind you of a very English version of a department store. They'll ship any of the Royal Doulton, Wedgwood, or Spode to anywhere in the world. Look especially for the displays of ginger jars, vases, and clocks manufactured by Moorcroft, and perfumes by London-based Floris. The most charming and unusual emporium in Bath, **Whittard of Chelsea,** 14 Union Passage (*©* **01225/483529**), supplies everything you'll need to duplicate the dearly held tea-drinking ritual. Ask for Monkey-Picked Oolong, a Chinese tea from plants so difficult to reach that leaves can be gathered only by trained monkeys. The most important gallery of contemporary art in Bath, **Beaux Arts Gallery,** 13 York St. (*©* **01225/464850**), specializes in well-known British artists. The gallery occupies a pair of interconnected, stone-fronted Georgian houses, set close to Bath Abbey.

BATH AFTER DARK

To gain a very different perspective of Bath, you may want to take the **Bizarre Bath Walking Tour** (*©* **01225/335124**), a 1½-hour improvisational tour of the streets during which the tour guides pull pranks, tell jokes, and behave in a humorously annoying manner toward tour-goers and unsuspecting residents. Running nightly at 8pm from Easter to September, it requires no reservations; just show up, ready for anything, at the Huntsman Inn at North Parade Passage. The tour costs £5 ($8) for adults, £4 ($6.40) for students and children.

After your walk, you may want to check out the local club scene. At **The Bell,** 103 Walcot St. (*©* **01225/460426**), music ranges from jazz and country to reggae and blues on Monday and Wednesday nights and Sunday at lunch. On music nights, the band performs in the center of the long, narrow, 400-year-old room. The two-story **Hat and Feather,** 14 London St. (*©* **01225/425672**), has live musicians or DJs playing funk, reggae, or dance music nightly.

France

by Darwin Porter & Danforth Prince

Though France covers only 342,513 sq. km (212,741 sq. miles), making it slightly smaller than Texas, no other country has such a diversity of sights and scenery in such a compact area. A visitor can travel to Paris, one of the world's great cities; drive among the Loire Valley's green hills; or head south to sunny Provence and the French Riviera. Discover the attractions (and transport, lodging, and dining offerings) in each of these regions in this chapter.

1 Paris ⊛⊛⊛

Discovering the City of Light and making it your own has always been the most compelling reason to visit Paris. If you're a first-timer, everything, of course, will be new to you. If you've been away for a while, expect changes: Taxi drivers may no longer correct your fractured French but address you in English—tantamount to a revolution. Paris, aware of its role within a united Europe, is an international city. Parisians are attracted to foreign music, videos, and films, especially those from America. Security is tighter than ever in the wake of the terrorist attacks in New York and Washington, D.C., on September 11, 2001. Expect to see far more police in bulletproof vests at all transport hubs and government buildings, as well as at high-profile sites such as the Eiffel Tower.

As Paris and the country itself move deeper into the new millennium, there is a fear among the French of a loss of identity. France continues to attract record numbers of immigrants from its former colonies. Though Paris is in flux culturally and socially, it lures travelers for the same reasons it always has. You'll still find classic sights like the Tour Eiffel, Notre-Dame, the Arc de Triomphe, Sacré-Coeur, and all those atmospheric cafes, as well as trendy new projects like the Grand Arche de La Défense, the Cité des Sciences et de l'Industrie, and the Cité de la Musique. And don't forget the parks, gardens, and squares; the Champs-Elysées and other grand boulevards; the River Seine and its quays. Paris's beauty is still overwhelming, especially at night, when it truly is the City of Light.

ESSENTIALS

GETTING THERE   By Plane   Paris has two international airports: Aéroport Roissy-Charles de Gaulle, 23km (14¼ miles) northeast of the city; and Aéroport d'Orly, 14km (8½ miles) south. A shuttle (14€) makes the 50- to 75-minute journey between the two airports about every half hour.

At **Charles de Gaulle Airport (Roissy; ⌀ 01-48-62-22-80)**, foreign carriers use Aérogare 1, while Air France wings into Aérogare 2. From Aérogare 1, you take a moving walkway to the passport checkpoint and the Customs area. The two terminals are linked by a *navette* (shuttle bus).

The shuttle also transports you to the **Roissy rail station,** from which fast RER (Réseau Express Régional) trains leave every 15 minutes for such Métro stations as Gare du Nord, Châtelet, Luxembourg, Port-Royal, and Denfert-Rochereau. A typical fare from Roissy to any point in central Paris is 12€ in first class, 8€ in second class.

You can also take an **Air France shuttle bus** to central Paris for 12€. It stops at the Palais des Congrès (Port Maillot), and then continues on to place Charles-de-Gaulle-étoile, where subway lines can carry you to any point in Paris. That ride, depending on traffic, takes between 45 and 55 minutes. The shuttle departs about every 12 minutes between 5:40am and 11pm.

Another option is the **Roissybus** (© **01-48-04-18-24**), departing the airport daily from 5:45am to 11pm and costing 7.30€ for the 45- to 50-minute ride. Departures are about every 15 minutes, and the bus will take you near the corner of rue Scribe and place de l'Opéra in the heart of Paris.

A **taxi** from Roissy into the city will cost about 40€, but from 8pm to 7am the fares are 40% higher. Long lines for taxis form outside each of the airport's terminals and are surprisingly orderly.

Orly Airport (© **01-49-75-15-15**) has two terminals—Orly *Sud* (south) for international flights and Orly *Ouest* (west) for domestic flights. They're linked by a free shuttle bus (trip time: 15 min.).

Air France buses leave from Exit E of Orly Sud and from Exit F of Orly Ouest every 12 minutes between 5:45am and 11pm for Gare des Invalides; the fare is 7.20€. Returning to the airport, buses leave the Invalides terminal for Orly Sud or Orly Ouest every 15 minutes, taking about 30 minutes.

Another way to get to central Paris is via the free **shuttle bus** that leaves both of Orly's terminals about every 15 minutes for the nearby Métro and RER train station (Pont-de-Rungis/Aéroport-d'Orly). RER trains take 35 minutes for rides into the city center. A trip to Les Invalides, for example, is 8€.

A **taxi** from Orly to central Paris costs about 5.50€, more at night. Don't take a meterless taxi from Orly—it's much safer (and usually cheaper) to hire one of the metered cabs, which are under the scrutiny of a police officer.

By Train   Paris has six major stations: **Gare d'Austerlitz,** 55 quai d'Austerlitz, 13e (servicing the southwest with trains to and from the Loire Valley, Bordeaux, the Pyrénées, and Spain); **Gare de l'Est,** place du 11-Novembre-1918, 10e (servicing the east with trains to and from Strasbourg, Reims, and beyond to Zurich and Austria); **Gare de Lyon,** 20 bd. Diderot, 12e (servicing the southeast with trains to and from the Côte d'Azur [Nice, Cannes, St-Tropez], Provence, and beyond to Geneva and Italy); **Gare Montparnasse,** 17 bd. Vaugirard, 15e (servicing the west with trains to and from Brittany); **Gare du Nord,**

Tips   The Paris Airport Shuttle

Cheaper than a taxi for one or two people but more expensive than airport buses and trains, the **Airport Shuttle** (© **01-43-21-06-78**; fax 01-43-21-35-68; www.paris-anglo.com/clients/ashuttle.html) will pick you up in a minivan at Charles de Gaulle or Orly and take you to your hotel for 20€ for one person or 16€ per person for parties of two or more. It'll take you to the airports from your hotel for the same price. The **Paris Airport Service** (© **01-49-62-78-78**; fax 01-49-62-78-79) offers a similar service. It charges 24€ for one person or 30€ for two or more going to Charles de Gaulle, and 18€ for one person or 21€ for two or more to Orly. Both companies accept Visa and MasterCard, with 1-day advance reservations required.

France

18 rue de Dunkerque, 15e (servicing the north with trains to and from London, Holland, Denmark, and northern Germany); and **Gare St-Lazare,** 13 rue d'Amsterdam, 8e (servicing the northwest with trains to and from Normandy). Buses operate between the stations. Each has a Métro stop, making the whole city accessible. For train information and to make reservations, call ℭ **08-36-35-35-35** between 7am and 8pm daily. One-way to Tours costs 27€; one-way to Strasbourg 35€.

Warning: The stations and surrounding areas are usually seedy and frequented by pickpockets, hustlers, hookers, and addicts. Be alert, especially at night.

By Bus Most buses arrive at the **Eurolines France** station at 28 av. du Général-de-Gaulle, in Bagnolet (ℭ **08-36-69-52-52;** Métro: Gallieni).

By Car Driving in Paris is *not* recommended. Parking is difficult and traffic dense. If you drive, remember that Paris is encircled by a ring road, the *périphérique.* Always obtain detailed directions to your destination, including the name of the exit on the *périphérique* (exits aren't numbered). Avoid rush hours.

The major highways into Paris are A1 from the north; A13 from Rouen, Normandy, and other points northwest; A10 from Spain and the southwest; A6 and A7 from the French Alps, the Riviera, and Italy; and A4 from eastern France.

VISITOR INFORMATION The **main tourist information office** is at 127 av. des Champs-Elysées, 8e (ℭ **08-36-68-31-12;** Métro: George-V), where you can get details about Paris and the provinces. It's open April through October, daily from 9am to 8pm (closed May 1), and November through March, daily from 11am to 6pm (closed Dec 25). There are branches in the base of the Eiffel Tower (open only May–Oct Mon–Sat 8am–8pm) and within the arrivals hall of the Gare de Lyon (Mon–Sat 8am–8pm). Any of the above-mentioned tourist offices will give you free copies of English-language leaflets *Time Out* and *Paris Users' Guide.*

Welcome Offices in the city's rail stations (except Gare St-Lazare) and at the Eiffel Tower can give you free maps, brochures, and *Paris Selection,* a French-language monthly listing current events and performances.

WEBSITES   Surf these recommended websites for information on the City of Light: Bonjour Paris, **www.bparis.com**, is one of the most comprehensive and fun sites about life in Paris, written from an American expatriate point of view. Paris Digest, **www.parisdigest.com**, is an independent website containing articles that link to restaurants, hotels, museums, monuments, parks, and activities. It includes city history and tips for getting around. Paris France Guide, **www. parisfranceguide.com**, has lots of useful information, such as articles and current listings for nightlife, events, theater, and music. Paris Tourist Office, **www. paris-touristoffice.com**, offers information on city events arranged by week, month, favorites, and year, plus the closest Métro stops for museums, lodgings, restaurants, and nightlife.

CITY LAYOUT   Paris is surprisingly compact. Occupying 696 sq. km (432 sq. miles), it's home to more than 10 million people. The River Seine divides Paris into the **Rive Droite (Right Bank)** to the north and the **Rive Gauche (Left Bank)** to the south. These designations make sense when you stand on a bridge and face downstream (west)—to your right is the north bank, to your left the south. A total of 32 bridges link the Right Bank and the Left Bank, some providing access to the two islands at the heart of the city—**Ile de la Cité,** the city's birthplace and site of Notre-Dame; and **Ile St-Louis,** a moat-guarded oasis of 17th-century mansions.

The "main street" on the Right Bank is, of course, **avenue des Champs-Elysées,** beginning at the Arc de Triomphe and running to place de la Concorde. Avenue des Champs-Elysées and 11 other avenues radiate like the arms of an asterisk from the Arc de Triomphe, giving it its original name, place de l'étoile (*étoile* means "star"). It was renamed place Charles-de-Gaulle following the general's death; today, it's often referred to as place Charles-de-Gaulle-étoile.

Maps   If you're staying more than 2 or 3 days, purchase an inexpensive pocket-size book called *Paris par arrondissement,* at newsstands and bookshops; prices start at 6.10€. This guide provides you with a Métro map, a foldout map of the city, and maps of each arrondissement, with all streets listed and keyed.

Arrondissements in Brief   The heart of medieval Paris was the **Ile de la Cité** and the areas immediately surrounding it. As Paris grew, it absorbed many of the once-distant villages, and today each of these *arrondissements* (districts) retains a distinct character. They're numbered 1 to 20 starting at the center and progressing in a clockwise spiral. The key to finding any address in Paris is to look for the arrondissement number, rendered either as a number followed by "e" or "er" (1er, 2e, and so on). If the address is written out more formally, you can tell what arrondissement it's in by looking at the postal code. For example, the address may be written with the street name, then "75014 Paris." The last two digits, 14, indicate that the address is in the 14th arrondissement, Montparnasse.

⟮*Value* **Save on Travel**

When purchasing Métro tickets, a *carnet* is the best buy—10 tickets for 9.25€. You can also purchase a **Paris-Visite**, a tourist pass valid for 1, 2, 3, or 5 days on the public transportation system, including the Métro, buses, and RER (Réseau Express Régional) trains. (The RER has both 1st- and 2nd-class compartments, and the pass lets you travel in 1st class.) As a bonus, the funicular ride to the top of Montmartre is included. A 1-day pass costs 8.35€, a 2-day pass 14€, a 3-day pass 18€, and a 5-day pass 27€. The card is available at RATP (Régie Autonome des Transports Parisiens), tourist offices, or the main Métro stations (⟮℃ **08-36-68-77-14**).

There are other discount passes as well, though most are available only to French residents with government ID cards and proof of taxpayer status. One available to temporary visitors is **Carte Mobilis,** which allows unlimited travel on all bus, subway, and RER lines during a 1-day period. The 1-day pass costs 5€. Ask for it at any Métro station. The pass is valid only within the 20 arrondissements.

On the Right Bank, the **1er** is home to the Louvre, place Vendôme, rues de Rivoli and St-Honoré, Palais Royal, and Comédie-Française—an area filled with grand institutions and grand stores. At the center of the **2e** is the Bourse (Stock Exchange), making it the city's financial center. Most of the **3e** and the **4e** is referred to as the Marais, the old Jewish quarter that in the 17th century was home to the aristocracy—today it's a trendy area of boutiques and restored mansions as well as the center of Paris's gay and lesbian community. On the Left Bank, the **5e** is known as the Latin Quarter, home to the Sorbonne and associated with the intellectual life that thrived in the 1920s and 1930s. The **6e,** known as St-Germain-des-Prés, stretches from the Seine to boulevard du Montparnasse. It is associated with the 1920s and 1930s and known as a center for art and antiques; it boasts the Palais and Jardin du Luxembourg. The **7e,** containing both the Tour Eiffel and Hôtel des Invalides, is a residential district for the well heeled.

Back on the Right Bank, the **8e** epitomizes monumental Paris, with the triumphal avenue des Champs-Elysées, the Elysées Palace, and the fashion houses along avenue Montaigne and the Faubourg St-Honoré. The **18e** is home to Sacré-Coeur and Montmartre and all that the name conjures of the bohemian life painted most notably by Toulouse-Lautrec. The **14e** incorporates most of Montparnasse, including its cemetery, whereas the **20e** is where the city's famous lie buried in Père-Lachaise and where today the recent immigrants from North Africa live. Beyond the arrondissements stretch the vast *banlieue,* or suburbs, of Greater Paris, where the majority of Parisians live.

GETTING AROUND   Paris is a city for strollers, whose greatest joy is rambling through unexpected alleys and squares. Given a choice of conveyance, try to make it on your own two feet whenever possible.

By Metro (Subway)   The **Métro** (⟮℃ **08-36-68-77-14**) is the fastest, most efficient means of transportation in Paris. All lines are numbered, and the final destination of each line is clearly marked on subway maps, in the underground passageways, and on the train cars. The Métro runs daily from 5:30am to 1:15am. It's reasonably safe at any hour, but beware of pickpockets.

Note: To familiarize yourself with Paris's Métro, check out the **color map** on the inside front cover of this book.

To make sure you catch the correct train, find your destination on the map, then follow the rail line it's on to the end of the route and note the name of the final destination—this final stop is the direction. In the station, follow the signs labeled with your direction in the passageways until you see it labeled on a train.

Transfer stations are *correspondances*—some require long walks; Châtelet is the most difficult—but most trips require only one transfer. When transferring, follow the orange CORRESPONDANCE signs to the proper platform. Don't follow a SORTIE (exit) sign or you'll have to pay another fare to get back on the train.

Many of the larger stations have maps with push-button indicators that light up your route when you press the button for your destination.

By Bus   Buses are much slower than the Métro, and the majority run from 7am to 8:30pm (a few operate until 12:30am, and 10 operate during early-morning hours). Service is limited on Sunday and holidays. Bus and Métro fares are the same; you can use the same tickets on both. Most bus rides require one ticket, but some destinations require two (never more than two within the city limits).

At certain stops, signs list the destinations and numbers of the buses serving that point. Destinations are usually listed north to south and east to west. Most stops are also posted on the sides of the buses. During rush hours, you may have to take a ticket from a dispensing machine, indicating your position in the line at the stop.

If you intend to use the buses a lot, pick up an RATP bus map at the office on place de la Madeleine, 8e, or at the tourist offices at RATP headquarters, 53 bis quai des Grands-Augustins, 6e. For detailed recorded information (in English) on bus and Métro routes, call ✆ **08-36-68-41-14.**

The same organization that runs the Métro and the buses, **RATP** (✆ **08-36-68-77-14**), also offers the **Balabus,** big-windowed orange-and-white motor coaches that run during limited hours: Sundays and national holidays from noon to 9pm, from April 15 to the end of September. Itineraries run in both directions between Gare de Lyon and the Grande Arche de La Défense, encompassing some of the city's most beautiful vistas. It's a great deal—two Métro tickets for 2.60€ will carry you the entire route. You'll recognize the bus and the route it follows by the *Bb* symbol emblazoned on each bus's side and on signs posted beside the route it follows.

By Taxi   It's impossible to get one at rush hour, so don't even try. Taxi drivers are organized into a lobby that keeps their number limited to 15,000.

Watch out for common rip-offs. Always check the meter to make sure you're not paying the previous passenger's fare. Beware of cabs without meters, which often wait outside nightclubs for tipsy patrons, or settle the tab in advance. You can hail regular cabs on the street when their signs read LIBRE. Taxis are easier to find at the many stands near Métro stations.

The flag drops at 2.15€, and from 7am to 7pm you pay .60€ per kilometer. From 7pm to 7am, you pay 1.15€ per kilometer. On airport trips, you're not required to pay for the driver's empty return ride.

You're allowed several pieces of luggage free if they're transported inside and are less than 5 kilograms (11 lb.). Heavier suitcases carried in the trunk cost 1.50€ to 2€ apiece. Tip 12% to 15%—the latter usually elicits a *"Merci."* For radio cabs, call ✆ **08-25-16-50-50** or 01-44-52-23-58—note that you'll be charged from the point where the taxi begins the drive to pick you up.

By Car   Don't even consider driving in Paris. The streets are narrow and parking is next to impossible.

By Bicycle   In recent years, the city has added many miles of right-hand lanes designated for cyclists as well as hundreds of bike racks. Cycling is especially popular in the larger parks and gardens.

Paris-Vélos, 2 rue du Fer-à-Moulin, 5e (© **01-43-37-59-22;** Métro: Censier-Daubenton), rents bicycles by the day (15€–26€), weekend (27€–35€), or week (72€–98€). You must leave a 400€ deposit. It's open Monday through Saturday from 10am to 12:30pm and 2 to 7pm.

By Boat   The **Batobus** (© **01-44-11-33-99**) is a 150-passenger ferry with big windows. Every day between May and September, the boats operate along the Seine, stopping at points of interest: the **Eiffel Tower,** the **Musée d'Orsay,** the **Louvre, Notre-Dame,** and the **Hôtel de Ville.** Transit from one stop to another is 3.05€, and departures are every 15 to 25 minutes from 10am to 7pm. The views are panoramic, but the Batobus isn't really a sightseeing tour (there's no recorded commentary); it simply offers a way to move from one attraction to another.

 ### *FAST FACTS:* Paris

American Express   With a Paris office at 11 rue Scribe, 9e (© **01-47-14-50-00;** Métro: Opéra, Chaussée-d'Antin, or Havre-Caumartin; RER: Auber), Amex is quite busy. It's open Monday through Friday from 9am to 6pm. On Saturday the bank is open from 9am to 5:30pm, but the mail-pickup window is closed. A less-busy office is at 38 av. de Waqram, 8e (© **01-42-27-58-80;** Métro: Ternes), open Monday through Friday from 10am to 5pm.

Area Code   All French telephone numbers now consist of 10 digits, the first two of which are like an area code. If you're calling anywhere in France from within France, just dial all 10 digits—no additional codes are needed. If you're calling from the United States, drop the initial 0 (zero).

Currency   In 2002, France abandoned the French franc and fell under the euro umbrella along with most other European Union countries. At press time, US$1 = 1.12€.

Currency Exchange   American Express (see above) can fill most banking needs. Most banks in Paris are open Monday through Friday from 9am to 4:30pm, but a few are open Saturday; ask at your hotel for the location of the one nearest you. For the best exchange rate, cash your traveler's checks at banks or foreign-exchange offices, not at shops and hotels. Most post offices will change traveler's checks or convert currency. Currency exchanges are also found at Paris airports and train stations and along most of the major boulevards. A small commission is charged.

Dentists   For emergency dental service, call **S.O.S. Dentaire,** 87 bd. du Port-Royal, 13e (© **01-43-37-51-00;** Métro: Port-Royal), Monday through Friday from 8pm to midnight and Saturday and Sunday from 9:30am to midnight. You can also call or visit the **American Hospital,** 63 bd. Victor-Hugo, in the suburb of Neuilly-sur-Seine outside Paris (© **01-46-41-25-25;** Métro: Pont-de-Levallois or Pont-de-Neuilly; bus: 82).

Doctors Some large hotels have a doctor on staff. You can also try the **American Hospital,** 63 bd. Victor-Hugo, Neuilly (© **01-46-41-25-25**; Métro: Pont-de-Levallois or Pont-de-Neuilly; bus: 82), which operates a 24-hour emergency service. The bilingual staff accepts Blue Cross and other American insurance plans.

Drugstores After regular hours, have your concierge contact the Commissariat de Police for the nearest 24-hour pharmacy. French law requires one pharmacy in any given neighborhood to stay open 24 hours. You'll find the address posted on the doors or windows of all other drugstores.

Embassies & Consulates Call before you go, as they often keep strange hours and observe both French and home-country holidays. The embassy of the **United States,** at 2 av. Gabriel, 8e (© **01-43-12-22-22**; Métro: Concorde), is open Monday through Friday from 9am to 6pm. The embassy of **Canada,** at 35 av. Montaigne, 8e (© **01-44-43-29-00**; Métro: Franklin D. Roosevelt or Alma-Marceau), is open Monday through Friday from 9am to noon and 2 to 4pm. The embassy and consulate of the **United Kingdom,** at 35 rue du Faubourg St-Honoré, 8e (© **01-44-51-31-00**; Métro: Concorde or Madeleine), is open Monday through Friday from 9:30am to 12:30pm and 2:30 to 5pm. The embassy of **Australia,** at 4 rue Jean-Rey, 15e (© **01-40-59-33-00**; Métro: Bir Hakeim), is open Monday through Friday from 9:15am to noon and 2 to 4:30pm. The embassy of **New Zealand,** at 7 ter rue Léonard-de-Vinci, 16e (© **01-45-01-24-11**; Métro: Victor Hugo), is open Monday through Friday from 9am to 1pm and 2:30 to 6pm. The embassy of **Ireland** is at 4 rue Rude, 16e (© **01-44-17-67-00**; Métro: Charles de Gaulle-étoile). Hours are Monday through Friday from 9:30am to noon. The embassy of **South Africa** is at 59 quai d'Orsay, 7e (© **01-53-59-23-23**; Métro: Invalides). Hours are Monday through Friday from 9am to noon.

Emergencies For the police, call © **17**; to report a fire, call © **18.** For an ambulance, call the fire department at © **01-45-78-74-52**; a fire vehicle rushes cases to the nearest emergency room. **SAMU** is an independently operated, privately owned ambulance company; call © **15.**

Police In an emergency, call © **17.** For non-emergency situations, the principal Préfecture is at 9 bd. du Palais, 4e (© **01-53-73-53-71** or 01-53-73-53-73; Métro: Cité).

Post Office The **Bureau de Poste,** 52 rue du Louvre, 75001 Paris (© **01-40-28-76-00**; Métro: Louvre-Rivoli), is open 24 hours a day for the sale of stamps and expedition of faxes and telegrams. For other financial services such as the sale of money orders, hours are Monday through Friday from 8am to 5pm and Saturday from 8am to noon. Your mail can be sent to this post office *poste restante* (general delivery) for a small fee. Take an ID such as a passport. Airmail letters to North America cost .65€; to other European countries .45€; to Australia and New Zealand .80€.

Safety Beware of child pickpockets, who prey on visitors around sites such as the Louvre, Eiffel Tower, Notre-Dame, and Montmartre, and who like to pick pockets in the Métro, often blocking the entrance and exit to the escalator. Women should hang on to their purses.

Telephones The country code for France is **33.** All phone numbers in France have 10 digits, and this includes the **area code** (or regional prefix).

For example, the phone number for the Hôtel Regina, 01-42-60-38-09, contains the area code **(01)** for Paris and the Ile de France. To make a **long-distance call within France,** you would just dial this 10-digit number. **When calling from outside France,** dial the international prefix for your country **(011** for the United States and Canada), the country code for France, and then the last 9 digits of the number, dropping the 0 (zero) from the regional prefix.

Public phone booths are found in cafes, restaurants, Métro stations, post offices, airports, and train stations, and sometimes on the streets. Finding a coin-operated phone in France may be an arduous task; a simpler option is to use a *télécarte,* a prepaid calling card available for purchase at most post offices, Métro stations, and tobacco shops.

From a *télécabine,* using a *télécarte,* a 3-minute local call will cost around .30€; a call to the United States will cost around .45€ per minute. *Note:* these rates apply to public phone booths; hotels will add surcharges. *Télécartes* are sold in denominations of 7.60€ to 30€. Access codes for the major U.S.-based carriers are as follows: **AT&T,** ℰ **0800-99-00-11; MCI,** ℰ **0800-99-00-19; Sprint,** ℰ **0800-99-00-87.**

Tipping By law, all bills show *service compris,* which means the tip is included; additional gratuities are customarily given as follows: For **hotel staff,** tip the porter .90€ to 1.50€ per item of baggage, and tip the chambermaid 1.50€ per day. You're not obligated to tip the concierge, doorman, or anyone else unless you use his or her services. In **cafes** and **restaurants,** waiter service is usually included, though you can leave a couple of francs. Tip **taxi drivers** 12% to 15% of the amount on the meter.

WHERE TO STAY

Although Paris hotels are quite expensive, there is some good news. Scores of lackluster Paris lodgings have been renovated and offer much better value in the moderate-to-inexpensive price range. The most outstanding example is in the **7th arrondissement,** where several good-value hotels have blossomed from dives.

Hot weather doesn't last long in Paris, so most hotels except the deluxe ones don't provide air-conditioning. To avoid the noise problem when you have to open windows, request a room in the back when making a reservation.

Most hotels offer a continental breakfast of coffee, tea, or hot chocolate; a freshly baked croissant and roll; and limited quantities of butter and jam or jelly. The word "breakfast" in the following entries refers to this continental version.

Service and value-added tax are included in rates quoted, unless otherwise specified. Unless otherwise specified, all hotel rooms have a private bathroom.

RIGHT BANK: 1ST ARRONDISSEMENT
Very Expensive

Hôtel Ritz ℱℱℱ   The Ritz is Europe's greatest hotel, an enduring symbol of elegance on one of Paris's most beautiful and historic squares. César Ritz, the "little shepherd boy from Niederwald," converted the Hôtel de Lazun into a luxury hotel in 1898. With the help of the culinary master Escoffier, he made the Ritz a miracle of luxury. In 1979, the Ritz family sold the hotel to Mohammed al Fayed, who refurbished it and added a cooking school. Two town houses were annexed, joined by an arcade lined with display cases representing 125 of Paris's leading

Paris Accommodations

Hôtel de la Place des Vosges **22**	Hôtel Ritz **8**
Hôtel du Globe **15**	Hôtel Saint-Merry **23**
Hôtel du Jeu de Paume **19**	Hôtel Sofitel Trocadero Dokhan's **1**
Hôtel du Quai-Voltaire **10**	Hôtel St-Louis **20**
Hôtel du 7e Art **21**	Hôtel-Résidence St-Christophe **18**
Hôtel Le Clos Médicis **16**	L'Hôtel **12**
Hôtel Montalembert **7**	Relais Christine **14**
Hotel Pershing Hall **3**	Timhôtel Louvre **9**

boutiques. The public salons are furnished with museum-caliber antiques. Each guest room is uniquely decorated, most with Louis XIV or XV reproductions; all have fine rugs, marble fireplaces, tapestries, brass beds, and more.

15 place Vendôme, 75001 Paris. © 800/223-6800 in the U.S. and Canada, or 01-43-16-30-30. Fax 01-43-16-36-68. www.ritzparis.com. 175 units. 630€–730€ double; from 1,210€ suite. AE, DC, MC, V. Parking 40€. Métro: Opéra, Concorde, or Madeleine. **Amenities:** 2 restaurants; 2 bars; pool; health club; 24-hr. room service; in-room massage; laundry/dry cleaning; cooking school. *In room:* A/C, TV, minibar, hair dryer, safe.

Moderate

Hôtel Britannique *Value*   Conservatively modern and plush, this is a much-renovated 19th-century hotel near Les Halles and Notre-Dame. The place is not only British in name, but seems to have cultivated an English graciousness. The guest rooms are small but immaculate and soundproof, with comfortable beds and well-maintained bathrooms with shower-tub combinations. A satellite receiver gets U.S. and U.K. television shows. The reading room is a cozy retreat.

20 av. Victoria, 75001 Paris. © 01-42-33-74-59. Fax 01-42-33-82-65. www.hotel-britannic.com. 39 units. 157€–180€ double. AE, DC, MC, V. Parking 20€. Métro: Châtelet. **Amenities:** Limited room service. *In room:* TV, minibar, hair dryer, safe.

Hôtel Burgundy *✦ Value*   The Burgundy is one of the best values in this expensive area. The frequently renovated building began as two adjacent town houses in the 1830s, one a pension where Baudelaire wrote poetry in the 1860s, the other a bordello. The houses were linked by British-born managers who insisted on using the English name. Renovated in 1992, with improvements in 2001, the hotel hosts many North and South Americans and features conservatively decorated rooms, each with a bathroom with full tub and shower.

8 rue Duphot, 75001 Paris. © 01-42-60-34-12. Fax 01-47-03-95-20. www.burgundyhotel.com. 89 units. 163€–170€ double; 250€ suite. AE, DC, MC, V. Métro: Madeleine or Concorde. **Amenities:** Restaurant; bar; room service (7–10:30am); babysitting. *In room:* TV, minibar, hair dryer.

Inexpensive

Timhôtel Louvre *Kids*   This hotel and its sibling, the Timhôtel Palais-Royal, are mirror images, at least inside; they're part of a new breed of two-star family-friendly hotels cropping up in France. These Timhôtels share the same manager and temperament. Though the rooms at the Palais-Royal branch are a bit larger than the ones here, this branch is so close to the Louvre it's almost irresistible. The ambience is modern, with monochromatic rooms and wall-to-wall carpeting.

4 rue Croix des Petits-Champs, 75001 Paris. © 01-42-60-34-86. Fax 01-42-60-10-39. www.timhotel.fr. 56 units. 120€–150€ double. Children under 12 stay free in parent's room. AE, DC, MC, V. Métro: Palais Royal. The 56-unit **Timhôtel Palais-Royal** is at 3 rue de la Banque, 75002 Paris (© 01-42-61-53-90; fax 01-42-60-05-39; Métro: Bourse). **Amenities:** Babysitting; laundry/dry cleaning. *In room:* A/C, TV.

RIGHT BANK: 3RD, 4TH & 8TH ARRONDISSEMENTS
Very Expensive

Four Seasons Hotel George V *✦✦✦*   In its latest reincarnation, with all its glitz and glamour, this hotel is one of the best in the world—and its history is as gilt-edged as they come. It opened in 1928 in honor of George V of England. During the liberation of Paris, it housed Dwight D. Eisenhower. After its acquisition by Saudi Prince Al Waleed and a 2-year renovation, it was reopened under the banner of Toronto-based Four Seasons. The guest rooms are about as close as you'll come to residency in a well-upholstered private home where teams of decorators have lavished vast amounts of attention and money. It's deluxe all the way. The renovation reduced the number of units from 300 to 245, which now come in three sizes. The largest are magnificent; the smallest are, in the words of a spokesperson, *"très agreeable."* Security is tight—a fact appreciated by its sometimes notorious guests.

31 av. George V, 75008 Paris. © 800/332-3442 in the U.S. or Canada, or 01-49-52-70-00. Fax 01-49-52-70-10. www.fourseasons.com. 245 units. 670€–900€ double; from 1,600€ suite. Parking 40€. AE, DC, MC, V. Métro: George-V. **Amenities:** Restaurant; 2 lounges; pool; fitness center; spa; 24-hr. room service. *In room:* A/C, TV, minibar, hair dryer, safe.

Hotel Pershing Hall ★★★   Set on a hyper-stylish street that parallels the avenue Montaigne, this hotel was created when a late-19th-century town house was radically altered by one of France's most celebrated modern designers, Andrée Putnam. Admittedly, she had fascinating raw materials: The five-story town house was built in 1890 by the comte de Paris, at the time the heir apparent to the French monarchy had it been fully restored, as a home for his mistress. During World War I, it was transformed into the Paris headquarters of American Gen. John Pershing. Today, the walls of the soaring courtyard are draped in lush tropical plants from Southeast Asia that thrive in the microclimate of the courtyard. Inside, don't expect homage to the imperial days of the French monarchy, as it's all been replaced in favor of the warm but artfully spartan and rectilinear style favored by Putnam, the woman behind the original decor of Air France's Concorde.

49 rue Pierre Charron, 75001 Paris. © 01-58-36-58-00. Fax 01-58-36-58-01. www.pershing-hall.com. 26 units. 380€–500€ double; 720€–1,000€ suite. AL, DC, MC, V. Metro: Georges V. **Amenities:** Restaurant; bar; health club and sauna; babysitting; laundry/dry cleaning; courtyard terrace. *In room:* A/C, TV, minibar, hair dryer, safe.

Expensive

Hôtel du Jeu de Paume ★   This hotel is small-scale and charming, with a layout that includes a pair of 17th-century town houses accessible via a timbered passageway from the street outside. The rooms are a bit larger than those within some of the nearby competitors. Originally, the hotel was a "clubhouse" used by members of the court of Louis XIII, who amused themselves with *les jeux de paume* (an early form of tennis) nearby. Public areas are outfitted in a simple version of Art Deco. Guest rooms, some under a wooden beamed ceiling, are freshly decorated with sleek contemporary styling, each with elegant materials such as oaken floors and fine craftsmanship.

54 rue St-Louis en l'Ile, 75004 Paris. © 01-43-26-14-18. Fax 01-40-46-02-76. www.jeudepaumehotel.com. 30 units. 220€–250€ double; 450€ suite. AE, DC, MC, V. Métro: Pont-Marie. **Amenities:** Sauna; limited room service; laundry/dry cleaning. *In room:* TV, minibar, hair dryer, safe.

Hôtel St-Louis ★ *Value*   Proprietors Guy and Andrée Record maintain a charming family atmosphere at this antique-filled hotel in a 17th-century town house. Despite a renovation completed in 1998, it represents an incredible value considering its prime location on Ile St-Louis. Expect cozy, slightly cramped rooms, each with a small private bathroom containing a shower-tub combination. Beds have fine mattresses of medium thickness. With mansard roofs and old-fashioned moldings, the top-floor units sport tiny balconies with sweeping views. The breakfast room is in the cellar, with 17th-century stone vaulting.

75 rue St-Louis-en-l'Ile, 75004 Paris. © 01-46-34-04-80. Fax 01-46-34-02-13. www.hotelsaintlouis.com. 19 units. 130€–145€ double; 210€ suites. Breakfast 9€. MC, V. Métro: Pont Marie or St-Michel. **Amenities:** Room service (7:30–10am); babysitting. *In room:* TV, hair dryer, safe.

Moderate

Galileo Hotel ★ *Finds*   This is one of the 8th's most charming hotels, run by Roland and Elisabeth Buffat. A short walk from the Champs-Elysées, the town house is the epitome of French elegance and charm. The rooms are medium and a study in understated taste, decorated in cocoa and beige. The most spacious are room nos. 100, 200, 501, and 502, each with a glass-covered veranda you can use even in winter.

54 rue Galilée, 75008 Paris. © **01-47-20-66-06.** Fax 01-47-20-67-17. www.hotel-ile-saintlouis.com. 27 units. 149€ double. AE, DC, MC, V. Parking 23€. Métro: Charles de Gaulle-étoile or George-V. **Amenities:** Limited room service (8am–9pm); babysitting; laundry/dry cleaning. *In room:* A/C, TV, minibar, hair dryer, safe.

Hôtel Saint-Merry 𝔸 *Finds*   The rebirth of this once-notorious brothel as a charming, upscale hotel is an example of how the area has been gentrified. It contains only a dozen rooms, each relatively small, but accented with neo-Gothic detail, exposed stone, 18th-century ceiling beams, and lots of quirky architecture. Suites, much larger than doubles, have upgraded furnishings and more comfort. According to the staff, the clientele here is about 50% gay males; the other half is straight and involved in the neighborhood arts scene. Before it became a bordello, it was conceived as the presbytery of the nearby Church of Saint-Merry.

78 rue de la Verrerie, 75004 Paris. © **01-42-78-14-15.** Fax 01-40-29-06-82. www.hotelmarais.com. 12 units. 146€–210€ double; 305€ suite. Metro: Hôtel de Ville or Châtelet. **Amenities:** Breakfast lounge. *In room:* Hair dryer, safe.

Inexpensive

Hôtel de la Place des Vosges 𝔸 *Value*   Built about 350 years ago, during the same era as the construction of the majestic square for which it's named (a 2-min. walk away), this well-managed, small-scale property has reasonable prices and lots of charm. The structure was once used as a stable for the mules of Henri IV. Many of the small guest rooms have beamed ceilings, tiled bathrooms (with tub or shower), small TVs hanging from the ceiling, and a sense of cozy, well-ordered efficiency. The most desirable and expensive accommodation is top-floor room no. 60, overlooking the rooftops of Paris, with a luxurious private bathroom.

12 rue de Birague, 75004 Paris. © **01-42-72-60-46.** Fax 01-42-72-02-64. www.bparis.com. 16 units. 101€–120€ double; 130€ room no. 60. AE, MC, V. Métro: Bastille. *In room:* TV, hair dryer.

Hôtel du 7e Art   The hotel is in one of the many 17th-century buildings in this neighborhood classified as historic monuments. Don't expect grand luxury: Guest rooms are cramped but clean and outfitted with the simplest of furniture, relieved by 1950s-era movie posters. Each unit has white walls, and some—including those under the sloping mansard-style roof—have exposed ceiling beams. All have small bathrooms with either a tub or shower. The hotel has a lobby bar and a breakfast room, but no elevator—and it's a five-story building. The hotel is named after the 7th Art, a French reference to filmmaking.

20 rue St-Paul, 75004 Paris. © **01-44-54-85-00.** Fax 01-42-77-69-10. 23 units. 120€ double. AE, DC, MC, V. Métro: St-Paul. **Amenities:** Health club; laundromat. *In room:* TV, hair dryer, safe.

RIGHT BANK: 16TH ARRONDISSEMENT
Expensive

Hôtel Sofitel Trocadero Dokhan's 𝔸𝔸   If not for the porters walking through its public areas carrying luggage, you might suspect that this well-accessorized hotel is a private home. It's housed in a stately 19th-century building vaguely inspired by Palladio, and contains accessories like antique paneling, Regency-era armchairs, chandeliers, and a pervasive sense of upper-bourgeois taste. Each guest room has a different decorative style, with antiques or good reproductions, lots of personalized touches, triple-glazed windows, and beautifully maintained bathrooms with shower-tub combinations.

117 rue Lauriston, 75116 Paris. ℂ **01-53-65-66-99.** Fax 01-53-65-66-88. hotel.trocadero.dokhans@ wanadoo.fr. 45 units. 400€–700€ double; 1,100€ suite. Parking 17€. Métro: Trocadero. AE, DC, MC, V. **Amenities:** Restaurant (lunch only); champagne bar. *In room:* A/C, TV, fax, minibar, hair dryer, CD player.

LEFT BANK: 5TH ARRONDISSEMENT
Moderate
Hôtel-Résidence St-Christophe   This hotel, in one of the Latin Quarter's undiscovered areas, offers a gracious English-speaking staff. It was created in 1987 when an older hotel was connected to a butcher shop. All the small- to medium-size rooms were renovated in 1998, with Louis XV–style furniture and carpeting. Half of the bathrooms have tubs in addition to showers.

17 rue Lacépède, 75005 Paris. ℂ **01-43-31-81-54.** Fax 01-43-31-12-54. www.charme-hotel-paris.com. 31 units. 86€–123€ double. AE, DC, MC, V. Métro: Place Monge. *In room:* TV, minibar, hair dryer.

Inexpensive
Familia-Hôtel   As the name implies, this hotel has been family-run for decades. Many personal touches make the place unique. The walls of 14 rooms are graced with finely executed sepia-colored frescoes of Parisian scenes. Eight units have restored stone walls, and seven boast balconies with delightful views over the Latin Quarter. Half of the bathrooms come with tubs as well as showers. Thanks to a dynamic family-ownership that likes to keep this place humming, the guest rooms are renovated as often as needed to maintain a high level of comfort.

11 rue des Ecoles, 75005 Paris. ℂ **01-43-54-55-27.** Fax 01-43-29-61-77. www.hotel-paris.familia.com. 30 units. 76€–106€ double. Rates include breakfast. AE, DC, MC, V. Métro: Jussieu or Maubert-Mutualité. **Amenities:** Car-rental desk. *In room:* TV, minibar, hair dryer.

LEFT BANK: 6TH ARRONDISSEMENT
Very Expensive
Relais Christine 🌟🌟   This hotel welcomes you into what was a 16th-century Augustinian cloister. From a cobblestone street, enter a symmetrical courtyard to find an elegant reception area with Renaissance antiques. Each room is uniquely decorated with wooden beams and Louis XIII–style furnishings. Extras include mirrored closets, plush carpets, and thermostats. Some units have balconies facing the courtyard. The least attractive rooms are those in the interior.

3 rue Christine, 75006 Paris. ℂ **01-40-51-60-80.** Fax 01-40-51-60-81. www.relais-christine.com. 51 units. 320€–410€ double; 460€–700€ duplex or suite. AE, DC, MC, V. Free parking. Métro: Odéon. **Amenities:** Honor bar in lobby; massage; babysitting; laundry/dry cleaning. *In room:* A/C, TV, minibar, hair dryer, safe.

Expensive
Hôtel de Fleurie 🌟 *Kids*   Off boulevard St-Germain on a colorful little street, the Fleurie is one of the best of the "new" old hotels; its statuary-studded facade recaptures a 17th-century elegance, and the stone walls have been exposed in the salon. All the guest rooms have been recently renovated. Many have elaborate draperies and antique reproductions. Because some of the rooms are larger than others and contain an extra bed for kids, the hotel has long been a family favorite.

32–34 rue Grégoire-de-Tours, 75006 Paris. ℂ **01-53-73-70-00.** Fax 01-53-73-70-20. www.hotel-de-fleurie. tm.fr. 29 units. 167€–198€ double; 297€–343€ family room. Children 12 and under stay free in parent's room. AE, DC, MC, V. Métro: Odéon or St-Germain-des-Prés. **Amenities:** Bar; car rental; room service (breakfast only); laundry/dry cleaning. *In room:* A/C, TV, minibar, hair dryer, safe.

L'Hôtel 🌟   Ranking just a notch below the Relais Christine, this is one of the Left Bank's most charming boutique hotels. It was once a 19th-century fleabag whose major distinction was that Oscar Wilde died here. But today's guests aren't anywhere near poverty row. The guest rooms all have nonworking fireplaces and fabric-covered walls. In 2000, superstar aesthete Jacques Garcia redecorated the hotel, retaining its Victorian-baroque sense but outfitting each room differently. Expect to be lodged amid themes that reflect China, Russia, Japan, India, or high-camp Victorian. The Cardinal room is all scarlet, and the room where Wilde died is stately looking, Victorian, respectful, and nostalgia-laden.

13 rue des Beaux-Arts, 75006 Paris. (✆ 01-44-41-99-00. Fax 01-43-25-64-81. www.l-hotel.com. 20 units. 259€–580€ double; from 687€ suite. AE, DC, MC, V. Métro: St-Germain-des-Prés or Mabillon. **Amenities:** Restaurant; pool; steam room; limited room service; babysitting; laundry/dry cleaning. *In room:* A/C, TV, mini-bar, hair dryer.

Moderate

Hôtel Aviatic   Completely remodeled, this is a bit of old Paris in an interesting section of Montparnasse, with an inner courtyard and a vine-covered wall lattice, surrounded by cafes popular with artists, writers, and musicians. It has been a family-run hotel for a century and has an English-speaking staff. The reception lounge boasts marble columns, chandeliers, antiques, and a petite salon. The guest rooms were renovated throughout the 1990s; each comes with a shower or tub/shower combo, and new beds are quite comfortable.

105 rue de Vaugirard, 75006 Paris. (✆ 01-53-63-25-50. Fax 01-53-63-25-55. www.aviatic.fr. 43 units. 127€–160€ double; 245€ suite. AE, DC, MC, V. Parking. 20€. Métro: Montparnasse–Bienvenue or St-Placide. **Amenities:** Limited room service; babysitting; laundry/dry cleaning. *In room:* A/C, TV, minibar, hair dryer, safe.

Hôtel Le Clos Médicis   The location of this hotel across from the Jardin du Luxembourg is a major advantage. You'll find a garden with lattices and stone walls, a lobby with modern spotlights and simple furniture, and a multilingual staff. The warmly colored rooms, small to medium in size, are comfortable, and each comes with a neatly tiled bathroom with combination tub and shower. Book one of the multi-level suites with spacious living areas and tasteful furnishings.

56 rue Monsieur-le-Prince, 75006 Paris. (✆ 01-43-29-10-80. Fax 01-43-54-26-90. www.select-paris.com/hotels. 38 units. 165€–180€ double; 240€ duplex suite. AE, DC, MC, V. Parking 23€. Métro: Odéon. RER: Luxembourg. **Amenities:** Room service (7–11am); laundry/dry cleaning. *In room:* A/C, TV, minibar, hair dryer, safe.

Inexpensive

Hôtel du Globe   This 17th-century building is on an evocative street; inside you'll find most of the original stonework and dozens of original timbers and beams. There's no elevator (and a very narrow antique staircase) and no breakfast area (trays are brought to your room). Each guest room is decorated with old-fashioned flair. The rooms with tubs are almost twice as large as those with shower stalls. The largest and most desirable are nos. 1, 12 (with a baldachin-style bed), 14, 15, and 16. The room without a bathroom is a single that goes for 50€.

15 rue des Quatre-Vents, 75006 Paris. (✆ 01-46-33-62-69. Fax 01-46-33-62-69. 15 units. 84€–100€ double. Breakfast 8€. MC, V. Closed Aug. Métro: Mabillon, Odéon, or St-Sulpice. **Amenities:** 24-hr. room service. *In room:* TV.

LEFT BANK: 7TH ARRONDISSEMENT
Very Expensive

Hôtel Montalembert   Unusually elegant for the Left Bank, the Montalembert dates from 1926, when it was built in the beaux arts style. Its decor borrows elements of Bauhaus and postmodern design in beiges, creams, and golds. The guest rooms are spacious, except for some standard doubles, which are small unless you're a very thin model. Frette linens decorate roomy beds topped with cabana-stripe duvets crowning deluxe French mattresses. The bathrooms are luxurious, with deep tubs, Cascais marble, and tall pivoting mirrors.

3 rue de Montalembert, 75007 Paris. (C) 800/786-6397 in the U.S. and Canada, or 01-45-49-68-68. Fax 01-45-49-69-49. www.montalembert.com. 56 units. 300€–450€ double; 680€ suite. AE, DC, MC, V. Parking 16€. Métro: Rue du Bac. **Amenities:** Restaurant; bar; privileges at nearby health club; 24-hr. room service; babysitting; laundry/dry cleaning. In room: A/C, TV, minibar, hair dryer, safe.

Moderate

Hôtel de l'Université ✪   Long favored by well-heeled parents of North American students studying in Paris, this 300-year-old, antiques-filled town house enjoys a location in a discreetly upscale neighborhood. Room no. 54 is a favorite, containing a rattan bed and period pieces. Another charmer is room no. 35, which has a fireplace and opens onto a courtyard with a fountain. The most expensive unit has a small terrace overlooking the surrounding rooftops. Beds have plush comfort and discreet French styling. You'll sleep well here.

22 rue de l'Université, 75007 Paris. (C) 01-42-61-09-39. Fax 01-42-60-40-84. www.hoteluniversite.com. 27 units. 150€–290€ double. AE, MC, V. Métro: St-Germain-des-Prés. **Amenities:** Laundry/dry cleaning. In room: A/C, TV, hair dryer, safe.

Inexpensive

Hôtel du Quai-Voltaire   Built in the 1600s as an abbey, then transformed into a hotel in 1856, the Quai-Voltaire is best known for its illustrious guests, like Wilde, Richard Wagner, and Baudelaire, who occupied room nos. 47, 55, and 56, respectively. Camille Pissarro painted Le Pont Royal from the window of his fourth-floor room. Many guest rooms in this modest inn have been renovated; most overlook the bookstalls and boats of the Seine.

19 quai Voltaire, 75007 Paris. (C) 01-42-61-50-91. Fax 01-42-61-62-26. 33 units. 122€–145€ double; 145€ triple. AE, DC, MC, V. Parking 18€ nearby. Métro: Musée d'Orsay or Rue du Bac. **Amenities:** Bar; limited room service; laundry. In room: TV, hair dryer.

WHERE TO DINE

Our best piece of advice—even if your budget is lean—is to splurge on one grand French meal. (And make reservations well in advance!) A meal at a place such as **La Tour d'Argent** ✪✪✪, **Taillevent** ✪✪✪, **Alain Ducasse** ✪✪✪, or **Violon d'Ingres** ✪✪✪ will be a memory you'll always carry.

In the past, suits and ties were a given, and women always wore smart dresses or suits. Well, you can kiss your suits *au revoir*—these days. Except in first-class and deluxe places, attire is more relaxed. Relaxed doesn't mean sloppy jeans and workout clothes! Parisians still value style, even when dressing informally.

Restaurants are required by law to post their menus outside, so peruse them carefully. The prix-fixe menu remains a solid choice if you want to have some idea of what your bill will be when it's presented by the waiter (whom, by the way, you should call *monsieur,* not *garçon*).

RIGHT BANK: 1ST ARRONDISSEMENT
Very Expensive

Carré des Feuillants ✪✪✪ MODERN FRENCH   This is a bastion of perfection, an enclave of haute gastronomy between the place Vendôme and the Tuileries. When chef Alain Dutournier turned this 17th-century convent into a restaurant, it was an overnight success. The interior is like an early-1900s bourgeois house with several salons opening onto a sky-lit courtyard, across from a glass-enclosed kitchen. You'll find a sophisticated reinterpretation of cuisine from France's southwest, using seasonally fresh ingredients and lots of know-how. Examples are roasted veal kidneys cooked in their own fat; and grilled wood pigeon with chutney and polenta. Lighter dishes are scallops wrapped in parsley-infused puff pastry served with cabbage and truffles, and mullet-studded risotto with lettuce. For dessert, try the pistachio cream cake with candied tangerines.

14 rue de Castiglione (near place Vendôme and the Tuileries). ℂ **01-42-86-82-82.** Fax 01-42-86-07-71. Reservations required far in advance. Main courses 80€–100€; fixed-price lunch 138€. AE, DC, MC, V. Mon–Fri noon–2:30pm; Mon–Sat 7:30–10pm. Closed Aug. Métro: Tuileries, Concorde, Opéra, or Madeleine.

Expensive

Goumard 🤏🤏🤏 SEAFOOD   Opened in 1872, this landmark is one of Paris's leading seafood restaurants. It's so devoted to the fine art of preparing fish that other food is banned from the menu (the staff will verbally present a limited roster of meat dishes). The decor consists of a collection of Lalique crystal fish in artificial aquariums. Even more unusual are the men's and women's restrooms, classified as historic monuments; the commodes were designed by the Art Nouveau master cabinetmaker Majorelle in the early 1900s. Much of the seafood is flown in from Brittany daily. Examples are a *craquant* (crisp-cooked) crayfish in its own herb salad, lobster soup with coconut, and a grilled turbot salad on a bed of artichokes with tarragon. In all these dishes, nothing (no excess butter, spices, or salt) is allowed to interfere with the natural flavor of the sea. Be prepared for some unusual food—the staff will help translate the menu items for you.

9 rue Duphot. ℂ **01-42-60-36-07.** Fax 01-42-60-04-54. www.goumard.com. Reservations required far in advance. Main courses 29€–75€; fixed-price lunch 40€. AE, DC, MC, V. Daily noon–2:30pm and 7:30–10:30pm. Closed 2 weeks in Aug. Métro: Madeleine or Concorde.

Moderate

Il Cortile 🤏🤏 ITALIAN/MEDITERRANEAN   Flanking the verdant courtyard of a small hotel, this much-talked-about restaurant serves the best Italian food in Paris. In warm weather, tables are set up in an enclosed patio—a luxury in this congested neighborhood. The cuisine is fresh, inventive, and seasonal. Dishes are from throughout Italy, with emphasis on the north. Look for items like farfalle pasta with squid ink and fresh shellfish, fettuccine with *pistou* (pasta in a soup made from vegetables), and an award-winning guinea fowl (spit-roasted and served with artfully shaped slices of the bird's gizzard, heart, and liver, it comes with polenta). The service is flawless: The Italian-speaking staff is diplomatic and good-humored. If you want to see what's cooking, ask for a seat in the dining room with a view of the rotisserie, where hens and guinea fowl slowly spin.

In the Hôtel Castille, 37 rue Cambon. ℂ **01-44-58-45-67.** Reservations recommended. Main courses 30€–35€; fixed-price menu 40€. AE, DC, DISC, MC, V. Mon–Fri noon–2:30pm and 7:30–10:30pm. Métro: Concorde or Madeleine.

Inexpensive

La Fermette du Sud-Ouest 🤏 SOUTHWESTERN FRENCH   This restaurant, which occupies the site of a 1500s convent, is in the heart of one of Paris's oldest neighborhoods. After the Revolution, the convent was converted into a coaching inn, preserving the original stonework and massive beams. La Fermette prepares rich, savory stews and confits celebrating agrarian France, serving them on the ground floor and on a mezzanine resembling a choir loft. Menu items include an age-old but ever-popular magret of duckling with flap mushrooms, *andouillette* (chitterling sausages), and a sometimes startling array of *cochonailles* (pork products and by-products) you probably need to be French to appreciate. Cassoulet and pot-au-feu are enduring specialties.

31 rue Coquillière. ⓒ 01-42-36-73-55. Reservations recommended. Main courses 14€–20€; fixed-price lunch 15€; set menu 25€. MC, V. Mon–Sat noon–2pm and 7:30–10pm. Métro: Les Halles.

RIGHT BANK: 3RD ARRONDISSEMENT (LE MARAIS)
Inexpensive
L'Ambassade d'Auvergne ☞ AUVERGNAT/FRENCH   You enter this rustic tavern through a bar with heavy oak beams, hanging hams, and ceramic plates. This favorite showcases the culinary generosity of France's most isolated region, the Auvergne, whose pork products are widely celebrated. Try a chicory salad with apples and pieces of country ham; pork braised with cabbage, turnips, and white beans; or grilled tripe sausages with mashed potatoes and cantal cheese with garlic. Non-pork specialties are pan-fried duck liver with gingerbread, perch steamed in verbena tea, and roasted rack of lamb with wild mushrooms. Dessert might be a poached pear with crispy almonds and caramel sauce.

22 rue de Grenier St-Lazare. ⓒ 01-42-72-31-22. Reservations recommended. Main courses 12€–16€; fixed-price menu 27€. AE, MC, V. Daily noon–2pm and 7:30–11pm. Métro: Rambuteau.

RIGHT BANK: 4TH ARRONDISSEMENT
Moderate
Bofinger ☞ ALSATIAN/FRENCH   Opened in the 1860s, Bofinger is the oldest Alsatian brasserie in town and one of the best. It's a Belle Epoque dining palace, resplendent with brass and stained glass. Weather permitting, you can dine on an outdoor terrace. Affiliated with La Coupole, Julien, and Brasserie Flo, the restaurant has updated its menu, retaining the most popular of its traditional dishes, like sauerkraut and sole meunière. Recent additions include roasted leg of lamb with a fondant of artichoke hearts and a purée of parsley; grilled turbot with a *brandade* of fennel; and stingray with chives and burnt-butter sauce. Shellfish, including fresh oysters and lobster, is almost always available in season.

5–7 rue de la Bastille. ⓒ 01-42-72-87-82. Reservations recommended. Main courses 14€–30€. AE, DC, MC, V. Mon–Fri noon–3pm and 6:30pm–1am; Sat–Sun noon–1am. Métro: Bastille.

Georges ☞ INTERNATIONAL   The Centre Pompidou is again in the spotlight; all of artsy Paris is talking about this place. Georges is in a large space on the top floor of Paris's most comprehensive arts complex, with views through bay windows over most of the city. The decor is minimalist and postmodern, with lots of brushed aluminum and stainless steel. Tables are made from sandblasted glass, lit from below, and accessorized with hypermodern cutlery. Menu items are mostly Continental, with hints of Asia. Some combinations come as a surprise—macaroni with lobster, for example. Others seem exotic, including roasted ostrich steak. Aside from these dishes, some of the best items on the menu are the roasted scallops with lemon butter and a tuna steak spiced up with coriander. There's also a luscious version of sole meunière. (May that dish never go out of style!)

On the 6th floor of the Centre Georges Pompidou, 19 rue Beaubourg. ⓒ 01-44-78-47-99. Reservations imperative for dinner, recommended for lunch. Main courses 18€–32€. AE, DC, MC, V. Wed–Mon 11am–2am. Métro: Châtelet or Rambuteau.

Inexpensive
Chez Jo Goldenberg ☞ JEWISH/CENTRAL EUROPEAN   This is the best-known restaurant on the "Street of the Rose Bushes." Albert Goldenberg, the doyen of Jewish restaurateurs in Paris, moved to choicer surroundings (69 av. de Wagram, 17e), but his brother, Joseph, has remained. Dining is on two levels, one for nonsmokers. Look for the collection of samovars, the fantail pigeon in a wicker

cage, and the paintings. The *carpe farcie* (stuffed carp) is a preferred selection, but the beef goulash is also good. We like the eggplant moussaka and the pastrami. The menu offers Israeli wines, but M. Goldenberg admits they're not as good as French wines. Live Yiddish music is presented every night beginning at 9pm, and special menus are offered during Jewish holidays—reservations are a must.

7 rue des Rosiers. © 01-48-87-20-16. Reservations required. Main courses 11€–18€. AE, DC, MC, V. Daily 11am–1am. Métro: St-Paul.

RIGHT BANK: 8TH ARRONDISSEMENT
Very Expensive

Pierre Gagnaire 𝕬𝕬𝕬 MODERN FRENCH   If you're able to get a reservation, it's worth the effort. The menus are seasonal to take advantage of France's rich bounty; owner Pierre Gagnaire demands perfection, and the chef has a dazzling way with flavors and textures. Stellar examples are crayfish cooked tempura-style with thinly sliced flash-seared vegetables and sweet-and-sour sauce; and turbot cooked in a bag and served with fennel and Provençal lemons. Chicken with truffles is part of a two-tiered service—first the breast in a wine-based aspic, second the thighs chopped into roughly textured pieces. For dessert, try the chocolate soufflé served with a frozen parfait and pistachios.

6 rue Balzac. © 01-58-36-12-50. Fax 01-58-36-12-51. Reservations are imperative and difficult to get. Main courses 60€–110€. Fixed-price menu 120€ lunch, 200€ dinner. AE, DC, MC, V. Mon–Fri noon–1:30pm and 7–10pm. Métro: George-V.

Restaurant Plaza Athénée (Alain Ducasse) 𝕬𝕬𝕬 MODERN & TRADITIONAL FRENCH   Few other chefs have been catapulted to international fame as quickly as Alain Ducasse. The most recent setting for his cuisine is a world-renowned hotel, the Plaza Athénée. There's a lot of glitzy marketing involved, but what you'll find is a lobby-level hideaway that top-notch decorator Patrick Jouin transformed with layers of pearl-gray paint and yards of translucent organdy. The five-star Michelin chef divides his time between Paris and Monaco, though he insists he doesn't repeat himself in either of his famous eateries. He seeds his dishes with produce from every corner of France—rare local vegetables, fish from the coasts—and dishes incorporate cardoons, turnips, celery, turbot, cuttlefish, and Bresse fowl. Though many dishes are light, Ducasse isn't afraid of lard, as he proves by his thick, oozing slabs of pork grilled to a crisp.

In the Hotel Plaza Athénée, 25 av. Montaigne. © 01-53-67-66-65. Fax 01-53-67-65-12. Reservations required 6 weeks in advance. Main courses 150€–190€; fixed-price menus 250€–280€. AE, DC, MC, V. Thurs–Fri noon–2pm; Mon–Fri 8–10:30pm. Closed mid-July to Aug 29 and Dec 21–31. Métro: Alma-Marceau.

Taillevent 𝕬𝕬𝕬 MODERN & TRADITIONAL FRENCH   This is the Parisian *ne plus ultra* of gastronomy. Taillevent opened in 1946 and has climbed steadily in excellence; today it ranks as Paris's outstanding all-around restaurant, challenged only by Lucas-Carton and Pierre Gagnaire. It's in a grand 19th-century town house off the Champs-Elysées, with paneled rooms and crystal chandeliers. The place is small, as the owner wishes, since it permits him to give personal attention to every facet of the operation and maintain a discreet atmosphere. You might begin with a *boudin* (sausage) of Breton lobster a la Nage, cream of watercress soup with sevruga caviar, or duck liver with spice bread and ginger. Main courses include red snapper with black olives, Scottish salmon cooked in sea salt with a sauce of olive oil and lemons, and cassoulet of crayfish.

15 rue Lamennais. © 01-44-95-15-01. Fax 01-42-25-95-18. Reservations required 4–6 weeks in advance. Main courses 44€–102€, *menu dégustation* 130€. AE, DC, MC, V. Mon–Fri noon–2:30pm and 7–10pm. Closed Aug. Métro: George-V.

Expensive
Buddha Bar ✦ FRENCH/PACIFIC RIM   This place remains Paris's restaurant of the moment, even though it's been around for a while. A location near the Champs-Elysées and place de la Concorde, and an allegiance to a fusion of French, Asian, and Californian cuisines, attract trendy diners devoted to the whims of fashion. The vast dining room is presided over by a giant Buddha, and the culinary theme combines Japanese sashimi, Vietnamese spring rolls, lacquered duck, sautéed shrimp with black bean sauce, grilled chicken skewers with orange sauce, sweet-and-sour spareribs, and crackling squab a l'orange. There are two seatings for dinner: 7 to 9pm and 10:30pm to 12:30am. Many come here just for a drink in the carefully lacquered bar, upstairs from the street-level dining room.

8 rue Boissy d'Anglas. ℂ 01-53-05-90-00. Reservations required far in advance. Main courses 60€–72€. AE, MC, V. Mon–Fri noon–3pm; daily 7pm–12:30am. Métro: Concorde.

L'Angle du Faubourg ✦✦ FRENCH   Throughout the 1980s and early 1990s, a reservation at the Restaurant Taillevent was sought after by diplomats, billionaires, and *demi-mondains* from around Europe. In 2001, the owner and chef, M. Vrinat, opened a cost-conscious bistro that capitalized on Taillevent's reputation, but at much lower prices. Lunches here tend to be efficient, relatively quick, and businesslike, while dinners are more leisurely, even romantic. Expect an ultra-modern dining room in tones of soft red and pink, additional seating in the cellar, and a menu that simplifies the lofty culinary ideas of Taillevent. The best examples include cream of beet soup; marinated salmon; a risotto whose ingredients change; and a grilled, low-fat version of *daurade,* served with a sweet-and-sour sauce, appreciated by the many diet-conscious *photo-modèles* who stop in between bouts of shopping. Dessert might be an old-fashioned rice pudding.

195 rue du Faubourg St-Honoré. ℂ 01-40-74-20-20. Reservations required. Main courses 30€–40€; fixed-price menu 60€. AE, DC, MC, V. Mon–Fri noon–2:30pm and 7 10:30pm. Métro: Terne.

Spoon, Food & Wine ✦ INTERNATIONAL   This hypermodern venture of star chef Alain Ducasse is hailed as a "restaurant for the millennium" and condemned by some as surreal and a bit absurd. Despite that, there can be a wait of 2 weeks for a dinner reservation. The prevailing sense is that this upscale but relatively affordable restaurant might be the least pretentious and most hip of any of Ducasse's ventures. The décor of the somewhat claustrophobic dining room has both Parisian and Californian references, and the cuisine—whose menu changes every 2 months—roams the world. Examples include grilled tuna steak with satay sauce; deliberately undercooked grilled squid (part of it will evoke a sushi dish) with curry sauce; and roasted pigeon with an Italian *dolce-forte* (sweet-and-sour) sauce. Vegetarians appreciate stir-fried dishes in which you can mix and match up to 15 ingredients. Desserts feature Parisian versions of such U.S.–inspired dishes as cheesecake and doughnuts drenched with bitter chocolate.

In the Hôtel Marignan-Elysée, 14 rue Marignan. ℂ 01-40-76-34-44. Reservations recommended 2 weeks in advance. Main courses 50€–70€. Mon–Fri noon–2pm and 7–11pm. AE, DC, V. Métro: Franklin-D.-Roosevelt.

RIGHT BANK: 9TH, 10TH & 12TH ARRONDISSEMENTS
Expensive
Au Trou Gascon ✦✦✦ GASCONY   One of Paris's most acclaimed chefs, Alain Dutournier lures fashionable palates to an un-chic area. His parents mortgaged their Gascony inn to allow Dutournier to open an early-1900s bistro in a little-known part of the 12th. Word spread of a savant in the kitchen who practiced authentic *cuisine moderne.* Dutournier's wife, Nicole, is the welcoming

hostess. You can start with duck foie gras cooked in a terrine or Gascony-cured ham. The best main courses include fresh tuna with braised cabbage, a superb cassoulet, and chicken from the Chalosse region of Landes, which Dutournier roasts and serves in its own drippings.

40 rue Taine. ℂ 01-43-44-34-26. Reservations required far in advance. Main courses 15€–20€; fixed-price lunch 36€. AE, DC, MC, V. Mon–Fri noon–2pm; Mon–Sat 7:30–10pm. Closed Aug. Métro: Daumesnil.

Wally Le Saharien ALGERIAN   Head to this dining room—lined with desert photos and tribal artifacts crafted from clay, wood, and weavings—for an insight into the spicy, slow-cooked cuisine that fueled the colonial expansion of France into North Africa. The fixed-price dinner menu begins with a trio of starters: a spicy soup, stuffed and grilled sardines, and a savory *pastilla* of pigeon in puff pastry. This can be followed by any of several kinds of couscous or a *méchouia* (slow-cooked tart) of lamb dusted with an optional coating of sugar, according to your taste. *Merguez,* the cumin-laden spicy sausage of the North African world, factors importantly into any meal, as do homemade (usually honey-infused) pastries. End your meal with traditional mint-flavored tea.

36 rue Rodier. ℂ 01-42-85-51-90. Reservations recommended. A la carte main courses (available only at lunch) 12€–15€; fixed-price dinner 29€. MC, V. Tues–Sat noon–2pm; Mon–Sat 7–10pm. Métro: Anvers.

Moderate

Brasserie Flo 🎰 ALSATIAN   This remote restaurant is hard to find, but once you arrive (after walking through passageway after passageway), you'll see that *fin-de-siècle* Paris lives on. The restaurant opened in 1860 and has changed its decor very little since. The specialty is *la formidable choucroute* (a mound of sauerkraut with boiled ham, bacon, and sausage) for two. The onion soup and sole meunière are always good, as are the warm foie gras and guinea hen with lentils. Look for the *plats du jour,* ranging from roast pigeon to veal fricassee with sorrel.

7 cour des Petites-Ecuries. ℂ 01-47-70-13-59. Reservations recommended. Main courses 15€–27€. Fixed-price menus 26€ lunch, 31€ dinner. AE, DC, MC, V. Daily noon–3pm and 7pm–1:30am. Métro: Château d'Eau or Strasbourg-St-Denis.

RIGHT BANK: 17TH ARRONDISSEMENT
Very Expensive

Guy Savoy 🎰🎰 TRADITIONAL FRENCH   One of the hottest chefs in Europe, Guy Savoy serves the kind of food he likes to eat, prepared with consummate skill. Although the superb meals comprise as many as nine courses, portions are small; you won't necessarily be satiated at the end. The menu changes with the seasons but may include a cream soup of lentils and crayfish; duckling foie gras with aspic and gray salt; or sea bass grilled in a salt shell and served with a sauce of sweet herbs. If you come in the right season, you may have a chance to order game. Savoy is fascinated with mushrooms, serving, for example, a delectable pan-fried combination of mussels and wild mushrooms.

18 rue Troyon. ℂ 01-43-80-40-61. Fax 01-43-80-36-22. Reservations required 1 week in advance. Main courses 52€–105€; *menu dégustation* (tasting menu) 250€. AE, DC, MC, V. Mon–Fri noon–2pm; Mon–Sat 7:30–10:30pm. Métro: Charles de Gaulle-étoile or Ternes.

LEFT BANK: 5TH ARRONDISSEMENT
Very Expensive

La Tour d'Argent 🎰🎰 TRADITIONAL FRENCH   This penthouse restaurant, a national institution, serves up a panoramic view over the Seine and Notre-Dame. Although its reputation as the best in Paris has been eclipsed, dining here remains an unsurpassed event. A restaurant of some sort has stood on this site since 1582: Mme de Sévigné refers to a cafe here in her letters, and Dumas used it in one of his novels. The fame of La Tour d'Argent spread during its ownership by Frédéric Delair, who started the practice of issuing certificates to diners who ordered *caneton* (pressed duckling). The birds are numbered: The first was served to Edward VII in 1890, and now they number over one million! Under the sharp eye of owner Claude Terrail, the cooking is superb and the service impeccable. A good part of the menu is devoted to duck, but the kitchen knows how to prepare other dishes. Start with the pheasant consommé or pikeperch quenelles André Terrail; follow either with the ravioli with foie gras or filet of sole Cardinal with shrimp sauce.

15–17 quai de la Tournelle. ℰ 01-43-54-23-31. Fax 01-44-07-12-04. Reservations required far in advance. Main courses 45€–97€; fixed-price lunch 65€. AE, DC, MC, V. Tues–Sun noon–1:15pm and 7:30–9pm. Métro: St-Michel or Pont Marie.

Moderate

Marty ⊛ *(Finds* MODERN FRENCH Charming, with a stone-trimmed decor that's authentic to the era (1913) it was established, this restaurant has been "discovered" by new generations of restaurant-goers. Named after its founders, Etienne and Marthe Marty, its fame now extends beyond the 5th arrondissement. Food is savory, satisfying, and unfussy. If someone opts to seat you on one of the hideaway tables on the mezzanine, don't resist, since views from here sweep over the entire Human Comedy unfolding above and below you. Begin your meal with a tartare of sea bream flavored with anise and lime; lobster ravioli with sherry vinegar; or fresh oysters. Continue with a *suprême* of guinea fowl with a vegetable moussaka; a platter that combines grilled squid with grilled strips of red mullet; or perhaps a brochette of hake and salmon, served with a mustard-flavored olive tapenade. Dessert might be a soup of red fruit with orange-flavored liqueur.

20 av. des Gobelins. ℰ 01-43-31-39-51. Main courses 20€–50€. Set menu 33€. AE, DC, MC, V. Daily noon–midnight. Métro: Gobelins.

Inexpensive

Coco de Mer ⊛ *(Finds* SEYCHELLE ISLANDS The theme of this restaurant tugs at the emotions of those Parisians who have spent their holidays on the beaches of the Seychelles in the Indian Ocean. It contains several dining rooms, one of which is outfitted like a beach, with a sand-covered floor, replicas of palm trees, and a scattering of conch shells. Menu items feature such exotic dishes as tartare of tuna flavored with ginger, olive oil, salt, and pepper; and smoked swordfish, served as a carpaccio or in thin slices with mango mousse and a spicy sauce. Main courses focus on fish, including a species of red snapper *(boirzoes)* imported from the Seychelles. Dessert might be a *crème de banana gratiné.*

34 bd. St-Marcel. ℰ 01-47-07-06-64. Reservations recommended. Main courses 19€–23€; set menus 24€–28€. AE, DC, MC, V. Tues–Sat noon–3pm; Mon–Sat 7:30pm–midnight. Métro: Les Gobelins or St-Marcel.

LEFT BANK: 6TH ARRONDISSEMENT
Expensive

Restaurant d'Hélène/Salon d'Hélène ⊛⊛⊛ SOUTHWESTERN FRENCH Hélène d'Arroze is the most famous female chef in Paris, a Basque-born *wunderkind* whose southwestern French cuisine is a superb modern take on a classic. Be very clear before you enter this restaurant about what you want: The upstairs dining room (Le Restaurant d'Hélène, where tables are round and outfitted with elaborate napery) is more formal, expensive, and sedate than the bistro (Le Salon d'Hélène). In both areas, expect a pop-influenced decor of bright colors and relatively slow service. Upstairs, menus are artfully composed and presented as part of fixed-price meals that contain, among others, a confit of foie gras with grilled apples; a salad of white beans and clams; and roast wild duck stuffed with foie gras and truffles. On street level, food focuses on an array of *plats du jour* (skate Grenobloise with lemon and capers) and tapas, which might include raw marinated tuna with Basque-derived red pepper sauce, or cannelloni gratineed with Basque sheep's-milk cheese and smoked Basque ham.

4 rue d'Assas. ℂ **01-42-22-00-11.** Reservations required. In restaurant: fixed-price menus 65€–135€. In Salon: fixed-price lunch 35€; plat du jour 30€; tapas 7€–15€. AE, MC, V. Tues–Sat 12:30–2:15pm and 7:30–10pm. Métro: Sèvres-Babylone.

Moderate
Ze Kitchen Galerie ⭐ *Finds* FRENCH/INTERNATIONAL   The owner and head chef of this restaurant was trained in the lofty plateau of *haute* Parisian gastronomy under the directive of culinary czar Guy Savoy. Since William Ledeuil established the place in 2001, he's attracted the likes of First Lady Laura Bush, who dined here in 2002, accompanied by a daunting staff of security guards. The setting is a loft space in an antique building, with an open-to-view "showcase"-style kitchen, and a color scheme of bold, primary colors. Main courses are divided into meats and fish that are usually cooked *"a la plancha"* (on a flat-top grill). The best examples include platters of oysters, mussels, and sea urchins served with an herb sauce and *crostini;* or grilled shoulder of wild boar with tamarind sauce.

4 rue des Grands-Augustins. ℂ **01-44-32-00-32.** Reservations recommended. Main courses 18€–23€; set-price lunch, with wine, 21€–32€. AE, DC, MC, V. Metro: Saint-Michel.

Inexpensive
Crémerie-Restaurant Polidor ⭐ *Kids* TRADITIONAL FRENCH   Crémerie Polidor is the most traditional bistro in the Odéon area, serving *cuisine familiale.* Its name dates from the early 1900s, when it specialized in frosted cream desserts, but the restaurant can trace its history back to 1845. The Crémerie was André Gide's favorite, and Joyce, Hemingway, Valéry, Artaud, and Kerouac also dined here. The place is still frequented by students and artists, who head for the rear. Peer beyond the lace curtains and brass hat racks to see drawers where repeat customers lock up their cloth napkins. Overworked but smiling waitresses serve the 19th-century cuisine. Try the pumpkin soup followed by *boeuf bourguignon,* Basque-style chicken, or *blanquette de veau.* For dessert, get a chocolate, raspberry, or lemon tart—the best in all Paris.

41 rue Monsieur-le-Prince. ℂ **01-43-26-95-34.** Main courses 7€–15€. Fixed-price menus (Mon–Fri) 9€ lunch, 18€ dinner. No credit cards. Daily noon–2:30pm and 7pm–12:30am; Sun 7–11pm. Métro: Odéon.

LEFT BANK: 7TH & 14TH ARRONDISSEMENTS
Very Expensive
L'Arpège ⭐⭐⭐ MODERN FRENCH   L'Arpège is best known for Alain Passard's specialties—no restaurant in the 7th serves better food. Amid a modern decor of etched glass, burnished steel, monochromatic oil paintings, and pearwood paneling, you can enjoy specialties like a couscous of vegetables and shellfish; lobster braised in the yellow wine of the Jura; pigeon roasted with almonds and honey-flavored mead; and carpaccio of crayfish with a caviar-flavored cream sauce. While Passard is loathe to include red meat on his menus, it does appear from time to time, in dishes of Japan-derived Kobe beef; and venison during late autumn and early winter. But he focuses on fish, shellfish, poultry, and—his current passion—vegetables. These, he elevates to levels unequalled by any other

The Top Cafes

Whatever your pleasure—reading, meeting a lover, writing your memoirs, or drinking yourself into oblivion—you can do it at a French cafe.

Across from the Centre Pompidou, avant-garde **Café Beaubourg,** 100 rue St-Martin, 4e (☎ **01-48-87-63-96;** Métro: Rambuteau or Hôtel-de-Ville), boasts soaring concrete columns and a minimalist decor by the architect Christian de Portzamparc. In summer, tables are set on the sprawling terrace. The cafe is open Sunday through Thursday from 8am to 1am and Friday and Saturday from 8am to 2am.

Next door, the legendary **Deux Magots,** 6 place St-Germain-des-Prés, 6e (☎ **01-45-48-55-25;** Métro: St-Germain-des-Prés), is still the hangout for sophisticates and a tourist favorite in summer. Inside are two Asian statues that give the cafe its name. It's open daily from 7:30am to 1:30am.

Fouquet's, 99 av. des Champs-Elysées, 8e (☎ **01-47-23-50-00;** Métro: George-V), is the premier cafe on the Champs-Elysées. Outside, cafe tables are separated from the sidewalk by a barricade of potted flowers. Inside are a grill room and a restaurant. The cafe and grill room are open daily from 8am to 2am; the restaurant is open daily from noon to 3pm and 7pm to midnight.

Does today's generation have a cafe to equal the Lost Generation's La Coupole? Perhaps it's the ultramodern **Café Cosmos,** 101 bd. Du Montparnasse, 6e (☎ **01-43-26-74-36;** Métro: Vavin). Here you might rub elbows with a French film star or a movie executive. The cafe features wooden tables, black leather chairs, and black clothing in winter—the perfect backdrop for smoked salmon or a light meal. It's open daily from 8am to 2am.

chef in Paris. The signature dessert is a candied tomato stuffed with 12 kinds of dried and fresh fruit, served with anise-flavored ice cream.

84 rue de Varenne. ☎ **01-47-05-09-06.** Fax 01-44-18-98-39. Reservations required far in advance. Main courses 40€–160€; *menu dégustation* (tasting menu) 300€. AE, DC, MC, V. Mon–Fri 12:30–2:30pm and 8–10pm. Métro: Varenne.

Expensive

Le Violon d'Ingres ★★★ TRADITIONAL & MODERN FRENCH   This restaurant is Paris's pièce de résistance. Chef/owner Christian Constant is "the new Robuchon." Those fortunate enough to dine in Violon's warm atmosphere rave about the artistic dishes. They range from pan-fried foie gras with gingerbread and spinach salad to more elegant main courses like lobster ravioli with crushed vine-ripened tomatoes; roasted veal in a light and creamy milk sauce served with tender spring vegetables; and even a selection from the rotisserie, like spit-roasted leg of lamb rubbed with fresh garlic and thyme. A well-chosen selection of wine is offered. The service is charming and discreet.

135 rue St-Dominique. ☎ **01-45-55-15-05.** Fax 01-45-55-48-42. Reservations required at least 3–4 days in advance. Main courses 40€–47€; *menu dégustation* (tasting menu) 110€. AE, MC, V. Mon–Sat 12:30–2:30pm and 7:30–11:30pm.

Moderate

La Cagouille ☆ *Finds* FRENCH/SEAFOOD Don't expect to find meat at this temple of seafood—owner Gérard Allamandou refuses to feature it. Everything about La Cagouille is a testimonial to a modern version of the culinary arts of La Charente, the flat sandy district on the Atlantic south of Bordeaux. In a trio of oak-sheathed dining rooms, you'll sample seafood prepared as naturally as possible, with no fancy sauces or elaborate cooking techniques. Allamandou's preferred fish is red mullet, which might appear sautéed in a bland oil or baked in rock salt. The name of the place derives from the regional symbol of La Charente: the sea snail, whose preparation here is elevated to a fine culinary art.

10–12 place Constantine-Brancusi, 23 rue de l'Ouest. ℂ **01-43-22-09-01.** Reservations recommended. Main courses 20€–35€; fixed-price menu 25€–40€. AE, V. Daily noon–2:30pm and 5:30–10:30pm. Métro: Gaîté.

SEEING THE SIGHTS IN THE CITY OF LIGHT

The best way to discover Paris is on foot. Walk along the grand avenue des Champs-Elysées, tour the quays of the Seine, wander around Ile de la Cité and Ile St-Louis, browse through the countless shops and stalls, wander through the famous squares and parks. Each turn will open a new vista.

SIGHTSEEING SUGGESTIONS FOR FIRST-TIME VISITORS

If You Have 1 Day Get up early and find a cafe for a typical Parisian breakfast of coffee and croissants. The two most popular museums are the **Louvre** and the **Musée d'Orsay;** the three most enduring monuments are the **Eiffel Tower,** the **Arc de Triomphe,** and **Notre-Dame.** If it's a toss-up between the Louvre and the d'Orsay, we'd make it the Louvre if you're a first-timer; if it's a toss-up between monuments, we'd make it the Eiffel Tower, for the view of the city. If your day is too short to visit museums, then spend your time strolling—the streets of Paris are live theater. The most elegant place for a walk is Ile St-Louis, filled with 17th-century mansions. On the **Left Bank,** wander St-Germain-des-Prés or around place St-Michel, the heart of the student quarter. As the sun sets over Paris, head for **Notre-Dame** along the banks of the Seine, and watch the shadows fall over Paris and the lights come on for the night.

If You Have 2 Days Spend your second day taking in the Right Bank. Begin at the **Arc de Triomphe** and stroll down the **Champs-Elysées,** the main boulevard of Paris, until you reach the Egyptian obelisk at the **place de la Concorde.** The place de la Concorde— where some of France's most notable figures met the guillotine— affords terrific views of the **Madeleine,** the **Palais Bourbon,** the Arc de Triomphe, and the Louvre. Then we'd suggest a rest stop in the **Jardin de Tuileries,** or lunch in a Right Bank bistro. After exploring the heart of elegant, monumental Paris, why not go for a walk on the seedy side? Our favorite is a stroll along rue des Rosiers in the **Marais,** a street that's the heart of the Jewish community. After a rest, follow Hemingway's footsteps and head down to **Montparnasse** for a lively dinner.

If You Have 3 Days This is the day to follow your special interests.

Many will want to select the **Centre Pompidou.** You might explore the **Musée Picasso** as well, along with some of the galleries of the Marais. At midday, head for lunch to Paris's most charming square, **place des Vosges.** Reserve the afternoon for the **Ile de la Cité,** where you can see the **Conciergerie,** where Marie Antoinette and others were held prisoner, and the **Sainte-Chapelle** in the Palais de Justice with its stunning stained glass. For dinner, we suggest a bistro in Le Marais.

If You Have 4 or 5 Days On your fourth day, go on your own or take an organized tour to **Versailles.** Then head back to the city for dinner and an evening stroll in the **Latin Quarter.** On your fifth day, devote at least a morning to **Montmarte,** on top of the highest of Paris's seven hills. Visit the **Basilica du Sacré-Coeur,** for the view if nothing else.

THE TOP MUSEUMS

Musée du Louvre ⚜⚜⚜   The Louvre is one of the world's largest and greatest museums. The $1.2-billion Grand Louvre Project, a 15-year-long project, is officially complete, but refurbishment of individual galleries and paintings continues. For up-to-the-minute data on what is open or about to open, you can check out the Louvre's website at www.louvre.fr. The collection is staggering. You'll have to resign yourself to missing some masterpieces because you simply can't see everything. People on one of those "Paris-in-a-day" tours race to glimpse the *Mona Lisa* and the *Venus de Milo.* Those with an extra 5 minutes go in pursuit of *Winged Victory.* The good news is that after 2 centuries of living here, the *Mona Lisa* has her own special room.

To enter the Louvre, you pass through the 21m (71-ft.) **I. M. Pei glass pyramid** in the courtyard. *Tips on tickets:* If you don't want to wait in line at the entrance of the pyramid or use the automatic ticket machines, you can order tickets over the phone (see below) with a credit card. You can also order advance tickets (and take a virtual tour of the museum) at the website. Tickets can be mailed to you in the U.S., or you can pick them up at any FNAC (a Barnes & Noble–type books, music, and electronics chain) location in Paris.

Pressed for time? Take a **guided tour** (in English), which lasts about 90 minutes. These start under the pyramid at the station marked ACCEIL DES GROUPES.

The collections are divided into seven departments: Asian antiquities; Egyptian antiquities; Greek, Etruscan, and Roman antiquities; sculpture; paintings; prints and drawings; and objets d'art. **The Grand Galerie,** a 180m (600-ft.) hall opening onto the Seine, is dedicated to mostly Italian paintings from the 1400s to the 1700s, including works by Raphael and Leonardo da Vinci.

The **Richelieu Wing** houses the collection of northern European and French paintings, decorative arts, French sculpture, Asian antiquities (a rich collection of Islamic art), and the grand salons of Napoléon III. Of the Greek and Roman

---

Tips **The Handy Museum Pass**

La Carte Musées et Monuments (Museum and Monuments Pass) is available at any of the museums that honor it or at any branch of the Paris Tourist Office. It offers entrance to the collections of 70 monuments and museums in Paris and the Ile de France. A 1-day pass is 15€, a 3-day pass 30€, and a 5-day pass 45€.

Paris Attractions

Arc de Triomphe **5**
Basilique du Sacré-Coeur **24**
Bois de Boulogne **2**
Cathédrale Notre-Dame **17**
Centre Pompidou **20**
Cemetière du Père-Lachaise **22**
Conciergerie **19**

Eiffel Tower **3**
Hôtel des Invalides **1**
Jardin des Tuileries **8**
Jardin du Luxembourg **12**
Latin Quarter **14**
Montmartre **23**
Musée National d'Art Moderne **4**

Musée d'Orsay **9**
Musée du Louvre **10**
Musée National du Moyen
 Age/Musée de Cluny **11**
Musée Picasso **21**
Panthéon **13**
Parc Monceau **6**

Place de la Bastille **15**
Place de la Concorde **7**
Place des Vosges **16**
Ste-Chapelle **18**

ⓘ Information
⊠ Post Office
— Railway

antiquities, the most notable (aside from *Venus* and *Winged Victory*) are fragments of the Parthenon's frieze.

When you tire of strolling the galleries, you might like a pick-me-up at the Richelieu Wing's **Café Richelieu** or **Café Marly,** 93 rue de Rivoli, 1er (☎ **01-49-26-06-60**). Boasting Napoléon III opulence, the Marly offers a perfect oasis. Try a cafe crème, a club sandwich, a pastry, or something from the bistro menu.

34–36 quai du Louvre, 1er. Main entrance in the glass pyramid, cour Napoléon. ☎ **01-40-20-53-17;** 01-40-20-51-51 for recorded message; 08-03-80-88-03 for advance credit-card sales. www.louvre.fr. Admission 7.50€ before 3pm, 5€ after 3pm and on Sun, free for children 17 and under, free 1st Sun of every month. Mon and Wed 9am–9:45pm; Thurs–Sun 9am–6pm. (Parts of the museum begin to close at 5:30pm.) 1½-hr. English-language tours leave Mon (short tour only) and Wed–Sat at various times for 3€; free for children 12 and under with museum ticket. Métro: Palais Royal-Musée du Louvre.

Musée d'Orsay ✯✯✯

The neoclassical Gare d'Orsay train station has been transformed into one of the world's great museums. It contains an important collection devoted to the pivotal years from 1848 to 1914. Across the Seine from the Louvre and the Tuileries, it is a repository of works by the Impressionists as well as the Symbolists, Pointillists, Realists, and late Romantics. Artists represented include van Gogh, Manet, Monet, Degas, and Renoir. It houses thousands of sculptures and paintings across 80 galleries, plus Belle Epoque furniture, photographs, objets d'art, architectural models, and a cinema.

One of Renoir's most joyous paintings is here: *Moulin de la Galette* (1876). Another celebrated work is by James McNeill Whistler—*Arrangement in Gray and Black: Portrait of the Painter's Mother.* The most famous piece in the museum is Manet's 1863 *Déjeuner sur l'herbe* (Picnic on the Grass).

1 rue de Bellechasse or 62 rue de Lille, 7e. ☎ **01-40-49-48-14.** www.musee-orsay.fr. Admission 7€ adults, 5€ ages 18–24 and seniors, free for children 17 and under. Tues–Wed and Fri–Sat 10am–6:30pm; Thurs 10am–9:45pm (June 20–Sept 20 9am–6:30pm); Sun 9am–6:30pm. Métro: Solférino. RER: Musée d'Orsay.

Musée Picasso ✯✯✯

This museum offers an unparalleled view of the artist's career, including his fabled gaunt blue figures and harlequins. The world's greatest Picasso collection, acquired by the state in lieu of $50 million in inheritance taxes, consists of 203 paintings, 158 sculptures, 16 collages, 19 bas-reliefs, 88 ceramics, and more than 1,500 sketches and 1,600 engravings, plus 30 notebooks. These works span some 75 years of Picasso's life and changing styles. The range of paintings includes a 1901 self-portrait and embraces such masterpieces as *Le Baiser* (The Kiss). Another masterpiece is *Reclining Nude and the Man with a Guitar.*

In the Hôtel Salé, 5 rue de Thorigny, 3e. ☎ **01-42-71-25-21.** www.paris.org/Musees/Picasso. Admission 5€ adults, 3€ ages 17–25 and seniors, free for children 18 and under. Year-round Wed–Mon 9:30am–5:30pm. Métro: St-Paul, Filles du Calvaire, or Chemin Vert.

Centre Pompidou ✯✯✯

Relaunched in 2000, in what was called in the 1970s "the most avant-garde building in the world," the newly restored Pompidou Centre is packing in the art-loving crowds again. This center for 20th-century art, designed by Richard Rogers and Renzo Piano, opened in 1977 and became the focus of controversy. Its bold exoskeletal architecture and the brightly painted pipes and ducts crisscrossing its transparent facade (green for water, red for heat, blue for air, and yellow for electricity) were jarring in the old Beaubourg neighborhood. The Centre Pompidou encompasses four separate attractions. Of them, the **Musée National d'Art Moderne (National Museum of Modern Art)** offers a large collection of 20th-century art. With some 40,000 works, this is the big draw, although only some 850 works can be displayed at one time. If you want to view some real charmers, see Alexander Calder's 1926 *Josephine Baker*, one of his earlier versions of the mobile, an art form he invented. Marcel Duchamp's *Valise* is a collection of miniature reproductions of his fabled Dada sculptures and drawings; they're displayed in a carrying case.

Finally, you can visit a re-creation of **l'Atelier Brancusi,** the jazz-age studio of Romanian sculptor Brancusi; it's configured as a mini-museum slightly separate from the rest of the action.

Place Georges-Pompidou, 4e. © **01-44-78-12-33.** www.centrepompidou.fr. Admission 6€ adults, 4€ students, free for under age 18. Special exhibits 7€ adults, 5€ students, free for under age 13. Wed–Mon 11am–9pm. Métro: Rambuteau, Hôtel de Ville, or Châtelet–Les Halles.

ON THE CHAMPS-ELYSEES

Arc de Triomphe ★★★   At the western end of the Champs-Elysées, the Arc de Triomphe is the largest triumphal arch in the world, about 49m (163 ft.) high and 44m (147 ft.) wide. Don't try crossing the square to reach it! Take the underground passage. With a dozen streets radiating from the "Star," the traffic circle is vehicular roulette. Commissioned by Napoléon in 1806 to commemorate his Grande Armée's victories, the arch wasn't completed until 1836, under Louis-Philippe. Of the sculptures decorating the monument, the best known is Rude's *Marseillaise*, also called *The Departure of the Volunteers*. J. P. Cortot's *Triumph of Napoléon in 1810*, along with the *Resistance of 1814* and *Peace of 1815*, both by Etex, also adorn the facade. The arch is engraved with the names of hundreds of generals who commanded troops in Napoléonic victories. You can take an elevator or climb the stairway to the top, where there's an exhibition hall with lithographs and photos depicting the arch throughout its history. From the observation deck, you have a panoramic view of the Champs-Elysées as well as such landmarks as the Louvre, the Eiffel Tower, and Sacré-Coeur.

Place Charles de Gaulle-étoile, 16e. © **01-55-37-73-77.** www.monuments.fr Admission 6.50€ adults, 5€ ages 18–25, free for ages 17 and under. Apr–Sept daily 9:30am–11pm; Oct–Mar daily 10am–10:30pm. Métro: Charles de Gaulle-étoile. Bus: 22, 30, 31, 52, 73, or 92.

ILE DE LA CITE: WHERE PARIS WAS BORN

Medieval Paris, that architectural blending of grotesquerie and Gothic beauty, began on this island in the Seine. Explore as much of it as you can, but if you're in a hurry, try to visit at least Notre-Dame, the Sainte-Chapelle, and the Conciergerie.

Notre-Dame ★★★   For 6 centuries, it has stood as a Gothic masterpiece of the Middle Ages. You'll have to walk around the entire structure to appreciate this "vast symphony of stone" with its classic flying buttresses. Better yet, cross the bridge to the Left Bank and view it from the quay. From the square parvis (the courtyard in front), you can view the trio of 13th-century sculpted portals. On the left, the Portal of the Virgin depicts the signs of the zodiac and the Virgin's coronation. The central Portal of the Last Judgment is divided into three levels: the first shows Vices and Virtues; the second, Christ and his Apostles; and the third, Christ in triumph after the Resurrection. On the right is the Portal of Ste-Anne, depicting such scenes as the Virgin enthroned with Child. It's Notre-Dame's most perfect piece of sculpture. Over the central portal is a remarkable rose window, 9m (31 ft.) in diameter, forming a showcase for a statue of the Virgin and Child. Equally interesting is the Cloister Portal (around on the left), with its 13th-century Virgin, a unique survivor of many that originally adorned the facade. (Unfortunately, the Child she's holding is decapitated.)

If possible, view the interior at sunset. Of the three giant medallions that warm the austere cathedral, the north rose window in the transept, from the mid–13th century, is best. To visit those gargoyles immortalized by Victor Hugo (where Quasimodo lurked), you have to scale steps leading to the twin square towers, rising to a height of 68m (225 ft.). Once here, you can inspect those devils (some sticking out their tongues), hobgoblins, and birds of prey.

Approached through a garden behind Notre-Dame is the **Memorial des Martyrs Français de la Déportation.** This memorial honors the French martyrs of World War II, deported to camps like Auschwitz and Buchenwald. In blood red are the words (in French): "Forgive, but don't forget." It's open Monday through Friday from 8:30am to 9:45pm, Saturday and Sunday from 9am to 9:45pm. Admission is free.

6 place du parvis Notre-Dame, 4e. ℂ 01-42-34-56-10. www.paris.org/Monuments/NDame. Free admission to cathedral; towers 5€ adults, 4€ ages 18–25 and seniors, free for children under 18; treasury 3€ adults, 2€ ages 12–25 and seniors, free for children under 12. Cathedral open year-round daily 8am–6:45pm. Towers and crypt Apr–Sept daily 9:30am–6pm; Oct–Mar daily 10am–5:15pm. Museum Wed and Sat–Sun 2:30–5pm. Treasury Mon–Sat 9:30–11:30am and 1–5:45pm. Métro: Cité or St-Michel. RER: St-Michel.

Sainte Chapelle ✦✦✦   Come here if for no other reason than to see one of the world's greatest examples of Flamboyant Gothic architecture—"the pearl among them all," as Proust called it—and brilliant stained-glass windows with a lacelike delicacy. Sainte Chapelle is Paris's second most important monument of the Middle Ages (after Notre-Dame); it was erected to enshrine relics from the First Crusade, including the Crown of Thorns, two pieces from the True Cross, and the Roman lance that pierced the side of Christ.

Viewed on a bright day, the 15 stained-glass windows depicting Bible scenes seem to glow ruby red and Chartres blue. The walls consist almost entirely of the glass. Built in only 5 years, beginning in 1246, the chapel has two levels. You enter through the lower chapel, supported by flying buttresses and ornamented with fleurs-de-lis. The servants of the palace used the lower chapel, and the upper chamber was for the king and his courtiers; the latter is reached by ascending a narrow spiral staircase. Ste-Chapelle stages **concerts** in summer, with tickets at 19€ to 25€. Call ℂ 01-42-77-65-65 from 11am to 6pm daily for details.

Palais de Justice, 4 bd. du Palais, 1er. ℂ 01-53-73-78-50. www.monum.fr. Free admission. Apr–Sept daily 9:30am–6:30pm; Oct–Mar daily 10am–5pm. Métro: Cité, St-Michel, or Châtelet–Les Halles. RER: St-Michel.

THE EIFFEL TOWER & ENVIRONS ✦✦✦

From place du Trocadéro, you can step between the wings of the Palais de Chaillot and gaze out on a panoramic view. At your feet lie the Jardins du Trocadéro. Directly in front of you, the Pont d'Iéna spans the Seine, leading to the immensity of the Tour Eiffel. Beyond, stretching as far as your eye can see, is the Champ-de-Mars, a garden with arches, grottoes, lakes, and cascades.

Eiffel Tower ✦✦✦   This may be the single most recognizable structure in the world—it's the symbol of Paris. Gustave-Alexandre Eiffel built it for the Universal Exhibition of 1889. The tower, including its 17m (55-ft.) TV antenna, is 317m (1,056 ft.) tall. Its open-framework construction ushered in the almost-unlimited possibilities of steel construction, paving the way for skyscrapers.

You can visit the tower in three stages: Taking the elevator to the first landing, you'll have a view over the rooftops of Paris. There's a cinema, museum, restaurants, and a bar open year-round. The second landing provides a panoramic look at the city (on this level is Le Jules Verne restaurant). The third landing offers the best view, allowing you to identify monuments and buildings.

To get to **Le Jules Verne** (© 01-45-55-61-44), take the private south foundation elevator. You can enjoy an aperitif in the piano bar, then take a seat at one of the dining room's tables, all of which provide an inspiring view. Reservations are recommended. *Insider tip:* The least expensive way to see the tower is to walk up the first two floors for 3€. You also bypass the long lines for the elevator.

Champ de Mars, 7e. © 01-44-11-23-23. www.tour-eiffel.fr. Admission to 1st landing 3.65€, 2nd landing 6.90€, 3rd landing 9.90€. Stairs to 2nd floor 3€. Sept–May daily 9:30am–11pm; June–Aug daily 9am–midnight. Fall and winter, stairs open only to 6:30pm. Métro: Trocadéro, Ecole Militaire, or Bir-Hakeim. RER: Champ de Mars–Tour Eiffel.

Hôtel des Invalides (Napoléon's Tomb) ✮✮✮

The glory of the French military lives on in the **Musée de l'Armée.** Included in the collections (begun in 1794) are Viking swords, Burgundian basinets, 14th-century blunderbusses, Balkan khandjars, American Browning machine guns, war pitchforks, salamander-engraved Renaissance serpentines, musketoons, and grenadiers. As a sardonic touch, there's even General Daumesnil's wooden leg. There are suits of armor worn by kings and dignitaries. The famous "armor suit of the lion" was made for François I. The displays of swords are among the world's finest.

Crossing the Cour d'Honneur (Court of Honor), you'll come to **Eglise du Dôme,** designed by Hardouin-Mansart for Louis XIV. He began work on the church in 1677, though he died before its completion. In the Napoléon Chapel is the hearse used at the emperor's funeral on May 9, 1821. To accommodate the Tomb of Napoléon—made of red porphyry, with a green granite base—architect Visconti had to redesign the high altar. First buried at St. Helena, Napoléon's remains were returned to Paris in 1840.

Place des Invalides, 7e. © 01-44-42-37-72. Admission to Musée de l'Armée, Napoléon's Tomb, and Musée des Plans-Reliefs (a museum in the Hôtel des Invalides containing scale models of French fortresses and fortified towns of the 17th and 18th c.): 6.50€ adults, 4.60€ children 12–17, free for children 11 and under. Oct–Mar daily 10am–5pm; Apr–May and Sept daily 10am–6pm; June–Aug daily 10am–7pm. Closed Jan 1, May 1, Nov 1, and Dec 25. Métro: Latour-Maubourg, Varenne, or Invalides.

IN MONTMARTRE ✮✮✮

From the 1880s to just before World War I, Montmartre enjoyed its golden age as the world's best-known art colony, where *la vie de bohème* reigned supreme.

Before its discovery, Montmartre was a sleepy farming community, with windmills dotting the landscape. Those who find the trek up to Paris's highest elevations too much of a climb may prefer to ride **Le Petit Train de Montmartre,** which passes all the major landmarks; it seats 55 passengers and offers English commentary. Board at place Blanche (near the Moulin Rouge); the fare is 5€ adults, 3€ children 12 and under. From June to September, trains run daily from 10am to 10pm; off season, daily from 10am to 6pm. For information, contact **Promotrain,** 131 rue de Clignancourt, 18e (© 01-42-62-24-00).

The simplest way to reach Montmartre is to take the Métro to Anvers, then walk up rue du Steinkerque to the funicular, which runs to the precincts of Sacré-Coeur every day from 5:30am to 12:30am. Except for Sacré-Coeur, Montmartre has only minor attractions; it's the architecture and the atmosphere that are compelling.

Specific attractions to look for include the **Bateau-Lavoir (Boat Warehouse),** on place Emile-Goudeau. Although gutted by fire in 1970, it has been reconstructed. Picasso once lived here and, in the winter of 1905 to 1906, painted one of the world's most famous portraits, *The Third Rose* (Gertrude Stein).

Espace Montmartre Salvadore-Dalí, 11 rue Poulbot, 18e (© 01-42-64-40-10), presents Dalí's phantasmagorical world with 330 original works, including his 1956 *Don Quixote* lithograph. It's open daily from 10am to 6:30pm; admission is 7€ for adults, 6€ for seniors, and 5€ for ages 8 to 26. It's free for children 7 and under.

Basilique du Sacré-Coeur ✸✸✸   Montmartre's crowning achievement is Sacré-Coeur, though its view of Paris takes precedence over the basilica itself. Its gleaming white domes and *campanile* (bell tower) tower over Paris like a Byzantine church of the 12th century. But it's not that old: After France's defeat by the Prussians in 1870, the basilica was planned as an offering to cure the country's misfortunes; rich and poor alike contributed. Construction began in 1873, but the church wasn't consecrated until 1919. The interior is decorated with mosaics, the most striking of which are the ceiling depiction of Christ and the mural of the Passion at the back of the altar. The crypt contains what some believe is a piece of the sacred heart of Christ—hence the church's name. On a clear day, the vista from the dome can extend for 56km (35 miles).

Place St-Pierre, 18e. Ⓒ **01-53-41-89-00.** www.paris.org/Monuments/Sacre.Coeur. Free admission to basilica; joint ticket to dome and crypt 5€ adults. Basilica open daily 7am–11pm; dome and crypt daily 9am–7pm. Métro: Abbesses; take the elevator to the surface and follow the signs to the funicular, which goes up to the church for the price of a Métro ticket.

Cimetière de Montmartre ✸   Novelist Alexandre Dumas and Russian dancer Vaslav Nijinsky are just a few of the famous composers, writers, and artists interred here. The remains of the great Stendhal are here, along with Hector Berlioz, Heinrich Heine, Edgar Degas, Jacques Offenbach, and even François Truffaut.

20 av. Rachel (west of the Butte Montmartre and north of bd. de Clichy), 18e. Ⓒ **01-43-87-64-24.** Sun–Fri 8am–6pm; Sat 8:30am–6pm (closes at 5:30pm in winter). Métro: La Fourche.

IN THE LATIN QUARTER ✸✸

This is the Left Bank precinct of the **University of Paris (the Sorbonne).** Rabelais called it the Quartier Latin, because of the students and professors who spoke Latin in the classrooms and on the streets. The sector teems with belly dancers, restaurants from Vietnamese to Balkan, sidewalk cafes, bookstalls, and smoky cellars.

A good starting point is **place St-Michel** (Métro: St-Michel), where Balzac used to get water from the fountain when he was a youth. The quarter centers around **boulevard St-Michel,** to the south (the students call it "Boul Mich").

Musée National du Moyen Age (Musée de Cluny) ✸✸   There are two reasons to come here: the world's finest collection of art from the Middle Ages, including jewelry and tapestries; and the well-preserved manor house built atop Roman baths in which the collection is displayed. The Cluny was the mansion of a 15th-century abbot. By 1515, it was the home of Mary Tudor, the widow of Louis XII and daughter of Henry VII of England and Elizabeth of York. Most people come to see the **Unicorn Tapestries** ✸✸✸, discovered a century ago in the Château de Boussac in the Auvergne. Five seem to deal with the senses (one depicts a unicorn looking into a mirror held by a maiden). The sixth shows a woman under an elaborate tent, her pet dog resting on an embroidered cushion beside her. The lovable unicorn and its friendly companion, a lion, hold back the flaps. Downstairs are the ruins of the Roman baths, dating from around A.D. 200.

Insider tip: Just inaugurated is a new garden that's a return to the Middle Ages. It was inspired by the luxuriant detail of the museum's most fabled treasure, the 15th-century tapestry of *The Lady of the Unicorn.* It's small, but richly planted.

In the Hôtel de Cluny, 6 place Paul-Painlevé, 5e. (*C*) **01-53-73-78-15**. Admission 5.50€ adults, 4€ ages 18–25, free for ages 17 and under. Wed–Mon 9:15am–5:45pm. Métro: Cluny–La Sorbonne.

HISTORIC GARDENS & SQUARES

GARDENS   Bordering place de la Concorde, the statue-studded **Jardin des Tuileries** ✪✪ (*C* **01-44-50-75-01**; Métro: Tuileries) are as much a part of Paris as the Seine. They were designed by Le Nôtre, Louis XIV's gardener and planner of the Versailles grounds. **Jardin du Luxembourg** ✪✪, 6e (*C* **01-44-61-20-89**; Métro: Odéon; RER: Luxembourg), has always been associated with artists, though students from the Sorbonne and children predominate nowadays. The gardens are the best on the Left Bank (if not in all of Paris).

SQUARES   In **place de la Bastille** ✪ on July 14, 1789, a mob of Parisians attacked the Bastille and thus sparked the French Revolution. Nothing remains of the historic Bastille, built in 1369. Many prisoners were kept within its walls, the best known being the "Man in the Iron Mask." Bastille Day is celebrated with great festivity on July 14. In the center of the square is the Colonne de Juillet (July Column), but it doesn't commemorate the revolution. It honors the victims of the 1830 July revolution, which put Louis-Philippe on the throne.

   Place des Vosges ✪✪✪, 4e (Métro: St-Paul or Chemin Vert), is Paris's oldest square and once the most fashionable. In the heart of the Marais, it was called the Palais Royal in the days of Henri IV, who planned to live here—but his assassin, Ravaillac, had other ideas. Henry II was killed while jousting on the square in 1559. Its grand siècle redbrick houses are ornamented with white stone. Its covered arcades allowed people to shop at all times, even in the rain—quite an innovation at the time.

   The Champs-Elysées begins at **place de la Concorde** ✪✪✪, an octagonal traffic hub built in 1757 to honor Louis XV and one of the world's grandest squares. The statue of the king was torn down in 1792 and the name of the square changed to place de la Révolution. Floodlit at night, it's dominated now by an Egyptian obelisk from Luxor, the oldest man-made object in Paris; it was carved around 1200 B.C. and presented to France in 1829 by the viceroy of Egypt. During the Reign of Terror, Dr. Guillotin's little invention was erected on this spot and claimed thousands of lives.

   For a spectacular sight, look down the Champs-Elysées—the view is framed by Coustou's Marly horses, which once graced the gardens at Louis XIV's Château de Marly (these are copies—the originals are in the Louvre).

HISTORIC PARKS & A CEMETERY

PARKS   One of the most spectacular parks in Europe is the **Bois de Boulogne** ✪✪✪, Porte Dauphine, 16e (*C* **01-40-67-90-82**; Métro: Les-Sablons, Porte-Maillot, or Porte-D'Autevil). Horse-drawn carriages traverse it, but you can also drive through. Many of its hidden pathways, however, must be discovered by walking. The park was once a forest kept for royal hunts. When Napoléon III gave the grounds to the city in 1852, they were developed by Baron Haussmann. Separating Lac Inférieur from Lac Supérieur is the Carrefour des Cascades (you can stroll under its waterfall). The Lower Lake contains two islands connected by a footbridge.

   Parc Monceau ✪, 17e (*C* **01-42-27-08-64**; Métro: Monceau or Villiers), is ringed with 18th- and 19th-century mansions, some evoking Proust's *Remembrance of Things Past*. It was built in 1778 by the duc de Charties (or Philippe Egalité, as he became known). Parc Monceau was laid out with an Egyptian-style obelisk, a thatched alpine farmhouse, a Chinese pagoda, a Roman temple, an enchanted grotto, various chinoiseries, and a waterfall. The park was opened to the public during Napoléon III's Second Empire.

A CEMETERY **Cemetière du Père-Lachaise** 🗺🗺, 16 rue de Repos, 20e (© **01-55-25-82-10;** Métro: Père-Lachaise), contains more illustrious dead than any other cemetery. When it comes to name-dropping, this cemetery knows no peer—it's been called the "grandest address in Paris." Everybody from Sarah Bernhardt to Oscar Wilde is buried here. So are Balzac, Delacroix, and Bizet. Colette's body was taken here in 1954, and her pink and black granite slab always sports flowers (legend has it that cats replenish the red roses). In time, the "little sparrow," Edith Piaf, followed. Marcel Proust's black tombstone rarely lacks a bunch of violets. Some tombs are sentimental favorites—Jim Morrison's reportedly draws the most visitors. Another stone is marked Gertrude Stein on one side and Alice B. Toklas on the other. The cemetery is open Monday through Friday from 8am to 6pm, Saturday from 8:30am to 6pm, and Sunday from 9am to 6pm (closes at 5:30pm Nov–Mar).

ORGANIZED TOURS

BY BUS The most popular get-acquainted tour in Paris is offered by **Cityrama,** 149 rue St-Honoré, 1er (© **01-44-55-61-00;** Métro: Palais-Royal–Musée-du-Louvre). On a double-decker bus you're taken on a 2-hour ride through the city. You don't go inside any attractions, but you get a look at the outside of Notre-Dame and the Eiffel Tower, among other sights. There's commentary in 10 languages on earphones. Tours depart daily at 9:30am, 10:30am, 1:30pm, and 2:30pm. There are additional tours every Saturday and Sunday at 11:30am, and between March and October, there are two additional tours every day at 3:30 and 4:30pm. A 2-hour orientation tour is 25€. A morning tour with interior visits to Notre-Dame and the Louvre costs 50€. A tour of the nighttime illuminations leaves daily at 10pm in summer, 7pm in winter, and costs 25€; it tends to be touristy.

The **RATP** (© **08-36-68-41-14**) operates the **Balabus,** a fleet of orange-and-white big-windowed motor coaches. The only drawback is their limited operating hours: Sunday only, from noon to 9pm (and some national holidays). Itineraries run in both directions between Gare de Lyon and the Grand Arche de La Défense. Three Métro tickets will carry you along the entire route. You'll recognize the bus, and its route, by the *Bb* symbol on its side and on signs posted along its route.

BY BOAT **Bateaux-Mouche** (© **01-40-76-99-99;** Métro: Alma-Marceau) cruises depart from the Right Bank of the Seine, adjacent to Pont de l'Alma, and last about 75 minutes. Tours leave daily at 20- to 30-minute intervals from 10am to 11:30pm between May and October. Between November and April, there are at least nine departures daily between 11am and 9pm, with a schedule that changes according to demand and the weather. Fares are 7€ for adults and 4€ for children 5 to 15. Dinner cruises depart daily at 8:30pm, last 3 hours, and cost 85€ to 125€, depending on which of the fixed-price menus you order. On dinner cruises, jackets and ties are required for men.

Batobus (© **01-44-11-33-99**) boats are 150-passenger ferries with big windows. Daily between April and November, they operate east–west along the Seine, stopping at eight points en route. Departures occur at 15- to 25-minute intervals (depending on the season and time of day) from 10am to 7pm (until 9pm June–Aug). Stops include the Eiffel Tower, Musée d'Orsay, points on both the Left Bank and the Right Bank opposite the Louvre, Notre-Dame, and the

Hôtel de Ville. There's no recorded commentary. The fare between any two stops is 3.05€ for the first segment, and 2€ for each segment after that, though we consider the Batobus an expensive way to cross a river that's already criss-crossed with many bridges. More appealing is to pay 10€ per adult or 5.50€ per child 11 and under (children under 3 ride free) for a day ticket. The views are panoramic, and the boat allows you to move from one history-rich neighborhood to another while bypassing the Métro and street traffic.

THE SHOPPING SCENE

The City of Light is one of the rare places in the world where you don't go anywhere in particular to shop—shopping surrounds you on almost every street. You don't have to buy anything—just peer in the *vitrines* (display windows), absorb cutting-edge ideas, witness trends—and take home an education in style.

Shops are usually open Monday through Saturday from 10am to 7pm, but the hours vary. Paris doesn't run at full throttle on Monday morning, when small shops sometimes take a 2-hour lunch break. While most stores open at 10am, some open at 9:30am or even 11am. Thursday is the best day for late-night shopping, with stores open until 9 or 10pm.

THE BEST BUYS

Perfumes and **cosmetics,** including such famous brands as Guerlain, Chanel, Schiaparelli, and Jean Patou, are almost always cheaper in Paris than in the United States. Paris is also a good place to buy Lalique and Baccarat **crystal.** They're expensive but still priced below international market value.

Of course, many people come to Paris just to shop for **fashions.** From Chanel to Yves Saint Laurent, Nina Ricci to Sonia Rykiel, the city overflows with fashion boutiques, ranging from haute couture to the truly outlandish. Fashion accessories, such as Louis Vuitton and Céline, are among the finest in the world. Smart Parisians know how to dress in style without mortgaging their condos: They head for discount and resale shops. **Anna Lowe,** 104 rue du Faubourg St-Honoré, 8e (© **01-42-66-11-32;** Métro: Miromesnil), is one of the top boutiques for women who wish to purchase a Chanel or a Versace at a discount, *bien sur.* Many clothes are runway samples; some have been gently worn. French film stars often shop at **Défilé des Marques,** 171 rue de Grenelles, 7e (© **01-45-55-63-47;** Métro: Latour-Maubourg), but anyone can pick up discounted Laurent, Dior, Lacroix, Prada, Chanel, Versace, Hermès, and others at a fraction of the price.

Lingerie is another great French export. All the top lingerie designers are represented in boutiques as well as in the major department stores, Galeries Lafayette and Le Printemps.

Chocolate lovers will find much to tempt them in Paris. **Christian Constant,** 37 rue d'Assas, 6e (© **01-53-63-15-15;** Métro: Rennes), produces some of Paris's most sinfully delicious chocolates. Racks and racks of chocolates are priced individually or by the kilo at **Maison du Chocolat,** 225 rue du Faubourg St-Honoré, 8e (© **01-42-27-39-44;** Métro: Ternes), though it'll cost you nearly 76€ for a kilo. There are five other branches around Paris.

GREAT SHOPPING AREAS

1er & 8e   Because these two adjoin each other and form the heart of what is Paris's best Right Bank shopping, they really function as one shopping neighborhood. This area includes the famed **rue du Faubourg St-Honoré,** where the big designer houses are, and **avenue des Champs-Elysées,** where the mass-market and teen scenes are hot.

> ⌒*Value* **Paris Shopper's Secret**
>
> For bargain cosmetics, try out French dime-store (such as **Monoprix** and **Prisunic**) brands. Other brands to look for include **Bourjois** (made in the same factories as Chanel cosmetics), **Lierac,** and **Galenic. Vichy,** famous for its water, has a complete skin-care and make-up line.

At one end of the 1st is the **Palais Royal,** where an arcade of boutiques flanks the garden of the former palace. At the other side of town, at the end of the 8th, lies **avenue Montaigne** (Métro: Franklin D. Roosevelt or Alma Marceau), 2 blocks of the fanciest shops in the world, where you float from big name to big name. You'll find fabulous perfumes at **Parfums Caron** (✆ **01-47-23-40-82**). The shop, which was founded in 1904, can be visited at no. 34.

3e & 4e The difference between these two arrondissements gets fuzzy, especially around **place des Vosges**—center stage of Le Marais. Even so, they offer several dramatically different shopping experiences.

On the surface, the shopping includes the real-people stretch of **rue de Rivoli** (which becomes **rue St-Antoine**). Two department stores are in this area. **La Samaritaine,** 19 rue de la Monnaie (✆ **01-40-41-20-20;** Métro: Pont Neuf), occupies four architecturally noteworthy buildings erected between 1870 and 1927. Of special interest are the annual sales that go on here during October and November, when much, but not all, of the merchandise is reduced by between 20% and 40%. **BHV (Bazar de l'Hôtel de Ville),** which was first opened in 1856, has seven floors loaded with merchandise. It lies adjacent to Paris's City Hall at 52–64 rue de Rivoli (✆ **01-42-74-90-00;** Métro: Hôtel de Ville).

In the Marais is a medieval warren of tiny twisting streets chockablock with cutting-edge designers and up-to-the-minute fashions and trends. Start by walking around place des Vosges for art galleries, designer shops, and fabulous little finds, then dive in and get lost in the area leading to the Musée Picasso.

Place de la Bastille—an up-and-coming area for artists and galleries—is in the 4th arrondissement (leading to the 12th), as is the Ile St-Louis. One of the best galleries, the **Viaduc des Arts,** 147 av. Daumesnil, 12e (✆ **01-44-75-80-66**), begins at Bastille but stretches to the 12th arrondissement. This is a complex of boutiques and craft workshops, occupying the vaulted spaces beneath one of the 19th-century railway access routes into the Gare de Lyon.

6e & 7e While the 6th arrondissement is one of the most famous shopping districts—it's the soul of the Left Bank—a lot of the good stuff is hidden in the zone that becomes the wealthy 7th. **Rue du Bac,** stretching from the 6th to the 7th in a few blocks, stands for all that wealth and glamour can buy. The street is jammed with art galleries, home-decorating stores, and gourmet-food shops.

9e To add to the fun of shopping the Right Bank, the 9th arrondissement sneaks in behind the 1st, so if you don't choose to walk toward the Champs-Elysées and the 8th, you can head to the big department stores in a row along **boulevard Haussmann** in the 9th. These stores include not only the mammoth French icons, **Au Printemps,** 64 bd. Haussmann, 9e (✆ **01-42-82-50-00;** Métro: Havre–Caumartin; RER: Auber), and **Galeries Lafayette,** 40 bd. Haussmann, 9e (✆ **01-42-82-34-56;** Métro: Chausée d'Antin–La Fayette; RER: Auber), but a large branch of Britain's **Marks & Spencer** at 35 bd. Haussmann, 9e (✆ **01-47-42-42-91;** Métro: Chausée-d-Antin–La Fayette; RER: Auber).

PARIS AFTER DARK
THE PERFORMING ARTS

Announcements of shows, concerts, and operas are on kiosks all over town. You can find listings in *Pariscope,* a weekly entertainment guide, or the English-language *Boulevard,* a bimonthly magazine.

There are many ticket agencies in Paris, but most are near the Right Bank hotels. *Avoid them if possible.* You can buy the cheapest tickets at the theater box office. Tip the usher who shows you to your seat in a theater or movie house.

Several agencies sell tickets for cultural events and plays at discounts of up to 50%. One is the **Kiosque Théâtre,** 15 place de la Madeleine, 8e (no phone; Métro: Madeleine), offering leftover tickets for about half price on the day of performance. Tickets for evening performances are sold Tuesday through Friday from 12:30 to 8pm and Saturday from 2 to 8pm. For matinees, tickets are sold Saturday from 12:30 to 2pm and Sunday from 12:30 to 4pm.

For easy access to tickets for festivals, concerts, and the theater, try one of two locations of the **FNAC** department-store chain: 136 rue de Rennes, 6e (© 01-49-54-30-00; Métro: St. Placide), or in the Forum des Halles, 1–7 rue Pierre-Lescot, 1er (© 01-40-41-40-00; Métro: Châtelet or Les-Halles).

Even those with only a modest understanding of French can delight in a sparkling production of Molière at the **Comédie-Française,** 2 rue de Richelieu, 1er (© 01-44-58-15-15; Métro: Palais-Royal–Musée-du-Louvre), established to keep the classics alive and to promote important contemporary authors. The box office is open daily from 11am to 6pm, but the hall is dark from July 21 to September 5. In 1993, a Left Bank annex was launched, the **Comédie-Française-Théâtre du Vieux-Colombier,** 21 rue du Vieux-Colombier, 4e (© 01-44-39-87-00; Métro: Sèvres-Babylone, Saint-Sulpice). Although its repertoire can vary, it's known for presenting some of the most serious French dramas in town.

The **Opéra Bastille,** place de la Bastille, 120 rue de Lyon, 12e (© 08-92-69-78-68; Métro: Bastille), was inaugurated in July 1989 (for the Revolution's bicentennial), and on March 17, 1990, the curtain rose on Hector Berlioz's *Les Troyens.* Since its much-publicized opening, the opera house has presented works like Mozart's *Marriage of Figaro* and Tchaikovsky's *Queen of Spades.* The main hall is the largest of any French opera house, with 2,700 seats, but music critics have lambasted the acoustics. The building contains two additional concert halls, including an intimate room seating 250, usually used for chamber music. Both traditional opera performances and symphony concerts are presented here. There are sometimes free concerts on French holidays; call before your visit.

Opéra Garnier, place de l'Opéra, 9e (© 08-92-69-78-68; Métro: Opéra), is the premier stage for dance and opera. Because of the competition from the Opéra Bastille, the original opera has made great efforts to present more up-to-date works. Charles Garnier designed this rococo wonder in the heyday of the empire. The facade is adorned with marble and sculpture, including *The Dance* by Carpeaux. Restoration has returned the Garnier to its former glory, the ceiling (painted by Marc Chagall) has been cleaned, and air-conditioning has been added. The box office is open Monday through Saturday from 11am to 6:30pm.

Conceived by the Mitterrand administration, **Cité de la Musique,** 221 av. Jean-Jaurès, 19e (© 01-44-84-45-00, or 01-44-84-44-84 for tickets and information; Métro: Porte-de-Pantin), has been widely applauded. At the city's northeastern edge in what used to be a run-down neighborhood, the $120-million stone-and-glass structure, designed by Christian de Portzamparc, incorporates a network of concert halls, a library and research center, and a museum. The complex hosts a variety of concerts, ranging from Renaissance to 20th-century programs.

For the best orchestra performances in France, try **Maison de Radio France,** 116 av. du Président-Kennedy, 16e (② **01-56-40-15-16;** Métro: Passy-Ranelagh), which offers top-notch concerts with guest conductors. It's the home of the Orchestre Philharmonique de Radio France and the Orchestre National de France. The box office is open Monday through Saturday from 11am to 6pm.

NIGHTCLUBS & CABARETS

Folies-Bergère Folies-Bergère is a Paris institution; foreigners have been flocking here since 1886. Josephine Baker became "the toast of Paris" here. Since the naughty Belle Epoque days when the can-can was likely to be performed by women who didn't necessarily wear underpanties, Folies-Bergère has witnessed many changes, many modernizations, and an attempt in the mid-1990s to become a "legitimate" dramatic theater. (It didn't work particularly well—audiences preferred the cabaret revues that had made the place famous.)

In 2002, Folies-Bergère reverted to its original role, wherein 2-hour revues within a state-of-the-art 1,600-seat theater showcase an appreciation for the (partially unclothed) elegance and allure of *"la femme."* Be prepared for G-strings and brassieres which management refers to as *"léger, léger"* (very light), lots of feathers and sequins, and all the ooh-la-la razzmatazz you'd expect. Each show includes two female singers performing in a mixture of French and English, a juggler, and lots of mostly female flesh. Shows are usually presented Tuesday through Sunday at 9pm. 34 rue Richer, 9e. ② 01-44-79-98-98. www.foliesbergere. com. Tickets 34€–64€; set-price dinner, with access to show included, 80€ per person. Metro: Grands Boulevards or Cadet.

Moulin Rouge This is a camp classic. The establishment that Toulouse-Lautrec immortalized is still here, but the artist would probably have a hard time recognizing it. Colette created a scandal here by offering an on-stage kiss to Mme de Morny, but shows today have a harder time shocking audiences. Try to get a table, as the view is much better on the main floor than from the bar. What's the theme? Strip routines and the saucy sexiness of la Belle Epoque, and permissive Paris between the wars. Handsome men and girls, girls, girls, virtually all topless, keep the place going. Dance finales usually include two dozen of the belles ripping loose with a topless can-can. Revues take place nightly at 9 and 11pm. Place Blanche, 18e. ② 01-53-09-82-82. Cover including champagne 82€–90€; cover for seats at the bar (including 2 drinks) 63€; 7pm dinner and show 125€. Métro: Blanche.

LIVE MUSIC & DANCING

JAZZ The great jazz revival is still going strong here. Most clubs are on the Left Bank near the Seine, between rue Bonaparte and rue St-Jacques. For the latest details, see *Jazz Hot, Jazz Magazine,* or *Pariscope.* **Au Duc des Lombards** (42 rue des Lombards, 1er; ② **01-42-33-22-88;** Métro: Châtelet) is comfortable and appealing. Performers begin playing nightly at 9pm and continue (with breaks) for 5 hours, touching on everything from free jazz to more traditional forms like hard bop. Cover is 19€. **Le Bilboquet/Club St-Germain** (13 rue St-Benoît, 6e; ② **01-45-48-81-84**) is a restaurant/jazz club/piano bar offering some of the best music in the city. Jazz is featured on the upper level in the restaurant, Le Bilboquet, a wood-paneled room with a copper ceiling, brass-trimmed bar, and Victorian candelabra. There's no cover in Bilboquet, but there is one of 21€ for Club St-Germain, a downstairs disco, and drinks cost a rather steep 8€ to 15€. Hours are Tuesday through Saturday from 8:30pm to 2am; jazz music 9:30pm to 2am. Métro: St-Germain-des-Prés.

DANCE CLUBS   The area around the Eglise St-Germain-des-Prés is full of dance clubs. For the most up-to-date information, see *Time Out, Pariscope,* or *L'Officiel des Spectacles.* **Batofar** (facing 11 quai François Mauriac, 13e; © **01-56-29-10-33;** Métro: Quai de la Gare) is proud of its status as a club that everybody views as hip. It sits within a converted barge that floats on the Seine, sometimes with hundreds of gyrating dancers, most of whom are in their twenties and thirties. House, garage, techno, and live jazz from groups that hail from (among other places) Morocco, Senegal, and Germany sometimes add to the mix. Come here for an insight into late-night Paris at its most raffish and counterculture. The cover ranges from 7€ to 16€. Tapas can be ordered starting at 4€ each, and beer costs around 7€ a bottle. Hours are Tuesday through Saturday from 6pm to 3 or 4am, depending on business. It's closed November through March.

ROCK   **Bus Palladium** (6 rue Fontaine, 9e; © **01-53-21-07-33;** Métro: Blanche or Pigall) is set in a single room with a long bar, a rock 'n' roll temple with varnished hardwoods and fabric-covered walls that barely absorb the reverberations of nonstop recorded music. It's rock 'n' roll for hard-core, mostly heterosexual, rock wannabes ages 25 to 35. Alcoholic drinks of any kind cost 13€, except for women on Tuesday, when they can drink for free. The cover is 20€ all the time for men, and Friday and Saturday only for women.

GAY & LESBIAN BARS   **Banana Café,** 13 rue de la Ferronnerie, 1er (© **01-42-33-35-31;** Métro: Châtelet or Les Halles), is the most popular gay bar in the

 Native Behavior

Call adult males *Monsieur* (meaning sir). Addressing women isn't so easy as you have to determine a woman's marital status. When the English say "Mrs.," the French say *Madame.* If you're talking to an unmarried woman, call her Mademoiselle. When in doubt, go with the Madame.

After you get to know someone, if only briefly, kisses (called *bises* in French) are freely exchanged. Women kiss women and men kiss women, and often men kiss each other, one kiss for each cheek. If you're not at the kissing stage, handshaking will do.

The French believe that "going Dutch"—that is, splitting the bill—is best left for the Dutch. If you invite someone for drinks or dinner, you are expected to pay the bill. Don't ask the waiter to split the tab. The French would view that as "barbaric."

If invited to someone's home, bring a gift. Wine will do, but not a cheap bottle. Flowers are also good to carry along, but never chrysanthemums: They're reserved for paying your respects to the dead.

If you can, do as the Parisians do and avoid Paris in summer. As Catherine Deneuve once noted, "That is the time we turn the city over to American tourists and pickpockets."

Marais. Occupying two floors of a 19th-century building, it has dim lighting and a well-publicized policy of raising the price of drinks after 10pm. There's a street-level bar and a dance floor in the cellar featuring a live pianist and recorded music. On many nights, go-go dancers perform from spot-lit platforms. The bar is open daily from 4pm to around 5:30am.

Le Pulp, 25 bd. Poissonnière, 2e (© **01-40-26-01-93;** Métro: Grand Blvd.), is one of the most visible and popular lesbian discos in Paris. New management has outfitted the disco like a burgundy-colored 19th-century French music hall, and made its seedy past a distant memory. Today it's fun, trendy, and chic. It's best to show up before midnight. The venue, as the French like to say, is very cool, with all types of cutting-edge music played in a setting that just happens to discourage the presence of men. Le Pulp is open Thursday through Saturday from 11:30pm to at least 5am. Cover ranges from 7.60€ to 12€.

Le Red Light, 34 rue du Depart, 14e (© **01-55-34-73-60;** Metro: Montparnasse), is Paris's newest blockbuster on Friday and Saturday nights, in one of the cellars beneath the city's tallest building, La Tour Montparnasse. Inside, you'll find two dance floors, each with its own bars and sound system,. A clientele of up to 2,500 mostly gay men, ages 18 to 38, roils and mingles restlessly between the two rooms, where house and techno music reign and where specific evenings might be themed after prominent gay bars in, say, Ibiza or London. The cover is 20€ per person, the first drink included. Hours are 11pm to 10am.

DAY TRIPS FROM PARIS: THE ILE DE FRANCE

VERSAILLES 𝄞𝄞𝄞   Within 50 years the **Château de Versailles** (© **01-39-24-88-88;** www.chateauversailles.fr) was transformed from Louis XIII's simple hunting lodge into an extravagant palace. What you see today is the greatest living museum of a vanished way of life. Begun in 1661, the construction of the château involved 32,000 to 45,000 workmen, some of whom had to drain marshes—often at the cost of their lives—and move forests. Louis XIV set out to create a palace that would awe all Europe, and the result was a symbol of pomp and opulence that was to be copied, yet never quite duplicated.

The six magnificent **Grands Appartements** 𝄞𝄞𝄞 are in the Louis XIV style; each takes its name from the allegorical painting on its ceiling. The most famous room is the 72m (236-ft.) **Hall of Mirrors** 𝄞𝄞𝄞. Begun by Mansart in 1678 in the Louis XIV style, it was decorated by Le Brun with 17 large arched windows matched by beveled mirrors in simulated arcades.

Spread across 100 hectares (250 acres), the **Gardens of Versailles** 𝄞 were laid out by the great landscape artist André Le Nôtre. A long walk across the park will take you to the **Grand Trianon** 𝄞𝄞𝄞, in pink-and-white marble, designed by Hardouin-Mansart for Louis XIV in 1687. Traditionally it's been a place where France has lodged important guests. Gabriel, the designer of place de la Concorde in Paris, built the **Petit Trianon** 𝄞𝄞 in 1768 for Louis XV; its construction was inspired by Mme de Pompadour, who died before it was completed. In time, Marie Antoinette adopted it as her favorite residence.

The latest attraction is the **Grande Ecourie,** the newly reopened stables of Louis XIV. For 2 centuries, these historic stables have been closed to the public. They once housed more than 600 horses of the king. Today they are home to 20 cream-colored Lusitanian horses from Portugal. Visitors are taken on a brief guided tour and then witness morning dressage demonstrations. Ten advanced equestrian students direct the horses, and costumed riders demonstrate equestrian choreography performed to music.

Three main avenues radiate from place d'Armes in front of the palace. The **tourist office** is at 2 bis av. de Paris, 78000 Versailles (✆ **01-39-24-88-88**).

The château is open from May 2 to September 30, Tuesday through Sunday from 9am to 6:30pm (5:30pm the rest of the year). It's closed December 25 and January 1. Call or visit the website for a complete fee schedule (which varies, depending on which attractions you visit). The grounds are open daily from dawn to dusk. The individual attractions may have earlier opening and closing times.

An unguided visit to the Grands Appartements is 7.50€ per person (free for those under 18). A group tour, with commentary in English and French, including the Opera House and the Chapel, is an additional 4.50€ or 7€, depending on whether you take a 60-minute or a 90-minute tour. You can also rent a portable cassette player, with a recorded tour in English or French, for 12€.

Getting There   To get to Versailles, catch the **RER** line C at the Gare d'Austerlitz, St-Michel, Musée d'Orsay, Invalides, Pont de l'Alma, Champ de Mars, or Javel stops and take it to the Versailles Rive Gauche station, from which there's a shuttle bus to the château. Priced at 4.90€ round-trip, the trip takes 35 to 40 minutes. Eurailpass holders travel free on the RER, but you'll need to show your Eurailpass at the kiosk near any RER entrance for a ticket.

Alternatively, you can take one of the frequent **SNCF trains** from Gare St-Lazare or Gare Montparnasse. Trains departing from Gare St-Lazare arrive at the Versailles Rive Droite station; trains departing from Gare Montparnasse arrive at Versailles Chantiers. Both are a 10-minute walk from the château, and we highly recommend the walk as a means of orienting yourself with the town, its geography, its scale, and its architecture. You can also take bus B, bus H, or (in midsummer) a shuttle bus marked CHATEAU from any of the three stations directly to the château for a fee of 2€ each way, per person. However, the vagaries of the bus schedules are another reason we highly recommend the walk. Directions to the château are clearly marked from each of the three railway stations. If you're **driving**, take Route N-10 and park on the place d'Armes in front of the château.

CHARTRES ★★★   The architectural aspirations of the Middle Ages reached their highest expression in the **Cathédrale Notre-Dame de Chartres,** 16 Cloître Notre-Dame (✆ **02-37-21-59-08**). A mystical light seems to stream through this stained glass, which gave the world a new color—Chartres blue. One of the greatest of the world's high Gothic cathedrals, Chartres contains some of the oldest (some of it created as early as the 12th c.) and most beautiful medieval stained glass anywhere. It was spared in both World Wars; the glass was removed painstakingly piece by piece for storage and safekeeping.

The cathedral you see today dates principally from the 13th century. It was the first to use flying buttresses, giving it a higher and lighter construction. French sculpture in the 12th century broke into full bloom when the Royal Portal was added; the sculptured bodies are elongated and formalized, but the faces are amazingly lifelike. Admission is free; the cathedral is open Monday through Saturday from 7:30am to 7pm and Sunday from 8:30am to 7pm. The crypt can only be visited on a guided tour, costing 1.65€ adults or 1.20€ for students and children. From April to October, there are five tours daily; off season, there are two per day. Inquire locally about tour times, as they change frequently. If you feel fit enough, climb to the top of the **New Bell Tower.** Open the same hours as the cathedral, except for a closing from noon to 2pm, it charges an admission fee of 4€ for adults and 3€ for students.

Getting There   From Paris's Gare Montparnasse, **trains** run directly to Chartres in under an hour. **By car,** take A10/A11 southwest from the *périphérique* and follow the signs to Le Mans and Chartres.

Visitor Information   The **tourist office** is on place de la Cathédrale (© 02-37-18-26-26).

2 The Loire Valley Châteaux ⋆⋆⋆

Bordered by vineyards, the Loire Valley cuts through the land of castles in France's heart. When royalty and nobility built châteaux throughout this valley during the Renaissance, sumptuousness was uppermost in their minds. An era of excessive pomp reigned until Henri IV moved his court to Paris.

The Loire is blessed with abundant attractions—there's even the castle that inspired the fairy tale *Sleeping Beauty.* Tours is the traditional gateway; once here you can explore either east or west, depending on your interests. From Paris, you can reach Tours by autoroute (take A-10 southwest).

In general, Loire Valley **tourist offices** are open October through March, Monday through Saturday from 9am to 6:30pm and Sunday from 10am to noon; the rest of the year, hours are Monday through Saturday from 9am to 7pm and Sunday from 9:30am to 12:30pm.

TOURS

Tours, 232km (144 miles) southwest of Paris and 113km (70 miles) southwest of Orléans, is at the junction of the Loire and Cher rivers. The devout en route to Santiago de Compostela in northwest Spain once stopped here to pay homage to St. Martin, the Apostle of Gaul, bishop of Tours in the 4th century. Tours is the traditional place to begin your exploration of the medieval Loire Valley.

ESSENTIALS

GETTING THERE   **Trains** to Tours depart Paris from the Gare Montparnasse and the Gare d'Austerlitz. The quickest are usually from Gare Montparnasse, departure point for up to 10 TGV (very fast) trains per day, charging 46€ for the 70-minute transit. Most conventional trains to Tours depart from the Gare d'Austerlitz. Taking about 2¼ hours for the trip, they cost from 31€ to 40€, based on the time of day and day of the week you travel. Trains arrive at place du Maréchal-Leclerc, 3 rue Edouard-Vaillant (© 08-36-35-35-35 for information). If you're **driving,** take Highway A10 to Tours.

GETTING AROUND   It's easy to **walk** from one end of central Tours to the other. For taxi service, call **Allo Taxi** at © 02-47-20-30-40. There are several car rental offices in or near the train station, including **Avis** (inside the station; © 02-47-20-53-27), open daily from 8am to noon and 1:15 to 7pm; and **Hertz** (57 rue Marcel-Tribut; © 02-47-75-50-00), open daily from 8am to noon and 2 to 7pm. You can rent a bike at **Vélomania** (109 rue Colbert; © 02-47-05-10-11) for 15€ a day. It's open Monday from 3:30 to 7:30pm, Tuesday through Friday from 10:30am to 1:30pm and 2:30 to 7:30pm, and Saturday and Sunday from 10:30am to 7:30pm.

VISITOR INFORMATION   The **Office de Tourisme** is at 78 rue Bernard-Palissy (© 02-47-70-37-37; www.ligeris.com).

WHERE TO STAY

Best Western Le Central *Value*   This old-fashioned hotel is within walking distance of the river and cathedral, surrounded by gardens, lawns, and trees.

Built in 1850, it is a modest, economical choice. The Tremouilles family offers comfortable rooms at reasonable rates. Accommodations come in a variety of shapes and sizes; a renovation in 1999 improved them and updated the plumbing. Half the guest rooms have bathrooms with shower/tub combos; the other bathrooms have showers.

21 rue Berthelot, 37000 Tours. ℂ **800/528-1234** in the U.S. or Canada, or 02-47-05-46-44. Fax 02-47-66-10-26. bestwestern.centralhotel@wanadoo.fr. 39 units. 73€–91€ double. AE, DC, MC, V. Parking 8.50€. Bus: 1, 4, or 5. **Amenities:** Bar; limited room service; babysitting; laundry/dry cleaning. *In room:* A/C, TV, minibar, hair dryer.

Clarion Hôtel de l'Univers   This hotel was erected in 1853, making it the oldest in town. It has recently been upgraded to a government-rated four-star status, with its midsize rooms redecorated and made more upscale. Bathrooms with shower and tub have also been renewed. On weekdays, it's filled with business travelers; on weekends, it hosts many area brides and bridegrooms.

5 bd. Heurteloup, 37000 Tours. ℂ **02-47-05-37-12.** Fax 02-47-61-51-80. www.hotel-univers.loirevalley.com. 85 units. 195€ double. AE, DC, MC, V. Parking 9.50€. Bus 1, 4, or 5. **Amenities:** Restaurant; bar; limited room service; babysitting; laundry/dry cleaning. *In room:* A/C, TV, minibar, hair dryer.

Hôtel du Manoir   On a quiet street with shops and restaurants, this 19th-century residence provides guests with a comfortable place to stay. The cheerful reception area is an indication of the quality of the rooms. Though small to average in size, all units have windows that let in lots of light and afford views of the neighborhood or the hotel's courtyard.

2 rue Traversière, 37000 Tours. © 02-47-05-37-37. Fax 02-47-05-16-00. manoir37@aol.com. 20 units. 40€–49€ double. AE, DC, MC, V. Parking 3€ per day. Bus: 3, 70. *In room:* A/C, TV.

WHERE TO DINE

Chateau Belmont (Jean Bardet) ✿ MODERN FRENCH   Set in three rooms of a 19th-century château, this restaurant is the creation of the Michelin two-star chef Jean Bardet, who considers all meals here "an orchestration of wines, alcohol, food, and cigars." That's not to say that you must partake of all four to have one of the best meals in the region. Specialties include a lobster ragout, sliced sea bass with a confit of tomatoes and artichoke hearts, and scallops with a purée of shallots and truffle cream. The duck giblets and lobster accompanied by a red wine and orange sauce is reason enough to visit.

57 rue Groison. © 02-47-41-41-11. Fax 02-47-51-68-72. www.jeanbardet.com. Reservations recommended. Main courses 40€–65€; set-price menus 61€–128€. AE, DC, MC, V. Daily noon–2pm and 7:30–9:30pm. Closed Jan–Apr and Nov–Dec Sun night and Mon all day; closed Apr–Nov Mon lunch.

La Roche le Roy ✿✿ MODERN FRENCH   One of the hottest chefs in town, Alain Couturier blends new and old techniques in a steep-gabled 15th-century manor south of the town center. Couturier's repertoire includes scalloped foie gras with lentils, cod with saffron cream, and pan-fried scallops with a truffle vinaigrette. His masterpiece is suprême of pigeon with "roughly textured" sauce, and a matelote of eel with Chinon or Bourgeuil wine. For dessert, try his mélange of seasonal fruit with zabaglione made from Vouvray Valley wine.

55 rte. St-Avertin. © 02-47-27-22-00. Reservations recommended. Main courses 13€–28€; fixed-price menu 29€ lunch only. AE, MC, V. Tues–Sat 12:30–1:45pm and 7:30–10pm. Closed 3 weeks in Aug and 2 weeks in Feb. From the center of town, take av. Grammont south (follow signs to St-Avertin–Vierzon). The road crosses a bridge, but doesn't change names. The restaurant is beside that road, on the southern periphery of Tours.

Les Tuffeaux *Value* TRADITIONAL FRENCH   This 18th-century house contains one of the best restaurants in Tours. Menu items change about once a month, depending on the inspiration of chef Gildas Marsollier, who prepares a roster of classics but also experiments with noisettes of roasted rabbit with bacon and almonds, fricassee of chicken livers with raspberry vinegar, and braised turbot with a gratineed *viennoise* of Comté cheese. Roasted filet of pigeon with pink grapefruit is an enduring favorite.

19 rue Lavoisier. © 02-47-47-19-89. Reservations required. Main courses 19€–35€; fixed-price menu 35€–40€. AE, MC, V. Tues–Sat noon–2pm; Mon–Sat 7:30–9:30pm. Bus: 1, 4, or 5.

EXPLORING TOURS

The heart of town is **place Jean-Jaurès. Rue Nationale** is the principal street (the valley's Champs-Elysées), running north to the Loire River. Head along rue du Commerce and rue du Grand-Marché to reach La Vieille Ville, the old town.

One of the best ways to get an overview of Tours is a ride aboard a rubberwheeled **train** that operates between July and September, daily at 10am and 11am, and again every hour on the hour between 2 and 6pm, for a per-person price of 5€ adults and 2.50€ children under 12. Rides last about 50 minutes each, depart and return from in front of the tourist office (78–82 rue Bernard Palissy; © 02-47-70-37-37), and incorporate the city's historic core. You can buy your tickets at the tourist office or aboard the train.

Cathédrale St-Gatien   The cathedral's flamboyant Gothic facade is flanked by towers with bases from the 12th century, though the lanterns are Renaissance. The choir is from the 13th century, and each century through the 16th saw new additions. Some of the glorious stained-glass windows are from the 13th century.

5 place de la Cathédrale. ☎ **02-47-70-21-00.** Free admission. Daily 9am–7pm. Bus: 3.

Musée des Beaux-Arts   This fine provincial museum is housed in the Palais des Archevêques. It's worth visiting for its lovely rooms and gardens. There are works by Degas, Delacroix, Rembrandt, and Boucher, and sculpture by Houdon and Bourdelle.

18 place François-Sicard. ☎ **02-47-05-68-73.** Museum 4.55€ adults, 2.30€ students and those over 65, free for ages 12 and under. Gardens free. Both museum and gardens Wed–Mon 9am–12:45pm and 2–6pm. Bus: 3.

VILLANDRY ✸✸✸

The extravagant 16th-century-style gardens of the Renaissance **Château de Villandry,** 37510 Joué-les-Tours (☎ **02-47-50-02-09**), are celebrated throughout the Touraine. Forming a trio of superimposed cloisters, with a water garden on the highest level, the gardens were purchased in a decaying state and restored by Spanish doctor/scientist Joachim Carvallo, the present owner's great-grandfather. The grounds contain 17km (10½ miles) of boxwood sculpture, which the gardeners must cut to style in only 2 weeks in September. Every square of the gardens seems like a geometric mosaic. The borders represent the many faces of love: for example, tender, tragic (with daggers), or crazy, the last evoked by a labyrinth that doesn't get you anywhere.

A feudal castle originally stood at Villandry, but in 1536 Jean Lebreton, the chancellor of François I, built the present château; the buildings form a U and are surrounded by a two-sided moat.

Admission to the gardens with a guided tour of the château costs 7.50€ for adults, 5€ for ages 8 to 18, and free for children under 8. Visiting the gardens separately, without a guide, costs 5€ for adults, 3.50€ for ages 8 to 18, and free for children under 8. Year-round, the gardens are open daily from 9am to between 5:30 and 7:30pm, depending on the hour of sunset; and year-round, the château is open daily from 9am to between 5 and 6:30pm, depending on a complicated seasonal schedule. Tours are conducted in French with leaflets in English.

ESSENTIALS
GETTING THERE   There is no train service to Villandry. The nearest connection from Tours is at the town of Savonnières. From Savonnières, you can walk along the Loire for 3km (2 miles) to reach Villandry, rent a **bike** at the station, or take a **taxi.** You can also **drive,** following D7 from Tours.

WHERE TO STAY & DINE
Le Cheval Rouge MODERN FRENCH   This is a well-known lunch stopover near the château, in spite of a sometimes difficult staff. Set in a conservatively decorated dining room about 90m (300 ft.) from the banks of the Cher, it won't offer you your most memorable meal in the Loire Valley. Specialties include lobster thermidor, and medallions of veal with morels. The inn also rents 18 rooms, all with private bathroom and telephone. A double is 46€. Parking is free.

Villandry, 37510 Joué-les-Tours. ℭ **02-47-50-02-07.** Fax 02-47-50-08-77. Reservations recommended. Main courses 15€–32€. Fixed-price menus 16€–30€. MC, V. Tues–Sun noon–2pm and 7:30–9pm. Closed Feb to mid-Mar.

AZAY-LE-RIDEAU ✹✹✹
This château's machicolated towers and blue-slate roof pierced with dormers shimmer in the moat, creating a reflection like a Monet painting. But the defensive medieval look is all for show; the **Château d'Azay-le-Rideau,** 37190 Azay-le-Rideau (ℭ **02-47-45-42-04**), was created during the Renaissance at an idyllic spot on the Indre River. Gilles Berthelot, François I's finance minister, commissioned the castle, and his spendthrift wife, Philippa, supervised its construction. So elegant was the creation that the chevalier king grew jealous. In time, Berthelot was forced to flee and the château reverted to the king.

Before entering, circle the château, enjoying the perfect proportions of this crowning achievement of the Renaissance in Touraine. Its most fanciful feature is a bay enclosing a grand stairway with a straight flight of steps. The Renaissance interior is a virtual museum.

The château is open daily July and August from 9:30am to 7pm; April through June and September through October from 9:30am to 6pm; and November through March from 9:30am to 12:30pm and 2 to 5:30pm. Admission is 5.50€ for adults and 3.50€ for ages 18 to 25, free for under 18. Allow 2 hours for a visit. From May to July, *son et lumière* (sound and light) performances, about an hour in length, with recorded music and lights beaming on the exterior of the château, begin at 10:30pm; during August they begin at 10pm;

and in September at 9:30pm. Tickets are 9€ for adults and 5€ for ages 18 to 25; free for those under 18.

ESSENTIALS

GETTING THERE   To reach Azay-le-Rideau, take the **train** from either Tours or Chinon. Trip time is about 30 minutes; the one-way fare is 4.25€. Both Tours and Chinon have express service to Paris. For SNCF bus and rail schedules to Azay-le-Rideau from anywhere, call ⓒ **08-36-35-35-35.** If you're **driving** from Tours, take D759 southwest to Azay-le-Rideau.

VISITOR INFORMATION   The **Syndicat d'Initiative** (tourist office) is on place de l'Europe (ⓒ **02-47-45-44-40**).

WHERE TO DINE

L'Aigle d'Or *(Kids)* TRADITIONAL FRENCH   The owners, Jean-Luc and Ghislaine Fèvre, work in the kitchens and dining room of this century-old house, the best restaurant in town for nearly 2 decades. Their restaurant is in the village center, about .3km (¼-mile) from the château. The service is professional, the welcome charming, and the food the best in Azay. In a dining room accented with ceiling beams, a fireplace, and pastel colors, you'll enjoy dishes including crayfish with foie gras, and a *blanquette* (stew) of Loire Valley whitefish prepared with one of the region's white wines. Desserts are made fresh daily. In summer, the party expands onto an outdoor terrace.

10 av. Adélaïde-Riché. ⓒ 02-47-45-24-58. Reservations recommended. Main courses 25€–40€; set lunch 40€–56€; children's menu 10€. V. Thurs–Tues noon–2pm and 7:30–9:30pm. Closed Sun nights year-round and Tues nights off season.

AMBOISE ✸✸✸

On the banks of the Loire, Amboise is in the center of vineyards known as Touraine Amboise. Leonardo da Vinci spent his last years in this city. Dominating the town is the **Château d'Amboise** ✸✸ (ⓒ **02-47-57-00-98**), the first in France to reflect the Italian Renaissance. A combination of both Gothic and Renaissance, this 15th-century château is mainly associated with Charles VIII.

You enter via a ramp, opening onto a panoramic terrace fronting the river. At one time, buildings surrounded this terrace, and fêtes were staged in the enclosed courtyard. After the revolution, the castle declined, and little remains of the once-sprawling edifice. First you come to the flamboyant Gothic Chapelle St-Hubert, distinguished by its lacelike tracery. It allegedly contains da Vinci's remains; actually the great artist was buried in the castle's Collegiate Church, which was destroyed between 1806 and 1810. Today the walls of the château are hung with tapestries and the rooms furnished grandly. The *Logis du Roi* (king's apartment) escaped destruction and can be visited.

The château is open daily, July and August from 9am to 8pm; April through June from 9am to 6:30pm; September and October from 9am to 6pm; November 1 to 15 from 9am to 5:30pm; November 16 through January 31 from 9am to noon and 2 to 4:45pm; and February through March from 9am to noon and 1:30 to 5:30pm. Admission is 7€ adults, 6€ students, 4€ children ages 7 to 14, free for children under 7.

You might also wish to visit **Clos-Lucé** ✸, 2 rue du Clos-Lucé (ⓒ **02-47-57-62-88**), a 15th-century manor that contains a museum devoted to Leonardo da Vinci. In what had been an oratory for Anne de Bretagne, François I installed "the great master in all forms of art and science," Leonardo da Vinci. Venerated by the chevalier king, Leonardo lived here for 3 years, dying at the manor in

1519. (Those paintings of Leonardo dying in François's arms are symbolic; the king was supposedly away at the time.) The manor's interior contains furniture from his era, sketches, and models that were faithfully executed for his flying machines, bridges, cannon, and even a primitive example of a machine gun. Clos-Lucé is open daily year-round: January from 9am to 5pm; February and March from 9am to 6pm; April through June from 9am to 7pm; July through August from 9am to 8pm; September and October from 9am to 7pm; and November and December from 9am to 6pm. Admission is 6.50€ adults, 3.50€ students and children 6 to 15, free for ages 5 and under.

ESSENTIALS

GETTING THERE Amboise is on the Paris–Blois–Tours rail line, with 14 **trains** per day from both Tours and Blois. The trip from Tours takes 20 minutes and costs 4.50€ one-way; from Blois, it takes 20 minutes and costs 5.30€. About five conventional trains a day leave from Paris's Gare d'Austerlitz (trip time: 2½ hr.), and several high-speed TGV trains depart from the Gare Montparnasse for St-Pierre-des-Corps, less than a kilometer from Tours. From St-Pierre-des-Corps, you can transfer to a conventional train for Amboise. Fares from Paris to Amboise cost from 22€. For information, call ℭ **08-36-35-35-35.**

If you prefer to travel by bus, **Autocars de Touraine** (ℭ **02-47-57-00-44**), which operates out of the Gare Routière in Tours, just across from the town's railway station, runs about six **buses** every day between Tours and Amboise. Each takes about 40 minutes and costs 2€ one-way.

If you're **driving** from Tours, take N152 east to D32 and then turn south, following the signs to Amboise.

VISITOR INFORMATION The **Office de Tourisme** is on quai du Général-de-Gaulle (ℭ **02-47-57-09-28;** www.amboise-valdeloire.com).

WHERE TO STAY

Le Choiseul ★★★ There's no better address in Amboise and no better place for cuisine than this 18th-century hotel, in the valley between a hillside and the Loire. Guest rooms, 16 of which are air-conditioned, are luxurious; though modernized, they've retained their old-world charm. The small bathrooms contain combination tub/showers. The formal dining room has a view of the Loire and welcomes nonguests who phone ahead. The cuisine is better than that in Tours or the surrounding area; it is deluxe, international, classic French, and regional, utilizing the freshest ingredients. On the grounds is a garden with flowering terraces.

36 quai Charles-Guinot, 37400 Amboise. ℭ **02-47-30-45-45.** Fax 02-47-30-46-10. www.lechoiseul.com. 32 units. 128€–325€ double; 230€–285€ suite. AE, DC, MC, V. Closed Dec 20–Feb 6. **Amenities:** Restaurant; bar; pool; tennis court; limited room service; babysitting; laundry/dry cleaning. *In room:* A/C, TV, minibar, hair dryer.

Le Vieux Manoir ★★ *Finds* Gloria and Bob Belknap, an American couple, fell in love with France and this 18th-century manor, which they restored and turned into an elegant B&B. They now welcome guests to their beautifully furnished guest rooms with country antiques, exposed oak beams, stone walls, and tile floors; a glass conservatory overlooks a garden. Guests are also housed in a 17th-century structure with old oak beams and exposed stone walls. This latter accommodation with its fully equipped kitchen is ideal for families. Each bathroom is lined with locally made tiles in a different hue, such as one of the streaky golds of Monet's dining room at Giverny. Bathrooms are the finest in Amboise, with period mirrors and washstands, and heavy German fixtures with tub-and-shower combinations. Accommodations are named after various legends, everybody from Georges Sand and Colette to Joséphine and Mme du Barry. The house is set in manicured gardens of stately elegance.

13 rue Rabelais, 37400 Amboise. ℂ **02-47-30-41-27.** Fax 02-47-30-41-27. www.le-vieux-manoir.com. 6 units, 2-bedroom cottage. 125€–175€ double; 250€–335€ cottage for 4. No credit cards. Rates include breakfast. **Amenities:** Garden; conservatory.

WHERE TO DINE

The finest dining choice is **Le Choiseul** (see "Where to Stay," above).

Le Manoir St-Thomas ✸ TRADITIONAL FRENCH   The best food in town outside of Le Choiseul is served at this Renaissance house in the shadow of the château. Set in a garden, the dining room is decorated with a polychrome ceiling and a massive stone fireplace. Owner and chef François Le Coz's specialties include truffles with foie gras, lamb filet with port, and red mullet filet with cream of sweet pepper sauce. The saddle of hare is perfectly flavored. Some unique delights are the goose liver paté wrapped in a combination of truffles and wild black mushrooms, and duck flavored with honey, cinnamon, and ginger.

Place Richelieu. ℂ **02-47-57-22-52.** Reservations required. Main courses 13€–46€; fixed-price menu 29€–48€. AE, DC, MC, V. Tues 7:30–9:30pm; Wed–Sat 12:15–2:30pm and 7:15–9:30pm; Sun 12:15–2:30pm. Closed Jan 15–Mar 15.

BLOIS ✸✸

Blois is the most attractive of the major Loire towns. It rises on the right bank of the Loire, its skyline dominated by its château, where the duc de Guise was assassinated on December 23, 1588, on orders of his archrival, Henri III. Several French kings lived here, and the town has a rich architectural history.

The murder of the duc de Guise is only one of the memories evoked by the **Château de Blois** ✸✸✸ (ℂ **02-54-90-33-32**), begun in the 13th century by the comtes de Blois. Charles d'Orléans (son of Louis d'Orléans, assassinated by the Burgundians in 1407) lived at Blois after his release from 25 years of English captivity. In his seventies, Charles became the father of the future Louis XII. Blois was then launched in its new role as a royal château. In time it was to be called the second capital of France, with Blois, the city of kings.

However, Blois soon became a palace of banishment. Louis XIII got rid of his interfering mother, Marie de Médici, by sending her here; but this plump matron escaped by sliding into the moat down a mound of dirt left by the builders. Then in 1626 the king sent his conspiring brother, Gaston d'Orléans, here; he stayed.

If you stand in the courtyard, you'll find that the château is like an illustrated storybook of French architecture. The Hall of the Estates-General is a 13th-century work; the Charles d'Orléans gallery was actually built by Louis XII from 1498 to 1501, as was the Louis XII wing. The Gaston d'Orléans wing was constructed by Mansart between 1635 and 1638. The most remarkable is the François I wing, a masterpiece of the French Renaissance, containing a spiral staircase with elaborately ornamented balustrades and the king's symbol, the salamander.

The château is open daily, mid-October through mid-March from 9am to 12:30pm and 2 to 5:30pm; mid-March through June and September from 9am to 6:30pm; and July and August from 9am to 7:30pm. Admission is 6€ adults, 4€ students 12 to 20, 3€ children 6 to 11, free for children 5 and under. A *son et lumière* presentation is sponsored nightly May through September, beginning between 9:30 and 10:30pm. The presentation is usually in French except on Wednesday, when it's in English. The show costs 9.50€ for adults, 4.50€ for children 7 to 15.

ESSENTIALS
GETTING THERE   The Paris–Austerlitz line via Orléans delivers six **trains** per day from Paris (trip time: 2 hr.), costing 20€ one-way; from Tours, five trains arrive per day (trip time: 30 min.), at a cost of 8.40€ one-way. For information, call © **08-36-35-35-35**. The station is at place de la Gare. Once here, you can take a **bus** (© 02-54-90-41-41) to tour various châteaux, including Chambord, Chaumont, Chenonceau, and Amboise. Buses depart from the train station from June to September only. If you're **driving** from Tours, take RN152 east to Blois. If you'd like to explore the area by **bike**, go to **Cycles Le Blond**, 44 levée des Tuileries (© **02-54-74-30-13**), where rentals range from 6€ to 13€ per day, depending on the model. You have to leave your passport, a credit card, a driver's license, or a deposit of between 76€ and 228€, depending on the value of the bike.

VISITOR INFORMATION   The **Office de Tourisme** is in the Pavillon Anne-de-Bretagne, 3 av. Jean-Laigret (© **02-54-90-41-41;** www.loiredes chateaux.com).

WHERE TO STAY
Hôtel le Savoie   This modern 1930s-era hotel is both inviting and livable, from its courteous staff to its guest rooms, which are small but nonetheless quiet and cozy. They were last renovated in 2000. Bathrooms are small but have sufficient shelf space; each comes with a shower. In the morning, a breakfast buffet is set up in the bright dining room.

6–8 rue du Docteur-Ducoux, 41000 Blois. © **02-54-74-32-21**. Fax 02-54-74-29-58. 26 units. 39€–46€ double. MC, V. *In room:* TV, hair dryer.

Mercure Centre ✿   This is the newest and best-located hotel in Blois—three stories of reinforced concrete and big windows beside the quays of the Loire, a 5-minute walk from the château. Rooms never rise above the chain-style format and are very roadside-motel in look, but they are roomy and soundproof. Bathrooms come with a combination shower and tub.

28 quai St-Jean, 41000 Blois. © **02-54-56-66-66**. Fax 02-54-56-67-00. www.mercure.blois.fr. 96 units. 82€–99€ double. AE, DC, MC, V. Bus: Quayside marked PISCINE. **Amenities:** Restaurant; bar; indoor pool; Jacuzzi; sauna; limited room service; babysitting; laundry/dry cleaning. *In room:* A/C, TV, minibar, hair dryer.

WHERE TO DINE
Le Médicis ✿ TRADITIONAL FRENCH   Christian and Annick Garanger maintain one of the most sophisticated inns in Blois—ideal for a gourmet meal or an overnight stop. Fresh fish is the chef's specialty. Typical main courses are asparagus in mousseline sauce, scampi ravioli with saffron sauce, and supreme of perch with morels. Chocolate in many manifestations is the dessert specialty.

2 allée François-1er, 41000 Blois. © **02-54-43-94-04**. Fax 02-54-42-04-05. www.le-medicis.com. Reservations required. Main courses 21€–30€; fixed-price menus 22€, 30€, 38€, 45€, and 65€. AE, MC, V. Daily noon–2pm and 7–9pm. Closed Jan and Sun night Nov–Mar. Bus: 2.

L'Orangerie du Château ✿✿✿ TOURAINE   Next to the château, this is the grandest and best restaurant in the area. You approach the restaurant through a gated courtyard, which sets the elegant tone. Chef Molveaux invites you into his floral-themed dining room, where he'll dazzle you with an intriguing array of specialties. His faithful customers, along with the most discerning foodies visiting Blois, take delight in his filet mignon with truffles, everything tasting better with a Sauvignon de Touraine. You can also sample his lovely medley of shellfish and nuts in a cream sauce or his perfectly roasted monkfish flavored with fresh thyme. For dessert, our special favorite is his melted chocolate and pistachio with crème fraîche. Prepare to make an evening of it if you dine here.

1 av. Jean-Laigret. ℭ **02-54-78-05-36.** Reservations required. Main courses 22€–34€. Fixed-price menus 40€–59€. Children's menu 13€. MC, V. Thurs–Tues 12:10–1:45pm and 7:15–9:15pm. Closed Sun night and sometimes Tues night, and mid-Feb to mid-Mar.

CHAMBORD

When François I used to say, "Come on up to my place," he meant the **Château de Chambord** ✮✮✮, 41250 Bracieux (ℭ **02-54-50-40-00**). Some 2,000 workers began to piece together "the pile" in 1519. What emerged after 20 years was the pinnacle of the French Renaissance, the largest château in the Loire Valley. It was ready for the visit of Charles V of Germany, who was welcomed by nymphets in transparent veils gently tossing wildflowers in his path. French monarchs like Henri II and Catherine de Médici, Louis XIV, and Henri III came and went from Chambord.

The château is set in a park of more than 5,200 hectares (13,000 acres), enclosed within a wall stretching some 32km (20 miles). Looking out a window in one of the 440 rooms, François is said to have carved these words on a pane with a diamond ring: "A woman is a creature of change; to trust her is to play the fool." Four huge towers dominate Chambord's facade. The keep has a spectacular terrace on which the ladies used to stand to watch for the return of their men from the hunt.

The château is open daily (except Jan 1, May 1, and Dec 25) from 9am to 6:30pm (last entrance at 5:45pm). Admission is 6€ for adults, 4.50€ for ages 18 to 25, and free for children 17 and under. At the tourist office, you can pick up tickets for the summer *son-et-lumière* presentation, *Jours et Siècles* (Days and Centuries). The price is 12€.

ESSENTIALS

GETTING THERE It's best to **drive** to Chambord. Take the D951 northeast from Blois to Ménars, turning onto the rural road to Chambord. You can also rent a **bicycle** in Blois and ride the 18km (11 miles) to Chambord, or take one of the **tours** to Chambord leaving from Blois in summer. From June 15 to September 15, **Transports du Loir et Cher** (ℭ **02-54-58-55-61**) operates bus service to Chambord, leaving Blois at 9am and again at 1:30pm, with returns at 1 and 6pm.

VISITOR INFORMATION The **Office de Tourisme** on place St-Michel (ℭ **02-54-20-34-86**) is open only from April to September.

WHERE TO STAY & DINE

Hôtel du Grand-St-Michel Across from the château, and originally built as a kennel for the royal hounds, this inn is the only one of any substance in town. Try for a front room overlooking the château, which is dramatic when floodlit at night. Accommodations are plain but comfortable, with provincial decor and shower-only private bathrooms. The regional dishes are complemented by a marvelous collection of Loire wines so good they almost overshadow the cooking. High points include a stew of wild boar (in late autumn and winter), breast of duckling in a green peppercorn sauce, and several of the local patés and terrines, including the coarsely textured and very flavor-filled rillettes of regional pork.

103 place St-Michel, 41250 Chambord, near Bracieux. © **02-54-20-31-31.** Fax 02-54-20-36-40. 39 units. 49€–62€ double. Main courses 19€–25€. MC, V. Free parking. Closed Nov 13–Dec 21. **Amenities:** Restaurant; lounges. *In room:* TV.

CHEVERNY

The *haut monde* still come to the Sologne area for the hunt as if the 17th century had never ended. However, 20th-century realities, like taxes, are *formidable* here—hence the **Château de Cheverny** ★★★ (© **02-54-79-96-29**) must open some of its rooms for inspection by paying guests.

Unlike most of the Loire châteaux, Cheverny is actually lived in by the descendants of the original owner, the vicomte de Sigalas. The family's lineage can be traced back to Henri Hurault, the son of the chancellor of Henri III and Henri IV, who built the château here in 1634. Designed in classic Louis XIII style, it boasts square pavilions flanking the central pile.

Inside, the furnishings, tapestries, decorations, and objets d'art are impressive. A 17th-century artist, Jean Mosnier, decorated the fireplace with motifs from the legend of Adonis. In the Guards' Room is a collection of medieval armor.

The château is open daily, November through February, from 9:30am to noon and 2:15 to 5pm; March and October, from 9:30am to noon and 2:15 to 5:30pm; April through June and September, from 9:15am to 6:15pm; and July and August, from 9:15am to 6:45pm. Admission is 5.80€ for adults, 2.80€ for children 7 to 14, free for children 6 and under.

ESSENTIALS

GETTING THERE   Cheverny is 19km (12 miles) south of Blois, along D765. It's best reached by **car** or on a **bus tour** from Blois with **Transports du Loir et Cher** (© **02-54-58-55-61**). From the railway station at Blois, a bus departs for Cheverny once a day at noon, returning to Blois 4 hours later, according to an oft-changing schedule that varies by the season and the day of the week. Frankly, most visitors find it a lot easier to take their own car or a **taxi** from the railway station at Blois.

WHERE TO STAY & DINE

Les Trois Marchands TRADITIONAL FRENCH   This coaching inn, more comfortable than St-Hubert, has been handed down for many generations. Today, Jean-Jacques Bricault owns the three-story building with awnings, a mansard roof, a glassed-in courtyard, and sidewalk tables with umbrellas. In the tavern-style dining room, the menu might include foie gras, lobster salad, frogs' legs, fresh asparagus in mousseline sauce, or fish cooked in a salt crust. The inn rents 37 well-furnished, comfortable rooms for 42€ to 55€ double.

Place de l'Eglise, 41700 Cour-Cheverny. © **02-54-79-96-44.** Fax 02-54-79-25-60. Main courses 15€–30€; fixed-price menu 25€–46€. AE, DC, MC, V. Tues–Sun noon–2:15pm and 7:30–9:15pm. Closed Feb 1–Mar 15. **Amenities:** 2 restaurants. *In room:* TV.

St-Hubert TRADITIONAL FRENCH   About 450m (1,500 ft.) from the château, this inn was built in the 1950s in the provincial style. The least expensive menu might include terrine of quail, pikeperch with beurre blanc, some cheeses, and a fruit tart. The most expensive may offer lobster, an aiguillette of duckling prepared with grapes, salmon braised in white wine, a casserole of seafood with shellfish sauce, and, in season, thigh of roebuck in pepper sauce. The St-Hubert offers 19 conservatively decorated rooms with bathroom, for 44€ to 54€ double.

Rte. Nationale, 41700 Cour-Cheverny. ⓒ **02-54-79-96-60.** Fax 02-54-79-21-17. Main courses 13€–16€; fixed-price menu 15€–37€. AE, MC, V. Daily 12:15–2pm and 7:30–9:30pm. Closed Feb and Sun nights off season. **Amenities:** Restaurant. *In room:* TV.

CHENONCEAUX

A Renaissance masterpiece, the **Château de Chenonceau** 🐾🐾🐾 (ⓒ **02-47-23-90-07;** www.chenonceau.com) is best known for the *dames de Chenonceau* who have occupied it. (Note that the town is spelled with a final x, but the château is not.) Originally it was owned by the Marqués family. Thomas Bohier, the comptroller-general of finances in Normandy, began buying land around the château. The extravagant Marqués family was eventually forced to sell to Bohier, who tore down Chenonceau, preserving only the keep and building the rest in the emerging Renaissance style.

Many of the château's walls are covered with Gobelin tapestries, including one depicting a woman pouring water over the back of an angry dragon. The chapel contains a marble *Virgin and Child,* plus portraits of Catherine de Médici in her traditional black and white. There's even a portrait of stern Catherine in the former bedroom of her rival, Diane de Poitiers. In François I's Renaissance bedchamber, the most interesting portrait is that of Diane de Poitiers as the huntress Diana.

The history of Chenonceau is related in 15 tableaux in the **Musée de Cire** (wax museum), located in a Renaissance-era annex a few steps from the château. Open during the same hours as the château, it charges a general admission fee of 3€. Diane de Poitiers, who, among other activities, introduced the artichoke to France, is depicted in three tableaux. One portrays Catherine de Médici tossing out her husband's mistress.

The château is open daily from 9am to 7pm (except Jan 1 and Dec 25). Admission is 6.50€ for adults and 6.10€ for students and children 7 to 15. A *son-et-lumière* show, *The Era of the Ladies of Chenonceaux,* is staged daily in July and August at 10:15pm; admission is 7.60€ for adults, 6.10€ for students and children ages 7 to 15, free for children 6 and under. Allow 2 hours to see this château.

ESSENTIALS

GETTING THERE   There are four daily **trains** from Tours to Chenonceaux (trip time: 30 min.), costing 5.50€ one-way. The train deposits you at the base of the château; from there, you can either walk or take a taxi.

VISITOR INFORMATION   The **Syndicat d'Initiative** (tourist office) is at 1 rue Bretonneau (ⓒ **02-47-23-94-45**), open from Easter to September.

WHERE TO STAY

Hôtel du Bon-Laboureur et du Château 🐾🐾   This inn is your best bet for a comfortable night's sleep and some of the best cuisine in the Loire Valley. Founded in 1786, the hotel maintains the flavor of that era, thanks to thick walls, solid masonry, and a scattering of antiques. Most guest rooms are small, especially those on the upper floors, and each comes with a private bathroom with shower or tub. The rear garden has a guesthouse and formally planted roses. The place is noted for its restaurant, which receives fewer bus groups than many competitors. In fair weather, tables are set up in the courtyard, amid trees and flowering shrubs. Fixed-price menus are 30€ to 65€.

6 rue du Dr. Bretonneau, Chenonceaux, 37150 Bléré. ⓒ **02-47-23-90-02.** Fax 02-47-23-82-01. www. amboise.com/laboureur. 24 units. 70€–125€ double; 145€–165€ suite. AE, DC, MC, V. Closed Nov 15–Dec

20. **Amenities:** Restaurant; bar; pool; limited room service; babysitting; laundry/dry cleaning. *In room:* A/C, TV, kitchenette, hair dryer, safe.

La Roseraie *(★ (Value* La Roseraie is the most charming hotel in Chenonceaux, with individually decorated rooms and well-kept gardens. Each unit contains a small bathroom with shower. In the 1940s, its guests included Winston Churchill, Eleanor Roosevelt, and Harry Truman. Some of the finest meals in town are served at lunch and dinner in the restaurant, which is open to the public. Our favorites include house-style foie gras; magret of duckling with pears and cherries; and an unusual and delicious invention—*emincée* (a dish made with braised meat) of rump steak with wine-marinated pears.

7 rue du Dr. Bretonneau, Chenonceaux, 37150 Bléré. ℂ **02-47-23-90-09.** Fax 02-47-23-91-59. 17 units. 53€–90€ double; 72€–120€ for 4; 168€ for apt. MC, V. Closed Dec to mid-Feb. **Amenities:** Restaurant; bar; pool; laundry/dry cleaning. *In room:* TV, hair dryer.

WHERE TO DINE

Note that **La Renaudière,** 24 rue du Dr. Bretonneau (ℂ **02-47-23-90-04**), and **La Roseraie** (see above) boast very good restaurants.

Au Gateau Breton TRADITIONAL FRENCH   The terrace in back of this Breton-type inn, a short walk from the château, is a refreshing place for dinner or tea. Gravel paths run among beds of pink geraniums and lilacs, and the red tables are adorned with bright umbrellas. In cool months, meals are served in the rustic dining rooms. Make a meal of the home cooking and cherry liqueur—a specialty of the region. Specialties include small chitterling sausages of Tours, chicken with Armagnac sauce, and *coq au vin.* Tasty pastries are sold in the front room.

16 rue du Dr. Bretonneau. ℂ **02-47-23-90-14.** Fax 02-47-23-92-57. Reservations required July–Aug. Fixed-price menu 15€–22€. AE, MC, V. Mar–Oct daily noon–2:30pm and Thurs–Mon 7–10pm; Nov–Feb Thurs–Tues only noon–2:30pm.

CHINON ★

In the film *Joan of Arc,* Ingrid Bergman sought out the dauphin as he tried to conceal himself among his courtiers—an action whose real-life equivalent took place at the Château de Chinon. Charles VII, mockingly known as the king of Bourges, centered his government at Chinon from 1429 to 1450. In 1429, with the English besieging Orléans, the Maid of Orléans, that "messenger from God," prevailed on the weak dauphin to give her an army. The rest is history. The seat of French power stayed at Chinon until the Hundred Years' War ended.

Chinon retains a medieval atmosphere. It consists of winding streets and turreted houses, many built in the 15th and 16th centuries. For the best view, drive across the river, turning right onto quai Danton. From that vantage point, you'll have the best perspective, seeing the castle in relation to the village and the river. The most typical street is **rue Voltaire,** lined with 15th- and 16th-century town houses. This is one of the most medieval-looking streets in the entire Loire Valley. At no. 44, Richard the Lion-Hearted died on April 6, 1199, after being mortally wounded while besieging Chalus in Limousin. In the heart of Chinon, the **Grand Carroi** lies at the intersection of an ancient Roman road that was later joined by a medieval road. The village of Chinon evolved from this crossroad.

The most famous son of Chinon, François Rabelais, the earthy and often bawdy Renaissance writer, lived on the rue de la Lamproie; today a plaque marks the spot where his father practiced law and maintained a prosperous home and office. The cottage 6km (3½ miles) west of Chinon where he was born is the site of the **Musée de la Devinière,** 37500 Seuilly (ℂ **02-47-95-91-18**). Admission is 3.75€ adults, 2.70€ children or students 6 to 25 and seniors, free for children

5 and under. It's open daily, January 1 through March 13 and October 1 through December 31, from 9:30am to 12:30pm and 2 to 5pm; March 15 through April 30 daily 9:30am to 12:30am and 2 to 6pm; May 1 through September 14 daily 10am to 7pm. To reach it from Chinon, follow the road signs pointing to Saumur and the D-17. Along the way, make a stop at the **Church of Notre Dame in Rivière;** admission is free (© **02-47-93-07-53**). It's the most visible building in the agrarian hamlet of Rivière and one of the oldest buildings in the Loire Valley, a small and stocky-looking Romanesque church originally built between the 10th and 11th centuries.

Château de Chinon 🏰🏰 (© **02-47-93-13-45**) includes three separate strongholds, once badly ruined. Today at least two of the buildings, the Château du Milieu and the Château du Coudray, have been restored, with the exception of their roofs, which are relatively unobtrusive modern constructions that don't necessarily adhere to the original designs. Some of the grim walls from other edifices remain, though many of the buildings—including the Great Hall where Joan of Arc sought out the dauphin—have been torn down. Demolished in the 17th and 18th centuries, the Château de St Georges was built by Henry II of England, who died here in 1189. The Château du Milieu dates from the 11th century to the 15th century; it contains the keep and the clock tower, where the Musée Jeanne d'Arc has been installed. The Château du Coudray contains the Tour du Coudray, where Joan of Arc stayed during her time at Chinon. In the 14th century the Knights Templar were imprisoned here before meeting their violent deaths.

January through March and October through December, the chateau is open daily from 9:30am to 12:30pm and 2 to 5:30pm. April through September, it's open daily from 9am to 7pm. Admission is 4.60€ adults, 1.20€ ages 7 to 18, and free for ages 6 and under.

ESSENTIALS

GETTING THERE   The SNCF runs about 10 **trains** and four **buses** every day to Chinon from Tours (trip time: about an hour for either). Call © **08-36-35-35-35** for information and schedules. Both buses and trains arrive at the train station, which lies at the edge of this very small town. If you're **driving** from Tours, take D759 southwest through Azay-le-Rideau to Chinon.

VISITOR INFORMATION   The **Office de Tourisme** is at place Hoffheim (© **02-47-93-17-85**).

WHERE TO STAY

Hôtel Diderot 🏰 *Finds*   This sprawling aristocratic house from the 1700s offers a calm elegance. Off place Jeanne d'Arc with its black slate roof and white limestone walls, the hotel maintains a regal air. The staff helps you settle into the large guest rooms, which have hardwood floors, exposed beams, antique furniture, and cushy beds, plus tidily kept bathrooms, 17 of which come with both tub and shower. A sense of the past is preserved in the exposed beams and supports, the 18th-century staircase, and the 15th-century fireplace in the dining room, where breakfast is served. As a bonus, guests have use of a private garden and patio.

4 rue Buffon, 37500 Chinon. © **02-47-93-18-87**. Fax 02-47-93-37-10. www.hoteldiderot.com. 27 units. 56€–69€ double. AE, DC, MC, V. **Amenities:** Bar. *In room:* TV.

WHERE TO DINE

Au Plaisir Gourmand 🏰🏰 TRADITIONAL FRENCH   This is the premier restaurant in the area, owned by Jean-Claude Rigollet. The 18th-century building contains a dining room with a limited number of tables. Menu items are likely to include roast rabbit in aspic with foie gras sauce, oxtail in a Chinon red-wine sauce, and sautéed crayfish with a spicy salad. For dessert, try the prunes stuffed in puff pastry.

2 rue Parmentier. ℂ **02-47-93-20-48.** Reservations required. Main courses 12€–25€; tasting menus 39€ and 59€. AE, V. Tues–Sun noon–3:30pm; Tues-Sat 7:30–8:30pm. Closed mid-Jan to mid-Feb.

ANGERS ✹✹✹

Once the capital of Anjou, Angers straddles the Maine River. Although it suffered extensive damage in World War II, it has been considerably restored, somehow blending provincial charm with the suggestion of sophistication. The town is often used as a base for exploring the château district to the west.

The moated **Château d'Angers** ✹✹✹ (ℂ **02-41-87-43-47**) from the 9th century was once the home of the comtes d'Anjou. After the castle was destroyed, it was reconstructed by St. Louis. From 1230 to 1238 the outer walls and 17 massive towers were built, creating a fortress well prepared to withstand invaders. The château was favored by "Good" King René; until he was forced to surrender Anjou to Louis XI, a brilliant court life flourished. Louis XIV turned the château into a prison. During World War II, the Nazis used it as a munitions depot. Allied planes bombed it in 1944.

The castle displays the **Apocalypse Tapestries** ✹✹✹, masterpieces of medieval art. (This series of tapestries wasn't always so highly regarded; they once served as a canopy for orange trees to protect the fruit from unfavorable weather, and at another time to cover the damaged walls of a church.) Nicolas Bataille, master weaver, created the tapestries. The series illustrates the Book of St. John in 77 pieces that stretch 102m (335 ft.). One scene is called *La Grande Prostituée,* and another shows Babylon invaded by demons.

You can tour the fortress, including the courtyard of the nobles, prison cells, ramparts, windmill tower, 15th-century chapel, and royal apartments. The château and its tapestries can be visited daily year-round from 10am to 7pm.

Admission to the château and exhibits is 5.45€ adults, 3.50€ seniors and students 19 to 25, free for ages 18 and under. Once you've paid, you can participate in one of the guided tours on the architecture and history of the château. They depart every day at 10am, 11:30am, 1:15pm, 2:30pm, and 3:30pm. Guided tours that focus on the tapestries begin every day at 10:15am and 3:45pm. Each tour lasts about 75 minutes and is conducted mostly in French, with foreign-language leaflets (in English and several other languages) available.

ESSENTIALS

GETTING THERE   Three **trains** per day leave Paris's Gare de Montparnasse for the 2- to 4-hour trip; the cost is 40€ to 51€ one-way. From Tours, seven trains per day make the 1-hour trip; a one-way ticket is 13€. The Angers train station, at place de la Gare, is a convenient walk from the château. For train information, call ℂ **08-36-35-35-35.** There are three **bus** connections a day from Saumur, from Monday to Saturday (1½ hr.). Buses arrive at place de la République. Call ℂ **02-41-33-64-64** for schedules. If you're **driving** from Tours, take N152 southwest to Saumur, and turn west on D952.

VISITOR INFORMATION   The **Office de Tourisme,** on place du Président-Kennedy (ℂ **02-41-23-50-00**), is opposite the entrance to the château.

WHERE TO STAY

Hôtel d'Anjou   Next to a park, this hotel is the best choice for overnighting in the area. Although comparable in price to the Quality Hôtel de France, it has more upscale appointments and amenities, along with a better restaurant. The guest rooms closer to the ground have higher ceilings and are more spacious.

1 bd. Foch, 49100 Angers. ℭ **800/528-1234** in the U.S. or Canada, or 02-41-88-24-82. Fax 02-41-87-22-21. 53 units. 80€–127€ double. AE, DC, MC, V. Parking 8€. **Amenities:** Restaurant; bar; laundry/dry cleaning. *In room:* TV, minibar.

Quality Hôtel de France   This 19th-century hotel, one of the most respected in town, has been run by the Bouyers since 1893. It's the best choice near the railway station. Rooms are soundproof, and many were renovated in the late 1990s. Bathrooms are very small with bathtubs.

8 place de la Gare, 49100 Angers. ℭ **02-41-88-49-42.** Fax 02-41-86-76-70. www.destination-anjou. com/hoteldefrance. 55 units. 72€–102€ double. AE, DC, MC, V. Parking 6.80€. **Amenities:** 2 restaurants; bar; limited room service; laundry/dry cleaning. *In room:* A/C, TV, minibar, hair dryer.

WHERE TO DINE

Hôtel d'Anjou (see below) boasts the town's best restaurant.

Le Salamandre ℱ CLASSIC FRENCH   Any educated French person can tell you that the salamander was the symbol of King François I, and in this formal and elegant restaurant you'll see portraits of, and references to, that strategist everywhere. Beneath massive ceiling beams, beside a large wooden fireplace, you'll enjoy the most impeccable service and the best food in town. Shining examples include filet of red snapper in a lime-flavored cream sauce; scallops in a mushroom cream sauce; and squid stuffed with crayfish and served with a shellfish-flavored cream sauce.

In the Hotel d'Anjou, 1 bd. Foch. ℭ **02-41-88-99-55.** Reservations recommended. Main courses 17€–28€. Set-price meals 25€–42€ lunch, 34€–45€ dinner. AE, DC, MC, V. Mon–Sat noon–2pm and 7:30–9:30pm.

3 Provence & the Côte d'Azur

Provence has been called a bridge between the past and the present, which blend in a quiet, often melancholy way. Peter Mayle's *A Year in Provence* and its sequels have played a large role in the popularity of this sunny corner of France.

The Greeks and Romans filled the landscape with cities boasting baths, theaters and arches. Romanesque fortresses and Gothic cathedrals followed. In the 19th century, the light and landscapes attracted painters like Cézanne and van Gogh.

Provence has its own language and customs. The region is bounded on the north by the Dauphine, the west by the Rhône, the east by the Alps, and the south by the Mediterranean. We cover the northern area of this region, what's traditionally thought of as Provence, and then head down to the southern part, what's known as the Côte d'Azur, or French Riviera.

The Riviera has been called the world's most exciting stretch of beach and "a sunny place for shady people." Each resort—be it Beaulieu by the sea or eagle's-nest Eze—has a unique flavor and special merits. Glitterati and eccentrics have always been drawn to this narrow strip of fabled real estate. A trail of modern artists, attracted to the brilliant light, have left a rich heritage: Matisse in his chapel at Vence, Cocteau at Menton and Villefranche, Picasso at Antibes and seemingly everywhere else, Léger at Biot, Renoir at Cagnes, and Bonnard at Le Cannet. The best art collection of all is at the Maeght Foundation in St-Paul-de-Vence.

The Riviera's high season used to be winter and spring only. However, with changing tastes, July and August have become the most crowded months, and reservations are imperative. The average summer temperature is 75°F (24°C); the average winter temperature, 49°F (10°C).

The Corniches of the Riviera, featured in countless films, stretch from Nice to Menton. The Alps drop into the Mediterranean and roads were carved along the way. The lower road, about 32km (20 miles) long, is the **Corniche Inférieure.** Along this road are Villefranche, Cap-Ferrat, Beaulieu, and Cap-Martin. Built between World War I and the beginning of World War II, the **Moyenne Corniche** (Middle Road), 30km (19 miles) long, also runs from Nice to Menton, winding in and out of tunnels and through mountains. The highlight is at Eze. The **Grande Corniche**—the most panoramic—was ordered built by Napoléon in 1806. La Turbie and Le Vistaero are the principal towns along the 32km (20-mile) stretch, which reaches more than 488m (1,600 ft.) high at Col d'Eze.

In general, **tourist offices** in Provence are open from April to September, Monday through Friday from 9am to 1pm and 2 to 6pm, and Saturday and Sunday from 9am to 1pm and 2 to 5pm (closed Sun the rest of the year).

AVIGNON ✦✦✦

In the 14th century, Avignon was the capital of Christendom. The pope lived here during what the Romans called the Babylonian Captivity. The legacy left by that court makes Avignon one of the most beautiful of Europe's medieval cities.

Today, this walled city of some 100,000 residents is increasingly known as a cultural center. Artists and painters have been moving here; experimental theaters, galleries, and cinemas have brought diversity to the inner city.

ESSENTIALS

GETTING THERE The fastest and easiest way to get here is to fly from Paris's Orly Airport to **Aéroport Avignon–Caumont** (© **04-90-81-51-51**), 8km (5 miles) southeast of Avignon (trip time: 1 hr.). Taxis from the airport to the center cost 15€ to 20€. From Paris, TGV **trains** depart from Gare de Lyon, taking 2 hours and 38 minutes. A one-way fare costs 101€ in first class, 75€ in second class. Trains arrive frequently from Marseille, taking 70 minutes and costing 15€; and from Arles, taking 30 minutes and costing 5.60€. For train information and reservations, call © **08-36-35-35-39.**

If you're **driving** from Paris, take A6 south to Lyon; then take A7 south to Avignon. If you'd like to explore the area by **bike,** go to **Cycles Peugeot,** 80 rue Guillaume-Puy (© **04-90-86-32-49**), which rents all sorts of bikes for around 16€ to 19€ per day, including 10-speed road bikes and mountain bikes. A deposit of 152€ is required, either in the form of cash or a credit-card imprint.

VISITOR INFORMATION The **Office de Tourisme** is at 41 cours Jean-Jaurès (© **04-32-74-32-74;** www.avignon-tourism.com).

WHERE TO STAY

Clarion Hotel Cloître St-Louis ✦ This hotel is in a former Jesuit school built in the 1580s. Much of the original premises remain, including the baroque facade, the wraparound arcades, and the soaring ceiling vaults. Guest rooms are rather dull as a result of renovations. Rooms range from medium to spacious, and some have sliding-glass doors overlooking the patio. Each unit has modern decor without a lot of extras; all but three have a combination tub/shower.

20 rue Portail Boquier, 84000 Avignon. © **800/CLARION** in the U.S., or 04-90-27-55-55. Fax 04-90-82-24-01. www.cloitre-saint-louis.com. 80 units. 113€–275€ double; 275€ suite. AE, MC, V. Parking 8€. **Amenities:** Restaurant; bar; outdoor pool; limited room service; dry cleaning. *In room:* A/C, TV, minibar, hair dryer, safe.

Hôtel d'Angleterre   This Art Deco structure in the heart of Avignon is the city's best budget hotel, with the advantage of being located inside the city ramparts. It was built in 1929 in a three-story format of gray stone, emulating the style that local builders imagined was native to most English houses. The rooms are on the small side, but they are comfortably furnished. All except one come with a compact shower-only bathroom. Breakfast is the only meal served.

29 bd. Raspail, 84000 Avignon. ℂ **04-90-86-34-31.** Fax 04-90-86-86-74. www.hoteldangleterre.fr. 40 units, 39 with private bathroom. 55€–74€ double. Breakfast 7€. MC, V. Parking 7€. Closed Dec 20–Jan 20. **Amenities:** Laundry/dry cleaning. *In room:* TV.

La Mirande ✦✦✦   In the heart of Avignon (behind the Palais des Papes), this 700-year-old town house is one of France's grand little luxuries. In 1987, Achim and Hannelore Stein transformed this place into a citadel of opulence. The hotel treats you to 2 centuries of decorative art: from the 1700s Salon Chinois to the Salon Rouge, with its striped walls in Rothschild red. Room no. 20 is the most sought-after, as its lavish premises open onto the garden. All the rooms are stunning, with exquisite decor, hand-printed fabrics on the walls, antiques, bedside controls, and huge bathtubs. The restaurant, among the finest in Avignon, deserves its one Michelin star. Chef Daniel Hébet has a light, sophisticated touch.

4 place Amirande, 84000 Avignon. ℂ **04-90-85-93-93.** Fax 04-90-85-26-85. www.la-mirande.fr. 20 units. 300€–430€ double; 614€–875€ suite. AE, DC, V. Parking 15€. **Amenities:** Restaurant; bar; limited room service; babysitting; laundry service; dry cleaning. *In room:* A/C, TV, minibar, hair dryer, safe.

WHERE TO DINE

Christian Etienne ★★★ PROVENÇAL   The stone house containing this restaurant was built in 1180, around the same time as the Palais des Papes (next door). Owner Christian Etienne continues to reach new culinary heights. His dining room contains early-15th-century frescoes honoring the marriage of Anne de Bretagne to the French king in 1491. Several of the fixed-price menus feature specific themes: Two present seasonal tomatoes, mushrooms, or vegetables; one offers preparations of lobster; and the priciest relies on the chef's imagination *(menu confiance)* to come up with unique combinations. In summer, look for the vegetable menu in which every course is based on ripe tomatoes; the main course is a mousse of lamb, eggplants, tomatoes, and herbs. A la carte specialties include filet of red snapper with black-olive coulis, and a dessert of fennel sorbet with saffron-flavored English cream sauce. The vegetable menus aren't completely vegetarian; they're flavored with meat, fish, or sometimes meat drippings.

10 rue Mons. ℂ **04-90-86-16-50.** Reservations required. Main courses 25€–30€; set-price menus 26€–70€. AE, DC, MC, V. Mon–Sat noon–2:30pm and 8–10:30pm.

La Fourchette *(Value* TRADITIONAL & MODERN FRENCH   This bistro offers creative cooking at a moderate price, although it shuts down on the weekends. There are two dining rooms, bright and airy thanks to large bay windows that flood the inside with light. You might begin with fresh sardines flavored with citrus, ravioli filled with haddock, or a parfait of chicken livers with a spinach flan and a confit of onions. For a main course, we recommend the stew of monkfish with endive, or daube of beef with a gratin of macaroni.

7 rue Racine. ℂ **04-90-85-20-93.** Main courses 15€–24€; set-price dinner 27€. MC, V. Mon–Fri noon–2:30pm and 7:30–10pm. Bus: 11.

EXPLORING THE TOWN

Even more famous than the papal residency is the ditty *"Sur le pont d'Avignon, l'on y danse, l'on y danse,"* echoing through every French nursery and around the world. Ironically, **Pont St-Bénézet** ★★ (ℂ **04-90-85-60-16**) was far too narrow for the *danse* of the rhyme, inspired, according to legend, by a vision a shepherd named Bénézet had while tending his flock. Spanning the Rhône and connecting Avignon with Villeneuve-lèz-Avignon, the bridge is now only a fragmented ruin. Built between 1177 and 1185, it suffered various disasters from then on; in 1669 half of it toppled into the river. On one of the piers is the two-story Chapelle St-Nicolas—one story in Romanesque style, the other Gothic. The remains of the bridge are open daily from 9am to 6:30pm. Admission is 3.50€ for adults and 3€ for students and seniors, free for ages 7 and under.

Dominating Avignon from a hill is the **Palais des Papes,** place du Palais-des-Papes (ℂ **04-90-27-50-00**). You're shown through on a guided tour, usually lasting 50 minutes. Most of the rooms have been stripped of their finery; the exception is the Chapelle St-Jean, known for its frescoes of scenes from the lives of John the Baptist and John the Evangelist, attributed to the school of Matteo Giovanetti, painted between 1345 and 1348. The Grand Tinel, or banquet hall, is about 41m (135 ft.) long and 9m (30 ft.) wide, and the pope's table stood on the southern side. The pope's bedroom is on the first floor of the Tour des Anges. It's open daily, November through March from 9:30am to 5:45pm; April through June and August through October from 9am to 7pm; and in July from 9am to 8pm. Admission (including tour with guide or cassette) is 9.50€ adults, 7.50€ students and seniors, free for ages 7 and under.

Near the palace is the 12th-century **Cathédrale Notre-Dame,** place du Palais-des-Papes (© **04-90-86-81-01**), containing the flamboyant Gothic tomb of Pope John XXII, who died at age 90. Benedict XII is also buried here. The cathedral's hours vary, but generally it's open daily from 9am to noon and 2 to 6pm; admission is free. From the cathedral, enter the promenade du Rocher-des-Doms to stroll through its garden and enjoy the view to Villeneuve-lèz-Avignon.

ST-REMY-DE-PROVENCE 🦋

Nostradamus, the French physician/astrologer and author of over 600 obscure verses, was born here in 1503. In 1922, Gertrude Stein and Alice B. Toklas found St-Rémy after "wandering around everywhere a bit," as Stein once wrote to Cocteau. But St-Rémy is mainly associated with van Gogh, who committed himself to an asylum here in 1889 after cutting off his left ear. Between moods of despair, he painted such works as *Olive Trees* and *Cypresses* here. The town lies 26km (16 miles) northeast of Arles and 13km (8 miles) north of Les Baux.

ESSENTIALS
GETTING THERE   Local **buses** from Avignon (between four and nine per day) take 40 minutes and cost around 6€ one-way. In St-Rémy, buses pull into the place de la République, in the town center. For bus information, call © **04-90-82-07-35.** If you're **driving,** head south from Avignon along D571.

VISITOR INFORMATION   The **Office de Tourisme** is on place Jean-Jaurès (© **04-90-92-05-22**).

WHERE TO STAY

Château de Roussan ✦✦ *Finds*   Although other château hotels are more stylish, this one is more evocative of another time. Its most famous resident, the psychic Nostradamus, lived in an outbuilding a few steps from the front door. Today, you'll pass beneath an archway of 300-year-old trees leading to the neoclassical facade, built in 1701. Most rooms are spacious. Expect old-fashioned plumbing with combination tub/showers. History will envelop you as you wander the grounds, especially when you come upon the sculptures lining a basin, fed by a stream. Be warned that the staff can be off-putting, but the sense of mysticism and the historical importance of this place usually compensate for any crabbiness.

Rte. de Tarascon, 13210 St-Rémy-de-Provence. © **04-90-92-11-63.** Fax 04-90-92-50-59. 21 units. 70€–120€ double. Half board 30€. AE, MC, V. **Amenities:** Restaurant; bar; laundry service. *In room:* Hair dryer.

WHERE TO DINE

La Maison Jaune ✦✦ FRENCH/PROVENÇAL   One of the most enduringly popular restaurants in St-Rémy is in the former residence of an 18th-century merchant. Today, in a pair of dining rooms occupying two floors, you'll appreciate cuisine prepared and served with flair by François and Catherine Perraud. In nice weather, additional seats are available on a terrace overlooking the Hôtel de Sade. Menu items include pigeon roasted in wine from Les Baux; grilled sardines served with candied lemon and raw fennel; artichoke hearts marinated in white wine and served with tomatoes; and a succulent version of roasted rack of lamb served with a tapenade of black olives and anchovies.

15 rue Carnot. © **04-90-92-56-14.** Reservations required. 3 prix-fixe menus for lunch and dinner: 29€, 44€, and 52€. June–Sept Wed–Sun noon–2pm, Tues–Sun 7:30–9:30pm; Oct–May Tues–Sat noon–2pm, Mon–Sat 7:30–9:30pm.

EXPLORING ST-REMY & ENVIRONS

One interesting activity is visiting the cloisters of the asylum van Gogh made famous in his paintings at the 12th-century **Monastère de St-Paul-de-Mausole.** Now a psychiatric hospital for women, the former monastery is east of D-5, a short drive north of Glanum (see below). You can't visit the cell in which van Gogh was confined, but it's still worth a visit to explore the Romanesque chapel and cloisters with their circular arches and columns. November through March, the cloisters are open daily from 10:30am to 1pm and 1:30 to 5pm. April through October, they're open Monday through Friday from 9:30am to 7pm, Saturday and Sunday from 10:30am to 7pm. On your way to the church, you'll see a bust of van Gogh. Admission is 2€ adults, 1€ students and children 12 to 16, free for children 11 and under. There's no public number for the monastery, but you can call the nearby clinic (© **04-90-92-77-00**) for information.

Just south of St-Rémy on D-5 is **Ruines de Glanum** ✦, avenue Vincent-van-Gogh (© **04-90-92-23-79**), a Gallo-Roman city (follow the signs to Les Antiques). Its monuments include an Arc Municipal (a triumphal arch dating from the time of Julius Caesar) and a cenotaph called the Mausolée des Jules. Garlanded with sculptured fruits and flowers, the arch dates from 20 B.C. and is the oldest in Provence. The mausoleum was raised to honor the grandsons of Augustus and is the only extant monument of its type. In the area are entire streets and foundations of private residences from the 1st-century town. Some remains are from an even earlier Gallo-Greek town dating from the 2nd century B.C. Admission is 5€ adults, 3.50€ students and ages 12 to 25, free for children 11 and under. April through September, the excavations are open daily from 9am to 7pm; the rest of the year they're open daily from 9am to noon and 2 to 5pm (closed Jan 1, May 1, Nov 1, Nov 11, and Dec 25).

LES BAUX 🕸🕸🕸

What Cardinal Richelieu called "a nesting place for eagles" lies 19km (12 miles) north of Arles and 80km (50 miles) north of Marseille and the Mediterranean. Once it was the citadel of the seigneurs of Les Baux; today, in its lonely position on a windswept plateau overlooking the southern Alpilles, Les Baux is a ghost of its former self. Still, there is no more dramatically situated town in Provence than this one nestled in a valley surrounded by mysterious, shadowy rock formations.

ESSENTIALS

GETTING THERE There's no rail station in Les Baux, so most **train** passengers get off at Arles, where there are four **buses** daily that stop at Les Baux (trip time: 25 min.) and more that stop in Maussane-les-Alpilles, 3km (2 miles) south. The bus makes fewer runs between November and March. For information, call Ste. Ceyte Tourism Mediterranée at ℭ **04-90-93-74-90** in Arles.

VISITOR INFORMATION The **Office de Tourisme** is on Maison du Roy, near the northern entrance to the old city (ℭ **04-90-54-34-39**).

WHERE TO STAY & DINE

Oustau de Baumanière 🕸🕸🕸 This Relais & Châteaux member is one of southern France's most legendary hotels. Raymond Thuilier bought the farmhouse in 1945, and by the 1950s and 1960s, it was a rendezvous for the glitterati. Today, managed by its founder's grandson, it's not as glitzy, but the three stone houses, draped in flowering vines, are still charming. The plush rooms evoke the 16th and 17th centuries. All units contain large sitting areas, and no two are alike. If there's no vacancy in the main building, the hotel will assign you to one of the annexes. If this is the case, request Le Manor, the most appealing. The spacious bathrooms contain tub/showers. In the stone-vaulted dining room, the chef serves specialties like ravioli of truffles with leeks, a *rossini* (stuffed with foie gras) of veal with fresh truffles, and roasted duckling with olives. The award-winning *gigot d'agneau* (lamb) *en croûte* has become this place's trademark.

Les Baux, 13520 Maussane-les-Alpilles. ℭ **04-90-54-33-07.** Fax 04-90-54-40-46. www.oustaudebaumaniere. com. 27 units. 250€–275€ double; 400€–430€ suite. Restaurant fixed-price menus 75€–112€. AE, DC, MC, V. Closed Jan 3–Mar 4. Restaurant closed Wed Oct–Apr 1. **Amenities:** Restaurant; bar; outdoor pool; limited room service; laundry service; dry cleaning. *In room:* A/C, TV, minibar, hair dryer.

EXPLORING LES BAUX

Some one million visitors a year flock here to wander the feudal ruins, inspect the foundation of a demolished castle, and explore the facades of restored Renaissance homes. The **Château des Baux** (ℭ **04-90-54-55-56**) is carved out of the rocky mountain peak; the site of this former castle covers an area at least five times that of Les Baux itself below. As you stand here, you can look out over the **Val d'Enfer (Valley of Hell).** At the castle you can enjoy panoramas from Tour Paravel and Tour Sarascenes. Admission to the castle is 6.50€ for adults, 5€ for students, and 3.50€ for children 7 to 17 (under 7 free). The site is open daily, from 9am to 8:30pm in July and August; from 9am to 6:30pm in March and September through October; and from 9am to 5pm during other months.

ARLES ✲✲✲

Arles, 35km (22 miles) southwest of Avignon and 88km (55 miles) northwest of Marseille, has been called "the soul of Provence," and art lovers, archaeologists, and historians alike are attracted to this town on the Rhône. Van Gogh left Paris for Arles in 1888 and painted some of his most celebrated works here—*Starry Night, The Bridge at Arles, Sunflowers,* and *L'Arlésienne* among others. Many of these luminous scenes remain to delight visitors today.

Arles isn't quite as charming as Aix-en-Provence, but it has first-rate museums, excellent restaurants, and summer festivals, such as an international photography festival in early June. Though not as lovely as it was when Picasso came here, Arles has enough antique Provençal flavor to keep the appeal alive.

ESSENTIALS

GETTING THERE   **Trains** leave from Paris's Gare de Lyon and arrive at Arles's **Gare SNCF** (av. Paulin-Talabot), a short walk from the town center. One high-speed direct TGV travels from Paris to Arles each day (4½ hr.; 92€ 1st class, 68€ 2nd). For other trains, you must change in Avignon. There are hourly connections between Arles and Avignon (15 min.; 8.40€ 1st class, 5.60€ 2nd), Marseille (1 hr.; 17€ 1st class, 11€ 2nd), and Aix-en-Provence (1¾ hr., change in Marseille; 22€ 1st class, 14€ 2nd). For rail schedules and information, call ✆ **08-36-35-35-39.** If you're **driving,** head south along D570 from Avignon.

VISITOR INFORMATION   The **Office de Tourisme** is on esplanade Charles-de-Gaulle (✆ **04-90-18-41-20**).

WHERE TO STAY

Hôtel Jules César et Restaurant Lou Marquês ✲✲✲   This 17th-century Carmelite convent is now a country hotel with the best restaurant in town. Although it's in a noisy neighborhood, most rooms face the cloister. You'll wake to the scent of roses and the sounds of birds singing. Throughout, you'll find a blend of antique neoclassic architecture and modern amenities. The decor is luxurious, with antique Provençal furnishings. The interior rooms are the most tranquil and also the darkest, though enlivened by bright fabrics. Most of the downstairs units are spacious, and although the upstairs rooms are small, they have a certain old-world charm. The rooms in the modern extensions are comfortable but lack character. Each bathroom comes with a combination tub/shower.

9 bd. des Lices, 13631 Arles CEDEX. ✆ 04-90-52-52-52. Fax 04-90-52-52-53. www.hotel-julescesar.fr. 58 units. 120€–215€ double; 345€–375€ suite. AE, DC, MC, V. Parking 12€. Closed Nov 12–Dec 24. **Amenities:** 2 restaurants; bar; limited room service; laundry service. *In room:* TV, minibar, hair dryer.

WHERE TO DINE

L'Olivier ✲   PROVENÇAL/FRENCH   On the western edge of the old town is one of the most charming restaurants in Arles, occupying a house whose foundations date from the 12th century. Inside, you'll find a pair of dining rooms with beamed ceilings, fireplaces, terra-cotta tiles, ladder-backed chairs, and the kinds of antiques your French grandmother might have had in her home. Menu items vary with the season, but the best examples include fresh local asparagus garnished with sweetbreads on a bed of roasted tomatoes; fava bean soup with garlic croutons and saffron-flavored rouille; codfish steak with a bouillon of garlic and fresh herbs; and baby pigeon roasted with foie gras–flavored butter.

1 bis rue Réattu. ✆ **04-90-49-64-88.** Reservations recommended. Main courses 15€–25€; set menus 28€–55€. MC, V. Tues–Sat noon–2:30pm and 7:30–9:30pm.

EXPLORING ARLES

At the tourist office (see "Essentials"), buy a *billet global* 🅡, a pass that admits you to the town's museums, Roman monuments, and major attractions; it costs 10€ adults, 5€ students and ages 17 and under.

The town is full of Roman monuments. The general vicinity of the old Roman forum is occupied by **place du Forum,** shaded by plane trees. Once, the Café de Nuit, immortalized by van Gogh, stood on this square. Two Corinthian columns and pediment fragments from a temple can be seen at the corner of the Hôtel Nord-Pinus. South of here is **place de la République** (also known as the place de l'Hôtel de Ville), the principal plaza, dominated by a 15m (50-ft.) blue porphyry obelisk. On the north is the impressive Hôtel-de-Ville (town hall) from 1673, built to Mansart's plans and surmounted by a Renaissance belfry.

On the east side is the **Eglise St-Trophime** 🅡 (© 04-90-49-33-53), noted for its 12th-century portal, one of the finest achievements of southern Romanesque style in all of France. In the pediment Christ is surrounded by the symbols of the Evangelists. The cloister, designed in both the Gothic and Romanesque styles, is noted for its medieval carvings. Admission to the church is free; for the cloister, it's 3.05€ adults, 2.30€ students and ages 12 to 18, free for ages 11 and under. The church is open daily from 8:30am to 6:30pm; the cloister from mid-June to mid-September daily from 9am to 12:30pm and 2 to 7pm.

The city's two great classical monuments are the **Théâtre Antique,** rue du Cloître (© **04-90-96-93-30**), and the Amphitheater (see below). The Roman theater begun by Augustus in the 1st century was mostly destroyed, and only two Corinthian columns remain. Now rebuilt, the theater is the setting for an annual drama festival in July. The theater was where the Venus of Arles was discovered in 1651. Take rue de la Calade from the town hall. The theater is open daily, as follows: November through February from 10 to 11:30am and 2 to 4:30pm; March and April from 9 to 11:30am and 2 to 6:30pm; May through September from 9am to 6:30pm; and during October from 9am to 11:30pm and 2 to 5:30pm. Admission costs 3€ for adults, 2.20€ for students and ages 12 to 18. It's free for children under 12.

Nearby, the **Amphitheater** 🅡🅡, Rond-Point des Arènes (© **04-90-49-36-36**), also built in the 1st century, seats almost 25,000 and still hosts bullfights in summer. The government warns you to visit the old monument at your own risk, because of the worn and uneven masonry. For a good view, you can climb the three towers that remain from medieval times, when the amphitheater was turned into a fortress. Hours are daily as follows: November through February from 10am to 4:30pm; March, April, and October from 9am to 5:30pm; and May through September from 9am to 6:30pm. Admission costs 3€ for adults, 2.50€ for students and ages 18 and under.

The most memorable sight in Arles is **Nécropoledes Alyscamps** 🅡, rue Pierre-Renaudel (© **04-90-49-36-87**), once a necropolis established by the Romans, converted into a Christian burial ground in the 4th century. As the latter, it became a setting for legends in epic medieval poetry and was mentioned in Dante's *Inferno.* Today, it's lined with poplars and the remaining sarcophagi: a cool oasis in hot weather. Hours are the same as for the Théâtre Antique (see above). Admission is 3.50€ adults, 2.60€ ages 12 to 18, free for ages 11 and under.

AIX-EN-PROVENCE 🅡🅡

Founded in 122 B.C. by Roman general Caius Sextius Calvinus, who named it Aquae Sextiae after himself, Aix evolved from a Roman military outpost to a

Moments   Aix Through the Eyes of Cézanne

The best experience in Aix is a walk along the *route de Cézanne* (D17), which winds eastward through the countryside toward Ste-Victoire. From the east end of cours Mirabeau, take rue du Maréchal-Joffre across boulevard Carnot to boulevard des Poilus, which becomes avenue des Ecoles-Militaires and finally D17. The stretch between Aix and the hamlet of Le Tholonet is full of twists and turns where Cézanne often set up his easel to paint. The entire route is a lovely 5.5km (3½-mile) stroll. Le Tholonet has a cafe or two where you can refresh yourself while waiting for one of the frequent buses back to Aix.

provincial administrative capital, the seat of an archbishop, and the official residence of the medieval comtes de Provence.

The celebrated son of this faded university town is Paul Cézanne. Montagne Ste-Victoire looms over the town today just as it did in Cézanne's time, though a string of high-rises has cropped up. Aix is 80km (50 miles) southeast of Avignon and 32km (20 miles) north of Marseille.

ESSENTIALS

GETTING THERE   The city is easily accessible from Marseille, with 21 trains arriving daily. The trip takes 35 minutes and costs 5.70€ one-way. Eight trains arrive from Nice, the trip taking 3 to 4 hours and costing 28€ one-way. There are eight trains per day from Cannes, taking 3½ hours and costing 25€ one-way. A newer train station designed for the high-speed TGV trains is at Vitrolle, 24km (15 miles) to the west of Aix. Bus links cost 3.60€ one-way into the center of Aix. For more information, call © **08-36-35-35.** Buses from Marseille arrive at the rate of one every 10 minutes, or else five per day from Avignon, plus two per day from Nice. For more information, call © **04-42-91-26-80.** If **driving** to Aix from Avignon or other points north, take A7 south to RN7 and follow it into town. From Marseilles or other points to the south, take A51 north into town.

VISITOR INFORMATION   The **Office de Tourisme** is at 2 place du Général-de-Gaulle (© **04-42-16-11-61;** fax 04-42-16-11-62; www.aixenprovence tourism.com).

WHERE TO STAY

Hôtel Cardinal *Value*   Not everything is state of the art here, but for many travelers, the Cardinal is still the best value in Aix. Lying on the other side of the cours in the Mazarin quarter, it is distinguished by a lingering air of fragility and nostalgia. Guests stay in simply furnished rooms either in the main building or in the high-ceilinged 18th-century annex up the street, site of most of the hotel's suites. Bathrooms tend to be small but each has a good shower.

54 rue Cardinale, 13100 Aix-en-Provence. © **04-42-38-32-30.** Fax 04-42-26-39-05. 29 units. 50€–60€ double; 73€ suite. MC, V. *In room:* A/C, TV, kitchenette (suites), hair dryer.

Villa Gallici ★★★   This elegant, relentlessly chic inn is the most stylish hotel in town. The rooms, richly infused with the decorative traditions of Aix, are subtle and charming. Some rooms boast a private terrace or garden, and each comes with a combination tub/shower. The villa sits in a large enclosed garden in the heart of Aix, close to one of the best restaurants, **Le Clos de la Violette** (see "Where to Dine," below). It's only a 5-minute walk to the town center.

Av. de la Violette (impasse des Grands Pins), 13100 Aix-en-Provence. ℂ **04-42-23-29-23**. Fax 04-42-96-30-45. www.villagallici.com. 22 units. 270€–500€ double; 550€–600€ suite. AE, DC, MC, V. **Amenities:** Restaurant; bar; pool; 24-hr. room service; babysitting; laundry. *In room:* A/C, TV, minibar, hair dryer, safe.

WHERE TO DINE

Le Bistro Latin ★★ *Value* PROVENÇAL   The best little bistro in Aix-en-Provence (for the price) is run by Gilles Holtz, who prides himself on his fixed-price menus. Guests dine in two intimate rooms: a street-level space and a cellar-level space decorated in Greco-Latin style. The staff is young and enthusiastic. Try the chartreuse of mussels, one of the meat dishes with spinach-and-saffron cream sauce, the scampi risotto, or the crepe of hare with basil sauce. We've enjoyed the classic cuisine on all our visits.

18 rue de la Couronne. ℂ **04-42-38-22-88**. Reservations recommended. Main courses 16€–21€. Fixed-price menus 15€ lunch, 14€–17€ dinner. MC, V. Mon–Sat noon–2pm and 7–10:30pm.

Le Clos de la Violette ★★★ MODERN FRENCH   This innovative restaurant is a few steps from Villa Gallici (see "Where to Stay," above), in an elegant neighborhood that most visitors reach by taxi. The Provençal villa has an octagonal reception area and several dining rooms. Menu items are stylish and seasonal, and include a medley of dishes highlighting the flavors of Provence. Examples include an upside-down tart of snails with parsley juice; braised sea wolf with beignets of fennel; onion brioche with a fig-flavored vinaigrette and balsamic vinegar; and roasted Provençal lamb in puff pastry. An absolutely superb dessert is a "celebration" of Provençal figs—an artfully arranged platter containing a galette of figs, a tart of figs, a parfait of figs, and a sorbet of figs.

10 av. de la Violette. ℂ **04-42-23-30-71**. Reservations required. Main courses 30€–45€; fixed-price lunch 54€; tasting menu 117€. AE, V. Apr–Oct Tues and Thurs–Sat noon–1:30pm, Tues–Sat 7:30–9:30pm. Nov–Mar Tues–Sat noon–2:30pm and 7:30–10pm. Closed late Dec to early Jan, Feb and early Aug.

EXPLORING THE CITY

The main street, **cours Mirabeau** ★★, is one of the most beautiful in Europe. Plane trees act like umbrellas, shading the street from the sun and filtering the light into shadows that play on the rococo fountains. On one side are shops and sidewalk cafes, on the other embellished sandstone *hôtels particuliers* (mansions) from the 17th and 18th centuries. The street, which honors Mirabeau, the revolutionary and statesman, begins at the 1860 fountain on place de la Libération.

Nearby in a former archbishop's palace is the **Musée des Tapisseries,** 28 place des Martyrs de la Résistance (ℂ **04-42-23-09-91**). Lining its gilded walls are three series of tapestries from the 17th and 18th centuries collected by the archbishops: *The History of Don Quixote* by Natoire, *The Russian Games* by Leprince, and *The Grotesques* by Monnoyer. In addition, the museum exhibits rare furnishings from the 17th and 18th centuries as well as contemporary exhibitions. It's open Wednesday through Monday from 10 to 11:45am and 2 to 5:15pm. Admission is 2€ adults, free for ages 25 and under.

Up rue Cardinale is the **Musée Granet** ★, place St-Jean-de-Malte (ℂ **04-42-38-14-70**), which owns a not-very-typical collection of Cézannes. Matisse donated a nude in 1941. Housed in the former center of the Knights of Malta, the gallery contains works by Van Dyck, Van Loo, and Rigaud; portraits by Pierre and François Puget; and (the most interesting) a Jupiter and Thetis by Ingres. Ingres also did an 1807 portrait of the museum's namesake, François Marius Granet. Granet's own works abound. On the grounds are archaeological finds of the vestiges of Aix-en-Provence during the Roman Empire. The museum is open Wednesday through Monday from 10am to noon and 2:30 to

6pm. (It's closed Jan 1, May 1, May 21, July 14, Aug 15, Nov 1, Nov 11, Dec 25, and Dec 31.) Admission is 2€ adults, free for ages 24 and under.

Outside town, at 9 av. Paul-Cézanne, is the **Atelier de Cézanne** (𝒞 **04-42-21-06-53**), the studio of the painter who was the major forerunner of cubism. Surrounded by a wall, the house was restored by American admirers. Repaired again in 1970, it remains much as Cézanne left it in 1906. It's open daily from 10am to noon and 2 to 6pm (to 5pm Oct–May). Admission is 3.80€ adults, 2.75€ students and children.

ST-TROPEZ 𝒜𝒜

Sun-kissed lasciviousness is rampant in this carnival town, 76km (47 miles) southwest of Cannes, but "we can be classy, too," one native insisted. Creative people in the arts and ordinary folk create a compelling mixture.

Colette lived here for many years. Diarist Anaïs Nin posed on the beach in 1939 in a Dorothy Lamour bathing suit. Earlier, St-Tropez was known to Guy de Maupassant, Matisse, and Bonnard. Today, artists, composers, novelists, and the film colony come to St-Tropez in summer. Trailing them is a line of humanity unmatched anywhere else on the Riviera for sheer flamboyance.

ESSENTIALS

GETTING THERE The nearest **rail** station is in St-Raphaël, a neighboring resort. At the Vieux Port, four or five **boats** per day between April and October leave the **Gare Maritime de St-Raphaël,** rue Pierre-Auble (𝒞 **04-94-95-17-46**), for St-Tropez (trip time: 50 min.), at a cost of 10€ each way. Year-round, between 10 and 15 Sodetrav **buses** per day leave from the Gare Routière in St-Raphaël (𝒞 **04-94-97-88-51**) and go to St-Tropez, taking 1½ to 2¼ hours, depending on the bus and the traffic, which during midsummer is usually horrendous. A one-way ticket costs 8.30€. Buses run directly to St-Tropez from Toulon and Hyères. Buses also run directly to St-Tropez from the nearest airport at Toulon-Hyères, 56km (35 miles) away.

If you **drive,** note that parking in St-Tropez is very difficult. You can park in the **Parc des Lices** (𝒞 **04-94-97-34-46**), beneath place des Lices, whose entrance is on avenue Paul-Roussel. This lot charges 2€ to 3.50€ per hour, depending on the season. Many visitors prefer it, as it's more secure than any other lot. If you don't use it, you'll have to squeeze your car into tiny parking spaces wherever you find them. To get here from **Cannes,** drive southwest along the coastal highway (RD98), turning east when you see the signs to St-Tropez.

VISITOR INFORMATION The **Office de Tourisme** is on quai Jean-Jaurès (𝒞 **04-94-97-45-21;** www.saint-tropez.st).

WHERE TO STAY

Hôtel Byblos 𝒜𝒜𝒜 The builder said he created "an anti-hotel, a place like home." That's true if your home resembles a palace in Beirut with salons decorated with Phoenician gold statues from 3000 B.C. On a hill above the harbor, this complex boasts intimate patios and courtyards and retreats filled with antiques and objects like polychrome carved woodwork, marquetry floors, and a Persian-rug ceiling. Every room is unique and might feature a fireplace on a raised hearth or a bed recessed on a dais. The rooms range from medium to spacious, often with high ceilings and antiques or reproductions and each with an elegant French bed. Le Hameau contains 10 duplex suites built around a small courtyard with an outdoor spa. Some rooms have balconies overlooking an inner courtyard; others open onto a terrace of flowers. You can dine by the pool,

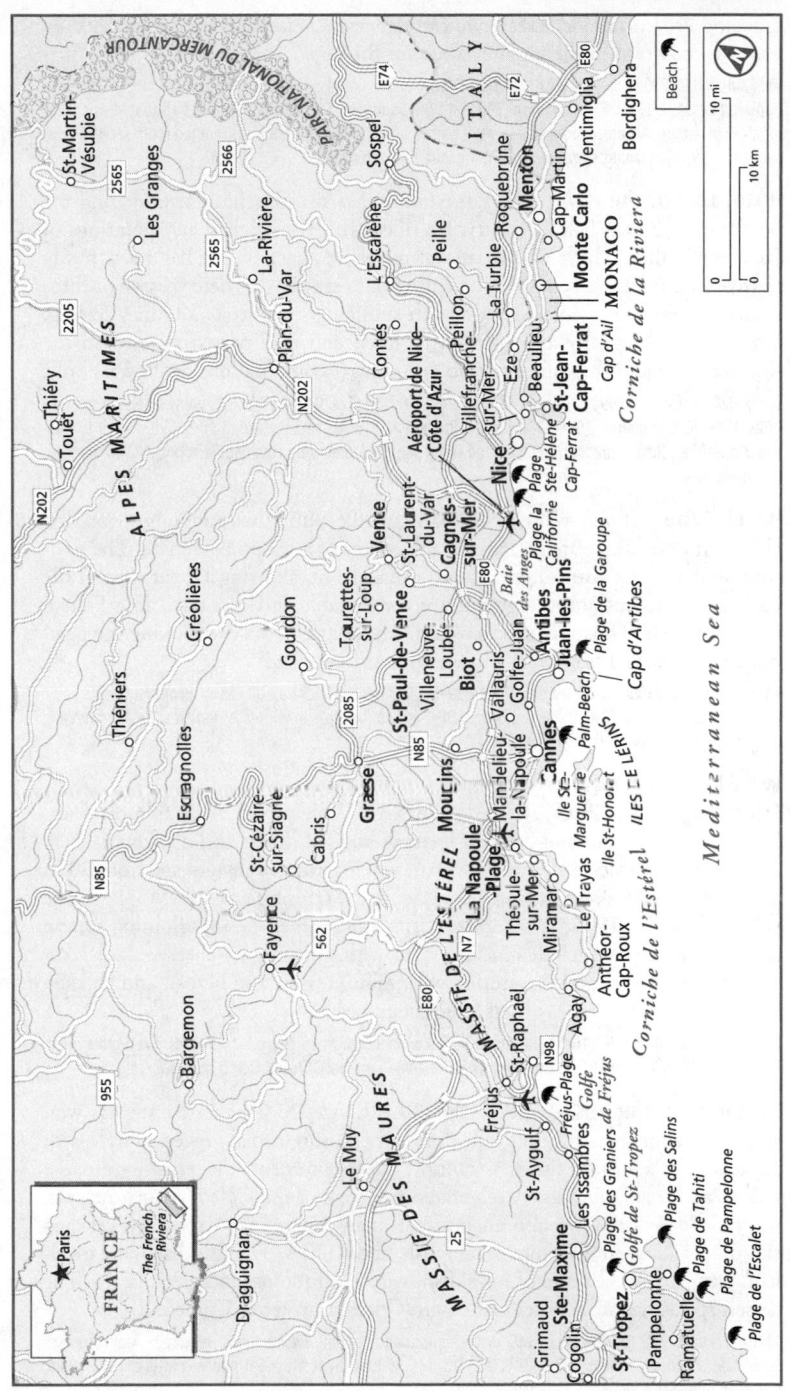

The French Riviera

Beach

10 mi

10 km

PARC NATIONAL DU MERCANTOUR

ITALY

St-Martin-Vésubie
2565
Les Granges
2566
La-Rivière
2565
Thiéry
Touët
Plan-du-Var
L'Escarène
Sospel
Peille
Peillon
La Turbie
Roquebrûne
Menton
Cap-Martin
Ventimiglia
Bordighera

ALPES MARITIMES

N202

N202

Gréolières

Théniers

Escragnolles

Contes

Eze

Villefranche-sur-Mer

Beaulieu

St-Jean-Cap-Ferrat

Monte Carlo

MONACO

Corniche de la Riviera

Aéroport de Nice–Côte d'Azur

Nice

Plage Ste-Hélène

Cap-Ferrat

Cap d'Ail

Gourdon

Tourettes-sur-Loup

Vence

St-Laurent-du-Var

Cagnes-sur-Mer

Plage la Californie

Baie des Anges

St-Paul-de-Vence

Villeneuve-Loubet

Biot

Golfe-Juan

Antibes

Juan-les-Pins

Plage de la Garoupe

Cap d'Antibes

St-Cézaire-sur-Siagne

Cabris

Grasse

2085

Moucins

Vallauris

Cannes

Palm-Beach

Plage de l'Estérel

N85

Fayence

562

MASSIF DE L'ESTÉREL

La Napoule-Plage

Théoule-sur-Mer

Miramar

Ile Ste-Marguerite

Ile St-Honorat

ÎLES DE LÉRINS

Bargemon

Le Trayas

Anthéor-Cap-Roux

Corniche de l'Estérel

Mediterranean Sea

955

E80

St-Raphaël

Agay

N98

Fréjus

Fréjus-Plage

MASSIF DES MAURES

St-Aygulf

Les Issambres

Golfe de Fréjus

Le Muy

25

Draguignan

Grimaud

Cogolin

Ste-Maxime

Plage des Graniers de St-Tropez

Golfe de St-Tropez

St-Tropez

Pampelonne

Plage des Salins

Plage de Tahiti

Ramatuelle

Plage de Pampelonne

Plage de l'Escalet

FRANCE

Paris

The French Riviera

N7

E80

E74

E72

E80

359

enjoying Provençal food. Later, you can dance on a circular floor surrounded by bas-relief columns in the nightclub, **Caves du Roy.**

Av. Paul-Signac, 83990 St-Tropez. (€) **04-94-56-68-00.** Fax 04-94-56-68-01. www.byblos.com. 98 units, 10 duplex suites. 430€–510€ double; from 790€–1,550€ suite. AE, DC, MC, V. Closed Oct 15 to mid-Apr. Parking 24€ in garage. **Amenities:** 2 restaurants; 2 bars; nightclub; outdoor pool; spa; limited room service; massage; laundry/dry cleaning. *In room:* A/C, TV, minibar, hair dryer, safe.

Hôtel La Ponche ★★ The same family has run this hotel overlooking the port for more than half a century. It's filled with the original airy paintings of Jacques Cordier, which add to the atmosphere. Each room has been newly redecorated and is well equipped, opening onto sea views. There are two or three rooms per floor. Sun-colored walls with subtle lighting evoke a homey feeling. The beds are elegantly appointed with linen and quality mattresses, and the midsize to large bathrooms have tub and shower combinations or showers only.

3 rue des Remparts, 83990 St-Tropez. (€) **04-94-97-02-53.** Fax 04-94-97-78-61. www.laponche.com. 18 units. 125€–295€ double; 195€–340€ suite. Breakfast 17€. AE, MC, V. Parking 18€. Closed Nov to mid-Feb. **Amenities:** Restaurant; bar; pool; limited room service; laundry/dry cleaning. *In room:* A/C, TV, minibar, hair dryer, safe.

Hôtel Sube If you want to be right on the port, this might be your first choice. It's over the Café de Paris in the center of a shopping arcade. The two-story lounge has a beamed ceiling and a glass front, allowing a great view of the harbor. The rooms aren't large but are comfortable and decorated in a French Provincial style. The more expensive units have nice views overlooking the port. Each comes with a private bathroom with a shower stall.

15 quai Suffren, 83900 St-Tropez. (€) **04-94-97-30-04.** Fax 04-94-54-89-08. www.nova.fr/sube. 28 units. 120€–250€ double. AE, MC, V. Parking nearby 30€ in summer, free in winter. **Amenities:** Restaurant/cafe; bar; limited room service. *In room:* A/C, TV.

WHERE TO DINE

Chez Maggi ★★ PROVENÇAL/ITALIAN This is St. Tropez's most flamboyant gay restaurant and bar, but it draws straight diners and drinkers as well. At least half its space is devoted to a bar, where patrons range in age from 20 to 60. There are no tables in front. Consequently, cruising at Chez Maggi, in the words of loyal patrons, is *très crazée.* Meals are served in an adjoining dining room. Menu items include chicken salad with ginger, goat-cheese salad, *petits farcis provençaux* (vegetables stuffed with minced meat and herbs), and chicken curry with coconut milk, capers, and cucumbers.

7 rue Sibille. (€) **04-94-97-16-12.** Reservations recommended. Main courses 14€–27€; fixed-price menu 30€. MC, V. Daily 7pm–midnight (restaurant); daily 7pm–3am (bar). Closed Oct to mid-Mar.

Leï Mouscardins ★★★ FRENCH/PROVENÇAL This restaurant has won awards for culinary perfection. The dining room is in formal Provençal style with an adjoining sunroom under a canopy. We recommend the *moules* (mussels) *marinières* for an appetizer. A celebrated fish stew of the Côte d'Azur is offered, *bourride Provençale,* and also an unusual main-course menu specialty, crushed chestnuts garnished with morels, crayfish, and truffles. The fish dishes are excellent, particularly the sauté of monkfish, wild mushrooms, and green beans. The dessert specialties are soufflés made with Grand Marnier or Cointreau.

1 rue Portalet. (€) **04-94-97-29-00.** www.leimouscardins.com. Reservations required. Main courses 30€–42€. Fixed-price menus 58€–78€. AE, DC, MC, V. June–Sept Mon–Sat noon–2pm and 7:30–10pm; Oct–May Tues–Sat noon–2pm and 7:30–9:30pm.

Spoon Byblos ✿✿ FRENCH/INTERNATIONAL   This is one of the latest statements of Alain Ducasse, considered by some to be the world's greatest chef—at least the most acclaimed. Originally launched in Paris, Spoon has traveled everywhere from London to the Riviera. Within the Hotel Byblos, Spoon serves the cuisines of many cultures with produce mainly from the Mediterranean. Special inspiration is drawn from the food of Catalonia, Andalusia, and Morocco, and there are more than 300 wines from around the world. The restaurant opens onto a circular bar of blue-tinted glass and stainless steel. Dig into the shrimp and squid consommé with a hint of jasmine and orange, or the spicy king prawns on a skewer. A delectable lamb couscous is served, and you might enjoy spit-roasted John Dory. You might top off a meal with the chef's favorite cheesecake.

In the Hotel Byblos, av. Paul-Signac. ✆ **04-94-56-68-00.** Reservations required. Main courses 30€–38€. Summer daily 8pm–2am. Off season daily 7:30pm–12:30am.

EXPLORING ST-TROPEZ & ENVIRONS

Near the harbor is the **Musée de l'Annonciade (Musée St-Tropez),** at place Georges-Grammont (✆ **04-94-97-04-01**), in the former chapel of the Annonciade. As a legacy from the artists who loved St-Tropez, the museum shelters one of the finest modern art collections on the Riviera. Many of the artists, including Paul Signac, depicted the port of St-Tropez. Opened in 1955, the collection includes such works as Van Dongen's *Women of the Balustrade* and paintings and sculpture by Bonnard, Matisse, Braque, Utrillo, Seurat, Derain, Maillol, and Van Dongen. The museum is open from June to September, Wednesday through Monday from 10am to noon and 3 to 7pm; October and December through May, Wednesday through Monday from 10am to noon and 2 to 6pm. It's closed in November, December 25, January 1, and May 1. Admission is 5.35€ adults, 3.10€ children.

HITTING THE BEACH & OTHER OUTDOOR ACTIVITIES

BEACHES   St-Tropez has the Riviera's best beaches. The best for families are those closest to the town center, including the amusingly named **Bouillabaisse** and **Plage des Graniers.** The more daring beaches are the 10km (6-mile) sandy crescents at **Plage des Salins** and **Plage de Pampelonne,** beginning some 4km (2 miles) from the town center and best reached by bike (see below) if you're not driving. If you ever wanted to go topless, go bottomless, or wear a truly daring bikini, this is the place! Bouillabaisse and Plage des Graniers are public beaches, with free access. Parts of Plage des Salins and Plage de Pampellone are private, and parts are public. Both have areas reserved for guests of hotels and beach clubs.

BICYCLING & MOTOR-SCOOTERING   The largest outfitter for bikes and motor scooters is **Louis Mas,** 5 rue Josef-Quaranta (✆ **04-94-97-00-60**). You'll be required to leave a deposit of 153€ to 229€, payable with a major credit card, plus 8€ to 12€ per hour for a bike, 30€ to 45€ per hour for a motor scooter, depending on its size.

BOATING   The highly recommended **Suncap Company,** 15 quai de Suffren (✆ **04-94-97-11-23**), rents boats from 5.5m to 12m (18 ft.–40 ft.) long. The smallest can be rented to qualified sailors without a captain, but the larger ones come with a captain at the helm. Prices begin at 475€ per day.

SCUBA DIVING   A team of dive enthusiasts who are ready, willing, and able to show you the azure-colored depths off the coast of St-Tropez operate from the *Octopussy I* and *II.* Both are aluminum-sided, yellow-painted dive boats.

They're based year-round in St-Tropez's Nouveau Port. Experienced divers pay from 30€ to 44€ for a one-tank "exploration" dive, depending on how much of their own equipment they use; novices are charged 45€ for a *baptême* that includes one-on-one supervision and a descent to a depth of around 5m (15 ft.). Except for people who sign up for the *baptême,* where supervision for neophyte divers is enhanced, and where you'll be expected to show strong swimming skills in advance, you have to have a license to participate in any of the conventional dives. For reservations and information, call or write *Les Octopussys,* quartier de Bertaud, Gassin, 83900 St-Tropez (② **04-94-56-53-10;** fax 04-94-56-46-59).

TENNIS　Anyone who phones in advance can use the eight courts (both artificial grass and "Quick," a form of concrete) at the **Tennis-Club de St-Tropez,** route des Plages, in St-Claude (② **04-94-97-80-76**), about half a mile from the resort's center. Open year-round, the courts rent for 15€ per hour from 10am to 5pm, and 20€ per hour after 5pm.

ST-TROPEZ AFTER DARK

On the lobby level of the Hôtel Byblos, **Les Caves du Roy,** avenue Paul-Signac (② **04-94-56-68-00**), is the most self-consciously chic nightclub in St-Tropez. Entrance is free, but drinks begin at a whopping 18€. It's open nightly from 11:30pm till dawn, from May to late September.

　　Le Papagayo, in the Résidence du Nouveau-Port, rue Gambetta (② **04-94-97-76-70**), is one of the largest nightclubs in town. The decor was inspired by the psychedelic 1960s. Entrance is 17€ and includes the first drink. Next to Le Papagayo is **Le VIP Room,** in the Résidence du Port (② **04-94-97-14-70**), where patrons pay about 16€ per cocktail for the chance to (demurely or not) whoop it up. Expect an active bar, a dance floor, and the kind of posturing and preening that can be amusing or not depending on your point of view.

　　Le Pigeonnier, 13 rue de la Ponche (② **04-94-97-84-26**), rocks, rolls, and welcomes a crowd that's mostly gay, male, and between the ages of 20 and 50. Most of the socializing revolves around the long, narrow bar, where menfolk from all over Europe seem to enjoy chitchatting. There's also a dance floor.

CANNES ✶✶✶

When Coco Chanel came here and got a suntan, returning to Paris bronzed, she startled the milk-white society ladies. However, they quickly began copying her. Today the bronzed bodies—clad in nearly nonexistent swimsuits—that line the beaches of this chic resort continue the late fashion designer's example.

　　Something is always happening at Cannes, except in November, traditionally a dead month. Popular with celebrities, Cannes is at its most frenzied during the **International Film Festival** at the Palais des Festivals on promenade de la Croisette, in the spring.

　　Cannes, sheltered by hills, lies 26km (16 miles) southwest of Nice. For many it consists of only one street, **promenade de la Croisette,** curving along the coast and split by islands of palms and flowers. The seafront is lined with hotels, apartment houses, and boutiques. Many of the bigger hotels claim parts of the beaches for the private use of their guests. However, there are also public areas.

ESSENTIALS

GETTING THERE　**Trains** arrive frequently throughout the day. Cannes is 15 minutes by train from Antibes and 35 minutes from Nice. The TGV from Paris via Marseille also services Cannes (from Paris to Cannes via TGV takes about 6 breathless hr.) For rail information and schedules, call ② **08-36-35-35-35.**

The **Nice international airport** (© 08-20-42-33-33) is a 20-minute drive northeast. **Buses** pick up passengers at the airport every 40 minutes during the day, delivering them to the Gare Routière, place de l'Hôtel de Ville (© 04-93-45-20-08). Service to Cannes is also available from Antibes by one bus every half hour.

By **car,** Cannes can be easily approached by two cities along the Riviera. From Marseille, take A51 north to Aix-en-Provence, continuing along A8 east to Cannes. From Nice, follow A8 southwest to Cannes.

VISITOR INFORMATION   The **Office de Tourisme** is in the Palais des Festivals, esplanade Georges-Pompidou (© 04-93-39-24-53; www.cannes.fr).

WHERE TO STAY

Although hotels in Cannes might elect to have their own e-mail address, there is a shared and collective e-mail address for all hotels in the city: infos@cannes.hotel.com.

Hôtel Carlton Inter-Continental 🎭🎭🎭   Cynics say that one of the most amusing sights in Cannes is the view from under the grand gate of the Carlton. Here you'll see vehicles of every description dropping off huge amounts of baggage and numbers of fashionable (and sometimes not-so-fashionable) guests. It's the epitome of luxury and has become such a part of the city's heartbeat that to ignore it would be to miss the resort's spirit. The twin gray domes at either end of the facade are often the first things recognized by starlets planning their grand entrances, grand exits, and grand scenes in the hotel's public and private rooms.

Shortly after it was built in 1912, the Carlton attracted the most prominent members of Europe's *haut monde.* Today the hotel is more democratic, hosting conventions and motor-coach tour groups; however, in summer (especially during the film festival) the public rooms still are filled with all the voyeuristic and exhibitionistic fervor that seems so much a part of the Riviera. Guest rooms are plush and a bit airier than you might expect. The most spacious rooms are in the west wing, and many upper-floor rooms open onto waterfront balconies.

58 bd. de la Croisette, 06400 Cannes. © **04-93-06-40-06.** Fax 04-93-06-40-25. http://cannes.interconti. com. 338 units. 370€–750€ double; from 1,070€ suite AE, DC, MC, V. Parking 36€. **Amenities:** 2 restaurants; bar; indoor pool; health club; 24-hr. room service; laundry/dry cleaning; casino. *In room:* A/C, TV, minibar, hair dryer, safe.

Hôtel le Fouquet's 🎭 *Finds*   This is an intimate hotel drawing a discreet clientele, often from Paris, who'd never think of patronizing the grand hotels. Very "Riviera French" in design and decor, it's several blocks from the beach. Each of the cozy guest rooms is outfitted differently, just a bit, from its neighbor. Each has pastel colors and contemporary furniture. The personality of the owner, who's often on-site, is very palpable, making it feel a bit like an intimate B&B. Bathrooms, although small, are efficiently organized, with showers.

2 rond-point Duboys-d'Angers, 06400 Cannes. © **04-92-59-25-00.** Fax 04-92-98-03-39. www.le-fouquets. com. 10 units. 115€–190€ double. AE, DC, MC, V. Parking 12€. Closed Nov to mid-Mar. Bus: 1. **Amenities:** Limited room service; laundry/dry cleaning. *In room:* A/C, TV, minibar, hair dryer, safe.

Hôtel Gray-d'Albion 🎭🎭   The smallest of the major hotels isn't on La Croisette. But the rooms are outfitted with all the luxury a modern hotel can offer. Some consider the Gray-d'Albion among the most luxurious hotels in France. Groups form a large part of its clientele, but it also caters to the individual. All rooms are medium in size, blending contemporary and traditional furnishings; the generous-sized bathrooms have tub and shower combinations.

Each unit has a balcony but the views aren't notable, except for views of the Mediterranean from rooms on the eighth and ninth floors.

38 rue des Serbes, 06400 Cannes. ℂ **04-92-99-79-79**. Fax 04-93-99-26-10. www.lucienbarriere.com. 189 units. 185€–405€ double; 510€–1,450€ suite. AE, DC, MC, V. Bus: 1. **Amenities:** Restaurant; bar; salon; 24-hr. room service; babysitting; laundry/dry cleaning. *In room:* A/C, TV, minibar, hair dryer, safe.

Hotel Splendid ℛ (Value)   Opened in 1871, this is a favorite of scholars, politicians, actors, and musicians. The Splendid's ornate white building with wrought-iron accents looks out onto the sea, the old port, and a park. The rooms boast antique furniture and paintings as well as videos; about half have kitchenettes. Each comes with a good bed and a small but efficient bathroom with a combination tub and shower. The more expensive rooms have sea views.

Allée de la Liberté (4 and 6 rue Félix-Faure), 06400 Cannes. ℂ **04-97-06-22-22**. Fax 04-93-99-52-02. hotel.splendid.cannes@wanadoo.fr. 64 units. 119€–246€ double; 199€–250€ suite. Breakfast 15€. AE, MC, V. Parking 8€. **Amenities:** Room service for breakfast. *In room:* A/C, TV.

Hôtel Villa de l'Olivier (Finds)   Charming and personal, this is a hideaway with a low-key style. In the 1930s, it was a villa; in the 1960s it was transformed into a hotel with a six-unit annex in the garden. Today, you'll find buildings with lots of glass overlooking a pool and a decor combining the French colonial tropics with the late 19th century and Provence. The rooms are outfitted with upholstered walls, each in a different color and pattern, and lots of Provençal accessories. Bathrooms come in a variety of sizes, each with a combination tub and shower.

5 rue des Tambourinaires, 06400 Cannes. ℂ **04-93-39-53-28**. Fax 04-93-39-55-85. www.hotelolivier.com. 24 units. 120€–140€ double; 244€ suite. AE, DC, MC, V. Parking 10€. Closed 3 weeks in Dec. **Amenities:** Pool; limited room service (drinks only).; laundry. *In room:* A/C, TV.

WHERE TO DINE

La Palme d'Or ℛℛℛ MODERN FRENCH   Movie stars on the see-and-be-seen circuit head here during the film festival. It's a sophisticated rendezvous point that also serves one of the Riviera's finest hotel cuisines. The light wood–paneled Art Deco marvel has bay windows, a winter garden theme, and terraces overlooking the pool, the sea, and La Croisette. Menu items change with the seasons but are likely to include warm foie gras with fondue of rhubarb; filets of fried red mullet with a beignet of potatoes, zucchini, and olive-cream sauce; and a medley of crayfish, clams, and squid marinated in peppered citrus sauce. A modernized version of a niçoise staple includes three parts of a rabbit with rosemary sauce, fresh vegetables, and chickpea rosettes. The most appealing dessert is wild strawberries from Carros, with a Grand Marnier–flavored *nage* and a "cream sauce of frozen milk." The service is worldly without being stiff.

In the Hôtel Martinez, 73 bd. de la Croisette. ℂ **04-92-98-74-14**. Reservations required. Main courses 45€–120€. Fixed-price menus 47€–140€ lunch Mon–Sat, 70€–135€ dinner. AE, DC, MC, V. Wed–Sun 12:30–2pm and 7:30–10:30pm (also Tues 7:30–10:30pm mid-June to mid-Sept). Closed Nov 15–Dec 20.

Le Festival ℛ TRADITIONAL FRENCH   Screen idols and sex symbols flood the terrace during the film festival. Almost every chair is emblazoned with the names of movie stars (who may or may not have graced it with their bottoms), and tables are among the most sought-after in town. You can choose from the Restaurant or the less formal Grill Room. Meals in the Restaurant may include *bourride Provençale; soupe des poissons* (fish soup) with *rouille;* simply grilled fresh fish (perhaps with aioli); bouillabaisse with lobster; and sea bass flambéed with fennel. Items in the Grill are more in the style of an elegant brasserie, served without as much fuss but at generally the same prices.

> ### *Finds* Provençal Olives for Sale
>
> A charmingly old-fashioned shop, **Cannolive,** 16–20 rue Vénizelos ((0) **04-93-39-08-19**), is owned by the Raynaud family, who founded the place in 1880. It sells Provençal olives and their by-products—*tapenades* (pastes) that connoisseurs refer to as "Provençal caviar," black "olives de Nice," and green "olives de Provence," as well as olive oil from regional producers. Oils and food products are dispensed from no. 16, while gift items (fabrics, porcelain, and Provençal souvenirs) are sold next door.

---

55 bd. de la Croisette. (0) **04-93-38-04-81.** Reservations required. Main courses 27€–35€; fixed-price menu from 40€. AE, DC, MC, V. Daily 11:30am–3pm and 7:30–10pm. Until 11pm during film festival and July–Aug. Closed Nov 18–Dec 26.

Le Monaco *Value* FRENCH/ITALIAN/PROVENÇAL   Restaurant tabs on La Croisette often resemble the GNP of a small country. But believe it or not, pricey Cannes has working people who have to eat, and they go to Le Monaco, a blue-collar eatery with great food served bistro style. Menu choices include osso buco with sauerkraut, spaghetti Bolognese, paella, couscous, roast rabbit with mustard sauce, mussels, trout with almonds, and minestrone with basil. Another specialty is grilled sardines, which many restaurants won't serve, considering them too messy and old-fashioned. Dessert might be a slice of orange tart.

15 rue du 24-Août. (0) **04-93-38-37-76.** Reservations required. Main courses 10€–24€; fixed-price menu 20€. MC, V. Mon–Sat noon–2:30pm and 7–10:30pm. Closed Nov 10–Dec 10.

EXPLORING CANNES

Above the harbor, the old town of Cannes sits on Suquet Hill, where you'll see a 14th-century tower that the English dubbed the Lord's Tower.

The **Musée de la Castre** *⚜*, in the Château de la Castre, Le Suquet ((0) **04-93-38-55-26**), contains paintings, sculpture, decorative arts, and a section on ethnography, which includes objects from the Pacific islands to Southeast Asia, including Peruvian and Mayan pottery. There's also a gallery devoted to relics of Mediterranean civilizations, from the Greeks to the Romans, from the Cypriots to the Egyptians. Five rooms are devoted to 19th-century paintings. The museum is open Wednesday through Monday: April through June from 10am to noon and 2 to 6pm, July through September from 10am to noon and 3 to 7pm, and October through March from 10am to noon and 2 to 5pm. Admission is 3€, free for students and children 14 and under.

HITTING THE BEACH & OTHER OUTDOOR PURSUITS

BEACHES   Looking for a free public beach? Head for **Plage du Midi,** just west of the Vieux Port ((0) **04-93-39-92-74**); or **Plage Gazagnaire,** just east of the Port Canto (no phone). Here you'll find greater numbers of families with children and lots of caravan-type vehicles parked nearby. Between these two public beaches are many private ones where you can gain entrance by paying a fee that includes a mattress and sun umbrella.

BICYCLING & MOTOR-SCOOTERING   Despite the roaring traffic, the flat landscapes between Cannes and satellite resorts like La Napoule are well suited for riding a bike or motor scooter. At **Cycles Daniel,** 2 rue du Pont Romain ((0) **04-93-99-90-30**), *vélos tout terrain* (mountain bikes) cost 15€ a day. Renters of motorized bikes and scooters will pay 35€ per day and must be at least 14 years old. For the larger of the scooters, potential renters must present a valid driver's license. Another purveyor of bikes is **Mistral Location,** 4 rue Georges Clémenceau (℃ **04-93-39-33-60**), which charges 11€ per day.

BOATING   Several companies can rent you a boat of any size, with or without a crew, for a day, a week, or a month. An outfit known for its short-term rentals of small craft, including motorboats, sailboats, and canoes, is **Elco Marine,** 110 bd. du Midi (℃ **04-93-47-12-62**). For access to larger boats, including motor-driven and sailing yachts and craft suitable for deep-sea fishing, try **MS Yachts,** 57 La Croisette (℃ **04-93-99-03-51**), or **Mediterranée Courtage** (Agence Y.P.), 22 quai Port Marseille (℃ **04-93-38-30-40**).

CANNES AFTER DARK

CASINOS   There is a pair of world-class casinos in Cannes. The better established is the **Casino Croisette,** in the Palais des Festivals, 1 jetée Albert-Edouard (℃ **04-92-98-78-00**). A well-respected fixture in town since the 1950s, it's a competitor of the newer **Palm Beach Casino,** place F. D. Roosevelt (Pointe de la Croisette; ℃ **04-97-06-36-90**), on the southeast edge of La Croisette. Originally inaugurated in 1933 and rebuilt in 2002, it features three restaurants, an Art Deco decor, and a format that's glossier, newer, and a bit hungrier (and trying harder) for new business. Both casinos offer slot machines that operate daily from 11am to 5am. Suites of rooms devoted to *les grands jeux* (blackjack, roulette, and chemin de fer) open nightly from 8pm to 5am. Both casinos charge 11€ and require a passport or ID card for access to *les grands jeux.*

CLUBS   In the cellar of the Hotel Grey d'Albion is the nightlife staple, the disco **Jane's,** 38 rue des Serbes (℃ **04-92-99-79-79**). It isn't considered ultra-hip or even particularly cutting edge, but you can have a lot of fun. There's a cover of between 10€ and 15€, depending on the night of the week, and a policy of allowing women in free every Friday and Saturday before midnight. At the Casino Croisette is the nightclub **Jimmy's** (℃ **04-92-98-78-78**), with a 16€ cover.

JUAN-LES-PINS ⊕

This suburb of Antibes is a resort developed in the 1920s. In the 1930s Juan-les-Pins drew a chic winter crowd. Today it attracts young Europeans from many economic backgrounds, in pursuit of sex, sun, and sea, in that order.

Juan-les-Pins is often called the "Coney Island of the Riviera," but anyone who calls it that hasn't seen Coney Island in a long time. One writer said that Juan-les-Pins is "for the young and noisy." Even F. Scott Fitzgerald decried it as a "constant carnival." If he could see it now, he'd know he was a prophet.

The town has some of the best nightlife on the Riviera, and the action reaches its frenzied height during the **Festival International de Jazz,** which usually begins July 15 and lasts for about 10 to 12 days. For more information on the festival, contact the tourist office. The pines sweep down to a good beach, crowded with summer sunbathers, most often in skimpy swimwear.

ESSENTIALS

GETTING THERE   Juan-les-Pins is connected by **rail** and bus to most other coastal resorts, especially Nice (trip time: 30 min.). For rail information, call ℃ **08-36-35-35-35. Buses** arrive from Nice and its airport at 40-minute intervals throughout the day. A bus leaves for Juan-les-Pins from Antibes at place Guynemer (℃ **04-93-34-37-60**) daily every 20 minutes and costs 1.50€ one-way (trip time: 10 min.). To **drive** to Juan-les-Pins from Nice, take N7 south; from Cannes, follow the signposted roads. Juan-les-Pins is just outside of Cannes.

VISITOR INFORMATION   The **Office de Tourisme** is at 51 bd. Charles-Guillaumont (© **04-92-90-53-05;** www.riviera.fr/tourisme.htm).

WHERE TO STAY

Hôtel Cecil *Value*   A stone's throw from the beach, this well-kept small hotel is one of the best bargains in Juan-les-Pins. It originated in 1929 when a 19th-century villa was enlarged with another story and transformed into a hotel. The traditionally furnished rooms are well worn yet clean, ranging from small to midsize, each with a compact tiled bathroom with shower. Owner/chef Michel Courtois provides a courteous welcome and good meals. In summer, you can enjoy his food on a patio.

Rue Jonnard, 06160 Juan-les-Pins. © **04-93-61-05-12.** Fax 04-93-67-09-14. www.hotelcecilfrance.com. 21 units. Apr–Sept 40€–70€ double. AE, DC, MC, V. Parking 8€. Closed Oct–Mar. **Amenities:** Restaurant; bar. *In room:* TV.

Hôtel des Belles-Rives *★★★*   This is one of the Riviera's fabled addresses. Once it was a holiday villa occupied by Zelda and F. Scott Fitzgerald. In the following years, it hosted the illustrious, like the duke and duchess of Windsor, Josephine Baker, and Edith Piaf. A 1930s aura lingers through recent renovations. Double-glazing and air-conditioning help a lot. As befits a hotel of this age, rooms come in a variety of shapes and sizes, from small to spacious, but each is fitted with a luxurious bathroom with a combination tub and shower. The lower terraces are devoted to garden dining rooms, an aquatic club with a snack bar and lounge, and a jetty. The beach is private. Dinners are served in the romantic setting at **La Terrasse** with a panoramic bay view.

33 bd. Baudoin, 06160 Juan-les-Pins. © **04-93-61-02-79.** Fax 04-93-67-43-51. www.bellesrives.com. 45 units. 180€–500€ double; 545€ suite. AE, DC, DISC, MC, V. Free parking. Closed mid-Oct to Mar. **Amenities:** Restaurant; bar; courtesy car; limited room service; babysitting; laundry/dry cleaning; landing dock. *In room:* A/C, TV, minibar, hair dryer, safe.

WHERE TO DINE

La Terrasse *★★★* FRENCH/MEDITERRANEAN   Chef Christian Morisset cooks with a light, precise, and creative hand. His cuisine is among the finest along the Riviera. The setting is lively and sophisticated, with a modern decor overlooking the garden and a glassed-in terrace whose roof opens for ventilation and a view of the stars. Menu items are steeped in the flavors of Provence. Examples include raviolis stuffed with fresh crayfish and olive-flavored essence of shellfish; and a rack of lamb from the salt marshes of Pauillac cooked in a clay pot, served with stuffed zucchini flowers and Provençal herbs. Dessert might be a napoleon of wild strawberries with mascarpone cream sauce.

In the Hôtel Juana, La Pinède, av. Gallice. © **04-93-61-20-37.** Reservations required. Main courses 40€–65€. Fixed-price menus 48€ lunch, 80€–107€ dinner. AE, MC, V. July–Aug daily 12:30–2pm and 7:30–10:30pm; Apr–June and Sept–Oct Tues and Thurs–Sun 12:30–2pm, Thurs–Mon 7:30–10:30pm. Closed Nov–Mar.

ANTIBES & CAP D'ANTIBES *★★*

On the other side of the Baie des Anges (Bay of Angels), across from Nice, is the port of Antibes. This town has a quiet charm unique on the Côte d'Azur. Its harbor is filled with fishing boats and yachts, and in recent years it has emerged as a new hot spot. The marketplaces are full of flowers. If you're in Antibes in the evening, you can watch fishers playing the popular Riviera game of *boule.*

Spiritually, Antibes is totally divorced from Cap d'Antibes, a peninsula studded with the villas of the super-rich. In *Tender Is the Night,* Fitzgerald described it as a place where "old villas rotted like water lilies among the massed pines."

ESSENTIALS

GETTING THERE   **Trains** from Cannes arrive at the rail station, on place Pierre-Semard, every 20 minutes (trip time: 10 min.), at a one-way fare of 3€. Trains from Nice arrive every 30 minutes (trip time: 18 min.), charging a one-way fare of around 4€. For information, call © **08-36-35-35-35.**

If you're **driving,** follow E1 east from Cannes and take the turnoff to the south for Antibes. From Nice, take E1 west until you come to the turnoff for Antibes. From the center of Antibes, follow the coastal road, boulevard Leclerc, south until you come to Cap d'Antibes.

VISITOR INFORMATION   The **Office de Tourisme** is at 11 place du Général-de-Gaulle (© **04-92-90-53-00;** fax 04-92-90-53-01; www.Antibesjuan lespins.com).

WHERE TO STAY

Auberge de la Gardiole 🖈   This is a country inn run with a personal touch. The large villa, surrounded by gardens, is in an area of private estates. The charming rooms are on the upper floors of the inn and in the little buildings in the garden; they come in a variety of shapes and sizes, each furnished with a certain charm and an eye on comfort. Half the units come with showers, and half with combination tub/showers. The cheerful dining room, serving French and Provençal cuisine, has a fireplace and hanging pots and pans; in good weather you can dine under a wisteria-covered trellis.

Chemin de la Garoupe, 06160 Cap d'Antibes. © **04-93-61-35-03.** Fax 04-93-67-61-87. www.hotel-la garoupe-gardiole.com. 17 units. 90€–130€ double; from 165€–200€ suite. AE, MC, V. Closed Nov–Mar. Bus: A2. **Amenities:** Restaurant; bar; pool; limited room service; laundry. *In room:* A/C (in 15), TV, minibar, safe.

Castel Garoupe ⟨*Value*⟩   We highly recommend this Mediterranean villa, which was built in 1968 on a private lane in the center of the cape, because it offers tastefully furnished spacious rooms with fine beds and compact bathrooms with showers and tubs. Many of the rooms have private balconies, and each has shuttered windows. There's a tranquil garden on the premises.

959 bd. de la Garoupe, 06160 Cap d'Antibes. © **04-93-61-36-51.** Fax 04-93-67-74-88. www.castelgaroupe. com. 28 units. 118€–146€ double; 140€–168€ studio apt with kitchenette. Rates include breakfast. AE, MC, V. Closed Nov to mid-Mar. Bus: A2. **Amenities:** Outdoor pool; exercise room; room service (8am–10pm); babysitting. *In room:* A/C, TV, kitchenette, fridge, hair dryer, safe.

Hôtel du Cap-Eden Roc 🖈🖈🖈   Legendary for the glamour of its setting and its clientele, this Second Empire hotel, opened in 1870, is surrounded by gardens. It's like a country estate, with spacious public rooms, marble fireplaces, paneling, and chandeliers. The guest rooms are among the most sumptuous on the Riviera, with deluxe beds. Bathrooms are spacious with brass fittings and tub and shower combinations. Even though the guests snoozing by the pool, which was blasted out of the cliffside at enormous expense, might appear undraped during the day, evenings are upscale, with lots of emphasis on clothing and style. The famous Pavillon Eden Roc, near a rock garden apart from the hotel, has a panoramic sea view. Venetian chandeliers, Louis XV chairs, and elegant draperies add to the drama. Lunch is served on a terrace, under umbrellas and an arbor.

Bd. J.-F.-Kennedy, 06600 Cap d'Antibes. ℂ 04-93-61-39-01. Fax 04-93-67-76-04. www.edenroc-hotel.fr. 140 units. 420€–510€ double; 670€–1,100€ suite. No credit cards. Closed mid-Oct to Apr. Bus: A2. **Amenities:** Restaurant; 2 bars; pool; gym; sauna; secretarial service; limited room service; massage; babysitting; laundry/dry cleaning. *In room:* A/C, TV, hair dryer, safe.

WHERE TO DINE

La Taverne du Saffranier *(Value* PROVENÇAL   Earthy, irreverent, and occupying a century-old building in the Provençal motif, this brasserie serves a medley of local specialties. Portions are savory and generous. Examples are a platter of *petits farcis* (stuffed vegetables); *céviche,* the cold raw fish in hot sauce that's refreshing on a hot day; and a medley of grilled fish (including sardines) served with a dash of fresh lemon. The kitchen can prepare its own version of bouillabaisse if you give a day's notice. Lunch hours are very limited.

Place du Saffranier. ℂ 04-93-34-80-50. Reservations recommended. Main courses 12€–25€; fixed-price menu 15€. No credit cards. Tues–Sun noon–12:30pm; Tues–Sat 7–10:30pm.

Restaurant de Bacon 𝕱𝕱𝕱 SEAFOOD   The Eden Roc restaurant at the Hôtel du Cap is more elegant, but Bacon serves the best seafood around. This restaurant on a rocky peninsula offers a panoramic coast view. Bouillabaisse aficionados claim that Bacon offers the best in France. In its deluxe version, saltwater crayfish float atop the savory brew; we prefer the simple version—a waiter adds the finishing touches at your table. If bouillabaisse isn't to your liking, try fish soup with the garlic-laden *rouille* sauce, fish terrine, or something from a collection of fish unknown in North America. These include sar, pageot, and denti.

Bd. de Bacon. ℂ 04-93-61-50-02. Reservations required. Main courses 16€–110€. Fixed-price menu 45€–65€. AE, MC, V. Wed–Sun noon–2pm and Tues–Sun 8–10pm. Closed Oct–Jan.

A MUSEUM WORTH VISITING

On the ramparts above the port is the Château Grimaldi, once the home of the princes of Antibes of the Grimaldi family, who ruled the city from 1385 to 1608. Today it houses the **Musée Picasso** 𝕱𝕱, place du Château (ℂ **04-92-90-54-20**), one of the world's great Picasso collections. Picasso came to town after the war years and stayed in a small hotel at Golfe-Juan until the museum director at Antibes invited him to work and live at the museum. He spent 1946 painting here. When he departed, he gave the museum all the work he'd done: 24 paintings, 80 pieces of ceramics, 44 drawings, 32 lithographs, 11 oils on paper, 2 sculptures, and 5 tapestries. In addition, there's a gallery of contemporary art exhibiting Léger, Miró, Ernst, and Calder, among others. Admission is 4.60€ adults, 2.30€ students and ages 7 to 26, free for ages 6 and under. The museum is open from October to May, Tuesday through Sunday from 10am to noon and 2 to 6pm (June–Sept Tues–Sun 10am–6pm).

ST-PAUL-DE-VENCE 𝕱𝕱

Of all the perched villages of the Riviera, St-Paul-de-Vence is the best known. It was popularized in the 1920s when many artists lived here, occupying the 16th-century houses flanking the cobblestone streets. Its ramparts (allow about 30 min. to circle them) overlook a setting of flowers and olive and orange trees. They haven't changed much since they were constructed from 1537 to 1547 by order of François I. From the north ramparts you can look out on Baou de St-Jeannet, a sphinx-shaped rock that was painted into the landscape of Poussin's *Polyphème.*

ESSENTIALS

GETTING THERE   The nearest **rail** station is in Cagnes-sur-Mer. Some 20 **buses** per day leave from Nice's Gare Routière, dropping passengers off in

St-Paul-de-Vence, then in Vence. For information, call the Société SAP at © 04-93-58-37-60. If you're **driving** from Nice, take the coastal A8 highway east, turn inland at Cagnes-sur-Mer, and follow the signs north to St-Paul-de-Vence.

VISITOR INFORMATION   The **Office de Tourisme** is at Maison Tour, 2 rue Grande (© **04-93-32-86-95**; www.stpaulweb.com).

EXPLORING ST-PAUL-DE-VENCE

Fondation Maeght ★★★ (© **04-93-32-81-63**)   On a hill in pine-studded woods, Fondation Maeght is like a Shangri-La. Nature and the creations of men and women blend harmoniously in this unique achievement of the architect José Luis Sert. Its white concrete arcs give the impression of a giant pagoda.

A stark Calder rises on the lawn. In a courtyard, the bronze works of Giacometti form a surrealistic garden. Sculpture is displayed inside, but the museum is at its best in a natural setting of terraces and gardens. It's built on several levels, its many glass walls providing an indoor-outdoor vista. The foundation, a gift "to the people" from Aimé and Marguerite Maeght, also provides a showcase for new talent. Everywhere you look, you see 20th-century art: mosaics by Chagall and Braque, Miró ceramics in the "labyrinth," and Ubac and Braque stained glass in the chapel. Bonnard, Kandinsky, Léger, Matisse, Barbara Hepworth, and many other artists are well represented.

Fondation Maeght is open from July to September, daily from 10am to 7pm; from October to June, daily from 10am to 12:30pm and 2:30 to 6pm. Admission is 9€ adults, 7.50€ students and ages 10 to 25, free for children under 10.

North of St-Paul-de-Vence, you can visit the sleepy old town of Vence, with its **Vieille Ville (Old Town).** If you're wearing comfortable shoes, the narrow, steep streets are worth exploring. The **cathedral** on place Godeau is unremarkable except for some 15th-century choir stalls. If it's a Tuesday or Thursday, however, most visitors pass through the narrow gates of this once-fortified walled town on their way to the **Chapelle du Rosaire** ★★, 466 av. Henri-Matisse (© **04-93-58-03-26**), created by Henri Matisse. Matisse was 77 when he set out to create this masterpiece, of which he spoke as "the culmination of a whole life dedicated to the search for truth." From the front you might find the chapel of the Dominican nuns of Monteils unremarkable—until you spot a 12m (40-ft.) crescent-adorned cross rising from a blue-tile roof. The light inside picks up the coloring in the simply rendered leaf forms and abstract patterns: sapphire blue, aquamarine, and lemon yellow. In black-and-white ceramics, St. Dominic is depicted in a few lines. The Stations of the Cross are also black-and-white tile, with Matisse's self-styled "tormented and passionate" figures. Year-round, the chapel is open Monday through Thursday and Saturday from 2 to 5:30pm. Every Tuesday and Thursday, it's also open from 10 to 11:30am. It's closed November through mid-December. Admission is 2.50€ for adults, 1€ for ages 16 and under; contributions to maintain the chapel are welcomed.

NICE ★★★

Nice is the capital of the Riviera. It's also one of the country's most ancient cities, founded by the Greeks, who called it Nike (Victory). By the 19th century, the Victorian upper class and tsarist aristocrats flocked here. These days it's not as chichi and expensive, especially compared to Cannes. Of all the major resorts of France, Nice is the most affordable. It's also the best place to base yourself on the Riviera, especially if you're dependent on public transportation. From the Nice airport, the second largest in France, you can travel by train or bus along the entire coast.

⌒ *Value* Bus Passes for Easy Travel

If you plan on traveling via the city's buses, consider buying a **Sun Pass,** available from tobacco stands and newspaper kiosks throughout the city. Valid for 1, 5, or 7 days, the pass allows unlimited transit on any municipal bus during the pass's validity. The price is 5€ for a 1-day pass, 12€ for a 5-day pass, and 19€ for a 7-day pass. For additional information, call **Société SunBus (CQ)** at ℂ **04-92-17-52-52.**

Because of its brilliant sunshine and relaxed living, Nice has attracted artists and writers, among them Matisse, Dumas, Nietzsche, Apollinaire, Flaubert, Hugo, Stendhal, and Mistral.

ESSENTIALS

GETTING THERE   **Trains** arrive at Gare Nice-Ville, avenue Thiers (ℂ **08-36-35-35-35**). From there you can take trains to Cannes, Monaco, and Antibes, with easy connections to anywhere else along the Mediterranean coast. There's a small-scale tourist center at the train station, open Monday through Saturday from 8am to 6:30pm and Sunday from 8am to noon and 2 to 5:30pm. If you face a long delay, you can eat at the cafeteria and even take showers at the station.

Transatlantic and inter-continental flights land at **Aéroport Nice–Côte d'Azur** (ℂ **08-20-42-33-33**). From here, municipal bus nos. 23 and 99 depart at 20-minute intervals from the airport for the bus station, **Gare Routière,** promenade du Paillon (ℂ **04-93-85-61-81**), charging 3.50€ per person, each way. A more luxurious mode of transport involves a yellow-sided shuttle bus *(la navette de l'aéroport)* that charges 4.50€ for a ride between the airport and Nice's main bus station. A taxi ride from the airport into the city center will cost at least 25€ to 30€ each way. Trip time is about 30 minutes.

GETTING AROUND   Most of the local buses in Nice create connections with one another at their central hub, the **Station Central,** 10 av. Félix-Faure (ℂ **04-93-13-53-13**), a very short walk from the place Masséna. Municipal buses each charge 2€ for a ride within Greater Nice. To save money, consider buying a five-ticket *carnet* for 13€. Bus nos. 2 and 12 make frequent trips to the beach. Long-distance buses making the trek, say, between Nice and such destinations as Monaco, Cannes, St-Tropez, and other parts of France and Europe, depart from the **Gare Routière,** 5 bd. Jean-Jaurès (ℂ **04-93-85-61-81**).

The best place to rent bikes and mopeds in Nice is from **Cycles Arnaud,** 5 rue François 1e (ℂ **04-93-87-88-55**), just behind the place Grimaldi. Open Tuesday through Saturday from 9am to noon and 2 to 7pm, it charges 15€ per day for both bikes and mopeds, and requires a deposit of at least 304€ or more, depending on the value of the machine you rent. Somewhat less appealing, but useful for the days when Cycles Arnaud is closed, is **Nicea Rent,** 12 rue de Belgique (ℂ **04-93-82-42-71**), which charges about the same rates, but whose staff isn't always on the premises. (They maintain a somewhat erratic mobile phone service at ℂ **06-12-44-15-37**.)

WHERE TO STAY
Very Expensive

Hôtel Negresco ★★★   The Negresco is one of the Riviera's super-glamorous hotels. Jeanne Augier has taken over the place and has triumphed. This Victorian wedding-cake hotel is named after its founder, Henry Negresco, a Romanian who died franc-less in Paris in 1920. It was built on the seafront, in the French château style, with a mansard roof and domed tower. Its decorators scoured Europe to gather antiques, tapestries, and art. Some of the guest rooms are outfitted in homage to the personalities who stayed here: the Coco Chanel Room, for example. Suites and public areas are even grander, as is the case with the Louis XIV salon, reminiscent of the Sun King, and the Napoléon III suite, where swagged walls, a leopard-skin carpet, and a half-crowned canopy in pink create a sense of majesty. The most expensive rooms with balconies face the Mediterranean. The staff wears 18th-century costumes. The beach is private. The featured restaurant—one of the Riviera's greatest—is Chantecler (see below).

37 promenade des Anglais, 06007 Nice CEDEX. © **04-93-16-64-00.** Fax 04-93-88-35-68. www.hotel-negresco-nice.com. 150 units. 213€–460€ double; 585€–1,410€ suite. AE, DC, MC, V. Parking 24€. **Amenities:** 2 restaurants; bar; fitness center; secretarial service; room service; massage; babysitting; laundry/dry cleaning. *In room:* A/C, TV, minibar, hair dryer.

Expensive

La Pérouse ⊛ *(Finds* Once a prison, La Pérouse is now a unique Riviera hotel. Set on a cliff, it's built right into the gardens of an ancient château-fort. There's no hotel in Nice with a better view over both the old city and the Baie des Anges. Many people stay here for the view alone. Inside, the hotel is like an old Provençal home, with low ceilings, white walls, and antiques. Most of the lovely rooms have loggias overlooking the bay. The spacious rooms are beautifully furnished, often with Provençal fabrics. The bathrooms are large and done in Boticino marble, all with tubs and showers.

11 quai Rauba-Capéu, 06300 Nice. © **04-93-62-34-63.** Fax 04-93-62-59-41. www.hroy.com/la-perouse. 63 units. 163€–376€ double; from 686€ suite. AE, DC, MC, V. Parking 14€. **Amenities:** Restaurant; outdoor pool; exercise room; Jacuzzi; sauna; limited room service; laundry/dry cleaning. *In room:* A/C, TV, minibar, hair dryer.

Moderate

Château des Ollières ⊛ *(Finds* This most appealing and unusual hotel made its debut as a hotel in 1996, and as a restaurant a year later. The villa was recently expanded with modern and beautiful rooms. It's within a 5-minute walk of the Negresco and the promenade des Anglais. The setting is one of the largest tracts of privately owned land in Nice—an 8-hectare (20-acre) park. The centerpiece is a beaux arts villa built in the 1870s by a Russian prince. Inside, you'll find a noteworthy collection of oil paintings and "neo-Napoléonienne" and Empire-inspired antiques. One of the highlights is a set that was custom-made for the dining room, when the villa was being constructed. The high-ceilinged guest rooms are outfitted in the same ornate style as the public areas. Bathrooms are quite luxurious, with tub and shower combinations. The hotel restaurant occupies both the villa's original dining room as well as a garden wing. Menus change weekly, according to the inspiration of the chef and the availability of fresh ingredients.

39 av. des Baumettes, 06000 Nice. © **04-92-15-77-99.** Fax 04-92-15-77-98. www.chateaudesollieres.com. 34 units. 140€–370€ double; 180€–500€ suite. AE, MC, V. Bus: 38. **Amenities:** Restaurant; bar; limited room service; babysitting; laundry/dry cleaning. *In room:* A/C, TV, minibar, hair dryer.

Inexpensive

Hôtel de la Mer *(Value* In the center of Old Nice, this place was built around 1910, transformed into a hotel in 1947, and renovated in 1993. Despite that, it manages to keep its prices low. Ms. Feri Forouzan, the owner, welcomes you with a personal charm. Most guest rooms are of good size, each with a small bathroom with shower. From the hotel it's a 2-minute walk to the promenade des Anglais and the seafront. Breakfast is served in one of the public salons or in your room.

4 place Masséna, 06000 Nice. © **04-93-92-09-10**. Fax 04-93-85-00-64. hotel-mer@wanadoo.fr. 12 units. 50€–70€ double. AE, MC, V. Bus: 1, 2, 5, 15, or 17. **Amenities:** Room service; massage. *In room:* A/C, TV, minibar (in some).

WHERE TO DINE

Chantecler ✸✸✸ TRADITIONAL/MODERN FRENCH   This is Nice's most prestigious and best restaurant. Its walls are covered with panels removed from a château in Puilly-Fussé; a Regency-style salon was installed for before- or after-dinner drinks; and a collection of 16th-century paintings was imported. A much-respected chef, Alain Llorca, revised the menu to include the most sophisticated and creative dishes in Nice. They change almost weekly but may include turbot filet served with a purée of broad beans, sun-dried tomatoes, and asparagus; roasted suckling lamb served with beignets of fresh vegetables and ricotta-stuffed ravioli; and a melt-in-your-mouth fantasy of marbled hot chocolate drenched in almond-flavored cream sauce.

In the Hôtel Negresco, 37 promenade des Anglais. © **04-93-16-64-00**. Reservations required. Main courses 43€–65€. Fixed-price menus 45€–55€ lunch, 90€–130€ dinner. AE, MC, V. Daily 12:30–2pm and 8–10pm. Closed mid-Nov to mid-Dec. Bus: 8, 9, 10, or 11.

La Merenda ✸✸ *Finds* NIÇOISE   Since there's no phone, you have to go by this place twice: once to make a reservation and once to dine. It's worth the effort. Forsaking his chef's crown at Chantecler (above), Dominique Le Stanc opened this tiny bistro serving a sublime cuisine. Though he was born in Alsace, his heart and soul belong to the Mediterranean, the land of black truffles, wild morels, sea bass, and asparagus. His food is a lullaby of gastronomic unity, with texture, crunch, richness, and balance. Look for his specials on a chalkboard. Perhaps you'll find stuffed cabbage, fried zucchini flowers, or oxtail flavored with fresh oranges. Lamb from the Sisteron is cooked until it practically falls from the bone. Raw artichokes are paired with a salad of mâche. Service is discreet and personable. We wish we could dine here every day.

4 rue Terrasse. No phone. Reservations required. Main courses 28€–38€. No credit cards. Mon–Fri noon–2pm and 7–9.30pm. Closed Aug 4–18, Dec 24–Jan 4, and Feb 16–22. Bus: 8.

La Zucca Magica ✸ *Finds* VEGETARIAN/ITALIAN   The chef at this popular harborside restaurant was recently selected best Italian chef in Nice. That this honor should go to a vegetarian restaurant was the most startling part of the news. Chef Marco certainly has a fine pedigree—he's a relative of Luciano Pavarotti. He serves refined cuisine at reasonable prices, using recipes from Italy's Piedmont region and updating them with no meat or fish. The pink and green decor will put you in the mood for the creative cuisine. You'll have to trust Marco, though, because everyone is served the same meal. You can count on savory cuisine using lots of herbs, Italian cheeses, beans, and pasta. Lasagna is a specialty.

4 bis quai Papacino. © **04-93-56-25-27**. Reservations recommended. Menus 16€ lunch, 25€ dinner. No credit cards. Tues–Sat 12:30–2:30pm and 7:30–10:30pm.

Restaurant L'Estocaficada *Finds* NIÇOISE   *Estocaficada* is the Provençal word for stockfish, Europe's ugliest fish. There might be a dried-out, balloon-shaped version on display in the cozy dining room. Brigitte Autier is the owner and chef, and her kitchens are visible from everywhere in the dining room. Descended from a matriarchal line (since 1958) of mother-daughter teams who've managed this place, she's devoted to the preservation of recipes prepared by her Niçoise grandmother. Examples are gnocchi, beignets, several types of *farcies* (tomatoes, peppers, or onions stuffed with herbed fillings), grilled sardines, and bouillabaisse served as a main course or in a mini-version.

2 rue de l'Hôtel-de-Ville. (℃) **04-93-80-21-64.** Reservations recommended. Main courses 12€–18€; fixed-price menus 17€, 21€, and 25€. AE, MC, V. Tues–Sat noon–2pm and 7–9:30pm. Bus: 1, 2, or 5.

IN & AROUND NICE

The wide **boulevard des Anglais** fronts the bay. Split by "islands" of palms and flowers, it stretches for about 6km (4 miles). Fronting the beach are rows of grand cafes, the Musée Masséna, villas, and hotels—some good, others decaying.

In the east, the promenade becomes **quai des Etats-Unis,** lined with some of the best restaurants in Nice, each specializing in bouillabaisse. Rising sharply on a rock is the site known as **Le Château,** where the ducs de Savoie built their castle, torn down in 1706. The hill has been turned into a garden of pines and exotic flowers. To reach the site, many prefer to take an elevator; actually, many prefer to take the elevator up, then walk down. The park is open daily from 8am to 7:30pm.

The center of Nice is **place Masséna,** with pink buildings in the 17th-century Genoese style and the **Fontaine du Soleil (Fountain of the Sun)** by Janoit. Stretching from the main square to the promenade is the **Jardin Albert-Ier,** with an open-air terrace and a Triton Fountain. Palms and exotic flowers make this the most relaxing oasis at the resort.

A PAIR OF MUSEUMS WORTH A LOOK

Musée des Beaux-Arts ☆☆ The collection is housed in the former residence of the Ukrainian Princess Kotchubey. There's a gallery devoted to the masters of the Second Empire and the Belle Epoque. The gallery of sculptures includes works by J. B. Carpeaux, Rude, and Rodin. Note the important collection by a dynasty of painters, the Dutch Vanloo family. One of its best-known members, Carle Vanloo, born in Nice in 1705, was Louis XV's premier *peintre.* A fine collection of 19th- and 20th-century art is displayed, including works by Ziem, Raffaelli, Boudin, Renoir, Monet, Guillaumin, and Sisley.

33 av. des Baumettes. (℃) **04-92-15-28-28.** Admission 3.80€ adults, 2.30€ students, free for children under 18. Tues–Sun 10am–6pm. Bus: 3, 9, 12, 22, 23, or 38.

Musée International d'Art Naïf Anatole-Jakovsky (Museum of Naïve Art) ☆ This museum is housed in the Château Ste-Hélène in the Fabron district. The collection was once owned by the museum's namesake, for years one of the world's leading art critics. His 600 drawings and canvases were turned over to the institution and made accessible to the public. Artists from more than two dozen countries are represented here—from primitive painting to 20th-century works.

Av. Val-Marie. (℃) **04-93-71-78-33.** Admission 3.80€ adults, 2.30€ students and seniors, free for children 18 and under. Wed–Mon 10am–6pm. Bus: 9, 10, or 12; the walk from the bus stop takes 10 min.

A MUSEUM IN NEARBY CIMIEZ ☆☆

Founded by the Romans, who called it Cemenelum, Cimiez, a hilltop suburb, 4.8km (3 miles) north of Nice, was the capital of the Maritime Alps province. Take bus nos. 15 or 17 from place Masséna.

Musée Matisse ☆ This museum honors the artist, who died in Nice in 1954. Seeing his nude sketches today, you'll wonder how early critics could have denounced them as "the female animal in all her shame and horror." The museum has several permanent collections. These include *Nude in an Armchair with a Green Plant* (1937), *Nymph in the Forest* (1935–42), and a chronologically arranged series of paintings from 1890 to 1919. The most famous of these is *Portrait of Madame Matisse* (1905), usually displayed near a portrait of the artist's wife by Marquet, painted in 1900. There's also an ensemble of drawings and designs *(Flowers and Fruits)* he prepared as practice sketches for the Matisse Chapel at Vence. The most famous works are *The Créole Dancer* (1951), *Blue Nude IV* (1952), and around 50 dance-related sketches he did between 1930 and 1931.

In the Villa des Arènes-de-Cimiez, 164 av. des Arènes-de-Cimiez. 📞 04-93-53-40-53. Admission 3.80€ adults, 2.30€ students, free for ages 18 and under. Wed–Mon 10am–6pm. Closed Jan 1, May 1, and Dec 25.

HITTING THE LINKS & OTHER OUTDOOR PURSUITS

GOLF   The oldest golf course on the Riviera is about 16km (10 miles) from Nice: **Golf Bastide du Roi** (also known as the Golf de Biot) is at avenue Michard Pellissier, Biot (📞 **04-93-65-08-48**). Open daily, this is a flat, not particularly challenging sea-fronting course. (It's necessary to cross a highway midway through to complete the full 18 holes.) Tee times are from 8am to 6pm; you can play until the sun sets. Reservations aren't necessary, though on weekends you should probably expect a delay. Greens fees are 40€ for 18 holes; club rental is 10€.

SCUBA DIVING   The best outfit is the **Centre International de Plongée de Nice,** 2 ruelle des Moulins (📞 **06-09-52-55-57** or 04-93-55-59-50), adjacent to the city's old port, between quai des Docks and boulevard Stalingrad. A *baptême* (initiatory dive for first-timers) costs 24€. A one-tank dive for experienced divers, equipment included, is 30€; a license is required.

TENNIS   The oldest tennis club in Nice is the **Nice Lawn Tennis Club,** Parc Impérial, 5 av. Suzanne-Lenglen (📞 04-92-15-58-00). It's open daily from 8:30am to 9:30pm (mid-Oct to mid-Apr) and charges 19€ per person for 2 hours of court time, or a reduced rate of 55€ per person for unlimited access to the courts for 1 week. The club has a cooperative staff, loyal clientele, 13 clay courts, and six hard-surfaced courts. Reserve a court the night before.

NICE AFTER DARK

Nice has some of the most active nightlife along the Riviera; pick up a copy of *La Semaine de Spectacles,* which outlines the week's nighttime diversions, for clues to what's hot. The major cultural center is the **Opéra de Nice,** 9 rue Terrasse (📞 **04-92-17-40-40;** bus: 15), with a busy season in winter. A full repertoire is presented, including both operas and the popular French Opéra Comique. The opera hall is also the major venue for concerts and recitals. Tickets are available up to about a day or two prior to any performance. You can show up at the box office (Tues–Fri 10am–5:30pm) or buy tickets in advance with a major credit card by phoning 📞 04-92-17-40-40. Tickets run 10€ for nosebleed (and we mean it) seats to 60€ for front-and-center seats on opening night.

Cabaret du Casino Ruhl, in the Casino Ruhl, 1 promenade des Anglais (📞 04-97-03-12-77), is Nice's answer to the cabaret glitter that appears in more ostentatious forms in Monte Carlo and Las Vegas. It includes just enough flesh to titillate; lots of spangles, feathers, and sequins; a medley of cross-cultural jokes and nostalgia for the old days of French *chanson;* and an acrobat or juggler. The cover of 16€ includes the first drink; dinner and the show, complete with a bottle of wine per person, costs 46€. Shows are presented every Friday and Saturday at 10:30pm. No jeans or sneakers are allowed.

The casino contains an area exclusively for slot machines, open daily from noon to 4am, entrance to which is free. A more formal gaming room (jacket required, but not a tie), with blackjack, baccarat, chemin de fer, and 21 tables, is open nightly, at a fee of 11€ per person, Monday through Friday from 8pm to 4am and Saturday and Sunday from 5pm to 5am.

Near the Hôtel Negresco and promenade des Anglais, **Le Blue Boy,** 9 rue Spinetta (© 04-93-44-68-24), is the oldest gay disco on the Riviera. With two bars and two floors, it's a vital stop for passengers aboard the all-gay cruises that call at Nice. The cover varies from free to 10€. A newer club is **Le Klub,** 10 rue Halevy (© 04-93-16-27-56); no cover.

ST-JEAN-CAP-FERRAT ⚜

Of all the oases along the Côte d'Azur, no place has the snob appeal of Cap-Ferrat. It's a 15km (9-mile) promontory sprinkled with luxurious villas, outlined by sheltered bays, beaches, and coves. The vegetation is lush. In the port of St-Jean, the harbor accommodates yachts and fishing boats.

The cape hosts the **Musée Ile-de-France** ⚜⚜, avenue Denis-Séméria (© 04-93-01-33-09), in one of the Côte d'Azur's most legendary villas. Its owner, Baronne Ephrussi de Rothschild, died in 1934, leaving the Italianate building and its gardens to the Institut de France. The wealth of her collection is preserved: 18th-century furniture; Tiepolo ceilings; Savonnerie carpets; screens and panels from the Far East; tapestries from Gobelin, Aubusson, and Beauvais; Fragonard drawings; canvases by Boucher; Sèvres porcelain; and more. The sprawling gardens contain fragments of statuary from churches, monasteries, and palaces. An entire section is planted with cacti.

Admission is 10€ adults, 7.50€ students and persons 7 to 18. The museum is open from November to February, Monday through Friday from 2 to 6pm and Saturday and Sunday from 10am to 6pm; from March to October, it's open daily from 10am to 6pm.

ESSENTIALS

GETTING THERE   Most visitors drive or take a **bus** or **taxi** from the rail station at nearby Beaulieu. Buses at Beaulieu depart hourly for Cap-Ferrat. There's also bus service from Nice. For bus information, call © **04-93-85-64-44.** By **car,** St-Jean-Cap-Ferrat is best reached from Nice along N7 east.

VISITOR INFORMATION   The **Office de Tourisme** is on avenue Denis-Séméria (© **04-93-76-08-90;** www.riviera.fr/tourisme.htm).

WHERE TO STAY

Grand Hôtel du Cap-Ferrat ⚜⚜⚜   This early-1900s palace is at the tip of the peninsula in the midst of a 5.6-hectare (14-acre) garden. It has been the retreat of the international elite since 1908. Parts of the exterior have open loggias and big arched windows; you can also enjoy the views from the elaborately flowering terrace over the sea. Accommodations look as if the late Princess Grace might settle in at any minute. They're generally spacious and open to sea views, and each comes with a sumptuous bathroom with tub and shower. Rates include admission to the pool, Club Dauphin. The beach is accessible via funicular from the main building. The hotel is open year-round.

Bd. du Général-de-Gaulle, 06230 St-Jean-Cap-Ferrat. © 04-93-76-50-52. Fax 04-93-76-04-52. www.grand-hotel-cap-ferrat.com. 53 units. 580€–1,100€ double; 1,680€–2,550€ suite. Rates include breakfast. AE, MC, V. Indoor parking 75€; outdoor parking free. Closed Jan–Feb. **Amenities:** 2 restaurants; 2 bars; Olympic-size heated pool; 2 tennis courts; sauna; hotel bicycles; limited room service; babysitting; laundry/dry cleaning. *In room:* A/C, TV, minibar, hair dryer, safe.

Hôtel Clair Logis *(Value)*   This B&B was created by the grandmother of the present owners when she added two outbuildings to the grounds of her early-1900s villa, about a 10-minute walk from the beach. The hotel's most famous guest was de Gaulle, who stayed in a room called *Strelitzias* (Bird of Paradise). The pleasant rooms, each named after a flower, are scattered over three buildings in the confines of the garden. The most romantic and spacious are in the main building; the seven in the annex are the most modern but have the least character and are smaller and cheaper. Each comes with a small bathroom with shower.

12 av. Centrale, 06230 St-Jean-Cap-Ferrat. © 04-93-76-51-81. Fax 04-93-76-51-82. www.hotel-clair-logis.fr. 18 units. 110€–125€ double. AE, DC, MC, V. Closed Jan 10 to mid-Mar and Nov to Dec 15. *In room:* TV, minibar, hair dryer.

WHERE TO DINE
Le Provençal *(★)* FRENCH/PROVENÇAL   Near the top of Nice's highest peak, it has the most panoramic view. Many of the menu items are credited to the inspiration of "the Provençal" in the kitchens. Menu items include marinated artichoke hearts beside half a lobster, a *tarte fine* of potatoes with deliberately undercooked foie gras, rack of lamb with local herbs and tarragon sauce, and crayfish with asparagus and black-olive tapenade. The best way to appreciate the desserts is to order the sampler, *les cinq desserts du Provençal*—five desserts that usually include macaroons with chocolate and crème brûlée. With the passage of years, the cooking seems more inspired than ever.

2 av. Denis-Séméria. © 04-93-76-03-97. Reservations required. Main courses 40€–56€; fixed-price menu 68€. AE, MC, V. Apr–Sept daily noon–2:30pm and 7:30–11pm; Oct–Mar Wed–Sun noon–2:30pm and 7:30–11pm.

MONACO *(★★★)*
Monaco—or rather its capital, Monte Carlo—has for a century been a symbol of glamour. Its legend was enhanced by the 1956 marriage of its Prince Rainier III to American actress Grace Kelly. Although not always happy in her role, Princess Grace soon won the respect and adoration of her people. The Monégasques still mourn her death in a 1982 car accident.

Monaco became a property of the Grimaldi clan, a Genoese family, as early as 1297. With shifting loyalties, it has maintained something resembling independence ever since. In a fit of impatience, the French annexed it in 1793, but the ruling family recovered it in 1814, though the prince at the time couldn't bear to tear himself away from the pleasures of Paris for "dreary old Monaco."

ESSENTIALS
GETTING THERE   Monaco has rail, bus, and highway connections from other coastal cities, especially Nice. **Trains** arrive every 30 minutes from Cannes, Nice, Menton, and Antibes. For information, call © **08-36-35-35-35.** Monaco's railway station (Gare SNCF) is on avenue Prince Pierre. It's a long walk uphill from the station to Monte Carlo. If you'd rather take a **taxi,** call © **377/93-50-56-28** or 93-15-01-01. There are no border formalities when entering Monaco from mainland France. If you're on the Riviera, **drive** from Nice along N7 northeast. It's only 19km (12 miles), but with traffic, the drive can take 30 minutes.

VISITOR INFORMATION   The **Direction du Tourisme** is at 2A bd. des Moulins (© **377/92-16-61-16;** www.monaco-congres.com).

WHERE TO STAY

Columbus Monaco Hotel 🏰🏰 *Value*   In the Fontvieille sector of Monaco is a stylish and contemporary hotel. Owner Scotsman Ken McCulloch is called the "champion of high style at low prices." Facing Princess Grace's former rose garden and the sea, this first-class hotel is open from April to October. Guest rooms are done in "Hybrid Hip," evocative of both Miami and London. The decor of dark wardrobes and tables, brown, gray, and off-white, is lightened with the occasional use of lavender blue. McCulloch dictated many of the features of the hotel himself: Lartigue photos of the Riviera, high-tech cabinets filled with video games, and chocolate leather furnishings. Details include deluxe bed linens and Frette bathrobes. Each unit comes with a first-class tiled bathroom with tub and shower. The pool is shared with residents of the condo complex in which the hotel is situated. But guests are carried in a boat to a tranquil sandy beach nearby.

The on-site brasserie serves a fabulous antipasti buffet along with savory pastas and pizzas; and the bar, Downstairs, is lively with lounge music. A hip crowd of locals and visitors are attracted to it, including Prince Albert.

23 av. des Papalins, 98000 Monaco. ℭ 377/92-05-90-00. Fax 92-05-91-67. www.columbushotels.com. 181 units. 200€–295€ double; 350€–450€ suite. AE, MC, V. Parking 23€. **Amenities:** Restaurant; bar; outdoor pool; fitness room; business center; salon/barber; 24-hr. room service; babysitting; laundry/dry cleaning. *In room:* A/C, TV, minibar, hair dryer, safe.

Hôtel de Paris 🏰🏰🏰   On the resort's main plaza, opposite the casino, this is one of the world's most famous hotels. The facade has marble pillars, and the lounge has an Art Nouveau rose window at the peak of the dome. The hotel is furnished with a decor that includes marble pillars, statues, crystal chandeliers, Louis XVI chairs, and a wall-size mural. The guest rooms come in a variety of styles, with a period decor or a contemporary one. Some are enormous. Elegant fabrics, rich carpeting, and classic accessories make this a favorite among the world's most discerning guests. Note that the rooms opening onto the sea aren't as spacious as those in the rear. Bathrooms are large with marble and elegant brass fittings, plus tub and shower combinations. The hotel's most famous dining options are Le Louis XV and Le Grill. Both benefit from a collection of rare fine wines kept in a dungeon chiseled out of the rocks. The Thermes Marins spa, connected to both the Hôtel de Paris and the Hôtel Hermitage, offers cures of thalassotherapy under medical supervision.

Place du Casino, 98000 Monaco. ℭ 377/92-16-26-26. Fax 93-16-38-50. www.montecarloresort.com. 197 units. 365€–685€ double; from 680€–5,370€ suite. Breakfast 30€–35€. AE, DC, MC, V. Valet parking 25€. **Amenities:** 3 restaurants; bar; large indoor pool; fitness center; Thermes Marins spa; 2 saunas; concierge; salon; 24-hr. room service; babysitting; laundry/dry cleaning. *In room:* A/C, TV, hair dryer, safe.

Hôtel Mirabeau 🏰🏰   In the heart of Monte Carlo, the Mirabeau combines modern design with a refined atmosphere. Large mirrors, lighted closets, and sumptuous beds make living here idyllic; many rooms have terraces with views over the Mediterranean. Although the newest rooms are as fine as those in the main building, many guests prefer older ones for their old-fashioned decor and street-front exposures. Bathrooms are well appointed, with tub/shower combos.

1 av. Princesse-Grace, 98000 Monaco. ℭ 377/92-16-65-65. Fax 377/93-50-84-85. www.montecarloresort. com. 103 units. 250€–425€ double; from 600€ suite. AE, DC, MC, V. Parking 21€. **Amenities:** Restaurant; bar; pool; limited room service; babysitting; laundry/dry cleaning. *In room:* A/C, TV, minibar, hair dryer, safe, robes.

WHERE TO DINE

Le Louis XV 🏰🏰🏰 FRENCH/ITALIAN   In the Hôtel de Paris, the Louis XV offers what one critic called "down-home Riviera cooking within a Fabergé egg."

To ↑
Grande
Corniche

BEAUSOLEIL

av. de Villaini

To Menton ↑

FRANCE

av. P. Doumer

bd. Princesse-Charlotte

bd. des Moulins

MONTE
CARLO

bd. Larvotto
av. Princesse-Grâce

FRANCE
MONACO

MONEGHETTI

i

la Costa

MONACO

pl. du
Casino 5

Plage
de
Larvotto

← To Nice

bd. du Jardin-Exotique

bd. de Belgique

Rainier-III

av. de

av. d'Ostende

quai des Etats-Unis

PARC
PRINCESSE
ANTOINETTE

Grimaldi

bd. Albert-1er

Stade Nautique
Rainier-III

Port de Monaco

rue

LA
CONDAMINE

❶
JARDIN
EXOTIQUE bd.

❷

Station

pl. du
Canton Charles-III

bd.

quai Antoine-1er

av. de la Porte-Neuve

❸

pl. du
Palais

MONACO-
VILLE

Heliport

FONTVIEILLE

av. St-Martin

❹

JARDINS
ST-MARTIN

0   1/5 mile
0   200 meters

N

★Paris

FRANCE

MONACO ■

0   100 mi
0   100 km

Jardin Exotique **2**
Monte Carlo Casino **5**
Musée d'Anthropologie Préhistorique **1**
Musée de l'Océanographie **4**
Palais du Prince **3**

✝ Church
ⓘ Information
✉ Post Office
— Railway

When it lost one of its three Michelin stars in 2001, it made headlines. However, don't fear—the cuisine is as refined and elegant as it always was. Star chef Alain Ducasse creates a refined but not overly adorned cuisine, served by the finest staff in Monaco. Everything is light and attuned to the seasons, with an intelligent, modern interpretation of Provençal and northern Italian dishes. You'll find chargrilled breast of baby pigeon with sautéed duck liver, and everything from truffles and caviar to the best stewed salt cod on the coast.

In the Hôtel de Paris, place du Casino. ✆ **377/92-16-30-01.** Reservations recommended. Jacket and tie required for men. Main courses 80€–92€. Fixed-price dinner menus 160€–180€. AE, MC, V. Thurs–Mon 12:15–1:45pm and 8–9:45pm. Also open Wed for lunch July–Aug.

Rampoldi ⚐ FRENCH/ITALIAN   More than any other restaurant in Monte Carlo, Rampoldi is linked to the charming but somewhat dated interpretation of *La Dolce Vita.* Opened in the 1950s and staffed with a mix of old and new, it has a spirit that's more Italian than French. It also serves some of the best cuisine in

Monte Carlo from a location at the edge of the Casino Gardens. Menu items include an array of such pastas as tortelloni with cream and white truffle sauce; sea bass roasted in a salt crust; ravioli stuffed with crayfish; and veal kidneys in Madeira sauce. Crêpes suzette makes a spectacular finish.

3 av. des Spélugues. (C) 377/93-30-70-65. Reservations required. Main courses 25€–40€; fixed-price menu 23€–45€. AE, MC, V. Daily 12:15–2:30pm and 7:30–11:30pm. Closed Feb 3–18.

EXPLORING MONACO

The second-smallest state in Europe (Vatican City is the tiniest), Monaco consists of four parts: The old town, **Monaco-Ville,** is on a promontory, The Rock, 60m (200 ft.) high, and is the seat of the royal palace and the government building, as well as the home of the Oceanographic Museum. To the west of the bay, **La Condamine,** the 19th-century home of the Monégasques, is at the foot of the old town, forming its harbor and port sector. Up from the port (walking is steep in Monaco) is **Monte Carlo,** once the playground of European royalty and still the center for the wintering wealthy; it's the setting for the casino and its gardens and the deluxe hotels. The fourth part, **Fontvieille,** is a neat industrial suburb.

Ironically, **Monte-Carlo Beach,** at the far frontier, is on French soil. It attracts a chic crowd, including movie stars. The resort has a freshwater pool, an artificial beach, and a sea-bathing establishment.

The home of Monaco's royal family, the **Palais du Prince** ★, dominates the principality from "The Rock." When touring Les Grands Appartements du Palais, place du Palais ((C) 377/93-25-18-31), you're shown the Throne Room and some of the art collection, including Brueghels and Holbeins, as well as Princess Grace's stunning state portrait. The palace was built in the 13th century and part of it is from the Renaissance. The ideal time to arrive is 11:55am to watch the 10-minute changing of the guard. A combination ticket including admission to the **Musée du Palais du Prince (Souvenirs Napoléoniens et Collection d'Archives)** is 6€ adults, 3€ children 8 to 14, free for children under 8. The palace is open from June 1 to September 31 daily from 9:30am to 6pm and in the month of October from 10am to 5pm. It's closed to visitors from October 31 to May 31.

Jardin Exotique ★★, boulevard du Jardin-Exotique ((C) 377/93-15-29-80), was built on the side of a rock and is known for its cactus collection. The gardens were begun by Prince Albert I in 1933; he was both a naturalist and a scientist. He spotted some succulents growing in the palace gardens, and knowing that these plants were normally found only in Central America or Africa, he created the garden from them. You can also explore the grottoes here, as well as the **Musée d'Anthropologie Préhistorique** ((C) 377/93-15-80-06), which is surrounded by the gardens. The view of the principality is splendid. Entrance to both the gardens and the museum costs 6.50€ adults, 3.20€ ages 6 to 18, free for children ages 5 and under. The gardens and museum are open daily: mid-May through September 16 and November through December from 9am to 5pm; September 16 through October 31 from 9am to 6:30pm; January from 9am to 5:30pm; February and March from 9am to 6pm; and April through mid-May from 9am to 6:30pm.

Musée de l'Océanographie ★★★, avenue St-Martin ((C) 377/93-15-36-00), was founded by Albert I, great-grandfather of the present prince. In the main rotunda is a statue of Albert dressed as a sea captain. Displayed are specimens he collected during 30 years of oceanographic expeditions. The aquarium, one of the

---

Finds **Fabulous & Fake**

Bijoux Marlene, Les Galeries du Metropole, 207 av. des Spélugues (© 93-50-17-57), sells only imitation gemstones. They're shamelessly copied from the real McCoys sold by Cartier and Van Cleef & Arpels. Made in Italy of gold-plated silver, the fake jewelry (the staff refers to it as *Les Bijoux Fantaisies*) costs between 10€ and 300€ per piece.

---

finest in Europe, has more than 90 tanks, including Le Lagoon, a large holding tank for sharks. Hours are daily, April through June and September from 9am to 7pm; July and August from 9am to 8pm; and October through March from 10am to 6pm. Admission is 11€ adults, 6€ students and children 6 to 18, free for children under 6.

TAKING A DIP & OTHER OUTDOOR ACTIVITIES

BEACHES/SWIMMING   Monaco offers swimming and sunbathing at the **Plage de Larvotto,** off avenue Princesse-Grace (© 93-30-63-84). There's no charge to enter this strip of beach, whose sands are frequently replenished with sand hauled in by barge. It is open to the public at all hours.

You can also try the **Monte-Carlo Beach Club** adjoining the Monte-Carlo Beach Hotel, 22 av. Princesse-Grace (© 04-93-28-66-66). The beach club has thrived for years as an integral part of Monaco's social life. The sand is replenished at regular intervals, and you'll find two large pools (one for children), cabanas, a restaurant, a cafe, and a bar. As the temperature drops in late August, it closes for the winter. The admission charge of 40€ grants you access to the changing rooms, toilets, restaurants, and bar. A day's use of a cubicle, where you can lock up your street clothes, costs an extra 15€. A full day's rental of a mattress for sunbathing costs 16€. A fee of 175€ will get you a day's use of a private cabana. Most socializing occurs around the pool's edges. On the premises are bars and three restaurants. As usual, topless is *de rigueur,* but bottomless isn't.

GOLF   The prestigious **Monte Carlo Golf Club,** route N7, La Turbie (© 04-93-41-09-11), on French soil, is a par-72 golf course with scenic panoramas. Certain perks (including use of electric golf carts) are reserved for members. In order to play, nonmembers are asked to show proof of membership in another club and provide evidence of their handicap. Greens fees for 18 holes are 85€ Monday through Friday and 100€ Saturday and Sunday. Clubs can be rented for 15€. The course is open daily from 8am to sunset.

SPA TREATMENTS   In 1908, the Société des Bains de Mer launched a seawater (thalassotherapy) spa in Monte Carlo, inaugurated by Prince Albert I. However, it was bombed during World War II and didn't reopen until 1996. **Les Thermes Marins de Monte-Carlo,** 2 av. de Monte-Carlo (© 92-16-40-40), is one of the largest spas in Europe. Spread over four floors are a pool, a Turkish *haman,* a diet restaurant, a juice bar, two tanning booths, a fitness center, a beauty center, and private treatment rooms. A day pass, giving access to the sauna, steam rooms, fitness facilities, and pools, costs 65€. Massages cost 55€ for a 30-minute session and 100€ for a 60-minute session.

GAMBLING & OTHER AFTER-DARK DIVERSIONS

CASINOS   **Sun Casino,** in the Monte Carlo Grand Hôtel, 12 av. des Spélugues (© 93-50-65-00), is a huge room filled with one-armed bandits. It also features blackjack, craps, and American roulette. Additional slot machines are available on the roof starting at 11am—for those who want to gamble with a wider view of the sea. The rooms with slot machines open daily from 11am to 4am, and gaming tables are open daily from 5pm to 4am. Admission is free.

A speculator, François Blanc, developed the **Monte-Carlo Casino,** place du Casino (© **92-16-21-21**), into the most famous in the world. The architect of Paris's Opéra Garnier, Charles Garnier, built the oldest part of the casino, and it remains an example of the 19th century's most opulent architecture. It's divided into an area devoted to the casino and other areas for different kinds of nighttime entertainment, including a theater presenting opera and ballet. Baccarat, roulette, and chemin-de-fer are the most popular games, though you can play *le craps* and blackjack as well. Admission is 10€ to 20€.

Salle Américaine, containing only slot machines, opens at noon, as do doors for roulette and *trente-quarente.* A section for roulette and chemin-de-fer opens at 3pm. Most of the facilities inside are operational by 4pm, when additional rooms open with more roulette, craps, and blackjack. The gambling continues until very late/early, depending on the crowd. The casino classifies its "private rooms" as the more demure, nonelectronic areas devoid of slot machines. To enter the casino, you must carry a passport, be at least 21, and pay an admission of between 8€ and 17€, depending on where you want to go. In lieu of a passport, an ID card or driver's license will suffice. After 9pm, the staff will insist that gentlemen wear jackets and neckties for entrance into the private rooms.

The premises also contain a **Cabaret** in the Casino Gardens, where the show is preceded by the music of a well-rehearsed orchestra. A cabaret featuring feathers, glitter, jazz dance, ballet, and Riviera-style seminudity is presented at 11pm Tuesday through Sunday, mid-September through June. For reservations, call © **92-16-36-36.** Entrance to the cabaret costs 45€ and includes a first drink.

Theoretically, the **Opéra de Monte-Carlo,** whose patron is Prince Rainier, is headquartered within the lavish Belle Epoque **Salle Garnier** of the casino that, regrettably, will be closed for renovations until at least 2004. In the meanwhile, venues for concerts, ballets, and operas are either the **Salle du Canton,** Les Terrasses, avenue de Fontvieille (© **92-16-22-99** for tickets and information), or the **Grimaldi Forum,** 10 av. Princesse-Grace (© **99-99-30-00** for tickets and information). At both the Salle du Canton and the Grimaldi Forum, tickets to ballets cost between 7.60€ and 26€; tickets to concerts cost 15€ to 30€; and tickets to operas cost 25€ to 105€.

7

Germany

by Darwin Porter & Danforth Prince

The rebuilding of Berlin for the 21st century comes at a rapid pace as the city solidifies its position as the capital of a unified Germany. What was once the city's biggest tourist attraction, the Berlin Wall, is now a bicycle path where Berliners push baby strollers. Restored baroque Munich, in the south, known as Germany's "secret capital," is the gateway to the Bavarian Alps and colorful alpine villages. For a taste of medieval Germany, explore the untouched towns of the Romantic Road and Ludwig II's fairy-tale castle of Neuschwanstein.

1 Berlin ★★★

When Heinrich Heine arrived in Berlin in 1819, he exclaimed, "Isn't the present splendid!" Were he to arrive today, he might make the same remark. Visitors who come by plane to Berlin see a splendid panorama. Few metropolitan areas are blessed with as many lakes, woodlands, and parks—these cover one-third of the city's area, and small farms with fields and meadows still exist in the city limits.

Berlin today is an almost completely modern city. Regrettably, Berlin is hardly the architectural gem that old time visitors remember from the pre-Nazi era; it wasn't rebuilt with the same kind of care lavished on Munich and Cologne. But in spite of its decades-long "quadripartite status," it's a vibrant city, always receptive to new ideas, a major economic and cultural center, and a leader in development and research. Because of its excellent facilities, it is a favored site for trade fairs, congresses, and conventions.

Berlin today is shedding its dark history and reinventing itself as Europe's "capital of cool." Suddenly, it's hip to claim, *"Ich bin ein Berliner."* Nothing dramatizes the change more than the once dreary Potsdamer Platz, the so-called Times Square of Berlin. No longer a Cold War relic, it has blossomed into a showcase of modern architecture, dominated by the 25-story DaimlerChrysler building, whose viewing platform can be reached in only 20 seconds from the ground.

"No city on earth has gone through such a roller-coaster ride—from villain to victim, from horrors to heroics," said Richard Holbrooke, former U.S. ambassador to Germany. Today Berlin is the fourth-most-popular tourist destination in Europe, having surged past Madrid.

ESSENTIALS

GETTING THERE By Plane Tegel Airport is the city's busiest, serving most flights from the west. Historic **Tempelhof Airport,** made famous as the city's lifeline during the Berlin Airlift, has declined in importance. **Schönefeld,** the airport in the eastern sector, is used primarily by Russian and eastern European airlines. Private bus shuttles among the three airports operate constantly so you can make connecting flights at different airports. Buses from each airport

will also take you into the city center. For information on all three airports, call
© **0180/500-01-86** or visit www.berlin-airport.de.

By Train   Frankfurt and Hamburg, among other cities, have good rail connections to Berlin. From Frankfurt to Berlin takes about 4 hours. Hamburg is now
closer than ever, thanks to a new, high-speed InterCity Express train running
between the two cities nonstop in 2 hours and 8 minutes. Eurailpass and Ger-
manRail passes are valid. Most arrivals from western European and western German cities are at the **Bahnhof Zoologischer Garten** (© **0810/599-66-33**), the
main train station, called "Bahnhof Zoo," in western Berlin. In the center of the
city, close to the Kurfürstendamm, it's well connected for public transportation.
Facilities include a tourist information counter dispensing free maps and tourist
brochures, open daily from 5am to 11pm. The staff will make same-day hotel
reservations for 2.55€.

Berlin has two other train stations, the **Berlin Hauptbahnhof** and **Berlin
Lichtenberg.** Call the main station at © **0810/599-66-33** or visit http://bahn.
hafas.de for information.

By Bus   The operations center for several independent bus operators is headquartered within a central arrivals and departures point, the **ZOB Omnibus-
bahnhof am Funkturm,** Messedamm 6 (© **030/301-03-80**). Call for departure
times and fare information for routes to and from other parts of Europe.

By Car   From Frankfurt, take A-66 to Bad Herzfeld, and either go east on A-4
to pick up A-9 to Berlin, or continue on A-7 to Braunschweig and east on A-2
toward Berlin. North of Nürnberg, A-9 leads to Berlin. From Leipzig, take A-14
in the direction of Halle; at the intersection of A-9, head northeast into Berlin.
From Dresden, head northeast on A-13 into Berlin. Expect heavy traffic delays on
Autobahnen, especially on weekends and sunny days when everyone is out touring.

VISITOR INFORMATION   Tourist Office   For tourist information and
hotel bookings, head for the **Berlin Tourist Information Center,** in the
Europa-Center near the Memorial Church, entrance on the Budapesterstrasse
side (© **030/25-00-25;** www.berlin-tourism.de), open Monday through Saturday from 8am to 8pm and Sunday from 10am to 6:30pm.

Websites   Visit **www.berlin-info.de** for a virtual tour of Berlin's sights, but be
aware that some of the links go to German-only pages. The site **www.hotel
stravel.com/germany.html** not only provides detailed listings for hotels in
Germany but also has links to related sites, like Ritz-Carlton and Relais &
Châteaux, that offer lodging and general travel info. The definitive dining guide
www.eat-germany.net lets you search the site for restaurants or view its Top 10
for each city. The restaurants are selected by users who rate them, giving an aura
of objectivity. With lots of detail about type of food, hours, locations, and kinds
of patrons, searches can be narrowed by nation, state, or city.

CITY LAYOUT   The center of activity in the western part of Berlin is the 3km
(2-mile) long **Kurfürstendamm,** called the Ku'damm by Berliners. Along this
wide boulevard you'll find the best hotels, restaurants, theaters, cafes, nightclubs,
shops, and department stores. The huge **Tiergarten,** the city's largest park, is
crossed by Strasse des 17 Juni, which leads to the famed **Brandenburg Gate
(Brandenburger Tor);** just north is the Reichstag. On the southwestern
fringe of the Tiergarten is the **Zoologischer Garten (Berlin Zoo).** From the
Ku'damm you can take Hardenbergstrasse, crossing Bismarckstrasse and traversing Otto-Suhr-Allee, which leads to **Schloss Charlottenburg,** one of your major

sightseeing goals. The **Dahlem Museums** are on the southwestern fringe, often reached by going along Hohenzollerndamm.

The Brandenburg Gate is the start of Berlin's most celebrated street, **Unter den Linden,** the cultural heart of Berlin before World War II. The famous street runs from west to east, cutting a path through the city. It leads to **Museumsinsel (Museum Island),** where the most outstanding museums of eastern Berlin, including the Pergamon, are situated. As it courses along, Unter den Linden crosses another major Berlin artery, **Friedrichstrasse.** If you continue south along Friedrichstrasse, you'll reach the former location of **Checkpoint Charlie,** the famous border-crossing site of the Cold War days.

Unter den Linden continues east until it reaches **Alexanderplatz,** the center of eastern Berlin, with its TV tower (Fernsehturm). A short walk away is the restored **Nikolaiviertel (Nikolai Quarter),** a neighborhood of bars, restaurants, and shops that evoke life in the prewar days.

GETTING AROUND   By Public Transportation   The Berlin transport system consists of buses, trams, and U-Bahn and S-Bahn trains. The network is run by the **BVG (© 030/1-94-49; www.bvg.de),** which operates an information booth outside the Bahnhof Zoo on Hardenbergplatz, open daily from 8am to 10pm. The staff will provide details about which U-Bahn (underground) or S-Bahn (elevated railway) line to take to various locations and the ticket options. You can also purchase tickets, including discount cards.

Western Berlin

Post Office ⊠

S-Bahn stop Ⓢ

Berlin U-Bahn & S-Bahn

S1	Wannsee/ Oranienburg	S6	Zeuthen/ Warschauer Str.	S25	Zeuthen/ Warschauer Str.
S2	Blankenfelde/ Waidmannslust	S7	Potsdam Stadt/ Ahrenfelde	S45	Westend/Flughafen Berlin-Schönefeld/
S3	Westkreuz/ Erkner	S8	Blankenburg/ Grünau	S46	Westend/ Königs Wusterhausen
S4	Westhafen/ Bernau (b Berlin)	S9	Flughafen Berlin-Schönefeld/Westkreuz	S75	Spandau/ Wartenberg
S5	Spandau/ Strausberg Nord	S10	Birkenwerder (b Bln)/ Spindlerfeld		

(Value The Welcome Card

If you're going to be in Berlin for 3 days, you can purchase a **WelcomeCard** for 19€, entitling holders to 72 free hours on public transportation in Berlin and Brandenburg. You also get free admission or price reductions up to 50% on sightseeing tours, museums, and other attractions. Reductions of 25% are granted at 10 of the city's theaters as well. It's valid for one adult and up to three children 13 or younger.

The **BVG standard ticket** *(Einzelfahrschein)* is 2.40€ and is valid for 2 hours of transportation in all directions, transfers included. Also available at counters and vending machines is a 24-hour ticket; the price is 6.30€. On buses, only standard tickets can be purchased, and tram tickets must be purchased in advance. Tickets should be kept until the end of the journey; otherwise, you'll be liable for a fine of 31€.

By Taxi Taxis are available throughout Berlin. The meter starts at 3.05€, plus 1.55€ per kilometer after that. Visitors can flag down taxis that have a T-sign illuminated. For a taxi, call © **21-02-02,** 69-41-099, or 24-63-25-63.

By Car Touring Berlin by car isn't recommended. Free parking places are difficult to come by.

 FAST FACTS: Berlin

American Express Reiseland American Express offices at Alte Potsdamer Strasse 7 (© 030/25-29-74-74; U-Bahn: Hüttenweg), Am Borsigturm 2 (© 030/21-47-62-92; U-Bahn: Borischverger), Bayreuthstrasse 37–38 (© 030/30-17-400; U-Bahn: Wittenbergplatz), and Friedrichstrasse 172 (© 030/20-17-40-12; U-Bahn: Friedrichstrasse), are all open Monday through Friday from 9am to 7pm.

Business Hours Most **banks** are open Monday through Friday from 9am to 1 or 3pm. Most other **businesses** and **stores** are open Monday through Friday from 9 or 10am to 6 or 6:30pm and Saturday from 9am to 2pm. On *langer Samstag,* the first Saturday of the month, shops stay open until 4 or 6pm. Some stores observe late closing on Thursday, usually at 8:30pm.

Currency The long-standing German mark faded into history on January 1, 2002, giving way to the euro. Currently, the U.S. dollar and the European euro are trading for par value, with slight daily fluctuations.

Currency Exchange You can exchange money at all airports, major department stores, any bank, and the American Express offices (above).

Dentists/Doctors The Berlin tourist office in the Europa-Center (see "Visitor Information," above) keeps a list of English-speaking dentists and doctors in Berlin. In case of a medical emergency, call © **030/31-00-31.**

Drugstores If you need a pharmacy *(Apotheke)* at night, go to one on any corner. There you'll find a sign in the window giving the address of the nearest drugstore open at night; such posting is required by law. A central pharmacy is **Europa-Apotheke,** Tauentzienstrasse 9–12 (© **030/2-61-41-42;**

U-Bahn: Kurfürstendamm), by the Europa-Center. It's open Monday through Friday from 9am to 8pm and Saturday to 6pm.

Embassies & Consulates The embassy of the **United States** is at Neustaedtische Kirchstrasse 4–5 (*©* **030/2-38-51-74**; U-Bahn: Friedrichstrasse), and a consulate at Clayallee 170 (*©* **030/8-32-92-33**; U-Bahn: Hüttenweg). Hours are Monday through Friday from 8:30am to 4pm. The embassy of the **United Kingdom** is at Wilhelmstrasse 70 (*©* **030/20-45-70**; U-Bahn: Friedrichstrasse). Hours are Monday through Friday from 9am to noon and 2 to 4pm. The embassy of **Australia** is on Kempinski Plaza, at Friedrichstrasse 200 (*©* **030/8-80-08-80**; U-Bahn: Friedrichstrasse). Hours are Monday through Friday from 9am to noon. **Canada** maintains a consulate at Friedrichstrasse 95 (*©* **030/20-31-20**; U-Bahn: Friedrichstrasse). Hours are Monday through Friday from 9am to noon and 1:30 to 4pm by appointment. The embassy of **New Zealand** is at Friedrichstrasse 60 (*©* **030/20-62-10**; U-Bahn: Friedrichstrasse). Hours are Monday through Friday from 9am to 1pm and 2 to 5:30pm. The consulate of **Ireland** is at Friedrichstrasse 200 (*©* **030/22-07-20**; U-Bahn: Friedrichstrasse). Hours are Monday through Friday from 9:30am to 12:30pm and 2:30 to 4:45pm.

Emergencies Call the police at *©* **110**; dial *©* **112** to report a fire or to call an ambulance.

Internet Access If you're feeling out of touch, visit **Karstadt Sports,** Joachimstalerstrasse 5–6 (*©* **030/8802-41-89**; U-Bahn: Banhof Zoologischer Garten), open Monday through Saturday from 10am to 8pm.

Post Office The post office at the Bahnhof Zoo is open Monday through Saturday from 6am to midnight and Sunday from 8am to midnight. If you have mail sent here, have it marked Hauptpostlagernd, Postamt 120, Bahnhof Zoo, D-10612, Berlin. There's also a post office at Hauptbahnhof, open Monday through Friday from 7am to 8pm and Saturday from 8am to 1pm. For postal information, call *©* **030/31-00-80**. You can make long-distance calls at post offices at far cheaper rates than at hotels.

Safety Germany is a reasonably safe country in which to travel, although neo-Nazi skinheads have sometimes attacked black or Asian travelers, especially in the eastern part of the country. One of the most dangerous places, especially at night, is around the large railway stations of large cities, such as Berlin. Some beer halls get rowdy late at night.

Taxes As a member of the European Union, Germany imposes a tax on most goods and services known as the **value-added tax (VAT)** or, in German, *Mehrwertsteuer.* Nearly everything is taxed at 15%, including vital necessities such as gas or luxury items like jewelry. VAT is included in the price of restaurants and hotels. Note that goods for sale, such as cameras, also have the 15% tax already factored into the price; but the listed prices of services, such as having a mechanic fix your car, don't include VAT, so an extra 15% will be tacked on to your bill. Stores that display a TAX FREE sticker will issue you a Tax-Free Shopping Check at the time of purchase. You can then get a refund at one of the Tax-Free Shopping Service offices in the major airports and many train stations (and some of the bigger ferry terminals). Otherwise, send checks to Tax-Free Shopping Service, Mengstrasse 19, 23552 Lübeck, Germany.

Telephone The **country code** for Germany is **49**; the **city code** for Berlin is **30** for calls from outside Germany or **030** if you're calling within the country.

If you're going to make a lot of phone calls or wish to make an international call from a phone booth, you'll probably want to purchase a **phone card.** Phone cards are sold at post offices and newsstands. The 6.15€ card offers about 40 minutes, and the 26€ card is useful for long-distance calls. Simply insert them into the telephone slot. Phone cards are becoming so popular in Germany that many public phones no longer accept coins.

To make a **collect or calling-card call,** dial one of the following access numbers to reach an operator or an English-language voice prompt: **AT&T** (© **0130-0010**), **MCI** (© **0130-0012**), or **Sprint** (© **0130-0013**). To call the U.S. direct, dial **001** followed by the area code and phone number.

Tipping If a restaurant bill says *Bedienung,* that means a service charge has already been added, so just round up to the nearest euro. If not, add 10% to 15%. Round up to the nearest euro for taxis. Bellhops get 1€ per bag, as does the doorperson at your hotel, restaurant, or nightclub. Room cleaning staffs get small tips in Germany, as do concierges who perform some special favors such as obtaining hard-to-get theater or opera tickets. Tip hairdressers or barbers 5% to 10%.

WHERE TO STAY
ON OR NEAR THE KURFÜRSTENDAMM
Very Expensive

Grand Hotel Esplanade ☆☆☆   The Esplanade rivals the Kempinski for supremacy in Berlin. Rooms are spacious, bright, and cheerfully decorated, with sound insulation. Beds are large with quality linens and duvets. Bathrooms, which contain tub/shower combos, are among the city's most luxurious. When reserving, ask for one of the corner rooms, as they're the biggest and have the best views. Even if you don't stay here, stop in for a drink at the elegant Harry's New York Bar, or go native at the traditional German EckKneipe.

Lützowufer 15, D-10785 Berlin. © **030/25-47-80.** Fax 030/265-11-71. www.esplanade.de. 400 units. 110€–305€ double; from 420€ suite. AE, DC, MC, V. Parking 16€. U-Bahn: Kurfürstenstrasse, Nollendorfplatz, or Wittenbergplatz. **Amenities:** Harlekin restaurant (see "Where to Dine," below); 2 bars; indoor pool; sauna; whirlpool; solarium; room service; babysitting; laundry/dry cleaning; nonsmoking rooms. *In room:* A/C, TV/VCR, minibar, hair dryer, bathrobes.

Kempinski Hotel Bristol Berlin ☆☆☆   The legendary Kempinski, or "Kempi," is matched in style only by the Grand Hotel Esplanade. Rooms range in size from medium to spacious. Furnishings are elegant and the mattresses firm. The cheapest (and smallest) rooms are called the Berlin rooms. The high category Bristol rooms are larger and better appointed, and the finest accommodations of all are refined Kempinski rooms. Each room has a spacious bathroom with tub/shower combos, dual basins, scales, shoehorns, and deluxe toiletries.

Kurfürstendamm 27, D-10719 Berlin. © **800/426-3135** in the U.S., or 030/88-43-40. Fax 030/88-360-75. www.kempinski.com. 301 units. 135€–312€ double; from 180€ suite. AE, DC, MC, V. Parking 21€. U-Bahn: Kurfürstendamm. **Amenities:** 3 restaurants; indoor pool; fitness center; sauna; solarium; room service; massage; babysitting; laundry/dry cleaning. *In room:* A/C, TV, minibar, hair dryer.

Expensive

Brandenburger Hof Relais & Châteaux ⭐⭐⭐ Rooms at this white-fronted classic, though perhaps too severe and minimalist for some tastes, are among the most stylish in the city. This is authentic Bauhaus—torchier lamps, black leather upholstery, and platform beds. French doors open to small balconies, but not on the top floors. Bathrooms are spacious, with large tub/shower combos. Housekeeping is among the finest in Berlin, and there's state-of-the-art security.

Eislebener Strasse 14, D-10789 Berlin. ℭ **030/21-40-50.** Fax 030/21-40-51-00. www.brandenburger-hof. com. 82 units. 240€–280€ double; from 450€ suite. Rates include breakfast buffet. AE, DC, MC, V. Parking 18€. U-Bahn: Kurfürstendamm or Augsburger Strasse. S-Bahn: Zoologischer Garten. **Amenities:** 2 restaurants; piano bar; room service; babysitting; laundry/valet. *In room:* TV, minibar, hair dryer.

Savoy ⭐ If you don't demand the full-service facilities of the grander choices, this is the hotel for you. In general, rooms are a bit small but they are comfortable nonetheless, with such amenities as double-glazed windows and fine furnishings. Bathrooms are decent sizes, are maintained spotlessly, and contain tub/shower combos. For a nightcap, try the cozy Times Bar.

Fasanenstrasse 9–10, D-10623 Berlin. ℭ **800/223-5652** in the U.S. and Canada, or 030/3-11-0-30. Fax 030/3-11-03-333. www.savoy-hotels.com. 125 units. 182€–242€ double; 212€–459€ suite. Children under 12 stay free in parent's room. AE, DC, MC, V. Parking 10€. U-Bahn: Kurfürstendamm. **Amenities:** Restaurant; bar; fitness club; sauna; room service; babysitting; laundry. *In room:* TV, minibar, hair dryer, safe, trouser press.

Moderate

Art Nouveau On the fourth floor of an Art Nouveau apartment house, this little-known hotel is an atmospheric choice. Even the elevator is a historic gem of the upmarket and desirable neighborhood. Art Nouveau was fully renovated in 1998. The comfortable mid-size rooms are pleasantly decorated and high ceilinged, with excellent beds and bathrooms with shower-tub combinations. Rooms in the rear are more tranquil except when the schoolyard is full of children. There's an honor bar in the lobby where guests keep track of their own drinks. A generous breakfast is the only meal served.

Leibnizstrasse 59, D-10629 Berlin. ℭ **030/3-27-74-40.** Fax 030/327-744-40. www.hotelartnouveau.de. 16 units. 110€–165€ double; 175€–230€ suite. Parking 4€. Rates include breakfast. U-Bahn: Adenauerplatz. *In room:* TV, hair dryer.

Bleibtreu Hotel ⭐ Hidden away from the bustle of Berlin, this is a trend-conscious choice. Its tiny lobby is accessible via an alleyway that leads past a garden and a big-windowed set of dining and drinking facilities. The setting is the labyrinthine premises of what was built long ago as a Jugendstil-era apartment house. Rooms are small, minimalist, and furnished in carefully chosen natural materials. Bathrooms are cramped but well designed with tub/shower combos.

Bleibtreustrasse 31, D-10707 Berlin (1 block south of the Kurfürstendamm). ℭ **800/223-5652** for reservations in the U.S. and Canada, or 030/88474-0. Fax 030/88474-444. www.bleibtreu.com. 60 units. 192€–242€ double; 302€–352€ suite. AE, MC, V. U-Bahn: Kurfürstendamm. **Amenities:** Restaurant; bar; room service; laundry. *In room:* TV, minibar, hair dryer, safe.

Inexpensive

Hotel-Pension Bregenz This dignified pension occupies the fourth and sunniest floor of a four-story turn-of-the-19th-century apartment building, accessible by elevator. The owner, Mr. Zimmermann, works hard to maintain the cleanliness and charm of his comfortably furnished, relatively large rooms. Double doors help minimize noise from the public corridors outside. A continental breakfast is served each morning in a small dining area. The staff assists guests in reserving tickets for shows and tours.

Bregenzer Strasse 5, D-10707 Berlin. © **030/8-81-43-07**. Fax 030/8-82-40-09. 14 units, 11 with bathroom (shower only). 60€ double without bathroom; 88€ double with bathroom. Rates include breakfast. MC, V. Parking 3€. S-Bahn: Savignyplatz. U-Bahn: Adenauerplatz. *In room:* TV, minibar, hair dryer, safe.

Pension München This pension occupies only part of the third floor of a massive four-story building (with an elevator) erected as an apartment house in 1908. It offers a simple but tasteful decor of modern furnishings accented with fresh flowers. The small rooms are clean and color-coordinated, with bathrooms containing shower stalls, contemporary furnishings, and prints and engravings by local artists. Look for sculptures by the owner, an artist, in some of the public areas as well. Note that if no rooms are available at this place, you're likely to be recommended to a similar pension.

Guntzelstrasse 62 (close to Bayerischer Platz), 10717 Berlin. © **030/8-57-91-20**. Fax 030/85-79-12-22. 8 units. 75€ double. AE, DC, MC, V. Parking is available on the street. U-Bahn: Guntzelstrasse. *In room:* TV.

NEAR THE MEMORIAL CHURCH & ZOO
Expensive
Palace Berlin ⊱ The stylish and comfortable Palace is much improved over recent years. However, in some rooms, the double-glazing on the windows is unable to deafen the noise from the adjacent Europa-Center. Rooms range from medium to spacious, each with deluxe bed. The best are in the more recent Casino Wing. Bathrooms are medium size, most often with tub/shower combo (sometimes with shower only).

In the Europa-Center, Budapesterstrasse 45, D-10787 Berlin. © **800/457-4000** in the U.S., or 030/2-50-20. Fax 030/2502-1161. www.palace.de. 282 units. 225€–300€ double; from 455€ suite. AE, DC, MC, V. Parking 21€. U-Bahn: Zoologischer Garten. **Amenities:** 3 restaurants (see First Floor, "Where to Dine," below); 2 bars; large health club; nonsmoking rooms. *In room:* A/C, TV, minibar, hair dryer, safe, trouser press.

Sorat Art'otel ⊱ Those partial to the more famous and highly regarded Brandenburger Hof (above) also like this tasteful, discreet hotel. Chic and avant-garde, the Sorat is unlike any other hotel in Berlin. Rooms, all medium size, are minimalist, with a touch of industrial design. Although they will not please clients seeking a traditional Berlin hotel, modernists will be at home with the pedestal tables evoking cable spools and chrome-legged furnishings, and everyone will appreciate the large beds. Bathrooms are generously proportioned with showers.

Joachimstalerstrasse 29, D-10719 Berlin. © **030/88-44-70**. Fax 030/88-44-77-00. www.sorat-hotels.com. 133 units. 147€–267€ double. Rates include buffet breakfast with champagne. Parking 11€. AE, DC, MC, V. U-Bahn: Kurfürstendamm. **Amenities:** Restaurant; room service; laundry. *In room:* A/C, TV, minibar, hair dryer.

Moderate
Hecker's Hotel This hotel is near the Ku'damm and the many bars, cafes, and restaurants around the Savignyplatz. Rooms range from small to medium, but are fairly routine despite good beds and frequently renewed mattresses. There's a sterility here but also up-to-date comfort and top-notch maintenance. Bathrooms are small, with shower units.

Grolmanstrasse 35, D-10623 Berlin. © **030/8-89-00**. Fax 030/8-89-02-60. www.heckers-hotel.de. 69 units. 150€–200€ double; 300€–330€ suite. AE, DC, MC, V. Parking 11€. U-Bahn: Uhlandstrasse. Bus: 109 from Tegel Airport to Uhlandstrasse or 119 from Tempelhof Airport. **Amenities:** Small restaurant; bar (roof dining in summer); room service; dry cleaning/laundry; nonsmoking rooms. *In room:* TV, minibar, hair dryer, safe.

Hotel Sylter Hof Berlin This hotel offers rich trappings at good prices. The main lounges are warmly decorated in old-world style. The well-maintained rooms, most of which are singles, may be too small for most tastes, but the staff pay special attention to your comfort. Bathrooms are cramped but efficiently arranged, with tub/shower combos.

Kurfürstenstrasse 116, D-10787 Berlin. ℂ 030/2-12-00. Fax 030/214-28-26. www.sylterhof-berlin.de. 161 units. 125€–140€ double; from 180€ suite. Rates include buffet breakfast. AE, DC, MC, V. Parking 11€. U-Bahn: Wittenbergplatz. Bus: 119, 129, 146, or 185. **Amenities:** Restaurant; bar; coffee bar; nightclub next door. *In room:* TV, minibar, hair dryer.

IN BERLIN-MITTE
Very Expensive

Hotel Adlon 👁👁👁   Only steps from the Brandenburg Gate, this hotel is one of Berlin's premier addresses and is famous among celebrities. The large, beautifully appointed rooms contain king-size or twin beds. Bathrooms are spacious with tub/shower combos, deluxe toiletries, and a phone.

Unter den Linden 77, D-10117 Berlin. ℂ **800/426-3135** in the U.S., or 030/22-61-0. Fax 030/22-61-11-16. www.hotel-adlon.de. 337 units. 280€–620€ double; 375€–415€ junior suite. AE, DC, MC, V. Parking 23€. S-Bahn: Unter den Linden. **Amenities:** 3 restaurants; bar; health club; spa; room service; babysitting; laundry/dry cleaning. *In room:* A/C, TV, CD player, minibar, hair dryer, safe.

Westin Grand 👁👁👁   Many hotels call themselves grand—this one truly is, rivaled only by the Kempinski. Since taking over, Westin has spent a fortune in making the rooms among the finest in the city. All are spacious and tastefully decorated. Bathrooms are also large and state-of-the-art with tub/shower combos and deluxe toiletries.

Friedrichstrasse 158–164, D-10117 Berlin. ℂ **888/625-5144** in the U.S., or 030/2-02-70. Fax 030/20-27-33-62. www.westin.com/berlin. 364 units. 286€–302€ double; from 455€ junior suite; from 920€ apt suite. AE, DC, MC, V. Parking 20€. U-Bahn: Französische Strasse. S-Bahn: Friedrichstrasse. **Amenities:** Restaurant; bar; pool; fitness club; sauna; solarium; 24-hr. room service; massage; babysitting; laundry/dry cleaning. *In room:* A/C, TV, minibar, hair dryer.

Expensive

Four Seasons 👁👁👁   One of Berlin's most opulent hotels was built in 1996 on the site of a bombed-out parking lot about a block from the Gendarmenmarkt. From the look of things, you'd never realize the venue is new, as everything about the place evokes Versailles and an undeniable sense of well-established and very plush prosperity. Rooms are furnished with timeless taste and elegance, with very large bathrooms that have walk-in showers, deep tubs, and a selection of toiletries.

Charlottenstrasse 49, 10117 Berlin. ℂ **800/332-3442** in the U.S., or 030/2-03-38. Fax 030/203-36-009. www.fourseasons.com. 204 units. 300€–360€ double; from 395€ suite. AE, MC, V. Parking 21€. U-Bahn: Französische Strasse. **Amenities:** Restaurant; bar; health club; 24-hr. room service; massage; babysitting; dry cleaning/laundry. *In room:* A/C, TV, minibar, hair dryer, safe.

Moderate

Hotel Hackescher Markt 👁   You'd never know this nugget of charm had been newly built in 1998, as everything about it evokes a late 19th-century landmark. Rooms are soothing, partially oak-paneled, and outfitted with comfortable and practical furniture. Standard singles tend to be just a bit small—a better bet might be one of the more upscale doubles. Bathrooms have heated floors and almost all contain tub/shower combos. Some guests appreciate the romantic overtones of bedrooms on the uppermost floor, whose walls are angled thanks to the building's mansard roof.

Grosse Präsidentenstrasse 8, D-10178 Berlin. ℂ **030/28-00-30.** Fax 030/28-00-31-11. www.hackeschermarkt.com. 31 units. 135€–170€ double; 174€–199€ suite. AE, MC, V. U-Bahn: Hackescher Markt. **Amenities:** Bar; room service; laundry. *In room:* TV, minibar, hair dryer, safe.

Hotel Luisenhof *⚚* One of the most desirable small hotels in Berlin's eastern district, the Luisenhof occupies a dignified 1822 house. Five floors of high-ceilinged rooms will appeal to those desiring to escape modern Berlin's sterility. Rooms range greatly in size, but each is equipped with good queen or twin beds. Bathrooms, though small, are beautifully appointed, with shower stalls (often with a large tub).

Köpenicker Strasse 92, 10179 Berlin. *✆* **030/2-41-59-06.** Fax 030/2-79-29-83. www.luisenhof.de. 27 units. 136€ double; from 195€ suite. Rates include breakfast. AE, DC, MC, V. U-Bahn: Märkisches Museum. **Amenities:** Restaurant; room service (6am–midnight); laundry/dry cleaning. *In room:* TV, minibar, hair dryer.

WHERE TO DINE

For food on the run, try one of the dozens of kabob stalls *(Imbisse)* that dot the streets. Some 200,000 Turks live in Berlin, and the food that they've introduced—meat- or *Scharfskäse-* (sheep's cheese, virtually identical to feta) stuffed pitas—make a filling, cheap meal—but watch out for the cascades of cabbage. Good sit-down Turkish restaurants are harder to find, but one of the best is **Hitit,** Knobelsdorffstrasse 35 (*✆* **030/322-45-57**), near Charlottenburg Schloss, with a full array of Turkish specialties, some 150 dishes in all. It's open Monday through Saturday from 5pm to midnight, Sunday from 11am to midnight.

ON OR NEAR THE KURFÜRSTENDAMM
Expensive

Harlekin *⚚⚚* FRENCH/INTERNATIONAL Chefs at traditional favorite restaurants were chagrined at this spot's success. The menu is perfectly balanced between tradition and innovation. Appetizers are likely to include such dishes as calves' consommé with crayfish or osso buco consommé with lobster spaetzle. For your main course, you might be won over by the saddle of lamb baked in a spring roll or turbot roasted with mixed root vegetables.

In the Grand Hotel Esplanade, Lützowufer. *✆* **030/254-78-858.** Reservations recommended. Main courses 25€–32€; 4- to 6-course fixed-price menu 68€–86€. AE, DC, MC, V. Tues–Sat 6:30–11pm. Closed 3½ weeks in July (dates vary). U-Bahn: Nollendorfplatz or Wittenbergplatz.

Paris Bar *⚚* FRENCH This French bistro has been a local favorite since the postwar years, when two Frenchmen established the restaurant to bring a little Parisian cheer to the dismal gray of bombed-out Berlin. The place is just as crowded with elbow-to-elbow tables as a Montmartre tourist trap, but you'll find it a genuinely pleasing little eatery. It's a true restaurant on the see-and-be-seen circuit between Savignyplatz and Gedächtniskiche. The food is invariably fresh and well prepared but not particularly innovative.

Kantstrasse 152. *✆* 030/313-80-52. Reservations recommended. Main courses 13€–35€. AE. Daily noon–3am. U-Bahn: Uhlandstrasse.

Moderate

Istanbul TURKISH Vegetarians patronize Berlin's oldest Turkish restaurant for its selection of hot and cold appetizers. The dark and lavishly decorated interior evokes old Constantinople (as do the belly dancers performing in a back room). Try the stuffed grape leaves or the hummus (chickpeas with garlic), or the meat-topped Turkish pizza. Shish kabob is the most popular item, and there's a wide array of succulent lamb dishes. A chef's specialty is veal grilled on a roasting spit.

Knesebeckstrasse 77. *✆* 030/883-27-77. Main courses 12€–25€. AE, DC, MC, V. Daily noon–midnight. S-Bahn: Savignyplatz.

Marjellchen ⭐ EAST PRUSSIAN This is the only restaurant in Berlin specializing in the cuisine of Germany's long-lost province of East Prussia, along with the cuisines of Pomerania and Silesia. Amid a Bismarckian ambience of still lifes, vested waiters, and oil lamps, you can enjoy a savory version of red-beet soup with strips of beef, East Prussian potato soup with crabmeat and bacon, *falscher Gänsebraten* (pork spareribs stuffed with prunes and bread crumbs), and *mecklenburger Kümmelfleisch* (lamb with chives and onions).

Mommsenstrasse 9. ℂ **030/883-26-76.** Reservations required. Main courses 12€–22€. AE, DC, MC, V. Mon–Sat 5pm–midnight. Closed Dec 23, 24, and 31. U-Bahn: Adenauerplatz or Uhlandstrasse. Bus: 109, 119, or 129.

Restaurant Mario NORTHERN ITALIAN Named for its owner, this restaurant serves some of the most imaginative northern Italian food in Berlin. It was created by an East Berliner who'd never been to Italy but wanted to "cook Italian," nevertheless. Today the chefs are fully grounded in the repertoire of Italy. The innovative and refreshing dishes might include platters of the most delectable antipasti in town or else carpaccio. At least two different kinds of pastas are offered nightly, including a favorite made with a green pepper pesto. Savory ravioli and rigatoni appear several different ways.

Carmerstrasse 2. ℂ **030/312-31-15.** Reservations recommended. Main courses 10€–18€; fixed-price menus 14€–35€. AE, DC, MC, V. Mon–Fri noon–midnight; Sat 4pm–1am. S-Bahn: Savignyplatz.

Inexpensive

Hard Rock Cafe AMERICAN This is the local branch of the familiar worldwide chain that mingles rock 'n' roll nostalgia with American food. Menu choices range from a veggie burger to a "pig" sandwich (hickory smoked pork barbecue) that you might find in rural Georgia. The food is unexceptional, but service is friendly.

Meinekestrasse 21. ℂ 030/00-40-20. Reservations accepted for groups of 10 or more. Main courses 9€–20€. AE, MC, V. Sun–Thurs noon–midnight; Fri–Sat noon–1am. U-Bahn: Kurfürstendamm.

 Cafe Society

At the turn of the 19th century, the **Café Adlon,** Kurfürstendamm 69 (ℂ **030/883-76-82;** U-Bahn: Adenauerplatz), was one of the most prestigious cafes in its neighborhood. It still offers charming summer vistas from its sidewalk tables and a view of Berlin kitsch from its interior. You'll find a huge selection of cakes. The cafe is open daily from 8am to 11pm.

The family-owned **Café/Bistro Leysieffer,** Kurfürstendamm 218 (ℂ **030/885-74-80;** U-Bahn: Kurfürstendamm), opened in the early 1980s within what had been the Chinese embassy. The street level contains a pastry and candy shop, but most clients climb the flight of stairs to a marble- and wood-sheathed cafe with a balcony overlooking the busy Ku'damm. The breakfast menu is one of the most elegant in town: Parma ham, smoked salmon, a fresh baguette, French butter, and—to round it off—champagne. Hours are Sunday through Thursday from 10am to 8pm, Friday and Saturday from 10am to 10pm.

Lubitsch CONTINENTAL   Its conservative chic reputation was enhanced in 1999 when Chancellor Schröder dropped in for lunch and a photo-op, causing ripples of energy to reverberate through the neighborhood. Menu items include lots of cafe drinks and steaming pots of afternoon tea, but if you drop in for a meal, expect platters of chicken curry salad with roasted potatoes; Berlin-style potato soup; braised chicken with salad and fresh vegetables; a roulade of suckling pig; and Nürnberger-style wursts. Expect brusque service, a black and white decor with Thonet-style chairs, and a somewhat arrogant environment that, despite its drawbacks, is very, very *Berliner.*

Bleibtreustrasse 47. © 030/882-37-56. Main courses 6€–21€. AE, DC, MC, V. Mon–Sat 9am–midnight. U-Bahn: Kurfürstendamm.

NEAR THE MEMORIAL CHURCH & ZOO
Very Expensive
First Floor ★★ REGIONAL GERMAN/FRENCH   This is the showcase restaurant within one of the most spectacular hotels ever built near the Tiergarten. Set one floor above street level, it features a perfectly orchestrated service and setting that revolve around the cuisine of a master chef. Winning our praise are such dishes as a terrine of veal with arugula-flavored butter; sophisticated variations of Bresse chicken; guinea fowl stuffed with foie gras and served with a truffle vinaigrette sauce; a cassoulet of lobster and broad beans in a style vaguely influenced by the culinary precepts of southwestern France; filet of sole with champagne sauce; and a mascarpone mousse with lavender-scented honey.

In the Palace Berlin, Budapesterstrasse 42. © 030/25-02-10-20. Reservations recommended. Main courses 28€–39€. Set menus 42€ at lunch only; 68€–105€ at lunch and dinner. AE, DC, MC, V. Daily noon–2pm and 8–11pm. U-Bahn: Zoologischer Garten.

TIERGARTEN
Expensive
Paris-Moskau INTERNATIONAL   The grand days of the 19th century are alive and well at this restaurant in the beautiful Tiergarten area, where good dining spots are scarce. Menu items are both classic and more cutting-edge. The fresh tomato soup is excellent. Some of the dishes are mundane—the grilled filet of beef in mushroom sauce comes to mind—but other, lighter dishes with delicate seasonings are delightful. We recommend the grilled North Sea salmon with herbs accompanied by basil-flavored noodles. The chef should market his recipe for saffron sauce, which accompanies several dishes. You'll receive attentive service from the formally dressed staff.

Alt-Moabit 141. © 030/3-94-20-81. Reservations recommended. Main courses 16€–26€; fixed-price menus 56€–80€. No credit cards. Daily 6–11:30pm. S-Bahn: Bellevue.

IN & AROUND CHARLOTTENBURG
Expensive
Alt-Luxemburg ★★ CONTINENTAL/FRENCH/GERMAN   Bamberger Reiter may be the leader among Berlin restaurants, but the Alt-Luxemburg is nipping at its heels. Chef Karl Wannemacher is one of the most outstanding chefs in eastern Germany. Known for his quality and market-fresh ingredients, he prepares a seductively sensual plate. Everything shows his flawless technique, especially the stuffed veal or the saddle of venison with elderberry sauce. Taste his excellent lacquered duck breast with honey sauce or saddle of lamb with stewed peppers. Alt-Luxemburg offers a finely balanced wine list, and service is both unpretentious and gracious.

Windscheidstrasse 31. ℰ **030/323-87-30**. Reservations required. Fixed-price 4-course menu 68€; fixed-price 5-course menu 76€. AE, DC, MC, V. Mon–Sat 5–11pm. U-Bahn: Sophie-Charlotteplatz.

Moderate

Bierhaus Luisen-Bräu GERMAN   Luisen-Bräu brewery established this restaurant in 1987. The decor includes enormous stainless-steel vats of the fermenting brew, from which the waiters refill your mug. There's no subtlety of cuisine here; it's robust and hearty fare. You serve yourself from a long buffet table. The seating is indoor or outdoor, depending on the season, at long picnic tables that encourage a sense of beer-hall *Bruderschaft* (camaraderie).

Luisenplatz 1, Charlottenburg (close to Charlottenburg Castle). ℰ **030/3-41-93-88**. Reservations recommended on weekends. Main courses 6.80€–15€. AE, MC, V. Sun–Thurs 9am–1am; Fri–Sat 9am–2am. U-Bahn: Richard-Wagner-Platz.

Ponte Vecchio ✿ TUSCAN   We've dined here many times before and were moderately pleased, but the kitchen is so improved that we now view this as the finest Italian restaurant in Berlin. Market-fresh ingredients produce a winning cuisine with a Tuscan focus. If you don't opt for the excellent fresh fish of the day, you'll find any number of other tempting dishes, such as several variations on veal. Shellfish is deftly handled according to Tuscan style, with fresh basil and olive oil. For savory, succulent pasta, we'd recommend the *penne all'arrabiata* (spicy tomato sauce), that old Roman favorite.

Spielhagenstrasse 3. ℰ **030/3-42-19-99**. Reservations required. Main courses 18€–35€. DC. Wed–Mon 6.30–11pm. Closed 4 weeks in summer. U-Bahn: Bismarckstrasse.

IN BERLIN-MITTE
Expensive

Langhans ✿✿ ITALIAN/JAPANESE   Few other Berlin restaurants combine the culinary traditions of Italy and Japan with such skill and style. Named after the 18th-century designer of the Brandenburg Gate, and created by Detlef Bernhardt, a German-born longtime resident of Japan, it's in a grand building that flanks the Gendarmenmarkt. Downstairs is a convivial and hip bar, serving Spanish-inspired tapas. Upstairs, there's a long, gracefully minimalist dining room. Here, a team of international craftspersons produces dishes whose flavors are as intriguing as they are delicious. Our favorites are carpaccio of veal with sesame and arugula, braised dorado with green curry and mango, and a superb version of free-range hen with ginger-flavored risotto and sukiyaki sauce.

Charlottenstrasse 59. ℰ **030/20-94-50-70**. Reservations recommended. Main courses 7.50€–19€; set-price menus 26€–29€. AE, MC, V. Daily 10am–2am. U-Bahn: Gendarmenmarkt.

Restaurant VAU ✿✿ GERMAN   This restaurant is the culinary showcase of master chef Kolja Kleeberg. Choices include terrine of salmon and morels with rocket salad; aspic of suckling pig with sauerkraut; salad with marinated red mullet, mint, and almonds; crisp-fried duck with marjoram; ribs of suckling lamb with thyme-flavored polenta; and desserts such as woodruff soup with champagne-flavored ice cream. The wine list is international and well chosen.

Jägerstrasse 54 (near the Four Seasons Hotel and the Gendarmenmarkt). ℰ **030/202-9730**. Reservations recommended. Main courses 26€–36€. Set-price lunches 48€–52€; set-price dinners 75€–100€. AE, DC, MC, V. Mon–Sat noon–2:30pm and 7–10:30pm. U-Bahn: Hausvoigteiplatz.

Schwarzengraben ✿ ITALIAN   "Black Crows" (its English name) evokes a SoHo-style restaurant in New York. This is the watering hole of the Berlin *Schickeria*, or chic crowd. One Berlin paper defined these trendies as "media honchos and their overblond dates." The see-and-be-seen scene might be more important than the cuisine, but two Italian brothers, Ivo and Rudolf Girolo, succeed admirably with super-fresh ingredients that are well prepared. Sea bass is baked between slices of eggplant, and it's a most credible dish, as is the Italian gnocchi with sausage and green olives. Remarkably, the kitchen is prepared to make on short notice some 300 pasta dishes. Our dining companion for the evening hailed the gnocchi with rabbit ragout and truffles as "orgasmic." We're fond of the duck and rabbit *pastele*. The main dining is upstairs; downstairs is for whiskey and cigars.

Neue Schonbauswer Schonhauser Strasse 13. ℂ **030/2839-1698.** Reservations recommended. Main courses 14€–23€. AE, MC, V. Mon–Sat 10am–3:30pm and 6:30pm–midnight. U-Bahn: Weinmeister.

Moderate

Guy ✿ INTERNATIONAL   At this top-notch restaurant, anticipate a strong sense of gastronomy as theater. Proceed to any of three separate balconies, each supporting at least one row of artfully decorated tables. The overall effect can be compared to the balconies and private boxes of an old-fashioned opera house. The cuisine is very *haute*, even to the point of seeming experimental. Examples change frequently, but might include a medley of marinated quail and goose liver; mussels served on a purée of arugula; lobster and sweetbreads cooked in puff pastry with tarragon-flavored cream sauce; and braised breast of goose with a roulade of potatoes and herbs.

Jägerstrasse 59–60. ℂ **030/20-94-26-00.** Reservations recommended. Main courses 26€–30€. Set-price lunches 15€–20€; set-price dinners 51€–74€. AE, MC, V. Mon–Fri noon–3pm and 6pm–1am; Sat 6pm–1am. U-Bahn: Stadtmitte or Französischer Strasse.

Restaurant Borchardt INTERNATIONAL   This restaurant is elegant, light-hearted, and fashionable among the city's artistic movers and shakers. You can order anything from a simple salad (as supermodel Claudia Schiffer often does) to the more substantial cream of potato soup with bacon and croutons; filet of carp prepared with Riesling and herbs and finished with champagne; foie gras served with caramelized apples; chicken stuffed with morels and served with cream-and-herb sauce; and a pistachio mousse garnished with essence of fresh fruit.

Französische Strasse 47. ℂ **030/2038-7110.** Reservations recommended. Daily special menu 48€; main courses 20€–30€. AE, V. Daily noon–2am (kitchen closes at midnight). U-Bahn: Französische Strasse.

Inexpensive

Dressler CONTINENTAL   No other bistro along Unter den Linden so successfully re-creates Berlin's pre-war decor and style. Designed to resemble an arts conscious bistro of the sort that might have amused and entertained tuxedo-clad clients in the 1920s, it's outfitted with leather banquettes, tile floors, mirrors, and film memorabilia from the great days of early German cinema. Waiters scurry around, carrying trays of everything from caviar to strudel, as well as three kinds of oysters and hefty portions of lobster salad. Substantial menu items include perfectly prepared turbot with champagne vinaigrette; pheasant breast with Riesling sauce; local salmon trout with white-wine sauce and braised endive; stuffed breast of veal; and calves' liver with apples.

Unter den Linden 39. ℂ **030/204-44-22.** Reservations recommended. Main courses 19€–23€. AE, DC, MC, V. Daily 8am–midnight. S-Bahn: Unter den Linden.

La Gaiola CONTINENTAL   It's crowded, it's hip, and its decor evokes the 1930s allure of what might have been a coffee plantation in the highlands of Africa. Many clients come here just for its bar scene, but if you're hungry, the food is firmly based on what's cooking in the area that stretches between North

Germany and southern Austria, and is served in generous portions. Come here for a chance to meet unattached residents of the surrounding neighborhood, a dialogue with a hip Berliner or two, and good-tasting food items that include beef filet with braised arugula; all manner of fresh fish; homemade salmon with apples, roasted potatoes, and horseradish; and drinks that include raspberry daiquiris.

Monbijouplatz 11–12. ℭ 030/28-53-98-90. Reservations recommended. Main courses 10€–18€. AE, MC, V. Mon–Sat 6pm–midnight. U-Bahn: Hackescher Markt.

Mutter Hoppe GERMAN   This cozy, wood-paneled restaurant still serves the solid Teutonic cuisine favored by a quasi-legendary matriarch (Mother Hoppe) who used to churn out vast amounts of *gütbergerlich* cuisine to members of her extended family and entourage. Within a quartet of old-fashioned dining rooms, you'll enjoy heaping portions of such rib-sticking fare as sauerbraten with roasted potatoes; creamy goulash with wild mushrooms; filets of zander with dill-flavored cream sauce; and braised filets of pork in mushroom-flavored cream sauce. Wine is available, but most guests opt for at least one foaming mug of beer.

Rathausstrasse 21, Nikolaiviertel. ℭ 030/241-56-25. Reservations recommended. Main courses 9€–20€. MC, V. Daily 11:30am–midnight. U- and S-Bahn: Alexanderplatz.

StäV ⓐ *Finds* RHENISH   For years, this upscale tavern entertained the politicians and journalists whose business involved the day-to-day running of the German government from Germany's former capital of Bonn. Although its owners at first opposed the re-inauguration of Berlin as the German capital, when the switch was made, they valiantly pulled out of the Rhineland and followed their clientele to new digs within a 5-minute walk of the Brandenburg Gate near the Friedrichstrasse Bahnhof. The only beer served is Kölsch, a brew more closely associated with the Rhineland than any other beer. Rhenish food items include a mass of apples, onions, and blood sausage known as *Himmel und Ärd* ("heaven and hell"); braised beef with pumpernickel and raisin sauce; and Rhineland sauerbraten with noodles. Other items, many influenced by the culinary traditions of Berlin, include braised liver with bacon and onions; a crisp version of Alsatian pizza known as *Flammenküche;* and a potato cake topped with apples and shredded beets or with smoked salmon and sour cream.

8 Schiffbauerdamm. ℭ 030/282-3965. Reservations recommended. Main courses 7€–13€. AE, DC, MC, V. Daily 10am–1am. U-Bahn: Friedrichstrasse.

SEEING THE SIGHTS
SIGHTSEEING SUGGESTIONS FOR FIRST-TIME VISITORS

If You Have 1 Day Get up early and visit the **Brandenburg Gate,** symbol of Berlin, then walk down **Unter den Linden** and have coffee and pastry at the Operncafé. Visit the **Gemäldegalerie** to see some of the world's greatest masterpieces. Afterward, go to **Charlottenburg** to view the celebrated bust of Queen Nefertiti in the **Egyptian Museum.** In the evening, walk along the Kurfürstendamm, visit the **Kaiser Wilhelm Memorial Church,** and dine in a local restaurant.

If You Have 2 Days On day 2, visit the **Pergamon Museum** on Museum Island, seeing the Pergamon Altar. Explore the **National Gallery,** then head for Alexanderplatz. Take the elevator up for a view from its TV tower, before exploring the **Nikolai Quarter** on foot. Spend an hour in the evening walking around the newly rebuilt **Potsdamer Platz.**

If You Have 3 Days On day 3, go to **Potsdam** (see "Day Trips from Berlin," later in this chapter).

If You Have 4 or 5 Days On day 4, visit the new **Judisches Museum Berlin.** In the afternoon return to Charlottenburg Palace and explore the **Historical Apartments,** and in the evening visit the **Europa-Center** for drinks and dinner. On day 5, see some of the sights you might have missed. Take some walks through Berlin and stop at the Cold War's **Checkpoint Charlie,** with its museum. If time remains, visit the **Berlin Zoo,** stroll through the **Tiergarten,** and attend a cabaret in the evening.

THE TOP MUSEUMS
In the Tiergarten

Gemäldegalerie 𝄞𝄞𝄞 Opening in its new home in 1998, this is one of Germany's greatest painting galleries. Several rooms are devoted to early German masters, with altarpieces dating from the 13th to 15th centuries. Note the panel of *The Virgin Enthroned with Child* (1350), surrounded by angels that resemble the demons so popular in the later works of Hieronymus Bosch. Eight paintings make up the Dürer collection in adjacent rooms.

Another gallery is given over to Italian painting. Here are five Raphael Madonnas; and works by Titian *(The Girl with a Bowl of Fruit),* Fra Filippo Lippi, Botticelli, and Correggio *(Leda with the Swan).* There are also early Netherlandish paintings from the 15th and 16th centuries (van Eyck, Van der Weyden, Bosch, and Bruegel). Several galleries are devoted to Flemish and Dutch masters of the 17th century, with no fewer than 20 works by Rembrandt, including the *Head of Christ.*

Stauffenbergstrasse (entrance is at Mattäiskirchplatz 4). ✆ **030/20-90-55-55.** Admission 6€ adults, 3€ children. Tues–Sun 10am–6pm (Thurs to 10pm). U-Bahn: Potsdamer Platz, then bus 148. Bus: 129 from Ku'-damm (plus a 4-min. walk).

Neue Nationalgalerie (New National Gallery) 𝄞 In its modern glass-and-steel home designed by Ludwig Mies van der Rohe, the Neue Nationalgalerie is a sequel of sorts to the art at Dahlem. It contains a continually growing collection of modern European and American art. Here you'll find works of 19th-century artists, with a stellar concentration on French Impressionists. German art starts with Adolph von Menzel's paintings from about 1850. The 20th-century collection includes works by Max Beckmann, Edvard Munch, and E. L. Kirchner *(Brandenburger Tor),* as well as a few paintings by "the usual suspects," Bacon, Picasso, Ernst, Klee, and American artists such as Barnett Newman. There's food service in the cafe on the ground floor. Hot meals are served from 11am to 5pm.

Potsdamerstrasse 50 (just south of the Tiergarten). ✆ **030/2-66-26-62.** Permanent collection, 6€ adults, 3€ children; temporary exhibitions, 3€. Tues–Fri 10am–6pm; Sat–Sun 11am–6pm. U-Bahn: Kurfürstenstrasse. S-Bahn: Potsdamer Platz.

Museumsinsel (Museum Island)

Pergamon Museum 𝄞𝄞𝄞 The Pergamon Museum houses several departments, but if you have time for only one exhibit, go to the central hall of the U-shaped building to see the **Pergamon Altar** 𝄞𝄞𝄞. This Greek altar (180–160 B.C.) has a huge room all to itself. Some 27 steps lead up to the colonnade. Most fascinating is the frieze around the base, tediously pieced together over a 20-year period. Depicting the struggle of the Olympian gods against the Titans as told in Hesiod's *Theogony,* the relief is strikingly alive, with figures projecting as much as a foot from the background. This, however, is only part of the collection of Greek and Roman antiquities, housed in the north and east wings. You'll also find a Roman market gate discovered in Miletus, and sculptures from many Greek and Roman cities, including a statue of a goddess holding a pomegranate (575 B.C.), found in southern Attica. The **Near East Museum** , in the south wing, contains one of the largest collections anywhere of antiquities discovered in the lands of ancient Babylonia, Persia, and Assyria. Among the exhibits is the Processional Way of Babylon with the Ishtar Gate (580 B.C.).

Kupfergraben, Museumsinsel. ℂ **030/2090-55-55**. Admission 6€ adults, 3€ children; free the 1st Sun of the month. Tues, Wed, Fri, Sat, and Sun 10am–6pm, Thurs 10am–10pm. U-Bahn/S-Bahn: Friedrichstrasse. Tram: 1, 2, 3, 4, 5, 13, 15, or 53.

Altes Museum Karl Friedrich Schinkel, the city's greatest architect, designed this structure, which resembles a Greek Corinthian temple, in 1822. On its main floor is the **Antikensammlung** or Museum of Greek and Roman Antiquities. This great collection of world-famous works of antique decorative art was inaugurated in 1960. It's rich in pottery; Greek, Etruscan, and Roman bronze statuettes and implements; ivory carvings, glassware, objects in precious stone, and jewelry of the Mediterranean region, as well as gold and silver treasures; mummy portraits from Roman Egypt; wood and stone sarcophagi; and a few marble sculptures. The collection includes some of the finest Greek vases of the black- and red-figures style dating from the 6th century to the 4th century B.C. The best known is a large Athenian wine jar (amphora) found in Vulci, Etruria, dating from 490 B.C., which shows a satyr with a lyre and the god Hermes.

Bodestrasse 13, Museumsinsel. ℂ **030/20-90-55-55**. Admission 6€ adults, 3€ children. Tues–Sun 10am–6pm. U-Bahn/S-Bahn: Friedrichstrasse. Bus: 100 to Lustgarten, 147, 157, 257.

✐ Native Behavior

Traditional Germans enjoy their big meal at noon and, in the evening, satisfy hunger with deli cold cuts, open-faced sandwiches, sour pickles, and liver sausage, among other food. To be truly native, you'll begin your *Mittagessen* (main noonday meal) with *Leberknodel-suppe* (liver dumpling).

Germany is a land that welcomes all serious beer drinkers. The country is home to about 40% of the world's breweries, the largest concentration found in Bavaria. The best and most plentiful beer gardens and beer halls are in Munich.

In general the German people are rather candid, especially if they don't agree with something. Whereas this might appear argumentative to foreigners, locals might counterclaim that they are "merely being honest, not hypocritical."

Many young Germans seemed obsessed with all things Yankee; yet, almost in contradiction, they possess deeply felt anti-American sentiments. You must wander carefully through the maze of politics, if the subject comes up at all.

As a rule, expect more formality in Germany than in America or even Britain. By all means, if you have an appointment, show up on time!

Alte Nationalgalerie 🕭 At last open for business, this museum is known for its collection of 19th-century German art as well as for its French Impressionists. A feature of the museum is the world's largest collection of the works of one of the best known of all Berlin artists, Adolph von Menzel (1815–1905). We especially like his *Das Balkonzimmer.* Other paintings include a galaxy of art representing the romantic and classical movements as well as the Biedermeier era. Allow at least an hour and a half to take in canvasses by everybody from Pissarro to Cézanne, from Delacroix to Degas, and from van Gogh to Monet. We are especially fond of the works of Max Liebermann and Max Beckmann. The collection would have been far greater than it is had not the Nazis either sold or destroyed so many early 20th-century works they viewed as "degenerate."

Museumsinsel. ⓒ 030/20905555. Admission 6€ adults, 3€ children. Tues–Sun 10am–6pm. S-Bahn: Hackescher Markt or Friedrichstrasse. Tram: 1, 2, 3, 4, 5, 6, or 53.

In Charlottenburg

Charlottenburg is the quarter of Berlin just west of the Tiergarten. In addition to viewing the exhaustive collections in Charlottenburg Palace, you can enjoy a relaxing ramble through Schlossgarten Charlottenburg. The gardens have been restored and landscaped much as they were in the days of Friedrich Wilhelm II.

Schloss Charlottenburg (Charlottenburg Palace) 🕭🕭 Napoléon exaggerated a bit in comparing Schloss Charlottenburg to Versailles when he invaded Berlin in 1806, but in its heyday this palace was the most elegant residence for Prussian rulers outside the castle in Potsdam. Begun in 1695 as a summer palace for the Electress Sophie Charlotte, patron of philosophy and the arts and wife of King Frederick I (Elector Frederick III), the little residence got out of hand until it grew into the massive structure you see today. The main wing contains the apartments of Frederick I and his "philosopher queen." The **new wing,** known as the Knobelsdorff-Flügel and built from 1740 to 1746, shelters the apartments of Frederick the Great, which now houses a collection of paintings, many of which were either collected or commissioned by the king.

Luisenplatz. ⓒ **030/320-91-275.** Combined ticket for all buildings and historical rooms 7€ adults, 5€ children under 14 and students. Palace, Tues–Fri 9am–5pm, Sat–Sun 10am–5pm; museum, Tues–Fri 10am–6pm; gardens (free admission) daily 6:30am–8pm. U-Bahn: Sophie-Charlotte-Platz or Richard-Wagner-Platz. Bus: 109, 121, 245, or 204.

Ägyptisches Museum (Egyptian Museum) 🕭 The western Berlin branch of the Egyptian Museum is housed in the east guardhouse built for the king's bodyguard. It's worth the trip just to see the famous colored bust of **Queen Nefertiti** 🕭🕭🕭, dating from about 1340 B.C. The bust, stunning in every way, is all by itself in a dark first-floor room, illuminated by a spotlight. It is believed that the bust never left the studio in which it was created but served as a model for other portraits of the queen. The left eye was never drawn in. In addition, look for the head of Queen Tiy and the world-famous head of a priest in green stone. The monumental Kalabasha Gateway was built by Emperor Augustus around 30 B.C. Other displays feature jewelry, papyrus, tools, and weapons, as well as objects relating to the Egyptian belief in the afterlife.

Schlossstrasse 70. ⓒ **030/32-09-11.** Admission 6€ adults, 3€ children; free admission 1st Sun of each month. Tues–Fri 10am–6pm; Sat–Sun 11am–6pm. U-Bahn: Sophie-Charlotte-Platz or Richard-Wagner-Platz. Bus: 109, 110, or 145.

Die Sammlung Berggruen: Picasso und Seine Zeit (The Berggruen Collection: Picasso and his Era) 🕭 *Finds* One of the most unusual private museums in Berlin has accumulated the awesome collection of respected art and antiques dealer Heinz Berggruen. A native of Berlin who fled the Nazis in 1936, he later established antiques dealerships in Paris and California before returning, with his collection, to his native home in 1996. The setting is a renovated former army barracks designed by noted architect August Stüler in 1859. Although most of the collection is devoted to Picasso; there are also works by Cézanne, Braque, Klee, and van Gogh. Some 60 or more works in all, the Picasso collection alone is worth the trip, ranging from his teenage efforts to all of his major periods.

Schlossstrasse 1. (© **030/326-95815**. Admission 6.15€ adults, 2.05€ students and children. Tues–Fri 10am–6pm; Sat–Sun 11am–6pm. U-Bahn: Richard-Wagner-Platz, followed by a 10-min. walk. Bus: 21, 109, 110, or 145.

Bröhan Museum   This wonderful museum specializes in decorative objects of the Art Nouveau (*Jugendstil* in German) and Art Deco periods (1889–1939), with exquisite vases, glass, furniture, silver, paintings of artists belonging to the Berlin Secession, and other works of art arranged in drawing-room fashion, including an outstanding porcelain collection.

Schlossstrasse 1a. (© **030/3269-0600**. Admission 6€ adults, 3€ students/children. Tues–Sun 10am–6pm. U-Bahn: Sophie-Charlotte-Platz. Bus: 109 or 145 to Luisenplatz/Schloss Charlottenburg.

OTHER MUSEUMS
Deutsche Guggenheim Berlin 🏛   Opened in autumn 1997, this state-of-the-art museum is devoted to organizing and presenting exhibitions of modern

and contemporary art. The Guggenheim Foundation conceives, organizes, and installs several exhibitions annually, and also presents exhibitions of newly commissioned works created specifically for this space by world-renowned artists. In addition to contemporary artists, exhibition subjects in the past have ranged from Picasso and Cézanne to Andy Warhol.

Unter den Linden 13–15. ℂ 030/2020-930. Admission 3€ adults, 2€ children. Free on Mon. Daily 11am–8pm (Thurs to 10pm). S-Bahn: Unter den Linden.

Judisches Museum Berlin ✪✪
The most talked-about museum in Berlin, the Jewish Museum is housed in a building that is one of the most spectacular in Berlin. Called "the silver lightning bolt," it was designed by architect Daniel Libeskind. To some viewers, the building suggests a shattered Star of David by its building plan and the scarring in the zinc-plated facade. Odd-shaped windows are haphazardly embedded in the building's exterior.

Inside, the spaces are designed to make the visitor uneasy and disoriented, simulating the feeling of those who were exiled. A vast hollow cuts through the museum to mark what is gone. When the exhibits reach the rise of the Third Reich, the hall's walls, ceiling, and floor close in as the visitor proceeds. A chillingly hollow Holocaust Void, a dark, windowless chamber, evokes much that was lost.

The exhibits concentrate on three themes: Judaism and Jewish life, the devastating effects of the Holocaust, and the post–World War II rebuilding of Jewish life in Germany. The on-site Liebermanns Restaurant features world cuisine, with an emphasis on Jewish recipes—all strictly kosher.

Lindenstrasse 9–14. ℂ 030/25-99-33. Admission 5.10€; free for kids 5 and under. Family ticket 10€ for 2 adults, 4 children. Mon 10am–10pm; Tues–Sun 10am–8pm. U-Bahn: Hallesches Tor or Kochstrasse.

Käthe-Kollwitz Museum ✪
More than any other museum in Germany, this one reflects the individual sorrow of the artist whose work it contains. Some visitors call it a personalized revolt against the agonies of war, as well as a welcome change from the commercialism of the nearby Ku'damm. Established in 1986, it was inspired by Berlin-born Käthe Kollwitz, an ardent socialist, feminist, and pacifist whose stormy social commentary led to the eventual banning of her works by the Nazis. Many Kollwitz works show the agonies of wartime separation of mother and child, inspired in part by her loss of a son in Flanders during World War I and a grandson during World War II.

Fasanenstrasse 24. ℂ 030/882-52-10. Admission 5€ adults, 2.50€ children and students. Wed–Mon 11am–6pm. U-Bahn: Uhlandstrasse or Kurfürstendamm. Bus: 109, 119, 129, 219, or 249.

Märkisches Museum
The full cultural history of Berlin is displayed in one of the most prominent buildings on the banks of the Spree; 42 rooms contain collections of artifacts from excavations, plus such art treasures as Slav silver items and Bronze Age finds. You can learn about Berlin's theaters and literature, the arts in Berlin and Brandenburg, and the life and work of Berlin artists. Most visitors like the array of mechanical musical instruments that can be played Sunday from 11am to 2pm, for an extra 1€.

Am Köllnischen Park 5. ℂ 030/30-86-60. Admission 4.10€ adults, 2.05€ children. Tues–Sun 10am–6pm. U-Bahn: Märkisches Museum. Bus: 147, 240, or 265.

Museum für Gegenwart
This Museum of Contemporary Art opened in 1996 north of the Spree in the old Hamburger Bahnhof. The structure was the terminus for trains from Hamburg. Today, the station no longer receives trains but is a premier storehouse of postwar art, a sort of Musée d'Orsay of Berlin.

Traces of its former function are still evident in the building, including the high roof designed for steam engines. The modern art on display is some of the finest in Germany, the nucleus of the collection, a donation from the Berlin collector Erich Marx (no relation to Karl Marx). A multimedia event, you can view everything from Andy Warhol's now legendary *Mao* to an audiovisual Joseph Beuys archive. The museum houses one of the best collections of Cy Twombly. Other works on display are by Rauschenberg, Lichtenstein, and Dan Flavin. The conceptual artist Beuys is also represented by 450 drawings.

Invalidenstrasse 50–51. ℭ 030/20-90-55-55. Admission 6€ adults, 3€ children. Tues–Fri 10am–6pm; Sat–Sun 11am–6pm. U-Bahn: Zinnowitzer Strasse. Bus: 157, 245, 248, or 340.

Museum Haus am Checkpoint Charlie   This small building houses exhibits depicting the tragic events leading up to and following the erection of the former Berlin Wall. You can see some of the instruments of escape used by East Germans. Photos document the construction of the wall, escape tunnels, and the postwar history of both parts of Berlin from 1945 until today, including the airlift of 1948 and 1949. One of the most moving exhibits is the display on the staircase of drawings by schoolchildren who, in 1961 and 1962, were asked to depict both halves of Germany in one picture.

Friedrichstrasse 44. ℭ 030/253-72-50. Admission 7€ adults, 4€ children. Daily 9am–10pm. U-Bahn: Kochstrasse or Stadtmitte. Bus: 129.

Kunstgewerbe Museum (Museum of Applied Arts)   This museum, next to the Gemäldegalerie in a modern redbrick edifice built for the collection, is devoted to European applied arts from the early Middle Ages to the present, including the Renaissance, baroque, rococo, Jugendstil (German Art Nouveau), and Art Deco periods. Displayed are glassware, porcelain, silver, furniture, jewelry, and clothing. The collection of medieval goldsmiths' works is outstanding, as are the displays of Venetian glass, early Meissen and KPM porcelain, and Jugendstil vases, porcelain, furniture, and objects.

Matthäiskirchplatz. ℭ 030/2662-902. Admission 3.05€ adults, 1.55€ students/children. Tues–Fri 10am–6pm; Sat–Sun 11am–6pm. U-Bahn/S-Bahn: Potsdamer Platz. Bus: 129 from Ku'damm to Potsdamer Brücke.

The Story of Berlin   This multimedia extravaganza portrays 8 centuries of the city's history through photos, films, sounds, and colorful displays. Beginning with the founding of Berlin in 1237, it chronicles the plague, the Thirty Years' War, Frederick the Great's reign, military life, the Industrial Revolution and the working poor, the Golden 1920s, World War II, divided Berlin during the Cold War, and the fall of the Wall. Lights flash in a media blitz as you enter the display on the fall of the Wall, making you feel like one of the first East Berliners to wonderingly cross to the West. Conclude your tour on the 14th floor with a panoramic view over today's Berlin. Though the displays are a bit jarring and the historical information is too jumbled to be truly educational, the museum does leave a lasting impression. Allow at least 2 hours.

Ku'damm-Karree, Kurfürstendamm 207–208 (at the corner of Uhlandstrasse). ℭ 01805/99-20-10. Admission 9.30€ adults, 7.50€ students/children, 21€ families. Daily 10am–8pm (you must enter by 6pm). S-Bahn: Uhlandstrasse.

HIGHLIGHTS OF BERLIN-MITTE

Reichstag (Parliament)   On the night of February 17, 1933, a fire broke out in the seat of the German parliament, the Reichstag. It was obviously set by the Nazis, but the German Communist Party was blamed. That was all the excuse Hitler's troops needed to begin mass arrests of "dissidents and enemies of the lawful government." During World War II, the Reichstag faced massive Allied bombardment. Today it's once again the home of Germany's parliament. A new glass dome, designed by English architect Sir Norman Foster, now crowns the neo-Renaissance structure originally built in 1894. You can go through the west gate for an elevator ride up to the dome, where a sweeping vista of Berlin opens before you. There's both an observation platform and a rooftop restaurant (the view is better than the food).

Platz der Republik 1. ✆ 030/2273-2152. Free admission. Daily 8am–midnight (last entrance at 10pm). S-Bahn: Unter den Linden. Bus: 100.

Brandenburger Tor (Brandenburg Gate) ✪✪ This triumphal arch stood for many years next to the Wall, symbolizing the divided city. Today it represents the reunited German capital. Six Doric columns hold up an entablature inspired by the Propylaea of the Parthenon at Athens. Surrounded by the famous and much photographed Quadriga of Gottfried Schadow from 1793, the gate was designed by Carl Gotthard Langhans in 1789. Napoléon liked the original Quadriga so much he ordered them taken down and shipped to Paris, but they were returned to Berlin in 1814. In Berlin's heyday before World War II, the gate marked the grand western extremity of the "main street," Unter den Linden. In the Room of Silence, visitors still gather to meditate and reflect on Germany's past.

Pariser Platz. Free admission. Room of Silence daily 11am–6pm. S-Bahn: Unter den Linden. Bus: 100.

A PARK & A ZOO

Tiergarten ✪ Tiergarten, the largest green space in central Berlin, covers just under 2.5 sq. km (1 sq. mile), with more than 23km (14 miles) of meandering walkways. Late in the 19th century, partially to placate growing civic unrest, it was opened to the public, with a layout formalized by one of the leading landscape architects of the era, Peter Josef Lenné. The park was devastated during World War II, and the few trees that remained were chopped down for fuel as Berlin shuddered through the winter of 1945 and 1946. Beginning in 1955, trees were replanted and alleyways, canals, ponds, and flower beds rearranged in their original patterns through the cooperative efforts of many landscape architects.

The park's largest monuments include the Berlin Zoo, described below, and the **Siegessäule (Victory Column),** which perches atop a soaring red-granite pedestal from a position in the center of the wide boulevard (Strasse des 17 Juni) that neatly bisects the Tiergarten into roughly equivalent sections.

From the Bahnhof Zoo to the Brandenburger Tor. Bus: 100, 141, or 341 to Grosser Stern.

Zoologischer Garten Berlin (Berlin Zoo) ✪ *Kids* Occupying most of the southwest corner of Tiergarten is Germany's oldest and finest zoo. Founded in 1844, it's a short walk north from the Ku'damm. Until World War II, the zoo boasted thousands of animals of every imaginable species and description—many familiar to Berliners by nicknames. The tragedy of the war struck here as well, and by the end of 1945, only 91 animals remained. Since the war, the city has been rebuilding its large and unique collection; today more than 13,000 animals are housed here. The zoo has Europe's most modern birdhouse, with more than 550 species. The most valuable inhabitants here are giant pandas.

Hardenbergplatz 8. ✆ 030/25-40-10. Zoo, 8€ adults, 4€ children. Zoo and aquarium, 13€ adults, 6.50€ children. Zoo, Apr–Oct daily 9am–5pm; Nov–Mar daily 9am–5:30pm. Aquarium, year-round, daily 9am–6pm. S-Bahn/U-Bahn: Zoologischer Garten.

Berlin-Mitte

Legend:
- ✚ Church
- Ⓢ S-Bahn Stop

Scale: 0 – 200 meters / 0 – 1/5 mile

ACCOMMODATIONS ■
- Four Seasons **1**
- Hotel Adlon **4**
- Hotel Hackescher Markt **7**
- Hotel Luisenhof **11**
- Westin Grand **13**

ATTRACTIONS ●
- Alte Nationalgalerie **6**
- Altes Museum **15**
- Brandenburg Gate (Brandenburger Tor) **2**
- Deutche Guggenheim Berlin **14**
- Fernsehturm **8**
- Märkisches Museum **9**
- Museum Haus am Checkpoint Charlie **12**
- Nikolai Quarter **10**
- Pergamon Museum **5**
- Reichstag (Parliament) **3**

Area of detail — BERLIN — CHARLOTTEN-BURG — TIERGARTEN — Spree

ORGANIZED TOURS

BUS & BOAT TOURS   Some of the best tours are operated by **Severin+ Kühn,** Kurfürstendamm 216 (© 030/880-41-90), which offers half a dozen tours of Berlin and its environs. Their 2-hour **"14 Stops City Tour"** departs at 30-minute intervals November through April daily 10am and 3pm, May through October 10am and 4pm. Priced at 18€ per person, the tour passes most of the important attractions using buses equipped with taped commentaries in eight languages. Among the attractions visited are the Europa-Center, the Brandenburg Gate, and Unter den Linden.

You can supplement this bus tour with a 2-hour boat ride on the Spree, which will carry you past the riverbanks and among some of the backwater harbors that are difficult to access except by water. The boat-tour supplement is available only May through October, with departures from 10am to 1pm daily for 26€ per person. The Severin+Kühn drivers and staff, at the end of the bus tour portion of the experience, will deposit you at the appropriate quays (either adjacent to the Berliner Dom or in the Nicolaiviertel, depending on the day of your visit) in time for the boat's departure.

More appealing and personalized is the 3-hour **"Big Berlin Tour,"** which departs 10am and 2pm daily, costs around 22€ per person, and—depending on the itinerary—usually incorporates sights not included on the shorter tour. Among the attractions is a section of the Grünewald Forest.

One interesting tour lasts 4 hours and visits Potsdam and Sans Souci Palace, former residence of Frederick the Great. The price is 35€ per person. Departures are Tuesday, Thursday, Saturday, and Sunday at 10am; May and October, there are additional departures Friday, Saturday, and Sunday at 2:15pm.

THE SHOPPING SCENE

The central shopping destinations are **Kurfürstendamm, Tauentzienstrasse, Am Zoo,** and **Kantstrasse.** You might also want to walk up streets that intersect with Tauentzienstrasse: Marburger, Ranke, and Nürnberger. Most stores are open Monday through Friday from 9 or 10am to 6 or 6:30pm. Many stores stay open late on Thursday evening, usually until about 8:30pm. Saturday hours for most stores are from 9 or 10am to 2pm.

One of Berlin's largest indoor shopping centers, topped by the Mercedes-Benz logo, is the **Europa-Center,** Breitscheidplatz Tauentzienstrasse (© **030/348-0088;** U-Bahn: Kurfürstendamm), in the heart of the western city. You'll find a number of restaurants and cafes, in addition to an array of shops offering wide-ranging merchandise.

The city's newest and largest shopping and entertainment complex is the **Potsdamer Platz Arkaden,** Alte Potsdamer Strasse 7 (© **030/2559-270**), where you'll find nearly 150 shops, cafes, and restaurants on three different levels. The square is also home to the Grand Hyatt Berlin and a movie complex as well as the new Berlin casino.

TWO STORES WORTH A LOOK

Known popularly as KaDeWe (pronounced kah-*day*-vay), **Kaufhaus des Westens,** Wittenbergplatz (© 030/21-21-0; www.kadewe.de; U-Bahn: Wittenberg-platz), is about 2 blocks from the Kurfürstendamm. The huge luxury store, whose name means "department store of the west," was established some 75 years ago. Displaying extravagant items, it's known mainly for its sixth-floor food department. It's been called the greatest food emporium in the world. More than 1,000 varieties of German sausages are displayed, and delicacies from all over the world are shipped in.

Despite its abbreviated name, **KPM,** Wegelystrasse 1 (© **030/39-00-90;** S-Bahn: Tiergarten), is one of Europe's most prestigious emporiums of luxury dinnerware. Königliche Porzellan Manufaktur was founded in 1763 when Frederick the Great invested his personal funds in a lackluster porcelain factory and elevated it to royal status. Each item is hand painted, hand decorated, and hand packed in almost unbreakable formats that can be shipped virtually anywhere.

BERLIN AFTER DARK

The German *Zitty* and *Tip* include some listings in English, and keep you informed about various nightlife and cultural venues. Both *Berlin Programm* and *Kultur!news* also contain theater listings and other diversions. Performance arts are also covered in *Berlin,* a quarterly published in both English and German. These pamphlets and magazines are available at news kiosks.

THE PERFORMING ARTS

The **Berliner Philharmonisches Orchester (Berlin Philharmonic)** is one of the world's premier orchestras. Its home, **the Philharmonie,** in the Kulturforum, Herbert-von-Karajan Strasse 1 (© **030/254-88-0;** www.berlin-philharmonic. com; U-Bahn: Potsdamer Platz), is a significant piece of modern architecture; you may want to visit even if you do not attend a performance. None of the 2,218 seats are more than 30m (100 ft.) from the rostrum. The box office is open Monday through Friday from 3:30 to 6pm and Saturday and Sunday from 11am to 2pm. You can place orders by phone at © **030/25-48-89-99.** If you're staying in a first-class or deluxe hotel, you can usually get the concierge to obtain seats for you. Tickets are 15€ to 51€; special concerts 26€ to 128€.

The famed **Deutsche Oper Berlin (Berlin Opera),** Bismarckstrasse 35 (© **030/34-384-01;** www.deutsche-oper.berlin.de; U-Bahn: Deutsche Oper, S-Bahn: Charlottenburg), performs in one of the world's great opera houses, built on the site of the prewar opera house in Charlottenburg. A ballet company performs once a week. Concerts, including *Lieder* evenings, are also presented on the opera stage. Tickets are 15€ to 102€.

Deutsche Staatsoper (German State Opera), Unter den Linden 7 (© **030/ 20-35-45-55;** www.staatsoper-berlin.org; U-Bahn: Französische Strasse), presents some of the finest opera in the world, along with a regular repertoire of ballet and concerts. Its home was rebuilt within the walls of the original 1740s Staatsoper, destroyed in World War II. The box office generally is open Monday through Friday from 10am to 6pm and Saturday and Sunday from noon to 6pm. Concert tickets are 7.65€ to 61€; opera tickets are 11€ to 82€. The opera closes from late June to the end of August.

Komische Oper Berlin, Behrensstrasse 55–57 (© **030/20-26-00;** www. komische-oper-berlin.de; U-Bahn: Französische Strasse, S-Bahn: Friedrichstrasse or Unter den Linden), lies in the middle of the city near Brandenburger Tor. Over the years, it has become one of the most innovative theater ensembles in Europe, presenting many avant-garde productions. The box office is open Monday through Saturday from 11am to 7pm and Sunday from 1pm until 1½ hours before the performance. Tickets are 7.65€ to 54€.

LIVE-MUSIC CLUBS

A-Trane, Pestalozzistrasse 105 (© **030/313-25-50;** S-Bahn: Savignyplatz), is a small and smoky jazz house where virtually everyone seems to have a working

---

Moments Come to the Cabaret!

If you know how to sing "Life is a cabaret, old chum," in German no less, you may enjoy an evening in this postwar "Porcupine." Like its namesake, **Die Stachelschweine,** Tauentzienstrasse and Budapester Strasse (in the basement of the Europa-Center; ℂ 030/261-47-95; U-Bahn: Kurfürstendamm), pokes prickly fun at German, and often American, politicians. Get a ticket early, because the Berliners love this one. The box office is open Tuesday through Friday from 11am to 2pm and 3 to 7:30pm, and Saturday from 10am to 2pm and 3 to 8:45pm. Shows are presented from Tuesday to Friday at 7:30pm and Saturday at 6 and 9pm. Cover is 11€ to 24€. The cabaret is closed during July.

Opened in 1893 as one of the most popular purveyors of vaudeville in Europe, the **Wintergarten,** Potsdamer Strasse 96 (ℂ 030/230-88-230; U-Bahn: Kurfürstenstrasse), operated in fits and starts throughout the war years, until it was demolished in 1944 by Allied bombers. In 1992, a modernized design reopened. Today, it's the largest and most nostalgic Berlin cabaret, laden with schmaltzy reminders of yesteryear and staffed with chorus girls; magicians from America, Britain, and countries of the former Soviet bloc; circus acrobats; political satirists; and musician/dancer combos. Shows begin at 8pm Monday through Friday, at 6pm Saturday, and at 6 and 10pm Sunday. Shows last around 2¼ hours. The box office is open daily from 7pm to midnight. Cover Friday and Saturday is 47€ to 53€, Sunday through Thursday 37€ to 43€, depending on the seat. The price includes your first drink.

---

familiarity with great names from the jazz world's past and present. The name is a hybrid of the old Duke Ellington standard, "Take the 'A' Train," with the "ane" in "Trane" derived from the legendary John Coltrane's name. It's open daily at 9pm; music begins around 10pm. Closing hours vary. Cover is 7.65€ to 15€, depending on who's playing.

With its kitschy knickknacks, colored lights, and wine-red walls, **Wild at Heart,** Wienerstrasse 20 (ℂ 030-6-11-70-10; U-Bahn: Görlitzer Bahnhof), is dedicated to the rowdier side of rock. Hard-core punk, rock, and rockabilly bands from Germany and elsewhere are featured. Live performances take place from Wednesday to Saturday nights. It's open Monday through Friday from 8pm to 3am, and Saturday and Sunday from 8pm to 10am (yes, you may miss breakfast). Cover is 8€.

Hyper-trendy, **Oxymoron,** in the courtyard at Rosenthaler Strasse 40–41 (ℂ 030/283-91-88-6; S-Bahn: Hackenschen Höfe), is a lot of fun on most nights. The setting is a high-ceilinged room with old-fashioned proportions and enough battered kitsch to remind you of a century-old coffeehouse in Franz-Josef's Vienna. Local wits refer to it as a *Gesamtkunstwerk*—a self-obsessed, self-sustaining work of art that might have been appreciated by Wagner. On Friday and Saturday after around 11pm, a slightly claustrophobic, much-used annex room—all black with ghostly flares of neon—opens as a disco, usually with a clientele that's about 75% hetero and 100% iconoclastic. If live bands appear at all, it will usually be on Thursday. The restaurant is open daily from 11am to 2am. Cover is 5.10€ to 10€.

Large and artfully drab, **Far Out,** Kurfürstendamm 156 (ℂ **030/320-00-717; U-Bahn:** Adenauerplatz), plays danceable rock from the 1970s to the 1990s that manages to get hundreds of high-energy dancers up and out on the floors. Clientele includes lots of students and artists, who dress up in artfully bizarre clothing that has lots of punk-rock overtones. It occasionally imports celebrity DJs from other disco-crazed cities of Europe. The place only really comes alive after midnight. It's open Tuesday through Sunday from 10pm to between 4 and 6am, depending on the crowd. Cover is 5.10€ to 7.65€.

Knaack-Klub, Greifswalderstrasse 224 (ℂ **030/442-7060;** S-Bahn: Alexanderplatz), features a live music venue, two floors of dancing, and a floor dedicated to games. There are usually four live rock shows a week, with a fairly even split between German and international touring bands. The music ranges from techno to hip-hop to 1980s. Disco music is played on Wednesday, Friday, and Saturday nights. The club is open nightly from 10pm. Cover is 2.55€ to 5.10€.

The premises that contain **Opernschänke,** in the Opernpalais, Unter den Linden 5 (ℂ **030/20-26-83;** U-Bahn: Friedrichstrasse), were built in 1762, a fact that seems to add a certain importance to a setting that's undeniably historic, and to the artists who perform their music live. For the most part, this is a restaurant serving Continental food every day from noon to midnight, with the last order accepted at 11:30pm. Main courses cost 10€ to 18€. The food is augmented with live music, usually jazz, Thursday, Friday, and Saturday nights from 6pm to 1am, as well as Sunday afternoon from 11am to 2pm, as part of set-price "Jazz Brunch" costing 26€. After the end of the jazz brunch, the restaurant remains open till 7pm for food and drink.

DANCE CLUBS

Gays, straights, and everybody in between show up at **SO 36,** Oranienstrasse 190 (ℂ **030/61-40-13-06;** U-Bahn: Görlitzer Bahnhof), for wild action and frantic dancing into the wee hours. A young, vibrant Kreuzberg crowd is attracted to this joint where the scene changes nightly. On Wednesday it's strictly gay and lesbian disco. On Friday and Saturday the parties "get really wild, man," as the bartender accurately promised. Some nights are devoted to themes such as James Bond where you can show up looking like a Cold War spy. Wednesdays and Sundays are generally all gay. Hours are Wednesday through Saturday from 10pm until "we feel like closing," and Sunday from 5 to 11pm. Cover is 5.10€ to 13€.

Metropole, Nollendorfplatz 5, Schöneberg (ℂ **030/217-36-80;** U-Bahn: Nollendorfplatz), one of the leading dance clubs in Berlin, opens only on weekends and attracts patrons ages 18 to 38. Built as a theater around a century ago, Metropole hosts live concerts and special events for gay people. It's open Tuesday through Saturday from 9pm to 6am. Cover is 6€ to 8€.

One of Berlin's most rocking techno venues, **Tresor Globus,** Leipzigerstrasse 126A (ℂ **030/229-06-11;** U-Bahn: Mohrenstrasse), has been packing 'em in since 1991. The building was once part of Globus Bank. Downstairs there's a bunkerlike atmosphere with prison-type metal bars and harsh acoustics. The spacious dance floor upstairs has lighter house sounds. There's also a bar in the back when you want to chill out. In summer, tables are placed outside, with lights strung among the shrubbery. The club is open Wednesday through

Sunday at 11pm; it often closes at 6am. Cover on Wednesday is 2.55€, Friday 5.10€, Saturday and Sunday 7.65€ to 13€.

DAY TRIPS FROM BERLIN

POTSDAM ✯✯✯   Of all the tours possible from Berlin, the best attraction is the baroque town of Potsdam, 24km (15 miles) southwest of Berlin on the Havel River, often called Germany's Versailles. From the beginning of the 18th century it was the residence and garrison town of the Prussian kings. World attention focused on Potsdam from July 17 to August 2, 1945, when the Potsdam Conference shaped postwar Europe.

West of the historic core lies **Sans Souci Park,** with its palaces and gardens. Northwest of Sans Souci are the New Garden and the Cecilienhof Palace, on the Heiliger See.

Getting There   There are 29 daily connections by rail from Bahnhof Zoo (trip time: 23 min.) and Berliner Hauptbahnhof (54 min.). For rail information in Potsdam, call ✆ **018/05-99-66-33.** Potsdam can also be reached by S-Bahn (30 min.). Car access is via the E-30 autobahn east and west or the E-53 north and south.

Visitor Information   **Potsdam-Information,** Friedrich-Ebert-Strasse 5 (✆ **0331/ 275580**), is open April through October, Monday through Friday from 9am to 7pm, Saturday and Sunday from 9am to 4pm; November through March, Monday through Friday from 10am to 6pm, Saturday and Sunday from 10am to 4pm.

Exploring Potsdam   With its palaces and gardens, **Sans Souci Park** ✯✯✯, Zur historischen Mühle (✆ **0331/96-94-202;** tram: 94 or 95; bus: 612, 614, 631, 632, 692, or 695), was the work of many architects and sculptors. The park covers about a square mile. Once at Potsdam, a complete tour costs 33€. For information on English-speaking tours, call ✆ **0331/96-94-200.**

Frederick II ("the Great") chose Potsdam rather than Berlin as his permanent residence. The style of the buildings he ordered erected is called Potsdam rococo, an achievement primarily of Georg Wenzeslaus von Knobelsdorff. Knobelsdorff built **Sans Souci Palace** ✯✯✯, with its terraces and gardens, as a summer residence for Frederick II. The palace, inaugurated in 1747, is a long one-story building crowned by a dome and flanked by round pavilions. The music salon is the supreme example of the rococo style, and the elliptical Marble Hall is the largest in the palace. As a guest of the king, Voltaire visited in 1750. Sans Souci is open April through October from 9am to 5pm; November through March from 9am to 4pm; closed Monday. Admission is 8€ adults and 5€ children.

Schloss Charlottenhof ✯, south of Okonomieweg (✆ **0331/969-42-00;** tram: 1 or 4), was designed by Karl Friedrich Schinkel, the great neoclassical master, and built between 1826 and 1829. He erected the palace in the style of a villa and designed most of the furniture inside. It's open May through October daily from 10am to 5pm; also November through April Tuesday through Sunday from 9am to 4pm. Admission is 5.10€ adults and 4€ children.

North of the 80-hectare (200-acre) park, the **Cecilienhof Palace** ✯, Im Neuer Garten (✆ **0331/969-42-44;** bus: 694), was built in the style of an English country house by Kaiser Wilhelm II between 1913 and 1917. The 176-room mansion became the new residence of Crown Prince Wilhelm of Hohenzollern. It was occupied as a royal residence until March 1945, when the crown prince and his family fled to the West, taking many of their possessions.

Tips **A Fabulous Place to Dine in Potsdam**

In 1878, a courtier in the service of the Prussian monarch built an elegant villa on the shore of the Heiliger See. During the 1920s, author Bernhardt Kellerman wrote some of his best work here. After a Cold War stint as a base for Russian officers, it now functions as the most talked-about restaurant in Potsdam: **Villa Kellerman,** Mangerstrasse 33–36 (© **0331/29-15-72**; bus: 695). The classical Italian cuisine might include marinated carpaccio of whitefish; a mixed platter of antipasti; spaghetti with scampi, herbs, and garlic; or John Dory in butter-and-caper sauce. Reservations are recommended. American Express and Visa are accepted. It's open Tuesday through Thursday from 4 to 11pm, Friday through Sunday from noon to midnight.

Cecilienhof was the headquarters of the 1945 Potsdam Conference. It's open year-round, Tuesday through Sunday, as follows: April through October from 9am to 5pm; November through March from 9am to 4pm. Between November and March, adults pay 4€, and children under 7 and students pay 3€; visitors must visit the palace as part of a guided tour, which is included in the entrance price. Between April and October, adults pay 5€, and children under 7 and students pay 4€. During that period, visitors may choose to participate or not participate in the guided tour.

2 Munich ✶✶✶ & the Bavarian Alps ✶✶

Sprawling Munich, home of some 1.3 million people and such industrial giants as Siemens and BMW, is the pulsating capital and cultural center of Bavaria. One of Germany's most festive cities, Munich exudes a hearty Bavarian *Gemütlichkeit.*

Longtime resident Thomas Mann wrote: "Munich sparkles." Although the city he described was swept away by some of the most severe bombing of World War II, Munich continues to sparkle, as it introduces itself to thousands of new visitors annually.

The Munich cliché as a beer-drinking town of folkloric charm is marketed by the city itself. Despite a roaring gross national product, Munich likes to present itself as a large, agrarian village peopled by jolly beer drinkers who cling to rustic origins despite the presence on all sides of symbols of the computer age, high-tech industries, a sophisticated business scene, a good deal of Hollywood-style glamour, and fairly hip night action. Bavarians themselves are a minority in Munich—more than two-thirds of the population comes from other parts of the country or from outside Germany—but everybody buys into the folkloric charm and schmaltz.

ESSENTIALS

GETTING THERE   By Plane   The **Munich International Airport** (© **089/ 97-52-13-13;** www.munich-airport.de) lies 27km (17 miles) northeast of central Munich at Erdinger Moos.

S-Bahn (© **089/41-42-43-44**) trains connect the airport with the Hauptbahnhof (main railroad station) in downtown Munich, with departures every 20 minutes for the 40-minute trip. The fare is 8€; Eurailpass holders ride free. A

Munich

To Olympiapark

Berlin
GERMANY
Munich

To Nymphenburg
(see inset top right)

Zieblandstr.
Schellingstrasse
Theresien- strasse
Hess-Strasse
Luisenstrasse
Schleissheimerstrasse
Augustenstr.
Gabelsbergerstrasse
Arcisstrasse
Barerstrasse

Brienner Strasse
Königs-
platz
Karolinen-
platz
Dachauerstrasse
Augustenstrasse
Seidlstrasse
Karlstrasse
Meiserstrasse
Max-Joseph-Strasse
Barerstrasse

Marsstrasse
Luisenstrasse
Sophienstrasse
ALTER
BOTANISCHER
GARTEN
Lenbach-
platz
Maximilians-
platz
Arnulfstrasse
Elisenstrasse
Bahnhof-
platz
Prielmayerstrasse
Maxburgstrasse

Hauptbahnhof
Schützenstr.
Karls-
platz
Neuhauserstrasse
Herzogspitalstr.
Bayerstr.
Senefelder-
strasse
Adolf-Kolping-Str.
Sonnenstr.
Sonnenstr.
Josephspitalstr.
Hotterstr.
Sendlingerstr.

Schwanthalerstrasse
Landwehrstrasse
Goethestrasse
Schillerstrasse
Mathildenstrasse
Herzog-Wilhelm-Strasse

Pettenkofer-
strasse
Sendlingertor-
platz
Beethoven-
platz
Nussbaumstrasse
Matthäus-
kirche
Blumen- strasse
Müller- strasse
Lindwurmstrasse
Unterer Anger
Jahnstrasse

Thalkirchnerstrasse
ST. STEFAN'S
CEMETERY

† Church
ⓘ Information
✉ Post Office
Ⓢ S-Bahn
Ⓤ U-Bahn

10 min walk

416

NYMPHENBURG

15 Kleiner See
16
Nymphenburger Kanal
Schloss 17
SCHLOSSPARK
18
19
Grosser See
20
21

Zuccalistrasse
Richildenstrasse
Hirschgartenstr

Akademiestrasse
Blütenstrasse
Adalbertstrasse
Schack-strasse
Schellingstrasse
Türkenstrasse
University
Prof.-Huberplatz
Veterinärstr.
Amalienstrasse
Theresienstrasse
Ludwigstrasse
Kaulbachstrasse
Königinstrasse

ENGLISCHER GARTEN

Türkenstrasse
Schönfeldstrasse
Von-der-Tann Strasse
Oskar-von-Miller-Ring
Prinzregentenstrasse
Briennerstrasse
Galeriestrasse
Theater-museum
22
23
Lerchenfeldstrasse
24
Oettingenstrasse

Odeons-platz
HOFGARTEN
26
Hofgartenstrasse
Unsöldstrasse
K.Scharnagl-Ring
'Mag'müllerstr.

Promenade-platz
Kard-Faulhaber-Strasse
Theatinerstrasse
Residenzstr
Residenz
Cuvilliés Theater
28
Christophstr.
St.-Anna-Platz
25
Liebigstrasse
Reitmorstrasse

Frauen-platz
Max Joseph-Platz
Nationaltheater
Marstallstrasse
Bürkleinstr.
Thierschstr.
Sternstr.
Widenmayrstrasse
Isar

Weinstr.
29
Am Kosttor-Platz
40
Museum für Völkerkunde
Maximilianstrasse
Maximilians-brücke

31
30
Dienerstr.
Pfisterstrasse
Jüdisches Museum München
39
38
Steinsdorfstrasse

Kaufingerstr.
S U
17
Marien-platz
33
Im Tal
Knöbelstrasse
Th.-Wimmer-Ring

34
35
Viktualienmarkt
Westenriederstrasse
Isartor-platz
S
Kanal-strasse
Thierschstrasse
Isar

Blumenstr.
Frauenstrasse
Zweibrücken-strasse

Corneliusstrasse
Rumfordstr.
Morassistrasse

Müllerstr.
Gärtner-platz
Baader-platz
Ludwigs-brücke
Innere Wiener Strasse
Kellerstrasse
Rosenheimerstr.

Klenzestrasse
Fraunhoferstr.
Reichenbachstrasse
Baaderstrasse
Erhardtstrasse
Deutsches Museum
37
Zeppelinstrasse
Lilienstrasse
Hochstrasse
S

36
Isar

417

taxi into the center costs about 56€ to 72€. Airport buses also run between the airport and the center.

By Train   Munich's main rail station, the **Hauptbahnhof,** on Bahnhofplatz, is one of Europe's largest. Near the city center, it contains a hotel, restaurants, shopping, car parking, and banking facilities. All major German cities are connected to this station, most with service every hour. For information about long-distance trains, call ℂ **01805/99-66-33.**

By Bus   Munich is a focal point for bus service that fans out across Bavaria and the rest of Germany. The West-Wing Starnberger Bahnhof, on Arnulfstrasse within the Hauptbahnhof, is the point of arrivals and departures for most of the bus lines servicing the city. For schedules, information, and reservations, call ℂ **089/545-8700.**

VISITOR INFORMATION   Tourist Office   There are two tourist offices in the center of Munich. One is at the Bahnhofplatz 2 (ℂ **089/23-33-02-72**), the main train station. It's open Monday through Saturday from 9:30am to 6:30pm, Sunday from 10am to 6pm. The other office is at Marienplatz im Neuen Rathaus (ℂ **089/23-33-02-72**), open Monday through Friday from 10am to 8pm and Saturday from 10am to 4pm.

Websites   Updated for each year's Oktoberfest, **www.munich-tourist.de** from the Munich Tourist Office includes a program of events, a guide to various beer tents, and images from past festivals. Descriptions of hotel packages and discount voucher packages are added. All things Bavarian are touched on at **www.bavaria.com**, such as Mad King Ludwig's castle and an Oktoberfest beer and music raft ride down the river Isar. There's advice on shopping, getting around, and enjoying the Alps, among many other nuggets.

CITY LAYOUT   Munich's Hauptbahnhof lies just west of the town center and opens onto Bahnhofplatz. From the square, you can take Schützenstrasse to **Karlsplatz** (nicknamed Stachus), one of the major centers of Munich. Many tram lines converge on this square. From Karlsplatz, you can continue east along the pedestrians-only Neuhauserstrasse and Kaufingerstrasse until you reach Marienplatz, where you'll be deep in the Altstadt (Old Town) of Munich.

From **Marienplatz,** the center and heart of the city, you can head north on Dienerstrasse, which will lead you to Residenzstrasse and finally to **Max-Joseph-Platz,** a landmark square, with the National Theater and the former royal palace, the Residenz. East of this square runs **Maximilianstrasse,** the most fashionable shopping and dining street of Munich. Between Marienplatz and the National theater is the **Platzl** quarter, where you'll want to head for nighttime diversions, as it's the seat of some of the finest (and some of the worst) restaurants in Munich, along with the landmark Hofbräuhaus, the most famous beer hall in Europe.

North of the old town is **Schwabing,** the university and former Bohemian section whose main street is Leopoldstrasse. The large, sprawling municipal park grounds, the Englischer Garten, are found due east of Schwabing.

GETTING AROUND   By Public Transportation   The city's efficient rapid-transit system is the **U-Bahn,** or Untergrundbahn, one of the most modern subway systems in Europe. The **S-Bahn** rapid-transit system, a 420km Euro (260-mile) network of tracks, provides service to various city districts and outlying suburbs. The city is also served by a network of **trams** and **buses.** The same ticket entitles you to ride the U-Bahn, the S-Bahn, trams, and buses. For more information, call ℂ **089/41-42-43-44.**

Munich U-Bahn & S-Bahn

419

(*Value* **A Money-Saving Tip**

Munich's S-Bahn is covered by Eurail, so if you have a railpass, don't buy a separate ticket.

A single-journey ticket for a ride within the city's central zone—a large area that few tourists ever leave—costs 2€. If you go to the outermost zones of the subway system, your ride could cost as much as 8€. One of the best things about Munich's transit system is that you can make as many free transfers between subways, buses, and trams as you need to reach your destination.

More economical than single-journey tickets is the ***Streifencarte,*** a strip-ticket that contains 10 units, two of which are annulled for each zone of the system you travel through. A Streifencarte costs 9€. Children ages 6 to 14 can purchase a ***Kinderstreifencarte*** for 3.80€. With this type of ticket, you can travel in one continuous direction during any 2-hour time period with unlimited transfers. You can also use it for multiple passengers (for two people to ride two zones, simply stamp four strips).

An even better deal may be the ***Tageskarte*** (day ticket), which for 4.50€ gives you unlimited access within the central zone for a full day. Double the price for access to all of Greater Munich—an 80km (50-mile) radius.

By Taxi   Cabs are relatively expensive—you'll pay 2.55€ when you get inside, plus 1.35€ per kilometer; add 1€ if you call for pickup. In an emergency, call *©* **089/2161-0** or 089/194-10 for a radio-dispatched taxi.

By Car   Driving in the city, which has an excellent public transportation system, is not advised. The streets around Marienplatz in the Altstadt are pedestrian-only. If you are interested in renting a car locally, try **Sixt Autovermietung,** Einsteinstrasse 106 (*©* **089/550-24-47**), or look under *Autovermietung* in the Munich yellow pages.

By Foot & Bicycle   Of course, the best way to explore Munich is by foot, since it has a vast pedestrian zone in the center. Many of its attractions can, in fact, be reached only by foot. Pick up a good map and set out.

The tourist office sells a pamphlet that outlines itineraries for touring Munich by bicycle called *Radl-Touren für unsere Gäste,* costing .40€. One of the most convenient places to rent a bike is **Radius Bikes** (*©* **089/59-61-13**), at the far end of the Hauptbahnhof, near lockers opposite tracks 30 and 31. The charge is 6.15€ per 2 hours, or else 13€ from 10am to 6pm. Mountain bikes are rented for about 25% more. A deposit of 51€ is assessed; students and Eurailpass holders are granted a 10% discount. The store is open May through early October daily from 10am to 6pm; it's closed November through April.

 FAST FACTS: **Munich**

American Express The American Express Foreign Exchange Service, Kaufingerstrasse 24 (*©* **089/228-013-87**), is open Monday through Friday from 9am to 6pm, Saturday from 10am to 3pm. Reisland American Express, Promenadeplatz 6 (*©* **089/290-900;** U-Bahn: Marienplatz), is open for mail pickup and check cashing Monday through Friday from 9am to 6pm, Saturday from 9:30am to 12:30pm.

Business Hours Most **banks** are open Monday through Friday from 8:30am to 12:30pm and 1:30 to 3:30pm (many stay open until 5:30pm on Thurs). Most **businesses** and **stores** are open Monday through Friday from 9am to 6pm and Saturday from 9am to 2pm. On *langer Samstag* (1st Sat of the month), stores remain open until 6pm. Many observe an 8 or 9pm closing on Thursday.

Consulates There's a **United States** consulate at Känigstrasse 5 ((C) **089/288-80; U-Bahn: Universität**); hours are Monday through Friday from 8am to 11am. The Consulate General Office for the **United Kingdom** at Bürkleinstrasse 10 ((C) **089/21-10-90; U-Bahn: Isartor**) is open Monday through Friday from 8:30 to 11:30am and 1 to 3:15pm.The consulate of **Ireland** at Denninderstrasse 15 ((C) **089/20-80-59-90; bus: 87**) is open Monday through Friday from 9 to 11am. The consulate of **Canada** at Tal Strasse 29 ((C) **089/219-95-70; U-Bahn: Marienplatz**) is open Monday through Thursday from 9am to noon and 2 to 5pm, Friday from 9am to noon and 2:30 to 3:30pm. The governments of Australia and New Zealand do not maintain offices in Munich.

Currency See "Fast Facts: Berlin," earlier in this chapter.

Currency Exchange You can get a better rate at a bank than at your hotel. On weekends or at night, you can exchange money at the Hauptbahnhof exchange, open daily from 6am to 11:30pm.

Dentists/Doctors For an English-speaking dentist, go to **Klinik und Poliklinik für Kieferchirurgie der Universität München,** Lindwurmstrasse 2A ((C) **089/51-60-0; U-Bahn: Goetheplatz**). It deals with emergency cases and is always open. The American, British, and Canadian consulates keep a list of recommended English-speaking physicians. For dental or medical emergencies, call **Notfallpraxis,** Elisenstrasse 3 ((C) **089/55-17-71; bus: 69**). It's open Monday, Tuesday, and Thursday from 7pm to midnight; Wednesday and Friday from 2pm to midnight; and Saturday, Sunday, and holidays from 8am to midnight.

Drugstores For an international drugstore where English is spoken, go to **Bahnhof Apotheke,** Bahnhofplatz 2 ((C) **089/59-41-19; U-Bahn/S-Bahn: Hauptbahnhof**), open Monday through Friday from 8am to 6:30pm and Saturday from 8am to 2pm. If you need a prescription filled during off-hours, call (C) **089/55-76-61** for information about what's open. The information is recorded and in German only, so you may need to get someone from your hotel staff to assist you.

Emergencies For emergency medical aid, phone (C) **089/55-77-55.** Call the police at (C) **110.**

Internet Access You can send e-mails or check your messages at the **Internet-Café,** Bayer-Strasse 10A ((C) **089/55-08-800; bus: 2, 19, 20, or 29**). This is also the site of a cafe, bar, bistro, pastry shop, and pizzeria. It's open daily from 7am to 1am.

Post Office The most central post office is found at Bahnhofplatz ((C) **59-90-87-16; U-Bahn/S-Bahn: Hauptbahnhof**), opposite the main train station exit. It's open Monday through Friday from 7am to 8pm, Saturday from 9am to 4pm, and Sunday from 10am to 3pm. You can have your mail sent here Poste Restante (general delivery), but include the zip code D-80335. You'll need a passport to reclaim mail.

Telephone The **country code** for Germany is **49.** The **city code** for Munich is **89.** Use this code when you're calling from outside Germany; if you're within Germany, use **089.** For more information on making calls from Germany, see "Fast Facts: Berlin," earlier in this chapter.

WHERE TO STAY
VERY EXPENSIVE
Bayerischer Hof & Palais Montgelas ★★★   A Bavarian version of New York's Waldorf-Astoria, this hotel is in a swank location, opening onto a little tree-filled square. Rooms range from medium to extremely spacious, each with plush duvets; many beds are four-posters. Decor ranges from Bavarian provincial to British country house chintz. The large bathrooms have tub/shower combos, private phones, and state-of-the-art luxuries.

Promenadeplatz 2–6, D-80333 München. ✆ **800/223-6800** in the U.S., or 089/2-12-00. Fax 089/21-20-906. www.bayerischerhof.de. 399 units. 235€–385€ double; from 425€–1,070€ suite. AE, DC, MC, V. Parking 19€. Tram: 19. **Amenities:** 3 restaurants; 4 bars; nightclub; rooftop pool and garden; gym; sauna; room service; massage; babysitting; laundry; sun terrace. *In room:* TV, minibar, hair dryer, safe.

Hotel Vier Jahreszeiten München ★★★   This grand hotel, with a tradition dating from 1858, is the most elegant place to stay in Munich. Rooms range from medium to very spacious. Bedside controls, luxury furnishings, and Oriental rugs, plus spacious bathrooms with showers, will keep any guest comfortable. The restaurant is one of the most esteemed in Germany.

Maximilianstrasse 17, D-80539 München. ✆ **800/426-3135** in the U.S., or 089/2125-2000. Fax 089/2125-2777. www.kempinski-vierjahreszeiten.de. 316 units. 345€–495€ double; from 1,000€ suite. AE, DC, MC, V. Parking 20€. Tram: 19. **Amenities:** Restaurant; bistro; indoor pool; sauna; solarium; room service; babysitting; laundry; sun terrace. *In room:* A/C, TV, minibar, hair dryer, safe, bathrobe.

EXPENSIVE
Eden-Hotel-Wolff ★   If you must stay near the train station, this is your best bet. With some exceptions, most rooms are spacious, their styles ranging from modern to rustic Bavarian. Rooms have luxurious appointments and double-glazed windows; and the large bathrooms have tub/shower combos. Some rooms are hypoallergenic with special beds and a private ventilation system.

Arnulfstrasse 4–8, D-80335 München. ✆ **089/55-11-50.** Fax 089/551-15-555. www.ehw.de. 216 units. 169€–282€ double; 256€–358€ suite. 1 child up to age 6 stays free in parent's room. Rates include buffet breakfast. AE, DC, MC, V. Parking 14€. U-Bahn/S-Bahn: Hauptbahnhof. **Amenities:** Restaurant; bar; room service; babysitting; laundry. *In room:* TV, minibar, hair dryer, safe.

MODERATE
Advokat Hotel   This hotel occupies a 1930s apartment house. Its streamlined interior borrows in discreet ways from Bauhaus and minimalist models. The rooms look as if Philippe Starck had gone on a shopping binge at Ikea. All come with neatly kept bathrooms with tub/shower combination. The result is an aggressively simple, clean-lined, and artfully spartan hotel with very few extras and facilities.

Baaderstrasse 1, 80469 München. © 089/21-63-10. Fax 089/21-63-190. www.hotel-advokat.de. 50 units. 185€ double. Rates include breakfast. AE, DC, MC, V. S-Bahn: Isartor. *In room:* TV, minibar, hair dryer.

An der Oper ⍟

Just off Maximilianstrasse, near Marienplatz, this is a superb choice for sightseeing or shopping in the traffic-free malls, just steps from the Bavarian National Theater. Built in the 1970s, it's one of the best-run hotels in this price category. Recently renovated rooms, which range from small to medium, have such amenities as double-glazed windows, firm beds, a small sitting area, and a table for those who want breakfast in their rooms. Bathrooms are medium in size and beautifully maintained, with tub/shower combos.

Falkenturmstrasse 11, D-80331 München. © 089/290-02-70. Fax 089/290-02-729. www.hotelanderoper.de. 68 units. 150€–215€ double. Rates include buffet breakfast. AE, MC, V. Tram: 19. *In room:* TV, minibar, hair dryer.

Gästehaus Englischer Garten ⍟

This oasis of charm and tranquility, close to the Englischer Garten, is one of our preferred stopovers. The decor of the rooms might be termed "Bavarian grandmother." Bathrooms are small and not one of the hotel's stronger features. In an annex across the street are 15 small apartments, each with a shower-only bathroom and a tiny kitchenette. Try for room nos. 16, 23, 26, or especially 20; all are more spacious, are better furnished, and have better views. In fair weather, breakfast is served in a rear garden.

Liebergesellstrasse 8, D-80802 München-Schwabing. © 089/38-39-41-0. Fax 089/38-39-41-33. 25 units, 16 with bathroom. 70€–103€ double without bathroom; 103€–115€ double with bathroom; 79€–105€ apt. AE, DC, MC, V. Parking 8€. U-Bahn: Münchner Freiheit. *In room:* TV, minibar.

Hotel Exquisit ⍟

One of the most appealing hotels in the Sendlinger Tot neighborhood lies behind a wine-colored facade on a quiet residential street that seems far removed from the heavy traffic and bustle of the nearby theater district. Built in 1988, it has a paneled lobby whose focal point is a lounge that gets busy around 6 or 7pm. Staff is pleasant, offering a genuine welcome and ushering you up to rooms that are spacious and comfortably furnished. About half overlook an ivy-draped garden, others look over the street. Bathrooms are efficient, with a tiled shower unit.

Pettenkoferstrasse 4, D-80336 München. © 089/55-19-900. Fax 089/199-499. www.augustiner-restaurant. com. 50 units. 160€–195€ double; 195€–240€ suite. Rates include breakfast. AE, DC, MC, V. U-Bahn: Sendlinger Tor. **Amenities:** Restaurant; bar; room service; laundry/dry cleaning; private garden. *In room:* TV, minibar, hair dryer, safe.

Hotel Mark *(Value)*

This hotel near the Hauptbahnhof's south exit is known for comfort and moderate prices. The rooms are functionally furnished, although a bit cramped, and furnishings were recently renewed, so you should sleep in peace. Bathrooms are small but tidily maintained, each with a shower unit. Breakfast is the only meal served.

Senefelderstrasse 12, D-80336 München. © 089/55-98-20. Fax 089/559-82-333. www.heh.de. 95 units. 107€–177€ double. Rates include buffet breakfast. AE, DC, MC, V. Parking 9.50€. U-Bahn/S-Bahn: Hauptbahnhof. *In room:* TV, minibar, hair dryer, safe.

Hotel Opera ⍟

This charming little gem (not to be confused with the An der Oper) is filled with comfort and an authentic Bavarian atmosphere so lacking in many postwar Munich hotels. Each mid-size guest room is beautifully and individually decorated, often with antiques from the countryside. Rooms are thoughtfully laid out; some contain French doors leading to small balconies. Bathrooms are relatively small but well maintained, each with a shower unit. The rooms at the rear on the third and fourth floors are more tranquil, although they're slightly smaller than those fronting the street.

St-Anna Strasse 10, 80538 München. ℂ **089/210-49-40.** Fax 089/21-04-94-77. www.hotel-opera.de. 25 units. 150€–210€ double; 265€–295€ suite. Rates include breakfast. AE, MC, V. Parking 21€ nearby. U-Bahn: U5 to Lehel. **Amenities:** Bar; 24-hr. room service; laundry/dry cleaning; roof garden; garden terrace. *In room:* TV, hair dryer.

INEXPENSIVE

Am Markt This popular but basic Bavarian hotel stands in the heart of the older section. You're likely to find yourself surrounded by opera and concert artists who stay here to be close to where they perform. The rooms are trim, neat, and small—space to store your stuff is at a minimum. Private bathrooms are also small, and corridor bathrooms are kept quite fresh; all with shower units.

Heiliggeiststrasse 6, D-80331 München. ℂ **089/22-50-14.** Fax 089/22-40-17. 32 units, 16 with bathroom (shower only). 68€–95€ double without bathroom; 88€–145€ double with bathroom. Rates include continental breakfast. MC, V. Parking 8€. U-Bahn/S-Bahn: Marienplatz. *In room:* TV.

Hotel Jedermann *Value* This pleasant spot's central location and value make it a good choice. It's especially good for families, as both cribs and cots are available. Rooms are generally small and old fashioned, but are cozy and comfortable. Private bathrooms with shower stalls are also small. A generous breakfast buffet is served in a charming room.

Bayerstrasse 95, D-80335 München. ℂ **089/54-32-40.** Fax 089/54-32-41-11. www.hotel-jedermann.de. 56 units. 67€–149€ double; 102€–179€ triple. Rates include buffet breakfast. MC, V. Parking 7.65€. U-Bahn/S-Bahn: Hauptbahnhof. *In room:* TV, hair dryer, private safe (in most units).

Pension Westfalia Facing the meadow where the annual Oktoberfest takes place, this town house near Goetheplatz is another of Munich's top pensions. Rooms range from small to medium, but the owner takes great pride in seeing that they are well maintained and comfortable. Private bathrooms with shower stalls are small, and corridor bathrooms are well maintained and do the job just as well.

Mozartstrasse 23, D-80336 München. ℂ **089/53-03-77.** Fax 089/54-39-120. www.pension-westfalia.de. 20 units, 14 with bathroom (shower only). 50€–55€ double without bathroom; 65€–75€ double with bathroom. Rates include buffet breakfast. AE, MC, V. Parking, when available, is free on the street. U-Bahn: Goetheplatz. Bus: 58. *In room:* TV.

Uhland Garni In a residential area, just a 10-minute walk from the Hauptbahnhof, the Uhland could easily become your home in Munich. It offers friendly, personal service. The stately town mansion, built in Art Nouveau style, stands in its own small garden. Its rooms are soundproof, snug, traditional, and cozy. The bathrooms contain shower units. Only breakfast is served.

Uhlandstrasse 1, 80336 München. ℂ **089/54-33-50.** Fax 089/54-33-52-50. www.hotel-uhland.de. 30 units. 77€–165€ double. Rates include buffet breakfast. AE, DC, MC, V. Free parking. U-Bahn/S-Bahn: Theresienwiese. Bus: 58. *In room:* TV, minibar, hair dryer, safe.

WHERE TO DINE

For beer halls serving plenty of low-priced food, see the box "What's Brewing at the Beer Halls?" later in this chapter.

VERY EXPENSIVE

Boettner's INTERNATIONAL The restaurant today is housed in Orlandohaus, a Renaissance structure in the very heart of Munich. Culinary fans from yesterday will recognize its wood-paneled interior, which was dismantled from a previous site and moved here. The cookery is lighter and more refined, and seems better than ever. Try the lobster stew in a cream sauce and almost any dish with white truffles. Pike balls appear delectably in a Chablis herb sauce, and succulent lamb or venison appear enticingly in a woodsy morel sauce. Desserts are as sumptuous as ever. The French influence is very evident, as are many traditional Bavarian recipes.

Pfisterstrasse 9. ℂ **089/22-12-10**. Reservations required. Main courses 24€–31€. AE, DC, MC, V. Summer Mon–Sat 11:30am–3pm and 6–10pm. Oct–May Mon–Sat 11:30am–10pm. U-Bahn/S-Bahn: Marienplatz.

Gasthaus Glockenbach ⟨⟩⟨⟩⟨⟩ MODERN CONTINENTAL   The setting is a 200-year-old building, close to a tributary (the Glockenbach) of the Isar. The dignified country-baroque interior is accented with vivid modern paintings and the most elegant table settings in town. Cuisine changes with the season. Examples include imaginative preparations of venison and pheasant in autumn, lamb and veal dishes in springtime, preparations of whatever shellfish is seasonal at the time, and a medley of ultrafresh vegetables and exotica imported from local farms and from sophisticated purveyors throughout Europe and the world.

Kapuzinerstrasse 29, corner of Maistrasse. ℂ **089/53-40-43**. Reservations recommended. Main courses 22€–36€; fixed-price menu 75€. AE, MC, V. Tues–Fri noon–1:30pm (last order); Tues–Sat 7–11pm (last order). Closed for 1 week at Christmas. U-Bahn: Goetheplatz.

Restaurant Königshof ⟨⟩⟨⟩ INTERNATIONAL   On the top floor of this deluxe hotel, this is Munich's best shot at hotel dining. You're rewarded not only with a fine cuisine, but with a view of the city. Appetizers are sometimes pleasantly startling in their originality, as exemplified by the delicately diminutive rib and loin chops, liver, and rolled duck in a sweet and sour ice wine, the flavor enhanced by a pumpkin vinaigrette. Instead of the typical lasagna, you get a pasta layered with morels and crayfish, a real delicacy. The city's best veal dishes are served here; veal sweetbreads rest on a bed of fresh vegetables, including beets and green beans. The wine list is one of the finest in Germany, though it may take you a good hour just to read it.

In the Hotel Königshof, Karlsplatz 25 (Am Stachus). ℂ **089/55-13-60**. Reservations required. Main courses 24€–35€; fixed-price menus 75€–98€. AE, DC, MC, V. Tues–Sat noon–2:30pm and 7–9pm. S-Bahn: Karlsplatz. Tram: 19, 20, or 21.

Tantris ⟨⟩⟨⟩⟨⟩ FRENCH/INTERNATIONAL   Tantris serves Munich's finest cuisine. Hans Haas was voted the top chef in Germany in 1994, and, if anything, he has refined and sharpened his culinary technique since. Once inside, you're transported into an ultramodern atmosphere with fine service. The food is a treat to the eye as well as to the palate. You might begin with a terrine of smoked fish served with green cucumber sauce, then follow with classic roast duck on mustard-seed sauce, or perhaps a delightful concoction of lobster medallions on black noodles. These dishes show a refinement and attention to detail that you find nowhere else in Munich. And just when you think you've had the perfect meal, the dessert arrives, and you're hungry again as you sample the gingerbread soufflé with chestnut sorbet.

Johann-Fichte-Strasse 7, Schwabing. ℂ **089/3-61-95-90**. Reservations required. Fixed-price 5-course lunch 85€; fixed-price dinner 128€ for 7 courses, 136€ for 8 courses. AE, DC, MC, V. Tues–Sat noon–2pm and 6:30–10pm. Closed public holidays; annual holidays in Jan and May. U-Bahn: Dietlindenstrasse.

EXPENSIVE

Alois Dallmayr ⟨⟩ CONTINENTAL   Munich's most famous restaurant traces its history back to 1700. Near the Rathaus, it is the best-known delicatessen in all of Germany. The upstairs dining room serves a subtle German version of Continental cuisine, owing a heavy debt to France. The food array is dazzling, ranging from the best herring and sausages we've ever tasted to such rare treats as perfectly vine-ripened tomatoes flown in from Morocco, and papayas from Brazil. Also shipped in is the famous French *poulet de Bresse,* believed by many gourmets to be the world's finest.

Dienerstrasse 14–15. ✆ **089/213-51-00.** Reservations required. Main courses 22€–28€. AE, DC, MC, V. Mon–Wed 9:30am–7pm; Thurs–Fri 9:30am–8pm; Sat 9am–3pm. Tram: 19.

Spatenhaus ✿ BAVARIAN/INTERNATIONAL One of Munich's best-known beer restaurants has wide windows overlooking the opera house on Max-Joseph-Platz. Of course, to be loyal, you should accompany your meal with the restaurant's own beer, Spaten-Franziskaner-Bier. You can sit in an intimate, semiprivate dining nook or at a big table. The Spatenhaus has old traditions, offers typical Bavarian food, and is known for generous portions and reasonable prices. If you want to know what all this fabled Bavarian gluttony is about, order the "Bavarian plate," which is loaded down with various meats, including lots of pork and sausages.

Residenzstrasse 12. ✆ **089/290-70-60.** Reservations recommended. Main courses 13€–25€. AE, MC, V. Daily 10:30am–2:30pm and 5:30pm–midnight. U-Bahn: Odeonsplatz or Marienplatz.

MODERATE

Buon Gusto (Talamonti) ✿ ITALIAN Some of Munich's best Italian food is served here in the rustic-looking bistro, or in the more formal and more upscale-looking dining room. Menu items and prices are identical in both. Owned and managed by an extended family, the Talamontis, the restaurant emphasizes fresh ingredients, strong and savory flavors, and food items inspired by the Italian Marches and Tuscany. Stellar examples include ravioli stuffed with mushrooms and herbs, roasted lamb with potatoes, lots of scaloppine, and fresh fish that seems to taste best when served simply, with oil or butter and lemon. Especially appealing are the array of risottos whose ingredients change with the seasons. During Oktoberfest and trade fairs, the place is mobbed.

Hochbruckenstrasse 3. ✆ **089/296-383.** Reservations recommended. Main courses 15€–21€. AE, MC, V. Tues–Sat 11am–11pm. Closed Dec 23–Jan 3. U-Bahn/S-Bahn: Marienplatz.

Der Tisch ✿ MEDITERRANEAN Its minimalist name, "the table," doesn't suggest the allure of this bistro, one of the best and most fashionable in Munich. You can stop in for a pre-dinner beer at the Münchener Lowenbrau brewery and beer hall across the street before heading to this 36-seat dining room. Presented on a clipboard, the daily-changing menu is eclectic and well chosen. The cookery is resolutely contemporary—start with the eggplant mousse with a perfectly balanced tomato vinaigrette or something simpler: tuna flavored with tomato sauce and accompanied by olives and capers. The main courses are always imaginative and satisfying, especially the pikeperch on a mound of cabbage, sprinkled with a beet-flavored pink sauce. In autumn, opt for venison in a red-wine sauce.

Maxvorstadt, Nymphenburger Strasse 1. ✆ **089/557-154.** Reservations required. Main courses 12€–25€. AE DC, MC, V. Mon–Fri 11:30am–2:30pm and 6pm–midnight. U-Bahn: Stiglmeier Platz.

Hunsiger's Pacific ✿ SEAFOOD Despite the name, don't expect the menu to be devoted exclusively to Pacific Rim cuisine. Fish is the premier item here. Preparation is based on classic French-inspired methods, but the innovative flavors come from Malaysia (coconut milk), Japan (wasabi), Thailand (lemon grass), and India (curry). You could begin with a tuna carpaccio with sliced plum, fresh ginger, and lime. Main courses include a succulent version of bouillabaisse with aioli, which you might follow with cold melon soup garnished with a dollop of tarragon-flavored granita. Fried monkfish in the Malaysian style and turbot in chile and ginger sauce are evocative of Hawaii. Prices here are relatively low compared to those of its competitors.

Maximiliansplatz 5 (entrance on Max-Joseph-Strasse). (C) **089/5502-9741.** Main courses 18€–40€. AE, DC, MC, V. Mon–Sat noon–3pm and 6–11pm. Closed Sun May–Sept. U-Bahn: Stachus/Odeonsplatz.

Pfistermühle BAVARIAN   The country comes right into the heart of Munich at this authentic and old-fashioned place. A warm welcome and a refreshing cuisine await you here. Many of the dishes would be familiar to your Bavarian grandmother, and portions are generous and most satisfying. Come here for some of the most perfectly prepared roasts in the city. You can also opt for a fine array of fresh fish from the lakes and rivers of Bavaria, especially the delectable salmon trout or brown trout. Most fish dishes come with chive-flecked sour cream and a potato pancake. The fish is also simply prepared, such as pikeperch sautéed in butter. Finish with a pyramid of vanilla custard served with a fresh berry sauce, followed by a glass of wild cherry schnapps.

In the Platz Hotel, Pfistermühle 4. (C) **089/2370-3865.** Reservations recommended. Main courses 13€–20€; set menus 34€–45€. AE, DC, MC, V. Mon–Sat noon–midnight. U-Bahn: Marienplatz.

Ratskeller München BAVARIAN   Go here for the old Bavarian ambience at one of the best town hall cellars in the country. The decor is typical: lots of dark wood and carved chairs. The most interesting tables, the ones staked out by in-the-know locals, are the semiprivate dining nooks in the rear, under the vaulted painted ceilings. Bavarian music adds to the ambience. The menu, a showcase of regional fare, includes many vegetarian choices, which is unusual for a rathskeller. Some of the dishes are a little heavy and too porky, but you can find lighter fare if you search the menu.

Im Rathaus, Marienplatz 8. (C) **089/219-98-90.** Reservations required. Main courses 9€–22€. AE, MC, V. Daily 10am–midnight. U-Bahn/S-Bahn: Marienplatz.

INEXPENSIVE

Andechser am Dom GERMAN   Set on two floors of a postwar building erected adjacent to the back side of the Frauenkirche, this restaurant and beer hall serves copious amounts of a beer brewed in a monastery near Munich (Andechser) as well as generous portions of German food. Order a snack, a full meal, or just a beer, and enjoy the frothy fun of it all. Menu items include such dishes as veal schnitzels, steaks, turkey croquettes, roasted lamb, fish, and several kinds of sausages that taste best with tangy mustard. During clement weather, tables are set up on the building's roof and on the sidewalk in front, both of which overlook the back of one of the city's most evocative churches.

Weinstrasse 7A. (C) **089/29-84-81.** Reservations recommended. Main courses 10€–18€. AE, DC, MC, V. Daily 10am–1am. U-Bahn/S-Bahn: Marienplatz.

Donisl BAVARIAN/INTERNATIONAL   This is one of Munich's oldest beer halls, dating from 1715. The seating capacity of this relaxed and comfortable restaurant is about 550, and in summer you can enjoy the hum and bustle of Marienplatz while dining in the garden area out front. The standard menu offers traditional Bavarian food, as well as a weekly changing specials menu. The little white sausages, Weisswürst, are a decades-long tradition here.

Weinstrasse 1. (C) **089/22-01-84.** Reservations recommended. Main courses 7€–12€. AE, DC, MC, V. Daily 9am–midnight. U-Bahn/S-Bahn: Marienplatz.

Hundskugel BAVARIAN   The city's oldest tavern, Hundskugel dates back to 1440, and apparently serves the same food as it did back then. If it was good a long time ago, why mess with the menu? Built in an alpine style, the tavern is within easy walking distance of Marienplatz. Perhaps half the residents of Munich have at one time or another made their way here to enjoy the honest Bavarian cookery that has no pretensions. Although the chef specializes in *Spanferkel* (roast suckling pig with potato noodles), you might prefer *Tafelspitz* (boiled beef) in dill sauce, or roast veal stuffed with goose liver.

Hotterstrasse 18. ℂ **089/26-42-72.** Reservations required. Main courses 9.10€–20€. No credit cards. Daily 11am–midnight. U-Bahn/S-Bahn: Marienplatz.

Nürnberger Bratwurst Glöckl Am Dom BAVARIAN   In the coziest and warmest of Munich's local restaurants, the chairs look as if they were made by some Black Forest woodcarver, and the place is full of memorabilia—pictures, prints, pewter, and beer steins. Upstairs through a hidden stairway is a dining room decorated with reproductions of Dürer prints. The restaurant has a strict policy of shared tables, and service is on tin plates. The homesick Nürnberger comes here just for one dish: *Nürnberger Schweinwurstl mit Kraut* (little sausages with kraut). Last food orders go in at midnight.

Frauenplatz 9. ℂ **089/29-52-64.** Reservations recommended. Main courses 8€–22€. No credit cards. Daily 10am–1am. U-Bahn/S-Bahn: Marienplatz.

SEEING THE SIGHTS
SIGHTSEEING SUGGESTIONS FOR FIRST-TIME VISITORS

If You Have 1 Day Local tourist tradition calls for a morning breakfast of Weisswürst; head for **Donisl** (see "Where to Dine," above). A true Münchener downs them with a mug of beer. Then walk to **Marienplatz,** with its glockenspiel and **Altes Rathaus (Old Town Hall).** Later, stroll along **Maximilianstrasse,** one of Europe's great shopping streets. In the afternoon, visit the **Neue Pinakothek** and see at least some exhibits at the **Deutsches Museum.** Cap the evening with a night of Bavarian food, beer, and music at the **Hofbräuhaus am Platzl.**

If You Have 2 Days In the morning of day 2, visit the **Bayerisches Nationalmuseum (Bavarian National Museum),** with three vast floors devoted to Bavaria's artistic and historical riches. If the weather's right, plan a lunch in one of the beer gardens of the **Englischer Garten.** In the afternoon, visit the **Nymphenburg Palace,** summer residence of the Wittelsbach dynasty, longtime rulers of Bavaria.

If You Have 3 Days Pass your third day exploring the sights you've missed so far: the **Residenz,** the **Antikensammlungen (Museum of Antiquities),** and the **Glyptothek.** If you have any more time, return to the Deutsches Museum. Enjoy dinner or at least a drink at **Olympiapark,** along with a panoramic view of the Alps.

If You Have 4 or More Days As fascinating as Munich is, tear yourself away on day 4 for an excursion to the **Royal Castles** once occupied by the "mad king" Ludwig II (see "Organized Tours," below and "The Romantic Road," later in this chapter). On day 5, take an excursion to **Dachau,** the notorious World War II concentration camp, and in the afternoon visit **Mittenwald** for a taste of the Bavarian Alps.

EXPLORING THE ALTSTADT (OLD TOWN)

Marienplatz, dedicated to the patron of the city whose statue stands on a huge column in the center of the square, is the heart of the Altstadt. On its north side is the **Neues Rathaus (New City Hall)** built in 19th-century Gothic style. Each day at 11am, and also at noon and 5pm in the summer, the **Glockenspiel** on the facade performs a miniature tournament, with enameled copper figures moving in and out of the archways. Since you're already at the Rathaus, you may wish to climb the 55 steps to the top of its tower (an elevator is available if you're conserving energy) for a good overall view of the city center. The **Altes Rathaus (Old City Hall),** with its plain Gothic tower, is to the right. It was reconstructed in the 15th century, after being destroyed by fire.

MUSEUMS & PALACES

Alte Pinakothek ★★★   This is one of the most significant art museums in Europe. The paintings represent the greatest European artists of the 14th through the 18th centuries. Begun as a small court collection by the royal Wittelsbach family in the early 1500s, the collection has grown and grown. There are two floors with exhibits, but the museum is immense. Albrecht Altdorfer, landscape painter par excellence of the Danube school, is represented by no fewer than six monumental works. Albrecht Dürer's works include his greatest—and final—*Self-Portrait* (1500). Here the artist has portrayed himself with almost Christ-like solemnity. Also displayed is the last great painting by the artist, his two-paneled work called *The Four Apostles* (1526).

Barer Strasse 27. ⓒ **089/238-050-216.** Admission 5€ adults, 3.50€ students, free for children 15 and under. Combination ticket to Neue Pinakothek, Alte Pinakothek, Pinakothek der Moderne, and Schack-Galerie, 12€ adults, 7€ students and seniors, free for children 15 and under. Tues and Thurs 10am–8pm; Wed, Fri, Sat, Sun 10am–5pm. U-Bahn: Theresienstrasse. Tram: 27. Bus: 53.

Bayerisches Nationalmuseum (Bavarian National Museum) ★★   Three vast floors of sculpture, painting, folk art, ceramics, furniture, textiles, and scientific instruments demonstrate Bavaria's artistic and historical riches. Entering the museum, turn to the right and go into the first large gallery, called the **Wessobrunn Room.** Devoted to early church art from the 5th to the 13th centuries, this room holds some of the oldest and most valuable works. The desk case contains ancient and medieval ivories, including the so-called Munich ivory, from about A.D. 400. The **Riemenschneider Room** is devoted to the works of the great sculptor Tilman Riemenschneider (ca. 1460–1531) and his contemporaries. The second floor contains a fine collection of stained and painted glass—an art in which medieval Germany excelled—baroque ivory carvings, Meissen porcelain, and ceramics.

Prinzregentenstrasse 3. ⓒ **089/211-2401.** Admission 3.05€ adults, 2€ students and seniors, free for children under 15. Free on Sun. Tues–Sun 10am–5pm. U-Bahn: Lehel. Tram: 17. Bus: 53.

Deutsches Museum (German Museum of Masterpieces of Science and Technology) ★★★
On an island in the Isar River is the largest technological museum of its kind in the world. Its huge collection of priceless artifacts and historic originals includes the first electric dynamo (Siemens, 1866), the first automobile (Benz, 1886), the first diesel engine (1897), and the laboratory bench at which the atom was first split (Hahn, Strassmann, 1938). There are hundreds of buttons to push, levers to crank, and gears to turn, as well as a knowledgeable staff to answer questions and demonstrate how steam engines, pumps, or historical musical instruments work. Among the most popular displays are those on mining, with a series of model coal, salt, and iron mines, as well as the electrical

power hall, with high-voltage displays that actually produce lightning. There are many other exhibits, covering the whole range of science and technology.

Museumsinsel 1. ℂ **089/2-17-91.** Admission 7.50€ adults, 5€ seniors, 3€ students, free for children 6 and under. Daily 9am–5pm (closes at 2pm the 2nd Wed in Dec). Closed major holidays. S-Bahn: Isartor. Tram: 18.

Glyptothek ☆   The Glyptothek supplements the pottery and smaller pieces of the main museum with an excellent collection of ancient Greek and Roman sculpture. Included are the famous pediments from the temple of Aegina, two marvelous statues of *kouroi* (youths) from the 6th century B.C., the colossal figure of a *Sleeping Satyr* from the Hellenistic period, and a splendid collection of Roman portraits.

Königsplatz 3. ℂ **089/28-61-00.** Admission 3.05€ adults, 1.80€ students and seniors, 1.55€ children. Combination ticket to the Museum of Antiquities and the Glyptothek, 5.10€ adults, 2.55€ students and children, free for children under 14. Tues–Sun 10am–5pm. U-Bahn: Königsplatz.

Neue Pinakothek ☆☆   This gallery is a showcase of Munich's most valuable 18th- and 19th-century art, an artistic period that was hardly the Renaissance but has its artistic devotees nonetheless. Across Theresienstrasse from the Alte Pinakothek, the museum has paintings by Gainsborough, Goya, David, Manet, van Gogh, and Monet. Among the more popular German artists represented are Wilhelm Leibl and Gustav Klimt. Note particularly the genre paintings by Carl Spitzweg.

Barer Strasse 29. ℂ **089/23-80-51-95.** Admission 5€ adults, 3.50€ students and seniors, free for children 15 and under. Combination ticket to Neue Pinakothek, Alte Pinakothek, Pinakothek der Moderne, and Schack-Galerie 12€ adults, 7€ students and seniors, free for children 15 and under. Mon 10am–5pm; Thurs 10am–10pm; Wed–Sun 10am–5pm. U-Bahn: Theresienstrasse. Tram: 27. Bus: 53.

Pinakothek der Moderne ☆☆   In 2002, one of the world's largest museums devoted to the visual arts of the 19th and 20th centuries opened in Munich, just minutes from the Alte and Neue Pinakothek. Four major collections have been brought together under one roof, making this the most vast display of fine and applied arts in the country. It's Munich's version of the Tate Gallery in London or the Pompidou in Paris.

Wander where your interest dictates: the **Staatsgalerie Moderner Kunst (State Gallery of Modern Art)** ☆☆☆, with paintings, sculpture, photography, and video; **Die Neue Sammlung,** which constitutes the national museum of applied art featuring design and craftwork; the **Architekturmuseum der Technischen Universität (University of Architecture Museum),** with architectural drawings, photographs, and models; and the **Staatliche Grapische Sammlung,** with its outstanding collection of prints and drawings.

Whenever we visit, we spend most of our time in the modern art collection, lost in a world of some of our favorite artists: Picasso, Magritte, Klee, Kandinsky, even Francis Bacon, de Kooning, and Warhol. The museum also owns 400,000 drawings and prints from Leonardo da Vinci to Cézanne up to contemporary artists. They are presented as alternating exhibits.

The architectural galleries hold the largest specialist collection of its kind in Germany, comprising some 350,000 drawings, 100,000 photographs, and 500 models. The applied arts section features more than 50,000 items. You go from the beginnings of the Industrial Revolution up to today's computer culture, with exhibitions of Art Nouveau and Bauhaus along the way.

Barerstrasse 40. ℂ **089/23805-118.** Admission 10€ adults, 6€ students and ages 17 and under. Tues–Sun 10am–5pm. Combination ticket to Neue Pinakothek, Alte Pinakothek, Pinakothek der Moderne, and Schack-Galerie 12€ adults, 7€ students and seniors, free for children 15 and under. U-Bahn: Odeonsplatz.

Residenz ⚲ The official residence of Bavaria's rulers from 1385 to 1918, the complex is a conglomerate of various styles of art and architecture. Depending on how you approach the Residenz, you might first see a German Renaissance hall (the western facade), a Palladian palace (on the north), or a Florentine Renaissance palace (on the south facing Max-Joseph-Platz). The Residenz has been completely restored since its almost total destruction in World War II and now houses the Residenz Museum, a concert hall, the Cuvilliés Theater, and the Residenz Treasure House.

Residenzmuseum comprises the southwestern section of the palace, some 120 rooms of art and furnishings collected by centuries of Wittelsbachs. There are two guided tours, one in the morning and the other in the afternoon, or you may visit the rooms on your own.

If you have time to view only one item in the **Schatzkammer (Treasure House)** ⚲⚲, make it the 16th-century Renaissance statue of *St. George Slaying the Dragon.* The equestrian statue is made of gold, but you can barely see the precious metal for the thousands of diamonds, rubies, emeralds, sapphires, and semiprecious stones embedded in it.

From the Brunnenhof, you can visit the **Cuvilliés Theater** ⚲, whose rococo tiers of boxes are supported by seven bacchants. The huge box, where the family sat, is in the center. In summer, this theater is the scene of frequent concert and opera performances. Mozart's *Idomeneo* was first performed here in 1781.

Max-Joseph-Platz 3. ✆ **089/29-06-71.** Combination ticket for Residenzmuseum and Schatzkammer 7.15€ adults, 3.05€ students/seniors, free for ages 15 and under. Ticket for either Schatzkammer or Residenzmuseum 4.10€ adults, 2.55€ seniors/students, free for ages 16 and under. Daily 10am–4pm. U-Bahn: Odeonsplatz.

Schack-Galerie To appreciate this florid and romantic overdose of sentimental German paintings of the 19th century, you've got to enjoy fauns and elves at play in picturesque, even magical, landscapes. Such art has its devotees. Obviously, if you're a Picasso Cubist, you'd be better off going elsewhere. But this once-private collection adheres to the baroque tastes of Count Adolf Friedrich von Schack of Schwerin (1815–94), who spent a rich life acquiring works by the likes of Spitzweg, Schwind, Fuerbach, and others, many others, some of whom frankly should have been assigned to the dustbin of art history. Still, in all, we find a visit here fun, at least on a rainy, gray day. It's like wandering back to a lost world and getting absorbed in the taste of yesterday.

Prinzregentenstrasse 9. ✆ **089/23805-224.** Admission 5€ adults, 3.50€ children. Combination ticket to Neue Pinakothek, Alte Pinakothek, Pinakothek der Moderne, and Schack-Galerie 12€ adults, 7€ students and seniors, free for children 15 and under.

Schloss Nymphenburg ⚲⚲ In summer, the Wittelsbachs would pack up their bags and head for their country house, Schloss Nymphenburg. A more complete, more sophisticated palace than the Residenz, it was begun in 1664 in Italian villa style and went through several architectural changes before completion.

The main building's great hall, decorated in rococo colors and stuccos with frescoes by Zimmermann (1756), was used for both banquets and concerts. Concerts are still presented here in summer. From the main building, turn left and head for the arcaded gallery connecting the northern pavilions. The first room in the arcade is the Great Gallery of Beauties. More provocative, however, is Ludwig I's Gallery of Beauties in the south pavilion (the apartments of Queen Caroline). Ludwig commissioned no fewer than 36 portraits of the most beautiful women of his day. The paintings by J. Stieler include the *Schöne Münchnerin*

(Lovely Munich Girl) and a portrait of Lola Montez, the dancer whose "friendship" with Ludwig I caused a scandal that factored into the Revolution of 1848.

To the south of the palace buildings, in the rectangular block of low structures that once housed the court stables, is the **Marstallmuseum.** In the first hall, look for the glass coronation coach of Elector Karl Albrecht, built in Paris in 1740. From the same period comes the elaborate hunting sleigh of Electress Amalia, adorned with a statue of Diana, goddess of the hunt; even the sleigh's runners are decorated with shellwork and hunting trophies. The coaches and sleighs of Ludwig II are displayed in the third hall.

One of Nymphenburg's greatest attractions is the **park** 🎔. Stretching for 200 hectares (500 acres) in front of the palace, it's divided into two sections by the canal that runs from the pool at the foot of the staircase to the cascade at the far end of the English-style gardens.

Within the park are a number of pavilions. The guided tour begins with **Amalienburg** 🎔🎔, whose plain exterior belies the rococo decoration inside. Built as a hunting lodge for Electress Amalia (in 1734), the pavilion carries the hunting theme through the first few rooms and then bursts into salons of flamboyant colors, rich carvings, and wall paintings. The most impressive room is the Hall of Mirrors, a symphony of silver ornaments on a faint blue background.

Other attractions include the **Porzellansammlung,** or museum of porcelain, which is above the stables of the Marstallmuseum. Some of the finest pieces of porcelain in the world, executed in the 18th century, are displayed here, along with an absolute gem—extraordinarily detailed miniature porcelain reproductions of some of the grand masterpieces in the Old Pinakothek, each commissioned by Ludwig I.

The **Botanischer Garten (Botanical Gardens)** 🎔🎔 is among the most richly planted in Europe. It's worth a spring trip to Munich for garden lovers to see this great mass of vegetation burst into bloom.

Schloss Nymphenburg 1. ℂ **089/17-908-668.** Admission to all attractions 7.65€ adults, free for children 6 and under. Separate admissions: 3.60€ Schloss Nymphenburg or 2.55€ to either Marstallmuseum, Amalienburg, or Porzellansammlung; free for children 15 and under. Mon–Fri 8am–6pm. Parking beside the Marstallmuseum. U-Bahn: Rotkreuzplatz, then tram 17 to Botanischergarten. Bus: 41.

CHURCHES

When the smoke cleared from the 1945 bombings, only a fragile shell remained of Munich's largest church, the **Frauenkirche (Cathedral of Our Lady)** 🎔, Frauenplatz 1 (ℂ **089/290-08-20;** U-Bahn/S-Bahn: Marienplatz). Workers and architects who restored the 15th-century Gothic cathedral used whatever remains they could find in the rubble, along with modern innovations. The overall effect of the rebuilt Frauenkirche is strikingly simple yet dignified. The twin towers, which remained intact, have been a city landmark since 1525. Instead of the typical flying buttresses, huge props on the inside that separate the side chapels support the edifice. The Gothic vaulting over the nave and chancel is borne by 22 simple octagonal pillars. Except for the tall chancel window, when you enter the main doors at the west end, you don't notice windows; they're hidden by the enormous pillars. According to legend, the devil laughed at the notion of hidden windows and stamped in glee at the stupidity of the architect—you can still see the strange footlike mark called "the devil's step" in the entrance hall.

Peterskirche (St. Peter's Church), Rindermarkt 1 (ℂ **089/260-48-28;** U-Bahn/S-Bahn: Marienplatz), is Munich's oldest church (1180). Its tall steeple is worth the climb in clear weather for a view as far as the Alps. In its gilded baroque interior are murals by Johann Baptist Zimmermann. The **Asamkirche** 🎔,

Sendlinger Strasse (U-Bahn/S-Bahn: Sendlingertor), is a remarkable example of rococo, designed by the Asam brothers, Cosmas Damian and Edgar Quirin, in 1733 to 1746. The **Michaelskirche,** Neuhauser Strasse 52 (U-Bahn/S-Bahn: Karlsplatz), has the distinction of being the largest Renaissance church north of the Alps. The lovely **Theatinerkirche,** Theatinerstrasse 22 (U-Bahn/S-Bahn: Odeonsplatz), with its graceful fluted columns and arched ceilings, is the work of the court architect, François Cuvilliés and his son.

ORGANIZED TOURS

The easiest, and fastest, ways to gain an overview of Munich is on a guided tour. One of the largest organizers of these is **Panorama Tours** (an affiliate of Gray Line), Arnulfstrasse 8 (© 089/550-28995; U-Bahn/S-Bahn: Hauptbahnhof), just north of the Hauptbahnhof. At least a half-dozen touring options are available, ranging from a quickie 1-hour overview of the city to full-day excursions to such outlying sites as Berchtesgaden, Oberammergau, and Hohenschwangau, site of three of Bavaria's most stunning palaces.

City tours encompass aspects of both modern and medieval Munich, and depart from the main railway station aboard blue-sided buses. Departures, depending on the season and the tour, occur between two and eight times a day, and tours are conducted in both German and English. Most tours don't last more than 2½ hours, with the exception of a scientific odyssey that focuses on the technological triumphs of Munich as witnessed by various museums that include the Deutsches Museum. That experience usually lasts for a minimum of 4 hours, plus whatever time you spend wandering through museums at the end of your tour.

Depending on the tour, adults pay 11€ to 23€; children under 14 pay 6€ to 12€. Advance reservations for most city tours aren't required, and you can buy your ticket from the bus driver at the time you board.

If you want to participate in any tour that covers attractions outside the city limits, advance reservations are required, especially if you want the bus to pick you up at any of Munich's hotels. Travel agents in Munich, as well as the concierge or reception staff at your hotel, can book any of these tours, but if you want to contact Panorama Tours directly, they're open year-round Monday to Friday 9am to 6pm and Saturday 9am to 1pm.

Pedal pushers will want to try Mike Lasher's **Mike's Bike Tour** (© 089/651-4275; www.mikesbiketours.com). His bike rentals for 22€ include maps and locks, child and infant seats, and helmets at no extra charge. English and bilingual tours of central Munich run from March to November, leaving daily at 12:30pm (call to confirm). The cost of the tour is included in the rental fee.

THE SHOPPING SCENE

The most interesting shops are concentrated on Munich's pedestrians-only streets between **Karlsplatz** and **Marienplatz.**

Handmade crafts can be found on the fourth floor of Munich's major department store, **Ludwig Beck am Rathauseck,** Am Marienplatz 11 (© 089/236-910; U-Bahn/S-Bahn: Marienplatz). **Wallach,** Residenzstrasse 3 (© 089/22-08-71; U-Bahn/S-Bahn: Odeonplatz), is a fine place to obtain handcrafts and folk art, both new and antique. Shop here for a memorable object to remind you of your trip. You'll find antique churns, old hand-painted wooden boxes and trays, painted porcelain clocks, and many other items.

Dirndl-Ecke, Am Platzl 1/Sparkassenstrasse 10 (© 089/22-01-63; U-Bahn/S-Bahn: Marienplatz), 1 block up from the famed Hofbräuhaus, gets our unreserved recommendation as a stylish place specializing in dirndls, feathered alpine hats, and all the clothing associated with the alpine regions. Everything is of the best quality—there's no tourist junk. Bavarian clothing for children is also available.

On the grounds of Schloss Nymphenburg at Nördliches Schlossrondell 8, you'll find **Nymphenburger Porzellan-manufaktur** (© **089/17-91-970;** U-Bahn: Rotkreuzplatz, then tram no. 17 toward Amalienburgstrasse; bus: 41), one of Germany's most famous porcelain makers. You can visit the exhibition and sales rooms; shipments can be arranged if you make purchases. There's also a branch in Munich's center, at Odeonsplatz 1 (© **089/28-24-28;** U-Bahn/ S-Bahn: Odeonplatz).

MUNICH AFTER DARK

To find out what's happening in the Bavarian capital, go to the tourist office and buy a copy of "Monats-programm." This pamphlet contains complete information about what's going on in Munich and how to purchase tickets.

THE PERFORMING ARTS

Nowhere else in Europe, other than London and Paris, will you find so many musical and theatrical performances. And the good news is the low cost of the seats—you'll get good tickets if you're willing to pay anywhere from 10€ to 43€.

A part of the Residenz (see "Museums & Palaces," earlier), **Altes Residenztheater (Cuvilliés Theater),** Residenzstrasse 1 (© **089/2185-19-40;** U-Bahn: Odeonsplatz), is a sightseeing attraction in its own right, and Germany's most outstanding example of a rococo tier-boxed theater. During World War II, the interior was dismantled and stored. You can tour it Tuesday through Friday from 2 to 4pm and Sunday from 11am to 5pm. **Bavarian State Opera** and the **Bayerisches Staatsschauspiel (State Theater Company;** © **089/2185-1920)** perform smaller works here in keeping with the tiny theater's intimate character. Box-office hours are Monday through Friday from 10am to 6pm, plus 1 hour before performances; Saturday from 10am to 1pm only. Opera tickets are 15€ to 130€; theater tickets 10€ to 51€; building tours 2.55€.

The regular season of the **Deutsches Theater,** Schwanthalerstrasse 13 (© **089/552-34-444;** www.deutsches-theater.de; U-Bahn: Karlsplatz/Stachus), lasts year-round. Musicals, operettas, ballets, and international shows are performed here. During carnival season (Jan–Feb) the theater becomes a ballroom for more than 2,000 guests. Tickets are 18€ to 51€, higher for special events.

Gasteig München GmbH, Rosenheimer Strasse 5 (© **089/48-09-80;** www.gasteig.de; S-Bahn: Rosenheimerplatz; tram: 18; bus: 51), is the home of the **Münchner Philharmoniker** (www.muenchnerphilharmoniker.de), founded in 1893. Its present home opened in 1985 and shelters the Richard Strauss Conservatory and the Munich Municipal Library. The orchestra performs in Philharmonic Hall. Purchase tickets Monday through Friday from 9am to 6pm, Saturday from 9am to 2pm, for 10€ to 51€. The Philharmonic season runs mid-September to July.

Practically any night of the year, except from August to mid-September, you'll find a performance at the **Nationaltheater,** Max-Joseph-Platz 2 (© **089/21-85-01;** www.staatstheater.bayern.de; U-Bahn/S-Bahn: Marienplatz or Odeonsplatz), home of the **Bavarian State Opera,** one of the world's great opera companies. The productions are beautifully mounted and presented, and sung by famous singers. Hard-to-get tickets may be purchased Monday through Friday from 10am to 6pm, plus 1 hour before performance; Saturday from 10am to 1pm. The Nationaltheater is also home to the **Bavarian State Ballet.** Opera tickets are 13€ to 240€; ballet tickets, 7.65€ to 66€.

THE CLUB & MUSIC SCENE

You'll find some of Munich's most sophisticated entertainment at **Bayerischer Hof Night Club,** in the Hotel Bayerischer Hof, Promenadeplatz 2–6 (© **089/ 212-00;** tram: 19). Within one very large room is a piano bar where a musician plays melodies every night except Monday from 7 to 10pm. Behind a partition that disappears at 10pm, there's a bandstand for live orchestras, which play to a crowd of dancing patrons until 3 or 4am. The piano bar is free, but there's a nightclub cover charge of 10€ to 20€. Daily happy hour is from 7 to 8:30pm in the piano bar.

Jazzclub Unterfahrt, Einsteinstrasse 42 (© **089/448-27-94;** U-Bahn/ S-Bahn: Ostbahnhof), is Munich's leading jazz club, lying near the Ostbahnhof in the Haidhausen district. The club presents live music Tuesday through Sunday from 8:30pm to 1am (it opens at 8pm). Wine, small snacks, beer, and drinks are sold as well. Sunday night there's a special jam session for improvisation. Cover from Tuesday to Saturday is 9.20€ to 14€, Sunday jam session 15€. Club members pay half the regular cover. Small, dark, and popular with blues and jazz aficionados, **Mister B's,** Herzog-Heinrichstrasse 38 (© **089/534901;** U-Bahn: Goetheplatz), hosts a slightly older, mellower crowd than the rock and dance clubs. It's open Tuesday through Sunday from 8pm to 3am. Blues, jazz, and rhythm-and-blues combos take the stage Thursday through Saturday. Cover is 5€ to 7.50€.

Set in a huge factory warehouse, **Nachtwerk,** Landesbergerstrasse 185 (© **089/578-3800;** S-Bahn: Donnersbergerbrücke), is a mostly straight dance club that also books bands. It's a festive place that's not nearly as pretentious as other more "exclusive" discos (the doorman won't send you away for wearing the wrong shoes or pants). The club is open Thursday from 10pm to 4am; Friday and Saturday from 10:30pm. Cover is 6.15€.

Parkcafé, Sophienstrasse 7 (© **089/59-83-13;** U-Bahn: Lebachplatz), contains three distinct subdivisions, each catering to the food, beverage, and socializing needs of the young, the restless, and the occasionally cutting-edge residents of Munich. Come here for a drink, snack, or coffee at the **Parkcafé,** and perhaps extend the venue into a full meal at the immediately adjacent premises of the **Parkcafé Kitchen.** Both are open Sunday through Thursday from 10am to 1am; Friday and Saturday from 10am to 6pm. And if you're in the mood to dance, surrounded by nocturnal denizens of Munich who might be dressed in Teutonic punk or leather and perhaps heavily pierced, come here every night of the week from 11pm to 4am for access to the **Parkcafé Club,** where hipster music blares and entrance costs from 8€ to 11€, depending on the night of the week.

THE BAR & CAFE SCENE

Once a literary cafe, **Alter Simpl,** Türkenstrasse 57 (© **089/272-30-83;** U-Bahn: University), attracts a diverse crowd of locals, including young people. The real fun begins after 11pm, when the iconoclastic artistic ferment becomes more reminiscent of Berlin than Bavaria. It's open Sunday through Thursday from 11am to 3am, Friday and Saturday from 11am to 4am.

Nachtcafé, Maximilianplatz 5 (© **089/59-59-00;** tram: 19), hums, thrives, and captures the nocturnal imagination of everyone—no other nightspot in Munich attracts such an array of soccer stars, film celebrities, literary figures,

What's Brewing at the Beer Halls?

The world's most famous beer hall, **Hofbraühaus am Platzl,** Am Platzl 9 (© **089/22-16-76;** U-Bahn/S-Bahn: Marienplatz), is a legend. Visitors with only 1 night in Munich usually target the Hofbräuhaus as their top nighttime destination. Owned by the state, the present Hofbräuhaus was built at the end of the 19th century, but the tradition of a beer house on this spot dates from 1589. In the 19th century it attracted artists, students, and civil servants and was known as the Blue Hall because of its dim lights and smoky atmosphere. When it grew too small to contain everybody, architects designed another in 1897. This one was the 1920 setting for the notorious meeting of Hitler's newly launched German Workers Party. Today, 4,500 beer drinkers can crowd in on a given night. Several rooms are spread over three floors, including a top-floor room for dancing. The ground floor, with its brass band (which starts playing at 11am), is exactly what you'd expect of a beer hall—here it's eternal Oktoberfest. It's open daily from 10am to midnight.

In a century-old house northwest of Schwabing at the edge of Luitpold Park, **Bamberger Haus,** Brunnerstrasse 2 (© **089/308-89-66;** U-Bahn: Scheidplatz), is named after the city most noted for the quantity of beer its residents drink. Bavarian and international specialties served in the street-level restaurant include well-seasoned soups, grilled steak, veal, pork, and sausages. If you only want to drink, visit the rowdier and less expensive beer hall in the cellar, where a large beer is 2.80€ to 3.30€. The restaurant is open daily noon to midnight and the

and, as one employee put it, "ordinary people, but only the most sympathetically crazy ones." Waves of patrons appear at different times of the evening: at 11pm, when live concerts begin; at 2am, when the restaurants close; and at 4am, when die-hard revelers seek a final drink in the predawn hours. The music is jazz, blues, funk, and soul, and the decor is updated 1950s. There's a cover only rarely and for special entertainment. It's open daily from 9pm to 6am.

Schumann's, Maximilianstrasse 36 (© **089/22-90-60;** tram: 19), doesn't waste any money on decor—it depends on the local *beau monde* to keep it looking chic. In warm weather the terrace spills onto the street. Schumann's is known as a "thinking man's bar." Charles Schumann, author of three bar books, wanted a bar that would be an artistic, literary, and communicative social focus of the metropolis. Popular with the film, advertising, and publishing worlds, his place is said to have contributed to a remarkable renaissance of bar culture in the city. It's open Sunday from 6pm to 3am, Monday through Friday from 5pm to 3am; closed on Saturday.

GAY & LESBIAN CLUBS

Much of Munich's gay and lesbian scene takes place in the blocks between the Viktualienmarkt and Gärtnerplatz, particularly on Hans-Sachs-Strasse.

A virtual communications center of gay and lesbian Munich, the **Stadtcafe,** St. Jakobsplatz 1 (© **089/266-949;** U-Bahn: Marienplatz), attracts creative people, often in the arts. By Munich nightlife standards, it closes relatively early;

beer hall daily 5pm to 1am; in summer, weather permitting, a beer garden is open daily from 11am to 11pm.

Englischer Garten, the park between the Isar River and Schwabing, is the biggest city-owned park in Europe. It has a main restaurant and several beer gardens, of which the **Biergärten Chinesischer Turm,** Englischer Garten 3 (© **089/38-38-730;** U-Bahn: Giselastrasse), is our favorite. It takes its name from its location at the foot of a pagoda-like tower. Plenty of beer and cheap Bavarian food are what you get here. A large glass or mug of beer (ask for *ein mass Bier*), enough to bathe in, costs 5.60€. Homemade dumplings are a specialty, as are all kinds of tasty sausage. Oompah bands often play. It's open daily from 10am to midnight (closed Jan 11–Feb 5).

On the principal pedestrian-only street of Munich, **Augustinerbrau,** Neuhäuserstrasse 27 (© **089/260-4106;** U-Bahn/S-Bahn: Stachus), offers generous helpings of food, good beer, and a mellow atmosphere. It's been around for a little less than a century, but beer was first brewed on this spot in 1328. The cuisine is not for dieters: It's hearty, heavy, and starchy, but it sure soaks up that beer. Hours are daily from 9am to midnight. **Waldwirtschaft Grosshesslohe,** George-Kalb-Strasse 3 (© **089/74-99-4030;** tram: 7), is a popular summertime rendezvous seating some 2,000 drinkers. The gardens are open daily from 10am to 10pm (they have to close early because neighborhood residents complain). Music ranges from Dixieland to English jazz to Polish bands. Entrance is free and you bring your own food. It's above the Isar River in the vicinity of the zoo.

night owls drift on to other late-night venues. Expect lots of chitchat from table to table, and there's sure to be someone scribbling away at his or her unfinished story (or unfinished novel). It's open Sunday through Thursday from 11am to midnight, Friday and Saturday from 11am to 1am, and Sunday from 10:30am to midnight. **Soul City,** Maximilianplatz 5 (© **089/595272;** U-Bahn: Karlsplatz), is *the* gay dance club in Munich. Scattered nooks allow conversation sheltered from one of the best sound systems in the city, as well as offer a brief respite from the throng on the dance floor and at the bar. The 5.10€ cover charge on Thursday and Friday includes free drinks, and on Saturday you get discounted drink coupons. The club is open Thursday through Saturday from 10pm to 6am.

DAY TRIPS FROM MUNICH

HERRENCHIEMSEE ⋆ & NEUES SCHLOSS ⋆⋆   Known as the "Bavarian Sea," Chiemsee is one of the Bavarian Alps' most beautiful lakes in a serene landscape. Its main attraction lies on the island of Herrenchiemsee, where "Mad" King Ludwig II built one of his fantastic castles.

Neues Schloss, begun in 1878, was never completed because of the king's death in 1886. The castle was to have been a replica of the grand palace of Versailles that Ludwig so admired. One of the architects was Julius Hofmann, whom the king had also employed for the construction of his alpine castle, Neuschwanstein. When work was halted in 1886, only the center of the

Outdoors in the Bavarian Alps

HITTING THE SLOPES & OTHER WINTER ACTIVITIES The winter **skiing** here is the best in Germany. A regular winter snowfall in January and February measures 30cm to 50cm (12–20 in.), which in practical terms means about 2m (6 ft.) of snow in the areas served by ski lifts. The great **Zugspitzplatt** snowfield can be reached in spring or autumn by a rack railway. The Zugspitze, at 2,960m (9,720 ft.) above sea level, is the tallest mountain peak in Germany. Ski slopes begin at a height of 2,650m (8,700 ft.).

The second great ski district in the Alps is **Berchtesgadener Land,** with alpine skiing centered on Jenner, Rossfeld, Götschen, and Hochschwarzeck, and consistently good snow conditions until March. Here you'll find a cross-country skiing center and many miles of tracks kept in first-class condition, natural toboggan runs, one artificial ice run for toboggan and skibob runs, artificial ice skating, and ice-curling rinks. Call the local "Snow-Telefon" at ℂ **08652/9670** for current snow conditions.

From October to February, you can use the world-class **ice-skating** rink in Berchtesgaden (the Eisstadion). Less reliable, but more evocative of Bavaria's wild open spaces, it involves skating on the surface of the Hintersee Lake once it's sufficiently frozen. Rarer is an ice-skating experience on the Königsee, whose surface freezes to the degree that you can skate on average only once every 10 winters. A particularly cozy way to spend a winter's night is to huddle with a companion in the back of a **horse-drawn sled.** For a fee of 46€ to 72€ per hour, this can be arranged by calling ℂ **08652/1760.**

HIKING & OTHER SUMMER ACTIVITIES In summer, **alpine hiking** is a major attraction—climbing mountains, enjoying nature, watching animals in the forest. Hikers are able at times to observe endangered species firsthand. One of the best areas for hiking is the 1,237m (4,060-ft.) **Eckbauer** lying on the southern fringe of Partenkirchen (the tourist office at Garmisch-Partenkirchen will supply maps and details). Many visitors come to the Alps in summer just to hike through the **Berchtesgaden National Park,** bordering the Austrian province of Salzburg. The 2,466m (8,091-ft.) Watzmann Mountain, the Königssee (Germany's cleanest, clearest lake), and parts of the Jenner—the pride of Berchtesgaden's four ski areas—are within the boundaries of the national park, which has well-mapped trails cut through protected areas, leading the hiker along spectacular flora and fauna. Information about hiking in the park is provided by the **Nationale Parkverwaltung,** Franciscanalplatz 7, D-83471 Berchtesgaden (ℂ **08652/64343**). It's open Monday through Saturday from 9am to 5pm.

From Garmisch-Partenkirchen, serious hikers can embark on full-day or, if they're more ambitious, overnight alpine treks, following clearly marked footpaths and staying in isolated mountain huts maintained by the German Alpine Association (Deutscher Alpenverein/DAV). Some huts are staffed and serve meals. For the truly remote unsupervised huts, you'll be provided with information on how to gain access and your responsibility in leaving them tidy after your visit. For information, inquire at the local tourist office or write to the **German Alpine Association,** Am Franciscanalplatz 7, D-83471, Berchtesgaden (ℂ **08652/64343**).

At the same address and phone number, you'll also be routed to staff members of a privately owned tour operator, the **Summit Club,** an outfit devoted to the organization of high-altitude expeditions throughout Europe and the world.

If you're a true outdoors person, you'll briefly savor the somewhat touristy facilities of Garmisch-Partenkirchen, and then use it as a base for exploring the rugged **Berchtesgaden National Park,** which is within an easy commute of Garmisch. You can also stay at one of the inns in Mittenwald or Oberammergau and take advantage of a wide roster of sporting diversions within the wild open spaces. Any of the outfitters below will provide directions and link-ups with their sports programs from wherever you decide to stay. Street maps of Berchtesgaden and its environs are usually available for free from the **Kurdirektion** (the local tourist office) at Berchtesgaden (© 08652/967-0), and more intricately detailed maps of the surrounding alpine topography are available for a fee.

In addition to hill climbing and rock climbing, summertime activities include **ballooning,** which, weather permitting, can be arranged through **Outdoor Club Berchtesgaden,** Am Gmundberg (© 08652/9776-0), open from Monday through Friday from 8am to 6pm. Local enthusiasts warn that ballooning is not a sport for the timid or anyone who suffers unduly in the cold: Warm thermal currents that prevail around Berchtesgaden in summer limit the sport to the cold-weather months. Consequently, the seasonal heyday for ballooning is from December to February.

Cycling and **mountain biking,** available through the rental facilities of **Para-Taxi,** Maximilianstrasse 16 (© 08652/948450), give outdoor enthusiasts an opportunity to enjoy the outdoors and exercise their leg muscles simultaneously. It's open Monday through Friday from 9am to 12:30pm and 2 to 6pm, Saturday from 9am to 12:30pm.

Anglers will find plenty of **fishing** opportunities (especially salmon, pikeperch, and trout) at Lake Hintersee and the rivers Ramsauer Ache and Königsseer Ache, although in most cases it's best to obtain a fishing permit. To acquire one, contact the Kurdirektion (tourist office) at Berchtesgaden, which will direct you to any of four different authorities, based on where you want to fish. For fishing specifically within the Hintersee, contact officials at the **Kurverwaltung,** Im Tal 2 (© 08657/98-89-20) at Ramsau, 12km (7½ miles) from Berchtesgaden.

Despite its obvious dangers, **hang gliding** or **para gliding** from the vertiginous slopes of Mount Jenner can be thrilling. To arrange it, contact **Para-Taxi,** Maximilianstrasse 15 (© 08652/948450). The headquarters for a loosely allied group of parasailing enthusiasts, the **Berchtesgaden Gleitschirmflieger** (© 08652/23-63) sometimes arranges communal paragliding excursions to which qualified newcomers are invited. Practice your **kayaking** or **white-water rafting** techniques on one of the many rivers in the area, such as the Ramsauer, Königisser, Bischofswiesener, and Berchtesgadener Aches. For information and options, contact the above-mentioned **Outdoor Club Berchtesgaden.**

enormous palace had been completed. The palace and its formal gardens remain one of the most fascinating of Ludwig's adventures, in spite of their unfinished state.

The splendid Great Hall of Mirrors most authentically replicates Versailles. The 17 door panels contain enormous mirrors reflecting the 33 crystal chandeliers and the 44 gilded candelabra. The vaulted ceiling is covered with 25 paintings depicting the life of Louis XIV. The dining room is a popular attraction because of "the little table that lays itself." A mechanism in the floor permitted the table to go down to the room below to be cleared and relaid between courses.

You can visit Herrenchiemsee at any time of the year. April through September, tours are given daily from 9am to 5pm; off season, from 10am to 4pm. Admission—in addition to the 5.10€ for the round-trip boat fare—is 6.50€ adults, 5.50€ students, and free for children under 17.

Getting There   Take the train to Prien am Chiemsee (trip time: 1 hr.). For information, call © **18051/99-66-33.** There's also regional bus service offered by **RVO Regionalver-kehr Oberbayern** (© **08021/948274**). Access by car is via A-8 Autobahn.

From Prien, lake steamers make the trip to Herrenchiemsee. They are operated by **Chiemsee-Schiffahrt Ludwig Fessler** (© **08051/60-90**). The round-trip fare is 5.10€. For visitor information, contact the **Kur und Verkehrsamt,** Alte Rathausstrasse 11, in Prien am Chiemsee (© **08051/69050**), open Monday through Friday from 8:30am to 6pm. March through September, the office is also open on Saturday from 8:30am to 6pm.

GARMISCH-PARTENKIRCHEN ✹✹✹
In spite of its urban flair, Garmisch-Partenkirchen, Germany's top alpine resort, has maintained the charm of an ancient village. Even today, you occasionally see country folk in traditional costumes, and you may be held up in traffic while the cattle are led from their mountain grazing grounds down through the streets of town. Garmisch is about 88km (55 miles) southwest of Munich.

ESSENTIALS
GETTING THERE   By Train   The **Garmisch-Partenkirchen Bahnhof** lies on the major Munich–Weilheim–Garmisch–Mittenwald–Innsbruck rail line with frequent connections in all directions. Twenty trains per day arrive from Munich (trip time: 1 hr. 22 min.). For rail information and schedules, call © **01805/99-66-33.**

By Bus   Both long-distance and regional buses through the Bavarian Alps are provided by **RVO Regionalverkehr Oberbayern** in Garmisch-Partenkirchen (© **08821/948-274** for information).

By Car   Access is via A-95 Autobahn from Munich; exit at Eschenlohe.

VISITOR INFORMATION   For tourist information, contact the **Kurver-waltung und Verkehrsamt,** Richard-Strauss-Platz (© **08821/720-688**), open Monday through Saturday from 8am to 6pm, Sunday from 10am to noon.

GETTING AROUND   An unnumbered municipal bus services the town, depositing passengers at Marienplatz or the Bahnhof, from where you can walk to all central hotels. This free bus runs every 15 minutes.

WHERE TO STAY
Gästehaus Trenkler   For a number of years, Frau Trenkler has made travelers feel well cared for in her quiet, centrally located guesthouse. She rents four

doubles, each with shower and sink. Each duvet-covered bed is equipped with a good mattress. Rooms range from small to medium, and corridor bathrooms are adequate and tidily maintained.

Kreuzstrasse 20, D-82467 Garmisch-Partenkirchen. © 08821/34-39. Fax 08821/15-67. www.gaestehaus-trenkler.de. 4 units with shower. 60€ double. Rates include continental breakfast. No credit cards. Free parking. Bus: Eibsee no. 1. In room: No phone.

Post-Hotel Partenkirchen ⭐

This is one of the town's most prestigious hotels, especially with the asset of its unusually fine restaurant (see "Where to Dine," below). The U-shaped and handsomely furnished rooms are generally medium size. Duvets rest on comfortable beds, mostly doubles or twins. Bathrooms are handsomely maintained with tub/shower combos and deluxe toiletries. The balconies overlook a garden and offer a view of the Alps.

Ludwigstrasse 49, D-82467 Garmisch-Partenkirchen. © 08821/9363-0. Fax 08821/9363-2222. www.post-hotel.de. 57 units. 90€–150€ double; 150€–180€ suite. Rates include buffet breakfast. AE, DC, MC, V. **Amenities:** 2 dining rooms; bar; nearby golf, tennis, swimming, and mountain climbing; laundry. In room: TV, minibar, hair dryer, safe.

Reindl's Partenkirchner Hof ⭐⭐

This special Bavarian retreat maintains a high level of luxury and hospitality. The annexes have balconies, and the main building has wraparound verandas, giving each room an unobstructed view of the mountains and town. All rooms have a cozy charm. The best are suites opening onto panoramic views of mountains or the garden. Rustic pine furniture adds to the allure of this place. Bathrooms are spacious with a tub/shower combo.

Bahnhofstrasse 15, D-82467 Garmisch-Partenkirchen. © 08821/943870. Fax 08821/9438-7250. www.reindls.de. 63 units. 94€–136€ double; 166€–264€ suite. AE, DC, MC, V. Parking 8€. Closed Nov 15–Dec 15. **Amenities:** Restaurant (see "Where to Dine," below); 2 bars; covered pool; health club; sauna; massage; room service; laundry; sunroom; open terrace; 2 gardens. In room: TV, minibar, hair dryer, safe

Romantik-Hotel Clausing's Posthotel ⭐

This hotel in the heart of town was originally built in 1512 as a tavern and has retained its *gemütlich* antique charm. In the early 1990s, it was radically upgraded. Rooms range from rather small and cozy Bavarian nests to spacious. The owners have installed comfortable furnishings, and bathrooms are beautifully kept and have tub/shower combos.

Marienplatz 12, D-82467 Garmisch-Partenkirchen. © 08821/7090. Fax 08821/70-92-05. www.clausings-posthotel.de. 47 units. 95€–205€ double. DC, MC, V. Free parking. **Amenities:** 2 restaurants; historic tavern; bar; room service. In room: TV, minibar, hair dryer.

WHERE TO DINE

Flösserstuben INTERNATIONAL   Regardless of the season, a bit of the Bavarian Alps always seems to flower amid the wood-trimmed nostalgia of this intimate restaurant close to the town center. You can select a seat at a colorful wooden table or on an ox yoke–inspired stool in front of the spliced saplings that decorate the bar. Moussaka and souvlakia, as well as sauerbraten and all kinds of Bavarian dishes, are abundantly available. You can also order Mexican tacos and tortillas or even *Tafelspitz* (boiled beef) from the Austrian kitchen. The menu isn't imaginative but is soul satisfying, especially on a cold night.

Schmiedstrasse 2. © 08821/28-88. Reservations recommended. Main courses 8€–17€. AE, MC, V. Daily 11:30am–3pm and 5–11pm. Town bus.

Post-Hotel Partenkirchen ⭐ CONTINENTAL   This hotel dining room is renowned for its distinguished cuisine. The interior rooms are rustic, with lots of mellow, old-fashioned atmosphere. You could imagine meeting Dürer here. Everything seems comfortably subdued, including the guests. The best way to dine is to order one of the fixed-price menus, which change daily, depending on the availability of seasonal produce. The a la carte menu is extensive, featuring game in the autumn. The Wiener schnitzel served with a large salad is the best we've had in the resort.

Ludwigstrasse 49. ⓒ 08821/5-93-630. Reservations required. Main courses 11€–30€; fixed-price menus 15€–26€. AE, DC, MC, V. Daily noon–2pm and 6–10pm.

Reindl's Restaurant ⓖ CONTINENTAL   Reindl's is first class all the way. The seasonal menu comprises *cuisine moderne* as well as regional Bavarian dishes. Among main dishes, we recommend *coq au Riesling* (chicken with wine) with noodles, or a perfect veal roasted with *Steinpilzen,* a special mushroom from the Bavarian mountains. For dessert, try the spectacular Grand Marnier zabaglione with strawberry and vanilla ice cream, or try a *Salzburger Nockerln* (a feathery light soufflé made of eggs, flour, butter, and sugar) for two.

In the Partenkirchner Hof, Bahnhofstrasse 15. ⓒ 08821/5-80-25. Reservations required. Main courses 14€–23€; fixed-price menus 24€–29€. AE, DC, MC, V. Daily noon–2pm and 6:30–10:30pm. Closed Nov 10–Dec 15.

SEEING THE SIGHTS IN TOWN
The symbol of the city's growth and modernity is the **Olympic Ice Stadium,** built for the 1936 Winter Olympics and capable of holding nearly 12,000 people. On the slopes at the edge of town is the much larger **Ski Stadium,** with two ski jumps and a slalom course. In 1936 more than 100,000 people watched the events in this stadium. Today it's still an integral part of winter life in Garmisch—the World Cup Ski Jump is held here every New Year.

Garmisch-Partenkirchen is a center for winter sports, summer hiking, and mountain climbing. In addition, the town environs offer some of the most panoramic views and colorful buildings in Bavaria. The **Philosopher's Walk** in the park surrounding the pink and silver 18th-century pilgrimage **Chapel of St. Anton** is a delightful spot to enjoy the views of the mountains around the low-lying town.

Exploring the Environs
One of the most beautiful of the alpine regions around Garmisch is the **Alpspitz region,** which hikers and hill climbers consider uplifting and healing for both body and soul. Here, you'll find alpine meadows, masses of seasonal wildflowers, and a rocky and primordial geology whose savage panoramas might strike you as Wagnerian. Ranging in altitude from 1,200m to 1,800m (4,000 ft.–6,000 ft.) above sea level, the Alps around Garmisch-Partenkirchen are accessible via more than 30 ski lifts and funiculars, many of which run year-round.

The most appealing and panoramic of the lot includes the Alpspitz (Osterfelderkopf) cable car that runs uphill from the center of Garmisch to the top of the Osterfelderkopf peak, at a height of 1,980m (6,500 ft.). It makes its 9-minute ascent at least every hour, year-round, from 8am to 5pm. The round-trip cost is 25€ adults, 14€ persons ages 16 to 18, and 12€ children ages 4 to 15. After admiring the view at the top, you can either return directly to Garmisch, or continue your journey into the mountains via other cable cars. If you opt to continue, take the Hochalm cable car across the high-altitude plateaus above Garmisch. At its terminus, you'll have two options, both across clearly marked alpine trails. The 20-minute trek will take you to the uppermost station of the Kreuzbergbahn, which will carry you back to Garmisch. The 75-minute trek will carry you to the upper terminus of the Hausbergbahn, which will also carry you back to Garmisch.

Another of the many cable car options within Garmisch involves an eastward ascent from the center of Partenkirchen to the top of the 1,780m (5,850-ft.) Wank via the Wankbahn, for a round-trip price of 16€ adults, 11€ persons ages 16 to 18, and 9.50€ children. From here, you'll get a sweeping view of the plateau upon which the twin villages of Garmisch and Partenkirchen sit. In winter, the top of the Wank is a favorite departure point for many downhill ski runs. It's also, however, a favorite with the patrons of Garmisch's spa facilities because the plentiful sunshine makes it ideal for the *Liegekur* (deck-chair cure).

If you plan on pursuing any of these options, it's to your advantage to invest in a day pass, the **Classic Garmisch Pass,** with which you'll be able to ride most of the cable cars in the region (including those to the above-recommended Alpspitz, Kreuzeck, and Wank, as well as several others that fan out over the Eckbauer and the Ausberg) as many times as you like within the same day. Priced at 27€ per person, the pass is available from any of the town's cable car stations. For information on all the cable car schedules and itineraries within the region, call © **08821/7970.**

Another option for exploring the environs of Garmisch involves an ascent to the top of the **Zugspitze,** at 2,960m (9,720 ft.) the tallest mountain in Germany, with a base set astride the Austrian frontier. Ski slopes begin at 2,650m (8,700 ft.). For a panoramic view over both the Bavarian and Tyrolean Alps, go to the summit. The first stage begins in the center of Garmisch by taking the cog railway to an intermediary alpine plateau (Zugspitzplatz). Trains depart hourly throughout the year from 7:39am to 2:39pm, although we recommend that you begin by 1:39pm (and preferably earlier) and not wait until the cog railway's final ascent from Garmisch. At Zugspitzplatz, you can continue uphill on the same cog railway to the debut of a high-speed, 4-minute ride aboard the Gletscherbahn cable car, the high-altitude conveyance you'll ride to the top of the Zugspitz peak. (The distance between Zugspitzplatz and debut of the Gletscherbahn can also be transited aboard a secondary cable car, the Eibsee-Seilbahn, but this will require that you walk uphill for part of the route.) Regardless of the exact route you follow, round-trip transit between the center of Garmisch and the top of the Zugspitz costs 42€ adults, 29€ persons 16 to 17, and 25€ children 5 to 15. Children under 4 ride free. Note that the price of the ascent to the Zugspitz is not included in the above-mentioned Classic Garmisch Pass, as it forms part of an independent network of cable cars that's not associated with the other cable cars within the region. For more information, call © **08821/720-688.**

MITTENWALD ⍟
Seeming straight out of *The Sound of Music,* the year-round resort of Mittenwald lies in a pass in the Karwendel Range, 18km (11 miles) southeast of Garmisch-Partenkirchen. Especially noteworthy and photogenic are the painted Bavarian houses with overhanging eaves. Even the baroque church tower is covered with frescoes. On the square stands a monument to Mathias Klotz, who introduced violin making to Mittenwald in 1684. The town is a major international center for this highly specialized craft.

ESSENTIALS
GETTING THERE   By Train   Mittenwald lies on the express rail line between Munich and Innsbruck and can be reached by almost hourly train service from Munich (trip time: 1½–2 hr.). Call © **01805/99-66-33** for information.

By Bus   Regional bus service from Garmisch-Partenkirchen and nearby towns is frequent; call **RVO Regionalverkehr Oberbayern** at Garmisch (© **08821/ 94-82-74** for information).

By Car   Access by car is via A-95 Autobahn from Munich.

VISITOR INFORMATION   Contact the **Kurverwaltung und Verkehrsamt,** Dammkarstrasse 3 (© **08823/3-39-81**), open Monday through Friday from 8am to noon and 1 to 5pm, Saturday from 10am to noon.

WHERE TO STAY

Alpenrose   In the village center at the foot of a rugged mountain, this inn is covered with decorative designs and window boxes holding flowering vines. The main building, a former 14th-century monastery, is much more desirable than the more functionally furnished annex, the Bichlerhof. Rooms in the main building are very charming, with their old-fashioned farmhouse cupboards and dark wood paneling. The private bathrooms are well kept but a bit small, with shower stalls.

Obermarkt 1, D-82481 Mittenwald. © **08823/92-700.** Fax 08823/37-20. www.hotel-alpenrose-mittenwald.de. 18 units. 75€–95€ double; 105€ triple. Rates include buffet breakfast. AE, DC, MC, V. Free parking. **Amenities:** Restaurant; bar; room service. *In room:* TV, minibar, hair dryer.

Gästehaus Franziska *Value*   The Kufler family labors to make this the most personalized guesthouse in town. Each small room is comfortably furnished and beautifully maintained—first-rate beds feature crisp linen duvets. All have balconies with mountain views. Bathrooms are a bit small but inviting and tidy, with shower stalls. Breakfast is the only meal served. It's extremely difficult to obtain bookings from June 20 to October 2.

Innsbrucker-Strasse 24, D-82481 Mittenwald. © **08823/92030.** Fax 08823/3893. 19 units. 78€–92€ double; from 95€ suite. Rates include buffet breakfast. AE, MC, V. Free parking. Closed Nov to Dec 15. *In room:* TV, minibar, tea/coffeemaker (suites only), safe.

Hotel Post ✦   Dating from 1632, this hotel remains Mittenwald's finest address. A delightful breakfast is served on the sun terrace, with a view of the Alps; in cool weather you can enjoy a beer in the snug lounge-bar with its open fireplace. Rooms are comfortable but standard. Beds (twin or double) and mattresses are among the best in town. Bathrooms are small and contain shower stalls. The maids are especially helpful if you need something extra.

Obermarkt 9, D-82481 Mittenwald. © **08823/938-2333.** Fax 08823/938-2999. www.posthotel-mittenwald. de. 90 units. 86€–140€ double; 118€–170€ suite. Rates include buffet breakfast. MC, V. Free parking. **Amenities:** Wine tavern/restaurant; bar/lounge; indoor pool; sauna; massage. *In room:* TV, minibar, hair dryer, safe.

WHERE TO DINE

Restaurant Arnspitze BAVARIAN   Housed in a modern chalet hotel on the outskirts, this is the finest dining room in town. The restaurant is decorated in the old style; the cuisine is solid, satisfying, and wholesome. You might order sole with homemade noodles or veal steak in creamy smooth sauce, then finish with one of the freshly made desserts. There's an excellent fixed-price lunch.

Innsbruckerstrasse 68. © **08823/24-25.** Reservations required. Main courses 15€–23€; fixed-price lunch 22€; fixed-price dinner 45€–52€. AE. Thurs–Mon noon–2pm; Wed–Mon 6–9pm; closed Tues all day and Wed for lunch. Closed Oct 25–Dec 15. Bus: RVO.

SEEING THE SIGHTS

The town's museum has exhibits devoted to the evolution of violins and other string instruments. The **Geigenbau-und Heimatmuseum,** Ballenhausgasse 3

(© **08823/25-11**), is open Tuesday through Friday from 10am to 1pm and 3 to 6pm, Saturday and Sunday from 10am to 1pm. Admission is 2.50€ adults and 1.50€ children. The museum is closed from November 1 to December 20.

In the countryside, you are constantly exposed to the changing scenery of the Wetterstein and Karwendel ranges. Horse and carriage trips are available as well as coach tours from Mittenwald to nearby villages. In the evening there's typical Bavarian entertainment, often consisting of folk dancing and singing, zither playing, and yodeling, but you also have your choice of concerts, dance bands, discos, and bars. Mittenwald has good spa facilities, in large gardens landscaped with tree-lined streams and trout pools. Concerts during the summer are held in the music pavilion.

OUTDOOR ACTIVITIES

In winter, the town is a skiing center, but it remains equally active throughout the summer. Some 130km (80 miles) of paths wind up and down the mountains around the village, with chairlifts making the hiking trails readily accessible. Of course, where there are trails, there's mountain biking. A biking map is available from the tourist office (see above), and mountain climbing expeditions are also available. You can always go swimming to cool off on a hot summer's day—the Lautersee and Ferchensee are brisk waters that, even in summer, might be forfeited by the fainthearted for the heated adventure pool in Mittenwald.

OBERAMMERGAU 🔾

A visit to Oberammergau, 19km (12 miles) north of Garmisch-Partenkirchen, is ideal in summer or winter. It stands in a wide valley surrounded by forests and mountains, with sunny slopes and meadows. The world-famous **Passion Play** is presented here, usually every 10 years; the next one is scheduled for 2010. It has also long been known for the skill of its woodcarvers. Here in this village right under the Kofel, farms are still intact, and tradition prevails.

ESSENTIALS

GETTING THERE   By Train   The Oberammergau Bahnhof is on the Murnau–Bad Kohlgrum–Oberammergau rail line, with frequent connections in all directions. Murnau has connections to all major German cities. Daily trains from Munich take 2 hours. For information, call © **01805/99-66-33.**

By Bus   Regional bus service to nearby towns is offered by **RVO Regionalverkehr Oberbayern** in Garmisch-Partenkirchen (© **08821/948-274**). An unnumbered bus travels between Oberammergau and Garmisch-Partenkirchen.

By Car   Take A-95 Munich–Garmisch-Partenkirchen Autobahn and exit at Eschenlohe (trip time: 1½ hr.).

VISITOR INFORMATION   Contact the **Oberammergau Tourist Information Office,** Eugen-Papst-Strasse 9A (© **08822/92310**), open Monday through Friday from 9am to 6pm, Saturday from 9am to noon.

SEEING THE SIGHTS

Oberammergau's most respected citizens include an unusual group, the woodcarvers, many of whom have been trained in the village's woodcarver's school. In the **Pilatushaus,** Ludwigthomstrasse (© **08822/92310**), you can watch local artists at work, including woodcarvers, painters, sculptors, and potters. Hours are May through October, Monday through Friday from 1 to 5pm. You'll see many examples of these art forms throughout the town, on the painted cottages and inns and in the churchyard. Also worth seeing when strolling through the village are the houses with 18th-century frescoes by Franz Zwink that are named after fairy-tale characters, such as "Hansel and Gretel House" and the "Little Red Riding Hood House."

Heimatmuseum, Dorfstrasse 8 (© **08822/94136**), has a notable collection of Christmas crèches, all hand carved and painted, dating from the 18th century through the 20th century. It's open mid-April to mid-October, Tuesday through Saturday from 2 to 6pm; off season, only on Saturday from 2 to 6pm. Admission is 2.50€ adults and 1.50€ children.

NEARBY ATTRACTIONS   The Ammer Valley, with Oberammergau in the (almost) center, offers easy access to many nearby attractions. **Schloss Linderhof** 🏰🏰 (© **08822/920321**), designed as a French rococo palace, the smallest of Ludwig II's constructions, is open year-round. This is in many ways the most successful of his palaces. The gardens and smaller buildings here are even more elaborate than the two-story main structure. Especially outstanding is a Hall of Mirrors, set in white and gold panels, decorated with gilded woodcarvings. The king's bedchamber overlooks a Fountain of Neptune and the cascades of the garden. The palace is open daily April through September from 9am to 5:30pm, October through March from 10am to 4pm. Admission is 6€, free for children under 15. Buses arrive from Garmisch-Partenkirchen throughout the day. Motorists can leave Oberammergau following the road signs to Ettal, 5km (3 miles) away. From Ettal, follow the signs for another 5km (3 miles) to Draswang, at which point the road into Schloss Linderhof is signposted.

OUTDOOR ACTIVITIES

Numerous **hiking trails** lead through the mountains around Oberammergau to hikers' inns such as the **Kolbenalm** and the **Romanshohe.** You can, however, simply go up to the mountaintops on the Laber cable railway or the Kolben chairlift. Oberammergau also offers opportunities to tennis buffs, minigolf players, cyclists, swimmers, hang-gliding enthusiasts, and canoeists. The recreation center **Wellenberg,** with its large alpine swimming complex with open-air pools, hot water and fountains, sauna, solarium, and restaurant, is one of the Alps' most beautiful recreation centers.

WHERE TO STAY & DINE

Alte Post   This provincial inn in the village center with a wide overhanging roof, green-shuttered windows, and tables set on a sidewalk under a long awning, is the village social hub. The interior has storybook charm, with a ceiling-high green ceramic stove, alpine chairs, and shelves of pewter plates. Most of the rustic rooms have views. Wide, comfortable beds with giant posts range in size from cozy to spacious. Bathrooms are medium size with a shower stall. Nonresidents are welcome to the thriving and excellent Bavarian restaurant.

Dorfstrasse 19, D-82487 Oberammergau. © **08822/91-00.** Fax 08822/910-100. 32 units. 68€–86€ double. Rates include buffet breakfast. AE, DC, MC, V. Parking 3.60€. Closed Oct 29–Dec 17. Bus: 30. **Amenities:** Restaurant; bar. *In room:* TV.

Hotel Café–Restaurant Friedenshöhe *Value*   This 1906 villa enjoys a beautiful location and is among the town's best bargains. Well-maintained rooms range from rather small singles to spacious doubles. Corner rooms are bigger, but bathrooms tend to be small, each with a shower stall. Even nonresidents join the townspeople who head for one of the four dining rooms, which has both indoor and outdoor terraces opening onto panoramic views, and serves Bavarian favorites.

König-Ludwig-Strasse 31, D-82487 Oberammergau. ℂ **08822/35-98.** Fax 08822/43-45. www.friedenshöhe. com. 16 units. 52€–84€ double. Rates include buffet breakfast. AE, DC, MC, V. Closed Nov to Dec 14. **Amenities:** Restaurant; bar. *In room:* TV on request.

Hotel Restaurant Böld A stone's throw from the river, this well-designed chalet hotel is one of the town's premier choices. Rooms in both the main building and the annex have equally good beds, usually doubles or twins. Most rooms open onto balconies. The spotless bathrooms are medium size with shower stalls. A tranquil atmosphere and attentive service await you here. The restaurant serves Bavarian and international fare.

König-Ludwig-Strasse 10, D-82487 Oberammergau. ℂ **08822/91-20.** Fax 08822/71-02. 57 units. 95€–120€ double. Rates include continental breakfast. AE, MC, V. Free outside parking; 5.50€ in the garage. **Amenities:** Restaurant; bar; sauna; solarium; whirlpool. *In room:* TV, minibar, hair dryer.

3 The Romantic Road ★★

No area of Germany is more aptly named than the Romantische Strasse. Stretching 290km (180 miles) from Würzburg to Füssen in the foothills of the Bavarian Alps, it passes through untouched medieval villages and 2,000-year-old towns.

The best way to see the Romantic Road is by car, stopping whenever the mood strikes you and then driving on through vineyards and over streams until you arrive at the alpine passes in the south. Frankfurt and Munich are convenient gateways. Access is by A-7 Autobahn from north and south, or A-3 Autobahn from east and west; A-81 Autobahn has links from the southwest. You can also explore the Romantic Road by train or bus, or by organized tour.

ROTHENBURG OB DER TAUBER ★★★

This city was first mentioned in written records in 804 as Rotinbure, a settlement above *(ob)* the Tauber River that grew to be a free imperial city, reaching its apex of prosperity under a famous Burgermeister, Heinrich Toppler, in the 14th century.

The place is such a gem and so well known that its popularity is its chief disadvantage—tourist hordes march through here, especially in summer, and the concomitant souvenir peddlers hawk kitsch. Even so, if your time is limited and you can visit only one town on the Romantic Road, make it Rothenburg.

Contemporary life and industry have made an impact, and if you arrive at the railroad station, the first things you'll see are factories and office buildings. But don't be discouraged. Inside those undamaged 13th-century city walls is a completely preserved medieval town, relatively untouched by the passage of time.

ESSENTIALS

GETTING THERE By Train Rothenburg lies on the Steinach–Rothenburg rail line, with frequent connections to all major German cities, including Nürnberg and Stuttgart. Daily trains arrive from Frankfurt (trip time: 3 hr.), Hamburg (5½ hr.), or Berlin (7 hr.). For information, call ℂ **01805/99-66-33.**

By Bus The bus that traverses the length of the Romantic Road is EB189 or EB189E, operated by **Deutsche Touring Frankfurt** (ℂ **069/790-3261**). Two buses operate along this route every day, but only from April to October. Know in advance that although you'll see a lot of romantic color en route, travel time to Rothenburg from Frankfurt via these buses is 6½ hours because of frequent stops en route. Any travel agent in Germany or abroad can book you a seat on any of these buses, each of which stops at Würzburg, Augsburg, Füssen, and Munich.

Regional bus service that's limited to towns and hamlets within the vicinity of Rothenburg and the rest of the Romantic Road is provided by **OVF Omnibusverkehr Franken GmbH,** Kopernikusplatz 5, 90159 Nürnberg (✆ **0911/43-90-60**).

VISITOR INFORMATION   Contact **Stadt Verkehrsamt,** Marktplatz (✆ **09861/40-492**), open Monday through Friday from 9am to noon and 1 to 5pm, Saturday and Sunday from 10am to 3pm (Nov–Mar it closes at 5pm weekdays).

WHERE TO STAY
Expensive

Burg Hotel ✿   This old-fashioned timbered house at the end of a cul-de-sac is out of the Brothers Grimm. Its Tauber Valley view, picket fences, and window boxes exude German charm. Rooms are spread across three floors (no elevator). Extras include spacious bathrooms with tub/shower combos and large mirrors. Any room is likely to please, but if you want a view, ask for nos. 7, 12, or 25.

Klostergasse 1–3, D-91541 Rothenburg o.d.T. ✆ **09861/94-89-0.** Fax 09861/94-89-40. www.burghotel. rothenburg.de. 15 units. 110€–140€ double; from 150€ suite. Rates include buffet breakfast. MC, V. Parking 7.50€. *In room:* TV, minibar, hair dryer, safe.

Eisenhut ✿✿   The most celebrated inn on the Romantic Road, Eisenhut is also one of the finest small hotels in Germany. Four medieval patrician houses were joined to make this distinctive inn. Demand for rooms is great, and the staff appears forever overworked. No two rooms are alike—yours may contain hand-carved, monumental pieces or have a 1940s Hollywood touch with a tufted satin headboard. All are enhanced by comforters and pillows piled high on state-of-the-art German beds. Extras include bedside controls, and spacious bathrooms outfitted with tub/shower combos and twin basins. The three-story galleried dining hall is one of the most distinctive in Germany, with a multi-tiered flagstone terrace on the Tauber.

Herrngasse 3–5, D-91541 Rothenburg o.d.T. ✆ **09861/70-50.** Fax 09861/70-545. www.eisenhut.com. 79 units. 155€–205€ double; 280€–340€ suite. AE, DC, MC, V. Parking 9€. Closed Jan 3–Feb 28. **Amenities:** Restaurant; piano bar; Bavarian beer garden; room service; dry cleaning/laundry. *In room:* TV, minibar, hair dryer.

Hotel Tilman Riemenschneider ✿   This hotel's half-timbered facade rises directly above one of Rothenburg's busy historic streets. Its rear courtyard, adorned with geraniums, offers a cool and calm oasis from the heavy pedestrian traffic in front. Most rooms are medium size though a few are small. All have well-kept bathrooms with tub/shower combos.

Georgengasse 11–13, D-91541, Rothenburg o.d.T. ✆ **09861/9790.** Fax 09861/29-79. www.tilman-riemenschneider.de. 60 units. 125€–205€ double. Rates include buffet breakfast. AE, DC, MC, V. Parking 6€. **Amenities:** Restaurant (see "Where to Dine," below); lounge; fitness center; sauna; solarium; two whirlpools; room service; laundry/dry cleaning. *In room:* TV, hair dryer.

Romantik Hotel Markusturm ✿✿   This is one of the charming nuggets of Rothenburg, without the facilities and physical plant of the Eisenhut, but a winner in its own right. When this hotel was constructed in 1264, one of Rothenburg's defensive walls was incorporated into the building. Some rooms have four-poster beds, and about half the bathrooms have tubs and showers. Many guests request room no. 30, a cozy attic retreat. The hotel employs one of the most helpful staffs in town.

The Romantic Road

Aschaffenburg
E41
Schweinfurt
Bamberg
Harburg
20 mi
20 km
Castle

Werthelm
E45
Wiesentheid
Forchheim

Mittenberg
47
Würzburg
27
3

Amorbach
E43
8
Erlangen
E45

27
Tauberbischofsheim
Lauda-königshofen
Röttingham
290
Bad Mergentheim
Creglingen
Fürth
Nürnberg
73

Weikersheim
25
Rothenburg o.d.T.
Schillingfürst
Schwabach

HOHENLOHER EBENE
Ansbach
E50
Roth
2

E50
Feuchtwangen
Gunzenhausen
FRÄNKISCHE ALB

Heilbronn
Crailsheim
25
Dinkelsbühl
Ellingen
E45

Murrhardt
E43
Ellwangen
(Jagst)

Backnang
19
Wallerstein
2

Winnenden
29
Nördlingen

Schwäbisch
Gmund
Aalen
29
Harburg
Ingolstadt

ALBUCH
Donauwörth
16
Neuberg-an-
der-Donau

Goppingen
Heidenheim an
der Brenz
16
ROMANTIC ROAD

Kirchheim
unter Teck
Dillingen an
der Donau
2

Nürtingen
28
E52
E43
16

Berlin
28
Ulm
Augsburg
17
To
Munich

GERMANY
Ehingen
(Donau)
Friedberg
E52

Area of detail
30
Krumbach
(Schwaben)
Olching

312
Biberach
an der Riß
E43
Fürstenfeldbruck
Landsberg
E54

Herbertingen
312
Mindelheim
E54
Landsberg
am Lech
Starnberg

32
Memmingen
Ammersee
Starnberger-
see

30
Weingarten
Kaufbeuren
17
Hohenfurch

Ravensburg
Leutkirch
im Allgäu
Markt-
oberdorf
Schongau
Peiting
Penzberg

Wangen im
Allgäu
E43/54
Kempten
25
Wildsteig
Rottenbuch

Bodensee
Immenstadt
im Allgäu
17
Steingaden

Lindau
Schwangau
Neuschwanstein

SWITZERLAND
Sonthofen
Füssen
Hohenschwangau
Garmisch-
Partenkirchen

AUSTRIA
LECHTALER ALPEN
AUSTRIA

Rödergasse 1, D-91541 Rothenburg o.d.T. ⓒ **09861/9-42-80.** Fax 09861/9-42-81-13. www.markusturm.de.
25 units. 125€–190€ double. Rates include buffet breakfast. AE, DC, MC, V. Free parking. **Amenities:** Tennis
court; room service; babysitting; dry cleaning/laundry. *In room:* TV, hair dryer.

Moderate
Hotel Gasthof Glocke *Value*   South of the town center off Wenggasse, this
hotel does not have the charm and style of the premier inns, but it's a good
choice for those who want plain, simple, affordable rooms; a family atmosphere;
and good food. The small rooms, though a bit institutional, are nonetheless
comfortable and a good value for pricey Rothenburg. Bathrooms are exceedingly
small, each with a shower stall.

Am Plönlein 1, D-91541 Rothenburg o.d.T. ⓒ **09861/95899-0.** Fax 09861/95899-22. 24 units. 89€–105€
double. Rates include continental breakfast. AE, DC, MC, V. Parking 4.50€. Closed Dec 24–Jan 11. **Amenities:** Restaurant (see "Where to Dine," below). *In room:* TV, hair dryer, safe.

Hotel Reichs-Küchenmeister *&*   We consider this hotel, one of Rothen-
burg's oldest structures, near St. Jakobskirche, comparable with Tilman Riemenschneider and the Goldener Hirsch. The owners take special care with the guests'
comfort. Rooms are nicely furnished with painted wooden furniture. Bathrooms
are a bit small, each with a shower stall. An extra 25 rooms are available in the
duller annex across the street.

Kirchplatz 8, D-91541 Rothenburg o.d.T. ⓒ **09861/9700.** Fax 09861/86-965. www.reichskuechenmeister.
com. 45 units. 75€–135€ double; 135€ suite for 2; 215€ suite for 5. Rates include buffet breakfast. AE, DC,
MC, V. Parking 5€ in lot, 6.50€ in garage. **Amenities:** Restaurant (see "Where to Dine," below); wine bar;
sauna; solarium; Turkish bath; whirlpool. *In room:* TV.

Inexpensive
Bayerischer Hof   This little place, midway between the Bahnhof and the
medieval walled city, doesn't even try to compete with the grand inns. And why
should it? It's found a niche as a B&B, and although the outside looks rather
sterile, many cozy warm Bavarian touches grace the interior. Beds are comfortable, and rooms are small; bathrooms come with shower stalls. Housekeeping is
excellent, and the staff is most hospitable.

Ansbacherstrasse 21, D-91541 Rothenburg o.d.T. ⓒ **09861/60-63.** Fax 09861/86-56-1. www.bayerischerhof.
com. 9 units. 64€–84€ double. Rates include breakfast. MC, V. Free parking. Closed Jan. **Amenities:** Restau-
rant/bar. *In room:* TV.

Gasthof Goldener Greifen *&*   This is one of the very best B&Bs in town if
you want Bavarian home-style warmth. Fine furnishings, tidy housekeeping,
and a willing staff make this patrician 1374 house off Marktplatz extremely
comfortable. Corridor bathrooms are adequate, and generally spruced up after
use. Those in rooms with private shower-only bathrooms will find them small
but well maintained. You can order your morning coffee in the garden amid
roses and geraniums.

Obere Schmiedgasse 5, D-91541 Rothenburg o.d.T. ⓒ **09861/22-81.** Fax 09861/86-374. www.gasthof-greifen.
rothenburg.de. 21 units (20 with bathroom). 60€ double without bathroom; 77€–82€ double with shower
or bathroom. Rates include buffet breakfast. AE, MC, V. Closed Aug 22–Sept 2 and Dec 22 to Jan. *In room:*
No phone.

WHERE TO DINE
Expensive
Louvre *&* NEW GERMAN   Chef Berhard Reiseer is a man of multiple tal-
ents, and he has brought a lighter touch to the kitchens of Rothenburg with his
Neuer Küche (new cuisine) style of cookery. His appetizers are dazzling,

especially the goose liver terrine with huckleberries and white port, or our favorite, consommé of crayfish with ravioli. For a main course, try the perfectly cooked halibut with a potato sauce or else the roulade of guinea fowl with herb-infused cabbage and white-flour dumplings. The elegant cuisine is served against a mainly black decor with high-tech lighting and paintings on display. The wine list, for the most part, is good and fairly priced.

Klingengasse 15. © 09861/87809. Reservations required. Main courses 21€–28€; fixed-price menu 50€–74€. AE, MC, V. Daily 6pm–1am.

Moderate

Baumeisterhaus ☞ FRANCONIAN Right off Marktplatz, the Baumeister-haus is housed in an ancient patrician residence, built in 1596. It has Rothen-burg's most beautiful courtyard (which only guests can visit), with colorful murals, serenely draped by vines. Frankly, although the menu is good, the romantic setting is better. The food, for the most part, is rib-sticking fare beloved of Bavarians, including roast suckling pig with potato dumplings, and one of the chef's best dishes, *sauerbraten* (braised beef marinated in vinegar), served with *spaetzle* (small flour dumplings).

Obere Schmiedgasse 3. © 09861/94-700. Reservations required for courtyard tables. Main courses 8.60€–24€. AE, DC, MC, V. Daily 9am–9pm.

Ratsstube FRANCONIAN This restaurant enjoys a position right on the market square, one of the most photographed spots in Germany. It's a bustling center of activity throughout the day—a day that begins when practically every Rothenburger stops by for coffee. Inside, a true tavern atmosphere prevails with hardwood chairs and tables, vaulted ceilings, and pierced copper lanterns. Downstairs you'll find a newly constructed wine bar offering live music nightly. The a la carte menu of Franconian wines and dishes includes sauerbraten and venison, both served with fresh vegetables and potatoes. For dessert, you can order homemade Italian ice cream and espresso. This is a longtime favorite of those who prefer typical Franconian cookery without a lot of fuss and bother. If you arrive at 9am, the staff will serve you an American breakfast.

Marktplatz 6. © 09861/55-11. Reservations recommended. Main courses 10€–22€. MC, V. Mon–Sat 9am–11pm; Sun 9am–6pm. Closed Jan 7 to Feb.

Reichs-Küchenmeister FRANCONIAN The main dishes served here are the type Bavarians have loved for years, including sauerbraten, or pork tender-loin; white herring and broiled salmon are also available. The *Lebensknodel* (liver dumpling) or goulash soup is perfect for cold days. The chef makes one of the best Wiener schnitzels in town. The restaurant is near St. Jakobskirche and has a typical Weinstube decor, along with a garden terrace and a *Konditorei* (cake shop). Service is warm and efficient.

Kirchplatz 8. © 09861/9700. Reservations required. Main courses 8.50€–21€. AE, DC, MC, V. Daily 7am–9:30pm.

Inexpensive

Hotel Gasthof Glocke FRANCONIAN This traditional hotel and guest-house serves good-tasting regional specialties along with a vast selection of local wine. Meals emphasize seasonal dishes and range from a simple vegetarian plate to lobster. If your expectations aren't too high, you'll probably enjoy this good regional cookery. Service is polite and attentive.

Am Plönlein 1. © 09861/958-990. Reservations recommended. Main courses 7.50€–22€. AE, DC, MC, V. Daily 11am–2pm; Mon–Sat 6–9:30pm. Closed Dec 24–Jan 6.

Tilman Riemenschneider FRANCONIAN   This traditional old Weinstube is housed in one of Rothenburg's finest hotels. The old-fashioned cookery is served in generous portions. You might begin with air-dried beef or smoked filet of trout, then follow it with poached eel, halibut steak, or loin of pork. Everything is served in generous portions with good results.

Georgengasse 11. ⓒ 09861/9790. Main courses 13€–30€; fixed-price menu 20€–28€. AE, DC, MC, V. Daily 11:30am–2pm and 6–9pm.

EXPLORING THE MEDIEVAL TOWN

The **Rathaus (Town Hall)** 🏛 on the Marktplatz (ⓒ 09861/404-92), along with the Jakobskirche, are the outstanding attractions, along with the medieval walls. The town hall consists of two sections: The older, Gothic section dates from 1240. From the 50m (165-ft.) tower of the Gothic hall, you get an overview of the town. The belfry has quite a history—in 1501, fire destroyed part of the building, and after that the belfry became a fire watchtower. Guards had to ring the bell every quarter hour to prove they were awake and on the job. The newer Renaissance section, built in 1572, is decorated with intricate friezes, an oriel extending the building's full height, and a large stone portico opening onto the square. The octagonal tower at the center of the side facing the square contains a grand staircase leading to the upper hall. On the main floor is the large courtroom.

Admission to the tower is 1€ adults, .50€ children. The Rathaus is open Monday through Friday from 8am to 6pm. The tower is open April through October, daily from 9:30am to 12:30pm and 1 to 5pm; November through March, Saturday, Sunday, and holidays only, from noon to 3pm.

St. Jakobskirche (Church of St. James), Klostergasse 15 (ⓒ **09861/70-06-20**), contains the famous *Altar of the Holy Blood* 🏛🏛 (west gallery), a masterpiece of the Würzburg sculptor and woodcarver Tilman Riemenschneider (1460–1531). The Rothenburg Council commissioned the work in 1499 to provide a worthy setting for the *Reliquary of the Holy Blood*. The relic is contained in a rock-crystal capsule set in the reliquary cross (about 1270) in the center of the shrine, and beneath it the scene of *The Last Supper* makes an immediate impact on the viewer—Jesus is giving Judas the morsel of bread, marking him as the traitor. The altar wings show (left) the *Entry of Christ into Jerusalem* and (right) *Christ Praying in the Garden of Gethsemane*.

The vertical Gothic church has three naves. The choir, dating from 1336, is the oldest section and has fine late Gothic painted-glass windows. To the left is the tabernacle (1390–1400), which was recognized as a "free place," a sanctuary for condemned criminals where they could not be touched. It's open April through October, Monday through Saturday from 9am to 5:30pm, Sunday from 11am to 5:30pm. In December, it's open daily from 10am to 5pm. In November and January through March, it's open daily from 10am to noon and 2 to 4pm. Admission costs 1.55€ adults, and .75€ children under 6 and students of any age.

Also of interest is the **Reichsstadtmuseum** 🏛, Klosterhof 5 (ⓒ **09861/939-043**). This is Rothenburg's historical collection, housed in a 13th-century Dominican nunnery with well-preserved cloisters. You'll find on display here an enormous tankard that holds 3.5 liters (3½ qt.), whose story has echoes all over the city. In 1631, during the Thirty Years' War, the Protestant city of Rothenburg was captured by General Tilly, commander of the armies of the Catholic League. He promised to spare the town from destruction if one of the town burghers would drink the huge tankard full of wine in one draught. Burgermeister Nusch accepted the challenge and succeeded, and so saved Rothenburg. There's a festival every spring at Whitsuntide to celebrate this event. Among the exhibits is the 1494 *Rothenburg Passion* series, 12 pictures by Martinus Schwartz, and works by English painter Arthur Wasse (1854–1930), whose pictures managed to capture in a romantic way the many moods of the city. Admission to the museum is 3€ adults, 2€ children; a family card costs 5.50€. The museum is open daily April through October from 9:30am to 5:30pm; November through March from 1 to 4pm.

Kriminal Museum, Burggasse 3 (℘ **09861/53-59**), is the only one of its kind in Europe. The museum's four floors display 10 centuries of legal history and provide insight into the life, laws, and punishments of medieval days. You'll see chastity belts, shame masks, a shame flute for bad musicians, and a cage for bakers who baked bread too small or too light. It's open daily April through October from 9:30am to 6pm; November and January through March from 2 to 4pm; and December from 10am to 4pm. Admission is 3.20€ adults and 1.70€ children under 13.

DINKELSBÜHL ✶

Still surrounded by medieval walls and towers, Dinkelsbühl is straight out of a Brothers Grimm story, even down to the gingerbread, which is one of its main products. Behind the ancient 10th-century walls is a town that retains its quiet, provincial ambience in spite of the many tourists who come here. The cobblestone streets are lined with fine 16th-century houses, many with carvings and paintings depicting biblical and mythological themes. In the center of town, on Marktplatz, is the late Gothic **Georgenkirche** (1448–99). It contains a carved Holy Cross Altar and pillar sculptures.

ESSENTIALS

GETTING THERE   By Train   The nearest train station is in Ansbach, which has several trains arriving daily from Munich and Frankfurt (trip time: 2½–3 hr.), Nürnberg, and Stuttgart. From Ansbach, Dinkelsbühl can be reached by bus. For information, call ℘ **01805/99-66-33.**

By Bus   For long-distance bus service along the Romantic Road, see "Rothenburg," earlier. Regional buses link Dinkelsbühl with local towns. There are three to five buses a day to Rothenburg and five or six to Nördlingen.

By Car   Take B-25 south from Rothenburg.

VISITOR INFORMATION   Contact **Stadt Verkehrsamt,** Marktplatz (℘ **09851/9-02-40**). April through October, hours are Monday through Friday from 9am to noon and 2 to 6pm, Saturday from 9am to 1pm and 2 to 4pm, and Sunday from 10am to 1pm. November through March, it's open only on Saturday from 2 to 5pm.

SPECIAL EVENTS   The **Kinderzeche (Children's Festival),** held for 10 days in July, commemorates the saving of the village by its children in 1632. According to the story, the children pleaded with conquering Swedish troops to leave their town without pillaging and destroying it—and got their wish. The pageant includes concerts given by the local boys' band dressed in historic military costumes.

WHERE TO STAY & DINE

Blauer Hecht   The inn is the best of a lackluster lot. The elegant ocher 17th-century building was once a brewery tavern, and the owners still brew in the backyard. The mid-size rooms are tranquil and sunny. Most rooms have bedside controls. Bathrooms are routine but well maintained, each with a shower stall. Good regional meals are served in the hotel restaurant/bar open to nonresidents.

Schweinemarkt 1, D-91150 Dinkelsbühl. © **09851/5810.** Fax 09851/581170. 44 units. 85€–115€ double. Rates include continental breakfast. AE, DC, MC, V. Free parking. **Amenities:** Restaurant/bar. *In room:* TV.

Deutsches Haus   The facade of Deutsches Haus, which dates from 1440, is rich in painted designs and festive woodcarvings. Rooms are unique; you may find yourself in one with a ceramic stove or in another with a Biedermeier desk. For the tradition-minded, there're no finer rooms in town. Bathrooms are spotless, often with a tub/shower combo. The Altdeutsches Restaurant, one of the finest in Dinkelsbühl, is intimate and convivial, serving regional dishes.

Weinmarkt 3, D-91550 Dinkelsbühl. © **09851/60-58.** Fax 09851/79-11. www.deutsches-haus-dkb.de. 9 units. 75€–115€ double; 135€ suite. Rates include continental breakfast. AE, MC, V. Parking 8€. Closed Dec 23–Feb 1. **Amenities:** Restaurant. *In room:* TV, minibar, hair dryer.

Eisenkrug   This is a hit-or-miss choice, letting you stay in traditional style or sterile modernity. The stylish rooms are filled with engaging old furniture. A newer wing contains the most contemporary rooms, all rather standard and modern, each medium in size. The older rooms offer more charm, although some tend to be smaller. Some beds are canopied, and housekeeping and maintenance are top-notch. Bathrooms vary from small to spacious; all but one have a shower instead of a tub. Consider Mediterrano for your dining choice even if you're a nonresident. The chef invents his own recipes and carefully selects ingredients that go into his market-fresh cuisine. His is an indigenous Franconian-Swabian approach, with many innovative touches. The superior wine cellar has some really unusual vintages.

Dr.-Martin-Luther-Strasse 1, D-91550 Dinkelsbühl. © **09851/57700.** Fax 09851/577070. www.hotel-eisenkrug.de. 23 units. 88€–110€ double. Rates include continental breakfast. MC, V. Free parking. **Amenities:** Restaurant. *In room:* TV, minibar, hair dryer.

Goldene Rose *(Value*   A landmark in the heart of this village since 1450, the intricately timbered Goldene Rose rises three stories, with a steeply pitched roof and overflowing window boxes. Although it doesn't match the impressive standards of the Eisenkrug, it is one of Dinkelsbühl's best values. The small- to medium-size rooms have been modernized in a style more institutional and functional than traditional Bavarian. The more expensive rooms offer more charm. Bathrooms are rather small, but 10 have full tub and shower. The dining rooms are country-inn style. The a la carte menu (in English) offers such tempting items as tenderloin of wild hare flavored with hazelnuts, and rump steak. This is another good choice to consider even if you're a nonresident.

Marktplatz 4, D-91550 Dinkelsbühl. © **09851/57-750.** Fax 09851/57-75-75. www.akzent.de/dinkelsbuhl. 34 units. 70€–125€ double. Rates include continental breakfast. AE, DC, MC, V. Parking 4€ in lot, 8€ in garage. **Amenities:** Restaurant, bar. *In room:* TV, minibar, hair dryer.

NÖRDLINGEN ⑂

One of the most irresistible and perfectly preserved medieval towns along the Romantic Road, Nördlingen is still completely encircled by its well-preserved 14th- to 15th-century **city fortifications.** You can walk around the town on the covered parapet, which passes 11 towers and five fortified gates set into the walls.

Things are rather peaceful around Nördlingen today, and the city still employs sentries to sound the message, *"So G'sell so"* ("All is well"), as they did in the Middle Ages. However, events around here weren't always so peaceful. The valley sits in a gigantic crater, the Ries. The Ries was once thought to be the crater of an extinct volcano; it is now known that a large meteorite was responsible. It hit the ground at more than 100,000 mph, the impact having the destructive force of 250,000 atomic bombs. Debris was hurled as far as Slovakia, and all plant and animal life within a radius of 160km (100 miles) was destroyed. This momentous event took place some 15 million years ago. Today it is the best-preserved and most scientifically researched meteorite crater on earth. The American Apollo 14 and 17 astronauts had their field training in the Ries in 1970.

ESSENTIALS
GETTING THERE   By Train   Nördlingen lies on the main Nördlingen-Aalen-Stuttgart line, with frequent connections in all directions (trip time: 2 hr. from Stuttgart and Nürnberg, 1 hr. from Augsburg). Call ☎ **01805/99-66-33** for information.

By Bus   The long-distance bus that operates along the Romantic Road includes Nördlingen; see "Rothenburg," earlier.

By Car   Take B-25 south from Dinkelsbühl.

VISITOR INFORMATION   Contact the **Verkehrsamt,** Marktplatz 2 (☎ **09081/43-80**). The office is open Easter through October, Monday through Thursday from 9am to 5pm and Friday from 9am to 3:30pm. The rest of the year, hours are Monday through Thursday from 9am to 6pm, Friday from 9am to 4:30pm, and Saturday from 9:30am to 1pm.

WHERE TO STAY
Astron Hotel Klösterle ⚓   This is the best place to stay in town. In 1991, this 13th-century former monastery was renovated, a new wing added, and the entire complex transformed into the town's most luxurious hotel. Rated four stars by the government, it offers elevator access and a hardworking, polite staff. Rooms have excellent furnishings, lots of electronic extras, and large bathrooms with tub/shower combos and deluxe toiletries.

Am Klösterle 1, D-86720 Nördlingen. ☎ 09081/88-054. Fax 09081/870-8100. www.euro-hotels.com. 97 units. 142€ double; 155€ suite. Rates include breakfast. AE, DC, MC, V. Parking 7.70€. Amenities: Restaurant; bar; fitness center; sauna; room service; laundry. In room: TV, minibar, hair dryer, safe.

Kaiser Hotel Sonne ⚓   Next to the cathedral and the Rathaus is the Sonne, an inn since 1405. Among its guests have been Frederick III, Maximilian I, Charles V, and, in more recent times, the American Apollo astronauts. Many of the mid-size rooms contain hand-painted four-posters to bring out the romantic in you. Others are regular doubles or twins. Goethe may have complained of the lack of comfort he found here, but you'll fare well. Bathrooms are fresh and immaculate, with tub/shower combos.

Marktplatz 3, D-86720 Nördlingen. ☎ 09081/50-67. Fax 09081/23-999. 43 units (35 with bathroom). 86€ double without bathroom; 100€ double with bathroom; 130€ suite. Rates include breakfast and parking. AE, DC, MC, V. Amenities: Restaurant; bar; room service; babysitting; laundry/dry cleaning. In room: TV, minibar, hair dryer.

WHERE TO DINE
Meyer's Keller CONTINENTAL   The conservative, modern decor here seems a suitable setting for the restrained *neue Küche* of talented chef and owner Joachim Kaiser, adroit with both rustic and refined cuisine. The menu changes according to availability of ingredients and the chef's inspiration; typical selections are likely to include roulade of sea wolf and salmon with baby spinach and

wild rice, or—a perfect delight—John Dory with champagne-flavored tomato sauce. The wine list is impressive, with many bottles quite reasonably priced.

Marienhöhe 8. ℂ 09081/44-93. Reservations required. Main courses 15€–26€; fixed-price meals 48€–60€. AE, MC, V. Wed–Sun 11am–2pm; Tues–Sun 6–10pm. Local bus to Marktplatz.

SEEING THE SIGHTS

At the center of the circular Altstadt within the walls is **Rübenmarkt.** If you stand in this square on market day, you'll be swept into a world of the past— the country people have preserved many traditional customs and costumes here, which, along with the ancient houses, create a living medieval city. Around the square stand a number of buildings, including the Gothic **Rathaus.** An antiquities collection is displayed in the **Stadtmuseum,** Vordere Gerbergasse 1 (ℂ **09081/273-8230**), open Tuesday through Sunday from 1:30 to 4:30pm; closed November through February. Admission is 2.55€ adults and 1.55€ children.

The 15th-century Hallenkirche, the **Church of St. George,** on the square's northern side, is the town's most interesting sight and one of its oldest buildings. Plaques and epitaphs commemorating the town's more illustrious 16th- and 17th-century residents decorate the fan-vaulted interior. Although the original Gothic altarpiece by Friedrich Herlin (1470) is now in the Reichsstadt Museum, a portion of it, depicting the crucifixion, remains in the church. Above the high altar today stands a more elaborate baroque altarpiece. The church's most prominent feature, however, is the 90m (295-ft.) French Gothic tower, called the "Daniel." At night, the town watchman calls out from the steeple, his voice ringing through the streets. The tower is open daily April through October from 9am to 8pm. Admission is 1.55€ adults and 1€ children.

Rieskrater-Museum, Hintere Gerbergasse (ℂ **09081/273-8220**), documents the impact of the stone meteorite that created the Ries. Examine fossils from Ries Lake deposits and learn about the fascinating evolution of this geological wonder. Hours are Tuesday through Sunday from 10am to noon and from 1:30 to 4:30pm. Admission is 3€ adults; 1.50€ students, seniors, and large groups. Tours of the crater are possible through the museum.

EN ROUTE TO AUGSBURG

After Nördlingen, B-25 heads south to Augsburg. After a 19km (12-mile) ride you can stop to visit **Schloss Harburg** ℛ (it's signposted), one of the best-preserved medieval castles in Germany. It once belonged to the Hohenstaufen emperors and contains treasures collected by the family over the centuries. It is open mid-March through September, Tuesday through Sunday from 10am to 5pm; October, Tuesday through Sunday from 10am to 4pm. Admission is 3.50€ adults and 2.50€ children, including a guided tour. For information call ℂ **09080/969930.**

After exploring the castle, continue 11km (7 miles) south to the walled town of **Donauwörth** ℛ, where you can stop to walk through the oldest part of the town, on an island in the river, connected by a wooden bridge. Here the Danube is only a narrow, placid stream. The town's original walls overlook its second river, the Woernitz.

After a brief stopover, continue your southward trek for 48km (30 miles) to Augsburg, the largest city on the Romantic Road.

AUGSBURG ℛℛ

Augsburg is near the center of the Romantic Road and the gateway to the Alps and the south. Founded 2,000 years ago by the Roman emperor Augustus, for whom it was named, it once was the richest city in Europe. Little remains from the early Roman period. However, the wealth of Renaissance art and architecture is staggering. Over the years, Augsburg has boasted an array of famous native sons, including painters Hans Holbein the Elder and Hans Holbein the Younger, and playwright Bertolt Brecht. It was here in 1518 that Martin Luther was summoned to recant his 95 theses before a papal emissary. Only 15% of the city was left standing after World War II, but there's still much here to intrigue. Today, Augsburg is an important industrial center on the Frankfurt–Salzburg autobahn, and Bavaria's third largest city after Munich and Nürnberg.

ESSENTIALS

GETTING THERE   By Train   About 90 Euro and InterCity trains arrive here daily from all major German cities. For information, call ℂ **01805/99-66-33.** There are 60 trains a day from Munich (trip time: 30–50 min.), and 35 from Frankfurt (3–4½ hr.).

By Bus   Long-distance buses (lines EB190 and 190A, plus line 189) service the Romantic Road. The buses are operated by **Deutsche Touring GmbH** at Am Römerhof in Frankfurt (ℂ **069/790-350** for reservations and information).

VISITOR INFORMATION   Contact **Tourist-Information,** Bahnhofstrasse (ℂ **0821/50-20-70**), Monday through Friday from 9am to 5pm, Saturday at Rathausplatz from 10am to 2pm; closed Sunday.

GETTING AROUND   The public transportation system in Augsburg consists of four tram and 31 bus lines covering the inner city and reaching into the suburbs. Public transportation operates daily from 5am to midnight.

WHERE TO STAY
Very Expensive
Steigenberger Drei Mohren ★★   This is one of the premier choices for a stopover along the Romantic Road and one of the top inns if you didn't book into the Eisenhut at Rothenburg. The original hotel, dating from 1723, was renowned in Germany before its destruction in an air raid. In 1956, it was rebuilt in a modern style. Decorators worked hard to create a decor that was both comfortable and inviting, with thick carpets, subdued lighting, and double-glazing at the windows. Rooms vary in size and appointments, however, ranging from some economy specials that are a bit small with narrow twin beds and showers (no tubs) to spacious, luxurious rooms with full shower and tub. Many rooms are smoke free, and most bathrooms are fairly spacious.

Maximilianstrasse 40, D-86150 Augsburg. ℂ **800/223-5652** in the U.S. and Canada, or 0821/5-03-60. Fax 0821/15-78-64. www.augsburg.steigenberger.de. 106 units. 164€–197€ double; 282€–640€ suite. Rates include buffet breakfast. AE, DC, MC, V. Parking 12€. Tram: 1. **Amenities:** Restaurant; bar; golf by arrangement; room service; babysitting; laundry/dry cleaning. *In room:* TV, minibar, hair dryer, trouser press.

Moderate
Dom Hotel   Although it may not have the decorative flair of the more expensive hotels such as Drei Mohren, the low rates and an indoor pool make this one of the most appealing choices in town. The hotel is a half-timbered structure, next to Augsburg's famous cathedral, and was built in the 15th century. Rooms on most floors are medium size and nicely appointed, although we prefer the smaller attic accommodations where you can rest under a beamed ceiling and enjoy a panoramic sweep of the rooftops of the city. Bathrooms are small, with tub and shower combos. Only breakfast is served but it's a treat in a garden beside the town's medieval fortifications.

Frauentorstrasse 8, D-86152 Augsburg. ℂ **0821/34-39-30.** Fax 0821/34-39-32-00. www.domhotel-augsburg.de. 50 units. 73€–117€ double. Rates include buffet breakfast. AE, DC, MC, V. Free parking or 7€ garage. Tram: 2. *In room:* TV, minibar, hair dryer, safe.

Hotel Am Rathaus *Value*   Many repeat guests consider this hotel's location just behind the town hall to be its best asset. Built in a three-story contemporary format in 1986, it offers comfortable, mid-size rooms but small bathrooms with well-maintained showers. The hotel serves a very generous breakfast buffet. It may be short on style but it's long on value.

Am Hinteren Perlachberg 1, D-86150 Augsburg. ℂ **0821/34-64-90.** Fax 0821/346-49-99. www.hotel-am-rathaus-augsburg.de. 32 units. 90€–110€ double. Rates include breakfast. AE, DC, MC, V. Parking 9€. Tram: 1. **Amenities:** Bar. *In room:* TV, minibar, hair dryer.

Romantik Hotel Augsburger Hof *☆☆*   Its main competitor, the Drei Mohren, still has more flair, but this hotel enjoys a comfortable runner-up slot. Originally built in 1767 in a solid, thick-walled design with exposed beams and timbers, the hotel was carefully restored in 1988. In the town center, it's a favorite for its traditional atmosphere and excellent food. In spite of the Renaissance interior, the rooms are completely up to date and not as romantic as the name of the hotel suggests. They range from cozy to spacious, each with a fine bed. Those overlooking the calm inner courtyard are more expensive than ones facing the street. Some bathrooms seemed crowded in as an afterthought, but each is beautifully maintained, containing a shower stall.

Auf dem Kreuz 2, D-86152 Augsburg. ℂ **0821/34-30-50.** Fax 0821/343-0555. www.augsburger-hof.de. 36 units. 90€–133€ double. Rates include buffet breakfast. AE, DC, MC, V. Parking 6€. Tram: 2. **Amenities:** Restaurant; bar; room service; dry cleaning/laundry. *In room:* TV, minibar, hair dryer.

Inexpensive
Hotel Garni Weinberger   One of the best budget accommodations in the area lies about 3km (2 miles) from the center along Augsburgerstrasse in the western sector. Rooms are small but well kept with good beds. The bathrooms are rather cramped with shower stalls, but housekeeping is excellent. The place is well patronized by bargain-hunting Germans and has a very popular cafe and bar.

Bismarckstrasse 55, D-86391 Stadtbergen. ℂ **0821/24-39-10.** Fax 0821/43-88-31. 31 units. 70€ double. Rates include buffet breakfast. AE, MC, V. Closed Aug 15–30. Tram: 3. **Amenities:** Restaurant; bar. *In room:* Clock radio.

WHERE TO DINE
Die Ecke *☆* FRENCH/SWABIAN   Dripping with atmosphere, this place seemingly dates from the Last Supper. Well, almost. At least it was founded in the year Columbus sighted the New World, and its guests have included Hans Holbein the Elder, Wolfgang Amadeus Mozart, and, in more contemporary times, Bertolt Brecht, whose sharp-tongued irreverence tended to irritate diners of more conservative political leanings. The Weinstube ambience belies the skilled cuisine of the chef, which wins us over year after year. Breast of duckling might be preceded by paté, and the filet of sole in Riesling is deservedly a classic. Venison dishes in season are a specialty—the best in town.

Elias-Holl-Platz 2. ℂ **0821/51-06-00.** Reservations required. Main courses 15€–30€; fixed-price dinner 40€ for 4 courses, 60€ for 6 courses. AE, DC, MC, V. Daily 11am–2pm and 5:30pm–midnight. Tram: 2.

Fuggerei Stube GERMAN/SWABIAN   Not as atmospheric as Die Ecke, this is nonetheless a local and enduring favorite with good food and decent prices. The large dining room, suitable for 60 persons, has welcomed diners

since 1946, with very little change in the menu, the decor, or the ambience. Expect generous portions of well-prepared food such as sauerbraten, roasted pork, pork schnitzel; game dishes such as venison, pheasant, and rabbit; and fish such as filet of sole served with boiled potatoes and parsley. The beer foaming out of the taps here is Storchenbräu, and most visitors find that it goes wonderfully with the conservative German specialties.

Jakoberstrasse 26. ℂ **0821/3-08-70.** Reservations recommended. Main courses 8.50€–18€; set-price menu 22€. AE, MC, V. Tues–Sun 11:30am–2:30pm; Tues–Sat 5:30–11pm.

Oblinger ✪ CONTINENTAL   Near the cathedral, in the heart of the historic section, Oblinger is the best restaurant within the city. It's a charming, intimate, 20-seat choice offering a changing array of seasonal specialties. The surroundings are unpretentious, the waiters attentive, and there's a superb collection of wine. You can savor the goose-liver terrine with mushrooms and cabbage, then go on to an equally well-prepared sole roulade with crepes. The turbot with chanterelles and the stuffed Bresse pigeon are also successes—quite simply, the cuisine has personality.

Pfäarrle 14. ℂ **0821/345-83-92.** Reservations required. Main courses 14€–25€. AE, DC, MC, V. Daily 11am–2pm; Tues–Sat 6–11pm. Closed Aug 1–19. Tram: 12.

SEEING THE SIGHTS IN TOWN

Rathaus   In 1805 and 1809, Napoléon visited the Rathaus, built by Elias Holl in 1620. Regrettably, it was also visited by an air raid in 1944, leaving a mere shell of the building that had once been a palatial eight-story monument to the glory of the Renaissance. Its celebrated "golden chamber" was left in shambles. Now, after costly restoration, the Rathaus is open to the public.

Am Rathausplatz 2. ℂ **0821/3249-180.** Admission 1.55€ adults, .75€ children 7–14. Daily 10am–6pm. Tram: 1.

Dom St. Maria   The cathedral of Augsburg has the distinction of containing the oldest stained-glass windows in the world. Those in the south transept, dating from the 12th century, depict Old Testament prophets in a severe but colorful style. They are younger than the cathedral itself, which was begun in 944. You'll find the ruins of the original basilica in the crypt beneath the west chancel. Partially Gothicized in the 14th century, the church stands on the edge of the park, which also fronts the **Episcopal Palace,** where the basic Lutheran creed was presented at the Diet of Augsburg in 1530. The 11th-century bronze doors, leading into the three-aisle nave, are adorned with bas-reliefs of biblical and mythological characters. The cathedral's interior, restored in 1934, contains side altars with altarpieces by Hans Holbein the Elder and Christoph Amberger.

Hoher Weg. ℂ **0821/31-66-353.** Free admission. Mon–Sat 7am–4pm; Sun noon–4pm. Tram: 1.

Church of St. Ulrich and St. Afra ✪   This is the most attractive church in Augsburg. It was constructed between 1476 and 1500 on the site of a Roman temple. The church and the dom, one Protestant, one Catholic, stand side by side, a tribute to the 1555 Peace of Augsburg, which recognized the two denominations, Roman Catholic and Lutheran. Many of the church's furnishings, including the three altars representing the birth and resurrection of Christ and the baptism of the church by the Holy Spirit, are baroque. In the crypt are the tombs of the Swabian saints, Ulrich and Afra.

Ulrichplatz 19. ℂ **0821/34-55-60.** Free admission. Daily 9am–6pm. Tram: 1.

Schaezlerpalais Facing the Hercules Fountain is the Schaezlerpalais, home to the city's art galleries. Constructed as a 60-room mansion between 1765 and 1770, it was willed to Augsburg after World War II. Most of the paintings are Renaissance and baroque. One of the most famous is Dürer's portrait of Jakob Fugger the Rich, founder of the dynasty that was once powerful enough to influence the elections of the Holy Roman emperors. Other works are by local artists Hans Burgkmair and Hans Holbein the Elder; Rubens, Veronese, and Tiepolo are also represented.

Maximilianstrasse 46. ✆ 0821/324-4125. Admission 3.05€ adults, 1.55€ children. Wed–Sun 10am–4pm. Tram: 1.

NEUSCHWANSTEIN ✹✹✹ & HOHENSCHWANGAU ✹✹: THE ROYAL CASTLES

The 19th century saw a great classical revival in Germany, especially in Bavaria, mainly because of the enthusiasm of Bavarian kings for ancient art forms. Beginning with Ludwig I (1786–1868), who was responsible for many Greek Revival buildings in Munich, this royal house ran the gamut of ancient architecture in just 3 short decades. It culminated in the remarkable flights of fancy of "Mad" King Ludwig II, who died under mysterious circumstances in 1886. In spite of his rather lonely life and controversial alliances, both personal and political, he was a great patron of the arts.

Although the name "Royal Castles" is limited to Hohenschwangau (built by Ludwig's father, Maximilian II) and Neuschwanstein, the extravagant king was responsible for the creation of two other magnificent castles, Linderhof (near Oberammergau) and Herrenchiemsee (on an island in Chiemsee).

In 1868, after a visit to the great castle of Wartburg, Ludwig wrote to his good friend, composer Richard Wagner: "I have the intention to rebuild the ancient castle ruins of Hohenschwangau in the true style of the ancient German knight's castle." The following year, construction began on the first of a series of fantastic edifices, a series that stopped only with Ludwig's death in 1886, only 5 days after he was deposed because of alleged insanity.

The nearest towns to the castles are **Füssen,** 3km (2 miles) away at the very end of the Romantic Road, and **Schwangau,** where accommodations can be found.

ESSENTIALS

GETTING THERE **By Train** There're frequent trains from Munich (trip time: 2½ hr.) and Augsburg (3 hr.) to Füssen. For information, call ✆ **01805/ 99-66-33.** Frequent buses travel to the castles.

By Bus Long-distance bus service into Füssen from other parts of the Romantic Road, including Würzburg, Augsburg, and Munich, is provided by the **Deutsche Touring GmbH** bus EB189 or EB189E. For information and reservations, call ✆ **069/790-30** in Frankfurt, or look on the Web at www.deutsche-touring.com. Regional service to villages around Füssen is provided by **RVA Regionalverkehr Allgau GmbH** in Füssen (✆ **08362/939-0505**). Its most important routing, at least for visitors to Füssen, includes about 14 orange, yellow, or white-sided buses that depart every day from Füssen's railway station for the village of Hohenschwangau, site of both Hohenschwangau Palace and Neuschwanstein Palace, a 10-minute ride. The cost of a one-way ticket to the village or to either of the two palaces is 3€. For more information, contact the Füssen tourist office.

By Car Take B-17 south to Füssen, then head east from Füssen on B-17.

HotelBergruh 2.5 r
116/night
Neuschwanstein
expedia.
com
THE ROMANTIC ROAD **461**
Alte Steigel6
Füssen

VISITOR INFORMATION   For information about the castles and the region in general, contact the **Kurverwaltung,** Kaiser-Maximilian-Platz 1, Füssen (℃ **08362/938-50**), open Monday through Friday from 8am to noon and 2 to 5pm, Saturday from 10am to noon. Information is also available at the Kurverwaltung, Rathaus, Münchenerstrasse 2, Schwangau (℃ 08362/8-19-80). It's open Monday through Friday from 8am to 12:30pm and 1:30 to 5pm.

WHERE TO STAY
In Hohenschwangau   *$110.00*
Hotel Lisl and Jägerhaus   This graciously styled villa and its annex across the street sit in a narrow valley, surrounded by their own gardens. Most rooms have a view of at least one of the two royal castles, and some rooms open onto views of both. We prefer the rooms in the main building to the more sterile annex, but all are comfortable and have good furnishings. Bathrooms, though small, are adequate, with shower stalls.

Neuschwansteinstrasse 1–3, D-87645 Hohenschwangau. ℃ 08362/88-70. Fax 08362/81-107. www. neuschwanstein-hotels.de. 47 units. 110€–160€ double; 200€ suite. AE, DC, MC, V. Free parking. Closed Dec 20–26 and New Year's. **Amenities:** 2 restaurants; bar. *In room:* TV.

Hotel Müller Hohenschwangau   As if the yellow walls, green shutters, and gabled alpine detailing of this hospitable inn weren't incentive enough, its location near the foundation of Neuschwanstein Castle makes it even more alluring. Mid-size rooms are inviting and have a bit of Bavarian charm, each with a good bed. The shower-only bathrooms are spotless. Nature lovers usually enjoy hiking the short distance to nearby Hohenschwangau Castle.

Alpseestrasse 16, D-87645 Hohenschwangau. ℃ 08362/8-19-90. Fax 08362/81-99-13. www.hotel-mueller.de. 41 units. 120€–160€ double; 165€–310€ suite. Rates include buffet breakfast. AE, DC, MC, V. Free parking. Closed Jan–Feb. **Amenities:** 4 restaurants; bar; room service. *In room:* TV, hair dryer.

In or Near Füssen
AlstadHotel Zum Hechten   Family owners have maintained this impeccable guesthouse for generations—it's one of the oldest (and most comfortable) in town. In spring, you'll open your window to a flower box of geraniums, and feel like Gretel (or Hansel) getting ready to milk the cows. Rooms are small to medium size; the bathrooms are spotless but a bit cramped, containing shower stalls. Corridor bathrooms are adequate and well maintained.

Ritterstrasse 6, D-87629 Füssen. ℃ 08362/91-600. Fax 08362/91-6099. www.hotel-hechten.com. 35 units, 33 with bathroom. 58€–75€ double without bathroom; 74€–84€ double with bathroom. Rates include buffet breakfast. AE, V. Free parking. **Amenities:** 2 restaurants. *In room:* TV.

Hotel Christine   The Christine, 5 minutes by taxi from the train station in Füssen, is one of the best local choices for accommodation. The staff spends the winter months refurbishing the rooms so they'll be fresh and sparkling for spring visitors. A Bavarian charm pervades the hotel, and rooms are cozy, though hardly fit for King Ludwig. Each is well maintained and supplied with decent furnishings. The shower-only bathrooms are a bit cramped. Breakfast, the only meal offered, is served on beautiful regional china as classical music plays in the background.

Weidachstrasse 31, D-87629 Füssen. ℃ 08362/72-29. Fax 08362/94-05-54. 13 units. 95€–130€ double. Rates include breakfast. No credit cards. Closed Jan 15–Feb 15. *In room:* TV, minibar.

Seegasthof Weissensee   The hotel is good but the view is better. The paneled rooms at this hotel have sliding glass doors opening onto a balcony overlooking the lake, 6.5km (4 miles) from central Füssen on B-310. Each room has a minibar stocked with beer, wine, and champagne. Owners are extra careful about the comfort of their guests, offering comfortable furnishings in the small but very well-maintained rooms. Bathrooms, also small, are well kept with shower stalls. Breakfast is an appetizing and generous meal of cheese, cold cuts, bread, pastry, eggs, and beverages.

An der B-310, D-87629 Füssen-Weissensee. ℂ 08362/91780. Fax 08362/917888. 19 units. 64€–80€ double. Rates include breakfast. No credit cards. Free parking. **Amenities:** Restaurant. In room: TV, minibar.

Steig Mühle ⟨ Value   Owners and hosts Gunter and Nedwig Buhmann like things to be cozy, and their chaletlike guesthouse is almost a cliché of Bavarian charm. The rooms open onto views of the lake or the mountains, and many have their own balconies. Each room has been outfitted with double or twin beds. Private bathrooms (shower only) are well kept. There aren't a lot of frills, but the place offers one of the most exceptional hotel values in the area.

Alte Steige 3, D-87629 Weissensee-Oberkirch. ℂ 08362/91-76-0. Fax 08362/31-48. www.steigmuehle.de. 24 units. 52€–64€ double. Rates include buffet breakfast. No credit cards. Free outside parking; 2.50€ in garage. From Füssen, take Rte. B310 north toward Kempten, a 5-min. drive. In room: TV.

WHERE TO DINE

Fischerhütte SEAFOOD   In Hopfen am See, at the edge of the lake within sight of dramatic mountain scenery 5km (3 miles) northwest of Füssen, lie four old-fashioned dining rooms, plus a terrace in summer. As the name "Fisherman's Cottage" suggests, the establishment specializes in an array of international fish dishes: half an Alaskan salmon (for two); a garlicky version of French bouillabaisse; fresh alpine trout, pan-fried or with aromatic herbs in the style of Provence; North Atlantic lobster; and grilled halibut. A few meat dishes are also offered, as well as tempting desserts. The food is well-prepared and top rate.

Uferstrasse 16, Hopfen am See. ℂ 08362/91-97-0. Reservations recommended. Main courses 13€–25€. AE, DC, MC, V. Daily 10am–2pm and 6–10:30pm.

Zum Schwanen SWABIAN/BAVARIAN   This small, old-fashioned restaurant serves a conservative yet flavor-filled blend of Swabian and Bavarian specialties. Good-tasting and hearty specialties include homemade sausage, roast pork, lamb, and venison. Expect robust flavors and a crowd of cheery diners who don't believe in the Weight Watchers packaged dinner.

Brotmarkt 4, Füssen. ℂ 08362/61-74. Reservations required. Main courses 6.60€–17€. MC, V. Tues–Sun noon–2pm; Tues–Sat 5:30–10pm. Closed Nov.

VISITING THE ROYAL CASTLES

There are often very long lines in summer, especially in August. With 25,000 people a day visiting, the wait in peak summer months can be as long as 4 or 5 hours for a 20-minute tour. For more information on Neuschwanstein, call ℂ **08362/8-10-35** or visit the website at **www.neuschwanstein.com**. For information on Hohenschwangau, call ℂ **08362/8-11-27** or visit the website at **www.hohenschwangau.de.**

Neuschwanstein ⟨⟨⟨

This is the fairy-tale castle of Ludwig II. Construction went on for 17 years, until the king's death, when all work stopped, leaving a part of the interior uncompleted. Ludwig lived here on and off for about 6 months from 1884 to 1886.

The doorway off the left side of the vestibule leads to the king's apartments. The study, like most of the rooms, is decorated with wall paintings showing scenes from the Nordic legends (which inspired Wagner's operas). The theme of the study is the Tannhäuser saga, painted by J. Aigner. The curtains and chair coverings are in hand-embroidered silk, designed with the Bavarian coat of arms.

From the vestibule, you enter the throne room through the doorway at the opposite end. This hall, designed in Byzantine style by J. Hofmann, was never completed. The floor, a mosaic design, depicts the animals of the world. The columns in the main hall are the deep copper red of porphyry.

The king's bedroom is the most richly carved and decorated in the entire castle—it took 4½ years to complete. Aside from the mural showing the legend of Tristan and Isolde, the walls are decorated with panels carved to look like Gothic windows. In the center is a large wooden pillar completely encircled with gilded brass sconces. The ornate bed is on a raised platform with an elaborately carved canopy.

The fourth floor of the castle is almost entirely given over to the **Singer's Hall,** the pride of Ludwig II and all of Bavaria. Modeled after the hall at Wartburg, where the legendary song contest of Tannhäuser supposedly took place, this hall is decorated with marble columns and elaborately painted designs interspersed with frescoes depicting the life of Parsifal.

The castle is open year-round, and in September, visitors have the additional treat of hearing Wagnerian concerts and other music in the Singer's Hall. For information and reservations, contact the tourist office in Schwangau, **Verkehrsamt,** at the Rathaus (**© 08362/93-85-23**). The castle, which is seen by guided tour, is open daily April through September from 9am to 6pm; October through March from 10am to 4pm. Admission is 7€ adults, 4.60€ students and seniors over 65, free for children under 14.

Reaching Neuschwanstein involves a steep 1km (½-mile) climb from the parking lot of Hohenschwangau Castle—about a 25-minute walk for the energetic, an eternity for anybody else. To cut down on the climb, you can take a bus to Marienbrücke, a bridge that crosses over the Pollat Gorge at a height of 93m (305 ft.). From that vantage you, like Ludwig, can stand and meditate on the glories of the castle and its panoramic surroundings. If you want to photograph the castle, don't wait until you reach the top, where you'll be too close. It costs 2.05€ for the bus ride up to the bridge or 1€ if you'd like to take the bus back down the hill. From the Marienbrücke Bridge it's a 10-minute walk to Neuschwanstein over a very steep footpath that is not easy to negotiate for anyone who has trouble walking up or down precipitous hills.

The most colorful way to reach Neuschwanstein is by horse-drawn carriage, costing 5.50€ for the ascent, 3€ for the descent. However, some readers have objected to the rides, complaining that too many people are crowded in.

Hohenschwangau ★★

Not as glamorous or spectacular as Neuschwanstein, the neo-Gothic Hohenschwangau Castle nevertheless has a much richer history. The original structure dates back to the 12th-century knights of Schwangau. When the knights faded away, the castle began to do so too, helped along by the Napoleonic Wars. When Ludwig II's father, Crown Prince Maximilian (later Maximilian II), saw the castle in 1832, he purchased it and 4 years later had completely restored it. Ludwig II spent the first 17 years of his life here and later received Richard Wagner in its chambers, although Wagner never visited Neuschwanstein on the hill above.

The rooms of Hohenschwangau are styled and furnished in a much heavier Gothic mode than those in Ludwig's castle and are typical of the halls of medieval knights' castles. Also unlike Neuschwanstein, this castle has a comfortable look about it, as if it actually were a home, not just a museum. The small chapel, once a reception hall, still hosts Sunday Mass. The suits of armor and the Gothic arches set the stage. Among the most attractive chambers is the **Hall of the Swan Knight,** named for the wall paintings that tell the saga of Lohengrin.

Hohenschwangau is open daily March 15 through mid-October from 8:30am to 5:30pm, off season from 9:30am to 4pm. Admission is 7.15€ adults, 4.60€ children 12 to 15 and seniors over 65, free for children under 12. Several parking lots nearby enable you to leave your car while visiting both castles. For ticket information for either castle, call ℂ **08362/930-830.**

OUTDOOR ACTIVITIES IN THE AREA

Most visitors come to Füssen for views of its magnificent Bavarian castles, testimonials to the megalomania of a demented king. But if you want to get away from the grandeur of his dreams, nearby Forggensee and Hopfensee provide lots of opportunities for windsurfing, swimming, and sailing. The focal points for all of these include the Forggensee's **Yachtschule Forggensee,** Seestrasse 10, 87669 Rieden (ℂ **08367/471**), and the Hopfensee's **Selbach Bootsvermietung,** Höhenstrasse 51, 87629 Hopfen (ℂ **08364/1487**). At both of these sites, instruction for, and rentals of, windsurfers and sailboats are available.

There's also a limited amount of mid-winter skiing available in the area, at lower altitudes and with less reliable snowfall, than that which prevails at more visible resorts such as Garmisch. About 6.5km (4 miles) from Füssen, the **Schigebiet Tegelberg,** near the hamlet of Schwangau (ℂ **08362/98-36-0**), provides a half-dozen lifts and a cable car that ascend the slopes of the Tegelberg.

Frankly, your best bet for recreation, diversion, and distraction will probably involve hiking and hill climbing in the foothills around Füssen and Schwangau. Maps, guide services, and hiking-related information of all kinds are available from the local tourist offices.

Greece

by Sherry Marker

Greeks are gearing up to welcome visitors from around the world to the 2004 Summer Olympics, to be held August 13 to 29 in and around Athens, the first home of the Olympic Games. But the "glory that was Greece" continues to lure visitors year-round to such attractions as the Acropolis in Athens; Olympia, where the games began; Delphi, with the magnificent temple of Apollo; Mycenae, where Agamemnon met his bloody death when he returned home from Troy; and Epidauros, with its astonishingly well-preserved ancient theater. There's also a profusion of less well-known ancient sites such as Nemea, home to a carefully restored stadium and a handsome 4th-century-B.C. temple, currently undergoing restoration. In addition, Greece has a wealth of Byzantine monuments, including the churches of Daphni, just outside Athens, and Osios Loukas, near Delphi. But its myths and monuments are only one aspect of the country's allure: Greece is also the quintessential vacation land of glorious beaches and scenic peaks. After sightseeing, you can laze the day away on a perfect beach—and then dance the night away in a cafe at the foot of the Acropolis or on one of the breathtakingly beautiful "isles of Greece."

1 Athens

Athens is the city that Greeks love to hate. They complain that it's too expensive, too crowded, and too polluted. The city does seem to be bursting at the seams: Some 40% of Greece's population lives here, with five million inhabitants, a rumored 17,000 taxis, and streets so congested you'll suspect that each of those five million Athenians has a car. Work on the Metro continues, with handsome stations open in central Athens at Syntagma, Acropolis, and Omonia. No one really knows when the tunneling and construction that have disrupted traffic in much of central Athens will end and the entire system will be up and running. Hopes are high that when the Metro is finished, Athens's perpetual gridlock and endemic *nefos* (smog) will be substantially alleviated. Already, pedestrians are enjoying the new network of walkways that will eventually link the major archaeological sites—although pedestrianizing important roads such as Dionyssiou Areopagitou has increased congestion on once-tranquil side streets. In short, as always in Athens, things are in a state of flux. So, why are you here? Because you, too, will probably soon develop a love-hate relationship with the city. You'll snarl at the traffic and resent the construction, all the while marveling at the view of the Acropolis as you stroll on Dionyssiou Areopagitou. You may find yourself fuming at a taxi driver who tries to overcharge you—and moments later thanking the stranger who realizes you're lost and walks several blocks out of his way to take you where you're going.

Allow yourself some time to make haste slowly in Athens. Your best moments may come at a small cafe, sipping a tiny cup of the sweet sludge that Greeks call coffee, or in the Plaka, getting hopelessly lost—only to find yourself in the shady courtyard of an old church. With a little planning, you should enjoy a comfortable stay in a good hotel, eat well in convivial restaurants, and leave Athens expecting to return, as the Greeks say, *tou chronou:* next year.

ESSENTIALS

BY PLANE The new **Athens International Airport Eleftherios Venizelos** (© 210/353-0000; www.aia.gr), 27km (17 miles) northeast of Athens at Spata, opened in 2001. The good news is that this is a large, modern facility, with ample restrooms, interesting shops, and acceptable restaurants. The bad news is that unlike Hellinikon airport, which was virtually in Athens, the new airport is a serious slog from Athens (allow an hour). The airport's website and official publications cannot always be relied on for accurate, up-to-date information. The airport has shops (including a good bookstore, and stores carrying attractively priced perfumes and colognes) and restaurants (including the inevitable McDonald's). Although the direct six-lane link road to Athens is now officially complete, not all exits, entrances, and feeder roads have been completed, nor are they accurately signposted. Depending on whom you listen to, the Metro link into Athens will (or will not) be completed in time for the 2004 Summer Olympics. At present, allow at least an hour for the journey from the airport to Athens (and vice-versa) by bus or taxi; you may be pleasantly surprised that you need less time, but you may find yourself glad you allowed the full hour. A taxi into central Athens usually costs around 15€ to 25€, depending on the time of day and traffic. Bus service to Syntagma Square or to Piraeus costs about 4€. Officially, there's one bus to Syntagma and one to Piraeus every 20 minutes. Bus and taxi stations are signposted at the airport.

When planning your carry-on luggage for the Athens airport, keep in mind that you may have quite a trek from your arrival point to the baggage-claim area. Tourist information, currency exchange, a post office, baggage storage (left luggage), and car rentals are available at the Arrivals level of the Main Terminal. ATMs, telephones, toilets, and luggage carts (1€) are available at the baggage-claim area. There are also several free phones from which you can call for a porter. *Note:* Porters' fees are highly negotiable.

There have been frequent complaints that adequate information on arrivals, departures, cancellations, delays, and gate changes is not always posted on the flight information screens. Nonetheless, it is important to check these screens and at the information desks, as there are currently no flight announcements. Arrive at your gate as early as possible; gates are sometimes changed at the last minute, necessitating a considerable scramble to reach the new gate in time.

Tips Taxi Savvy

If you decide to take a taxi, ask an airline official or a policeman what the fare should be, and let the taxi driver know you've been told the official rate before you begin your journey. If you're taking a taxi to the airport, try to have the desk clerk at your hotel order it for you well in advance of your departure. Many taxis refuse to go to the airport, fearing that they'll have a long wait before they get a return fare.

BULGARIA

Tirane

ALBANIA

Kilkis, Serrai, Drama, Komotini
Edhessa, **MACEDONIA**, Kavala, **THRACE**
Kastoria, Thessaloniki, Alexandroupolis
Kozani, Veroia, Thasos, Samothraki
Poliyiros

Sea of Marmara

ZAGORI

Mt. Olympus

Kerkira, Ioannina, Larisa, Limnos, TURKEY
Igoumenitsa, **EPIRUS**, **THESSALY**
Arta, Kardhitsa, Volos
Preveza, **NORTHERN**
Levkas, Lamia, **SPORADES**
CENTRAL GREECE, **EVVIA**, Skiros, Aegean, Lesvos
Mesolongion, Delphi, Khalkis, Sea
Kefallinia, Patrai, Khios

Corinth, Athens, Andros, Samos
Zakinthos, Pirgos, Olympia, Ikaria
Tripolis, Navplion
Kalamata, **PELOPONNESE**, Sparta, Syros, Tinos, **CYCLADES**, **DODECANESE**
Yithion, Sifnos, Naxos, Kos
Santorlnl. (Thira), Rhodes
Kithira, Sea of Crete, Karpathos

Ionian Sea

Khania, Rethimnon, Ayios Nikolaos, Mediterranean Sea
CRETE, Iraklion, Sitia

0 — 100 mi
0 — 100 km

BY TRAIN   There are two train stations in central Athens; both are just off Dilyianni, about 1.5km (1 mile) northwest of Omonia Square. Trains from the west, including Eurail connections via Patra, arrive at the **Stathmos Peloponnissou (Peloponnese Station),** about 1.5km (1 mile) northwest of Omonia Square. Trains from the north arrive 3 blocks north at the **Stathmos Larissis (Larissa Station),** on the opposite side of the tracks from the Peloponnese Station. If you are making connections from one station to the other, allow 10 to 15 minutes for the walk. Both stations have currency-exchange offices usually open daily from 8am to 9:15pm; and luggage-storage offices charging 4€ per bag per day, open daily from 6:30am to 9:30pm. The cafe and waiting room are often closed. A **taxi** into the center of town should cost about 5€. For information on schedules and fares, contact the **Greek Railroad Company (OSE;** © **210/512-4913** or 210/529-7777; www.ose.gr).

BY BOAT   **Piraeus,** the main harbor of Athens's main seaport, 11km (7 miles) southwest of central Athens, is a 15-minute subway (Metro) ride from Monastiraki and Omonia squares. The subway runs from about 5am to midnight and costs 1€. The far-slower bus no. 040 runs from Piraeus to central Athens (with a stop at Filellinon off Syntagma Sq.) every 15 minutes between 5am and 1am and hourly from 1am to 5am, for .50€.

     You might prefer to take a **taxi** to avoid what can be a long hike from your boat to the bus stop or subway terminal. Be prepared for some serious bargaining.

Athens

The normal fare on the meter from Piraeus to Syntagma should be about 7€ to 10€, but many drivers simply offer a flat fare, which can be as much as 20€. Pay it if you're desperate, or walk to a nearby street, hail another taxi, and insist that the meter be turned on.

If you travel to Piraeus by hydrofoil *(Flying Dolphin)*, you'll probably arrive at the **Zea Marina** harbor, about a dozen blocks south across the peninsula from the main harbor. Even our Greek friends admit that getting a taxi from Zea Marina into Athens can involve a wait of an hour or more—and that drivers usually drive a hard (and exorbitant) bargain. To avoid both the wait and the big fare, walk up the hill from the hydrofoil station and catch bus no. 905 for .50€; it connects Zea to the Piraeus subway station, where you can complete your journey into Athens. You must buy a ticket at the small ticket stand near the bus stop or at a newsstand before boarding the bus. *Warning:* If you arrive late at night, you might not be able to do this, as both the newsstand and the ticket stand may be closed.

VISITOR INFORMATION   Tourist Office   In 2003, the **Greek National Tourism Organization** (**GNTO** or **EOT,** also known as the Hellenic Tourism Organization) closed its main office just off Syntagma Square at 2 Amerikis. The new main office is at 7 Tsochas St., Ambelokipi (© **210/870-0000;** www. gnto.gr), well out of central Athens. The office is open Monday through Friday from 8am to 3pm and is closed weekends. No sign identifies the building as an EOT office, but there's a round sign with an I above the door. Information about Athens, free city maps, transportation schedules, hotel lists, and booklets on other regions of Greece are available in Greek, English, French, and German, although many publications on popular sights seem to be perpetually out of print.

Websites   Sites include **www.greece.gr**, **www.culture.gr**, **www.phantis.com**, and **www.ellada.com** for Athens and Greece in general; **http://city.net** (Athens information); **www.athensnews.gr** (*The Athens News,* Greece's English-language newspaper); **www.eKathimerini.com** (an insert of translations from the Greek press sold with the *International Herald Tribune*); **www.all-hotels.gr/intro.asp** (information on hotels); **www.dilos.com** (travel information, including discounted hotel prices); **www.gtp.gr** (information on ferry service); **www.greek islands.gr** (information on the islands); **www.greektravel.com** (a helpful site on all aspects of Greece run by American Matt Barrett); **www.ancientgreece.com** and **www.perseus.tufts.edu** (an excellent source about ancient Greece); and **www.greekbooks.com**, **www.book.culture.gr**, **www.nbc.gr**, and **www.greek books.gr** (useful sites for information on books on many aspects of Greece).

Tips Personal Safety

In June 2003, The "Personal Safety Survey" done annually by the Mercer Human Resource Consulting Group listed Athens as the 10th worst-rated holiday destination in terms of personal safety. Pickpocketing, especially in the Plaka area, and even on the Acropolis, has become a real problem. Visitors, especially during the Olympics, are advised to exercise all the usual precautions of only carrying their passport, large sums of money, or credit cards with them on the street if these valuables are in a secure place.

Tips **Olympics Info**

If you want to find out more about the upcoming Summer Olympics in Greece in August 2004, check out **www.athens.olympic.org**, **www.athens 2004.com**, and **www.forthnet.gr/olympics**.

CITY LAYOUT   If you, like the Greek mathematician Euclid, find it easy to imagine geometric forms, it will help you to think of central Athens as an almost perfect equilateral triangle, with its points at **Syntagma (Constitution) Square, Omonia (Harmony) Square,** and **Monastiraki (Little Monastery) Square,** near the **Acropolis.** In government jargon, the area bounded by Syntagma, Omonia, and Monastiraki squares is defined as the commercial center, from which cars are banned (in theory, if not in practice) except for several cross streets. Most Greeks consider Omonia the city center, but visitors usually get their bearings from Syntagma, where the House of Parliament is. Few Athenians have been enchanted with Omonia's "facelift" in honor of the Olympics. Twenty-seven months and two million euros later, it is now possible, somewhat safely, to walk across Omonia Square—on lots of cement. The promised trees, at least at press time, had not appeared. Omonia and Syntagma squares are connected by the parallel **Stadiou Street** and **Panepistimiou Street,** also called **Eleftheriou Venizelou.** West from Syntagma Square, ancient **Ermou Street** and broader **Mitropoleos Street** lead slightly downhill to **Monastiraki Square.** Here you'll find the **flea market,** the **Ancient Agora (Market)** below the Acropolis, and the **Plaka,** the oldest neighborhood, with many street names and a scattering of monuments from antiquity. A special bonus: **Adrianou,** the main drag in Plaka, which once teemed with traffic, is now pedestrianized. From Monastiraki Square, **Athinas Street** leads north past the modern market (the Central Market) to Omonia Square. Bustling with shoppers in the daytime, Athinas Street is less savory and avoided at night, when prostitutes and drug dealers tend to hang out here.

In general, finding your way around Athens is easy, except in the Plaka, at the foot of the Acropolis. This labyrinth of narrow, winding streets can challenge even the best navigators. Don't panic: The area is small enough that you can't go far astray, and its side streets, with small houses and neighborhood churches, are so charming that you won't mind being lost. One excellent map may help: the Greek Archaeological Service's **Historical Map of Athens,** which includes the Plaka and the city center and shows the major archaeological sites. The map costs about 4€ and is sold at many bookstores, museums, ancient sites, and newspaper kiosks.

GETTING AROUND   By Public Transportation   The **blue-and-white buses** run regular routes in Athens and its suburbs every 15 minutes daily from 5am to midnight. The **orange electric trolley buses** serve areas in the city center daily from 5am to midnight. The **green buses** run between the city center and Piraeus every 20 minutes daily from 6am to midnight, then hourly to 6am. At press time, tickets cost .50€ and must be bought in advance, usually in groups of 10, from any news kiosk or special bus ticket kiosks at the main stations. When you board, validate your ticket in the automatic machine. Hold onto it: Uniformed and plainclothes inspectors periodically check tickets and can levy a basic fine of 5€ or a more punitive fine of 20€, on the spot.

(*Tips* **Ride the Metro & View Artifacts**

Allow a little extra time when you catch the Metro in central Athens. Two stations—**Syntagma Square** and **Acropolis**—handsomely display finds from the subway excavations in what amounts to Athens's newest small museums. For more on the Athens Metro, go to **www.ametro.gr**.

The **Athens map** distributed by the Greek National Tourist Organization indicates major public transportation stops and routes. Keep in mind that the buses are usually very crowded and their schedules are erratic. Furthermore, construction on the Metro, as well as the opening of new Metro stops, is affecting bus routes and schedules.

The major bus stations in Athens are: Suburban bus terminal at Areos Park; Long Distance Bus Terminal A, 100 Kiffissou (reached by bus no. 051 from Zinonos and Menandrou sts., off Omonia Sq.); and Long Distance Bus Terminal B, 260 Liossion (reached by bus no. 024 from Amalias Ave., Syntagma Sq.). Keep in mind that the numbers of buses serving these routes may have changed by the time you visit Athens.

The original **Metro** line linked Piraeus, Athens's seaport; central Athens itself; and Kifissia, an upscale northern suburb. A second line, with its main station in Syntagma Square, links the Defense Ministry on Mesogheion Avenue with central Athens and the northwest suburb of Sepolia. Original plans for the entire 21-station Metro to be running by the end of 2002 have been changed to target the August 2004 Summer Olympics. (Now if someone would just figure out how to build adequate parking lots near the new Metro stops so that commuters can leave their cars there rather than park them on every available inch of the sidewalks.) In the city center, the main stops are **Syntagma, Acropolis, Monastiraki, Omonia,** and **Viktorias (Victoria).** Trains run about every 5 to 15 minutes daily from 5am to midnight. At present, tickets on the old line cost .60€; tickets on the new line cost .75€; and a day pass costs 3€—but don't be surprised if these prices have gone up by the time you arrive. Validate your ticket in the machine as you enter the waiting platform, or risk a fine. Metro and bus tickets are not interchangeable.

By Taxi   Supposedly there are 17,000 taxis in Athens, but finding one empty is almost never easy. Especially if you have travel connections to make, it's a good idea to pay the 2€ surcharge and reserve a radio taxi. The minimum fare in a taxi is 2€.

When you get into a taxi, check to see that the meter is turned on and set on "1" rather than "2"; it should be set on "2" (double fare) only from midnight to 5am or if you take a taxi outside the city limits. (If you plan to do this, try to negotiate a flat rate in advance.) Unless your cab is caught in very heavy traffic, a trip to the center of town from the airport between 5am and midnight shouldn't cost more than 15€ to 25€. Don't be surprised if your driver picks up other passengers en route; he'll work out everyone's share, and probably the worst that will happen is you'll get less of a break on the shared fare than you would if you spoke Greek. Most Greek passengers at least round out the fare—for example, from 2.90€ to 3€—and some give a bit more of a tip.

There are about 15 radio taxi companies, including **Athina** (© 210/921-7942), **Express** (© 210/993-4812), **Kosmos** (© 210/645-7000), **Parthenon**

(© 210/581-4711), and **Piraeus** (© 210/418-2333-5). If you're trying to make travel connections or traveling during rush hours, the service will be well worth the 2€ surcharge.

If you suspect you've been overcharged, ask for help at your hotel or other destination before you pay the fare. Keep in mind that your driver may have difficulty understanding your pronunciation of your destination. If you are taking a taxi from your hotel, a staff member can tell the driver your destination or write down the address for you to show to the driver. If you carry a business card from your hotel, you can show it to the driver when you return. Most restaurants will call for a taxi at no charge.

By Foot Most of what you probably want to see and do in Athens is in the city center, allowing you to sightsee mostly on foot. *Warning:* All visitors should keep in mind that here, as in many busy cities, a red traffic light or stop sign is no guarantee that cars will stop for pedestrians. The pedestrian zones in sections of the Plaka, the commercial center, and Kolonaki make strolling, window-shopping, and sightseeing infinitely more pleasant than on other, traffic-clogged streets.

> **⌒Tips A Taxi Warning**
>
> There are increasing numbers of unlicensed cab drivers in Athens and Piraeus. Usually, these pirate cabbies (many from eastern Europe) drive not the standard gray Athens taxi but a gray car you might mistake for an Athens cab. It's always a good idea to make sure your cab driver has a meter and a photo ID. Many of the unlicensed cab drivers are uninsured and unfamiliar with the metropolitan area.

By Car Parking is so difficult and traffic so heavy in Athens that you should use a car only for trips outside the city. Keep in mind that on any day trip (to Sounion or Daphni, for example), you'll spend at least several hours leaving and reentering central Athens.

Car-rental agencies in the Syntagma Square area include **Avis,** 48 Amalias Ave. (© **800/331-1084** in the U.S., or 210/322-4951); **Auto Europe,** 29 Hatz-ihristou, right off Syngrou (© **800/223-5555** in the U.S., or 210/924-2206); and **Budget,** 8 Syngrou Ave. (© **800/527-0700** in the U.S., or 210/921-4711). Remember: You almost always get the best deal if you arrange the rental before leaving home. You will usually get the worst possible deal if you arrive in Athens and want a car for only 1 day. *Warning:* Be sure to take full insurance and ask if the price you are quoted includes everything. Often the price quoted doesn't include all taxes, a drop-off fee, gasoline charges, and so on. Be particularly vigilant if you intend to collect or return your car at an airport: Many companies charge—but do not mention it when you reserve your car—a hefty fee for this.

 FAST FACTS: Athens

American Express The office at 2 Ermou, near the southwest corner of Syntagma Square (© **210/324-4975**; fax 210/322-7893), offers currency exchange and other services weekdays from 8:30am to 4pm and Saturday from 8:30am to 1:30pm.

Business Hours **Banks** are generally open Monday through Thursday from 8am to 2pm and Friday from 8am to 1:30pm. In winter, shops are generally open Monday and Wednesday from 9am to 5pm; Tuesday, Thursday, and Friday from 10am to 7pm; and Saturday from 8:30am to 3:30pm. In summer, shops are generally open Monday, Wednesday, and Saturday from 8am to 3pm; and Tuesday, Thursday, and Friday from 8am to 1:30pm and 5:30 to 10pm. Note that many shops geared to visitors keep especially long hours, but some close from about 2 to 5pm. Most **food stores** and the **Central Market** are open Monday and Wednesday from 9am to 4:30pm, Tuesday from 9am to 6pm, Thursday from 9:30am to 6:30pm, Friday from 9:30am to 7pm, and Saturday from 8:30am to 4:30pm.

Currency On January 1, 2002, the monetary unit in Greece became the euro €. At press time, the euro and the dollar were almost equal in value.

Currency Exchange Most banks have currency-exchange counters that use the rates set daily by the government, which are usually more favorable than those offered at unofficial exchange bureaus. It's worth doing a little comparison shopping for the best rate of exchange; for example, many hotels offer rates (usually only for cash) that are better than the official bank rates. ATM cash dispensers are increasingly common in Athens, and the National Bank of Greece operates a 24-hour ATM next to the tourist information office on Syntagma Square. It's not a good idea to rely on using ATMs exclusively in Athens because the machines are often out of service on holidays or during bank strikes.

Dentists & Doctors If you need an English-speaking doctor or dentist, call your embassy for advice; or try **SOS Doctor** (© **210/331-0310** or 210/331-0311). The English-language *Athens News* lists some American- and British-trained doctors and hospitals offering emergency services. Most of the larger hotels have doctors whom they can call for you in an emergency.

Drugstores Pharmakia, identified by green crosses, are scattered throughout Athens. Hours are usually from 8am to 2pm on weekdays. In the evening and on weekends most are closed, but they usually post a notice listing the names and addresses of pharmacies that are open or will open in an emergency. The English-language *Athens News* (published on Fri) often lists pharmacies open outside regular hours.

Embassies/Consulates These may be found at the following locations: **United States,** 91 Leoforos Vas. Sofias (© 210/721-2951; emergency number 210/729-4301); **Canada,** 4 Ioannou Yenadiou (© 210/727-3400 or 210/725-4011); **United Kingdom,** 1 Ploutarchou (© 210/723-6211); **Ireland,** 7 Vas. Konstantinou (© 210/723-2771); **Australia,** 37 Leoforos Dimitriou Soutsou (© 210/645-0404-5); **New Zealand,** 24 Xenias, Ambelokipi (© 210/771-0112); **South Africa,** 60 Kifissias, Maroussi (© 210/680-6645). Be sure to phone ahead before you go to any embassy. Most are only open for business Monday through Friday from 9am to noon and are usually closed on their own country's holidays as well as Greek holidays.

Emergencies In an emergency, dial © **100** for fast police assistance and © **171** for the **Tourist Police.** Dial © **199** to report a **fire** and © **166** for an **ambulance** and **hospital.**

Internet Access Most cybercafes charge about 6€ an hour. The very efficient and helpful **Sofokleous.com Internet C@fe** ⚡, 5 Stadiou, a block off Syntagma Square (ⓒ/fax **210/324-8105**), is open daily from 10am to 10pm. The **Astor Internet Cafe,** 27 Patission, a block off Omonia Square (ⓒ **210/ 523-8546**), is open Monday through Saturday from 10am to 10pm and Sunday from 10am to 4pm. Across from the National Archaeological Museum is the **Museum Internet Cafe,** 28 Octobriou (the street is also called Patission; ⓒ **210/883-3418;** www.museumcafe.gr), open daily from 9am to 11pm. In the Plaka, **Plaka Internet World,** 29 Pandrossou, Monastiraki, is usually open from 11am to 11pm.

Post Office The main **post offices** in central Athens are at 100 Eolou, just south of Omonia Square, and in Syntagma Square on the corner of Mitropoleos Street. They're open Monday through Friday from 7:30am to 8pm, Saturday from 7:30am to 2pm, and Sunday from 9am to 1pm. All the post offices can accept small parcels. The **parcel post office,** 4 Stadiou, inside the arcade (ⓒ **210/322-8940**), is open Monday through Friday from 7:30am to 8pm. Parcels must be open for inspection before you seal them (bring your own tape and string) at the post office.

Telephone/Telegrams/Telefaxes The country code for Greece is **30.** The city code for Athens is **210.**

Many of the city's public phones now accept only **phone cards,** available at newsstands and OTE offices in several denominations starting at 5€. Some kiosks still have **metered phones;** you pay what the meter records. Local phone calls cost about .05€. North Americans can phone home directly by contacting **AT&T** at ⓒ 00-800-1311, **MCI** at ⓒ 00-800-1211, or **Sprint** at ⓒ 00-800-1411; calls can be collect or billed to your phone charge card. You can send a telegram or fax from offices of the **Telecommunications Organization of Greece (OTE).** The three main OTE offices in central Athens are at 15 Stadiou, near Syntagma; Omonia Square; and Victoria Square at 85 Patission.

Tipping Restaurants include a service charge in the bill, but many visitors add a 10% tip. Most Greeks don't give a percentage tip to taxi drivers but round the fare up to the nearest euro, adding more for a higher fare.

WHERE TO STAY

Virtually all Greek hotels are clean and comfortable; few are charming, elegant, or memorable. Most, in fact, are monotonous, with one guest room a bit larger, another a bit smaller—and few have any individual touch to warm the traveler's heart. (I've noted those hotels that are truly distinctive in the listings below.) Keep in mind that, in the absence of clearly distinguishing characteristics, location is often the most important factor in choosing your hotel.

A few suggestions: If shower and tub facilities are important to you, be sure to have a look at the bathroom. Many Greek tubs are tiny, and the showers are hand held. Don't assume that just because a hotel says it has air-conditioning, the air-conditioning is working—and be sure to see if the hotel has adequately functioning central heating in the winter.

Although many guidebooks do, I don't recommend staying in any of the luxury hotels on Syngrou Avenue. Sure, the Metropolitan, the Leda Marriott, and the Athenaem-Intercontinental have all the creature comforts, but Syngrou Avenue is ugly, noisy, and away from everything you want to see in Athens. In short, the Syngrou hotels are just fine for the businesspeople here for conferences who never leave their hotels—but not for visitors here to see the sights.

Warning: Hotel prices were accurate at press time, but price increases of 20% and more are rumored as hoteliers gear up for the Summer Olympics. Once the Olympics are on, horrific price hikes of between 50% and an unbelievable 300% are rumored.

IN PLAKA
Expensive
Electra Palace 𝒢𝒢   Just a few blocks southwest of Syntagma Square, the Electra is the most modern and stylish Plaka hotel; it even has a decent restaurant, and the rooftop pool is a real bonus. Rooms are a good size and have balconies. The top floors (5–7) are where you want to be, both for the Acropolis view and to escape traffic noise. And that's the problem: the Electra won't guarantee you a top-floor room when you reserve, and if you sit on your balcony on one of the lower floors, you'll inhale lots of fumes, hear lots of traffic noise, and have a view of the building across the street. Still, you can always retreat to the rooftop pool and take in the Acropolis view there.

18 Nikodimou, Plaka, 105 57 Athens. ✆ 210/324-1401 or 210/324-1407. Fax 210/324-1875. 106 units. 140€–200€ double. Rates include breakfast. AE, DC, MC, V. **Amenities:** Restaurant; bar; rooftop pool. *In room:* A/C, TV, minibar, hair dryer.

Moderate
Acropolis House Hotel   Try to get room no. 401 or 402 for an Acropolis view in this small hotel in a renovated 150-year-old villa. The relatively quiet pedestrianized Plaka side street is a real plus, although motorcycles can be a problem. The newer wing (only 65 years old) isn't architecturally special, but the toilets (one for each room but across the hall) are fully tiled and modern. There's a washing machine (for a small fee; free after a 4-day stay). If the Acropolis House is full, try the less appealing Adonis or (still less appealing) Kouros.

6–8 Kodrou, 105 58 Athens. ✆ 210/322-2344. Fax 210/324-4143. 25 units, 15 with bathroom. 50€ double without bathroom; 75€ double with bathroom. 10€ surcharge for A/C. Rates include continental breakfast. V. Walk 2 blocks out of Syntagma Sq. on Mitropoleos and turn left on Voulis, which becomes pedestrianized Kodrou. *In room:* A/C.

Byron Hotel   Every year I come close to eliminating the Byron, where the indifferent-at-best service is a real drawback. Still, it offers one real plus: the relatively quiet central Plaka location just off recently pedestrianized Dionyssiou Areopagitou Street. The price is fair (and often negotiable). That said, if you don't remember the dingy Byron before its remodeling 3 years ago, the new decor, which lacks charm, might not impress you. I've also had reports that the air-conditioning is temperamental at best. Alas, the same can be said for the service, which is haphazard and often curt.

19 Vyronos, 105 58 Athens. ✆ 210/325-3554. Fax 210/323-0327. 20 units. 80€ double. Rates include breakfast. No credit cards. From Syntagma Sq., walk south on Amalias Ave. past Hadrian's Arch, stay right, and turn right on Dionyssiou Areopagitou; Vyronos ("Byron" in Greek) is the 2nd street on the right, and the hotel (with a portrait of Lord Byron by the door) is on the right. **Amenities:** Bar. *In room:* A/C.

Hotel Nefeli 𝒢   The little Nefeli, just steps from the main Plaka shopping and restaurant streets, was completely redecorated in 1998, with new beds and furniture. The rooms (all now with air-conditioning) are small but comfortable, the quietest overlooking pedestrianized Angelikis Hatzimihali Street (although illegal motorcycle traffic can be a real problem at night). I've found the staff courteous and helpful, and friends who've stayed here say the same. I was, therefore, surprised by one reader's report of curt service, sleep interrupted by a noisy tour group, and a grubby bathroom.

16 Iperidou, 105 58 Athens. ✆ 210/322-8044. Fax 210/322-5800. 18 units (5 with shower only). 70€ double. Rates include continental breakfast. AE, V. Walk 2 blocks west from Syntagma Sq. on Mitropoleos, turn left on Voulis, cross Nikodimou, and turn right on Iperidou. **Amenities:** Breakfast room. *In room:* A/C, TV.

Hotel Plaka ★★ This 10-year-old hotel—popular with Greeks, who prefer its modern conveniences to the old-fashioned charms of most other hotels in the Plaka area—has a terrific location and fair prices. Many rooms have balconies. Fifth- and sixth-floor rooms in the rear (where it's usually quieter) have views of the Plaka and the Acropolis, also splendidly visible from the roof-garden bar (open in summer). Friends who stayed here recently weren't charmed by the service but loved the Plaka's central and relatively quiet location and the blue-and-white color scheme. Rates here are usually considerably cheaper off season.

Mitropoleos and 7 Kapnikareas, 105 56 Athens. ✆ 210/322-2096. Fax 210/322-2412. plaka@tourhotel.gr. 67 units (38 with shower only). 75€–115€ double. Rates include breakfast. AE, MC, V. Follow Mitropoleos out of Syntagma Sq. past the cathedral and turn left onto Kapnikareas. **Amenities:** Bar; roof garden. *In room:* A/C, TV, minibar, hair dryer.

NEAR MONASTIRAKI SQUARE
Moderate

Attalos Hotel ★ The six-story Attalos is well situated for those wanting to take in the frenzied daytime street life of the nearby Central Market and the exuberant nighttime scene at the cafes and restaurants of the Psirri district. The rooms here are plain, but pleasant; 40 have balconies and 12 have Acropolis views. Unusual for Greece, nonsmoking rooms are available, and all rooms have lock boxes. The roof garden offers fine views of the city and the Acropolis. The Attalos (whose staff is usually very helpful) often gives a 10% discount to Frommer's readers.

29 Athinas, 105 54 Athens. ✆ 210/391-2801. Fax 210/324-3124. atthot@hol.gr. 80 units. 70€–80€ double. Rates include buffet breakfast. AE, MC, V. From Monastiraki Sq., walk about 1½ blocks north on Athinas. **Amenities:** Luggage storage. *In room:* A/C, TV, hair dryer (most rooms).

Jason Inn Hotel ★★ *Value* If you don't mind walking a few extra blocks to Syntagma, this is one of the best values in Athens, with a staff that's usually very helpful. You're just out of the Plaka, around the corner from the newly fashionable Psirri district and steps from bustling Athinas Street. The hotel is redecorated on a regular basis and has bright, attractive, decent-sized rooms with modern amenities and double-paned windows to keep out traffic noise. If the

---

⎛*Value* Planning Ahead

Keep in mind that the 2004 Summer Olympics will make getting a hotel room *very* difficult. Do not go to Athens from June through August 2004 without a hotel reservation. In general, if you plan to visit Athens in the summer, when the best-value hotels tend to be full, write or fax in advance for reservations. If you visit Athens in the off season, especially in winter, you may be pleasantly surprised at the not-always-publicized low rates available in even the most expensive hotels.

Jason is full, the staff may be able to find you a room in one of its other hotels: the similarly priced Adrian, in the Plaka; or the slightly less expensive King Jason or Jason, both a few blocks from Omonia Square.

12 Ayion Assomaton, 105 53 Athens. © **210/325-1106.** Fax 210/324-3123 or 210/523-4786. Douros@hotel net.gr. 57 units. 85€–90€ double. Rates include American buffet breakfast. AE, MC, V. From Monastiraki Sq., head west on Ermou, turn right at Thisio Metro station, pass the small below-ground-level church, and bear left. *In room:* A/C, TV, minibar.

ON & AROUND SYNTAGMA SQUARE
Very Expensive

Grande Bretagne ✹✹✹   The legendary Grande Bretagne, one of Athens's most distinguished 19th-century buildings, is back after a year-and-a-half $70-million renovation. The exquisite beaux arts lobby has been preserved, indoor and outdoor swimming pools have been added, and the rooms that were once grand—and then rather dingy for too many years—are once again very grand indeed. If you decide to stay at the hotel where everyone from Winston Churchill to Sting has been a guest, be sure to insist on a room (or a suite, if you can swing it!) with a balcony overlooking Syntagma Square, the Parliament building, and the Acropolis.

Syntagma Sq., 105 64 Athens. © **210/333-000.** Fax 210/333-0160. www.grandebretagne.gr. 290 units, 38 suites. 350€–800€ double/suite. AE, DC, MC, V. **Amenities:** 2 restaurants; 2 bars; indoor and outdoor swimming pools; health club with spa and Jacuzzi; concierge; airport pickup arranged; business center; shopping arcade; salon; 24-hr. room service; same-day laundry/dry cleaning services; nonsmoking rooms. *In room:* AC, TV, minibar, hair dryer.

N. J. V. Athens Plaza ✹   The Athens Plaza, managed by the Grecotel group, reopened its glitzy doors in March 1998 after a complete remodeling. Many of the guest rooms—most with two king-size beds, armchairs, a desk, and a table—are larger than substantial living rooms, and many have balconies overlooking Syntagma Square. In short, this is a modern, up-to-date hotel with a superb location, good restaurants, a congenial bar, and an expansive lobby. Hardly a place where you'd expect bare wires dangling from the ceiling in your bathroom, or a bedside table with a small hole cut out of its side and covered with aluminum foil. Mysterious.

Syntagma Sq., 105 64 Athens. © **210/325-5301.** Fax 210/323-5856. 207 units. 325€–400€ double. AE, DC, MC, V. **Amenities:** 2 restaurants; 2 bars; exercise room; concierge; business center; 24-hr. room service; same-day dry cleaning/laundry. *In room:* A/C, TV, minibar, hair dryer.

Expensive

Electra Hotel ✹ *Value*   If Ermou Street remains pedestrianized and the Electra sticks to its present rates, this hotel is excellent value, with a location that's both central (steps from Syntagma Sq.) and quiet (despite the presence of lots of tour groups). Most rooms, although not large, come with comfortable armchairs, large windows, and modern bathrooms; about half have balconies. The front desk is sometimes understaffed, but the service is generally acceptable. Off-season prices are usually considerably lower.

5 Ermou, 105 63 Athens. © **210/322-3223.** Fax 210/322-0310. electrahotel@ath.forthnet.gr. 110 units. 150€ double. Rates include buffet breakfast. AE, DC, MC, V. The Electra is about 2 blocks down on the left as you walk along Ermou with Syntagma Sq. behind you. **Amenities:** Restaurant; bar. *In room:* A/C, TV, minibar, hair dryer.

Moderate

Athens Cypria ✹✹   After extensive renovations, the former Diomia Hotel was reborn in 2000 as the Athens Cypria. Gone are the Diomia's gloomy lobby and rooms, but the very convenient central location on a street with (usually) no traffic and the splendid Acropolis views from room nos. 603 to 607 remain (as do the less-than-enchanting views of walls and rooftops from other rooms). The bathrooms are freshly tiled with all new fixtures. The breakfast buffet offers hot and cold dishes from 7 to 10am in a mirrored dining room. The Cypria is an excellent addition to Athens's moderately priced hotels in a neighborhood where most hotels are seriously expensive.

5 Diomias, 105 62 Athens. (✆) 210/323-8034. Fax 210/324-8792. 71 units. 85€ double. Reductions possible off season. Rates include buffet breakfast. AE, MC, V. Take Karayioryi Servias out of Syntagma Sq.; Diomias is on the left, after Lekka. **Amenities:** Bar and snack bar; luggage storage. *In room:* A/C, TV, minibar, hair dryer.

Hotel Achilleas   The Achilleas (Achilles) has a great location on a relatively quiet side street steps from Syntagma Square and was completely renovated in 2001. Rooms are a good size and light. Some rear ones have small balconies. Several rooms on the fifth floor can be used as interconnecting family suites. The very central location and fair prices make this hotel a good choice, and the breakfast room is pleasant. Guest rooms here are sometimes heavily discounted off season.

21 Lekka, 105 62 Athens. (✆) 210/323-3197. Fax 210/322-2412. achilleas@tourhotel.gr. 34 units. 110€ double. Rates include breakfast. AE, DC, MC, V. With Hotel Grande Bretagne on your right, walk 2 blocks out of Syntagma Sq. on Karayioryi Servias and turn right into Lekka. **Amenities:** Snack bar. *In room:* A/C, TV, minibar; hair dryer and safe in most units.

Inexpensive
Hotel Carolina 𝕲𝕲   The friendly family-owned and -operated Carolina, on the outskirts of the Plaka, a brisk 5-minute walk from Syntagma, has always been popular with students. In the last few years, the hotel has undertaken extensive remodelings and now attracts a wide range of frugal travelers. Guest rooms have double-glazed windows and air conditioning; many, like room nos. 407 and 308, have large balconies. Several rooms, such as no. 308, have four or five beds, which makes them popular with families and students.

55 Kolokotroni, 105 60 Athens. (✆) 210/324-3551. Fax 210/324-3350. hotelcarolina@galaxnet.gr. 31 units. 75€ 89€ double; breakfast 5€. MC, V. Take Stadiou out of Syntagma Sq. to Kolokotroni St. (on left). **Amenities:** Breakfast room. *In room:* A/C, TV.

IN KOLONAKI
Very Expensive
Saint George Lycabettus Hotel 𝕲𝕲   Kolonaki is a fashionable residential and shopping neighborhood northeast of Syntagma at the foot of Mount Likavitos. As yet, the Saint George Lycabettus does not get many tour groups, which contributes to the tranquil tone here. The rooftop pool is a real plus, as are the two excellent restaurants, and the hotel is just steps from the chic Kolonaki restaurants and shops—but keep in mind that when you head back to the hotel, those steps are steeply uphill. The distinctively appointed rooms (different floors have different decorative motifs, from baroque to Italian modern) look toward Mount Likavitos or a small park. Some have views of both Likavitos and the Acropolis. In short, this is a distinctive and classy hotel (much-used by wealthy Greeks for private events), although the surrounding street traffic keeps it from being an absolute oasis of calm.

2 Kleomenous, 106 75 Athens. (✆) 210/729-0711. Fax 210/721-0439. www.sglycabettus.gr. 167 units. 225€–300€ double. Breakfast 20€. AE, DC, MC, V. From Kolonaki Sq., take Patriarchou Ioachim to Loukianou; follow Loukianou uphill to Kleomenous; turn left on Kleomenous; the hotel overlooks Dexamini Park. **Amenities:** 2 restaurants; 2 bars; pool; concierge; 24-hr. room service. *In room:* A/C, TV, minibar.

Moderate

Athenian Inn 🏛️   The Athenian Inn is on a relatively quiet side street 3 blocks from Kolonaki Square's cafes, restaurants, and shops. The inn has a loyal following, including many teachers, despite its small rooms (many of which do have small balconies). Between stays, I tend to forget how small the rooms are here, which suggests to me that the staff is doing a good job of making guests feel comfortable. A quote from the guest book: "At last the ideal Athens hotel, good and modest in scale but perfect in service and goodwill." Breakfast is served in the small ground-floor lounge, which has a fireplace, piano, and TV. Keep in mind that if you stay here, you will do a good deal of walking (some of it fairly steep) to get to and from the central attractions. Neighborhood doves coo vigorously at night, a sound you will probably find either soothing or infuriating.

22 Haritos, Kolonaki, 106 75 Athens. © 210/723-8097. Fax 210/724-2268. 28 units. 115€ double. Rates include breakfast. AE, DC, V. From Syntagma Sq., go east on Vasilissis Sofias Ave. to Loukianou; turn left on Loukianou and take it 6 blocks uphill to Haritos. **Amenities:** Breakfast room. *In room:* A/C.

IN THE EMBASSY DISTRICT
Very Expensive

Andromeda Hotel 🏛️🏛️🏛️   The city's only boutique hotel is easily the most charming in Athens, with a staff that makes you feel that this is your ideal home away from home, on a quiet residential street by the American ambassador's garden, not far from the Megaron Musikis (Athens Concert Hall). Rooms are large and elegantly decorated, the service is superb, and the breakfast buffets are lavish. The only drawbacks: It's a serious hike (20–30 min.) or a 10-minute taxi ride to Syntagma; and there are relatively few restaurants in this residential neighborhood, although the superb Vlassis is just around the corner. If you're planning a long stay in Athens, check out the Andromeda's new (and very lovely) service apartments just across the street.

22 Timoleontos Vassou (off Plateia Mavili), 115 21 Athens. © 210/641-5000. Fax 210/646-6361. Reservations@andromedaathens.gr. 42 units. 435€–450€ double. Breakfast included in rates. Special rates sometimes available. AE, DC, MC, V. **Amenities:** Restaurant; breakfast room; bar. *In room:* A/C, TV, minibar, hair dryer, wall safe; all rooms fully wired for Internet.

NEAR THE ACROPOLIS (MAKRIYANNI & KOUKAKI DISTRICTS)
Very Expensive

Divani Palace Acropolis 🏛️🏛️   Just 3 blocks south of the Acropolis, in a quiet residential neighborhood (there's a handy SPAR supermarket a block away at 4 Parthenonos, as well as a shop at 7 Parthenonos that sells American and English newspapers), the Divani Palace Acropolis does a brisk tour business but welcomes independent travelers. The blandly decorated rooms are large and comfortable, with generously sized bathrooms. (The breakfast buffet is more than generous.) A section of Athens's 5th-century-B.C. defense wall is preserved behind glass in the basement. The same hotel group operates the **Divani Caravel Hotel,** near the National Art Gallery and Hilton Hotel at 2 Vas. Alexandrou Ave. (© **210/725-3725;** fax 210-723-6683).

19–25 Parthenonos, Makriyanni, 117 42 Athens. © **210/928-0100.** Fax 210/921-4993. www.divanicaravel.gr. 253 units. 200€–300€ double. AE, DC, MC, V. From Syntagma Sq., take Amalias Ave. to pedestrianized Dionyssiou Areopagitou; turn left into Parthenonos; the hotel is on your left after about 3 blocks. **Amenities:** Restaurant; 2 bars; small pool; concierge; business center; 24-hr. room service; roof garden. *In room:* A/C, TV, minibar, hair dryer.

Moderate

Acropolis View Hotel ✿   This nicely maintained hotel is on a residential side street off Robertou Galli, not far from the Herodes Atticus theater. The usually quiet neighborhood, at the base of Philopappos Hill, is a 10- to 15-minute walk from the heart of the Plaka. Rooms (most freshly painted each year) are small but clean and pleasant, with good bathrooms; 16 have balconies. Some, like no. 405, overlook Philopappos Hill, and others, like no. 407, face the Acropolis.

Robertou Galli and 10 Webster, 117 42 Athens. ⓒ **210/921-7303.** Fax 210/923-0705. www.acropolisview.gr. 32 units. 115€ double. Rates include buffet breakfast. Substantial reductions Nov to Apr 1. AE, MC, V. From Syntagma Sq. take Amalias Ave. to Dionyssiou Areopagitou; head west past Herodes Atticus theater to Robertou Galli. Webster (Gouemster on some maps) is the little street intersecting Robertou Galli between Propilion and Garibaldi. **Amenities:** Breakfast room; bar. *In room:* A/C, TV, minibar.

Art Gallery Hotel ✿   As you might expect, this small hotel—in a half-century-old house that has been home to several artists—has an artistic flair (and a nice old-fashioned cage elevator). Customers tend to be loyal, many of them on repeat visits, greeting old friends and cordial to newcomers. Rooms are small and plain but comfortable, some with ceiling fans, although all now have air-conditioning. There's a nice Victorian-style breakfast room on the fourth floor.

5 Erechthiou, Koukaki, 117 42 Athens. ⓒ **210/923-8376.** Fax 210/923-3025. ecotec@otenet.gr. 22 units. 45€–70€ double. Rates include generous breakfast. Hotel sometimes closed Nov–Mar; when open then, prices reduced. AE, MC, V. *In room:* A/C, TV.

Austria Hotel ✿   This very well-maintained hotel at the base of wooded Philopappos Hill is operated by a Greek-Austrian family, who can point you to local sights (including a convenient neighborhood laundry!). The Austria's guest rooms and bathrooms are rather spartan (the linoleum floors aren't enchanting) but are more than acceptable—and the very efficient staff is a real plus here. There's a great view over Athens and out to sea (I could see the island of Aegina) from the rooftop, where you can sun or sit under an awning.

7 Mousson, Filopappou, 117 42 Athens. ⓒ **210/923-5151.** Fax 210/924-7350. Austria@austriahotel.com. 36 units (11 with shower only). 110€ double. Rates include breakfast. AE, DC, MC, V. Follow Dionyssiou Areopagitou around south side of Acropolis to where it meets Robertou Galli; take Garibaldi around base of Filopappou Hill until you reach Mousson. **Amenities:** Breakfast room; rooftop terrace. *In room:* A/C, fax.

Parthenon Hotel   This recently redecorated hotel has an excellent location just steps from the Plaka and the Acropolis. The Parthenon is one of the AirOtel group of four Athenian hotels; if it's full, the management will try to get you a room at the Christina, a few blocks away, or at the Riva or Alexandros, near the Megaron (Athens Concert Hall). One warning: On occasion I've found the desk staff less than helpful and infuriatingly vague about room prices.

6 Makri, 115 27 Athens. ⓒ **210/923-4594.** Fax 210/644-1084. 79 units. 90€ double. MC, V. From Syntagma, take Amalias into Dionyssiou Areopagitou; Makri is the 2nd street on the left. **Amenities:** Restaurant; bar; garden. *In room:* A/C, TV.

Inexpensive

Marble House Pension ✿✿   Named for its marble facade, usually covered by bougainvillea, this small hotel, whose front rooms offer balconies overlooking quiet Zinni Street, is famous among budget travelers (including many teachers) for its friendly staff. Over the last several years, the pension has been remodeled and redecorated, gaining all-new bathrooms and guest room furniture. There are two easy-access ground-floor guest rooms, two guest rooms with kitchenettes, and nine guest rooms with air-conditioning. If you're spending more than a few days in Athens and don't mind being out of the center, this is a homey base.

35 A. Zinni, Koukaki, 117 41 Athens. © **210/923-4058.** Fax 210/922-6461. 16 units, 12 with bathroom. 40€ double without bathroom; 45€ double with bathroom. 9€ supplement for A/C. Monthly rates available off season. No credit cards. From Syntagma Sq. take Amalias Ave. to Syngrou Ave; turn right onto Zinni; the hotel is in the cul-de-sac beside the small church. **Amenities:** Luggage storage. *In room:* TV, minibar.

WHERE TO DINE

Athens has an astonishing number of restaurants and tavernas (and a growing number of fast-food joints) offering everything from good, cheap Greek food in plain surroundings to fine Greek, French, Asian, and other international cuisines served in luxurious surroundings.

Most restaurants have menus in Greek and English, but many don't keep their printed (or handwritten) menus up to date. If a menu is not in English, there's almost always someone working at the restaurant who will either translate or rattle off suggestions for you in English. That may mean you'll be offered some fairly repetitive suggestions because restaurant staff members tend to suggest what most tourists request. In Athens, that means *moussaka* (baked eggplant casserole, usually with ground meat), *souvlakia* (chunks of beef, chicken, pork, or lamb grilled on a skewer), *pastitsio* (baked pasta, usually with ground meat and béchamel sauce), or *dolmadakia* (grape leaves, stuffed usually with rice and ground meat). Although all these dishes can be delicious, all too often restaurants catering to tourists serve profoundly dull moussaka and unpleasantly chewy souvlakia.

Mezedes (appetizers served with bread) are one of the great delights of Greek cuisine, and often can be enjoyed in lieu of a main course. Some perennial favorites include *tzatziki* (garlic, cucumber, dill, and yogurt dip), *melitzanosalata* (eggplant dip), *skordalia* (garlic sauce), *taramosalata* (fish roe dip), *keftedes* (crispy meatballs), *kalamaria* (squid), *gigantes* (large white beans in tomato sauce), *loukanika* (little sausages), and *oktopodi* (octopus).

If you're wondering what to use to wash all this down with, the best-known Greek table wine is **retsina.** It's usually white, although sometime rosé or red, and flavored with pine resin. In theory, the European Union now controls the amount of resin added, so you're less likely to come across the harsh retsina that some compare to turpentine. If you don't like the taste of retsina, try *aretsinato* (wine without resin).

If you want to find out more about the wide range of excellent Greek wines, pick up a copy of Dimitri Hadjinicolaou's *The A to Z Guide of Greek Wines* (Oenos O Agapitos Publisher). This handy pocket-size Greek/English guide has illustrations of labels and information on vintages, and sells for about 9€.

Tips Don't Count on Credit Cards

One of my most humiliating travel moments happened a number of years ago when I was taking Athenian friends out to dinner—and planning to pay with a credit card. The restaurant took only cash, and my friends ended up having to take me to dinner. Much has changed in Athens since then—but, amazingly, my friends are still speaking to me. One thing that has not changed is that many Athenian restaurants still do not accept credit cards. Consider yourself warned.

> **Tips** **Eating Well**
>
> To avoid the ubiquitous favorites-for-foreigners, tell your waiter you'd like to have a look at the food display case, often positioned just outside the kitchen, and then point to what you'd like to order. Many restaurants are perfectly happy to have you take a look in the kitchen itself, but it's not a good idea to do this without checking first. Not surprisingly, you'll get the best value and the tastiest food at establishments serving a predominantly Greek, rather than a transient tourist, clientele.

When it comes time for dessert or a mid-afternoon infusion of sugar, Greeks usually head to a *zaharoplastion* (sweet shop). Consequently, most restaurants don't offer a wide variety of desserts. Almost all do serve fruit (stewed in winter, fresh in season), and, increasingly, many serve sweets such as *baklava* (pastry and ground nuts with honey), *halva* (sesame, chopped nuts, and honey), and *kataifi* (shredded wheat with chopped nuts and lots of honey). All these sweets are seriously sweet. If you want coffee with your dessert, keep in mind that for Greeks, regular coffee usually includes a mere teaspoon of sugar. Sweet coffee seems to be about a fifty-fifty mixture of coffee and sugar. Watch out for the grounds in the bottom of the cup.

Greek **brandy** is a popular after-dinner drink (although—you guessed it—it's a bit sweet for non-Greek tastes), but the most popular Greek hard drink is *ouzo.* The anise-flavored liqueur is taken either straight or with water, which turns it cloudy white. You may see Greek men drinking quarter- and even half-bottles of ouzo with their lunch; if you do the same, you'll find out why the after-lunch siesta is so popular. There are many cafes *(ouzeri,)* where ouzo, wine, and a selection of mezedes are served from breakfast to bedtime.

IN THE PLAKA

Some of the most charming old restaurants in Athens are in the Plaka—as are some of the worst tourist traps. Here are a few things to keep in mind when you head off for a meal.

Some Plaka restaurants station waiters outside who don't just urge you to come in and sit down, but virtually pursue you down the street with an unrelenting sales pitch. The hard sell is almost always a giveaway that the place caters to tourists.

In general, it's a good idea to avoid places with floor shows; many charge outrageous amounts (and levy surcharges not always openly stated on menus) for drinks and food. If you get burned, stand your ground, phone the **Tourist Police** (© **171**), and pay nothing before they arrive. Often the mere mention of the Tourist Police has the miraculous effect of causing a bill to be lowered.

Expensive

Daphne's ✸✸✸ ELEGANT GREEK/NOUVELLE   This lovingly restored neoclassical 1830s town house has frescoes on the walls, a shady garden with bits of ancient marble found when the restaurant was built, and sophisticated Athenians at many tables. The cuisine here gives all the old favorites (try the zesty eggplant salad) new distinctions, employing familiar ingredients in innovative ways (delicious hot pepper and feta cheese dip). I could cheerfully just eat the hors d'oeuvres all night, but I have also enjoyed the *stifado* (stew) of rabbit in *mavrodaphne* (sweet wine) sauce and the tasty prawns with toasted almonds.

Most nights, a pair of strolling musicians entertains with a repertoire that ranges from Greek favorites to "My Darling Clementine." The staff is attentive, encouraging, endearing, and beyond excellent.

4 Lysikratous. ✆/fax **210/322-7971**. Reservations recommended. Main courses 14€–25€, with some fish priced by the kilo. AE, DC, MC, V. Daily 8pm–1am. Closed Dec 20–Jan 15. From Syntagma Sq., head south on Amalias to Lysikratous (across from Hadrian's Gate).

Moderate

Eden Vegetarian Restaurant ✿ VEGETARIAN
You can find vegetarian dishes at almost every Greek restaurant, but if you want to experience organically grown products, soy (rather than eggplant) moussaka, mushroom pie with a whole-wheat crust, freshly squeezed juices, and salads with bean sprouts, join the young Athenians and Europeans who patronize the Eden. The prices are reasonable, if not cheap, and the decor is engaging, with 1920s-style prints and mirrors and wrought-iron lamps.

12 Lissiou. ✆/fax **210/324-8858**. Main courses 6€–12€. AE, MC, V. Daily noon–midnight. Closed Tues and usually closed Aug. From Syntagma Sq., head south on Filellinon or Nikis to Kidathineon, which intersects Adrianou; turn right on Adrianou and take Mnissikleos up 2 blocks toward the Acropolis to Lissiou.

Platanos Taverna ✿✿ TRADITIONAL GREEK
This taverna on a quiet pedestrian square has tables outdoors in good weather beneath a spreading plane tree (*Platanos* means "plane tree"). Inside, where locals congregate to escape the summer sun at midday and the tourists in the evening, you can enjoy looking at the old paintings and photos on the walls. The Platanos has been serving good *spitiko fageto* (home cooking) since 1932 and has managed to keep steady customers happy while enchanting visitors. If artichokes or spinach with lamb are on the menu, you're in luck: They're delicious. The house wine is tasty, and there's a wide choice of bottled wines from many regions of Greece. If possible, plan to come here and relax, not rush, through a meal.

4 Dioyenous. ✆ **210/322-0666**. Fax 210/322-8624. Main courses 5€–10€. No credit cards. Mon–Sat noon–4:30pm and 8pm–midnight; Sun in Mar, Apr, May, Sept, and Oct noon–4:30pm. From Syntagma Sq., head south on Filellinon or Nikis to Kidathineon; turn right on Adrianou, and take Mnissikleos up 1 block toward the Acropolis; turn right on Dioyenous.

Taverna Xinos ✿ TRADITIONAL GREEK
Despite the forgivable spelling lapse, Xinos's business card says it best: "In the heart of old Athens there is still a flace [sic] where the traditional Greek way of cooking is upheld." In summer, you can dine at tables in the courtyard; in winter, you can warm yourself by the coal-burning stove. While the strolling musicians may not be as good as the Three Tenors, they do sing wonderful Greek golden oldies, accompanying themselves on the guitar and bouzouki. (If you're serenaded, you may want to give the musicians a tip. If you want to hear the theme from *Never on Sunday,* ask for "Ena Zorbas.") Most evenings, tourists predominate until after 10pm, when locals begin to arrive.

4 Geronta. ✆ **210/322-1065**. Main courses 6€–15€. No credit cards. Daily 8pm–anytime from 11pm–1am; sometimes closed Sun, usually closed part of July and Aug. From Syntagma Sq., head south on Filellinon or Nikis to Kidathineon; turn right on Geronta and look for the sign for Xinos in the cul-de-sac.

Inexpensive

Damigos (The Bakaliarakia) ✿✿✿ GREEK/CODFISH
Since 1865, Damigos has been serving delicious deep-fried codfish and eggplant, as well as chops and stews for inveterate meat-eaters. This basement taverna serves wine from family vineyards. (If you wish, you can usually buy a bottle to take away.) There are few pleasures greater than sipping the white or rosé retsina while

watching the cook turn out unending meals in his absurdly small kitchen. Don't miss the delicious *skordalia* (garlic sauce), equally good with cod, eggplant, bread—well, you get the idea.

41 Kidathineon. ℂ 210/322-5084. Main courses 4€–10€. No credit cards. Daily 7pm–anytime from 11pm–1am. Usually closed June–Sept. From Syntagma Sq., head south on Filellinon or Nikis to Kidathineon; Damigos is downstairs on the left just before Adrianou.

Kouklis Ouzeri (To Yerani) ⚜ GREEK/MEZEDES Besides Kouklis Ouzeri and To Yerani, Greeks call this popular old favorite with its winding staircase to the second floor the "Skolario" because of the nearby school. Sit down at one of the small tables and a waiter will present a large tray with about a dozen plates of *mezedes*—appetizer portions of fried fish, beans, grilled eggplant, taramos alata, cucumber-and-tomato salad, olives, fried cheese, sausages, and other seasonal specialties. Accept the ones that appeal. If you don't order all 12, you can enjoy a tasty and inexpensive meal, washed down with the house *krasi* (wine). No prices are posted, but the waiter will tell you what everything costs if you ask. Now if only the staff could be just a bit more patient when foreigners are trying to decide what to order.

14 Tripodon. ℂ 210/324-7605. Appetizers 2€–10€. No credit cards. Daily 11am–2am. From Syntagma Sq., head south on Filellinon or Nikis to Kidathineon; take Kidathineon across Adrianou to Thespidos and climb toward Acropolis; Tripodon is the 1st street on the right after Adrianou.

NEAR MONASTIRAKI SQUARE
Moderate
Abyssinia Cafe ⚜ GREEK This small cafe in a ramshackle building has a nicely restored interior featuring lots of gleaming dark wood and polished copper. It faces a lopsided square where furniture restorers ply their trade. You can sit inside or outside and have just a coffee, but it's tempting to snack on cheese Abyssinia (feta cheese scrambled with spices and garlic), mussels and rice pilaf, or *keftedes* (meatballs).

Plateia Abyssinia. ℂ 210/321-7047. Appetizers and main courses 4€–12€. No credit cards. Tues–Sun 10:30am–2pm (often open evenings as well). Usually closed for a week at Christmas and Easter, sometimes closed part of Jan and Feb and mid-July to mid-Aug. Abyssinia Sq. is just off Ifaistou (Hephaistos) across from the entrance to Ancient Agora on Adrianou.

Taverna Sigalas ⚜ TRADITIONAL GREEK This longtime family- owned and -run Plaka taverna, housed in a vintage 1879 commercial building, boasts that it is open 365 days a year. Its lively interior has huge old retsina kegs in the back and dozens of black-and-white photos of Greek movie stars on the walls. After 8pm nightly, there's Greek Muzak. At all hours, Greeks and tourists wolf down large portions of stews, moussaka, grilled meatballs, baked tomatoes, gyros, and other hearty dishes, washed down with the house red and white retsinas.

Plateia Monastiraki 2. ℂ 210/321-3036. Main courses 5€–12€. AE, DC, M/C, V. Daily 7pm–2am. Across Monastiraki Sq. from the Metro station.

Inexpensive
Diporto *(Finds* GREEK This little place, sandwiched between olive shops, serves up salads, stews, and delicious *revithia* (chickpeas), a Greek winter dish popular among stall owners, shoppers, and Athenians who make their way to the market for cheap and delicious food. If you like Diporto, try Papandreou, also in the Central Market, and famous for its restorative tripe soup, a Greek remedy for hangovers.

Athens Central Market. No phone. Dishes 4€–8€. No credit cards. Mon–Sat 6am–6pm. From Syntagma Sq., follow Hermou to Athinas; the Central Market is on the right side of the street.

Thanasis ★★ *Value* GREEK/SOUVLAKIA   Thanasis serves individual souvlakia, souvlakia and pita sandwiches, and plates heaped with sliced gyro (grilled lamb) and exceptionally good fries, both to go and at its outdoor and indoor tables; as always, the prices are higher if you sit down. On weekends, it often takes the strength and determination of an Olympic athlete to get through the door and place an order. It's worth the effort: This is both a great budget choice and a great place to take in the local scene, which often includes a fair sprinkling of Gypsies, including some cute and very determined child beggars.

69 Mitropoleos. ✆ 210/324-4705. Main courses 2€–8€. No credit cards. Daily 9am–2am. On northeast corner of Monastiraki Sq. Hermou leads directly from Syntagma Sq. to Monastiraki Sq.

NEAR SYNTAGMA SQUARE
Expensive

Aigli ★★ INTERNATIONAL   For years, the bistro in the Zappeion Gardens was a popular meeting spot, and when it closed in the 1970s, it was sorely missed. Now it's back, along with a cinema and fine restaurant. Once more, chic Athenian families head here, in the cool of the Zappeion Gardens, for the foie gras, oysters, Chinese ravioli, rich profiteroles, and delicious yogurt crème brûlée. You can sit at tables indoors, or outdoors by the trees, where you can relax with a morning cup of coffee and watch the balloon sellers tempt families with their wares. In the evening, take in a movie at the open-air cinema here before dinner, or have a drink and snack at one of several cafes. In short, this is a wonderful spot to while away an afternoon or evening.

Zappeion Gardens (adjacent to the National Gardens fronting Vas. Amalias Blvd.). ✆ 210/336-9363. Main courses 10€–25€. Reservations recommended. Daily 10am–12am. Sometimes closed in Aug.

Inexpensive

Neon ★ *Value* GREEK/INTERNATIONAL   If you're tired of practicing your restaurant Greek, the Neon restaurants are good places to eat, since most items are self-service. This centrally located member of the chain is convenient, albeit not as pleasant as the original on Omonia Square. There is also a very handy Neon a block north of Kolonaki Square at Tsakalof and Iraklitou. You're sure to find something to your taste—maybe a Mexican omelet, spaghetti Bolognese, a salad bar, or sweets ranging from Black Forest cake to tiramisu.

3 Mitropoleos (on the southwest corner of Syntagma Sq.). ✆ 210/322-8155. Snacks1€–3€; sandwiches 3€–6€; main courses 4€–20€. No credit cards. Daily 9am–midnight.

IN KOLONAKI
Expensive

To Kafeneio ★★ GREEK/INTERNATIONAL   This is hardly a typical *kafeneio* (coffee shop/cafe). If you relax, you can easily run up a substantial tab (50€ for lunch or dinner for two is easy), but you can also eat more modestly and equally elegantly. If you have something light, like the artichokes a la polita, leeks in crème fraîche, or onion pie (one, not all three!), washed down with draft beer or the house wine, you can finish with profiteroles and not put too big a dent in your budget. I've always found this an especially congenial spot when I'm eating alone (perhaps because I love people-watching and profiteroles).

26 Loukianou. ✆ 210/722-9056. Reservations recommended. Main courses 6€–25€. No credit cards. Mon–Sat 11am–midnight or later. Closed Sun and most of Aug. From Kolonaki Sq., follow Patriarkou Ioakim several blocks uphill to Loukianou and turn right on Loukianou.

Moderate

Filipou ★ TRADITIONAL GREEK   This longtime Athenian favorite almost never disappoints. The traditional dishes such as stuffed cabbage, stuffed vine leaves, vegetable stews, and fresh salads are consistently good. In the heart of Kolonaki, near the very fashionable George Lykabettus Hotel, this is a place to head for when you want good *spitiko* (home) cooking in the company of the Greeks and resident expatriates who prize the food here.

19 Xenokratous. (C) 210/721-6390. Main courses 7€–15€. No credit cards. Mon–Fri 8:30pm–midnight; Sat lunch (call for hours); closed Sun. From Kolonaki Sq., take Patriarch Ioakim to Ploutarchou, turn left on Ploutarchou, and then turn right on Xenokratous.

Rhodia 🦋 TRADITIONAL GREEK   This respected taverna in a handsome old Kolonaki house has tables in its small garden in good weather—although the interior, with its tile floor and old prints, is so charming that you might be tempted to eat indoors. The Rhodia is a favorite of visiting archaeologists from the nearby British and American Schools of Classical Studies, as well as of Kolonaki residents. It may not sound like just what you'd always hoped to have for dinner, but the octopus in mustard sauce is terrific, as are the veal and *dolmades* (stuffed grape leaves) in egg-lemon sauce. The house wine is excellent, as is the halva, which manages to be both creamy and crunchy.

44 Aristipou. (C) 210/722-9883. Main courses 6.50€–13€. No credit cards. Mon–Sat 8pm–2am. From Kolonaki Sq., take Patriarkou Ioakim uphill to Loukianou; turn left on Loukianou, climb steeply uphill to Aristipou, and turn right.

To Ouzadiko 🦋🦋 GREEK/MEZEDES   This ouzo bar has at least 40 kinds of ouzo and as many mezedes, including fluffy *keftedes* (meatballs) that make all others taste leaden. To Ouzadiko is very popular with Athenians young and old who come to see and be seen while having a snack or a full meal, often after concerts and plays. A serious foodie friend of mine comes here especially for the wide variety of *horta* (greens), which she says are the best she's ever tasted. If you see someone at a nearby table eating something you want and aren't sure which of the bean or eggplant dishes it is, ask your waiter, and it will appear for you—sometimes after a bit of a wait, as the staff here is often seriously overworked.

25–29 Karneadou (in the Lemos International Shopping Center), Kolonaki. (C) 210/729-5484. Reservations recommended. Mezedes and main courses 7€–16€. No credit cards. Tues–Sat 1pm–12:30am. From Kolonaki Sq., take Kapsali across Irodotou into Karneadou The Lemos Center is the mini-skyscraper on your left

To Prytaneion 🦋 GREEK/INTERNATIONAL   The trendy bare stone walls here are decorated with movie posters and illuminated by baby spotlights. Waiters with cellphones serve customers with cellphones tempting plates of some of Athens's most expensive and eclectic mezedes, including beef carpaccio, bruschetta, and shrimp in fresh cream, as well as that international favorite, the hamburger. This place is so drop-dead chic that it comes as a pleasant surprise to learn that it functioned as a neighborhood hangout during the 1999 earthquake and the 2001 snowstorm that shut down Athens.

7 Milioni, Kolonaki. (C) 210-364-3353 or 210/364-3354. www.prytaneion.gr. Reservations recommended. Mezedes and snacks 7€–25€. No credit cards. Mon–Sat 10am–3am. From Kolonaki Sq., head downhill a (pedestrianized) block or 2 until you hit Milioni on your right. To Prytaneion is on your left.

AROUND OMONIA SQUARE & THE NATIONAL ARCHAEOLOGICAL MUSEUM
Moderate

Athinaikon 🦋🦋 GREEK/OUZERI   Not many tourists come to this favorite haunt of lawyers and businesspeople working in the Omonia Square area. You can have just some appetizers (technically, this is an *ouzeri*) or a full meal. Obviously, the way to have a reasonably priced snack is to stick to the appetizers, including delicious *loukanika* (sausages) and *keftedes* (meatballs), and pass on the pricier grilled shrimp or seafood paella. Whatever you have, you'll enjoy taking in the old photos on the walls, the handsome tiled floor, the marble-topped tables and bentwood chairs, and the regular customers, who combine serious eating with animated conversation.

2 Themistokleous. © 210/383-8485. Appetizers and main courses 4€–14€. No credit cards. Mon–Sat 11am–midnight. Closed Sun and usually in Aug. From Omonia Sq., take Panepistimou a block to Themistokleous; the Athinaikon is almost immediately on your right.

Ideal ⚡ GREEK TRADITIONAL   The oldest restaurant in the heart of Athens, today's Ideal has an Art Deco decor and lots of old favorites, from egg-lemon soup to stuffed peppers, pork with celery, and lamb with spinach. This is a favorite of businesspeople, and the service is usually brisk, especially at lunchtime. It may not be the place for a quiet rendezvous, but it's definitely the spot for good, hearty Greek cooking.

46 Panepistimiou. © 210/330-3000. Reservations recommended. Main courses 8€–12€. AE, DC, MC, V. Mon–Sat noon–midnight. From Omonia or Syntagma, take Panepistimiou (the Ideal is just outside Omonia Sq.).

Inexpensive

Taygetos ⟨Value⟩ GREEK/SOUVLAKIA   This is a great place to stop for a quick meal on your way to/from the National Archaeological Museum. The service is swift, and the souvlakia and fried potatoes are excellent, as are the grilled lamb and chicken (priced by the kilo). The menu sometimes includes delicious *kokoretsi* (grilled entrails). The Ellinikon Restaurant next door is also a good value.

4 Satovriandou. © 210/523-5352. Main courses 5€–9€. No credit cards. Mon–Sat 9am–1am. From Omonia Sq. take Patission (28 Oktovriou) toward National Museum; Satovriandou is 3rd major turn on your left.

NEAR THE ACROPOLIS
Moderate

Socrates' Prison/Samaria ⚡ GREEK/CONTINENTAL   This longtime visitors' favorite has moved around the corner to a new location (and a new name that not everyone uses), where it remains an excellent place to head when you want good food near the Plaka but want to avoid the frenzy of the central Plaka. The new place has a roof garden with an Acropolis view, a real plus for summer evenings. Greeks, as well as American and European expats living in Athens, love this place, with its tables outdoors in good weather and in the pleasant rooms year-round. In addition to the usual Greek meat dishes, the menu includes tasty veggie croquettes, *salade niçoise* and—for those who can't decide between veggies and meat—vegetable-stuffed pork roll. The retsina is excellent, and there's a wide choice of bottled wines and beers.

17 Robertou Galli. © 210/922-3434. Main courses 10€–15€. AE, DC, MC, V. Mon–Sat 11am–4pm and 7pm–1am. Closed Aug. From Syntagma Sq., take Amalias Ave. to pedestrianized Dionyssiou Areopagitou, walk away from Temple of Zeus on the side of Dionyssiou Areopagitou across from Acropolis, and turn left onto Mitseon and right onto Robertou Galli.

Strofi ⚡ GREEK   The rooftop terrace here has a drop-dead view of the Acropolis and the Herodes Atticus theater. After performances, actors and members of the audience cross the street to Strofi to dine on grills, stews, good salads, and *horta* (greens). The cooking can be a bit rough and ready and the waiters a bit rushed, but the Acropolis view makes this place pretty irresistible.

25 Robertou Galli, Makriyianni (across from the Herodes Atticus theater). © 210/921-4130. Main courses 8€–18€. DC, MC, V. Mon–Sat 8pm–1am. Closed Sun. From Syntagma Sq., take Amalias Ave. to pedestrianized Dionyssiou Areopagitou, walk away from Temple of Zeus on the side of Dionyssiou Areopagitou across from Acropolis, and turn left onto Mitseon and right onto Robertou Galli.

HERE & THERE
Very Expensive

Varoulko ★★★ SEAFOOD/NOUVELLE   In an unlikely location on a side street in Piraeus, chef-owner Lefteris Lazarou has created what many consider not just the city's finest seafood restaurant, but the finest restaurant in the greater Athens area. I had one of the best meals in my life here—smoked eel; artichokes with fish roe; crayfish with sun-dried tomatoes; monkfish livers with soy sauce, honey, and balsamic vinegar—and the best sea bass and monkfish I have ever eaten. The bare-brick walls of the restaurant are softened with artwork, and the food is beautifully presented and absolutely delicious.

14 Deligeorgi, Piraeus. ✆ **210/411-2043.** Fax 210/422-1283. Reservations necessary (arrange several days in advance). Dinner for 2 from about 120€; fish priced by the kilo. No credit cards. Mon–Sat about 8pm–midnight. Closed Sun and most of June–Sept, when it often relocates outdoors at the Peace and Friendship Stadium. We recommend taking a taxi to this restaurant, which is hard to find and not in central Piraeus.

Expensive

Boschetto ★★ ITALIAN/INTERNATIONAL   Tucked away in the garden below the Evangelismos Hospital, just across from the Hilton Hotel, Boschetto serves up some of the best Italian cuisine in Athens. If you don't want shrimp cannelloni or any of the other pastas, there's fresh fish (sea bass is usually on the menu) and squid, duck, sweetbreads, and excellent beef dishes. This surprisingly tranquil spot just feet from the hubbub of central Athens often attracts an almost entirely Athenian clientele that appreciates the excellent food, careful service, and indoor/outdoor dining here. There's an excellent wine list.

Alsos Evangelismos (Garden of Evangelismos Hospital). ✆ **210/721-0893.** Reservations recommended. Main courses 15€–30€. AE, V. Mon–Sat 8pm–midnight. Usually closed in Aug. From Syntagma, take Vas. Sophias Blvd. to the Evangelismos Garden. If you come to Gennadiou, you've gone too far.

Moderate

Vlassis ★★★ TRADITIONAL GREEK   Greeks call this kind of food *paradisiako:* traditional, but paradisiacal is just as good a description. This very reasonably priced food is fit for the gods: delicious fluffy vegetable croquettes, eggplant salad that tastes like no other, hauntingly tender lamb in egg-lemon sauce. It's a sign of Vlassis's popularity with Athenians—each time I eat here, I seem to be the only obvious foreigner—that there's not even a discreet sign announcing its presence in a small apartment building on hard-to-find Paster. Figure the price of a taxi (no more than 10€) into your meal tab; you may feel so giddy with delight after eating you won't mind the half-hour walk back to Syntagma.

8 Paster (off Plateia Mavili). ✆ **210/646-3060.** Reservations recommended. Main courses 7€–20€. No credit cards. Mon–Sat 8pm–1am. Closed much of June–Sept. From Syntagma Sq., take Vasilissis Sophias Ave. to Plateia Mavili, and follow D. Tsoustou out of Plateia Mavili to Chatzikosta; Paster is the cul-de-sac on the left after you turn right onto Chatzikosta.

Zeidoron ★★ GREEK/MEZEDES   This *mezedopolio* (hors d'oeuvres place) is one of a number of restaurants springing up in the old warehouse district of Psirri, now well on its way to being transformed into a neighborhood of chic restaurants, cafes, and galleries. There are lots of delicious mezedes to choose from, including vegetable croquettes, several eggplant dishes, and some heartier meat dishes, like pork in mustard. You can have a varied and delicious meal—and keep the price tab reasonable—by avoiding the more expensive mezedes like shrimp. There's a wide variety of wines, beers, and ouzos. And you can take in the passing scene, which gets more and more lively as the night wears on and Athens's beautiful young people hit the street with their cellphones and Prada gear.

10 Taki and Ayios Anaryiron. ℂ **210/321-5368.** Reservations recommended. Main courses 7€–18€ (appetizers 5€–15€). No credit cards. Mon–Sat 11am till at least midnight. Closed Aug. From Syntagma Sq. take Ermou to Navarchou Apostoli, which runs into Taki, which intersects Ayios Anaryiron.

SEEING THE SIGHTS
SIGHTSEEING SUGGESTIONS FOR FIRST-TIME VISITORS

If You Have 1 Day Try to be at the **Acropolis** as soon as it opens (or in the hour before it closes) so that you can take in the site and enjoy seeing the **Parthenon** and the **Acropolis Museum** with as few people around as possible. Afterward, walk downhill to visit the **Ancient Agora** and then head into **Monastiraki** and the **Plaka,** where you can window-shop and relax over lunch or dinner. Keep an eye out for the Plaka **tram.** The half-hour ride begins in Palia Agora Square, loops through the Plaka, and passes the Acropolis on Dionyssiou Areopagitou Boulevard before heading back into the Plaka (10am–10pm in summer; 3€). It's a great (and relaxing) way to get a sense of what you may want to explore on foot in the Plaka.

If You Have 2 Days It's worth spending several hours of day 2 at the **National Archaeological Museum**—but call to make sure it's open during your visit. The museum closed for renovations in 2002; it is slated to reopen in May 2004 in time for the August 2004 Summer Olympics. Try to arrive the minute it opens to beat the crowds; or choose the hour before it closes, when there are fewer visitors.

If the archaeological museum is closed, check out some of Athens's smaller museums, or, if you prefer a change of pace, head up **Mount Likavitos** on the funicular that leaves from the top of Ploutarchou Street (2€), 10am to midnight, about every 20 minutes in summer. If the *nefos* (smog) isn't too bad, you'll have a wonderful view of Athens, Piraeus, and the Saronic Gulf. If you have an extra hour, stroll down one of the paths from the summit, enjoying the scent of pine trees and the changing views of the city.

If You Have 3 Days or More For the rest of your stay, visit more of the museums listed below, or consider a day trip to one of the great sights of antiquity, such as Delphi or **Sounion;** or a day excursion to **Corinth, Mycenae,** and **Epidauros** (best done on a bus tour). If you don't want to go home without seeing one of the "isles of Greece," take a day trip by boat from Piraeus to one of the islands of the Saronic Gulf. **Aegina (Egina), Poros,** and **Hydra (Idra)** are all feasible day trips—but they are best not done the day before you leave Athens, lest bad weather strands you on an island.

Tips **The Ups & Downs of Ticket Prices**

At press time, ticket prices for many monuments and museums were in flux. The prices listed in this guide are based on the prices available at press time and "guesstimates" offered by some museums. As if that is not sufficiently confusing, keep in mind that virtually all the major attractions plan to raise their admission fees "sometime" in 2003 and 2004. As there is—surprise!—no fixed policy on cheaper tickets for students and seniors, be sure to ask about a discounted ticket if you are a senior or a student.

THE TREASURES OF ANTIQUITY

The Acropolis ✦✦✦   *Note:* At press time, the monuments of the Acropolis were undergoing extensive renovation. The Temple of Nike had been entirely dismantled for restoration. The Propylaia and Parthenon were encased in scaffolding. I have attempted to describe what you should see when the renovations are completed, supposedly in 2003/2004, in time for the Summer Olympics.

When you climb up the Acropolis—the heights above the city—you'll realize why people seem to have lived here as long ago as 5000 B.C. The sheer sides of the Acropolis make it a superb natural defense, just the place to avoid enemies and to be able to see invaders coming across the sea or the plains of Attica. And, of course, it helped that in antiquity there was a spring here, ensuring a steady supply of water.

In classical times, when Athens's population had grown to around 250,000, people lived on the slopes below the Acropolis, which had become the city's most important religious center. Athens's civic and business center, the Agora, and its cultural center, with several theaters and concert halls, bracketed the Acropolis; when you peer over the sides of the Acropolis at the houses in the Plaka and the remains of the ancient **Agora** and the **Theater of Dionysos,** you'll see the layout of the ancient city. Syntagma and Omonia squares, the heart of today's Athens, were well out of the ancient city center.

Even the Acropolis's height couldn't protect it from the Persian invasion of 480 B.C., when most of its monuments were burned and destroyed. You may notice some immense column drums built into the Acropolis's walls. When the great Athenian statesman Pericles ordered the monuments rebuilt, he had the drums from the destroyed Parthenon built into the walls lest Athenians forget what had happened—and so they would remember that they had rebuilt what they had lost. Pericles' rebuilding program began about 448 B.C.; the new Parthenon was dedicated 10 years later, but work on other monuments continued for a century.

The **Parthenon** ✹✹✹—dedicated to Athena Parthenos (the Virgin), patron goddess of Athens—was the most important religious monument, but there were shrines to many other gods and goddesses on the Acropolis's broad summit. As you climb up, you pass through first the **Beule Gate,** built by the Romans and now known by the name of the French archaeologist who discovered it in 1852. Next comes the **Propylaia** ✹, the monumental 5th-century-B.C. entranceway. You'll notice the little **Temple of Athena Nike (Athena of Victory)** ✹ perched above the Propylaia; the beautifully proportioned Ionic temple was built in 424 B.C. Off to the left of the Parthenon is the **Erechtheion** ✹✹, which the Athenians honored as the tomb of Erechtheus, a legendary king of Athens. A hole in the ceiling and floor of the northern porch indicates the spot where Poseidon's trident struck to make a spring (symbolizing control of the sea) gush forth during his contest with Athena to be the city's chief deity. Athena countered with an olive tree (symbolizing control of the rich Attic plain); the olive tree planted beside the Erechtheion reminds visitors of her victory. Give yourself a little time to enjoy the delicate carving on the Erechtheion, and be sure to see the original **caryatids** (the monumental female figures who served as columns on the Erechtheion's porch) in the Acropolis Museum.

However charmed you are by these elegant little temples, you're probably still heading resolutely toward the **Parthenon,** and you may be disappointed to realize that visitors are not allowed inside, both to protect the monument and to allow ongoing restoration work to proceed safely. If you find this frustrating, keep in mind that in antiquity only priests and honored visitors were allowed in to see the monumental 11m (36-ft.) statue of Athena designed by the great Phidias, who supervised Pericles' building program. Nothing of the huge gold-and-ivory statue remains, but there's a small Roman copy in the National Archaeological Museum—and horrific renditions on souvenirs ranging from T-shirts to ouzo bottles.

The Parthenon's entire roof and much of the interior were blown to smithereens in 1687, when a party of Venetians attempted to take the Acropolis from the Turks. A shell fired from nearby Mouseion Hill struck the Parthenon—where the Turks were storing gunpowder and munitions—and caused appalling damage to the building and its sculptures. Most of the remaining sculptures were carted off to London by Lord Elgin in the first decade of the 19th century. Those surviving sculptures—known to most of the world as **Elgin Marbles,** but known here as the **Parthenon Marbles**—are on display in the British Museum, causing ongoing pain to generations of Greeks, who continue to press for their return.

The Parthenon originally had sculpture in both its pediments, as well as a frieze running around the entire temple. Alternating **triglyphs** (panels with three incised grooves) and **metopes** (sculptured panels) made up the frieze. The message of most of this sculpture was the triumph of knowledge and civilization (read: Athens) over the forces of darkness and barbarians. An interior frieze showed scenes from the Panathenaic Festival each August, when citizens walked in procession through the streets, bringing a new *peplos* (tunic) for the statue of Athena. Only a few fragments of any of the sculptures remain in place, and every visitor will have to decide whether it's a good or a bad thing that Lord Elgin removed so much before the smog spread over Athens and ate away at the remaining sculpture.

If you're lucky enough to visit the Acropolis on a smog-free and sunny day, you'll see the golden and cream tones of the Parthenon's handsome Pentelic marble at their most subtle. It may come as something of a shock to realize that the Parthenon, like most other monuments here, was painted in antiquity, with gay colors that have since faded, revealing the tones of the marble.

The **Acropolis Archaeological Museum** 𝕮𝕮 hugs the ground to detract as little as possible from the ancient monuments. Inside, you'll see the four original caryatids from the Erechtheion that are still in Athens (one disappeared during the Ottoman occupation, and one is in the British Museum). Other delights here include sculpture from the original Parthenon burned by the Persians, statues of *korai* (maidens) dedicated to Athena, figures of *kouroi* (young men), and a wide range of finds from the Acropolis.

Those interested in learning more about the Acropolis should check to see if the **Center for Acropolis Studies,** on Makriyanni Street just southeast of the Acropolis (𝕮 **210/923-9381**), has reopened. If so, it should be open daily from 9am to 2:30pm; admission is free. On display are artifacts, reconstructions, photographs, drawings, and plaster casts of the Elgin Marbles (see above). A museum is being built here to house the marbles when (if) they're returned to Athens. Construction has been slowed by the discovery of important Byzantine remains here.

You'll probably want to spend half a day on the Acropolis.

Dionyssiou Areopagitou. 𝕮 210/321-0219. Admission 12€ adults. Free Sun. This ticket, which is valid for 1 week, includes admission to the Acropolis, Acropolis Museum, Ancient Agora, Theater of Dionysos, Karameikos Cemetery, Roman Forum, Tower of the Winds, and Temple of Olympian Zeus. It is still possible to buy individual tickets at the other sites. The Acropolis is usually open summer daily 8am–7pm; winter daily 8:30am–2:30pm. The Acropolis Museum usually closes at least half an hour earlier than the Acropolis. From Syntagma Sq., take Amalias Ave. into pedestrianized Dionyssiou Areopagitou, and follow the marble path up to the Acropolis. The ticket booth, along with a small post office and a snack bar, are slightly below the Acropolis entrance.

Ancient Agora 𝕮𝕮   The Agora was Athens's commercial and civic center, with buildings used for a wide range of political, educational, philosophical, theatrical, and athletic purposes—which may be why what remains seems such a jumble. This is a nice place to wander and enjoy the views up toward the Acropolis; take in the herb garden and flowers planted around the 5th-century-B.C. **Theseion (Temple of Hephaistos);** peek into the heavily restored 11th-century church of **Ayii Apostoli (Holy Apostles);** and admire the 2nd-century-B.C. **Stoa of Attalos,** totally reconstructed in the 1950s.

The museum in the Stoa's ground floor has finds from 5,000 years of Athenian history, including sculpture and pottery, as well as a voting machine and a child's potty seat, all with labels in English. The museum (which, by the way, has excellent toilet facilities) closes 15 minutes before the site.

You'll want to spend at least 2 hours here.

Below the Acropolis on the edge of Monastiraki (entrance on Adrianou, near Ayiou Philippou Sq., east of Monastiraki Sq. and on Ay. Apostoli, the road leading down into Plaka from the Acropolis). © 210/ 321-0185. Admission (includes museum) 4€.

Cemetery of Keramikos This ancient cemetery, where **Pericles** gave his famous funeral oration, is a short walk from the Ancient Agora and not far from the presumed site of **Plato's Academy.** There are a number of well-preserved funerary monuments and the remains of the colossal **Dipylon Gate,** the main entrance to the ancient city of Athens. In 2002, the well-preserved marble figure of a *kouros* (youth) was found in excavations here, a hint of what treasures remain to be found. For now, you can see the substantial remains of the 5th-century-B.C. fortifications known as the "Long Walls" that ran from Athens to Piraeus. The Keramikos is seldom crowded, which makes it a pleasant spot to sit and read. If you like cemeteries, be sure to take in Athens's enormous **First Cemetery,** near the Athens Stadium, where notables such as former prime minister George Panandreou are buried beneath elaborate monuments. Both are pleasant spots in which to spend a few hours.

148 Ermou. © 210/346-3553. Admission 2€. Tues–Sun 8:30am–3pm. Walk west from Monastiraki Sq. on Ermou past Thisio Metro station; cemetery is on the right.

THE TOP MUSEUMS

The National Archaeological Museum ✮✮✮   *Note:* The museum closed for renovations in 2002; it is slated to reopen in May 2004 in time for the August 2004 Summer Olympics. The second floor of the museum, where most of the extensive collection of Greek vases was housed, had already been closed since 1999, when an earthquake shook Athens. It was not known at press time where objects would be displayed; therefore, for now, we can only detail the museum's main attractions, not where they will be displayed. Be sure to call ahead for updated opening times.

This is an enormous and enormously popular museum; try to arrive as soon as it opens (or the hour before it closes) so that you can see the exhibits and not just the other visitors' backs. The collection includes objects from the Neolithic to the Roman eras. Don't miss the stunning gold masks, cups, dishes, and jewelry unearthed from the site of Mycenae by Heinrich Schliemann in 1876; the elegant marble Cycladic figurines (ca. 2000 B.C.); and the famous marble and bronze statues. The museum's extensive collection of black-and-red figure vases is, not surprisingly, the finest in the world. The museum shop has reproductions and books on aspects of the collection. You'll probably want to spend a minimum of 3 hours here—and wish you'd spent more.

44 Patission. © 210/821-7717. protocol@eam.culture.gr. Admission 6€. Mon 12:30–6pm; Tues–Fri 8am– 6pm; Sat–Sun and holidays 8:30am–3pm. From Omonia Sq., walk about a half-kilometer (⅓ mile or 10 min.) north on the road officially named 28 Oktovriou (Oct 28) Ave. but usually called Patission.

N. P. Goulandris Foundation Museum of Cycladic Art ✮✮✮   This handsome new museum houses the largest collection of Cycladic art outside the National Archaeological Museum. See if you agree with those who have compared

---

(Tips Online Museum Updates

You can get information on most Greek museums and archaeological sites by logging onto **www.culture.gr**.

> **Tips Museum Cafe with a View**
>
> Dine with a spectacular view over Athens at the excellent rooftop cafe of the **Benaki Museum** (see below), which offers a buffet supper (25€) Thursday evenings, when the museum remains open until midnight.

the faces of the Cycladic figurines to the works of the Italian painter Modigliani. Be sure to go through the courtyard into the museum's newest acquisition: an elegant 19th-century house with some of its original furnishings and visiting exhibits. The museum shop has a wide variety of books and reproductions—and a wildly unhelpful staff. You'll want to spend at least 3 hours here; be sure to give yourself a break in the garden or in the cafe.

4 Neophytou Douka. ✆ 210/722-8321. www.cycladic-m.gr. Admission 4€. Mon and Wed–Fri 10am–4pm; Sat 10am–3pm. From Syntagma Sq., walk 7 blocks east along Vasilissis Sofias Ave., then 1/2 block north on Neophytou Douka.

Benaki Museum ★★ This stunning private collection includes treasures from the Neolithic era to the 20th century. The folk art collection (including magnificent costumes and icons) is superb, as are the two entire rooms from 18th-century northern Greek mansions, ancient Greek bronzes, gold cups, Fayum portraits, and rare early Christian textiles. A new wing doubles the exhibition space of the original 20th-century neoclassical town house that belonged to the wealthy Benaki family. The museum shop is excellent, and new galleries will house special exhibitions. This is a very pleasant place to spend several hours.

Koumbari 1 (at Leoforos Vasilissis Sofias, Kolonaki, 5 blocks east of Syntagma Sq.). ✆ 210/367-1000. www.benaki.gr. Admission 6€; free on Thurs. Mon, Wed, Fri, Sat 9am–5pm; Thurs 9am midnight; Sun 9am–3pm; closed Tues.

Byzantine Museum ★ If you love icons (paintings, usually of saints, usually on wood) or want to find out about them, this is the place to go. As its name makes clear, this museum, in a 19th-century Florentine-style villa, is devoted to the art and history of the Byzantine era (roughly 4th–15th c. A.D.). Selections from Greece's most important collection of icons and religious art—along with sculptures, altars, mosaics, religious vestments, Bibles, and a small-scale reconstruction of an early Christian basilica—are exhibited on several floors around a courtyard. Allow at least an hour for your visit; 2 hours is better. If there is a special exhibit, try to allow 3 hours or more.

22 Vasilissis Sofias Ave. ✆ 210/723-1570 or 210/721-1027. Admission 4€. Tues–Sun 8:30am–3pm. From Syntagma Sq., walk along Queen Sophias Ave. for about 15 min. The museum is on your right. If you come to the Hilton Hotel, you have gone too far.

Greek Folk Art Museum ★★ *Kids* This endearing small museum has dazzling embroideries and costumes, carved wooden furniture and tools, and ceramic and copper utensils from all over the country, plus a small room with zany frescoes of gods and heroes done by eccentric artist Theofilos Hadjimichael, who painted in the early part of the 20th century. Lots of Greek schoolchildren visit here, and sometimes puppet shows are offered. It's a great place to spend several hours.

17 Kidathineon, Plaka. ✆ 210/322-9031. Admission 2€. Tues–Sun 10am–2pm. From Syntagma, take Filellinon to Kidathineon.

Hellenic Cosmos *(Kids)* This high-tech museum, housed in a former factory, has interactive displays showing the history of Greece from ancient to modern times, a cafe, an Internet cafe, and a museum shop. There's usually an English-speaking guide on duty, but if you call ahead, you can ensure that one is available.

254 Pireos, Tavros (near Kallithea Metro station). © 210/483-5300. www.hellenic-cosmos.gr. Admission 4€. Mon–Fri 9am–4pm; Sun 11am–3pm.

GALLERIES

One of the great (usually free) pleasures of visiting Athens is browsing in its small art galleries. Very occasionally a gallery will have an admission fee for a special exhibit, but usually there is no charge. This is a wonderful way to get a sense of the contemporary Greek art scene and possibly buy something to take home. Openings are usually not by invitation only, so if you see a notice of an opening, feel free to stop by. Here are some galleries to keep an eye out for in central Athens. The **Epistrofi Gallery,** 6 Taki (© 210/321-8640), in trendy **Psirri** (so trendy that it has its own website: www.psiri.gr/english), has occasional concerts as well as shows; the **Epikentro Gallery,** 10 Armodiou (© 210/331-2187), stages frequent exhibits in its improbable location in the Athens Central Market; the **Rebecca Kamhi Gallery,** Sophokleous 23 (© 210/321-0448), not far from the Central Market, and one of Athens's best-known galleries, is open by appointment only in August; **Bernier/Eliades Gallery,** 11 Eptachalkou, Theseion (© 210/341-3935), stages group exhibitions, as does **Kappatos,** Agias Irenes 6 (© 210/321-7931). There are also frequent shows at the **Melina Mercouri Cultural Center,** Iraklidon and Thessalonikis 66 (© 210/345-2150), not far from the Theseion and at the Melina Mercouri Foundation, Polygnotou 9–11 (© 210/331-5601), in the Plaka. The fashionable Kolonaki district is chockablock with galleries: the **Athens Art Center,** 4 Glyconos, Dexameni (© 210/721-3938); **Photohoros,** Tsakalof 44 (© 210/321-0448); and **Medussa,** Xenokratous 7 (© 210/724-4552), are three to look for. The **Athens Arts and Technology School** (© 210/381-3700) usually stages shows around Athens in July and August when many galleries close or move out of town. One just-out-of-town suburban gallery that's open year-round and well worth a visit (in part for its great cafe and shop) is **The Deste Foundation for Contemporary Art,** Omirou 8, Nea Psychico (© 210/672-9460; www.deste.gr), a 20-minute cab ride from Syntagma.

ORGANIZED TOURS

You can book tours of Athens through most hotels or any travel agency. A half-day tour of city highlights should cost about 50€. Night tours can include a sound-and-light show, Greek folk dancing at the Dora Stratou Dance Theater, or dinner and Greek dancing; the tours range from about 50€ to 100€. Since many Athenian nightclubs are clip joints, the safety-in-numbers aspect of a visit with a tour group may appeal to you.

Educational Tours & Cruises, 9 Irving, Medford, MA 02111 (© 800/275-4109; edtours@ars.nep.gr), and 1 Artemídos, Glyfáda 16674, Athens (© 210/898-1741), can arrange tours in Athens and throughout Greece, including individual tours with an emphasis on Greek culture. **CHAT Tours,** 9 Xenofondos (Syntagma, 4th floor; © 210/322-3137; fax 210/323-5270; chat@chatours.gr); and **Key Tours,** 4 Kalliroïs (© 210/923-3166; fax 210/923-2008), are reliable, established companies that offer tours of Athens and various day trips.

Destinations include the temple of Apollo at Sounion, Delphi (day trip or overnight visit), and the Peloponnese (day trip usually taking in Corinth, Mycenae, and Epidauros; 3-day trips of the major sites; and a 5-day trip, usually including Delphi).

THE SHOPPING SCENE

If you want to pick up retro clothes or old copper, try the **flea market,** a daily spectacle between the Plaka and Monastiraki Square. It's most lively on Sunday, but you can find the usual touristy trinkets, copies of ancient artifacts, jewelry, sandals, and various handmade goods, including embroideries, any day. Keep in mind that not everything sold as an antique is genuine, and that it's illegal to take antiquities and icons more than 100 years old out of the country without a hard-to-obtain export license.

Martinos, 50 Pandrossou, Monastiraki (✆ **210/321-2414**), has Venetian glass, woodcarvings (usually including some handsome chests and furniture), old jewelry, coins—and sometimes swords. In the Plaka–Monastiraki area, several shops with nicer-than-usual arts and crafts at fair prices include **Stavros Melissinos,** "the Poet-Sandalmaker of Athens," 89 Pandrossou (✆ **210/321-9247**); **Iphanta,** a weaving workshop, 6 Selleu (✆ **210/322-3628**); **Emanuel Masmanidis's Gold Rose Jewelry shop,** 85 Pandrossou (✆ **210/321-5662**); and the **Center of Hellenic Tradition,** 59 Mitropoleos and 36 Pandrossou sts. (✆ **210/321-3023**), which sells arts and crafts. Check to see if the **National Welfare Organization Arts and Crafts Shop** is still at 6 Ipatias and Apollonos streets, Plaka (✆ **210/324-0017**), or has moved to its new location on Filellinon Street (no phone available at press time). A portion of the proceeds from everything sold (including handsome woven and embroidered carpets) goes to the National Welfare Organization, which encourages traditional crafts. Finally, don't forget that most museums have excellent shops.

On your way there, you can ogle the window displays at **Lalaounis,** 6 Panepistimiou (✆ **210/362-1371**), and at **Zolotas,** 8 Pandrossou (Plaka; ✆ **210/322-1212**), Greece's two finest jewelers.

To window-shop for elegant clothes, luxury house goods, and designer chocolates along with the beautiful people, head up to **Kolonaki** (preferably on a Sat), and join the throngs strolling along the pedestrianized streets that run in and out of Patriarchou Ioakeim.

ATHENS AFTER DARK

Greeks enjoy their nightlife so much that they take an afternoon nap to rest up for it. The evening often begins with a leisurely *volta* (stroll); you'll see it in most neighborhoods, including the Plaka and Kolonaki Square. Most Greeks don't think of dinner until at least 9pm—when there's still no hurry. Around midnight the party may move on to a club for music and dancing. Feel free to try places on your own, although you may feel like the odd man out because Greeks seldom go anywhere alone. If you're a woman on your own and want to be left alone, you'll probably find hitting the bars and dance clubs uncongenial.

Check the daily *Kathimerini* insert in the *International Herald-Tribune* or the *Athens News,* both sold at most major newsstands, for current cultural and entertainment events, including films, lectures, theater, music, and dance. The weekly *Hellenic Times* and *Athenscope* and the monthly *Now in Athens* list nightspots, restaurants, movies, theater, and much more. The weekly Greek publication *Athinorama* has comprehensive listings of events.

Best of all, if you have a Greek friend, ask for pointers on what's currently on. If you ask a taxi driver, he's likely to take you to either his cousin George's joint or the place that gives him a kickback for bringing you. Be especially wary of heading out of the city to the places that spring up each summer on the airport road; these spots are usually overpriced and often unsavory. That said, the **Asteria Club** (✆ 210/894-4558) and the **Bio-Bio Club** (✆ 210/894-1300) in Glyfada were popular during the summer of 2002, as was **Riba's** (✆ 210/965-5555) in Varkiza and **Gefira** (✆ 210/940-9221) at 26–28 Posidonos, Tzitzifies. In Athens itself, Kolonaki's **Haritos** has a number of popular bars, as does the **Psirri district** and the **Thission district.** Expect to pay about 20€ for one or two drinks after paying an entrance charge of at least that much at all these live-music joints. (Also see below under "Live-Music Clubs.")

THE PERFORMING ARTS

Tickets for the **Athens, Lycabettus,** and **Epidauros festivals** are available at the **Hellenic Festival Box Office,** 39 Panepistimiou in the arcade (✆ 210/322-1459). Advance booking for the Athens and Epidauros festivals starts 3 weeks before each performance; 10 days before each event for the Lycabettus Festival. Ticket reservations and telephone booking are also possible by credit card (MasterCard or Visa) or by e-mail to **nikolaidis@greekfestival.gr** with exact date and performance, number and category of tickets, and number and expiration date of the credit card. Tickets (if available) are also on sale at the box offices at each theater 2 hours before each performance.

Additional information on the Hellenic Festival, including the Athens, Epidauros, and Lycabettus festivals, is available at the websites **www.hellenicfestival.gr**, **www.cultureguide.gr**, and **www.greektourism.com**. Many of these events, and others, are sponsored by the **Cultural Olympiad** (www.cultural-olympiad.gr), which is part of the buildup to the 2004 Summer Olympics.

The **Athens Festival** at the **Odeon of Herodes Atticus** features famous Greek and foreign artists performing music, plays, opera, and ballet from the beginning of June to the beginning of October in a beautiful open-air setting. The only drawbacks are that the stone seats are hard, with thin foam cushions, and that there are no backrests. Find out what's being presented through the English-language press or at the **Hellenic Festival Box Office,** 39 Panepistimiou in the arcade (✆ **210/322-1459,** 210/322-3111, or 210/322-3110, ext. 137). The office is open Monday through Saturday from 8:30am to 2pm and 5 to 7pm, and Sunday from 10am to 1pm. Tickets usually cost about 15€ to 50€. If they're available—and that's a big "if"—tickets can also be purchased at the **Odeon** (✆ 210/323-2771) several hours before a performance.

Information on performances (often of pop music) at the Lycabettus Festival, staged in a modern amphitheater on the slopes of Mount Lycabettus each summer, is available from the Hellenic Festival Box Office (see above).

Information on performances (primarily of ancient Greek drama, usually translated into modern Greek) in the ancient theater of Epidauros at the Epidauros Festival take place each summer; information is available from the Hellenic Festival Box Office (see above) and, if available, at the theater in Epidauros on the day of performances.

The acoustically marvelous new **Megaron Mousikis Concert Hall,** 89 Vasilissis Sofias Ave. (✆ **210/729-0391** or 210/728-2333), hosts a wide range of classical music programs that include chamber music, operas in concert, symphonic concerts, and recitals. The box office is usually open weekdays from

10am to 6pm, Saturday from 10am to 2pm, and Sunday from 6 to 10:30pm on performance nights only. Tickets, usually costing about 3€ to 50€, are also sold weekdays from 10am to 5pm in the Megaron's convenient downtown kiosk in the Spiromillios Arcade, 4 Stadiou (the arcade is in the courtyard off Stadiou). The Megaron has a limited summer season but is in full swing the rest of the year.

Most major jazz and rock concerts, as well as some classical performances, take place at the **Pallas Theater,** 1 Voukourestiou (© **210/322-8275**).

English-language theater and American-style music are performed at the **Hellenic American Union Auditorium,** 22 Massalias, between Kolonaki and Omonia squares (© **210/362-9886**); you can usually get a ticket for around 10€. Arrive early and check out the art show or photo exhibition at the adjacent gallery. The **Greek National Opera** performs at the **Olympia Theater,** 59 Akadimias, at Mavromihali (© **210/361-2461**).

The **Dora Stratou Folk Dance Theater,** which performs May through October on Philopappos Hill, is the best known of the traditional dance troupes. For several years there have been rumors of the company's closing, but thus far regional dances continue to be performed in costume with appropriate (if over-amplified) musical accompaniment nightly at 10:15pm, with additional shows at 8:15pm on Wednesday and Sunday (no performances on Mon). You can buy tickets for about 10€ to 20€ from 8am to 2pm at the box office, 8 Scholio, Plaka (© **210/924-4395**, or 210/921-4650 after 5:30pm).

Sound-and-light shows, seen from the Pnyx, the hill across Dionyssiou Areopagitou Street from the Acropolis, illuminate (sorry) Athens's history by focusing on the history of the Acropolis. Try to sit away from the (very) loud speakers, so you won't be deafened by the booming historical narrative and all-too-stirring music and can concentrate instead on the play of lights on the monuments of the Acropolis. Shows are held April through October. Performances in English begin at 9pm and last 45 minutes. Tickets can be purchased at the **Hellenic Festival Box Office,** 39 Panepistimiou in the arcade (© **210/322-1459**); or at the entrance to the sound-and-light show (© **210/922-6210**), which is signposted on the Pnyx. Ticket prices had not been set at press time, but should be about 7€.

LIVE-MUSIC CLUBS

Walk the streets of the Plaka on any night and you'll find lots of tavernas offering pseudo-traditional live music (usually at clip-joint prices) and a few offering the real thing. **Taverna Mostrou,** 22 Mnissikleos (© **210/324-2441**), is one of the largest, oldest, and best known for traditional Greek music and dancing. Shows begin about 11pm and usually last to 2am. The 20€ cover includes a fixed-price supper; a la carte fare is available but expensive. Nearby, **Palia Taverna Kritikou,** 24 Mnissikleos (© **210/322-2809**), is another lively open-air taverna with music and dancing. Other reliable tavernas with live traditional music are **Nefeli,** 24 Panos (© **210/321-2475**); **Dioyenis,** 3 Sellei (© **210/324-7933**); **Stamatopoulou,** 26 Lissiou (© **210/322-8722**); and **Xinou,** 4 Geronta (© **210/322-1065**).

Those interested in authentic *rebetika* (music of the urban poor and dispossessed) should consult their hotel receptionist or the current issue of *Athenscope* or *Athinorama* (in Greek) to see which clubs are featuring the best performers. Shows usually don't start until nearly midnight, and although there's usually no cover, a 15€ charge per drink isn't uncommon. Most clubs are closed in summer, and many are far from the town center, so budget at least another 15€ to 25€ for round-trip taxi fare.

One of the more central clubs is the **Stoa Athanaton,** 19 Sofokleous, in the Central Meat Market (© **210/321-4362**), which has live rebetika Monday through Saturday from 3 to 6pm and after midnight and serves good food; the minimum charge is 10€. **Taximi,** 29 Isavron, Exarchia (© **210/363-9919**), is consistently popular, with drinks costing about 10€. It's closed Sunday and July and August. **Frangosyriani,** 57 Arachovis, Exarchia (© **210/360-0693**), specializes in the music of rebetika legend Markos Vamvakaris; it's closed Tuesday and Wednesday. The downscale, smoke-filled **Rebetiki Istoria,** in a neoclassical building at 181 Ippokratous (© **210/642-4937**), features old-style rebetika music, played to a mixed crowd of older regulars and younger students and intellectuals. The music usually starts at 11pm, but arrive earlier to get a seat. The legendary Maryo I Thessaloniki (Maryo from Thessaloniki), sometimes described as the Bessie Smith of Greece, sometimes sings rebetika at **Perivoli t'Ouranou,** 19 Lysikratous in the Plaka (© **210/323-5517** or 210/322-2048); admission is around 25€.

A number of clubs and cafes specialize in jazz but also offer everything from Indian sitar music to rock and punk. **The Café Asante,** 78 Damareos in Pangrati (© **210/756-0102**), has music most nights from 11pm. As at most of these clubs and cafes, admission varies, but count on spending around at least 35€ at the Café Asante if you have a couple of drinks. The very popular **Half Note Jazz Club,** 17 Trivonianou, Mets (© **210/921-3310**), offers up everything from medieval music to jazz nightly. Performance times vary from 8 to 11pm and later; admission is usually around 15€ to 20€. At **The House of Art,** 4 Sahtouri and Sari (© **210/321-7678**), and at **Pinakothiki,** 5 Agias Theklas (© **210/324-7741**), both in newly fashionable Psyrri, you can often hear jazz from 11pm; admission is around 20€, including the first drink. **The Rodon Club,** 24 Marni, west of Omonia Square (© **210/523-6293**), also has jazz and pop concerts many nights from 10pm; admission is usually from 20€.

GAY & LESBIAN BARS

The gay scene is fairly low-key; get-togethers are sometimes advertised in the English-language press. Information is also available from the Greek national gay and lesbian organization **AKOE-AMPHI,** P.O. Box 26002, 10022 Athens.

The friendliest bar is **Aleko's Island,** 42 Tsakalof, Kolonaki (no phone), a fun place where you can actually have a conversation. **Granazi,** 20 Lembesi (© **210/325-3979**), attracts a loud and lively young crowd. The disco **Lambda,** 15 Lembesi and 9 Syngrou Ave. (© **210/922-4202**), is hip and trendy with the young locals. In Kolonaki, **Alexander's,** 44 Anagnostopoulou (© **210/364-6660**), is more sedate, with more variety. **Porta,** 10 Phalirou (© **210/924-3858**), and **Fairytale,** 25 Kolleti (© **210/330-1763**), are well-established lesbian bars.

DANCE CLUBS

Hidden on the outskirts of the Plaka, **Booze,** 57 Kolokotroni, second floor (© **210/324-0944**), blasts danceable rock to a hip student crowd. There's art on every wall, gelled stage lights, and two bars. If it's disco you're craving, head east to **Absolut,** 23 Filellinon (no phone); **Q Base,** 49 Evripidou, Omonia (© **210/321-8256**); or **R-Load,** 161 Ermou (© **210/345-6187**). If you feel a bit too old here, head north to Panepistimiou Street, where the **Wild Rose,** in the arcade at 10 Panepistimiou (© **210/364-2160**), and **Mercedes Rex,** at 48 Panepistimiou (© **210/361-4591**), usually have varied programs. Admission at all these clubs usually ranges from 7€ to 10€.

2 Delphi & the Northern Peloponnese

With the exception of the Acropolis in Athens, the most famous and beautiful ancient sites in Greece bracket the Gulf of Corinth. Apollo's sanctuary at Delphi is on the mainland north of the gulf, and Agamemnon's palace at Mycenae, the Mycenaean fortress of Tiryns, the spectacular 4th-century-B.C. theater of Epidauros, and Olympia, the birthplace of the Olympic Games, are south of the gulf in the northern Peloponnese.

EXPLORING THE REGION BY CAR   Thanks to the excellent road linking Athens and the Peloponnese at Corinth, and the frequent ferry service across the Gulf of Corinth between Rio and Anti-Rio, it's easy to combine a visit to Delphi with a tour of the most important ancient sites in the Peloponnese. Try to allow at least 4 days (spending 2 nights at Nafplion and 1 night each at Olympia and Delphi).

If traffic is light (and it almost never is), you can drive the 88km (55 miles) from Athens to Corinth on the National Road in an hour. After you take a look at the Corinth Canal and the sprawling site of ancient Corinth, an hour's drive (less if you take the new National Road to Argos and double back) through the farmland of Corinthia and Argolis will take you to Mycenae, 114km (70 miles) southwest of Athens. From Mycenae, an hour's drive will easily get you to Nafplion, 145km (90 miles) southwest of Athens. Generally considered the prettiest town in the Peloponnese, Nafplion is the perfect spot to spend the night before visiting Epidauros.

Although it's only 32km (20 miles) from Nafplion to Epidauros, the road is usually clogged with tour buses, especially when there are performances at the ancient theater; allow at least an hour for the drive. From Nafplion and Epidauros, two routes lead across the Peloponnese to Olympia. You can return to Corinth and join the National Road, which runs as far as Patras, where you take the good coast road on to Olympia. (Although there are signs in Patras pointing you toward Olympia, the heavy traffic in Patras means that you can easily spend an hour getting across town.)

If you want to avoid Patras, you can join the new National Road at Argos and drive through the Arcadian mountains via Tripolis to Olympia, 320km (199

Tips Driving Tips

Keep in mind that most Greek roads are quite good, but much of your journey to and around the Peloponnese will be on beautiful, but sometimes vertiginous, winding mountain and coastal roads that make distances deceptive. Plus, severe rains and flooding in the winter of 2003 damaged many roads; don't be surprised if you encounter detours as road repairs continue. Check road conditions with your rental-car agency in Athens when you pick up the car, or contact the **Greek Automobile Association (ELPA;** Athens Tower, 2–4 Mossogion, Athens 115 27; ☎ **210/779-1615),** which has a reciprocity arrangement with many foreign auto clubs. The ELPA emergency number is ☎ **104.** I've indicated how long you should expect each part of the trip to take, rather than give you a false sense of how quickly you can travel by just telling you how much distance you'll cover. Also keep in mind that only Portugal has more traffic fatalities each year than Greece, so buckle up and be careful out there!

miles) west of Athens. Either way, expect to spend at least 4 hours en route—and try to spend more, so that you can enjoy the coastal scenery or the mountain villages of Arcadia. Then, to reach Delphi from Olympia, simply head to Rio, just north of Patras, and catch one of the frequent ferries across the gulf to Anti-Rio, where a new road runs all the way to Delphi, 177km (110 miles) west of Athens. (If you want to avoid the ferry, check whether the new Rio–Anti-Rio bridge, linking the Peloponnese with the rest of mainland Greece, slated to be finished by Dec 2004, is in service.) Allow at least 5 hours for the trip from Olympia to Delphi, and 3 hours to get from Delphi to Athens.

THE NORTHERN PELOPONNESE & THE CLASSICAL SITES

One of the delights of visiting the northern Peloponnese is that it's relatively uncrowded when many of the Aegean islands are sagging under the weight of tourists each summer. That doesn't mean you'll have famous spots like Mycenae, Epidauros, and Olympia to yourself if you arrive at high noon in August. It does mean that if you arrive just as they open or just before they close, you may have an hour under the pine trees at Olympia or Epidauros virtually alone, and be able to stand in Mycenae's Treasury of Atreus with swallows as your only companions.

Because even the most avid tourists do not live by culture alone, it's good to know that one of the great delights of spending time in the northern Peloponnese comes from quiet hours spent in shady *plateias* (squares), watching fishers mend their nets while local families settle down for a leisurely meal. An hour in a seaside cafe watching the locals watching you watch them is the ideal way to unwind after a day's sightseeing.

Warning: If you visit here in the winter, make sure your hotel has functioning heating.

CORINTH

Corinth exported its pottery around the Mediterranean and dominated trade in Greece for much of the 8th century and 7th century B.C. It experienced a second golden age under the Romans in the 2nd century A.D. Today, as in antiquity, Corinth and Patras are the two major gateways to the Peloponnese. As you pause here, you'll want to leave the main highway (look for the turnoff for the Canal Tourist Area) to take a look at the Corinth Canal and visit ancient Corinth before heading deeper into the northern Peloponnese.

Essentials

GETTING THERE   By Train   Several trains a day run from Athens's Stathmos Peloponnisou to the Corinth station off Demokratias (© **2741/22-522**). The trains are almost invariably late, often taking 3 hours or more. Refreshments sometimes are available on board. For information on schedules and fares, contact **OSE** (© **210/512-4913** in Athens; www.ose.gr).

By Bus   At least 15 buses a day run to Corinth from the Stathmos Leoforia Peloponnisou, 100 Kifissou in Athens. For schedule and fare information, call © **210/512-8233** in Athens. Buses to and from Athens come and go from the **bus station** at Ermou and Koliatsou streets (© **2741/25-645**). Buses for Ancient Corinth sometimes leave from this station or from another bus stop on Koliatsou. Inquire upon arrival and allow 20 minutes for the bus ride to Archaia Korinthos (Ancient Corinth); buses usually run once an hour from about 8am to 8pm. Buses from Corinth for the Peloponnese leave from the station at the corner of Konstantinou and Aratou streets (© **2741/24-403**).

By Car Corinth is 88km (54 miles) west of Athens on the National Highway; the toll is 2€. The highway continues past the Corinth Canal; just after the canal, you'll see signs for Ancient Corinth (the splendid archaeological site), Epidauros, and Corinth (the architecturally uninteresting modern town).

FAST FACTS The police station is on Ermou Street (© **2741/22-143**).

The Corinth Canal

When the main road ran directly past the restaurants and cafes on either side of the canal, almost everyone used to stop here for a coffee, a souvlakia, and a look at the canal that separates the Peloponnese from the mainland. Now buses, trucks, and most cars stay on the new highway, but you can still take the exit for the Canal and Tourist Area to see the canal and have a snack. There's a small post office at the canal and a kiosk with postcards and English-language newspapers. Most of the large souvlakia places have surprisingly clean toilet facilities (and very tough souvlakia). One word of warning that's necessary here and almost nowhere else in Greece: *Be sure to lock your car door.* This is a popular spot for thieves to prey on unwary tourists.

The French engineers who built the Corinth Canal between 1881 and 1893 used lots of dynamite, blasting through 87m (285 ft.) of sheer rock to make this 6km (4-mile) long, 27m (89-ft.) wide passageway. The canal utterly revolutionized shipping in the Mediterranean; vessels that previously had spent days making their way around Cape Matapan, at the southern tip of the Peloponnese, could dart through the canal in hours.

Exploring Ancient Corinth

To reach Ancient Corinth, follow the signs after the Corinth Canal for Ancient and Old Corinth. It's a 20-minute bus ride from the train station or 10 minutes by taxi. A number of small restaurants and cafes are adjacent to the ancient site; frankly, we have had bad or mediocre meals at most of them and suggest you just have a light meal here—and, if you are heading for Nafplion, reward yourself with a good meal there.

Ancient Corinth ★★ Although Corinth's greatest period of prosperity was between the 8th and 5th centuries B.C., most of the ancient remains here are from the Roman period. Razed and destroyed when the Romans conquered Greece in 146 B.C., Corinth was refounded by Julius Caesar in 44 B.C. and began a second period of wealth and prosperity. When Paul visited here in A.D. 52, he found it all too sophisticated and chastised the Corinthians for their wanton ways.

By the 2nd century A.D., Corinth was much larger and more powerful than Athens. During the next hundred years, a series of barbarian invasions and attacks undermined Corinth's prosperity. Thereafter, although the long series of invaders fought for control of the strategic citadel of Acrocorinth, Corinth itself was a provincial backwater with a glorious past.

The most conspicuous—and the most handsome—surviving building at Ancient Corinth is clearly the 6th-century-B.C. **Temple of Apollo,** which stands on a low hill overlooking the extensive remains of the **Roman Agora** (forum or marketplace). Only seven of the temple's 38 monolithic Doric columns are standing, the others having long since been toppled by earthquakes.

Ancient Corinth's main drag, the 12m (40-ft.) wide marble-paved road that ran from the port of Lechaion into the heart of the marketplace, is clearly visible from the temple. Along the road, and throughout the Agora, are the foundations of hundreds of the stores that once stocked everything from spices imported from Asia Minor to jugs of wine made from Corinth's excellent grapes.

Two spots in the Agora are especially famous—the **Fountain of Peirene** and the **Bema.** In the 2nd century A.D., the famous Roman traveler Philhellene and benefactor Herodes Atticus encased the modest Greek fountain in an elaborate two-story building with arches, arcades, and the 5 sq. m (50-sq.-ft.) courtyard whose remains you see today. Peirene was a woman who wept so hard when her son died that she dissolved into the spring that still flows here. The Bema (public platform) was where Paul had to plead his case when the Corinthians, irritated by his constant criticisms, hauled him in front of the Roman governor Gallo in A.D. 52.

If you visit here in the summer, you may see archaeologists at work excavating more of Ancient Corinth. Usually, they are willing to be observed, less willing to chat. In 2002, work continued on an extensive Roman villa unearthed near the ancient Agora/forum.

Old Corinth. ✆ **2741/31-207.** Admission to archaeological site and museum 6€. Summer Mon–Fri 8am–7pm; Sat–Sun 8am–3pm. Winter Mon–Fri 8:45am–3pm; Sat–Sun 8:30am–3pm.

Archaeological Museum ✦ As you'd expect, this museum just inside the site entrance has a particularly fine collection of the famous Corinthian pottery, which is often decorated with charming red and black figures of birds and animals. There are also a number of statues of Roman worthies and several mosaics, including one in which Pan is shown piping away to a clutch of cows. The museum courtyard is a shady spot in which to sit and read up on the ancient site, which has virtually no shade. When you visit, be sure to see the handsome sculpture and vases stolen from the museum in 1990, found in Miami, Florida, in 1998, and officially handed over to Greece in 2001, again now on display.

Ancient Corinth, in the town of Old Corinth. ✆ **2741/31-207.** Admission to museum and archaeological site 6€. Summer Mon–Sun 8am–7pm; winter Mon–Sun 8am–5pm.

Acrocorinth ✦✦ (Moments It's hard to say what's more impressive here: the superb fortifications or the spectacular view across the plain of Corinth to the Gulf and beyond into central Greece. A winding dirt road runs from the site of Ancient Corinth to the summit of Acrocorinth, the rugged limestone sugarloaf mountain topped by centuries of fortifications that dominates the plain of Corinth. A superb natural acropolis, Acrocorinth was fortified first by the Greeks and later by the Byzantines, Franks, Venetians, and Turks. Extensive remains of the centuries of walls, turrets, and towers built here still remain. After you roam around enjoying the seemingly endless view over the rich plain below, you can relax at the small cafe just outside the site entrance.

Old Corinth. Free admission. Summer daily 8am–7pm; winter daily 8am–5pm.

NAFPLION ✦✦
With two hilltop Venetian fortresses, shady parks, an interesting assortment of small museums, and better-than-average hotels, restaurants, and shops—and even a miniature castle (the Bourtzi) in the harbor—this port town on the northeast coast of the Gulf of Argos is almost everyone's first choice as the most charming town in the Peloponnese. A good deal of Nafplion's appeal comes from the fact that for several years after the Greek War of Independence (1821–28), this was the country's first capital. Although the palace of Greece's young King Otto—a mail-order monarch from Bavaria—burned down in the 19th century, an impressive number of handsome neoclassical civic buildings

and private houses have survived, as have a scattering of Turkish fountains and several mosques.

Essentials

GETTING THERE   By Bus   At least a dozen buses a day run to Nafplion from the **Stathmos Leoforia Peloponnisou,** 100 Kifissou, Athens (© **210/513-4110** or 210/513-4588). The trip takes about 4 hours because the bus goes into Corinth and Argos before reaching Nafplion.

By Boat   *Flying Dolphin* hydrofoil service runs from Marina Zea, Piraeus, to Nafplion, Monday through Saturday, weather permitting. The hydrofoil makes a number of stops and takes almost as long as the bus to reach Nafplion. For fare and schedule information, call © **210/324-2281** or 210/453-6107 in Athens.

By Car   From Athens, head south to the Corinth Canal. Take the new Corinth–Tripolis road to the Argos exit and follow signs into Argos and Nafplion. You'll almost certainly get lost at least once in Argos, which has an abysmal system of directional signs. Allow at least 3 hours for the drive from Athens to Nafplion. When you reach Nafplion, park in the large, free municipal lot by the harbor. If you want to stop at Mycenae or Nemea, take the winding old road to Nafplion. If you want to stop at Epidauros, take the signposted turn for Epidauros just after the canal.

VISITOR INFORMATION   The **Greek National Tourist Organization (EOT)** office is at 16 Photomara (© **27520/28-131**), cater-corner across from the bus station in Plateia Nikitara. It's usually open weekdays from 9am to 2pm, but seems to have frequent unscheduled closings. The helpful brochure "Nafplion Day and Night" is sometimes available here, in shops, and in hotels.

FAST FACTS   The **post office** is open weekdays from 8am to 2pm, and the **OTE** telephone and telegraph office is open weekdays from 8am to 7pm. Both are signposted from the bus station. The **National Bank of Greece** has a branch on the main square, Syntagma Square. There are a number of **travel agencies** in Nafplion, including **Staikos Travel,** by the harbor (© **27520/27-950**). The best place to swim is at the **beach** beneath the Palamidi, a 15-minute walk (with the sea on your right) from the harborside cafes.

Where to Stay

Byron Hotel 🏆   The Byron was one of the first hotels here to attempt to add individual charm and creature comfort to a pleasant location. The hotel is in a quiet, breezy location overlooking the Church of Agiou Spiridona, a short but steep hike up from the main *plateia* (square). It has nice bits of Victoriana in the sitting rooms and guest rooms, as well as modern conveniences. Word has gotten out about the Byron's charm, and it's almost impossible to stay here in July or August without a reservation, especially on weekends, when the entire hotel can be taken over by Athenians. The cheapest rooms are quite small and have no view; for another 10€, you'll get a view of Nafplion—and enough space that you won't feel the burden of togetherness with your roommate.

2 Platonos, Plateia Agiou Spiridona, 211 00 Nafplion. © **27520/22-351.** Fax 27520/26-338. byronhotel@otenet.gr. 17 units. 50€–75€ double. AE, MC, V. **Amenities:** Breakfast room; terrace. *In room:* A/C, TV, minibar, hair dryer.

Epidauros Hotel   Rooms here are small but acceptable, with good, firm beds, small bathrooms, and wooden hanging cupboards large enough for a stay of at least a month. The location, on a quiet street just off the main square, is excellent and usually quiet, although adjacent nightclubs, restaurants, and bars can make things noisy on summer weekends. The staff here is neither wildly welcoming nor noticeably efficient. The Epidauros has an annex across the street, as well as nearby pension quarters at 30€ for a double.

2 Kokkinou (beside the Commercial Bank), 211 00 Nafplion. ©/fax **27520/27-541**. 30 units, 25 with full bathroom. 50€ double. No credit cards. **Amenities:** Bar.

Hotel Nafsimedon ⚘

This "boutique" hotel in a handsome mid-19th-century neoclassical house is a welcome addition to Nafplion's hotels. It's set back from the street and overlooks relatively quiet Kolokotronis Park. The exterior is a warm peach color, and the interior walls are peach and apricot (fashionably sponge-painted, of course). Rooms are attractively furnished, some with bits of Victoriana and four-poster beds; most are larger than those in most Greek hotels. The service was rather casual for a "boutique" hotel when we visited, but several letters from travelers praised the service, ambience, and comfort.

9 Sideras Merarhias (on Kolokotronis Park), 211 00 Nafplion. © **27520/25-060**. Fax 27520/26-913. www.nafsimedon.gr. 13 units. 80€ double. Reductions possible off season. No credit cards. **Amenities:** Breakfast room; bar; garden. *In room:* A/C, TV.

King Otho ⚘

This longtime favorite (we first stayed here in the early 1960s) was somewhat down at the heels before its complete and completely successful renovation in 2000. In 2002, the owners bought and restored another wonderful town house a few blocks up the hill on Staikopoulou. Now Nafplion has two small hotels contending for the honor of having the most breathtaking curved staircase in the Pelopponese. Both hotels have high ceilings (some with frescoes); wood floors; period furniture, including marble-topped baths; and all the modern amenities. The new Otho is more expensive, because every room is a room with a view (of Nafplion and of the harbor). Each hotel has a garden, a real plus for breakfast or a quiet hour's reading.

4 Farmakapoulou, 211 00 Nafplion. © **27520/27-585**. Fax 27520/27-595. 12 units. 85€ double. Rates include continental breakfast. No credit cards. **Amenities:** Breakfast room. *In room:* A/C, TV. 21 Staikopoulou, Nafplion 21100. © **27520/27-595**. Fax 27520/27-595. 10 units. 100€ double. Rates include continental breakfast. **Amenities:** Breakfast room. *In room:* A/C, TV.

Nafplia Palace *(Overrated)*

When this was built as the Xenia Palace Hotel in the 1970s, the disco, minibars, and in-bathroom telephones made it a relentlessly modern provincial hotel. By the 1990s, the hotel was sadly down at the heels (once when I opened my bathroom door, it came off the wall!) and soon thereafter underwent a thorough renovation. Unfortunately, when I visited, service was lax, the food was indifferent, the decor was bland, and there was no toilet paper in the restroom off the restaurant. Still, to its credit, this hotel has large guest rooms and the best views in town of the harbor and Bourtzi. We look forward to hearing from any readers who stay here.

Acronafplia, 210 00 Nafplion. © **27520/28-981** and 27520/752-99-555. Fax 27520/28-783. palace@nafplion hotels.gr. 51 units, 54 bungalows. 200€ double with demi-pensione; 160€ bungalow. Significant off-season reductions possible. AE, DC, MC, V. **Amenities:** Restaurant; bar; pool. *In room:* A/C, TV, minibar.

Omorfi Poli Pension ⚘⚘

What a lovely place! This small pension/hotel above the charming cafe by the same name (Beautiful City) has gone all out, giving guests the sense that you're staying in a Nafplion home—but with your own privacy. There's nothing to fault here—the beds are good, and the tile floors and prints on the walls are handsome. This makes a very pleasant base for touring the area. Families will like the rooms with fridges and sleeping lofts for children (80€), and the breakfasts with freshly baked bread.

Sofroni 5, 211 00 Nafplion. © 27520/21-565. Fax 27520/29-014. sofroni5@otenet.gr. 9 units (all with shower only). 60€ double; 80€ family suite for up to 5. Rates include breakfast. **Amenities:** Cafe. *In room:* A/C, TV, fridge.

Where to Dine

Oddly enough, the restaurants in and just off Syntagma Square are not the tourist traps you'd expect. Furthermore, you'll see a good number of Greeks at the big harborside cafes on Akti Miaoulis. In short, Nafplion has lots of good restaurants, and any number of ice-cream parlors selling elaborate gooey confections.

Antica gelateria di roma ★★ SWEETS/ICECREAM/COFFEES/DRINKS

What a wonderful addition to Nafplion! Marcello and Claudia Raffo make and sell the best ice creams and ices in the entire Peloponnese. You can have anything from a banana split to a tiny cup with just a taste. Flavors not to miss are hazelnut, lemon, mango, strawberry, chocolate—well, you get the idea. If you tire of ice cream, you can always have a freshly made *panini* (sandwich) with tomato and mozzarella and finish with a real espresso.

3 Pharmakopoulou and Komninou. © **27520/23-520.** spyde@tri.forthnet.gr. Sweets and sandwiches 1€–10€.

Hellas Restaurant ★ GREEK Kostas, the omnipresent host of the Hellas,

says that there's been a restaurant here for more than 100 years. Shady trees and awnings make this a cool spot to eat outdoors; there's also an inside dining room, where locals tend to congregate year-round. Excellent dolmades with egg-lemon sauce are usually on the menu, as well as stuffed tomatoes and peppers in season. Just about everyone in town passes through Syntagma Square, so this is a great spot to people-watch.

Syntagma Sq. © **27520/27-278.** Main courses 5€–10€. AE, MC, V. Daily 9am–midnight.

Karamanlis GREEK This pleasantly old-fashioned harbor-front taverna sev-

eral blocks east of the cluster of harbor-front cafes tends to get fewer tourists (and a good number of local businesspeople, lawyers, and civil servants) than most of the places in town. It serves good grills and several kinds of meatballs (*keftedes, sousoutakia,* and *yiouvarlakia*). If you like the food here, you'll probably enjoy the Kanares Taverna and the Hundalos Taverna, both also on Bouboulinas.

1 Leoforos Bouboulinas. © **27520/27-668.** Main courses 5€–10€; fish priced daily by the kilo. AE, MC, V. Daily 11am–midnight.

Noufara ★ ITALIAN/GREEK If you're not sure you can face another stuffed

tomato, head for the Noufara, which has a wide range of Italian dishes as well as the usual Greek favorites, snacks, sandwiches and ice cream. You can sit under the umbrellas and have a cool drink or a full meal—or you can retreat inside to the mildly air-conditioned dining room. The Noufara also has a branch with the same menu (but a wider offering of fish) just outside Nafplion on the shore in Nea Chios (© **27520/52-314**). Our only criticism: The Noufara seems to be resting a bit sluggishly on its laurels of late, and there's been a noticeable decline in the quality of the pasta dishes, perhaps as more and more people stick to the pizzas.

Plateia Syntagma, Nafplion. © **27520/23-648.** Fax 27520/23-945. Main courses 5€–17€. MC, V. Daily about 8am–1am.

Paleo Archontiko ✦✦ GREEK   This excellent restaurant in a nicely restored town house serves up tasty *stifado* (beef stew with onions), chops, and a wide range of popular favorites—but usually only in the evening. Live music is often offered here on Friday and Saturday, when half the customers may be Athenians down for the weekend; there's also often music on summer evenings. In good weather, tables are set up in the pedestrianized street outside the restaurant; in winter, the rooms indoors are cozy and congenial.

Corner of Siokou and Ipsilantou sts. ✆ 27520/27-704. Main courses 5€–10€. No credit cards. Hours irregular; usually open for dinner 8pm–midnight. Reservations recommended weekends.

Savouras Psarotaverna ✦✦ SEAFOOD   This harborside restaurant has been here more than 20 years, and its fresh fish attracts Greek day-trippers from Tripolis and even Athens. What you eat depends on what was caught that day—and it's always a good idea to check the price before ordering. Expect to pay at least 50€ (and easily more) for two fish dinners, a salad, and some house wine. On summer weekends this restaurant can be terribly crowded.

79 Leoforos Bouboulinas. ✆ 27520/27-704. Fish priced daily by the kilo. AE, MC, V. Daily noon–11pm.

Sokaki ✦ CREPES/SWEETS/BREAKFASTS/COFFEES   In the morning, tourists tuck into the full American breakfast here, while locals toy with a tiny cup of Greek coffee. In the evening, young men lounge here, some eyeing the women who pass by, others eyeing the men. This is a nice place to take a break and watch people watching people. The yogurt with honey and fresh fruit is delicious and the serving so generous that it is a meal in itself.

Corner of Eth. Antistaseos and Nafpleo sts. ✆ 27520/26-032. Drinks and snacks 2€–12€. Daily 9am–midnight (to about 8pm in winter).

Stathmos Cafe ✦ (Moments) DRINKS/SNACKS   This is a nice shady spot in which to sit and take a break from touring Nafplion, perhaps after visiting the Museum of Childhood next door. The old train station is decorated with a splendid painting of an old steam engine, and has elaborate wooden gingerbread trim, comfortable chairs under shady trees, and a cozy inside room for cold weather.

The old railroad station, Kapodistras Park. No phone. Coca-Cola 2€; assorted mezedes from 4€. No credit cards. Daily about 9am–midnight.

Exploring the Town

Nafplion is a stroller's delight, and one of the great pleasures here is simply walking through the parks, up and down the stepped side streets, and along the harbor. Don't make the mistake of stopping your harborside stroll when you come to the last of the large seaside cafes by the Hotel Agamemnon. If you continue, you can watch fishing boats putting in at the pier and explore several cliffside chapels. Nafplion is so small that you can't get seriously lost, so have fun exploring. Here are some suggestions on how to take in the official sights after you've had your initial stroll.

ACRONAFPLIA & THE PALAMIDI   Nafplion's two massive fortresses, Acronafplia and the Palamidi, dominate the skyline. There's no charge to visit the cliffs known as **Acronafplia,** where there are considerable remains of Greek, Frankish, and Venetian fortresses, as well as two modern hotels, undergoing renovations at press time (see the Nafplia Palace, above). This is not an easy walk if it is hot, and you may prefer to take a taxi up for 6€ and walk down. If you do walk up, follow signs in the lower town to the **Church of Saint Spyridon,** one of whose walls has the mark left by one of the bullets that killed Ianni

Kapodistria, the first governor of modern Greece. From Saint Spyridon, follow the signs farther uphill to the **Catholic Church of the Metamorphosis.**

This church is as good a symbol as any for Nafplion's vexed history. Built by the Venetians, it was converted into a mosque by the Turks and then reconsecrated as a church after the War of Independence. Inside, an ornamental doorway has an inscription listing Philhellenes who died for Greece, including nephews of Lord Byron and George Washington. As you continue to climb to Acronafplia, keep an eye out for several carvings of the winged lion that was the symbol of Mark, the patron saint of Venice.

Similarly, if you're not in the mood to climb the 800-plus steps to the summit of the **Palamidi** ✯, you can take a taxi up and then walk down. The Venetians spent 3 years building the Palamidi, only to have it conquered the next year (1715) by the Turks. You'll enter the fortress the way the Turkish attackers did, through the main gate to the east. Once inside, you can trace the course of the massive wall that encircled the entire summit and wander through the considerable remains of the five fortresses that failed to stop the Turkish attack. In June, concerts are sometimes held here in the evening. The Palamidi is open weekdays from 8am to 7pm in summer, from 8:30am to 5pm in winter. Admission is 3€.

NAFPLION'S MUSEUMS All four of Nafplion's museums are within easy walking distance of one another. Almost as soon as it opened in 1981, the **Folk Art Museum** ✯✯, also called the **Peloponnesian Folklore Foundation** (1 V. Alexandros; ✆ **27520/28-947;** fax 27520/27-960; pff@otenet.gr), with its superb collection of Greek costumes, won the European Museum of the Year Award. The display highlights "The Best of the Peloponnesian Folk Foundation," with exhibits from its more than 25,000-object collection, which includes coins, ceramics, furniture, and farm implements as well as all those costumes. The museum occupies three floors in an elegant 18th-century house with a shady courtyard and a welcome snack bar. Throughout, labels are in English as well as Greek, and a number of dioramas (my favorite shows nine elegant matrons in a 19th-c. parlor) help visitors imagine life in Greece, especially during the 19th century when the Western world impinged on the Greek world. The small gift shop is excellent, with fine ceramic and copper reproductions. This is a wonderful place to get an idea of life in Greece in the "good old days"—which still exist in many villages. It's open Wednesday through Monday from 9am to 3pm; closed Tuesday and the month of February. Admission is 4€.

The Museum of Childhood, Stathmos, Kolokotronis Park, an offshoot of the Folk Art Museum, has an eclectic collection of dolls, baby clothes, and toys. In theory, it's open year-round, Tuesday through Saturday from 10am to 2pm, Sunday from 11am to 2pm, but there are frequent unscheduled closings. Admission is 1.50€.

The Archaeological Museum, Syntagma Square (✆ **27520/27-502**), is housed in the handsome 18th-century Venetian arsenal that dominates Syntagma Square. The thick walls make it a deliciously cool place to visit on even the hottest day. Displays are from sites in the area and include pottery, jewelry, and some horrific Mycenaean terra-cotta idols, as well as a handsome bronze Mycenaean suit of armor. The museum is open Tuesday through Sunday from 8:30am to 1pm; admission is 2€.

If you like old prints and old photographs, not to mention muskets, you'll enjoy strolling through the exhibits at the **Military Museum** on Leoforos Amalias (✆ **27520/25-591**). It covers Greek wars from the War of Independence to

World War II. The museum is open Tuesday through Sunday from 9am to 2pm; admission is free.

The Shopping Scene

Nafplion has not escaped the invasion of T-shirt and mass-produced–souvenir shops that threatens to overwhelm Greece, but there are some genuinely fine shops. Many are on or just off Spiliadou, the street immediately above Plateia Syntagma. As in most Greek towns heavily dependent on tourism, many of the shops are closed in the winter.

There are lots of jewelry shops in Nafplion, but one that stands out is **Preludio,** 2 Vas. Constantinou (just off Syntagma Sq.), Nafplion (© **27520/25-277;** preludio@otenet.gr). Preludio has a surprisingly wide range of handsome earrings, necklaces, bracelets, and rings. Some designs are modern, some traditional; others are replicas of ancient and Byzantine styles (including some nice rings and necklaces with good reproductions of ancient coins). The staff speaks excellent English and is very helpful. Just two doors away at 4 Vas. Constantinou, Cleopatra Pomoni at **Morphes** (© **27520/29-022**) has handsome wooden chests, antique locks and keys, jewelry, and other objets d'art.

In her shop near the waterfront, **Helene Papadopoulou,** 5 Spiliadou (© **27520/25-842**), sells traditional weavings and dolls made from brightly painted gourds. Prices start at 20€. Next door, her husband and daughter have a wide collection of excellent-quality Greek costume dolls (from 40€), as well as some nice ceramic jewelry of Greek ships and flowers from 5€.

Konstantine Beselmes, 6 Athan Siokou (© **27520/27-274**), sells his own magical paintings of village scenes, sailing ships, idyllic landscapes, and family groups. Although new, the paintings are done on weathered boards, which gives them a pleasantly aged look. Prices begin at around 40€. The **Komboloi Museum,** 25 Staikopoulou, Nafplion (©/fax **27520/21-618**), is a fascinating shop with its own museum of *komboloi,* usually referred to as "worry beads." Both the shop and museum have examples of Muslim prayer beads, Catholic rosaries, and the secular Greek worry beads. Prices range from a few dollars into the thousands. Admission is 2€.

The Corner, Staikopoulou and Koletti, just off Syntagma Square (© **27520/21-359**), often has old photographs, prints, wood and copper items, and sometimes handsome old embroidered aprons and vests from traditional costumes. **The Wine Shop,** 5 Amalias, Nafplion (©/fax **27520/24-446**), is one of the best wine shops in the Peloponnese and an excellent place to head to if you want to browse and learn about Greek wines. Owner Dimitris Karonis is usually happy to talk to browsers about his wide selection of Greek wines, and he also stocks wines and spirits from Europe and North America. The **Odyssey Bookshop,** Syntagma Square (no phone), has a wide selection of newspapers, magazines, and books in English, as well as a collection of startling pornographic drink coasters.

A Day Trip from Nafplion

TIRYNS   The **archaeological site** of Tiryns is 5km (3 miles) outside Nafplion on the Argos road. (Before you visit here, check with the Greek National Tourism Association [GNTO] to make sure that the site is open. It has had several unscheduled closings recently due to damage from recent earthquakes.) From the moment you see it, you'll understand why Homer called this **citadel,** which may have been Mycenae's port, "well walled." Tiryns stands on a rocky outcropping 27m (87 ft.) high and about 302m (990 ft.) long, girdled by the massive walls that so impressed Homer—but that didn't keep Tiryns from being destroyed around 1200 B.C. Later Greeks thought that only the giants known as Cyclopes could have hefted the 14-ton red limestone blocks into place for the walls that archaeologists still call "Cyclopean." Even today, Tiryns's walls stand more than 9m (30 ft.) high; originally, they were twice as tall—and as much as 17m (57 ft.) thick. The citadel is crowned by the palace, whose **megaron** (great hall) has a well-preserved circular hearth and the base of a throne. This room would have been gaily decorated with frescoes (the surviving frescoes are now in the National Archaeological Museum in Athens).

The site is officially open daily, from 8am to 7pm in the summer, from 8am to 5pm in the winter. Admission is 2€. Visitors without cars can reach Tiryns from Nafplion by taxi (expect to pay about 20€ for a 1-hr. round-trip) or by the frequent (about every half-hour) Nafplion–Argos–Nafplion bus (about 2€; tell the driver you want to get off at Tiryns).

MYCENAE ★★★
Greek legend and the poet Homer tell us that King Agamemnon of Mycenae was the most powerful leader in Greece at the time of the Trojan War. In about 1250 B.C., Homer says, Agamemnon led the Greeks from Mycenae to Troy, where they fought for 10 years to reclaim fair Helen, the wife of Agamemnon's brother Menelaus, from the Trojan prince Paris. The German archaeologist Heinrich Schliemann, who found and excavated Troy, began to dig at Mycenae in 1874. Did Schliemann's excavations here prove that what Homer wrote was based on an actual event, not myth and legend? Scholars are suspicious, although most admit that Mycenae could have been built to order from Homer's descriptions of its palaces.

Essentials
GETTING THERE   By Bus   Buses run frequently from Athens's **Stathmos Leoforia Peloponnison**, 100 Kifissou (© 210/513-4100), to Corinth, Argos, and Nafplion. Allow 3 to 4 hours. From any of those places, allow an hour for the trip to Mycenae.

By Car   Mycenae is 114km (70 miles) southwest of Athens and 50km (31 miles) south of Corinth. From Corinth, take the old Corinth–Argos highway south for about 48km (30 miles), and then take the left turn to Mycenae, which is about 8km (5 miles) down the road. From Nafplion, take the road out of town toward Argos. When you reach the Corinth–Argos highway, turn right and then, after about 16km (10 miles), turn right again at the sign for Mycenae. If you're going to Nafplion when you leave Mycenae, try the pleasant back road that runs through villages and rich farmland. You'll see the sign for Nafplion on your left shortly after you leave Mycenae.

FAST FACTS   You can buy stamps and change money at the mobile **post office** at the ancient site weekdays from 8am to 2pm. This office is sometimes open on weekends and after 2pm, but don't count on it.

Where to Stay & Dine
Most of the restaurants specialize in serving set-price meals to groups. If you eat at one of the big, impersonal roadside restaurants, you're likely to be served a bland, lukewarm "European-style" meal of overcooked roast veal, underripe tomatoes and, even in summer, canned vegetables. You'll have better luck at the smaller restaurants at the hotels listed below.

La Belle Helene   The real reason to stay here is to add your name to those of Schliemann and other luminaries in the guest book and take in the photos of the archaeologists who rediscovered Agamemnon's palace. Tradition aside, this small hotel is usually quiet (although it does a brisk business with tour groups in its large restaurant), and the simple rooms are clean and comfortable. If you stay here, be sure to drive or walk up to the ancient site at night, especially if it's a full moon—it's magical.

Mycenae, 212 00 Argolis. ℂ **27510/76-225.** Fax 27510/76-179. 8 units, none with bathroom. 30€–55€ double. Rates include breakfast. Off-season discounts sometimes available. DC, V. On the main road to Mycenae, on the left as you approach the site. **Amenities:** Restaurant.

La Petite Planete   The bright, good-size rooms would make this a nice place to stay even without its swimming pool, which is irresistible after a hot day's trek around Mycenae. We've usually found it quieter here than at La Belle Helene, and friends who stayed here recently praised the restaurant (in the evening, not at lunch, which is aimed at tour groups) and enjoyed the view over the hills from their window.

Mycenae, 212 00 Argolis. ℂ **27510/76-240.** Fax 27510/76-610. 30 units. 70€ double. Rates include breakfast. Usually closed Dec–Apr. Off-season discounts sometimes available. AE, V. The hotel is on the main road to Mycenae, on the left as you approach the site. **Amenities:** Restaurant; bar; pool. *In room:* A/C.

Exploring Ancient Mycenae

The Citadel & the Treasury of Atreus 𝕒𝕒𝕒

Just as when you visit the Acropolis in Athens, when you walk uphill to Mycenae, you begin to get an idea of why people settled here as long ago as 5000 B.C. Mycenae straddles a low bluff between two protecting mountains and is a superb natural citadel overlooking one of the richest plains in Greece. By the time of the classical era, almost all memory of the Mycenaeans had been lost, and Greeks speculated that places like Mycenae and Tiryns had been built by the Cyclopes. Only such enormous giants, people reasoned, could have moved the huge rocks used to build the ancient citadels' defense walls.

You enter Mycenae through just such a wall, passing under the massive Lion Gate, whose two lions probably symbolized Mycenae's strength. The door itself (missing, like the lions' heads) probably was made of wood and covered with bronze for additional protection; cuttings for the doorjambs and pivots are clearly visible in the lintel. Soldiers stationed in the round **tower** on your right would have shot arrows down at any attackers who tried to storm the citadel.

One of the most famous spots at Mycenae is immediately ahead of the Lion Gate—the so-called **Grave Circle A,** where Schliemann found the gold jewelry now on display at the National Archaeological Museum in Athens. When archaeologist Heinrich Schliemann opened the tombs and found some 14 kilograms (30 lb.) of gold here, including several solid-gold face masks, he concluded he had found the grave of Agamemnon himself. However, recent scholars have concluded that Schliemann was wrong, and that the kings buried here died long before Agamemnon was born.

From the grave circle, head uphill past the low remains of a number of houses. Mycenae was not merely a palace, but a small village, with administrative buildings and homes on the slopes below the **palace.** The palace had reception rooms, bedrooms, a throne room, and a large megaron (ceremonial hall). You can see the imprint of the four columns that held up the roof in the megaron, as well as the outline of a circular altar on the floor.

If you're not claustrophobic, head to the northeast corner of the citadel and climb down the flight of stairs to have a look at Mycenae's enormous **cistern.** (You may find someone here selling candles, but it's a good idea to bring your own flashlight.) Along with Mycenae's great walls, this cistern, which held a water supply channeled from a spring 450m (1,500 ft.) away, helped make the citadel impregnable for several centuries.

There's one more thing to see before you leave Mycenae. The massive tomb known as the **Treasury of Atreus** is the largest of the tholos tombs (circular marble structures) found here. You'll see signs for the Treasury of Atreus on your right as you head down the modern road away from Mycenae. The Treasury of Atreus may have been built around 1300 B.C., at about the same time as the Lion Gate, in the last century of Mycenae's real greatness. The enormous tomb, with its 118-ton lintel, is 13m (43 ft.) high and 14m (47 ft.) wide. To build the tomb, workers first cut the 35m (115-ft.) passageway into the hill and faced it with stone blocks. Then the tholos chamber itself was built, by placing slightly overlapping courses of stone one on top of the other until a capstone could close the final course. As you look up toward the ceiling of the tomb, you'll see why these are called "beehive tombs." Once your eyes get accustomed to the poor light, you can make out the bronze nails that once held hundreds of bronze rosettes in place in the ceiling. This tomb was robbed even in antiquity, so we'll never know exactly what it contained, although the contents of Grave Circle A give an idea of what riches must have been here. If this was the family vault of Atreus, it's entirely possible that Agamemnon himself was buried here.

There's a good deal of up-and-down walking here, much on slippery terrain; give yourself at least 3 hours to absorb this magnificent and mysterious site.

🕐 **27510/76-585.** Admission 6€. Summer, Mon–Fri 8am–7:30pm; Sat–Sun 8am–3pm. Winter, Mon–Fri 8am–5pm; Sat–Sun 8:30am–3pm.

EPIDAUROS 🏛🏛

Epidauros, dedicated to the healing god Asclepios, was one of the most famous shrines in ancient Greece. Greeks came to the shrine of Asclepios in antiquity as they go to the shrine of the Virgin on the island of Tinos today, to give thanks for good health and in hopes of finding cures for their ailments. While at Epidauros, patients and their families could "take the waters" at any one of a number of healing springs and in the superb baths. Visitors could also take in a performance in the theater, just as you can today.

Essentials

GETTING THERE   By Bus   Two buses a day run from the **Stathmos Leoforia Peloponnisou,** 100 Kifissou, Athens (🕐 **210/513-4100**). The trip takes about 3 hours. There are three buses a day to Epidauros from the Nafplion bus station, off Plateia Kapodistrias (🕐 **27520/27-323**), with extra buses when there are performances at the Theater of Epidauros. The trip takes about an hour.

By Car   Epidauros is 63km (39 miles) south of Corinth and 32km (20 miles) east of Nafplion. If you're coming from Athens or Corinth, turn left at the sign for Epidauros immediately after the Corinth Canal and take the coast road to the Theatro (ancient theater), not to Nea Epidauros or Palaia Epidauros. From Nafplion, follow the signs for Epidauros. If you drive to Epidauros from Nafplion for a performance, be alert; the road will be clogged with tour buses and other tourists who are driving the road for the first time.

THEATER PERFORMANCES   Performances are often held at the ancient theater on Saturday and Sunday from June to September. Many are given by the National Theater of Greece, some by foreign companies. For information and ticket prices, contact the **Hellenic Festival Box Office,** 39 Panepistimiou in the arcade (© **210/322-1459**). Most of the travel agencies in Nafplion sell tickets, as does the theater itself, from 5pm on the day of a performance. The performance starts around 9pm. The ancient tragedies are usually performed in classical or modern Greek; programs cost 3€ and usually have a full translation or a synopsis of the play. The excellent Odyssey bookstore on Syntagma Square in Nafplion often has English translations of the plays being performed at Epidauros.

If you are in Epidauros in July, check out the **Musical July Festival** at the Little Theater of Ancient Epidauros. Performances in the past have ranged from chamber music to flamenco. Information on ticket prices and bus transportation from Athens is usually available from the **Athens Concert Hall** (Megaron Mousikis), 1 Kokkali and Vas, Sophias (© **210/728-2000**) in June.

Where to Stay & Dine

If you are not attending a performance at the theater, you may wish to take a look at the small hotels springing up in nearby Palea Epidauros, which is on the coast; the **Christina** (© 27530/41-451) and the **Verdelis Inn** (© 27530/41-332) are good choices. Keep in mind that Palea Epidauros (like many seaside resorts) can be quite noisy, especially on summer weekends.

Epidauros Xenia Hotel   Although the location beside the ancient site is charming, the hotel is not. Still, the convenience of staying here (especially if you are attending a performance at the theater) makes this (admittedly gloomy) hotel your best choice. Once everyone leaves, this is a lovely, quiet spot, in a pine grove beside the ancient site. The bungalow-like units (which could use some serious sprucing up and redecoration) go quickly, so reserve well in advance if you plan to be here the night of a performance. The restaurant serves bland but acceptable food, so you may want to try the **Leonidas Restaurant** (© 27520/22-115) in the village of Epidauros; it's usually packed (often with actors) after performances at the ancient theater.

Ligourio, Nafplias, Peloponnese. © 27530/22-003-5. 26 units, 12 with bathroom. 70€ double. Rates include breakfast. Off-season discounts sometimes available. No credit cards. **Amenities:** Restaurant.

Exploring the Ancient Site

The **excavation museum** at the entrance to the site helps put some flesh on the bones of the confusing remains of the Sanctuary of Asclepios. The museum has an extensive collection of architectural fragments from the sanctuary, including lovely acanthus flowers from the mysterious tholos, which you'll see when you visit the site. Also on view are an impressive number of votive offerings from pilgrims: The terra-cotta body parts show precisely what part of the anatomy was cured. The display of surgical implements will send you away grateful that you didn't have to go under the knife here, although hundreds of inscriptions record the gratitude of satisfied patients.

It's pleasant to wander through the shady **Sanctuary of Asclepios,** but it's not at all easy to decipher the scant remains. The Asclepion had accommodations for visitors, several large bathhouses, civic buildings, a stadium and gymnasium, and several temples and shrines. The remains are so meager that you might have to take this on faith. Try to find the round tholos, which you'll pass about halfway into the sanctuary. The famous 4th-century-B.C. architect Polykleitos, who built similar round buildings at Olympia and Delphi, was the designer here. If you wonder why the inner foundations of the tholos are so convoluted and labyrinthine, you're in good company—scholars still aren't sure what went on here, although some suspect that Asclepios's healing serpents lived in the labyrinth.

The museum and archaeological site (© **27530/23-009**) are open in summer, weekdays from 8am to 7pm and Saturday and Sunday from 8:30am to 3:15pm; in winter, weekdays from 8am to 5pm and Saturday and Sunday from 8:30am to 3:15pm. Admission (also covering the theater; see below) is 6€. Several kiosks sell snacks and cold drinks near the ticket booth.

The Theater

If you found the remains of the ancient sanctuary a bit of a letdown, don't worry—the **Theater of Epidauros** is one of the most impressive sights in Greece. Probably built in the 4th century B.C., possibly by Polykleitos, the architect of the tholos, the theater seats some 14,000 spectators. Unlike so many ancient buildings, and almost everything at the Sanctuary of Asclepios, the theater was not pillaged for building blocks in antiquity. As a result, it's astonishingly well preserved, and restorations have been minimal and tactful.

If you climb to the top, you can look down over the seats, divided into a lower section of 34 rows and an upper section with 21 rows. The upper seats were added when the original theater was enlarged in the 2nd century B.C. The theater's acoustics are famous; you'll almost certainly see someone demonstrating that a whisper can be heard all the way from the orchestra to the topmost row of seats. Just as the stadium at Olympia brings out the sprinter in many visitors, the theater at Epidauros tempts many to step center stage and recite poetry, declaim the opening of the Gettysburg Address, or burst into song. It's always a magical moment when a performance begins, as the sun sinks behind the orchestra and the first actor steps onto the stage.

The 6€ admission to the museum and archaeological site (see above) includes the theater; they keep the same hours.

If you're a theater buff, be sure to take in the new **Epidauros Festival Museum,** near the entrance to the site, with its displays of props, costumes, programs, and memorabilia from past performances. It's usually open daily from May 1 until September 30, when the site is open (and until 9pm on performance nights); entrance is free.

OLYMPIA ✫✫✫

With its shady groves of pine, olive, and oak trees, the considerable remains of two temples, and the stadium where the first Olympic races were run in 776 B.C., Olympia is the most beautiful major site in the Peloponnese. The archaeological museum is one of the finest in Greece, and you can easily spend a full day or more here. The straggling modern village of Olympia (confusingly known as Ancient Olympia) is bisected by its one main street, Leoforos Kondili. The town has the usual assortment of tourist shops as well as more than a dozen hotels and restaurants. The ancient site of Olympia lies a 15-minute walk south of the modern village, but if you have a car, you might as well drive; the road teems with tour buses, and the walk is less than relaxing.

Essentials

GETTING THERE   By Train   Several trains a day run from Athens to Pirgos, where you change to the train for Olympia. Information on schedules and fares is available from the **Stathmos Peloponnisou** (railroad station for the Peloponnese) in Athens (© **210/513-1601;** www.ose.gr).

By Bus   Three buses a day run to Olympia from the Stathmos Leoforia Peloponnisou, 100 Kifissou, Athens (© **210/513-4110**). There are also frequent buses from Patras to Pirgos, with connecting service to Olympia. In Patras,

> **Tips** **Summer Olympics Stampede**
>
> Visitors to Olympia during the summer of 2004 are urged to reserve rooms well in advance of your visit, even if you are not coming here during the Olympic Games, to be held in and around Athens August 13 to 29. Visitors should also be braced for possible very steep price hikes up to and at the time of the Summer Olympics.

KTEL buses leave from the intersection of Zaimi and Othonos streets (© 2610/273-694).

By Car   Olympia, 320km (198 miles) from Athens, is at least a 6-hour drive whether you take the coast road that links Athens to Corinth, Patras, and Olympia or head inland to Tripolis and Olympia on the new Corinth–Tripolis road. Heavy traffic in Patras, 159km (99 miles) south, means that the drive from Patras to Olympia can easily take 2 hours.

VISITOR INFORMATION   The office of the **Greek National Tourist Organization (EOT)** is on the way to the ancient site near the south end of Leoforos Kondili, the main street (© **26240/23-100** or 26240/23-125). It's usually open daily, from 9am to 10pm in the summer and from 11am to 6pm in the winter.

FAST FACTS   The **OTE telephone and telegraph office** on Praxitelous is open weekdays from 7:30am to 10pm. The **train station** is at the north end of town, one street off Leoforos Kondili. You can call © **26240/22-580** for a **taxi.**

Where to Stay

Olympia has more than 20 hotels, which means you can almost always find a room, although if you arrive without a reservation in July or August, you might not get your first choice. In the winter, many hotels are closed. If you're here in winter, check to see if the hotel you choose has central heating.

Hotel Europa ☆☆   The Europa is the best hotel in town—and one of the best in the Peloponnese. Part of the Best Western chain, it's a few minutes' drive out of town on a hill overlooking both the modern village and the ancient site. Most rooms overlook a large pool and garden, and several have views of a bit of the ancient site. Rooms are large, with extra-firm mattresses and sliding glass doors opening onto generous balconies. One drawback, pointed out to us by a recent visitor on crutches: Although there is an elevator, you have to use the stairs to get to the pool and the breakfast room.

270 65 Ancient Olympia, Peloponnese. © **800/528-1234** in the U.S., 26240/22-650, or 26240/22-700. Fax 26240/23-166. 80 units. 120€ double. Considerable reductions off season. Rates include breakfast. AE, DC, MC, V. **Amenities:** Restaurant; bar; pool. *In room:* A/C, TV, unstocked minifridge, hair dryer.

Hotel Neda   With a pleasant rooftop cafe, a comfortable lobby, a serviceable restaurant, and a distinctive red-and-white facade, the Neda (off the noisy main drag) offers good value. Rooms are large, with good bedside reading lamps. Some of the doubles have double beds, but most have twins, so specify which you want. Each room has a good-size balcony, and the bathrooms are better than those usually found in hotels in this price category (thanks to the presence of shower curtains, which help you avoid spraying the entire room). Rooms here are usually quieter than those in hotels on the main street.

Praxiteles, 270 65 Ancient Olympia, Peloponnese. ℂ **26240/22-563.** Fax 26240/22-206. 43 units. 50€ double. AE, V. **Amenities:** Restaurant; rooftop cafe bar; breakfast room.

Hotel Olympia Palace ⭐⭐

Back for a return engagement (for many years this was the Altis Hotel), the completely remodeled Olympia Palace is an excellent choice if you want to be poised on Olympia's main street to investigate the village. If you don't want to venture out, the hotel has restaurants, shops, and a pool. Rooms in the front can be noisy; rooms in the back have views over the countryside. The good-size guest rooms (each with a balcony) are very tastefully decorated (with nice rugs on the floor and attractive furniture); the bathrooms are modern and spacious. This hotel avoids the pallid anonymous colors so beloved of most Greek hotels.

2 Praxiteleous Kondili, 270 65 Ancient Olympia, Peloponnese. ℂ **26240/23-101.** Fax 26240/22-525. 60 units. 90€–120€ double. AE, MC, V. **Amenities:** 2 restaurants; bar; pool; shops. *In room:* A/C, TV, minibar, hair dryer.

Hotel Praxiteles

Just one street back from Olympia's main street, Spiliopoulou, this hotel has a nice neighborhood feel and is the best bargain in town—if you don't mind a no-frills approach. (Someone may, or may not, be on duty at the front desk, and there's neither air-conditioning nor central heating.) Rooms are small and spare, with narrow beds; those in front have balconies. If you want to avoid the sounds of conversation from the hotel's excellent restaurant (see below) on the sidewalk below the balconies, ask for a room at the back (and hope that the neighborhood dogs don't bark too much).

7 Spiliopoulou, 270 65 Ancient Olympia, Peloponnese. ℂ **26240/22-592.** 10 units. 35€ double. AE, V. **Amenities:** Restaurant.

Olympion Asty Hotel

This relatively new hotel has all the creature comforts, and all the good-size rooms have balconies or terraces. The only drawback: The Olympion Asty is a kilometer away from the village of Ancient Olympia and the ancient site. If you stay here and don't have a car, you will be tempted to take a taxi back and forth to Olympia (5€). The hotel's dining room is no worse (but more expensive) than most of the tourist traps in town. The Olympion hopes to do a brisk tourist business, which may mean that independent travelers will feel outnumbered here. Frommer's readers should receive a 10% discount if you show this guidebook.

270 65 Ancient Olympia, Peloponnese. ℂ **26240/23-665.** Fax 26240-23-123. olasty@otenet.gr. 30 units. 85€–95€ double. AE, MC, V. **Amenities:** Restaurant; pool; tennis court. *In room:* A/C, TV, minibar, hair dryer.

Where to Dine

There are almost as many restaurants as hotels in Olympia. The ones on and just off the main street with large signs in English and German tend to have indifferent food and service, although it's possible to get good snacks of yogurt or *tiropites* (cheese pies) in most of the cafes.

Taverna Ambrosia GREEK

This large restaurant with a pleasant outside veranda continues to attract locals, although it does a brisk business with tour groups. You'll find the usual grilled chops and souvlakia here, but the vegetable dishes (especially the vegetable casserole usually called *briam*) are unusually good, as is the lamb stew with lots of garlic and oregano. If you like rabbit, try the tasty stew with onions. The Ambrosia owners opened the Olympion Asty Hotel in 2002 (see above); unfortunately, the restaurant there doesn't hold a candle to the Ambrosia.

Behind the train station. ℂ **26240/23-414.** Main courses 4€–12€. AE, MC, V. Daily 8–11pm. Lunch served every weekend noon–3pm.

Taverna Kladeos ⭐⭐ GREEK   The charming Kladeos, a hearteningly traditional taverna in the midst of Olympia's growing throng of blah tourist places, has the best food in town. You may not be the only foreigner, but you'll probably find lots of locals here. In good weather, tables are set up under canvas awnings and roofs made of rushes. The menu changes according to what's in season. The lightly grilled green peppers, zucchini, and eggplant are especially delicious. The house wine, a light rosé, is heavenly. If you want to buy a bottle to take away with you, give your empty water bottle to the waiter and ask him to fill it with *krasi* (wine). There's lots of parking near the restaurant and plans for a pedestrian walkway here in time for the 2004 Summer Olympics.

Near the rear gate to the Archaeological Museum. ℂ **26240/23-322.** Main courses 6€–12€. MC, V. Daily 1:30–3pm and 6pm–1am. Usually closed Nov–Apr.

Taverna Praxiteles ⭐ *Value* GREEK   The reputation of the Hotel Praxiteles's excellent and reasonably priced restaurant has spread rapidly. It's packed almost every evening, first with foreigners eating unfashionably early, then with locals, who start showing up around 10pm. Although the entrees are very good—especially the rabbit stew with onions *(stifado)*—it's easy to make a meal of the delicious and varied appetizers. A sampling of mezedes costs about 6€ and may include octopus, eggplant salad, taramosalata, fried cheese, and a handful of olives. In good weather, tables are outside on the sidewalk; the rest of the year, meals are in the pine-paneled dining room.

7 Spiliopoulou (in the Hotel Praxiteles), Ancient Olympia. ℂ **26240/23-570** and 26240/22-592. Main courses 3€–12€. AE, V. Daily about 11am–3pm and about 7pm–midnight.

The Museums & the Ancient Site ⭐⭐⭐

Archaeological Museum   Even though you'll be eager to see the ancient site, it's a good idea to begin your visit with the museum, whose collection makes clear Olympia's astonishing wealth and importance in antiquity. Every victorious city and almost every victorious athlete dedicated a bronze or marble statue here. Nothing but the best was good enough for Olympia, and many of the superb works of art found since excavations began here more than 150 years ago are on view in the museum. Most of the exhibits are in galleries on either side of the main entrance and follow a chronological sequence, from severe Neolithic vases to baroque Roman imperial statues. The museum's superstars are in the central galleries directly ahead of the entrance.

The monumental images from the **Temple of Zeus** are probably the finest surviving examples of archaic Greek sculpture. The sculpture from the west pediment shows the battle of the Lapiths and Centaurs raging around the magisterial figure of Apollo. On the east pediment, Zeus oversees the chariot race between Oinomaos, king of Pisa, and Pelops, the legendary figure who wooed and won Oinomaos's daughter by the unsporting expedient of loosening his opponent's chariot pins. On either end of the room, sculptured metopes show scenes from the labors of Hercules, including the one he performed at Olympia: cleaning the Augean stables.

Just beyond the sculpture from the Temple of Zeus are the 5th-century-B.C. **Winged Victory** done by the artist Paionios and the 4th-century-B.C. figure of Hermes and the infant Dionysios known as the **Hermes of Praxiteles.** The Hermes has a room to itself—or would, if tourists didn't make a beeline to admire Hermes smiling with amused tolerance at his chubby half-brother Dionysios. In addition to several cases of glorious bronze heads of snarling griffins and the lovely terra-cotta of a resolute Zeus carrying off the youthful

Ganymede, the museum has a good deal of **athletic paraphernalia** from the ancient games. You'll see stone and bronze weights used for balance by long jumpers, bronze and stone discuses, and even an enormous stone with an inscription boasting that a weight lifter raised it over his head with only one hand.

Before you leave the museum, have a look at the two excellent **site models** just inside the main entrance. As the models make clear, a low wall divided ancient Olympia into two distinct parts: the Altis, or religious sanctuary, containing temples and shrines; and the civic area, with athletic and municipal buildings. Between festivals, Olympia was crowded only with its thousands of statues. Every 4 years, during the games, so many people thronged here that it was said by the time the games began, not even one more spectator could have wedged himself into the stadium. So if the site is crowded when you visit, just remember it would have been much worse in antiquity. You can easily spend a day at Olympia, wandering back and forth between the site and the museum, with a break for lunch.

(✆/fax **26240/22-529.** www.culture.gr. Admission 6€; museum and site 9€. Summer, Mon noon–7pm; Tues–Sun 8am–7pm. Winter, Mon noon–5pm; Tues–Fri 8am–5pm; Sat–Sun 8:30am–5pm. The museum is directly across the road from the Ancient Site (see below).

The Ancient Site   Olympia's setting is magical—pine trees shade the little valley, dominated by the conical Hill of Kronos that lies between the Alphios and Kladeos rivers. The handsome temples and the famous stadium are not at once apparent as you enter the site. Immediately to the left are the unimpressive low walls that are all that remain of the **Roman baths** where athletes and spectators could enjoy hot and cold plunge baths. The considerably more impressive remains with the slender columns on your right mark the **gymnasium** and **palestra,** where athletes practiced their footracing and boxing skills. The enormous gymnasium had one roofed track, precisely twice the length of the stadium, where athletes could practice in bad weather. Also on the right are the fairly meager remains of a number of structures, including a swimming pool and the large square **Leonidaion,** which served as a hotel for visiting dignitaries until a Roman governor decided it would do nicely as his villa. If you want, you can continue around the outskirts of the site, identifying other civic buildings, but you'll probably want to enter the sanctuary itself.

The religious sanctuary is dominated by two shrines: the good-size **Temple of Hera** and the massive **Temple of Zeus.** The Temple of Hera, with its three standing columns, is the older of the two, built around 600 B.C. If you look closely, you'll see that the temple's column capitals and drums are not uniform. That's because this temple was originally built with wooden columns, and as each column decayed, it was replaced; inevitably, the new columns had variations. The Hermes of Praxiteles was found here, buried under the mud that covered Olympia for so long, caused by the repeated flooding of the rivers. The Temple of Zeus, which once had a veritable thicket of 34 stocky Doric columns, was built around 456 B.C. The entire temple—so austere and gray today—was anything but plain in antiquity. Gold, red, and blue paint was everywhere, and inside the temple stood an enormous gold-and-ivory statue of Zeus seated on an ivory-and-ebony throne. The statue was so ornate that it was considered one of the Seven Wonders of the Ancient World—and so large that people joked that if Zeus stood up, his head would go through the temple's roof. In fact, the antiquarian Philo of Byzantium suggested that Zeus had created elephants simply so that the sculptor Phidias would have the ivory to make his statue.

Not only do we know that Phidias made the 13m (42-ft.) statue, we know where he made it: **The Workshop of Phidias** was on the site of the well-preserved brick building clearly visible west of the temple just outside the sanctuary. How do we know that this was Phidias's workshop? Because a cup with "I belong to Phidias" on it and artist's tools were found here. Between the Temples of Zeus and Hera you can make out the low foundations of a round building: This is all that remains of the **shrine** that Philip of Macedon, never modest, built here to pat himself on the back after conquering Greece in 338 B.C. Beyond the two temples, built up against the Hill of Kronos itself, are the curved remains of a once-elegant **Roman fountain** and the foundations of 11 **treasuries** where Greek cities stored votive offerings and money. In front of the treasuries are the low bases of a series of bronze statues of Zeus dedicated not by victorious athletes but by those caught cheating in the stadium. The statues would have been the last thing competitors saw before they ran through the vaulted tunnel into the stadium.

Admission 6€; site and museum 9€. Summer, Mon–Fri 7:30am–7pm; Sat–Sun 8:30am–3pm. Winter, Mon–Fri 8am–5pm; Sat–Sun 8:30am–3pm.

Museum of the Olympic Games   When you head back to town, try to set aside half an hour or so to visit the Museum of the Olympic Games. Not many tourists come here, and the guards are often glad to show visitors around. Displays include victors' medals, commemorative stamps, and photos of winning athletes, such as former King Constantine of Greece and the great American athlete Jesse Owens. It's a pleasant place to spend an hour.

© 26420/22-544. Admission 2€. Mon–Sat 8am–3:30pm; Sun and holidays 9am–2:30pm.

DELPHI ✿✿✿

Delphi, which the ancient Greeks believed was the center of the world, is the big enchilada of Greek sites. Even more than Olympia, it has everything: a long and glorious history as the scene of Apollo's famous oracle and the Pythian games; spectacular ancient remains, including the Temple of Apollo and the well-preserved stadium where the ancient games took place; a superb museum; and a heart-achingly beautiful location on the slopes of Mount Parnassus. Look up and you see the cliffs and crags of Parnassus; look down at Greece's most beautiful plain of olive trees stretching as far as the eye can see toward the town of Itea on the Gulf of Corinth.

Many tour groups offer day trips to Delphi, stopping at the Byzantine monastery of Osios Loukas (see "Organized Tours," earlier in this chapter). In the summer, tour groups clog Delphi's few streets by day, but many head elsewhere for the night, which means that hotel rooms are usually available— although often all the cheap rooms are gone by midmorning. In the winter, thousands of Greeks head here each weekend, not for the archaeological site, but for the excellent skiing on Mount Parnassus. Getting a room in the once-sleepy nearby hamlet of Arachova is virtually impossible without a reservation on winter weekends, and Delphi itself is often full.

ESSENTIALS

GETTING THERE   By Bus   Depending on the season, as many as five daily buses make the 3-hour trip to Delphi from the **Athens station,** 260 Liossion (© **210/831-7096**), north of Omnia Square.

By Car   Take the Athens–Corinth National Highway 74km (46 miles) west of Athens to the Thebes turnoff and continue 40km (25 miles) west to Levadia. If you want to stop at the monastery of Osios Loukas, take the Distomo turnoff for 9km (5½ miles). Return to Distomo and continue via Arachova for 26km (16 miles) to Delphi or via the seaside town of Itea for 64km (40 miles) to Delphi. The approach from Itea is well worth the time if you aren't in a hurry.

VISITOR INFORMATION   The **Greek National Tourism Organization (GNTO)** Office (© **22650/82-900**) in the town hall on the main street (Frederikis) is usually open from 8am to 3pm (sometimes later in summer).

FAST FACTS   Most services are available on Frederikis Street. The **post office** is usually open from 8am to 4pm, and sometimes Sunday from 9am to 1pm. The **OTE telephone and telegraph office** is open Monday through Saturday from 7:30am to 3pm and Sunday from 9am to 1pm. Both banks on Frederikis Street have **ATMs** (not always in service).

GETTING AROUND   The village of Delphi, with its handful of long, parallel streets connected by stepped side streets, is small enough that most visitors find it easiest to abandon their cars and explore on foot. If you have to drive to the site rather than make the 5- to 10-minute walk from town, be sure to set off early to get one of the few parking places. Whether you walk or drive, keep an eye out for the enormous tour buses that barrel down the center of the road—and for the not-terribly-well-marked one-way streets in the village.

WHERE TO STAY

There's no shortage of hotels in Delphi, and you can usually get a room even in July and August. Still, if you want a room in a specific price category or with a view, it's best to make a reservation. Finally, in summer (but not in winter when the skiers take over this hamlet), consider staying in nearby **Arachova,** where the hotels are usually less crowded (see "A Day Trip from Delphi," below). Be sure to check whether your hotel has functioning heating if you visit here in the winter.

Hotel Varonos ★ *Value*   This small, family-owned hotel has very clean, spare rooms (completely remodeled every few years) with fine views out over the olive plain. If you can, take in the rooftop view. This is a very welcoming place: we once arrived here with an ailing gardenia plant, and the entire family pitched in to make sure that it was well taken care of during our stay. If you want to have an early breakfast, mention it at the desk the night before. Be sure to check out the owners' shop next door, with local produce and crafts.

25 Vasileos Pavlou and Frederikis, 330 54 Delphi. ©/fax **22650/82-345.** 11 units (10 with shower, 1 with shower/tub). 70€ double. Rates include breakfast (although room without breakfast sometimes possible). Inquire about the 20% discount sometimes available. MC, V. **Amenities:** Breakfast room; lounge with fireplace. *In room:* A/C, TV.

Hotel Vouzas ★   The Vouzas has a cozy fireplace in the lobby, spectacular views from most rooms, and a wraparound veranda. It's a short walk from everything you've come to see—and it's the hotel closest to ancient Delphi itself. Guest rooms and bathrooms are very comfortable, and the balconies have not only a table and chairs but also, when we stayed there, a welcoming pot of basil. That said, on a recent visit the desk staff had no record of our reservation and, when that was sorted out, was supremely uninterested that our TV did not work—but with the view at Delphi, it's borderline criminal to watch TV.

1 Frederikis (at Vasileos Pavlou), 330 54 Delphi. © **22650/82-232.** Fax 22650/82-033. 59 units. 120€–130€ double. AE, DC, MC, V. **Amenities:** Restaurant; bar. *In room:* A/C, TV.

Kastalia Hotel   The Kastalia, an attractive white stucco building with projecting balconies on Delphi's main street, has been here since 1938. Most of the good-size rooms have hand-loomed rugs, and the rear ones have fine views over the olive plain. In 1999, the Kastalia added a wing, the 12-unit Villa Apollonia, whose rooms have air-conditioning and TV. Air-conditioning is almost never needed in Delphi; you can decide if you want to pay about 10% more for a room with TV.

13 Vasileos Pavlou and Frederikis sts., 330 54 Delphi. ℂ **22650/82-205.** Fax 22650/82-208. 26 units. 85€ double. Rates include breakfast. AE, DC, V. Usually closed weekdays Jan–Feb. **Amenities:** Restaurant.

WHERE TO DINE

You won't starve in Delphi, but there's no really outstanding restaurant, so you may prefer to head to the village of Arachova, 10km (6 miles) to the north (see "A Day Trip from Delphi," below). That said, in Delphi you might try **Topiki Gefsi,** Pavlou and 19 Frederikis (ℂ **22650/82-480**); the **Taverna Vakchos,** 31 Apollonos (ℂ **22650/82-448**); or the family-run **Taverna Lekaria,** 33 Apollonos (ℂ **22650/82-864**). Its main street location, periodic live music, and fine views probably make Topiki Gefsi the most expensive of the three (about 20€ per person). I've often enjoyed the simple food (and tasty toasted bread, sometimes topped with garlic and cheese) at the Lekaria, but this is not a good place to come to if you are in a hurry.

EXPLORING THE SITE

If possible, begin your visit when the site and museum open in the morning (both are sometimes relatively uncrowded in the hour before closing, too). If you begin your visit at the museum, you'll arrive at the site already familiar with many of the works of art that once decorated the sanctuary. As with Olympia, it's easy to spend a whole day here, taking in the site and museum, with a break for lunch.

Delphi Archaeological Museum ⭐⭐⭐   Each of the museum's rooms has a specific focus: sculpture from the elegant Siphnian treasury in one room, finds from the Temple of Apollo in two rooms, discoveries from the Roman period (including the Parian marble statue of the epicene youth Antinous, the beloved of the emperor Hadrian) in another. If you're lucky, the museum extension will have opened by the time you visit here and there'll be lots more to see. Keep an eye out for the impressively large 4th-century-B.C. marble egg, a symbol of Delphi's position as the center of the world. According to legend, when Zeus wanted to determine the earth's center, he released two eagles from Mount Olympus. When the eagles met over Delphi, Zeus had his answer. (You can still see eagles in the sky above Delphi, but as often as not, the large birds circling overhead are the less distinguished Egyptian vultures.)

> ### Museum Warning
> In June 2003, it was announced that the Delphi Archeological Museum would remain closed until the Olympics in August 2004, reopen for the Olympics (Aug 13–29, 2004), and close indefinitely thereafter.

The star of the museum, with a room to himself, is the famous 5th-century-B.C. **Charioteer of Delphi,** a larger-than-life bronze figure that was part of a group that originally included a four-horse chariot. It's an irresistible statue—don't miss the handsome youth's delicate eyelashes shading wide enamel and stone eyes or the realistic veins that stand out in his hands and feet.

Although the charioteer is the star of the collection, he's in good company. Delphi was chockablock with superb works of art given by wealthy patrons, such as King Croesus of Lydia, who contributed the massive silver bull that's on display. Many of the finest exhibits are quite small, such as the elegant bronzes in the museum's last room, including one that shows Odysseus clinging to the belly of a ram. According to Homer, this is how the wily hero escaped from the cave of the ferocious (but nearsighted) monster Cyclops.

© **22650/82-312.** Admission (which includes the site) 6€. Summer, Mon noon–5:30pm; Tues–Fri 7:30am–6:30pm; Sat–Sun 8:30am–3pm. Winter, usually daily 8:30am–3pm.

Sanctuary of Apollo, Castalian Spring & Sanctuary of Athena Pronaia

As you enter the **Sanctuary of Apollo,** just past the museum, you'll be on the marble **Sacred Way,** following the route that visitors to Delphi have taken for thousands of years. The Sacred Way twists uphill past the remains of Roman **stoas** (porticoes) and a number of **Greek treasuries** (including the Siphnian and Athenian treasuries, whose sculpture is in the museum). Take a close look at the treasury walls: You'll see not only beautiful dry-wall masonry, but countless inscriptions. The ancient Greeks were never shy about using the walls of their buildings as bulletin boards. Alas, so many contemporary visitors have added their own names to the ancient inscriptions that the Greek Archaeological Service no longer allows visitors inside the massive 4th-century-B.C. **Temple of Apollo,** which was built here after several earlier temples were destroyed.

From the temple, it's a fairly steep uphill climb to the remarkably well-preserved 4th-century-B.C. theater and the stadium, extensively remodeled by the Romans. In antiquity, contests in the Pythian festivals took place in both venues. Today the theater and stadium are used most summers for the Festival of Delphi—which, on occasion, has featured exceptionally nonclassical pop music.

Keep your ticket as you leave the Sanctuary of Apollo and begin the 10-minute walk along the Arachova–Delphi road to the Sanctuary of Athena (also called the Marmaria, which refers to all the marble found here). En route, you'll pass the famous **Castalian Spring,** where Apollo planted a laurel. Above are the rose-colored cliffs known as the Phaedriades (the Bright Ones), famous for the way they reflect the sun's rays. Drinking from the Castalian Spring has inspired legions of poets; however, poets now have to find their inspiration elsewhere because the spring is off-limits to allow repairs to the Roman fountain facade. Poets, be warned: Once an antiquity is closed in Greece, it often stays closed for quite a while.

A path descends from the main road to the **Sanctuary of Athena Pronaia,** goddess of wisdom, who shared the honors at Delphi with Apollo. The remains here are quite fragmentary, except for the large 4th-century-B.C. gymnasium, and you might choose simply to wander about and enjoy the site without trying too hard to figure out what's what. The round 4th-century-B.C. tholos with its three graceful standing Doric columns is easy to spot—but no one knows why the building was constructed, why it was so lavishly decorated, or what went on inside. Again, the oracle is silent.

© **22650/82-313.** Admission (which includes the museum) 6€. Summer, Mon–Fri 7:30am–6:30pm; Sat, Sun, holidays 8:30am–3pm. Winter, usually daily 8:30am–3pm.

Tips At Your Service

Delphi taxi driver **Elias Karatzogles** (© **22650/82-741;** mobile 093/202-3659) speaks English, drives an air-conditioned taxi, and will whisk you off to see Osios Loukas, Arachova, Mount Parnassos, or just about anywhere you want to go at competitive prices.

A DAY TRIP FROM DELPHI

ARACHOVA The mountain village of Arachova, 10km (6 miles) north of Delphi, clings to Mount Parnassus some 945m (3,100 ft.) above sea level. Arachova is famous for its hand-loomed *tagari* shoulder bags, heavy blankets, and fluffy *flokakia* rugs. When several tour buses stop here during the daytime, the tiny village can be seriously crowded. Don't despair—come in the evening, when the shops are still open and the cafes and restaurants allow you to escape from the tourist world of Delphi to the village world of Greece—except, of course, in winter, when Athenian skiers in full après-ski outfits roam the village. Year-round, in decent weather, there's usually an energetic evening *volta* (stroll) on the main street, and if you climb the steep stairs to the upper town, you'll find yourself on quiet neighborhood streets where children play and families sit in front of their homes.

On the main street, have a look at the weavings in Georgia Charitou's shop, **Anemi** (© 22670/31-701), which also offers some nice reproductions of antiques. **Katina Panagakou's shop,** on the main street (© 22670/31-743), has local crafts, too.

For lunch or dinner, try one of the restaurants strung along the main street with its lovely freshwater springs and cafes: **Taverna Karathanassi** (© 22670/31-360), **Taverna Dasargyri** (also known as Barba Iannis; © 22670/31-391), or **Taverna Kaplanis** (© 22670/31-891). The Dasargyri has tasty *loukanika* (sausages) and delicious *kokoretsi,* the stuffed entrails that are not perhaps to every traveler's taste. No credit cards are accepted; all are open daily approximately from noon to midnight but sometimes close from about 4 to 7pm. Dinner for two costs about 20€ to 30€ at all these restaurants.

If you want to stay in Arachova, the **Xenia Hotel** (© 22670/31-230; fax 22670/32-175) in town, with 42 rooms, each with a balcony (but charmless decor), has doubles at 70€. The very pleasant **Anemolia** (© 22670/31-640; fax 22670/31-642), with 52 rooms, on a hill just outside Arachova above the Delphi road, was originally a member of the Best Western chain, and its rooms are large and comfortable. Tentative prices for 2003 are 85€ for a double (sometimes as much as 20€–50€ higher on the weekend).

3 The Cyclades

When most people think of the "Isles of Greece," they're thinking of the Cyclades, the rugged (even barren) chain of Aegean islands whose villages of dazzling white houses look from a distance like so many sugar cubes. The Cyclades got their name from the ancient Greek word meaning "to circle," or surround, because the island chain encircles the sacred island of Delos. Today, especially in the summer, it's the visitors who circle these islands, taking advantage of the swift island boats and hydrofoils that link them.

Mykonos, with its dazzling architecture, superb tradition of weaving, and poverty—all of which made it susceptible to the tourist trade—was the first of the islands to become popular in the 1960s. Although the Beautiful People may have moved on, Mykonos remains a favorite, although expensive, island—especially in the summer, when reservations are imperative. The crescent of **Santorini (Thira),** with its black-sand beaches and blood-red cliffs, is all that remains of the island that was blown apart in antiquity by a volcano that still steams and hisses today. Santorini's exceptional physical beauty, dazzling relics, and elegant restaurants and boutiques cause people to call it "sophisticated."

The Cyclades

Ferry Route

Unfortunately, Santorini's charms draw so many day-trippers from cruise ships that the island almost sinks under the weight of tourists each summer. **Sifnos,** long popular with Athenians, increasingly draws summer visitors to its handsome whitewashed villages, which many consider to have the finest architecture in all the Cyclades. In the spring it's one of the greenest and most fertile of the islands.

The islands are crowded and expensive in the high season, roughly from mid-June to mid-September—and the season seems to get longer every year. If this doesn't appeal to you, visit the Cyclades in the off season; the best times are in the autumn (mid-Sept to Oct) or in the spring (Apr to early June, which can still be chilly in these islands). Although the restaurant you'd hoped to eat at may be closed and some of the chic shops shuttered in the off season, you'll be able to enjoy the islands without feeling that you're surrounded by other visitors—and pay much less for your hotel room. Should you visit in winter, keep in mind that many island hotels have minimal heating; make sure that your hotel conforms to your expectations for heating before you check in.

On most of these islands, the capital town has the name of the island itself. It's also sometimes called "Hora," or "Chora," a term meaning "the place" that's commonly used for the most important regional town. The capital of Paros, Parikia, is also called Hora, as is Apollonia, the capital of Sifnos.

One note of explanation: We've dropped our coverage of the island of Ios. Alas, in recent years some visitors have transformed Ios from a lively "party island" into an Aegean Animal House, complete with food fights in the tavernas. Let's hope that things calm down on the once-lovely island so that we can again recommend a visit.

GETTING TO THE CYCLADES

BY AIR   Olympic Airways (© **210/966-6666** or 210/936-9111 in Athens) has frequent daily service from Athens to Mykonos and Santorini; there's service several times a week from Mykonos or Santorini to Thessaloniki, Iraklio, Crete, and Rhodes. In addition, an increasing number of charter flights from all over Europe fly into the various islands. Several small, private Greek airlines serving the islands have gone in (and out) of business in recent years; you might check to see if **Aegean Air** (© **0801-2000;** www.aegeanair.com) is in service when you are traveling. *Note:* In the past, Aegean Air has offered 20% discounts for students and for travelers over 60.

BY SEA   Ferries leave daily from Athens's main port of Piraeus and from Rafina, the port east of Athens; contact the Piraeus Port Authority (© **210/451-1310** or 210/451-1311) or the Rafina Port Police (© **22940/22-300**) for schedules. The speedy **Seajet** (© **210/414-1250**) catamaran service also departs from Rafina and zips between Andros, Syros, Tinos, Mykonos, Paros, Naxos, and Santorini (Thira). **Ilio Lines** (© **210/422-4772** in Athens, or 22940/22-888 in Rafina) offers regular **hydrofoil** service from Rafina to a number of destinations.

It can take an hour for the 27km (17-mile) bus ride from Athens to Rafina (the most convenient port for Mykonos), but you save about an hour of sailing time and usually about 20% on the fare. Buses leave every 30 minutes from 6am to 10pm from 29 Mavromateon (© **210/821-0872**), near Areos Park north of the National Archaeological Museum (indicated on most city maps).

In the summer there's regular ferry service to Iraklio, Crete, from Piraeus, the port of Athens. There are also ferry and hydrofoil connections several times a week between Mykonos and Kos and Rhodes; twice a week between Mykonos and Skyros, Skiathos, and Thessaloniki; and two or three times a week between Syros and the Dodecanese.

Warning: In September 2000, the ferry *Express Samina* sank, with a loss of 82 lives, when it hit rocks entering the harbor at Paros. The subsequent investigation disclosed many oversights in safety precautions on the Samina and other Greek ferries. A word to the wise: When you travel by ferry, make sure you know where the exits are and where the lifeboats and life jackets are—and do not board any ferry that appears overcrowded. If you book a cabin, make sure that it is not located below the cargo deck. The excellent Thomas Cook guide *Island Hopping* (published annually) is a useful guide to the safety rating of Greek ferryboats.

GETTING AROUND THE CYCLADES

You are advised to double-check all ferry information in Greece. Although there is frequent ferry service between most of the islands, schedules can be erratic,

> ### Tips The Wind & the Sea
>
> The winds frequently complicate sea travel on the Aegean. For this reason, plan to arrive back in Athens from the islands at least 24 hours before you have to make any air or sea connections. In July the strong winds known as the *meltemi* usually kick up, often playing havoc with hydrofoil schedules. The larger ferries still run—although if you're prone to seasickness, take precautions. In the winter the strong north winds *(vorias)* frequently make sea travel impossible for days at a time.

and service diminishes suddenly at the end of the season. Changes in the line that serves an island can occur with little advance warning. Smaller excursion vessels are easily affected by high winds. To further complicate matters, a line will sometimes authorize only one agent to sell tickets or limit the number of tickets available to an agency, giving other agents little incentive to tout its service. You may want to visit several agents or inquire at the port authority. (For specifics, see "Getting There," under "Essentials," for each island.)

The easiest, most comfortable, and most expensive way to island-hop is on a **chartered yacht cruise;** you don't have to worry about ferry connections, hotel reservations, and most meals. **Viking Star Cruises,** 1 Artemidos, Glyfada, 166 74 Athens (© **210/898-0729;** fax 210/894-0952; vikings@forum.ars.net.gr or bjgh44a@prodigy.com), offers 7-day cruises beginning every Friday, from April to early November. The cruises stop at Tinos, Ios, Santorini, Paros, Naxos, Mykonos, and Delos. Last-minute discount fares are occasionally available.

If you want to cruise around the Cyclades (or elsewhere in Greece) for a week or two, and don't want to travel with strangers, put together your own group and contact **Arl Drivas Yachting** ((© **210/411-3194;** fax 210/411-4459; drivasy@ath.forthnet.gr). Choose among a stunning array of motor yachts and sailing vessels with from 2 to 24 cabins. Drivas prides itself on its superbly trained crews, which include excellent cooks.

For more information on cruises, contact the **Greek National Tourist Organization** ((© **212/421-5777** in New York; 020/7734-5997 in London; or 210/331-0437 or 210/331-0562 in Athens) or the **Greek Island Cruise Center** ((© **800/342-3030** in the U.S.). **Sea Cloud Cruises** ((© **888/732-2568** in the U.S.) uses a four-masted private yacht that takes up to 60 passengers on Aegean cruises.

MYKONOS

If you haven't been to Mykonos (pop. 15,000) for a number of years, you'll probably wander around muttering "ruined" when you arrive. Then you'll realize that once you're away from the shops, bars, and restaurants along the harbor, you're pleasantly surprised at how familiar many of the twisting back streets seem. You might even admit that it's not half bad to have such a wide choice of restaurants, shops, and bars. If this is your first visit, you'll find lots to enjoy—especially if you avoid July and August, when it seems that every one of the island's 800,000 annual visitors is here.

What makes this small (about 16km/10 miles long), arid island so popular? At least initially, it was the exceptionally handsome Cycladic architecture—and the fact that many on the poor island were more than eager to rent their houses to visitors. First came the jet-setters, artists, and expatriates (including a number of sophisticated gay visitors), as well as the mainland Greeks who opened many of the chic shops and restaurants—all followed by a curious mixture of jet-set wannabes and backpackers. Now, with cruise ships lined up in the harbor all summer and as many as 10 flights each day from Athens, it's easier to say who *doesn't* come to Mykonos than who does. That's why it's very important not to arrive here without reservations in the high season, unless you enjoy sleeping outdoors—and don't mind being moved from your sleeping spot by the police, who are not always charmed to find foreigners alfresco.

ESSENTIALS

GETTING THERE   By Air   Olympic Airways has as many as 10 flights daily between Athens and Mykonos. In addition, there's usually one flight daily between Mykonos and Iraklio (Crete), Rhodes, and Santorini, and three flights a week between Mykonos and Ios, Lesvos, and Samos. It's difficult to get a seat on any of these flights, so make reservations early and reconfirm them at the office in Athens (© **210/966-6666** or 210/936-9111) or Mykonos (© **22890/ 22-490** or 22890/22-237).

By Sea   From Piraeus, **Ventouris Lines** (© **210/482-5815;** 210/482-8001) has departures at least once daily, usually at 8am, with a second on summer afternoons. From Rafina, **Strintzis Lines** has daily ferry service; schedules can be checked with the **Port Police** (© **22940/28-888**). There are daily ferry connections between Mykonos and Andros, Paros, Syros, and Tinos; five to seven trips a week to Ios; four a week to Iraklio, Crete; several a week to Kos and Rhodes; and two a week to Ikaria, Samos, Skiathos, Skyros, and Thessaloniki. **Hellas Flying Dolphins** offers service from **Piraeus** (© **210/451-1311;** booking@mfd.gr) in summer.

On Mykonos, your best bets for getting boat information is to check at individual agents, or check if the **Port Authority** (© **22890/22-218;** by National Bank), **Tourist Police** (© **22890/22-482;** at the north end of the harbor), or **tourist office** (© **22890/23-990;** fax 22890/22-229; also on the harbor) has an up-to-date list of sailings.

Hydrofoil service to Crete, Ios, Paros, and Santorini is often irregular. For information, check at the **Port Authority** in Piraeus (© **210/451-1311**), Rafina (© **22940/23-300**), or Mykonos (© **22890/22-218**).

Note: Check each travel agent's current schedule, because most ferry tickets are not interchangeable. Reputable agents on the main square in Mykonos (Hora) town include: **Delia Travel** (© **22890/22-490;** fax 22890/24-440); **Sea & Sky Travel** (© **22890/22-853;** fax 22890/24-753); and the **Veronis Agency** (© **22890/22-687;** fax 22890/23-763).

VISITOR INFORMATION   The **Mykonos Accommodations Center,** at the corner of Enoplon Dhinameon and Malamatenias (© **22890/23-160;** mac@mac.myk.forthnet.gr), helps visitors find accommodations. It also functions as a tourist information center. Look for the free *Mykonos Summertime* magazine, available in cafes, shops, and hotels throughout the island.

TOWN LAYOUT   Legend has it that the streets of Mykonos town—which locals call Hora—were designed to confuse pirates, so your own confusion will be understandable. As you get off the ferry, you can see the main square south across the harbor beyond the small town beach and a cluster of buildings; we refer to it as **Taxi Square,** although it's officially called Plateia Manto Mavroyenous, after a local heroine. Here you'll find several travel agents, kiosks, snack bars, and, of course, the town's taxi stand. The map published by **Stamatis Bozinakis** is sold at most kiosks for 2€ and is quite decent; the excellent **Mykonos Sky Map** is free at some hotels and shops.

The main street, **Matoyanni,** leads south off Taxi Square behind the church; it's narrow, but you can hardly miss the bars, boutiques, and restaurants. Several "blocks" along it you'll find a "major" cross street, **Kaloyera,** and by turning right, you'll find several of the hotels and restaurants we recommend. If you get lost—and you will—remember that in Mykonos that's part of the fun.

GETTING AROUND   By Foot   One of Hora's greatest assets is the government decree that made the town an architectural landmark and prohibited motorized traffic on its streets. If you don't arrive with your donkey or bicycle, you can walk around town. Much of the rest of the island is served by local buses.

By Bus   Mykonos has one of the best bus systems in the Greek islands; the buses run frequently and on schedule. Depending on your destination, a ticket costs about .50€ to 3.50€ There are two bus stations in Hora: one near the archaeological museum and one near the Olympic Airways office (follow the helpful blue signs). Check at the tourist office to see which station the bus you want leaves from, or look for one of the schedules sometimes available in hotels. Bus information in English is sometimes available from the office of Greece's long-distance bus service, **KTEL (© 22890/23-360).**

> **Tips   Finding an Address**
>
> Although some shops hand out a map of Mykonos town, you'll probably do better finding restaurants, hotels, and attractions by asking people to point you in the right direction. Many streets do not have their names posted, and the map leaves off lots of small, twisting, streets— and Mykonos has almost nothing but small, twisting, streets!

By Boat   Weather permitting, excursion boats to **Delos** depart every day at 9am from the west side of the harbor near the tourist office. For more information, see "An Excursion to the Island of Delos," later in this chapter, or consult a travel agent; guided tours are available. Caïques (sailboats) to the beaches of **Super Paradise, Agrari,** and **Elia** depart from the town harbor every morning, weather permitting. Caïques to **Paradise, Super Paradise, Agrari,** and **Elia** also leave from **Plati Yialos** every morning, weather permitting. (Caïque service is almost continuous during the high season, when boats also depart from **Ornos Bay.**)

By Car & Moped   Rental cars and Jeeps are available from travel agents for about 60€ per day, including full insurance, during the high season, and for substantially less at other times if you bargain. Mopeds can be a fun way to get around if you know how to handle one and can negotiate the sometimes treacherous roads. Mopeds (around 15€–30€ a day) are available from shops near both bus stations.

Note: If you park in town or in a no-parking area, the police will remove your license plates, and you, not the rental office, will have to find the police station and pay a steep fine to get them back.

By Taxi   Getting a taxi in Hora is easy; walk to Taxi Square, near the statue, and get in line; a notice board gives rates for each destination for both high and low seasons. You can also phone (© **22890/22-400,** or 22890/23-700 for late-hour and out-of-town service). You'll be charged the fare from Hora to your pickup point plus the fare to your destination, so before calling, try to find an empty taxi returning to Hora or flag one down along the road. You can also take a moped taxi in Mykonos town, but only if you like to live dangerously.

 FAST FACTS: Mykonos

Banks The Commercial Bank and the National Bank of Greece are on the harbor a couple of blocks west of Taxi Square. Both are open weekdays from 8am to 2pm. The ATMs usually (but not always) function after hours. Traveler's checks can be cashed at the post office and at many travel agents and hotels, usually at a less favorable rate than at banks.

Hospital The **Mykonos Health Center** (© **22890/23-994** or **22890/23-996**) handles routine medical complaints; serious cases are usually airlifted to the mainland.

Internet Access Using the Internet is expensive on Mykonos. The **Mykonos Cyber Café,** 26 M. Axioti, on the road between the south bus station and the windmills (© **22890/27-684**), is usually open daily from 9am to 10pm and charges 15€ per hour or 4€ for 15 minutes. **Angelo's Internet Café,** on the same road (© **22890/24-106**), may have lower rates.

Police The **Tourist Police** office (© **22890/22-482**) is on the west side of the port near the ferries to Delos. The **Port Police** office (© **22890/22-218**) is on the east side of the harbor front near the post office. The local **police office** (© **22890/22-235**) is behind the grammar school.

Post Office The post office (© **22890/22-238**), on the east side of the harbor near the Port Police, is open weekdays from 7:30am to 2pm.

Telephone The **OTE telephone office** (© **22890/22-499**), on the east side of the harbor beyond the Hotel Leto, is usually open daily from 7:30am to 10pm.

WHERE TO STAY

In summer, if you arrive by ferry, you're met by a throng of people hawking rooms, some in small hotels, others in private homes. If you don't have a hotel reservation, one of these rooms may be very welcome. If you're pretty sure that won't suit your needs, be sure you have reserved a room 1 to 3 months in advance of your visit. Many hotels are fully booked all summer by tour groups or regular patrons. Keep in mind that Mykonos is an easier, more pleasant place to visit in the late spring or early fall, and that off-season hotel rates are sometimes half the quoted high-season rate. Also keep in mind that many small hotels (and restaurants and shops) close in winter, especially if business is slow.

The **Mykonos Accommodations Center (MAC),** Enoplon Dinameon 10 (© **22890/23-160** or 22890/23-408; fax 22890/24-137; http://mykonos-accommodation.com), will correspond, talk by phone, or meet with you to determine the best accommodation for your budget. The service is free when you book hotel stays of 3 nights or longer; check the current price for booking a shorter stay or budget accommodations (expect to pay around 20€).

In & Around Hora

Belvedere Hotel ⊛ The spiffy Belvedere, in part occupying a handsome and handsomely restored 1850s town house on the main road into town, has stunning views over the town and harbor, a few minutes' walk away. Rooms are nicely, if not distinctively, furnished. This is the place to stay if you want the creature comforts of Mykonos's beach resorts but prefer to be within walking distance of Hora. The in-house Remvi restaurant has a cellar with 5,000 bottles of wine, and is both excellent and pricey; there's also a sushi bar. In season, the hotel often offers massage, hairdresser, and barber services. Off season, there are often excellent specials, including a free jeep for a day if you stay 4 nights, or a fifth night free after a 4-night stay.

Hora, School of Fine Arts District, 846 00 Mykonos. ℂ 22890/25-122. Fax 22890/25-126. belvedere@ mykonos-accomodations.com. 48 units. 160€–450€ double. Rates include American buffet breakfast. Considerable off-season reductions usually available. AE, MC, V. **Amenities:** 2 restaurants; bar; pool; fitness center; Jacuzzi; sauna. *In room:* A/C, TV, dataport (10 rooms), minibar, hair dryer.

Cavo Tagoo ⊛⊛ This elegant hotel set into a cliff with spectacular views over Mykonos town is hard to resist—and consistently makes it onto *Odyssey* magazine's list of the 10 best Greek hotels. Cavo Tagoo's island-style architecture has won awards, and its gleaming marble floors, nicely crafted wooden furniture, queen- and king-size beds, and local-style weavings are a genuine pleasure. It's only a 15-minute walk to Hora's harbor, although you may find it hard to budge: A (saltwater) pool and a good restaurant are right here.

Hora, 846 00 Mykonos. ℂ 22890/23-692, 22890/23-693, or 22890/23-694. Fax 22890/24-923. cavotagoo@ mykonos-accomodation.com. 72 units. 180€–320€ double. Rates include buffet breakfast. AE, MC, V. Closed Nov–Mar. **Amenities:** Restaurant; bar; pool. *In room:* A/C, TV, minibar, hair dryer.

Matina Hotel ⊛ This small hotel set in a large garden is surprisingly quiet, given its central location. If you want to avoid the large, isolated hotels and enjoy the comings and goings in a Hora neighborhood, this may be the place for you. Rooms are a bit on the small side but are modern and comfortable, and the owner has been described by several readers as "very helpful." We agree.

3 Fournakion, Hora, 846 00 Mykonos. ℂ 22890/22 307. Fax 22090/24-501. www.matina.gr. 19 units. 90€ double. Rates include buffet breakfast. AE, MC, V. Closed Nov–Mar. **Amenities:** Breakfast room; garden.

Philippi Hotel Each room in this homey little hotel in the heart of Mykonos town is different, so you might want to have a look at several before choosing yours. The owner tends a lush garden that often provides flowers for her son's restaurant, the elegant Philippi (see "Where to Dine," below), which can be reached through the garden.

25 Kaloyera, Hora, 846 00 Mykonos. ℂ 22890/22-294. Fax 22890/24-680. 13 units. 60€ double. No credit cards. **Amenities:** Restaurant; breakfast room.

Around the Island

Although most visitors prefer to stay in Hora and commute to the beaches, there are hotels near many of the more popular island beaches.

There are private studios and simple pensions at Paradise and Super Paradise beaches, but rooms are almost impossible to get, and prices more than double in July and August. Contact the **Mykonos Accommodations Center** (ℂ **22890/ 23-160**)—or, for Super Paradise, **GATS Travel** (ℂ **22890/22-404**)—for information on the properties they represent. The tavernas at each beach may also have suggestions.

AT KALAFATI The sprawling **Aphrodite Hotel** (© **22890/71-367**) has a large pool, two restaurants, and 150 rooms. It's a good value in May, June, and October, when a double costs about 100€. This place is popular with tour groups and Greek families.

AT ORNOS BAY 🏨🏨 The elegant **Kivotos Club Hotel,** Ornos Bay, 846 00 Mykonos (© **22890/25-795**; fax 22890/22-844; www.kivotosclubhotel.gr), is a small luxury hotel where most of its 45 distinctively decorated units overlook the Bay of Ornos. If you don't want to walk that far for a swim, head for the salt-water pool, or for the Jacuzzi and sauna. Kivotos Clubhouse is small enough to be intimate and tranquil; the service (including frozen towels to cool poolside guests on hot days) gets raves from guests. Small wonder that this popular honeymoon destination has appeared on *Odyssey* magazine's annual list of the best hotels in Greece. If you ever want to leave (and you may not—it has several restaurants and bars), the hotel minibus will whisk you into town. Doubles cost from 225€; suites are priced as high as 800€. The **Santa Marina,** also at Ornos Bay (© **22890/23-200**; fax 22890/23-412; info@santa-marina.gr), has 90 suites and villas in 8 hectares (20 acres) of landscaping overlooking the bay. If you don't want to swim in the sea, two pools and spa facilities are available at the hotel, which also has its own restaurant. Doubles cost from 230€; suites and villas start at 350€.

AT PLATI YIALOS The 82 units at the **Hotel Petassos Bay,** Plati Yialos, 846 00 Mykonos (© **22890/23-737**; fax 22890/24-101), all have air-conditioning and minibars, and are large and comfortable. Doubles rent for about 170€. Each has a balcony overlooking the (relatively secluded) beach, which is less than 36m (120 ft.) away. The hotel has a good-size pool, sun deck, Jacuzzi, gym, and sauna, and offers free round-trip transportation from the harbor or airport, safety boxes, and laundry service. The new seaside restaurant has a great view and serves a big buffet breakfast (not included in the room rate).

AT AYIOS STEPHANOS This popular resort, about 4km (2½ miles) north of Hora, has a number of hotels. The 38-unit **Princess of Mykonos,** Ayios Stephanos, 846 00 Mykonos (© **22890/23-806**; fax 22890/23031), is the most elegant. The Princess has bungalows, a gym, a pool, and an excellent beach; doubles cost from 180€. The **Hotel Artemis,** Ayios Stephanos, 846 00 Mykonos (© **22890/22-345**), near the beach and bus stop, offers 23 units with bathroom from 115€ with breakfast included. The small **Hotel Mina,** Ayios Stephanos, 846 00 Mykonos (© **22890/23-024**), uphill behind the Artemis, has 15 doubles with bathroom that go for 70€. All these hotels are usually closed November through March.

AT PSARROU BEACH **Grecotel Mykonos Blu,** Psarrou Beach, 846 00 Mykonos (© **22890/27-900**; fax 22890/27-783; www.grecotel.gr), is another of the island's serious luxury hotels, with award-winning Cyclades-inspired architecture. Like Cavo Tagoo and Kivotos, this place is popular with wealthy Greeks, honeymooners, and jet-setters. The private beach, large pool, and in-house Poets of the Aegean restaurant allow guests to be just as lazy as you wish (although there is a fitness club and spa for the energetic). Doubles cost from 250€ to 400€.

WHERE TO DINE

Unfortunately, most restaurants here know that you're probably just passing through—hardly an incentive to offer the best in food or service. Restaurants also come and go, so if possible, check with other travelers or locals as to what's just opened and is getting good reviews.

As usual on the islands, most of the harborside tavernas are expensive and mediocre, although **Kounelas** 🍴 on the harbor (no phone; no credit cards) is still a good value for fresh fish—as the presence of locals dining here attests.

Antonini's GREEK   Antonini's is one of the oldest of Mykonos's restaurants, and it serves consistently decent stews, chops, and mezedes. Locals still eat here, although in summer they tend to leave the place to tourists.

Plateia Manto, Hora. 🕾 **22890/22-319.** Main courses 8€–15€ No credit cards. Daily noon–3pm and 7pm–1am in summer. Usually closed Nov–Mar.

Edem 🍴 GREEK/CONTINENTAL   This restaurant beside a pool in a garden has a quiet location—unless you have the bad luck to arrive here, as I once did, just before a raucous tour group occupied all the other tables. If that happens, console yourself with the food: the excellent appetizers, lots of tasty (and very pricey) seafood (usually including baked shrimp, something of a house specialty), and lamb stews with delicate seasonings that visitors have enjoyed here for more than 30 years.

Signposted off Matoyanni (near the church). 🕾 **22890/22-855.** Reservations recommended July–Aug. Main courses 10€–20€; fish priced by the kilo. AE, DC, MC, V. Daily noon–3pm and 7pm–midnight in summer (hours are flexible; sometimes open in winter).

Philippi 🍴🍴 GREEK/CONTINENTAL   This restaurant in the garden of the Hotel Philippi is a nice place in which to escape the hurly-burly of the harbor. Old Greek favorites share space on the menu with French dishes and a more than impressive wine list.

32 Kalogera, off Matoyanni. 🕾 **22890/22-294.** Reservations recommended July–Aug. Main courses 10€–20€. AE, MC, V. Daily 7pm–1am. Walk up the main street, past Kaloyera, and you'll find it on the right.

Sea Satin Market 🍴🍴 GREEK/SEAFOOD   Restaurants open and close on Mykonos, but this quite new (1999) place on the sea by Hora's famous cluster of windmills looks like a success. First, there's the location: a perfect spot to take in the sunset by the sea. And the food is more than tasty, specializing in fish, grills, and decent salads and vegetables.

On the beach below the windmills, Hora. 🕾 **22890/24-676.** Main courses 9€–20€; fish priced by the kilo. AE, V. Daily 6:30pm–12:30am.

Sesame Kitchen 🍴 GREEK/INTERNATIONAL/VEGETARIAN   This small, health-conscious taverna draws a big crowd with its spinach, vegetable, cheese, and chicken pies, all baked fresh daily. There's a large variety of salads, brown rice, and soy dishes, including an all-vegetable moussaka, lightly grilled and seasoned meat dishes, and a seafood paella.

Dinameon, Tria Pigadia Sq. 🕾 **22890/24-710.** Main courses 6€–20€. V. Daily 7pm–12:30am. Walk up the main street and turn right on Enoplon Dinameon; it's on the right next to the Nautical Museum.

EXPLORING THE ISLAND

Even if you're here for the beaches or to visit the island of Delos, you'll probably want to spend some time exploring Hora, enjoy the twists and turns of the narrow streets, and admire the harbor front's resident pelican. Try to remember to make haste slowly, and enjoy the unexpected sights you'll see when you (inevitably!) get lost in Hora's maze of streets.

The Archaeological Museum (🕾 **22890/22-325**), near the harbor, has finds from Delos; it's open Monday and Wednesday through Saturday from 9am to

3:30pm, Sunday and holidays from 10am to 3pm. Admission is 3€; free on Sunday. The **Nautical Museum of the Aegean** (© 22890/22-700), across from the park on Enoplon Dinameon Street, has just what you'd expect, including some handsome ship models. It's open daily from 10:30am to 1pm and 7 to 9pm; admission is 1€. The **Museum of Folklore** (© 22890/25-591), in a 19th-century sea captain's mansion near the quay, has examples of local crafts and furnishings and a re-created 19th-century island kitchen. It's usually open Monday through Saturday from 4 to 8pm; admission is free.

Hora also has the remains of a small **Venetian Kastro** (fortress) and the island's most famous church, the **Panagia Paraportiani (Our Lady of the Postern Gate),** a thickly whitewashed asymmetrical edifice made up of four small chapels. Beyond the Panagia Paraportiani is the Alefkandra quarter, better known as **Little Venice** *★★*, for its cluster of homes built overhanging the sea. Many buildings here have been converted into fashionable bars prized for their sunset views; you can sip a margarita and listen to Mozart most nights at the Montparnasse or Kastro bars (see "Mykonos After Dark," below).

Another nearby watering spot is at the famous **Tria Pigadia (Three Wells)** *★★*. Local legend says that if a virgin drinks from all three she is sure to find a husband, but it's probably not a good idea to test this hypothesis by drinking the brackish well water. After you visit the Tria Pigadia, you may want to take in the famous **windmills** of **Kato Myli** and enjoy the views back toward Little Venice.

THE SHOPS   Mykonos has a lot of shops, mostly selling overpriced souvenirs, clothing, and jewelry. The finest jewelry shop is **Lalaounis,** 14 Polykandrioti (© **22890/22-444**), associated with the famous Lalaounis museum and shops in Athens. It has superb reproductions of ancient and Byzantine jewelry as well as original designs. If you can't afford Lalaounis, you might have a look at the **Gold Store,** right on the waterfront (© **22890/22-397**), one of the island's oldest jewelry shops; **Delos Dolphins,** Matoyanni at Enoplon Dimameon (© **22890/22-765**), which specializes in copies of museum pieces; or **Vildiridis,** 12 Matoyanni (© **22890/23-245**), which also has designs based on ancient jewelry. If you want to see some serious works of art, try the **Scala Gallery,** 48 Matoyianni (© **22890/23-407;** fax 22890/26-993), which represents a wide range of contemporary Greek artists and frequently has exhibitions. When you finish your shopping, treat yourself to a local delicacy, almond biscuits from **Efthemios,** 4 Florou Zouganeli (© **22890/22-281**), off the harbor front.

THE BEACHES   If you've come to Mykonos to find a secluded beach, you have made a serious mistake. People come to Mykonos to see and be seen, whether in their best togs at cafes or naked on nudist beaches. If you want to hit the "in" beaches, take a little time to ask around, because beaches go in and out of favor quickly. Then catch the bus or a caïque to the beach of your choice. If you want a quick swim, the closest beach to Hora is **Megali Ammos (Big Sand),** about a 10-minute walk south of town, and usually very crowded. A better but still-crowded beach is 4km (2½ miles) farther north of Megali Ammos at **Ayios Stephanos,** a major resort center with watersports.

Plati Yialos is another favorite. It's served by a bus that runs every 15 minutes from 8am to 8pm, then every 30 minutes until midnight during the summer. If Plati Yialos is too crowded, you can catch a caïque there for the more distant beaches of Paradise, Super Paradise, Agrari, and Elia. **Paradise,** the island's most famous nude beach, remains beautiful, despite the crowds and activity, with especially clear water. Paradise is also easily reached by local bus or taxi.

Super Paradise (Plindri) is accessible only by a very poor road, footpath, or caïque, so it's less crowded. It's predominantly gay and nude, but clothed sunbathing by heterosexuals is tolerated. Farther east across the little peninsula is Agrari, a lovely cove (about to undergo serious overdevelopment) with good shade and a good little taverna.

Elia, a 45-minute caïque ride from Plati Yialos, is one of the island's best and largest beaches, attracting many nudists, gays—and, thanks to a Watermania, a theme park with a water slide—families with children (open daily in season 9am–midnight; 12€ adults, 6€ children under 12).

The next major beach, Kalo Livadi (Good Pasture), a beautiful spot in an idyllic farming valley, is accessible by a scramble over the peninsula east from Elia and by bus from the north station in the summer. There's even a nice restaurant.

The last resort area on the southern coast accessible by bus from the north station is at Kalafati, a fishing village that was once the port for the ancient citadel of Mykonos. It's now dominated by the large Aphrodite Beach Hotel complex. Several miles farther east, accessible by a fairly good road from Kalafati, is Lia, which has fine sand, clear water, bamboo windbreaks, and a small taverna.

Beaches to avoid on Mykonos because of pollution, noise, and crowds include Tourlos and Korfos Bay.

MYKONOS AFTER DARK

Mykonos has the liveliest, most abundant (and expensive), and most chameleon-like nightlife—especially gay nightlife—in the Aegean. New places open and shut here every season. Here I try to suggest a few durable favorites and some new places that were popular last year. I've given phone numbers where available; if you dial one of these places and get no reply, don't assume it's closed—when business is brisk, phones are often not answered.

Watching the sunset is a popular sport at the sophisticated bars in Little Venice. The Kastro (© 22890/23-072), near the Paraportiani Church, is famous for classical music and frozen daiquiris. This is a great spot to watch (or join in with) handsome young men flirting with each other. If you find it too crowded or tame, sashay up the block on Scarpa to Le Caprice, which also has a seaside perch; or Porta (© 22890/27-807), a popular gay cruising spot. The Montparnasse (© 22890/23-719), on the same lane, is cozier, with classical music and Toulouse-Lautrec posters. The Veranda (© 22890/23-290), in an old mansion overlooking the water with a good view of the windmills, is as relaxing as its name implies. Galeraki (© 22890/27-118) has a wide variety of exotic cocktails (and customers) and an in-house art gallery that gives this popular spot its name ("little gallery").

The decibel level is considerably higher along the harbor, where Pierro's (© 22890/22-177), popular with gay visitors, rocks all night long to American and European music; the adjacent Icarus is best known for its drag shows. The Anchor plays blues, jazz, and classic rock for its 30-something clients, as does Argo. Stavros Irish Bar and the Scandinavian Bar-Disco draw customers from Ireland, Scandinavia, and, quite possibly, as far away as Antarctica. If you'd like to sample some Greek music and dancing, try Thalami (© 22890/23-291), a small club underneath the town hall. If you'd like to relax at a movie, head for Cinemanto (© 22890/27-190), which shows films nightly around 9pm. Many films are American; most Greek films have English subtitles.

How much are you going to spend going out on the town for a drink or two in Mykonos? As little as 10€—and after that, the sky really is the limit here!

AN EXCURSION TO THE ISLAND OF DELOS ★★★

According to legend, Delos is the spot where Leto gave birth to the twins Artemis and Apollo. Why did Leto pick this tiny—less than 5 sq. km (2 sq. miles)—barren island as her nursery? Because she hoped to escape her lover Zeus's jealous spouse Hera by hiding on the smallest of the Cycladic islands. Although remote and tiny, Delos had an excellent harbor (long since silted up) that made it a vital way station for ancient ships plying the Aegean. The island was also a significant religious shrine in the cult of Apollo, with an oracle second in importance only to Delphi. When the Greeks banded together after defeating the Persians in 478 B.C., they called their association, with its headquarters at Delos, the Delian League. The Delian Festival held here every year was one of the most important ancient festivals, drawing visitors from across the Greek world. Less endearingly, in Roman times Delos was the most important slave market in the Aegean; there are reports of as many as 10,000 slaves being sold here in a single day. Today, the extensive ruins on Delos make the island rival Delphi and Olympia as one of the most impressive ancient sites in all Greece—although you'll long for the shady pine trees of Delphi and Olympia when you visit virtually shadeless Delos.

GETTING THERE   Delos can be visited only by sea, and many days the sea is too rough for boats to put in here. The site is usually open from 8:30am to 3pm and is always closed on Monday. Most people visit on excursion boats from nearby Mykonos, although there are excursions from other neighboring islands, and Delos is a prominent stop for cruise ships and yachts. Spending the night is not allowed. From Mykonos, organized guided and unguided excursions leave about four times a day from Tuesday to Sunday from the west end of the harbor; the trip takes about 40 minutes and costs about 10€ round-trip for transportation alone (departure from Mykonos around 8:30am; return to Mykonos around 3pm). **Yiannakis Tours** (② **22890/22-089**) offers guided tours for about 30€ that depart at 9 or 10am and return at 12:30 or 2pm.

Note: High seas can prevent boats going to Delos at any time of the year, so if you want to visit, don't put it off, as the weather can change unexpectedly. When you go, try to leave as early as possible in the morning, especially in the summer, when both the afternoon heat and the crowds are intense. Be sure to wear sturdy shoes, sunscreen, and a hat, and bring water and a snack. (There's a cafe near the museum, but the prices are high and the quality is poor.)

Exploring the Island

Delos flourished from the earliest days of Greek history through the Roman era, and the remains here attest to its life as the most important religious, maritime, and commercial center in the Aegean. Still, the 3 hours allotted by most excursion boats should be enough for all except the most avid archaeology enthusiasts to explore the site and museum.

Entrance to the site (which includes the museum) costs 6€ unless it was included in your tour; site plans and picture guides are sold at the ticket facility. If you intend to explore the sprawling remains, be sure to get a site plan. If you're energetic enough, climb **Mount Kythnos,** at 113m (371 ft.) the highest point on the island, for an overview of the site, the Sacred Lake (now dry), where Leto gave birth to Apollo, and near and distant islands.

French archaeologists have been excavating Delos since 1872, and there's a lot to see on and off the **Sacred Way,** the route that runs to the Sanctuary of Apollo—although little enough remains of the three temples here to Apollo.

Note that most visitors are more interested in the marble phalluses in the **Sanctuary of Dionysos** than in the remains of houses, stoas, and religious shrines here—although the marble lions along the **Avenue of the Lions** have their admirers. (Some lions may not be in place when you visit, having been taken off-island for restoration work.) If you've never seen ancient mosaics, be sure to take in the handsome pebble mosaics in the **House of the Dolphins, House of the Masks,** and **House of the Tridents.**

SANTORINI (THIRA) ⭐⭐⭐

Especially if you arrive by sea, you won't confuse Santorini with any of the other Cyclades—although you might be confused to learn that it's also known as Thira. Small ships arrive at Santorini (pop. 7,000; 240km/130 nautical miles southeast of Piraeus) in Skala, a spectacular harbor that's part of the enormous caldera (crater) formed when a volcano blew out the island's center around 1450 B.C. To this day, some scholars speculate that the destruction gave birth to the myth of the lost continent of Atlantis.

Your first choice upon disembarking at Skala will be to decide whether you want to ride the funicular (3€) or a donkey (3€) the 335m (1,100 ft.) up the sheer sides of the caldera to the island's capital, Fira. If you arrive on a large ship, you'll be spared this choice, as you'll dock at the new harbor at Athinios and grab a cab costing about 6€ into Fira. Once there, you may decide to reward yourself with a glass of the island's rosé wine before you explore the shops and restaurants of Fira, swim at the black volcanic beach of Kamari, or visit the dazzling site of Akrotiri, an Aegean Pompeii destroyed when the volcano erupted. In case you were wondering, the volcano is now officially dormant, so you don't have to fret about the plumes of steam you might see around the islands of Kamenes in the harbor.

ESSENTIALS

GETTING THERE   By Air   Olympic Airways has several (six in the high season) daily flights between Athens and the airport at Monolithos (© **22860/ 31-525**), which also receives European charters. There are also daily connections with Mykonos; three or four a week with Rhodes, two or three a week with Iraklion, Crete; and three a week during the high season with Thessaloniki. For schedule information and reservations, check with the Olympic Airways office on Ayiou Athanassiou Street (© **22860/22-493,** or 210/961-6161 or 210/ 966-6666 in Athens). **Aegean Airlines** (© **210/998-2888** in Athens), with an office at the Monolithos airport (© **22860/28-500**), also has several flights daily between Athens and Santorini.

By Sea   Several companies operate **ferry service** at least twice daily from Piraeus; the trip takes 10 to 12 hours and costs about 25€ one-way (deck). If you can book a day sailing, you'll see many of the Cyclades en route to Santorini. In summer, there are often daily ferry connections from Santorini to Ios, Mykonos, and Paros. **Excursion boats** go to and from Iraklion, Crete, almost daily. The fare is about 16€ one-way. Because this is an open-sea route, the trip can be an ordeal in bad weather. Check the schedules with the **Tourist Police** in Athens (© **171**) or with the **Port Authority** in Piraeus (© **210/451-1311**) or Santorini (© **22860/22-239**).

High-speed **hydrofoils** connect Santorini with Ios, Paros, Mykonos, and Iraklio, Crete, almost daily in the high season and three times weekly in the low season, if the winds aren't too strong.

VISITOR INFORMATION   There's no official government tourist office, but there are a number of travel agencies. Several travelers have written of good experiences dealing with **Kamari Tours,** 2 blocks south of the main square on the right (© **22860/31-390;** fax 22860/31-497; kamaritours@san.forthnet.gr). **Maria Tours** (© **22860/24-701;** fax 22860/23-848) often seems to offer car rentals and island tours at especially good prices. Other agencies include **Joint Travel Service** (© **22860/24-900;** fax 22860/24992; joint@otenet.gr), next to the Olympic Airways office in Fira; and **Nomikos Travel** (© **22860/23-660;** 22860/23-666), with offices in Fira, Karterados, and Perissa. Any of these agencies should be able to help you find accommodations, rent a car, get boat tickets, or book a tour. Expect to pay about 28€ to join a bus tour to Akrotiri or Ancient Thira.

GETTING AROUND   By Bus   Santorini has very good bus service. The island's central bus station is just south of the main square in Fira. Schedules and prices are posted on the wall of the office above it; most routes are serviced every half hour from 7am to 11pm in the summer, less frequently in the off season.

By Car   Most travel agents can help you rent a car. You might find that a local company such as **Zeus** (© **22860/24-013**) offers better prices than the big names, although the quality might be a bit lower. Of the better-known agencies, try **Budget Rent-A-Car,** a block below the bus stop square in Fira (© **22860/ 22-900;** fax 22860/22-887), where a small car should cost about 50€ a day, with unlimited mileage. If you reserve in advance through Budget in the United States (© **800/527-0700**), you should be able to beat that price.

By Moped   The roads on the island are notoriously treacherous, narrow, and winding; add local drivers who take the roads at high speed and visiting drivers who aren't sure where they're going, and you'll understand the island's high accident rate. If you're determined to use two-wheeled transportation, expect to pay about 25€ per day (less off season).

By Taxi   The taxi station is just south of the main square. In high season, you should book ahead by phone (© **22860/22-555** or 22860/23-951) if you want a taxi for an excursion; prices are standard from point to point. If you call for a taxi outside Fira, you'll be charged a pickup fee of at least 1.50€. The fare from Ia to Akrotiri, for example, is about 16€, not including additional charges for luggage, pickup, or late-night travel. If you call for a taxi outside Fira, you're required to pay the fare from there to your pickup point, although you can sometimes find a taxi that has dropped off a passenger. All bus service usually shuts down at midnight, so it's a good idea to book a taxi in advance if you need it after midnight. If you find yourself walking home, keep in mind that lots of drivers on the roads are newcomers to the island and may not know every twist and turn.

 FAST FACTS: Santorini

Area Code   The telephone area code for Santorini is **22860.**

Banks   The **National Bank** (open weekdays 8am–2pm; ATM) is a block south from the main square on the right near the taxi station. Many travel agents also change money; most are open daily from 8am to 9:30pm.

Hospital The **health clinic** (© 22860/22-237) is near the main Olympic Airways office.

Internet Access The **PC World Club** (© 22860/25-551) is in the main square, Fira. It's usually open Monday through Saturday from 9am to 2pm and 5 to 8pm; 4€ per hour for use.

Police The police station is on Dekigala Street (© 22860/22-649), several blocks south of the main square, on the left. The Port Authority can be reached at © 22860/22-239.

Post Office The post office (© 22860/22-238; fax 22860/22-698) is off to the right of the bus station. It's open weekdays from 8am to 1pm.

Telephone The **OTE telephone office** is just off Ypapantis Street, up from the post office. It's usually open Monday through Friday from 8am to 4pm.

WHERE TO STAY

Despite its growing number of hotels, efficiency apartments, and rooms-to-rent, Santorini is packed in July and August—and increasingly crowded year-round. If you plan a summer visit, make a reservation with a deposit at least 2 months in advance or be prepared to accept potluck. Don't accept rooms offered (sight unseen) at the port unless you're exhausted and don't care where you wake up possibly in a small room in a village in Santorini's interior plain, quite a distance from what you've come here to see. If you come between April and mid-June or in September or October, when the island is less crowded and far more pleasant, the rates can be considerably less than the high-season rates we quote. Keep in mind that off season many of the hotels, restaurants, shops, and bars here are closed. Most of the hotels recommended below don't have air-conditioning, but with cool breezes blowing through, you won't need it; if you take a room here in the winter, make sure that it offers working central heat or a serviceable room heater.

Two youth hostels, near Thira's main square, the **Thira Youth Hostel** (© 22860/22-387) and the **International Youth Hostel** (© 222860/24-472), usually offer the island's cheapest accommodations, at around 10€ per person. You don't have to be young to stay at these hostels, but it helps to be young-at-heart and relaxed about shared facilities and noise. About 2km (1¼ miles) outside Fira, the village of Karterados is in the throes of development. It has one budget choice that's worth a stay: the 20-unit **Pension George** ♠ (www.pensiongeorge.com), with a small pool; simple, attractive, and reasonably priced accommodations; and very helpful owners, George and Helen Halaris. Doubles run 30€ to 70€.

Astra Apartments ♠♠♠   Perched on a cliffside, with spectacular views, this is one of the nicest places to stay in all of Greece—in fact, friends who stayed here recently say that this was the highlight of their entire holiday! The Astra Apartments look like a tiny, whitewashed village (with an elegant pool) set in the village of Imerovigli, which is still much less crowded than Fira or Oia. Every detail here is perfect. Best of all, although each unit has its own kitchenette, breakfast is served on your private terrace or balcony, and you can order delicious salads and sandwiches from the bar day and night. Manager George Karayiannis is always at the ready to arrange car rentals, recommend a wonderful beach or restaurant—or even help you plan your wedding and honeymoon here. My only problem when I stayed here: I didn't want to budge from my terrace, especially at sunset, when the view over the offshore islands is dazzling. You may want to go whole hog, as it were, and book one of the new apartments or suites, two with private Jacuzzis, two with private pools.

Imerovigli, 847 00 Santorini. ℂ **22860/23-641.** Fax 22860/24-765. www.astra.gr. 25 units. 220€–310€ standard double apt; 370€–590€ suite. AE, MC, V. **Amenities:** Bar; pool. *In room:* A/C, TV, minibar, hair dryer, radio.

Katikies 𝒜𝒜 If you find a more spectacular pool anywhere on the island, let us know: This one runs virtually to the side of the caldera, so that you can paddle around and enjoy an endless view. (There's also a smaller pool intended for the use of guests who have suites.) The hotel's island-style architecture incorporates twists and turns, secluded patios, beamed ceilings, and antiques. If the people in the next room like to sing in the shower, you might hear them—but most people who stay here treasure the tranquillity. The top-of-the-line honeymoon suite has its own Jacuzzi, just in case you can't be bothered going to either outdoor pool. The new White Cave restaurant has only three tables, so be sure to book ahead!

Oia, 847 02 Santorini. ℂ **22860/71-401.** Fax 22860/71-129. www.katikies.com. 22 units. 175€–260€ double; 205€–305€ superior; 235€–1,050€ suite. Rates include breakfast. MC, V. **Amenities:** 2 restaurants; bar; 2 pools. *In room:* A/C, TV, minibar, hair dryer.

Loucas Hotel 𝒜 This is one of the oldest and best hotels on the caldera, with barrel-ceilinged "caves" built to prevent collapse during an earthquake. Rooms are newly renovated; some were enlarged and have arched ceilings and shared patios overlooking the pool and the caldera. The hotel is an excellent value for the location, amenities, and view, although it's sufficiently in the heart of things in Fira that it can be noisy here at night.

Fira, 847 00 Santorini. ℂ **22860/22-480** or 22860/22-680. Fax 22860/24-882. loucas@ath.forthnet.gr. 22 units. 110€–130€ double. Rates include breakfast. MC, V. **Amenities:** Restaurant, bar; pool. *In room:* A/C, TV, minibar.

Tsitouras Collection 𝒜 This top-of-the-line luxury hotel will either dazzle or dismay you—understatement is conspicuous by its absence here, where antiques and reproductions jostle for space in five separate themed villas (including the "House of Portraits" and the "House of Porcelain"). The villa you stay in is all yours (and your traveling companion's), which ensures blissful privacy. The absence of televisions helps ensure tranquillity; the absence of a pool in such a deluxe hotel seems more than odd. We're eager to hear readers' reports on Tsitouras Collection; thus far, we've had almost as many thumbs-down for the haphazard service as we have had raves for the serious luxury and quiet location.

Firostefani, 847 00 Santorini. ℂ **22860/23-747.** fax 22860/23-918. tsitoura@lotenet.gr. 5 villas (each villa can accommodate at least 4). 500€ for 2 sharing a villa; 150€ for each additional guest. MC, V. **Amenities:** Restaurant; cafe. *In room:* A/C, minibar, kitchenette.

WHERE TO DINE

Camille Stephani GREEK/INTERNATIONAL Even if you're not staying at Kamari, this restaurant on the north end of the beach, 460m (1,500 ft.) from the bus stop, will make the trip worthwhile. The house specialty is a tender beef filet with green pepper in Madeira sauce. You can take a moonlight stroll along the beach after dinner.

Kamari Beach. ℂ **22860/31-716.** Reservations recommended July–Sept. Main courses 14€–30€. AE, DC, MC, V. Daily 1–4pm and 6:30pm–midnight (but often open all day; often closed off season).

Katina Fish–Taverna *(Moments* SEAFOOD   One of the best places to eat in Oia isn't in town but down in the port of Ammoudi, which is best reached by donkey (ask in the village about hiring a donkey), or you can walk or take a taxi. Katina Pagoni is considered one of the very best local cooks, and the setting beside the glittering Aegean is romantic.

Port of Oia (Ammoudi). ℂ **22860/71-280.** Fish priced daily by the kilo. No credit cards. Daily 11am–1am.

Koukoumavolos *(((* NOUVELLE GREEK   This elegant restaurant was for many years in Oia, but it now overlooks the caldera in Fira. There's delicious fresh fish (wonderful monkfish!) and an adventurous menu of "nouvelle Greek" cuisine (dishes are lighter and less oil-saturated than is customary in Greece), and a wide selection of island and off-island wines and cheeses. The view over the caldera is fantastic—and so is the panacotta with yogurt and cherry sauce.

Fira (below the Atlantis Hotel). ℂ **22860/23-807.** Reservations recommended for dinner. Fish priced daily by the kilo. Main courses 18€–23€. AE, MC, V. Daily noon–3pm and 8pm–midnight.

Selene *(((* TRADITIONAL GREEK   The best restaurant on Santorini—and one of the best in all Greece—Selene uses local produce to highlight what owners Evelyn and George Hatziyiannakis call the "creative nature of Greek cuisine." The appetizers, including a delicious eggplant salad with octopus and tomato, mushrooms with crabmeat and cheese, and fluffy fava balls with caper sauce, are deservedly famous. Entrees include sea bass grilled with pink peppers; rabbit; quail; and saddle of lamb with yogurt and mint sauce. If you eat only one meal on Santorini, eat it here, in a truly distinguished restaurant with distinctive local architecture—and be sure to try the enormous local capers.

Fira (in the passageway between the Atlantis and Aressana hotels). ℂ **22860/22-249.** Fax 22860/24-395. Reservations recommended. Main courses 16€–20€. AE, MC, V. Mid-Apr to early Oct, daily 7pm–midnight. Closed late Oct to early Apr.

EXPLORING THE ISLAND

FIRA   If you're staying overnight on Santorini, take advantage of the fact that almost all the day-trippers from cruise ships leave in the late afternoon, and explore the capital in the evening. As you stroll, you may be surprised to discover that Fira has a Roman Catholic cathedral and convent in addition to the predictable Greek Orthodox cathedral, a legacy from the days when the Venetians controlled much of the Aegean. The name Santorini, in fact, is a Latinate corruption of the Greek for "Saint Irene." The **Megaron Gyzi Museum** (ℂ **22860/22-244**), by the cathedral, has church and local memorabilia, including some before-and-after photographs of the island at the time of the devastating earthquake of 1956. It's open Monday through Saturday from 10:30am to 1pm and 5 to 8pm, and Sunday from 10:30am to 4:30pm; admission is 3€. The small **Archaeological Museum** (ℂ **22860/22-217**) has both Minoan and classical finds. It's open Tuesday through Sunday from 8:30am to 3pm; admission is 3€. You might find it almost deserted, as most visitors head directly for Thira's shops. Before you do the same, stop at the **Thera Foundation** (ℂ **22860/230-16**), near the cable car station en route to Firostephani, to have a look at the spectacular reproductions and re-creations of the frescoes from Akrotiri. It's usually open Tuesday through Sunday from 8:30am to 3pm; admission is 3€. The **Museum of Prehistoric Thira** near the bus station has a small, but excellent, collection of prehistoric finds (mainly from Akrotiri). It's open Tuesday through Sunday from 8:30am to 3pm; admission is free.

VILLAGES   Two island villages well worth visiting are **Pirgos (Tower),** the oldest and highest settlement on the island, and **Oia** (also spelled **Ia**), on a cliff above the caldera. Badly damaged in a massive earthquake in 1956, Oia was virtually a ghost town until it was rebuilt in the 1960s and '70s and resettled. Now its chic shops (check out the **Art Gallery** and **Art Gallery Oia** on Oia's meandering main drag) and gorgeous sunsets make it an increasingly popular place to stay or to visit—especially with those who find Fira too frenetic. If you travel to either village (local buses run here from Fira, or you can take a taxi), keep a lookout for some of the island's cave dwellings (homes hollowed out of Santorini's soft volcanic stone).

BEACHES   Santorini does not have the soft sand beaches of Mykonos, but the black volcanic sand and pebble beach make **Kamari** a very nice place to swim, especially in the morning, before the all-day sunbathers arrive (and before the black sand gets seriously hot). Kamari also has the **Volcano Diving Center** (© 22860/33-177; www.scubagreece.com), which offers guided snorkel swims for around 20€ and scuba lessons from around 65€. On the way to or from Kamari from or to Fira by local bus or taxi, you can stop at the Antoniou, Roussos, or Boutari vintners to see how wine is made, have a free sample, and perhaps buy a bottle or two to sample later. Be warned: Vino Santo, Santorini's sweet wine, is *very* sweet. **Boutari,** Megalohori (© 22860/81-011), is the island's largest vintner. For about 6€ you can see the wine press, sample the wines, and snack on mezedes. The **Antoniou winery** (run by the same family who has the Antoniou jewelry in Fira) is especially charming, with the old wine press and barrels on display.

ANCIENT THIRA & AKROTIRI   Above Kamari beach on a rocky promontory are the ruins of **Ancient Thira** (© 02860/22-217 or 02860/22-366), settled in the 9th century B.C., although most of the scattered remains date from the Hellenistic era. At press time, it was open Tuesday through Friday from 8am to 2:30pm, Sunday and holidays from 8am to 2:30pm; it was also sometimes open on Saturday from 8am to 2:30pm. Admission is 6€. A good but alarmingly narrow road now runs almost to the summit, which can also be reached on foot or by donkey (for hire from some travel agents) by a path. The hilltop site is very fine, but if you have to choose between Ancient Thira and Akrotiri, head for Akrotiri.

The excavations at **Akrotiri,** the Minoan settlement destroyed when the volcano erupted around 1450 B.C., have unearthed buildings three stories tall that were lavishly decorated with frescoes. It's breathtaking to visit the Akrotiri site and walk down the streets and peek in the windows of houses in a town whose life was extinguished in a torrent of lava and ash so long ago. Most of the frescoes discovered were taken to the National Archaeological Museum in Athens. At press time, it was uncertain whether they would be on display when the museum reopens in 2004 or returned to Thira. At present, you can see several

---

Tips **Submerged Santorini**

There's a new way to explore Santorini: a 1-hour submarine ride under the surface of the caldera. Sink to 30m (100 ft.) below the surface and get a glimpse of the submerged volcanic crater. The trip costs 50€; information is available at © **22860/28-900** or at most local travel agencies.

Tips **Santorini Swings**

The height of the tourist season is also the height of the music season in Santorini: If you are here in July, you may want to take in the annual **Santorini Jazz Festival** (www.jazzfestival.gr), which has been bringing several dozen international jazz bands and artists here every summer since 1997. Many performances are on Kamari beach. In August and September, the 2-week **Santorini International Music Festival** (*©* **22860/23-166**), with international singers and musicians, gives performances of classical music at the Nomikos Centre in Fira. Admission to most events is from 15€.

---

frescoes from Akrotiri in the Museum of Prehistoric Thera in Fira. The **site** (*©* **22860/81-366**) is open Tuesday through Sunday from 8:30am to 3pm; admission is 6€. Akrotiri can be reached by public bus, taxi, or one of the bus tours available from island travel agents.

SANTORINI AFTER DARK

Most people will want to start the evening with a drink on the caldera watching the sunset. **Franco's** (*©* **22860/22-881**) is the most famous place for this magic hour, but drinks are expensive; the nearby **Tropical** (no phone) has almost as good a view and charges less. **Archipelago** (*©* **22860/23-673**) and the **Canava Cafe** (*©* **22860/22-565**) also have good views. For more reasonable prices and the same fantastic view, continue past the Loucas Hotel to the **Renaissance Bar** (*©* **22860/22-880**).

Most of the action is north and west of the main square. Underneath the square, the **Kirathira Bar** plays jazz at a level that permits conversation. The **Town Club** appeals to clean-cut rockers, while the **Two Brothers** pulls in the biggest, chummiest crowd on the island. For Greek music, find the **Apocalypse Club,** or **Bar 33** for bouzouki. Discos come and go; follow your ears to find them. The **Koo Club** is the biggest (with some five individual bars), and **Enigma** is popular with those interested in good dance music. In Oia, **Melissa's Piano Bar** and **Zorba's** are good spots for a drink at sunset.

None of the places recommended above have specific street addresses; it's best just to ask someone for directions. ***Remember:*** At virtually all of these places, you'll probably pay at least 10€ for one drink.

SIFNOS

Sifnos (pop. 2,500) is the most beautiful of the western Cyclades—although the port is bland and uninteresting. Just beyond the port, however, are the island's unusually green hills and valleys, and particularly lovely villages. Sifnos also has a reputation for especially good olive oil and distinguished cooking—although the influx of tourists has inevitably produced some cursory cuisine. Sifnos has long been a favorite summer retreat for Athenians, and now that foreign visitors have discovered Sifnos's charms, the island can be terribly crowded in July (especially around the feast day of the Prophet Elias, the patron saint of the island's most important monastery) and in August. If possible, don't visit then, unless you like your restaurants and beaches very busy—and very noisy.

ESSENTIALS

GETTING THERE   There's at least one boat daily from Piraeus, in addition to daily (twice daily in summer) connections to the other western Cyclades, Serifos and Milos, and less frequently to Kimolos and Kythnos. There are ferry connections four times a week with Santorini; three times a week with Folegandros, Ios, and Sikinos; and once a week with Andros, Crete, Mykonos, Paros, Rafina, Syros, and Tinos. In summer, there's a weekly connection with the Dodecanese islands of Karpathos, Kassos, Rhodes, and Symi. Contact the **Port Authority** in Piraeus (© **210/451-1311**) or in Sifnos (© **22840/31-617**) for information.

VISITOR INFORMATION   You can book a room, buy ferry tickets, rent a car or motorbike, arrange excursions, and usually leave your luggage at the **Aegean Thesaurus Travel and Tourism office** 🌟🌟 on the port (© **22840/ 32-152;** www.thesaurus.gr). Check to see if Aegean Thesaurus, which also has an office on the main square in Apollonia (© **22840-151;** fax 22840/332-190), still has its excellent information packet on Sifnos for 2€. Other useful travel agents include **Siphanto Travel** (© **22840/32-034;** fax 22840/31-024) and **Katzoulakis Tourist Agency** (© **22840/32-362**) on the port. At press time, **Ventouris Ferries** (© **22840/31-700**) in Kamares had the concession for tickets for most ferry lines, while Aegean Thesaurus handled hydrofoil *(Flying Dolphin)* tickets.

FAST FACTS   Tourist services are centered around the main square, Plateia Iroon (Heroes' Square), in Apollonia, the capital. The **post office** (© **22840/ 31-329**) is open weekdays from 8am to 3pm and, in the summer, Saturday and Sunday from 9am to 1:30pm. The **National Bank** (© **22840/31-317**) is open Monday through Thursday from 8am to 2pm and Friday from 8am to 1:30pm. The **OTE telephone office** is open daily from 8am to 3pm, and in summer from 5 to 10pm. The news kiosk on the square has a metered phone for after-hours calls. The **police station** (© **22840/31-210**), which also functions as an informal information center, is just east of the square; a nearby **first-aid station** handles **medical emergencies** (© **22840/31-315**).

GETTING AROUND   Many visitors come to Sifnos just for the wonderful hiking and mountain trails. A car or moped isn't really necessary, but cars can be rented at **Aegean Thesaurus** (© **22840/33-151**) in Apollonia; or at **Sifnos Car** (© **22840/31-793**) in Kamares. Apollonia has a few moped dealers; try **Yanni's** (© **22840/31-155**) on the main square, or **Easy Rider** (© **22840/31-001**) on the road circling the village. As always, exercise caution if you do decide to rent a car or moped; many drivers, like you, will be unfamiliar with the island roads. The daily rate for an economy car with full insurance is about 50€; a moped rents for about 22€.

By Bus   Apollonia's Heroes' Square (Plateia Iroon) is the central bus stop for the island. The system is fairly efficient; buses run regularly to and from the port at Kamares, north to Artemonas, east to Kastro, and south to Faros and Plati Yialos. A bus schedule is usually posted by the stop in Heroes' Square.

By Taxi   Apollonia's Heroes' Square is also the main taxi stand, although there aren't many of them on the island. Some mobile phone numbers for taxis are © **6940/642-680,** 6940/444-904, 6940/761-210, or 6940/936-111.

WHERE TO STAY

Many young Athenians vacation on Sifnos, particularly on summer weekends, when it can be virtually impossible to find a room. If you plan to be in Kamares during the high season, be sure to make reservations by May. If you're here off season, many of these hotels are closed, but several remain open year-round. The efficient **Aegean Thesaurus Travel Agency** (see "Visitor Information," above) can place you in a room in a private house with your own bathroom, in a studio with a kitchenette, or in other, more stylish accommodations.

Hotel Anthoussa   This hotel is located above the excellent and popular Yerontopoulos cafe and patisserie, on the right past Heroes' Square. Although street-side rooms offer wonderful views over the hills, they overlook the latenight sweet-tooth crowd and can be recommended only to night owls. Back rooms are quieter and overlook a beautiful bower of bougainvillea.

Apollonia, 840 03 Sifnos. ℂ **22840/31-431**. 15 units. 60€ double. MC, V. **Amenities:** Breakfast room. *In room:* A/C, TV.

Hotel Petali ⭐⭐   This hotel—situated on a relatively quiet side street not far (but all of it uphill) from Apollonia's main square, Plateia Iroon—would be a nice place to stay for a week. It has lovely views over Ano Petali (a suburb of Apollonia) to the sea; a large terrace with handsome, comfortable chairs; rooms furnished in Cycladic style; good beds; modern bathrooms; and a small restaurant that serves delicious Siphnian specialties. You may want to check if the pool and Jacuzzi promised for 2003 have materialized. Although the Hotel Petali does not accept credit cards, its managing office, Aegean Thesaurus Travel Agency (ℂ **22840/33-151;** fax 22840/32-190), accepts MasterCard and Visa.

Apollonia, 840 03 Sifnos. ℂ/fax **22840/33-024**. petali@par.forthnet.gr. 11 units. 110€ double. MC, V. **Amenities:** Restaurant; bar. *In room:* A/C, TV.

Hotel Platis Yialos ⭐ *Kids*   The island's best hotel is ideally situated overlooking the beach on the west side of the cove, set apart from the rest of the town's densely populated beach strip. This is a great place to stay if you are traveling with young children; I speak from experience. It was originally a government-owned Xenia hotel, its design functional rather than beautiful. The ground-floor guest rooms, with patios facing the garden and water, are especially desirable; rooms on the upper stories have balconies. A new suite contains flagstone floors, beamed ceilings, beds for up to six people, and two bathrooms, one with a Jacuzzi; it opens onto a small terrace with views of the bay. Frescoes and small paintings by a local artist are displayed throughout the hotel. The Platis Yialos's flagstone sun deck extends from the beach to a dive platform at the end of the cove; a bar and restaurant share the same Aegean views.

Platis Yialos, 840 03 Sifnos. ℂ **22840/31-324**, or 0831/22-626 in winter. Fax 22840/31-325, or 0831/55-042 in winter. 29 units. 150€ double; 200€ double. Rates include breakfast. No credit cards. Closed Oct–Mar. **Amenities:** Restaurant; bar. *In room:* A/C, minifridge.

Hotel Sifnos ⭐⭐   Many consider this family-owned and -operated hotel on a quiet pedestrianized street off the Plateia Iroon the most congenial in Apollonia. The hospitable owners have tried hard to make it reflect island taste, using local pottery and weavings in the good-size, bright rooms. It has an excellent indoor/outdoor restaurant that attracts locals.

Apollonia, 840 03 Sifnos. ℂ **22840/31-624**. 9 units. 60€ double. AE, MC, V. Usually open year-round. **Amenities:** Restaurant; bar. *In room:* A/C, TV.

WHERE TO DINE

Apostoli's Koutouki Taverna GREEK   Apollonia has several tavernas, and this one on the main pedestrian street is generally the best for Greek food. The service is leisurely at best. All the vegetable dishes, most made from locally grown produce, are tasty, but portions are on the skimpy side.

Apollonia. ℂ **22840/31-186**. Main courses 4€–15€. No credit cards. Daily noon–midnight.

Captain Andreas GREEK/SEAFOOD   This is a typical fish taverna, on the beach, with the catch of the day on the menu, as well as the usual chops and salads. Captain Andreas has many fans, although some find him a bit dour.

Kamares, on the town beach. ℂ **22840/32-356**. Main courses 3.50€–11€; fish priced by the kilo. No credit cards. Daily 1–5pm and 7:30pm–12:30am.

Sifnos Cafe-Restaurant ⋒ GREEK   You can start the day here with breakfast, including fresh fruit juice and your choice of a dozen coffees. Stop by later in the day for a snack, light meal, ouzo and mezedes, or dessert. This place (in the Hotel Sifnos, see above) often has delicious *rivithia* (chickpeas), a Siphnian specialty, on Sunday.

Apollonia. ℂ **22840/31-624**. Main courses 3€–15€. AE, MC, V. Daily 8am–midnight.

To Liotrivi (Manganas) ⋒⋒ GREEK   One of the island's favorite tavernas is in the pretty village of Artemona, just over a mile's walk from Apollonia. Taste for yourself why the Sifnians consider Yannis Yiorgoulis one of their best cooks. Try his delectable *kaparosalata* (minced caper leaves and onion salad), *povithokeftedes* (croquettes of ground chickpeas), or *ambelofasoula* (crisp local black-eyed peas in the pod). In short, there're lots of vegetarian delights here, but there's also a very tasty beef filet with potatoes baked in foil. This place usually has the excellent Siphnian specialty of chickpeas *rivithia* on Sundays.

Artemona. ℂ **22840/31-246**. Main courses 6€–17€. No credit cards. Daily noon–midnight.

EXPLORING THE ISLAND

Kamares, on the west coast, is the island's port and will be most visitors' introduction to Sifnos—a pity, because it has none of the charm of the capital, Apollonia, or the inland villages. Still, there's a good **sand beach** at Kamares, and the usual assortment of restaurants and shops, some of which sell the distinctive local pottery made from island clay.

From Kamares, you can catch a bus for the 5km (3-mile) trip to **Apollonia** (also called **Hora**), the largest of the island's seven villages. En route up the hill to Apollonia, you'll begin to get a sense of the island's handsome architecture, especially its stone paths and small, cubical, whitewashed houses, almost all with whitewashed containers of geraniums.

Apollonia's **Plateia Iroon (Heroes' Square)** is the site of a monument to Sifnos's World War II veterans. Home to a number of small cafes, restaurants, and shops, it's the transportation hub of the island, where its vehicular roads converge. There's also a **Museum of Folk Art** on the square. The museum is usually open July through mid-September from 10am to 1pm and 6 to 10pm; admission is 1.50€.

More and more asphalt roads are appearing on Sifnos, but you'll still be able to do most of your walking on the island's distinctive flagstone and marble paths. You'll probably see village women whitewashing the edges of the paving stones, transforming the monochrome paths into elaborate abstract patterns. Throughout the island, you'll see dovecotes, windmills, and small white chapels in amazingly remote spots.

Apollonia gleams with whitewash, as does the handsome village of **Kastro,** the former capital, where you can see remains of the walls of the medieval fortress *(kastro)*. A romantic ghost town well into the last century, Kastro now has a sprinkling of RENT ROOMS signs, as well as shops, restaurants, and discos. The small **Archaeological Museum** sometimes is, and sometimes is not, open Tuesday through Sunday from 8:30am to 3pm; free admission.

Most connoisseurs rank **Plati Yialos** on the island's south coast as Sifnos's best beach. Don't expect to be alone: A hotel and a campground are located on the popular, long crescent beach. There's also good swimming at **Heronissos, Vroulidia,** and **Faros,** a small resort on the east coast with some good budget accommodations and tavernas. **Apokofto** has a good sand beach, and you can often reach the lovely beach at **Vathy** by one of the caïques that leave from Kamares, or by bus on the new road. **Aegean Thesaurus Travel** (see "Visitor Information," above) has caïque excursions to a number of isolated beaches.

SIFNOS AFTER DARK

In Apollonia, the **Argo Bar, Botzi,** and **Volto,** on the main pedestrian street, are good for the latest European and American pop. At Kamares, the **Old Captain's Bar, Collage Bar, Mobilize Dance Club,** and **Follie-Follie,** all on the beach, compete most nights to see who can crank up the volume the loudest for disco music. If this doesn't appeal to you, check to see whether the **Cultural Society of Sifnos** has scheduled any concerts in Artemonas (usually only in summer).

9

Hungary

by Joseph S. Lieber & Christina Shea

The dramatic political changes of 1989 irreversibly altered life in Hungary. Awakened after its long slumber behind the Iron Curtain, Hungary is now one of Europe's hottest destinations. Poised between East and West, both geographically and culturally, it's at the center of the region's rebirth.

To best understand and appreciate Hungary, go beyond its stately capital, Budapest. Get to know the great river that runs through the country's heart. Take a slow boat (or a fast hydrofoil) up the Danube to the "Bend" towns of Szentendre, Esztergom, or Visegrád.

1 Budapest

Budapest came of age in the 19th century, at the start of which the two towns of Buda and Pest were little more than provincial outposts on the Danube. In 1867, Hungary finally came to terms with Austrian domination, agreeing to the formation of the Austro-Hungarian empire. The dawning of a modern Hungarian identity spawned the city's neoclassical development. The great post-1867 boom coincided with the rise of an eclectic style of architecture, and most of the historic inner city was created at this time. Indeed, Budapest, notwithstanding its long and tattered history of Roman, Mongol, and Turkish conquest, is very much a late-19th-century city, with its characteristic coffeehouse and music hall culture. The decades after World War I and the fall of the Hapsburg monarchy weren't kind to Hungary's charming capital, and Budapest's glory seemed irretrievably lost. However, the city has undergone a post–Cold War renaissance and is once again attracting visitors from far and wide at the start of the new century.

Budapest retains an exotic atmosphere seldom experienced in the better-known capitals of Europe. Explore it fully. Turn off any of the main boulevards and you'll quickly find yourself in a quiet residential neighborhood. The rich scent of a hearty *gulyás* (beef stew) wafts from a kitchen window, salamis hang in the window of the little grocer's shop, and cigarette smoke fogs the cave-like entry of the corner pub.

ESSENTIALS

GETTING THERE **By Plane** All flights arrive at **Ferihegy II** (© 1/296-7155 general info, 1/296-5052 arrivals, 1/296-5883 departures), located in the XVIII district in southeastern Pest.

The easiest way into the city is probably the **Airport Minibus** (© 1/296-8555; fax 1/296-8993), a service of the Budapest Airport Authority (LRI). The minibus, leaving every 10 or 15 minutes throughout the day, takes you directly to any city address at a cost of 1,800 Ft ($8.10). The trip takes 30 minutes to an hour, depending on how many stops are made before your own. The Airport Minibus desk is easily found in the main hall. Minibuses also provide the same efficient service returning to the airports; but be sure to arrange for your pickup a full day in advance.

Note: We strongly discourage the use of cabs from the **Airport Taxi** fleet (© 1/296-6534), which are notoriously overpriced. A ride downtown from one of these cabs could cost as much as twice the fare of a ride in a reasonably priced taxi. Alas, for reasons no one has been able to explain to us with a straight face, cabs from the Airport Taxi fleet are the only cabs permitted to wait for fares on the airport grounds. However, dozens of cabs from the cheaper fleets that we recommend are at all times stationed at roadside pullouts just off the airport property, a stone's throw from the terminal, waiting for radio calls from their dispatchers. You can phone any of these fleets from the terminal and a cab will be there for you in a few minutes. (See "By Taxi" in the "Getting Around" section, below, for other taxi fleet phone numbers.) For two or more people traveling together, a taxi from a recommended fleet to the city will generally be cheaper than the combined minibus fares, at about 3,000 Ft ($14). A taxi from the airport to downtown takes about 20 to 30 minutes.

It's also possible (and very cheap) to get to the city by public transportation; the bus-to-Metro-to-town trip takes about 1 hour total. Take the red-lettered **bus no. 93** to the last stop, Kőbánya–Kispest. From there, the Blue Metro line runs to the Inner City of Pest. The cost is two transit tickets, which are 220 Ft ($1); you can buy tickets from the automated vending machine at the bus stop (coins only) or from any newsstand at the airport.

By Train Budapest has three major train stations: Keleti pályaudvar (Eastern Station), Nyugati pályaudvar (Western Station), and Déli pályaudvar (Southern Station). The stations' names, curiously, correspond neither to their geographical location in the city nor to the origins or destinations of the trains serving them. Each has a Metro station beneath it and an array of accommodation offices, currency-exchange booths, and other services.

Most international trains pull into bustling **Keleti Station** (© 1/314-5010; Metro: Keleti pu.), a classic steel-girded European train station located in Pest's seedy Baross tér. In addition to the Metro, numerous bus, tram, and trolleybus

Budapest

ATTRACTIONS ●

Bazilika
  (St. Stephen's Church) **22**
Belvárosi
  Plébániatemplom **13**
Budapesti Történeti
  Múzeum **11**
Chain Bridge **10**
City Park **28**
Dohány Synagogue **20**
Gellért Hegy **15**
Hungarian State Opera
  House **23**
Károly krt. **19**
Margaret Island **1**
Mátyás Templom **8**
Nemzeti Galéria **11**
Nemzeti Múzeum **18**
Néprajzi Múzeum **4**
Parliament **3**
Széchényi Baths **14**
Vidám Park **29**
Zeneakadémia (Ferenc Liszt
  Academy of Music) **26**

ACCOMMODATIONS ■

Charles Apartment House **12**
Hilton Budapest **6**
Hotel Astra Vendégház **7**
Hotel Gellért **16**
Hotel Kulturinnov **5**
Hotel MEDOSZ **25**
Hotel Victoria **9**
K & K Hotel Opera **24**
King's Hotel **21**
Peregrinus ELTE Hotel **17**
Radio Inn **27**

-- Ⓜ Metro

lines serve Baross tér. Some international trains arrive at **Nyugati Station** (© 1/349-0115; Metro: Nyugati pu.), another classic of a station designed by the Eiffel company and built in the 1870s. Numerous tram and bus lines serve busy Nyugati tér. Few international trains arrive at **Déli Station** (© 1/375-6293; Metro: Déli pu.), an ugly modern building in central Buda.

Train-station phone numbers are good from 8pm to 6am. During the day, obtain **domestic train information** at © 1/461-5400 and **international train information** at © 1/461-5500. Purchase **tickets** at train-station ticket windows or from the MÁV Service Office, VI. Andrássy út 35 (© 1/322-8082), open Monday through Friday from 9am to 5pm. You can access a timetable on the Web at **http://elvira.mavinformatika.hu/index2.htm**. (As you must conduct your search in Hungarian, it's helpful to know that *honnan* means "from where," *hova* "to where," *ma* "today," *holnap* "tomorrow," and *keres* "ask" or, in this context, "search.")

MÁV operates a **minibus** that'll take you from any of the three stations to any point in the city for 1,300 Ft to 2,000 Ft ($5.85–$9) per person (depending on the distance); to the airport for 1,800 Ft ($8.10); or between stations for 900 Ft ($4.05) per person. To order the minibus, call © **1/353-2722** or 1/357-2617. Often, however, a taxi fare (from a recommended fleet) will be cheaper, especially for groups of two or more travelers.

By Bus   The **Népstadion Bus Station** is the city's recently renovated and expanded main bus terminal. It is located at the Népliget stop on the Blue Metro line. The central information center is located there (© **1/219-8080** for both in-land and international info). Buses to and from western, eastern, and central Europe, as well as from points in Hungary east of the Danube, arrive here. However, buses to/from the Danube Bend and other points north of Budapest arrive at the much smaller **Árpád híd Bus Station** (© 1/320-9229 or 1/317-9886; Metro: Árpád híd/Blue line). Note that the former main bus station, at Erzsébet tér in the Inner City of Pest, was permanently closed in 2002.

By Car   Vienna, 275km (170 miles) from Budapest, is connected to the Hungarian capital by the Austrian A4 superhighway, which becomes the M1 and feeds into the city via southern Buda. The border crossings from Austria and Slovakia are generally hassle-free. You may be requested to present your driver's license, vehicle registration, and proof of insurance (the number plate and symbol indicating country of origin are acceptable proof). Hungary doesn't require an international driver's license. Cars entering Hungary are required to have a decal indicating country of registration, a first-aid kit, and an emergency triangle.

By Hydrofoil   The Hungarian state shipping company **MAHART** operates hydrofoils on the Danube between Vienna and Budapest in spring and summer. It's an extremely popular route, so book your tickets well in advance. To book, contact your local Austrian National Tourist Board. In Vienna, contact MAHART, Handelskai 265 (© **0043/729-2161;** fax 0043/729-2163). The Budapest office of **MAHART** is at V. Belgrád rakpart (© **1/318-1880**). Boats and hydrofoils from Vienna arrive at the international boat station next door to the MAHART office on the **Belgrád rakpart,** which is on the Pest side of the Danube, between the Szabadság and Erzsébet bridges.

VISITOR INFORMATION   Tourist Offices   The city's best information source is **Tourinform,** V. Liszt Ferenc tér 11, in Pest (© **1/322-4098;** www.hungarytourism.hu; Metro: Opera/Yellow line; tram: Octogon, nos. 4–6). It's open daily in winter from 10am to 6pm, in summer from 9am to 7pm.

Another useful source is the **Vista Visitor Center,** V. Paulay Ede u. 7 (© **1/267-8603;** www.vista.hu; Metro: Deák tér). It's open Monday through Friday from 9am to 8pm and Saturday from 10am to 4pm.

Websites   The site **www.gotohungary.com** has a wealth of tourist information, as does **www.hungarytourism.hu.** Use the extensive collection of links at **www.hungary.org** as a jumping-off point to learn more about Hungary's history, culture, cuisine, and more. Go to **www.budapest.com** to view a virtual slide show, consult the shopping guide, or see what the city looked like a century ago. Current local news, entertainment listings, and the like can be found at either or **www.budapestweek.com.**

CITY LAYOUT   The city of Budapest was founded in 1873 by joining three cities: Buda, Pest, and Óbuda. Budapest, like Hungary itself, is defined by the River Danube (Duna), along which many historic sites are found. Eight bridges join the two banks; five of them are in the city center.

On the right bank lies **Pest,** the commercial and administrative center. Central Pest is that part of the city between the river and the semicircular **Nagykörút (Outer Ring Blvd.),** stretches of which take the names of former monarchs: Ferenc, József, Erzsébet, Teréz, and Szent István. The Outer Ring begins at the Pest side of the Petőfi Bridge in the south and wraps itself around the center, ending at the Margit Bridge in the north. Several of Pest's busiest squares are along the Outer Ring, and Pest's major east–west avenues bisect the Outer Ring at these squares.

Central Pest proper is defined by the **Kiskörút (Inner Ring).** It starts at **Szabadság híd (Freedom Bridge)** in the south and is alternately named Vámház körút, Múzeum körút, Károly körút, Bajcsy-Zsilinszky út, and József Attila utca before ending at the Chain Bridge (Széchenyi lánchíd). Inside this ring is the **Belváros,** the historic Inner City of Pest.

Váci utca is a popular pedestrian shopping street between the Inner Ring and the Danube. It spills into **Vörösmarty tér,** one of the best-known squares. The **Dunakorzó (Danube Promenade),** a popular evening stroll, runs along the river in Pest, between the Chain Bridge and the Erzsébet Bridge. The **historic Jewish district** of Pest is in the Erzsébetváros, between the two ring boulevards. **Margit-sziget (Margaret Island)** is in the middle of the Danube. Accessible by the Margaret Bridge or Árpád Bridge, it's a popular park without vehicular traffic.

On the left bank is **Buda;** to its north, beyond the city center, lies **Óbuda.** Buda is as hilly as Pest is flat. Buda's **Castle Hill** is widely considered the most beautiful part of Budapest. A number of steep paths, staircases, and small streets go up to Castle Hill, but no major roads. The easiest access is from **Clark Ádám tér** (at the head of the Chain Bridge) by funicular, or from **Várfok utca** (near Moszkva tér) by foot or bus. Castle Hill consists of the royal palace itself, home to numerous museums, and the so-called **Castle District,** a lovely neighborhood

---

⌒Tips A Note on Addresses

Budapest is divided into 22 districts called **kerülets** (abbreviated ker.). A Roman numeral followed by a period precedes every written address in Budapest, signifying the kerület; for example, XII. Csörsz utca 9 is in the 12th kerület. Because many street names are repeated in different parts of the city, it's very important to know which kerület a certain address is in.

of small, winding streets, centered on the Gothic Matthias Church. Below Castle Hill, along the Danube, is a long, narrow neighborhood, historically populated by fishermen and other river workers, known as the **Víziváros (Watertown)**. **Central Buda** is a collection of low-lying neighborhoods below Castle Hill. The main square is **Moszkva tér,** just north of Castle Hill. Beyond Central Buda, mainly to the east, are the Buda Hills.

Óbuda is also on the left bank of the Danube, north of Buda. Although the greater part of Óbuda is modern and drab, it features a beautiful old city center and impressive Roman ruins.

Getting Around   Budapest has an extensive and inexpensive public transportation system. However, except for 17 well-traveled bus and tram routes, all forms of transport shut down nightly at around 11:30pm; certain areas of the city, most notably the Buda Hills, are beyond the reach of the limited night service, so you'll have to take a taxi if you're out late. Be on the alert for pickpockets when on crowded public transportation. Keep your money and valuables inside your clothing in a money belt.

All forms of public transportation require the self-validation of pre-purchased **tickets** *(vonaljegy),* costing 110 Ft (50¢) apiece (children under 6 travel free). Single tickets can be bought at Metro ticket windows, newspaper kiosks, and the occasional tobacco shop. There are also automated machines in most Metro stations and at major transportation hubs, but the older ones among these are not too reliable. On weekends and at night it can be rather difficult to find an open ticket window, so buy enough tickets to avoid the trouble of constantly having to replenish your stock. For 1,000 Ft ($4.50) you can get a **10-pack** *(tizes csomag),* and for 1,950 Ft ($8.75) you can get a **20-pack** *(huszas csomag).* **Note:** During the process of validating tickets, you must keep the stack intact. Do not tear the individual tickets off as you use them.

Your best bet is to buy a day pass or multiday pass. Passes are inexpensive and only need to be validated once. A pass will probably save you some money too, as you're likely to be getting on and off public transportation all day long. **Day passes** *(napijegy)* cost 850 Ft ($3.80) and are valid until midnight of the day of purchase; **3-day passes** *(turistajegy)* cost 1,700 Ft ($7.65); and **7-day passes** *(hétibérlet)* cost 2,100 Ft ($9.45). You can buy these passes from Metro ticket windows; the clerk will validate the pass at the time of purchase.

Uniformed inspectors frequently come around checking for valid tickets, particularly at the top or bottom of the escalators to Metro platforms. On-the-spot fines (2,000 Ft/$9) are assessed to fare dodgers. All public transportation operates on rough schedules, posted at bus and tram shelters and in Metro stations. The Budapest Transport Authority (BKV térkép) produces a detailed transportation map, available at most Metro ticket windows for 380 Ft ($1.70).

By Metro   The Metro is clean and efficient, with trains running every 3 to 5 minutes from about 4:30am until about 11:30pm. The three lines are universally known by color——Yellow, Red, and Blue. Officially they have numbers as well, but all signs are color-coded. All three lines converge at the **Deák tér** station.

The **Yellow (1) line,** the oldest Metro on the European continent, was fully renovated in 1996. This easily accessible line, just a few steps underground, runs from Vörösmarty tér in the heart of central Pest, out the length of Andrássy út, past the Városliget (City Park), and ends at Mexikói út. Tickets for the Yellow line are validated on the train itself. The **Red (2)** and **Blue (3) lines** are modern Metros, deep underground and accessible by escalator. The Red line runs from eastern Pest, through the center, across the Danube to Déli Station. The Blue line runs from southeastern Pest, through the center, to northern Pest. Tickets must be validated at the automated time-stamp boxes before you descend the escalator. When changing lines at Deák tér, you must validate a new ticket at the orange machines in the hallway between lines.

By Bus   Many parts of the city, most notably the Buda Hills, are best accessed by bus *(busz)*. Most lines are in service from about 4:30am to about 11:30pm, with less frequent weekend service on some. A few buses run all night long (an *É*—with an accent—signifies *éjszaka,* meaning that the bus runs all night). You must validate your bus ticket on board at the mechanical red box found by each door. Tickets for Budapest buses cannot be purchased from the driver (though in smaller cities and towns the drivers generally do sell tickets). You can board the bus by any door.

Black-numbered local buses constitute the majority of the bus fleet. Red-numbered buses are express. If the red number on the bus is followed by an *E,* the bus runs nonstop between terminals (however, remember that an *É*—with an accent—signifies *éjszaka,* meaning that the bus runs all night). A few buses are labeled by something other than a number; one you'll probably use is the **Várbusz (Palace Bus),** a minibus that runs between Várfok utca, off Buda's Moszkva tér, and the Castle District.

By Tram   You'll find Budapest's bright-yellow trams (known as *villamos* in Hungarian) very useful, particularly the **4** and **6,** which travel along the Outer Ring (Nagykörút). You must validate your ticket on board. As with buses, tickets are valid for one ride, not for the line itself. Trams stop at every station, and all doors open, regardless of whether anyone is waiting to get on. ***Warning:*** The buttons near the tram doors are for emergency stops, not stop requests.

By Trolleybus   There are 14 trolleybus lines in Budapest, all in Pest. Of particular interest to train travelers is no. 73, the fastest route between Keleti Station and Nyugati Station. All the information in the "By Bus" section above on boarding and ticket validation applies to trolleybuses as well.

By HÉV   The HÉV is a suburban railway network that connects Budapest to various points along the city's outskirts. There are four HÉV lines; only one, the **Szentendre line,** is of serious interest to tourists. The terminus for the Szentendre HÉV line is Buda's Batthyány tér, also a station of the Metro Red line. To reach Óbuda's Fő tér (Main Sq.), get off at the Árpád híd (Árpád Bridge) stop. The HÉV runs regularly between 4am and 11:30pm. For trips within the city limits, you need one transit ticket, available at HÉV ticket windows at the Batthyány tér Station or from the conductor on board. These tickets are different from the standard transportation tickets and are punched by conductors on board. If you have a valid day pass, you do not need to buy a ticket for trips within the city limits.

By Taxi   Budapest taxis are largely unregulated, so fares vary tremendously. Perhaps because there are more taxi drivers than the level of business can support, many drivers are experts at fleecing foreigners. However, if you watch out, taxis are still a bit cheaper than in western Europe. Several fleet companies have good reputations, honest drivers, and competitive rates. We particularly recommend **Fő Taxi** (© 1/222-2222). Other reliable fleets are **Volántaxi** (© 1/466-6666), **City Taxi** (© 1/211-1111), **Tele5** (© 1/355-5555), and **6x6** (© 1/266-6666).

By Car   We don't recommend using a car for sightseeing in Budapest. You may, however, want to rent one for trips outside the capital. We recommend **Denzel**

Europcar InterRent, VIII. Üllői út 60–62 (© **1/477-1080;** fax 1/477-1099), where you can rent an Opel Corza or Fiat Punto for 95€ for the day, or for 68€ for 3 to 4 days (insurance included). They also have a rental counter at the airport (© **1/296-6610**), but there you pay a 12% airport tax.

 FAST FACTS: Budapest

American Express Budapest's Amex office is between Vörösmarty tér and Deák tér in central Pest, at V. Deák Ferenc u. 10, 1052 Budapest (© **1/235-4330** or 1/235-4300; fax 1/267-2028; Metro: Deák tér). It's open year-round on weekdays from 9am to 5:30pm and Saturday from 9am to 2pm. There is an American Express ATM on the street in front.

Business Hours **Banks** are usually open Monday through Thursday from 8am to 3pm and Friday from 8am to 1pm. Most **stores** are open Monday through Friday from 10am to 6pm (except shopping malls which remain open until 7pm) and Saturday from 9 or 10am to 1 or 2pm. Smaller shops close for an hour at lunch, and as a general rule only stores in central tourist areas are open Sunday. Many shops and restaurants close for 2 weeks in August.

Currency The basic unit of currency in Hungary is the **forint (Ft).** The rate of exchange used to calculate the dollar values given in this chapter is $1 = about 225 Ft (or 100 Ft = 45¢). At press time, the rate of exchange for the British pound was £1 = about 370 Ft (or 100 Ft = 27p). Note that exchange rates fluctuate from time to time and may not be the same when you travel to Hungary.

Note: Several hotels and pensions in Budapest list their prices in U.S. dollars and many list them in euros, the new currency of the European Union. This is done as a hedge against forint inflation. The euro is not the lawful currency of Hungary. Hungary is to become a member of the European Union in 2004 and may adopt the euro at that time. We have not converted the euro prices into dollar prices (or vice versa) because since the euro's inception, the U.S. dollar and the euro have traded almost on par (that is, $1 approximately equals 1€). But as this book went to press, 1€ was worth approximately $1.15 and gaining in strength, so your dollars might not go as far as you'd expect. For up-to-the minute exchange rates between the euro and the dollar, check the currency converter website www.xe.com/ucc.

Currency Exchange The best official rates for both cash and traveler's checks are obtained at banks. Exchange booths are located throughout the city center, in train stations, and in most luxury hotels, but they almost always offer lower rates than banks. This is particularly true of one chain called Inter Change, which offers a rate up to 20% lower than the going bank rate, depending on the amount you exchange. ATMs (Cirrus and PLUS networks) are found in front of banks throughout the city. Since 2001, with the full convertibility of the Hungarian forint, there are no longer any restrictions regarding re-exchange of forints back into your currency. Consequently, unlike in the past, you need not retain your currency exchange receipts as proof of exchange.

Doctors We recommend the **American Clinic,** in a modern building across from the Mammut shopping center at I. Hattyu u. 14 (© **1/224-9090;** Metro: Moszkva tér); it's a newly opened private outpatient clinic with two U.S. board–certified physicians and several English-speaking Hungarian doctors. Your best bet is to make an appointment. The clinic is open on weekdays from 8:30am to 7pm (to 6pm Fri). Check with Vista Visitor Center for discount coupons. For dental work, we recommend **Dr. Susan Linder,** II. Vihorlat u. 23 (© **1/335-5245;** bus: 5 or 29), the dentist for the U.S. and British embassies. She did her postdoctoral work at the University of California at San Francisco and speaks flawless English. Her office is open Monday, Tuesday, and Thursday.

Drugstores The Hungarian word for "drugstore" is *gyógyszertár* or *patika.* Generally, pharmacies carry only prescription drugs. Hotel "drugstores" are just shops with soap, perfume, aspirin, and other non-prescription items. There are a number of 24-hour pharmacies in the city— every pharmacy posts the address of the nearest one in its window, in case the one that you've gone to is not open at the time. Your best bet for 24-hour service throughout the year is **Oktogon Patika** on Teréz körút, next to Hotel Béke Radisson (off Oktogon Sq.; Metro: Yellow line; tram: 4 or 6).

Embassies The embassy of the **United States** is at V. Szabadság tér 12 (© **1/475-4400;** Metro: Kossuth tér). The embassy of **Canada** is at XII. Budakeszi út 32 (© **1/392-3360;** Metro: Moszkva tér, then tram 22). The embassy of the **United Kingdom** is at V. Harmincad u. 6 (© **1/266-2888;** Metro: Deák tér). The embassy of **Ireland** is at V. Szabadság tér 7 (© **1/302-9600;** Metro: Kossuth tér). The embassy of **Australia** is at XII. Királyhágo tér 8-9 (© **1/457-9777;** Metro: Déli pu.). The U.K. embassy handles matters for **New Zealand** citizens. Call for hours.

Emergencies Dial © **104** for an ambulance, © **105** for the fire department, or © **107** for the police.

Internet Access We generally use **Vista Visitor Center,** V. Paulay Ede u. 7 (© **1/267-8603;** Metro: Deák tér), with about 10 terminals costing 11 Ft (5¢) per minute. The wait here is sometimes pretty long. It's open Monday through Saturday from 10am to 10pm and Sunday from 10am to 8pm. Another option, with less risk of a wait, is the **Internet Café,** V. Kecskeméti u. 5 (© **1/328-0292;** Metro: Kálvin tér), with about 20 terminals, each costing 700 Ft ($3.15) per hour; pricing is by 30-minute intervals (except 10 min. or less, which costs 150 Ft or 65¢).

Post Office The main branch of the Magyar Posta (Hungarian Postal Service) is at V. Petőfi Sándor u. 17–19, 1052 Budapest, Hungary (© **36/1-318-3947** or 487-1100; Metro: Deák tér). This rather confusing office is open Monday through Friday from 8am to 8pm and Saturday from 8am to 2pm. The post office at VIII. Baross tér 11/c (© **36/1-322-9013;** Metro: Keleti pu.) is open Monday through Saturday from 7am to 9pm. The post office at VI. Teréz krt. 51 (© **36/1-312-1480;** Metro: Nyugati pu.) is open Monday through Friday from 7am to 9pm and Saturday from 8am to 8pm. At press time, an airmail postcard cost 130 Ft (60¢), and an airmail letter 190 Ft (85¢) and up, depending on size of envelope and weight.

Safety By U.S. standards, Budapest is a relatively safe city—muggings and violent attacks are rare. Nevertheless, foreigners are always prime targets. Though they're clearly less of a threat now than a few years ago, teams of professional pickpockets still plague Budapest, operating on crowded trams, Metros, and buses. Be particularly careful on bus no. 26 (Margaret Island) and tram nos. 4 and 6, or in any other crowded setting. The pickpockets' basic trick is to create a distraction to take your attention away from yourself and your own security. Avoid being victimized by wearing a money belt under your clothes instead of wearing a fanny pack or carrying a wallet or purse. No valuables should be kept in the outer pockets of a backpack.

Telephone The **country code** for Hungary is **36.** The **city code** for Budapest is **1;** use this code when you're calling from outside Hungary. If you're within Hungary but not in Budapest, first dial **06;** when you hear a tone, dial the city code and phone number. If you're calling within Budapest, simply leave off the code and dial only the regular seven-digit phone number.

Be aware that some Budapest phone numbers may change as MATÁV continues to upgrade its system. Note, for instance, that any number beginning with a "1" has been changed; try replacing the 1 with a 3 or 4. Usually, if the number you're dialing has changed, you'll get a recording first in Hungarian and than in English, indicating the new number. If further information is needed, dial ✆ **198** for domestic directory assistance and **199** for international queries.

The Hungarian phone company MATÁV provides much better service than in the past, but it still falls significantly short of Western standards. For best results, dial slowly and don't be too quick to trust a busy signal—try again.

Numbers beginning with **06-20, 06-30, 06-70,** or **06-80,** followed by a seven-digit number, are **mobile phone numbers.** If the mobile number you've been given has only six digits, it's incorrect; try adding a **9** before the other six digits. Be aware that you pay for a long-distance call when you call a mobile phone (except 06-80, which is toll-free).

Public **pay phones** charge varying amounts for local calls depending on the time of day you place your call. It's cheapest to call late in the evenings and on weekends. Public phones operate with 20, 50, and 100 Ft coins or with phone cards (in 50 or 120 units) you can buy from post offices, tobacco shops, newsstands, travel agencies, and any MATÁV customer service office (MATÁV Pont).

You can reach the **AT&T** operator at ✆ **00/800-01111,** the **MCI** operator at ✆ **00/800-01411,** and the **Sprint** operator at ✆ **00/800-01877.**

Tipping Tipping is generally 10%. Among those who welcome tips are waiters, taxi drivers, hotel employees, barbers, cloakroom attendants, toilet attendants, masseuses, and tour guides.

WHERE TO STAY

One of the nice developments of the post-1989 boom in Budapest is the proliferation of new pensions and small hotels. The better choices among these—and the less expensive—are usually outside the city center, but all the places we list can easily be reached by public transportation. Notwithstanding the arrival of these new places, Budapest retains its reputation as a city without enough guest beds. Indeed, in high season it can be difficult to secure a hotel or pension room or hostel bed, so make reservations and get written confirmation well ahead of time if possible. Since the previous edition of this book was written, parking meters have been introduced in practically all central areas of Budapest, and most of the parking spaces outside hotels are metered on weekdays from 8am to 6pm. The rate may vary in accordance with the centrality of the location.

Many hotels and pensions in Budapest list their prices in euros or U.S. dollars. This is done as a hedge against forint inflation; all hotels in Budapest accept payment in Hungarian forints as well as foreign currencies. We have listed lodging prices either in forints or euros, because since the euro's inception, the U.S. dollar and the euro have traded almost on par (that is, $1 approximately equals 1€). But as this book went to press, 1€ was worth approximately $1.15 and gaining in strength, so your dollars might not go as far as you'd expect. For up-to-the-minute exchange rates between the euro and the dollar, check the currency converter website **www.xe.com/ucc.**

An attractive accommodation alternative in Hungary is a room in a **private apartment.** Typically, you share the bathroom with the hosts or with other guests. An average room will cost about 3,500 Ft to 6,000 Ft ($16–$27) for two people or 3,800 Ft ($17) for one person. Breakfast isn't officially included, but the host will often offer a continental breakfast for 500 Ft to 750 Ft ($2.25–$3.40). You may have limited kitchen privileges (ask in advance). Some hosts will greet you when you arrive, give you a key, and seemingly disappear; others will want to befriend you, show you around, and cook for you. Most rooms are adequate, some are even memorable, but any number of reasons may cause you to dislike yours: Noisy neighborhoods, tiny bathrooms, and bad coffee are among the complaints we've heard. The great majority of visitors, though, appear to be very satisfied. Plus, staying in a private room provides a window into everyday Hungarian life that you might otherwise miss.

The most established agencies for hotel, pension, and apartment reservations are the former state-owned travel agents **Ibusz, Cooptourist,** and **Budapest Tourist.** Although newer, private agencies have proliferated, the older ones tend to have the greatest number of rooms listed. There are agencies at the airport, at all three major train stations, throughout central Pest, and along the main roads into Budapest for travelers arriving by car. The main **Ibusz reservations office**

 Native Behavior

When you are first introduced to someone, make sure to call him or her by the appropriate title (such as Dr., Mr., Mrs.) followed by the last name. When in doubt in Hungary, opt for formality in addressing people. Also remember that handshakes are common gestures of greeting, no matter how well you know someone.

On business cards and the like, the last name precedes the first name.

Expect to be offered plenty of food and drink when you enter someone's home. Always accept at least a modest serving of whatever is offered.

is at Ferenciek tere 10 (℃ **1/485-2700;** fax 1/318-2805; Metro: Ferenciek tere), open year-round Monday through Friday from 8:15am to 5pm. All major credit cards are accepted. **Cooptourist,** Nyugati Station (℃ **36/1-458-6200**), is open from 9am to 4:30pm Monday through Friday and does not accept credit cards. **Budapest Tourist,** Nyugati Station (℃ **36/1-318-6552**), is open from 9am to 5pm Monday through Friday, from 9am to 12pm Saturday, and does not accept credit cards.

IN THE INNER CITY & CENTRAL PEST
Very Expensive
K & K Hotel Opera ★★★ (Value   Operated by the Austrian K & K hotel chain, this tasteful, elegant establishment opened in 1994 and expanded in 1997. Directly across the street from the Opera House in central Pest, the hotel blends nicely with its surroundings. The interior is pleasing and the staff is uniformly friendly and helpful. Pets are welcome.

VI. Révay u. 24, 1065 Budapest. ℃ **1/269-0222.** Fax 1/269-0230. www.kkhotels.com. 205 units. 143€ double and 122€ single. Rates 5% lower in low season. Rates include breakfast. AE, DC, MC, V. Parking 10€. Metro: Opera/Yellow line. Pets accepted. **Amenities:** Fitness room; sauna; business center; nonsmoking rooms. *In room:* A/C, TV, minibar, safe.

Expensive
Peregrinus ELTE Hotel ★★ (Value   This is the guesthouse of Pest's ELTE University, ideally located in the heart of the Inner City of Pest. While many guests are affiliated with the university, the hotel is open to the public as well. You should reserve well in advance. The building dates from the turn of the 20th century and was renovated when it was opened in 1994. The rooms are simple but comfortable. Payment must be in cash in Hungarian forints.

V. Szerb u. 3, 1056 Budapest. ℃ **1/266-4911.** Fax 1/266-4913. 26 units. 99€ double; (81€ double in low season. Rates include breakfast. No credit cards. No parking. Metro: Kálvin tér/Blue line. *In room:* A/C (attic rooms), TV, minibar.

Moderate
King's Hotel ★★ (Finds   King's Hotel opened for business in 1995 in a beautifully renovated and restored fin de siècle building in the heart of Pest's Jewish district. The reception is friendly and helpful. Despite the somewhat drab modern furnishings, rooms retain a 19th-century atmosphere, many boasting small balconies overlooking the quiet residential street. Most, but not all, have a private bathroom. The kosher hotel restaurant is the only one of its kind in Budapest. *Note:* Meals are served on weekends and Jewish holidays in the hotel's restaurant by prior arrangement only.

VII. Nagydiófa u. 25–27 Budapest. ℃/fax **1/352-7675.** 80 units. 60€–80€ double; 140€ suite. Rates include breakfast. AE, DC, MC, V. Parking available on street for $10 per day. Metro: Astoria. **Amenities:** Restaurant (kosher). *In room:* A/C, TV.

Inexpensive
Hotel MEDOSZ ★ (Value   The MEDOSZ was formerly a trade-union hotel for agricultural workers. It is located on sleepy Jókai tér, in the heart of Pest's theater district, just across the street from the bustling Liszt Ferenc tér, Pest's most recent nightlife hub, a couple of blocks from the Opera House. This is as good as it gets off the river in central Pest. Although the hotel has not been renovated since privatization, it remains a great value given its location. The rooms are simple but clean. Next door to Hotel MEDOSZ is one of Budapest's special treats for children: a puppet theater *(bábszínház).*

> ### *Tips* Traveler's Tip
>
> Most hotels and pensions in Budapest divide the year into three seasons. **High season** is roughly from March or April to September or October and the week between Christmas and New Year's. **Mid-season** is usually considered March, and October and/or November. **Low season** is roughly from November to February, except Christmas week. Some hotels discount as much as 50% in low season, while others offer no winter discount. Be sure to inquire.

VI. Jókai tér 9, 1061 Budapest. ℂ 1/374-3000. Fax 1/332-4316. www.medoszhotel.hu. 67 units. 55€ double; 42€ single. Rates are 20% lower in low season. Rates include breakfast. No credit cards. Metered on-street parking very difficult in neighborhood. Metro: Oktogon. *In room:* TV.

JUST BEYOND CENTRAL PEST
Inexpensive
Radio Inn ⭐⭐ *(Value* As the official guesthouse of Hungarian National Radio, the Radio Inn houses many visiting dignitaries and offers apartments to individual tourists. The inn is in an exclusive embassy neighborhood (next door to the Chinese embassy), a stone's throw from City Park, and a block from Pest's grand Andrássy út. The Metro's Yellow line takes you into the center of Pest in 5 minutes; alternatively, it's a 30-minute walk. Behind the building, there's an enormous private courtyard full of flowers. The huge apartments (all with fully equipped, spacious kitchens) are comfortably furnished and painstakingly clean. Note that the toilets and bathrooms are separate, European style. The management is somewhat old-system (read: begrudging with information, slightly suspicious of foreigners), yet cordial enough.

VI. Benczúr u. 19, 1068 Budapest. ℂ 1/342-8347 or 1/322-8284. Fax 1/322-8284. www.hotels.hu/radio_inn budapest. 36 units. In high season 43€, 65€, and 84€ for 1, 2, and 3-person apartments, and 43€, 48€, and 61€ respectively in low season. Breakfast 5 € extra. MC, AE, MC, V. Parking available on street, but parking meter is 100 Ft (45¢) per hour 8am–6pm weekdays. Metro: Bajza utca/Yellow line. **Amenities:** Restaurant; bar; 24-hr. room service; laundry service; nonsmoking rooms. *In room:* TV, kitchen, minibar.

CASTLE DISTRICT & BUDA
Very Expensive
Hilton Budapest ⭐⭐⭐ Overlooking the river and Pest beyond, the Hilton, built in 1977, is widely considered the city's classiest hotel. Its location, on Hess András tér, next door to Matthias Church and the Fisherman's Bastion, is no less than spectacular. The award-winning design incorporates the ruins of a 13th-century Dominican church and the baroque facade of a 17th-century Jesuit college (the main entrance). More expensive rooms have views over the Danube, with a full Pest skyline; rooms on the other side of the hotel overlook the delightful streets of the Castle District.

I. Hess András tér 1–3, 1014 Budapest. ℂ 1/488-6600. Fax 1/488-6644. www.hilton.com. 322 units. 270€–350€ double in high season and 240€–320€ in low season; 250€–330€ single in high season and 220€–300€ in low season; add 15% tax. Children 17 and under stay free in parent's room. Breakfast 19€ extra. AE, DC, MC, V. Parking 5,600 Ft ($25) per day. Bus: "Várbusz" from Moszkva tér or 16 from Deák tér. **Amenities:** 2 restaurants; 2 bars; lounge; fitness room; concierge; tour desk; free airport minibus; full business center; salon; 24-hr. room service; babysitting; laundry service; doctor/dentist on call; nonsmoking rooms. *In room:* A/C, TV w/pay movies, dataport, minibar, hair dryer, safe.

Hotel Gellért ⭐⭐⭐ *(Kids* First opened in 1918, this splendid, sprawling Art Nouveau hotel, located in Buda at the base of Gellért Hill on the bank of the

Danube, has not seen a renovation since 1970. It's pretty run-down, but it's still one of the most charming hotels in Budapest. The quality and size of the rooms vary greatly—it seems to be hit or miss. Only 29 rooms have air-conditioning. Some rooms with balconies offer great views over the Danube, but these can be noisy since the hotel fronts loud and busy Gellért Square. The Gellért Baths are perhaps the most popular of Budapest's thermal baths.

XI. Gellért tér 1, 1111 Budapest. ℂ **1/385-2200.** Fax 1/466-6631. www.danubiusgroup.com. 234 units. 190€–205€ double; 250€–275€ suite. Rates include breakfast and spa access. AE, DC, MC, V. Parking 5€ per night. Tram: 47 or 49 from Deák tér. **Amenities:** 2 restaurants; bar; 2 swimming pools (1 indoor and 1 outdoor); spa facilities; tour desk; business center; 24-hr. room service; babysitting, laundry service. *In room:* A/C (some rooms), TV, minibar.

Expensive

Hotel Astra Vendégház ★★ *Finds*   This little gem of a hotel opened in 1996 inside a renovated 300-year-old building on a quiet side street in Buda's lovely Watertown neighborhood. The rooms are large, with wood floors and classic Hungarian-style furniture; the overall effect is a far more homey and pleasant space than that found in most Budapest hotel rooms. Indeed, the hotel is tasteful through and through, and the staff are friendly. Some rooms overlook the inner courtyard, while others face the street.

I. Vám u. 6, 1011 Budapest. ℂ **1/214-1906.** Fax 1/214-1907. hotelastra@euroweb.hu. 12 units. All rooms are double and cost 106€ for 2 people and 90€ for 1. Rates include breakfast. Rates 10% lower in low season. Parking available on street, but the meter is 40 Ft ($1.10) per hour 8am–6pm weekdays. Metro: Batthyány tér/Red line. **Amenities:** Restaurant; bar; car-rental desk; babysitting (on request). *In room:* A/C, TV, minibar.

Hotel Victoria ★★   The Hotel Victoria, located in Buda's lovely Watertown district, is separated from the Danube bank by the busy road that runs alongside the river. The narrow building has only three rooms on each of its nine floors. Two-thirds are corner rooms with large double windows providing great views over the river to Pest. Rooms are quite large, with spacious bathrooms. Middle rooms, though smaller than corner ones, also have windows facing the river. Unfortunately, noise from the busy road beneath your window may disturb your rest.

I. Bem rakpart 11, 1011 Budapest. ℂ **1/457-8080.** Fax 1/457-8088. www.victoria.hu. 27 units. 102€ double; 97€ single. Rates include breakfast. Rates 25% lower in low season. AE, DC, MC, V. Parking in garage 9€. Tram: 19 from Batthyány tér to the 1st stop. **Amenities:** Bar; sauna; limited room service; laundry service. *In room:* A/C, TV, dataport, minibar, hair dryer, safe.

Moderate

Hotel Kulturinnov ★★ *Finds*   This is the guesthouse of the Hungarian Culture Foundation, dedicated to forging ties with ethnic Hungarians in neighboring countries. It's open to the public, but few travelers know about it. The rooms are small and simple; nothing is modern, but everything works and the bathrooms are clean. One chagrined traveler reported a nocturnal battle with certain tiny insects living inside a mattress, but that has not been our experience. The hotel can be a bit hard to find; the entrance is unassuming and practically unmarked. Go through the iron grille door and pass through an exhibition hall, continuing up the grand red-carpeted staircase to the right.

I. Szentháromság tér 6, 1014 Budapest. ℂ **1/355-0122** or 1/375-1651. Fax 1/375-1886. 16 units. 70€ double. Rates almost 50% lower in low season. Rates include breakfast. AE, DC, MC, V. Bus: "Várbusz" from Moszkva tér or 16 from Deák tér. **Amenities:** 2 restaurants; 2 bars. *In room:* Fridge.

Inexpensive

Charles Apartment House ★ *Value*   Owner Károly Szombati has gradually amassed 70 apartments in a group of apartment buildings in a dull but convenient Buda neighborhood (near the Hotel Novotel). All are average Budapest apartments with full kitchens, but the furnishings are comfortable and clean. Hegyalja út is a very busy street, but only a few of the apartments face out onto it; the rest are in the interior of the buildings or on side streets. A nearby park has tennis courts and a track.

I. Hegyalja út 23, 1016 Budapest. ⓒ 1/212-9169. Fax 1/202-2984. www.charleshotel.hu. 70 units. 44€–120€ apt for 1–4 in low season; 48€–136€ in high season. Rates include breakfast. AE, DC, MC, V. Parking 1,700 Ft ($7.65) per day or for free on nearby side streets. Bus: 78 from Keleti pu. to Mészáros utca. **Amenities:** Restaurant; bar; bicycle rental; tour desk; business center; babysitting; laundry service. *In room:* A/C, TV, kitchen, minibar, hair dryer, safe.

IN THE BUDA HILLS
Inexpensive
Gizella Panzió ⓐ   This fine pension in the Buda Hills is a 10-minute walk from the tram station. Built on the side of a hill, it has a lovely view and a series of terraced gardens leading down to the swimming pool. The pension also features a solarium. Guest rooms are all unique but uniformly quaint and sunny. Owner Gizella Varga has good taste. A sightseeing car and driver can be arranged for guests upon request.

XII. Arató u. 42/b, 1121 Budapest. ⓒ/fax 1/249-2281. gazella@axelero.hu. 9 units. 65€ double; 75€ suite. Rates about 20%–25% lower in low season. Rates include breakfast. MC, V. Free parking. Tram: 59 from Moszkva tér to the last stop. **Amenities:** Bar; outdoor pool; exercise room; sauna; laundry service. *In room:* TV, minibar.

WHERE TO DINE
You can get more for your money dining in Budapest than you can anywhere in western Europe. The selection of international eateries is wide, and Hungarian cuisine is adventurous with spices.

Étterem is the most common Hungarian word for restaurant and is used for everything from cafeteria-style eateries to first-class restaurants. A *vendéglő*, or guesthouse, is a smaller, more intimate restaurant, often with a Hungarian folk motif; a *csárda* is a countryside vendéglő. An *étkezde* is an informal lunchroom open only in the daytime. An *önkiszolgáló* is a self-service cafeteria, typically open only for lunch. Stand-up *büfés* are often found in bus stations and near busy transport hubs. A *cukrászda* or *kávéház* is a classic central European coffeehouse, where lingering has developed into an art form. A *borozó* is a wine bar, and a *söröző* is a beer bar; sandwiches are usually available at both. Finally,

---

Tips The Etiquette of Paying & Tipping

In most restaurants, you'll have to initiate the paying and tipping ritual by summoning the waiter. The waiter usually brings the bill, nestled in a small booklet, to your table. Occasionally you'll be asked to confirm what you ordered. If you think your bill is incorrect, don't be embarrassed to call it into question; waiters readily correct bills when challenged. After handing over the bill, in most restaurants, the waiter will disappear. The tip (generally about 10%) should be included in the amount you place in the booklet. In smaller, less formal lunchroom-type places, waiters will often remain at your table after delivering the bill, waiting patiently for payment. In these face-to-face encounters, state the full amount you are paying (bill plus tip) and the waiter will make change. Hungarians never leave tips on the table.

a *kocsma* is a sort of roadside tavern; the Buda Hills are filled with them. Most kocsmas serve full (if greasy) dinners, but their kitchens close very early.

IN THE INNER CITY & CENTRAL PEST
Expensive
Légrádi & Társa Vendéglő ★★ HUNGARIAN   A very small (just nine tables) and inconspicuously marked restaurant on a surprisingly sleepy side street in the southern part of the Inner City, Légrádi & Társa is one of Budapest's most elegant and formal restaurants. The food is served on Herend china, the cutlery is sterling, and an excellent string trio livens the atmosphere with its repertoire of Hungarian classics. If you're on a budget, pass on the initial, pre-menu offer of hors d'oeuvres, which costs 1,800 Ft ($8.10). The cream of asparagus soup is a fine interpretation of a Hungarian favorite. The chicken paprika served with cheese dumplings seasoned with fresh dill will surpass any you've tried elsewhere, and the veal cavalier, smothered in a cauliflower-cheese sauce, is equally sumptuous.

V. Magyar u. 23. ℭ 1/318-6804. Reservations highly recommended. Soup 600 Ft–700 Ft ($2.70–$3.15); main courses 2,000 Ft–6,000 Ft ($9–$27). AE, MC, V. Mon–Fri 6pm–midnight. Metro: Kálvin tér.

Lou Lou ★ FRENCH   Located on a quiet side street not far from Parliament in the financial district, this is a handsome new addition to the Budapest dining scene. The decor is rustic and tasteful, with Roman yellow walls and a vaulted ceiling. They specialize in fresh fish dishes. Lou Lou features an extensive wine list, from 6,000 Ft ($27) and up per bottle. A very good house wine is also available by the carafe.

V. Vigyázó F. u. 4. ℭ 1/312-4505. Reservations recommended. Appetizers 1,400 Ft–2,400 Ft ($6.30–$11); main courses 2,100 Ft–4,500 Ft ($9.45–$20). AE, MC, V. Mon–Fri noon–3pm and 7–11pm; Sat 7pm–midnight. Closed Sun. Metro: Deák tér or Kossuth tér.

Moderate
Marquis de Salade ★★★ RUSSIAN/MIDDLE EASTERN   Vegetarians will feel right at home here. On the edge of Pest's theater district, this recently renovated restaurant employs an eclectic team of eight cooks from five different areas (Russia, Bangladesh, Hungary, Italy, and the Caucasus Mountains), who turn out an amazing assortment of exceptional dishes from a number of cuisines. The offerings are sophisticated yet earthy. Try the lamb with rice (Azerbaijan) or the borscht soup (Russian). A nonsmoking area is available, and tablecloths and tapestries are for sale.

VI. Hajós u. 43. ℭ 1/302-4086. Appetizers 750 Ft–2,500 Ft ($3.40–$11); main courses 1,500 Ft–2,800 Ft ($6.75–$13). V. Daily 11am–midnight. Metro: Arany János u.

Inexpensive
Kádár Étkezde ★★★ *Finds* HUNGARIAN   By 11:45am, Uncle Kádár's, in the heart of the Jewish district, is filled with regulars—from paint-spattered workers to elderly Jewish couples. Uncle Kádár, a neighborhood legend, personally greets them as they file in. From the outside, the only indication of the restaurant is a very small red sign saying KÁDÁR ÉTKEZDE. The place is no more than a lunchroom, but it has a great atmosphere: high ceilings, wood-paneled walls with photos (many autographed) of actors and athletes, and old-fashioned seltzer bottles on every table. The food is simple but hearty, and the service is friendly. Table sharing is the norm.

VII. Klauzál tér 9. ℭ 1/321-3622. Soup 300 Ft ($1.35); main courses 500 Ft–750 Ft ($2.25–$3.40). No credit cards. Tues–Sat 11:30am–3:30pm. Metro: Astoria or Deák tér.

Coffeehouse Culture

Imperial Budapest, like Vienna, was famous for its coffeehouse culture. Literary movements and political circles alike were identified in large part by which coffeehouse they met in. You can still go to several classic coffeehouses, all of which offer delicious pastries, coffee, and more in an atmosphere of splendor. Table sharing is common.

The best are **Gerbeaud's** 🌟🌟🌟, in the Inner City at V. Vörösmarty tér 7 (© **1/429-9000;** Metro: Vörösmarty tér/Yellow line); **Művész Kávéház** 🌟, across the street from the Opera House at VI. Andrássy út 29 (© **1/352-1337;** Metro: Opera); **Central,** at V. Károlyi Mihály u. 9. (© **1/266-2110;** Metro: Ferenciek tere/Blue line); **Ruszwurm Cukrászda** 🌟, in the Castle District at I. Szentháromság u. 7 (© **1/375-5284;** Várbusz [Castle Bus] from Moszva tér); and **Angelika Cukrászda** 🌟🌟, also in Buda, at I. Batthyány tér 7 (© **1/201-4847;** Metro: Batthyány tér).

JUST BEYOND CENTRAL PEST
Very Expensive
Gundel 🌟🌟 *Moments* HUNGARIAN/INTERNATIONAL   Budapest's fanciest and most famous historic restaurant, Gundel was reopened in 1992 by the well-known restaurateur George Lang, owner of New York's Café des Artistes. Located in City Park, Gundel has an opulent dining room and a large, carefully groomed garden. Lamb and wild-game entrees are house specialties. The menu highlights fruits and vegetables in season. In late spring, don't miss out on the asparagus served in hollandaise with grilled salmon. Gundel has an extensive wine list, and the waiters are well versed in its offerings. Homemade fruit ice cream served in the shape of the fruit makes for a delectable dessert, as does the famous Gundel torta, a decadently rich chocolate layer cake.

XIV. Állatkerti út 2. © **1/468-4040.** www.gundel.hu. Reservations highly recommended. Soup 1,000 Ft–1,500 Ft ($4.45–$6.75); main courses 4,000 Ft–7,400 Ft ($18–$33). AE, DC, MC, V. Daily noon–4pm and 7pm–midnight. Metro: Hősök tere.

IN CENTRAL BUDA
Expensive
Kacsa Vendéglő 🌟 HUNGARIAN   Kacsa (meaning "duck") is located on the main street of Watertown, the Buda neighborhood that lies between Castle Hill and the Danube. Here you'll find an intimate, elegant dining atmosphere, though the service seems overly attentive and ceremonious. Enticing main courses include roast duck with Morello cherries and haunch of venison with grapes. The vegetarian plate is the best we've had anywhere in town.

I. Fő u. 75. © **1/201-9992.** Reservations recommended. Soup 600 Ft–900 Ft ($2.70–$4.05); main courses 1,900 Ft–3,600 Ft ($8.55–$16). MC, V. Mon–Fri noon–3pm and 6pm–1am; Sat and Sun 6pm–1am. Metro: Batthyány tér.

Moderate
Le Jardin de Paris 🌟🌟 *Finds* FRENCH   This wonderful little French bistro is in the heart of Buda's Watertown, fittingly located just across the street from the Institut Français. A cozy cellar space, it's decorated with an eclectic collection of

graphic arts. A jazz trio entertains diners from 7 to 11pm daily. The menu contains nouvelle French specialties, and the wine list features French as well as Hungarian vintages. The presentation is impeccable and the waiters aren't overbearing. In summer there's outdoor seating in a garden area.

I. Fő u. 20. 🕿 **1/201-0047.** Reservations recommended. Appetizers 650 Ft–2,800 Ft ($2.90–$13); main courses 1,650 Ft–2,750 Ft ($7.40–$12). AE, DC, MC, V. Daily noon–midnight. Metro: Batthyány tér.

IN THE BUDA HILLS
Moderate

Náncsi Néni Vendéglője 🌟🌟 *Finds* HUNGARIAN   Decorated with photographs of early 1900s Budapest, this popular but remote restaurant is located high in the Buda Hills. There's outdoor garden dining in the summer, with live guitar music at night. The menu features classic Hungarian fare, prepared with great care.

II. Ördögárok út 80. 🕿 **1/397-2742.** Reservations recommended for dinner. Soup 700 Ft–750 Ft ($3.15–$3.40); main courses 1,500 Ft–2,500 Ft ($6.75–$11). MC, V. Daily noon–11pm. Metro: Moszkva tér, then tram 56 to last stop, then bus 63 to Széchenyi utca.

Szép Ilona 🌟🌟 HUNGARIAN   This cheerful, unassuming restaurant serves a mostly local crowd. There's a good selection of specialties: Try the *borjúpaprikás galuskával* (veal paprika) served with *galuska* (a typical central European style of dumpling). There's a small sidewalk garden for summer dining. Szép Ilona is in a pleasant Buda neighborhood; after your meal, take a stroll through the tree-lined streets.

II. Budakeszi út 1–3. 🕿 **1/275-1392.** Soup 300 Ft–720 Ft ($1.35–$3.40); main courses 780 Ft–2,800 Ft ($3.50–$13). MC, V. Daily 11:30am–10pm. Metro: Moszkva tér, then bus 158 (departs from Csaba utca, at the top of the stairs, near the stop from which the Várbusz departs for the Castle District).

IN NORTHERN BUDA & ÓBUDA
Expensive

Kis Buda Gyöngye 🌟🌟🌟 *Finds* HUNGARIAN/INTERNATIONAL   On a quiet side street in a residential Óbuda neighborhood, Kis Buda Gyöngye ("Little Pearl of Buda") is a favorite of Hungarians and visitors alike, serving impeccably prepared Hungarian standards. This cheerful place features an interior garden, which sits in the shade of a wonderful old gnarly tree. Inside, an eccentric violinist entertains diners. Consider the goose plate, an unspeakably rich combination platter including a roast goose leg, goose cracklings, and goose liver.

III. Kenyeres u. 34. 🕿 **1/368-6402** or **1/368-9246.** Reservations highly recommended. Soup 820 Ft–980 Ft ($3.70–$4.40); main courses 1,800 Ft–3,200 Ft ($8.10–$14). AE, DC, MC, V. Mon–Sat noon–midnight. Tram: 17 from Margit híd (Buda side).

SEEING THE SIGHTS

SIGHTSEEING SUGGESTIONS FOR FIRST-TIME VISITORS

If You Have 1 Day Spend a few hours in the morning exploring the **Inner City** and **central Pest.** Stroll along the Danube as far as the neo-Gothic **Parliament,** noting the **Chain Bridge** along the way. In the afternoon, visit the major sites of **Castle Hill** and meander the cobblestone streets of the **Castle District.**

If You Have 2 Days On day 1, head for Buda's **Gellért Hotel** and take a dip in its spa waters. Then hike up the stairs of **Gellért Hill** for an unparalleled panorama. Devote most of day 2 to the **Castle District** and the sites of **Castle Hill** and visit some of the smaller museums. Head back to Pest to see **Heroes' Square** and **City Park,** and in the evening stroll the length of grand **Andrássy út** back to the center of Pest.

If You Have 3 Days or More On day 3, take a boat up the Danube to visit **Szentendre,** a charming riverside town. On days 4 and 5, visit some of the central sites you may have missed, and after lunch cross the Chain Bridge to **Watertown** to explore Buda's historic riverside neighborhood. See **St. Anne's Church,** the **Capuchin Church,** and the **Király Bathrooms.** Check out Pest's indoor **market halls** and visit **Margaret Island.**

THE TOP ATTRACTIONS
In Pest

Néprajzi Múzeum (Ethnographical Museum)   Directly across from Parliament, the vast Ethnographical Museum features an ornate interior equal to that of the Opera House. A ceiling fresco of Justitia, the goddess of justice, by artist Károly Lotz, dominates the lobby. Although a third of the museum's holdings are from outside Hungary, most exhibits concentrate on the items from Hungarian ethnography. The fascinating permanent exhibition, *From Ancient Times to Civilization,* features everything from drinking jugs and razor cases to chairs and clothing.

V. Kossuth tér 12. ℂ **1/473-2440.** Admission 500 Ft ($2.25). Tues–Sun 10am–6pm. Metro: Kossuth tér.

Nemzeti Múzeum (Hungarian National Museum) 😊😊   This enormous neoclassical structure, built from 1837 to 1847, played a major role in the beginning of the Hungarian Revolution of 1848 and 1849. On its wide steps, on March 15, 1848, poet Sándor Petőfi and other young radicals are said to have exhorted the people of Pest to revolt against the Hapsburgs. The two main museum exhibits on view are *The History of the Peoples of Hungary from the Paleolithic Age to the Magyar Conquest* and *The History of the Hungarian People from the Magyar Conquest to 1989. The Hungarian Royal Insignia* is another permanent exhibit.

VIII. Múzeum krt. 14. ℂ **1/338-2122.** Admission 600 Ft ($2.70). Tues–Sun 10am–6pm (to 5pm in winter). Metro: Kálvin tér.

In Buda

Budapesti Történeti Múzeum (Budapest History Museum)   This museum, also known as the Castle Museum, is the best place to get a sense of the once-great medieval Buda. Even though the museum's descriptions are written in English, it's probably worth splurging for a guided tour—the history of the palace's repeated cycles of destruction and reconstruction is so arcane that it's difficult to understand what you're seeing without a guide.

I. In Buda Palace, Wing E, on Castle Hill. ℂ **1/225-7815** or 1/355-8849. Admission 700 Ft ($3.15). Guided tours by qualified staff in English for serious history buffs, 6,000 Ft ($27; open to negotiation), available on advance request. May 15–Sept 15 Wed–Mon 10am–6pm; Sept 16–May 14 Wed–Mon 10am–4pm. Metro: Moszkva tér, then bus "Várbusz"; or Metro stop Deák tér, then bus 16. Funicular: From Clark Ádám tér to Castle Hill.

Nemzeti Galéria (Hungarian National Gallery) 😊   Hungary has produced some fine artists, particularly in the late 19th century, and this is the place to view their work. The giants of the time are the brilliant but moody Mihály Munkácsy; László Paál, a painter of village scenes; Károly Ferenczy, a master of light; and Pál Szinyei Merse, a plein-air artist and contemporary of the early French Impressionists.

I. In Buda Palace, Wings B, C, and D, on Castle Hill. ✆ 1/375-5567. Admission 600 Ft ($2.70). Tues–Sun 10am–6pm. Metro: Moszkva tér, then bus "Várbusz"; or Metro Deák tér, then bus 16. Funicular: From Clark Ádám tér to Castle Hill.

MORE ATTRACTIONS

Vidám Park (Amusement Park) 🎡🎡🎡 *Kids* This is a must if you're traveling with kids, and two rides in particular aren't to be missed (even if you're not traveling with kids). The 100-year-old **Merry-Go-Round (Körhinta),** constructed almost entirely of wood, was recently restored to its original grandeur. The riders must actively pump to keep the horses rocking, and authentic Würlitzer music plays. As the carousel spins round and round, it creaks mightily. The **Ferris wheel (Óriáskerék)** is also wonderful, though it has little in common with rambunctious modern Ferris wheels. A gangly bright-yellow structure, it rotates at a liltingly slow pace, gently lifting you high for a remarkable view. The Vidám Park also features Europe's longest wooden roller coaster.

XIV. Állatkerti krt. 14–16. ✆ 1/363-2660. www.vidampark.hu. Admission 300 Ft ($1.35) adults, 100 Ft (45¢) children; rides 200 Ft–600 Ft (90¢–$2.70). Apr–Sept Mon–Fri 11am–7pm, Sat and Sun 10am–8pm; Oct–Mar Mon–Fri noon–6pm, Sat–Sun 10am–6:30pm. Metro: Széchenyi fürdő.

Historic Buildings

Magyar Állami Operaház (Hungarian State Opera House) 🎭 Completed in 1884, Budapest's Opera House boasts a fantastically ornate interior featuring frescoes by two of the best-known Hungarian artists of the day, Bertalan Székely and Károly Lotz. Home to both the State Opera and the State Ballet, the Opera House has a rich and evocative history.

VI. Andrássy út 22. ✆ 1/331-2550. Admission (by guided tour only) 1,500 Ft ($6.75). Tours daily at 3 and 4pm. Metro: Opera.

Parliament Budapest's great Parliament, an eclectically designed building, mixing the predominant neo-Gothic style with a neo-Renaissance dome, was completed in 1902. Standing proudly on the Danube bank, visible from almost any riverside point, it has from the outset been one of Budapest's symbols, though until 1989 a democratically elected government had convened here only once (just after World War II, before the Communist takeover). The main cupola is decorated with statues of Hungarian kings. On either side of the cupola are waiting rooms leading into the respective houses of Parliament. Here the MPs gather during breaks in the session to smoke and chat. The waiting room on the Senate side (blue carpet) is adorned with statues of farmers, peasants, tradesmen, and workers. The statues that decorate the waiting room on the representatives' side (red carpet) are of sailors, soldiers, postal officials, and so on. The interior decor is predominantly neo-Gothic. The ceiling frescoes are by Károly Lotz, Hungary's best-known artist of that genre. Note the purportedly largest handmade carpet in Europe, from the small Hungarian village of Békésszentandrás. The Parliament is also home to the legendary crown jewels of St. Stephen, which were moved here from the National Museum in 2000, as part of the Hungarian millennium celebration.

V. Kossuth tér. ✆ 1/441-4415. Admission (by guided tour only): 30-min. tour in English, 1,700 Ft ($7.65) adults, 800 Ft ($3.60) students. Tickets available at gate X, enter at gate XII. Tours Mon–Fri 8am–6pm; Sat 4pm; Sun 2pm. Closed when Parliament is in session, usually Tues and Wed. Metro: Kossuth tér.

Terror Háza Opened in 2001, the "Terror House" commemorates the abuse of power in Hungary during the Fascist and Communist regimes, the two major forms of totalitarian dictatorship in the 20th century. It is most appropriately located in the former headquarters of the Hungarian Nazi party (the "Arrow-Cross" party), which briefly ruled Hungary in the chaotic final year of World War II. The building was later the headquarters of the Hungarian Secret Police under the Stalinist regime of Mátyás Rákosi. The museum has attracted controversy since its opening, concerning what some critics consider the disproportionate emphasis on Communist abuses, and a disregard for the Hungarian role in supporting the Nazi genocide. Expect a long line outside the entrance.

VI. Andrássy u. 60. ℂ **1/374-2600.** www.terrorhaza.hu. Admission 3,000 Ft ($14); 1,000 Ft ($4.50) for Hungarian citizens. Wed–Mon 10am–6pm; closed Tues. Metro: Oktogon. Tram: 4 or 6.

Churches & Synagogues

Dohány Synagogue ★★ Built in 1859 and recently restored, this is said to be the largest synagogue in Europe and the second largest in the world. The architecture has striking Moorish and Byzantine elements; the interior is vast and ornate, with two balconies, and the unusual presence of an organ. The synagogue has a rich but tragic history. There's a Jewish museum next door that traces the origins of Hungarian Judaism and features exhibits of ceremonial Judaica throughout the centuries, including Torah covers, scholarly writings, and documents.

VII. Dohány u. 2–8. ℂ **1/342-8949.** Admission 600 Ft ($2.70). Open Tues–Thurs 10am–5pm; Fri 10am–2pm; Sun 10am–2pm. Metro: Astoria or Deák tér.

Bazilica (St. Stephen's Church) The country's largest church, this basilica took more than 50 years to build (the 1868 collapse of the dome caused significant delay) and was finally completed in 1906. Szent István Square, a once-sleepy square in front of the church, was elegantly renovated in the autumn of 2002, converted along with several neighboring streets into a pedestrian-only zone. In the Chapel of the Holy Right (Szent Jobb Kápolna), you can see Hungarian Catholicism's most cherished—and bizarre—holy relic: the preserved right hand of Hungary's first Christian king, Stephen I, whose crown jewels are on display in the Parliament building.

V. Szent István tér 33. ℂ **1/332-0873.** Church, free; treasury, 200 Ft (90¢); tower, 400 Ft ($1.80). Church, daily 7am–7pm, except during services; treasury, daily 9am–5pm (10am–4pm in winter); Szent Jobb Chapel, Mon–Sat 9am–5pm (10am–4pm in winter) and Sun 1–5pm; tower, daily Apr–May 10am–4:30pm, June–Aug 9:30am–6pm, and Sept–Oct 10am–5:30pm. Metro: Arany János utca or Bajcsy-Zsilinszky út.

Mátyás Templom (Matthias Church) ★★★ Officially named the Church of Our Lady, this symbol of Buda's Castle District is popularly known as Matthias Church after the 15th-century king who was twice married here. Though it dates from the mid–13th century, like other old churches in Budapest it has an interesting history of destruction and reconstruction, always being refashioned in the architectural style of the time. Current plans for renovation have been put on hold due to financial constraints.

I. Szentháromság tér 2. ℂ **1/355-5657.** Entrance 400 Ft ($1.80). Daily 9am–6pm (to 5pm in winter). Metro: Moszkva tér, then bus "Várbusz"; or Deák tér, then bus 16. Funicular: From Clark Ádám tér to Castle Hill.

PARKS & PANORAMAS

Gellért Hegy (Gellért Hill), towering 230m (750 ft.) above the Danube, offers the city's single best panorama (bus: 27 from Móricz Zsigmond körtér). It's named after the Italian Bishop Gellért, who assisted Hungary's first Christian king, Stephen I, in converting the Magyars. Gellért became a martyr when vengeful pagans, outraged at the forced and violent nature of Stephen's proselytizing, killed the bishop by rolling him in a barrel down the side of the hill on which his enormous statue now stands. On top of Gellért Hill you'll find the Liberation Monument, built in 1947 to commemorate the Red Army's liberation of Budapest from Nazi occupation. Also atop the hill is the Citadella, built by the Austrians shortly after they crushed the Hungarian War of Independence (1848–49).

Margit-sziget (Margaret Island) ★★★ has been a public park since 1908 (bus: 26 from Nyugati tér; tram: 4 or 6, which stop at the entrance to the island midway across the Margaret Bridge). The long, narrow island, connected to both Buda and Pest by the Margaret and Árpád bridges, is barred to most vehicular traffic. Facilities on the island include the Palatinus Strand open-air baths, which draw upon the famous thermal waters under Margaret Island; the Alfréd Hajós Sport Pool; and the Open Air Theater. Sunbathers line the steep embankments along the river, and bicycles are available for rent. Despite its popularity, Margaret Island is a quiet, tranquil place.

Városliget (City Park) ★ is an equally popular place to spend a summer day (Metro: Hósök tere/Heroes' Square and Széchenyi Fürdó). Heroes' Square, at the end of Andrássy út, is the most logical starting point for a walk in City Park. The lake behind the square is used for boating in summer and ice-skating in winter. The park's Zoo Boulevard (Állatkerti körút), the favorite street of generations of Hungarian children, is where the **zoo,** the **circus,** and the **amusement park** are all found. **Gundel,** Budapest's most famous restaurant, is also here, as are the **Széchenyi Baths.**

Károly kert (Charles Garden) ★★★, a little enclosed park in the southern half of the Inner City (Metro: Astoria/Red line), houses Budapest's most charming playground. To enter the park, you must pass through a gigantic wrought-iron gate. The equipment here might not be as modern or as varied as that of some of the city's other playgrounds, but the place has a distinct old-world charm and its location in the Inner City makes it a convenient destination.

ORGANIZED TOURS

BUS & BOAT TOURS   Ibusz (© 1/485-2700; fax 1/318-2805, V. Ferenczick tere 10), with decades of experience, sets the standard for organized tours in terms of quality and quantity. It offers 11 boat and bus tours, from basic city tours to special folklore-oriented tours. Ibusz tours operate year-round, with an abbreviated schedule off season. Bus tours leave from the Erzsébet tér bus station (Metro: Deák tér) and boat tours from the Vigadó tér landing on the Pest waterfront, between the Erzsébet Bridge and the Chain Bridge (Metro: Vörösmarty tér). There's also a free hotel pickup service 30 minutes before departure.

A boat tour is a great way to get your measure of the scope and scale of the Hungarian capital, and you can see the majority of the city's grand sights from the river. The Hungarian state company **MAHART,** V. Belgrád rakpart (© **1/484-4013** or 1/489-4013), operates daily sightseeing cruises on the Danube. Boats depart frequently from Vigadó tér on weekends and holidays in spring and every day in summer.

WALKING TOURS We recommend "The Absolute Walking Tour in Budapest" offered by a company called **Absolute Walking Tours** ★★ (© 06-30/211-8861; www.absolutetours.com). They have three different walks: the "Absolute Walk," the "Hammer and Sickle Walk," and the "Absolute Dark Side and Pub Crawl." Your best bet is the Absolute Walk, with tickets costing 3,500 Ft ($16); free for children under 12. Show this book (or the company's flyer, found at many tourist haunts, or print your own coupon from their website) and you'll get a 500 Ft ($2.25) discount. Buy your ticket from the guide at the start of the tour. From June to August, tours are daily at 9:30am and 1:30pm; from September to mid-December and from February to May, tours are daily at 10:30am; in January, tours are on weekends only. All three tours, conducted by knowledgeable and personable guides, start from Deák tér (Metro: Deák tér, all lines), in front of the church, or you can join them half an hour later on the front steps of the **Műcsarnok** (Metro: Hősök tere). Tours last anywhere from 3½ to 5 hours, depending on the mood of the group, and take you throughout central Pest and central Buda. You get quite a comprehensive introduction to the city, but be aware that it's practically an entire day on your feet.

THE SHOPPING SCENE

Year-round, shoppers fill the pedestrian-only street **Váci utca,** from the stately Vörösmarty tér, in the center of Pest, across the roaring busy street of Kossuth Lajos utca, all the way to Vámház krt (Yellow line). The **Castle District** in Buda, with many folk-art boutiques and galleries, is another popular area for souvenir hunters. Locals (and budget travelers) might window-shop in these two neighborhoods, but they do their serious shopping elsewhere. One popular street is Pest's **Nagykörút (Outer Ring);** another bustling shopping street is Pest's **Kossuth Lajos utca,** off the Erzsébet Bridge, and its continuation **Rákóczi út,** extending all the way out to Keleti Station.

BEST BUYS   Folkloric Objects   Hungary's famous folkloric objects are the most popular souvenirs among foreign visitors. The state-owned Folkart shops (Népművészeti Háziipar) have a great selection of handmade goods. Popular items include pillowcases, pottery, porcelain, dolls, dresses, skirts, and sheepskin vests. The main store, **Folkart Centrum,** now relocated in the upper end of the mall, is at V. Váci u. 58 (© 1/318-5840), and is open daily from 10am to 7pm. One outstanding private shop on Váci utca is **Vali Folklór,** in the courtyard of V. Váci u. 23 (© 1/337-6301). This cluttered shop is run by a soft-spoken man named Bálint Ács who travels the villages of Hungary and neighboring countries in search of authentic folk items and communist-era badges, pins, and medals.

Holló Folkart Gallery, at V. Vitkovics Mihály u. 12 (© 1/317-8103), is an unusual gallery selling handcrafted reproductions of folk-art pieces from various regions of the country. It is open Monday through Friday from 10am to 6pm and Saturday from 10am to 1pm.

Porcelain & Pottery   Another popular Hungarian item is porcelain, particularly from the country's two best-known producers, Herend and Zsolnay. Although both brands are available in the West, you'll find a better selection here and prices are about 50% lower.

You'll find world-renowned hand-painted Herend porcelain (www.herend. com), which was first produced in 1826 in the town of Herend near Veszprém in western Hungary, at the **Herend Shop,** V. József nádor tér 11 (© 1/317-2622). This shop has the widest Herend selection in the capital, and can arrange overseas shipping if you are dealing with them on the premises. If Herend porcelain isn't within your price range, you'll find lovely pottery at **Herend Village Pottery,** V. Váci u. 23 (© 1/318-3240). Delightfully gaudy Zsolnay porcelain from the southern city of Pécs is Hungary's second-most celebrated brand of porcelain; you'll find it at **Zsolnay Márkabolt,** V. Kígyó u. 4 (© 1/318-3712).

Hungarian Foods   Connoisseurs generally agree that **Pick Salami,** from the southeastern city of Szeged, is the best of the world-renowned Hungarian salamis, and it's easy to carry home without giving your clothes an unforgettable aroma. Chestnut paste *(gesztenye püré)*, found in a tin or block wrapped in foil, is rare abroad and used primarily as a pastry filling, but it can also top desserts and ice cream. Paprika paste *(pirosarany)* is also hard to find outside Hungary; it comes in a bright-red tube in hot *(csípős)*, deli-style *(csemege)*, and sweet *(édes)* varieties. All these can be found in grocery stores *(élelmiszer)* and delicatessens *(csemege)*.

Hungarian Wines   Fine, affordable Hungarian wines from the Szekszárd, Villány, Tokaj, and Eger regions are abundant. The most renowned red wines come from the region around Villány, a town to the south of Pécs by the Croatian border. As a result of the aggressive marketing strategy of the former Communist regime, many foreigners are familiar with the red wines from Eger, especially *Egri Bikavér* (Eger Bull's Blood). Eger wines, though rich and fruity, are markedly inferior to Villányi reds. The country's best white wines are generally believed to be those from the Lake Balaton region, though some Hungarians insist that white wines from the Sopron region (by the Austrian border) are better. *Tokaj* wines, especially *Szamorodni* and *Aszu*—both *száraz* (dry) or *édes* (sweet)—are popular as aperitifs and dessert wines.

MARKETS   Budapest has a handful of **vásárcsarnok (vintage market halls),** wonders of steel and glass, built in the 1890s in the ambitious grandiose style of the time. Three are still in use and provide a measure of local color you won't find in the grocery store. The **Központi Vásárcsarnok (Central Market Hall),** on IX. Vámház körút, is the largest and most spectacular market hall. In the Inner Ring (Kiskörút), on the Pest side of the Szabadság Bridge, this tri-level hall was impeccably reconstructed in 1995. Other vintage market halls include the **Belvárosi Vásárcsarnok (Inner City Market Hall),** on V. Hold utca, behind Szabadság tér in central Pest; and the **Józsefváros Vásárcsarnok,** on VIII. Rákóczi tér. Other active and lively markets are found in unspectacular buildings, such as the **Fehérvári úti Vásárcsarnok,** on XI. Fehérvári út, in front of the Buda Skála department store, just a block from the Móricz Zsigmond körtér transportation hub; and the **Fény utca Piac,** on II. Fény utca, just off Moszkva tér in Buda.

BUDAPEST AFTER DARK

The most complete schedule of mainstream performing arts events is found in the free bimonthly *Koncert Kalendárium* at the Central Philharmonic Ticket Office in Vörösmarty tér. *Koncert Kalendárium* lists events in English. The *Budapest Sun* is a good source, as are the new magazine *Look* and the *Budapest Week* website (www.budapestweek.com).

Színházak Központi Jegyiroda **(Central Theater Ticket Office),** VI. Andrássy út 18 (✆ 1/267-1267; Metro: Opera), sells tickets to just about everything, from theater and operetta to sports events and rock concerts; it's open Monday through Friday from 10am to 6pm. For **classical performances,** go to the National Philharmonic Ticket Office (Filharmónia Nemzeti Jegyiroda), V. Vörösmarty tér 1 (✆ 1/318-0281; Metro: Vörösmarty tér). For **opera and ballet,** go to the Hungarian State Opera Ticket Office (Magyar Állami Opera Jegyiroda), VI. Andrássy út 20 (entrance inside the courtyard; ✆ 1/353-0170; Metro: Opera). For events during the **Spring Festival,** go to the Festival Ticket Service, V. 1081 Rákóczi út 65 (✆ 1/486-3300; Metro: Blaha Lujza tér/Red line). For **rock and jazz concert** tickets, try Ticket Express, VI. Jókai u. 40 (✆ 1/353-0692; Metro: Opera/Yellow line).

Moments   **Music for a Summer Evening**

During the warm, lazy days of summer, you'll find several special venues for classical music. Tickets for these concerts are available at the **National Philharmonic Ticket** Office, V. Vörösmarty tér 1 (© **1/318-0281;** Metro: Vörösmarty tér).

The historic outdoor Dominican Courtyard, inside the Castle District's Hilton Hotel, I. Hess András tér 1–3 (© **1/488-6600;** Metro: Moszkva tér, then bus "Várbusz"; or Deák tér, then bus 16), is the site of a series of classical recitals during the summer. The district's beautiful **Mátyás Templom (Matthias Church),** next door at I. Szentháromság tér 2, holds a regular Tuesday- and Friday-night series of organ concerts from June to September. Concerts start at 7:30pm. Tickets can be purchased before the performance at the church entry.

Organ concerts are also held Monday evenings at 7pm during July and August at **Bazilica (St. Stephen's Church),** Hungary's largest church, V. Szent István tér 33 (© 1/317-2859; Metro: Arany János utca or Bajcsy-Zsilinszky út). You can buy tickets at the church entry before the performance.

The **Dohány Synagogue,** VII. Dohány u. 2–8 (© 1/342-8949; Metro: Astoria or Deák tér), is the venue for occasional concerts from May to September. Concerts begin at 7pm, but days are not regular. For information and tickets, call the **Central Theater Ticket Office** (© **1/267-1267;** Metro: Opera).

THE PERFORMING ARTS

Completed in 1884, the **Magyar Állami Operaház (Hungarian State Opera House),** VI. Andrássy út 22 (© **1/331-2550;** Metro: Opera), is Budapest's most famous performance hall and a tourist attraction in its own right. Hungarians adore opera, and a large percentage of seats are sold on a subscription basis; buy your tickets a few days ahead, if possible. The box office is open Monday through Friday from 11am to 6pm. Ticket prices range from 2,900 Ft to 9,800 Ft ($13–$44).

The Nagyterem (Great Hall) of the **Zeneakadémia (Ferenc Liszt Academy of Music),** VI. Liszt Ferenc tér 8 (© **1/341-4788, ext. 179;** Metro: Oktogon), is the city's premier music hall. The academy was built in the Art Nouveau style of the early 20th century with the best acoustics in the city. Box-office hours are from 2pm to showtime on the day of performance. Tickets range from 1,000 Ft to 6,000 Ft ($4.50–$27).

LIVE-MUSIC CLUBS

The club scene has found fertile ground since 1989's political changes—so much so, in fact, that clubs come in and out of fashion overnight. Check the *Budapest Sun* for up-to-the-minute club listings.

Fat Mo's Music Club is *the* place to be, at V. Nyári Pál u. 11 (© **1/267-3199;** Metro: Kálvin tér/Blue line).There is no cover. This spot is always crowded. Live jazz band concerts start at 9pm and dancing starts at 11pm. The best night is definitely Sunday, with Hot Jazz Band performing in the style of the 1920s and

'30s. Make sure you book a table if you wish to enjoy the superb food. The club offers the best succulent steaks in town.

TRAFO, XI. Liliom u. 41 (℃ **1/215-1600;** tram: 4 or 6 to Üllöi út), is an old electric power station that was recently renovated and transformed into a cultural center for young alternative artists. It also hosts the hippest disco in town. The hottest nights are Wednesday and Sunday with DJ Palotai, with the party starting at 10pm, but you can have a great time on Friday dancing to the 1960s and '70s greatest hits.

The **Fél 10 Jazz Klub,** VIII. Baross u. 30 (no phone; Metro: Kálvin tér), is a classy multilevel club. The place features live jazz performances nightly, while techno-free dance parties get going in the wee hours from Thursday to Saturday. It's open Monday through Friday from noon to 4am and Saturday and Sunday from 7pm to 4am. **Old Man's,** VIII. Akácfa u. 13 (℃ **1/322-7645;** Metro: Blaha Luzja tér), is the place to take in the best jazz and blues in Hungary. Hobo, the legendary figure of Hungarian beat music since the late 1960s, regularly plays here with his blues band. This very hip spot is open daily from 3pm to 3am.

BARS

The **Irish Cat Pub,** V. Múzeum krt. 41 (℃ **1/266-4085;** Metro: Kálvin tér), is an Irish-style pub with Guinness on tap and a whiskey bar. It's a popular meeting place for expatriates and travelers, serving a full menu, and is open Monday through Saturday from 10am to 2 am and Sunday from 5pm to 2am. **Morrison's Music Pub,** VI. Révay u. 25 (℃ **1/269-4060;** Metro: Opera), is a casual place packed by an almost-20-something crowd. There's a small dance floor, an eclectic variety of loud live music, and a number of beers on tap. It's open Wednesday through Saturday from 11am to 4am, Sunday from 5pm to 2am.

HUNGARIAN DANCE HOUSES

Recent years have seen the growth of an urban-centered folk revival movement known as the *tánchéz* (dance house). This interactive evening of **folk music** and **folk dancing,** held in community centers around town, is one of the best cultural experiences you can have in Hungary. The format usually consists of about an hour of dance-step instruction, followed by several hours of dancing accompanied by a live band, which might include some of Hungary's best folk musicians, in an authentic, casual atmosphere.

The leading Hungarian folk band Muzsikás hosts a tánchéz for children every Tuesday (except July and Aug) from 5:30 to 6:30pm for 180 Ft (80¢) at **Szakszervezetek Fővárosi Művelődési Háza (FMH Cultural House),** XI. Fehérvári út 47 (℃ **1/203-3868;** Metro: Deák tér, then tram 47). If you are a folk music or folk dance enthusiast, this is an event not to be missed. The **FMH Cultural House** also hosts Thursday-evening folk *csángó tánchéz* nights (but only Sept–May). Admission is 400 Ft ($1.80). The music is all on traditional instruments, and the dance is an authentic type of traditional Hungarian folk dance. The evening kicks off with a tánchéz hour for kids, at 5pm. Klezmer bands play on the first Saturday of the month, from 6:30 to 11pm, for 400 Ft ($1.80). You can also find some dance house activity at **Marczibányi tér Művelődésiház (Marczibányi Square Cultural House),** II. Marczibányi tér 5/a (℃ **1/212-0803;** Metro: Moszkva tér). Wednesday is dance house night, at 8pm for 500 Ft ($2.25). The bands vary.

DAY TRIPS ALONG THE DANUBE BEND

The delightful towns along the Bend—Szentendre, Esztergom, and Visegrád—are easy day trips from Budapest. The great natural beauty of the area, with forested hills looming over the river, makes it a welcome departure for the city weary.

GETTING THERE   By Boat & Hydrofoil   From April to September, **boats** run between Budapest and the towns of the Danube Bend. All boats leave Budapest's Vigadó tér boat landing, stopping to pick up passengers 5 minutes later at Buda's Batthyány tér landing, before continuing up the river.

Schedules and towns served are complicated, so contact **MAHART,** the state shipping company, at the Vigadó tér landing (© 1/318-1704) for information. Round-trip prices are 1,330 Ft ($6) to Szentendre, 1,390 Ft ($6.25) to Visegrád, and 1,460 Ft ($6.60) to Esztergom. Children ages 4 to 14 receive a 50% discount. Travel time is 2 hours to Szentendre, 3½ hours to Visegrád, and 5 hours to Esztergom.

By Train   To Szentendre: The HÉV suburban railroad connects Budapest's Batthyány tér with Szentendre. Trains leave daily, year-round, every 20 minutes or so from 4am to 11:30pm (trip time: 45 min.). The one-way fare is 320 Ft ($1.45); subtract 105 Ft (50¢) if you have a valid Budapest public transportation pass.

To Visegrád: There's no direct train service to Visegrád. Instead, take one of 20 daily trains departing from Nyugati Station for Nagymaros (trip time: 1 hr.). From Nagymaros, take a ferry across the river to Visegrád. The ferry dock (RÉV; © 06-80/406-611) is a 5-minute walk from the train station. A ferry leaves every hour throughout the day. The train ticket to Nagymaros costs 408 Ft ($1.85); the ferryboat ticket to Visegrád costs 200 Ft (90¢).

To Esztergom: Seventeen trains daily make the run between Budapest's Nyugati Station and Esztergom (trip time: 1¼ hr.). Train tickets cost 388 Ft ($1.75).

SZENTENDRE   Peopled in medieval times by Serbian settlers, Szentendre (pronounced *Sen*-ten-dreh), 21km (13 miles) north of Budapest, counts half a dozen Serbian churches among its rich collection of historical buildings. Since the turn of the century, Szentendre has been home to an artist's colony and has a wealth of museums and galleries. The town is an extremely popular tourist destination.

Visitor Information   The information office **Tourinform** is at Dumtsa Jenő u. 22 (© **26/317-965**); it offers maps of Szentendre (and the Danube Bend region), as well as concert and exhibition schedules. The office can also provide accommodations information. It's open April through October daily from 9:30am to 4:30pm; in the off season it's open Monday through Friday from 9:30am to 4:30pm. If you arrive by train, you'll come upon this office as you follow the flow of pedestrian traffic into town on Kossuth Lajos utca. If you arrive by boat, you may find the **Ibusz** office sooner, at the corner of Bogdányi út and Gőzhajó utca (© **26/310-181**). It's open April through October, Monday through Friday from 9am to 5pm and weekends from 10am to 2pm; November through March, weekdays only, 9am to 4pm. The Ibusz office provides decent information, but we recommend heading to the Tourinform office.

Exploring the Museums & Churches   The **Margit Kovács Museum** 𝒜𝒜𝒜, Vastagh György u. 1 (© **26/310-244**), is a must-see, displaying the exceptional and highly original work of Hungary's best-known ceramic artist. Her sculptures of elderly women and friezes of village life are particularly moving. The museum is open April through October Tuesday through Sunday from 9am to 5pm (Nov–Mar to 4pm). Admission is 400 Ft ($1.80). The **Blagovestenska church** at Fő tér 4 dates from 1752. A rococo iconostasis features paintings by Mihailo Zivkovic—notice that the eyes of all the icons are on you; the effect is extraordinary. Next door at Fő tér 6 (© **26/310-244**) is the **Ferenczy Museum** 𝒜𝒜, dedicated to the art of the prodigious Ferenczy family. The paintings of Károly Ferenczy, one of Hungary's leading Impressionists, are featured. It's open April through October Wednesday through Sunday from 10am to 5pm; November through March Friday through Sunday from 10am to 4pm. Admission is 300 Ft ($1.35).

The **Ámos and Anna Muzeum,** Bogdány u. 10 (© **26/310-790**), was the former home of artist couple Imre Ámos and Margit Anna, whose work represents the beginning of expressionist painting in Hungary. Opened after Anna's death in 1991, the collection is Szentendre's best-kept secret. It's open Monday through Sunday from 10am to 6pm (in winter 1–5pm), and admission is 300 Ft ($1.35).

Where to Dine   If you get hungry, **Aranysárkány Vendéglő (Golden Dragon Inn)** 𝒜, Alkotmány u. 1/a (© **26/301-479**), just east of Fő tér on Hunyadi utca, is always crowded, often with locals (a definitely good sign in a tourist town like Szentendre). Choose from such enticing offerings as alpine lamb, roast leg of goose, spinach cream, and venison ragout. A very tasty vegetarian plate is also offered. Various traditional Hungarian beers are on draft.

If you walk directly south from Fő tér, you'll find **Régimódi,** Futó u. 3 (© **26/ 311-105**). This elegant restaurant is in a former private home and serves Hungarian specialties, with an emphasis on game dishes. The wild-boar stew in red wine is particularly sumptuous. Be sure to stop at the **Dobos Museum & Café** ⟨★⟩, Bogdányi u. 2, for a slice of authentic *dobos torta,* a sumptuously rich layer cake named after pastry chef József Dobos, who experimented with butter frostings in the 19th century, and was appointed the Hapsburg emperor's official baker because of his success.

VISEGRÁD   Halfway between Szentendre and Esztergom, Visegrád (pronounced *Vee*-sheh-grod) is a sparsely populated, sleepy riverside village, which makes its history all the more fascinating and hard to believe. The Romans built a fort here, which was still extant when Slovak settlers gave the town its present name (meaning "High Castle") in the 9th or 10th century. After the Mongol invasion (1241–42), construction began on both the present ruined hilltop citadel and the former riverside palace. Eventually, Visegrád could boast one of the finest royal palaces ever built in Hungary. Only one king, Charles Robert (1307–42), actually used it as his primary residence, but monarchs from Béla IV, in the 13th century, through Matthias Corvinus, in the late 15th century, spent time in Visegrád and contributed to its development, the latter expanding the palace into a great Renaissance center known throughout Europe.

Visitor Information   **Visegrád Tours,** RÉV u. 15 (© **26/398-160**), is located across the road from the RÉV ferryboat landing (not to be confused with the MAHART boat landing, just down the road). It is open April through October, daily from 9am to 6pm; November through March, weekdays from 10am to 4pm.

Each summer on the second weekend in July, Visegrád hosts the **International Palace Tournament,** an authentic medieval festival replete with dueling knights on horseback, early music, and dance. If you cannot make it to this fabulous event, you can enjoy a tournament on a smaller scale combined with a medieval dinner at 6pm on Thursday in July and August, at the Renaissance Restaurant (see listing below). For more information, contact Visegrád Tours (see above).

Exploring the Palace & the Citadel   The **Royal Palace** covered much of the area where the MAHART boat landing and Fő utca (Main St.) are now found. Indeed, the entrance to its open-air ruins, called the **King Matthias Museum** ⟨★★⟩, is at Fő u. 27 (© **26/398-026**). Admission is 400 Ft ($1.80). The museum is open Tuesday through Sunday from 9am to 4:30pm. The buried ruins of the palace, having achieved a near-mythical status, were not discovered until this century. Almost all of what you see is the result of ongoing reconstruction, which has been rigorous in recent years. Because of the under-construction aspect of the place, you need to keep a close eye on the kids here.

The **Citadel** ⟨★★★⟩ (© **26/398-101**) on the hilltop above Visegrád affords one of the finest views you'll find over the Danube. Admission to the Citadel is 400 Ft ($1.80). It is open daily from 9am to 6pm. There are three buses a day to the Citadel, departing from the RÉV ferryboat terminal at 9:26am, 12:26pm, and 3:26pm. Otherwise, "City Bus," a van taxi that awaits passengers outside Visegrád Tours, takes people up the steep hill for the steep fare of 2,000 Ft ($9) apiece. Note that it is not a casual walk to the Citadel; consider it a day hike and pack accordingly.

Where to Dine   **Renaissance Restaurant,** at Fő u. 11, across the street from the MAHART boat landing (© **26/398-081**), specializes in authentic medieval cuisine. Food is served in clay crockery without silverware (only a wooden spoon) and guests are offered paper crowns to wear. The menu meal is 4,000 Ft ($18), but it's available for groups only. The restaurant is open daily from noon to 10pm. If you're big on the medieval theme, come for dinner on a Thursday (July–Aug), when a six-course "Royal Feast" is celebrated following a 45-minute duel between knights. No vegetarians, please! Tickets for this special evening are handled by Visegrád Tours (see above). The duel gets underway at 6pm sharp.

Don Vito Pizzeria *✦*, Fő u. 83 (© **26/397-230**), serves very good pizza in a pleasant, relaxed atmosphere. This is a good option if you're traveling with kids. Individual pan-size pizzas cost 550 Ft to 880 Ft ($2.50–$3.95). Try the "Don Vito," a delicious mushroom, goose liver, and apple pizza; or the equally tempting "Albino," a vegetarian pizza with a ricotta, garlic, and herb topping. A wide range of 14 different types of bottled beer and a more modest list of wine are also offered.

ESZTERGOM   Formerly a Roman settlement, Esztergom (pronounced *Ess*-tair-gome), 46km (29 miles) northwest of Budapest, was the seat of the Hungarian kingdom for 300 years. Hungary's first king, István I (Stephen I), crowned by the pope in A.D. 1000, converted Hungary to Catholicism, and Esztergom became the country's center of the early church. Although its glory days are long gone, the quiet town remains the seat of the archbishop-primate—the "Hungarian Rome."

Visitor Information   **Gran Tours,** Széchenyi tér 25 (© **33/502-001**), is the best source of information. Summer hours are Monday through Friday from 8am to 4pm and Saturday from 9am to noon; winter hours are Monday through Friday from 8am to 4pm.

Exploring the Town   The massive, neoclassical **Esztergom Cathedral** (© **33/411-895**), in Szent István tér on Castle Hill, is Esztergom's most popular attraction and one of Hungary's most impressive buildings. It was built in the last century to replace the cathedral ruined during the Turkish occupation. The cathedral **Kincstár (Treasury)** *✦* contains a stunning array of ecclesiastical jewels and gold works. Since Cardinal Mindszenty's body was moved to the crypt in 1991 (he died in exile in 1975), it has been a place of pilgrimage for Hungarians. If you brave the ascent of the cupola, you'll be rewarded at the top with unparalleled views of Esztergom and the surrounding Hungarian and Slovak countryside. The cathedral is open daily, summer from 8am to 6pm, winter from 9am to 4pm. The treasury, crypt, and cupola are also open daily, summer from 9am to 5pm, winter from 11am to 4pm. Admission to the cathedral and the crypt are free, but it costs 300 Ft ($1.35) to see the treasury and 200 Ft (90¢) to see the cupola.

It's definitely worthwhile to take a break from the crowds at the cathedral and stroll through the quiet cobblestone streets of **Víziváros (Watertown).** There you'll find the **Keresztény Múzeum (Christian Museum),** Mindszenty tér 2 (© **33/413-880**), in the neoclassical former archbishop-primate's palace. It houses Hungary's largest collection of religious art and the largest collection of medieval art outside the National Gallery. Hours are Tuesday through Sunday from 10am to 6pm, and admission is 300 Ft ($1.35).

Where to Dine   The food at **Szalma Csárda** *✦✦✦*, Nagy-Duna sétány 2 (© **33/315-336**), is absolutely first-rate, with everything made to order and served piping hot. The excellent house soups—fish soup *(halászlé),* goulash *(gulyásleves),* and bean soup *(babgulyás)*—constitute meals in themselves. It's open daily from noon to 10pm and doesn't accept credit cards.

10

Ireland

by Suzanne Rowan Kelleher

If you haven't been to Ireland in a decade or so, then you haven't been to Ireland. The scale and pace of change here since the mid-1990s has been dizzying. Once the donkey cart of the European Union, Ireland is now a pacesetter—a young, turbulent, venturesome nation that's slow to look back and quick to outreach itself. If you look for it, old Ireland lingers and, to be sure, the country remains a land of breathtaking beauty, whose people possess more than their share of wit and welcoming charm. What's new is that today's Ireland is the product of the economic boom known as the "Celtic Tiger," a renaissance that has made the country richer, more self-confident, and more sophisticated than before. Though the pace of that boom has slowed of late, Ireland remains one of the most prosperous and savvy spots in Europe. Regardless of whether you're looking for the old or new Ireland, you'll be joining six million annual visitors, many of whom come a long way to see it for themselves.

1 Dublin

"Seedy elegance" may have aptly described much, if not most, of Dublin until the mid-1990s, when the city's transformation from endearingly frumpy to cutting-edge cool began. The change was remarkably swift: In 1997 *Fortune* magazine named Dublin the number-one European city in which to do business—an accolade fueled, no doubt, by its reputation as the "Silicon Valley" of Europe and strategic Euro-headquarters for computer giants like Microsoft, Dell, Intel, and Sun Microsystems. Then, in 1998, Dublin became the fifth-most-visited city in Europe—nudging ahead of traditional tourist powerhouses like Rome and Amsterdam. More recently, in 2000 an annual survey of world cities ranked Dublin among the world's top-10 most livable cities—above New York, Boston, and Washington, D.C.

Dublin, indeed, is a great place to visit. The River Liffey may never be potable, but otherwise the sky seems to be the limit here. New hotels continue to sprout up in the race to keep up with tourist demand. Dublin is "ground zero" for the new Ireland, the lair of the "Celtic Tiger," and uncontestably the hottest spot on the island.

ESSENTIALS
GETTING THERE By Plane Dublin International Airport (© 01/814-1111; www.dublin-airport.com) is 11km (7 miles) north of the city center. A travel information desk located in the Arrivals Concourse provides information on public bus and rail services throughout the country.

An excellent airport-to-city bus service called **AirCoach** operates 24 hours a day, making runs at 15-minute intervals. AirCoach runs direct from the airport to Dublin's city center and south side, servicing O'Connell Street, St. Stephen's

Green, Fitzwilliam Square, Merrion Square, Ballsbridge, and Donnybrook—that is, all the key hotel and business districts. The one-way fare is €5 (round-trip costs €10); you buy your ticket from the driver. AirCoach is more expensive than the Dublin Bus (see below), but it is faster because it makes fewer intermediary stops and brings you right into the hotel districts. To confirm AirCoach departures and arrivals, call © **01/844-7118** or find it on the Web at **www. aircoach.ie.**

If you need to connect with the Irish bus or rail service, the **Airlink Express Coach** (© **01/873-4222;** www.dublinbus.ie) provides express coach service from the airport to the city's central bus station, **Busaras,** on Store Street, and on to the two main rail stations, **Connolly** and **Heuston.** Service runs daily from 7am until 11pm (till 8:30pm Sun), with departures every 20 to 30 minutes. The one-way fare is €5 for adults and €2 for children under age 12.

Finally, the main **Dublin Bus** (© **01/873-4222;** www.dublinbus.ie) service runs several routes between the airport and the city center from 6am to 11:30pm. The one-way trip takes about 30 minutes, and the fare is €2. The 16, 16A, 33A, 41, 41A, 41B, 41C all serve the city center from Dublin Airport.

For speed and ease—especially if you have a lot of luggage—a **taxi** is the best way to get directly to your hotel or guesthouse. Depending on your destination in Dublin, fares average between €15 and €20. Depending on traffic, a cab should take from 20 to 45 minutes to get into the city center. A 10% tip is standard. Taxis are lined up on a first-come, first-served taxi stand outside the arrivals terminal.

By Ferry Passenger/car ferries from Britain arrive at the **Dublin Ferryport** (© **01/855-2222**), on the eastern end of the North Docks; and at the **Dun Laoghaire Ferryport** (© **01/661-0511**), about 16km (10 miles) south of the city center. Call **Irish Ferries** (© **01/661-0511;** www.irishferries.ie) for bookings and information. There are bus and taxi services from both ports.

By Train Irish Rail (© **01/836-6222;** www.irishrail.ie) operates daily train service into Dublin from Belfast in Northern Ireland and all major cities in the Irish Republic, including Cork, Galway, Limerick, Killarney, Sligo, Wexford, and Waterford. Trains from the south, west, and southwest arrive at **Heuston Station,** Kingsbridge, off St. John's Road; from the north and northwest at **Connolly Station,** Amiens Street; and from the southeast at **Pearse Station,** Westland Row, Tara Street.

By Bus Bus Eireann (© **01/836-6111;** www.buseireann.ie) operates daily express coach and local bus services from all major cities and towns in Ireland into Dublin's central bus station, Busaras, on Store Street.

By Car If you are arriving by car from other parts of Ireland or via car ferry from Britain, all main roads lead into the heart of Dublin and are well signposted to An Lar (City Centre). To bypass the city center, the East Link (toll bridge €1.30) and West Link are signposted, and the M50 circuits the city on three sides.

VISITOR INFORMATION Tourist Offices Dublin Tourism (© **01/ 605-7700;** www.visitdublin.com) operates six year-round walk-in visitor centers in greater Dublin. The principal center is in the former Church of St. Andrew, on Suffolk Street, Dublin 2, open June through August Monday through Saturday from 8:30am to 6:30pm, Sunday and bank holidays from 10:30am to 3pm, and the rest of the year Monday through Saturday from 9am to 5:30pm. For accommodation reservations throughout Ireland by credit card, contact Dublin Tourism; for other information call **Bord Failte** (℘ **1850/230330** from within Ireland; www.travel.ireland.ie). Other services at the Suffolk Street Dublin Tourism office include a currency-exchange counter, an American Express services desk, a car-rental counter, bus and rail information desks, a gift shop, and a cafe. The other five Dublin Tourism centers are at the Arrivals Hall of **Dublin Airport;** Exclusively Irish, **O'Connell Street,** Dublin 1; **Baggot Street Bridge,** Baggot Street, Dublin 2; **The Square Towncentre,** Tallaght, Dublin 24; and the new ferry terminal, **Dun Laoghaire Harbor** (all telephone inquiries should be directed to the number listed above). All centers are open year-round with at least the following hours: Monday through Friday from 10am to 5pm.

In addition, an independent center offers details on concerts, exhibits, and other arts events in the **Temple Bar** section at 18 Eustace St., Temple Bar, Dublin 2 (℘ **01/677-2255;** www.temple-bar.ie), open year-round Monday through Friday from 9:30am to 5:30pm, and Saturday from 10am to 5pm.

At any of these centers you can pick up the free *Tourism News* or the free *Event Guide,* a biweekly entertainment guide (www.eventguide.ie). *In Dublin,* a biweekly arts-and-entertainment magazine selling for €3.70, is available at most newsstands.

Websites Your first stop should be **Dublin Tourism's www.visitdublin.com**. To tap into a nearly overwhelming breadth of listings, try **www.goireland.com,**

Dublin

To Airport ↗

CONNOLLY

Central Bus Station

Customs House

TARA ST.

PEARSE ST.

Four Courts

Dublin Castle

Trinity College

Leinster House

St. Stephen's Green

Merrion Square

Fitz-william Square

ATTRACTIONS ●

The Book of Kells **13**	Dublinia **27**	Kilmainham Gaol Historical
The Ceol—The Irish	GAA Museum **7**	Museum **1**
Traditional Music Centre **4**	Guinness Storehouse **6**	National Gallery **15**
Christ Church Cathedral **28**	Hugh Lane Municipal	National Museum **16**
Collins Barracks **3**	Gallery of Modern Art **9**	National History Museum **18**
Dublin Castle **25**	Irish Film Centre **31**	Old Jameson Distillery **5**
Dublin Writers Museum **8**	Irish Museum of Modern Art **2**	St. Patrick's Cathedral **24**
	James Joyce Centre **10**	Waterways Visitor Centre **14**

which offers more than 11,000 lodging listings (many with pictures) and thousands of restaurants (some with menus), although in some cases the info is pretty thin. Use the well-designed **www.ireland.travel.ie** for tips on getting around, places to stay, and things to do. Visit **www.shamrock.org** to learn about package vacations and find some special deals, such as off-peak fares on Aer Lingus.

CITY LAYOUT   Compared with other European capitals, Dublin is a relatively small metropolis; it's easy to get to know and easily traversed. The city center—identified in Irish as AN LAR—is bisected by the River Liffey flowing west to east into Dublin Bay, with 15 bridges linking the north and south banks. Canals ring the city center; the Royal Canal forms a skirt through the north half, and the Grand Canal the south half. True Dubliners, it is said, live between the two canals. Northside suburbs include Drumcondra, Glasnevin, Howth, Clontarf, and Malahide. Southside suburbs include Ballsbridge, Blackrock, Dun Laoghaire, Dalkey, Killiney, Rathgar, and Rathmines.

GETTING AROUND   By Bus   Dublin Bus operates a fleet of green double-decker buses, frequent single-deck buses, and minibuses (called "imps") throughout the city and its suburbs. Most buses originate on or near **O'Connell Street, Abbey Street,** or **Eden Quay** on the north side, and from **Aston Quay, College Street,** or **Fleet Street** on the south side. Destinations and bus numbers are posted above the front windows; buses destined for the city center are marked with the Irish Gaelic words AN LAR.

Bus service runs daily throughout the city, starting around 6am (10am on Sun), with the last bus at 11:30pm on most routes; on Thursday, Friday, and Saturday nights, the NiteLink service from city center to the suburbs extends bus hours to 3am. Schedules are posted on revolving notice boards at each bus stop. City bus fares are calculated on the distances traveled and run from a base fare of €.80 to €1.70. The NiteLink fare is a flat €4. Tickets should be purchased from a ticket machine as you enter the bus; exact change is welcomed but not required on most buses, but only coins are accepted. One-day, 4-day, and weekly passes are available at reduced rates. For more information, contact **Dublin Bus,** 59 Upper O'Connell St. (✆ **01/872-1000;** www.dublinbus.ie).

By DART   Although Dublin has no subway in the strict sense, there is an electrified-train rapid-transit system, known as the **DART (Dublin Area Rapid Transit),** Pearse Station, Dublin 2 (✆ **01/836-6222;** www.irishrail.ie). It links the city-center stations at **Connolly Station, Tara Street, Pearse Street,** and **Amiens Street** with suburbs and seaside communities as far as Balbriggan to the north and Greystones to the south. Service operates roughly every 10 to 20 minutes Monday through Saturday from 7am to midnight and Sunday from 9:30am to 11pm. The minimum fare is €1.20. One-day, 4-day, and weekly passes, as well as family tickets, are available at reduced rates.

By Tram   The newest addition to Dublin's public transportation network is the sleek light-rail tram known as **LUAS,** due for completion at the end of 2003 and the answer, many hope, to Dublin's congestion problems. Traveling at a maximum speed of 70 kilometers per hour (45 mph) and departing every 5 minutes in peak hours, LUAS brings the city's transportation into the 21st century. Three lines will link the city center at **Connolly Station** and **St. Stephen's Green** with the suburbs of Tallaght in the southwest and Dundrum and Sandyford to the south. Fares were not yet set at press time. For more information, contact **LUAS** (✆ **01/703-2029;** www.luas.ie).

By Taxi   It's very difficult to hail a taxi on the street; instead, taxis line up at ranks located outside all the leading hotels, at bus and train stations, and on prime thoroughfares such as Upper O'Connell Street, College Green, and the north side of St. Stephen's Green. You can also phone for a taxi. Some of the companies that operate a 24-hour radio-call service are **Co-Op** (© **01/676-6666), Shamrock Radio Cabs** (© **01/855-5444), and VIP Taxis** (© **01/478-3333).** (If you need a wake-up call, VIP even offers that service, along with especially courteous dependability.) Taxi rates are fixed by law and posted in each taxi. The minimum fare in central Dublin is €2.75 for the first .9km (½ mile); after that, it's €.15 for each additional .2km (⅑ mile). There's an additional charge for each extra passenger and for each suitcase of €.50, up to a maximum of two pieces of luggage. It costs an extra €1.50 for a dispatched pick-up. Some hotel or guesthouse staff, when asked to arrange for a taxi, tack on as much as €5 for their services, although this practice violates city taxi regulations.

By Bicycle   Riding a bike in Dublin isn't recommended. Traffic is very heavy, the streets are narrow, and pedestrians crowd every corner. For those determined to take to the streets on wheels, bicycle rental averages €13 per day, €50 per week, with a €65 deposit. In the downtown area, bicycles can be rented from **Raleigh Ireland,** Kylemore Road, Dublin 10 (© **01/626-1333;** Raleigh@iol.ie).

By Car   Unless you plan to do a lot of driving from Dublin to neighboring counties, it's not practical or affordable to rent a car. In fact, getting around the city and its environs is much easier without a car. If you must drive in Dublin, remember to keep to the *left-hand side of the road,* and don't drive in bus lanes. The most reliable and safest places to park are at surface parking lots or in multistory car parks in central locations, such as Kildare Street, Lower Abbey Street, Marlborough Street, and St. Stephen's Green West. The speed limit in the city is 46 kilometers per hour (30 mph), and seat belts must be worn at all times by driver and passengers.

By Foot   Small and compact, Dublin is ideal for walking, but be careful to look right and then left for oncoming traffic and to obey traffic signals. Each traffic light has timed "walk/don't walk" signals for pedestrians. Pedestrians have the right of way at specially marked, zebra-striped crossings; as a warning, there are usually two flashing lights at these intersections. For walking-tour suggestions, see "Organized Tours" under "Seeing the Sights," later in this chapter.

 FAST FACTS: Dublin

American Express   The Dublin office offers currency exchange, traveler's checks, and (for members) mail-holding. It's located opposite the Dublin Tourism Office, formerly the Church of St. Andrew, on Suffolk Street (© 01/605-7709). In an emergency, traveler's checks can be reported lost or stolen by dialing collect © 1800/282728.

Business Hours   Nearly all banks are open Monday through Friday from 10am to 4pm (to 5pm Thurs) and have ATMs that accept Cirrus network cards as well as MasterCard and Visa. **Post offices** (known as **An Post**) are open from 9am to 5:30pm Monday through Friday and from 9am to 1:30pm Saturday. The GPO on O'Connell Street is open from 8am to 8pm

Monday through Saturday, and from 10:30am to 6:30pm Sunday (for stamps only). **Museums** and **attractions** are generally open from 10am to 5pm Tuesday through Saturday, and from 2 to 5pm Sunday. **Shops** generally open from 9am to 6pm, Monday through Friday, with late openings on Thursday until 7pm or 8pm. In the city center, most department stores and many shops are open from noon to 6pm Sunday.

Currency   The official currency of Ireland is the **euro** (€).

Currency Exchange   Currency-exchange services, signposted as BUREAU DE CHANGE, are in all banks and at many branches of the Irish post office system, known as **An Post.** A bureau de change operates daily during flight arrival and departure times at Dublin airport; a foreign currency note-exchanger machine is also available on a 24-hour basis in the main arrivals hall. Some hotels and travel agencies offer bureau de change services, although the best rate of exchange usually results when you use your bank card at an ATM.

Dentist & Doctor   For medical or dental emergencies, contact the **Eastern Health Board Headquarters,** Dr. Steevens Hospital, Dublin 8 (© 01/679-0700). See also "Dental Surgeons" or "Doctors—Medical" in the Golden Pages (Yellow Pages) of the telephone book. The American Embassy (see "Embassies/Consulates," below) can provide a list of dentists in the city and surrounding areas.

Drugstores   Centrally located drugstores, known locally as pharmacies or chemist shops, include **Hamilton Long & Co.,** 5 Lower O'Connell St. (© 01/874-8456); and **Dame Street Pharmacy,** 16 Dame St., Dublin 2 (© 01/670-4523). A late-night chemist shop is **Byrne's Pharmacy,** 4 Merrion Rd., Dublin 4 (© 01/668-3287). It closes at 9pm on weekdays, 6pm on Saturday, and 1pm on Sunday.

Embassies/Consulates   The embassy of the **United States** is at 42 Elgin Rd., Ballsbridge, Dublin 4 (© 01/668-8777); the embassy of **Canada** is at 65/68 St. Stephen's Green, Dublin 2 (© 01/417-4100); the embassy of the **United Kingdom** is at 29 Merrion Rd., Dublin 2 (© 01/205-3700); and the embassy of **Australia** is at Fitzwilton House, Wilton Terrace, Dublin 2 (© 01/676-1517). Call for hours.

Emergencies   For the **Garda** (police), fire, or other emergencies, dial © **999.**

Hospitals   For emergency care, two of the most modern health-care facilities are **St. Vincent's Hospital,** Elm Park (© 01/269-4533), on the south side of the city; and **Beaumont Hospital,** Beaumont Road, Dublin 9 (© 01/837-7755 or 01/809-3000), on the north side.

Internet Access   In cyber-savvy Dublin, public access terminals are no longer hard to find, appearing in shopping malls, hotels, and hostels throughout the city center. Like all of Dublin's public libraries, the **Central Library,** in the ILAC Centre, off Henry Street, Dublin 1 (© 01/873-4333), has a bank of PCs with free Internet access. One of the most convenient and comfortable of the many cybercafes in town is **Betacafe@Arthouse,** Curved Street, Dublin 2 (© 01/605-6800; www.arthouse.ie), located above the Multimedia Centre for the Arts, in Temple Bar. Fifteen minutes online will set you back €2. It's open Monday through Friday from 9:15am to 5:30pm, Saturday from 9:15am to 2pm. Also in Temple Bar is the **Cyberia**

Cafe, Temple Lane South, Dublin 2 (② **01/679-7607;** www.cyberia.ie), where 15 minutes online costs €2, or €1.60 for students. It's open Monday through Thursday from 10am to 10pm and Friday and Saturday from 10am to 2pm. At both the **Central Cybercafe,** 6 Grafton St., Dublin 2 (② **01/677-8298**), and **Planet Cyber Café,** 13 St. Andrews St., Dublin 2 (② **01/670-5183**), 30 minutes online cost €3.50.

Post Office The **General Post Office (GPO)** is located on O'Connell Street, Dublin 1 (② **01/705-7000**). Hours are Monday through Saturday from 8am to 8pm, Sunday and holidays from 10:30am to 6:30pm. Branch offices, identified by the sign OIFIG AN POST/POST OFFICE, are open Monday through Friday from 9am to 5:30pm and Saturday from 9am to 1:30pm.

Taxes Sales tax is called VAT (value-added tax) and is often already included in the price quoted to you or shown on price tags. VAT rates vary—for hotels, restaurants, and car rentals, it's 12.5%; for souvenirs and gifts, it's 21%. If you're not a citizen of an EU country, you're entitled to have this money refunded. You can get your money back through **Global Refund** (② **800/566-9828;** www.globalrefund.ie), the world's largest private company offering VAT refunds. If a shop isn't part of the Global Refund network, get a full receipt at the time of purchase that shows the shop's name, address, and VAT paid. When you're ready to depart Ireland, go to the Customs office at the airport or ferry port and have your receipts stamped; then send the stamped receipts back to the store where you made your purchase, which will then mail you a VAT refund check.

Telephone The **country code** for the Republic of Ireland is **353.** The **city code** for Dublin is **01.** If you're calling from outside Ireland, drop the initial 0 (zero) from the city code. Thus, to call from the United States, you would dial ② 011-353-1, followed by the 7-digit local number. For direct-dial calls to the United States, dial the international access code (**00** from Ireland), and then the U.S. country code (**1**), followed by area code and number. To place a collect call to the United States from Ireland, dial ② **1-800/550-000** for USA Direct service. The toll-free international access codes are: AT&T ② **1-800-550-000,** Sprint ② **1-800-552-001,** and MCI ② **1-800-551-001.**

Local calls from a phone booth require a **Callcard,** a prepaid computerized card that you insert into the phone instead of coins. Callcards can be purchased in a range of denominations at phone company offices, post offices, and many retail outlets (such as newsstands). There's a local and international phone center at the General Post Office on O'Connell Street. If you have difficulty reaching a party, the Irish toll-free number for **directory assistance** is ② **11811.**

Tipping Most hotels and guesthouses add a service charge to the bill, usually 12.5% to 15%, although some smaller places add only 10% or nothing at all. If you feel the service charge is sufficient, there is no need for more gratuities. If, however, staff members have provided exceptional service, by all means tip them extra. For taxi drivers, tip as you would at home, 10% to 15%. For restaurants, the policy is usually printed on the menu—either a gratuity of 10% to 15% is automatically added to your bill or it's left up to you (always ask if you are in doubt). As a rule, bartenders do not expect a tip, except when table service is provided.

WHERE TO STAY
HISTORIC OLD CITY & TEMPLE BAR/
TRINITY COLLEGE AREA
Expensive
The Clarence ★★ Partly owned by members of the rock band U2, the Clarence is one of the finest and truly stylish hotels in Dublin. Situated beside the Liffey in Temple Bar, this mid-19th-century, Regency-style hotel was totally overhauled in 1996, trading antique charm for contemporary elegance. Each room features a rich color against cream walls and light Shaker-style oak furniture, including exceptionally firm beds. The Clarence's elegant **Tea Room** restaurant is one of the best places in town to dine on contemporary Irish cuisine, and after hours there's the **Kitchen,** one of the city's most glamorous nightspots.

6/8 Wellington Quay, Dublin 2. ℂ **01/407-0800.** Fax 01/407-0820. www.theclarence.ie. 50 units. €285– €305 double; €590 1-bedroom suite; €720 2-bedroom suite. Full Irish breakfast €20. AE, DC, MC, V. Bus: 51B, 51C, 68, 69, or 79. **Amenities:** Restaurant; bar; nightclub; concierge; salon; room service; babysitting; laundry/dry cleaning; nonsmoking rooms. *In room:* A/C, TV/VCR, dataport, minibar, hair dryer, safe.

Moderate
Eliza Lodge Opened in 2001, Eliza Lodge sits right beside the Liffey and embodies all the exuberance and zest of Temple Bar. If the Morgan is booked, this place is a good, moderately priced alternative. Rooms are very attractive, done up in neutral creams and blond woods, with big floor-to-ceiling windows—the better to take in the riverside vistas. At the top end, executive rooms (€203– €228) have Jacuzzi tubs and mod round bay windows perched over the quay. Even better value are the smaller penthouse doubles, which have balconies overlooking the river and are a comparative steal at €165 to €190.

23 Wellington Quay, Dublin 2. ℂ **01/671-8044.** Fax 01/671-8362. www.dublinlodge.com. 18 units. €152– €228 double. AE, MC, V. Bus: 51B, 51C, 68, 69, or 79. **Amenities:** Restaurant; bar; nonsmoking rooms. *In room:* A/C, TV, tea/coffeemaker, hair dryer, iron.

The Morgan ★ If you love Temple Bar but can't afford to stay at the Clarence, this is a fabulous second choice. In just a few short years, this stylized little boutique hotel has developed a cult following among folks in fashion and music. Rooms are airy and minimalist, featuring light beechwood furnishings and crisp white bedspreads against creamy neutral tones, with a smattering of modern artworks adding visual punch. Though it seems like a contradiction in terms, this place manages to be both trendy and a classic at the same time.

10 Fleet St., Dublin 2. ℂ **01/679-3939.** Fax 01/679-3946. www.themorgan.com. 61 units. €140–€240 double. AE, DC, MC, V. Bus: 78A or 78B. **Amenities:** Bar; cafe; fitness center; aromatherapy/masseuse; limited

---

⒯ Tips Room Booking Savvy

In general, rates for Dublin hotels don't vary as greatly with the seasons as they do in the Irish countryside. Hotels often charge higher prices, however, during special events, such as the Dublin Horse Show. For the best deals, try to reserve a room in Dublin over a weekend, and ask if there's a reduction or a weekend package in effect. Some Dublin hotels cut their rates by as much as 50% on Friday and Saturday nights, when business traffic is low. Also, significant reductions are sometimes available when rooms are booked from the States using the 800 numbers listed in this book.

room service; babysitting; laundry/dry cleaning; nonsmoking rooms. *In room:* TV/VCR, CD player, dataport, voice mail, tea/coffeemaker, iron, garment press, safe.

Inexpensive

Jurys Inn Christchurch *Value*   A good location in Old City, facing Christ Church Cathedral, makes this a solid choice in the budget category. Rooms are larger than you'd expect, refurbished regularly, and bright, though the decor has the same floral bedspreads and framed watercolors you see in every other chain hotel room. Make your reservations early and request a fifth-floor room facing west for a memorable view of Christ Church. *Tip:* Room nos. 501, 507, and 419 are especially spacious.

Christchurch Place, Dublin 8. © **800/44-UTELL** from the U.S., or 01/454-0000. Fax 01/454-0012. www.jurys.com. 182 units. €101 double. Breakfast €10. AE, DC, MC, V. Discounted parking available at adjacent lot. Bus: 21A, 50, 50A, 78, 78A, or 78B. **Amenities:** Restaurant; pub; babysitting; laundry/dry cleaning; nonsmoking rooms. *In room:* TV, tea/coffeemaker, hair dryer.

Self-Catering

25 Eustace Street *★★*   This wonderfully restored Georgian town house has an enviable location smack in the heart of Temple Bar. It's truly a privilege to stay here for even 1 night. The house has been faithfully reinstated to the gracious, slightly sober atmosphere of a house of its period, with its superb timber paneled staircase, fireplaces in every room, mainly mahogany furniture, and brass beds. You have the run of three entire floors of the house, including a huge drawing room with a baby grand piano, a dining room, an equipped galley kitchen, and three bedrooms (a double, a twin, and a triple). There are two bathrooms, one of which is enormous with an extra-roomy cast-iron claw-foot tub placed dead center. All this, and Temple Bar at your doorstep.

25 Eustace St., Dublin 2. Contact the Irish Landmark Trust, © **01/670-4733.** Fax 01/670-4887. Landmark@iol.ie. €768 per night, sliding up to €1,200 per week. **Amenities:** Kitchen; fridge; oven/stove; microwave; no phone.

ST. STEPHEN'S GREEN/GRAFTON STREET AREA
Very Expensive

Fitzwilliam *★*   Take an unbeatable location with stunning views over the Green, a fabulous restaurant, and cool, contemporary design by Terence Conran, and you have the makings of the Fitzwilliam. Conran has a knack for understated luxury, using clean lines and neutral colors throughout. Rooms are beautifully appointed and very relaxing. The **Citron** restaurant is downstairs, and you can also dine at the stylish **Inn on the Green** bar. If staying somewhere fashionable is important to you, this gets the nod over the Shelbourne (see below).

109 St. Stephen's Green, Dublin 2. © **01/478-7000.** Fax 01/478-7878. www.fitzwilliam-hotel.com. 130 units. €307–€373 double. AE, DC, MC, V. DART: Pearse. Bus: 10, 11A, 11B, 13, or 20B. **Amenities:** Restaurant; bar; concierge; room service; babysitting; laundry/dry cleaning; roof garden; nonsmoking rooms. *In room:* A/C, TV/VCR, fax, CD player, dataport, voice mail, minibar, tea/coffeemaker, hair dryer, garment press.

Shelbourne *★*   While the Fitzwilliam is all about cutting-edge style, the Shelbourne is all about tradition. Founded in 1824, this is Dublin's answer to the Grand Hotel, having played a significant role in Irish history—the constitution was drafted here in 1922, in room no. 112. Rooms vary in size, but all are beautifully appointed with antiques and period pieces. Ask for one that overlooks bucolic St. Stephen's Green. The public areas, replete with glowing fireplaces, Waterford chandeliers, and original artworks, are popular rendezvous spots for Dublin's movers and shakers. Service is impeccable, and you get to experience a slice of Irish heritage to boot.

27 St. Stephen's Green, Dublin 2. © **800/225-5843** from the U.S., or 01/663-4500. Fax 01/661-6006. www.shelbourne.ie. 190 units. €245–€273 double. Service charge 15%. AE, DC, MC, V. Limited free parking. DART: Pearse. Bus: 10, 11A, 11B, 13, or 20B. **Amenities:** 2 restaurants; 2 bars; tearoom; fitness center; concierge; room service; babysitting; laundry/dry cleaning. *In room:* A/C, TV, radio, minibar.

Expensive

Brownes Townhouse ⭐ If you love luxury but hate big chain hotels, look no further than this sumptuously restored Georgian town house with an unbeatable location on St. Stephen's Green. Downstairs is all Georgian splendor: comfy wingback chairs, rich upholsteries, and ornate ceiling plasterwork. The dozen guest rooms come in all shapes and sizes, but all are sumptuously decorated with period furnishings, four-poster king-size beds (some of them 2.4m/8 ft. wide!), marble bathrooms, and unique architectural details. When you book, voice your decor preferences, as rooms vary drastically according to masculine, feminine, classic, or eccentric tastes. If you splurge on the Thomas Leighton suite, you'll sleep on a magnificent king-size mahogany Murphy bed that once belonged to Marilyn Monroe. Downstairs, the elegant **Brasserie** serves up excellent traditional French fare.

22 St. Stephen's Green, Dublin 2. © **01/638-3939.** Fax 01/638-3900. www.brownesdublin.com. 12 units. €215–€245 double. No service charge. Rates include full breakfast. MC, V. DART: Pearse. Bus: 10, 11A, 11B, 13, or 20B. **Amenities:** Restaurant. *In room:* A/C, TV, fax, dataport, tea/coffeemaker, hair dryer.

Moderate

Number 31 ⭐ A plaque placed discreetly at an elegant gated entrance in the heart of Georgian Dublin is your only clue that what lies beyond is an award-winning town house B&B. The house is actually two beautifully renovated coach houses, featuring a striking sunken fireside seating area with mosaic tiles in the main lounge. In the main house, rooms range from grand, high-ceilinged affairs to cozier nests. The smaller coach house has lower ceilings, but some rooms have their own patios. All the rooms are a triumph of quiet good taste, decorated with fine fabrics against a cream backdrop. Breakfast is truly magnificent—think mushroom frittatas, cranberry bread, and scrumptious little potato cakes.

31 Leeson Close, Lower Leeson St., Dublin 2. © **01/676-5011.** Fax 01/676-2929. www.number31.ie. 20 units. €119–€183 double. Rates include breakfast. AE, MC, V. Bus: 11, 11A, 11B, 13, 13A, or 13B. **Amenities:** Lounge; bar; conservatory. *In room:* TV, hair dryer.

FITZWILLIAM/MERRION SQUARE AREA
Moderate

Kilronan House ⭐ This extremely comfortable B&B is set on a peaceful, leafy road just 5 minutes' walk from St. Stephen's Green. Much of the Georgian character remains, in the ceiling cornicing, hardwood parquet floors, and the fine staircase. The sitting room on the ground floor is particularly intimate, with a fire glowing through the cold months of the year. Rooms are brightly inviting in white and yellow, and those facing the front have commodious bay windows. There's no elevator, so consider requesting a room on a lower floor. The front rooms, facing Adelaide Street, are preferable to those in back, which face office buildings and a parking lot. Breakfast here is especially good, featuring home-made breads.

70 Adelaide Rd., Dublin 2. © **01/475-5266.** Fax 01/478-2841. www.dublinn.com/kilronan.htm. 15 units, 13 with private bathroom (shower only). €152 double. Rates include full breakfast. AE, MC, V. Bus: 14, 15, 19, 20, or 46A. **Amenities:** Nonsmoking rooms. *In room:* TV, tea/coffeemaker, hair dryer.

Longfields ⭐ Created from two 18th-century Georgian town houses, this award-winning hotel is a small, elegant alternative to the large upscale hotels in this area. Totally restored and recently refurbished, it combines authentic Georgian decor with quality reproduction period furnishings of dark woods and brass trim. Though some of the standard rooms are smallish, the superior doubles (at €210) are noticeably more spacious; and the best doubles (at €230) are even larger and feature four-poster beds. Longfields is centrally located yet remarkably quiet, an elegant yet unpretentious getaway 5 minutes' walk from St. Stephen's Green. The restaurant, simply known as **Number 10,** is beloved by foodies for its flavorful international cuisine.

10 Lower Fitzwilliam St., Dublin 2. ℂ **01/676-1367.** Fax 01/676-1542. www.longfields.ie. 26 units. €190–€230 double. No service charge. Rates include full breakfast. AE, DC, MC, V. No parking available. DART: Pearse. Bus: 10. **Amenities:** Restaurant; concierge; room service; babysitting; laundry/dry cleaning; non-smoking rooms. *In room:* TV, clock radio, dataport, hair dryer.

O'CONNELL STREET AREA
Very Expensive
The Morrison 🏵🏵   Just when it seemed that everything chic and hip happened south of the Liffey, the Hong Kong–born, Irish designer John Rocha opened the Morrison and pow!—the central Northside ain't so shabby after all. This stunning contemporary hotel is a 5-minute walk from O'Connell Street and across the river from Temple Bar. Rocha used clean minimalist lines, neutral colors, and natural elements to evoke a sensuous, luxurious feeling of space and relaxation. **Halo,** the atrium-style main restaurant, is one of the most exciting eateries in town. The upshot: The Morrison is just as stylish as the Clarence (Temple Bar) and the Fitzwilliam (St. Stephen's Green), with the sky-high rates to prove it.

Lower Ormond Quay, Dublin 1. ℂ **01/887-2400.** Fax 01/878-3185. www.morrisonhotel.ie. 93 units. €270–€445 double. AE, DC, MC, V. DART: Connolly. Bus: 70 or 80. **Amenities:** 2 restaurants; 2 bars. *In room:* A/C, CD player, dataport, voice mail, minibar, hair dryer, safe.

Moderate
Royal Dublin   Romantically floodlit at night, this hotel is near Parnell Square at the north end of Dublin's main thoroughfare, within walking distance of all the main theaters and Northside attractions. The contemporary, skylit lobby lies adjacent to lounge areas that were part of the original 1752 building. These Georgian-style rooms are elegant, with high molded ceilings, ornate cornices, crystal chandeliers, gilt-edged mirrors, and open fireplaces. Rooms are contemporary, featuring blond woods, bold checked bedspreads, and bay windows that extend over the busy street below. *Warning:* The price for a double room doubles in the summer to an outrageous €350, so save this for off-season trips.

40 Upper O'Connell St., Dublin 1. ℂ **800/528-1234** from the U.S., or 01/873-3666. Fax 01/873-3120. www.royaldublin.com. 120 units. €175–€350 double. Rates include full Irish breakfast and service charge. AE, DC, MC, V. Free parking. DART: Connolly. Bus: 36A, 40A, 40B, 40C, or 51A. **Amenities:** Restaurant; bar; lounge; concierge; car-rental desk; room service; babysitting; laundry. *In room:* TV, radio, tea/coffeemaker, hair dryer.

BALLSBRIDGE/EMBASSY ROW AREA
Situated south of the Grand Canal, this is the most prestigious part of town, known for its embassies, tree-lined streets, and historic buildings. If you're coming to Dublin specifically for a conference at the RDS show grounds or a match at the Lansdowne Rugby Ground, this neighborhood will put you right in the thick of things. The downside is that it's a good 20- to 30-minute walk to get into the city's best sightseeing and shopping areas.

Very Expensive

Four Seasons 👑👑   The 3-year-old drop-dead gorgeous Four Seasons hiked up its prices by a whopping 50% after its successful first year—so don't look for any sweet deals here. Still, if money is no object, the Four Seasons blows Dublin's other luxury hotels out of the water in terms of services and leisure facilities. The health club is state of the art. The public areas and guest rooms share a smart and very plush look, thanks to the liberal use of natural elements and fine fabrics. This is a fabulous place for families, with a babysitting service, complimentary cribs, childproof bedrooms, and a roster of children's activities to keep the kids occupied while you kick back and get some head space.

Simmonscourt Rd., Ballsbridge, Dublin 4. © **800/819-5053** from the U.S., or 01/665-4000. Fax 01/665-4099. www.fourseasons.com. 259 units. €375–€795 double. AE, DC, MC, V. Valet parking. DART: Sandymount (5-min. walk). Bus: 7, 7A, 7X, 8, or 45. **Amenities:** 2 restaurants; bar; lobby lounge; indoor pool; health club/spa; whirlpool; children's programs; concierge; room service; babysitting; laundry/dry cleaning; nonsmoking rooms; conservatory. *In room:* TV/VCR, radio, CD player available, dataport, voice mail, minibar, hair dryer, safe.

Expensive

Butler's Town House 👑   This beautifully restored and expanded Victorian town house B&B feels like a gracious family home into which you are lucky enough to be welcomed. The atmosphere is semi-formal yet invitingly elegant, class without the starched collar. Rooms are richly furnished with four-poster or half-tester beds. It's hard to elude comfort here—you're pampered by two-fold Egyptian cotton sheets, heavenly water pressure, and an especially solicitous staff. A bonus is the **Glendalough Room** restaurant, which requires early booking. The hotel offers free tea and coffee all day. Breakfast, afternoon tea, and high tea are served in the atrium dining room.

44 Lansdowne Rd., Ballsbridge, Dublin 4. © **800/44-UTELL** from the U.S., or 01/667-4022. Fax 01/667-3960. www.butlers-hotel.com. 20 units. €190 double. Rates include full breakfast. AE, DC, MC, V. Closed Dec 23–Jan 8. DART: Lansdowne Rd. Bus: 7, 7A, 8, or 45. **Amenities:** Dining room; limited room service; babysitting; laundry/dry cleaning. *In room:* A/C, TV, dataport, hair dryer.

Moderate

Waterloo House   These two adjacent Georgian town houses make up one of the most popular B&Bs in Dublin. Perhaps it's because Evelyn Corcoran and her staff take such good care of you, in a friendly but unobtrusive manner. The place is charming in an Old World kind of way, with classical music wafting through the lobby, and an elegant, high-ceilinged drawing room. Rooms are comfortable and large (some have two double beds), but some might find the traditional red-patterned carpet and box-pleated bedspreads a tad dated. The varied breakfast menu is a high point. This is a nonsmoking house.

8–10 Waterloo Rd., Ballsbridge, Dublin 4. © **01/660-1888.** Fax 01/667-1955. www.waterloohouse.ie. 17 units. €110–€140 double. Rates include full breakfast. MC, V. Closed Christmas week. DART: Lansdowne Rd. Bus: 5, 7, or 8. **Amenities:** Drawing room; breakfast room; nonsmoking house. *In room:* TV, tea/coffeemaker, hair dryer, garment press.

Inexpensive

Bewley's Hotel *Value*   Bewley's occupies what was once a 19th-century brick Masonic school building adjacent to the RDS show grounds and next to the British Embassy. A modern wing harmonizes well with the old structure and is indistinguishable in the interior. Rooms are spacious and well furnished—each has a writing desk, an armchair, and a large double bed. The studios have a bedroom with a double bed, plus an additional room with a foldout couch, a table (seats six), a pullout kitchenette/bar hidden in a cabinet, and an additional bathroom (shower only). The basement restaurant (**O'Connell's**) is run by the

Allen family of Ballymaloe fame, and offers very good food at reasonable prices; there's also an informal Bewley's tearoom. The hotel is an excellent value for families, but the big downside is its location outside the city center.

Merrion Rd., Ballsbridge, Dublin 4. © 01/668-1111. Fax: 01/668-1999. www.bewleyshotels.com. 220 units. €99 double; €175 studio. Rates include service charge and taxes. AE, DC, MC, V. DART: Sandymount (5-min. walk). Bus: 7, 7A, 7X, 8, or 45. **Amenities:** Restaurant; tearoom; nonsmoking rooms. *In room:* TV, dataport, kitchenette, tea/coffeemaker, hair dryer, safe, garment press.

WHERE TO DINE
HISTORIC OLD CITY & TEMPLE BAR/ TRINITY COLLEGE AREA
Expensive

Jacob's Ladder 🐝🐝 MODERN IRISH   Inspired cooking by chef-owner Adrian Roche and a stylish dining room with great views over Trinity College make this one of the most consistently packed places in town. Roche's forte is taking old Irish stalwarts and updating them into sublime signature dishes, like the delicious Dublin Coddle (seafood stew) and a braised wood pigeon that comes with a melt-away colcannon—potatoes and cabbage mashed together with plenty of butter. Service is terrific and you get great value for your money.

4–5 Nassau St., Dublin 2. © 01/670-3865. www.jacobsladder.ie. Reservations required. Main courses €27–€29; early-bird 2-course menu Tues–Fri 6–7pm €19; fixed-price dinner €32. AE, DC, MC, V. Tues–Sat 12:30–2:30pm; Tues–Fri 6–10pm; Sat 7–10pm. Closed Dec 24–Jan 4. DART: Pearse. Bus: 7, 8, 10, 11, or 46A.

Les Frères Jacques 🐝 FRENCH   The business crowd loves this friendly, upmarket French restaurant, which brings a touch of haute cuisine to the lower edge of the trendy Temple Bar district. The menu offers such entrees as daube of beef with root vegetables, rabbit lasagna with Madeira sauce, and rosette of spring lamb in meat juice zabaglione and tomato coulis with crispy potato straws. You might also try veal on rainbow pasta with garlic and basil sauce or grilled lobster (from the tank) flamed in whiskey.

74 Dame St., Dublin 2. © 01/679-4555. Fax 01/679-4725. www.lesfreresjacques.com. Reservations recommended. Main courses €23–€29; fixed 3-course dinner €34. AE, MC, V. Mon–Fri 12:15–2:30pm; Mon–Fri 7:15–10:30pm; Sat 7–10:30pm. Closed Dec 24–Jan 4. Bus: 50, 50A, 54, 56, or 77.

The Tea Room 🐝🐝 INTERNATIONAL   The ultra-smart restaurant of the ultra-smart Clarence Hotel is virtually guaranteed to deliver one of your best meals in Ireland. This gorgeous dining room's soaring lines are the perfect backdrop for Michael Martin's complex but controlled cooking. Start with the deep-fried potato and bacon cakes or pan-fried foie gras with onion tarte *tatin*. Follow with the mixed grill of fish and zucchini with olive roast couscous or, if you're very hungry, the pan-fried filet of beef in a red wine sauce with mushroom duxelles. Desserts are an indulgence not for the fainthearted.

The Clarence Hotel, 6/8 Wellington Quay, Dublin 2. © 01/670-9000. www.theclarence.ie. Reservations required. Main courses €20–€25; fixed 2-course dinner €40, 3-course dinner €50. AE, MC, V. Mon–Fri 12:30–2pm; Mon–Sun 6:30–9:45pm. Bus: 51B, 51C, 68, 69, or 79.

Moderate

Eden 🐝 INTERNATIONAL/MEDITERRANEAN   This is one of Temple Bar's hippest eateries, a cool minimalist dining room with an open-plan kitchen and a people-watching view of Meeting House Square. Chef Eleanor Walsh's cooking is highly influenced by Mediterranean flavors, as when her fresh hake comes served with black olives, sun-dried tomatoes, arugula (called rocket in Ireland), and a slab of pesto. Desserts are worth saving room for. The fixed-price lunch is particularly good value.

Meeting House Sq. (entrance on Sycamore St.), Dublin 2. ℭ **01/670-5372.** Main courses €16–€24; fixed-price lunch menu €19. AE, DC, MC, V. Daily 12:30–3pm and 6–10:30pm. Bus: 51B, 51C, 68, 69, or 79.

Mermaid Café 🎝🎝 INTERNATIONAL   This unassuming bistro has a loyal cult following with foodies like Michael Caine, who visited when in Dublin filming the 2003 movie *The Actors.* That's thanks to Ben Gorman's remarkable way of taking classic dishes and giving them a fresh, eclectic twist. Typical starters run along the lines of a beetroot, quail egg, and baby spinach salad or a paprika smoked chicken with avocado and cilantro. The New England crab cakes, grilled swordfish with mango relish, roast duck breast on curried noodles, and chargrilled monkfish are all flawlessly prepared and quite memorable. The wine list is one of the best in Ireland and the desserts divine.

69/70 Dame St., Dublin 2. ℭ **01/670-8236.** www.mermaid.ie. Reservations required. Dinner main courses €18–€30. Sunday brunch €8–€15. MC, V. Mon–Sat 12:30–2:30pm and 6–11pm; Sun brunch noon–3:30pm and dinner 6–9pm. Bus: 50, 50A, 54, 56A, 77, 77A, or 77B.

Inexpensive
Irish Film Centre Cafe Bar 🎝*Value* IRISH/INTERNATIONAL   In the lobby of the city's coolest place to grab a movie, the hip Cafe Bar features an excellent, affordable menu that changes daily. Vegetarian and Middle Eastern menus are available for both lunch and dinner. The weekend entertainment usually includes music or comedy.

6 Eustace St., Temple Bar, Dublin 2. ℭ **01/677-8788.** Lunch and dinner €7–€12. MC, V. Mon–Fri 12:30–3pm; Sat–Sun 1–3pm; daily 6–9pm. Bus: 21A, 78A, or 78B.

Leo Burdock's FISH AND CHIPS   Every visitor should go to a Dublin take-out "chipper" at least once, and you might as well do it at the best in town. Established in 1913 across from Christ Church, this quintessential Irish takeout shop remains a cherished Dublin institution, despite a devastating fire in 1998. Rebuilt from the ground up, Burdock's is back. Cabinet ministers, university students, and businesspeople alike can be found in the queue. There's no seating, but you can stroll down to the park at St. Patrick's Cathedral.

2 Werburgh St., Dublin 8. ℭ **01/454-0306.** Main courses €4–€7. No credit cards. Mon–Sat noon–midnight; Sun 4pm–midnight. Bus: 21A, 50, 50A, 78, 78A, or 78B.

ST. STEPHEN'S GREEN/GRAFTON STREET AREA
Expensive
Aya @ Brown Thomas 🎝🎝 JAPANESE   This buzzy, fashionable annex to Dublin's poshest department store is very much the good-time destination of the moment. Yes, the conveyor belt sushi bar has finally arrived, and Dubliners may never be the same. Beyond the trendiness, the food here is damn good. Lunch offers all the classics—tempura, gyoza, and, of course, plenty of sushi—while the dinner menu expands to include yakitori, steaks, and noodle salads. There's table seating, but it's cheaper to eat at the bar. Come for dinner Sunday through Tuesday, for the Sushi55 special: all you can eat, including one complimentary drink, for €24.

49–52 Clarendon St., Dublin 2. ℭ **01/677-1544.** Reservations recommended for dinner. Lunch averages €11; dinner averages €32. AE, DC, MC, V. Mon–Sat 10:30am–11pm; Sun noon–10pm. DART: Tara St. Bus: 16A, 19A, 22A, 55, or 83.

Moderate
Café Mao 🎝 ASIAN   This is where to go when you feel like dining on Asian cooking laced with a fun and exhilarating attitude. An exposed kitchen lines an entire wall, and the rest of the space is wide open—fantastic for people-watching

on weekends. The menu reads like a "best of Asia": Thai fish cakes, *nasi goreng* (fried rice), chicken hoi sin, salmon ramen. Everything is well prepared and delicious, so you can't go wrong.

2 Chatham Row, Dublin 2. © 01/670-4899. Reservations recommended. Main courses €10–€15. AE, MC, V. Mon–Thurs noon–11pm; Fri–Sat noon–11:30pm; Sun noon–10pm. DART: Pearse. Bus: 10, 11A, 11B, 13, or 20B.

Fitzer's Cafe INTERNATIONAL   This is one branch of a chain of winning cafes that serves excellent, up-to-date, and reasonably priced food. Nestled on a street known for its bookshops, this bright, airy Irish-style bistro has a multi-windowed facade and modern decor. Choices range from chicken breast with hot chili cream sauce or brochette of lamb tandoori with mild curry sauce to gratin of smoked cod. There are also tempting vegetarian dishes made with organic produce. Other Dublin locations include the National Gallery, Merrion Square West (© **01/661-4496**), and Temple Bar Square (© **01/679-0440**). You get the same menu, the same decor, and the same good service at each location.

51a Dawson St., Dublin 2. © **01/677-1155**. Fax 01/670-6575. www.fitzers.ie. Dinner main courses €13–€22. AE, DC, MC, V. Daily 12:30–11pm. Closed Jan 1 and Dec 25–26. DART: Pearse. Bus: 10, 11A, 11B, 13, or 20B.

Inexpensive

Bewley's Café TRADITIONAL CAFE/TEAROOM   Bewley's, a three-story landmark on Grafton Street, has been a staple of Dublin life since 1840, with a traditional interior of dark woods, amber glass, and deep red velvet banquettes. Go once, because Bewley's is a quintessential hit of real Dublin and the people-watching is good. But stick to coffee and tea, since the food can be mediocre. Most Bewley's establishments are self-service cafeterias, but Bewley's of Grafton Street also has several full-service tearooms. Other locations are at 11 Westmoreland St., Dublin 2; 13 S. Great George's St., Dublin 2; 40 Mary St., Dublin 1 (near the ILAC shopping center north of the Liffey); shopping centers in Dundrum, Stillorgan, and Tallaght; and Dublin Airport.

78/79 Grafton St., Dublin 2. © 01/677-6761. Homemade soup €3.50; lunch main courses €4–€9 and specials from €7; dinner main courses €15–€19. AE, DC, MC, V. Sun–Thurs 7:30am–11pm; Fri–Sat 7:30am–1am (continuous service for breakfast, hot food, and snacks). Bus: Any city-center bus

Café Bell (*Value*) IRISH/SELF-SERVICE   In the cobbled courtyard of early-19th-century St. Teresa's Church, this serene little place is one of a handful of dining options springing up in historic or ecclesiastical surroundings. With high ceilings and an old-world decor, Café Bell is a welcome contrast to the bustle of Grafton Street a block away and Powerscourt Town House Centre across the street. The menu includes very good homemade soups, sandwiches, salads, quiches, lasagna, sausage rolls, hot scones, and other baked goods.

St. Teresa's Courtyard, Clarendon St., Dublin 2. © 01/677-7645. All items €3–€6.50. No credit cards. Mon–Sat 9am–5:30pm. Bus: 16, 16A, 19, 19A, 22A, 55, or 83.

FITZWILLIAM/MERRION SQUARE AREA
Very Expensive

L'Ecrivain (*★★*) FRENCH   This is one of Dublin's truly exceptional restaurants, from start to finish. The atmosphere is relaxed, welcoming, and unpretentious, and chef Derry Clarke's food is extraordinary in its attention to detail. Each course consists of traditional "best of Irish" ingredients, prepared without dense sauces. The roast monkfish with citrus ravioli and the entrecôte with caramelized onion are not only perfectly prepared, but elegantly presented. For dessert, the crème brûlée here may be the best outside of France.

109 Lower Baggot St., Dublin 2. ℂ **01/661-1919.** www.lecrivain.com. Reservations required. Fixed-price 2-course lunch €27, 3-course lunch €35; fixed-price 4-course dinner €53. Main courses €34–€38. AE, DC, MC, V. Mon–Fri 12:30–2pm; Mon–Thurs 6:30–10:30pm; Fri–Sat 7–11pm. Bus: 10.

Restaurant Patrick Guilbaud ✵ FRENCH   Ireland's most lauded restaurant has a glowing Michelin-star reputation for fine food and artful service. The menu features such dishes as roasted West Cork turbot, veal sweetbreads with black truffles, wild sea bass with ragout of mussels, and a casserole of winter vegetables with wild mushrooms. Start with the open ravioli of lobster with coconut cream, follow with the sole and duck confit flavored with walnut liqueur, and finish with the *assiette gourmande au chocolat* (five small hot and cold chocolate desserts).

21 Upper Merrion St., Dublin 2. ℂ **01/676-4192.** www.merrionhotel.com/guilbaud.htm. Reservations required. Fixed-price lunch €28; dinner main courses €44–€49. AE, DC, MC, V. Tues–Sat 12:30–2pm and 7:30–10:15pm. DART: Westland Row. Bus: 10, 11A, 11B, 13, or 20B.

Moderate

Dobbins Wine Bistro BISTRO   Almost hidden in a lane between Upper and Lower Mount streets, this hip, friendly bistro is a haven for inventive Continental cuisine. The menu changes often, but usually includes such items as duckling with orange and port sauce; steamed paupiette of black sole with salmon, crab, and prawn filling; pan-fried veal kidneys in pastry; and filet of beef topped with herbed bread crumbs with shallot and Madeira sauce. You can sit in the bistro, with checkered tablecloths and sawdust on the floor, or on the atrium patio.

15 Stephen's Lane (off Upper Mount St.), Dublin 2. ℂ **01/676-4670.** www.dobbins-dublin.com. Reservations recommended. Dinner main courses €16–€25. AE, DC, MC, V. Mon–Fri 12:30–2:30pm; Tues–Sat 7:30–10:30pm. DART: Pearse. Bus: 5, 7A, 8, 46, or 84.

Inexpensive

National Museum Café *Value* CAFETERIA   This is a great place to step out of the rain, warm yourself, and wander among the nation's treasures. The cafe is informal but elegant, thanks to an elaborate mosaic floor, enameled fireplace, marble tabletops, chandelier, and tall windows that look across a cobbled yard toward the National Library. Everything is made fresh: beef salad, chicken salad, quiche, an abundance of pastries. The soup of the day is often vegetarian, and quite good. Admission to the museum is free, so you can visit at your own pace, as often as your curiosity (and appetite) demand.

National Museum of Ireland, Kildare St., Dublin 2. ℂ **01/662-1269.** Lunch main courses €5–€8. MC, V. Tues–Sat 10am–5pm; Sun 2–5pm. Bus: 7, 7A, 8, 10, 11, or 13.

O'CONNELL STREET AREA
Expensive

Halo ✵✵ FUSION   This is easily the hippest, hottest, coolest, most stylish place to eat in Dublin right now—so book your table before you leave home. Chef Jean-Michel Poulot's cooking is fusion at its best—snazzy, mind-blowing combinations of taste and texture that are elegant instead of merely out there. Consider the curried king scallops with lime potato, fennel, mizuna, and ginger vinaigrette. Or the baked goat's cheese wrapped in Parma ham with mizuna salad. Eating at Halo is an intense experience for all of your senses.

Morrison Hotel, Ormond Quay, Dublin 1. ℂ **01/878-2999.** www.morrisonhotel.ie. Reservations required. 2-course lunch menu €25; 3-course lunch menu €28. Dinner main courses €25–€30. AE, MC, V. Daily 12:30–2pm and 7–10:30pm. DART: Connolly. Bus: 70 or 80.

Moderate

101 Talbot ⟨R⟩ INTERNATIONAL   This modest, friendly, second-floor eatery over a camping shop is a bright beacon of great cooking in a neighborhood that's otherwise culinarily challenged. The menu features light, healthy foods, with a strong emphasis on vegetarian and vegan dishes. Main dishes include seared filet of tuna with mango cardamom salsa, roast duck breast with plum and ginger sauce, Halloumi cheese and mushroom brochette served with couscous and raita, and a blue cheese/pistachio cream sauce on pasta. The dining room is bright and casually funky, with contemporary Irish art on display, big windows, yellow rag-rolled walls, ash-topped tables, and newspapers to read. Espresso and cappuccino are always available, and there is a full bar.

101 Talbot St. (at Talbot Lane near Marlborough St.), Dublin 1. ℭ/fax **01/874-5011**. Reservations recommended. Main courses €15–€22. AE, DC, MC, V. Tues–Sat 5–11pm. DART: Connolly. Bus: 27A, 31A, 31B, 32A, 32B, 42B, 42C, 43, or 44A.

Inexpensive

Winding Stair ⟨Value⟩ HEALTH   This darling bookshop's self-service cafe is a great place to snack while browsing for secondhand gems. It has three floors— one smoke-free and each chock-full of used books (from novels to history, art, music, and sports) connected by a winding 18th-century staircase. Tall, wide windows provide expansive views of the Ha'penny Bridge and the River Liffey. The food is simple and healthy—sandwiches made with additive-free meats or fruits (such as banana and honey), organic salads, homemade soups, and natural juices. Evening events include poetry readings and recitals.

40 Lower Ormond Quay, Dublin 1. ℭ **01/873-3292**. All items €2.50–€7. AE, MC, V. Mon–Sat 10am–6pm; Sun 1–6pm. Bus: 70 or 80.

BALLSBRIDGE/EMBASSY ROW AREA

Expensive

Le Coq Hardi ⟨R⟩⟨R⟩ FRENCH   In a society obsessed with discovering the next big thing, this plush, 20-year-old gentlemen's-club-style restaurant continues to rank at the top of its class. Award-winning chef John Howard is a maestro at the classics, such as quail with foie gras, spring lamb with *pommes boulangères,* king scallops served with bacon, *darne* (steak) of Irish wild salmon on fresh spinach leaves, and filet of prime beef flamed in Irish whiskey. The 700-bin wine cellar is the best in Dublin.

35 Pembroke Rd., Ballsbridge, Dublin 4. ℭ **01/668-9070**. Reservations required. Lunch main courses €19–€21; dinner main courses €27–€30. AE, MC, V. Mon–Fri 12:30–2:30pm; Mon–Sat 7–10:45pm. DART: Lansdowne Rd. Bus: 18, 46, 63, or 84.

Moderate

Dish ⟨R⟩ INTERNATIONAL   Maybe it should call itself New Dish. After being a popular Temple Bar eatery for years, Dish moved last year to these Ballsbridge digs and instantly became a huge hit all over again. The chic, contemporary surroundings work well with the ambitious, eclectic cooking that awaits you. Chef Gerard Foote believes in organic ingredients and is a master at combining unlikely flavors for tantalizing results. The sweet-potato-and-pear bisque is perfect, as is the grilled salmon with avocado, papaya, and tequila-lime dressing. The desserts are nothing short of sensational.

146 Upper Leeson St., Dublin 4. ℭ **01/671-1249**. Reservations recommended. Fixed-price lunch €17. Dinner main courses €12–€23. AE, DC, MC, V. Daily 12:30–11:30pm. DART: Tara St. Bus: 21A, 46A, 46B, 51B, 51C, 68, 69, or 86.

Roly's Bistro ⭑⭑ IRISH/INTERNATIONAL   This shop-front restaurant has been a beloved Dublin institution for over a decade. Chef Paul Cartwright cooks the kind of excellent, tummy-warming food you never get tired of: confit of duck with garlic mash, chicken-and-bean-sprout spring roll, pan-fried Dublin Bay prawns, wild mushroom risotto. The main dining room, an airy affair with lots of windows, can be noisy when the house is full, but the no-smoking section has an enclave of booths laid out in an intimate Orient Express style.

7 Ballsbridge Terrace, Dublin 4. ℂ 01/668-2611. Reservations required. Main courses €15–€20. Fixed 2-course lunch €18. AE, DC, MC, V. Daily noon–3pm and 6–10pm. DART to Lansdowne Rd. Station. Bus: 5, 6, 7, 8, 18, or 45.

SEEING THE SIGHTS
SIGHTSEEING SUGGESTIONS FOR FIRST-TIME VISITORS

If You Have 1 Day Start at the beginning—Dublin's medieval quarter, the area around **Christ Church** and **St. Patrick's Cathedral.** Tour these great churches and then walk the cobblestone streets and inspect the nearby old city walls at **High Street.** From Old Dublin, take a turn eastward and see **Dublin Castle** and then **Trinity College** with the famous Book of Kells. Cross over the River Liffey to **O'Connell Street,** Dublin's main thoroughfare. Walk up this wide street, passing the landmark General Post Office (GPO), to Parnell Square and the picturesque Garden of Remembrance. If time permits, visit the **Dublin Writers Museum,** and then hop on a double-decker bus heading to the south bank of the Liffey for a relaxing stroll amid the greenery of **St. Stephen's Green.** Cap the day with a show at the **Abbey Theatre** and maybe a drink or two at a nearby pub.

If You Have 2 Days On your first day, get oriented with a sightseeing tour—the most fun is the amphibious **Viking Splash Tour,** though the **Dublin City Tour** gives a broader overview of the city, plus it goes to some of the leading sights on the edge of the city, such as the **Guinness Brewery,** the **Royal Hospital,** and **Phoenix Park.** Later in the day, head for **Grafton Street** for some shopping. If time allows, stroll around **St. Stephen's Green** and **Merrion Square** for a sampling of the best of Dublin's Georgian architecture. Spend the evening in Temple Bar and end up with a few pints in a pub. On your second day, follow the 1-day itinerary, above.

If You Have 3 Days Make day 3 a day for Dublin's artistic and cultural attractions—visit the **National Museum** and **National Gallery,** the **Guinness Hop Store,** or a special-interest museum, such as the **Writers Museum.** Save time to walk around **Temple Bar** by day, when the city's Left Bank district is all about art galleries and film studios, interesting secondhand shops, and casual eateries.

If You Have 4 Days On day 4, take a ride aboard DART to one of the southern suburbs, either **Dun Laoghaire** or medieval **Dalkey.** DART follows the rim of Dublin Bay, so you'll enjoy a scenic ride and get to spend some time in an Irish coastal village. Or take a trip to the **Boyne Valley** in nearby County Meath to visit the burial mounds at Newgrange, the site of the Battle of the Boyne, and King William's Glen. This trip is also worthwhile for the glimpses of Irish countryside it affords.

DUBLIN'S TOP ATTRACTIONS

The Book of Kells ✸✸✸   The jewel in Ireland's tourism crown is the Book of Kells, a magnificent manuscript of the four Gospels, written around A.D. 800, with elaborate scripting and illumination. This famous treasure and other early Christian manuscripts are on permanent public view at Trinity College, in the Colonnades, an exhibition area on the ground floor of the Old Library. Also housed in the Old Library is the **Dublin Experience** (see below; ℂ **01/ 608-1177**), an excellent multimedia introduction to the history and people of Dublin. The oldest university in Ireland, Trinity was founded in 1592 by Queen Elizabeth I. It occupies a beautiful 17-hectare (40-acre) site just south of the River Liffey, with cobbled squares, gardens, a picturesque quadrangle, and buildings dating from the 17th to the 20th centuries.

College Green, Dublin 2. ℂ **01/608-2320.** www.tcd.ie/library/kells.htm. Free admission to college grounds. Old Library/Book of Kells €6 adults, €5 seniors/students, €11 families, free for children under 12. Dublin Experience €4 adults, €3.25 seniors/students, €2 children, €8 family. Combination tickets also available. Library Mon–Sat 9:30am–5pm, Sun noon–4:30pm (opens at 9:30am June–Sept). Dublin Experience May–Sept daily 10am–5pm; closed Oct–Apr. Bus: All city center buses.

Ceol—The Irish Traditional Music Centre ✸✸   Ceol means "music" in Irish, and this is a must for any lover of Irish traditional music and dance. The beautifully designed ultra-high-tech center offers a plethora of interactive audiovisual displays and videos presenting the basic ingredients of Irish traditional music song, dance, story, and instruments. The climax of Ceol is the extraordinary film, shown in the 180-degree wide-screen main auditorium, titled *The Music of the People,* reason enough for going well out of your way to pay Ceol a visit. Plan on spending at least a couple of hours here; some visitors make it a day without even realizing it.

Smithfield Village, Dublin 7. ℂ **01/817-3820.** www.ceol.ie. €6.50 adults, €5 seniors and students, €4.50 children, €19 family. Mon–Sat 10am–6pm; Sun 11am–6pm (last film 45 min. before closing). Bus: 25, 25A, 67, 67A, 68, 69, 79, or 90.

Christ Church Cathedral ✸✸   Standing on high ground in the oldest part of the city, this is one of Dublin's finest historic buildings. It dates from 1038, when Sitric, Danish king of Dublin, built the first wooden Christ Church here. In 1171, the original foundation was extended into a cruciform and rebuilt in stone by Strongbow. The present structure dates mainly from 1871 to 1878, when a huge restoration took place. Highlights of the interior include magnificent stonework and graceful pointed arches, with delicately chiseled supporting columns. This is the mother church for the diocese of Dublin and Glendalough of the Church of Ireland. The new treasury in the crypt is now open to the public, and you can hear new bells pealing in the belfry.

Christchurch Place, Dublin 8. ℂ **01/677-8099.** cccdub@indigo.ie. Suggested donation €3 adults, €1.50 students and children under 15. Daily 10am–5:30pm. Closed Dec 26. Bus: 21A, 50, 50A, 78, 78A, or 78B.

Dublin Castle ✸✸   Built between 1208 and 1220, this complex represents some of the oldest surviving architecture in the city. It was the center of British power in Ireland for more than 7 centuries, until the new Irish government took it over in 1922. Film buffs might recognize the castle's courtyard as a setting in the Neil Jordan film *Michael Collins.* Highlights include the 13th-century Norman Tower; the State Apartments, once the residence of English viceroys; and the Chapel Royal, a 19th-century Gothic building with particularly fine plaster decoration and carved oak gallery fronts and fittings. The newest developments are the Undercroft, an excavated site on the grounds where an early Viking fortress stood, and the treasury, built between 1712 and 1715 and believed to be the oldest surviving office building in Ireland. Also here are a crafts shop, a heritage center, and a restaurant.

Palace St. (off Dame St.), Dublin 2. © 01/677-7129. www.dublincastle.ie. Admission €5 adults, €4 seniors and students, €2 children under 12. No credit cards. Mon–Fri 10am–5pm; Sat–Sun and holidays 2–5pm. Guided tours every 20–25 min. Bus: 50, 50A, 54, 56A, 77, 77A, or 77B.

Dublin Writers Museum ★★ Housed in a stunning 18th-century Georgian mansion with splendid plasterwork and stained glass, the museum is an impressive reminder of the grandeur of the Irish literary tradition. A fine collection of personal manuscripts and mementos that belonged to Yeats, Joyce, Beckett, Behan, Shaw, Wilde, Swift, and Sheridan are among the items that celebrate the written word. One of the museum's rooms is devoted to children's literature.

18–19 Parnell Sq. N., Dublin 1. © 01/475-0854. www.writersmuseum.com. Admission €5.50 adults, €5 seniors/students, €3 ages 3–11, €15 families (2 adults and up to 4 children). AE, DC, MC, V. Mon–Sat 10am–5pm (6pm June–Aug); Sun and holidays 11am–5pm. DART to Connolly Station. Bus: 11, 13, 16, 16A, 22, or 22A.

National Gallery ★★★ This museum houses Ireland's national art collection, as well as a superb collection of 14th- to 20th-century European art. Every major European school of painting is represented, including fine selections by Italian Renaissance artists, French Impressionists, and Dutch 17th-century masters. The Millennium Wing houses various temporary exhibitions as well as the Irish collection, which includes many mesmerizing works of Jack B. Yeats, brother of the poet William Butler Yeats. All public areas are wheelchair accessible. The museum has a fine gallery shop and an excellent self-service restaurant.

Merrion Sq. W., Dublin 2. © 01/661-5133. Fax 01/661-5372. www.nationalgallery.ie. Free admission. Mon–Sat 9:30am–5:30pm; Thurs 9:30am–8:30pm; Sun noon–5pm. Free guided tours (meet in the Shaw Room) Sat 3pm; Sun 2, 3, and 4pm. Closed Good Fri and Dec. 24–26. DART: Pearse. Bus: 5, 6, 7, 7A, 8, 10, 44, 47, 47B, 48A, or 62.

National Museum ★★★ Established in 1890, this museum is a reflection of Ireland's archaeological and historical heritage from 2000 B.C. to the present. It is the home of many of the country's greatest historical finds, including the Ardagh Chalice, Tara Brooch, and Cross of Cong. Other highlights range from the artifacts from the Wood Quay excavations of the Old Dublin Settlements to "Or," an extensive exhibition of Irish Bronze Age gold ornaments dating from 2200 to 700 B.C. The museum has a shop and a cafe. *Note:* The National Museum encompasses two other attractions, **Collins Barracks** and the **Natural History Museum;** see their separate listings below.

Kildare St. and Merrion St., Dublin 2. © 01/677-7444. www.museum.ie. Free admission. Tours (hours vary) €1.50 adults, free for seniors and children. MC, V. Tues–Sat 10am–5pm; Sun 2–5pm. DART: Pearse. Bus: 7, 7A, 8, 10, 11, or 13.

MORE ATTRACTIONS

Collins Barracks Officially part of the National Museum, Collins Barracks is the oldest military barracks in Europe. Even if it were empty, it's well worth a visit to see the structure itself, a splendidly restored early-18th-century masterwork by Col. Thomas Burgh, Ireland's chief engineer and surveyor general under Queen Anne. The collection focuses on the history of decorative arts. Most notable is the extraordinary display of Irish silver and furniture. It's a prime site for touring exhibitions, so consult *The Event Guide* for details. It also has a cafe and gift shop.

Benburb St., Dublin 7. ℭ **01/677-7444.** Free admission. Tours (hours vary) €2 adults, free for seniors and children. MC, V. Tues–Sat 10am–5pm; Sun 2–5pm. Bus: 34, 70, or 80.

Dublinia What was medieval Dublin like? This historically accurate presentation of the Old City from 1170 to 1540 is re-created through a series of theme exhibits, spectacles, and experiences. Highlights include an illuminated Medieval Maze, complete with visual effects, background sounds, and aromas that lead you on a journey through time from the arrival of the Anglo-Normans in 1170 to the closure of the monasteries in the 1530s. Another segment depicts everyday life in medieval Dublin with a diorama, as well as a prototype of a 13th-century quay along the banks of the Liffey.

St. Michael's Hill, Christ Church, Dublin 8. ℭ **01/679-4611.** www.dublinia.ie. Admission €5.75 adults; €4.50 seniors and students; €4.25 children; €15 family. AE, MC, V. Apr–Sept daily 10am–5pm; Oct–Mar Mon–Sat 11am–4pm, Sun 10am–4:30pm. Bus: 50, 78A, or 123.

GAA Museum On the grounds of Croke Park, principal stadium of the Gaelic Athletic Association, this museum dramatically presents the athletic heritage of Ireland. The Gaelic Games (Gaelic football, hurling, handball, and camogie) have long been held on an annual basis between teams representing the various regions of Ireland. Test your skills with interactive exhibits, and peruse the extensive video archive of football finals dating back to 1931. The 12-minute film *A Sunday in September* captures admirably the hysteria of the final match. *Note:* The museum is open only to those holding tickets in the new stands on match days.

Croke Park, Dublin 3. ℭ **01/855-8176.** Fax 01/855-8104. www.gaa.ie. Admission €5 adults, €3.50 seniors and students, €3 children. May–Sept daily 9:30am–5pm; Oct–Apr Tues–Sat 10am–5pm, Sun noon–5pm. Bus: 3, 11, 11A, 16, 16A, 51A, or 123.

Guinness Storehouse Founded in 1759, the Guinness Brewery is one of the world's largest breweries, producing the distinctive dark beer called stout, famous for its thick, creamy head. Although tours of the brewery are no longer allowed, visitors are welcome to explore the adjacent Guinness Storehouse, a converted 19th-century four-story building. It houses the World of Guinness Exhibition, an audiovisual presentation showing how the stout is made, and a bar where visitors can sample a glass. The brewery recently became home to the largest glass of stout in the world, roughly 60m (200 ft.) tall, whose head is in fact an observatory restaurant offering spectacular views of the city.

St. James's Gate, Dublin 8. ℭ **01/408-4800.** www.Guinness-storehouse.com. Admission €14 adults, €6.50 seniors and students, €3 children under 12, €28 family. AE, MC, V. Daily 9:30am–5pm. Guided tours every half hour. Bus: 51B, 78A, or 123.

Hugh Lane Municipal Gallery of Modern Art ⋆ Housed in a finely restored 18th-century building, this gallery is situated next to the Dublin Writers Museum. It's named after Hugh Lane, an Irish art connoisseur who died when the *Lusitania* sank in 1915 and who willed his collection (including works by Courbet, Manet, Monet, and Corot) to be shared between the government of Ireland and the National Gallery of London. This gallery also contains Impressionist and post-Impressionist paintings, Rodin sculptures, stained glass, and modern Irish works. In 2001 the museum opened the studio of Irish painter Francis Bacon. The bookshop is considered the best art bookshop in the city.

Parnell Sq. N., Dublin 1. ℭ **01/874-1903.** Fax 01/872-2182. www.hughlane.ie. Free admission to museum; Francis Bacon studio €7.50. MC, V. Tues–Thurs 9:30am–6pm; Fri–Sat 9:30am–5pm; Sun 11am–5pm. DART to Connolly or Tara stations. Bus: 3, 10, 11, 13, 16, or 19.

Native Behavior: The Art of Pouring Guinness

No trip to Ireland is complete without sampling the national beverage, whether you call it Guinness or simply "the black stuff." Despite its thick-as-pitch color, don't be afraid of it; Guinness isn't a heavy beer, only 11 calories per ounce or about 150 calories per pint, about the same as domestic beer. Draft Guinness is actually lower in alcohol than Coors Light. To the Irish, it's a classic "session beer," one with low alcohol and a great taste that can be enjoyed without leaving you feeling bloated. There are plenty of hops thrown in to give it a robust taste, and the Irish will vouch for the old advertising slogan that "Guinness is good for you."

Yet the Guinness ritual doesn't begin in the drinking; it starts in the pouring. And pouring the perfect pint is, as any respectable Irish barman will tell you, an art form known as the "two shot pour." Watch as he quickly fills the pint glass three-quarters of the way with swirling stout, then sets the glass on the counter for about a minute and a half so that the gas can break out. It's the 75% nitrogen to 25% carbon dioxide mix that builds the famous Guinness head. Next, the barman tops up the pint, and serves it while a sepia-colored storm brews inside. Patience, patience: No sipping until the pint has settled into a distinct line between the black stout and the honey-colored head. Classically, the head should stand "proud," just slightly above the rim of the glass and quite thick and mousse-y. And with a "Cheers!" or "Slainte!" (Irish for "To your health!") you're finally ready to enjoy your pint.

James Joyce Centre 🐦 Near Parnell Square and the Dublin Writers Museum, the Joyce center is in a restored 1784 Georgian town house, once the home of Denis J. Maginni, a dancing instructor who appears briefly in *Ulysses.* The Ulysses Portrait Gallery on the second floor has a fascinating collection of photographs and drawings of characters from *Ulysses* who had a life outside the novel. The Paul Leon Exhibition Room holds the writing table used by Joyce in Paris when he was working on *Finnegans Wake.* There are talks and audiovisual presentations daily. Guided walking tours through the neighborhood streets of "Joyce Country" in Dublin's north inner city are offered daily.

35 N. Great George's St., Dublin 1. © 01/878-8547. www.jamesjoyce.ie. Admission €4.50 adults, €3.50 seniors and students. Separate fees for walking tours and events. AE, MC, V. Mon–Sat 9:30am–5pm; Sun 12:30–5pm. Closed Dec 24–26. DART: Connolly. Bus: 3, 10, 11, 13, 16, 19, 22, 123.

The Joyce Tower Museum 🐦 Sitting on the edge of Dublin Bay about 10km (6 miles) south of the city center, this 12m (40-ft.) granite monument is one of a series of Martello towers built in 1804 to withstand an invasion threatened by Napoléon. The tower's great claim to fame is that James Joyce lived here in 1904. He was the guest of Oliver Gogarty, who had rented the tower from the Army for an annual fee of £8 ($11). Joyce, in turn, made the tower the setting for the first chapter of *Ulysses,* and it has been known as Joyce's Tower ever since. Its collection of Joycean memorabilia includes letters, documents, first and rare editions, personal possessions, and photographs.

Sandycove, County Dublin. ℂ/fax **01/280-9265**. joycetower@dublintourism.ie. Admission €5.50 adults, €5 seniors and students, €3 children, €15 family. AE, MC, V. Apr–Oct Mon–Sat 10am–1pm and 2–5pm; Sun 2–6pm. Closed Nov–Mar. DART: Sandycove. Bus: 59.

Kilmainham Gaol Historical Museum ✦   This is a key sight for anyone interested in Ireland's struggle for independence from British Rule. Within these walls political prisoners were incarcerated, tortured, and killed from 1796 until 1924, when former President Eamon de Valera left as its final prisoner. To walk along the corridors, through the exercise yard, or into the main compound is a moving experience that lingers hauntingly in the memory.

Kilmainham, Dublin 8. ℂ **01/453-5984**. www.heritageireland.ie. Guided tour €4.50 adults, €3.25 seniors, €2 children, €10 family. AE, MC, V. Apr–Sept daily 9:30am–4:45pm; Oct–Mar Mon–Fri 9:30am–4pm, Sun 10am–4:45pm. Bus: 51B, 78A, or 79 at O'Connell Bridge.

Natural History Museum   A division of the National Museum of Ireland, the recently renovated Natural History Museum is considered one of the finest traditional Victorian-style museums in the world. In addition to presenting the zoological history of Ireland, it contains examples of major animal groups from around the world, including many that are rare or extinct. The Blaschka glass models of marine animals are a big attraction.

Merrion St., Dublin 2. ℂ **01/677-7444**. Free admission. Tours (hours vary) €1.50 adults, free for seniors and children. MC, V. Tues–Sat 10am–5pm; Sun 2–5pm. DART: Pearse. Bus: 7, 7A, 8, or 13A.

Irish Film Centre ✦   This art house film institute is a hip hangout in Dublin's artsy Temple Bar district. The Irish Film Centre houses two cinemas, the Irish Film Archive, a library, a bookshop and cafe, and eight film-related organizations. Follow a movie with lunch in the cafe for a perfect midday outing.

6 Eustace St., Dublin 2. ℂ **01/679-5744** or 01/679-3477 for cinema box office. www.fii.ie. Free admission; cinema admission €6. Centre open daily 10am–11pm; cinemas daily 2–11pm; cinema box office daily 1:30–9pm. Bus: 21A, 78A, or 78B.

Irish Museum of Modern Art (IMMA) ✦ *Kids*   Housed in the splendidly restored 17th-century Royal Hospital, IMMA is a showcase of Irish and international art from the latter half of the 20th century. The buildings and grounds also provide a venue for theatrical and musical events. The galleries contain the work of Irish and international artists from the small but impressive permanent collection, with numerous temporary exhibitions. There's even a drawing room, where kids and parents can record their impressions of the museum with crayons. The formal gardens, an important early feature of this magnificent structure, are open to the public during museum hours. A new bookshop and a cafe are located in the former vaults of the building.

Military Rd., Kilmainham. ℂ **01/612-9900**. www.modernart.ie. Free admission. Tues–Sat 10am–5:30pm; Sun noon–5:30pm. Bus: 68, 68A, 69, 78A, 79, 123 and 90.

Old Jameson Distillery   This museum illustrates the history of Irish whiskey, known in Irish as *uisce beathectare* ("the water of life"). Housed in a former distillery warehouse, it consists of a short introductory audiovisual presentation, an exhibition area, and a whiskey-making demonstration. At the end of the tour, visitors can sample whiskey at an in-house pub, where an array of fixed-price menus (for lunch, tea, or dinner) is available. An added attraction here at Smithfield Village is **"The Chimney,"** a ride to the top of a 56m (185-ft.) brick chimney built in 1895 and converted to support an observation chamber from which you'll enjoy unparalleled views of the city.

Bow St., Smithfield Village, Dublin 7. ℂ **01/807-2355**. Admission €5 adults, €4 students and seniors, €2 children, €13 family. Daily 9:30am–6pm (last tour at 5pm). Chimney ascent €6 adults, €5 seniors and students, €4.50 children, €19 family. Mon–Sat 10am–6pm; Sun 11am–7pm. Bus: 67, 67A, 68, 69, 79, or 90.

St. Patrick's Cathedral It is said that St. Patrick baptized converts on this site, and consequently a church has stood here since A.D. 450, making it the oldest Christian site in Dublin. The present cathedral dates from 1190, but because of a fire and 14th-century rebuilding, not much of the original remains. It's mainly early English in style, with a square medieval tower that houses the largest ringing peal bells in Ireland and an 18th-century spire. The 90m (300-ft.) interior makes it the longest church in the country. Jonathan Swift was dean from 1713 to 1745, and his tomb lies in the south aisle. St. Patrick's is the national cathedral of the Church of Ireland.

21–50 Patrick's Close, Patrick St., Dublin 8. ℂ **01/475-4817**. Fax 01/454-6374. www.stpatrickscathedral.ie. Admission €3.50 adults, €2.50 students and seniors, €8 family. MC, V. Mon–Fri 9am–6pm year-round; Nov–Feb Sat 9am–5pm and Sun 9am–3pm. Closed except for services Dec 24–26 and Jan 1. Bus: 65, 65B, 50, 50A, 54, 54A, 56A, or 77.

Waterways Visitor Centre Heading south from Dublin on the DART, you'll see the tiny Waterways Visitor Centre, a brilliant white cube floating on the Grand Canal Basin amid massive derelict brick warehouses. This intriguing modern building is home to a fascinating exhibit describing the history of Ireland's inland waterways, a network of canals connecting Dublin westward and northward to the Shannon watershed. A series of displays describe aspects of canal design, and several interactive models attempt to demonstrate dynamically the daily operations of the canals. No longer used for transporting goods, the canals of Ireland are now popular among boaters and hikers, and the Visitor Centre offers information for those interested in these activities.

Grand Canal Quay, Ringsend Rd., Dublin 2. ℂ **01/677-7510**. Admission €3 adults, €2 seniors, €1.50 children or students, €6 families. No credit cards. June–Sept daily 9:30am–5:30pm; Oct–May Wed–Sun 12:30–5pm. DART: Pearse. Bus: 1 or 3.

PARKS & ZOOS
St. Stephen's Green 🎭 Preserved as an open space for Dubliners since 1690 and a short walk from most city center locations, this large park is popular for picnics, reading, a quiet stroll, and summertime concerts. While you're here, be sure to visit the **Iveagh Gardens** 🎭, a small garden hidden behind the National Concert Hall. Largely neglected by visitors, this is something of a hidden treasure within the city center. The main entrance is from Clonmel Street, off Harcourt Street, less than 5 minutes from Stephen's Green. The hours are the same as those for St. Stephen's Green.

St. Stephen's Green, Dublin 2. Mon–Sat 8am–dark and Sun 10am–dark. DART: Pearse. Bus: 10, 11A, 11B, 13, or 20B.

Phoenix Park 🎭 Dublin's 712-hectare (1,760-acre) playground (Europe's largest enclosed urban park) opened in 1747. Situated 3km (2 miles) west of the city center, it is traversed by a network of roads and quiet pedestrian walkways and is informally landscaped with ornamental gardens, nature trails, and broad expanses of grassland separated by avenues of trees, including oak, beech, pine, chestnut, and lime. The residences of the Irish president (see below) and the U.S. ambassador are on its grounds. Livestock graze peacefully on pasturelands, deer roam the forested areas, and horses romp on polo fields. The Phoenix Park Visitor Centre, adjacent to Ashtown Castle, offers exhibitions and an audiovisual presentation on the park's history. The cafe/restaurant is open from 10am to 5pm weekdays, from 10am to 6pm weekends. A shuttle bus runs on Saturday only from the visitor center, with stops throughout the park. One-day hop-on, hop-off service is €1.50 per person. On Saturdays only, tickets are issued at the Visitor Centre from 9:40am to 4:20pm for tours of **Aras an Uachtaráin** (**The President's Residence;** ℭ **01/670-9155**). Admission is free, and the tour lasts 1 hour. No advance booking is possible but it's advisable to arrive before noon, since only 525 tickets are available, first-come, first-served.

The **Dublin Zoo** (ℭ **01/677-1425;** www.dublinzoo.ie), also located here in Phoenix Park, was established in 1830 and is the third-oldest zoo in the world (after those in London and Paris). In the past few years, the zoo has doubled in size to about 25 hectares (60 acres) and provides a naturally landscaped habitat for more than 235 species of wild animals and tropical birds. Highlights for youngsters include the Children's Pets' Corner and a train ride around the zoo. There are playgrounds interspersed throughout the zoo, as well as several restaurants, coffee shops, and gift shops.

Phoenix Park, Dublin 8. ℭ **01/677-0095.** Visitor Centre: Admission €2.50 adults, €2 seniors, €1.50 students and children, €6.50 families. June–Sept 10am–6pm (call for off-season hours). Bus: 37, 38, or 39. Zoo: Admission €10 adults, €7.70 students, €6.30 seniors and children 3–16, free for children under 3, €25–€34 family, depending on number of children. V. Summer Mon–Sat 9:30am–6pm, Sun 10:30am–6pm. Bus: 10, 25, or 26.

National Botanic Gardens   Remember this quiet, lovely haven when you suddenly crave refuge from the bustle of the city. Established by the Royal Dublin Society in 1795 on a rolling 20-hectare (50-acre) expanse of land north of the city center, this is Dublin's horticultural showcase. The attractions include more than 20,000 different plants and cultivars, a Great Yew Walk, a bog garden, a water garden, a rose garden, and an herb garden. A variety of Victorian-style glass houses are filled with tropical plants and exotic species. All but the rose garden are wheelchair accessible.

Botanic Rd., Glasnevin, Dublin 9. ℭ **01/837-7596.** Free admission. Guided tour €2. Apr–Oct Mon–Sat 9am–6pm, Sun 11am–6pm; Nov–Mar Mon–Sat 10am–4:30pm, Sun 11am–4:30pm. Bus: 13, 19, or 134.

ORGANIZED TOURS

BUS TOURS   If you want to get a general feel for the city, **Dublin Bus** (ℭ **01/873-4222;** www.dublinbus.ie) operates a very good, 75-minute hop-on, hop-off **Dublin City Tour** that connects 10 major points of interest, including museums, art galleries, churches and cathedrals, libraries, and historic sites. It departs from the Dublin Bus office at 59 Upper O'Connell St., Dublin 1, daily from 9:30am to 6:30pm. Free pickup from many hotels is available for morning tours. Fares are €10 adults and €5 children under 14. You can buy your ticket from the bus driver or book in advance at the Dublin Bus office or at the Dublin Tourism ticket desk on Suffolk Street.

Gray Line (ℭ **01/605-7705;** www.guidefriday.com) operates its own hop-on, hop-off city tour, covering the same major sights as the Dublin Bus's Dublin City Tour. The tours are identical, so there's no reason to pay more for Gray Line. The first tours leave at 10am from 14 Upper O'Connell St., and at 10am from the Dublin Tourism Center on Suffolk Street, Dublin 2, and run every 10 to 15 minutes thereafter. The last departures are at 4pm from Suffolk Street, 4:30pm from O'Connell Street. You can also join the tour at any of a number of pickup points along the route and buy your ticket from the driver. Gray Line's Dublin City Tour costs €12 adults, €10 seniors and students, €4 children.

WALKING TOURS   You can set out on your own with a map, but the best way to avoid any hassles or missed sights is to follow one of the three signposted and themed **"tourist trails":** Old City Trail for historic sights; Georgian Trail for the landmark buildings, streets, squares, terraces, and parks; and Cultural Heritage Trail for a circuit of the top literary sites, museums, galleries, theaters, and churches. Each trail is mapped out with commentary in a handy booklet available at the tourist office or as a free printable guide from Dublin Tourism's website (www.visitdublin.com). There's also a "Rock 'n Stroll Guide" for a walking tour with a music theme, available for €4 from Dublin Tourism.

A number of firms offer guided tours led by knowledgeable locals. Tour times and charges vary, but many last about 2 hours and cost between €7 and €10. A complete listing of walking tours is available from Dublin Tourism, but here are some of the best:

Historical Walking Tours of Dublin (© 01/878-0227; €10) delivers your best introductory walk, an award-winning 2-hour primer on Dublin's historic landmarks, from medieval walls and Viking remains around Wood Quay to Christ Church, Dublin Castle, City Hall, and Trinity College. Guides are history graduates of Trinity College, and participants are encouraged to ask questions.

If you prefer an evening tour, there's the **Literary Pub Crawl** (© 01/670-5602; €10), a winner of the "Living Dublin Award." The tour follows in the footsteps of Joyce, Behan, Beckett, Shaw, Kavanagh, and other Irish literary greats to local pubs, with actors providing humorous performances and commentary between stops. Throughout the night, there is a Literary Quiz with prizes for the winners.

Zosimus Ghostly Experience (© 01/661-8646; €10) is the latest rage on the walking-tour circuit. Its creators describe it as a "cocktail mix" of ghosts, murderous tales, horror stories, humor, circus, history, street theater, and whatever's left, all set in medieval Dublin. Your storyteller is the blind and aging Zosimus, and you help guide him down the austere alleyways. It's essential to book this tour in advance, when you'll receive the where (gate of Dublin Castle, opposite the Olympia Theatre) and the when (7pm in winter, 9pm in summer). The experience lasts approximately 1½ hours.

HORSE-DRAWN CARRIAGE TOURS   If you don't mind being conspicuous, you can tour Dublin in style in a handsomely outfitted horse-drawn carriage while your driver points out the sights. To arrange a ride, consult with one of the drivers stationed with carriages on the Grafton Street side of St. Stephen's Green. Rides range from a short swing around the Green to an extensive half-hour Georgian tour or an hour-long Old City tour. Rides are available on a first-come, first-served basis from April to October (weather permitting) and cost anywhere from €15 to €60 for one to four passengers, depending on the duration of the ride.

LAND & WATER TOURS   The immensely popular **Viking Splash Tour** (© 01/855-3000; www.vikingsplashtours.com) brings you aboard a reconditioned World War II amphibious landing craft, or "duck." The tour begins on land (from Bull Alley St. beside St. Patrick's Cathedral) and eventually splashes into the Grand Canal. Passengers wear horned Viking helmets (a reference to the original settlers of the Dublin area) and are encouraged to issue war cries at appropriate moments. Tours last 75 minutes and depart roughly every half hour Monday through Saturday from 10am to 5pm and Sunday from 11am to 6:30pm. It costs €14 adults, €7.50 children under 12, €45 family. To book with a credit card by phone, call © **01/453-9185.**

THE SHOPPING SCENE

The hub of shopping south of the Liffey is the pedestrians-only **Grafton Street,** crowned by the city's most fashionable department store, Brown Thomas (known simply as BT), and most exclusive jeweler, Weirs. Sadly, many Irish specialty shops on Grafton Street have been displaced over the years by British chain shops (Principles, Jigsaw, Monsoon, Oasis, A–Wear, Next, Boots, Mothercare), so that it now resembles the average High Street in England. Pedestrianized Grafton Street tends to have a festive atmosphere thanks to street performers and sidewalk artists. But you'll find better shopping on the smaller streets radiating out from Grafton—Duke, Dawson, Nassau, and Wicklow—which have more Irish shops that specialize in small books, handcrafts, jewelry, gifts, and clothing. Two upscale shopping malls, the **Powerscourt Townhouse Centre** and **St. Stephen's Green Centre,** are examples of Dublin's ongoing renovation and gentrification.

A 2-minute walk northwest toward the river brings you to **Temple Bar,** the hub of Dublin's colorful, bohemian district and the setting for art and music shops, vintage clothing stores, and a host of other increasingly fine and interesting boutiques, cafes, and restaurants. Dublin's latest "it" shopping district is **Old City,** located just west of Temple Bar and roughly comprising the area between Castle Street and Fishamble Street. Though still under development, it already has a good mix of hip fashion, modern interior design, crafts, and leisure shops. The center of the action is a cobbled, pedestrianized street called Cow's Lane, which links Lord Edward Street with Essex Street West.

North of the Liffey, the **O'Connell Street** area is the main inner-city shopping nucleus, along with its nearby offshoots—Abbey Street for crafts, Moore Street for its open-air market, and, most notably, Henry Street, a pedestrian-only strip of chain stores, department stores, and indoor malls such as the ILAC Centre and the Jervis Shopping Centre.

BOOKS   This city of literary legends has quite a few good bookstores. For fine new and used books, including first editions of works by famous Irish authors, try **Hodges Figgis,** 57 Dawson St., Dublin 2 (© **01/677-4754**); more affordable used books can be found at **Greene's Bookshop,** 16 Clare St., Dublin 2 (© **01/676-2554**) and the **Winding Stair,** 40 Lower Ormond Quay, Dublin 1 (© **01/873-3292**).

CHINA & CRYSTAL   China Showrooms, 32/33 Abbey St. (© **01/878-6211;** www.chinashowrooms.ie), is a one-stop source of fine china such as Belleck, Aynsley, and Royal Doulton, and hand-cut crystal from Waterford, Tipperary, and Tyrone. The **Dublin Crystal Glass Company,** Brookfield Terrace, Carysfort Avenue, Blackrock (© **01/288-7932;** www.dublincrystal.ie), is Dublin's own distinctive hand-cut crystal business, founded in 1764 and revived in 1968. Dublin Crystal is a 15-minute walk from the Blackrock DART station.

CRAFTS & GIFTS   Whichcraft, 5 Castlegate, Lord Edward St. (© **01/670-9371**), is an essential stop for finding out what the best contemporary artisans from all over Ireland are doing. All kinds of crafts are represented, from wooden bowls to basketry to rocking horses to pottery to jewelry to ironmongery to batiks. A second Whichcraft shop recently opened on Cow's Lane in the burgeoning Old City.

HERALDRY   Heraldic Artists, 3 Nassau St. (© **01/679-7020**), has been known for helping visitors celebrate their family roots for over 20 years. In addition to tracing surnames, it also sells all the usual heraldic items, from parchments and mahogany wall plaques to crests, scrolls, and books on researching ancestry.

KNITWEAR **Blarney Woollen Mills,** 21–23 Nassau St. (© **01/671-0068**), known for its competitive prices, stocks a wide range of woolen knitwear made at its home base in Blarney, as well as crystal, china, pottery, and souvenirs. **Brown Thomas,** 88–95 Grafton St. (© **01/605-6666**), is the only place in town to find Dubliner Lainey Keogh's creative and sensuous knitwear—a far cry from the chunky Aran sweaters you see everywhere else. What *Vogue* magazine calls "amazingly organic knitwear" is a staple in the closets of such Hollywood celebrities as Demi Moore and Isabella Rossellini. Keogh works mostly with cashmere, and her pieces are predominantly made by expert hand-knitters, so prices are high. **Dublin Woollen Mills,** 41 Lower Ormond Quay (© **01/677-0301**), is on the north side of the River Liffey next to the Ha'penny Bridge, a leading source of Aran hand-knit sweaters as well as vests, hats, jackets, and tweeds. For cashmere, go to **Monaghan's,** 15–17 Grafton Arcade, Grafton Street (© **01/677-0823**), which has the best selection of colors, sizes, and styles for both men and women anywhere in Ireland. It's also located at 4–5 Royal Hibernian Way, off Dawson Street (© **01/679-4451**).

DUBLIN AFTER DARK

One general fact to keep in mind concerning Dublin's nightlife is that there are very few fixed points. Apart from a handful of established institutions, venues come and go, change character, open their doors to ballet one night and cabaret the next. Two publications, *In Dublin* and *The Event Guide,* offer the most thorough and up-to-date listings of what's happening in town. They can be found at any newsstand.

The award-winning website of the *Irish Times* (**www.ireland.com**) offers a "what's on" daily guide to cinema, theater, music, and whatever else you're up for. The *Dublin Events Guide* (**www.dublinevents.com**) also provides a comprehensive listing of the week's entertainment possibilities.

Advance bookings for most large concerts, plays, and so forth can be made through **Ticketmaster Ireland** (© **01/677-9409;** www.ticketmaster.ie), with ticket centers in most HMV stores, as well as at the Dublin Tourism Centre, Suffolk Street, Dublin 2.

THE PERFORMING ARTS
Concert & Performance Halls

National Concert Hall, Earlsfort Terrace, Dublin 2 (© **01/475-1572;** www. nch.ie), is home to the National Symphony Orchestra and Concert Orchestra, and is host to an array of international orchestras and performing artists. In addition to classical music, there are evenings of Gilbert and Sullivan, opera, jazz, and recitals. The box office is open Monday through Saturday from 10am to 3pm and from 6pm to the concert's close. Tickets are €10 to €40. Lunchtime concerts are €5.

For more than 90 years, the **Abbey Theatre,** Lower Abbey St., Dublin 1 (© **01/878-7222;** www.abbeytheatre.ie), has been the national theater of Ireland. The Abbey's artistic reputation within Ireland has risen and fallen many times and is at present reasonably strong. The box office is open Monday through Saturday from 10:30am to 7pm; performances begin at 8 or 8:15pm. Tickets are €15 to €26.

The Gate, 1 Cavendish Row, Dublin 1 (© **01/874-4368;** fax 01/874-5373), just north of O'Connell Street off Parnell Square, was founded in 1928 by Hilton Edwards and Michael MacLiammoir to provide a showing for a broad range of plays. This policy prevails today, with a program that includes a blend

Traditional Irish Entertainment

Culturlann Na hEireann, 32 Belgrave Sq., Monkstown (© 01/280-0295; www.comhaltas.com), is the home of Comhaltas Ceoltoiri Eireann, an Irish cultural organization that has been the prime mover in encouraging the renewal of Irish traditional music. An authentic fully costumed show featuring traditional music, song, and dance is staged mid-June through early September, Monday through Thursday at 9pm. No reservations are necessary. Year-round, ceili dances are performed Friday from 9pm to midnight; informal music sessions are held Wednesday, Friday, and Saturday at 9pm. Tickets for ceilis are €8; informal music sessions €3 from Friday to Saturday, free Wednesday; stage shows €8.

Jury's Irish Cabaret, Pembroke Road, Ballsbridge (© 01/660-5000), Ireland's longest-running show (over 30 years), offers a mix of traditional Irish music and Broadway classics, set dancing, humorous monologues, and audience participation. Shows take place May through October, Tuesday through Sunday, with dinner at 7:15pm and the show at 8pm. Dinner and show are €55; show with two drinks €35.

of modern works and the classics. Although less well known by visitors, the Gate is easily as distinguished as the Abbey. The box office is open Monday through Saturday from 10am to 7pm. Tickets are €21 to €25.

The **Andrews Lane Theatre,** 12–16 Andrews Lane, Dublin 2 (© 01/679-5720), has a growing reputation for fine theater. It consists of a main theater where contemporary works from home and abroad are presented, and a studio geared for experimental productions. The box office is open Monday through Saturday from 10:30am to 7pm. Tickets are €13 to €20.

With a seating capacity of 3,000, **The Point Depot,** East Link Bridge, North Wall Quay (© 01/836-3633), is one of Dublin's larger indoor theater/concert venues, attracting top Broadway-caliber shows and international stars such as Neil Young and Sarah Brightman. The box office is open Monday through Saturday from 10am to 6pm. Tickets are €20 to €65.

THE PUB SCENE
Pubs for Conversation & Atmosphere
The brass-filled and lantern-lit **Brazen Head,** 20 Lower Bridge St. (© 01/679-5186), has atmosphere in spades. It's a tad touristy, which isn't surprising when you consider that it's the city's oldest pub—licensed in 1661 and occupying the site of an earlier tavern dating from 1198. On the south bank of the River Liffey, it's at the end of a cobblestone courtyard and was once the meeting place of Irish freedom fighters such as Robert Emmet and Wolfe Tone.

Converted from an old merchant's warehouse, the **River Club,** in the Ha'penny Theatre, 48 Wellington Quay (© 01/677-2382), is a wine bar-cum-supper club with soaring ceilings, an enviable position overlooking the river, and contemporary furnishings for an overall feeling of easygoing sophistication. It's a favorite of Ireland's film glitterati for a late drink, so don't be surprised to spy author-screenwriter Roddy Doyle, Pierce Brosnan, or director Jim Sheridan.

Referred to as a "moral pub" by James Joyce in *Ulysses,* **Davy Byrnes,** 21 Duke St., just off Grafton Street (*©* **01/677-5217**), has drawn poets, writers, and lovers of literature ever since. Davy Byrnes first opened the doors in 1873; he presided here for more than 50 years and visitors today can still see his likeness on one of the turn-of-the-20th-century murals hanging over the bar.

Flannery's Temple Bar, 47–48 Temple Bar (*©* **01/497-4766**), in the heart of the trendy Temple Bar district on the corner of Temple Lane, was established in 1840. The decor is an interesting mix of crackling fireplaces, globe ceiling lights, old pictures on the walls, and shelves filled with local memorabilia. Tucked into a busy commercial street, **The Long Hall,** 51 S. Great George's St. (*©* **01/475-1590**), is one of the city's most photographed pubs, with a beautiful Victorian decor of filigree-edged mirrors, polished dark woods, and traditional snugs. The hand-carved bar is said to be the longest counter in the city.

Adjacent to the back door of the Gaiety Theatre, **Neary's,** 1 Chatham St., Dublin 2 (*©* **01/677-7371**), is a favorite with stage folk and theatergoers. Trademarks here are the pink-and-gray marble bar and the brass hands that support the globe lanterns adorning the entrance. Three generations of the Ryan family have contributed to the success of **J. W. Ryan,** 28 Parkgate St. (*©* **01/677-6097**), on the north side of the Liffey near Phoenix Park. The pub is a Victorian gem featuring a pressed tin ceiling and domed skylight, etched glass, brass lamp holders, a mahogany bar, and four old-style snugs.

Pubs with Traditional/Folk Music

Tucked between St. Stephen's Green and Merrion Street, **O'Donoghue's,** 15 Merrion Row, Dublin 2 (*©* **01/660-7194**), is a much-touristed, smoke-filled, kingpin of traditional music pubs. The Dubliners, one of Ireland's favorite traditional bands, got their start here, and impromptu music sessions are held almost every night. Situated in the heart of Temple Bar and named for one of Ireland's literary greats, **Oliver St. John Gogarty,** 57–58 Fleet St. (*©* **01/671-1822**), has an inviting old-world atmosphere, with shelves of empty bottles, stacks of dusty books, a horseshoe-shaped bar, and old barrels for seats. There are traditional music sessions every night from 9 to 11pm. A Saturday session is at 4:30pm, and a Sunday session from noon to 2pm.

THE CLUB & MUSIC SCENE

The club and music scene in Dublin is confoundingly complex and changeable. Jazz, blues, folk, country, traditional, rock, and comedy move from venue to venue, night by night. The same club could be a gay fetish scene one night and a traditional music hot spot the next, so you have to stay on your toes to find what you want. The first rule is to get the very latest listings and see what's on and where (see the introduction to "Dublin After Dark" above for suggested resources). Keeping all this in mind, a few low-risk generalizations might prove helpful to give you a sense of what to expect.

One fact unlikely to change is that the after-hours scene in Dublin is definitively young, averaging about 25. The hottest clubs have a "strict" (read: unfriendly) door policy of admitting only "regulars." It helps if you're a celebrity or a supermodel—or just look like one. But barring that, your chances of getting past the door increase if you go in smallish groups, and if you wear your hippest clothes and your coolest attitude.

Dozens of clubs and pubs all over town feature rock, folk, jazz, and traditional Irish music. This includes the so-called "late-night pubs"—pubs with an exemption allowing them to remain open past the usual closing time, mandated by law

(11pm in winter, 11:30pm in summer). Check *In Dublin* magazine or *The Event Guide* for club schedules. One of the most popular rock clubs is **Whelan's,** 25 Wexford St., Dublin 2 (© **01/478-0766**); you should also visit the new **Hot Press Irish Music Hall of Fame,** 57 Middle Abbey St., Dublin 1 (© **01/878-3345**), with music from Celtic to rock most nights; and the second-oldest pub in Dublin, **Bleeding Horse,** 24–25 Camden St., Dublin 2 (© **01/475-2705**). Other venues especially popular with the over-30 late crowd include: **Bad Bob's Backstage Bar,** East Essex Street, Dublin 2 (© **01/677-5482**); **Major Tom's,** South King Street, Dublin 2 (© **01/478-3266**); the **Baggot Inn,** Baggot Street, Dublin 4 (© **01/676-1430**); and **Sinnotts,** South King Street, Dublin 2 (© **01/478-4698**). All are open daily, with live music most nights. When there is a cover charge, it's usually €5 to €10.

The city's largest gay bar is the **George,** 89 S. Great George's St., Dublin 2 (© **01/478-2983**), a two-story venue where both the decor and clientele tend toward camp. It's open daily from 12:30pm to 2:30am; check listings magazines for theme nights, which start around 10pm.

2 Kerry & the Dingle Peninsula

For many first-time travelers to this island, Kerry is the Ireland they'd imagined in their mind's eye. To start with, it's picture-postcard gorgeous, with spectacular coastal vistas and vibrant towns. Spend a bit of time here, and you'll also see that Kerry is a place of disorienting contrasts, where the crassest tourist attractions coexist with some of Ireland's most spectacular scenic wonders. It's a rugged place for the most part, some of it so rugged that it's seldom visited and remains quite pristine; Ireland's two highest mountains, Carrantuohill and Mount Brandon, are examples of such places. You could be driving along—say, on the famous and much-trafficked Ring of Kerry, which traces the shores of the Iveragh Peninsula—make one little detour from the main road, and be in true wilderness. The transition can be startling.

Like many of Ireland's western counties, County Kerry has always been an outpost of Gaelic culture. Poetry and music are intrinsic to the lifestyle, as is a love of the outdoors and sports. Gaelic football is an obsession in this county, and "The Kingdom" wins more than their share of the national championships. You'll also find some of Ireland's best golf courses, and the fishing for salmon and trout is equally hard to resist.

GETTING TO COUNTY KERRY   By Train   Irish Rail (© **01/836-6222;** www.irishrail.ie) operates daily train service from Dublin, Limerick, Cork, and Galway to the **Killarney Railway Station** (© **064/31067**) on Railway Road, off East Avenue Road.

By Bus   Bus Eireann (© **01/836-6111;** www.buseireann.ie) operates daily express coach and local bus services to Killarney from Dublin and other parts of Ireland. The bus depot (© **064/34777**) is adjacent to the train station at Railway Road, off East Avenue Road. Once you're there, there's also limited daily service from Killarney to Caherciveen, Waterville, Kenmare, and other towns on the Ring of Kerry. Some private, Killarney-based companies offer daily sightseeing tours of the Ring of Kerry by bus.

By Car   Roads leading into Kerry include N6 from Dublin, N21 and N23 from Limerick, and N22 from Cork. The best way to do the Ring of Kerry (comprising the N70 and N71) is by car.

KILLARNEY TOWN

Killarney is the busiest beehive of tourism in Ireland, the Grand Central Station of the southwest, with all the positive and negative connotations that this implies. The town becomes one giant traffic jam of battling tour buses every summer and a mecca for pushy jaunting-car (horse-and-buggy) drivers. Tourism is more in-your-face here than perhaps anywhere else in Ireland, with generic souvenir shops and overpriced restaurants chock-a-block. If this doesn't sound like your bag, then resist Killarney's gravitational pull and base yourself in the incredibly scenic hinterlands that border the town on all sides. Then you can sneak into town at some point to sample the best of what this tourist megalopolis has to offer without experiencing the tourist trap in full gear.

It's important to remember that the reason Killarney draws millions of visitors a year has nothing to do with the town. It's all about the valley in which the town is nestled, a landscape of lakes and mountains that's so truly spectacular that Brendan Behan once said, "Even an ad man would be ashamed to eulogize it." And entering these wonders is ever so easy. Walk from the town car park toward the cathedral, and turn left into the national park (see below). During the summer, the evenings are long, the twilight is often indescribable, and you needn't share the lanes. Apart from deer and locals, the park is all yours until dark.

The lakes and the surrounding woodlands are part of the 65-sq.-km (25-sq.-mile) **Killarney National Park.** The ground is a soft carpet of moss and the air is fragrant with wildflowers. Cars are banned from most of the ferny trails, so take a hike or hire a "jarvey," an old-fashioned horse-and-buggy that's a holdover from the days when the Victorians waxed poetically about Killarney and brought it to the attention of the world.

ESSENTIALS

VISITOR INFORMATION   County Kerry's official tourism website is **www. kerry-tourism.com**. The **Killarney Tourist Office,** Aras Fáilte, is located at the Town Centre Car Park, Beech Road, Killarney (© **064/31633**). It's open January through April, Monday through Saturday from 9:15am to 1pm and 2:15 to 5:30pm; May, Monday through Saturday from 9:15am to 5:30pm; June, Monday through Saturday from 9am to 6pm, Sunday from 10am to 1pm and 2:15 to 6pm; July through August, Monday through Saturday from 9am to 8pm, Sunday from 10am to 1pm and 2:15 to 6pm; September, Monday through Saturday from 9am to 6pm, Sunday from 10am to 1pm and 2:15 to 6pm; October through December, Monday through Saturday from 9:15am to 1pm and 2:15 to 5:30pm. It offers many helpful booklets, including the "Tourist Trail" walking-tour guide and the "Killarney Area Guide" with maps.

Useful local publications include *Where: Killarney* (www.wherekillarney.com), a quarterly magazine distributed free at hotels and guesthouses. It's packed with all types of current information on tours, activities, events, and entertainment.

GETTING AROUND   The town is so small and compact that it's best traversed on foot. Taxicabs line up at the rank on **College Square** (© **064/31331**). You can also phone for a taxi from **John Burke** (© **064/32448**), **Dero's Taxi Service** (© **064/31251**), or **O'Connell Taxi** (© **064/31654**). You can drive to Killarney National Park (but not through it), or go by **jaunting car.** The horse-drawn jaunting cars line up at Kenmare Place, offering rides to Killarney National Park sites and other scenic areas.

County Kerry

Crag Cave **8**
Dingle Oceanworld **4**
Gallarus Oratory **3**
Gap of Dunloe **7**
Kerry the Kingdom **1**
Skellig Islands **5**
Staigue Fort **6**
Tralee Steam Railway **2**

KILLARNEY NATIONAL PARK ★★★

This is Killarney's centerpiece: a 10,000-hectare (25,000-acre) area of natural beauty. The park's three lakes are Killarney's main attraction. The first, the Lower Lake, is sometimes called "Lough Leane" or "Lough Lein," which means "the lake of learning." It's the largest, more than 6.5km (4 miles) long, and is dotted with 30 small islands. The second lake is aptly called the "Middle Lake" or "Muckross Lake," and the third simply "Upper Lake." Upper Lake, the smallest, is full of storybook islands covered with a variety of trees—evergreens, cedars of Lebanon, juniper, holly, and mountain ash.

The most noteworthy of Killarney's islands is **Innisfallen,** or "Fallen's Island," which seems to float peacefully in the Lower Lake. You can reach it by rowboat, available for rental at Ross Castle. St. Fallen founded a monastery here in the 7th century, and it flourished for 1,000 years. It's said that Brian Boru, the great Irish chieftain, and St. Brendan the Navigator were educated here. From 950 to 1320, the *Annals of Innisfallen,* a chronicle of early Irish history, was written at the monastery; it's now in the Bodleian Library at Oxford University. Traces of an 11th-century church and a 12th-century priory can still be seen today.

Found within the park's limits are two major demesnes, or estates, **Muckross** and **Knockreer,** and the remains of major medieval abbeys and castles. A profusion of foliage, such as rhododendrons, azaleas, magnolias, camellias, hydrangeas, and tropical ferns, blossoms in season. At almost every turn, you'll see Killarney's own botanical wonder, the arbutus, or strawberry tree, plus eucalyptus, redwoods, and native oak.

The park also contains a large variety of wildlife, including a rare herd of red deer. You can't drive through the park (car parks are available, however, if you want to drive *to* it), so touring is best done on foot, bicycle, or horse-drawn jaunting car. The park offers four signposted walking and nature trails along the lakeshore.

Access to the park is available from several points along the Kenmare road (N71), with the main entrance being at Muckross House, where a new visitor center features background exhibits on the park and a 20-minute film titled *Mountain, Wood, Water*. Admission is free, and the park is open year-round during daylight hours.

VIEWS & VISTAS   The journey through the **Gap of Dunloe** 🐴🐴 is a must. The winding and rocky mountain pass is situated amid mountains and lakelands about 10km (6 miles) west of Killarney. The route through the gap passes a kaleidoscope of craggy rocks, massive cliffs, meandering streams, and deep valleys. The route through the gap ends at Upper Lake. One of the best ways to explore the gap is by bicycle. Horse fanciers may want to take one of the excursions offered by **Castlelough Tours,** 7 High St. (© **064/31115**); **Corcoran's Tours,** Kilcummin (© **064/36666**); **Dero's Tours,** 22 Main St. (© **064/31251** or 064/31567), or **Tangney Tours,** Kinvara House, Muckross Road (© **064/33358**). Combination coach/horse/boat tours cost €37. If you'd rather have someone else handle the horse, you can take an 11km (7-mile) jaunting-car tour. Excursions go from Kate Kearney's Cottage through the Gap of Dunloe to Lord Brandon's Cottage and back.

Aghadoe Heights 🐴, on the Tralee Road (off N22), is a spectacular viewing point over the lakes and town. To your left is the ruin of the 13th-century Castle of Parkvonear, erected by Norman invaders and well worth a visit. In the nearby churchyard are the remains of a stone church and round tower dating from 1027.

MORE ATTRACTIONS
Muckross House and Gardens 🐴🐴   This estate is the focal point of the Middle Lake and, in many ways, of the entire national park. It's often called "the jewel of Killarney." The property consists of a gracious ivy-covered Victorian mansion and its elegant surrounding gardens. Dating from 1843, the 20-room Muckross House has been converted into a museum of County Kerry folk life, showcasing locally carved furniture, prints, maps, paintings, and needlework. Imported treasures like Oriental screens, Venetian mirrors, Chippendale chairs, Turkish carpets, and curtains woven in Brussels are on display. The cellars have been converted into craft shops, where local artisans demonstrate traditional trades such as bookbinding, weaving, and pottery. The adjacent mature gardens, known for their fine collection of rhododendrons and azaleas, are also worth exploring.

The ruin of the 15th-century **Muckross Abbey,** founded about 1448 and burned by Cromwell's troops in 1652, is also near the house. The abbey's central feature is a vaulted cloister around a courtyard that contains a huge yew tree, said to be as old as the abbey itself. There's a combination ticket available with Muckross Traditional Farms (see below).

Kenmare road (N71), Killarney, County Kerry. © 061/31440. www.muckross-house.ie. Admission €5 adults, €3.80 seniors, €2 students and children, €13 family. July–Aug daily 9am–7pm; mid-Mar to June and Sept–Oct daily 9am–6pm; Nov to mid-Mar daily 9am–5:30pm.

Muckross Traditional Farms 🎫 Located just across from Muckross House, this 28-hectare (70-acre) park is home to displays of traditional farm life and artisans' shops so authentically detailed that visitors feel they are dropping in on working farms and lived-in houses. It's a fascinating place, especially for families with children. You'll be able to watch sowing and harvesting or potato picking and hay making, depending on the season. Farmhands work in the fields and tend the animals, while the blacksmith, carpenter, and wheelwright ply their trades in the old manner. Women draw water from wells and cook meals in traditional kitchens with authentic household items. *Note:* A combination ticket allows you to visit Muckross House for €2.50 extra per person.

Kenmare road (N71), Killarney, County Kerry. (©) 064/31440. www.muckross-house.ie. Admission €5 adults, €3.80 seniors, €2 students and children, €13 family. Combination ticket with Muckross House €7.50 adults, €5.50 seniors, €3 students and children, €19 family. Mid-Mar to Apr and Oct Sat–Sun 1–6pm; May daily 1–6pm; June–Sept daily 10am–7pm. Closed Nov to mid-Mar.

Ross Castle This 15th-century restored fortress sits on the edge of the Lower Lake, 3km (2 miles) outside Killarney Town. Built by the O'Donoghue chieftains, this castle distinguished itself in 1652 as the last stronghold in Munster to surrender to Cromwell's forces. All that remains today is a tower house, surrounded by a fortified bawn (enclosure) with rounded turrets. The tower has been furnished in the style of the late 16th and early 17th centuries and offers a magnificent view of the lakes and islands from its top. Access is by guided tour only. A lovely lakeshore walk stretches for 1.6km (1 mile) between Killarney and the castle. Lake cruises are run from the castle (see "Boat Tours," below), including boats to **Innisfallen Island,** which has the ruins of a 7th-century monastery and a 12th-century oratory.

Ross Rd., off Kenmare road (N71), Killarney, County Kerry. (©) 064/35851. Admission €3.80 adults, €2.50 seniors, €1.50 students and children, €10 family. Apr daily 10am–5pm; May and Sept daily 10am–6pm; June Aug daily 9am–6.30pm, Oct Tues–Sun 10am–5pm. Last admission 45 min. before closing. Closed Nov–Mar.

SIGHTSEEING TOURS

BUS TOURS Dero's Tours, 7 Main St., Killarney ((©) **064/31251** or 064/31567, www.derostours.com), offers a 3-hour tour showing off Killarney's lakes from the best vantage points, including Aghadoe, the Gap of Dunloe, Ross Castle, Muckross House and Gardens, and Torc Waterfall. The tour is offered May through September daily at 10:30am, but schedules vary, so check in advance. It costs €11.

Castlelough Tours, 7 High St., Killarney ((©) **064/31115;** www.castlelough-tours.com), offers a tour through the spectacularly scenic Gap of Dunloe that includes a boat tour of the Killarney lakes for €20. It's offered May through September; call for current hours and bookings.

In addition to Killarney's main sights, some bus tours also venture into the two prime scenic areas nearby: the Ring of Kerry and Dingle Peninsula. From May to September, tours are offered daily; prices average €18 per person. Check the following companies if that's the kind of tour for you: **Bus Eireann,** Bus Depot, Railway Road, off East Avenue Road ((©) **064/34777;** www.buseireann. ie); **Castlelough Tours,** 7 High St. ((©) **064/31115**); **Corcoran's Tours,** 10 College St. ((©) **064/36666;** www.corcorantours.com); and **Dero's Tours,** 22 Main St. ((©) **064/31251** or 064/31567; www.derostours.com).

JAUNTING-CAR TOURS If you prefer walking or bicycling, just say no to the numerous jaunting-car drivers who will inevitably offer their services as you make your way around the Killarney lakes. These quaint horse-driven buggies are one of the main features of the landscape here, and if at some point you decide to give one a try, keep in mind that jaunting-car rates are set and carefully monitored by the Killarney Urban District Council. Current rates, all based on four persons to a jaunting car, run roughly from €16 to €40 per person round-trip, depending on destinations that may include Ross Castle, Muckross House and Gardens, Torc Waterfall, Muckross Abbey, Dinis Island, and Kate Kearney's Cottage, gateway to the Gap of Dunloe. To arrange a tour in advance, contact **Tangney Tours,** Kinvara House, Muckross Road, Killarney (© **064/33358**).

BOAT TOURS   There is nothing quite like seeing the sights from a boat on the Lakes of Killarney. Two companies operate regular boating excursions, with full commentary. **M.V. *Pride of the Lakes* Tours,** Scotts Gardens, Killarney (© **064/32638**), sails daily in an enclosed boat from the pier at Ross Castle from April to October at 11am, 12:30pm, 2:30pm, 4pm, and 5:15pm. The trip lasts just over an hour, and reservations are suggested. The cost is €8 adults, €4 children. **M.V. *Lily of Killarney* Tours,** 3 High St., Killarney (© **064/31068**), sails from April to October at 10:30am, noon, 1:45pm, 3:15pm, and 4:30pm for €8 adults, €4 children.

ENJOYING THE GREAT OUTDOORS

BICYCLING   The Killarney National Park is a paradise for bikers. Various types of bikes, from 21-speed touring bikes and mountain bikes to tandems, are available. Rental charges average €10 per day or €50 per week. Try **O'Neill's Cycle Shop,** 6 Plunkett St. (© **064/35357**), or **David O'Sullivan's Cycles,** Bishop Lane, New Street (© **064/31282**). Most shops are open year-round from 9am to 6pm daily, with extended hours to 7 or 8pm in the summer months.

One great ride beginning in Killarney takes you through the Gap of Dunloe along a dirt forest road, where you'll see some of the best mountain scenery in the area; it can be made into a 56km (35-mile) loop if you return on N71.

FISHING   Fishing for salmon and brown trout in Killarney's unpolluted lakes and rivers is a big attraction. Brown trout fishing is free on the lakes, but a permit is necessary for the rivers Flesk and Laune. A trout permit costs €4 to €14 per day.

Salmon fishing anywhere in Ireland requires a license; the cost is €4 per day or €14 for 21 days. In addition, some rivers also require a salmon permit, which costs €10 to €14 per day. Permits and licenses can be obtained at the Fishery Office at the **Knockreer Estate Office,** New Street, Killarney (© **064/31246**).

For fishing tackle, bait, rod rental, and other fishing gear, as well as permits and licenses, try **O'Neill's,** 6 Plunkett St., Killarney (© **064/35357**). This shop also arranges the hire of boats and ghillies (fishing guides) on the Killarney Lakes, leaving from Ross Castle.

GOLFING   Visitors are always welcome at the twin 18-hole championship courses of the **Killarney Golf & Fishing Club,** Killorglin Road, Fossa, Killarney (© **064/31034;** www.killarney-golf.com), located 5km (3 miles) west of the town center. Widely praised as one of the most scenic golf settings in the world, these courses, known as "Killeen" and "Mahony's Point," are surrounded by lake and mountain vistas. Greens fees are €70.

HORSEBACK RIDING   Many trails in the Killarney area are suitable for horseback riding. Hiring a horse costs about €20 per hour at **Killarney Riding**

Stables, N72, Ballydowney (℃ **064/31686**), and **Rocklands Stables,** Rockfield, Tralee Road (℃ **064/32592**). Lessons and weeklong trail rides can also be arranged.

WALKING Killarney is ideal for walking enthusiasts. On the outskirts of town, the Killarney National Park offers four signposted **nature trails.** Leaflets with maps of these four trails are available at the park's visitor center. For long-distance walkers, there is the 200km (125-mile) **"Kerry Way,"** a signposted walking route that extends from Killarney around the Ring of Kerry.

THE SHOPPING SCENE: KERRY GLASS & MORE

Shopping hours are normally Monday through Saturday from 9am to 6pm, but May through September most shops stay open to 9 or 10pm. Although there are more souvenir and crafts shops in Killarney than you can shake a stick (or shillelagh) at, here are a few of the best.

Blarney Woollen Mills, 10 Main St. (℃ **064/33222;** www.blarneywoollen mills.ie), a branch of the highly successful County Cork–based enterprise, occupies a beautiful shop front on the corner of Plunkett Street in the center of town. The wares range from hand-knit or hand-loomed sweaters to tweeds, crystal, china, pottery, and souvenirs of all sizes, shapes, and prices. **Quill's Woolen Market,** 1 High St. (℃ **064/32277**), is one of the best shops in town for hand-knit sweaters of all kinds, as well as tweeds, mohair, and sheepskins.

The **Mucros Craft Centre,** on the grounds of Muckross House (℃ **064-3144;** www.muckross-house.ie), is a studio-cum-shop carrying on many County Kerry craft traditions that features an on-premises weaver's workshop as well as a working pottery. There is also a wide selection of quality crafts from all over Ireland, and a skylit cafeteria overlooking the walled garden area. In town, **Serendipity,** 15 College St. (℃ **064/31056**), offers a wide range of unusual crafts from local artisans, such as hand-thrown pottery from the likes of Nicholas Mosse and Stephen Pearce, Jerpoint glass, and handcrafted jewelry.

WHERE TO STAY
Very Expensive

Killarney Park Hotel ✿ Voted by the Jameson Guide as "Hotel of the Year" for 2002, this handsome, neo-Georgian property is on the eastern edge of town, near the railway station. Public areas are posh and spacious and evoke a distinguished Victorian country house, with oil paintings, open fireplaces, and a sunlit conservatory-style lounge overlooking the gardens. Rooms have a traditional, conservative style, with quality provincial furnishings, designer fabrics, and marble-finished bathrooms.

Kenmare Place, Killarney, County Kerry. ℃ **064/35555.** Fax 064/35266. www.killarneyparkhotel.ie. 75 units. €220–€335 double; €320–€650 suite. No service charge. Rates include full breakfast. AE, DC, MC, V. **Amenities:** Restaurant; bar; indoor swimming pool; gym; Jacuzzi; sauna/steam room; concierge; room service; massage; babysitting; laundry service; library. *In room:* TV, minibar, hair dryer, garment press.

Expensive

Killarney Great Southern ✿✿ Set amid 15 hectares (36 acres) of gardens on the eastern edge of town, this ivy-covered mansion is the grande dame of Killarney hotels. It was built around the time of Queen Victoria's visit to Killarney and has since welcomed presidents, princes, and personalities from all over the world. The public areas hearken to yesteryear, with high ceilings, glowing fireplaces, and Waterford chandeliers. Rooms have a traditional decor and are quite spacious and comfortable. Train and bus terminals are opposite the hotel.

Railway Rd., off E. Avenue Rd., Killarney, County Kerry. © **800/44-UTELL** from the U.S., or 064/31262. Fax 064/31642. www.gsh.ie. 180 units. €200–€240 double. Rates include full breakfast. Service charge 13.5%. AE, DC, MC, V. **Amenities:** 2 restaurants; bar; lounge; indoor heated swimming pool; 2 tennis courts; gym; Jacuzzi; sauna/steam room; concierge; gift shop; salon; room service; laundry; dry cleaning. *In room:* TV, hair dryer, garment press.

Moderate

Earl's Court House ✦   Award-winning Earl's Court, a 5-minute walk from the town center, is among Killarney's most attractive guesthouses. On arrival, you'll be greeted with tea and scones in a lovely lounge. Rooms are spacious and stylishly furnished with Irish antiques. Some have half-tester beds, others have sitting areas, and nearly all have balconies. Rooms on the second floor have the best views of the mountains. The copious breakfast can be enjoyed in the gracious, formal dining room or, by request, in your room.

Signposted off N71, Woodlawn Junction, Muckross road, Killarney, County Kerry. © **064/34009.** Fax 064/34366. www.killarney-earlscourt.ie. 11 units, 1 single with shower only. €80–€128 double. Rates include full Irish breakfast and service charge. MC, V. Closed Nov 6 to Feb. Free parking. **Amenities:** Limited room service; nonsmoking rooms. *In room:* TV, radio, dataport, hair dryer.

Gleann Fia Country House   Although it's just a mile from town, this modern guesthouse feels pleasantly secluded, tucked away in 10 hectares (26 acres) of lawns and woodlands. Conor and Bridget O'Connell are thoughtful hosts whose presence makes this a highly personable place. The house has an airy conservatory with tea-making facilities, a guest lounge, and an unusually extensive breakfast menu. There is a nature walk along the stream by one side of the house.

Deerpark, Killarney, County Kerry. © **064/35035.** Fax 064/35000. www.gleannfia.com. 17 units. €80–€116 double. Rates include full breakfast. AE, MC, V. Closed Dec–Feb. Free parking. **Amenities:** Lounge; nonsmoking rooms; conservatory. *In room:* TV, hair dryer.

Kathleen's Country House   Of the many guesthouses in the area, this one stands out. About a mile north of town on 1.2 hectares (3 acres) of gardens next to a dairy farm, it's a two-story contemporary stone house with a modern mansard-style roof and many picture windows. Enthusiastic, efficient hostess Kathleen O'Regan-Sheppard offers totally refurbished guest rooms with antique pine furniture and light floral paisley fabrics, complemented by Kathleen's collection of contemporary pastels and paintings. Smoking is permitted only in the enclosed front foyer.

Madam's Height, Tralee road (N22), Killarney, County Kerry. © **064/32810.** Fax 064/32340. www.kathleens.net. 17 units. €90–€126 double. No service charge. Rates include full breakfast. AE, MC, V. Closed mid-Nov to early Mar. Free parking. **Amenities:** Nonsmoking rooms; drawing room; sunroom. *In room:* TV, tea/coffeemaker, hair dryer, garment press.

Randles Court   A former rectory, this attractive yellow gabled house is located just outside Killarney on the road to Muckross House. Since it opened as a hotel more than a decade ago, the Randle family has turned this into one of the most charming places to stay in Killarney. The public areas are rich with marble floors, fireplaces, chandeliers, gilt mirrors, tapestries, and old prints. Three of the rooms are in the original building and the rest are in a new wing. All have distinctive furnishings, including armoires, antique desks, or vanities.

Muckross road (N71), Killarney, County Kerry. © **800/4-CHOICE** from the U.S., or 064/35333. Fax 064/35206. www.randleshotels.com. 37 units. €110–€200 double. Rates include full breakfast and service charge. AE, DC, MC, V. Free parking. **Amenities:** Restaurant; bar; fitness center; limited room service; babysitting; laundry service. *In room:* TV, hair dryer.

WHERE TO DINE
Expensive
Gaby's Seafood Restaurant ✿✿ SEAFOOD   One of Killarney's longest established restaurants, this nautically themed place is a mecca for seafood lovers. Its walls are adorned with commendations and awards, which could be a tacky turnoff if the food weren't so good. Gaby's is known for its succulent lobster, served grilled or in a house sauce of cognac, wine, cream, and spices. Other choices include haddock in wine, a delectable tempura of prawns, and a giant Kerry shellfish platter—a feast of prawns, scallops, mussels, lobster, and oysters.

27 High St., Killarney, County Kerry. ✆ 064/32519. Reservations recommended. Main courses €16–€40. AE, DC, MC, V. Mon–Sat 6–10pm. Closed late Feb to mid-Mar and Christmas week.

Moderate
Bricín ✿✿ TRADITIONAL IRISH   Old-time Kerry boxty dishes (potato pancakes with various fillings, such as chicken, seafood, curried lamb, or vegetables) are the trademark of this restaurant above a very good crafts-and-book shop. The menu also offers a variety of fresh seafood, pastas, and Irish stew. Specials might include filet of pork with sage and apricot stuffing, or chicken Bricín (breast of chicken in a red-currant and raspberry sauce). Bricín is in one of Killarney's oldest buildings, dating from the 1830s, and boasts original stone walls, pine furniture, turf fireplaces, and—very rare in Ireland—a completely nonsmoking room that seats 40. Snacks and light fare are served during the day. In addition to the shop downstairs, the building houses the Bricín Art Gallery, which displays oils and watercolors by local artists.

26 High St., Killarney, County Kerry. ✆ 064/34902. Reservations recommended for dinner. Snacks €3–€8; dinner main courses €11–€20. AE, DC, MC, V. Year-round Tues–Sat 10am–4:30pm; Easter–Oct Mon–Sat 6–9:30pm.

Coopers Café and Restaurant ✿✿ MODERN CONTINENTAL   Coopers has clearly broken the mold here in Killarney, with its chic, industrial decor, making the most of glass, stone, aluminum, and sharp black/white contrasts. Overhead, the many-tendriled wire-sculpture chandeliers with flower-cup lights cast a magical fairylike illumination. The menu focuses on local Irish seafood and wild game, and includes wild pheasant cooked in Irish cream liqueur, escalope of venison, filet of wild pigeon, grilled swordfish and salmon, wild filet of sea trout, and baked cod Provençale. The alluring array of desserts includes crumbles, tarts, homemade ice creams, meringues, and crème brûlée.

Old Market Lane, off High St. (at New St.), Killarney, County Kerry. ✆ 064/37716. Reservations recommended. Main courses €11–€20. MC, V. Mon–Sat 12:30–3pm; Mon–Thurs 6:30–9:30pm; Fri–Sat 6:30–10pm; Sun 4–9:30pm.

IVERAGH PENINSULA/THE RING OF KERRY
For the majority of the literally millions of annual tourists to County Kerry, whose explorations follow the turn of a bus driver's wheel, the Iveragh Peninsula is synonymous with the Ring of Kerry. It's important to realize, however, that the Ring is a two-lane strip of tarmac measuring roughly 178km (110 miles), tracing the peninsula's shores and missing its tip altogether, while the Iveragh Peninsula itself is nearly 1,820 sq. km (700 sq. miles) of wild splendor, which you'll notice once you get off the tourist strip. Admittedly, almost everyone who gets this far feels compelled to "do" the Ring of Kerry; so, once it's done, why not take an unplanned turn, get truly lost, and let serendipity lead you to the unexpected and the unspoiled?

ESSENTIALS

MAKING THE DRIVE **By Bus** Bus Eireann (© **064/34777**) provides limited daily service from Killarney to Caherciveen, Waterville, Kenmare, and other towns on the Ring of Kerry.

By Car This is by far the best way to get around the Ring. For the most part, the route follows N70.

VISITOR INFORMATION Stop in at the **Killarney Tourist Office,** Aras Fáilte, at the Town Centre Car Park, Beech Road, Killarney (© **064/31633**), before you explore the area. For hours, see "Visitor Information" under "Killarney Town," earlier. The **Kenmare Tourist Office,** Market Square, Kenmare (© **064/41233**), is open daily Easter through September from 9:15am to 5:30pm, with extended hours in July and August. The rest of the year (Oct–Easter), it's open from Monday to Saturday.

EXPLORING THE RING

Although it's possible to circle the peninsula in as little as 4 hours, the only way to get a feel for the area and the people is to leave the main road, get out of your car, and explore some of the inland and coastal towns. **Portmagee** is a lovely seaside town, connected by a bridge to **Valentia Island,** which houses the informative Skellig Heritage Centre. **Caherdaniel** has a museum devoted to Daniel O'Connell, one of Ireland's great historical figures.

The most memorable and magical site to visit on the Iveragh Peninsula is **Skellig Michael,** a rocky pinnacle towering over the sea, where medieval monks built their monastery in ascetic isolation. The crossing to the island can be rough, so you'll want to visit on as clear and calm a day as possible. Seabirds nest here in abundance, and more than 20,000 pairs of gannets inhabit neighboring Little Skellig during the summer nesting season.

Kenmare is by far the most enchanting town on the Ring of Kerry route. Originally called Neidin (pronounced *Nay-deen,* meaning "little nest" in Irish), Kenmare is indeed a little nest of verdant foliage tucked between the River Roughty and Kenmare Bay. It's an ideal base for Kerry sightseeing, as it is well laid out and immaculately maintained—flower boxes in the windows, litter-free sidewalks—and full of excellent restaurants and places to stay.

From Kenmare to **Killarney,** the Ring road takes you through a scenic mountain stretch known as **Moll's Gap.** Killarney is best known for the natural beauty surrounding the town, and in particular for the spectacular **Killarney National Park** (see "Kerry & the Dingle Peninsula," earlier in the chapter), which includes the famous **Killarney Lakes** and the scenic **Gap of Dunloe.** The town itself, while colorful and bustling, has become a victim of its own success in recent years. Tourism is more in-your-face here than perhaps anywhere else in Ireland, with generic souvenir shops and overpriced restaurants chock-a-block.

Departing Killarney, follow the signs for **Killorglin.** When you reach this little town, you're on N70. You might want to stop and walk around Killorglin, a spot that's widely known for its annual mid-August horse, sheep, and cattle fair. It's officially called the **Puck Fair,** because local residents capture a wild goat (symbolizing the *puka* or *puki,* a mischievous sprite) from the mountains and enthrone it in the center of town as a sign of unrestricted merrymaking.

Continue on N70, and vistas of Dingle Bay will soon appear on your right. **Carrantuohill,** at 1,024m (3,414 ft.) Ireland's tallest mountain, is to your left. The open bog land constantly comes into view. From it, the local residents dig pieces of peat, or turf, to burn in their fireplaces. Formed thousands of years ago, the bog lands are mainly composed of decayed trees. They tend to be bumpy if you attempt to drive over them too speedily, so do be cautious.

The Ring winds around cliffs and the edges of mountains, with nothing but the sea below—another reason you will probably average only 48 kilometers per hour (30 mph), at best. As you go along, you'll notice the remains of many abandoned cottages. They date from the famine years, in the mid-1840s, when the Irish potato crop failed and millions of people starved to death or were forced to emigrate. This peninsula alone lost three-fourths of its population.

The next town on the Ring is **Glenbeigh,** a palm tree–lined fishing resort with a lovely duned beach called Rossbeigh Strand. You might want to stop here or continue the sweep through the mountains and along the sea's edge to **Cahirciveen.** From Cahirciveen, you can make a slight detour to see **Valentia** (which you may also see spelled "Valencia"). The offshore island is 11km (7 miles) long and one of Europe's westernmost points. Connected to the mainland by a bridge at Portmagee, this was the site from which the first telegraph cable was laid across the Atlantic in 1866. In the 18th century, the Valentia harbor was famous as a refuge for smugglers and privateers; it's said that John Paul Jones, the Scottish-born American naval officer in the War of Independence, often anchored here.

Head next for **Waterville,** an idyllic spot wedged between Lough Currane and Ballinskelligs Bay off the Atlantic. For years, it was known as the favorite retreat of Charlie Chaplin; today it's the home of the only Irish branch of Club Med.

If you follow the sea road north of town out to the Irish-speaking village of **Ballinskelligs,** at the mouth of the bay, you can catch a glimpse of the two Skellig Rocks. Continuing on N70, the next point of interest is **Derrynane,** at **Caherdaniel,** the home of Daniel O'Connell, remembered as "the Liberator" who freed Irish Catholics from the last of the English Penal Laws in 1829. Derrynane is now a national monument and park and a major center of Gaelic culture.

Watch for signs to **Staigue Fort,** about 3km (2 miles) off the main road. One of the best preserved of all ancient Irish structures, this circular fort is constructed of rough stones without mortar of any kind. The walls are 4m (13 ft.) thick at the base, and the diameter is about 27m (90 ft.). Not much is known of its history, but experts think it probably dates from around 1000 B.C.

Sneem, the next village on the circuit, is a colorful little hamlet with twin parklets. Its houses are painted in vibrant shades of blue, pink, yellow, purple, and orange, like a little touch of the Mediterranean plunked down in Ireland.

As you continue on the Ring, the foliage becomes lusher, thanks to the warming waters and winds of the Gulf Stream. When you begin to see lots of palm trees and other subtropical vegetation, you'll know you are in **Parknasilla,** once a favorite haunt of George Bernard Shaw.

WHERE TO STAY AROUND THE RING
Very Expensive
The Park Hotel Kenmare ✶✶✶ Ensconced in palm tree–lined gardens beside Kenmare Bay, this imposing limestone building was built at the end of the 19th century by the Great Southern Railway as a hotel for train travelers. The interior is rich in high-ceilinged sitting rooms and lounges, crackling open fireplaces, original oil paintings, tapestries, plush furnishings, and museum-worthy antiques (including an eye-catching cistern decorated with mythological figures and supported by gilded sea horses and dolphins).

The individually decorated guest rooms are decked out in a mix of Georgian and Victorian furnishings and rich upholsteries. Many have four-poster or canopy beds, hand-carved armoires, china lamps, curios, and luxurious extras like telephones in the bathroom and heated towel rails. Most rooms offer river and mountain vistas. Amid all the elegance, this hotel exudes an intrinsically welcoming atmosphere, and service is top-notch without being stuffy. The elegant dining room, with romantic views of the water and gardens, is one of the most acclaimed hotel restaurants in Ireland, meriting a Michelin star.

Kenmare, County Kerry. © **800/323-5463** from the U.S., or 064/41200. Fax 064/41402. www.parkkenmare. com. 49 units. €362–€498 double. No service charge. Rates include full breakfast. AE, DC, MC, V. Closed Nov to Dec 22 and Jan 3 to Mar. Free parking. **Amenities:** Restaurant; bar; 18-hole golf course; tennis court; joggers' trail; croquet lawn; salmon fishing; concierge; room service; babysitting; laundry service; nonsmoking rooms; drawing room; nightly turndown. *In room:* TV, CD player, minibar, hair dryer, garment press.

Expensive

Sheen Falls Lodge 🐾🐾🐾 Everything at Sheen Falls conspires to make you feel stress-free and pampered—the fabulous service, the faultless attention to detail—which is why it's a favorite getaway for Irish and Hollywood celebrities and *Condé Nast Traveler* magazine voted it the third-best hotel in Europe. Originally the 18th-century home of the Earl of Kerry, this salubrious resort sits beside a natural waterfall on 120 hectares (300 acres) of lawns and semitropical gardens where the River Sheen meets the Kenmare Bay estuary. The public areas are graceful, with pillars and columns, polished woodwork, open fireplaces, traditional furnishings, and original oil paintings. The staff make an effort to address guests by name, the bar feels like a drawing room, and the 1,000-volume library, with its green leather sofas and floor-to-ceiling bookshelves, hearkens back to a fine gentlemen's club. The guest rooms are spacious, decorated in elegant, contemporary style; each overlooks the falls (stunning when floodlit at night) or the bay. It all comes at a price, but Sheen Falls has the perfect Irish country house atmosphere: elegant yet relaxed.

Kenmare, County Kerry. © **800/537-8483** from the U.S., or 064/41600. Fax 064/41386. www.sheenfalls lodge.ie. 61 units. €240–€393 double; €413–€600 suite. No service charge. AE, DC, MC, V. Closed Dec 24–Feb 1. Free parking. **Amenities:** 2 restaurants; bar; indoor swimming pool; tennis; private salmon fishing; horseback riding; croquet; billiards room; gym; Jacuzzi; sauna/steam room; health and beauty treatments; concierge; room service; laundry/dry cleaning; library; helicopter pad; nightly turndown. *In room:* A/C, TV/VCR, radio, minibar, hair dryer, garment press.

Moderate

Sallyport House 🐾 This wonderful country house B&B won the Irish Automobile Association's "Guest Accommodation of the Year" award in 2000. It's got a great location, just 2 minutes on foot into Kenmare, yet it has extensive, well-kept grounds that run down to the Kenmare River. After spending years refurbishing her brother's B&B in California, Janey Arthur returned to Kenmare and did up her own handsome manor splendidly, giving it a sophisticated, uncluttered, and luxurious feel. The spacious, individually decorated guest rooms are furnished with well-chosen antiques, including very large beds and exceptionally grand bathrooms. Each room has a striking feature—extra-deep window seats that beg you to take in mountain views, an enormous king-size four-poster bed, or perhaps a lovely river view.

Glengarriff Rd., Kenmare, County Kerry. © **064/42066.** Fax 0646/42067. www.sallyporthouse.com. 5 units. €127 double. Rates include full breakfast and service charge. No credit cards Closed Nov to mid-Apr. Free parking. **Amenities:** Lounge; nonsmoking rooms. *In room:* TV, hair dryer.

Shelburne Lodge 🐾 Yet another fabulous, reasonably priced place to ink into your travel itinerary. This time, it's a Georgian farmhouse that the owners, Maura and Tom Foley, have transformed into one of the most original, stylish, and comfortable B&Bs on the island. Every room in the house has polished wood parquet floors, truly beautiful (and beautifully arranged) antique furnishings, contemporary artwork, and boldly colored walls that really pop. The guest rooms are all large and gorgeously appointed, with particularly sumptuous bathrooms (heated towel rails and handmade mirrors). The breakfasts are nothing short of decadent, and Maura and Tom really take care of you throughout your stay.

Killowen, Cork Rd., Kenmare, County Kerry. © **064/41013**. Fax 0646/42135. 9 units. €98–€122 double. Rates include full breakfast and service charge. MC, V. Closed Nov–Mar. Free parking. **Amenities:** Tennis court; drawing room. *In room:* TV.

WHERE TO DINE AROUND THE RING

Café Indigo ✹✹ MODERN CONTINENTAL/SEAFOOD   This ultra-hip, ultra-stylish restaurant has recently expanded the bar and added a grill, but the focus continues to be the talents of Vanessa Falvey, one of Ireland's hottest young chefs. Her cooking is a model of sophistication and simplicity, using a combination of fresh, local ingredients to bring one strong flavor to the fore. She's especially good with fish and seafood, as when she chooses sun-dried-tomato tapenade to complement oven-baked salmon, or celeriac purée to accent perfectly grilled sea scallops. The dining room is understated, the food is classy and memorable, and the crowd is happy.

The Square (above Square Pint pub), Kenmare, County Kerry. © **064/42356**. Reservations recommended. Main courses €18–€23; grill menu €10–€15. AE, DC, MC, V. Wed–Mon 7–11pm. Closed mid-Jan to mid-Mar.

d'Arcy's ✹ CONTINENTAL   In a two-story stone house at the top end of Kenmare, this restaurant has a big open fireplace and a homey atmosphere. The owner, Pat Gath, and head chef, James Mulchrone, make a great team, and d'Arcy's is a standout even in this restaurant-rich town. Using fresh local ingredients, the menu hits classics such as peppered filet of beef with crispy onions, and baked salmon with rosemary butter. Mulchrone's penchant for Mediterranean flavors is evident in dishes like goat's cheese with olive-and-tomato sauce or rack of lamb stuffed with garlic and sun-dried tomatoes. The homemade breads and desserts are also excellent.

Main St., Kenmare, County Kerry. © **064/41589**. Reservations recommended. Main courses €16–€23. MC, V. Wed–Mon 7–10pm (open daily in summer). Closed Jan to mid-Mar.

Lime Tree ✹ MODERN CONTINENTAL   Innovative cuisine is the focus at this restaurant, situated in an 1821 landmark renovated schoolhouse next to the grounds of the Park Hotel. Paintings by local artists line the stone walls, and the menu offers such dishes as goat's-cheese potato cake with balsamic glaze, oak-planked wild salmon, filet of Irish beef with colcannon (mashed potatoes with spring onions), and oven-roasted Kerry lamb.

Shelbourne Rd., Kenmare, County Kerry. © **064/41225**. Reservations recommended. Main courses €15–€23. MC, V. Apr–Nov daily 6:30–10pm.

Packie's ✹ BISTRO   If you're looking for a stylish place to have a great meal that won't break the bank, this little place is it. There's always a buzz here, and the smart crowd fits in perfectly with the bistro look—colorful window boxes, slate floor, stone walls filled with contemporary art, and dark oak tables and chairs. Everyone comes for chef-owner Maura Foley's tried-and-true favorites such as Irish stew, delicious potato pancakes, mint-infused rack of lamb, and crab claws in garlic butter. But there are also more creative combinations, such as gratin of crab and prawns, beef braised in Guinness with mushrooms, and curry zabaglione with Castletownberre prawns. Desserts are terrific, too.

Henry St., Kenmare, County Kerry. ℭ 064/41508. Reservations recommended. Main courses €14–€25. MC, V. Easter to mid-Nov Tues–Sat 5:30–10pm.

Purple Heather ☆ (Finds) IRISH   This lovely little eatery is *the* place to lunch in Kenmare. The food is all about tearoom classics with a gourmet twist—wild smoked salmon or prawn salad, smoked trout pâté, vegetarian omelets, and Irish cheese platters, as well as homemade soups.

Henry St., Kenmare, County Kerry. ℭ 064/41016. All items €3–€20. No credit cards. Mon–Sat 11am–7pm. Closed Christmas week.

SHOPPING IN KENMARE

The Green Note, 18 Henry St. (℗ **064/41212**), is a traditional Irish-music store selling banjos, harps, and tin whistles. The **Kenmare Bookshop,** Shelburne St. (℗ **064/41578**), specializes in books on Ireland, particularly Irish biographies and books by Irish writers, as well as maps and guides to the surrounding area, including ordinance survey maps, walking and specialist guides, and marine charts. **Nostalgia Linen and Lace,** 27 Henry St. (℗ **064/41389**), specializes in Irish linens and sells lace by the meter. **Cleo,** Shelburne Road (℗ **064/41410**), a branch of the long-established Dublin store of the same name, is a trendy women's-wear shop known for its beautiful, vibrantly colored tweed and linen fashions, as well as specialty items such as Kinsale cloaks. Perched in a most scenic setting, **Avoca Handweavers at Moll's Gap,** N71 (℗ **064/34720**), is a branch of the famous tweedmakers of County Wicklow. This outlet is set on a high mountain pass between Killarney and Kenmare. The wares range from colorful hand-woven capes, jackets, throws, and knitwear to pottery and jewelry. Oh, and it has an excellent coffee shop to boot.

TRALEE

Tralee is the commercial center of County Kerry; with its population of 22,000, it's three times the size of Killarney. This is more a functioning town than a tourist center, and locals outnumber visitors, except during the ever-popular **Rose of Tralee festival** in August (for more information, go to the website **www.roseoftralee.ie**). The town is the permanent home of the National Folk Theatre of Ireland, Siamsa Tíre, which operates year-round but is most active in July and August.

ESSENTIALS

GETTING THERE   By Air   Aer Lingus operates daily nonstop flights from Dublin into **Kerry County Airport,** Farranfore, County Kerry (℗ **066/976-4644**), about 24km (15 miles) south of Tralee.

By Bus   Buses from all parts of Ireland arrive daily at the **Bus Eireann Depot,** John Joe Sheehy Road (℗ **066/712-3566;** www.buseireann.ie).

By Train   Trains from major cities arrive at the **Irish Rail Station,** John Joe Sheehy Road (℗ **066/712-3522;** www.irishrail.ie).

By Car   Four major national roads converge on Tralee: N69 and N21 from Limerick and the north, N70 from the Ring of Kerry and points south, and N22 from Killarney, Cork, and the east.

VISITOR INFORMATION   The **Tralee Tourist Office,** Ashe Memorial Hall, Denny Street (℗ **066/712-1288**), offers information on Tralee and the

Dingle Peninsula. It is open weekdays from 9am to 1pm and 2 to 5pm, with weekend and extended hours in the spring and summer. It also has a first-rate cafe on the premises. For Tralee tourist information on the Web, visit **www. tralee-insight.com**.

SEEING THE SIGHTS

Believed to be more than a million years old, the limestone **Crag Cave** ⚜, 24km (15 miles) north of Killarney off N21, Castleisland (© **066/41244;** www.crag cave.com), was discovered and first explored in 1983. Guides accompany you 3,750m (12,510 ft.) into the passage on a well-lit tour revealing some of the largest stalactites in Europe. A crafts shop and a restaurant are on the premises. Admission costs €5 adults, €4 seniors and students, €2.50 children ages 6 to 17, €10 family (up to four children, children under 6 free). It's open daily mid-March through June and September through October from 10am to 6pm; July through August from 10am to 7pm.

Europe's westernmost railway, the restored **Tralee Steam Railway** ⚜⚜ train, Ballyard Station, Tralee (© **066/712-1064**), offers narrated, scenic 3km (2-mile) trips from Tralee to Blennerville. It uses equipment that was once part of the Tralee and Dingle Light Railway (1891–1953), one of the world's most famous narrow-gauge railways. Round-trip fare costs €4 adults, €3 students and seniors, €2 children, and €9 family. Trains run daily from May to October.

One of Ireland's largest indoor heritage centers, **Kerry the Kingdom** ⚜, Ashe Memorial Hall, Denny Street, Tralee (© **066/712-7777**), offers three separate attractions that give an in-depth look at 7,000 years of life in County Kerry. A 10-minute video, "Kerry in Colour," presents the seascapes and landscapes of Kerry; the Kerry County Museum chronologically examines the county's music, history, legends, and archaeology through interactive and hands-on exhibits; and the exhibit on Gaelic football is unique. Complete with lighting effects and aromas, a theme-park-style ride called "Geraldine Tralee" takes you through a re-creation of Tralee's streets, houses, and abbeys during the Middle Ages. Admission is €7 adults, €6.50 students, €4 children, €22 family. The center is open daily mid-March through July from 10am to 6pm, August from 10am to 7pm, September through October from 10am to 6pm, and November through December 22 from noon to 5pm.

WHERE TO STAY

Abbey Gate Hotel ⚜ This new three-story hotel brings much-needed quality lodging and a broader dimension of social activity to the center of Tralee town. The hotel is ideally located near Tralee's prime attractions, shops, and pubs. Guest rooms, like the public areas, are furnished with new reproductions, and fabrics, art, and accessories convey an air of Georgian and Victorian Tralee.

Maine St., Tralee, County Kerry. © **066/712-9888**. Fax 066/712-9821. www.abbeygatehotel.com. 100 units. €110–€140 double. No service charge. AE, DC, MC, V. Limited parking. **Amenities:** 2 restaurants; bar; room service; nonsmoking rooms. *In room:* TV, tea/coffeemaker, hair dryer.

Ballyseede Castle Hotel ⚜ Ballyseede Castle, a 15th-century castle complete with a live-in ghost, was once the chief garrison of the legendary Fitzgeralds, the earls of Desmond. The Blennerhassett family occupied it until 1966 and in 1985 turned it into a hotel. The lobby has Doric columns and a hand-carved oak staircase. Two drawing rooms are decorated with cornices of ornamental plasterwork and warmed by marble fireplaces. Guest rooms are spacious and elegantly appointed with period furnishings. The castle is 3.2km (2 miles) east of Tralee, on 12 hectares (30 acres) of parkland.

Tralee-Killarney road, Tralee, County Kerry. © **066/712-5799.** Fax 066/712-5287. 12 units. €180–€250 double. Service charge 13.5%. MC, V. Free parking. **Amenities:** Restaurant; piano lounge; library. *In room:* TV, hair dryer, garment press.

The Shores *Value*   This is a modern house, tastefully done over about 5 years ago, on the south side of Brandon Bay. It commands wonderful views of Tralee Bay and Mount Brandon. Annette O'Mahoney is an avid interior decorator and has extended a Victorian theme and a feeling of luxury throughout the house. Furnishings are lavish, with a canopy bed in one room and writing desks in three rooms. A downstairs room has a private entrance and a fireplace. All rooms have orthopedic beds, with crisp white cotton and cream lace linen. There's a sun deck and a beach for when the heavens are kind, and a guest library and video rentals for when they are not. Breakfast options are particularly extensive, with smoked salmon and waffles as alternatives to the standard fry. The latest addition is a new self-catering cottage.

.8km (½ mile) west of Stradbally on the Conor Pass Rd., Cappatigue, Castlegregory, County Kerry. © **066/ 713-9196.** 6 units. €56–€68 double. Rates include full breakfast. MC, V. Closed Dec–Jan. **Amenities:** Nonsmoking rooms; video library. *In room:* TV, tea/coffeemaker.

WHERE TO DINE

In addition to the recommendations below, you can get excellent pub grub, especially steaks, at **Kirby's Olde Brogue Inn,** Rock Street, Tralee (© **066/712-3357**). This pub has a barnlike layout, with an interior that incorporates farming memorabilia and rush-work tables and chairs. Sometimes traditional music and folk ballads are served up as well.

Larkin's 🐟 *Value* SEAFOOD   This bright, welcoming, Irish-country restaurant with antique pine furnishings is conveniently located and widely acclaimed for its catch of the day and roast rack of Irish lamb. The offerings are modestly priced and immodestly tasty. Proprietor Michael Fitzgibbon greets guests personally and generously provides information on the area.

Princes St., Tralee, County Kerry. © **066/976-7217.** Reservations recommended. Main courses €12–€21; set-price menu €19. DC, MC, V. Mon–Fri 12:30–2pm and 6:30–9:30pm; Sat 6:30–9:30pm.

The Tankard SEAFOOD   This is one of the few restaurants in the area that capitalizes on sweeping views of Tralee Bay. Situated on the water's edge, it has wide picture windows and sleek contemporary decor. The straightforward menu features local shellfish and seafood, such as lobster, scallops, prawns, and black sole. It also includes rack of lamb, duck, quail, and steak. This restaurant is at its best in the early evening, especially at sunset.

10km (6 miles) northwest of Tralee, Kilfenora, Fenit, County Kerry. © **066/713-6164.** Reservations recommended. Main courses €11–€20. AE, DC, MC, V. Daily: bar food 12:30–10pm; restaurant 6–10pm.

TRALEE AFTER DARK

Siamsa Tire, the National Folk Theatre of Ireland, is located at Town Park, Tralee (© **066/712-3055;** www.siamsatire.com). Founded in 1974, Siamsa (pronounced *Sheem*-sha) offers a mixture of music, dance, and mime. The scenes depict old folk tales and farmyard activities such as thatching a cottage roof, flailing sheaves of corn, and twisting a sugan (straw) rope.

In addition to these folk theater entertainments, Siamsa presents a full program of drama and musical concerts (from traditional to classical) performed by visiting amateur and professional companies. Admission is €16 adults; €14 seniors, students, and children. The schedule is Monday through Saturday from April to mid-October; curtain time is 8:30pm.

PUBS   Tralee pubs can be a little crowded and impersonal. **Olde Macs,** the Mall (© 066/712-1572), is an exception. From the delightful flowers in the hanging baskets outside to the dark-wood interior, the pub exudes atmosphere. Conversation is lighthearted, and the regulars are extremely friendly. The nicest location of any pub in the Tralee area belongs to the **Oyster Tavern,** Fenit Road (© 066/713-6102), 5km (3 miles) west of town overlooking Tralee Bay. The pub grub available includes seafood soups and platters.

THE DINGLE PENINSULA

Like the Iveragh Peninsula, Dingle has a spectacularly scenic peripheral road, and a substantially tacky tourist trade has blossomed along it. But as soon as you veer off the main roads or penetrate to such hinterlands of the peninsula as the Blasket Islands or Brandon Head, you'll discover extraordinary desolate beauty, seemingly worlds away from the tour buses and shamrock-filled shops. Dingle Town itself is definitely touristy, but it's smaller and less congested than Killarney and retains more traces of being a real, year-round town with an identity beyond the tourist trade. While the Dingle Peninsula is an ideal drive, it also makes a fine bicycling tour. Dingle village is a delightful place to stay (see below) while you explore the peninsula.

Don't miss **Slea Head,** at the southwestern extremity of the peninsula. It's a place of pristine beaches, great walks, and fascinating archaeological remains. The village of **Dunquin,** stunningly situated between Slea Head and Clogher Head, is home to the Blasket Centre. **Dunbeg Fort** sits on a rocky promontory just south of Slea Head, its walls rising from the cliff edge. Although much of the fort has fallen into the sea, the place is well worth a visit at the bargain-basement rate of €2 per person. From Slea Head, the Dingle Way continues east to Dingle Town (24km/15 miles) or north along the coast toward Ballyferriter.

Just offshore from Dunquin are the seven **Blasket Islands;** a ferry (© 066/915-6455) connects Great Blasket with the mainland when the weather permits. Alternatively, you can take a 3-hour cruise around the islands with **Blasket Island Tours** (© 066/915-6422), leaving from Dunquin Pier. The islands were abandoned by the last permanent residents in 1953 and now are inhabited only by a few summer visitors who share the place with the seals and seabirds. A magnificent 13km (8-mile) walk goes to the west end of Great Blasket and back, passing sea cliffs and ivory beaches; you can stop along the way at the only cafe on the island, which serves lunch and dinner.

East of Ballyferriter is **Gallarus Oratory,** one of the best-preserved early Christian church buildings in Ireland. With a shape much like an overturned boat, it's constructed of unmortared stone, yet is still completely watertight after more than 1,000 years.

DINGLE TOWN

With a charter dating back many centuries, Dingle was Kerry's principal harbor in medieval times. Even though it's just a small town (pop. 1,500), Dingle has more fine restaurants than many of Ireland's major cities, and is known for the traditional Irish music in its pubs.

EXPLORING THE TOWN

Despite the big-sounding name, **Dingle's Oceanworld Aquarium,** Dingle Harbour (© 066/915-2111; www.dingle-oceanworld.ie), is a relatively small aquarium with little to see to justify the ticket price. Admission costs €7.50 adults, €6 seniors and students, €4.50 children, €20 family. There are various sea critters behind glass in the aquarium's 29 tanks, and young staffers carry around live lobsters, crabs, starfish, and other "inner space" creatures and introduce them up close to visitors. During feeding times, children are allowed to hand out the grub. This is a compact, hands-on, interactive place that gets bonus points for effort, but in the end it doesn't provide the wow factor of many other aquariums. In addition, there are exhibits on Brendan the Navigator and the Spanish Armada, a cafe, and a gift shop. The aquarium is open September and June from 9:30am to 7pm; July through August from 9:30am to 8:30pm; and October through May from 9:30am to 6pm.

Forget Flipper. In Dingle, the name to know is Fungie the Dolphin. Every day, **Fungie the Dolphin Tours,** the Pier, Dingle (© 066/915-2626), ferry visitors out into the nearby waters to see the famous village mascot. Trips cost €10 for adults and €5 for children under 12. They last about 1 hour and depart regularly, roughly every 2 hours off season and as frequently as every half hour in high season. Fungie really does swim up to the boat, and the boatmen stay out long enough for ample sightings—and long, wonderful eyefuls of the gorgeous bay. If you want to get up close and personal with Fungie, you can also arrange an early-morning dolphin swim. Although Fungie can swim about 25 mph, he enjoys human company and is usually willing to slow down and swim with his new acquaintances. To arrange a dolphin encounter, contact Bridgit Flannery (© 066/915-1967), almost any day from 8am to 8pm. You book a swim the day before, when you rent your gear (semi-dry suit, mask, snorkel, boots, and fins, all in one duffel). The full overnight outfitting cost is €20 per person. Then you show up in your gear early the next morning to be brought out by boat to your aquatic rendezvous. The 2-hour escorted swim costs an additional €15. If you prefer, you can use your rented outfit and swim out on your own. Fungie also welcomes drop-ins. This outing is for teenagers on up, although smaller children will certainly enjoy watching.

ENJOYING THE GREAT OUTDOORS
BEACHES The Dingle Peninsula has some of the most dramatic beaches in Ireland. The most famous is **Inch Strand,** a 5km- (3-mile-) long dune-covered sandy spit—one of the largest dune fields in Ireland. Scenes from *Ryan's Daughter,* the 1969 David Lean production with Robert Mitchum and Sarah Miles, were filmed here.

If you've never seen a boulder beach, then **Kilmurray Bay at Minard** is a Lilliputian dream come to life. Here in the shadow of Minard Castle, giant sausage-shaped sandstone boulders form a beach unlike anything you've ever seen. If you want drama, **Trabeg Beach** features exquisite wave-sculptured maroon sandstone statues, sheer rock cliffs, and small sea caves lined with veins of crystalline quartz.

Some of the calmest beaches for swimming in this area are east of Castlegregory, on the west side of Tralee Bay. The beach at **Maherabeg** has a coveted European Blue Flag, and the beaches of **Brandon Bay** are exceptionally scenic and good for walking and swimming.

BICYCLING Mountain bikes can be rented at the **Mountain Man,** Strand Street, Dingle (© 066/915-1868), for €10 per day or €44 per week; rear panniers are included. Touring and mountain bikes are also available year-round from **Foxy John Moriarty,** Main Street, Dingle (© 066/915-1316). High-season prices start at €9 per day, €35 per week.

HORSEBACK RIDING At **Dingle Horse Riding,** Ballinaboula House, Dingle (© 066/915-2018), rides are available along nearby beaches or through the mountains; the cost is €24 for a 1-hour ride. Half-day, full-day, and 3- to 5-day packages including accommodation, meals, and riding can be arranged.

SAILING The **Dingle Sailing Club,** c/o Brenda Farrell, The Marina, Dingle Town (© **066/915-1984**), offers an array of sailing courses taught by certified instructors. Summer courses run €120 to €145. To charter a yacht, contact **Dingle Sea Ventures,** Dingle (© **066/915-2244;** www.charterireland.com). Yachts sleeping from 6 to 10 persons range in price from €1,200 to €2,700 per week. Skippers' fees are €70 per day.

SEA ANGLING For sea-angling packages and day trips, contact Nicholas O'Connor at **Angler's Rest,** Ventry (© **066/915-9947**); or Seán O'Conchúir (© **066/915-5429**), representing the **Kerry Angling Association.**

WALKING The **Dingle Way** begins in Tralee and circles the peninsula, covering 153km (95 miles) of gorgeous mountain and coastal landscape. The most rugged section is along Brandon Head, where the trail passes between Mount Brandon and the ocean; the views are tremendous, but the walk is long (about 24km/15 miles or 9 hr.) and strenuous, and should be attempted only when the sky is clear. The section between Dunquin and Ballyferriter follows an especially lovely stretch of coast. For more information, see *The Dingle Way Map Guide,* available in local tourist offices and shops.

WHERE TO STAY

Benners Hotel ⚐ *Value* One of the few hotels out here that stay open year-round, Benners is a good-value choice with character that's right in the heart of town. The lovely Georgian doorway with a fan light at the front entrance sets the tone. Dating from more than 250 years ago, the hotel blends old-world charm and modern comforts, thanks to a recent refurbishment and expansion. It's furnished with Irish antique pine furniture, including four-poster beds and armoires in the guest rooms. Special 2- and 3-night rates are available on the hotel's website.

Main St., Dingle, County Kerry. © 066/915-1638. Fax 066/915-1412. www.bennershotel.com. 52 units. €133–€222 double. Rates include full Irish breakfast and service charge. AE, DC, MC, V. **Amenities:** Restaurant; 2 bars. *In room:* TV, tea/coffeemaker, hair dryer.

The Captain's House ⚐ This friendly, dapper little B&B is smack in the middle of Dingle. The name is inspired less from the location (the house is land-locked, except for a river that runs through the well-manicured yard) than from the owner's former life as a sea captain. As in many town houses, rooms were built to a smallish scale, but the whole place is done up so delightfully that the overall effect is cozy rather than cramped. Returning guests often ask specifically to stay in room no. 10, which is tucked under the gables and has a sloping ceiling. Breakfasts here are exceptional.

The Mall, Dingle, County Kerry. © 066/915-1531. Fax 066/915-1079. 9 units. €80–€90 double. No service charge. Rates include full breakfast. AE, MC, V. Closed Dec–Jan. **Amenities:** Sitting room. *In room:* TV.

Doyle's Townhouse ⚐⚐ Sister to the successful Doyle's Seafood Restaurant next door, this three-story guesthouse is a favorite Dingle hideaway. It has a lovely Victorian fireplace in the drawing-room area, and many of the antique fixtures date from 250 years ago or more. Period pieces and country pine predominate in the guest rooms, although they're totally up-to-date with firm beds and good-size Italian marble bathrooms with towel warmers. Most are so spacious that they have a pullout couch that can accommodate a third person. Front rooms look out onto the town, and back rooms have a balcony or patio and face a garden, with mountain vistas in the background. Two ground-floor rooms are perfect for folks who have problems with stairs. Just down the road, off a little courtyard, are four little town houses—each with its own entrance and a sitting room downstairs, with a bedroom and bathroom on the upper level.

5 John St., Dingle, County Kerry. ⓒ **800/223-6510** from the U.S., or 066/915-1174. Fax 066/915-1816. www.doylesofdingle.com. 12 units. €105–€112 double. Service charge 10%. Rates include full breakfast. DC, MC, V. Closed Christmas and mid-Jan to mid-Feb. **Amenities:** Drawing room. *In room:* TV, hair dryer.

Greenmount House ⋆ *Value*   Perched on a hill overlooking Dingle Bay and the town, this modern bungalow-style B&B is a standout. It is a previous winner of the RAC (Royal Automobile Club—the British equivalent of AAA) "Small Hotel of the Year" for Ireland. It has all the comforts of a hotel at bargain prices, including spacious rooms, each with its own sitting area and large bathroom. Breakfasts, ranging from smoked-salmon omelets to ham-and-pineapple toasties, have won awards for proprietors Mary and John Curran.

John St., Dingle, County Kerry. ⓒ **066/915-1414.** Fax 066/915-1974. www.greenmounthouse.com. 12 units. €68–€108 double. No service charge. Rates include full breakfast. MC, V. Closed Dec 20–26. **Amenities:** Nonsmoking rooms; conservatory; sitting room. *In room:* TV, tea/coffeemaker.

Milltown House ⋆   You couldn't wish for a more picturesque Dingle setting than this bayside haven, which incorporates the amenities of a hotel with the informal warmth of a B&B. The spacious guest rooms—each uniquely designed—have sitting areas and firm beds. Half have sea views and nearly all have patios. The nonsmoking sitting room—all easy chairs and open fires—is elegant and comfortable, while the conservatory breakfast room (where you'll enjoy a lavish breakfast menu) looks out on Dingle Bay. A bit of film trivia: Robert Mitchum stayed in room no. 2 while filming *Ryan's Daughter*.

Milltown (off Ventry Rd.), Dingle, County Kerry. ⓒ **066/915-1372.** Fax 066/915-1095. http://indigo.ie/~milltown. 10 units. €84–€138. Rates include full breakfast. MC, V. **Amenities:** Conservatory; sitting room. *In room:* TV, tea/coffeemaker, hair dryer.

WHERE TO DINE

Beginish Restaurant ⋆⋆ SEAFOOD   If you're looking for the best seafood in Dingle, you've come to the right place. This delightful small restaurant exudes an atmosphere of unassuming elegance. A lovely conservatory overlooks the garden in back, with room for outdoor tables in summer. Although it offers lamb and beef dishes and a vegetarian special each night, the emphasis is on fish—the cooking is simple, traditional, and always wonderful. Among the starters, the smoked salmon with shallots, capers, and horseradish cream is exquisite—nothing fancy, just excellent ingredients combined in perfect proportions. You can't go wrong with any of the fish courses, be it old-fashioned fish chowder or cod on thyme-scented potatoes and sweet red peppers. Chef Pat Moore's hot rhubarb soufflé tart is legendary in these parts.

Green St., Dingle, County Kerry. ⓒ **066/915-1321.** Reservations recommended. Dinner main courses €16–€30. MC, V. Tues–Sun noon–2pm and 6–10pm. Closed Jan.

The Chart House ⋆⋆ MODERN COUNTRY   For several years now, this has been the hottest table in Dingle—in fact, it's quickly become a destination restaurant that draws folks from outside Kerry—so book ahead and prepare to enjoy. As the *Sunday Tribune* food critic gushed, "The food, the service, and the buzz all conspire to set this place apart." There's the ubiquitously inviting bistro-like atmosphere—complete with country half-door and chunky pine furniture—but everyone comes for Laura Boyce's confident, simple cooking. Think wonderful comfort food with a flair—filet of beef with garlicky mashed spuds; herb-marinated John Dory on a bed of citrus-infused couscous; roast monkfish with zucchini (called courgette in Ireland) and mustard sauce; home-smoked pork with apple frittatas. It's the kind of food you never tire of. And the service is, as the Irish would say, "spot on."

The Mall, Dingle, County Kerry. ℭ **066/915-2255.** Reservations required. Dinner main courses €15–€29. MC, V. Daily 6:30–10pm. Closed Jan 8–Feb 12.

Doyle's Seafood Bar ⭑ SEAFOOD   John Doyle meets the fishing boats each morning to select the best of the day's catch. The atmosphere is homey, with stone walls and floors, tweedy place mats, and old Dingle sketches. All the ingredients come from the sea, the Doyles' gardens, or nearby farms—and the Doyles even smoke their own salmon. Specialties include baked filet of lemon sole with prawn sauce; salmon filet in puff pastry with sorrel sauce; and a signature platter of seafood (sole, salmon, lobster, oysters, and crab claws).

4 John St., Dingle, County Kerry. ℭ **066/915-1174.** Reservations required. Main courses €15–€28. MC, V. Mon–Sat 6–10pm. Closed mid-Dec to mid-Feb.

DINGLE AFTER DARK

At night virtually every pub in Dingle offers live music from 9pm on. **An Droic-head Beag/The Small Bridge,** Lower Main Street (ℭ **066/915-1723**), is one of Dingle's most atmospheric pubs. It has a dark, cavernous interior that's filled with banter and laughter. Traditional Irish music takes place every night at 9pm. But be warned: It's popular, so get there early if you want a seat.

Although Richard "Dick" Mack died a few years ago, his family keeps up the traditions at **Dick Mack's "Haberdashery,"** Green Street (ℭ **066/915-1070**), where Dick handcrafted leather boots, belts, and other items in between pub chores. Corridors lined with old pictures and mugs lead into snug bars where locals and visitors stand around sipping stout and exchanging jokes and gossip. It's been a favorite pub with celebrities such as Robert Mitchum, Timothy Dalton, and Paul Simon, whose names are now commemorated with stars on the sidewalk just outside.

Italy

by Darwin Porter & Danforth Prince

Italy is a feast for the senses and the intellect. Any mention of Italy calls up visions of Pompeii, the Renaissance, and Italy's rich treasury of art and architecture. But some of the country's best experiences can involve the simple act of living in the Italian style, eating the regional cuisines, and enjoying the countryside.

1 Rome ★★★

The city of Rome is simultaneously strident, romantic, and sensual. And although the romantic poets would probably be horrified at today's traffic, pollution, overcrowding, crime, political discontent, and barely controlled chaos of modern Rome, the city endures and thrives in a way that is called "eternal."

It would take a lifetime to know a city filled with 27 centuries of artistic achievement. A cradle of Western civilization, Rome is timeless with its ancient history, art, and architecture, containing more treasures per square foot than any other city in the world. Caesar was assassinated here, Charlemagne crowned, and the list of the major events goes on and on.

In between all that absorption of culture and history, take time to relax and meet the Romans. Savor their succulent pastas while enjoying a fine glass of wine on one of the city's splendid squares where one of the reigning Caesars might have gone before you, or perhaps Michelangelo or Raphael.

ESSENTIALS

GETTING THERE   By Plane   Chances are that you'll arrive in Italy at Rome's **Leonardo da Vinci International Airport** (© **06-65951** or 06-65953640 for information; www.adr.it), popularly known as **Fiumicino,** 30km (18½ miles) from the city center. Domestic flights arrive at one terminal, international ones at the other. If you're flying by charter, you might arrive at Ciampino Airport.

To get into the city, there's a **shuttle service** known as the Leonardo Express that takes you directly from Fiumicino to Stazione Termini, the main train station. Upon leaving Customs, follow the signs marked TRENI. Trains go back and forth between the airport and the rail station daily from 7:07am to 11:37pm. A one-way ticket costs 9€. There's also a local train departing every 20 minutes and taking 45 minutes to reach the Tiburtina station. The cost is 4.75€ each way. But you'll have to change at the Piramide Metro stop, catching the B line into Termini for .75€. If you have luggage, this is a more awkward transit but cheaper, of course.

Taxis from Fiumicino to the city center are expensive—43€ and up, plus another 3€ or so for your luggage.

Should you arrive on a charter flight at **Ciampino Airport** (© **06-794941;** www.adr.it), take a COTRAL bus, departing every 20 minutes or so, which will deliver you to the Anagnina stop of Metropolitana (subway) line A. The one-way cost is 1€. At Anagnina you can take Metro line A to Stazione Termini, where you can make your final connections. The trip takes about 45 minutes and costs .75€.

By Train   Trains arrive in the center of old Rome at **Stazione Termini,** Piazza dei Cinquecento (© **1848-88088;** www.romatermini.it), the train and subway transportation hub for the city. For information and timetables, contact **FS** (© **848-888088;** www.trenitalia.it). Many hotels lie near the station, and you can walk to your hotel if you don't have too much luggage. Otherwise, an array of taxi, bus, and subway lines awaits you.

If you're taking the **Metropolitana (subway),** follow the illuminated M sign in red that points the way. To catch a bus, go straight through the outer hall of the Termini and enter the sprawling bus lot of Piazza dei Cinquecento. Taxis are also found here.

By Bus Arrivals are at the **Stazione Termini** (see "By Train," above).

By Car From the north, the main access route is **A-1 (Autostrada del Sole),** cutting through Milan and Florence; or you can take the coastal route, SS1 Aurelia, from Genoa. If you're driving north from Naples, take the southern lap of the **Autostrada del Sole (A-2).** All these autostradas join with the **Grande Raccordo Anulare,** a ring road that encircles Rome, channeling traffic into the city.

VISITOR INFORMATION Tourist Offices Information is available at three locations maintained by the **Azienda Provinciale di Turismo (APT):** a kiosk at **Leonardo da Vinci International Airport** (© 06-6595-6074), a kiosk at Stazione Termini, and the **administrative headquarters** at Via Parigi 5 (© 06-6595-6074; www.romaturismo.it). The Via Parigi 5 location is open Monday through Friday from 8:15am to 7:15pm, Saturday to 2pm. The airport and Stazione Termini kiosk are open daily from 8:15am to 7:15pm, but we've never found these locations to be great resources.

More helpful, stocking maps and brochures, are the offices maintained by the **Comune di Roma** at half a dozen sights around the city. You can identify them by their red-and-orange or yellow-and-black signs saying COMUNE DI ROMA— PUNTI DI INFORMAZIONE TURISTICA. The offices are staffed daily from 9am to 6pm and can be found in Piazza Pia, near the Castello Sant'Angelo (© 06-68809707); in Piazza San Giovanni in Laterano (© 06-77203598); along Largo Carlo Goldoni, near the intersection of Via del Corso and Via Condotti (© 06-68136061); on Via Nazionale, near the Palazzo delle Esposizioni (© 06-47824525); on Largo Corrado Ricci, near the Colosseum (© 06-69924307); and in Trastevere on Piazza Sonnino (© 06-58333457). The Stazione Termini office (© 06-48906300) is open daily from 8am to 9pm. Other offices have also opened, including Piazza 5 Lune, near Piazza Navona (© 06-68809240); Piazza Santa Maria Maggiore (© 06-4740955); and Piazza dei 500, outside Stazione Termini (© 06-47825194).

Websites Rome's official site, **www.romaturismo.it**, has a fair amount of info on most aspects of the Rome experience. Maintained by a private company, **www.enjoyrome.com** fills you in on useful information for visiting the city (they, after all, pen the official tourist office's "Info for Tourists" pamphlet) while promoting its walking tours in Rome, Florence, and Venice as well as guided trips to Pompeii.

The extensive **www.initaly.com** helps you find all sorts of accommodations (country villas, historic residences, convents, and farmhouses) and includes tips on shopping, dining, driving, and viewing works of art. Check out **www.italy tour.com** for coverage of the arts, culture, business, tours, entertainment, restaurants, lodging, media, shopping, sports, and major Italian cities. To stay up to date on trends in modern Italian culture, go to **www.dolcevita.com**, the self-proclaimed "insider's guide to Italy." It's all about style—as it pertains to fashion, cuisine, design, and travel.

CITY LAYOUT The drive into the city from the airport is rather uneventful until you pass through the still remarkably intact **Great Aurelian Wall,** begun in A.D. 271 to calm Rome's barbarian jitters. Suddenly, ruins of imperial baths loom on one side and great monuments can be seen in the middle of blocks.

Stazione Termini, the modern railroad station, faces the huge **Piazza dei Cinquecento,** named after 500 Italians who died heroically in a 19th-century battle in Africa.

The bulk of ancient, Renaissance, and baroque Rome lies on the east side of the **Fiume Tevere (Tiber River),** which meanders between 19th-century stone embankments. However, several important monuments are on the other side: **St. Peter's Basilica** and the **Vatican,** the **Castel Sant' Angelo** (formerly the tomb of the emperor Hadrian), and the colorful section known as **Trastevere.** The city's various quarters are linked by boulevards mostly been laid out since the late 19th century.

Major streets fan out from **Piazza Venezia** in front of the **Vittorio Emmanuele monument,** a highly controversial pile of snow-white Brescian marble. Running north to **Piazza del Popolo** and the city wall is **Via del Corso,** one of Rome's main streets. Called simply "Il Corso," it's noisy, congested, and always crowded with buses and shoppers. Going west across the Tiber toward St. Peter's is **Corso Vittorio Emanuele.** Running toward the Colosseum is **Via dei Fori Imperiali,** named for the excavated ruins of the imperial forums that flank this avenue. **Via Quattro Novembre** runs east and becomes **Via Nazionale** before terminating at **Piazza della Repubblica.**

GETTING AROUND   Much of the inner core of Rome is traffic-free—so you'll need to walk whether you like it or not. However, walking in many parts of the city is hazardous and uncomfortable because of overcrowding, heavy traffic, and very narrow and uneven sidewalks.

By Subway   The **Metropolitana,** or **Metro** for short, is the fastest means of transportation in Rome. It has two underground lines: **A** and **B.** A big red letter M indicates the subway entrance. The fare is .75€. Tickets are available from vending machines at all stations. Ticket booklets are available at *tabacchi* (tobacco) shops and in some terminals. *Tip:* Avoid riding the trains when the Romans are going to or from work or you'll be mashed flatter than fettuccine.

By Bus/Tram   Roman buses are operated by **ATAC (Azienda Tramvie e Autobus del Comune di Roma),** Via Volturno 65 (© 06-46951 for information). The service is quite good and you can ride to most parts of Rome for only .75€. The ticket is valid for 1¼ hours, and you can get on as many buses during that time period as you want, using the same ticket; you can also transfer free between the Metro and the bus within the 75 minutes of validity. Bus service runs from 5:30am to midnight and the night service is from 12:10 to 5:30am; an N after the line number defines buses running at night. A 2-hour bus tour of the city is offered by bus no. 110, leaving from Stazione Termini daily at 2:30pm.

> (*Value* **Traveler's Tip**
>
> At the Stazione Termini, you can purchase a special **tourist bus and subway pass,** which costs 3€ for 1 day or 12€ for a week.

By Taxi   Don't count on hailing a taxi on the street or even getting one at a stand. If you're going out, have your hotel call one. At a restaurant, ask the waiter or cashier to dial for you. If you want to call yourself, try one of these numbers: © **06-6645,** 06-3570, or 06-4994. The meter begins at 2.25€ for the first 3km, then .65€ per kilometer. On Sunday, a 1€ supplement is assessed, plus another 2.50€ supplement from 10pm to 7am. There's yet another 1€ supplement for every suitcase. The driver will expect a 10% tip.

By Car   You can rent a car from **Hertz,** near the parking lot of the Villa Borghese, Via Veneto 156 (© **06-3216831**); **Italy by Car,** Via Ludovisi 60

(© **06-4870010**); the local Italian company **Maggiore,** Via di Tor Cervara 225 (© **06-22935356**); or **Avis** at Stazione Termini (© **06-4814373**).

By Bicycle   You can rent bicycles at many places throughout Rome. Ask at your hotel for the nearest rental location, or else go to **I Bike Rome,** Via Veneto 156 (© **06-3225240**), which rents bicycles from the underground parking garage at the Villa Borghese. Most bikes cost 2€ per hour or 5€ per day. It's open daily from 9am to 7pm. Bring an ID card with you.

 FAST FACTS: Rome

American Express   The Rome offices are at Piazza di Spagna 38 (© **06-67641**; Metro: Spagna). The travel service is open Monday through Friday from 9am to 5pm, and Saturday from 9am to 12:30pm. Hours for the financial and mail services are Monday through Friday from 9am to 5pm. The tour desk is open during the same hours as those for travel services and also Saturday from 2 to 2:30pm (May–Oct).

Business Hours   In general, **banks** are open Monday through Friday from 8:30am to 1:30pm and 3 to 4pm. Most **stores** are open generally Monday from 3:30 to 7:30pm and Tuesday through Saturday from 9:30 or 10am to 1pm and from 3:30 to 7 or 7:30pm. Some shops are open on Monday mornings, however, and some shops don't close for the afternoon break.

Currency   On January 1, 2002, the euro (€), the new European currency, became the legal tender in place of the lira.

Currency Exchange   There are **exchange offices** throughout the city and at all major rail and air terminals, including Stazione Termini, where the **cambio** beside the rail information booth is open daily from 8am to 8pm. At some cambi, you'll have to pay commissions, often 1½%. Likewise, banks often charge commissions. **Automated teller machines (ATMs)—** with both the **Cirrus** (© **800/424-7787**; www.mastercard.com) and the **PLUS** (© **800/843-7587**; www.visa.com) networks represented—are prevalent in all Italian cities and even in smaller towns, and often offer a good exchange rate.

Dentists   There is a 24-hour **G. Eastman Dental Hospital,** Viale Regina Elena 287B (© **06-844831**; Metro: Policlinico).

Doctors/Hospitals   Call the U.S. embassy at © **06-46741** for a list of doctors who speak English. All big hospitals have a 24-hour first-aid service (go to the emergency room, *Pronto Soccorso*). You'll find English-speaking doctors at the privately run **Salvator Mundi International Hospital,** Viale delle Mura Gianicolensi 67 (© **06-588961**; bus: 44). For medical assistance, the **International Medical Center** is on 24-hour duty at Via Firenze 47 (© **06-4882371**; Metro: Razza Repubblica). You can also contact the **Rome American Hospital,** Via Emilio Longoni 69 (© **06-22551**), where English-speaking doctors are on duty 24 hours.

Drugstores/Pharmacies   A reliable pharmacy is **Farmacia Internazionale,** Piazza Barberini 49 (© **06-4825456**; Metro: Barberini), open day and night. Most pharmacies are open from 8:30am to 1pm and 4 to 7:30pm. In general, pharmacies follow a rotation system, so several are always open on Sunday.

Embassies/Consulates The embassy of the **United States,** Via Vittorio Veneto 119A (© **06-46741;** Metro: Barberini), is open Monday through Friday from 8:30am to 5:30pm. Consular and passport services for **Canada,** Via Zara 30 (© **06-445981;** Metro: Policlinico; bus: 36), are open Monday through Friday from 10am to 12:30pm; the embassy of Canada is at Via G. B. De Rossi 27 (© **06-445981;** bus: 36 or 60). The embassy of the **United Kingdom,** Via XX Settembre 80A (© **06-42200001;** Metro: Barberini), is open Monday through Friday from 9:15am to 1:30pm. The embassy of **Australia,** Via Alessandria 215 (© **06-852721;** Metro: Policlinico; bus: 36 or 60), is open Monday through Thursday from 8:30am to noon and 1:30 to 5pm and Friday from 9am to noon; the consulate of Australia is at Corso Trieste 25 (© **06-852721;** bus: 36 or 60), and is open Monday through Friday from 8:30am to noon and 1:30 to 4:15pm. The embassy of **New Zealand,** Via Zara 28 (© **06-4417171;** Metro: Policlinico; bus: 36 or 60), is open Monday through Friday from 8:30am to 12:45pm and 1:45 to 5pm. The embassy of **Ireland** is at Piazza di Campitelli 3 (© **06-697912;** Metro: Circo Massimo; bus: 46); for consular queries call © **06-69791211** (call for hours). In an **emergency,** embassies have a 24-hour referral service.

Emergencies Dial **113** for an ambulance or to call the police; to report a fire, call **115.**

Internet Access You can log onto the Web in central Rome at **Thenetgate,** Piazza Firenze 25 (© **06-87406008;** bus: 116). Summer hours are Monday through Saturday from 6am to noon and 3:30pm to midnight, and winter hours are daily from 10:40am to 8:30pm. A 20-minute visit costs 3€, and 1 hour costs 5€. Access is free on Saturday from 10:30 to 11am and 2 to 2:30pm.

Mail It's easiest just to buy stamps and mail letters and postcards at your hotel's front desk. Stamps *(francobolli)* can also be bought at tabacchi. You can buy special stamps at the **Vatican City Post Office,** adjacent to the information office in St. Peter's Square; it's open Monday through Friday from 8:30am to 7pm and Saturday from 8:30am to 6pm. Letters mailed at Vatican City reach North America far more quickly than mail sent from within Rome for the same cost.

Safety Pickpocketing is the most common problem. Men should keep their wallets in their front pocket or inside jacket pocket. Purse snatching is also commonplace, with young men on Vespas who ride past you and grab your purse. To avoid trouble, stay away from the curb; keep your purse on the wall side of your body and place the strap across your chest. Don't place anything valuable on tables or chairs, where it can be grabbed. Gypsy children have long been a particular menace, although the problem isn't as severe as in years past. If they completely surround you, you'll often literally have to fight them off. They might approach you with pieces of cardboard hiding their stealing hands. Just keep repeating a firm *"No!"*

Telephone The **country code** for Italy is **39.** The **city code** for Rome is **06,** which is the code you'll use every time you dial a party located within

Rome, regardless of whether you're within the city limits or not. To call **from one city code to another** within Italy, dial the city code, complete with the initial zero, then the local number. To **dial direct internationally,** dial **00,** then the country code for the country you are calling, then the area or city code, and then the local number. Direct-dial calls from the United States to Italy are usually cheaper than calls placed from an Italian hotel to most phones in North America, so if possible, try to arrange for friends and acquaintances to call you at your hotel at prearranged times.

To ring national **telephone information** (in Italian) in Italy, dial **12.** International information is available at **176,** but costs .60€ per request.

To make a **collect or calling-card call** from a public phone, drop in .10€ or insert a prepaid phone card (available from most tabacchi) and dial one of the following access numbers to reach an American operator or an English-language voice prompt: **AT&T** ✆ **172-10-11** (if calling a country other than the United States, after the access code dial 01, the country code of country you are calling, city code, and local number); **MCI** ✆ **172-10-22;** and **Sprint** ✆ **172-18-77.**

Tipping More and more restaurants automatically add a 15% service charge to your bill. Ask when you receive the bill; otherwise you might end up tipping twice. Add 15% if service is not included. It's customary to leave another .75€ or so on the table. Tip taxi drivers 10%.

WHERE TO STAY
NEAR STAZIONE TERMINI
Expensive

Hotel Artemide 👫👫 A refined government-rated four-star hotel, this establishment was transformed from a 19th-century palazzetto into an elegant hotel named for Artemis, the Greek goddess. Close to the Opera, it combines stylish simplicity with modern comforts against an Art Nouveau backdrop. The original stained-glass skylight dome was retained in the lobby. Rooms have good furnishings along with spacious bathrooms.

Via Nazionale 22, 00184 Roma. ✆ 06-489911. Fax 06-48991700. www.travel.it/roma/artemide. 85 units. 299€–320€ double; 372€ suite. Rates include breakfast. AE, DC, MC, V. Parking 15€. Metro: Piazza Repubblica. **Amenities:** Rooftop restaurant; bar; room service; laundry/dry cleaning. *In room:* A/C, TV, minibar, hair dryer, safe.

Hotel Mediterraneo 👫 A recent influx of cash has returned this golden oldie to some of its former glory. Located on the triumphant passageway through Rome, the hotel sports vivid Italian Art Deco styling. Its height, coupled with its position on one of Rome's hills, provides panoramic views from the most expensive rooms on the highest floors (some with lovely terraces) and from its roof garden/bar (open in May and especially charming at night). Views from here are far superior to those from the rooftop restaurant at the Artemide (see above).

Via Cavour 15, 00184 Roma. ✆ **800/223-9832** in the U.S., or 06-4884051. Fax 06-4744105. www.bettoja hotels.it. 267 units. 293€ double; from 675€ suite. Rates include buffet breakfast. AE, DC, MC, V. Parking 21€–26€. Metro: Termini. **Amenities:** 2 restaurants; bar; car-rental desk; room service; babysitting; laundry/dry cleaning. *In room:* A/C, TV, minibar, hair dryer, safe.

Moderate

Aberdeen Hotel   This completely renovated hotel near the Opera is centrally located for most landmarks and for rail and bus connections. It lies in front of the Ministry of Defense, in a rather quiet and fairly safe area of Rome. The recently renovated rooms are furnished in a modern style and sport neatly kept bathrooms with tub/shower combo.

Via Firenze 48, 00184 Roma. ℂ **06-4823920.** Fax 06-4821092. www.travel.it/roma/aberdeen. 27 units (19 with shower only). 140€–160€ double; 108€–165€ suite. Rates include buffet breakfast. AE, DC, MC, V. Parking 21€. Metro: Repubblica. Bus: 64 or 170. **Amenities:** Laundry/dry cleaning. *In room:* A/C, TV, minibar, hair dryer, iron, safe.

Hotel Columbia 🌟🌟 *(Finds)*   This is one of the newest hotels in the neighborhood, with a hardworking multilingual staff. A government-rated three-star choice, originally built around 1900, it underwent a successful, radical renovation in 1997. The interior contains Murano chandeliers and conservatively modern furniture. The compact and cozy guest rooms compare well against the accommodations in the best hotels nearby. The appealing roof garden has a view over the surrounding rooftops.

Via del Viminale 15, 00184 Roma. ℂ **06-4744289** or 06-4883509. Fax 06-4740209. www.venere.it/roma/columbia. 45 units. 144€–195€ double. Rates include buffet breakfast. AE, DC, MC, V. Parking nearby 20€. Metro: Repubblica. **Amenities:** Bar; room service; laundry service. *In room:* A/C, TV, minibar, hair dryer, safe.

Medici   The Medici, built in 1906, is a substantial hotel that has easy access to the shops along Via XX Settembre. Many of its better rooms overlook an inner patio garden. Rooms are a generous size and in a classic Roman style. The cheapest rooms are called standard; superior units offer air-conditioning, more antiques, and better furnishings. Breakfast is the only meal served.

Via Flavia 96, 00187 Roma. ℂ **06-4827319.** Fax 06-4740767. www.hotelmedici.com. 69 units (showers only). 150€–186€ double. Rates include breakfast. AE, DC, MC, V. Parking 20€ 40€. Metro: Piazza della Repubblica. **Amenities:** Bar; room service; laundry/dry cleaning. *In room:* A/C, TV, minibar, hair dryer, safe.

Inexpensive

Hotel Pavia 🌟   This is a popular choice on this quiet street near the gardens of the Baths of Diocletian. Established in the 1980s, it occupies a much-renovated century-old building. The front rooms tend to be noisy, but that's the curse of all Termini hotels. Nevertheless, the rooms are comfortable and fairly attractive, and were last renovated in 1998. Each comes with a neatly tiled shower bathroom.

Via Gaeta 83, 00185 Roma. ℂ **06-483801.** Fax 06-4819090. www.hotelpavia.com. 20 units (showers only). 100€–190€ double. Rates include breakfast. AE, DC, MC, V. Parking 11€. Metro: Termini. **Amenities:** Bar; room service. *In room:* A/C, TV, minibar, hair dryer, safe.

NEAR VIA VENETO & PIAZZA BARBERINI
Very Expensive

Hotel Eden 🌟🌟🌟   During the heyday of this ornate hotel, all the big names—Hemingway, Maria Callas, Ingrid Bergman, Fellini—checked in here. In 1994, it reopened after a 2-year (and $20-million) radical renovation that enhanced its original fin de siècle grandeur and added the modern amenities its government-rated five-star status calls for. Its hilltop position guarantees a panoramic city view from most rooms. Understated elegance is the rule.

Via Ludovisi 49, 00187 Roma. ℂ **800/225-5843** in the U.S., or 06-478121. Fax 06-4821584. www.hoteleden.it. 121 units. 452€–645€ double; from 679€–1,830€ suite. AE, DC, DISC, MC, V. Parking 30€. Metro: Piazza Barberini. **Amenities:** Restaurant; bar; health club; room service; babysitting; laundry/dry cleaning. *In room:* A/C, TV, minibar, hair dryer, iron, safe.

Rome Accommodations

Aberdeen Hotel **18**	Hotel delle Muse **8**	Hotel Pavia **17**
Alexandra **14**	Hotel de Russie **7**	Hotel Ponte Sisto **1**
Colosseum Hotel **22**	Hotel Eden **13**	Hotel Ranieri **16**
Hassler **12**	Hotel Gregoriana **11**	Medici **15**
Hotel Artemide **19**	Hotel Locarno **5**	Scalinata di Spagna **10**
Hotel Atlante Star **4**	Hotel Margutta **6**	Teatro di Pompeo **2**
Hotel Columbia **20**	Hotel Mediterraneo **21**	Trastevere Manara **1**
Hotel Columbus **3**	Hotel Parlamento **9**	

National Gallery
of Modern Art

8

Galleria
Borghese

*Piazza
di Siena*

**VILLA
BORGHESE/
PARIOLI**

Corso D'Italia

Via Campania
Via Sardegna
Via Sicilia
Via Boncompagni

*Piazzale di
Porta Pia*

Policlinico

15

Spagna | Spanish
Steps **13**

11

12

14 Barberini

VIA VENETO **16**

*Lgo. di
S. Susanna*

Via XX Settembre

**PIAZZA
BARBERINI**

18

Via Barberini

National Roman
Museum

*Piazza
Indipendenza* **17**

Castro Pretorio

9 *Via Tritone*

*Lg. de
Tritone*

*Piazza
Colonna*

Trevi
Fountain

Palazzo del
Quirinale

*Piazza d.
Quirinale*

*Piazza
Repubblica*

Repubblica **19**

*Piazza
Cinque-
cento*

20

Termini
Station

Termini

SAN
LORENZO

Palazzo
Doria
amphilj

Palazzo
Colonna

Teatro
dell'Opera

Via Giovanni Giolitti

21

*Piazza
dell'Esquilino*
Santa Maria
Maggiore

Palazzo
Venezia

Vittorio Emanuele
Monument

Capitoline
Museums

Via Cavour

22

*Piazza
Vittorio
Eman. II*

Vittorio Emanuele

ANCIENT ROME

Roman
Forum

San Pietro
in Vincoli

Colosseo

Golden House
of Nero

Manzoni

Colosseum

*Piazza d.
Colosseo*

Via di S. Giovanni in Laterano

*Piazza
Bocca
d. Verità*

**PALATINE
HILL**

Circus Maximus

San Giovanni
in Laterano

S. Giovanni

**AVENTINE
HILL**

Circo Massimo

*Piazza di
Pta. Capena*

Re di Roma

*Piazza
Albania*

Baths of
Caracalla

*Piazza di
Pla. Metronia*

Piramide

Information ⓘ
City Walls ━━━
Metro Ⓐ Ⓜ
Metro Ⓑ Ⓜ
Railway ┼┼┼┼┼

Venice
Florence
Rome
ITALY

Moderate

Alexandra ⭐ (Finds)   Here's where you can stay on Via Veneto without going broke. Set in what was originally a 19th-century private mansion, this hotel offers comfortable, well-kept accommodations filled with antique furniture and modern conveniences such as private bathrooms, some with shower and some with tub and shower. Rooms facing front are exposed to roaring traffic and animated street life; those in back are quieter but have less of a view. Breakfast is the only meal served. The garden-inspired breakfast room designed by Paolo Portoghesi is especially appealing.

Via Vittorio Veneto 18, 00187 Roma. ✆ 06-4881943. Fax 06-4871804. www.venere.it/roma/alexandra. 59 units (some with shower only). 217€ double; 336€ suite. Rates include buffet breakfast. AE, DC, MC, V. Parking 26€–31€. Metro: Piazza Barberini. **Amenities:** Laundry/dry cleaning. *In room:* A/C, TV, minibar, hair dryer, iron, safe.

IN PARIOLI
Inexpensive

Hotel delle Muse   A classic, family-run, government-rated three-star establishment, this hotel 1km (½ mile) north of the Villa Borghese is a winning but unheralded choice. Most rooms have been renovated but remain rather spartan. Each efficiently organized bathroom comes with a tub/shower combo.

Via Tommaso Salvini 18, 00197 Roma. ✆ 06-8088333. Fax 06-8085749. www.hoteldellemuse.com. 61 units (showers only). 78€–160€ double. Rates include buffet breakfast. AE, DC, MC, V. Parking 15€. Bus: 360. **Amenities:** Restaurant; bar; room service; babysitting; laundry/dry cleaning. *In room:* TV, hair dryer.

AROUND THE SPANISH STEPS & PIAZZA DEL POPOLO
Very Expensive

Hassler ⭐⭐⭐   The only deluxe hotel in this old part of Rome, it uses the Spanish Steps as its grand entrance. The crown worn by the Hassler is still in place after all these years; the hostelry has such a mystique that it prospers and endures in spite of high prices. Rooms, some of which are small, have a personalized look, with French windows, comfortable beds, and—the nicest touch of all—bowls of fresh flowers. Some have balconies with views of the city.

Piazza Trinità dei Monti 6, 00187 Roma. ✆ 800/223-6800 in the U.S., or 06-699340. Fax 06-6789991. www. hotelhasslerroma.com. 100 units. 545€–725€ double; from 1,626€ suite. AE, DC, MC, V. Parking 30€. Metro: Piazza di Spagna. **Amenities:** Restaurant; bar; gym; free use of bicycles; room service; massage; babysitting; laundry/dry cleaning. *In room:* A/C, TV, minibar, hair dryer, safe.

Hotel de Russie ⭐⭐⭐   This government-rated five-star deluxe hotel lies just off Piazza del Popolo. Lovers of *luxe* are deserting such traditional favorites as the Hassler to stay here. In one of the choicest platinum locations in Rome, it is lavishly furnished and was once a favorite of Russian dignitaries (hence, its name) and of such artists as Jean Cocteau, Picasso, and Stravinsky. In World War II, it was the spy center for Italy. About 30% of the spacious rooms are traditionally furnished, the others more minimalist with a strikingly contemporary motif. Bathrooms are elegantly tiled, with tub and shower.

Via del Babuino 9, 00187 Roma. ✆ 800/323-7500 in North America, or 06-328881. Fax 06-3288888. www. roccofortehotels.com. 125 units. 572€–797€ double; from 1,050€ suite. AE, DC, MC, V. Metro: Flaminia. **Amenities:** Lovely restaurant and bar; gym; spa; salon; room service. *In room:* A/C, TV, minibar, hair dryer, safe.

Expensive

Hotel Locarno ⭐ (Finds)   This little charmer is near Piazza del Popolo, said to be haunted by the imperial ghost of Nero, although that isn't expected to disturb your night's sleep. You can count on Rome's heavy traffic to do that. The hotel's most winning feature is its large roof terrace where you can take your breakfast while enjoying some of the major sights of Rome's skyline. If you'd like to go exploring, the Locarno will provide you with a bike. A 1920s aura pervades the hotel, as evoked by the wrought-iron elevator cage or the marble-topped walnut bar with its Tiffany-style lamp. Guest rooms and bathrooms with a tub/shower combo are completely up to date.

Via della Penna 25, 00186 Roma. ⓒ **06-3610841.** Fax 06-3215249. www.hotellocarno.com. 68 units. 190€–310€ double; 510€ suite. Rates include breakfast. AE, DC, MC, V. Parking 30€–40€. Metro: Flaminio. Bus: 116, 117. **Amenities:** Bar; lunch buffet; room service; laundry/dry cleaning. *In room:* A/C, TV, minibar, safe.

Scalinata di Spagna ⭐⭐ This upscale B&B near the Spanish Steps has always been one of the most sought-after in Rome. It's right at the top of the steps, directly across the small piazza from the deluxe Hassler. Decor varies radically from one room to the next; some have low beamed ceilings and ancient-looking wood furniture, others offer loftier ceilings and more average appointments. All rooms were renovated and upgraded in 1998, bathrooms— each with a tub and shower—receiving special attention. In season, breakfast is served on the rooftop garden terrace with its sweeping view of the dome of St. Peter's across the Tiber.

Via Belsiana, 00187 Roma. ⓒ **06-69380806.** Fax 06-69294231. www.hotelscalinata.com. 10 units. 180€– 350€ double; 200€–400€ triple. Rates include buffet breakfast. AE, DC, MC, V. Parking 30€. **Amenities:** Breakfast terrace; room service; laundry. *In room:* A/C, TV, minibar, hair dryer, safe.

Moderate

Hotel Gregoriana ⭐ Although surrounded by much more expensive neighbors like the pricey Hassler, the small Gregoriana in a former 17th-century convent has its fans—mainly members of the Italian fashion industry. Rooms are small but comfortable, each with a small, neatly organized private bathroom with tub and shower combo. The elevator cage is a black-and-gold Art Deco fantasy, and the door to each room has a reproduction of an Erté print whose fanciful characters indicate the letter designating that room.

Via Gregoriana 18, 00187 Roma. ⓒ **06-6794269.** Fax 06-6784258. 20 units. 217€ double. Rates include breakfast. No credit cards. Parking 25€. Metro: Spagna. **Amenities:** Room service; babysitting; laundry/dry cleaning. *In room:* A/C, TV, minibar, hair dryer, safe.

Inexpensive

Hotel Margutta Located on a cobblestone street near Piazza del Popolo, this hotel offers attractively decorated but exceedingly small rooms and cramped bathrooms, some with shower, some with a tub and shower combo. Its helpful staff makes it an enduring favorite, nonetheless. The best rooms are on the top floor; two of these share a terrace, and another larger room has a private terrace.

Via Laurina 34, 00187 Roma. ⓒ **06-3223674.** Fax 06-3200395. 24 units (showers only). 104€–115€ double; 140€–160€ triple. Rates include breakfast. AE, DC, MC, V. Metro: Flaminio. **Amenities:** Room service. *In room:* Hair dryer and iron on request.

Hotel Parlamento The Parlamento has a four-star government rating at two-star prices. Expect a friendly pensione-style reception. The furnishings are antiques or reproductions, and the firm beds are backed by carved wood or wrought-iron headboards. Fifteen rooms are air-conditioned, and the bathrooms were recently redone with heated towel racks, phones, and (in a few) even marble sinks. Rooms are different in style; the best are no. 82, with its original 1800s furniture, and nos. 104, 106, and 107, which open onto the roof garden.

Via delle Convertite 5 (at the intersection with Via del Corso), 00187 Roma. (℗ **06-6792082.** Fax 06-69921000. www.hotelparlamento.it. 23 units. 109€–125€ double. Rates include breakfast. AE, DC, MC, V. Parking 26€. Metro: Spagna. **Amenities:** Bar. *In room:* A/C (some), TV, hair dryer, safe.

NEAR CAMPO DE' FIORI
Moderate

Teatro di Pompeo ⭐ *Finds*   Built on the top of the ruins of the Theater of Pompey, which dates from about 55 B.C., this small charmer lies near the spot where Julius Caesar met his fate. Intimate and refined, it's on a quiet piazzetta near the Palazzo Farnese and Campo de' Fiori. Rooms, all doubles, are decorated in an old-fashioned Italian style with hand-painted tiles, and the beamed ceilings date from the days of Michelangelo. The tiled bathrooms are neatly kept, some with shower and some with a tub/shower combo. There's no restaurant, but breakfast is served.

Largo del Pallaro 8, 00186 Roma. (℗ **06-68300170.** Fax 06-68805531. 13 units (showers only). 180€–190€ double. Rates include breakfast. AE, DC, MC, V. Bus: 46, 62, or 64. **Amenities:** Bar; room service; babysitting; laundry/dry cleaning. *In room:* A/C, TV, minibar, hair dryer, safe.

NEAR VATICAN CITY
Very Expensive

Hotel Atlante Star ⭐⭐⭐   This is a first-class hotel near St. Peter's. The upper floors give the impression of being inside a luxuriously appointed ocean liner. Rooms are small but posh, outfitted with all the modern comforts, including tiled bathrooms with tub/shower combo. A royal suite features a Jacuzzi. The views of St. Peter's are the most striking of any hotel in Rome.

Via Vitelleschi 34, 00193 Roma. (℗ **06-6873233.** Fax 06-6872300. www.atlantehotels.com. 90 units. 170€–230€ double; from 375€ suite. Rates include buffet breakfast. AE, DC, MC, V. Parking 35€. Metro: Ottaviano. Bus: 23, 64, or 492. **Amenities:** Superb restaurant; cafe; room service; laundry/dry cleaning. *In room:* A/C, TV, minibar, hair dryer, safe.

Expensive

Hotel Columbus ⭐   In an impressive 15th-century palace, Hotel Columbus lies a few minutes' walk from St. Peter's. It was once the private home of a wealthy cardinal who later became Pope Julius II and had Michelangelo paint the Sistine Chapel. Rooms are considerably simpler than the tiled and tapestried salons. All are spacious; a few are enormous and still have such original details as decorated wood ceilings and frescoed walls. All units come with a well-organized private bathroom with tub/shower combo.

Via della Conciliazione 33, 00193 Roma. (℗ **06-6865435.** Fax 06-6864874. 92 units. 307€ double; 414€ suite. Rates include buffet breakfast. AE, DC, MC, V. Bus: 40, 62, or 64. **Amenities:** Restaurant; bar; room service; babysitting; laundry/dry cleaning. *In room:* A/C, TV, minibar, hair dryer, safe.

NEAR ANCIENT ROME
Inexpensive

Colosseum Hotel ⭐ *Finds*   Not far from the Santa Maria Maggiore, the Colosseum offers baronial living on a miniature scale. The tasteful hotel reflects the best of Italy's design heritage. Rooms are furnished with well-conceived antique reproductions. The drawing room, with its long refectory table, white walls, red tiles, and provincial armchairs, invites lingering. All the units contain a private bathroom with either a shower or a tub/shower combo.

Via Sforza 10, 00184 Roma. (℗ **06-4827228.** Fax 06-4827285. www.hotelcolosseum.com. 50 units (showers only). 130€–184€ double. Rates include breakfast. AE, DC, MC, V. Parking 30€. Metro: Cavour. **Amenities:** Lounge; room service; babysitting; laundry/dry cleaning. *In room:* A/C, TV, hair dryer, safe.

IN TRASTEVERE

Hotel Ponte Sisto ⓐ *Finds* Just steps from the River Tiber, this newly opened hotel lies on the most exclusive residential street in historic Rome at the gateway to Trastevere. The hotel is imbued with a bright, fresh look in contrast to some of the timeworn buildings surrounding it. Your windows will look out on the monumental core of Renaissance and baroque Rome. The 18th-century structure has been totally renovated with a certain class and elegance. Cool chic is achieved by the use of light pastels and marble floors, and the walls are highlighted with strips of black marble. If you can live in the small bedrooms (the singles are really cramped), you'll enjoy this choice address, with its cherrywood furnishings. Try for one of the upper-floor rooms with a greater panorama; some accommodations come with their own terrace. The most desirable room is the Belvedere, with two terraces, each with sweeping views of the city from north to south, including St. Peter's dome.

Via dei Pettinari 64, 00186 Roma. ⓒ 06-6863100. Fax 06-68301712. www.hotelpontesisto.it. 106 units. 310€ double; 420€ suite. Rates include breakfast. AE, DC, MC, V. Parking: 24€. Tram: 8. **Amenities:** Restaurant for guests only; breakfast-only room service; laundry/dry cleaning; garden. *In room:* A/C, TV, minibar.

WHERE TO DINE
NEAR STAZIONE TERMINI
Very Expensive

Agata e Romeo ⓐⓐ NEW ROMAN One of the most charming places near the Vittorio Emanuele Monument is this striking duplex restaurant in turn-of-the-century Liberty style. You'll enjoy the creative cuisine of Romeo Caraccio (who manages the dining room) and his wife, Agata (who prepares her own version of sophisticated Roman food). Look for pasta garnished with broccoli and cauliflower and served in skate broth, as well as a crisp *sformato* (a type of soufflé) loaded with eggplant, parmigiana, mozzarella, and fresh Italian herbs. There's a charming wine cellar with a wide choice of international and domestic wines. One of their most enduring dessert specialties is their own version of *millefoglie*—chantilly cream laced with liqueur and served in puff pastry.

Via Carlo Alberto 45. ⓒ 06-4466115. Reservations recommended. All main courses 26€. AE, DC, MC, V. Mon–Fri 1–2:30pm and 8–10:30pm. Metro: Vittorio Emanuele.

Moderate

Alvaro al Circo Massimo ⓐ ITALIAN Located at the edge of the Circus Maximus, Alvaro is the closest thing you'll find in Rome to a genuine provincial inn, right down to the hanging corncobs and rolls of fat sausages. The antipasti and pastas are fine, the meat courses are even better, and the fresh fish is never overcooked. Other specialties are tagliolini with mushrooms and truffles or briny roasted turbot with potatoes. Look for exotic seasonal mushrooms, including black truffles rivaling the ones you'd find in Spoleto. A basket of fresh fruit rounds out the meal. The atmosphere is comfortable and mellow.

Via dei Cerchi 53. ⓒ 06-6786112. Reservations required. Main courses 30€. AE, DC, MC, V. Tues–Sat 12:30–3:30pm and 7:30–11pm; Sun 12:30–3:30pm. Closed Aug. Metro: Circo Massimo.

Inexpensive

Il Dito e La Luna SICILIAN/ITALIAN At this charming, small restaurant, the menu is equally divided between traditional Sicilian recipes and more creative up-to-date recipes prepared with gusto and flair. The setting emulates an unpretentious bistro. Menu items include fresh orange-infused anchovies served on orange segments; a creamy flan of mild onions and mountain cheese; seafood

The Cafe Scene

Caffè de Paris, Via Vittorio Veneto 90 (© **06-4885284;** Metro: Barberini), rises and falls in popularity depending on the decade. In the 1950s, it was a haven for the fashionable and now it's a popular restaurant in summer where the tables spill out onto the sidewalk filled with patrons. It's open Wednesday through Monday from 8am to 1am. **Canova Café,** Piazza del Popolo 16 (© **06-3612231;** Metro: Flaminio), has a sidewalk terrace for people-watching, plus a snack bar, a restaurant, and a wine shop inside. In summer you'll have access to a courtyard with ivy-covered walls. Meals cost 18€ and up. It's open daily from 8am to midnight or later, depending on the crowd.

Since 1760, **Antico Caffè Greco,** Via Condotti 86 (© **06-6791700;** Metro: Spagna), has been Rome's most posh and fashionable coffee bar. It has for years enjoyed a reputation as the gathering place of the literati. In the front is a wooden bar, and beyond that a series of small salons, decorated in a 19th-century style. It's open daily from 8am to 8:30pm. **Caffè Sant'Eustachio,** Piazza Sant'Eustachio 82 (© **06-6861309;** bus: 116), is one of the city's most celebrated espresso shops, on a small square near the Pantheon. The water supply comes from a source outside Rome, which the emperor Augustus funneled into the city with an aqueduct in 19 B.C. Rome's most experienced espresso judges claim that the water plays an important part in the coffee's flavor. The caffè is open daily from 8:30am to 1:30pm.

couscous loaded with shellfish; and such succulent pastas as square-cut spaghetti *(tonnarelli)* prepared with mussels, bacon, tomatoes, and exotic mushrooms.

Via dei Sabelli 49–51, San Lorenzo. © 06-4940726. Reservations recommended. Main courses 13€–14€. No credit cards. Mon–Sat 8pm–midnight. Metro: Vittorio Emanuele.

NEAR VIA VENETO & PIAZZA BARBERINI
Very Expensive
Antico Bottaro 🐦🐦 *(Finds)* FRENCH/ITALIAN   There has been some kind of restaurant here for the past century or so, but in 2002, it got a huge kick forward when the administration and most of the staff of a well-known and very grand restaurant, Sans Souci, which lost its lease, moved onto its premises and conducted a radical transformation of both its decor and its cuisine. Today, it's an intimate setting with seats for about 65 people, with mustard-colored walls and carefully chiseled stone ceiling vaults. You'll enjoy well-prepared and imaginative French and Italian cuisine that's put this place on the city's culinary map.

Passegiata di Ripetta 15. © 06-3236763. Reservations required. Main courses 31€–34€; set-price menus 70€–75€. AE, MC, V. Tues–Sun 12:30–3pm and 8pm–midnight. Closed Aug 1–15. Metro: Flaminia or Piazza del Popolo.

Moderate
Césarina EMILIANA-ROMAGNOLA/ROMAN   This restaurant perpetuates the culinary traditions of the late Césarina Masi in a newer manifestation of the original hole-in-the-wall. Today, with three dining rooms and more than 200 seats, the restaurant serves excellent versions of *bollito misto* (an array of

well-seasoned boiled meats), rolled from table to table on a cart; and *misto Césarina*—three kinds of pasta, each handmade and served with a different sauce. Equally appealing is *saltimbocca* (veal with ham) and *cotoletta alla bolognese*(veal cutlet baked with ham and cheese).

Via Piemonte 109. (C) **06-4880828.** Reservations recommended. Main courses 25€–45€. AE, DC, MC, V. Mon–Sat 12:30–3pm and 7:30–11pm. Metro: Barberini. Bus: 52, 53, 63, or 80.

Colline Emiliane 🅖 EMILIANA-ROMAGNOLA This small restaurant right off Piazza Barberini serves *classica cucina bolognese*. It's a family-run place where everybody helps out. The owner is the cook and his wife makes the pasta, which, incidentally, is about the best you'll encounter in Rome. The house specialty is an inspired *tortellini alla panna* (cream sauce) with truffles. An excellent main course is *braciola di maiale*—boneless rolled pork cutlets that have been stuffed with ham and cheese, breaded, and sautéed. *Bollito misto* (mixed boiled meats) is another specialty.

Via Avignonesi 22 (off Piazza Barberini). (C) **06-4817538.** Reservations highly recommended. Main courses 11€–15€. MC, V. Sat–Thurs 12:45–2:45pm and 7:45–10:45pm. Closed Aug. Metro: Barberini.

NEAR VILLA BORGHESE
Moderate
Testa Food & Wine 🅖 *Finds* ITALIAN Near Villa Borghese, this restaurant draws discerning palates seeking food and wine at a reasonable price. Its *orecchiette* (ear-shaped pasta) gratinéed with broccoli and sautéed clams is one of the city's finest pasta dishes. Another excellent homemade pasta dish is *cacio e pepe* made with crunchy artichokes. The tuna steak with sun-dried tomatoes is a delight, as is the duck breast stuffed with foie gras, sprinkled with roasted almonds, and served with plums marinated in port. The bar features live jazz on Tuesday nights and has become one of the best places to be in Rome.

Via Tirso 30. (C) **06-85300692.** Main courses 14€–30€. Daily noon–3pm and 8pm–midnight (bar open until 3am). Closed Aug. Bus: 3 or 19.

IN PARIOLI
Very Expensive
Relais Le Jardin 🅖🅖🅖 ITALIAN/INTERNATIONAL For a traditional and creative cuisine in an elegantly romantic and classic setting, this is the place to go. A chichi crowd with demanding palates patronizes it nightly. The pasta and soups are among the best in town—the tonnarelli pasta with asparagus and smoked ham served with concassé tomatoes is delectable, as is the pasta with ricotta sauce, black olives, corn, and oregano. For your main course you face such selections as roast loin of lamb with artichoke romana, pork filet stuffed with crab, or grilled beef sirloin with hot chicory and sautéed potatoes.

In the Hotel Lord Byron, Via G. de Notaris 5. (C) **06-3613041.** Reservations required. Main courses 20€–30€. AE, DC, MC, V. Mon–Sat 12:30–3pm and 8–10:30pm. Bus: 26 or 52.

Moderate
Al Ceppo 🅖 *Finds* ROMAN This restaurant's somewhat hidden location (2 blocks from the Villa Borghese, near Piazza Ungheria) means that the clientele is likely to be Roman rather than foreign. At this longtime and enduring favorite, the cuisine is as good as it ever was in its heyday. "The Log" features an open fireplace where the chef prepares lamb chops, liver, and bacon to charcoal perfection. The beefsteak, which hails from Tuscany, is also succulent. Other dishes include *tagliolini monteconero* (made with clams and fresh tomatoes), and a savory version of spaghetti with pepperoni, fresh basil, and pecorino cheese.

Via Panama 2. ✆ **06-8419696.** Reservations recommended. Main courses 15€–23€. AE, DC, MC, V. Tues–Sun 12:30–3pm and 8–11pm. Closed last 2 weeks of Aug. Bus: 4, 52, or 53.

NEAR THE SPANISH STEPS & PIAZZA DEL POPOLO
Expensive
El Toulà ⋒ ROMAN/VENETIAN   This *luxe* restaurant offers quintessential Roman haute cuisine with creative flair in an elegant setting of vaulted ceilings and large archways. One menu section is devoted exclusively to culinary specialties of Venice, including Venice's classic dish, *fegato* (liver) *alla Veneziana;* calamari stuffed with vegetables; *baccalà* (codfish) mousse with polenta; and another Venetian classic, *broetto* (soup made with monkfish and clams). There's a charming bar. El Toulà usually isn't crowded at lunchtime.

Via della Lupa 29B. ✆ **06-6873498.** Reservations required for dinner. Main courses 20€–25€; 4-course *menu veneto* 57€; 5-course *menu degustazione* 68€. AE, DC, MC, V. Tues–Fri noon–3pm; Mon–Sat 7:30–11pm. Closed Aug. Bus: 81, 90, 90b, 628, or 913.

Moderate
Dal Bolognese ⋒ BOLOGNESE   If *La Dolce Vita* were being filmed now, this restaurant would be used as a backdrop, its patrons photographed in their latest Fendi drag. It's one of those rare dining spots that's not only chic, but noted for its food as well. To begin your meal, we suggest *misto di pasta*—four pastas, each flavored with a different sauce, arranged on the same plate. For your main course, specialties include *lasagne verdi, tagliatelle alla bolognese,* and a most recommendable *cotoletta alla bolognese* (veal cutlet topped with cheese). Although almond cake is the house specialty, it's hard to resist the fresh strawberry tart.

Piazza del Popolo 1–2. ✆ **06-3611426.** Reservations required. Main courses 14€–19€. AE, DC, MC, V. Tues–Sun 12:30–3pm and 8:15pm–1am (last dinner order at 11:15pm). Closed 20 days in Aug. Metro: Flaminio.

Inexpensive
Otello alla Concordia ROMAN   On a side street amid the glamorous boutiques near the northern edge of the Spanish Steps, this is a popular and consistently reliable restaurant. Diners choose a table (space permitting) in an arbor-covered courtyard or in a series of inner dining rooms. The *spaghetti alle vongole veraci* (spaghetti with clams) and the pasta with chickpeas are excellent, as are Roman-style *abbacchio arrosto* (roasted baby lamb), a selection of grilled or sautéed fish dishes, and classic eggplant parmigiana.

Via della Croce 81. ✆ **06-6791178.** Reservations recommended. Main courses 8€–15€; fixed-price menu 20€. AE, DC, MC, V. Mon–Sat 12:30–3pm and 7:30–11pm. Closed 2 weeks in Jan. Metro: Piazza di Spagna.

NEAR CAMPO DE' FIORI & THE JEWISH GHETTO
Expensive
Il Drappo ⋒ SARDINIAN   A favorite of the local artsy crowd, Il Drappo is on a narrow street near the Tiber and is run by a woman known to her regulars only as "Valentina." You have your choice of two tastefully decorated dining rooms festooned with patterned cotton draped from the ceiling. Flowers and candles are everywhere. Fixed-price dinners reflecting diverse choices might begin with wafer-thin *carte di musica* (sheet-music paper) topped with tomatoes, green peppers, parsley, and olive oil, and then be followed with fresh spring lamb in season, fish stew made with tuna caviar, or one of the strong-flavored regional specialties. For dessert, try the *seadas* (cheese-stuffed fried cake in special dark honey). Valentina's cuisine is a marvelous change of pace from the typical Roman diet, showing an inventiveness that keeps us coming back.

Vicolo del Malpasso 9. ℂ **06-6877365**. Reservations required. Main courses 9€–18€; fixed-price menu 35€. AE, DC, MC, V. Mon–Sat 7pm–midnight. Closed Aug 15–31. Bus: 46, 62, or 64.

Moderate

Da Giggetto ROMAN   Da Giggetto, in the old ghetto, is a short walk from the Theater of Marcellus. Romans flock to this bustling trattoria for their special traditional dishes. None are more typical than *carciofi alla giudea,* baby-tender fried artichokes. This is a true delicacy! The cheese concoction, mozzarella in carrozza, is another good choice, as are the zucchini flowers stuffed with mozzarella and anchovies, even the dried salted cod filet. Also sample shrimp sautéed in garlic and olive oil.

Via del Portico d'Ottavia 21/A. ℂ **06-6861105**. Reservations recommended. Main courses 11€–17€. AE, DC, MC, V. Tues–Sun 12:30–3pm and 7:30–11pm. Closed last week of July, 1st week of Aug. Bus: 62, 64, 75, 90, or 170.

Vecchia Roma ITALIAN/ROMAN   This charming, moderately priced trattoria is in the heart of the Jewish ghetto (a short walk from the Campidoglio). The owners are known for their selection of fresh seafood, and the minestrone of the day is made with fresh vegetables. An interesting selection of antipasti is always presented, including salmon and a vegetable antipasto. The pastas and risottos are also excellent; the "green" risotto with porcini mushrooms is invariably good. Lamb is a specialty of the chef.

Piazza di Campitelli 18. ℂ **06-6864604**. Reservations recommended. Main courses 12€–16€. AE, DC. Thurs–Tues 1–3:30pm and 8–11pm. Closed 10 days in Aug. Metro: Colosseo. Bus: 64, 90, 90b, 97, or 774.

NEAR PIAZZA NAVONA & THE PANTHEON
Very Expensive

Quinzi & Gabrieli ★★★ SEAFOOD   We've never found better, or fresher, seafood than that served here. Don't be put off by the rough and ready service, but be prepared to pay for the privilege, as fresh seafood is extremely expensive in Rome. Everything tastes natural and fresh, and heavy sauces aren't used to disguise old fish as they are in many restaurants. In fact, the restaurant is known for its raw seafood, such as a delicate carpaccio of swordfish, sea bass, and deep-sea shrimp. The house specialty is spaghetti with lobster, but all sorts of fish are served, including sea urchins, octopus, sole, and red mullet. Check out what's available in a special display on ice at the entrance. In summer French doors lead to a small dining terrace.

Via delle Coppelle 5–6, 00186 Roma. ℂ **06-6879389**. Reservations required as far in advance as possible. Main courses 25€–40€. AE, DC, MC, V. Mon–Sat 12:30-3pm and 7:30–11:30pm. Closed Aug. Bus: 44, 46, 55, 60, 61, 62, 64, or 65.

Expensive

Il Convivio ★★★ ROMAN/INTERNATIONAL   This is one of the most acclaimed restaurants in Rome, and one of the very few to be granted a coveted Michelin star. The Troiano brothers turn out an inspired cuisine based on shopping for the best and freshest ingredients at the market. To launch yourself, order their giant shrimp tossed with fresh greens. Among the pasta selections, their gnocchi stuffed with zucchini and dribbled with a well-seasoned seafood sauce delights, as does one of the chef's specialties—*petto di faraona,* stuffed chicken spiced up with fresh olives.

Vicolo dei Soldati 31. ℂ **06-6869432**. Reservations required. Main courses 29€–31€. AE, DC, MC, V. Mon–Sat 1–2:30pm and 8–11pm. Bus: 40 or 64.

Moderate

Bramante ROMAN   On a cobblestone street in back of the Piazza Navona, this cafe-restaurant opens onto a delightful small square of vine-draped taverns. Behind the ivy-covered facade the interior is completely hand painted, as white candles illuminate the marble bar, making for a cozy, inviting atmosphere. The owner, Mr. Giuseppe, tries to make visitors appreciate Italian food and traditions, and succeeds admirably. Recipes are simple but rich in Mediterranean flavor. You can taste wonderful pastas made just with fresh tomato sauce, garlic, and pasta, or else something heavier such as braised beef or tender grilled steak flavored with herbs and served with potatoes. They don't serve fish, however.

Via della Pace 25. ⓒ 06-68803916. Reservations recommended. Main courses 13€–17€. AE, DC, MC, V. Mon–Sat 5pm–2am; Sun noon–2am. Closed Dec 24. Bus: 44, 46, 55, 60, 61, 62, 64, or 65.

L'Eau Vive ⭐ *Finds* FRENCH/INTERNATIONAL   This discovery is run by lay missionaries who wear the dress of their native countries. The restaurant occupies the cellar and the ground floor of a 17th-century palace. In this formal atmosphere, at 10pm nightly, the waitresses sing religious hymns and "Ave Marias." Your gratuity for service will be turned over for religious purposes. Pope John Paul II used to dine here when he was still archbishop of Kraków. Specialties include hors d'oeuvres and frogs' legs. Main dishes range from guinea hen with onions and grapes in a wine sauce to couscous. Other selections include salade niçoise, several kinds of homemade paté, and beefsteak in wine sauce. A smooth finish is the chocolate mousse.

Via Monterone 85. ⓒ 06-68801095. Reservations recommended. Main courses 8.50€–26€; fixed-price menus 8.50€, 13€, 16€, and 27€. AE, MC, V. Mon–Sat 12:30–2:30pm and 7:30–10:30pm. Closed Aug 1–20. Bus: 46, 62, 64, 70, or 115.

Montevecchio ROMAN/ITALIAN   To find this place, you have to negotiate the winding streets of one of Rome's most confusing neighborhoods, near Piazza Navona. The heavily curtained restaurant on this Renaissance piazza is where both Raphael and Bramante had studios and where Lucrezia Borgia spun many of her intrigues. The entrance opens onto a high-ceilinged room filled with country-style decorations and bottles of wine. Your meal might begin with a strudel of porcini mushrooms followed by the invariably good pasta of the day, perhaps a *bombolotti* succulently stuffed with prosciutto and spinach. Then you might choose roebuck with polenta, roast Sardinian goat, or veal with salmon mousse. Each of these dishes is prepared with flair and technique, and the food takes advantage of the region's bounty.

Piazza Montevecchio 22A. ⓒ 06-6861319. Reservations required. Main courses 18€–25€. DC, MC, V. Tues–Sun 7:30pm–midnight. Closed Aug 10–25 and Jan 1–10. Metro: Spagna. Bus: 60 or 64.

Osteria dell'Antiquario ⭐ *Finds* INTERNATIONAL/ROMAN   Virtually undiscovered, this little Roman osteria lies a few blocks down the Via dei Coronari as you leave the Piazza Navona and head toward St. Peter's. It has three dining rooms and a terrace for fair-weather dining. We prefer to begin with a delectable appetizer of sautéed shellfish (usually mussels and clams), although you might opt for the risotto with porcini mushrooms. For a main course, you can go experimental with the filet of ostrich covered by a slice of ham and grated Parmesan, or else opt for shellfish flavored with saffron. The fish soup with fried bread is excellent, as is an array of freshly made soups and pastas. Veal rolls Roman style and turbot flavored with fresh tomatoes and basil are other excellent choices. This is dining in the classic Roman style.

Piazzetta di S. Simeone 26/27, Via dei Coronari. ✆ **06-6879694.** Reservations recommended. Main courses 10€–23€. AE, DC, MC, V. Mon–Sat 8–11pm. Closed 15 days in mid-Aug, Christmas, and Jan 1–15. Bus: 70, 87, or 90.

Inexpensive

Il Miraggio ROMAN/SARDINIAN/SEAFOOD   You might want to escape the roar of traffic along Via del Corso by ducking into this informal spot on a crooked side street (about midway between Piazza Venezia and Piazza Colonna). It's a cozy neighborhood setting where every dish has a rich and savory flavor. The risotto with scampi or the fettuccine with porcini mushrooms will have you begging for more. The grilled scampi is done to perfection, or you might prefer a steaming kettle of mussels flavored with olive oil, lemon juice, and fresh parsley. We're especially fond of the house specialty, spaghetti *alla bottarga* (with roe sauce), especially if it's followed by *spigola alla vernaccia* (sea bass sautéed in butter and Vernaccia wine from Tuscany).

Vicolo Sciarra 59. ✆ **06-6780226.** Reservations recommended. Main courses 8€–16€. AE, MC, V. Thurs–Tues 12:30–3:30pm and 7:30–11pm. Closed Nov 8–Dec 6. Metro: Barberini. Bus: 56, 60, 62, 81, 85, 95, 160, 175, 492, or 628.

Pizzeria Baffetto 🌟 *Kids* PIZZA   Our Roman friends always take out-of-towners here when they request the best pizza in Rome. Arguably, Pizzeria Baffetto fills the bill and has done so admirably for the past 80 years. Pizzas are sold as *piccolo* (small), *media* (medium), or *grande* (large). Most pizza aficionados order the Margherita, the simplest version with mozzarella and a delectable tomato sauce, but a wide range of toppings is served. The chef is preening proud of his pizza Baffetto, the house specialty. It comes with a topping of tomato sauce, mozzarella, mushrooms, onions, sausages, roasted peppers, and eggs. The pizza crusts are delightfully thin, and the pies are served piping hot from the intense heat of the ancient ovens.

Via del Governo Vecchio 114. ✆ **06-6861617.** Reservations not accepted. Pizza 3.50€–7.50€. No credit cards. Daily 6:30pm–1am. Closed last 2 weeks of Aug. Bus: 46, 62, or 64.

NEAR VATICAN CITY
Very Expensive

Les Etoiles 🌟🌟🌟 MEDITERRANEAN   Les Etoiles deserves all the stars it receives—both for its cuisine and for its panoramic view of Rome. At this garden in the sky you'll have an open window over the rooftops of Rome. In summer everyone wants a table outside, but in winter almost the same view can be seen through the picture windows. Refined Mediterranean cuisine, with perfectly balanced flavors, is served here. Dishes include quail cooked either with radicchio or in a casserole with mushrooms and herbs, artichokes stuffed with ricotta and pecorino cheese, Venetian-style risotto with squid ink, and roast suckling lamb with mint.

In the Hotel Atlante Star, Bitalleschi 34. ✆ **06-6873233.** Reservations required. Main courses 20€–35€. AE, DC, MC, V. Daily 12:30–2:30pm and 7:30–11pm. Metro: Ottaviano.

Moderate

Cesare ROMAN/TUSCAN   Cesare is a fine old-world dining room known for its deft handling of fresh ingredients. You can select your fresh fish from the refrigerated glass case at the entrance. We come here for the tender seafood salad, brimming with cuttlefish, shrimp, squid, mussels, and octopus, and dressed with olive oil, fresh parsley, and lemon. Our table was blessed with an order of *spaghetti all'amatriciana*—the spicy tomato sauce flavored with hot peppers and tiny bits of salt pork. The *saltimbocca alla romana,* that classic Roman dish, is a masterpiece as served here—butter-tender veal slices topped with prosciutto and fresh sage and sautéed in white wine.

Via Crescenzio 13, near Piazza Cavour. ℂ **06-6861227.** Reservations recommended. Main courses 13€–25€. AE, DC, MC, V. June 15–Aug 7 Mon–Sat 12:30–3pm and 7–11:30pm; Sun 12:30–3pm. Off season, Tues–Sat 12:30–3pm and 7–11:30pm; Sun 12:30–3pm. Closed Aug. Metro: Lepanto or Ottaviano. Bus: 23, 46, 49, or 62.

Girarrosto Toscano 𝔎 *Value* TUSCAN   You may have to wait for a table at this popular place near the Vatican. Under vaulted ceilings in a cellar setting, fine Tuscan specialties are served. Begin with an enormous selection of antipasti. You're then given a choice of pasta. *Bistecca alla fiorentina* (grilled steak seasoned with oil, salt, and pepper) is the best item to order, although it's expensive. Oysters and fresh fish from the Adriatic are also served daily. Meat and fish dishes are priced according to weight, and costs can run considerably higher than the prices quoted below.

Via Germanico 58. ℂ 06-39725717. Reservations required. Main courses 10€–16€. AE, DC, MC, V. Tues–Sun 12:30–3:30pm and 7:30–11pm. Metro: Ottaviano.

Inexpensive

Ristorante Giardinaccio ITALIAN/MOLISIAN/ROMAN   This popular restaurant is only 200 yards from St. Peter's. Unusual for Rome, it offers specialties from the provincial Molise region in southeast Italy, and is appropriately decorated in rustic country-tavern style. Flaming grills provide succulent versions of perfectly done quail, goat, and other dishes, but you might want to be adventurous and try the mutton goulash. Many pastas are featured, including *taconelle,* a homemade pasta with lamb sauce. Vegetarians and others will like the large self-service selection of antipasti.

Via Aurelia 53. ℂ **06-631367.** Reservations recommended, especially on weekends. Main courses 9€–20€; fixed-price menus 8€–20€. AE, DC, MC, V. Daily 12:15–3:15pm and 7:15–11:15pm. Bus: 46, 62, or 98.

IN ANCIENT ROME
Expensive

Trattoria San Teodoro 𝔎 *Kids* ROMAN   At last there's a good place to eat in the former gastronomic wasteland near the Roman Forum and Palatine Hill. The helpful staff welcomes you to a shady terrace or to a dimly lit dining room. The chef specializes in seafood, and does such exceedingly well, as reflected by his mini-size baby squid sautéed with Roman artichokes. His signature dish is seafood carpaccio made with tuna, turbot, or sea bass. Succulent meats such as medallions of veal in a nutmeg-enhanced cream sauce round out the menu at this family-friendly place. All the pastas are homemade.

Via dei Fienili 49–51. ℂ 06-6780933. Reservations recommended. All main courses 25€. AE, MC, V. Mon–Sat 12:30–3:30pm and 7:30pm–midnight. Closed Jan 15–Feb 15. Metro: Circo Massimo.

Moderate

F.I.S.H. 𝔎 *Finds* SEAFOOD   If you've got a dinner date with Madonna and Guy Ritchie, take them here. It's one of Rome's hottest new restaurants, managing to be both chic and good. Its initials stand for "Fine International Seafood House," and the restaurant lives up to its self-billing. It's tiny but choice, and count yourself lucky if you can get a table. The decor is sleek and minimalist, but with a touch of elegance. In the bar you can study the creatures in the tropical aquarium, perhaps contemplating one for your dinner.

Via dei Serpenti 16. ℂ 06-47824962. Reservations imperative. Main courses 12€–18€. AE, DC, MC, V. Tues–Sun noon–3pm and 7:45pm–1am. Closed Aug 7–26 and Dec 24–25. Metro: Colosseo.

Inexpensive
Hostaria Nerone ✦ ROMAN/ITALIAN   Built atop the ruins of the Golden House of Nero, this trattoria is run by the energetic de Santis family, who cook, serve, and handle the large crowds of hungry locals and visitors. Opened in 1929 at the edge of the Colle Oppio Park, it contains two compact dining rooms, plus a terrace lined with flowering shrubs that offers a view over the Colosseum and the Bath of Trajan. The copious antipasti buffet represents the bounty of Italy's fields and seas. The pastas include savory spaghetti with clams and, our favorite, pasta *fagioli* (with beans). You can also order grilled crayfish and swordfish or Italian sausages with polenta. Roman-style tripe is a local favorite, but maybe you'll skip it for the *osso buco* (braised veal shanks) with mashed potatoes and seasonal mushrooms. The wide list of some of the best Italian wines is reasonably priced.

Via Terme di Tito 96. ℂ **06-4817952.** Reservations recommended. Main courses 7.50€–13€. AE, DC, MC, V. Mon–Sat noon–3pm and 7–11pm. Metro: Colosseo. Bus: 75, 85, 87, 117, or 175.

IN TRASTEVERE
Expensive
Alberto Ciarla ✦✦ SEAFOOD   Alberto Ciarla is the best and most expensive restaurant in Trastevere, although it's not as chic as it was in the 1980s. It serves some of the most elegant fish dishes in the city. Specialties include a handful of ancient recipes subtly improved by Signor Ciarla, such as soup of pasta and beans with seafood. Original dishes include a delectable salmon Marcel Trompier with lobster sauce, as well as well-flavored sushi, a full array of shellfish, and filet of sea bass prepared in at least three different ways, including an award-winning version with almonds.

Piazza San Cosimato 40. ℂ **06-5818668.** Reservations required. Main courses 16€–28€; fixed-price menus 40€–70€. AE, DC, MC, V. Mon–Sat 8:30pm–12:30am. Closed 1 week in Jan and 1 week in Aug. Bus: 44, 75, 170, 280, or 718.

Moderate
La Cisterna ROMAN   This trattoria lies deep in the heart of Trastevere. For more than half a century it has been run by the Simmi family, who are genuinely interested in serving only the best as well as providing a good time for all guests. If you like traditional cookery based on the best of regional produce, come here. In summer you can inspect the antipasti—a mixed selection of hors d'oeuvres—right out on the street before going in. House specialties include Roman-style suckling lamb *(abbacchio),* rigatoni *all'amatriciana* (with diced bacon, olive oil, garlic, tomatoes, red peppers, and onions), and fresh fish—especially sea bass baked with herbs.

Via della Cisterna 13. ℂ **06-5812543.** Reservations recommended. Main courses 7€–12€. AE, DC, MC, V. Mon–Sat 7pm–1:30am. Bus: 44, 75, 170, 280, or 710.

EXPLORING THE ETERNAL CITY
Rome is studded with ancient monuments that silently evoke its history as one of the greatest centers of Western civilization—once all roads led to Rome, with good reason. It was the first cosmopolitan city in Europe, importing everything from slaves and gladiators to great art from the far corners of the empire. With all its carnage and mismanagement, it left a legacy of law and order and an uncanny lesson in how to conquer enemies by absorbing their cultures. But ancient Rome is only part of the spectacle. The Vatican also made the city a center of the world in art as well as religion. And although Vatican architects rifled much of the glory of the past for their projects, they also created the great Renaissance treasures we come to see today.

Rome Attractions

National Gallery
of Modern Art

Galleria
Borghese
8

Piazza
di Siena

**VILLA
BORGHESE/
PARIOLI**

Corso D'Italia

Piazzale di
Porta Pia

Via Campania
Via Sardegna
Via Sicilia
Via Boncompagni

Policlinico

Spagna Spanish
Steps
9
Piazza
di Spagna

VIA VENETO

Lgo. di
S. Susanna

National Roman
Museum
22
Piazza
Indipendenza

Castro Pretorio

Barberini

**PIAZZA
BARBERINI**
10

Via Barberini

Via XX Settembre

Via Tritone
Piazza
Colonna
Trevi
Fountain

Ly. de
Tritone

Palazzo del
Quirinale

Piazza d.
Quirinale

Piazza
Republica

Piazza
Cinque-
cento

Repubblica
21

Termini
Station

Termini

Palazzo
Doria
Pamphilj

Palazzo
Colonna

Via Nazionale

Teatro
dell'Opera

Piazza
dell'Esquilino
20

Via Principe Amedeo

Via Giovanni Giolitti

**SAN
LORENZO**

Palazzo
Venezia

Vittorio Emanuele
Monumont
11

Via Cavour

Santa Maria
Maggiore

Via Cavour

Vittorio Emanuele

Piazza
Vittorio
Eman. II

Capitoline
Museums
12   **13**

ANCIENT ROME

Roman
Forum

San Pietro
in Vincoli

Colosseo

Golden House
of Nero
19

Via di San Giovanni in Laterano

Manzoni

Piazza
Bocca
d. Verità

**PALATINE
HILL**

14
Colosseum
Piazza d.
Colosseo

Via Labicana
18

Circus Maximus

**AVENTINE
HILL**

Circo Massimo
Piazza di
Pta. Capena

17
San Giovanni
in Laterano

S. Giovanni

Piazza
Albania

Baths of
Caracalla
15

Re di Roma

Piramide

Piazza di
Pla. Metronia

Venice
Florence
ITALY
Rome

Via Gallia

16

655

Native Behavior

In *The Satyricon,* Petronius immortalized a dinner in which a boiled, fatted calf clad in a helmet was hauled in on a 200-pound platter. The animal was carved up with a sword, and the fleshy pieces of meat handed on the sword's sharp point to guests. We can't promise a bacchanal like that today, but the serving of food throughout Italy still remains grand theater.

In a country where Romans used to eat such prizes as the tongues of delicate songbirds, expect anything and everything to arrive on your plate, most of it savory. The Italians are among the greatest cooks in the world, so you can afford to lose some of your culinary inhibitions here and indulge your palate with everything from pasta with sardines, pine nuts, and sprigs of wild fennel, to stuffed pig's ear.

To be truly Italian, you have to love dropping into a caffè at any time of the day or night to order an *espresso.* A true Italian can lecture for an hour on the merits of espresso. What to avoid? *Caffè Americano,* which is watery and served in a big cup. Our favorite? *Caffè corretto* espresso, which is enhanced with a dash of grappa. If you don't want to be identified as a barbarian, never order *cappuccino* after a meal, only before lunch.

To go native, you have to develop an Italian sense of visual style, which today can mean virtually anything. As Versace once said, "It can't be explained. You just know it when you see it." Italians are miracle workers with materials and forms. "We express feeling through our clothes," Versace also said. "Clothes are like venting a whole range of pleasure and emotions expressed through what we wear."

Finally, in addition to talking with your hands, you must have a profound love of opera if you want to blend in with the natives. Perhaps you'll even shed tears when you hear beautiful renditions of the *oeuvres* of Rossini, Bellini, Verdi, Puccini, and Donizetti. From *Il Barbiere di Siviglia* to *La Bohème,* Italy remains the best place anywhere for hearing and appreciating opera.

SIGHTSEEING SUGGESTIONS FOR FIRST-TIME VISITORS

If You Have 1 Day Rome wasn't built in a day and you aren't likely to see it in a day either, but make the most of your limited time. You'll basically have to decide on the legacy of **Imperial Rome**—the Roman Forum, the Imperial Forum, and the Colosseum—or else St. Peter's and the **Vatican.** Walk along the **Spanish Steps** at sunset. At night go to **Piazza del Campidoglio** for a fantastic view of the Forum below. Have a nightcap on **Via Veneto,** which, although past its prime, is still appealing. Toss a coin in the **Trevi fountain** and promise yourself you'll return.

If You Have 2 Days If you elected to see the Roman Forum and the Colosseum on your first day, then spend the second day exploring St. Peter's and the **Vatican Museums** (or vice versa). Have dinner in a restaurant in **Trastevere.**

If You Have 3 Days In the morning go to the **Pantheon** in the heart of Old Rome; then, after lunch, explore the **Castel Sant'Angelo** and the **Etruscan Museum.** Have dinner at a restaurant in or around **Piazza Navona.**

If You Have 4 or 5 Days On day 4 head for the environs, notably **Tivoli,** where you can see the Villa d'Este and Hadrian's Villa. On Day 5 explore the ruins of **Ostia Antica,** return to Rome for lunch, and visit the **Capitoline Museum** and **Basilica di San Giovanni in Laterano** in the afternoon.

ST. PETER'S & THE VATICAN

Basilica di San Pietro (St. Peter's Basilica) ★★★ As you stand in Bernini's **Piazza San Pietro (St. Peter's Square),** you'll be in the arms of an ellipse; like a loving parent, the Doric-pillared colonnade reaches out to embrace the faithful. Holding 300,000 is no problem for this square. Inside, the size of this famous church is awe-inspiring—though its dimensions (about two football fields long) are not apparent at first. St. Peter's is said to have been built over the tomb of the crucified saint. The original church was erected on the order of Constantine, but the present structure is Renaissance and baroque; it showcases the talents of some of Italy's greatest artists.

In such a grand church, don't expect subtlety. But the basilica is rich in art. Under Michelangelo's dome is the celebrated **baldacchino** ★★★ by Bernini. In the nave on the right (the 1st chapel) is the best-known piece of sculpture, the *Pietà* ★★★ that Michelangelo sculpted while still in his early twenties. You can visit the **treasury** ★, filled with jewel-studded chalices, reliquaries, and copes. One robe worn by Pius XII strikes a simple note in these halls of elegance. The sacristy now contains a **Museo Storico (Historical Museum)** displaying Vatican treasures, including the large 1400s bronze tomb of Pope Sixtus V by Antonio Pollaiuolo and several antique chalices. In addition you can visit the **Vatican grottoes** ★★ with their tombs, both ancient and modern (Pope John XXII gets the most adulation).

The grandest sight is yet to come: the climb to **Michelangelo's dome** ★★★, which towers about 115m (375 ft.) high. Although you can walk up the steps, we recommend the elevator as far as it'll carry you. You can walk along the roof, for which you'll be rewarded with a panoramic view of Rome and the Vatican.

To tour the area around **St. Peter's tomb,** you must apply several days in advance to the excavations office (© **06-69885318**), open Monday through Saturday from 9am to 3:30pm. Pass under the arch to the left of the facade of St. Peter's to find it.

Piazza San Pietro. © **06-69884466** (for information on celebrations). Basilica (including grottoes), free; guided tour of excavations around St. Peter's tomb 8.75€ (children younger than 15 are not admitted); stairs to the dome 3.50€; elevator to the dome 4€; Sacristy (with Historical Museum) 4€. Basilica (including the

---

Tips **A St. Peter's Warning**

St. Peter's has a strict dress code: no shorts, no skirts above the knee, and no bare shoulders. You will not get in if you don't come dressed appropriately. In a pinch, men and women alike can buy a big cheap scarf from a nearby souvenir stand and wrap it around their legs as a long skirt or throw it over their shoulders as a shawl.

sacristy and treasury), Oct–Mar daily 9am–5:15pm; Apr–Sept daily 9am–6:15pm. Grottoes daily 8am–5pm. Dome, Oct–Mar daily 8am–5pm; Apr–Sept daily 8am–6pm. Metro: Ottaviano, then a long stroll. Bus: 46.

Vatican Museums & the Sistine Chapel ✦✦✦ The Vatican Museums contain a gigantic repository of treasures. You can follow one of four itineraries—A, B, C, or D—according to the time you have (1½–5 hr.) and your special interests. You can choose from the picture gallery, which houses paintings from the 11th century to the 19th century, the Egyptian collection, the Etruscan museum, Greek and Roman sculpture, and, of course, the **Sistine Chapel.** Consult the large panels at the entrance, then follow the letter and color of the itinerary chosen. Facilities for persons with disabilities are available.

⟨Tips⟩ A Vatican Tip

On the left side of Piazza San Pietro is the **Vatican Tourist Office** (✆ **06-69884866;** www.vatican.va), open Monday through Saturday from 8:30am to 7pm with maps and guides and reservations for Vatican Gardens tours.

Michelangelo labored for 4 years (1508–12) over the epic Sistine Chapel, now restored, although not without controversy, to its original glory. The work was so physically taxing that it permanently damaged his eyesight. Glorifying the human body as only a sculptor could, Michelangelo painted nine panels taken from the pages of Genesis, and surrounded them with prophets and sibyls. To get the best view of the Sistine Chapel's frescoes, bring binoculars. Also, visit the Stanze di Raphael, rooms decorated by Raphael when still a young man.

Viale Vaticano, Vatican City. ✆ 06-69883333. Admission 9€, free for everyone the last Sun of each month (be ready for a crowd). Mar 16–Oct 30 Mon–Fri 8:45am–3:30pm; Sat and the final Sun of the month 8:45am–12:30pm. Off season Mon–Sat and the final Sun of the month 8:45am–12:35pm. Closed religious holidays (except Easter week), and Aug 14–15. Metro: Ottaviano. The museum entrance is a long walk around the Vatican walls north from St. Peter's Square.

THE FORUM, THE COLOSSEUM & THE HIGHLIGHTS OF ANCIENT ROME

Foro Romano (Roman Forum) ✦✦✦ The Roman Forum was built in the marshy land between the Palatine and the Capitoline hills. It flourished as the center of Roman life in the days of the Republic, before it gradually lost prestige to the Imperial Forum. By day the columns of now-vanished temples and the stones from which long-forgotten orators spoke are mere shells. But at night, when the Forum is silent in the moonlight, it isn't difficult to imagine that Vestal Virgins still guard the sacred temple fire.

If you want the stones to have some meaning, you'll have to purchase a detailed plan, as the temples can be hard to locate. The best of the lot is the handsomely adorned **Temple of Castor and Pollux** ✦✦✦, erected in the 5th century B.C. in honor of a battle triumph. The **Temple of Faustina** ✦✦, with its lovely columns and frieze (griffins and candelabra), was converted into the San Lorenzo in Miranda Church. The **Temple of the Vestal Virgins** ✦✦✦ is a popular attraction; some of the statuary, mostly headless, remains.

A long walk up from the Roman Forum leads to the **Palatine Hill** ✦✦✦, one of the seven hills of Rome; your ticket from the Forum will admit you to this attraction (it's open the same hours). The Palatine, tradition tells us, was the spot on which the first settlers built their huts, under the direction of Romulus. In later years, the hill became a patrician residential district that attracted citizens

Ancient Rome & Attractions Nearby

0   1/8 mile
0   100 meters

Piazza Venezia

Imperial Forum

Via Cavour

Via dei Fori Imperiali

CAPITOLINE HILL

P.Fabricio

Via d. Teatro di Marcello

Roman Forum

Forum Entrance

Colosseo

Piazza d. Colosseo

Colosseum

P.Palatino

Piazza Bocca d. Verità

Via dei Cerchi

PALATINE HILL

Via di S. Gregorio

Circus Maximus

Via dei Circo Massimo

Lung. Aventino

AVENTINE HILL

Circo Massimo

Piazza di Pta. Capena

Via d. Terme di Caracalla

Viale Aventino

Metro B ═M═

like Cicero. It's worth the climb for the panoramic, sweeping view of both the Roman and Imperial forums, as well as the Capitoline Hill and the Colosseum. Of the ruins that remain, none is finer than the so-called **House of Livia** 🐦🐦 (the "abominable grandmother" of Robert Graves's *I, Claudius*).

When the glory that was Rome has completely overwhelmed you, you can enjoy a respite in the cooling **Farnese Gardens** 🐦, laid out in the 16th century, which incorporate some of Michelangelo's designs.

Via dei Fori Imperiali. 𝒞 **06-6990110.** Foro Romano free; Palatine Hill 6€. Apr–Sept daily 9am–8pm; Oct–Mar daily 9am–3:30pm; last admission 1 hr. before closing. Closed Dec 25, Jan 1, and May 1. Metro: Colosseo.

Colosseo (Colosseum) 🐦🐦🐦   In spite of the fact that it's a mere shell, the Colosseum remains the greatest architectural inheritance from ancient Rome. It was inaugurated by Titus in A.D. 80 with a weeks-long bloody combat between gladiators and wild beasts. At its peak, the Colosseum could seat 50,000 spectators; exotic animals—humans also—were shipped in from the far corners of the empire to satisfy their jaded tastes. Many historians now believe that one of the most enduring legends linked to the Colosseum—that Christians were fed to the lions here—is unfounded.

Next to the Colosseum is the **Arch of Constantine** 🐦🐦🐦, erected in honor of Constantine's defeat of the pagan Maxentius (A.D. 306).

Piazzale del Colosseo, Via dei Fori Imperiali. 𝒞 **06-7004261.** Admission 8€ all levels. Oct to Jan 15 daily 9am–3pm; Jan 16–Feb 15 daily 9am–4pm; Feb 16–Mar 17 daily 9am–4:30pm; Mar 18–Apr 16 daily 9am–5pm; Apr 17 to Sept daily 9am–7pm. Guided tours in English with an archaeologist 3 times per morning on Sun and holidays 3.50€. Tickets to Palatine Hill also sold at box office for 5€.

Domus Aurea (Golden House of Nero) 🐦   Nero's fabulous Golden House reopened in 1999 after a 15-year restoration. In A.D. 64, Rome was swept by a disastrous fire—contrary to gossip it has never been proven that Nero set the fire. The emperor did, however, seize more than 80 hectares (200 acres) of the burned-out historic core to create one of the most sumptuous palaces in history. Subsequent emperors, seeking to distance themselves from their unpopular predecessor, destroyed much of the place by using its vast network of rooms and walls as a foundation for new construction. Out of its original 250 rooms, 30 are now open to the public, decorated with some of the sculptures, mosaics, and frescoes that have survived the past 2,000 years. When Nero moved in, he shouted, "At last I can start living like a human being!"

Via della Domus Aurea. 𝒞 **06-39967700.** Admission 5€, plus 1€ for a reservation. Wed–Mon 9am–7:45pm. Last admission 1 hr. before closing. Metro: Colosseo.

Campidoglio (Capitoline Hill) 🐦🐦🐦   Of the Seven Hills of Rome, the Campidoglio is the most sacred—its origins stretch way back into antiquity (an Etruscan temple to Jupiter once stood on this spot). The approach to the Capitoline Hill is dramatic—climbing the long, sloping steps designed by Michelangelo. At the top is a perfectly proportioned square, Piazza del Campidoglio, also laid out by the Florentine artist.

One side of the piazza is open; the others are bounded by the **Senatorium (Town Council)** 🐦🐦, the statuary-filled **Palazzo dei Conservatori** 🐦🐦🐦, and the **Museo Capitolino (Capitoline Museum)** 🐦🐦 (see "More Attractions," below). The Campidoglio is dramatic at night (walk around to the back for a regal view of the floodlit Roman Forum).

Piazza del Campidoglio. Bus: 44, 89, 92, 94, or 716.

Castel Sant'Angelo ⭐⭐⭐   This overpowering structure, in a landmark position on the Tiber just east of Vatican City, was originally built in the 2nd century A.D. as a tomb for the emperor Hadrian; it continued as an imperial mausoleum until the time of Caracalla. It's an imposing and grim castle with thick walls and a cylindrical shape. If it looks like a fortress, it should, as that was its function in the Middle Ages. In the 14th century it became a papal residence. Its legend rests largely on its link with Pope Alexander VI, whose mistress bore him two children—Cesare and Lucrezia Borgia. Today the highlight of the castle is a trip through the Renaissance apartments with their coffered ceilings and lush decoration. Their walls have witnessed plots and intrigues that make up some of the arch-treachery of the High Renaissance. You can climb to the top terrace for another one of those dazzling views of the Eternal City.

Lungotevere Castello 50. ℭ **06-6819111**. Admission 5€. Tues–Sun 9am–7pm. Metro: Ottaviano, then a long stroll. Bus: 23, 46, 49, 62, 87, 98, 280, or 910.

Pantheon ⭐⭐⭐   Of all the great buildings of ancient Rome, only the Pantheon (All the Gods) remains intact today. It was built in 27 B.C. by Marcus Agrippa, and later reconstructed by the emperor Hadrian in the first part of the 2nd century A.D. This remarkable building is among the architectural wonders of the world because of its dome and its concept of space. The Pantheon was once ringed with niches containing white marble statues of Roman gods. Animals were sacrificed and burned in the center, and the smoke escaped through the only means of light, an opening at the top 8m (27 ft.) in diameter. Michelangelo came here to study the dome before designing the cupola of St. Peter's, whose dome is only .5m (2 ft.) smaller than the Pantheon's.

Piazza della Rotonda. ℭ **06-68300230**. Free admission. Mon–Sat 8:30am–7:30pm; Sun 9am–6pm. Bus: 46, 62, 64, 170, or 492 to Largo di Torre.

THE CATACOMBS OF THE APPIAN WAY

Of all the roads that led to Rome, Via Appia Antica—built in 312 B.C.—was the leader. It eventually stretched all the way from Rome to the seaport of Brindisi, through which trade with the colonies in Greece and the East was funneled.

Along the Appian Way the patrician Romans built great monuments above the ground, whereas Christians met in the catacombs beneath. The remains of both can be visited today. In some dank, dark grottoes (never stray too far from either your party or one of the exposed light bulbs), you can still discover traces of early Christian art.

Of the catacombs open to the public, those of St. Callixtus and of St. Sebastian are the most important. Both can be reached by bus no. 118, which leaves from near the Colosseo Metro station.

Catacombe di San Sebastiano ⭐⭐⭐ are at Via Appia Antica 136 (ℭ **06-7887035**; bus: 118). Today the tomb of the martyr is in the basilica, but it was originally in the catacomb under the building. From the reign of Valerian to that of Constantine, the bodies of Sts. Peter and Paul were hidden in these catacombs. The tunnels, if stretched out, would reach a length of 11km (7 miles). Admission is 4€ adults, 2€ children 6 to 15, free for children 5 and under. The catacombs are open April through October Monday through Saturday from 9am to noon and 2:30 to 5:30pm; January through March Monday through Saturday from 8:30am to noon and 2:30 to 5pm. They are closed from November 13 to December 11.

Catacombe di San Callisto (St. Callixtus) ⭐⭐⭐, Via Appia Antica 110 (ℭ **06-51301580**; www.catacombe.roma.it; bus: 118), comprise the first cemetery of the Christian community of Rome, burial place of 16 popes in the 3rd century. The catacombs bear the name of St. Callixtus, the deacon whom the pope St. Zephyrinus put in charge of them. Callixtus himself was later elected pope (217–22). The cemetery complex is made up of a network of galleries stretching for nearly 19km (12 miles), structured in five different levels, reaching a depth of about 20m (65 ft.). Admission is 4€ adults, 2€ children 6 to 15, free for children 5 and under. Hours are March through October Thursday through Tuesday from 8:30am to noon and 2:30 to 5:30pm; November through January Thursday through Tuesday from 8:30am to noon and 2:30 to 5pm; closed in February.

MORE ATTRACTIONS

Scalinata di Spagna (Spanish Steps) ★★★
The steps—filled in spring with azaleas and other flowers, flower vendors, jewelry dealers, and photographers snapping pictures of visitors—and the square take their names from the Spanish Embassy, which used to be headquartered here. Designed by Italian architect Francesco de Sanctis and built from 1723 to 1725, they were funded almost entirely by the French as a preface to Trinità dei Monti at the top. At the foot of the steps is a boat-shaped fountain designed by Pietro Bernini (not to be confused with his son, Giovanni Lorenzo Bernini, a far greater sculptor). The steps and the piazza below are always packed with a crowd: strolling, reading in the sun, browsing the vendors' carts, and people-watching.

Piazza di Spagna. Metro: Spagna.

Terme di Caracalla (Baths of Caracalla) ★★★
Named for the emperor Caracalla, the baths were completed in the early part of the 3rd century. The richness of decoration has faded and the lushness can only be judged from the shell of brick ruins that remain.

Via delle Terme di Caracalla 52. ℂ 06-5758626. Admission 5€. Oct to Mar 1 daily 9am–3:30pm; Mar 2– Mar 30 daily 9am–5pm; Apr–Sept 30 daily 9am–6pm. Last admission 1 hr. before closing. Closed holidays. Bus: 628.

Basilica di San Clemente ★★
From the Colosseum, head up Via di San Giovanni in Laterano, which leads to the Basilica of Saint Clement. In this church-upon-a-church, centuries of history peel away: A 4th-century church was built over a secular house from the 1st century A.D., beside which stood a pagan temple dedicated to Mithras; Normans destroyed the lower church, and a new one was built in the 12th century. Down in the eerie grottoes (which you can explore on your own—unlike the catacombs on the Appian Way), you'll discover well-preserved frescoes from the 1st to the 3rd centuries.

Via San Giovanni in Laterano at Piazza San Clemente, Via Labicana 95. ℂ 06-70451018. Basilica free; excavations 3€. Mon–Sat 9am–12:30pm and 3–6pm; Sun 10am–12:30pm and 3–6pm. Metro: Colosseo. Bus: 85, 87, or 810.

Basilica di San Giovanni in Laterano ★★★
This church—not St. Peter's—is the cathedral of the diocese of Rome. Catholics all over the world refer to it as their "mother church." Originally built in A.D. 314 by Constantine, the cathedral has suffered many vicissitudes and was forced to rebuild many times. The present structure is characterized by its 18th-century facade by Alessandro Galilei (statues of Christ and the Apostles ring the top). Borromini gets the credit—some say blame—for the interior, built for Innocent X.

The most unusual sight is across the street at the "Palace of the Holy Steps," called the **Santuario della Scala Santa** ★, Piazza San Giovanni in Laterano (ℂ 06-7726641). It's alleged that these were the actual steps that Christ climbed when he was brought before Pilate. These steps are supposed to be climbed only on your knees, which you're likely to see the faithful doing throughout the day. Visiting hours are daily from 6:15am to noon and 3:30 to 6:30pm. Admission is free.

Piazza San Giovanni in Laterano 4. © 06-69886433. Basilica free; cloisters 2€. Summer daily 9am–6:45pm (off season to 6pm). Metro: San Giovanni. Bus: 4, 16, 30, 85, 87, or 174.

Basilica di Santa Maria Maggiore (Saint Mary the Great) ✸✸✸ This
great church was originally founded by Pope Liberius in A.D. 358 but was rebuilt by Pope Sixtus III from 432 to 440. Its campanile, erected in the 14th century, is the loftiest in the city. Much doctored in the 18th century, the facade is not an accurate reflection of the treasures inside. The basilica is especially noted for the 5th-century Roman mosaics in its nave, as well as for its coffered ceiling, said to have been gilded with gold brought from the New World. In the 16th century Domenico Fontana built a now-restored "Sistine Chapel." The church contains the tomb of Bernini, Italy's most important architect during the flowering of the baroque in the 17th century.

Piazza Santa Maria Maggiore. © 06-483195. Free admission. Daily 7am–7pm. Metro: Termini.

Museo Capitolino ✸✸ and Palazzo dei Conservatori ✸✸✸ The Capi-
toline Museum was built in the 17th century, based on an architectural sketch by Michelangelo. In the first room is *The Dying Gaul,* a work of majestic skill; in a special gallery all her own is *The Capitoline Venus,* who demurely covers herself—this statue (a Roman copy of the Greek original) has been a symbol of feminine beauty and charm down through the centuries. The famous statue of *Marcus Aurelius* is the only bronze equestrian statue to have survived from ancient Rome. It was retrieved from the Tiber where it had been tossed by marauding barbarians. For centuries it was thought to be a statue of Constantine the Great; this mistake protected it further, since papal Rome respected the memory of the first Christian emperor.

The Palazzo dei Conservatori, across the way, is rich in classical sculpture and paintings. In the courtyard are fragments of a colossal statue of Constantine. One of the most notable bronzes is the *Spinario* (little boy picking a thorn from his foot), a Greek classic from the 1st century B.C. In addition, you'll find *Lupa Capitolina* (Capitoline She-Wolf), a rare Etruscan bronze possibly from the 5th century B.C. (Romulus and Remus, the legendary twins that the she-wolf suckled, were added at a later date.)

Piazza del Campidoglio 1. © 06-67102071. Admission (to both) 7.75€. Free on last Sun of each month. Tues–Sun 9am–7pm. Bus: 44, 81, 95, 160, 170, 715, or 780.

Galleria Borghese ✸✸✸ Closed for 14 years, this jewel-box collection of
masterworks is back in all its fabulous glory. The bad news is that it may be hard to get in because of limited access. This treasure trove of art in what was once the Borghese's summer residence includes such masterpieces as Bernini's *David, The Rape of Persephone,* and his *Apollo and Daphne;* Titian's *Sacred and Profane Love;* Raphael's *Deposition;* even Caravaggio's *Jerome.* One of the most viewed pieces of sculpture in today's gallery is Canova's life-size sculpture of Napoléon's sister, Pauline, in the pose of "Venus Victorious." When Pauline was asked if she felt uncomfortable about posing in the nude, she replied, "Why should I? The studio was heated."

Piazza Scipione Borghese, off Via Pinciano. © 06-328101 reservations (required), 06-8417645 information. Admission 6€. Tues–Sun 9am–7pm. Bus: 56 or 910. *Note:* No more than 300 visitors at a time are allowed on the ground floor, no more than 90 on the upper floor.

Galleria Nazionale d'Arte Antica ⊕⊕ The Palazzo Barberini, right off Piazza Barberini, is one of Rome's most magnificent baroque palaces. It was begun by Carlo Maderno in 1627 and completed in 1633 by Bernini, whose lavishly decorated rococo apartments are on view. The palace houses the Galleria Nazionale. The splendid array of paintings includes 13th- to 16th-century works by Simone Martini, Filippo Lippi, Andrea Solario, Francesco Francia, Il Sodoma, and Raphael. Since 1998, you can visit a newly restored 18th-century apartment decorated with frescoes from the school of Barberini. Admission is 1€, and hours are Tuesday through Sunday from 9am to 7pm.

Via delle Quattro Fontane 13. ℭ **06-4814430.** Admission to both museum and apt. 6€. Tues–Sun 9am–7pm. Metro: Piazza Barberini.

Museo Nazionale di Villa Giulia (Etruscan) ⊕⊕⊕ A 16th-century papal palace in the Villa Borghese shelters this priceless collection of art and artifacts of the mysterious Etruscans, who predated the Romans, and of whom little is known except for their sophisticated art and design. If you have time only for the masterpieces, head for Sala 7, which has a remarkable *Apollo* from Veio from the end of the 6th century B.C. (clothed, for a change). Two other widely acclaimed pieces of statuary in this gallery are *Dea con Bambino (Goddess with a Baby)* and a greatly mutilated, but still powerful, *Hercules* with a stag. In the adjoining Sala 8, you'll see the lions' sarcophagus from the mid–6th century B.C., which was excavated at Cerveteri, north of Rome. Finally, in Sala 9, is one of the world's most important Etruscan art treasures, the bride and bridegroom coffin from the 6th century B.C., also from Cerveteri.

Piazzale di Villa Giulia 9. ℭ **06-3201951.** Admission 4€. Tues–Sat 8:30am–7pm. Metro: Flaminio. Tram: 225.

MUSEO NAZIONALE ROMANO

Originally the museum occupied only the Diocletian Baths; today it's divided into four sections: Palazzo Massimo alle Terme; Terme di Diocleziano (Diocletian Baths); the Octagonal Hall annex; and Palazzo Altemps. A ticket including entry into any of the four sections is 7.50€.

Palazzo Massimo alle Terme ⊕ If you'd like to go wandering in a virtual garden of classical statues, head for this 19th-century palazzo built to resemble the patrician palaces from the baroque period. If you ever wanted to know what emperors looked like, this museum will make them live again, togas and all. In the central hall are works representing the political and social life of Rome at the time of Augustus. Other works include an altar from Ostia Antica, the ancient port of Rome, plus a statue of a wounded Niobid from 440 B.C. that is a masterwork of expression and character. Upstairs, stand in awe at frescoes, stuccoes, and mosaics from the 1st century B.C. to the Imperial Age. The most celebrated mosaic is of the Four Charioteers. In the basement are a rare numismatic collection and an extensive collection of Roman jewelry.

Largo di Villa Peretti 67. ℭ **06-48903500.** Admission 6€ (ticket includes Diocletian Baths). Tues–Sun 9am–7:45pm. Last admission 1 hr. before closing. Metro: Termini.

Palazzo Altemps ⊕ This branch of the National Roman Museum is housed in a 15th-century palace only a few steps from the Piazza Navona. It is home to the fabled Ludovisi Collection of Greek and Roman sculpture. Among the masterpieces of the Roman Renaissance, you'll find the *Ares Ludovisi,* a Roman copy of the original dated 330 B.C. and restored by Bernini. In the *Sala delle Storie di Mosè* is *Ludovisi's Throne,* representing the birth of Venus. The *Sala delle Feste* (The Celebrations Hall) is dominated by *Grande Ludovisi,* a sarcophagus depicting the

Romans fighting against the Ostrogoth Barbarians from the 2nd century A.D. Other outstanding art includes a 1st-century B.C. copy of Phidias's celebrated Athena that once stood in the Parthenon.

Piazza San Apollinare 44. ℂ 06-6833759. Admission 5€. Tues–Fri 9am–9pm; Sat 9am–midnight; Sun 9am–8pm. Last admission 1 hr. before closing. Metro: Termini.

Terme di Diocleziano (Diocletian Baths) and Aula Ottagona (Octagonal Hall) ⭐

This museum occupies part of the 3rd-century A.D. baths of Diocletian and part of a convent that may have been designed by Michelangelo. The Diocletian baths were the biggest thermal baths in the world. Nowadays they host a marvelous collection of funereal art and decorations from the Aurelian period. The Octagonal Hall occupies the southwest corner of the central building. Here you can see the *Lyceum Apollo*. This statue was found in the area surrounding the Trajan Baths. Worthy of a note is the *Aphrodite of Cyrene*, discovered in Cyrene, Libya.

Viale E. di Nicola 79. ℂ 06-4880. Admission to the Baths 4€ (ticket includes Palazzo Massimo alle Terme); Octagonal Hall, free. Terme di Diocleziano Tues–Sun 9am–7pm. Aula Ottagona Tues–Sat 9am–2pm and Sun 9am–1pm.

ORGANIZED TOURS

One of the leading tour operators (among the zillions of possibilities) is **American Express,** Piazza di Spagna 38 (ℂ **06-67641;** Metro: Spagna), open Monday through Friday from 9am to 5:30pm and Saturday from 9am to 12:30pm. One popular tour is a 4-hour orientation tour of Rome and the Vatican, which departs most mornings at 9:30am and costs 40€ per person. Another 4-hour tour, which focuses on ancient Rome (including visits to the Colosseum, the Roman Forum, the Imperial Palace, and the Church of San Pietro in Vincoli), costs 38€. Outside Rome, a popular excursion from April to October is a 5-hour bus tour to Tivoli, where visits are conducted of the Villa d'Este and its spectacular gardens and the ruins of the Villa Adriana, all for 45€ per person.

If your time in Italy is rigidly limited, you might opt for 1-day excursions to points farther afield on tours that are marketed (but not conducted) by American Express. A series of 1-day tours is offered to Pompeii and Sorrento for 100€ per person; to Florence for 105€; and to Capri and Sorrento for 115€. These trips, which include lunch, depart from Rome around 7am and return to your hotel sometime after 9 or 10pm.

THE SHOPPING SCENE

The posh shopping streets **Via Borgognona** and **Via Condotti** begin near Piazza di Spagna. For the most part, the merchandise on both is chic and very, very expensive. **Via Frattina** runs parallel to Via Condotti, its more famous sibling. **Via del Corso** doesn't have the image or the high prices of Via Condotti or Via Borgognona; the styles here are aimed at younger consumers. There are, however, some gems scattered amid the shops selling jeans and sporting equipment. The most interesting shops are on the section of the street nearest the fashionable cafes of Piazza del Popolo.

Beginning at the top of the Spanish Steps, **Via Sistina** runs to Piazza Barberini. The shops are small, stylish, and based on the personalities of their owners. The pedestrian traffic is less dense than on other major streets. Most shoppers reach **Via Francesco Crispi** by following Via Sistina 1 long block from the top of the Spanish Steps. Near the intersection of these streets are several shops full of unusual and less expensive gifts. Evocative of *La Dolce Vita,* **Via Veneto** is filled these days with expensive hotels and cafes and an array of relatively expensive stores selling shoes, gloves, and leather goods.

Traffic-clogged **Via Nazionale**—just crossing the street is no small feat—begins at Piazza della Repubblica and runs down almost to Piazza Venezia. Here you'll find an abundance of leather stores—more reasonable in price than those in many other parts of Rome—and a welcome handful of stylish boutiques.

Via dei Coronari, a good street for antiques, is buried in a colorful section of the Campus Martius and is an antiquer's dream, literally lined with magnificent vases, urns, chandeliers, breakfronts, chaises, refectory tables, and candelabra. To find the entrance to the street, turn left out of the north end of Piazza Navona, and pass the excavated ruins of Domitian's Stadium; the street will be just ahead of you. There are more than 40 antiques stores in the next 4 blocks.

A STORE WORTH SEEKING OUT

La Rinascente, Via del Corso 189 at the Piazza Colonna (✆ **06-6797691;** Metro: Barberini or Spagna), is Rome's most famous department store. Rather upscale, it has a little bit of everything: clothing, hosiery, perfume, cosmetics, housewares, and even furniture, plus its own line of clothing (Ellerre) for men, women, and children.

ROME AFTER DARK

There are few evening diversions quite as pleasurable as a stroll past the solemn pillars of old temples or the cascading torrents of Renaissance fountains glowing under the blue-black sky. Of the **fountains,** the Naiads (Piazza della Repubblica), the Tortoises (Piazza Mattei) and, of course, the Trevi are particularly beautiful at night. The **Capitoline Hill** is magnificently lit after dark, with its Renaissance facades glowing like jewel boxes. Behind the Senatorial Palace is a fine view of the **Roman Forum.** If you're staying across the Tiber, **Piazza San Pietro,** in front of St. Peter's Basilica, is impressive at night without tour buses and crowds. And a combination of illuminated architecture, Renaissance fountains, and frequent sidewalk shows and art expositions is at **Piazza Navona.** If you're ambitious and have a good sense of direction, try exploring the streets to the west of Piazza Navona, which look like a stage set when lit at night.

The mini-magazines *Metropolitan* and *Wanted in Rome* have listings of jazz, rock, and such and give an interesting look at expatriate Rome. The daily *Il Messaggero* lists current cultural news, especially in its Thursday magazine supplement, *Metro.* And *Un Ospite a Roma,* available free from the concierge desks of top hotels, is full of details on what's happening. Even if you don't speak Italian, you can generally follow the listings featured in *TrovaRoma,* a special weekly entertainment supplement published in the newspaper *La Repubblica* on Thursday.

THE PERFORMING ARTS

If you're in the capital for the opera season, usually from December to June, you can attend a performance at the historic **Teatro dell'Opera (Rome Opera House),** located off Via Nazionale, at Piazza Beniamino Gigli 1 (✆ **06-481601;** Metro: Repubblica). In the summer the venue switches to Piazza di Siena. The **Rome Opera Ballet** also performs at the Teatro dell'Opera. Look for announcements of classical concerts that take place in churches and other venues.

THE CLUB & MUSIC SCENE

Clubs are generally open Monday through Saturday from 9 or 10pm to 2 to 4am.

NIGHTCLUBS **Arciliuto,** Piazza Monte Vecchio 5 (✆ **06-6879419;** bus: 70, 81, or 87), reputedly the former studio of Raphael, is one of the most

---

---

romantic candlelit spots in Rome. From 10pm to 2am, Monday through Saturday, guests enjoy a musical salon ambience, listening to a guitarist, a pianist, and a violinist. The evening's presentation also includes live Neapolitan songs and new Italian madrigals, even current hits from Broadway or London's West End. Cover (including one drink) is 18€. Closed from July 20 to September 6.

One of Rome's largest and most energetic clubs, **Alpheus,** Via del Commercio 36 (© **06-5747826;** bus: 23 or 716), contains three sprawling rooms, each with a different musical sound and an ample number of bars. You'll find areas devoted to Latin music, rock, jazz, house, commercial, 1980s, whatever. Some Friday nights are devoted to hip hop or gay-themed parties. It's open Thursday through Sunday from 10pm to 4am; cover is 5€ to 13€.

JAZZ, SOUL & FUNK   Every night but Sunday **Alexanderplatz,** Via Ostia 9 (© **06-39742171;** Metro: Ottaviano), features live jazz. There's also a good restaurant here that serves everything from gnocchi alla romana to Japanese cuisine. A 1-month membership costs 6€. **Big Mama,** Vicolo San Francesco a Ripa 18 (© **06-5812551;** bus: 75 or 170), is a hangout for jazz and blues musicians; you're likely to meet the up-and-coming jazz stars of tomorrow. Sometimes the big names appear as well. It's closed from June to September. There's no cover for minor shows; cover for big acts is 10€ to 20€, plus 10€ for a seasonal membership.

Gilda, Via Mario dei Fiori 97 (© **06-6784838;** Metro: Spagna), is an adventurous combination of nightclub, disco, and restaurant known for the glamorous acts it books. The artistic direction assures first-class shows, a well-run restaurant, and disco music played between the live musical acts. The restaurant opens at 9:30pm and occasionally presents shows. International cuisine is featured as well, with meals beginning at 23€. The nightclub, opening at midnight, presents music of the 1960s as well as modern recordings. Cover (including one drink) is 20€.

L'Alibi, Via Monte Testaccio 44 (© **06-5743448;** bus: 95), is a year-round venue on many a gay man's agenda, and is one of the hottest clubs in Rome. The crowd, however, tends to be mixed, both Roman and international, straight and gay, male and female. Music ranges from garage to 1970s disco. One room is devoted to dancing. It's open Wednesday through Sunday from 11pm to 4am. Cover is 13€ Saturday, 7.50€ Friday; otherwise free.

SIDE TRIPS FROM ROME
TIVOLI   Tivoli, known as Tibur to the ancient Romans, was the playground of emperors. Today its reputation continues unabated: It's the most popular half-day jaunt from Rome.

While the **Villa d'Este,** Piazza Trento, Viale delle Cento Fontane (© **0774-312070**), is just a dank Renaissance palace with second-rate paintings that's hardly worth the trek from Rome, its **gardens** 🟊🟊🟊—designed by Pirro Ligorio—dim the luster of Versailles. Visitors descend a cypress-studded slope, and on their way are rewarded with everything from lilies to gargoyles spouting water, torrential streams, and waterfalls. The loveliest fountain—on this there's some agreement—is the **Fontana dell'Ovato,** designed by Ligorio. But nearby is the most spectacular achievement, the **hydraulic organ fountain,** dazzling visitors with its water jets in front of a baroque chapel, with four maidens who look tipsy. The best walk is along the promenade, which has 100 spraying fountains. Admission is 4.15€. The villa opens from Tuesday to Sunday at 9am; closing times vary according to the season (1 hr. before sunset). From November to January it closes at 4pm; closing times may be as late as 6:45pm in high season.

Whereas the Villa d'Este dazzles with artificial glamour, **Villa Gregoriana** 🟊, Largo Sant'Angelo (© **0774-311249**), relies more on nature. The gardens were built by Pope Gregory XVI in the 19th century. At one point on the circuitous walk carved along a slope, visitors stand and look out onto Tivoli's most panoramic waterfall (Aniene). The trek to the bottom on the banks of the Anio is studded with grottoes and balconies that open onto the chasm. From one belvedere, there's a panoramic view of the Temple of Vesta on the hill. Admission is 2.50€. It's open May through August daily from 10am to 7:30pm; September daily from 9:30am to 6:30pm; October through March daily from 9:30am to 4:30pm; and April daily from 9:30am to 6pm.

Of all the Roman emperors dedicated to *la dolce vita,* the globetrotting Hadrian spent the last 3 years of his life in the grandest style. Less than 6.5km (4 miles) from Tivoli he built his great estate—the **Villa Adriana (Hadrian's Villa)** 🟊🟊🟊, Via di Villa Adriana (© **0774-530203**)—and filled acre after acre with some of the architectural wonders he'd seen on his many trips. Hadrian directed the construction of much more than a villa—it's a self-contained world for a vast royal entourage, the guards required to protect them, and the hundreds of servants needed to bathe them, feed them, and satisfy their libidos. On the estate were theaters, baths, temples, fountains, gardens, and canals bordered with statuary. For a glimpse of what the villa once was, see the plastic reconstruction at the entrance. Admission is 6€. Hours are daily from 9am to 3:15pm (until about 6pm in summer).

Getting There   The town of Tivoli is 32km (20 miles) east of Rome on Via Tiburtina—about an hour's drive with traffic. You can also take public transportation: A bus marked TIVOLI leaves every 15 to 20 minutes during the day from Via Gaeta (west of Via Volturno), near the Stazione Termini. Buses also leave from the Rebibbia Metro station.

OSTIA ANTICA 🟊🟊   This major attraction is particularly interesting to those who can't make it to Pompeii. At the mouth of the Tiber, it was the port of ancient Rome. Through it were funneled riches from the far corners of the empire. It was founded in the 4th century B.C., and became a major port and naval base primarily under the emperors Claudius and Trajan. A thriving, prosperous city developed, full of temples, bathrooms, theaters, and patrician homes. Ostia Antica flourished for about 8 centuries before it began eventually to wither and the wholesale business of carting off its art treasures began.

Although a papal-sponsored commission launched a series of digs in the 19th century, the major work of unearthing was carried out under Mussolini's orders from 1938 to 1942. The city is only partially dug out today, but it's believed that all the chief monuments have been uncovered.

All the principal monuments are clearly labeled. The most important spot in the ruins is **Piazzale delle Corporazioni,** an early version of Wall Street. Near the theater, this square contained nearly 75 corporations; the nature of their businesses was identified by the patterns of preserved mosaics.

Ostia Antica is entered on Viale dei Romagnoli 717 (© **06-56358099**). Admission is 4€. It's open Tuesday through Sunday from 8:30am to 6pm in summer; off-season hours are Tuesday through Sunday from 8:30am to 5pm.

Getting There   Take the Metro to the Magliana stop, then change for the Lido train to Ostia Antica, about 26km (16 miles) from Rome. Departures are about every half hour, and the trip takes only 20 minutes. The train lets you off across the highway that connects Rome with the coast. It's just a short walk to the excavations.

HERCULANEUM & POMPEII   Both these ancient sights are more easily visited from Naples; however, many organized tours go here from Rome. **American Express,** Piazza di Spagna (© **06-67641;** Metro: Spagna), offers day tours to Pompeii, leaving Rome around 7am and returning between 9 and 10pm. You can also explore one—but rarely both—attractions on a day's drive here and back from Rome. Naples is about 2½ hours from Rome by frequent trains. For directions from Naples, see below.

The builders of **Herculaneum (Ercolano)** ✦✦ were still working to repair the damage caused by an A.D. 62 earthquake when Vesuvius erupted on that fateful August day in A.D. 79. Herculaneum, about one-fourth the size of Pompeii, didn't start to come to light again until 1709, when Prince Elbeuf launched the unfortunate fashion of tunneling through it for treasures. The prince was more intent on profiting from the sale of objets d'art than in uncovering a dead Roman town. Subsequent excavations at the site, **Ufficio Scavi di Ercolano,** Corso Resina, Ercolano (© **081-7390963**), have been slow. Herculaneum is not completely dug out today.

All the streets and buildings of Herculaneum hold interest, especially the baths *(terme),* divided between those at the forum and those on the outskirts (Terme Suburbane, near the more elegant villas). The municipal baths, which segregated the sexes, are larger, but the ones at the edge of town are more lavishly adorned. Important private homes to see include the **House of the Bicentenary** ✦, the **House of the Wooden Cabinet** ✦✦, and the **House of Poseidon (Neptune) and Amphitrite** ✦✦, the last containing what is the best-known mosaic discovered in the ruins. The finest example of how the aristocracy lived is provided by a visit to the **Casa dei Cervi** ✦✦, named the House of the Stags because of sculpture found inside.

The ruins may be visited daily April through October from 8:30am to 6pm, November through March from 8:30am to 3:30pm. Admission is 8€. To reach them, take the Circumvesuviana train from Stazione Centrale in Naples leaving about every half hour from Corso Garibaldi 387 for the 20-minute ride; or take bus no. 255 from Piazza Municipio. The excavations are a short walk from the train station. Otherwise, it's a 7km (4½-mile) drive on the autostrada to Salerno (turn off at Ercolano).

When Vesuvius erupted in A.D. 79, Pliny the Younger, who later recorded the event, thought the end of the world had come. Lying 24km (15 miles) south of Naples, the ruined Roman city of **Pompeii (Pompei)** ✦✦✦ has been dug out from the inundation of volcanic ash and pumice stone. At the excavations, the life of 19 centuries ago is vividly experienced.

The **Ufficio Scavi di Pompei** is entered at Piazza Esedra (© **081-8610744**). The most elegant of the patrician villas, the **House of Vettii** ✦✦✦ has a courtyard, statuary (such as a two-faced Janus), paintings, and a black-and-red Pompeiian dining room frescoed with cupids. The second important villa, the **Villa dei Misteri (House of Mysteries)** ✦✦✦ near the Porto Ercolano (Herculaneum Gate), lies outside the walls. What makes the villa exceptional are its remarkable frescoes. The **Casa del Fauno (House of the Faun)** ✦✦, so called because of a bronze statue of a dancing faun found there, takes up a city block and has four different dining rooms and two spacious peristyle gardens. In the center of town is the **Forum** ✦✦✦—although rather small, it was the heart of Pompeiian life.

Pompeii's ruins may be visited daily from 9am to 3:30pm. Admission is 8€. From Stazione Centrale in Naples, take the Sorrento-bound Circumvesuviana train leaving about every half hour and get off at the Pompei Scavi station; the excavations are across from the station. *Note:* Make sure your train is going to "Pompei Scavi," not "Pompei." Trains bound for Pompei stop at the modern town, not at the ruins.

2 Florence ★★★

No other city in Europe, with the exception of Venice, lives off its past the way Florence does. The Renaissance began here. Florence is a bit foreboding and architecturally severe; many of its *palazzi* (palaces), as was the Medici style, look like fortresses. But you must remember that when these structures were built, the aim was to keep foreign enemies at bay. And these facades guard treasures within, as the thousands of visitors who overrun the narrow streets know and appreciate.

Since the 19th century, Florence has been visited by seemingly half the world—the city has impressed some hard-to-impress people, including Mark Twain, who found it overwhelmed with "tides of color that make all the sharp lines dim and faint and turn the old city to a city of dreams."

It may appear that Florence is caught in a time warp—a Medici returning to the city from the past would have no trouble finding his way around. But Florence virtually pulsates with modern life. Students racing to and from the university quarter add vibrancy to the city, and it's amusing to watch the way many local businesspeople avoid the city's impossible traffic today, whizzing by on Vespas past cars stalled in traffic.

Florentines like to present *una bella figura* (a good appearance) to the rest of the world and are incredibly upset when that appearance is attacked, as in the case of the May 1993 bombing of the Uffizi. The entire city rallied to re-open this treasure trove of Renaissance art.

Try to visit this city, even on the most rushed of European itineraries. There's nothing like it anywhere else. Venice and Rome are too different from Florence to invite meaningful comparisons. Florence is also an ideal base from which to explore Tuscany. Though increasingly built up, Tuscany has enough old hill towns and rolling hills studded with olives and grapevines to attract the romantic. Florence and Siena are the chief drawing cards, but Fiesole and Pisa also have their allure.

ESSENTIALS

GETTING THERE   By Plane If you're flying from New York, a much-flown route is to Rome, where you can board a domestic flight to the **Galileo Galilei Airport** at Pisa (© 050-500707; www.pisa-airport.com), 93km (58 miles) west of Florence. **Alitalia** (© 050-20221 for the airport office; www.alitalia.it) also offers two flights a day from New York to Pisa with one stop in Rome. You can take an express train for the hour-long trip to Florence. There's also a small domestic airport, **Amerigo Vespucci,** on Via del Termine, near A-11 (© 055-373498; www.airport.florence.it), 6km (3½ miles) northwest of Florence, a 15-minute drive. This airport can be reached by ATAF bus no. 62, departing from the main Santa Maria Novella rail terminal. Domestic air service is provided by **Alitalia,** with offices in Florence at Lungarno degli Acciaiuoli 10–12R (© 055-27881).

By Train If you're coming north from Rome, count on a 2- to 3-hour trip, depending on your connection. **Santa Maria Novella rail station,** in Piazza della Stazione, adjoins Piazza di Santa Maria Novella. For information and timetables, contact **FS** (© 848-888088; www.trenitalia.it). Some trains into Florence stop at the **Stazione Campo di Marte,** on the eastern side of Florence. A 24-hour bus service (no. 91) runs between the two rail terminals.

Florence

(*i*) Information
— Railway

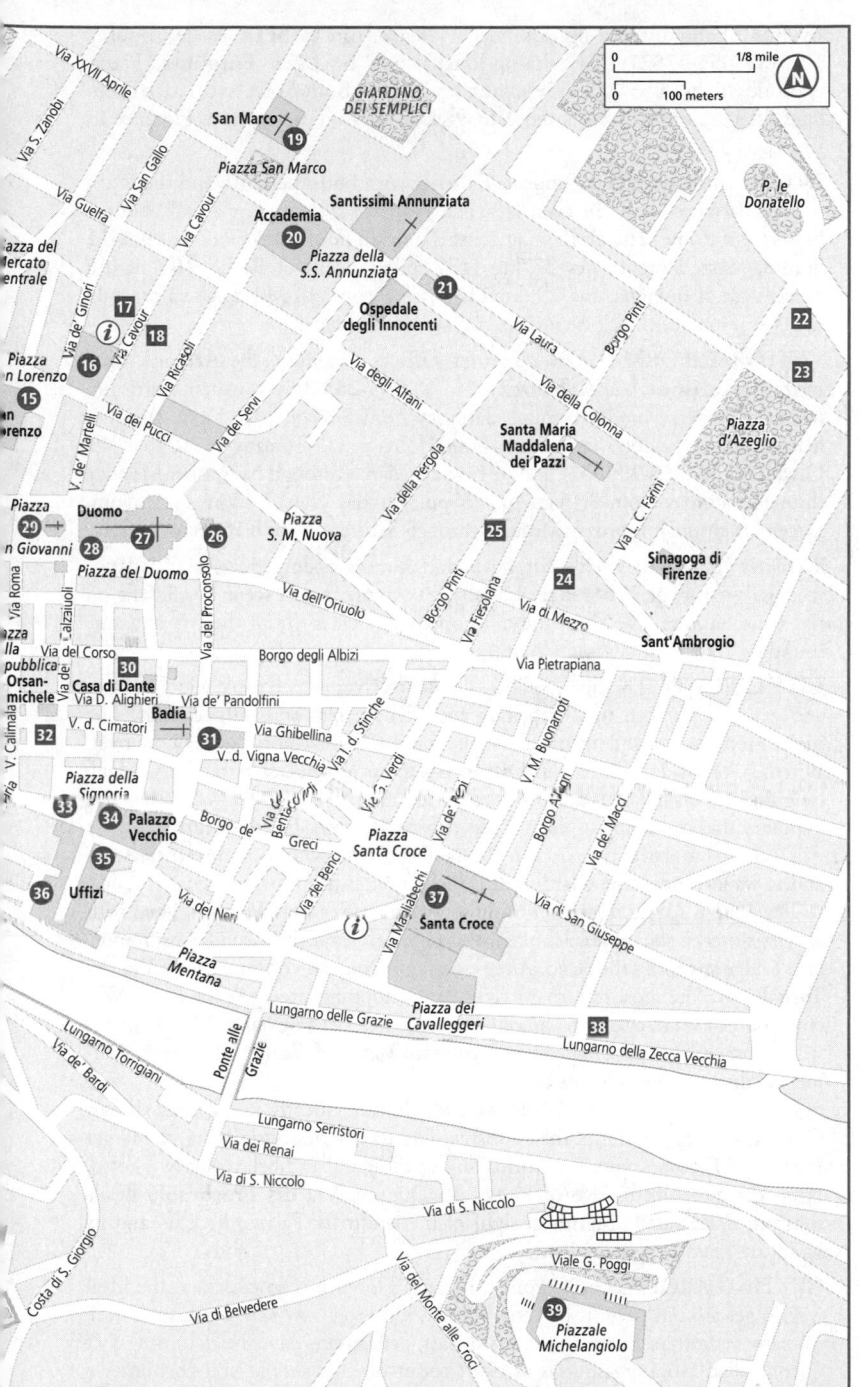

GIARDINO
DEI SEMPLICI

Via XXVII Aprile

Via S. Zanobi

Via Guelfa

Via San Gallo

Via Cavour

San Marco ✕
19

Piazza San Marco

Santissimi Annunziata

Accademia
20

Piazza della
S.S. Annunziata
21

P. le
Donatello

iazza del
lercato
entrale

Via di Ginori

17
(i)
18

Via Cavour

16

Via Ricasoli

Piazza
n Lorenzo

15

an
orenzo

V. de' Martelli

Via dei Pucci

Via dei Servi

Ospedale
degli Innocenti

Via Laura

Via degli Alfani

Via della Colonna

Borgo Pinti

22

23

Santa Maria
Maddalena
dei Pazzi

Piazza
d'Azeglio

Via della Pergola

Via L. C. Farini

Piazza
29 ✕
n Giovanni

Duomo
27

28

Piazza del Duomo

26

Piazza
S. M. Nuova

25

24

Borgo Pinti

Via Fiesolana

Via di Mezzo

Sinagoga di
Firenze

Via Roma

Via dell'Oriuolo

Sant'Ambrogio

Via Calzaiuoli

azza
lla
pubblica

Orsan-
michele

Via del Corso

Borgo degli Albizi

Via Pietrapiana

30
Casa di Dante

Via D. Alighieri

Via de' Pandolfini

V. Calimala

V. d. Cimatori

Badia

32

31

Via Ghibellina

Via d. Vigna Vecchia

Via de' Bentaccordi

Via I. d. Stinche

Via S. Verdi

Via de' Pepi

V. M. Buonarroti

Borgo Allegri

Via de' Macci

Piazza della
Signoria

33

34 Palazzo
Vecchio

35

Borgo de'
Greci

Via dei Benci

Piazza
Santa Croce

36
Uffizi

Via del Neri

(i)
Via Malfiabechi

37
Santa Croce

Via di San Giuseppe

Piazza
Mentana

Lungarno delle Grazie

Piazza dei
Cavalleggeri

38

Lungarno Torrigiani

Via de' Bardi

Ponte alle Grazie

Lungarno della Zecca Vecchia

Lungarno Serristori

Via dei Renai

Via di S. Niccolo

Via di S. Niccolo

Viale G. Poggi

Costa di S. Giorgio

Via di Belvedere

Via del Monte alle Croci

39
Piazzale
Michelangiolo

0 ———— 1/8 mile
0 ———— 100 meters
N

By Bus   Long-distance buses service Florence, run by **SITA,** Viale Cadorna 105 (© **055-47821;** www.sita-on-line.it), and by **Lazzi Eurolines,** Piazza Stazione 3R (© **055-215155;** www.eurolines.it). Both SITA and Lazzi Euro-lines offer transfers from Florence to Pisa. A one-way ticket from Florence to Pisa costs 5.60€.

By Car   Autostrada A-1 connects Florence with both the north and the south of Italy. It takes about an hour to reach Florence from Bologna and about 3 hours from Rome. The Tyrrhenian coast is only an hour from Florence on **A-11** heading west. Florence lies 277km (172 miles) north of Rome, 105km (65 miles) west of Bologna, and 298km (185 miles) south of Milan. Use a car only to get to Florence. Don't even contemplate its use once here.

VISITOR INFORMATION   Tourist Offices   Contact the **Azienda Pro-mozione Turistica,** Via A. Manzoni 16 (© **055-23320;** www.firenze.turismo. toscana.it), open Monday through Saturday from 8:30am to 1:30pm. Another helpful office, handling data about both Florence and Tuscany, is **APT** at Via Cavour 1R (© **055-290832**). Hours here are March through November Monday through Saturday from 8:15am to 7:15pm, Sunday from 8:15am to 1:45pm; December through February Monday through Saturday from 8:15am to 1:45pm.

Websites   Updated weekly for news and notices about concerts and dance recitals, **www.mega.it/florence** also lets you explore the art scene by clicking on the museum map. Switch to the monument version for both the city and sur-rounding regions, including Chianti.

CITY LAYOUT   The city is split by the **Arno River,** which usually looks serene and peaceful but can turn ferocious with floodwaters on rare occasions. The major monumental and historical core lies on the "right" (north) side of the river. But the "left" side—called the **Oltrarno**—is not devoid of attractions. Many longtime visitors frequent the Oltrarno for its tantalizing trattoria meals; they also maintain that the shopping here is less expensive. Even the most hurried visitor will want to cross over the Arno to see the Pitti Palace with its many art treasures and to walk through the Giardini di Boboli, a series of formal gardens.

The Arno is spanned by eight bridges, of which the **Ponte Vecchio,** lined with jewelry stores, is the most celebrated. **Ponte S. Trinità** is the second-most impor-tant bridge spanning the Arno. After crossing it you can continue along **Via dei Tornabuoni,** the most important right-bank shopping street. At the Ponte Vec-chio you can walk, again on the right bank, along **Via Por Santa Maria,** which will become Calimala. This will lead you into **Piazza della Repubblica,** a com-mercial district known for its cafes.

From here, you can take **Via Roma,** which leads directly into **Piazza di San Giovanni.** Here you'll find the baptistery and its neighboring sibling, the larger **Piazza del Duomo,** with the world-famous cathedral and bell tower by Giotto. From the far western edge of Piazza del Duomo, **Via del Proconsolo** heads south to **Piazza della Signoria,** sight of the landmark Palazzo Vecchio and its sculpture-filled Loggia dei Lanzi.

GETTING AROUND   By Foot   Because Florence is so compact, the ideal way to get around town is by foot—at times it's the only way, because there're so many pedestrian zones. In theory at least, pedestrians have the right of way at uncontrolled zebra crossings, but don't count on that should you encounter a speeding Vespa.

By Bus   You must purchase your bus ticket before boarding one of the public vehicles. For 1€, you can ride on any public bus in the city for a total of 60 minutes. A 3-hour pass costs 2€ and a 24-hour pass costs 4€. Bus tickets can be purchased from *tabacchi* (tobacconists' shops, marked by a white T) and news vendors. The local **bus station** (which serves as the terminal for ATAF city buses) is at Piazza della Stazione (© **055-56501**). Bus routes are posted at bus stops.

By Taxi Taxis can be found at stands at nearly all the major squares in Florence. If you need a radio taxi, call © **055-4390** or 055-4798.

By Car You'll need a car to explore the countryside of Tuscany in any depth. Cars are available at **Avis,** Borgo Ognissanti 128R (© **055-213629**); **Italy by Car,** Borgo Ognissanti 134R (© **055-287161**); and **Hertz,** Via del Termine 1 (© **055-307370**).

By Bicycle or Motor Scooter **Alinari** is near the rail station at Via Guelfa 85R (© **055-280500**). Depending on the model of bike you rent, it will cost 2€ to 2.50€ per hour or 10€ to 15€ per day. If you want to rent a scooter, it costs 7.50€ per hour, 25€ for 5 hours, 40€ per day. The shop is open Monday through Saturday from 9:30am to 1pm and 3 to 7:30pm, Sunday from 10am to 1pm and 3 to 7pm. November through February, the Sunday hours are 10am to 5pm.

 FAST FACTS: Florence

American Express The office is at Via Dante Alighieri 22R (© **055-50981**); it's open Monday through Friday from 9am to 5:30pm and Saturday from 9am to 12:30pm.

Business Hours Most **banks** are open Monday through Friday from 8:30am to 1:30pm and 2:45 to 3:45pm. **Shops** are generally open Monday from 4 to 7:30pm and Tuesday through Saturday from 9 or 10am to 1pm and 3:30 or 4 to 7:30pm. During the summer some shops are open Monday mornings. However, don't be surprised if shops close for several weeks in August, if not for the entire month.

Consulates The United States consulate is at Lungarno Amerigo Vespucci 38 ((© **055-2398276**), open Monday through Friday from 9am to 12:30pm and 2 to 3:30pm. The **United Kingdom** consulate is at Lungarno Corsini 2 (© **055-284133**), near Piazza Santa Trinità, open Monday through Friday from 9:30am to 12:30pm and 2:30 to 4:30pm. Citizens of other English-speaking countries, including **Canada, Australia,** and **New Zealand,** should contact their diplomatic representatives in Rome (see "Fast Facts: Rome," earlier).

Currency Exchange Local banks have the best rates, and most are open Monday through Friday from 8:30am to 1:30pm and 2:45 to 3:45pm. The tourist office (see "Visitor Information" under "Essentials," above) exchanges money at official rates when banks are closed and on holidays, but a commission is often charged. You can also go to the Ufficio Informazione booth at the rail station, open daily from 7:30am to 7:40pm. American Express (above) also exchanges money. One of the best places to exchange currency is the post office (below).

Dentists/Doctors For a list of English-speaking doctors or dentists, consult your consulate (above) or contact **Tourist Medical Service,** Via Lorenzo il

Magnifico 59 (© **055-475411**). Visits without an appointment are possible only Monday through Friday from 11am to noon and 5 to 6pm. After hours, an answering service gives names and phone numbers of dentists and doctors who are on duty.

Emergencies For fire, call © **115**; for an ambulance, call © **118**; for the police, call © **113**; and for road service, call © **116.**

Hospitals Call the **General Hospital** of Santa Maria Nuova, Piazza Santa Maria Nuova 1 (© **055-27581**).

Internet Access You can check your messages or send e-mail at **Internet Train,** Via dell'Orivolo 40R (© **055-2638968**; www.internettrain.it).

Pharmacies The **Farmacia Molteni,** Via Calzaiuoli 7R (© **055-215472**), is open 24 hours.

Police Dial © **113** in an emergency. English-speaking foreigners who want to see and talk to the police should go to the **Ufficio Stranieri station,** Via Zara 2 (© **055-49771**), where English-speaking personnel are available daily from 9am to 2pm.

Post Office The **Central Post Office** is at Via Pellicceria 3, off Piazza della Repubblica (© **055-27361** for English-speaking operators), open Monday through Saturday from 8:15am to 7pm. You can buy stamps and telephone cards at window nos. 21 and 22. A foreign exchange office is open Monday through Friday from 8:15am to 6pm. If you want to send packages of up to 20 kilograms (44 lb.), go to the rear of the building and enter at Piazza Davantati 4.

Safety Violent crimes are rare in Florence; most crime consists of pickpockets who frequent crowded tourist centers, such as corridors of the Uffizi Galleries. Members of group tours who cluster together are often singled out as victims. Car thefts are relatively common: Don't leave your luggage in an unguarded car, even if it's locked in the trunk. Women should be especially careful in avoiding purse-snatchers, some of whom grab a purse while whizzing by on a Vespa, often knocking the woman down. Documents such as passports and extra money are better stored in safes at your hotel, if available.

Telephone The **country code** for Italy is **39.** The **city code** for Florence is **055**; use this code when calling from *anywhere* outside or inside Italy— even within Florence itself (and you must now include the 0 every time, even when calling from abroad). See "Fast Facts: Rome," earlier, for details on how to call Italy, how to place calls within Italy, and how to call home once you're in Italy.

You can place **long-distance and international calls** at the Telecom office north of the Duomo at Via Cavour 21R (open daily 8am–9:45pm).

WHERE TO STAY
NEAR THE DUOMO
Very Expensive

Savoy Hotel ⭐⭐⭐ Everything is fresh and new again at Florence's most legendary hotel, which opened in 1896. Completely restored, it now takes its place just under the Excelsior and Grand in luxury. Refined Italian elegance is the hallmark of this landmark monument, which experienced years of decline after World War II. Rooms are decorated sumptuously. Bathrooms are beautifully tiled (some with shower only).

Piazza della Repubblica 7, 50123 Firenze. ℂ **055-27351**. Fax 055-2735888. www.roccofortehotels.com. 107 units (some with shower only). 420€–450€ double; from 750€ suite. AE, DC, MC, V. Parking 29€. Bus: 22, 36, or 37. **Amenities:** Restaurant; bar; room service; in-room massage; babysitting; laundry/dry cleaning. *In room:* A/C, TV, minibar, hair dryer, safe.

Expensive

Hotel J and J ⚐ This charming hotel, built in the 16th century as a monastery, lies a 5-minute walk from the church of Santa Croce. You'll find a flagstone-covered courtyard and a salon with vaulted ceilings and several preserved ceiling frescoes. Rooms combine an unusual mixture of modern furniture with the monastery's original beamed ceilings. Suites usually contain sleeping lofts and, in some cases, rooftop balconies overlooking the historic core. All units are filled with modern tiled bathrooms with tub/shower combos.

Via di Mezzo 20, 50121 Firenze. ℂ **055-263121**. Fax 055-240282. www.jandjhotel.com. 20 units. 282€–315€ double; 370€ junior suite; 430€–460€ suite. Rates include buffet breakfast. AE, DC, MC, V. Parking 30€. Bus: A. **Amenities:** Bar; room service; babysitting; laundry/dry cleaning. *In room:* A/C, TV, minibar, hair dryer.

Hotel Monna Lisa ⚐ This privately owned Renaissance palazzo is 4 blocks east of the Duomo. Most of the great old rooms overlook either an inner patio or a modest rear garden. Each of the salons is handsomely furnished. Rooms vary greatly—some are quite large, though no two are alike, and each comes with a tiled bathroom with tub/shower combos.

Borgo Pinti 27, 50121 Firenze. ℂ **055-2479751**. Fax 055-2479755. www.monnalisa.it. 30 units. 181€–284€ double; 232€–413€ triple. Rates include breakfast. AE, DC, MC, V. Parking 10€. Bus: A, 6, 31, or 32. **Amenities:** Room service; babysitting; laundry/dry cleaning. *In room:* A/C, TV, minibar, hair dryer, safe.

Hotel Porta Rossa ⚐ Reportedly, this is the second-oldest hotel in Italy, dating from 1386. The place is a bit dark, but on a hot Tuscan summer day you welcome that in lieu of air-conditioning. Since it isn't as well known or publicized as some of its competitors such as the Hermitage or Tornabuoni, you stand a better chance of getting a reservation. In spite of its antiquity, the hotel has kept abreast of the times, installing modern conveniences, good beds, and ample bathrooms, some with shower, others with tub. The managers have resisted making two new rooms out of one of the old spacious ones from centuries ago. Breakfast is the only meal served, and a little terrace offers a panoramic view.

Via Porta Rossa 19, 50123 Firenze. ℂ **055-287551**. Fax 055-282179. 79 units (some with shower only, some with tub only). 165€ double. Rates include breakfast. AE, DC, MC, V. Parking 20€–33€. Bus: A. **Amenities:** Bar; laundry/dry cleaning. *In room:* A/C, TV, minibar, hair dryer, safe.

NEAR THE PONTE VECCHIO
Moderate

Hermitage Hotel ⚐ The offbeat, intimate Hermitage is a charming place, with a sun terrace on the roof providing a view. You can take your breakfast under a leafy arbor surrounded by potted roses and geraniums. The small rooms are pleasantly furnished. Bathrooms are superb and contain lots of gadgets; some units come with shower, others with tub. Some recently restored ones have hydro-massage tubs. Those rooms overlooking the Arno offer the most scenic view, and they've been fitted with double-glazed windows.

Vicolo Marzio 1, Piazza del Pesce I, 50122 Firenze. ℂ **055-287216**. Fax 055-212208. www.hermitagehotel. com. 28 units. 195€–245€ double; 230€–299€ triple; 245€–310€ family room. Rates include breakfast.

MC, V. Parking 20€–40€. Bus: B. **Amenities:** Bar; tour desk; room service; baby-sitting; laundry/dry cleaning. *In room:* A/C, TV, hair dryer, safe.

NEAR PIAZZA SANTA TRINITÀ
Moderate
Hotel Tornabuoni Beacci   Near the Arno and Piazza S. Trinità, on the princi-pal shopping street, this pensione occupies the top three floors of a 14th-century palazzo. The renovated hotel still bears an air of old-fashioned gentility. The rooms are moderately well furnished, each with a tub and shower combination. The roof terrace is for breakfast or late-afternoon drinks. The view of the nearby churches, towers, and rooftops is worth experiencing.

Via Tornabuoni 3, 50123 Firenze. ℂ 055-212645. Fax 055-283594. www.bthotel.it. 30 units. 185€–220€ double; 240€–360€ suite. Rates include buffet breakfast. AE, DC, MC, V. Parking 24€–30€. Bus: B, 6, 11, or 36. **Amenities:** Restaurant; bar; room service; babysitting; laundry/dry cleaning. *In room:* A/C, TV, minibar, hair dryer.

NEAR PIAZZA SAN LORENZO & THE MERCATO CENTRALE
Inexpensive
Hotel Casci   Casci is a well-run little hotel, near the Piazza del Duomo and the main rail station. The building dates from the 14th century, and some of the public rooms feature frescoes. The hotel is both traditional and modern, and the English-speaking reception staff is attentive. Rooms are comfortably furnished, and each year four or five are upgraded and renovated. The small bathrooms come with tub/shower combo or shower only.

Via Cavour 13, 50129 Firenze. ℂ 055-211686. Fax 055-2396461. www.hotelcasci.com. 25 units. 90€–140€ double; 120€–180€ triple; 150€–220€ quad. Rates include buffet breakfast. AE, DC, MC, V. Parking 20€–25€. Bus: 1, 7, 25, or 33. **Amenities:** Bar; tour desk; babysitting; laundry/dry cleaning. *In room:* A/C, TV, minibar, hair dryer, safe.

Hotel Europa   Two long blocks north of the Duomo, this hotel in a 16th-cen-tury building has functioned as a family-run hotel since 1925. Homey touches remind newcomers of its ongoing administration by members of the Gassim family. All but four rooms overlook the back and usually open onto a view of the campanile and dome of the Duomo. Those that face the street are noisier but benefit from double-glazing. Each unit comes with a tub/shower combo.

Via Cavour 14, 50129 Firenze. ℂ 055-2396715. Fax 055-210361. 20 units (shower only). 90€–140€ dou-ble; 190€–220€ triple. Rates include buffet breakfast. AE, MC, V. Parking 20€ in nearby garage. Bus: 1, 7, 25, or 33. **Amenities:** Bar; babysitting; laundry/dry cleaning. *In room:* A/C, TV, hair dryer, safe.

NEAR PIAZZA SANTA MARIA NOVELLA & THE TRAIN STATION
Very Expensive
Grand Hotel Villa Medici 𝒞𝒞   This old-time favorite occupies an 18th-cen-tury Medici palace 2 blocks southwest of the train station. Of all the govern-ment-rated five-star hotels of Florence, it is the only one with its own pool and health club. It generally appeals more to Europeans than to Americans, who might want more up-to-date facilities, although it was renovated in 2001 (when the guest rooms were spruced up and given such extras as electronic safes). Most rooms have twin beds. The most peaceful rooms front the garden, but during the day there's noise from the convent school next door.

Via il Prato 42, 50123 Firenze. ℂ 055-2381331. Fax 055-2381336. www.villamedicihotel.com. 103 units. 450€–470€ double; 750€–950€ suite. AE, DC, MC, V. Parking 18€–23€. Bus: 1, 9, 14, 17, 23, 36, or 37. **Amenities:** Restaurant (including a romantic dining room and outdoor dining in summer); elegant piano bar;

pool; fitness center with sauna; room service; babysitting; laundry/dry cleaning. *In room:* A/C, TV, dataport, minibar, hair dryer, safe.

Expensive

Hotel Albani Firenze ✶   In 1993, a respected nationwide chain transformed a run-down pensione, a 10-minute walk from the Duomo and close to the train station, into one of Florence's most appealing luxury hotels, set in a structure that was built around 1900 as a private villa. Today, you'll find up-to-date comforts, artwork, and architectural embellishments. The high-ceilinged interiors, outfitted in tones of soft terra cottas and browns, sometimes verge on the theatrical but are never forbidding. The guest rooms, ranging from medium to spacious, possess style and grace, with mahogany beds.

Via Fiume 12, 50123 Firenze. ✆ **055-26030.** Fax 055-211045. www.hotelalbani.it. 100 units. 325€–345€ double; from 680€ suite. Rates include breakfast. AE, DC, MC, V. Valet parking 20€. Bus: 10, 12, 25, 31, or 32. **Amenities:** Restaurant; bar; room service; babysitting; laundry/dry cleaning. *In room:* A/C, TV, minibar, hair dryer, safe.

Moderate

Hotel Mario's ✶ *Value*   Two blocks from the rail station, this is a winning choice. It's on the first floor of an old building that has been a hotel since 1872, when the *Room with a View* crowd started arriving in search of the glory of the Renaissance. Mario Noce is the gracious host, and he and his staff speak English. Although you'll find cheaper inns in Florence, the service and hospitality make Mario's worth your euros. The guest rooms aren't very large but are furnished with taste; wrought-iron headboards frame firm beds. Several rooms open onto a small private garden.

Via Faenza 89, 50123 Firenze. ✆ **055-216801.** Fax 055-212039. www.hotelmarios.com. 16 units (shower only). 95€–165€ double; 125€–220€ triple. Rates include breakfast. AE, DC, MC, V. Valet parking 18€–23€. Bus: 10, 13, 17. **Amenities:** Bar; laundry. *In room:* A/C, TV, hair dryer, safe.

Inexpensive

Hotel Nuova Italia ✶ *Finds*   This little hotel has been welcoming Frommer's readers since 1958, when folks arrived with their dog-eared copies of *Europe on $5 a Day.* A Canadian guest, Eileen, met and fell in love with Luciano Viti, then a bellhop. Today they own the hotel and are grandparents with a new generation of Vitis waiting to take over one day. The guest rooms are pleasantly furnished and decorated with paintings and posters. The Vitis, who serve a fantastic cappuccino, will help you figure out how to get around Florence and offer tips on where to shop and what to do.

Via Faenza 26, 50123 Firenze. ✆ **055-287508.** Fax 055-210941. www.hotelnuovaitalia.com. 20 units (shower only). 125€ double; 145€ triple. Rates include breakfast. AE, MC, V. Parking 20€ nearby. Bus: 10, 12, 25, 31, 32, or 91. **Amenities:** Tour desk; car-rental desk; bike rentals; in-room massage; babysitting; laundry/dry cleaning. *In room:* A/C, TV.

ON PIAZZA OGNISSANTI

Piazza Ognissanti is a fashionable but car-clogged Renaissance square opening onto the Arno. It's home to two of the most legendary hotels in the city.

Very Expensive

Grand Hotel ✶✶✶   The Grand is a bastion of luxury, although neither it nor the Excelsior are as exclusive as the Regency. A hotel of history and tradition, the Grand is known for its halls and salons. Rooms and suites have a refined elegance, and the most desirable overlook the Arno. Each comes with a luxurious bathroom with tub/shower combos. A highlight of the hotel is the Winter Garden, an enclosed court lined with arches where regional and international dishes are served.

Piazza Ognissanti 1, 50123 Firenze. (C) **800/325-3589** in the U.S. and Canada, or 055-288781. Fax 055-217400. www.luxurycollection.com/grandflorence. 107 units. 555€–620€ double; from 1,099€–1,273€ suite. AE, DC, MC, V. Parking from 30€. Bus: 6 or 17. **Amenities:** Restaurant; 2 bars; room service; babysitting; laundry/dry cleaning; valet. *In room:* A/C, TV, minibar, hair dryer, safe.

Westin Excelsior ☆☆☆   The Excelsior, a former patrician mansion, is the ultimate in luxury. Cosmopolitan and sophisticated, it has the best-trained staff in town. If you like glamour and glitz, stay here. The opulent rooms have 19th-century Florentine antiques and sumptuous fabrics. Some of the more desirable rooms open onto views of the Arno. In these old palaces, expect the accommodations to come in a variety of configurations. All contain luxurious bathrooms with tub/shower combos.

Piazza Ognissanti 3, 50123 Firenze. (C) **800/325-3535** in the U.S. and Canada, or 055-264201. Fax 055-210278. www.westin.com/excelsiorflorence. 171 units. 456€–853€ double; from 1,426€ junior suite. AE, DC, MC, V. Parking 30€. Bus: 6 or 17. **Amenities:** Restaurant; bar; children's program; room service; in-room massage; babysitting; laundry/dry cleaning; valet. *In room:* A/C, TV, minibar, hair dryer, safe.

ON OR NEAR PIAZZA MASSIMO D'AZEGLIO
Piazza Massimo d'Azeglio is a 12-minute walk northeast of the historic core of Florence.

Very Expensive
Hotel Regency ☆☆☆   The Regency is an intimate villa of taste and exclusivity. This well-built old-style villa, a member of Relais & Châteaux, has its own garden across from a park in a residential area. It's a luxurious hideaway, and offers exquisitely furnished rooms with state-of-the-art bathrooms with tub/shower combos. The dining room, Relais le Jardin, is renowned for its *alta cucina.*

Piazza Massimo d'Azeglio 3, 50121 Firenze. (C) 055-245247. Fax 055-2346735. www.regency-hotel.com. 34 units. 300€–400€ double; 610€–800€ suite. Rates include buffet breakfast. AE, DC, MC, V. Parking 26€. Bus: 6, 31, or 32. **Amenities:** Restaurant; bar; tour desk; room service; in-room massage; babysitting; laundry/dry cleaning. *In room:* A/C, TV, minibar, hair dryer, safe.

Inexpensive
Albergo Losanna   A good choice, Albergo Losanna is a tiny family-run place off Viale Antonio Gramsci, between Piazzale Donatello and Piazza Massimo d'Azeglio. It offers utter simplicity and cleanliness. Rooms are homey and well kept, but the furnishings are simple and a bit tired. Each unit comes with a small bathroom with shower.

Via Vittorio Alfieri 9, 50121 Firenze. (C)/fax **055-245840.** www.albergolosanna.com. 8 units, 3 with bathroom (shower only). 52€ double without bathroom; 68€ double with bathroom. Rates include breakfast. AE, MC, V. Parking 18€. Bus: 6. *In room:* No phone.

ALONG THE ARNO
Moderate
Ritz Hotel ☆ *(finds)*   Don't be misled by the name "Ritz" and grab to hold onto your wallet. The Ritz of Florence has nothing to do with the *luxe* palaces of London, Paris, or Madrid. The local Ritz is a family-run hotel whose youthful owners have upgraded it and turned it into a reasonably priced alternative in a lethally priced city. They offer well-furnished, medium-size rooms. Some bathrooms have a tub/shower combo, others have a shower. A visit here is like a call on your favorite Florentine aunt back in 1870 but with more modern amenities than she had. Breakfast is the only meal served.

Lugarno Zeccia Vecchia 24, 50122 Firenze. (C) **055-2340650.** Fax 055-240863. www.florenceitaly.net. 32 units (some with shower only). 110€–180€ double; 170€–280€ suite. Rates include breakfast. AE, DC, MC, V. Bus: 23. **Amenities:** Bar; room service; babysitting; laundry/dry cleaning. *In room:* A/C, TV, minibar, hair dryer, safe.

ACROSS THE ARNO
Expensive
Hotel Villa Carlotta ✿ *Finds*   This hotel from the Edwardian age was built as a villa and bought in the 1950s by Carlotta Schulmann. Her lavish renovations have transformed it into one of Florence's most charming smaller hotels. It's still very homey and stands in a residential neighborhood. Rooms have silk wallpaper and bedspreads, reproduction antiques, safes, and crystal chandeliers; each has a view of the garden. The bathrooms are exceedingly well maintained. The hotel is only a 10-minute walk from the Ponte Vecchio; by taxi, it's a 5-minute ride.

Via Michele di Lando 3, 50125 Firenze. ℂ 055-220530. Fax 055-2336147. www.hotelvillacarlotta.it. 32 units (some with shower only). 150€–270€ double; 170€–305€ triple. Rates include buffet breakfast. AE, DC, MC, V. Free parking. Bus: 11, 36, or 37. **Amenities:** Restaurant; bar; lounge; car-rental desk; room service; babysitting; laundry/dry cleaning. *In room:* A/C, TV, minibar, hair dryer, safe.

Moderate
Pensione Annalena ✿ *Finds*   Most of the simply furnished rooms in this historic hotel overlook a secret garden; five face an open-air galleria on the loggia, evoking an idyllic landscape that might have been painted by Gozzoli. Don't be put off by the lack of air-conditioning; the high ceilings and thick masonry walls almost guarantee a relatively comfortable temperature in summer. The bathrooms are small but have adequate shelf space. The pensione is about a 5-minute walk from the Pitti and 10 minutes from the Ponte Vecchio.

Via Romana 34, 50125 Firenze. ℂ 055-222402. Fax 055-222403. www.hotelannalena.lt. 20 units. 126€–166€ double. Rates include breakfast. AE, DC, MC, V. Parking 21€. Bus: C, 11, 36, or 37. **Amenities:** Lounge; room service; laundry/dry cleaning. *In room:* TV, hair dryer.

WHERE TO DINE
NEAR THE DUOMO
Moderate
Il Cavallino TUSCAN/ITALIAN   A local favorite since the 1930s, Il Cavallino is the kind of discreetly famous restaurant where Florentines invariably go to be with one another. It's on a tiny street (which probably won't even be on your map) that leads off Piazza della Signoria at its northern end, not far from the equestrian statue. Menu items are typical hearty Tuscan fare, including an assortment of boiled meats in green herb sauce, grilled filet of steak, breast of chicken Medici style, and the inevitable Florentine spinach.

Via della Farine 6R. ℂ 055-215818. Reservations recommended. Main courses 10€–16€. AE, DC, MC, V. Mar–Oct daily noon–3pm and 7–10:30pm; off season Thurs–Tues noon–3pm, Thurs–Mon 7–10:30pm. Bus: B.

Paoli ✿ TUSCAN/ITALIAN   Paoli, between the Duomo and Piazza della Signoria, is one of Florence's finest restaurants. It turns out a host of specialties, but could be recommended almost solely for its medieval-tavern atmosphere. All pastas are homemade, and the fettuccine alla Paoli is served piping hot and full of flavor. The chef also does a superb *rognoncino trifolato* (thinly sliced kidney cooked with oil, garlic, and parsley) and sole meunière. A recommendable side dish is *piselli* (garden peas) in the Florentine style.

Via dei Tavolini 12R. ℂ 055-216215. Reservations required. Main courses 10€–18€. AE, DC, MC, V. Wed–Mon noon–2:30pm and 7–10:30pm. Closed 3 weeks in Aug. Bus: A.

NEAR THE PONTE VECCHIO
Inexpensive
Buca dell'Orafo ✿ *Finds* FLORENTINE   This little dive is one of many cellars or *buca*-type establishments beloved by Florentines. The trattoria is usually stuffed with regulars so if you want a seat, go early. Over the years the chef has

made little concession to the foreign palate, turning out genuine Florentine specialties, like tripe and mixed boiled meats with a green sauce, and *stracotto e fagioli* (beef braised in a sauce of chopped vegetables and red wine), served with beans in a tomato sauce.

Via Volta dei Girolami 28R. (② **055-213619**. Main courses 10€–18€. No credit cards. Tues–Sat 12:30–2:30pm and 7:30–10:30pm. Closed Aug and 2 weeks in Dec. Bus: B.

NEAR PIAZZA SAN LORENZO & THE MERCATO CENTRALE
Inexpensive
Le Fonticine TUSCAN/BOLOGNESE   Owner Silvano Bruci took this former convent and its adjoining garden and turned it into one of the most hospitable restaurants in Florence. He and his wife use recipes she collected from her childhood in Bologna. The food, served in copious portions, is both traditional and delectable. Begin with a platter of fresh antipasti, then enjoy samplings of three of the most excellent pasta dishes of the day. This might be followed by veal scaloppini, or stewed wild boar.

Via Nazionale 79R. (② **055-282106**. Reservations recommended for dinner. Main courses 8.50€–19€. AE, DC, MC, V. Tues–Sat noon–3pm and 7–10pm. Closed Jan 1–15 and Aug. Bus: 7, 10, 11, 12, 25, 31, 33, or 70.

Trattoria Antellesi ☆ *(Finds* TUSCAN   On the ground floor of a 15th-century historic monument, a few steps from the Medici Chapel, this restaurant is devoted almost exclusively to Tuscan recipes that have stood the test of time. The restaurant prepares at least seven *piatti del giorno* that change according to the availability of the ingredients. Menu items may include tagliatelle with porcini mushrooms or with braised arugula, *crespelle alla fiorentina* (a Tuscan Renaissance cheesy spinach crepe), market-fresh fish (generally on Fri), and delicious Valdostana chicken.

Via Faenza 9R. (② **055-216990**. Reservations recommended. Main courses 10€–16€. AE, DC, MC, V. Daily noon–3pm and 7–10:30pm. Closed Tues Dec–Apr. Bus: 1, 6, 7, 11, 17, 33, 67, or 68.

NEAR PIAZZA SANTA MARIA NOVELLA & THE TRAIN STATION
Expensive
I Quattro Amici ☆ SEAFOOD   Opened in 1990 by four Tuscan entrepreneurs, this restaurant occupies the street level of a modern building near the rail station. The place serves endless quantities of fish. Specialties include such dishes as pasta with fish sauce and sausage; fish soup; fried shrimp and squid in the style of Livorno; and grilled, stewed, or baked versions of all the bounty of the Mediterranean. The roast sea bass and roast snapper, flavored with Mediterranean herbs, are among the finest dishes, as is the fresh lobster with mixed vegetables.

Via degli Orti Oricellari 29. (② **055-215413**. Reservations recommended. Main courses 15€–25€. AE, DC, MC, V. Daily noon–2:30pm and 7–10:30pm. Bus: D, 26, 27, or 35.

Moderate
Buca Lapi ☆ TUSCAN   Buca Lapi, a cellar restaurant under the Palazzo Antinori, is big on glamour, good food, and the enthusiasm of fellow diners. Its decor alone makes it fun: Vaulted ceilings are covered with travel posters from all over the world. The cooks know how to turn out the most classic dishes of the Tuscan kitchen with superb finesse. Specialties include paté, cannelloni, *scampi giganti alla griglia* (a supersize shrimp), and *bistecca alla fiorentina* (local beefsteak), still cooked over coals in the old-fashioned way. In season, the *fagioli toscani all'olio* (Tuscan beans in the native olive oil) are a delicacy. Owner and

chef Luciano Ghinasi's cookbook, available in English, reveals some of his secrets in preparing succulent Tuscan dishes.

Via del Trebbio 1R. ℂ 055-213768. Reservations required for dinner. Main courses 15€–25€. AE, DC, MC, V. Tues–Sat 12:30–2:30pm; Mon–Sat 7:30–10:30pm. Closed 2 weeks in Aug. Bus: 6, 11, 36, or 37.

Don Chisciotte ⭐ ITALIAN/SEAFOOD   This restaurant is known for its creative cuisine and changing array of very fresh fish. Creative menu items are produced with a flourish from the kitchens. Examples include red taglierini with clams, pesto, and cheese; risotto of broccoli and baby squid; and black ravioli colored with squid ink and stuffed with a puree of shrimp and crayfish. Chefs also prepare one of the city's most flavor-filled Florentine steaks along with a succulent medley of boiled meats with fresh herb seasonings.

Via Ridolfi 4R. ℂ 055-475430. Reservations recommended. Main courses 18€–25€; *menu degustazione* 52€. AE, DC, MC, V. Mon 5–10:30pm; Tues–Sat 1–2:30pm and 8–10:30pm. Bus: 20.

Sabatini ⭐ FLORENTINE   Despite its location near the rail station, Sabatini has long been extolled by Florentines and visitors alike as the finest of the restaurants characteristic of the city. To celebrate our return visit every year, we order the same main course—boiled Valdarno chicken with savory green sauce. Other main courses are also delicious, especially the veal scaloppini with artichokes. Of course, you can always order a good sole meunière and the classic beefsteak Florentine.

Via de'Panzani 9A. ℂ 055-211559. Reservations recommended. Main courses 13€–24€. AE, DC, MC, V. Tues–Sun 12:30–2:30pm and 7:30–10:30pm. Bus: 1, 6, 14, 17, or 22.

Inexpensive
Ristorante Otello FLORENTINE   Beside the train station, Ristorante Otello is a long-established comfortable Florentine dining room. Its antipasto Toscano is one of the best in town, an array of appetizing hors d'oeuvres that practically becomes a meal in itself. The waiter urges you to *"Mangi, mangi, mangi!"* ("Eat, eat, eat!"). Order one of the succulent pasta dishes, such as spaghetti with baby clams or pappardelle with garlic sauce. The meat and poultry dishes are equally delectable, including sole meunière and veal pizzaiola with lots of garlic.

Via degli Orti Oricellari 36R. ℂ 055-216517. Reservations recommended. Main courses 9€–18€. AE, DC, MC, V. Daily noon–2:30pm and 7:30–10:30pm. Bus: D, 14, 17, 23, 26, 27, or 35.

Sostanza ⭐ *Finds* FLORENTINE   Sostanza is a tucked-away little trattoria where working people have gone since 1869 to get excellent, reasonably priced food. It's the city's oldest and most revered trattoria. The small dining room has crowded family tables. The rear kitchen is open, its secrets exposed to diners. Specialties include breaded chicken breast and a succulent T-bone steak. You might also want to try tripe the Florentine way—cut into strips and baked in a casserole with tomatoes, onions, and Parmesan.

Via del Porcellana 25R. ℂ 055-212691. Reservations recommended. Main courses 9€–18€. No credit cards. Mon–Fri 12:30–2:10pm and 7:30–10:45pm. Closed Aug and 2 weeks at Christmas. Bus: 12.

NEAR PIAZZA GOLDONI
Moderate
Harry's Bar ⭐ INTERNATIONAL/ITALIAN   Harry's Bar, in a prime position on the Arno, is an enclave of expatriate and well-heeled visiting Yankees that deserves its reputation. A specialty is risotto or tagliatelle with ham, onions, and cheese. Harry has created his own *tortellini* (stuffed pasta), but Harry's hamburger and his club sandwich are the most popular items. The chef also prepares

about a dozen specialties every day, like breast of chicken "our way," grilled giant-size scampi, and lean broiled sirloin.

Lungarno Vespucci 22R. ⓒ **055-2396700**. Reservations required. Main courses 18€–30€. AE, MC, V. Mon–Sat noon–3pm and 7–11pm. Closed 1 week in Aug and Dec 18–Jan 8. Bus B.

Trattoria Coco Lezzone FLORENTINE   In Florentine dialect, the establishment's name refers to the sauce-stained apron of the extroverted chef who established this place more than a century ago. Today, this remains a good place to sample the nearby food of the Tuscan countryside. Go before the rush begins if you want a seat in this bustling trattoria. The rib-sticking fare includes generous portions of boiled meats with a green sauce, pasta *fagiole* (with beans), *osso buco* (beef or veal knuckle braised in wine, butter, garlic, and lemon), tripe, and beefsteak Florentine, which is super-expensive, although most dishes are very moderate in price.

Via del Parioncino 26R. ⓒ **055-287178**. Reservations accepted only for groups of 10 or more. Main courses 9€–23€. No credit cards. Mon–Sat noon–2:30pm; Mon and Wed–Sat 7–10pm. Closed last week of July to Aug and Dec 25–Jan 6. Bus: 27 or 31.

NEAR PIAZZA SANTA CROCE
Expensive

Cibrèo ⓡ *Finds* MEDITERRANEAN   Cibrèo is one of the largest eateries in the neighborhood, with both a formal restaurant and a less expensive trattoria on-site. The *New York Times* called the chef and owner, Fabio Picchi, a poet for how he talks and a magician for how he cooks. The kitchens are noteworthy for not containing a grill and not serving pastas. They specialize in foodstuffs cooked in a wood-burning oven and cold marinated dishes, especially vegetables. Menu items include *sformato* (soufflé made from potatoes and ricotta, served with Parmesan and tomato sauce) and flan of Parmesan, veal tongue, and artichokes. A favorite dish of the chef is roast pigeon flavored with a fruity mustard. Among his classic recipes are *zuppa di cavolo* (cabbage soup), *polenta alle erbe* (polenta flavored with seasonal herbs), and *insalata di fave* (fava bean salad with parmigiana flakes).

Via Andrea del Verrocchio 8R. ⓒ **055-2341100**. Reservations recommended in the restaurant, not accepted in the trattoria. All main courses 30€ in the restaurant,15€ in the trattoria. AE, DC, MC, V (restaurant only). Tues–Sat 12:30–2:30pm and 7–11pm. Closed late July to early Sept. Bus: A.

Moderate/Inexpensive

Osteria del Caffè Italiano ⓡ *Value* WINE BAR/TUSCAN   Housed in the 13th-century Palazzo Salviati, this wine bar/trattoria is the brainchild of Umberto Montano. Beneath a wrought-iron chandelier hanging from the vaulted 6m (20-ft.) ceiling, you can sample delicious choices from the short menu. Look for the fresh *mozzarella di bufala,* specially couriered from a private supplier in Naples (not available June–Aug). Stop by any time the restaurant isn't serving meals for a by-the-glass introduction to Montano's renowned wine cellar and an assortment of Tuscan *salumi.* Or come back in the evening to dine in the elegant restaurant in the back room and splurge on excellently prepared entrees from the grill and a more serious sampling of wine.

Via Isola delle Stinche 11–13R (2 blocks west of Piazza Santa Croce). ⓒ **055-289368**. Reservations for restaurant (not wine bar) suggested. Wine bar: Small plates 8€–11€. Restaurant: Main courses 15€–21€. DC, MC, V. Tues–Sun noon–1am. Bus: A or 14.

EXPLORING THE RENAISSANCE CITY
Florence was the fountainhead of the Renaissance, the city of Dante and Boccaccio. Florentines are noted for their cunning, as represented by Machiavelli;

however, they're not noted for their religious zeal, as evoked by Savonarola, who might have found a better reception in Geneva. For 3 centuries, Florence was dominated by the Medici family, patrons of the arts and masters of assassination. But it's chiefly through its artists that we know of the apogee of the Renaissance: Ghiberti, Fra Angelico, Donatello, Brunelleschi, Botticelli, and the incomparable Leonardo da Vinci and Michelangelo.

Piazza della Signoria ★★★, though never completed, is one of the most beautiful in Italy. On the square is the Fountain of Neptune. Nearby is the spot where Savonarola walked his last mile. This zealous monk was a fire-and-brimstone reformer who rivaled Dante in conjuring up the punishment hell would inflict on sinners. For centuries Michelangelo's *David* stood in this piazza before it was moved to the Accademia. The work you see here today is a copy.

On the piazza, the 14th-century **Loggia dei Lanzi** ★★ (sometimes called the Loggia della Signoria) is a gallery of sculpture that often depicts fierce, violent scenes. The best piece is a rare work by Benvenuto Cellini, the goldsmith and tell-all autobiographer. Critics have said that his exquisite *Perseus,* who holds the severed head of Medusa, is the most significant Florentine sculpture since Michelangelo's *Night* and *Day.*

For a view of the wonders of Florence below and Fiesole above, climb aboard bus no. 13 from the central station and head for **Piazzale Michelangelo** ★, a 19th-century belvedere with a view seen in many a Renaissance painting. It's best at dusk, when the purple-fringed Tuscan hills form a frame for Giotto's bell tower, Brunelleschi's dome, and the towering stones sticking up from the Palazzo Vecchio. Another copy of Michelangelo's *David* dominates the square.

SIGHTSEEING SUGGESTIONS FOR FIRST-TIME VISITORS

If You Have 1 Day You'll have to accept the inevitable—you can only visit a small fraction of Florence's stellar attractions. Go to the **Uffizi Galleries** as soon as they open and concentrate only on some of the masterpieces or your favorite artists. Have lunch on **Piazza della Signoria,** dominated by the Palazzo Vecchio, and admire the statues in the Loggia dei Lanzi. After lunch, visit the **Duomo** and **Baptistery,** before continuing north to see Michelangelo's *David* at the **Accademia.** Next, head back south toward the Arno and the Ponte Vecchio. On the way do a little shopping at the fabled **Mercato Nuovo (Straw Market).** Sunset should find you at the landmark **Ponte Vecchio.** Finish your very busy day with a hearty Tuscan dinner in one of Florence's many *bucas* (cellar restaurants).

If You Have 2 Days On day 2, you can spend the morning visiting the **Bargello** to see some of the Renaissance, including another version of Michelangelo's *David.* A short walk will take you to the **Palazzo Vecchio,** where you can explore the Hall of the 500 to see the Vasari Renaissance frescoes. Then, in the afternoon, visit the **Pitti Palace,** on the other side of the Arno, and wander through the Galleria Palatina, with its 16th- and 17th-century masterpieces, including 11 works by Raphael alone. After a visit, stroll through the adjoining **Boboli Gardens.** At sunset, go again to the Duomo and the Baptistery for a much better look.

If You Have 3 Days In the morning of day 3, head for the **Medici Chapels** adjacent to the Basilica of San Lorenzo. Look especially for

Michelangelo's figures of *Dawn* and *Dusk*. Later in the morning you can go to the **Museo di San Marco,** a small museum that's a monument to the work of Fra Angelico. After lunch, visit the **Museo dell'Opera del Duomo,** with its sculptural masterpieces from the Duomo, including Donatello's *Mary Magdalene.*

If You Have 4 Days or More On day 4, begin with a morning visit to the **Palazzo Medici-Riccardi,** near the Duomo, to view the mid-15th-century frescoes by Benozzo Gozzoli in the Medici Chapel. Later that morning pop into **Santa Maria Novella,** one of Florence's most distinguished churches, with its Gondi Chapel containing Brunelleschi's wooden Christ on the Cross. Before it closes at 6:30pm, call at the **Basilica di Santa Croce,** with its two restored chapels by Giotto. On day 5, leave Florence, as fascinating as it is, and head south to yet another fascinating art city, **Siena,** the most important of the Tuscan hill towns.

THE TOP MUSEUMS

Galleria degli Uffizi ✶✶✶ This is one of the world's outstanding museums and Italy's finest collection of art. The Uffizi is nicely grouped into periods or schools to show the progress of Italian and European art. The Botticelli rooms contain his finest works, including *The Birth of Venus.* In another room you'll see Leonardo da Vinci's unfinished but brilliant *Adoration of the Magi* and Verrocchio's *Baptism of Christ,* not a very important painting but noted because Leonardo painted one of the angels when he was 14. Also in this salon hangs Leonardo's *Annunciation.* In the rooms that follow are works by Perugino, Dürer, Mantegna, Bellini, Giorgione, and Correggio. Finally, you can view Michelangelo's *Holy Family,* as well as Raphael's *Madonna of the Goldfinch.*

Piazzale degli Uffizi 6. ✆ 055-23885. www.uffizi.firenze.it. Admission 8.05€. Tues–Sun 8:15am–7pm (last entrance 45 min. before closing). Bus: A, B, 23, or 71.

Galleria dell'Accademia ✶✶ This museum boasts many paintings and sculptures, but they're completely overshadowed by one work: Michelangelo's colossal ***David*** ✶✶✶, unveiled in 1504. It first stood in Piazza della Signoria but was moved to the Accademia in 1873 and placed beneath the rotunda of a room built exclusively for its display. When he began work, Michelangelo was just 29. In the connecting picture gallery is a collection of Tuscan masters, such as Botticelli, and Umbrian works by Perugino (teacher of Raphael).

Via Ricasoll 60. ✆ 055-2388609. Admission 8.50€. Tues–Sun 8:15am–6:20pm. Bus: B, D, or 12.

Palazzo Pitti and Giardini di Boboli (Boboli Gardens) ✶✶ The Pitti, built in the mid–15th century (Brunelleschi was the original architect), was once the residence of the powerful Medici family. Today it contains several museums, the most important of which is the **Galleria Palatina** ✶✶, a repository of old masters. This gallery houses one of Europe's great art collections, with masterpieces hung one on top of the other, as in the days of the Enlightenment. In the **Sala di Saturno,** look for Raphael's *Madonna of the Canopy* and *Madonna of the Chair,* his best-known interpretation of the Virgin.

Other museums are the **Appartamenti Reali,** which the Medici family once called home; the **Museo degli Argenti** (✆ 055-294883), 16 rooms devoted to displays of the "loot" acquired by the Medici dukes; the **Coach and Carriage Museum;** the **Galleria d'Arte Moderna** (✆ 055-2388601); the **Museo delle Porcellane** (porcelain); and the **Galleria del Costume.**

> **Tips Reserving Tickets for the Uffizi & Other Museums**
>
> Finally, you can bypass the hours-long ticket line at the **Uffizi Galleries** by reserving a ticket and an entry time in advance for a 1.50€ fee by calling ℭ **055-294883** or going to **www.arca.net/uffizi**. By March, entry times can already be booked up over a week in advance. You can also reserve for the **Accademia Gallery** (another interminable line), as well as the **Galleria Palatina** in the Pitti Palace and the **Bargello** (you don't really need it for those last two) and several others. There's a nominal fee (worth every penny).

Behind the Pitti Palace are the **Boboli Gardens** ⊛, Piazza de'Pitti 1 (ℭ **055-2651838**), through which the Medici romped. The gardens were laid out in the 16th century by the great landscape artist, Triboli. The Boboli is ever popular for a promenade or an idyllic interlude in a pleasant setting. The gardens are filled with fountains and statuary, such as a Giambologna *Venus* in the "Grotto" of Buontalenti. You can climb to the top of the Fortezza di Belvedere for a dazzling city view.

Piazza Pitti, across the Arno. ℭ 055-2388611. Palatina 8.50€; Modern Art Gallery 5€; 4€ for both Argenti and Boboli Gardens. Galleria Palatina and Appartamenti Reali Tues–Sun 8:15am–6:45pm. Museo degli Argenti and Modern Art Gallery daily 8:30am–1:30pm; closed the 1st, 3rd, and 5th Mon and the 2nd and 4th Sun of each month. Boboli Gardens June–Sept daily 8:30am–7:45pm; Apr–May and Oct daily 8:30am–6:45pm; Nov–Mar daily 9am–5:45pm; closed the 1st and last Mon of each month. Ticket office closes 1 hr. before the gardens. Bus: D, 11, 36, 37, or 68.

Cappelle dei Medici (Medici Chapels) ⊛⊛

The Medici tombs are adjacent to the Basilica of San Lorenzo (see "Other Churches," below). Working from 1521 to 1534, Michelangelo created the Medici tomb in a style that foreshadowed the baroque. Lorenzo the Magnificent was buried near Michelangelo's uncompleted *Madonna and Child* group. Ironically, the finest groups of sculpture were reserved for two Medici "clan" members, who (in the words of Mary McCarthy) "would better have been forgotten." They're represented as armored, idealized princes. The other two figures on Lorenzo's tomb are most often called *Dawn* (represented as woman) and *Dusk* (as man). The best-known figures are *Night* (chiseled as a woman in troubled sleep) and *Day* (a man of strength awakening to a foreboding world) at the feet of Giuliano, the duke of Nemours.

Piazza Madonna degli Aldobrandini 6. ℭ 055-294883. Admission 5.50€. Tues–Sun 8:15am–4:30pm; Sun 8:30am–1:50pm. Closed 2nd and 4th Sun, and 1st, 3rd, 5th Mon of each month.

Museo Nazionale del Bargello ⊛⊛⊛

The National Museum, a short walk from Piazza della Signoria, is a 13th-century fortress palace whose dark underground chambers once resounded with the cries of the tortured. Today it's a vast repository of some of the most important Renaissance sculpture, including works by Michelangelo and Donatello. Here you'll see another Michelangelo *David* (formerly referred to as *Apollo*), chiseled perhaps 25 to 30 years after the figure in the Accademia. The Bargello *David* is totally different—even effete when compared to its stronger brother. Among the more significant sculptures is Giambologna's *Winged Mercury.* The Bargello displays two versions of Donatello's *John the Baptist.* Look for two more *Davids*—Donatello's and Verrocchio's. The Bargello contains a large number of terra-cotta works by the della Robbia clan.

Via del Proconsolo 4. ℭ 055-294883. Admission 5€. Daily 8:30am–1:50pm; 2nd and 4th Sun and 1st and 3rd Mon of the month 8:30am–1:50pm. Closed Jan 1, May 1, and Christmas. Bus: A, 14, or 23.

Museo di San Marco ★★★   This state museum is a handsome Renaissance palace whose cell walls are decorated with 15th-century frescoes by the mystical Fra Angelico. In the days of Cosimo dei Medici, San Marco was built as a Dominican convent. It originally contained bleak, bare cells, which Angelico and his students then brightened considerably. One of his better-known paintings here is *The Last Judgment,* which depicts people with angels on the left dancing in a circle and lordly saints towering overhead. On the second floor— at the top of the hall—is Angelico's masterpiece, *The Annunciation.*

Piazza San Marco 1. ℂ 055-294883. Admission 4.15€. Tues–Sun 8:30am–1:50pm. Ticket office closes 30 min. before the museum. Closed 1st, 3rd, and 5th Mon of the month; 2nd and 4th Sun of the month; Jan 1, May 1, and Christmas. Bus: 1, 6, 7, 10, 11, 17, or 20.

THE DUOMO, CAMPANILE & BAPTISTERY
Cattedrale di Santa Maria del Fiore (Duomo) ★★★   The Duomo, graced by Brunelleschi's dome, is the crowning glory of Florence. But don't rush inside too quickly, as the view of the exterior, with its geometrically patterned bands of white, pink, and green marble, is, along with the dome, the best feature. One of the world's largest churches, the Duomo represents the flowering of the "Florentine Gothic" style. Begun in 1296, it was finally consecrated in 1436, yet finishing touches on the facade were applied as late as the 19th century.

Inside, the overall effect is bleak, except when you stand under the cupola, frescoed in part by Vasari. Some of the stained-glass windows in the dome were based on designs by Donatello (Brunelleschi's friend) and Ghiberti (Brunelleschi's rival). If you resist scaling Giotto's bell tower (below), you may want to climb Brunelleschi's ribbed dome. The view is well worth the trek.

Piazza del Duomo. ℂ 055-2302885. Cathedral free; excavations 3€; cupola 6€. Mon–Fri 8:30am–6:30pm; Sat 8:30am–5pm. Bus: 1, 6, 17.

Campanile (Giotto's Bell Tower) ★★★   Giotto left to posterity the most beautiful campanile (bell tower) in Europe, rhythmic in line and form. The 84m (274-ft.) tower, a "Tuscanized" Gothic, with bands of colored marble, can be scaled for a panorama of the sienna-colored city. The view will surely rank among your most memorable—it encompasses the enveloping hills and Medici villas.

Piazza del Duomo. ℂ 055-2302885. Admission 6€. Daily 8:30am–6:50pm. Closed Jan 1, Easter, Sept 8, and Christmas. Bus: 1, 6, 17.

Battistero San Giovanni (Baptistery) ★★★   Named after the city's patron saint, Giovanni (John the Baptist), the present octagonal Battistero dates from the 11th and 12th centuries. The oldest structure in Florence, the baptistery is a highly original interpretation of the Romanesque style, with its bands of pink, white, and green marble. Visitors from all over the world come to gape at its three sets of bronze doors. The east door is a copy; the other two are originals. In his work on two sets of doors, Lorenzo Ghiberti reached the pinnacle of his artistry in *quattrocento* Florence. The gilt panels—representing scenes from the New Testament, including the *Annunciation,* the *Adoration,* and Christ debating the elders in the temple—make up a flowing, rhythmic narration in bronze.

Piazza San Giovanni. ℂ 055-2302885. Admission 3€. Oct–June daily 8:30am–7pm; July–Sept daily 12:30–7pm. Bus: 1, 6, 17.

OTHER CHURCHES
Basilica di San Lorenzo ★★★   This is Brunelleschi's 15th-century Renaissance church, where the Medici used to attend services from their nearby palace on Via Larga, now Via Camillo Cavour. Most visitors flock to see Michelangelo's

Medici Chapels (see "The Top Museums," above), but Brunelleschi's handiwork deserves some time, too. Built in the style of a Latin cross, the church is distinguished by harmonious grays and rows of Corinthian columns.

Biblioteca Medicea Laurenziana ✦✦ (✆ 055-210760) is entered separately at Piazza San Lorenzo 9 and was designed by Michelangelo to shelter the expanding library of the Medici. Beautiful in design and concept, and approached by exquisite stairs, the library is filled with some of Italy's greatest manuscripts—many of which are handsomely illustrated. Hours are Monday through Saturday from 9am to 1pm. Admission is free; the only time you'll be charged is if there's a special exhibition.

Piazza San Lorenzo. ✆ 055-214443. Free admission; 2.60€ for special exhibitions. Fri–Mon and Tues–Thurs 10am–5pm. Bus: 1, 6, 7, 11, 17, 33, 67, or 68.

Basilica di Santa Croce ✦✦ The Pantheon of Florence, this church shelters tombs or monuments of everyone from Michelangelo to Machiavelli, from Dante to Galileo. Santa Croce was the church of the Franciscans. In the right nave (1st tomb) is the Vasari-executed monument to Michelangelo, whose body was smuggled back to his native Florence from its original burial place in Rome. The Trecento frescoes are reason enough for visiting Santa Croce—especially those by Giotto to the right of the main chapel.

Piazza Santa Croce 16. ✆ 055-244619. Church free; cloisters and church museum 4€. Church Mon–Sat 9am–5:30pm, Sun 1–5:30pm. Museum and cloisters Thurs–Tues 9am–5:30pm. Bus: B, 13, 23, or 71.

Basilica di Santa Maria Novella ✦✦ Near the railway station is one of Florence's most distinguished churches, begun in 1278 for the Dominicans. Its geometric facade, with bands of white and green marble, was designed in the late 15th century by Leon Battista Alberti, an aristocrat and true Renaissance man. The church borrows from and harmonizes the Romanesque, Gothic, and Renaissance styles. In the left nave as you enter (the 3rd large painting) is Masaccio's *Trinity,* a curious work that has the architectural form of a Renaissance stage setting, but whose figures—in perfect perspective—are like actors in a Greek tragedy. Head straight up the left nave to the Gondi Chapel for a look at Brunelleschi's wooden *Christ on the Cross,* said to have been carved to compete with Donatello's same subject in Santa Croce.

Piazza Santa Maria Novella. ✆ 055-215918. Church free; Spanish Chapel and cloisters 2.60€. Church Mon–Fri 7am–noon and 3–6pm. Spanish Chapel and cloisters Sat–Thurs 8am–2pm. Bus: A, 6, 9, 11, 36, 37, or 68.

PALACES

Palazzo Vecchio ✦✦✦ The secular "Old Palace" is without doubt the most famous and imposing palace in Florence. It dates from the closing years of the 13th century. Its remarkable architectural feature is its 94m (308-ft.) tower. Once home to the Medici, the Palazzo Vecchio is occupied today by city employees, but much of it is open to the public. The 16th-century Dei Cinquecento (Hall of the 500), the most outstanding part of the palace, is filled with Vasari and Co. frescoes as well as sculpture. As you enter the hall, look for Michelangelo's *Victory.* Later you can stroll through the apartments and main halls. You can also visit the private apartments of Eleanor of Toledo, wife of Cosimo I, and a chapel that was begun in 1540 and frescoed by Bronzino.

Piazza della Signoria. ✆ 055-2768325. Admission 6€. Mon–Wed and Fri–Sun 9am–7pm; Thurs 9am–2pm. July 15–Sept 15 Mon and Fri 9am–11pm. Ticket office closes 1 hr. before palace. Bus: A, B, 23, or 71.

Palazzo Medici-Riccardi ✦✦ A short walk from the Duomo, this 15th-century palace was the home of Cosimo dei Medici before he took his household to the Palazzo Vecchio. The brown stone building was also the scene, at times, of the court of Lorenzo the Magnificent. Art lovers visit today chiefly to see the Chapel of the Magi with its mid-15th-century frescoes by Benozzo Gozzoli, which depict the *Journey of the Magi.*

Via Camillo Cavour 1. ⟨⟩ 055-2760340. Admission 4€. Thurs–Tues 9am–7pm. Bus: 1, 6, 7, 11, 17, 67, or 68.

OTHER MUSEUMS

Museo Archeologico ⟨⟩ The Archaeological Museum, a short walk from Piazza della Santissima Annunziata, houses one of Europe's most outstanding Egyptian and Etruscan collections. Egyptian mummies and sarcophagi are on the first floor, along with Etruscan works. Pause to look at the lid of the coffin of a fat Etruscan. Look for the bronze Chimera, a lion with a goat sticking out of its back, a masterpiece of Etruscan art.

Via della Colonna 38. ⟨⟩ 055-23575. Admission 4€. Nov–Aug Mon 2–7pm; Tues–Fri 9am–7pm; Sat–Sun 9am–2pm. Sept also Sat 9pm–midnight. Bus: 6, 31, or 32.

Museo dell'Opera del Duomo ⟨⟩ Museo dell'Opera del Duomo, behind the cathedral, is beloved by connoisseurs of Renaissance sculptural works. It shelters the sculpture removed from the campanile and the Duomo. A major attraction of this museum is Michelangelo's unfinished *Pietà,* carved between 1548 and 1555 when the artist was in his seventies. Also look for the marble choirs *(cantorie)* of Donatello and Luca della Robbia. The Luca della Robbia choir is more restrained, but it still "praises the Lord" in marble—with clashing cymbals and sounding brass that constitute a reaffirmation of life.

Piazza del Duomo 9. ⟨⟩ 055-2302885. Admission 5€. Mon–Sat 9:30am–6:30pm; Sun 9am–1pm.

THE SHOPPING SCENE

Skilled craftsmanship and traditional design unchanged since the days of the Medici have made Florence a destination for serious shoppers. Florence is noted for its hand-tooled **leather goods** and its **straw merchandise,** as well as superbly crafted **gold jewelry.** Its reputation for fashionable custom-made clothes is no longer what it was, having lost its position of supremacy to Milan.

Florence is not a city for bargain shopping. Most visitors interested in gold or silver jewelry head for the **Ponte Vecchio** and its tiny shops. It's difficult to tell one from the other, but you really don't need to since the merchandise is similar. If you're looking for a charm or souvenir, these shops are fine. But the heyday of finding gold jewelry bargains on the Ponte Vecchio is long gone.

The street for antiques in Florence is **Via Maggio;** some of the furnishings and objets d'art here are from the 16th century. Another major area for antiques shopping is **Borgo Ognissanti.**

Florence's Fifth Avenue is **Via dei Tornabuoni.** This is the place to head for the best-quality leather goods, the best clothing boutiques, and stylish but costly shoes. Here you'll find everyone from Armani to Ferragamo. You'll find better shops on **Via Vigna Nuova, Via Porta Rossa,** and **Via degli Strozzi,** too. You might also stroll on the Lungarno along the Arno. For some of the best buys in leather, check out **Via del Parione,** a short narrow street of Tornabuoni.

FLORENCE'S FAMOUS MARKETS

After checking into their hotels, the most intrepid shoppers head for **Piazza del Mercato Nuovo (Straw Market),** called "Il Porcellino" by the Italians because of the bronze statue of a reclining wild boar here. Tourists pet its snout (which is well worn) for good luck. The market stands in the monumental heart of Florence, an easy stroll from the Palazzo Vecchio. It sells not only straw items but leather goods as well, along with an array of typically Florentine merchandise—frames, trays, hand embroidery, table linens, and hand-sprayed and painted boxes in traditional designs. Market hours are Monday through Saturday from 9am to 7pm.

However, even better bargains await those who make their way through push-carts to the stalls of the open-air **Mercato Centrale** (also called the Mercato San Lorenzo), in and around Borgo San Lorenzo, near the train station. If you don't mind bargaining, which is imperative here, you'll find an array of merchandise, including raffia bags, Florentine leather purses, salt-and-pepper shakers, straw handbags, and art reproductions.

FLORENCE AFTER DARK

For theatrical and concert listings, pick up a free copy of *Welcome to Florence,* available at the tourist office. This helpful publication contains information on recitals, concerts, theatrical productions, and other cultural presentations.

Many cultural presentations are performed in churches. These might include open-air concerts in the cloisters of the Badia Fiesolana in Fiesole (the hill town above Florence) or at the Ospedale degli Innocenti, the foundling "hospital of the innocents" (on summer evenings only).

THE PERFORMING ARTS

Teatro Comunale di Firenze, Corso Italia 16 (© **055-211158;** bus: B), is the main theater in Florence, with an opera and ballet season presented from September to December, and a concert season from January until April. This is also the venue for the **Maggio Musicale Fiorentino** (www.maggiofiorentino.com), Italy's oldest and most prestigious festival. It takes place from May to July and offers opera, ballet, concerts, recitals, and cinema productions. The box office is open Tuesday through Friday from 10am to 4:30pm, Saturday from 10am to 1pm, and 1 hour before curtain. Tickets are 20€ to 80€. During the Maggio Musicale, tickets usually range from 23€ to 100€.

You'll have to understand Italian to appreciate most of the plays presented at **Teatro della Pergola,** Via della Pergola 18 (© **055-2479651;** bus: 6, 14, or 23). Plays are performed year-round except during the Maggio Musicale, when the theater becomes the setting for the many musical presentations of the festival. Performances are Tuesday through Saturday at 8:45pm and Sunday at 3:45pm. The box office is open October through June Tuesday through Saturday from 9:30am to 1pm and 3:30 to 6:45pm, Sunday from 10am to 12:15pm. In July, it's open Tuesday through Friday from 9:30am to 1pm and 4 to 7pm, Saturday from 10am to 12:30pm, Sunday from 10am to 12:15pm. It's closed in August. Tickets are 12€ to 25€.

MUSIC & DANCE CLUBS

Contained in the cellar of an antique building in the historic heart of town, the well-known **Full-Up,** Via della Vigna Vecchia 23–25R (© **055-293006;** bus: A or 14), attracts college students from the city's many universities, although older clients usually feel at ease, too. One section contains a smallish dance floor and recorded dance music; another is devoted to the somewhat more restrained ambience of a piano bar. Full-Up is open Tuesday through Saturday from 11pm to 4am; no cover.

PUBS & BARS

If you ask whether **Dublin Pub,** Via Faenza 27R (© **055-293049;** bus: 7, 10, 11, 12, 25, 31, or 70), is an Italian pub, the all-Italian staff will respond rather grandly that such a concept doesn't exist, and that pubs are by definition Irish. And once you get beyond the fact that virtually no one on the staff here has ever been outside of Tuscany, and that there's very little to do here except drink and perhaps practice your Italian, you might settle down and have a rollicking old (very Latin) time. Beers, at least, are appropriately Celtic, and include Harp, Guinness, Kilkenny, and Strong's on tap. The pub is near the Santa Maria Novella train station and is open daily from 5pm to 2am (closed 2 weeks in Aug). After an initial success in Rome, **Fiddler's Elbow,** Piazza Santa Maria Novella 7R (© **055-215056;** bus: A), also located near the train station, has now invaded the city of Donatello and Michelangelo. It has quickly become one of the most popular bars in Florence. It's open Monday through Friday from 5pm to 1am, Saturday and Sunday from 2pm to 2am.

ArciGay/Lesbica (aka Azione Gay e Lesbica), Italy's largest and oldest gay organization, has a center in Florence at Via Manara 12 (© **055-671298;** www. azionegayelesbica.it). It's open Monday through Thursday from 6 to 8pm.

A SIDE TRIP TO FIESOLE ⍟

This town, once an Etruscan settlement, is the most popular outing from Florence. Bus no. 7, which leaves from Piazza San Marco, brings you here in 25 minutes and gives you a panoramic view along the way. You'll pass fountains, statuary, and gardens strung out over the hills like pieces of a scrambled jigsaw puzzle.

You won't find anything as dazzling here as the Renaissance treasures of Florence—the charms of Fiesole are more subtle. Fortunately, all major sights branch out within walking distance of the main piazza, beginning with the **Cattedrale di San Romolo** ⍟. Dating from 1000, it was much altered during the Renaissance. In the Salutati Chapel are important sculptural works by Mino da Fiesole. It's open daily from 7:30am to noon and 4 to 7pm.

The ecclesiastical **Bandini Museum,** Via Dupre 1 (© **055-59477**), around to the side of the Duomo, belongs to the Fiesole Cathedral Chapter. On the ground floor are della Robbia terra-cotta works, as well as art by Michelangelo. March through October, hours are daily from 9:30am to 7pm; November through February, Wednesday through Monday from 9:30am to 5pm. Admission is 6€. The ticket is valid 24 hours and includes admission to the Teatro Romano e Museo Civico (see below).

The hardest task you'll have in Fiesole is to take the steep goat-climb up to the **Museo Missionario Francescano Fiesole,** Via San Francesco 13 (© **055-59175**). The church was consecrated in 1516. Inside are many paintings by well-known Florentine artists. In the basement is the ethnological museum. Begun in 1906, the collection has a large section of Chinese artifacts, including ancient bronzes, as well as Etruscan, Roman, and Egyptian objects. Admission is free (donation expected). It's open Tuesday through Friday from 10am to noon and 3 to 5:30pm, Saturday and Sunday from 3 to 7pm in summer (closes at 6pm off season).

On the site of the **Teatro Romano e Museo Civico,** Via Portigiani 1 (© **055-59477**), is the major surviving evidence that Fiesole was an Etruscan city 6 centuries before Christ, then later a Roman town. In the 1st century B.C., a theater was built, the restored remains of which you can see today. Near the theater are the skeleton-like ruins of the baths, which may have been built at the same time. The Etruscan-Roman museum contains many interesting finds that date from the days when Fiesole, not Florence, was supreme (a guide is on hand to show you through). For admission and hours, see the Bandini Museum above.

3 Highlights of the Tuscan & Umbrian Countryside

Rome may rule Italy, but **Tuscany** presides over its heart. The Tuscan landscapes, little changed since the days of the Medicis, look just like Renaissance paintings, with cypress trees, olive groves, evocative hill towns, and those fabled Chianti vineyards.

Tuscany was the place where the Etruscans first appeared in Italy. The Romans followed, absorbing and conquering them, and by the 11th century, the region had evolved into a collection of independent city-states, such as Florence and Siena, each trying to dominate the other. Although the Renaissance was immensely popular in Florence, it was slow to spread into the surrounding region.

When the Renaissance did arrive, however, with its titans of art, like Giotto, Michelangelo, and Leonardo, critics claim that Western civilization was "rediscovered" in Tuscany. According to D. H. Lawrence, Tuscany became "the perfect center of man's universe." Art flourished under the patronage of the powerful Medicis, and the legacy remains through Masaccio, della Francesca, Signorelli, Raphael, Donatello, Botticelli, and countless others. Tuscany also became known for its men of letters, like Dante, Petrarch, and Boccaccio (who wrote in the vernacular rather than in Latin).

Umbria, a small region at the heart of the Italian peninsula, is associated mainly with saints, like St. Francis of Assisi, founder of the Franciscan order, but Umbrian painters (such as Il Perugino) also contributed to the glory of the Renaissance. The landscape is as alluring as that of Tuscany, with fertile plains of olive groves and vineyards.

SIENA ✹✹✹

In Rome you see classicism and the baroque; in Florence, the Renaissance; but in the walled city of Siena you stand solidly planted in the Middle Ages. On three sienna-colored hills in the center of Tuscany, Sena Vetus lies in Chianti country, 34km (21 miles) south of Florence. Preserving its original character more markedly than any other Italian city, it's a showplace of the Italian Gothic.

ESSENTIALS

GETTING THERE   Trains arrive hourly from both Florence and Pisa. **TRAIN,** Piazza San Domenico 1 (© 0577-204245), in Siena, offers bus service to all of Tuscany, with air-conditioned coaches. The one-way fare between Florence and Siena is 6€. Motorists can head south from Florence along the Firenze-Siena autostrada, a superhighway through Poggibonsi linking the cities.

VISITOR INFORMATION   The **tourist information office** is at Piazza del Campo 56 (© 0577-280551), open Monday through Saturday from 8:30am to 7:30pm, Sunday from 9am to 3pm. November through March, hours are Monday through Saturday from 8:30am to 1pm and 3 to 7pm.

Tips Tuscan Tours

If you love to walk or bike, **I Bike Italy** (© 055-2342371 Mon–Fri; www.ibikeitaly.com) books guided bike rides through the countryside from March to November. **Country Walks in Italy** can be booked with the same outfit year-round. If you want to see Italy as did the Romans and the Renaissance *condottieri,* you can book a horseback trek through **Equitours** (© 800/545-0019 in the U.S.; www.ridingtours.com).

Tuscany & Umbria

WHERE TO DINE

Al Marsili (Ristorante Enoteca Gallo Nero) ⭐ SIENESE/ITALIAN   The beautiful Al Marsili is the best in Siena, standing between the Duomo and Via della Città. You dine beneath crisscrossed ceiling vaults whose russet-colored brickwork was designed centuries ago. Specialties include roast boar with tomatoes and herbs, *ribollita* (savory vegetable soup in the Sienese style), spaghetti with a sauce of seasonal mushrooms, and veal scaloppini with tarragon and tomato sauce.

Via del Castoro 3. ℂ 0577-47154. Reservations recommended. Main courses 12€–18€. AE, DC, MC, V. Tues–Sun 12:30–2:30pm and 7:30–10:30pm. Bus: A.

EXPLORING SIENA

Start in the heart of Siena, the shell-shaped **Piazza del Campo (Il Campo)** ⭐⭐⭐, described by Montaigne as "the finest of any city in the world." Pause to enjoy the Fonte Gaia, with embellishments by Jacopo della Quercia (the present sculptured works are reproductions; the badly battered original ones are found in the town hall).

Museo Civico and Torre del Mangia ⭐⭐⭐   The Palazzo Pubblico dates from 1288 to 1309 and is filled with important art works by some of the leaders in the Sienese school of painting and sculpture. Upstairs in the Museo Civico is the **Sala della Pace,** painted from 1337 to 1339 by Ambrogio Lorenzetti, whose allegorical frescoes show the idealized effects of good and bad government. Accessible

Siena

San Francesco

Piazza S. Francesco

Train Station

Piazza Gramsci

Stadio Comunale

Piazza Matteotti

Piazza Salimbeni

Via del Giglio

Via dei Baroncelli

Piazza P. Salvani

Casa di S. Caterina

Palazzo Tolomei

Via Refenero

Via S. Bandini

San Domenico

Loggia di Mercanzia

Via Banchi di Sotto

Palazzo Piccolomini

Piazza del Campo **1**

i

Palazzo Pubblico

Santo Spirito

4 Duomo

3

Museo d. Opera

Palazzo Chigi-Safacini

Piazza del Mercato

Piazza del Duomo

Via del Porrione

Via S. Martino

Porta Romana

2 Pinacoteca Nazionale

Sant' Agostino

Via di Fontanella

Siena • ITALY

★ Rome

Information **i**

Battistero **4**
Duomo **3**
Museo Civico &
    Torre del Mangia **1**
Pinacoteca Nazionale **2**

0   1/8 mile
0   100 meters
N

from the courtyard of the palazzo is the 102m (335-ft.) **Torre del Mangia,** from the 14th century. If you climb the tower, you'll be rewarded with a drop-dead view of the city skyline and Tuscan landscape.

In the Palazzo Pubblico, Piazza del Campo. ✆ **0577-292263.** Admission 6€. Museo and Torre: Apr–Oct daily 10am–7pm; Nov–Mar daily 10am–6:30pm. Bus: A, B, or N.

Il Duomo ✦✦✦   With its bands of colored marble, the Sienese cathedral is an original and exciting building, erected in the Romanesque and Italian Gothic styles during the 12th century. The dramatic facade—designed in part by Giovanni Pisano—dates from the 13th century, as does the Romanesque bell tower. The zebralike interior, with its black-and-white stripes, is equally stunning. The floor consists of various embedded works of art, many of which are roped off to preserve the richness in design, depicting both biblical and mythological subjects. The octagonal 13th-century pulpit is by Nicola Pisano (Giovanni's father), who was one of the most significant Italian sculptors before the dawn of the

Renaissance (see his pulpit in the baptistery at Pisa). The Siena pulpit is his masterpiece; it reveals in relief such scenes as the slaughter of the innocents and the Crucifixion.

Piazza del Duomo, southeast of Piazza del Campo. ✆ 0577-283048. Free admission. Cathedral: Mar 17 to Oct daily 7:30am–7:30pm; the rest of the year, daily 10am–1pm and 2–5pm.

Battistero (Baptistery) ✮
The Gothic facade of the Baptistery, left unfinished by Domenico di Agostino, dates from the 14th century. But you don't come to see that—you come to see the lavish frescoes inside. In the center of the interior is the star of the place, a baptismal font by Jacopo della Quercia that contains some bas-reliefs by Donatello and Ghiberti.

Piazza San Giovanni (behind the Duomo). ✆ 0577-283048. Admission 2€. Mar 16 to Sept daily 9am–7:30pm; Oct daily 9am–6pm; Nov–Mar 15 daily 10am–1pm and 2:30–5pm. Closed Jan 1 and Dec 25.

Pinacoteca Nazionale (Picture Gallery) ✮✮
Housed in the 14th-century Palazzo Buonsignori, the Pinacoteca contains a collection of the Sienese school of painting, which once rivaled that of Florence. Displayed are some of the giants of the pre-Renaissance. The principal treasures are on the second floor, where you'll contemplate the artistry of Duccio. The gallery is rich in the art of the 14th-century Lorenzetti brothers, Ambrogio and Pietro. Ambrogio is represented by an *Annunciation* and a *Crucifix*, but one of his most celebrated works is an almond-eyed *Madonna and Bambino* surrounded by saints and angels. Pietro's most important entry is an altarpiece—*The Madonna of the Carmine*—made for a church in Siena in 1329. Simone Martini's *Madonna and Child* is damaged but still one of the best-known paintings here.

Via San Pietro 29, near Piazza del Campo. ✆ 0577-281161. Admission 4€. Mon 8:30am–1:30pm; Tues–Sat 8:15am–7:15pm.

PISA ✮✮✮
Few buildings in the world have captured imaginations as much as the **Leaning Tower of Pisa,** one of the most instantly recognizable buildings in the world. The Leaning Tower is a landmark powerful enough to entice visitors to call at Pisa, and once here, they find many other sights to explore as well.

ESSENTIALS
GETTING THERE   Trains link Pisa and Florence every hour (trip time: 1 hr.); one-way fare is 4.15€. From Florence, motorists take the autostrada west (A-11) to the intersection (A-12) going south to Pisa.

VISITOR INFORMATION   The **tourist information office** is at Via Carlo Cammeo 2 (✆ 050-560464), open March through October Monday through Saturday from 9am to 7pm; off season, Monday through Saturday from 9am to 6pm. There's another office at Piazza della Stazione (✆ 050-42291), open daily from 9am to 7pm.

WHERE TO DINE
Al Ristoro dei Vecchi Macelli ✮ INTERNATIONAL/PISAN   Near Piazzetta di Vecchi Macelli is the best restaurant in Pisa. After selecting from a choice of two dozen varieties of seafood antipasti, you can enjoy a homemade pasta with scallops and zucchini or fish-stuffed ravioli in shrimp sauce. Other dishes are gnocchi with pesto and shrimp, and roast veal with a velvety truffle-flavored cream sauce.

Via Volturno 49. ✆ 050-20424. Reservations required. Main courses 10€–15€; fixed-price menu 42€. AE, DC, MC, V. Thurs–Sun noon–3pm and 8–10:30pm. Bus: 1.

SEEING THE SIGHTS

In the Middle Ages, Pisa reached the apex of its power as a maritime republic before it eventually fell to its rivals, Florence and Genoa. Its greatest legacy remains at **Piazza del Duomo** ★★★, which D'Annunzio labeled Piazza dei Miracoli (miracles). Here you'll find an ensemble of the top three attractions—original "Pisan-Romanesque" buildings, including the Duomo, the Baptistery, and the Leaning Tower itself.

La Torre di Pisa (Leaning Tower) ★★★ Construction of this eight-story campanile began in 1174 by Bonanno, and a persistent legend is that the architect deliberately intended the bell tower to lean (that claim is undocumented). Another legend is that Galileo let objects of different weights fall from the tower, then timed their descent to prove his theories on bodies in motion. The tower floats on a sandy base of water-soaked clay; it leans at least 5m (16 ft.) from perpendicular. If it stood up straight, the tower would measure about 56m (185 ft.) tall. In 1990, the government closed the Tower and began measures to keep it from falling. The tower was reopened in 2001 to guided tours (see "Climbing the Leaning Tower," below).

Piazza del Duomo 17. ✆ 050-560547. Phone for reservation, fax 050-560505, or use the Web at www. duomo.pisa.it. Admission 15€. Only a group of 30 admitted at a time. Open daily 9am–4:20pm.

Il Duomo ★★ Dating from 1063, the Duomo was designed by Buschetto, though Rainaldo in the 13th century erected the unusual facade with its four layers of open-air arches that diminish in size as they ascend. The cathedral is marked by three bronze doors—rhythmic in line—that replaced those destroyed in a fire in 1596. In the restored interior, the chief art treasure is the pulpit by Giovanni Pisano, finished in 1310. There are other treasures, too: Galileo's lamp (according to unreliable tradition, the Pisa-born astronomer used the chandelier to formulate his laws of the pendulum); mosaics in the apse said to have been designed by Cimabue; the tomb of Henry VII of Luxembourg; *St. Agnes* by Andrea del Sarto; *Descent from the Cross* by Il Sodoma; and a Crucifix by Giambologna.

Piazza del Duomo 17. ✆ **050-560547.** Admission 2€. Mar–Oct Mon–Sat 10am–12:45pm and 1–4:45pm. Sightseeing visits are discouraged during Mass and religious rites. Bus: 1.

Battistero (Baptistery) ★★★ Begun in 1153, the Baptistery is like a Romanesque crown. Although it's most beautiful on the exterior, with its arches and columns, venture inside to see the hexagonal pulpit made by Nicola Pisano in 1260. Supported by pillars resting on the backs of three marble lions, the pulpit contains bas-reliefs of the Crucifixion, the Adoration of the Magi, the Presentation

---

⌐Tips Climbing the Leaning Tower

Late in 2001, the **Leaning Tower** reopened to guided tours of up to 30 visitors each. The 40-minute tour takes you up a narrow, winding, 294-step staircase to the summit. As the number of visitors is strictly limited, it is strongly suggested you purchase tickets in advance. Reservations are available via e-mail (primaziale@sirius.pisa.it) and may be available through the Tower's website **(http://torre.duomo.pisa.it)**. For up-to-date information, check with the **Italian Government Tourist Board (www.italiantourism. com), www.pisaonline.it**, or the very useful Unofficial Leaning Tower of Pisa website **(www.endex.com/gf/buildings/ltpisa/ltpisa.html)**.

of the Christ Child at the Temple, and the Last Judgment (many angels have lost their heads over the years).

Piazza del Duomo. ℂ **050-560547**. Admission 5€. Apr–Sept daily 8am–8pm; Oct–Mar daily 9am–5pm. Closed Dec 25–Jan 1. Bus: 1.

Museo Nazionale di San Matteo ★★   Near Piazza Mazzini, the National Museum contains a good assortment of paintings and sculpture, many dating from the 13th century to the 16th century. In the museum are statues by Giovanni Pisano; Simone Martini's *Madonna and Child with Saints,* a polyptych; Nino Pisano's *Madonna de Latte,* a marble sculpture; Masaccio's *St. Paul,* painted in 1426; Domenico Ghirlandaio's two *Madonna and Saints* depictions; works by Strozzi and Alessandro Magnasco; and old copies of works by Jan and Pieter Bruegel.

Piazza San Matteo 1 (near Piazza Mazzini). ℂ **050-541865**. Admission 4€. Tues–Sat 8:30am–7:30pm; Sun 8:30am–1pm. Bus: 1.

SAN GIMIGNANO ★★★
The golden lily of the Middle Ages is called the Manhattan of Tuscany since it preserves 13 of its noble towers, giving it a skyscraper skyline. It lies 42km (26 miles) northwest of Siena and 55km (34 miles) southwest of Florence. Since you'll want to spend as much time here as possible, an overnight stay is recommended.

ESSENTIALS
GETTING THERE   Poggibonsi, serviced by regular trains from Florence and Siena, is the **rail** station nearest to San Gimignano. At Poggibonsi, buses depart from in front of the station at frequent intervals to the center of San Gimignano. For information, call ℂ **0577-204111. Buses** operated by **TRA-IN** (ℂ **0577-204111**) service San Gimignano from Florence with a change at Poggibonsi (trip time: 75 min.). The same company also operates service from Siena, with a change at Poggibonsi (50 min.). In San Gimignano, buses stop at Piazzale Montemaggio, outside Porta San Giovanni, the southern gate. You'll have to walk into the center, as vehicles aren't allowed in most of the town's core.

If you've got a **car,** leave Florence (trip time: 1½ hr.) or Siena (1¼ hr.) by the Firenze–Siena autostrada and drive to Poggibonsi, where you'll need to cut west along a secondary route (S324) to San Gimignano.

VISITOR INFORMATION   Go to **Associazione Pro Loco,** Piazza del Duomo 1 (ℂ **0577-940008;** www.sangimignano.com), open November through February daily from 9am to 1pm and 2 to 6pm (Mar–Oct to 7pm).

WHERE TO STAY
Hotel Bel Soggiorno *Value*   Though it's no longer the town's best, this hotel is still a good affordable alternative. The Gigli family has run it since 1886 (there's not as much antique charm as you'd think, though). The rear guest rooms and dining room open onto the lower pastureland and the bottom of the village. The medium-size rooms have beds verging on the over-soft, but the management is quite friendly. The best 10 rooms are those with private balconies. All the tiled bathrooms have tub/shower combos. In summer you'll be asked to have your meals at the hotel (the cuisine is excellent). Medieval in style, the dining room boasts murals depicting a wild boat hunt (see "Where to Dine," below).

Via San Giovanni 91, 53037 San Gimignano. ℂ **0577-940375**. Fax 0577-907521. www.hotelbelsoggiorno. it. 22 units. 94€ double; 170€ suite. AE, DC, MC, V. Parking 10€. Closed Jan–Feb. **Amenities:** Restaurant; bar; wine cellar; laundry. *In room:* A/C, TV, minibar, hair dryer.

Relais Santa Chiara ⭐ This solid, comfortable hotel lies in a residential neighborhood about a 10-minute walk south of the medieval ramparts. It's the most prestigious place to stay. It's surrounded with elegant gardens and a pool, and its spacious public rooms contain Florentine terra-cotta floors and mosaics. Though the hotel is relatively new, the furnishings and ambience blend harmoniously with the Tuscan countryside. Each unit comes with a well-organized private bathroom with tub and shower.

Via Matteotti 15, 53037 San Gimignano. ℂ 0577-940701. Fax 0577-942096. www.rsc.it. 41 units (some with shower only). 134€–215€ double; 186€–255€ suite. Rates include buffet breakfast. AE, DC, MC, V. Free parking. **Amenities:** Restaurant; bar; pool; gym; sauna; room service; babysitting; laundry/dry cleaning. *In room:* A/C, TV, minibar, hair dryer, safe.

WHERE TO DINE

Ristorante Bel Soggiorno TUSCAN Thanks to windows overlooking the countryside and a devoted use of fresh ingredients from nearby farms, you'll get a strong sense of Tuscany's agrarian bounty here. Two of the most appealing specialties (available only late summer to late winter) are roasted wild boar with red wine and mixed vegetables, and pappardelle pasta garnished with a savory ragout of pheasant.

In the Hotel Bel Soggiorno, Via San Giovanni 91. ℂ **0577-940375**. Reservations recommended. Main courses 14€–16€; fixed-price menu 36€. AE, DC, MC, V. Thurs–Tues 12:30–2:30pm and 7:30–10pm.

Ristorante Le Terrazze TUSCAN The newer of this restaurant's two dining rooms has large windows overlooking the old town and the Val d'Elsa. The setting is one of a country inn, and the food features an assortment of produce from the surrounding farms. Soups and pastas make fine beginnings, and specialties of the house include delectable items like sliced filet of wild boar with polenta and Chianti, breast of goose with walnut sauce, *vitello alla Cisterna* (veal with buttered beans), and Florence-style steaks.

In La Cisterna, Piazza della Cisterna 24. ℂ **0577-940328**. Reservations required. Main courses 13€–19€. AE, DC, MC, V. Wed 7:30–10pm; Thurs–Mon 12:30–2:30pm and 7:30–9:30pm. Closed Jan 7–Mar 10.

EXPLORING THE TOWN

In the town center is the palazzo-flanked **Piazza della Cisterna** ⭐⭐, so named because of the 13th-century cistern in its heart. Connected with the irregularly shaped square is its satellite, **Piazza del Duomo** ⭐⭐, whose medieval architecture—towers and palaces—is almost unchanged. It's the most beautiful spot in town. On the square, the **Palazzo del Popolo's Torre Grossa** ⭐, at 54m (178 ft.), is believed to have been the tallest "skyscraper" in town.

Note: A combination ticket, available at any of the sites below, allows admission to all of them for 10€.

Duomo Collegiata o Basilica di Santa Maria Assunta ⭐ Residents of San Gimignano still call this a Duomo (cathedral), even though it was demoted to a "Collegiata" once the town lost its bishop. Plain and austere on the outside, it's richly decorated inside. Retreat inside to a world of tiger-striped arches and a galaxy of gold stars. Head for the north aisle, where in the 1360s Bartolo di Fredi depicted scenes from the Old Testament. Two memorable ones are *The Trials of Job* and *Noah with the Animals*. In the right aisle, panels trace scenes from the life of Christ—the Kiss of Judas, the Last Supper, the Flagellation, and the Crucifixion. The chief attraction is the **Chapel of Santa Fina,** designed by Giuliano and Benedetto da Maiano. Michelangelo's fresco teacher, Domenico Ghirlandaio, frescoed it with scenes from the life of a local girl, Fina, who became the town's patron saint.

Piazza del Duomo. ℂ **0577-940316.** Church free; chapel 3.50€ adults, free for children 5 and under. Mar–Oct daily 9:30am–7pm; Nov–Feb Mon–Sat 9:30am–5pm and Sun 1–5pm.

Museo Civico (Civic Museum) ✪   This museum is installed upstairs in the Palazzo del Popolo (town hall). Most notable is the **Sala di Dante,** where the White Guelph–supporting poet spoke out for his cause in 1300. Look for one of the masterpieces of San Gimignano—the *Maestà* (Madonna enthroned) by Lippo Memmi (later touched up by Gozzoli). The first large room upstairs contains another masterpiece: a *Madonna in Glory,* with Sts. Gregory and Benedict, painted by Pinturicchio. On the other side of it are two depictions of the *Annunciation* by Filippino Lippi.

Passing through the Museo Civico, you can scale the **Torre Grossa** and be rewarded with a bird's-eye view of this most remarkable town. The tower, the only one in town you can climb, is open March through October daily from 9:30am to 7:30pm; off season, daily from 10am to 5:30pm. Admission is 4€.

In the Palazzo Pubblico, Piazza del Campo. ℂ **0577-292263.** Admission 6.50€. Mid-Mar to Oct daily 10am–7pm; Nov to mid-Mar daily 10am–5pm. Bus: A, B, or N.

ASSISI ✪✪✪
Ideally placed on the rise to Mount Subasio, watched over by the medieval **Rocca Maggiore,** this purple-fringed Umbrian hill town retains a mystical air. The site of many a pilgrimage, Assisi is forever linked in legend with its native son, St. Francis. The gentle saint founded the Franciscan order and shares honors with St. Catherine of Siena as the patron saint of Italy. But he's remembered by many, even non-Christians, as a lover of nature (his preaching to an audience of birds is one of the legends of his life). Dante compared him to John the Baptist. St. Francis put Assisi on the map, and making a pilgrimage here is one of the highlights of a visit to Umbria.

ESSENTIALS
GETTING THERE   Although there's no rail station in Assisi, the town, which lies 177km (110 miles) north of Rome and 24km (15 miles) southeast of Perugia, is but a 30-minute bus or taxi ride from the nearby Santa Maria degli Angeli rail station. Buses depart at 30-minute intervals for Piazza Matteotti, in the heart of Assisi. **Trains** between Florence and Assisi usually require a transfer at Terontola. Frequent **buses** connect Perugia with Assisi (trip time: 1 hr.). One bus a day arrives from Rome. Two buses pull in from Florence (2½ hr.).

If you have a **car,** you can be in Assisi in 30 minutes from Perugia by taking S3 southwest. At the junction of Route 147, just follow the signs toward Assisi. But you'll have to park outside the town's core, as it's usually closed to traffic.

VISITOR INFORMATION   The **tourist office** is at Piazza del Comune 12 (ℂ **075-812534**), open Monday through Friday from 8am to 2pm and 3:30 to 6:30pm, Saturday from 9am to 1pm and 3:30 to 6:30pm, and Sunday from 9am to 1pm. The office is closed December 25 and January 1.

WHERE TO STAY
Space in Assisi tends to be tight, so reservations are vital. For such a small town, however, it has a good number of accommodations.

Albergo Ristorante del Viaggiatore *Value*   This ancient town house is among the tops for value. It's been totally renovated, though the stone walls and arched entryways of the lobby hint at its age. The high-ceilinged rooms are spacious and very contemporary, with shower-only bathrooms.

Assisti

ITALY
Florence •
Rome ★

Information ⓘ

1/8 mile
100 meters

Basilica di San Francesco 1
Basilica di Santa Chiara 5
Duomo di San Rufino 4
Prisons' Hermitage 6
Rocca Maggiore 2
Temple of Minerva 3

Via San Antonio 14, 06081 Assisi. © 075-816297 or 075-812424. Fax 075-813051. 16 units (showers only). 69€ double. Half-board 50€ per person. Rates include breakfast. DC, MC, V. **Amenities:** Restaurant; bar. *In room:* A/C, TV, hair dryer.

Hotel dei Priori   Opened in 1923, this hotel keeps up with the times. It occupies one of the town's most historic buildings, the 17th-century Palazzo Nepis. A homelike, somewhat old-fashioned Umbrian atmosphere prevails. Marble staircases and floors, terra-cotta vaulted ceilings, and stone-arched doorways remain from its seigniorial palazzo heyday. Many of the rooms are a bit small, however. Most of the tiled private bathrooms contain tubs; others have showers.

Corso Mazzini 15, 06081 Assisi. © 075-812237. Fax 075-816804. www.assisihotel.net. 34 units. 101€–190€ double; 150€–170€ suite. Rates include breakfast. AE, DC, MC, V. Parking 10€ nearby. **Amenities:** Restaurant (only for hotel guests; closed Nov–Mar); bar; room service; babysitting; laundry/dry cleaning. *In room:* A/C, TV, minibar, hair dryer, safe.

Hotel Sole   For Umbrian hospitality and a general down-home feeling, the Sole is a winner in the heart of medieval Assisi—comfortable but traditional, a bit tattered but affordable. Rooms are rather basic and feature aging bathrooms, half with tub, half with shower. We prefer the rooms in the 15th-century palazzo as opposed to those in the more sterile and nondescript annex, although the latter is serviced by an elevator.

Corso Mazzini 35, 06081 Assisi. © 075-812373 or 075-812922. Fax 075-813706. www.italyhotels.it. 38 units (showers only). 62€ double; 83€ triple. Half-board (Apr–Nov) 50€ per person. AE, DC, MC, V. **Amenities:** Well-recommended restaurant (closed Dec–Mar); bar; room service. *In room:* TV, coffeemaker, safe.

WHERE TO DINE

Il Medioevo 🕭 UMBRIAN/INTERNATIONAL   Assisi's best restaurant is an authentic medieval gem. Alberto Falsinotti and his family prepare superb versions of Umbrian recipes whose origins are as old as Assisi itself. Specialties are *tortelloni* (a kind of dumpling) stuffed with minced turkey, veal, and beef and served with butter and Parmigiano Reggiano; gnocchi stuffed with ricotta and spinach and sprinkled with Parmigiano Reggiano; roasted rabbit with red-wine sauce and truffles; roast lamb with rosemary, potatoes, and herbs; homemade pasta stuffed with black truffles; and grilled filet of veal with herb sauce.

Via Arco dei Priori 4B. © 075-813068. Reservations recommended. Main courses 9€–14€. AE, DC, MC, V. Thurs–Tues noon–2:30pm and 7:30–10pm. Closed Jan 7–Feb 7 and July 1–20.

Ristorante Buca di San Francesco UMBRIAN/ITALIAN   Hospitable and evocative of the Middle Ages, this restaurant occupies a cave near the foundation of a 12th-century palace. There're about 100 seats in the dining room and another 60 in the garden, overlooking Assisi's historic center. Menu items change frequently, but what you're likely to find are spaghetti *alla buca* (with exotic mushrooms and meat sauce); *umbricelli* (big noodles) with asparagus sauce; *cannelloni* (stuffed pasta tubes baked in the oven) with ricotta, spinach, and tomatoes; *carlacca* (baked crepes stuffed with cheese, prosciutto, and roasted veal); and *piccione alla sisana* (roasted pigeon with olive oil, capers, and aromatic herbs).

Via Brizi 1. © 075-812204. Reservations recommended. Main courses 8.50€–16€. AE, DC, MC, V. Tues–Sun noon–2:30pm and 7–10pm. Closed July 1–15.

EXPLORING THE TOWN

In the heart of Assisi, **Piazza del Comune** 🕭 is a dream for a lover of architecture from the 12th century to the 14th century. On the square is a pagan structure, with six Corinthian columns, called the **Tempio di Minerva (Temple of Minerva)** 🕭, from the 1st century B.C. With Minerva-like wisdom, the people of Assisi turned it into a baroque church inside so as not to offend the devout. Adjoining the temple is the 13th-century **Torre (Tower)**, built by Ghibelline supporters. The site is open daily from 7am to noon and 2:30pm to dusk. In the wake of the earthquakes, the tower can no longer be visited.

Basilica di San Francesco ✮✮✮   This great basilica, with both an upper and a lower church, houses some of the most important cycles of frescoes in Italy, including works by such pre-Renaissance giants as Cimabue and Giotto. The basilica and its paintings form the most significant monument to St. Francis. Disaster struck in 1997 when a series of devastating earthquakes hit Umbria, causing much damage. After a major restoration effort, involving some of Europe's greatest restorers, the basilica reopened to the public late in 1999.

Giotto's most celebrated frescoes, St. Francis preaching to the birds, can be seen on the entrance wall. In the nave is the cycle of 27 frescoes, some by Giotto, though the authorship of the entire cycle is a subject of controversy. Many frescoes are almost surrealistic, like stage sets that allow you to see the actors inside. In the cycle, you can see pictorial evidence of the rise of humanism that led to Giotto's and Italy's split from the rigidity of Byzantium.

The upper church also contains the damaged masterpiece by Cimabue, his *Crucifixion*. Time and quakes have robbed the fresco of its former radiance, but its power and ghostlike drama remain at least on video. The cycle of badly damaged frescoes in the transept and apse are other works by Cimabue and his helpers. Rather tragically, art experts spend hours daily sorting through boxes of rubble, trying to piece together the jigsaw puzzle caused by the quakes. There's a debate about whether the Cimabue and Giotto frescoes will ever be in good-enough condition to be restored to their historic place.

From the transept of the upper church, proceed down the stairs through the two-tiered cloisters to the lower church. In the south transept, look for Cimabue's faded but masterly *Virgin and Child* with four angels and St. Francis looking on from the far right; it's often reproduced in detail as one of Cimabue's greatest works. You'll also find works here by Giotto, Pietro Lorenzetti, and Simone Martini.

Piazza. San Francesco 2. ⓒ **075-819001**. Free admission. July–Sept daily 8.30am–7pm, off season daily 8:30am–6pm.

Eremo delle Carceri (Prisons' Hermitage) ✮✮   Eremo delle Carceri dates from the 14th and 15th centuries. The "prison" isn't a penal institution but rather a spiritual retreat. It's believed that St. Francis retired to this spot for meditation and prayer. Out back is a moss-covered gnarled ilex (live oak) more than 1,000 years old, where St. Francis is believed to have blessed the birds, after which they flew in the four major compass directions to symbolize that Franciscans, in coming centuries, would spread from Assisi all over the world. The friary contains some faded frescoes. One of the handful of friars who still inhabit the retreat will show you through.

About 4km (2½ miles) east of Assisi, on Via Eremo delle Carceri. ⓒ **075-812301**. Free admission (donations accepted). Apr–Oct daily 7am–7pm; Nov–Mar daily 7am–5pm.

Basilica di Santa Chiara (Clare) ✮✮   This basilica is dedicated to "the little plant of Blessed Francis," as St. Clare liked to describe herself. Born in 1193 into one of the noblest families of Assisi, Clare gave all her wealth to the poor and founded, together with St. Francis, the Order of the Poor Clares. She was canonized by Pope Alexander IV in 1255, and Pope Pius XII declared her

Patroness of Television in 1958. She merited that last designation because, in her later years, when she was too infirm to attend Mass, she reportedly saw an image of the service broadcast on a wall in her room. Though many of the frescoes that once adorned the basilica have been completely or partially destroyed, much remains that's worthy of note. The basilica also houses the remains of St. Clare as well as the crucifix under which St. Francis received his command from above.

Piazza del Duomo. ✆ **0577-940316.** Church free; chapel 3.50€ adults, free for children 5 and under. Mar–Oct daily 9:30am–7pm; Nov–Feb Mon–Sat 9:30am–5pm and Sun 1–5pm.

4 Venice ★★★

Venice is a preposterous monument to both the folly and the obstinacy of humankind. It shouldn't exist, but it does, much to the delight of thousands of tourists, gondoliers, lace makers, hoteliers, restaurateurs, and glassblowers.

Fleeing the barbarians centuries ago, Venetians left dry-dock and drifted out to a flotilla of "uninhabitable" islands in the lagoon. Survival was difficult enough, but no Venetian has ever settled for mere survival. The remote ancestors of today's inhabitants created the world's most beautiful and unusual city.

However, it's sinking at a rate of about 6cm (2½ in.) per decade, and it's estimated that one-third of the city's art will have deteriorated hopelessly within the next few decades if action isn't taken to save it. Clearly, Venice is in peril, under assault by uncontrolled tides, pollution, atmospheric acid, and old age.

This is one of the most enchantingly evocative cities on earth, but you must pay a price for all this beauty. In the sultry heat of the Adriatic in summer, the canals become a smelly stew. Steamy, overcrowded July and August are the worst times to visit; May and June or September and October are much more ideal.

ESSENTIALS

GETTING THERE   All roads lead not necessarily to Rome but, in this case, to the docks of mainland Venice. The arrival scene at the unattractive Piazzale Roma is filled with nervous expectation, and even the most veteran traveler can become confused. Whether you arrive by train, bus, car, or airport limousine, there's one common denominator—everyone walks to the nearby docks to select a method of transport to his or her hotel. The cheapest way is by vaporetto, the more expensive by gondola or motor launch.

By Plane   You'll land at Mestre, with its **Marco Polo Aeroporto** (✆ **041-2606111;** www.veniceairport.it). **Boats** depart every hour directly from the airport, taking you to a terminal near Piazza San Marco. The fare is 9.50€.

It's less expensive to take a **bus** from the airport to Piazzale Roma (✆ **041-5287886**), a trip of less than 8km (5 miles); one-way fare is 2€. Departures are usually every 30 minutes (trip time: 30 min.). Once at Piazzale Roma, you can make transportation connections to most parts of Venice, including the Lido.

By Train   Trains pull into the **Stazione di Santa Lucia,** at Piazzale Roma, from Rome (trip time: 5¼ hr.), Milan (3½ hr.), Florence (4 hr.), and Bologna (2 hr.). For information and timetables, contact **FS** (✆ **848-888088;** www.trenitalia.it). The best and least expensive way to get from the station to the rest of town is to take a vaporetto, which departs near the main entrance to the station.

By Bus   Buses arrive from points on the mainland of Italy at **Piazzale Roma.** For information about schedules, contact **ACTV** at Piazzale Roma (✆ **041-5287886;** www.actv.it). If you're coming from a distant city in Italy, it's better to take the train.

By Car   Venice has autostrada links with the rest of Italy, with direct routes from such cities as Trieste (driving time: 1½ hr.), Milan (3 hr.), and Bologna (2 hr.). Bologna is 151km (94 miles) southwest of Venice; Milan, 265km (165 miles) west of Venice; and Trieste, 156km (97 miles) east. Rome is 526km (327 miles) to the southwest.

If you arrive by car, there're several multi-tiered parking areas at the terminus where the roads end and the canals begin. One of the most visible is the **Garage San Marco,** Piazzale Roma (© **041-5235101**), near the vaporetto, gondola, and motor-launch docks. You'll be charged 18€ for 12 hours, 24€ for 24 hours.

VISITOR INFORMATION   You can get information at the **Azienda di Promozione Turistica,** Castello 4421 (© **041-5298711;** www.turismovenezia.it). There's another office at Santa Lucia railway station. Both are open daily from 9am to 1pm and 1:30 to 5pm.

CITY LAYOUT   Venice, 4km (2½ miles) from the Italian mainland and 2km (1¼ miles) from the Adriatic, is an archipelago of some 117 islands. Most visitors, however, concern themselves only with **Piazza San Marco** and its vicinity. In fact, the entire city has only one piazza: San Marco. Venice is divided into six quarters that locals call *sestieri*. These include the most frequented, San Marco, but also Santa Croce, San Polo, Castello, Cannaregio, and Dorsoduro, the last of which has been compared to New York's Greenwich Village.

Many of the so-called streets of Venice are actually **canals,** some 150 in all. A canal is called a *rio,* and a total of 400 bridges span these canals. If Venice has a main street, it's the **Grand Canal,** which is spanned by three bridges: the Rialto, the Academy Bridge, and the stone Railway Bridge. The canal splits Venice into two unequal parts.

South of the section called Dorsoduro, which is south of the Grand Canal, is the **Canale della Giudecca,** a major channel separating Dorsoduro from the large island of La Giudecca. At the point where the Canale della Giudecca meets the Canale di San Marco, you'll spot the little **Isola di San Giorgio Maggiore,** with a church by Palladio. The most visited islands in the lagoon, aside from the **Lido,** are **Murano, Burano,** and **Torcello.**

Once you land and explore Piazza San Marco and its satellite, Piazzetta San Marco, you can head down **Riva degli Schiavoni,** with its deluxe and first-class hotels, or follow the signs along the **Mercerie,** the major shopping artery, which leads to the Rialto, site of the market area.

GETTING AROUND   Walking is the only way to explore Venice unless you plan to see it from a boat on the Grand Canal. Everybody walks in Venice—there's no other way.

By Vaporetto   The motorboats, or *vaporetti,* of Venice provide inexpensive and frequent, if not always fast, transportation in this canal-riddled city. An *accelerato* is a vessel that makes every stop and a *diretto* makes only express stops. The average fare is 3€. In summer, the vaporetti are often fiercely crowded. Pick up

---

Tips Finding an Address

The system of addresses in Venice is so confusing it's probably known only to the postman, if that. The best thing to do is to arm yourself with a good map, such as the **Falk** map of Venice, which is pocket size and available in many kiosks and bookstores.

Venice

To Train ↑
Station

San
Giovanni
Decollato

Fondego
dei Turchi

To Jewish ↑
Ghetto

**SANTA
CROCE**

San
† Giacomo
■ dell' Orio

Campo S.
Giacomo
dell'Orio

Santa Maria
Mater Domini

Rio della S.

Casa
Zane

Rio di S. Agostino

Scuola di San
Giovanni Evangelista

Rio di S. Polo

**SAN
POLO**

Rio terra S. Toma

Palazzo Corner
Mocenigo

Campo di
San Polo

† San
■ Rocco

Campo
dei
Frari

‡San Polo

Rio di San Polo

Frari

6

Scuola Grande
di S. Rocco

Palazzo Centani
(Museo Goldoni)

Palazzo
Griman

Rio della Frescada

S. Angelo

Palazzo Corner-
Spinelli

†S. Tomà

Rio

Ca' Foscari

Ca' Mocenigo

Ca' Foscari

4

Saliz S. Samuele

C. Crosera

Palazzo
Grassi

S.
Samuele

Campo
S. Stefano/
F. Morosini

Ca' Rezzonico

5

Rio di IS. Barnaba

Canal Grande

Rio del IDuca

C. Vetturi

Rio Malpaga

Ca' d'
Duca

Rio di IS. Vidal

Campo
San Vidal

Palazzo Loredan

Rio della Toletta

Palazzo Contarini
d. Zaffo

3

Ponte dell'
Accademia

4

Palazzo
Loredan

San
Trovaso

2
Accademia

Palazzo
Brandolin Rota

Rio di S. Vio

Squero di
San Trovaso

DORSODURO

1
↓

> **_Tips_ Getting Around by Gondola**
>
> When riding in a **gondola,** two major agreements have to be reached: the price of the ride and the length of the trip. The official rate is 60€, but virtually no one pays that amount; prices really start at about 75€ for up to 50 minutes. Two major stations at which you can hire gondolas are Piazza San Marco (℃ **041-5200685**) and the Ponte Rialto (℃ **041-5224904**). Both organize gondola tours, lasting about 50 minutes and costing from 60€ to 75€ per person.

a map of the system from the tourist office. There's frequent service daily from 7am to midnight, then hourly from midnight to 7am.

Visitors to Venice may avail yourselves of discount passes, which must be validated before use and shown together with the matrix (the last ticket of the booklet). An all-day ticket costs 9€ and goes up to 18€ for 3 days, or 30€ for 1 week.

By Water Taxi/Motor Launch   The city's many private motor launches are called *taxi acquei.* You may or may not have the cabin of one of these sleek vessels to yourself, since the captains fill their boats with as many passengers as the law allows before taking off. The price of a transit by water taxi from Piazzale Roma (the road and rail terminus) to Piazza San Marco begins at 40€ for one to six passengers, or else 70€ from the airport. You can also call for a taxi acquei—try **Cooperativa San Marco** at ℃ **041-5222303.**

 FAST FACTS: Venice

American Express   The office is at Salizzada San Moisè, San Marco 1471 (℃ **041-5200844**; vaporetto: San Marco). The staff can arrange city tours and mail handling. From May to October, hours are Monday through Saturday from 8am to 8pm for currency exchange, and 9am to 5:30pm for all other transactions; from November to April, hours are Monday through Friday from 9am to 5:30pm, and Saturday from 9am to 12:30pm.

Consulates   The **United Kingdom** consulate is at Dorsoduro 1051, at the foot of the Accademia Bridge (℃ **041-5227207**; vaporetto: Accademia), open Monday through Friday from 10am to noon and 2 to 3pm. The **United States, Canada,** and **Australia** have consulates in Milan, about 3 hours away by train.

Currency Exchange   There are many banks in Venice where you can exchange money. You might try the **Banco Commerciale Italiana,** Via XXII Marzo, San Marco 2188 (℃ **041-5296811**; vaporetto: San Marco), or **Banco San Marco,** Calle Larga San Marco, San Marco 383 (℃ **041-5293711**; vaporetto: San Marco). Hours are Monday through Friday from 8:30am to 1:30pm and 2:45 to 4pm.

Dentist/Doctor   Your best bet is to have your hotel set up an appointment with an English-speaking dentist or doctor. The American Express office and the British consulate also have lists. Also see "Hospitals," below.

Drugstores If you need a drugstore in the middle of the night, call ℂ **192** for information about which one is open (pharmacies take turns staying open late). A well-recommended central one is **International Pharmacy,** Via XXII Marzo, San Marco 2067 (ℂ **041-5222311;** vaporetto: San Marco).

Emergencies Call ℂ **113** for the police, ℂ **118** for an ambulance, or ℂ **115** to report a fire.

Hospitals Contact the **Ospedale Civile Santi Giovanni e Paolo,** Campo Santi Giovanni e Paolo in Castello (ℂ **041-785111;** vaporetto: San Toma), staffed with English-speaking doctors 24 hours a day.

Post Office The main post office is at Fondaco dei Tedeschi (ℂ **041-2717111;** vaporetto: Rialto), near the Rialto Bridge. It's open Monday through Saturday from 8:15am to 5pm. For information call ℂ **160.**

Safety The curse of Venice is the pickpocket. Violent crime is rare, but because of the overcrowding on vaporetti and even on the small, narrow streets, it's easy to pick pockets. Purse snatchings are commonplace as well. Secure your valuables, and if your hotel has safes, keep them locked there when not needed.

Telephones The **country code** for Italy is **39.** The **city code** for Venice is **041,** which is the code you'll use every time you dial a party located within Venice, regardless of whether you're within the city limits or not. We emphasize that newly imposed technologies will require the use of the "0" and then "41" for calls to parties in Venice, regardless of whether you're within the city limits of Venice or not. For additional information, see "Fast Facts: Rome," earlier in this chapter.

WHERE TO STAY
NEAR PIAZZA SAN MARCO
Very Expensive

Gritti Palace ✦✦✦   In a stately setting on the Grand Canal, Gritti Palace is the renovated palazzo of the 15th-century doge Andrea Gritti. It's a bit starchy but is topped only by the Cipriani in terms of prestige. "Our home in Venice" to Ernest Hemingway, it has for years drawn a clientele of theatrical, literary, political, and royal figures. The range and variety of the rooms seem almost limitless, from elaborate suites to relatively small singles. But in every case the stamp of glamour is evident. For a splurge, ask for Hemingway's old suite or the Doge Suite, once occupied by Somerset Maugham. All accommodations come with luxurious bathrooms with tub/shower combos.

Campo Santa Maria del Giglio, San Marco 2467, 30124 Venezia. ℂ **800/325-3535** in the U.S., 416/947-4864 in Canada, or 041-794611. Fax 041-5200942. www.luxurycollection.com/grittipalace. 93 units. 705€–995€ double; from 1,640€ suite. Rates include breakfast. AE, DC, MC, V. Vaporetto: Santa Maria del Giglio. **Amenities:** Elegant restaurant and bar; 24-hr. concierge and butler service; private boat launches and sightseeing tours; salon; 24-hr. room service; babysitting; laundry/dry cleaning. *In room:* A/C, TV, minibar, hair dryer, safe.

Expensive

Hotel Concordia ✦   The Concordia is the only hotel in Venice that has rooms overlooking St. Mark's Square. A series of gold-plated marble steps takes you to the lobby, where you'll find a comfortable bar area. All rooms are decorated in a Venetian antique style and contain hand-painted furnishings and small Murano chandeliers, plus small bathrooms with tubs.

Calle Larga, San Marco 367, 30124 Venezia. ℂ **041-5206866.** Fax 041-5206775. 57 units (some with shower only). 300€–400€ double; 400€–500€ suite. Rates include buffet breakfast. AE, DC, MC, V. Vaporetto: San Marco. **Amenities:** Restaurant; bar; room service; babysitting; laundry/dry cleaning. *In room:* A/C, TV, minibar, hair dryer, safe.

Hotel la Fenice et des Artistes ✫   This hotel offers widely varying accommodations in two connected buildings. One building is rather romantic yet timeworn, with overly decorated rooms. Your satin-lined room may have an inlaid desk and a wardrobe painted in the Venetian manner to match a baroque bed frame. The carpets might be thin, however, and the fabrics aging. Bathrooms, still a little cramped, were renewed in 1999; each has a tub and shower. Chambers in the other building are far less glamorous. The older of the two has no elevator.

Campiello de la Fenice, San Marco 1936, 30124 Venezia. ℂ 041-5232333. Fax 041-5203721. fenice@ fenicehotels.it. 69 units. 135€–218€ double; 200€–295€ suite. Rates include breakfast. AE, DC, MC, V. Vaporetto: San Marco. **Amenities:** Restaurant; bar; room service; babysitting; laundry/dry cleaning. *In room:* A/C, TV, hair dryer, safe.

Moderate

Hotel Do Pozzi   Small, modernized, and centrally located just a short stroll from the Grand Canal and Piazza San Marco, this place is more like a country tavern than a hotel. Its original structure is 200 years old, and it opens onto a paved front courtyard with potted greenery. The sitting and dining rooms are furnished with antiques (and near antiques) mixed with utilitarian modern decor. A major refurbishing has given everything a fresh touch, including the shower-only bathrooms.

Corte do Pozzi, San Marco 2373, 30124 Venezia. ℂ 041-5207855. Fax 041-5229413. www.hoteldopozzi.it. 35 units (some with shower only). 125€–196€ double. Rates include breakfast. AE, DC, MC, V. Vaporetto: Santa Maria del Giglio. **Amenities:** Dining room; bar; babysitting; laundry/dry cleaning. *In room:* TV, minibar, hair dryer.

Hotel Montecarlo   Although still unremarkable, this hotel is in a vastly improved 17th-century building, just 2 minutes from Piazza San Marco. The upper halls are lined with paintings by Venetian artists. The guest rooms are decorated with Venetian-style furniture and Venetian-glass chandeliers. Some are quite dark, the curse of many Venetian hotels. All have well-kept bathrooms.

Calle dei Specchieri, San Marco 463, 30124 Venezia. ℂ 041-5207144. Fax 041-5207789. www.venicehotel montecarlo.com. 48 units. 108€ standard double; 400€ deluxe double. Rates include buffet breakfast. AE, DC, MC, V. Vaporetto: San Marco. **Amenities:** Restaurant; bar; room service; babysitting; laundry. *In room:* A/C, TV, hair dryer, safe.

IN THE DORSODURO
Moderate

American Hotel ✫ *Value*   Set on a small waterway, the American Hotel (there's nothing American about it) is one of your best budget bets. The modest lobby is filled with murals, warm colors, and antiques, and the location is perfect for anyone wanting to avoid the crowds that descend in summer. Rooms are comfortably furnished in a Venetian style, but vary in size; some of the smaller ones are a bit cramped. Many rooms with private terraces face the canal. Each contains a small bathroom with tub. On the second floor is a beautiful terrace where guests relax over drinks.

Campo San Vio, Accademia 628, 30123 Venezia. ℂ 041-5204733. Fax 041-5204048. www.hotelamerican. com. 29 units. 130€–268€ double; 150€–310€ triple. Rates include buffet breakfast. AE, MC, V. Vaporetto: Accademia. **Amenities:** Breakfast room; lounge; room service; babysitting; laundry/dry cleaning. *In room:* A/C, TV, hair dryer, safe.

Pensione Accademia *(Value)*   This is the most patrician of the pensioni, in a villa whose garden extends into the angle created by the junction of two canals. Iron fences, twisting vines, and neoclassical sculpture are a part of the setting. There's an upstairs sitting room and a formal rose garden that's visible from the breakfast room. The recently renovated rooms are spacious and decorated with 19th-century furniture. The small tiled bathrooms contain showers.

Fondamenta Bollani, Dorsoduro 1058, 30123 Venezia. © **041-5237846.** Fax 041-5239152. www.pensione accademia.it. 27 units (showers only). 179€–225€ double. Rates include breakfast. AE, DC, MC, V. Vaporetto: Accademia. **Amenities:** Bar; room service; babysitting; laundry/dry cleaning. *In room:* A/C, TV, hair dryer, safe.

Inexpensive

Locanda Montin *(Finds)*   The well-recommended Locanda Montin is an old-fashioned Venetian inn whose adjoining restaurant is one of the most loved in the area. The hotel is officially listed as a fourth-class hotel because of its lack of in-room amenities aside from a phone, but the accommodations are considerably larger and better than that rating suggests. Reservations are virtually mandatory, because of the reputation of this locanda. Marked only by a small carriage lamp etched with the name of the establishment, the inn is a little difficult to locate but worth the search.

Fondamenta di Borgo, Dorsoduro 1147, 31000 Venezia. © **041-5227151.** Fax 041-5200255. 11 units, 5 with bathroom. 105€ double without bathroom; 130€ double with bathroom. AE, DC, MC, V. Vaporetto: Accademia. **Amenities:** Restaurant; bar; laundry/dry cleaning.

IN SANTA CROCE
Moderate

Hotel San Cassiano Ca'Favretto *(Value)*   San Cassiano Ca'Favretto was once the studio of 19th-century painter Giacomo Favretto. The views from the hotel's gondola pier and from the dining room's porch encompass the lacy facade of the Ca' d'Oro, the most beautiful building in Venice. The hotel was constructed in the 14th century as a palace. The present owner has worked closely with Venetian authorities to preserve the original details. Fifteen of the conservatively decorated rooms overlook one of two canals, and each comes with a neatly kept bathroom with tub.

Calle della Rosa, Santa Croce 2232, 30135 Venezia. © **041-5241768.** Fax 041-721033. www.sancassiano.it. 35 units. 200€–310€ double. Rates include breakfast. AE, DC, MC, V. Vaporetto: San Stae. **Amenities:** Dining room; bar; room service; babysitting. *In room:* A/C, TV, hair dryer, safe.

IN CANNAREGIO
Expensive

Locanda ai Santi Apostoli *(Value)*   If you can't afford the Gritti Palace (and few can), but still fantasize about living in a palazzo overlooking the Grande Canal, near the Rialto, here is a possibility. The Locanda knows the advantage of its location, however, and doesn't come cheap. But it's a lot less expensive than the grand palaces nearby. It's situated on the top floor of a 15th-century building, and the rooms, although simple, are rather inviting. Naturally, the two rooms actually opening onto the Grand Canal are the most requested. Even if you don't have one of these, there's a view from the main salon. All rooms come with a tiled bathroom with shower. Breakfast is the only meal served.

Strada Nuova, Cannaregio 4391, 30131 Venezia. © **041-5212612.** Fax 041-5212611. www.veneziaweb. com/santiapostoli. 11 units (showers only). 180€–223[eu double; 290€ double with Grand Canal view; 390€ suite. Rates include breakfast. AE, DC, MC, V. Vaporetto: Ca d'Oro. **Amenities:** Lounge; babysitting; laundry/dry cleaning. *In room:* A/C, TV, minibar, hair dryer.

ON ISOLA DELLA GIUDECCA
Very Expensive
Cipriani ✴✴✴ Isolated, security-conscious, and elegant, the Cipriani occupies a 16th-century cloister on the residential island of Giudecca. This refined, tranquil, and sybaritic resort hotel was established in 1958 by the late Giuseppe Cipriani, the founder of Harry's Bar and the one real-life character in Hemingway's Venetian novel. Rooms have different decors—ranging from tasteful contemporary to antique—but all have splendid views. The bathrooms with tub and shower are among the most luxurious in Venice. The hotel also runs a 24-hour motorboat shuttle to and from San Marco.

Isola della Giudecca 10, 30133 Venezia. ⓒ **800/992-5055** in the U.S., or 041-5207744. Fax 041-5207745. www.orient-expresshotels.com. 110 units. 767€–1,177€ double; from 1,998€ suite. Rates include breakfast. AE, DC, MC, V. Closed Nov–Mar. Vaporetto: Zitelle. **Amenities:** 2 superb and very expensive restaurants; 3 bars (including a piano bar); Olympic-size swimming pool; Venice's only tennis court; fitness center; Turkish bath and sauna; private boat shuttle; room service; massage; babysitting; laundry/dry cleaning. *In room:* A/C, TV, minibar, hair dryer, safe.

WHERE TO DINE
NEAR PIAZZA SAN MARCO
Very Expensive
Harry's Bar ✴✴✴ VENETIAN Harry's Bar serves the best food in Venice, though Quadri and the Antico Martini (see below) have more elegant atmospheres. Its fame was spread by Ernest Hemingway. A. E. Hotchner, in *Papa Hemingway,* quoted the writer as saying, "We can't eat straight hamburger in a Renaissance palazzo on the Grand Canal." So he ordered a 5-pound "tin of beluga caviar" to, as he said, "take the curse off it." Hemingway would skip the place today, fleeing from the foreign visitors, and the prices would come as a shock even to him. You can have your choice of dining in the bar downstairs or in the room with a view upstairs. We recommend the Venetian fish soup, followed by scampi thermidor with rice pilaf or seafood ravioli.

Calle Vallaresso, San Marco 1323. ⓒ **041-5285777.** Reservations required. Main courses 50€–100€. AE, DC, MC, V. Daily 10:30am–1am. Vaporetto: San Marco.

Expensive
Antico Martini ✴✴✴ VENETIAN/INTERNATIONAL As the city's leading traditional restaurant, Antico Martini, located near La Fenice, elevates Venetian cuisine to its highest level. The courtyard is favored in summer. An excellent beginning to your meal is the *risotto di frutti di mare,* creamy Venetian-style risotto with plenty of fresh seafood. For a main dish, try the *fegato alla Veneziana,* which is tender liver fried with onions and served with polenta, a yellow cornmeal mush. The chefs are better at regional dishes than they are with those of the international kitchen.

Campo San Fantin, San Marco 1983. ⓒ **041-5224121.** Reservations required. Main courses 24€–64€; 4-course fixed-price menu 46€–51€; 6-course *menu degustazione* 79€. AE, DC, MC, V. Wed 7–11:30pm; Thurs–Mon noon–2:30pm and 7–11:30pm. Vaporetto: San Marco or Santa Maria del Giglio.

Da Ivo ✴ TUSCAN/VENETIAN Da Ivo has such a faithful clientele that you'll think at first you're in a semiprivate club. The rustic atmosphere is both cozy and relaxing, with candles on the well-set tables. Homesick Florentines go here for fine Tuscan cookery; regional Venetian dishes are also served. In season, game, according to an ancient tradition, is cooked over an open charcoal grill. On one cold day, our hearts and plates were warmed when we ordered homemade tagliatelle. It came topped with slivers of tartufi bianchi, the pungent

The Cafe Scene

Venice's most famous cafe is the **Florian,** Piazza San Marco, San Marco 56–59 (☎ **041-5205641;** vaporetto: San Marco). It was built in 1720 and remains romantically and elegantly decorated—pure Venetian salons with red plush banquettes, elaborate murals under glass, and Art Nouveau lighting and lamps. Hours are Thursday through Tuesday from 9:30am to midnight. It's closed the first week of December and the first week of January.

   Quadri, Piazza San Marco, San Marco 120–124 (☎ **041-5222105;** vaporetto: San Marco), stands opposite the Florian. Founded in 1638, it's elegantly decorated in an antique style. Wagner used to drop in for a drink when he was working on *Tristan und Isolde*. The restaurant on the second floor offers refined Venetian cuisine. It's open April through October daily from 9am to midnight; off season, Tuesday through Sunday from 9am to midnight.

white truffle from the Piedmont district that's unforgettable to the palate. You'll also find delicacies like giant scampi with cherry tomatoes and black pepper, or beef carpaccio covered with arugula and parmigiana flakes.

Calle dei Fuseri, San Marco 1809. ☎ **041-5285004.** Reservations required. Main courses 30€–40€. AE, DC, MC, V. Mon–Sat noon–2:30pm and 7pm–midnight. Closed Jan 6–31. Vaporetto: San Marco.

Quadri ⭐⭐⭐ VENETIAN/INTERNATIONAL   One of Europe's famous restaurants, the deluxe Quadri evokes the world of its former patrons, Marcel Proust and Stendhal. Many diners come here just for the setting and are often surprised when they're treated to high-quality cuisine and impeccable service. You pay for all this nostalgia, however. The Venetian cuisine has been acclaimed—at least by one food critic—as "befitting a doge," though we doubt if those old doges ate as well. The chef is likely to tempt you with such dishes as octopus in fresh tomato sauce, salt codfish with polenta, or sea bass with crab sauce. Try the "baked" ice cream for dessert.

Piazza San Marco, San Marco 120–124. ☎ **041-5289299.** Reservations required. Main courses 33€–43€. AE, DC, MC, V. Tues–Sun noon–2:30pm (except July–Aug) and 7–10:30pm. Vaporetto: San Marco.

Moderate

Ristorante da Raffaele ⭐ *Value* ITALIAN/VENETIAN   This place is a 5-minute walk from Piazza San Marco and a minute from the Grand Canal. It has long been a favorite canal-side stop. It's often overrun with tourists, but the veteran kitchen staff holds up well. The food is excellent, beginning with a choice of tasty antipasti or well-prepared pastas. Seafood specialties include scampi, squid, or a platter of deep-fried fish from the Adriatic. The grilled meats are also succulent and can be followed by rich, tempting desserts.

Calle Larga XXII Marzo (Fondamenta delle Ostreghe), San Marco 2347. ☎ **041-5232317.** Reservations recommended Sat–Sun. Main courses 12€–24€. AE, DC, MC, V. Fri–Wed noon–3pm and 7–10:30pm. Closed Dec 10 through Jan. Vaporetto: San Marco or Santa Maria del Giglio.

Taverna la Fenice ⭐⭐ ITALIAN/VENETIAN   Opened in 1907, when Venetians were flocking in record numbers to hear the *bel canto* performances in the opera house nearby, this restaurant is one of Venice's most romantic dining spots. The interior is suitably elegant, but the preferred spot in clement weather is out beneath a canopy, a few steps from the burned Teatro La Fenice. The service is smooth and efficient. You might enjoy risotto with scampi and arugula, or freshly made tagliatelle with cream and exotic mushrooms. Among the wide selection of fresh fish, you may be tempted by the exquisite simplicity of the sea bream garnished with seasonal herbs. For pasta lovers the choice ranges from traditional black tagliolini with squid ink and crabmeat, to the more creative tagliatelle with a combination of scampi and artichokes.

Campiello de la Fenice, San Marco 1938. ℂ 041-5223856. Reservations required. Main courses 14€–40€. AE, DC, MC, V. Mon–Sat noon–3pm and 7–11pm. Vaporetto: San Marco.

Trattoria La Colomba * VENETIAN/INTERNATIONAL   This is one of
the most distinctive and popular trattorie in town, with a history going back at least a century. Menu items are likely to include at least five daily specials based exclusively on the time-honored cuisine of Venice. Otherwise, you can order *risotto di funghi del Montello* (risotto with mushrooms from the local hills of Montello) or *baccalà alla vicentina* (milk-simmered dry cod seasoned with onions, anchovies, and cinnamon, then served with polenta). If you're a meat fan, try the chateaubriand accompanied by steamed vegetables and almost a dozen different sauces.

Piscina Frezzeria, San Marco 1665. ℂ **041-5221175.** Reservations recommended. Main courses 23€–40€. AE, DC, MC, V. Daily noon–3pm and 7–11pm. Closed Wed Nov–Apr. Vaporetto: San Marco or Rialto.

Vini da Arturo * *Finds* VENETIAN   Vini da Arturo attracts many devoted
regulars, including artists and writers. Here you get some of the most delectable local cooking—and not just the standard cliché Venetian dishes, and not seafood, which may be unique for a Venetian restaurant. Instead of ordering plain pasta, try a tantalizing dish called *spaghetti alla Gorgonzola.* The beef is also good, especially when prepared with a cream sauce flavored with mustard and freshly ground pepper. The salads are made with crisp, fresh ingredients, often in unusual combinations. The place is small and contains only seven tables; it's between the Fenice Opera House and St. Mark's Square.

Calle degli Assassini, San Marco 3656. ℂ **041-5286974.** Reservations recommended. Main courses 21€–31€. No credit cards. Mon–Sat noon–2:30pm and 7–10:30pm. Closed Aug. Vaporetto: San Marco or Rialto.

Inexpensive
Da Bruno VENETIAN   Da Bruno is like a country tavern in the center of
Venice. On a narrow street about halfway between the Rialto Bridge and Piazza San Marco, this restaurant attracts its crowds by grilling meats on an open-hearth fire. Get your antipasti at the counter and watch your prosciutto being prepared—paper-thin slices of spicy flavored ham wrapped around breadsticks (*grissini*). In the right season, da Bruno does some of the finest game specialty dishes in Venice. If it's featured, try *capriolo* (roebuck) or *fagiano* (pheasant). Another great dish is veal scaloppini with wild mushrooms. If you feel more in a pasta mood, try the "black spaghetti" with tomato sauce.

Calle del Paradiso San Lio, Castello 5731. ℂ **041-5221480.** Main courses 8€–15€; fixed-price menu 14€. AE, DC, MC, V. Daily noon–3pm and 7–11pm. Vaporetto: San Marco or Rialto.

Sempione VENETIAN   This century-old restaurant does an admirable job
of feeding local residents and visitors. Set adjacent to a canal near St. Mark's Square, it contains three dining rooms outfitted in a soothingly traditional style,

a well-trained staff, and a kitchen that focuses on preparations of traditional Venetian cuisine. Examples include grilled fish, spaghetti with crabmeat, risotto with fish, fish soup, and a timeless and delectable version of Venetian calves' liver. If you like surprises, try spaghetti with crabmeat flavored with a mysterious sauce whose ingredients the chef doesn't want to reveal. Try for a table by the window so you can watch the gondolas slide by.

Ponte Beretteri, San Marco 578. ℭ 041-5226022. Reservations recommended. Main courses 8€–17€. AE, DC, MC, V. Wed–Mon 11:30am–3pm and 6:30–10pm. Closed Thurs Nov–Dec. Vaporetto: Rialto.

Trattoria alla Madonna VENETIAN   This restaurant, opened in 1954 and named after *another* famous Madonna, is one of the most popular and characteristic trattorie of Venice, specializing in traditional recipes and an array of grilled fresh fish. A suitable beginning may be the antipasto *frutti di mare*. Pastas, polentas, risottos, meats (including *fegato alla Veneziana,* liver with onions), and many kinds of irreproachably fresh fish are widely available.

Calle della Madonna, San Polo 594. ℭ 041-5223824. Reservations recommended but not always accepted. Main courses 10€–14€. AE, MC, V. Thurs–Tues noon–3pm and 7:15–10pm. Closed Dec 24 to Jan and Aug 4–17. Vaporetto: Rialto.

EAST OF PIAZZA SAN MARCO
Moderate
Ristorante Corte Sconta SEAFOOD   This restaurant lies on a narrow alley, whose name is shared by at least three other streets in Venice (this particular one is near Campo Bandiere Moro and San Giovanni in Bragora). The modest restaurant has become well known as a sophisticated gathering place for artists, writers, and filmmakers. It serves a variety of flawlessly grilled fish (much of the "catch" is largely unknown in North America). It's also flawlessly fresh—the gamberi, for example, is placed live on the grill. Begin with marinated salmon with arugula and pomegranate seeds in rich olive oil. If you don't like fish, a tender filet of beef is available.

Calle del Pestrin, Castello 3886. ℭ 041-5227024. Reservations required. Main courses 15€–30€; fixed-price menus 55€–60€. MC, V. Tues–Sat 12:30–2:30pm and 7:30–9:30pm. Closed Jan 7–Feb 7 and July 15–Aug 15. Vaporetto: Arsenale.

Inexpensive
Nuova Rivetta (Value) SEAFOOD   Nuova Rivetta is an old-fashioned Venetian trattoria where you eat well without having to pay a lot. The restaurant stands in the monumental heart of the old city. Many find it best for lunch during a stroll around Venice. The most representative dish to order is *frittura di pesce,* a mixed fish fry from the Adriatic, which includes squid or various other "sea creatures" that turned up at the market that day. Other specialties are gnocchi stuffed with Adriatic spider crab, pasticcio of fish (a main course), and spaghetti flavored with squid ink.

Campo San Filippo, Castello 4625. ℭ 041-5287302. Reservations required. Main courses 7.75€–14€. AE, MC, V. Tues–Sun noon–10pm. Closed July 23–Aug 20. Vaporetto: San Zaccaria.

NEAR THE PONTE DI RIALTO
Moderate
Il Sole Sulla Vecia Cavana ★ (Finds) SEAFOOD   This restaurant is off the tourist circuit and well worth the trek through the winding streets. A *cavana* is a place where gondolas are parked, a sort of liquid garage, and the site of this restaurant was such a place in the Middle Ages. When you enter, you'll be greeted by brick arches, stone columns, terra-cotta floors, framed modern paintings, and

a photo of 19th-century fishermen relaxing after a day's work. The menu specializes in seafood, such as a mixed grill from the Adriatic, fried scampi, fresh sole, squid, and three types of risotto. The food is authentic and seems prepared for the Venetian palate—not necessarily for the visitor's.

Rio Terà SS. Apostoli, Cannaregio 4624. ℭ 041-5287106. Reservations recommended. Main courses 16€–22€; fixed-price menu 20€. AE, DC, MC, V. Tues–Sun noon–3pm and 6:30–10:30pm. Vaporetto: Ca' d'Oro.

Poste Vechie ⭐ SEAFOOD   This is one of Venice's most charming restaurants near the Rialto fish market and connected to the rest of the city by a small, privately owned bridge. It was established in the early 1500s as the local post office—food was served to the mail carriers to fortify them for their deliveries. Today, it's one of the oldest restaurants in town. Menu items include a super fresh array of fish from the nearby markets; a salad of shellfish and exotic mushrooms; a spicy soup of Adriatic fish; tagliolini flavored with squid ink, crabmeat, and fish sauce; and the restaurant's pièce de résistance, *seppie* (cuttlefish) *alla Veneziana* with polenta. If you don't like fish, calves' liver or veal shank with ham and cheese are also well prepared. The desserts come rolling to your table on a trolley and are usually sumptuous.

Pescheria Rialto, San Polo 1608. ℭ 041-721822. Reservations recommended. Main courses 12€–24€. AE, DC, MC, V. Wed–Mon noon–3:30pm and 7–10:30pm. Vaporetto: Rialto.

IN SAN POLO
Expensive
Osteria da Fiore ⭐ *Finds* SEAFOOD   This restaurant serves only fish, and has done so since 1910. You'll find everything from scampi (a sweet Adriatic prawn, cooked in as many different ways as there are chefs) to granzeola, a type of spider crab. Try such dishes as *capelunghe alla griglia* (razor clams opened on the grill), *masenette* (tiny green crabs that you eat shell and all), and *canoce* (mantis shrimp). For your wine, we suggest Prosecco, which has a distinctive golden-yellow color and a bouquet that's refreshing and fruity.

Calle del Scaleter, San Polo 2202. ℭ 041-721308. Reservations required. Main courses 34€–43€. AE, DC, MC, V. Tues–Sat 12:30–2:30pm and 8–10:30pm. Closed 3 weeks in Aug and Dec 25–Jan 14. Vaporetto: San Tomà.

IN THE DORSODURO
Expensive
La Furatola SEAFOOD   La Furatola (an old Venetian word meaning "restaurant") is very much a Dorsoduro neighborhood hangout, but it has captured the imagination of local foodies. You'll need a good map and a lot of patience to find it. The specialty is fish brought to your table in a wicker basket so you can judge its size and freshness by its bright eyes and red gills. A display of seafood antipasti is set out near the entrance. A standout is the baby octopus boiled and eaten with a drop of red-wine vinegar.

Calle Lunga San Barnaba, Dorsoduro 2870A. ℭ 041-5208594. Reservations required. Main courses 20€–25€. AE, DC, MC, V. Fri–Sun 12:20–3pm and Fri–Mon 7:30–10:30pm. Closed Aug and Jan. Vaporetto: Ca' Rezzonico.

Inexpensive
Locanda Montin ⭐ INTERNATIONAL/ITALIAN   Since this restaurant opened just after World War II, its famous patrons have included Ezra Pound, Jackson Pollock, Mark Rothko, and Peggy Guggenheim's artist friends. The inn is owned and run by the Carretins. Today the arbor-covered garden courtyard of

this 17th-century building is filled with regulars. The menu includes a variety of salads, grilled meats, and fish caught in the Adriatic. Specialties include fresh crab with virgin olive oil and lemon, *tortelloni* (a kind of dumpling) stuffed with artichokes and covered in a scampi cream sauce, and seasonal fish often served in a Barolo red wine sauce.

Fondamenta di Borgo, Dorsoduro 1147. © 041-5227151. Reservations recommended. Main courses 14€–20€. AE, DC, MC, V. Thurs–Tues 12:30–2:30pm; Thurs–Mon 7:30–10pm. Closed 10 days in mid-Aug and 20 days in Jan. Vaporetto: Accademia.

SEEING THE SIGHTS IN VENICE

Unlike Florence, Venice would reward you with treasures even if you never ducked inside a museum or church. In the city on the islands, the frame eternally competes with the picture inside.

SIGHTSEEING SUGGESTIONS FOR FIRST-TIME VISITORS

If You Have 1 Day Get up early and watch the sun rise over **Piazza San Marco,** as the city wakes up. The pigeons will already be here to greet you. Have an early morning cappuccino on the square, then visit the **Basilica of San Marco** and the **Palazzo Ducale.** We recommend a lunch stop at **Poste Vecchie,** at Pescheria Rialto, San Polo 1608 (© 041-721822; vaporetto: Rialto). This restaurant near the fish market is the oldest in Venice, open Wednesday through Monday from noon to 3pm and 7 to 10:30pm. Ride the **Grand Canal** in a gondola 2 hours before sunset and spend the rest of the evening wandering the narrow streets of this strangely unreal and most fascinating city. Apologize to yourself for such a short visit and promise to return.

If You Have 2 Days On day 2 it's time for more concentrated sightseeing. Begin at Piazza San Marco (viewing it should be a daily ritual, regardless of how many days you have in Venice), then head for the **Accademia,** in the morning. In the afternoon, visit the **Collezione** **Peggy Guggenheim** (modern art) and perhaps the **Ca' d'Oro** and **Ca' Rezzonico.**

If You Have 3 Days Begin day 3 by having a cappuccino on Piazza San Marco, then inspect the **Campanile di San Marco.** Later in the morning visit the **Museo Correr.** In the afternoon, go to the **Scuola Grande di San Rocco** to see the works of Tintoretto. Spend the rest of the day strolling the streets of Venice and ducking into shops that capture your imagination. Even if you get lost, you'll eventually return to a familiar landmark, and you can't help but see the signs pointing you back to Piazza San Marco. Have dinner in one of the most typical of Venetian trattorie, such as **Locanda Montin.**

If You Have 4 or 5 Days On day 4 plan to visit the islands of the lagoon, including **Murano, Burano,** and **Torcello.** All three can be covered, at least briefly, on 1 busy day. On day 5, relax and stroll the streets; serendipity may await around the corner.

THE GRAND CANAL ★★★

Peoria may have its Main Street, Paris its Champs-Elysées—but Venice, for uniqueness, tops them all with its **Canal Grande (Grand Canal).** Lined with *palazzi* (palaces)—many in elegant Venetian-Gothic style—this great road of water is today filled with vaporetti, motorboats, and gondolas. Along the canal, the boat moorings are like peppermint sticks. It begins at Piazzetta San Marco on one side and Longhena's Salute Church on the opposite bank. At midpoint it's spanned by the Rialto Bridge. Eventually the canal winds its serpentine course to the railway station. We can guarantee that there's not a dull sight en route.

THE BASILICA, DOGES' PALACE & CAMPANILE

Piazza San Marco (St. Mark's Square) ★★★ was the heartbeat of La Serenissima (the Serene Republic) in the heyday of its glory as a seafaring state, the crystallization of its dreams and aspirations. If you have only 1 day for Venice, you need not leave the square, as the city's major attractions, such as the Basilica of St. Mark and the Doges' Palace, are centered here or nearby. Thanks to Napoléon, the square was unified architecturally. The emperor added the Fabbrica Nuova, thus bridging the Old and New Procuratie. Flanked with medieval-looking palaces, Sansovino's Library, elegant shops, and colonnades, the square is now finished—unlike Piazza della Signoria in Florence.

If Piazza San Marco is the drawing room of Europe, then its satellite, **Piazzetta San Marco** ★★, is the antechamber. Hedged in by the Doges' Palace, Sansovino's Library, and a side of St. Mark's Basilica, the tiny square faces the Grand Canal. One of the two tall granite columns in the piazzetta is surmounted by a winged lion, which represents St. Mark. The other is topped by a statue of a man taming a dragon, supposedly the dethroned patron saint Theodore. Both columns came from the East in the 12th century.

Basilica di San Marco ★★★ This so-called "Church of Gold" dominates Piazza San Marco, and is one of the world's greatest and most richly embellished churches—in fact, it looks as if it had been moved intact from Istanbul. The basilica is a conglomeration of styles, yet it's particularly indebted to Byzantium. It incorporates other schools of design, such as Romanesque and Gothic, with free-wheeling abandon. Like Venice itself, it's adorned with booty from every corner of the city's once far-flung mercantile empire—capitals from Sicily, columns from Alexandria, porphyry from Syria, sculpture from Constantinople. The basilica is capped by a dome that, like a spider plant, sends off shoots, in this case, a quartet of smaller-scale cupolas. Spanning the facade is a loggia, surmounted by replicas of the four famous St. Mark's horses—the *Triumphal Quadriga.*

If you look back at the aperture over the entryway, you can see a mosaic, the dance of Salome in front of Herod and his court. Wearing a star-studded russet-red dress and three white fox tails, Salome dances under a platter holding John's head. Her glassy face is that of a Madonna, not an enchantress. Proceed up the right nave to the doorway to the *tesoro* **(treasury).** The entrance to the **presbytery** is nearby. On the high altar, the alleged sarcophagus of St. Mark rests under a green marble blanket and is held up by four sculptured alabaster Corinthian columns. The Byzantine-style **Pala d'Oro,** from Constantinople, is the rarest treasure at St. Mark's—made of gold and studded with precious stones.

On leaving the basilica, head up the stairs in the atrium for the **Marciano Museum** and the Loggia dei Cavalli. The star attraction of the museum is the

---

Tips **A St. Mark's Warning**

St. Mark's has a strict **dress code:** no shorts, no skirts above the knee, and no bare shoulders. *They will not let you in if you don't come dressed appropriately.* You also must remain silent and cannot take photographs.

world-famous *Quadriga,* four horses looted from Constantinople by Venetian crusaders in the sack of that city in 1204. This is the only quadriga (a quartet of horses yoked together) to have survived from the classical era.

Piazza San Marco. ℂ **041-5225205.** Basilica free; treasury 2€; presbytery 1.50€; Marciano Museum 1.50€. Basilica and presbytery Apr–Sept Mon–Sat 9:30am–5:30pm, Sun 2–5:30pm; Oct–Mar Mon–Sat 10am–4:30pm, Sun 2–4:30pm. Treasury Mon–Sat 9:30am–5pm; Sun 2–5pm. Marciano Museum Apr–Sept Mon–Sat 10am–5:30pm, Sun 2–4:30pm; Oct–Mar Mon–Sat 10am–4:30pm, Sun 2–4:30pm. Vaporetto: San Marco.

Palazzo Ducale 🎭🎭🎭   You enter the Palace of the Doges through the magnificent 15th-century Porta della Carta on the piazzetta. It's somewhat like a frosted birthday cake in pinkish red marble and white Istrian stone. The Venetian–Gothic palazzo—with all the architectural intricacies of a doily—gleams in the tremulous Venetian light. The grandest civic structure in Italy, it dates back to 1309, though a fire in 1577 destroyed much of the original.

After climbing the Sansovino stairway of gold, proceed to the Anti-Collegio salon, which houses the palace's greatest artworks—notably Veronese's *Rape of Europa,* to the far left on the right wall. Tintoretto is well represented with his *Three Graces* and *Bacchus and Ariadne.* Some critics consider the latter his supreme achievement.

Now trek downstairs through the once-private apartments of the doges to the grand Maggior Consiglio, with its allegorical *Triumph of Venice* on the ceiling, painted by Veronese. What makes the room outstanding, however, is Tintoretto's *Paradise,* over the Grand Council chamber—said to be the largest oil painting in the world.

Re-enter the Maggior Consiglio and follow the arrows on their trail across the **Bridge of Sighs** 🎭, linking the Doges' Palace with the Palazzo delle Prigioni, where the cellblocks are found, the ones that lodged the prisoners who felt the quick justice of the Terrible Ten. The "sighs" in the bridge's name stemmed from the sad laments of the numerous victims led across it to certain torture and possible death.

Piazzetta San Marco. ℂ **041-5224951.** Admission 9.50€ adults, 5€ students ages 14–28, 2.50€ students ages 6–13 (schedule visit in advance), free for children under 6. Mar–Oct daily 9am–5:30pm; Nov–Feb daily 9am–5pm. Vaporetto: San Marco.

Campanile di San Marco 🎭🎭   One summer night back in 1902, the bell tower of the Basilica of St. Mark on Piazza San Marco, which was suffering from years of rheumatism in the damp Venetian climate, gave out a warning sound that sent the fashionable crowd scurrying from the Florian Caffè in a dash for their lives. But the campanile gracefully waited until the next morning, July 14, before it tumbled into the piazza. The Venetians rebuilt their belfry, and it's now safe to ascend. A modern elevator takes you up for a pigeon's view of the city. It's a particularly good vantage point for viewing the cupolas of St. Mark's Basilica.

Piazza San Marco. ℂ **041-5224064.** Admission 6€. Oct–Feb daily 9:30am–4pm; Mar–June daily 9am–7pm; July–Sept daily 9am–9pm. Closed Jan 7–31. Vaporetto: San Marco.

MUSEUMS & GALLERIES

Galleria dell'Accademia 🎭🎭🎭   The pomp and circumstance, the glory that was Venice, lives on in this remarkable collection of paintings spanning the 14th century to the 18th century. The hallmark of the Venetian school is color and more color. From Giorgione to Veronese, from Titian to Tintoretto, with a Carpaccio cycle thrown in, the Accademia has samples—often their best—of its most famous sons.

You'll first see works by such 14th-century artists as Paolo and Lorenzo Veneziano, who bridged the gap from Byzantine art to Gothic (see the latter's *Annunciation*). Next, you'll view Giovanni Bellini's *Madonna and Saint* (poor Sebastian, not another arrow), and Carpaccio's fascinating yet gruesome work of mass crucifixion. Two of the most important works with secular themes are Mantegna's armored *St. George,* with the dragon slain at his feet, and Hans Memling's 15th-century portrait of a young man. Giorgione's *Tempest* is the most famous painting at the Accademia.

Campo della Carità, Dorsoduro. © 041-5222247. Admission 6.50€. Mon 8:15am–2pm; Tues–Sun 8am–7:15pm. Vaporetto: Accademia.

Collezione Peggy Guggenheim 🕆🕆🕆 This is one of the most comprehensive and brilliant modern-art collections in the Western world, and it reveals the foresight and critical judgment of its founder. The collection is housed in an unfinished palazzo, the former home of Peggy Guggenheim. In the tradition of her family, Guggenheim was a lifelong patron of contemporary painters and sculptors. As her private collection increased, she decided to find a larger showcase and selected Venice. Displayed here are works not only by Pollock and Ernst but also by Picasso (see his cubist *The Poet* of 1911), Duchamp, Chagall, Mondrian, Brancusi, Delvaux, and Dalí, plus a garden of modern sculpture that includes works by Giacometti.

In the Palazzo Venier dei Leoni, Calle Venier dei Leoni, Dorsoduro 701. © 041-2405411. Admission 8€ adults; 4€ children/students; free for children under 9. Wed–Mon 10am–6pm. Vaporetto: Accademia.

Ca' d'Oro 🕆🕆🕆 This is one of the most handsomely embellished palaces along the Grand Canal. Although it contains the important **Galleria Giorgio Franchetti,** the House of Gold (so named because its facade was once gilded) competes with its own paintings. Built in the first part of the 15th century in the ogival style, it has a lacy look. Baron Franchetti, who restored the palace and filled it with his collection of paintings, sculpture, and furniture, presented it to Italy during World War I. In a special niche reserved for the masterpiece of the Franchetti collection is Andrea Mantegna's icy-cold *St. Sebastian,* the central figure of which is riddled with what must be a record number of arrows.

Cannaregio 3931–3932. © 041-5238790. Admission 3€. Mon 8am–2pm; Tues–Sun 8:15am–7:15pm. Closed Jan 1, May 1, and Dec 25. Vaporetto: Ca' d'Oro.

Museo Civico Correr 🕆🕆 This museum traces the development of Venetian painting from the 14th century to the 16th century. On the second floor are the red and maroon robes once worn by the doges, plus some fabulous street lanterns. There's also an illustrated copy of *Marco Polo in Tartaria.* You can see Cosmé Tura's *La Pietà,* a miniature of renown from the genius in the Ferrara School. This is one of his more gruesome works, depicting a bony, gnarled Christ sprawled on the lap of the Madonna. Farther on, search out a Schiavone *Madonna and Child* (no. 545), our candidate for ugliest bambino ever depicted on canvas (no wonder the mother looks askance). One of the most important rooms at the Correr is filled with three masterpieces: Antonello da Messina's *Pietà*, Hugo van der Goes's *Crucifixion,* and Dieric Bouts's *Madonna and Child.* The star attraction of the Correr is the Bellini salon, which includes works by founding padre Jacopo and his son, Gentile. But the real master of the household was the other son, Giovanni.

In the Procuratie Nuove, Piazza San Marco. © 041-5225625. Admission (including admission to the Ducal Palace above) 9.50€. Mar–Oct daily 9am–7pm; Nov–Feb daily 9am–5pm. Vaporetto: San Marco.

Ca' Rezzonico ✮✮   This 17th- and 18th-century palace along the Grand Canal is where Robert Browning set up his bachelor headquarters. Pope Clement XIII also stayed here. It's a virtual treasure house, known for its baroque paintings and furniture. You first enter the Grand Ballroom with its allegorical ceiling, then proceed through lavishly embellished rooms with Venetian chandeliers, brocaded walls, portraits of patricians, tapestries, gilded furnishings, and touches of chinoiserie. At the end of the first walk is the Throne Room, with its allegorical ceilings by Giovanni Battista Tiepolo.

Upstairs you'll find a survey of 18th-century Venetian art. Head for the first salon on your right (facing the canal) that contains paintings from the brush of Pietro Longhi. His most famous work, *The Lady and the Hairdresser,* is the first canvas to the right on the entrance wall.

Fondamenta Rezzonico, Dorsoduro 3136. ℂ **041-2410100.** Admission 6.50€ adults, 2.50€ children under 14. Wed–Mon 10am–6pm. Closed Tues. Vaporetto: Ca' Rezzonico.

THE SCUOLE
Scuola di San Rocco ✮✮✮   Of Venice's *scuole* (in the Renaissance, scuole were centers used by social and religious organizations affiliated with the local parish), none are as richly embellished as the Scuola di San Rocco, filled with epic canvases by Tintoretto. By a clever trick, he won the competition to decorate the darkly illuminated early 16th-century building. He began painting in 1564 and the work stretched on until his powers as an artist waned. The paintings sweep across the upper and lower halls, mesmerizing the viewer with a kind of passion play. In the grand hallway, they depict New Testament scenes, devoted largely to episodes in the life of Mary (*Flight into Egypt* is among the best). In the top gallery are works illustrating the Old and New Testaments, the most renowned devoted to the life of Christ. In a separate room is Tintoretto's masterpiece—a mammoth *Crucifixion,* one of the world's most celebrated paintings.

Campo San Rocco, San Polo. ℂ **041-5234864.** Admission 5.50€ adults, 1.50€ children. Mar 28–Nov 2 daily 9am–5:30pm; Nov 3–30 and Mar 1–27 daily 10am–4pm; Dec–Feb Mon–Sat 7:30am–12:30pm, Sun 7:30am–12:30pm and 2–4pm. Closed Easter and Dec 25–Jan 1. Ticket office closes 30 min. before last entrance. Vaporetto: San Tomà.

Scuola di San Giorgio degli Schiavoni ✮✮   At the Fondamenta dei Furlani (St. Antonino Bridge) is the second important scuola to visit in Venice. Between 1502 and 1509, Vittore Carpaccio painted a pictorial cycle here of exceptional merit and interest. Of enduring fame are his works of St. George and the dragon—these are our favorite pieces of art in all of Venice and certainly the most delightful. In one frame, St. George charges the dragon on a field littered with half-eaten bodies and skulls. Gruesome? Not at all. Any moment you expect the director to call "Cut!"

Calle dei Furiani, Castello. ℂ **041-5228828.** Admission 2.50€. Nov–Mar Tues–Sat 10am–12:30pm and 3–6pm; Sun 10am–12:30pm. Apr–Oct Tues–Sat 9:30am–12:30pm and 3:30–6:30pm; Sun 9:30am–12:30pm. Last entrance 30 min. before closing. Vaporetto: San Zaccaria.

ORGANIZED TOURS
Daily at 9:10am, **American Express,** San Marco 1471 (ℂ **041-5200844;** vaporetto: San Marco), offers a 2-hour guided tour of the city costing 23€. Sights include St. Mark's Square, the basilica, the Doges' Palace, the prison, the bell tower, and, in some cases, a demonstration of the art of Venetian glass blowing. Monday through Saturday at 3pm, a 2-hour guided tour incorporates visits to the exteriors of several palaces along Campo San Benetto and other sights of

the city. The tour eventually crosses the Grand Canal to visit the Church of Santa Maria dei Frari, which contains an *Assumption* by Titian. The tour continues by gondola down the canal to visit the Ca' d'Oro and ends at the Rialto Bridge. The cost of the afternoon tour is 29€.

The **Evening Serenade Tour,** at 30€ per person, allows a nocturnal view of Venice accompanied by the sound of singing musicians in gondolas. From April to October there are two daily departures, at 7:30pm and 8:30pm, leaving from Campo Santa Maria del Giglio, but from November to March there's just one departure at 3:30pm. Five to six occupants fit in each gondola as a singer and a handful of musicians perform throughout the Venetian evening. The experience lasts 50 minutes.

The **Islands Tour** is a 3-hour tour of Murano, Burano, and Torcello for 15€ per person. Departures are at 2:30pm year-round and also at 9:30am from March 15 to October.

THE SHOPPING SCENE

Venetian **glass** and **lace** are known throughout the world. However, selecting quality products in either craft requires a shrewd eye, as there's much that is tawdry and shoddily crafted. Some of the glassware hawked isn't worth the cost of shipping it home. Yet other pieces represent some of the world's finest artistic and ornamental glass. Murano is famous for its handmade glass, but you can find little glass animal souvenirs in shops all over Venice. If you're looking for an heirloom, stick to such award-winning houses as **Pauly & Co.** or **Venini** (see below).

For lace, head to Burano, where the last of a long line of women put in painstaking hours to produce some of the finest lace in the world. *The* name in Venetian lace is **Jesurum** (see below), which has stood for quality since the last century.

SHOPPING STROLLS   All the main shopping streets of Venice, even the side streets, are touristy and overrun. The greatest concentration of shops is around Piazza San Marco and around the Rialto Bridge. Prices are much higher at San Marco, but the quality of merchandise is better. There are two major shopping strolls in Venice. First, from Piazza San Marco you can stroll through Venice toward the spacious square of **Campo Morosini.** You just follow one shop-lined street all the way to its end (although the name will change several times along the way). You begin at Salizzada San Moisè, which becomes Via 22 Marzo and then Calle delle Ostreghe before it opens onto Campo Santa Maria Zobenigo. The street then narrows again and changes its name to Calle Zaguri before widening once more into Campo San Maurizio, finally becoming Calle Piovan before it reaches Campo Morosini. The only deviation from this tour is a detour down Calle Vallaressa, between San Moisè and the Grand Canal, which is one of the major shopping arteries with some of the biggest designer names in the business.

The other great shopping stroll in Venice wanders from Piazza San Marco to the Rialto in a succession of streets collectively known as **The Mercerie.** It's virtually impossible to get lost because each street name is preceded by the word *merceria,* such as Merceria dell'Orologio, which begins near the clock tower in Piazza San Marco. Many commercial establishments, mainly shops, line the Mercerie before it reaches the Rialto, which then explodes into one vast shopping emporium.

SOME SHOPS WORTH A LOOK

At **Pauly & Co.,** Ponte Consorzi, San Marco (© **041-5209899;** www.pauly glassfactory.com; vaporetto: San Zaccaria), you can wander through 21 salons, enjoy an exhibition of artistic glassware, and later see a furnace in full action. Pauly's production, which is mainly made-to-order, consists of continually renewed patterns, subject to change and alteration based on customer desire. The Venetian glass of **Venini,** Piazzetta Leoncini, San Marco 314 (© **041-5224045;** vaporetto: San Zaccaria), has won collector fans all over the globe. The store sells lamps, bottles, and vases, but not ordinary ones. Many are works of art, representing the best of Venetian craftsmanship. Their best-known glass has a distinctive swirl pattern in several colors, which is called a *venature.*

The elegant **Jesurum,** Mercerie del Capitello, San Marco 4857 (© **041-5206177;** www.jesurum.it; vaporetto: Rialto), the best place in Venice for serious lace purchases, has been in a 12th-century church since 1868. You'll find Venetian hand- or machine-made lace and embroidery on table, bed, and bath linens; and hand-printed bathing suits. **Laboratorio Artigiano Maschere,** Barbaria delle Tole, Castello 6657 (© **041-5223110;** vaporetto: Rialto), is one of the best places to purchase carnival masks handcrafted in papier-mâché or leather. The masks carry names and symbols, the best known being the birdlike luck bringer, called *Buonaventura* in Italian.

VENICE AFTER DARK

The tourist office distributes a free pamphlet (part in English, part in Italian), called *Un Ospite di Venezia.* A section of this useful publication lists events, including any music and opera or theatrical presentations, along with art exhibitions and local special events.

In addition, classical concerts are often at various churches, such as the Chiesa di Vivaldi. To see if any **church concerts** are being presented at the time of your visit, call **Kele and Teo Travel Agency** (© 041-5208722) for information.

THE PERFORMING ARTS

The city's main venue for performing arts, the fabled **La Fenice** at Campo San Fantin, has been a blackened shell since 1996. However, you can still see performances of the Orchestra and Caro della Fenice in a temporary venue, **PalaFenice,** in the Tronchetto parking facilities near Piazzale Roma (© **041-786500** for information; www.teatrolafenice.it; vaporetto: Tronchetto). Tickets for most events range from 15€ to 100€, but this can vary. The **box office** is open Monday through Friday from 8:30am to 1:30pm and 1 hour before the performance (© 041-5210161).

Teatro Goldoni, Calle Goldoni, near Campo San Luca (© **041-2402011;** vaporetto: Rialto), close to the Ponte Rialto in the San Marco district, honors Carlo Goldoni (1707–93), the most prolific—critics say the best—Italian playwright. The theater presents a changing repertoire of productions, often plays in Italian, but musical presentations as well. The box office is open Monday through Saturday from 10am to 1pm and 4:30 to 7pm. Tickets are 13€ to 25€.

PIANO BARS & DANCE CLUBS

The pub **Il Piccolo Mondo,** Calle Contarini Corfu 1056A (© **041-5200371;** vaporetto: Accademia), near the Accademia, is open during the day, and at night features disco dancing and organized parties. The crowd is often young, and dance music prevails. Hours are daily from 10pm to 4am, but the action doesn't begin until after midnight. Cover (including the 1st drink) ranges from 6€ to 9€.

Martini Scala Club, Campo San Fantin, San Marco 1980 (© **041-5224121;** vaporetto: San Marco or Santa Maria del Giglio), is an elegant restaurant with a piano bar that has functioned as some kind of an inn since 1724. You can enjoy its food and wine until 2am—it's the only kitchen in Venice that stays open late. After 10pm, you can come here to enjoy the piano bar. The restaurant is open March through November, Wednesday through Monday from 7 to 11:30pm; December through February, Wednesday through Monday from noon to 2:30pm and 7 to 11:30pm. The bar, which offers a piano bar and food, is open every day but Tuesday from 10pm to 3am, and is closed in July and August.

DAY TRIPS FROM VENICE

MURANO 🎭🎭   On this island, **glass blowers** have for centuries performed oral gymnastics to turn out those fantastic chandeliers that Victorian ladies used to prize so highly. They also produce heavily ornamented glasses so ruby red or so indigo blue you can't tell if you're drinking blackberry juice or pure wood grain. Happily, the glass blowers are still plying their trade, though increasing competition, notably from Sweden, has compelled a greater degree of sophistication in design. You can combine a tour of Murano with a trip along the lagoon. To reach it, take vaporetto 5 at Riva degli Schiavoni, a short walk from Piazzetta San Marco. The boat docks at the landing platform at Murano, where the first furnace conveniently awaits. It's best to go Monday through Friday from 10am to noon if you want to see glass-blowing action.

BURANO 🎭🎭   Burano became world famous as a center of **lace making,** a craft that reached its pinnacle in the 18th century. If you can spare a morning to visit this island, you'll be rewarded with a charming little fishing village far removed in spirit from the grandeur of Venice, but lying only half an hour away by ferry. Boats leave from Fondamente Nuove, overlooking the Venetian graveyard (which is well worth the trip all on its own). Take vaporetto 12 or 52 from Riva degli Schiavoni, get off at Fondamente Nuove, and catch boat 12, marked BURANO.

Once at Burano, you'll discover that the houses of the islanders come in varied colors—sienna, robin's-egg or cobalt blue, barn-red, butterscotch, grass green. **Scuola Merietti** stands in the center of the fishing village on Piazza Baldassare Galuppi. The Burano School of Lace was founded in 1872 as part of a resurgence movement aimed at restoring the age-old craft that had earlier declined, giving way to such other lace-making centers as Chantilly and Bruges. By going up to the second floor you can see the lace makers, mostly young women, at painstaking work and can purchase hand-embroidered or handmade lace items.

After visiting the lace school, you can walk across the square to the **Duomo** and its leaning campanile (inside, look for a *Crucifixion* by Tiepolo). However, walk quickly; the bell tower is leaning so precariously it looks as if it may topple at any moment.

TORCELLO 🎭🎭   Of all the islands of the lagoon, Torcello—the so-called Mother of Venice—offers the most charm. If Burano is behind the times, Torcello is positively antediluvian. You can follow in the footsteps of Hemingway and stroll across a grassy meadow, traverse an ancient stone bridge, and step back into that time when the Venetians first fled from invading barbarians to create a city of Neptune in the lagoon. To reach Torcello, take vaporetto 12 from Fondamenta Nuova on Murano. The trip takes about 45 minutes.

Cattedrale di Torcello, also called the Church of Santa Maria Assunta Isola di Torcello (*©* **041-730119**), was founded in A.D. 639 and was subsequently rebuilt. It stands in a lonely, grassy meadow beside a campanile dating from the 11th century. It's visited chiefly because of its Byzantine mosaics. Clutching her child, the weeping Madonna in the apse is a magnificent sight, whereas on the opposite wall is a powerful *Last Judgment.* It's open daily April through October from 10:30am to 6; November through March from 10am to 5pm. Admission is 2.50€.

While on the island, you can dine in Venice's most idyllic luncheon stopover, **Locanda Cipriani** *✿✿*, Piazza San Fosca 29 (*©* **041-730150**), operated by Bonifacio Brass, nephew of Harry Cipriani of Hotel Cipriani and Harry's Bar fame. This low-key, deliberately rustic locanda serves an authentic Venetian cuisine, everything from a succulent risotto made from fresh vegetables and herbs from the family garden to filet of John Dory in the style of Carla, a late and much-revered matriarch here (the fish is flavored with tomatoes and capers). Main courses run from 15€ to 25€. Hours are Wednesday through Monday from noon to 3pm and Saturday from 7 to 10pm; closed from January 15 to February 15. American Express, Diners Club, MasterCard, and Visa are accepted.

The Netherlands

by George McDonald

Easygoing, prosperous Amsterdam, full of canals, bridges, and world-class museums, and enveloped in the afterglow of its 17th-century golden age, is the natural focus of a visit to the Netherlands.

From here you can make day trips to historic Haarlem; brash Zandvoort on the North Sea coast; the pretty conservation village of Zaanse Schans; and the traditional IJsselmeer lakeside villages of Volendam and Marken. Also, you should visit Delft, famous for its royal connections and blue-and-white porcelain, and Leiden, known for its associations with the Pilgrim Fathers.

1 Amsterdam

The Dutch capital has never entirely shed its twofold reputation as a hippie haven and a tulips-and-windmills landmark, even with an economy that has moved far beyond these clichés. Powered more by business than by the combustion of semilegal exotic plants, prosperity has settled like a North Sea mist around the graceful cityscape of canals and 17th-century town houses.

The historic center recalls Amsterdam's golden age as the command post of a vast trading network and colonial empire, when wealthy merchants constructed gabled residences along neatly laid-out canals.

A delicious irony is that the placid old structures also host brothels, smoke shops, and some extravagant nightlife. The city's inhabitants, proud of their live-and-let-live attitude, which is based on pragmatism as much as a long history of tolerance, have decided to control what they cannot effectively outlaw. They permit licensed prostitution in the Red Light District and the sale of hashish and marijuana in designated "coffee shops."

But don't think Amsterdammers drift around town in a drug-induced haze. They are too busy whizzing around on bicycles, jogging through Vondelpark, feasting on arrays of ethnic dishes, or simply watching the parade of street life from a sidewalk cafe. A new generation of entrepreneurs has revitalized old neighborhoods like the Jordaan, turning some of the distinctive houses into offbeat stores and bustling cafes, hotels, and restaurants.

Between dips into Amsterdam's artistic and historical treasures, be sure to take time out to absorb the freewheeling spirit of Europe's most vibrant city.

ESSENTIALS

GETTING THERE   By Plane   If you fly into Amsterdam, you arrive at the efficient, single-terminal **Amsterdam Airport Schiphol** (© **0900/0141** for flight information; www.schiphol.nl), 18km (11 miles) south of the city. You exit from Customs into Schiphol Plaza, a combined arrivals hall and mall, with currency-exchange offices, ATMs, bars, restaurants, and shops. You can get questions answered and make hotel reservations at the **Holland Tourist Information** desk, open daily from 7am to 10pm.

A **train** from Schiphol Station, a floor below Schiphol Plaza, connects the airport with Amsterdam's Centraal Station. The fare is 2.95€ one-way in second class and the trip takes 15 minutes.

A **KLM hotel bus** shuttles between the airport and the city center on a circular route directly connecting 16 top hotels that are close to many others. A bus leaves from in front of Schiphol Plaza every 20 minutes from 7am to 6pm and every 30 minutes from 6 to 9:30pm. The fare is 8€ one-way. Bus no. 197 connects the airport with the city center every half hour and costs 3.40€ one-way. A **taxi** from the airport to the city center costs 35€.

By Train Whether you arrive by Thalys high-speed train from Brussels or Paris, by ordinary international train, or by a train from elsewhere in the Netherlands, you'll likely find yourself deposited at **Centraal Station,** built over 100 years ago on a man-made island. For information on trains (and other public transportation) in the Netherlands, call © **0900/9292;** for international trains, call © **0900/9296.** Inside the station is a currency-exchange counter, train info center, and VVV Amsterdam tourist office. Right in front of the station is another branch of VVV Amsterdam, an array of tram and bus stops, a Metro station (downstairs), and a ticket office where you can buy a *strippenkaart* or *dagkaart* for trams, the Metro, and buses (see "Getting Around," below). You

Amsterdam

- - - - Ferry route
———— Railway

buy these cards for less money here than if you buy them from tram conductors and bus drivers.

By Bus Coaches from London, Paris, Brussels, and other cities, operated by **Eurolines** (✆ 020/560-8788; www.eurolines.com), arrive at the bus station adjoining Amstel train station in the south of the city.

By Car European expressways E19, E35, E231, and E22 converge on Amsterdam from France and Belgium to the south and from Germany to the north and east.

VISITOR INFORMATION The **VVV Amsterdam tourist office,** Stationsplein 10 (✆ **0900/400-4040;** fax 020/625-2869; www.visitamsterdam.nl; tram: 1, 2, 4, 5, 9, 13, 16, 17, 20, 24, 25), is in front of Centraal Station in a small white building that also has a cafe and boat dock. It's open daily from 9am to 5pm (to 4:30pm Nov–Mar). Another office, on Platform 1 in the train station, is open Monday through Saturday from 8am to 8pm and Sunday from 8:30am to 4:30pm. Both offices provide maps, brochures, and details about the city, reserve hotels and tours, and sell theater and concert tickets. A VVV information center at Leidseplein 1 (tram: 1, 2, 5, 6, 7, 10, 20) is open Monday through Saturday from 9am to 8pm and Sunday from 9am to 5pm.

Be sure to pick up a copy of *What's On in Amsterdam* for 1.80€. This monthly magazine is full of details about art exhibits, concerts, and theater performances, and lists bars, dance clubs, and restaurants.

For more details on cultural events and to reserve and purchase tickets for almost every venue in the city, stop by the **Amsterdam Uit Buro (AUB),** on the corner of Leidseplein and Marnixstraat (✆ **020/621-1211;** tram: 1, 2, 5, 6, 7, 10, 20), open Monday through Saturday from 10am to 6pm.

Websites The official website of the Netherlands Board of Tourism (**www. visitholland.com**) has useful advice for upcoming events, bicycling, and culture—and it even lets you know when the tulips bloom. Amsterdam's most comprehensive website, **www.visitamsterdam.nl,** lays out the details on sightseeing, walking routes, wining and dining, shopping for antiques, and current events. There's even a page warning you about streets that can be dangerous at night. For information on many of Amsterdam's more than 40 museums, go to **www. hollandmuseums.nl.** To find an extensive "A–Z Index" with listings for museums, hotels, transportation, and other categories, visit **www.go-amsterdam.org.** One of the best virtual tours on the Net is **www.channels.nl**—the images are clear, you can direct your own tour, and you can chat with others about Amsterdam. Visitors give their impressions of restaurants, hotels, museums, and hash houses. At **www.amsterdamhotspots.nl,** they mean "hot." Here are *the* places to fill your nights, from eating and drinking to where to toke, what the top gay bars are, and where to see those famous working girls on display behind picture windows. Good eating-out info is available from **www.dinner-in-amsterdam. nl.** And if you're interested in an American expat's experience of the city, go to **www.homepage-amsterdam.com.**

CITY LAYOUT Although Amsterdam center is small enough that residents think of it as a village, it can be confusing until you get the hang of it. A map like the handy VVV Amsterdam Map, available from VVV tourist offices for 1.80€, is essential.

When you step out of Centraal Station's main entrance, you're facing south toward the center. From here the **Old City** is laid out along five concentric semicircles of canals: **Singel, Herengracht, Keizersgracht, Prinsengracht,** and

Singelgracht (*gracht* means "canal"). Along this necklace of man-made waterways, wealthy 17th-century merchants built their elegant homes, most of which are still standing. Within these canals are many smaller canals and connecting streets, radiating from the center.

Damrak, a busy tourist street, leads from Centraal Station to the **Dam,** once the location of the original dam on the Amstel River that gave the city its name and now a large open square on which stands the Royal Palace. To the left is the famous **Red Light District,** where government-licensed prostitutes sit in their windows, waiting for customers. A block to the right of Damrak is **Nieuwendijk** (which becomes **Kalverstraat** when it crosses the Dam), a pedestrianized shopping street. If you follow Kalverstraat to the end, you'll be at **Muntplein** (*plein* means "square"), identified by the old Mint Tower. Cross Singel and continue in the same direction to reach **Rembrandtplein,** one of the main nightlife areas. Beyond Rembrandtplein is **Waterlooplein,** which hosts the Muziektheater and a great flea market.

At the heart of another important nightlife zone is **Leidseplein,** on Singelgracht. Leidseplein is at the end of Leidsestraat, a pedestrians-only shopping street. **Museumplein,** where you find Amsterdam's three most famous museums—the Rijksmuseum, Van Gogh Museum, and modern art Stedelijk Museum—is a short walk along Singelgracht from Leidseplein.

The **Jordaan,** a fast-developing old neighborhood now filled with inexpensive restaurants, unusual stores, and small galleries, lies between Prinsengracht, Brouwersgracht, Singelgracht, and Rozengracht. Turn right off Damrak at any point between Centraal Station and the Dam, and when you cross Prinsengracht, you're in the Jordaan.

GETTING AROUND   By Tram, Bus & Metro   Public transportation begins around 6am and the regular service ends around midnight. After that, there are infrequent night buses. Riding the distinctive yellow **trams (streetcars)** is the most convenient means of getting around; they're fast, cheap, and fun, and provide a great view of the sights. Of 17 tram routes in the city, 11 begin and end at Centraal Station.

The **Circle Tram,** no. 20, is a special line that makes 30 stops at most of the important museums and attractions and Centraal Station, making this a convenient option for a heavy sightseeing day. Prices are the same as for the *dagkaart* (see below) and include a useful map, and a Circle Tram ticket is valid for all other transportation. The tram runs daily from 9am to 6pm.

An extensive **bus** network complements the trams and reaches many points the trams don't cover.

The city's four **Metro** (subway) lines don't serve most areas you'll want to visit, being used mainly to get people to and from the suburbs, but from Centraal Station you can use Metro trains to reach Nieuwmarkt and Waterlooplein, both stops in the central zone.

Maps showing the transportation network and fare zones are posted at most tram/bus shelters and all Metro stations. A detailed map is available from VVV tourist offices and **GVB/Amsterdam Municipal Transportation** (© 0900/ 9292) ticket booths on Stationsplein in front of Centraal Station.

You can buy tickets from drivers, conductors, ticket dispensers, GVB/Amsterdam Municipal Transportation ticket booths, VVV tourist offices, and many news vendors. An *enkeltje* (single-journey ticket) costs 1.35€ to 3.40€, depending on how many zones you travel through. Tourists rarely travel outside the central zone.

A *dagkaart* (day ticket) is good for unlimited travel in all city zones for up to 9 days. A 1-day card is 5.45€ from the GVB/Amsterdam Municipal Transportation ticket booths. Also available are day tickets valid for 2 to 9 days, priced from 7.25€ to 19€. You need to use public transportation a lot for these passes to be worthwhile.

If you plan to walk a lot and only occasionally take trams around the center, you're probably better off with a *strippenkaart* (strip card) that you can use throughout your stay. You can buy an eight-strip card for 5.60€ from drivers and conductors, or the more cost-effective 15-strip card for 5.90€ and the 45-strip card for 16€ from the locations referred to above. Before boarding a tram or bus, determine how many zones you'll be traversing. Fold your strip card so that one more box than the number of zones is facing up, and stick this end into the yellow box near the door as you enter. The machine stamps your card (some trams have a conductor who stamps the card). On buses, have the driver stamp your card. The ticket includes transfers to other tram, bus, and Metro lines within 1 hour of the time stamped.

Keep in mind that inspectors, sometimes undercover, may demand to see your ticket at any time. If you haven't paid the proper fare, you'll be fined 30€ plus the fare for the ride.

By Bike   Follow the Dutch example and pedal. A bike is one of the best ways of getting around in this flat city where too many cars clog the narrow streets. You see children barely old enough to walk, their great-grandparents, and even business-women in high heels pedaling through the city in any kind of weather. Sunday, when the city is quiet, is a good day to pedal through the parks and to practice riding on cobblestones and dealing with trams before venturing into a rush-hour fray.

Warning: Watch out for unpredictable car drivers and always lock your bike and its front wheel to something fixed and solid—theft is common.

Bike-rental rates average 6€ per day or 30€ per week, with a deposit required. The following outfits are located in the city center and have good rates and service: **Take a Bike,** in the basement of Centraal Station, to the right of the main entrance as you face the station (© **020/624-8391;** tram: 1, 2, 4, 5, 9, 13, 16, 17, 20, 24, 25); **Damstraat Rent-a-Bike,** Damstraat 22–24 (© **020/625-5029;** tram: 4, 9, 14, 16, 20, 24, 25); **MacBike,** Mr. Visserplein 2 (© **020/620-0985;** tram: 4, 9, 14, 20); **MacBike Too,** Marnixstraat 220 (© **020/626-6964;** tram: 10, 17, 20); and **Bike City,** Bloemgracht 70 (© **020/626-3721;** tram: 13, 14, 17, 20).

By Taxi   Officially, you can't simply hail a cab, but they'll often stop if you do. You can get a taxi in front of any major hotel and at Centraal Station, the Dam, Leidseplein, Rembrandtplein, and other locations. To phone for a cab, call **Taxi Centrale** (© **020/677-7777**). Rates start at 2.65€ and increase by 1.30€ per kilometer, or about 2.10€ per mile.

By Boat   The **Museumboot** (© **020/622-2181**) operates canal buses near virtually all Amsterdam's museums and attractions. The boats leave from in front of Centraal Station every 30 minutes daily from 10am to 5pm. Tickets are available at the Lovers Canal Cruises counter near the dock. A day ticket is 12€ adults and 7€ after 1pm for seniors or children 13 and under. The ticket allows reduced admission to most of the museums on the route. There are English-speaking guides on the boats.

The **Canal Bus** (© **020/623-9886**) boats operate daily from 10am to 5pm on three fixed routes—Green, Red, and Blue—that connect important museums and shopping and entertainment districts, with two buses an hour at peak times. A day pass, valid until noon the next day and including a museum admission discount, costs 13€ adults and 7.95€ children 13 and under.

A water taxi, from a dock outside Centraal Station, takes up to eight passengers, at 60€ per half hour and with a 25€ pick-up charge. If you feel like a splurge, call **Watertaxi** (✆ 020/530-1090).

By Rental Car   Don't drive in Amsterdam. The city is a jumble of one-way streets, narrow bridges, and trams and cyclists darting every which way. Tough measures are in place to make driving as difficult as possible. No-parking zones are rigorously enforced and the limited parking spaces are expensive. Car break-ins are common.

Outside the city, driving is a different story and you may want to rent a car to see the nearby countryside. All the top international firms rent here: **Avis,** Nassaukade 380 (✆ **020/683-6061;** tram: 1, 6); **Budget,** Overtoom 121 (✆ **020/612-6066;** tram: 1, 6); **Europcar,** Overtoom 197 (✆ **020/683-2123;** tram: 1, 6); and **Hertz,** Overtoom 333 (✆ **020/612-2441;** tram: 1, 6). All of these firms also have desks at the airport. Rates begin at around 45€ for a small car with unlimited mileage. The smallest car at **Diks,** Van Ostadestraat 278–280 (✆ **020/662-3366;** tram: 3, 4, 20), is 43€ per day, including unlimited mileage, insurance, and tax.

Remember: You get the best deal if you arrange the rental before leaving home.

By Foot   When looking at a map of Amsterdam, you might think the city is too large to explore by foot. This isn't true: It's possible to see almost every important sight in the Old City on a 4-hour walk.

By Swimming   Believe it or not, some folks (perhaps influenced by too many trips to the "coffee shop") think this is a good way to get around the canals. It isn't. Swallow so much as one mouthful of that witch's brew and a session on a hospital stomach pump will lie in your immediate future.

 ## *FAST FACTS:* Amsterdam

American Express   The offices at Damrak 66 (✆ 020/504-7777; tram: 4, 9, 14, 16, 24, 25) and Van Baerlestraat 39 (✆ 020/673-8550; tram: 2, 3, 5, 12) are open Monday through Friday from 9am to 5pm and Saturday from 9am to noon. The Damrak office provides currency exchange and books tours; the Van Baerlestraat office only books tours.

Business Hours   **Banks** are open Monday through Friday from 9am to 4 or 5pm, and some to 7pm on Thursday. Hours for **offices** are Monday through Friday from 9 or 10am to 4 or 5pm. Regular **shopping** hours are Monday from 10 or 11am to 6pm; Tuesday, Wednesday, and Friday from 9am to 6pm; Thursday from 9am to 9pm; and Saturday from 9am to 5pm. Some stores are open Sunday from noon to 5pm.

Currency   The Netherlands uses the **euro** (€).

Currency Exchange   The best options for changing money are the VVV tourist offices, banks, and, if you carry American Express traveler's checks, **American Express** (see above). Other fair-deal options are **Thomas Cook,** Damrak 125 (✆ 020/620-3236; tram: 4, 9, 14, 16, 29, 24, 25), Dam 23–25 (✆ 020/625-0922; tram: 4, 9, 14, 16, 29, 24, 25), and Leidseplein 31A (✆ 020/626-7000; tram: 1, 2, 5, 6, 7, 10); and the **Grenswisselkantoor (GWK)** exchanges at Schiphol Airport (✆ 020/653-5121), at Centraal Station (✆ 020/627-2731), and at some international border crossings and main train stations. These organizations can provide cash advances for holders of American Express, Diners Club, MasterCard, and Visa credit and charge cards. GWK can arrange money transfers through **Western Union.**

Hotels and bureaux de change (currency-exchange offices), which are open regular hours plus evenings and weekends, often charge a low commission (or none at all) but may give a low exchange rate—always know *exactly* how much you are going to get in your hand before agreeing to the transaction.

Among the centrally located **automated teller machines (ATMs),** accessible by cards linked to the Cirrus and PLUS networks and by the major credit cards and charge cards, are those at **ABN-AMRO Bank,** Dam 2 (tram: 4, 9, 14, 16, 24, 25), and at Leidsestraat 1 (tram: 1, 2, 5) at Leidseplein; **Rabobank,** Dam 16 (tram: 4, 9, 14, 16, 24, 25); and **Fortis Bank,** Singel 548 (tram: 4, 9, 14, 16, 24, 25), at the Flower Market.

Dentists/Doctors Call the **Central Medical Service** (© 020/592-3434).

Drugstores/Pharmacies For such items as toothpaste, deodorant, and razor blades, go to a *drogerij* (drugstore) or a supermarket. For both prescription and non-prescription medicines, go to an *apotheek* (pharmacy). All pharmacies have the name and address of an all-night and Sunday pharmacy posted on the door.

Embassies & Consulates The **United States** consulate at Museumplein 19 (© 020/575-5309; tram: 3, 5, 12, 16, 20) is open Monday through Friday from 8:30am to noon and 1:30 to 3:30pm; the U.S. embassy is at Lange Voorhout 102, The Hague (© 070/310-9209). The **United Kingdom** Consulate-General at Koningslaan 44 (© 020/676-4343; tram: 2) is open Monday through Friday from 9am to noon and 2 to 4pm; the British embassy is at Lange Voorhout 10, The Hague (© 070/364-5800).

Citizens of other English-speaking countries should contact their embassies in The Hague: **Australia,** Carnegielaan 14, Den Haag (© 070/ 310-8200); **Canada,** Sophialaan 7, Den Haag (© 070/311-1600); **Ireland,** Dr. Kuyperstraat 9, Den Haag (© 070/363-0993); **New Zealand,** Mauritskade 25, Den Haag (© 070/346-9324); and **South Africa,** Wassenaarseweg 40, Den Haag (© 070/392-4501).

Emergencies For police assistance, an ambulance, or the fire department, call © **112.**

Holidays The following holidays are observed in Amsterdam: January 1 (New Year's Day); Good Friday; Easter Monday; April 30 (Queen's Day/*Koninginnedag*); Ascension Day; Pentecost Monday; December 25 (Christmas Day) and December 26. The dates for Easter, Ascension, and Pentecost change each year.

Hospitals Two hospitals with emergency services are the **Onze Lieve Vrouwe Gasthuis,** Eerste Oosterparkstraat 179 (© 020/599-9111; tram: 3, 7, 10), in Amsterdam Oost; and the giant **Academisch Medisch Centrum (AMC),** Meibergdreef 9 (© 020/566-3333; Metro: Holendrecht), in Amsterdam Zuidoost.

Internet Access In the city center, **easyEverything** (www.easyevery thing.com) has two locations: Damrak 33 (© 020/320-8082; tram: 1, 2, 4, 5, 9, 13, 16, 17, 24, 25); and Reguliersbreestraat 22 (© 020/320-6291; tram:

4, 9, 14). Both are open 24 hours a day, and access begins at 1.15€ per hour. A less-crowded choice is the **Internet Café**, Martelaarsgracht 11 (*©* **020/627-1052;** info@internetcafe.nl; tram: 1, 2, 5, 13, 17), open Sunday through Thursday from 9am to 1am, Friday through Saturday from 9am to 3am; access is 2.75€ an hour.

Mail Most **post offices** are open Monday through Friday from 9am to 5pm. The office at Singel 256, at the corner of Raadhuisstraat (tram: 13, 14, 17, 20), is open Monday through Friday from 9am to 6pm (to 8pm Thurs), Saturday from 9am to 3pm. Postage for a postcard or ordinary letter to the U.S., Canada, Australia, New Zealand, or South Africa is .75€; to the U.K. or Ireland it's .45€.

Safety Random violent crime is not common in Amsterdam, though it does happen. Nonviolent crimes like pickpocketing and theft from cars are common and tourists in particular are targets. Muggings are more rare, but you need to watch out in some places and circumstances, like strolling through the Red Light District or along a deserted canal-side at night.

Taxes A **value-added tax (BTW)** of 6% is tacked onto hotel and restaurant bills (19% on beer, wine, and liquor), and 6% or 19% (the amount depends on the product) is added to purchases. For information on how to recover some of the 19% on purchases, see "The Shopping Scene," later in this chapter.

Telephone The **country code** for the Netherlands is **31**. The **city code** for Amsterdam is **20;** use this code when you're calling from outside the Netherlands. If you're within the Netherlands but not in Amsterdam, use **020**. If you're calling within Amsterdam, simply leave off the code and dial only the regular seven-digit phone number.

Both local and long-distance calls from a pay phone are .25€ per minute. International calls, per minute, are: **U.S.** and **Canada** .30€; **U.K.** and **Ireland** .25€; **Australia** and **New Zealand** .40€; **South Africa** 2€. You can use pay phones in booths all around town with a KPN *telekaart* (phone card), selling for 5€, 13€, and 25€ from post offices, train ticket counters, and newsstands. Some pay phones take coins of .05€, .10€, .20€, .50€, and 1€. For information inside the Netherlands, call *©* **0900/ 8008;** for international information, call *©* **0900/8418.**

To charge a call to your calling card, dial **AT&T** (*©* **0800/022-9111**); **MCI** (*©* **0800/022-9122**); **Sprint** (*©* **0800/022-9119**); **Canada Direct** (*©* **0800/ 022-9116**); or **British Telecom** (*©* **0800/022-9944**).

Tipping A 15% service is included in the price of the meals at almost all restaurants (if it isn't, it will generally say so on the menu), so it's not necessary to leave a tip. But waitstaff do appreciate tips and if the service was good you might want to leave a small one by rounding up in cash, not on a credit card slip, to the nearest euro or the nearest 5€, depending on the price of the meal (in an expensive restaurant you might feel obliged to go up to the nearest 10€). Taxi fares are high and include a service charge; though drivers appreciate a tip, it's not really necessary to give one unless you want to.

WHERE TO STAY

Most Amsterdam hotels, whatever their cost, are clean and tidily furnished, and in many cases they've been recently renovated or redecorated. Even if you don't stay in a canal-house hotel, you'll most likely stay in a building built 250 to 350 years ago during Amsterdam's golden age.

In most cases, a Dutch breakfast is included with the room rate. It usually includes ham, cheese, a boiled egg, several types of bread, butter, milk, and sometimes chocolate sprinkles, which are very popular.

Booking ahead is always advised. The Dutch hotel industry runs a free hotel-booking service, the **Netherlands Reservation Center,** P.O. Box 404, 2260 AK Leidschendam (ℰ **070/419-5500;** fax 070/419-5519; or book online at www. hotelres.nl). If you arrive in Amsterdam without a reservation, consult the **VVV tourist offices** (see "Visitor Information," earlier in this chapter). Or contact the VVV's **Amsterdam Reservation Center** (ℰ **0777/000-888;** reservations@ amsterdamtourist.nl). In summer, it's imperative you look for a room early in the day—by late afternoon many hotels are already full. Try to avoid arriving after dark, since this makes finding a place to stay difficult.

If you need to stay close to the airport, try the **Sheraton Amsterdam Airport,** Schiphol Blvd. 101, 1118 BG Schiphol Airport (ℰ **800/325-3535** in the U.S. and Canada, or 020/316-4300; fax 020/316-4399; www.sheraton.com/ amsterdam). You will have all the comfort you would expect from a top-flight Sheraton. Doubles cost 325€ to 395€. A less expensive option is the **Dorint Schiphol Amsterdam,** Sloterweg 299, 1171 VB Badhoevedorp (ℰ **020/658-8111;** fax 020/658-8100; www.dorint.de). Doubles cost 175€ to 210€.

NEAR THE DAM & CENTRAAL STATION
Very Expensive

Hôtel de l'Europe ✦✦✦   On a stretch of prime riverside real estate in the city center, this elegant old establishment is a member of the Leading Hotels of the World. Its red and white facade, at the point where the Amstel River flows into the city's canal network, is an iconic element in the classic view of the city. Built in 1896, the de l'Europe has a grand style and a sense of ease, a smooth combination of aged dignity and modern comforts. Guest rooms and bathrooms are spacious and bright, furnished with classic good taste. Some rooms have mini-balconies overlooking the river, and all boast marble bathrooms.

Nieuwe Doelenstraat 2–8 (facing Muntplein), 1012 CP Amsterdam. ℰ 800/223-6800 in the U.S. and Canada, or 020/531-1777. Fax 020/531-1778. www.leurope.nl. 100 units. 335€–415€ double; suites from 445€; add 5% city tax. AE, DC, MC, V. Valet and self-parking 38€. Tram: 4, 9, 14, 16, 24, or 25 to De Munt. **Amenities:** 2 restaurants; 2 bars; heated indoor pool; health club; sauna; concierge; 24-hr. room service; massage; babysitting; laundry service; dry cleaning; nonsmoking rooms. *In room:* A/C, TV w/pay movies, dataport, minibar, hair dryer, safe.

Expensive

Die Port van Cleve ✦✦   Oozing history and class, one of the city's oldest hotels began its life in 1864 as the first Heineken brewery. Behind the ornamental facade, complete with turrets and alcoves, rooms, though on the small side, are comfortably furnished in modern yet cozy style. You won't eat better Dutch food than in the hotel's character-rich restaurant Brasserie De Poort, and you can drink in the equally notable bar De Blauwe Parade, which is watched over by Delft Blue tiles.

Nieuwezijds Voorburgwal 176–180 (behind the Royal Palace), 1012 SJ Amsterdam. ℰ 020/624-4860. Fax 020/622-0240. www.dieportvancleve.com. 120 units. 215€–295€ double; 350€–525€ suite; add 5% city

---

Tips **Booking a Room at a B&B**

An alternative to hotels is a bed-and-breakfast. Contact **Bed & Breakfast Holland,** Theophile de Bockstraat 3, 1058 TV Amsterdam (© 020/615-7527; fax 020/669-1573). Rates per person range from 18€ to 32€, depending on amenities and location. There's a 2-night minimum stay.

---

tax. AE, DC, MC, V. No parking. Tram: 1, 2, 5, 13, or 17 to the Dam. **Amenities:** Restaurant; bar; cafe; concierge; business center; limited room service; executive rooms; nonsmoking rooms. *In room:* TV w/pay movies, hair dryer, safe.

Moderate

Avenue Hotel 🔆 About 2 minutes from Centraal Station, this recently renovated and expanded establishment has some of the style and amenities of its neighbor, the Crowne Plaza (see below), at less than half the price. Part of the premises is a converted warehouse from the city's golden age that belonged to the V.O.C., the United East India Company. The rooms aren't huge, but they are bright and have clean furnishings and good-size bathrooms, some with a double sink.

Nieuwezijds Voorburgwal 33 (near Centraal Station), 1012 9599 Amsterdam. © 020/530-9530. Fax 020/530-39-46. www.emb.hotels.nl. 78 units. 105€–164€ double. Rates include buffet breakfast. AE, DC, MC, V. Limited street parking. Tram: 1, 2, 5, 13, or 17 to Nieuwezijds Kolk. **Amenities:** Bar/brasserie; bike rental; dry cleaning. *In room:* TV w/pay movies, dataport, hair dryer.

Inexpensive

Amstel Botel 🔆 Where better to experience a city built on water than on a moored boat-hotel? Built in 1993, Amsterdam's only floating hotel has become quite popular, largely because of its location, seemingly adventurous nature, and rates. The rooms, on four decks connected by an elevator, are furnished in a nononsense but comfortable modern style; the showers are small. To get here, leave the station and turn left, passing the bike rental—the Botel is painted white and is directly in front of you. Be sure to ask for a room with a view on the waterside, not on the uninspiring quayside.

Oosterdokskade 2–4 (at Centraal Station), 1011 AE Amsterdam. © 020/626-4247. Fax 020/639-1952. 175 units. 75€–86€ double. AE, DC, MC, V. Limited street parking. Tram: 1, 2, 4, 5, 9, 13, 16, 17, 24, or 25 to Centraal Station. *In room:* TV.

ALONG THE RING CANALS
Expensive

Ambassade 🔆🔆 Perhaps more than any other hotel in Amsterdam, this one, in ten 17th- and 18th-century canal houses on the Herengracht and Singel canals, re-creates the feeling of living in an elegant canal house. The pastel-toned rooms are individually styled, their size and shape varying according to the character of the individual houses. Everyone who stays at the Ambassade enjoys the view each morning with breakfast in the bi-level, chandeliered breakfast room or each evening in the adjoining parlor, with Persian rugs and a stately grandfather clock ticking away.

Herengracht 335–353 (near Spui), 1016 AZ Amsterdam. © 020/555-0222. Fax 020/555-0277. www.ambassade-hotel.nl. 59 units. 180€ double; 250€–315€ suite; 285€ apt. AE, DC, MC, V. Limited street parking. Tram: 1, 2, or 5 to Spui. **Amenities:** Bike rental; 24-hr. room service; massage at nearby float center; babysitting; laundry service; dry cleaning. *In room:* TV, hair dryer, safe.

Moderate

Amsterdam Wiechmann It takes only a moment to feel at home in this hotel's antiques-adorned lobby. Owned for years by American T. Boddy and his Dutch wife, Nicky, the Wiechmann, which has no elevator, is comfortable and casual. Like a good wine, it gets better with age, and the location is one of the best you'll find in this or any price range. Most rooms are furnished in modern style, with twin or double beds, and some have big bay windows. Higher-priced doubles have antique furnishings, and many have a canal view.

Prinsengracht 328–332 (at Looiersgracht), 1016 HX Amsterdam. © **020/626-3321**. Fax 020/626-8962. www.hotelwiechmann.nl. 40 units. 120€–140€ double. Rates include continental breakfast. MC, V. Limited street parking. Tram: 1, 2, or 5 to Prinsengracht. *In room:* TV, safe.

Canal House A contemporary approach to re-establishing the elegant canal-house atmosphere has been taken by the owner of this small hotel, in an effort to create a home away from home. Three adjoining houses dating from 1630 were rebuilt to provide private bathrooms, and then filled with antiques, quilts, and Chinese rugs. Room no. 26 has a panoramic view of the canal. The beds, some with drapes, have new and comfortable mattresses on antique frames. An elegant breakfast room, seemingly unchanged since the 17th century, overlooks the back garden, and there's a cozy Victorian-style saloon.

Keizersgracht 148 (near Leliegracht), 1015 CX Amsterdam. © **020/622-5182**. Fax 020/624-1317. www.canalhouse.nl. 26 units. 150€–190€ double. Rates include continental breakfast. DC, MC, V. Limited street parking. Tram: 13, 14, or 17 to Westermarkt. **Amenities:** Lounge; limited room service. *In room:* Hair dryer.

Inexpensive

Hoksbergen *(Kids)* At a tranquil point on the historic Singel canal, this inexpensive hotel in a 300-year-old canal house is neither flashy nor elegant, but it's bright and fresh and recently renovated, which makes it appealing to budget-conscious travelers who don't want to swap creature comforts for euros. Its central location makes it easy to get to all the surrounding sights and attractions. Rooms at the front have canal views.

Singel 301 (near Spui), 1012 WH Amsterdam. © **020/626-6043**. Fax 020/638-3479. www.hotelhoksbergen. om. 14 units. 76€–90€ double. Rates include continental breakfast. AE, DC, MC, V. Limited street parking. Tram: 1, 2, or 5 to Spui. *In room:* TV.

ON & NEAR LEIDSEPLEIN
Very Expensive

Crowne Plaza Amsterdam–American A fanciful, castlelike mix of Venetian Gothic and Art Nouveau, the American has been both a prominent landmark and a popular meeting place for Amsterdammers since 1900. While the exterior must always remain a protected architectural treasure of turrets, arches, and balconies, the interior (except that of the cafe, which is also protected) is modern and chic, though at times a bit gaudy. Rooms are subdued, refined, and superbly furnished, and while some have a view of the Singelgracht, others overlook kaleidoscopic Leidseplein.

Tips **A Canal-House Warning**

Be prepared to climb hard-to-navigate stairways if you want to save money on lodging in Amsterdam. Narrow and steep as ladders, these stairways were designed to conserve space in the narrow houses along the canals. If you have difficulty climbing stairs, ask for a room on a lower floor.

Leidsekade 97 (at Leidseplein), 1017 PN Amsterdam. ℂ **020/556-3000.** Fax 020/556-3001. www.amsterdam-american.crowneplaza.com. 174 units. 290€–405€ double; 470€–505€ suite; add 5% city tax. AE, DC, MC, V. No parking. Tram: 1, 2, 5, 6, 7, or 10 to Leidseplein. **Amenities:** Restaurant; bar; exercise room; sauna; concierge; 24-hr. room service; in-room massage; laundry service; same-day dry cleaning. *In room:* A/C, TV w/pay movies, dataport, minibar, coffeemaker, hair dryer, iron, safe.

Expensive

Dikker & Thijs Fenice 👁   Small and homey, this hotel reveals a cozy character behind its stylish facade. Spacious rooms, tastefully styled in a modern version of Art Deco, are clustered in groups of two or four around small lobbies, which makes the hotel feel more like an apartment building. Double-glazed windows eliminate the noise from Leidsestraat. Rooms at the front have a great view of Prinsengracht.

Prinsengracht 444 (at Leidsestraat), 1017 KE Amsterdam. ℂ **020/620-1212.** Fax 020/625-8986. www.dtfh. nl. 42 units. 195€–345€ double. Rates include buffet breakfast. AE, DC, MC, V. Limited street parking. Tram: 1, 2, 5 to Prinsengracht. **Amenities:** Restaurant; bar; bike rental; concierge; room service; in-room massage; babysitting; laundry service; dry cleaning; nonsmoking rooms. *In room:* TV, dataport, minibar, hair dryer.

ON & NEAR REMBRANDTPLEIN
Expensive

NH Schiller Hotel 👁👁   A historic Amsterdam gem, now fully restored, this hotel boasts a blend of Art Nouveau and Art Deco in its public spaces, a theme that is reflected in the tasteful furnishings in the rooms. Its sculpted facade, wrought-iron balconies, and stained-glass windows stand out on the often brash Rembrandtplein. Brasserie Schiller is a gracious oak-paneled dining room, and Café Schiller is one of Amsterdam's few permanent sidewalk cafes.

Rembrandtplein 26–36, 1017 CV Amsterdam. ℂ **020/554-0700.** Fax 020/624-0098. www.nh-hotels.nl/ nhschiller. 92 units. 220€–270€ double; from 300€ suite. AE, DC, MC, V. Limited street parking. Tram: 4, 9, or 14 to Rembrandtplein. **Amenities:** Restaurant, 2 bars; health club; 24-hr. room service; babysitting; laundry service; dry cleaning. *In room:* TV, minibar, coffeemaker, hair dryer.

Moderate

Seven Bridges 👁👁   Each huge room at this fine hotel is unique, with antique furnishings, plush carpets, and reproductions of modern art; one room even has a bathroom with a skylight and wooden walls similar to those in a sauna. Decor includes handmade Italian drapes, hand-painted tiles, and wood-tiled floors. Some attic rooms have sloped ceilings and exposed beams. There's no elevator. The front rooms overlook a small canal, and the rear rooms overlook a garden. Proprietors Pierre Keulers and Gunter Glaner are extremely helpful.

Reguliersgracht 31 (at Keizersgracht), 1017 LK Amsterdam. ℂ **020/623-1329.** 8 units. 110€–200€ double. Rates include full breakfast. AE, MC, V. Limited street parking. Tram: 16, 24, 25 to Keizersgracht. *In room:* TV, hair dryer.

NEAR MUSEUMPLEIN
Expensive

Bilderberg Hotel Jan Luyken 👁👁   In a residential neighborhood 1 block from Pieter Cornelisz Hooftstraat's classy stores, this is best described as a small hotel with many of the amenities and facilities of a big one. Rooms are classically furnished, bathrooms modern. The owners are proud of the setting they've created and are constantly improving the hotel's facilities.

Jan Luykenstraat 58 (near the Rijksmuseum), 1071 CS Amsterdam. ℂ **800/641-0300** in the U.S. and Canada, or 020/573-0730. Fax 020/676-3841. www.janluyken.nl. 62 units. 180€–295€ double; add 5% city tax. AE, DC, MC, V. Limited street parking. Tram: 2 or 5 to Hobbemastraat. **Amenities:** Wine bar; spa; concierge; 24-hr. room service; in-room massage; babysitting; laundry service; dry cleaning; nonsmoking rooms. *In room:* A/C, TV, dataport, minibar, hair dryer, iron, safe.

Moderate

De Filosoof ⚹⚹　On a quiet street of brick houses near Vondelpark, this extraordinary, elegant hotel should at least make you think. One of the owners, a philosophy professor, has decorated rooms with posters, framed quotes, and unusual objects chosen to represent philosophical and cultural themes. Ponder the meaning of life in rooms dedicated to thinkers like Goethe, Wittgenstein, Nietzsche, Marx, and Einstein, or motifs like Eros, the Renaissance, or astrology. You can even consult your private bookshelf of philosophical works or join in a weekly philosophy debate. The rooms in an annex across the street are larger; some open onto a private terrace.

Anna van den Vondelstraat 6 (off Overtoom, at Vondelpark), 1054 GZ Amsterdam. ⓒ **020/683-3013.** Fax 020/685-3750. www.hotelfilosoof.nl. 38 units. 92€–122€ double. Rates include buffet breakfast. AE, MC, V. Limited street parking. Tram: 1 or 6 to Jan Pieter Heijestraat. **Amenities:** Lounge. *In room:* TV, hair dryer, safe.

Inexpensive

Piet Hein ⚹　Occupying a villa close to the city's most important museums, the Piet Hein is named after a Dutch folk hero, a 17th-century admiral who captured a Spanish silver shipment. Rooms are spacious and well furnished, and the staff friendly and professional. Half the rooms overlook the park; two second-floor doubles have semicircular balconies; and there is a honeymoon suite with a waterbed. Lower-priced rooms are in an annex.

Vossiusstraat 52–53 (off Van Baerlestraat), 1071 AK Amsterdam. ⓒ **020/662-7205.** Fax 020/662-15-26. www.hotelpiethein.com. 65 units. 115€–155€ double. Rates include continental breakfast. AE, DC, MC, V. Limited street parking. Tram: 3, 5, or 12 to Van Baerlestraat. **Amenities:** Bar; concierge; limited room service; laundry service; dry cleaning; nonsmoking rooms. *In room:* TV w/pay movies.

IN SOUTH AMSTERDAM
Expensive

Bilderberg Garden Hotel ⚹⚹⚹　This is the smallest and most personal five-star hotel in town. Because of its excellent Mangerie de Kersentuin restaurant, the Garden considers itself a "culinary hotel," an idea that extends to the rooms, whose color schemes are salad-green, salmon-pink, cherry-red, and grape-blue—and you can choose whichever suits you best. The rooms themselves are furnished and equipped to the highest standards and with refined taste.

Dijsselhofplantsoen 7 (at Apollolaan), 1077 BJ Amsterdam. ⓒ **0800/641-0300** in the U.S. and Canada, or 020/570-5600. Fax 020/570-5654. www.gardenhotel.nl. 124 units. 325€ double; 370€ executive double; add 5% city tax. AE, DC, MC, V. Limited street parking. Tram: 5 or 24 to Apollolaan. **Amenities:** Restaurant; bar; access to nearby health club; concierge; business center; 24-hr. room service; in-room massage; babysitting; laundry service; same-day dry cleaning; executive rooms; nonsmoking rooms. *In room:* A/C, TV w/pay movies, fax, dataport, minibar, hair dryer, safe.

Moderate

Apollofirst ⚹　Intimate and elegant, this family-owned hotel, set amid the Amsterdam School architecture on Apollolaan, advertises itself as the "best quarters in town in the town's best quarter." That boast may be open to discussion, but all rooms are quiet, spacious, and grandly furnished. Those at the back overlook well-kept gardens as well as the summer terrace where guests can have a snack or a cocktail. Other amenities include the elegant French restaurant Chambertin.

Apollolaan 123 (off Minervalaan), 1077 AP Amsterdam. ⓒ **020/673-0333.** Fax 020/675-0348. www. apollofirstl.nl. 40 units. 125€–170€ double; 275€ suite. Rates include continental breakfast. AE, DC, MC, V. Limited street parking. Tram: 5 or 24 to Apollolaan. **Amenities:** Bar; 24-hr. room service. *In room:* TV.

Inexpensive

Bicycle Hotel ⚹⚹　The young proprietors of this establishment have hit on an interesting idea: They cater to visitors who wish to explore Amsterdam on bikes and can help you plan biking routes through and around the city. You can rent bikes for 5€ daily, no deposit, and stable your trusty steed indoors. The recently renovated rooms have new carpets and plain but comfortable modern furnishings; some have kitchenettes and small balconies, and there are large rooms for families.

Van Ostadestraat 123 (off Ferdinand Bolstraat), Amsterdam 1072 SV. © **020/679-3452.** Fax 020/671-5213. www.bicyclehotel.com. 16 units, 8 with bathroom. 99€ double with bathroom; 61€–70€ double without bathroom. Rates include continental breakfast. No credit cards. Parking 20€. Tram: 24 or 25 to Ceintuurbaan. **Amenities:** Bike rental. *In room:* TV.

WHERE TO DINE

As a trading and gateway city that positively revels in its status as a melting pot, Amsterdam has absorbed culinary influences from far and wide. You find dozens of ethnic eateries serving everything from Argentine to Yugoslavian food. Indonesian food is extremely popular, notably the *rijsttafel* (see "Spice of Life," below). Many of these ethnic places serve hearty and delicious meals at very reasonable prices. And there's plenty of traditional Dutch restaurants.

Amsterdam's favorite lunch is a *broodje,* a small sandwich made with a soft roll or French bread and filled with meat or fish. You find these inexpensive tasty sandwiches at sandwich counters and street stands all over. An especially popular street food is *broodje haring,* raw herring and chopped onions in a soft bun for around 2.75€. The traditional method for eating herring is to tip your head back and lower the fish headfirst (well, where the head would be if it hadn't already been cut off) into your mouth. Another traditional Dutch lunch is an *uitsmijter* (pronounced *out*-smayter; the name means "bouncer"): two pieces of toast topped with ham or cheese and two fried eggs, often served with a small salad.

In general, with the exception of late-night restaurants, kitchens in Amsterdam take their last dinner orders at 10 or 11pm. Restaurants with outside terraces are always in big demand on pleasant summer evenings, and few take reservations. One way to combat escalating dinner tabs is to take advantage of the low-cost *dagschotel* (plate of the day) many restaurants serve. Two great areas for discovering new restaurants are around **Leidseplein** and in the **Jordaan.**

NEAR CENTRAAL STATION
Expensive
De Silveren Spiegel ☆ TRADITIONAL DUTCH/CLASSICAL FRENCH
The two houses forming the premises were constructed in 1614 for wealthy soap-maker Laurens Jansz Spieghel. It's typically Old Dutch inside, with the bar downstairs and more dining rooms where the bedrooms used to be. There's a garden in back, and the place emanates a traditionally Dutch tidiness that's very

---

Moments Spice of Life

You haven't really eaten in Amsterdam until you've had an **Indonesian** *rijsttafel.* This traditional "rice table" banquet consists of as many as 20 succulent and spicy foods served in tiny bowls. Pick and choose from among the bowls and add your choice to the pile of rice on your plate. It's almost impossible to eat all the food set on your table, but give it a shot— it's delicious and a true taste of multicultural Amsterdam. For an abbreviated version served on one plate, try *nasi rames.* At lunch, the standard Indonesian fare is *nasi goreng* (fried rice with meat and vegetables) or *bami goreng* (fried noodles prepared in the same way).

welcoming. The updated menu has finely prepared seafood and meat dishes like baked sole filets with wild spinach, and Texel lamb with *ratatouille;* traditional Zaanse mustard is always available.

Kattengat 4–6 (off Singel). ℂ **020/624-6589.** Main courses 25€–30€; fixed-price menus 38€–45€. AE, MC, V. Daily 6–11pm (open for lunch by reservation). Tram: 1, 2, 5, 13, or 17 to Martelaarsgracht.

Moderate
Amsterdam 🏵🏵🏵 *Finds* CONTINENTAL   Think of it as *Amsterdam: The Restaurant,* because it's quite a performance. Based in a century-old water-pumping station, complete with diesel-powered engine, the Amsterdam has taken this monument of Victorian industrial good taste and made of it a model of contemporary good eats. Service is friendly, and the food is good and moderately priced. If you're feeling flush, spring for a double starter of half lobster with six Zeeland oysters. The Amsterdam is a little bit out from the center, but easily worth the tram ride.

Watertorenplein 6 (off Haarlemmerweg). ℂ **020/682-2666.** Reservations recommended on weekends. Main courses 9.50€–20€. AE, DC, MC, V. Daily 11am–midnight. Tram: 10 to Van Hallstraat.

De Belhamel 🏵🏵 *Finds* CONTINENTAL   Classical music complements Art Nouveau in a graceful setting overlooking the Herengracht and Brouwersgracht canals. The menu changes seasonally, and game is a specialty. You can expect such menu dishes as puffed pastries layered with salmon, shellfish, crayfish tails, and *chervil beurre-blanc* to start; and beef tenderloin in Madeira sauce with zucchini *rösti* and puffed garlic for a main course. They serve vegetarian dishes, too.

Brouwersgracht 60 (at Herengracht). ℂ **020/622-1095.** Main courses 18€–20€; fixed-price menu 32€. AE, MC, V. Sun–Thurs 6–10pm; Fri–Sat 6–10:30pm. Tram: 1, 2, 5, 13, or 17 to Martelaarsgracht.

Inexpensive
Café Luxembourg 🏵🏵 INTERNATIONAL   "One of the world's great cafes," wrote the *New York Times* about this stylish, grand cafe. Unlike other cafes in Amsterdam, which often draw a distinctive clientele, the Luxembourg attracts all kinds of people with its amazingly large portions of food at reasonable prices. Soups, sandwiches, and such dishes as meatloaf are available. A special attraction: You may find such exotica as Chinese dim sum and *satay ajam* (Indonesian grilled chicken in a peanut sauce) on the menu.

Spui 22–24 (at Spui). ℂ **020/620-6264.** Salads and specials 8.50€–11€; lunch 4€–8.50€; main courses 8€–18€. AE, DC, MC, V. Sun–Thurs 9am–1am; Fri–Sat 9am–2am. Tram: 1, 2, or 5 to Spui.

ALONG THE RING CANALS
Expensive
Christophe 🏵🏵 MODERN FRENCH   The star of this show is owner and chef Jean-Christophe Royer, who offers sensuous, sophisticated food served up in an elegant setting that features dark cherrywood paneling, thick carpets, rice-paper lamp shades, stately cacti by the windows, and floral paintings by contemporary Dutch artist Martin van Vreden. The food is similarly refined, using traditional Mediterranean ingredients—figs, truffles, olives, and saffron—in exciting new ways. Try the roasted milk-fed Pyrenean lamb, or roasted turbot in a light curry sauce, and finish with a light tart of prunes in Armagnac.

Leliegracht 46 (between Prinsengracht and Keizersgracht). ℂ **020/625-0807.** Main courses 28€–33€; fixed-price menus 43€–53€. AE, DC, MC, V. Tues–Sat 6:30–10:30pm. Tram: 13, 14, or 17 to Westermarkt.

Moderate
Bolhoed 🏵 VEGETARIAN   Forget the wholesome, dull, corn-sheaf-and-brown-rice image of vegetarian dining—Bolhoed adds a touch of spice to its

health food formula with its Latin style, world music background, candlelight in the evenings, and fine view of the canal from its twin rooms beside the Prinsengracht. Service is zestful and friendly. Try such veggie delights as the *ragoût croissant* (pastry filled with leeks, tofu, seaweed, and curry sauce), or *zarzuela*. If you want to go whole hog, so to speak, and eat vegan, most of Bolhoed's dishes can be so prepared on request, and in any case most are made with organically grown produce.

Prinsengracht 60–62 (near Noordermarkt). © 020/626-1803. Main courses 12€–15€. No credit cards. Sun–Fri noon–11pm; Sat 11am–11pm. Tram: 13, 14, or 17 to Westermarkt.

Inexpensive

De Prins ⭐⭐ *Value* MODERN DUTCH/CONTINENTAL   In a 17th-century canal house, this companionable brown cafe/restaurant opposite the Anne Frankhuis serves the kind of food you'd expect from a much more expensive place. The clientele is loyal, so the relatively few tables fill up quickly. It's a quiet neighborhood restaurant—nothing fancy or trendy, but quite appealing, with the bar on a slightly lower level than the restaurant and a sidewalk terrace for drinks in summer.

Prinsengracht 124 (at Leliegracht). © 020/624-9382. Main courses 6€–13€; dish of the day 9.90€; specials 24€–28€. AE, DC, MC, V. Daily 10am–1am. Tram: 13, 14, or 17 to Westermarkt.

Pancake Bakery ⭐ *Kids* PANCAKES   In a 17th-century canal warehouse is this two-story restaurant with winding staircases and exposed beams, serving some of the most delicious and unusual pancakes you'll ever taste. There are several dozen varieties, almost all of which make for a full meal. Choices include salami and cheese, cheese and ginger, honey nuts and whipped cream, and ice cream and *advokaat* (a Dutch eggnoglike cocktail). One of the bestsellers is what they call the American pancake: with fried chicken, sweet corn, peppers, carrots, Cajun sauce, and salad.

Prinsengracht 191 (at Prinsenstraat). © 020/625-1333. Reservations required for large groups. Pancakes 4€–10€. AE, MC, V. Daily noon–9:30pm. Tram: 13, 14, or 17 to Westermarkt.

NEAR SPUI
Expensive

D'Vijff Vlieghen ⭐ MODERN DUTCH   Touristy? Yes, but the "Five Flies" is one of Amsterdam's most famous restaurants, and the food is authentic stick-to-the-ribs Dutch fare. The chef is passionate about an updated form of Dutch cuisine he calls "the new Dutch kitchen." The menu has a selection of seasonal fish and game often marinated with fresh herbs and served with unusual vegetables like chard, wild spinach, and Brussels sprouts. If you're feeling adventurous, try the wild boar with sweet chestnuts and *jenever* sauce. The restaurant is a kind of Dutch theme park, with seven dining rooms in five canal houses decorated with artifacts from Holland's golden age. Don't miss the four original Rembrandt etchings in the Rembrandt Room and the collection of handmade glass in the Glass Room.

Spuistraat 294–302 (at Spui). © 020/530-4060. Main courses 21€–30€; seasonal menu 31€–52€. AE, DC, MC, V. Daily 5:30pm–midnight. Tram: 1, 2, or 5 to Spui.

Moderate

Haesje Claes TRADITIONAL DUTCH   If you're yearning for a cozy Old Dutch environment and hearty Dutch food at moderate prices, this is the place to go. It's inviting and intimate, with lots of nooks and crannies and with brocaded benches and traditional Dutch hanging lamps. The menu covers a lot of ground, ranging from canapés to caviar, but you'll be happiest with such Dutch stalwarts as omelets, tournedos, *hutspot* (stew), *stampot* (mashed potatoes and cabbage), or various fish stews, including those with IJsselmeer *paling* (eel).

Spuistraat 273–275 (at Spui). ℂ 020/624-9998. Main courses 14€–20€; tourist menu 19€. AE, DC, MC, V. Daily noon–10pm. Tram: 1, 2, or 5 to Spui.

Kantjil en de Tijger 🛪 INDONESIAN Unlike Indonesian restaurants that wear their ethnic origins on their sleeve, the "Antelope and the Tiger" is modern and cool. Two bestsellers are *nasi goreng Kantjil* (fried rice with pork kabobs, stewed beef, pickled cucumbers, and mixed vegetables) and the 20-item *rijsttafel* (rice with meat, seafood, and vegetables) for two. Other choices are stewed chicken in soya sauce, tofu omelet, shrimp with coconut dressing, Indonesian pumpkin, and mixed steamed vegetables with peanut-butter sauce. Finish with the cinnamon layer cake or the coffee with ginger liqueur and whipped cream.

Spuistraat 291 (beside Spui). ℂ 020/620-0994. Reservations recommended on weekends. Main courses 12€–16€; *rijsttafels* 38€–48€ for 2. AE, DC, MC, V. Daily 4:30–11pm. Tram: 1, 2, or 5 to Spui.

ON & NEAR LEIDSEPLEIN
Expensive
De Oesterbar SEAFOOD De Oesterbar, which is more than 50 years old, is the best-known and most popular fish restaurant in Amsterdam. Its seafood is delivered fresh twice daily. The decor is a delight: all white tiles with fish tanks bubbling at your elbows on the street level, and Victorian brocades and etched glass in the more formal dining room upstairs. The menu is a directory of Dutch seafood dishes, but it also includes a few meat selections. Choices include sole Danoise with the tiny Dutch shrimps; sole Véronique with Muscadet grapes; stewed eel in wine sauce; and the assorted fish plate of turbot, halibut, and fresh salmon.

Leidseplein 10. ℂ 020/623-2988. Main courses 24€–33€. AE, DC, MC, V. Daily noon–1am. Tram: 1, 2, 5, 6, 7, 10 to Leidseplein.

Moderate
Café Américain 🛪 INTERNATIONAL This is a national monument of Dutch Jugendstil and Art Deco. Mata Hari held her wedding reception here in her pre-espionage days, and since its 1900 opening, this has been a haven for Dutch and international artists, writers, dancers, and actors. Leaded windows, newspaper-littered reading tables, bargello-patterned velvet upholstery, frosted-glass chandeliers from the 1920s, and tall, carved columns are all part of the dusky sit-and-chat setting. Menu dishes include monkfish, perch, rack of Irish lamb, and rosé breast of duck with creamed potatoes. Jazz lovers can stock up on good music at a Sunday jazz brunch.

In the American Hotel, Leidsekade 97 (at Leidseplein). ℂ 020/556-3232. Main courses 16€–21€. AE, DC, MC, V. Daily 10:30am–midnight. Tram: 1, 2, 5, 6, 7, 10 to Leidseplein.

NEAR REMBRANDTPLEIN
Moderate
Brasserie Schiller 🛪🛪 CLASSIC FRENCH/DUTCH Beamed and paneled in well-aged oak and graced with etched-glass panels and stained-glass skylights, this 100-plus-year-old Art Nouveau landmark (not to be mistaken for the equally notable Café Schiller next door) is a splendid sight. Paintings by Frits Schiller, the artist who built the hotel, adorn the walls. Former chefs supplied the restaurant with the exact recipes and techniques used in the old days. On the

classic menu you find everything from stewed eel and potato-and-cabbage casserole to T-bone steak, roast leg of lamb with mint sauce, and spaghetti Bolognese.

In the NH Schiller Hotel, Rembrandtplein 26–36. (C) 020/554-0723. Main courses 18€–23€; fixed-price menu 30€. AE, DC, MC, V. Daily 7am–10:30pm. Tram: 4, 9, 14 to Rembrandtplein.

Inexpensive

Falafel Koning *(Finds* MIDDLE EASTERN   This tiny gem of a restaurant really needs a category all to itself: "Almost Cost-Free" comes to mind. The specialty of the house will set you back a mere 3€. It's falafel, but don't laugh—it's probably the best falafel this side of the River Jordan: mashed chickpeas mixed with herbs, rolled in a ball along with what must be some magic ingredient, fried, and served in pita bread with salad. The snack bar is capable of seating about eight people at a push, plus more at a few tables outside when the sun shines.

Regulierssteeg 2 (off Reguliersstraat, opposite the Theater Tuschinski). (C) 020/421-1423. Snacks and light meals 3€–6€. Daily 10am–1am. Tram: 4, 9, 14 to Rembrandtplein.

NEAR MUSEUMPLEIN
Expensive

Bodega Keyser *(★★)* TRADITIONAL DUTCH   Whether or not you attend a concert at the Concertgebouw, you may want to plan a visit to its next-door neighbor. An Amsterdam landmark since 1903, the Keyser has enjoyed a colorful joint heritage with the world-famous concert hall. There's an elegance here that combines traditional dark-and-dusky decor and highly starched pink linens. The menu leans heavily toward local fish and, in season, game specialties such as hare and venison.

Van Baerlestraat 96 (beside the Concertgebouw). (C) 020/671-1441. Main courses 20€–35€; fixed-price menu 33€. AE, DC, MC, V. Mon–Sat 9am–midnight; Sun 11am–midnight. Tram: 2 to Willemsparkweg; 3, 5, 12 to Van Baerlestraat; 16 to De Lairessestraat.

IN AMSTERDAM EAST
Moderate

Gare de l'Est *(★★)* *(Value)* TRADITIONAL FRENCH/MEDITERRANEAN The detached, distinctive house, with a recently added conservatory and a large sidewalk terrace, was originally a coffeehouse for workers at the Eastern Dock. Service is both relaxed and knowledgeable, and as the fixed-price menu is excellent value for money, any surprises appear on your plate rather than on the check. The strict five-course formula (starter, salad, main course of meat or fish, cheese, and dessert) leaves no room for choice—except for the main course. How does this sound—*pulpo stofado* with *risotto nero* (inkfish stew with black risotto) as a starter, and roast lamb with gazpacho sauce and farfalle pasta as a main course?

Cruquiusweg 9 (at the East Harbor). (C) 020/463-0620. Reservations recommended on weekends. Fixed-price menu 28€. No credit cards. Daily 6–11pm. Tram: 7, 10 to Zeeburgerdijk.

Tips **Sweet Talk**

If you have a sweet tooth, be sure to try some traditional Dutch desserts, like *poffertjes* (miniature pancakes), *oliebollen* (like powdered sugar–covered doughnut holes), or pancakes. All these come with various fillings or toppings, many of which contain a liqueur of some sort. Traditional *poffertje* restaurants are garish affairs that look as though they're part of a circus. There's one on Weteringcircuit west of Leidseplein.

NEAR AMSTEL STATION
Moderate

De Kas ★★ CONTINENTAL   A converted 1926 greenhouse with a smoke-stack on open ground is the setting for this bright, spacious new place to see and be seen, with an atmosphere that's maybe a tad too precious. You get just a couple of variations on a three-course, daily-changing, fixed menu, with cheese board extra. Mediterranean-style greens and herbs come fresh from an adjacent working hothouse and the restaurant's own farm, and meat is sourced daily from nearby animal-friendly eco-producers. Service is attentive enough that the wait-staff seems to be acquainted personally with every item on your plate.

Kamerlingh Onneslaan 3 (close to Amstel Station). ℂ 020/462-4562. Reservations required. Fixed-price lunch 27€; fixed-price dinner 35€. AE, DC, MC, V. Mon–Fri noon–3pm and 6:30–10pm; Sat 6:30–10pm. Tram: 9 to Hogeweg.

SEEING THE SIGHTS

Amsterdam has an almost bewildering embarrassment of riches. There are 160 canals to cruise, with a combined length of 76km (47 miles), spanned by 1,281 bridges; hundreds of narrow streets to wander; almost 8,000 historic buildings to see in the city center; more than 40 museums of all types to visit; diamond cutters and craftspeople to watch as they practice generations-old skills . . . the list is as long as every visitor's individual interests—and then some.

SIGHTSEEING SUGGESTIONS FOR FIRST-TIME VISITORS

If You Have 1 Day For the perfect introduction to the city, take a **canal cruise** and admire the many gabled merchants' houses and almost 1,200 bridges. In the afternoon, stroll through **Vondelpark** and return to the center through lively **Leidseplein.** In the evening, dine at a traditional restaurant or opt for an Indonesian *rijsttafel,* and end your day by dropping into a **brown cafe** (a traditional Amsterdam bar).

If You Have 2 Days Begin by going early to the **Anne Frank House.** Then, stroll along the central canals until lunchtime. In the afternoon, continue exploring the historic center on foot, visiting the **Dam** and the **Royal Palace** and ending up at bustling **Rembrandtplein.** In the evening, attend a concert at the nearby **Concertgebouw,** or opera or dance at the **Muziektheater.**

If You Have 3 or More Days Visit the **Van Gogh Museum** in the morning. Relax over coffee at the **Café Américain** on Leidseplein,

with its stunning Art Nouveau interior. Look into some **street markets,** either the Albert Cuyp market, the floating Flower Market, or the Waterlooplein flea market. In the evening, take a walk in the **Red Light District** (if this isn't your idea of an edifying experience, consider instead the alternative dining option from day 1).

If You Have 4 or 5 Days Broaden your experience by mixing a focused perusal of interesting areas of Amsterdam with short out-of-town trips. For example, one morning you can tour **De Wallen,** the oldest part of the city, which includes the Red Light District (a far different kind of place during the daylight hours), before going by bus to **Volendam** and **Marken** on the IJsselmeer lake. On the other day, tour the **Jordaan** district in the morning (taking in a street market if you go on Mon or Sat), and take a breath of sea air at **Zandvoort** in the afternoon.

THREE KEY MUSEUMS

Anne Frankhuis ✶✶ A teenage Jewish girl, Anne Frank wrote her famous diary here while she and seven other Jewish refugees hid from the Nazis in a secret annex at the back of this large canal house. On July 6, 1942, the Franks and another Jewish family went into hiding to avoid being deported to Nazi concentration camps. Anne, the youngest Frank daughter, had been given a diary for her 13th birthday in 1942. With the eyes of a child and the writing skills of a girl who hoped one day to be a writer, she chronicled the almost-silent life in hiding of the *onderduikers* (divers or hiders), the continued persecution of Jews by Hitler, the progress of the war, and her personal growth as a young woman. The cramped, gloomy hiding place, where they were forced to maintain nearly total silence, kept them safe for more than 2 years until they were betrayed and pro-German Dutch police raided their refuge on August 4, 1944. Anne died of typhus in March 1945 at Bergen-Belsen, tragically close to the war's end; six of the others also died in concentration camps.

Although the rooms here contain no furniture and are as bare as they were when Anne's father Otto, the only survivor, returned, the exhibits, including a year-by-year chronology of Anne's life, fill in the missing details—a former employee gave him Anne's diary, which had been left behind when the police arrested the family. This lack of distraction allows you to project yourself into Anne's claustrophobic, fear-filled world. A new wing next door mounts temporary exhibits on themes such as intolerance and racism.

The museum is operated by the Anne Frank Foundation, an organization founded to eliminate anti-Semitism, fascism, and neo-Nazism and continue Anne's struggle for a better world. Anne achieved her dream of being a famous writer: Today more than 13 million copies of *The Diary of Anne Frank* have been sold, in 50 languages.

Note: Lines here can be very long, especially in summer—try going on a weekday morning. Once you're inside, an hour should do it, though many people linger.

Prinsengracht 263 (beside Westermarkt). ✆ 020/556-7100. Admission 6.50€ adults, 3€ children 10–17, children under 10 free. Apr–Aug, daily 9am–9pm; Sept–Mar, daily 9am–7pm; Jan 1 and Dec 25 noon–5pm. Closed Yom Kippur. Tram: 13, 14, 17 to Westermarkt.

Stedelijk Museum ✶✶ *Note:* The Stedelijk is due to close from January 1, 2003, to March 2005, for renovation and the construction of two new wings. This review stands in case something should happen to delay these plans. During the period of any closure, elements from the museum's collection can be viewed at other venues in the city. Architect Alvaro Siza has drawn up plans for restoring the old building as closely as possible to its original 1895 neo-Renaissance appearance.

Tips Rijksmuseum Renovations

Amsterdam's world-class **Rijksmuseum** ✶✶✶ is due to be closed for a whopping 5 years, from late 2003 to mid-2008, for renovation. During the period of partial closure, key paintings and other pieces, such as ceramics and gold and silverware, from the 17th-century Dutch Golden Age collection can be viewed in the museum's own Philips Wing, and other elements of the collection will likely be on view at other venues in the city. Throughout the period of renovation, our full review of the Rijksmuseum can be found on our website (**www.frommers.com**).

The city's modern art museum is the place to see works by such Dutch painters as Karel Appel, Willem de Kooning, and Piet Mondrian, alongside works by the French artists Chagall, Cézanne, Picasso, Renoir, Monet, and Manet and by the Americans Calder, Oldenburg, Rosenquist, and Warhol. The Stedelijk centers its collection around the De Stijl, Cobra, post-Cobra, Nouveau Réalisme, pop art, color-field painting, zero, minimalist, and conceptual schools of modern art. It houses the largest collection outside Russia of the abstract paintings of Kasimir Malevich.

In the museum cafe is a giant Appel mural. Mondrian is represented by, among other works, his *Composition in Red, Black, Blue, Yellow, and Gray* (1920) and, by way of variation, *Composition in Blue, Red, Black, and Yellow* (1922)— the gray's still there, in fact, but he chose not to mention it in the title.

Paulus Potterstraat 13 (at Museumplein). ℂ 020/573-2737. Admission 5€ adults, 2.50€ seniors/children 7–17, children under 7 free. Daily 11am–5pm. Closed Jan 1. Tram: 2 or 5 to Van Baerlestraat; 3, 12, or 16 to Museumplein.

Van Gogh Museum 🐸🐸🐸 Anyone who has ever responded to van Gogh's vibrant colors and vivid landscapes will find walking through the rooms of this rather stark contemporary building a moving experience. The museum displays, in chronological order, more than 200 van Gogh paintings. As you move through the rooms, the canvases reflect the artist's changing environment and much of his inner life, so that gradually van Gogh himself becomes almost a tangible presence standing at your elbow. You'll see the early, brooding *The Potato Eaters* and *The Yellow House,* as well as the painting known around the world simply as *Sunflowers,* though van Gogh actually titled it *Still Life with Fourteen Sunflowers.* By the time you reach the vaguely threatening painting of a flock of black crows rising from a waving cornfield, you can almost feel the artist's mounting inner pain.

In addition to the paintings, there are nearly 600 drawings by van Gogh, which will be on permanent display in the museum's new wing. This free-standing, multistory, half-oval structure, designed by the Japanese architect Kisho Kurokawa, is constructed in a bold combination of titanium and gray-brown stone, and is connected to the main building by a subterranean walkway.

Audio tours with mobile phone–type units are available. A bunch of flat-panel iMacs on a table are used as information kiosks—some people use them for their serious purpose, while others seem content to play with the movable screens. From February 14 to June 15, 2003, the Van Gogh Museum celebrates the 150th anniversary of Vincent's birth (Mar 30, 1853) with a special exhibit of his favorite paintings.

Paulus Potterstraat 7 (at Museumplein). ℂ 020/570-5200. Admission 7€ adults, 2.50€ children 13–17, free for children under 13. Daily 10am–6pm. Tram: 2, 3, 5, or 12 to Van Baerlestraat.

MORE TOP MUSEUMS & GALLERIES

Amsterdams Historisch Museum 🐸🐸 In a huge 17th-century former orphanage, now housing exhibits covering nearly 700 years of the city's history, this fascinating museum gives you a better understanding of everything you see as you explore the city. Gallery by gallery, century by century, you learn how a fishing village became a major world trading center. The main focus is on the city's 17th-century golden age, a period when Amsterdam was the richest city in the world, and some of the most interesting exhibits are of the trades that made it rich. You can also view many famous paintings by Dutch masters. Next to the museum is the **Schuttersgalerij (Civic Guard Gallery),** a narrow, skylit chamber bedecked

---

Value **Passport to Amsterdam**

One of the best discounts in town is the **Amsterdam Pass,** available at VVV tourist offices for 26€ for 1 day, 36€ for 2 days, and 46€ for 3 days. It provides up to 136€ in savings, offering free or discounted admission to 38 museums and attractions (including the Rijksmuseum, Rembrandthuis, and Oude Kerk), a free canal cruise, and discounts on selected restaurants and stores. A free 1-, 2-, or 3-day transport ticket is included.

---

with 17th-century group portraits of militiamen. The hours are the same as for the museum, and admission is free.

Jonas Daniël Meijerplein 2–4 (facing Waterlooplein). (⟡ **020/626-9945.** www.ahm.nl. Admission 5€ adults, 2.50€ children 13–18, 1.50€ children 6–12, free for children under 6. Daily 11am–5pm. Tram: 9, 14, 20 to Waterlooplein.

Joods Historisch Museum ⟡   Housed in the four restored 17th- and 18th-century synagogues of the beautiful Ashkenazi Synagogue complex, the Jewish Historical Museum tells the intertwining stories of Jewish identity, religion, culture, and history of the Jewish Dutch community. Inside are objects, photographs, artworks, and interactive displays. Jewish religious artifacts are a major focus. An exhibit covers the persecution of Jews in the Netherlands and throughout Europe under Hitler. The synagogues stand at the heart of a neighborhood that was the Jewish quarter for 300 years until the Nazi occupation during World War II emptied the city of its Jewish population. The oldest of the four, built in 1670, is the oldest public synagogue in western Europe; the newest dates from 1752.

Jonas Daniël Meijerplein 2–4 (at Waterlooplein). (⟡ 020/626-9945. Admission 5€ adults, 3€ seniors, 2.50€ children 13–17, 1.50€ children 6–12, free for children under 6. Daily 11am–5pm. Closed Yom Kippur. Tram: 9 or 14 to Waterlooplein.

Museum Het Rembrandthuis ⟡⟡   When Rembrandt van Rijn moved into this three-story house in 1639, he was already a well-established wealthy artist. However, the cost of buying and furnishing the house led to his financial downfall in 1656. When Rembrandt was declared insolvent, an inventory of the house's contents listed more than 300 paintings by Rembrandt and some by his teacher, Pieter Lasteman, and his friends Peter Paul Rubens and Jan Lievens. In 1658, Rembrandt was forced to sell the house and most of his possessions to meet his debts. He remained there until 1660, then moved to much less grandiose accommodations on Rozengracht, in the Jordaan.

The museum houses a nearly complete collection of Rembrandt's etchings, and the artist's printing press. Of the 300 prints he made, 250 are here, with around half hanging on the walls at any one time. Rembrandt's prints show amazing detail, and you can see his use of shadow and light for dramatic effect. Wizened patriarchs, emaciated beggars, children at play, Rembrandt himself in numerous self-portraits, and Dutch landscapes are the subjects you'll long remember after a visit here. Temporary exhibits are mounted in an adjacent house that belonged to Rembrandt's wife, Saskia.

Jodenbreestraat 4 (behind Waterlooplein). (⟡ **020/520-0400.** www.rembranthuis.nl. Admission 7€ adults, 5€ students, 1.50€ children 6–15, free for children under 6. Mon–Sat 10am–5pm; Sun and holidays 1–5pm. Tram: 9 or 14 to Waterlooplein.

Scheepvaartmuseum (Maritime Museum) 🔭🔭   A bonanza for anyone who loves the sea, the Netherlands Maritime Museum is housed in a former arsenal of the Amsterdam Admiralty dating from 1656 and appropriately overlooks the busy harbor. Around the inner courtyard are 25 rooms with exhibits: ship models, charts, instruments, maps, prints, and paintings—a chronicle of Holland's abiding ties to the sea through commerce, fishing, yachting, navigational development, and war. Old maps include a 15th-century Ptolemaic atlas and a sumptuously bound edition of the *Great Atlas* by Jan Blaeu, master cartographer of Holland's golden age. Among the historic papers on display are several pertaining to Nieuwe Amsterdam (New York City) and Nieuwe Nederland (New York State).

A full-size replica of the Dutch East India Company *Amsterdam,* which in 1749 foundered off Hastings on her maiden voyage to the fabled Spice Islands (Indonesia), is moored at the museum's wharf, as is a recently completed replica of the *Stad Amsterdam,* a three-masted iron clipper from 1854. Other ships include a steam icebreaker, a motor lifeboat, and a herring lugger. Environmentalists will be interested in going aboard Greenpeace's *Rainbow Warrior,* a trojan of environmental protection on the high seas. You can reach this museum by taking a 20-minute walk along the historical waterfront, the Nautisch Kwartier (Nautical Quarter).

Kattenburgerplein 1 (at the Eastern Dock). © 020/523-2222. www.generali.nl/scheepvaartmuseum. Admission 7€ adults, 4€ children 6–17, free for children 5 and under. Tues–Sat 10am–5pm (also Mon mid-June to mid-Sept); Sun noon–5pm. Bus: 22 or 32 to Kattenburgerplein.

Tropenmuseum (Tropical Museum) 🔭 *(Kids)*   One of Amsterdam's finest and most unusual museums, the Tropical Museum is dedicated to presenting the tropics to people living in a far different climate. Although founded in the 19th century by the Royal Tropical Institute as a monument to the nation's colonial empire, in particular the Dutch East Indies, today's Indonesia, the museum now focuses on contemporary culture and problems in tropical areas.

On the three floors surrounding the spacious main hall are numerous life-size tableaux depicting life in tropical countries. There are displays of beautiful handicrafts and antiquities from these regions, but the main focus is the life of the people today. There are hovels from the ghettoes of Calcutta and Bombay, and mud-walled houses from the villages of rural India. Bamboo huts from Indonesia and crowded little stores no bigger than closets show you how people live in such areas as Southeast Asia, Latin America, and Africa. Sound effects play over hidden speakers: dogs bark, children scream, car horns blare, frogs croak, and vendors call out their wares.

In the **Kindermuseum (Children's Museum) TM Junior,** youngsters 6 to 12 can explore and participate in all sorts of activities (one adult is allowed to accompany each child).

Finds **The World's Smallest Art Museum**

Amsterdam boasts the world's smallest art museum, **Reflex,** Weteringschans 79A (© **020/627-2832;** tram: 6, 7, 10), opposite the Rijksmuseum. It's only 13 sq. m (140 sq. ft.) and displays 1,500 miniature paintings, graphics, sculptures, and pictures, including works by Picasso, Lichtenstein, Oldenburg, and Christo. Admission is free, and it's open Tuesday through Saturday from 10am to 6pm.

Linnaeusstraat 2 (at Mauritskade). ℭ 020/568-8215. Admission 6.80€ adults, 3.40€ children 6–17, free for children under 6. Daily 10am–5pm. Closed Jan 1, Apr 30, May 5, Dec 25. Tram: 7, 9, 10, or 14 to Mauritskade.

MORE MUSEUMS

Museum Amstelkring   Although Amsterdam has been known as a tolerant city for many centuries, just after the Protestant Reformation, Roman Catholics fell into disfavor. Forced to worship in secret, they devised ingenious ways of gathering for Sunday services. In an otherwise ordinary-looking 17th-century canal house in the middle of the Red Light District is the most amazing of these clandestine churches, known to the general public as "Our Lord in the Attic." Built in the 1660s by a wealthy Catholic merchant, the three houses making up this museum were designed specifically to house a church. Today they're furnished much as they would have been in the mid—18th century. Nothing prepares you for the mini-cathedral you come upon when you climb the last flight of stairs into the attic. A large baroque altar, religious statuary, pews to seat 150, an 18th-century organ, and an upper gallery complete this miniature church.

Oudezijds Voorburgwal 40 (near the Oude Kerk). ℭ **020/624-6604.** Admission 7.50€ adults, 3.40€ children and seniors. Mon–Sat 10am–5pm; Sun and holidays 1–5pm. Closed Jan 1, Apr 30. Tram: 1, 2, 4, 5, 9, 13, 16, 17, 24, 25 to Centraal Station.

Museum Willet-Holthuysen   For a glimpse of what life was like for Amsterdam's wealthy merchants during the 18th and 19th centuries, pay a visit to this elegant canal-house museum. Each room is furnished much as it would have been 200 years ago. In addition, there's an extensive collection of ceramics, china, glass, and silver. Of particular interest are the large old kitchen and the formal garden in back.

Herengracht 605 (at the Amstel). ℭ 020/523-1870. Admission 4€ adults, 3€ seniors, 2€ children 16 and under. Mon–Fri 10am–5pm; Sat–Sun 11am–5pm. Tram: 4, 9, 14, 20 to Rembrandtplein.

Theatermuseum   Splendid marble corridors, wall and ceiling frescoes, and ornate plasterwork make this patrician canal house one of the city's most beautiful. Richly ornamented roof gables of different styles were a sign of wealth during Amsterdam's Golden Age, and crowning this building is the oldest extant example of an ornate neck gable. It's worth visiting this museum simply to see how the wealthy once lived, but there are also many interesting exhibits on theater in the Netherlands over the centuries. Be sure to press the buttons of the miniature stage sets: You'll see how waves once rolled across the stage and other equally dramatic effects.

Herengracht 168 (at Leliegracht). ℭ 020/551-3300. Admission 3.85€ adults, 1.95€ seniors/children 7–16, free for children under 7. Tues–Fri 11am–5pm; Sat–Sun 1–5pm. Tram: 13, 14, 17 to the Dam.

HISTORIC BUILDINGS & MONUMENTS

Only steps from busy shopping streets, the **Begijnhof** ⊛, at Spui (tram: 1, 2, 5), is the city's most tranquil spot. Hidden behind a nondescript facade is a 14th-century courtyard with a central garden ringed with restored almshouses formerly occupied by *begijns,* pious laywomen of the order of the Beguines. Most of the tiny 17th- and 18th-century buildings house elderly widows, and you should respect their privacy, especially after sunset. In the southwest corner of the cloister, at no. 34, stands **Het Huyten Huys,** one of Amsterdam's pair of surviving timber houses, built in 1477. (The authorities prohibited construction of timber houses in 1452 after a series of disastrous fires.) The complex includes a clandestine Roman Catholic church and the former Beguine church from 1419, donated

---

Finds **Gay Remembrance**

The *Homomonument,* Westermarkt (tram: 13, 14, 17, 20), a sculpture group of three pink granite triangles near the Anne Frankhuis, is dedicated to the memory of gays and lesbians killed during World War II, or as a result of oppression and persecution because of their sexuality. People also visit to remember those who have died of AIDS.

---

by the city's Protestant rulers to Scottish Presbyterian exiles in 1607, and now misnamed slightly as the Engelse Kerk (English Church). Allow an hour.

Koninklijk Paleis (Royal Palace)   The 17th-century neoclassical Royal Palace, built on top of 13,659 wooden pilings to prevent it from sinking into the soft Amsterdam soil, was Amsterdam's town hall for 153 years. It was first used as a palace during Napoléon's rule in the early 19th century, when from 1806 to 1810 the French emperor's brother Louis Bonaparte was king of the Netherlands. You can visit its high-ceilinged Citizens' Hall, Burgomasters' Chambers, and Council Room, as well as the Vierschaar—a marble tribunal where in the 17th century death sentences were pronounced. Although this is the monarch's official palace, Queen Beatrix rarely uses it for more than occasional receptions or official ceremonies.

Dam. ℂ **020/620-4060.** Admission 4€ adults, 3€ children 5–12, free for children under 5. Easter and June–Oct daily 11am–5pm; Nov to mid-Dec and mid-Feb to May generally Tues–Thurs 12:30–5pm (opening days and hours are highly variable; check before going). Closed mid-Dec to mid-Feb. Tram: 1, 2, 4, 5, 9, 13, 14, 16, 17, 24, 25 to the Dam.

HISTORIC CHURCHES

Nieuwe Kerk   This church across from the Royal Palace is new in name only. Construction on this late-Gothic structure began about 1400, but much of the interior, including the organ, dates from the 17th century. Since 1815, all Dutch kings and queens have been crowned here. Today the church is used primarily as a cultural center where special art exhibits are held. Regular performances on the church's huge organ are held in summer.

Dam. ℂ **020/638-6909.** Admission and opening hours vary depending on the exhibit or event. Tram: 1, 2, 4, 5, 9, 13, 14, 16, 17, 20, 24, 25 to the Dam.

Oude Kerk ⚿   This Gothic church from the 13th century is the city's oldest, and its many stained-glass windows are particularly beautiful. It now stands smack dab in the middle of the Red Light District, surrounded by old almshouses turned into prostitutes' rooms. Inside are monumental tombs, including that of Rembrandt's wife, Saskia van Uylenburg. The organ, built in 1724, is played regularly in summer; many connoisseurs believe it has the best tone of any organ in the world. During summer, you can climb the 70m (230-ft.) tower for an excellent view of old Amsterdam.

Oudekerksplein (at Oudezijds Voorburgwal). ℂ **020/625-8284.** Admission 1.50€ adults, 1€ seniors/students. Mon–Sat 11am–5pm; Sun 1–5pm. Metro: Nieuwmarkt.

Westerkerk ⚿   Built between 1620 and 1630, this church is a masterpiece of Dutch Renaissance style. At the top of the 84m (275-ft.) tower, the highest, most beautiful tower in Amsterdam, is a giant replica of the imperial crown of Maximilian of Austria. Somewhere in this church (no one knows where) is

Checking Out the Red Light District

You might want to study the quaint gabled architecture along the narrow canals of De Wallen (The Walls), the oldest part of the city—oh, yes, you might also notice certain ladies watching the world go by through their red-fringed windows.

The warren of streets east of the Dam, around Oudezijds Achterburgwal and Oudezijds Voorburgwal, is the *Rosse Buurt* (Red Light District), one of the most famous features of Amsterdam sightseeing (Metro: Nieuwmarkt). It's extraordinary to see women of all nationalities dressed in exotic underwear and perched in windows waiting for customers. With radios and TVs blaring, they knit, brush their hair, or just slink enticingly in their seats.

The Red Light District has now become a major attraction, not only for customers of storefront sex but also for sightseers. If you do choose to look around, you need to exercise some caution. Watch out for pickpockets. In a neighborhood where anything seems permissible, the one no-no is taking pictures. Violate this rule and your camera could be removed from you and broken.

Rembrandt's grave. During summer, regular organ concerts are played on a 300-year-old instrument. You can climb the tower or go by elevator to the top for a great view.

Westermarkt. ℂ **020/624-7766.** Church free admission; tower 1.50€. May 15–Sept 15 Mon–Sat 11am–3pm. Tram: 13, 14, 17, 20 to Westermarkt.

OTHER SIGHTS & ATTRACTIONS

Artis ★★ *(Kids*   The oldest zoo in the Netherlands, established in 1838, houses more than 6,000 animals. Also on the extensive property are a planetarium, aquarium, geological and zoological museum, and children's farm. The aquarium, constructed in 1882 and renovated in the late 1990s, is well presented, particularly the exhibits on the Amazon River, coral reefs, and Amsterdam's canals, with their fish and garbage.

Plantage Kerklaan 38–40. ℂ **020/523-3400.** Admission 13€ adults, 9€ children 4–11, free for children under 4. Daily 9am–5pm. Tram: 9 or 14 to Plantage Middenlaan.

Holland Experience   A multidimensional film and theater show takes you through the landscapes and culture of the Netherlands at different historical periods up to the present. Exhibitions include farming and fishing scenes. A simulated dike collapse, during which 80,000 liters of water pour toward you, gives a taste of what would happen if the sea should ever break through the coastal defenses. The toilets (I can vouch only for the men's) look like the deck of a ship passing along the Dutch coast, and even sport marine sound effects and a salty breeze.

Waterlooplein 17. ℂ **020/422-2233.** Admission 10€ adults, 8€ seniors, free for children 12 and under. Daily 10am–10pm. Tram: 9 or 14 to Waterlooplein.

PARKS & GARDENS

When the sun shines in Amsterdam, people head for the parks. The most popular and conveniently located of Amsterdam's 20 parks is the 49-hectare (122-acre)

Vondelpark 🐸🐸 (tram: 1, 2, 3, 5, 6, 7, 10, 12, 20), home to skateboarding, Frisbee-flipping, in-line skating, model-boat sailing, soccer, softball, basketball, open-air concerts and theater, smooching in the undergrowth, parties, picnics, crafts stalls, topless sunbathing—you name it. Its lakes, ponds, and streams are surrounded by meadows, trees, and colorful flowers. Vondelpark lies generally southwest of Leidseplein and has entrances all around; the most popular is adjacent to Leidseplein, on Stadhouderskade. Watch out for the tasty-looking "gateau" they sell here, or you might find yourself floating above the trees: Drug-laced "space cake" is an acquired taste. This park, open daily from 8am to sunset, is extremely popular in summer with young people from all over the world; admission is free.

To enjoy scenery and fresh air, head out to the giant **Amsterdamse Bos** (tram: 6, 16, 24 to Stadionplein, and then any bus, except the no. 23, south on Amstelveenseweg to the main entrance), in the Amstelveen southern suburb. Nature on the city's doorstep, the park was laid out during the Depression years as a public works project. By now the trees, birds, insects, and small animals are firmly established. From the entrance, follow a path to the **Roeibaan,** a rowing course 2km (1¼ miles) long. Beyond its western end, at the **Bosmuseum** (© **020/676-2152**), you can trace the park's history and learn about its wildlife. The museum is open daily from 10am to 5pm; admission is free. Nearby is a big pond called the **Grote Vijver,** where you can rent boats (© **020/644-5119**), and the **Openluchttheater (Open-Air Theater),** which often has performances on summer evenings. In 2000, the **Kersenbloesempark (Cherry Blossom Park)** opened in the Amsterdamse Bos. Its 400 cherry trees, donated by the Japan Women's Club, marked 400 years of cultural ties between the Netherlands and Japan. The Bos is open 24 hours; admission is free.

Established in 1682, **Hortus Botanicus,** Plantage Middenlaan 2A (© **020/ 625-9021;** tram: 9, 14, 20), Amsterdam's Botanical Garden, near Artis Zoo, is a medley of color and scent, containing 250,000 flowers and 115,000 plants and trees from 8,000 different varieties. It owes its origins to the treasure trove of tropical plants the Dutch found in their colonies—Indonesia, Surinam, and the Antilles—and its popularity to the Dutch love affair with flowers. Among highlights are the **Semicircle,** which reconstructs part of the original design from 1682; the **Mexico–California Desert House; Palm House,** with one of the world's oldest palm trees; and the **Tri-Climate House,** which displays tropical, subtropical, and desert plants. Hortus is open April through September Monday through Friday from 9am to 5pm, Saturday and Sunday from 11am to 5pm; October through March Monday through Friday from 9am to 4pm, Saturday and Sunday from 11am to 4pm. Admission is 5€ for adults, 3€ for children 5 to 14, free for children under 5.

ORGANIZED TOURS

Although you could see most of Amsterdam's important sights in one long walking tour, it's best to break the city into shorter walks. Luckily, the **VVV Amsterdam** tourist office has done that. For 1.80€, you can buy a brochure outlining one of four walking tours: *Voyage of Discovery Through Amsterdam, A Walk Through Jewish Amsterdam, A Walk Through the Jordaan,* and *A Walk Through Maritime Amsterdam.*

A **canal-boat cruise** 🐸🐸 is the best way to view the old houses and warehouses. If you have to choose among a walking tour, a bus tour, and a boat tour, definitely take a boat. This is a city built on the shipping trade, so it's only fitting you should see it from the water, just as the Golden Age merchants saw their city. There are several canal-boat jetties, all of which have signs stating the time of the next tour. The greatest concentration of canal-boat operators is along Damrak and Rokin from Centraal Station; another cluster is on Singelgracht, near Leidseplein. Most tours last 1 hour and cost 6€ to 8€ for adults, 5€ to 6€ for children 4 to 13, free for children under 4. Since the tours are all basically the same, simply pick the one that's most convenient for you. Some cruises include snacks and drinks, with floating candlelit dinners extra.

You can take a self-guided, self-powered tour on a **canal bike.** These small pedal boats for two to four are available from **Canal Bike** (© 020/626-5574) at Leidseplein near the Rijksmuseum (tram: 1, 2, 5, 6, 7, 10, 20), at Westerkerk (tram: 13, 14, 17, 20), and on Keizersgracht near Leidsestraat (tram: 1, 2, 5). Canal bikes are available daily from 10am to 4pm in spring and autumn (to 10pm in summer). The hourly rate is 7.50€ a head for one or two people and 6€ a head for three or four. There's a 25€ refundable deposit. You can pick one up at one jetty and drop it off at another.

A 3-hour **bus tour** costs around 20€ and includes tickets for a canal cruise. Children 4 to 13 are usually charged half-price. Tour companies include **The Best of Holland,** Damrak 34 (© 020/623-1539); **Holland International Excursions,** Dam 6 (© 020/551-2800), **Holland Keytours,** Dam 19 (© 020/624-7304); and **Lindbergh Excursions,** Damrak 26 (© 020/622-2766).

THE SHOPPING SCENE

Strolling Amsterdam's streets, you could get the impression the city is one giant outdoor mall. Everywhere you look are stores ranging in price and variety from the Jordaan's used-clothing stores and bookstores to Pieter Cornelisz Hooftstraat's designer boutiques. Alas, most stores have little in the way of bargains. However, many typically Dutch souvenirs and gift items might appeal to you and can be real bargains if you shop around.

Note: Look for the TAX-FREE SHOPPING sign in some store windows. These stores provide visitors who are not resident in the European Union the check they need for recovering the **value-added tax (BTW)** when they leave the EU. This refund amounts to 13.5% of the total cost of purchases of more than 137€ in a participating store. When you're leaving by air, present the check to Customs, along with your purchases and receipts; they will stamp it and you can get an immediate refund from the ABN-Amro bank at Schiphol Airport.

Best buys in Amsterdam include special items produced by the Dutch to perfection, or produced to perfection in the past and that now retail as antiques—Delftware, pewter, crystal, and old-fashioned clocks—or commodities in which they have significantly cornered a market such as diamonds. If cost is an important consideration, remember the Dutch also produce inexpensive specialties such as cheese, flower bulbs, and chocolate.

For jewelry, trendy clothing, and athletic gear, try the department stores and specialized stores around the Dam. On the long, pedestrianized Nieuwendijk–Kalverstraat shopping street and on Leidsestraat, you find inexpensive clothing stores and souvenir stores. For designer boutiques and upscale fashion and accessories, shop on Pieter Cornelisz Hooftstraat and Van Baerlestraat. Pricey antiques and art dealers congregate on Nieuwe Spiegelstraat. For fashion boutiques and funky little specialty stores, or a good browse through a flea market or secondhand store, roam the streets of the Jordaan. The Red Light District specializes in stores selling erotic clothing, sex aids and accessories, and pornographic books and magazines.

STORES WORTH A VISIT

The city's top department store, with the best selection of goods and a great cafe, is **De Bijenkorf,** Dam 1 (© 020/621-8080; tram: 4, 9, 14, 16, 20, 24, 25). You can find almost everything there is to buy in Amsterdam at **Magna Plaza** (tram: 1, 2, 5, 13, 14, 17, 20), a splendid three-story mall in the old main post office building, behind the Dam at the corner of Nieuwezijds Voorburgwal and Raadhuisstraat.

Focke & Meltzer, Pieter Cornelisz Hooftstraat 65–67 (© **020/664-2311;** tram: 2, 5, 20), is the best one-stop store for authentic Delft Blue and Makkumware porcelain, Hummel figurines, Leerdam crystal, and a world of other fine china, porcelain, silver, glass, and crystal.

Diamond showrooms offering free individual and small-group tours of their diamond-cutting and -polishing facilities include: **Amsterdam Diamond Center,** Rokin 1 (© **020/624-5787;** tram: 4, 9, 14, 16, 20, 24, 25), just off the Dam; **Coster Diamonds,** Paulus Potterstraat 2–6 (© **020/676-2222;** tram: 2, 5, 20), near the Rijksmuseum; and **Van Moppes Diamonds,** Albert Cuypstraat 2–6 (© **020/676-1242;** tram: 4), at the street market.

A MARKET

Buying flowers at the **Bloemenmarkt (Flower Market)** 🎇, on a row of barges permanently moored along Singel between Muntplein and Leidsestraat (tram: 1, 2, 4, 5, 9, 14, 16, 20, 24, 25), is an Amsterdam ritual. The market is open Monday through Saturday from 9am to 5pm.

AMSTERDAM AFTER DARK

Nightlife centers on Leidseplein and Rembrandtplein, and you'll find dozens of bars, nightclubs, cafes, dance clubs, and movie theaters around these two squares. More cultured evening entertainment can be found in other parts of the city.

For listings of performances, consult the monthly magazine *What's On in Amsterdam,* available for 1.80€ from VVV Amsterdam tourist offices. *De Uitkrant,* a free monthly magazine in Dutch, has an even more thorough listing of events (which is not hard for English speakers to follow) and is available from performance venues, clubs, and VVV offices.

For tickets to theatrical and musical events (including rock concerts), contact **Amsterdam Uit Buro (AUB) Ticketshop,** Leidseplein 26 (© **020/621-1211**), which can book tickets for almost every venue in town. VVV offices also book tickets, for a 2.25€ fee.

THE PERFORMING ARTS

CLASSICAL MUSIC The renowned **Koninklijk Concertgebouworkest** is based at the **Concertgebouw** 🎇, Concertgebouwplein 2–6 (© **020/671-8345;**

tram: 3, 5, 12, 16, 20), which has an ornate Greek Revival facade and some of the best acoustics of any hall in the world. Performances, by this and other orchestras, are held almost every night in the building's two halls. There are free concerts on Wednesdays at 12:30pm. The box office is open daily from 10am to 7pm, with tickets from 12€ to 90€.

The **Nederlands Philharmonisch Orkest** (the "NedPho") and the **Nederlands Kamer Orkest** both perform at the impressive **Beurs van Berlage,** Damrak 243 (℗ **020/627-0466;** tram: 4, 9, 14, 16, 20, 24, 25), which was once the Amsterdam stock exchange, and now houses two concert halls for symphonies and chamber music. The box office is open Tuesday through Friday from 12:30 to 6pm and Saturday from noon to 5pm, with tickets at 7.50€ to 25€.

OPERA & DANCE   The **Nederlands Opera** and **Het National Ballet** both perform regularly at the modern **Muziektheater,** Waterlooplein (℗ **020/625-5455;** tram: 9, 14, 20); the innovative **Nederlands Dans Theater** from The Hague is a frequent visitor. The box office is open Monday through Saturday from 10am to 8pm and Sunday from 11:30am to 6pm, with tickets from 15€ to 60€. Music and dance performances are occasionally held at the **Stadsschouwburg** (see "Theater," below).

THEATER   The **Koninklijk Theater Carré,** Amstel 115–125 (℗ **020/622-5225;** Metro: Weesperplein), a huge old domed former circus-theater on the Amstel River near the Magere Brug (Skinny Bridge), occasionally presents touring shows from New York's Broadway or London's West End. The box office is open Monday through Saturday from 10am to 7pm and Sunday from 1 to 7pm, and tickets go for 12€ to 53€. At the Dutch Renaissance **Stadsschouwburg,** Leidseplein 26 (℗ **020/624-2311;** tram: 1, 2, 5, 6, 7, 10, 20), from 1894, performances include plays in Dutch and, occasionally, English, plus music and dance performances by international companies. The box office is open daily 10am through 6pm, with tickets at 7€ to 35€.

Compared by *Time* magazine to Chicago's famous Second City troupe, **Boom Chicago Theater,** Leidsepleintheater, Leidseplein 12 (℗ **020/530-7300;** tram: 1, 2, 5, 6, 7, 10, 20), puts on great improvisational comedy, and Dutch audiences have no problem with the English sketches. You can have dinner and a drink while enjoying the show at a candlelit table. It's open daily in summer, closed Sunday in winter. Tickets are 15€. The restaurant opens at 7pm, and meals cost 10€ to 13€.

THE LIVE-MUSIC SCENE

Amsterdam's biggest and most popular clubs book up-and-coming acts and always charge admission. Plenty of smaller clubs in cafes showcase local bands and charge no admission.

Housed in an old canal-side warehouse, **Bimhuis** ⚘, Oude Schans 73–77 (℗ **020/623-3373;** Metro: Nieuwmarkt), is Amsterdam's premier jazz club. Music workshops are on Tuesday at 8pm (participants only). During the rest of the week jazz musicians from all over Europe, and occasionally from the States, perform. It's open Wednesday through Sunday from 8pm to 1am, with a 10€ to 15€ cover.

You can impress your ears with a never-routine mix of electronic music, avant-garde jazz, and anything else that goes out on a musical limb, in the small concert hall at **De IJsbreker,** Weesperzijde 23 (℗ **020/668-1805;** Metro: Weesperplein), a pleasant cafe with an outdoor terrace on the banks of the Amstel. Cover is 7€ to 12€.

A regular crowd frequents the small, intimate **Alto Jazz Café,** Korte Leidsedwarsstraat 115 (© **020/626-3249**), for nightly performances by both regular and guest combos. Check out also the **Bamboo Bar,** Lange Leidsedwarsstraat 64 (© **020/624-3993**), and funky **Bourbon Street,** Leidsekruisstraat 6–8 (© **020/ 623-3440**), for late-night blues and rock. All three bars are near Leidseplein, reached by tram 1, 2, 5, 6, 7, 10, 20.

THE BAR SCENE

There are countless bars—or cafes, as they're called here—in the city, many around **Leidseplein** and **Rembrandtplein.** Many of them don't start to get busy until at least 8pm, but they usually open at noon and stay open all day. The most popular drink is draft Pilsener served in small glasses with two fingers of head on top. Also popular is *jenever* (Dutch gin) available in *jonge* (young) and *oude* (old) varieties—*oude* is stronger, more refined in taste, and higher in alcoholic content.

BROWN CAFES   Particularly old and traditional bars often earn the appellation of *bruine kroeg* (brown cafe), a name said to have been derived as much from the preponderance of wood furnishings as from the browning of the walls from years of dense tobacco smoke. Some have been around since Rembrandt's time. At these warm and friendly (and smoky) cafes you can sit and sip a glass of beer or a mixed drink; at some you can even get a cheap meal.

Papeneiland, Prinsengracht 2, at the corner of Brouwersgracht (© **020/624-1989;** tram: 1, 2, 5, 13, 17, 20), is Amsterdam's oldest cafe: Since 1600 or thereabouts, folks have been dropping by for shots of *jenever* and glasses of beer. Originally a tasting house where people could try liqueurs distilled and aged on the premises, **De Drie Fleschjes,** Gravenstraat 18, between the Nieuwe Kerk and Nieuwendijk (© **020/624-8443;** tram: 1, 2, 4, 5, 9, 13, 14, 16, 17, 20, 24, 25), has been in business for more than 300 years. It's popular with businesspeople and journalists, who stop by to sample the wide variety of *jenevers.*

The dark walls, low ceilings, and old wooden furniture at **Hoppe,** Spui 18–20 (© **020/420-4420;** tram: 1, 2, 5), one of Amsterdam's oldest and most popular brown cafes, have literally remained unchanged since the cafe opened in 1670. It has become a tourist attraction, but locals love it too, often stopping for a drink on their way home. There's usually standing-room-only and the crowds overflow onto the sidewalk.

In a medieval alley, wood-paneled **In de Wildeman,** Kolksteeg 3 (© **020/ 638-2348;** tram: 1, 2, 5, 13, 17, 20), serves more than 200 kinds of beer. The tile floor and rows of bottles and jars behind the counters are remnants from its early days as a distillery's retail store.

MODERN CAFES   Flea-market tables, armchairs left over from the 1970s, and rotating exhibits of rather puzzling artwork have made **Café Schuim,** Spuistraat 189 (© **020/638-9357;** tram: 1, 2, 5), the cafe of the moment in the Dam area. The rumpled surroundings attract an assortment of creative types who debate and discuss during the week and try to avoid being crushed by mobs on weekends.

The concept of the Grand Cafe—combining drinks and food in elegant surroundings—has taken Amsterdam by storm. One of the best is **Grand Café Luxembourg,** Spuistraat 24 (© **020/620-6264;** tram 1, 2, 5), a chic rendezvous that takes some of its menu dishes from top eateries around town. Whether you're in jeans or theater attire, you'll feel comfortable at **Royal Café De Kroon,** Rembrandtplein 15 (© **020/625-2011;** tram: 4, 9, 14, 20), on the second floor of a building overlooking the square, amid a decor of Louis XVI–style fittings and tropical plants.

On summer evenings, trendies head to the terrace of **Café Vertigo,** Vondelpark 3 (© **020/612-3021;** tram: 2, 5, 20), in Vondelpark, for one of the liveliest scenes in town. The low arched ceilings, subtle lighting, and unobtrusive music set a mood of casual sophistication.

THE GAY & LESBIAN SCENE

Amsterdam bills itself as the gay capital of Europe, proud of its open and tolerant attitude toward homosexuality. To find out more about the gay and lesbian scenes, stop by **COC,** Rozenstraat 14 (© **020/623-4079;** tram: 13, 14, 17, 20), 2 blocks off Westerkerk. It houses a cafe open Monday through Saturday from 11pm to 4am as well as a dance club. The dance club is primarily for men on Fridays and primarily for women on Saturdays. Sundays attract a mixed crowd. You can also call the **Gay and Lesbian Switchboard** at © **020/623-6565,** open daily from 10am to 10pm.

Gay News Amsterdam, a new monthly newspaper in English, is available free in gay establishments throughout Amsterdam. Of course, you find the best coverage of the Gay Capital of Europe in *Frommer's Gay & Lesbian Europe.*

"COFFEE SHOPS"

Amsterdam is a mecca for the marijuana smoker and seems likely to remain that way. Visitors often get confused about "smoking" coffee shops and how they differ from "nonsmoking" ones. Well, to begin with, "smoking" and "nonsmoking" don't refer to cigarettes—they refer to cannabis. "Smoking" coffee shops not only sell cannabis, most commonly in the form of hashish, but also provide somewhere patrons can sit and smoke it all day if they so choose. Generally, these smoking coffee shops are the only places in Amsterdam called "coffee shops"—regular cafes are called *cafes* or *eetcafes.*

You are allowed to buy only 5 grams (.2 oz.) of soft drugs at a time for personal use, but you're allowed to be in possession of 30 grams (1.2 oz.) for personal use.

> **Tips   Toker's Tips**
>
> Don't buy on the street. You stand a fair chance of being ripped off, the quality is doubtful, and there may be unpleasant additives. *Mellow Pages,* a guide in English available from many bookstores for 7.95€, has reviews of coffee shops.

Coffee shops are not allowed to sell alcohol, so they sell coffee, tea, and fruit juices. You won't be able to get any food (except maybe drug-laced "space cake"), so don't expect to grab a quick bite. You're even allowed to smoke your own stuff in the coffee shop, so long as you buy a drink.

Some of the most popular smoking coffee shops are **The Rookies,** Korte Leidsedwarsstraat 145–147 (© **020/694-2353;** tram: 1, 2, 5); **Borderline,** Amstelstraat 37 (© **020/622-0540;** tram: 9, 14, 20); and, with tourists, the shops of the **Bulldog** chain, which has branches around the city. The **Bulldog Palace** is at Leidseplein 15 (© **020/627-1908;** tram: 1, 2, 5).

2 Environs of Amsterdam

If Amsterdam is your only stop in the Netherlands, try to make at least one excursion into the countryside. Dikes, windmills, and some of Holland's quaintest villages await you just beyond the city limits. And you don't need to travel much farther to reach one of the many historic art towns.

HAARLEM 🕸🕸

Just 20km (12 miles) west of Amsterdam, Haarlem is a graceful town of winding canals and medieval neighborhoods that also holds several fine museums. The best time to visit is Saturday, for the market on the Grote Markt, or in tulip season (Mar to mid-May), when the city explodes with flowers.

ESSENTIALS

GETTING THERE   Haarlem is 20 minutes from Amsterdam by train, and two or three leave every hour from Centraal Station. A round-trip ticket is 5.25€. There are also frequent buses from outside Centraal Station. By car, take N5 and then A5 west.

VISITOR INFORMATION   VVV Haarlem, Stationsplein 1, 2011 Haarlem (© **0900/61-61-600;** fax 023/534-0537; www.vvvzk.nl), just outside the train station, is open Monday through Friday from 9:30am to 5:30pm, Saturday from 10am to 2pm.

SEEING THE SIGHTS

Haarlem is where Frans Hals, Jacob van Ruysdael, and Pieter Saenredam were living and painting their famous portraits, landscapes, and church interiors while Rembrandt was living and working in Amsterdam.

Handel and Mozart made special visits just to play the magnificent organ of **Sint-Bavokerk,** also known as the **Grote Kerk** 🕸, Oude Groenmarkt 23 (© **023/532-4399**). Look for the tombstone of painter Frans Hals (ca. 1580–1666) and for a cannonball that has been embedded in the church's wall ever since it came flying through a window during the 1572 to 1573 siege of Haarlem. And, of course, don't miss seeing the famous **Christian Müller Organ,** built in 1738. You can hear it at one of the free concerts given on Tuesday and Thursday from April to October. It has 5,068 pipes and is nearly 30m (98 ft.) tall. The woodwork was done by Jan van Logteren. Mozart played the organ in 1766 when he was just 10 years old. St Bavo's is open Monday through Saturday from 10am to 4pm. Admission is 1.25€ adults, .75€ children under 14.

From St. Bavo's, it's a short walk to the oldest and perhaps the most unusual museum in the Netherlands, the **Teylers Museum,** Spaarne 16 (© **023/531-9010**). It contains a curious collection: Drawings by Michelangelo, Raphael, and Rembrandt; fossils, minerals, and skeletons; instruments of physics; and an odd assortment of inventions, including a 19th-century radarscope. It's open Tuesday through Saturday from 10am to 5pm and Sunday from 1 to 5pm. Admission is 3.75€ adults; 2.50€ students, seniors, and children 5 to 15; free for children under 5.

Saving the best for last, visit the **Frans Halsmuseum** 🕸🕸, Groot Heiligland 62 (© **023/516-4200**), where the galleries are the halls and furnished chambers of a former pensioners' home, and famous paintings by the masters of the Haarlem school hang in settings that look like the 17th-century homes they were intended to adorn. It's open Monday through Saturday from 11am to 5pm, Sunday from 1 to 5pm. Admission is 4€ adults, 2€ children 10 to 17, free for children under 10.

An ideal way to tour the city is by **canalboat cruise,** operated by Woltheus Cruises from their Spaarne River jetty, Gravensteenbrug (© **023/535-7723**). Cruises are from April through October at 10:30am, noon, 1:30, 3, and 4:30pm.

WHERE TO DINE

De Pêcherie Haarlem aan Zee ⚓ SEAFOOD   You can just about smell the fresh North Sea breeze at this fine seafood restaurant facing Haarlem's Grote Kerk. You sit in wooden booths on chairs that have brightly colored canvas backings, like deck chairs. The menu features oysters, crab, prawns, and various fish dishes, all of which go well with the crisp house white wine. Try the grilled Portuguese sardines in a *ravigotte* sauce as a starter, and the fried or poached filet of turbot as a main course.

Oude Groenmarkt 10. ℭ **023/531-4848.** Main courses 13€–19€. MC, V. Mon–Sat noon–midnight; Sun 5pm–midnight.

Jacobus Pieck ⚓ DUTCH/INTERNATIONAL   This popular cafe-restaurant has a lovely shaded terrace in the garden for fine-weather days, while inside is bustling but crisply stylish. Friendly service and good food for reasonable prices draw in a local clientele. Main dinner courses range from wholesome Dutch standards to pastas and Middle Eastern dishes.

Warmoesstraat 18. ℭ **023/532-6144.** Main courses 6.75€–13€; snacks from 2.95€. AE, MC, V. Open Mon–Sat 10am–11pm; Sun noon–11pm.

ZANDVOORT

If you feel like a breath of sea air, do what Amsterdammers do: Head for **Zandvoort,** 26km (16 miles) west of Amsterdam, on the North Sea coast. Zandvoort is 30 minutes from Amsterdam by train, and one leaves Amsterdam Centraal Station every hour. Usually you need to transfer at Haarlem, but during summertime extra trains go direct. Journey time is 30 minutes and a round-trip ticket is 6.75€. There are also frequent buses from outside Centraal Station. You can go by car via Haarlem on N5, then on A5, but during summer there are frequent traffic jams.

There's not much more to Zandvoort than its **beach** ⚓, but what a beach. Seemingly endless sands are lined in summertime with beach cafes and discos, and the conditions are good for windsurfing. Down from the mainstream beaches are gay and nudist beaches.

You'll find tranquility in the **Kennemer Duinen** and **Amsterdamse Waterleiding Duinen,** protected zones of sand dune and vegetation that play an important role in sea defense. Stroll along paths through woods on the eastern side and across dunes leading west toward the sea.

One of 10 legal casinos in the Netherlands, **Holland Casino Zandvoort,** Badhuisplein 7 (ℭ **023/574-0574**), has roulette, blackjack and more. Dress code is "correct" (collar and tie for men), the minimum age is 18, and you need your passport. It's open daily from 1:30pm to 2am. Admission is 3€.

There are plenty of eating and drinking possibilities in the town.

ZAANSE SCHANS ⚓

A visit to the beautiful little village of **Zaanse Schans,** on the banks of the Zaan River, 24km (15 miles) north of Amsterdam, makes a great short excursion.

The best way to get here is by **train** from Amsterdam's Centraal Station. There are departures every 30 minutes and the trip takes 15 minutes. Take a train bound for Alkmaar that makes local stops, and get off at the Koog–Zaandijk station; from the station, follow the signs to the village. It's about an 8-minute walk. The round-trip fare is 4.50€.

An excursion ticket, for 12€, includes round-trip train fare, a 45-minute cruise on the river, coffee and a pancake in the De Kraai pancake restaurant, and admission to the Zaandam Clockwork Museum. For information, call © 075/16-8218. If you're **driving,** take A10 in the direction of Zaanstad, then A7 in the direction of Leeuwarden, following the signs to Zaanse Schans.

Along the riverbank are six windmills, two of which are still operating and can be visited. Surrounding the village are pastures where cows graze, and the nearby cocoa factory fills the air with the smell of chocolate. The windmill museum (© 075/616-8218) is open daily from April to November 1, and on weekends only during the rest of the year.

VOLENDAM & MARKEN

One of these neighboring villages on the IJsselmeer lake is on the mainland, the other on a former island; one is Catholic, the other Protestant; in one, women wear white caps with wings, and in the other, caps with ribbons—but they are often combined on bus-tour itineraries.

There are separate, hourly buses to Volendam and Marken from outside Amsterdam's Centraal Station. The fare is 3.75€ round-trip; the trip takes 35 minutes to Volendam and 45 minutes to Marken.

Geared for tourism, **Volendam,** 18km (11 miles) northeast of Amsterdam, has souvenir stores, boutiques, and restaurants. Its boat-filled harbor, tiny streets, and traditional houses have an undeniable charm. If you want a snapshot of yourself surrounded by fishermen wearing little caps and balloon-legged pants, Volendammers will gladly pose. They understand that the traditional costume is worth preserving, as is the economy of a small town that lost most of its fishing industry when the Zuiderzee enclosure dam cut it off from the North Sea. You can visit attractions like the fish auction, a diamond cutter, a clog maker, and a house with a room entirely wallpapered in cigar bands.

A causeway now connects the onetime island of **Marken** ⚓, 16km (10 miles) northeast of Amsterdam, with the mainland, but it remains as insular as ever. Quieter than Volendam, with a village of green-painted houses on stilts around a tiny harbor, it is also more rural. Clusters of farmhouses dot the *polders* (the reclaimed land from the sea that makes up two-thirds of the Netherlands), and a candy-striped lighthouse stands on the IJsselmeer shore.

Marken does not gush over tourists, but it will feed and water them, and let them wander around its pretty streets. Villagers wear traditional costume, as much to preserve the custom as to appease the tourists who pour in daily. The

---

 The IJsselmeer

Only in the Netherlands could you say, "This used to be a sea." The IJsselmeer (pronounced "*Eye*-sselmeer"), a large freshwater lake on Amsterdam's doorstep, actually was once a sea, the Zuiderzee, until the Dutch decided they didn't want a sea any longer, because it was always threatening to flood Amsterdam (and Amsterdammers don't like water in their *jenever*).

So in the 1930s, workers blocked off the mouth of the Zuiderzee with a massive dike, the Afsluitdijk (Enclosing Dike), from Noord-Holland to Friesland, and that was that. The IJsselmeer is (usually) well behaved, and a tour of its long shoreline, called the "Golden Circle," makes a scenic excursion from Amsterdam.

Marken Historisch Museum, Kerkbuurt 44 (© **0299/601-904**), is a typical house open as a museum from Good Friday to the end of October, Monday through Saturday from 10am to 5pm and Sunday from noon to 4pm. Admission is 2€ adults and 1€ children.

3 Delft & Leiden

These two historic art towns are close enough from Amsterdam to be visited on separate day trips, and if you start out early enough, you'll have time to explore them quite thoroughly.

DELFT ✸✸

Yes, Delft, 54km (34 miles) southwest of Amsterdam, is the town of the famous blue-and-white porcelain. And, yes, you can visit the factory of Koninklijke Porceleyne Fles. But don't let Delftware be your only reason to visit. Not only is this one of the prettiest small cities in the Netherlands, but Delft is also important as a cradle of the Dutch Republic and the traditional burial place of the royal family. Plus, it was the birthplace, and inspiration, of the 17th-century master of light and subtle emotion, painter Jan Vermeer. Delft remains a quiet little town, with flowers in its flower boxes and linden trees bending over its gracious canals.

ESSENTIALS

GETTING THERE   There are several trains per hour from Amsterdam's Centraal Station to Delft Station, which is southwest of the town center. The trip takes about 1 hour and costs 15€ round-trip. If you go by car, take A4 (E19) in the direction of The Hague and watch for the Delft exit.

VISITOR INFORMATION   VVV Delft, Markt 83–85, 2611 GS Delft (© **015/212-6100;** fax 015/215-8695; www.delft.com), is open April through September, Monday through Saturday from 9am to 5:30pm, Sunday from 11am to 3pm; October through March, Monday through Friday from 9am to 5:30pm, Saturday from 9am to 5pm.

SEEING THE SIGHTS

Vermeer's house is long gone from Delft, as are his paintings. Instead, you can visit the **Oude Kerk,** Roland Holstlaan 753 (© **015/212-3015**), where he's buried; from April to October, it's open Monday through Saturday from 10am to 5pm. You might want to visit also the **Nieuwe Kerk** ✸, Markt (© **015/212-3025**), where Prince William of Orange and other members of the House of Orange–Nassau are buried, and to climb its tower, which is 109m (357 ft.) high. Both churches are open April through October, Monday through Saturday from 9am to 6pm; November through March, Monday through Friday from 11am to 4pm, Saturday from 11am to 5pm. Separate admission to each is 2.70€ adults, .90€ for children under 14; separate admission to the Nieuwe Kerk tower is 1.80€ adults, .80€ for children under 14.

The **Prinsenhof Museum** ✸, Sint-Agathaplein 1 (© **015/260-2358**), on the nearby Oude Delft canal, is where William I of Orange (William the Silent) lived and had his headquarters in the years during which he helped found the Dutch Republic. It's also where he was assassinated in 1584 (you can still see the musket-ball holes in the stairwell). Today the Prinsenhof is a museum of paintings, tapestries, silverware, and pottery. It's open Tuesday through Saturday from 10am to 5pm, Sunday from 1 to 5pm. Admission is 4€ adults, 3€ children 12 to 15, and free for children under 15.

In the same neighborhood you can see a fine collection of old Delft tiles displayed in the wood-paneled setting of a 19th-century mansion museum called **Lambert van Meerten,** Oude Delft 199 (© **015/260-2358**). It's open Tuesday through Saturday from 10am to 5pm, Sunday from 1 to 5pm. Admission is 2.80€ adults, 2.20€ children 12 to 15, and free for children under 12.

WHERE TO DINE

Spijshuis de Dis ⭐ DUTCH   Fine Dutch cooking that's traditional at heart but given a modern accent is served up at this atmospheric old restaurant. Among the top dishes are *bakke pot*—a stew made from beef, chicken, and rabbit; VOC mussels (named after the Dutch initials for the East India Company), prepared with garlic, ginger, and curry; and asparagus in season (May–June). The steaks and the pork and lamb filet dishes are great. Don't miss the homemade mushroom soup.

Beestenmarkt 36 (off the Markt). © **015/213-1782.** Main courses 8.75€–16€; 4-course menu 23. AE, DC, MC, V. Thurs–Tues 5–10:30pm.

Stadsherberg De Mol TRADITIONAL DUTCH   Food is served here in the medieval manner—in wooden bowls from which you eat with your hands. Prices are moderate and quantities copious, and there is fun, too, with live music and dancing.

Molslaan 104 (off Beestenmarkt). © **015/212-1343.** Fixed-price menu 19€. MC, V. Tues–Sun 6–11pm.

LEIDEN ⭐⭐

Students of U.S. history may know that the Pilgrim Fathers lived in this town, 36km (22½ miles) southwest of Amsterdam, for 11 years before sailing for North America on the *Mayflower.* Leiden's proudest homegrown moment came in 1574, when it was the only Dutch town to withstand a full-blown siege by the Spanish invaders. This was the birthplace of the Dutch tulip trade, and of the painters Rembrandt and Jan Steen, and it is the home of the oldest university in the Netherlands. Finally, with 14 museums, covering subjects ranging from antiquities, natural history, and anatomy to clay pipes and coins, Leiden seems perfectly justified in calling itself *Museum Stad* (Museum City).

ESSENTIALS

GETTING THERE   There are several trains an hour from Amsterdam Centraal Station to Leiden Station, which is northwest of the town center (about a 10-min. walk). If you go by car, take A4 (E19) in the direction of The Hague and watch for the Leiden exit.

VISITOR INFORMATION   VVV Leiden, Stationsweg 2D, 2312 AV, Leiden (© **0900/222-2333;** fax 071/516-1227; www.leidenpromotie.nl), outside the train station, is open Monday through Friday from 9:30am to 6pm, Saturday from 10am to 4:30pm.

SEEING THE SIGHTS

Among the spectacular antiquities housed at the **Rijksmuseum van Oudheden** ⭐⭐, Rapenburg 28 (© **071/516-3163**), is the 1st century A.D. Temple of Taffeh, presented by the Egyptian government as a gift to the Dutch nation for its assistance in saving monuments prior to the construction of the Aswan High Dam. The museum is open Tuesday through Friday from 10am to 5pm, Saturday and Sunday from noon to 5pm. Admission is 4€ adults, 3€ seniors and children 6 to 18, and free for children under 6.

To touch base with those courageous but humble Pilgrim Fathers, pick up the VVV tourist office's brochure *A Pilgrimage Through Leiden: A Walk in the Footsteps of the Pilgrim Fathers.* The walk starts at the **Lodewijkskerk,** which was used as a meeting place by the cloth guild. William Bradford, who later became governor of New Plymouth, was a member of this guild. The walk takes you past the house on William Brewstersteeg (formerly Herensteeg) where William Brewster's Pilgrim Press published the religious views that angered the Church of England. Plaques at **Sint-Pieterskerk** (in a small square off Kloksteeg) memorialize the Pilgrims, in particular Rev. Jon Robinson, who was forced to stay behind because of illness and is buried in this church (an almshouse, the Jean Pesijnhofje, in Kloksteeg, now occupies the house in which he died). Special Thanksgiving Day services are held each year in honor of the little band of refugees who worshipped here.

At the **American Pilgrim Museum** ✮, Beschuitsteeg 9 (© **071/512-2413**), you can hear a recorded commentary on the Pilgrims and see photocopies of documents relating to their 11-year residence in Leiden. The museum is open Wednesday through Saturday from 1 to 5pm. Admission is 2€ for adults and children 5 and over, free for children under 5.

On the other side of town, visit the **Stedelijk Museum de Lakenhal** ✮, Oude Singel 28–32 (© **071/516-5360**), to view works by local heroes Rembrandt and Jan Steen, and others, plus period rooms from the 17th to 19th centuries. Also on parade is Leiden's pride and joy: a copper stew pot said to have been retrieved by a small boy who crawled through a chink in the city wall just minutes after the lifting of the Spanish siege. He found this very pot full of boiling stew in the enemy's camp and brought it back to feed the starving inhabitants. Ever since, stew has been a national dish and is still traditionally prepared for the Leiden city holiday, October 3, which is the anniversary of its liberation. Each year on this day *haring en witte brood* (herring and white bread) are distributed, just as they were in 1574. The museum is open Tuesday through Friday from 10am to 5pm; Saturday, Sunday, and holidays (except Christmas and New Year's Day) from noon to 5pm. Admission is 3€ for adults, 1.50€ for children 6 to 18, and free for children under 6.

WHERE TO DINE

Annie's Verjaardag DUTCH/CONTINENTAL   This lively, water-level restaurant has vaulted cellars that are a favorite eating spot for both students and locals, who spill out onto the canal-side terrace (and occasionally *into* the canal) in fine weather. When the canals are frozen, the view is enchanting, as skaters practice their turns. The dinner menu is simple but wholesome, and during the day you can snack on sandwiches and *tapas.*

Oude Rijn 1A. © 071/512-6358. Main courses 8.75€–16€. No credit cards. Sun–Thurs 10am–1am; Fri–Sat 10am–2am.

Stadscafé van der Werff ✮ CONTINENTAL   This relaxed cafe-restaurant in a grand 1930s villa on the edge of the old town is popular with the town's students and ordinary citizens alike. Even if you're not having dinner, and enjoying dishes like a basic Indonesian *saté,* or their surf and turf *kalfsbiefstukje met gebakken gambas en een kreeftensaus* (beef steak with fried prawns in a lobster sauce), you can still while away the evening just having a drink and reading a paper.

Steenstraat 2. © 071/513-0335. Main courses 8.95€–17€. AE, DC, MC, V. Daily 10:30am–5pm and 6–10pm (cafe to 1am).

13

Norway

by Darwin Porter & Danforth Prince

Norway is a land of tradition, as exemplified by its rustic stave churches—look for these mysterious, dark structures with steep gables surmounted by dragons' heads and pointed steeples—and folk dances stepped to the airs of a fiddler. But Norway is also modern, a technologically advanced nation that's rich in petroleum and hydroelectric energy. One of the world's last great natural frontiers, Norway is a land of astonishing beauty; its steep and jagged fjords, salmon-rich rivers, glaciers, mountains, and meadows invite exploration. In winter, the shimmering Northern Lights beckon; in summer, the midnight sun shines late and warm.

1 Oslo

After World War II, Oslo grew to 450 sq. km (175 sq. miles), making it one of the 10 largest capitals in the world in sheer area, if not in urban buildup. The city is one of the most heavily forested on earth, and fewer than half a million Norwegians live and work here.

One of the oldest Scandinavian capital cities, founded in the mid–11th century, Oslo has never been a mainstream tourist site. But the city is culturally rich with many diversions—enough to fill at least 3 or 4 busy days. It's also the center for many easy excursions along the Oslofjord or to towns and villages in its environs, both north and south.

In recent years Oslo has grown from what even the Scandinavians viewed as a Nordic backwater to one of Europe's happening cities. Restaurants, nightclubs, cafes, shopping complexes, and other venues keep on opening. A kind of Nordic joie de vivre permeates the city; the only drawback is that all this fun is going to cost you—Oslo ranks as one of Europe's most expensive cities.

ESSENTIALS

GETTING THERE   By Plane   Since the recent closing of a small-scale, relatively outmoded airport named Fornebu, Oslo has learned to cope with all of its air traffic being funneled into the **Oslo International Airport** in Gardermoen (© **81-55-02-50**), about 50km (31 miles) east of downtown Oslo, a 45-minute drive from the center. All domestic and international flights coming into Oslo arrive through this much-upgraded airport, including aircraft belonging to SAS, British Airways, and Icelandair.

There's frequent bus service, departing every 15 to 30 minutes throughout the day, into downtown Oslo. It's maintained by both SAS (whose buses deliver passengers to the Central Railway station and to most of the SAS hotels within Oslo) and the **Norwegian Bus Express** (© **81-54-44-44**), whose buses head for the main railway station. Both companies charge 110NOK ($15) per person, each way. There's also 20-minute high-speed railway service between Gardermoen and Oslo's main railway station, priced at 180NOK ($24) per person each way. If you want to take a taxi, be prepared for a lethally high charge of around 500NOK ($67) for up to four passengers plus their luggage. If you need a "maxi-taxi," a minivan that's suitable for between 5 and 15 passengers, plus their luggage, you'll be assessed 800NOK ($106).

By Train   The first high-speed train between Oslo and Stockholm has reduced travel time to 4 hours and 50 minutes between these two once remotely linked Scandinavian capitals. Depending on the day, there are two to three trains daily in each direction. This high-speed train now competes directly with air travel. Trains from the Continent, Sweden, and Denmark arrive at **Oslo Sentral-stasjon (Central Station),** Jernbanetorget 1 (© 81-50-08-88 for train information). It's at the beginning of Karl Johans Gate, in the center of the city. The station is open daily from 7am to 11pm. From the Central Station, trains leave for Bergen, Stavanger, Trondheim, Bodø, and all other rail links in Norway. You can also take trams to all major parts of Oslo.

By Car   If you're driving from mainland Europe, the fastest way to reach Oslo is to take the car-ferry from Frederikshavn, Denmark (see below). You can also

Oslo

BYGDØY PENINSULA

To Bygdøy Peninsula (see inset above)

NORWAY
SWEDEN
Oslo

ACCOMMODATIONS ■

Cochs Pensjonat **10**
First Hotel Millennium **16**
Grand Hotel **14**
Golden Tulip Rainbow Hotel Stefan **12**
Hotel Bristol **13**
Tulip Inn Rainbow Munch **11**
White House **8**

take a car-ferry from Copenhagen (see below) or drive from Copenhagen by crossing over to Helsingborg, Sweden, from Helsingør, Denmark. Once at Helsingborg, take E-6 north all the way to Stockholm. If you're driving from Stockholm to Oslo, follow E-18 west all the way (trip time: 7 hr.). Once you near the outskirts of Oslo from any direction, follow the signs into the SENTRUM, or city center.

By Ferry   Ferries from Europe arrive at the Oslo port, a 15-minute walk (or a short taxi ride) from the city center. From Denmark, Scandinavia's link with the Continent, ferries depart for Oslo from Copenhagen, Hirtshals, and Frederikshavn.

From Strømstad, Sweden, in the summer, the daily crossing to Sandefjord, Norway, takes 2½ hours; from Sandefjord, it's an easy drive or train ride north to Oslo.

VISITOR INFORMATION   Assistance and information for visitors are available at the **Tourist Information Office,** Vestbaneplassen 1, N-0250 Oslo (© **22-83-00-50;** bus: 27). Free maps, brochures, sightseeing tickets, and guide services are available. The office is open June through August, daily from 9am to 7pm; May and September, Monday through Saturday from 9am to 5pm; October through April, Monday through Friday from 9am to 4pm.

There's also an Oslo-only **information office** at the Oslo Sentralstasjon (Central Station), Jernbanetorget 1, at the beginning of Karl Johans Gate (no phone), open daily from 8am to 11pm.

For information online, try the Norwegian Tourist Board **(www.visitnorway. com)** or Virtual Oslo **(www.oslorightnow.com).**

CITY LAYOUT   Oslo is at the mouth of the 95km (60-mile) Oslofjord. Opening onto the harbor is **Rådhusplassen (City Hall Square),** dominated by the modern City Hall, a major attraction. Guided bus tours leave from this square, and the launches that cruise the fjords depart from the pier facing the municipal building. (You can catch ferries to the Bygdøy Peninsula from the quay at Rådhusplassen.)

Out on a promontory to the east is the **Akershus Castle.** At **Bygdøy,** the much larger peninsula that juts out to the west, are four of Oslo's major attractions: the Viking ships, the Polar Ship *Fram* Museum, the *Kon-Tiki* Museum, and the Folk Museum.

Karl Johans Gate, Oslo's main street (especially for shopping and strolling) is north of City Hall Square. This boulevard begins at Oslo **Sentralstasjon (Central Station)** and stretches all the way to the 19th-century **Royal Palace** at the western end. A short walk from the palace is the famed **Student's Grove** (the University of Oslo is nearby), where everybody gathers on a summer day to socialize. Dominating this area is the **National Theater.** South of the theater and near the harbor is **Stortingsgaten,** another shopping street.

The main city square is **Stortorvet,** although it's no longer the center of city life, which has now shifted to Karl Johans Gate.

At a subway stop near the National Theater you can catch an electric train to **Tryvannstårnet,** the loftiest lookout in Scandinavia, and to the **Holmenkollen Ski Jump.**

GETTING AROUND   The **Oslo Card (Oslo-Kortet)** can help you become acquainted with the city at a fraction of the usual price. It allows free travel on public transportation, free admission to museums and other top sights, discounts on sightseeing buses and boats, a rebate on your car rental, and special treats in restaurants. You can buy the card at hotels, fine stores, and tourist offices; from travel agents; and in the branches of Sparebanken Oslo Akershus. Adults pay 180NOK ($24) for a 1-day card, 270NOK ($36) for 2 days, and 410NOK ($55) for 3 days. Children's cards cost 60NOK ($8), 80NOK ($11), and 110NOK ($15).

The 24-hour **Tourist Ticket (Turistkort)** lets you travel anywhere in Oslo by bus, tram, subway, local railway, or boat, including the Bygdøy ferries in the summer. The Tourist Ticket costs 40NOK ($5.30) for adults, half price for children 4 to 15; children under 4 travel free. The ticket is stamped when it's used for the first time and is good for the next 24 hours.

By Bus, Tram & Subway   Jernbanetorget, in front of the Central Station, is the major bus and tram terminal in Oslo. Most buses and trams passing through the heart of town stop at Wessels Plass, next to the Parliament (Stortinget), or at Stortorvet, the main marketplace. Many also stop at the National Theater or University Square on Karl Johans Gate.

The **T-banen** (subway) has four main lines running to the east of Oslo and four lines running to the west. The most heavily traveled routes by tourists are the eastern lines. The western lines take in Holmenkollen and residential and recreational areas west and north of the city.

For schedule and fare information, call **Trafikanten** (© **22-05-70-37**). Drivers sell single-trip tickets for 22NOK ($2.95); children travel for half fare. Automated machines cancel tickets. An eight-coupon Maxi card costs 135NOK ($18), half price for children. Maxi cards can be used for unlimited transfers for 1 hour from the time the ticket was stamped.

By Car   Driving is not a practical way to get around Oslo because parking is limited. The efficient network of public transportation makes a private car unnecessary. You can reach even the most isolated areas by public transportation.

By Taxi   If you need a taxi, call © **22-38-80-90,** 24 hours a day. Reserve at least an hour in advance. The approximate fare from Oslo International Airport to the center of Oslo is 500NOK ($67). All taxis have meters, and Norwegian cab drivers are generally honest. When a cab is available, a roof light goes on. Taxis can be hailed on the street, provided they're more than 90m (300 ft.) from a taxi rank. The worst times to hail a taxi are Monday through Friday from 8:30 to 10am and 3 to 5pm, and Saturday from 8:30 to 10am.

By Ferry   Beginning in mid-April, ferries depart for Bygdøy from Pier 3 in front of the Oslo Rådhuset. For schedules, call **Båtservice** (© **23-35-68-90**). The ferry or bus to Bygdøy is a good choice, because parking there is limited. Other ferries leave for various parts of the Oslofjord. Inquire at the **Tourist Information Office,** Vestbaneplassen 1 (© **22-83-00-50**).

By Bicycle   **Den Rustne Eike,** Vestbaneplassen 2 (© **22-83-52-08**), rents bikes at moderate rates, complete with free maps of interesting routes in Oslo and its environs. The cost is 265NOK ($35) per day or 800NOK ($106) per week, with a 1,000NOK ($133) deposit required. It's open May through October, daily from 10am to 6:30pm; in the off season, Monday through Friday from 10am to 6pm.

FAST FACTS: Oslo

American Express **American Express Reisebyrå,** Karl Johans Gate (© **22-98-37-00),** is open Monday through Friday from 8am to 4pm.

Business Hours Most **banks** are open Monday through Friday from 8:15am to 3:30pm (Thurs to 5pm). Most **businesses** are open Monday through Friday from 9am to 4pm. **Stores** are generally open Monday through Friday from 9am to 5pm (many stay open late on Thurs to 6 or 7pm) and Saturday from 9am to 1 or 2pm. Sunday closings are observed.

Currency You'll pay your way in Norway with Norwegian kroner or crowns, which are universally abbreviated NOK. There are 100 øre in 1 krone. The exchange rate used in this chapter is US$1 = 7.5NOK (or 1NOK = 13¢). At press time, £1 = approximately 11.5NOK (or 1NOK = 8.7 pence). Note that Norway is not a member of the EU.

Currency Exchange **Banks** will exchange most foreign currencies or cash traveler's checks. Bring your passport for identification. If banks are closed, try automated machines at the Oslo Sentralstasjon to exchange currency. You can also exchange currency at the **Bureau de Change** at the main Oslo post office, Dronningensgatan 15 (© **22-97-60-00).**

Dentists/Doctors For a dental emergency, contact the **Tøyen Senter,** Kolstadgate 18 (© **22-67-30-00;** T-banen: Groønen), open daily from 11am to 2pm and 7 to 10pm. For private dentists, look under *Tannleger* ("tooth doctors") in volume 1B of the telephone directory; there's rarely a language barrier.

Some larger hotels have arrangements with doctors in case a guest becomes ill. You can also try the 24-hour **Oslo Kommunale Legavakten,** Storgata 40 (© **22-93-22-93).** A privately funded alternative is **Oslo Akutten,** Nedre Vollgate 8 (© **22-00-81-60).** For more routine medical assistance, you can contact the biggest hospital in Oslo, **Ullaval,** Kirkeveien 166 (© **22-11-80-80).** To consult a private doctor (nearly all of whom speak English), check the telephone directory or ask at your hotel for a recommendation.

Drugstores A 24-hour pharmacy is **Jernbanetorvets Apotek,** Jernbanetorget 4A (© **22-41-24-82;** T-banen: Jernbanetorget).

Embassies & Consulates The embassy of the **United States** is at Drammensveien 18, N-0255 Oslo 2 (© **22-44-85-50;** T-banen: Nationaltheatret). The embassy of the **United Kingdom** is at Thomas Heftyes Gate 8, N-0264 Oslo 2 (© **23-13-27-00;** T-banen: Nationaltheatret). The embassy of **Canada** is at Oscarsgate 20, N-0244 Oslo 3 (© **22-99-53-00;** T-banen: Nationaltheatret). Visitors from Ireland and New Zealand should contact the British embassy. Australians should contact the Canadian embassy. Call for hours.

Emergencies Dial the Oslo **police** at © **112;** report a **fire** at © **110;** call an **ambulance** at © **113.**

Internet Access You can tap in free at the **Rådhuset,** the City Hall on Rådhusplassen (© **23-46-16-00).** Hours are May through September, Monday through Saturday from 9am to 5pm, Sunday from noon to 5pm; October through April, Monday through Saturday from 9am to 4pm, Sunday from noon to 4pm.

Post Office The **Oslo General Post Office** is at Dronningensgatan 15 (© 23-14-90-00 for information). Enter at the corner of Prinsensgate. It's open Monday through Friday from 8am to 5pm, Saturday from 9am to 2pm; closed Sunday and public holidays. You can arrange for mail to be sent to the main post office c/o General Delivery. The address is Poste Restante, P.O. Box 1181-Sentrum, Dronningensgatan 15, N-0101 Oslo, Norway. You must show your passport to collect it.

Safety Of the four Scandinavian capitals, Oslo is widely considered the safest. However, don't be lulled into a false sense of security. Oslovians no longer leave their doors unlocked. Be careful, and don't carry your wallet visibly exposed or sling your purse over your shoulder.

Taxes Oslo has no special city taxes. Norway imposes a 19.4% value-added tax (VAT) on most goods and services, which is figured into your final bill. If you buy goods in any store bearing the tax-free sign, you're entitled to a cash refund of up to 18.7% on purchases costing over 310NOK ($41). Ask the shop assistant for a tax-free shopping check, and show your passport to indicate that you're not a resident of Scandinavia. You may not use the articles purchased before leaving Norway, and they must be taken out of the country within 3 months of purchase. Complete the information requested on the back of the check you're given at the store; at your point of departure, report to an area marked by the tax-free sign, not at Customs. Your refund check will be exchanged there in *kroner* for the amount due you. Refunds are available at airports, ferry and cruise-ship terminals, borders, and train stations.

Telephone The country code for Norway is **47,** and the city code for Oslo is **22** (in some rare cases, **23**). For operator assistance in English, dial © **115.**

International calls can be made from **Telenor's Telecommunications Office,** Kongensgate 21 (© **81-07-70-00;** T-banen: Stortinget), open Monday through Friday from 9am to 8pm, Saturday from 10am to 5pm, and Sunday from noon to 6pm. The entrance is on Prinsensgate. Toll-free international access codes are: **AT&T** (© **800/CALL-ATT**), **MCI** (© **800/888-8000**).

Tipping Hotels add a 10% to 15% service charge to your bill, which is sufficient unless someone has performed a special service. Most bellhops get at least 10NOK ($1.10) per suitcase. Nearly all restaurants add a service charge of up to 15% to your bill. Barbers and hairdressers usually aren't tipped, but toilet attendants and hatcheck people expect at least 3NOK (35¢). Don't tip theater ushers. Taxi drivers don't expect tips unless they handle heavy luggage.

WHERE TO STAY
VERY EXPENSIVE

Grand Hotel 𝒦𝒦𝒦   Norway's leading hostelry is on the wide boulevard that leads to the Royal Palace. The stone-walled hotel with its mansard gables and copper tower has been an integral part of Oslo life since 1874. Famous guests have included Arctic explorer Roald Amundsen, Edvard Munch, Gen. Dwight

Eisenhower, Charlie Chaplin, Henry Ford, and Henrik Ibsen. Frankly, although it's still the grande dame of Norway hotels, we feel the Grand's stuffiness has cost it its cutting edge. Renovated in 1996, the guest rooms are in the 19th-century core or one of the modern additions. Newer rooms contain plush facilities and electronic extras, but many guests prefer the old-fashioned accommodations in the older section, which have also been modernized. Most of the old-fashioned bathrooms are done in marble or tile and have shower-tub combinations. Among the hotel's restaurants, the Grand Café (see below) is the most famous in Oslo.

Karl Johans Gate 31, N-0101 Oslo. © **800/223-5652** in the U.S., or 23-21-20-00. Fax 23-21-21-00. www.grand-hotel.no. 289 units. Summer 1,200NOK ($160) double; 2,160NOK–22,000NOK ($287–$2,926) suite. Fall, winter, spring 1,935NOK ($257) double; 2,740NOK–22,000NOK ($364–$2,926) suite. Rates include buffet breakfast. AE, DC, MC, V. Parking 240NOK ($32). T-banen: Stortinget. **Amenities:** 3 restaurants; 2 bars; nightclub; pool; health club; sauna; boutiques; massage; room service; laundry/dry cleaning. In room: A/C, TV, minibar, hair dryer.

EXPENSIVE

Hotel Bristol 👑👑👑   Loaded with character, and the source of many entertaining anecdotes, this 1920s-era hotel competes aggressively and gracefully with other historic hotel "dragons" of Oslo, including the Grand (see above) and the Continental. Of the three, the Bristol consistently emerges as the most liberal, the hippest, and the most accessible. Set in the commercial core of Oslo, a block north of Karl Johans Gate, it's warm, inviting, rich with tradition, and comfortable. It's becoming the preferred hotel of the media, arts, and show-biz communities, with a sense of playfulness that's unmatched by either of its more formal rivals.

In 2001, the hotel almost doubled its room count, thanks to the annexation and conversion of an office building next door. Guest rooms are comfortable and dignified, each with a tiled or marble bathroom with a tub/shower combination. Lavish public areas evoke the Moorish-inspired Art Deco style in which they were built. There's enormous life and energy in this hotel, thanks to active restaurants, piano bars, and a sense of elegant yet unpretentious conviviality.

Kristian IV's Gate 7, N-0164 Oslo 1. © **22-82-60-00.** Fax 22-82-60-01. www.bristol.no. 252 units. Mon–Thurs 1,350NOK–1,960NOK ($180–$261) double. Fri–Sun year-round and late June to early Aug 1,195NOK ($159) double. Year-round 4,000NOK–8,000NOK ($532–$1,064) suite. AE, DC, MC, V. Tram: 10, 11, 17, or 18. **Amenities:** 3 restaurants; 3 bars; live pianist in the lobby; nightclub/dance bar; small-scale exercise room and health club; room service; babysitting; laundry/dry cleaning. In room: A/C, TV, minibar, hair dryer, trouser press.

MODERATE

First Hotel Millennium 👑 *Finds*   One of Oslo's newest large-scale hotels is housed in what was originally a 12-floor 1930s Art Deco office building. This is one of the "personality" hotels of Oslo, known for its atmosphere and character, and noted for a stylish kind of functional minimalism. It's within walking distance of virtually everything in central Oslo. Rooms are among the most spacious in town, with many Art Deco touches. Extras include two phone lines and large bathrooms with both tub and shower. Some accommodations are suitable for persons with disabilities. Primo Ciaou-Ciaou is one of Oslo's best restaurants.

Tollbugate 25, N-0157 Oslo. © **21-02-28-00.** Fax 21-02-28-30. www.firsthotels.com. 112 units. Mon–Thurs 1,103NOK–1,510NOK ($147–$201) double; Fri–Sun 703NOK–853NOK ($94–$113) double. AE, DC, MC, V. Tram: 30 or 42. **Amenities:** Restaurant; bar; room service; babysitting; laundry/dry cleaning. In room: TV, minibar, hair dryer.

Golden Tulip Rainbow Hotel Stefan   In an excellent location in the center of the city, this hotel is comfortable and unpretentious. Built in 1952, it has been modernized and much improved, with a partial renovation in 1996. Rooms are traditional in style and well furnished and maintained, with small but adequate bathrooms with showers. Two offer facilities for people with disabilities. From May to September 1, weekend rates are granted only to those who make reservations less than 48 hours before arrival. The restaurant is known for its Norwegian buffets.

Rosenkrantzgate 1, N-0159 Oslo 1. © **23-31-55-00.** Fax 23-31-55-55. www.rainbow-hotels.no. 139 units. Sun–Thurs 1,015NOK ($135) double; Fri–Sat 735NOK ($98) double. Rates include breakfast. AE, DC, MC, V. Parking 180NOK ($24). Tram: 10, 11, 17, or 18. **Amenities:** Restaurant; bar; room service; babysitting; laundry/dry cleaning. *In room:* TV, minibar, hair dryer, safe.

Tulip Inn Rainbow Munch   This hotel is somewhat like a bed-and-breakfast, and it's just 5 minutes north of Karl Johans Gate. Built in 1983, the solid, nine-floor hotel offers comfortably furnished, well-maintained guest rooms, decorated with reproductions of Edvard Munch's paintings. Although not overly large, the rooms are cozy and comfortable. The bathrooms are tiny but come equipped with shower-tub combinations. If you don't plan to spend a lot of time in your room, this is an adequate choice, charging a fair price for what it offers.

Munchsgaten 5, N-0130 Oslo 1. © **23-21-96-00.** Fax 23-21-96-01. www.rainbow-hotels.no. 180 units. Mon–Thurs 1,145NOK ($152) double; Fri–Sun 720NOK ($96) double. Rates include breakfast. AE, DC, MC, V. Parking 140NOK ($19). T-banen: Stortinget. Tram: 7 or 11. Bus: 37. **Amenities:** Lounge; laundry/dry cleaning. *In room:* TV, minibar, hair dryer, safe.

INEXPENSIVE

Cochs Pensjonat *(Value*   Built more than a century ago, with an ornate facade that curves around a bend in a boulevard that flanks the northern edge of the Royal Palace, this clean, well-conceived, inexpensive hotel represents excellent value. In 2002, major renovations added a postmodern gloss to many of the guest rooms, with the remainder scheduled for overhauls sometime between 2003 and 2004. The result is a comfortable but simple lodging whose newer rooms have high ceilings and birch furniture, and a spartan but pleasant appearance. Expect very few, if any, amenities and services at this hotel—none of the rooms have TV or telephone, and no meals are served, but because of the in-room kitchens and a nearby restaurant that offers hotel guests a 25% discount on meals, no one really seems to mind.

Parkveien 25, N-0350 Oslo. © **23-33-24-00.** Fax 23-33-24-10. booking@cochs.no. 88 units, 78 with bathroom and kitchenette. Rooms with bathroom and kitchenette 600NOK–660NOK ($80–$88) double, 735NOK–795NOK ($98–$106) triple, 860NOK ($114) quad. Rooms without kitchenette and without private bathroom 500NOK ($67) double, 615NOK ($82) triple, 740NOK ($98) quad. AE, DC, MC, V. Tram: 11 or 12. *In room:* No phone.

WHERE TO DINE

Norwegians are as fond of *smørbrød* (smorgasbord) as the Danes (you'll see it offered everywhere for lunch), except they spell it differently. Basically, this is an open-faced sandwich that can be stacked with virtually anything, including ham with a peach slice resting on top or perhaps a mound of dill-flavored shrimp.

VERY EXPENSIVE

Restaurant Julius Fritzner ✾✾✾ NORWEGIAN/CONTINENTAL   This is one of the best and most impressive restaurants in Oslo. It opened in 1995 to rave reviews, and the accolades keep coming. It's one floor above street level in Norway's most prestigious hotel. The venue is appropriately conservative, with a battalion of impeccably trained waiters who maintain their humor and personal touch despite the sophisticated setting. The dishes, all made with the finest Scandinavian ingredients, change with the season and the chef's inspiration. Examples include pan-fried turbot, lobster and caviar sauce, crispy fried cod with sautéed vegetables, poached halibut with vermouth sauce, filet of veal with crispy fried sweetbreads, and roast saddle of lamb with rosemary. The restaurant, incidentally, is named after the controversial entrepreneur who established the Grand Hotel in 1874.

In the Grand Hotel, Karl Johans Gate 31. ℃ **23-21-20-00.** Reservations recommended. Main courses 220NOK–300NOK ($29–$40); 3-course fixed-price menu 470NOK ($63); 4-course fixed-price menu 550NOK ($73); 6-course fixed-price menu 640NOK ($85). AE, DC, MC, V. Mon–Sat 5–10:30pm. Closed July to Aug 5. T-banen: Stortinget.

EXPENSIVE

Babette's Gjestehus ⌨ SCANDINAVIAN   Named for the heroine of the film *Babette's Feast*—which almost every Scandinavian has seen at least once—this restaurant is decorated in the style of a turn-of-the-20th-century Norwegian home. Walls are blue, antiques are genuine, curtains are lace, and there's a scattering of old paintings. Menu items are authentic as well, with such time-tested favorites as filet of reindeer with lingonberries, breast of pheasant with mushroom sauce, and pan-fried breast of duck with creamed cabbage. The masterful chefs use seasonal products to produce reliable, good-tasting food all year.

Rådhuspassasjen, Roald Amundsensgate 6. ℃ **22-41-64-64.** Reservations recommended. Main courses 249NOK–265NOK ($33–$35). AE, DC, MC, V. Mon–Sat 5–11pm. T-banen: Centrum.

MODERATE

A Touch of France ⌨ FRENCH   This aptly named place is one of Oslo's best French bistros. In summer tables spill out onto the sidewalk. The decor is that of a typical French brasserie, the kind you find alongside the road in Alsace. A Touch of France is known for serving the freshest oysters in town. On our most recent visit, we opted for the traditional salt-baked leg of duck that was served in a beautifully made garlic sauce. On other occasions we've enjoyed classic calves' liver with mushrooms, spinach, and bacon. Bouillabaisse is a specialty but that grand dish loses something in translation this far north. The dessert trolley is loaded with such temptations as crème brûlée or a chocolate and almond cake.

Øvre Slottsgate 16. ℃ **23-10-01-60.** Reservations recommended. Main courses 185NOK–285NOK ($25–$38). AE, DC, MC, V. Mon–Sat noon–11:30pm. Bus: 27, 29, 30, 41, or 61.

Grand Café ⌨⌨ NORWEGIAN   This traditional cafe is an Oslo legend. A large mural on one wall depicts Ibsen (a fan of whale steaks), Edvard Munch, and many other patrons. A postcard sold at the reception desk identifies the mural's subjects. You can order everything from a napoleon with coffee to a full meal with reindeer steaks. Sandwiches are available for 80NOK ($11) and up. The atmosphere and tradition here are sometimes more compelling than the cuisine. The menu, nonetheless, relies on Norwegian country traditions. (How many places still serve elk stew?) If you like solid, honest flavors, this is the place to visit.

In the Grand Hotel, Karl Johans Gate 31. ℃ **24-14-53-00.** Reservations recommended. Main courses 145NOK–280NOK ($19–$37). AE, DC, MC, V. Mon–Sat 11am–11pm; Sun noon–11pm. T-banen: Stortinget.

Lipp INTERNATIONAL   Stylish and lighthearted, this restored brasserie is the Oslovian version of Paris in the 1920s. Painted a canary yellow, it employs a traditionally dressed, bistro-style, black-vested staff. On our last visit the dish of the day was roasted grouse served with a wild mushroom pie with crisp bacon. The menu changes about every 5 weeks and is seasonally adjusted, using the finest of produce from the field, not to mention river and lake. You might face a savory salmon in a white-wine sauce or reindeer in a mushroom sauce. Lighter fare is offered as well—perhaps an array of freshly made salads or grilled fish dishes.

In the Hotel Continental, Stortingsgaten 24. © **22-82-40-60.** Reservations recommended. Main courses 172NOK–255NOK ($23–$34). AE, DC, MC, V. Daily 4–11:30pm. T-banen: Nationaltheatret.

INEXPENSIVE

Engebret Café NORWEGIAN   A favorite since 1857, this restaurant is directly north of Akershus Castle in two landmark buildings. It has an old-fashioned atmosphere—it was formerly a bohemian literati haunt—and good food. During lunch, a tempting selection of open-faced sandwiches is available. The evening menu is more elaborate; you might begin with a terrine of game with blackberry port-wine sauce, or Engebret's fish soup. Main dishes include red wild boar with whortleberry sauce, Norwegian reindeer, salmon Christiania, or Engebret's big fish pot. For dessert, try the cloudberry parfait.

Bankplassen 1. © **22-33-66-94.** Reservations recommended. Main courses 265NOK–590NOK ($35–$78). AE, DC, MC, V. Mon–Sat 11am–11pm. Bus: 27, 29, or 30.

Mamma Rosa *Kids* ITALIAN   Established by two Tuscan brothers, this trattoria enjoys a popularity that's a good indication of Norwegians' changing tastes. The second-floor dining room is decorated in "reproduction rococo." You can order 15 kinds of pizza, fried scampi and squid, rigatoni, pasta Mamma Rosa (three kinds of pasta with three sauces), grilled steaks, and gelato. Frankly, some of the dishes have lost a bit of flavor on the trip this far north, but Mamma Rosa is nonetheless a marvelous change of taste and texture.

Øvre Slottsgate 12. © **22-42-01-30.** Main courses 91NOK–210NOK ($12–$28); pizzas from 97NOK ($13). DC, MC, V. Mon–Sat noon–11:30pm; Sun 3–10:30pm. T-banen: Stortinget.

SEEING THE SIGHTS
IN THE BYGDØY PENINSULA

Vikingskiphuset (Viking Ship Museum) 🔆🔆🔆   Displayed here are three Viking burial vessels that were excavated on the shores of the Oslofjord and preserved in clay. The most spectacular find is the 9th-century *Oseberg* 🔆, discovered near Norway's oldest town. This 20m (64-ft.) dragon ship features a wealth of ornaments and is the burial chamber of a Viking queen and her slave. The *Gokstad* find is an outstanding example of Viking vessels because it's so well preserved. The smaller *Tune* ship was never restored. Look for the *Oseberg* animal-head post, the elegantly carved sleigh used by Viking royalty, and the *Oseberg* four-wheeled cart.

Huk Aveny 35, Bygdøy. © **22-43-83-79.** Admission 40NOK ($5.30) adults, 20NOK ($2.65) children. Apr daily 11am–4pm; May–Aug daily 9am–6pm; Sept daily 11am–5pm; Oct daily 11am–6pm; Nov–Mar daily 11am–3pm. Ferry: From Pier 3 facing the Rådhuset (summer only). Bus: 30 from the National Theater.

Polar Ship Fram (Frammuseet)   A long walk from the Viking ships, the Frammuseet contains the sturdy polar exploration ship *Fram,* which Fridtjof

Nansen sailed across the Arctic (1893–96). The vessel was later used by Norwegian explorer Roald Amundsen, the first man to reach the South Pole (1911).

Bygdøynesveien. © 23-28-29-50. Admission 30NOK ($4) adults, 15NOK ($2) children. Mar–Apr Mon–Sun 11am–3:45pm; May 1–15 and Sept daily 10am–4:45pm; May 16 to Aug daily 9am–5:45pm; Oct–Nov Mon–Fri 11am–2:45pm, Sat–Sun 11am–3:45pm; Dec–Feb Sat–Sun 11am–3:45pm. Ferry: From Pier 3 facing the Rådhuset (summer only). Bus: 30 from the National Theater.

Kon-Tiki Museum   *Kon-Tiki* is the world-famed balsa-log raft in which the young Norwegian scientist Thor Heyerdahl and his five comrades sailed for 7,000km (4,300 miles) in 1947—all the way from Callao, Peru, to Raroia, Polynesia. Besides the raft, there are exhibits from Heyerdahl's subsequent visit to Easter Island, including an Easter Island family cave, with a collection of sacred lava figurines.

Bygdøynesveien 36. © 23-08-67-67. Admission 35NOK ($4.65) adults, 20NOK ($2.65) children, 90NOK ($12) family. Apr–May and Sept daily 10:30am–5pm; June–Aug daily 9:30am–5:45pm; Oct–Mar daily 10:30am–4pm. Ferry: From Pier 3 facing the Rådhuset (summer only). Bus: 30 from the National Theater.

Norsk Sjøfartsmuseum (Norwegian Maritime Museum)   This museum, which contains a complete ship's deck with helm and chart house, and a three-deck-high section of the passenger steamer *Sandnaes,* chronicles the maritime history and culture of Norway. The Boat Hall features a fine collection of original small craft. The fully restored polar vessel *Gjoa,* used by Roald Amundsen in his search for America's Northwest Passage, is also on display. The three-masted 1916 schooner *Svanen (Swan)* now belongs to the museum and is used as a training vessel.

Bygdøynesveien 37. © 22-43-82-40. Admission to museum and boat hall 40NOK ($5.30) adults, 20NOK ($2.65) children. May–Sept daily 10am–6pm; Oct–Apr Mon and Fri–Sat 10:30am–4pm, Tues–Thurs 10:30am–6pm. Ferry: From Pier 3 facing the Rådhuset (summer only). Bus: 30 from the National Theater.

Norwegian Folk Museum ⭐⭐   From all over Norway, 140 original buildings have been transported and reassembled on 14 hectares (35 acres) on the Bygdøy Peninsula. This open-air folk museum includes a number of medieval buildings, such as the Raulandstua, one of the oldest wooden dwellings still standing in Norway, and a stave church from about 1200. The rural buildings are grouped together by region of origin, while the urban houses have been laid out in the form of an old town.

Museumsveien 10. © 22-12-37-00. Admission 70NOK ($9.30) adults, 20NOK ($2.65) children under 17. Jan 1–May 14 and Sept 15–Dec 31 Fri–Sat 11am–3pm, Sun 11am–4pm; May 15–June 14 and Sept 1–Sept 14 daily 10am–5pm; June 15–Aug 31 daily 10am–6pm. Ferry: From Pier 3 facing the Rådhuset (summer only). Bus: 30 from the National Theater.

IN WESTERN OLSO

Vigelandsparken ⭐⭐   The lifetime work of Gustav Vigeland, Norway's greatest sculptor, is displayed inside the museum as well as throughout the nearby 30-hectare (75-acre) Frogner Park in western Oslo. Nearly 211 sculptures in granite, bronze, and iron can be admired. See in particular his four granite columns, symbolizing the fight between humanity and evil (a dragon, the embodiment of evil, embraces a woman). *The Angry Boy* is the most photographed statue in the park, but the really celebrated work is the 16m (52-ft.) monolith, composed of 121 figures of colossal size—all carved into one piece of stone.

Frogner Park, Nobelsgate 32. © 22-54-25-30. Free admission to park. Museum, 40NOK ($5.30) adults, 30NOK ($4) children. Park, daily 24 hr. Museum, May–Sept Tues–Sat 10am–6pm, Sun noon–7pm; Oct–Apr Tues–Sat noon–4pm, Sun noon–4pm. Tram: 12 or 15. Bus: 20, 45, or 81.

IN EASTERN OSLO

Edvard Munch Museum   Devoted exclusively to the works of Edvard Munch (1863–1944), Scandinavia's leading painter, this exhibit (Munch's gift to the city), traces his work from early realism to his latter-day expressionism. The collection comprises 1,100 paintings, some 4,500 drawings, around 18,000 prints, numerous graphic plates, six sculptures, and important documentary material.

Tøyengate 53. ℂ 23-24-14-00. Admission 60NOK ($8) adults, 30NOK ($4) children. June to mid-Sept daily 10am–6pm; mid-Sept to May Tues–Wed and Fri–Sat 10am–4pm, Thurs and Sun 10am–6pm. T-banen: Tøyen. Bus: 20.

IN THE CITY CENTER

Akershus Castle   One of the oldest historical monuments in Oslo, Akershus Castle was built in 1300 by King Haakon V Magnusson. It was a fortress and a royal residence for several centuries. A fire in 1527 devastated the northern wing, and the castle was rebuilt and transformed into a Renaissance palace under the Danish-Norwegian king Christian IV. Now it's used for state occasions. A few rooms, including the chapel, are open to the public. In the rectangular court, markings show where the massive medieval keep used to stand. You can wander through two large halls (Olav's and Christian IV's), which occupy the top floor of the north and south wings, respectively. For many, the most interesting part is the dungeon, which includes an "escape-proof room" built for a prisoner, Ole Pedersewn Hoyland. After he was placed in the chamber and realized there was no way he could ever escape, he killed himself.

Festnings-Plassen. ℂ 22-41-25-21. Admission 30NOK ($4) adults, 10NOK ($1.35) children, 70NOK ($9.30) family. April 15–Sept 15 Mon–Sat 10am–4pm, Sun 12:30–4pm. Closed Sept 16–Apr 14. Tram: 10 or 12. Bus: 60.

ATTRACTIONS NEARBY

Tryvannstårnet (Lookout Tower)   This is the loftiest lookout tower in Scandinavia—the gallery is approximately 580m (1,900 ft.) above sea level and offers a view of the Oslofjord with Sweden to the east. A walk down the hill takes you to the famous restaurant Frognerseteren. You can take another 20-minute walk down the hill to the Holmenkollen ski jump, the site of the 1952 Olympic competitions, as well as the Holmenkollen Ski Festival, when skiers compete in downhill, slalom, giant slalom, cross-country ski races, and jumping.

Voksenkollen. ℂ 22-14-67-11. Admission 40NOK ($5.30) adults, 20NOK ($2.65) children. May and Sept daily 10am–5pm; June daily 10am–7pm; July–Aug daily 9am–8pm; Oct–Apr Mon–Sun 10am–4pm. T-banen: Frognerseteren SST Line 1 from near the National Theater to Voksenkollen (30-min. ride), then an uphill 15-min. walk.

Henie-Onstad Kunstsenter (Henie-Onstad Art Center) 🌟🌟   On a site beside the Oslofjord 11km (7 miles) west of Oslo, ex-movie star and skating champion Sonja Henie and her husband, Niels Onstad, a shipping tycoon, opened a museum to display their art collection. This especially good 20th-century collection includes some 1,800 works by Munch, Picasso, Matisse, Léger, Bonnard, and Miró. Henie's Trophy Room is impressive, with 600 trophies and medals, including three Olympic gold medals—she was the star at the 1936 competition—and 10 world skating championships.

Høkvikodden, Baerum. ℂ 67-80-48-80. Admission 75NOK ($10) adults, 45NOK ($6) ages 15–25, free for children 14 and under. June–Aug Mon 11am–6pm, Tues–Fri 10am–9pm, Sat–Sun 11am–6pm; Sept–May Tues 10am–9pm, Sat–Mon 11am–5pm. Bus: 151, 152, 251, or 261.

ORGANIZED TOURS

H. M. Kristiansens Automobilbyrå, Hegdehaugsveien 4 (© **22-20-82-06**), has been showing visitors around Oslo for more than a century. Both of their bus tours are offered daily year-round. The 3-hour "Oslo Highlights" tour is offered at 10am and 1:30pm. It costs 250NOK ($33) for adults, 130NOK ($17) for children. The 2-hour "Oslo Panorama" tour costs 170NOK ($23) for adults, 90NOK ($12) for children. It departs at 10am and 5:30pm. The starting point is the Norway information center, Vestbaneplassen 1; arrive 15 minutes before departure. Tours are conducted in English by trained guides.

THE SHOPPING SCENE

Near the marketplace and the Oslo Domkirche (cathedral), **Den Norske Husfliden,** Møllergata 4 (© **22-42-10-75;** T-banen: Stortinget; bus: 17)—or Husfliden, as it's called—is the display and retail center for the Norwegian Association of Home Arts and Crafts, founded in 1891. Today it's almost eight times larger than any of its competitors, with two floors displaying the very finest of Norwegian design in ceramics, glassware, furniture, and woodworking. You can also purchase souvenirs, gifts, textiles, rugs, knotted Rya rugs, embroidery, wrought iron, and fabrics by the yard. Goods are shipped all over the world.

Norway's largest department store, **Steen & Strøm,** Kongensgate 23 (© **22-00-40-00;** T-banen: Stortinget), is a treasure house with hundreds of Nordic items spread through 58 individual departments. Look for hand-knit sweaters and caps, hand-painted wooden dishes reflecting traditional Norwegian art, and pewter dinner plates made from old molds. **Heimen Husflid,** Rosenkrantzgate 8 (© **22-41-40-50;** T-banen: Nationaltheatret), about a block from Karl Johans Gate, carries folk costumes, antiques, and reproductions. Hand-knit sweaters in traditional Norwegian patterns are a special item, as are pewter and brass items.

William Schmidt, Karl Johans Gate 41 (© **22-42-02-88;** T-banen: Stortinget), established in 1853, is a leading purveyor of unique souvenirs, including pewter items (everything from Viking ships to beer goblets), Norwegian dolls in national costumes, woodcarvings (the troll collection is the most outstanding in Oslo), and sealskin moccasins. The shop specializes in hand-knit cardigans, pullovers, gloves, and caps; sweaters are made from mothproofed 100% Norwegian wool.

OSLO AFTER DARK

To find out what's happening when you're visiting, pick up *What's On in Oslo,* which details concerts and theaters and other useful information.

Theater, ballet, and opera tickets are sold at various box offices and also at **Billettsentralen,** Karl Johans Gate 35 (© **81-53-31-33;** T-banen: Stortinget)— although this service costs quite a bit more than your typical box office. Tickets to sports and cultural events can now be purchased easily and more cheaply via computer linkup at any post office in the city, so when you buy a stamp you can also buy a voucher for a ticket to the ballet, theater, or hockey game.

THE PERFORMING ARTS

Home to the National Theater Company, the **National Theater,** Johanne Dybwads Plass 1 (© **81-50-08-11;** T-banen: Nationaltheatret), opens in August, so it may be of interest to off-season drama lovers who want to hear Ibsen and Bjørnson in the original. Avant-garde productions go on up at the **Amfiscenen,** in the same building. There are no performances in July and August. Guest companies often perform plays in English. Tickets range from 150NOK to 220NOK ($20–$29) adults, 85NOK to 170NOK ($11–$23) students and seniors.

Two blocks from the National Theater, **Oslo Konserthus,** Munkedamsveien 14 (© **23-11-31-11;** T-banen: Stortinget), is the home of the widely acclaimed Oslo Philharmonic. Performances are given from autumn to spring, on Thursday and Friday. Guest companies from around the world often appear on other nights. The hall is closed from June 20 until mid-August, except for occasional performances by folkloric groups. Tickets run from 200NOK to 700NOK ($27–$93).

Originally a movie theater, the 1931 building at Storgaten 23 was adapted for better acoustics and dedicated in 1959 to the **Den Norske Opera** (© **23-31-50-00;** T-banen: Jernbanetorget). It's also the leading venue for ballet—the companies alternate performances About 20 different operas and operettas are staged every year. There are no performances from mid-June to August. Tickets are generally available to nonsubscribers; seats can be reserved in advance and paid for with a credit card. Tickets range from 170NOK to 320NOK ($23–$43) except for galas.

Norwegian Folk Museum, on Bygdøy (ferry: Pier 3 near the Rådhuset), often presents folk-dance performances by its own ensemble on summer Sunday afternoons at the museum's open-air theater. Admission to the museum includes admission to the dance performance.

THE CLUB & MUSIC SCENE
Smuget, Rosenkrantzgate 22 (© **22-42-52-62;** T-banen: Nationaltheatret), is the most talked-about nightlife joint in the city, and has the long lines (especially on weekends) to prove it. It's in a 19th-century building in back of the City Hall and has a restaurant, an active dance floor, and a stage where live bands perform. It's open Monday through Saturday from 8pm to 3am; the cover ranges from 60NOK to 70NOK ($8–$9.30).

Buddha Bar, Klingenberggata 4 (© **22-82-86-50**), is the bar and nightclub in Oslo that everyone clamors to get into. Long lines form outside this place, composed of hipsters whose occasional aggression seems to fade once they reach the incense-scented interior of a suite of rooms dotted with iconic statues of Lord Buddha. Bruce Springsteen was spotted here, along with various members of the Rolling Stones. There's a dining area (Restaurant Fogo) shoved off into a side room, where set menus cost from 400NOK to 650NOK ($53–$86). But most people come here just to drink, meet other like-minded extroverts, and perhaps dance. The minimum age for entrance, unless you're very, very cool and irresistibly attractive, is 28. There might be a cover charge of 70NOK ($9.30),

---

Tips Native Behavior

Although Norwegians love their beer, note that buying a round is virtually unheard of in a Norwegian pub. In this independent country, both men and women pay for their own libations. During the week, never ask someone you meet "out for a drink." He or she will think you're a drunk. On Friday or Saturday night, it's different. Anything goes. Beer taverns are wild and riotous, and few patrons are satisfied with a mere 10 beers.

but often it's waived, depending on business and the mood of the security staff. The bar is open Tuesday through Sunday from 7pm till 3am.

DAY TRIPS FROM OSLO

The best 1-day excursion from Oslo includes visits to Fredrikstad and Tønsberg, which gives you a chance to explore the scenic highlights of the Oslofjord. A trip to Fredrikstad, in Østfold on the east bank of the Oslofjord, can easily be combined in 1 day with a visit to the port of Tønsberg on the west bank, by crossing over on the ferry from Moss to Horten, then heading south.

Getting There To reach the first stop, Fredrikstad, take E-6 south from Oslo toward Moss. Continue past Moss until you reach the junction of Route 110, which is signposted south of Fredrikstad. About six buses per day depart for the town from the Central Station in Oslo. Trains from Oslo's Central Station depart from Fredrikstad about every 2 hours during the day (trip time: 30 min.).

FREDRIKSTAD 𝕱 In recent years Fredrikstad, 95km (60 miles) south of Oslo, has become a major tourist center, thanks to its Old Town and 17th-century fortress. Across the river on the west is a modern industrial section, and although a bridge links the two sections, the best way to reach Old Town is by ferry, which costs 6NOK (80¢). The departure point is about 4 blocks from the Fredrikstad railroad station—simply follow the crowd out the main door of the station, make an obvious left turn, and continue down to the shore of the river. It's also possible to travel between the two areas by bus nos. 360 or 362, although most pedestrians opt for the ferry.

SEEING THE SIGHTS

Visitor Information **Fredrikstad Turistkontor** is on Turistsenteret, Østre Brohode in Gamle Fredrikstad (℃ **69-30-46-00**). From June to September, it's open Monday through Friday from 9am to 6pm and Saturday from 10am to 4pm; from October to May, it's open Monday through Friday from 9am to 4pm.

Fredrikstad was founded in 1567 as a marketplace at the mouth of the River Glomma. **Gamlebyen (Old Town)** became a fortress in 1663 and continued in that role until 1903, boasting some 200 guns in its heyday. It still serves as a military camp. The main guardroom and old convict prison are now the **Fredrikstad Museum,** Gamleslaveri (℃ **69-30-68-75**), open from May to September, Tuesday through Friday from noon to 5pm, Saturday from 11am to 5pm, and Sunday from noon to 5pm. Admission is 30NOK ($4) adults and 10NOK ($1.35) children.

Outside the gates of Old Town is **Kongsten Fort,** on what was first called Gallows Hill, an execution site. When Fredrikstad Fortress was built, it was provisionally fortified in 1677, becoming known as Svenskeskremme (Swede Scarer). Present-day Kongsten Fort with its 20 cannons, underground chambers, passages, and countermines, eventually replaced it.

Since Fredrikstad's heyday as a trading port and merchant base, Old Town has attracted craftspeople and artisans, many of whom create their products in the Old Town's historic houses and barns. Many of these glass blowers, ceramic artists, and silversmiths choose not to display or sell their products at their studios, preferring instead to leave the sales aspect to local shops.

En Route to Tønsberg You can drive back north from Fredrikstad to the town of Moss, where you can take a ferry to Horten. Once at Horten, signs will point the way south for the short drive to Tønsberg. Tønsberg is about 1½ hours from Oslo, with some 20 trains arriving daily.

TØNSBERG 🍂 Bordering the western bank of the Oslofjord, Tønsberg, 100km (64 miles) south of Oslo, is Norway's oldest town. It's divided into a historic area, filled with old clapboard-sided houses, and the commercial center, where the marketplace is located.

SEEING THE SIGHTS

Visitor Information   Tourist Information is at Nedre Langgate 36B, N-3100 Tønsberg (℡ 33-35-02-00). It's open in July daily from 10am to 5:30pm; from August to June, Monday through Friday from 8:30am to 4pm.

Tønsberg was founded a year before King Harald Fairhair united parts of the country in 872, and this Viking town became a royal coronation site. Svend Foyn, who invented modern whaling and seal hunting, was born here.

Slottsfjellet, a huge hill fortress directly ahead of the train station, is touted as "the Acropolis of Norway." But it has only some meager ruins, and people mostly come here for the view from the lookout tower. Built in 1888, the **Slottsfjelltårnet** (℡ 33-31-18-72) is open from May 18 to June 23, Monday through Friday from 10am to 3pm; from June 24 to August 18, daily from 11am to 6pm; from August 19 to September 15, Saturday and Sunday from noon to 5pm; and from September 16 to 29, Saturday and Sunday from noon to 3pm. Admission is 20NOK ($2.65) adults and 10NOK ($1.35) children.

Nordbyen is the old and scenic part of town, with well-preserved houses. **Haugar** cemetery, at Møllebakken, is right in the town center, with the Viking graves of King Harald's sons, Olav and Sigrød.

Sem Church, Hageveien 32 (℡ 33-36-93-99), the oldest in Vestfold, was built of stone in the Romanesque style around 1100. It's open Tuesday through Friday from 9am to 2pm; ask at the vestry. Admission is free.

You should also see **Fjerdingen,** a street of charming restored houses. Tønsberg was also a Hanseatic town during the Middle Ages, and some houses have been redone in typical Hanseatic style.

In the **Vestfold Folk Museum** 🍂, Frammannsveien 30 (℡ 33-31-29-19), there are many Viking and whaling treasures. One of the biggest thrills is the skeleton of a blue whale. A real Viking ship is displayed, the *Klastad* from Tjolling, built about A.D. 800. Admission is 30NOK ($4) adults, 20NOK ($2.65) children. It's open from mid-May to mid-September, Monday through Saturday from 10am to 5pm, Sunday and holidays from noon to 5pm; closed mid-September through mid-May.

2 Bergen & the Fjords

In western Norway the landscape takes on an awesome beauty, with iridescent glaciers; deep fjords that slash into rugged, snowcapped mountains; roaring waterfalls; and secluded valleys that lie at the end of corkscrew-twisting roads. From Bergen the most beautiful fjords to visit are the **Hardanger** (best at blossom time, May and early June), to the south; the **Sogne,** Norway's longest fjord, immediately to the north; and the **Nordfjord,** north of that. A popular excursion on the Nordfjord takes visitors from Loen to Olden along rivers and lakes to the Brixdal Glacier.

If you have time, on the Hardangerfjord you can stop over at one of the fjord resorts, such as Ulvik or Lofthus. The Folgefonn Glacier, Norway's second-largest ice field, which spans more than 250 sq. km (100 sq. miles), can be seen from many vantage points.

Bergen, with its many sightseeing attractions; good hotels and restaurants; and excellent boat, rail, and coach connections, is the best center for touring the fjord district. This ancient city looms large in Viking sagas. Until the 14th century, it was the seat of the medieval kingdom of Norway. The Hanseatic merchants established a major trading post here, holding sway until the 18th century.

BERGEN: GATEWAY TO THE FJORDS
ESSENTIALS
GETTING THERE   By Plane   The **Bergen Airport** at Flesland, 19km (12 miles) south of the city, offers frequent flights to Copenhagen and London, through which most international flights are routed.

There is frequent airport bus service from the airport to the SAS Royal Hotel, Braathens airlines' office at the Hotel Norge, and the city bus station. Buses depart every 20 minutes from Monday to Friday and every 30 minutes Saturday and Sunday. The one-way fare is 60NOK ($8). Taxis are readily available at the airport, or call © **55-99-70-00.** A ride to the city center costs 262NOK ($35).

By Train   Day and night trains arrive from Oslo (trip time: 6–8½ hr.). For information, call the Bergen train station at © **55-96-69-00.**

By Bus   Express buses travel to Bergen from Oslo in 11 hours. For long-distance bus information, call © **55-55-90-70.**

By Car   A toll is charged on all vehicles driven into the city center Monday through Friday from 6am to 10pm. A single ticket costs 10NOK ($1.35); a book of 20 tickets, 90NOK ($12).

The trip from Oslo to Bergen is a mountainous drive filled with dramatic scenery. Because mountains split the country, there's no direct road. The southern route, E76, takes you through mountain passes until the junction with Route 47; then you head north to Kinsarvik and make the ferry crossing to E16 leading to Bergen. It's quickest to take the northern route following E16 west. For the first time it's possible to make a ferry-free road connection to Bergen. In 2001 the world's longest tunnel opened, going as deep as 1,470m (4,900 ft.) beneath one of Norway's most scenic mountain areas beginning 300km (185 miles) northwest of Oslo. The 40km (25-mile) Laerdal Tunnel surpasses the 17km (11-mile) St. Gothard Tunnel in the Swiss Alps. It takes 20 minutes to go through the tunnel.

To reduce driving time, motorists can use a tunnel—almost 11km (7 miles), the longest in northern Europe—that goes between Flåm and Gudvangen. From Gudvangen, follow E16 southwest to Bergen.

VISITOR INFORMATION   Tourist Information, Bryggen 7 (© **55-32-14-80;** www.visitbergen.com), provides information, maps, and brochures about Bergen and the rest of the region. It's open from June to August daily from 8:30am to 10pm; May and September daily from 9am to 8pm; from October to April Monday through Saturday from 9am to 4pm.

SPECIAL EVENTS   The annual **Bergen Festival,** generally held the last 2 weeks in May (the 2003 festival was held May 21–June 1), features performances by regional, national, and international orchestras, dance ensembles, and theater groups. The complete festival schedule is usually available by February of each year. For festival and ticket information, contact the **Bergen Festival Office** (© **55-21-06-30;** www.festspillene.no).

GETTING AROUND **By Bus** The **Bystasjonen (Central Bus Station),** Strømgaten 8 (© **55-55-90-70**), is the terminal for all buses serving the Bergen and the Hardanger area, as well as the airport bus. Gaia Traffic runs a network of yellow-sided **city buses** (© **55-55-44-00**) that serve the city center.

By Taxi Sightseeing by taxi costs about 390NOK ($52) per hour.

WHERE TO STAY
Expensive

Clarion Admiral Hotel ⟨ƙ⟩ When it was built in 1906, this building was one of the largest warehouses in Bergen, with six sprawling floors peppered with massive trusses and beams. In 1987, it became a comfortable, tastefully appointed hotel, and in 1998, it was enlarged and renovated into the bustling establishment you'll see today. Rooms are a bit smaller than you might hope (with small bathrooms equipped with shower-tub combinations), but they are comfortable and have excellent beds. Many rooms lack water views, but the ones that open onto flower-bedecked balconies have the best harbor views in town.

Christian Sundts Gate 9, N-5004 Bergen. © **55-23-64-00.** Fax 55-23-64-64. www.admiral.no. 211 units. Mon–Thurs 1,695NOK ($225) double; 1,895NOK–4,000NOK ($252–$532) suite. Fri–Sun 950NOK ($126) double; 1,150NOK–2,550NOK ($153–$339) suite. AE, DC, MC, V. Bus: 2, 4, or 11. **Amenities:** 2 restaurants; bar; room service; laundry/dry cleaning. *In room:* TV, minibar, hair dryer, safe.

First Hotel Marin ⟨ƙ⟩⟨ƙ⟩ In the heart of Bergen, this first-class hotel is one of Bergen's most modern and streamlined. The brown brick building is set on a steep hillside. The bedrooms are moderate to spacious in size, and each is handsomely furnished in functional, stylish Nordic modern, with immaculately kept tiled bathrooms equipped with shower-tub combinations. For Bergen, the hotel offers a large number of suites—34 deluxe ones in all—the best of which are a

---

Value The Bergen Card

The **Bergen Card** entitles you to free bus transportation and (usually) free museum entrance throughout Bergen, plus discounts on car rentals, parking, and some cultural activities. Ask for it at the tourist office (see "Visitor Information," above). A 24-hour card costs 165NOK ($22) for adults, 80NOK ($11) for children 3 to 15. A 48-hour card is 245NOK ($33) for adults, 120NOK ($16) for children 3 to 15. Children under 3 generally travel or enter free.

---

trio of penthouse units with views so panoramic they encompass all seven mountains surrounding Bergen. Many accommodations are reserved for nonsmokers, and the finest units are in front, overlooking the harbor.

Rosenkrantzgaten 8, N-5003 Bergen. ℂ **53-05-15-00**. Fax 53-05-15-01. www.firsthotels.com. 131 units. 1,450NOK–1,670NOK ($193–$222) double; 2,210NOK ($294) suite. AE, DC, MC, V. Bus: 1, 5, or 9. **Amenities:** Restaurant; bar; fitness center; sauna; room service; laundry/dry cleaning. *In room:* TV, minibar, hair dryer, safe.

Moderate

Augustin Hotel *⋆* *Finds* The Augustin has one of the best locations in Bergen—right in the harbor's shopping district—with front rooms that have terrific harbor views. Constructed in 1909 in the Jugend or Art Nouveau style, Augustin has been in the same family for four generations. In 1995 it more than doubled in size by adding a new wing, with modern new rooms designed by award-winning Bergen architect Aud Hunskår. Bathrooms in both sections have both showers and tubs. The hotel is decorated with lots of art, many pieces from well-known contemporary Norwegian artists. Special accommodations are available for nonsmokers, wheelchair users, and allergy sufferers.

Carl Sundts Gate 24, N-5004 Bergen. ℂ **55-30-40-40**. Fax 55-30-40-10. www.augustin.no. 109 units. Mon–Thurs 1,550NOK ($206) double; 1,890NOK ($251) suite. Fri–Sun 800NOK ($106) double; 1,290NOK ($172) suite. AE, DC, MC, V. Bus: 2 or 4. **Amenities:** Restaurant; bar; babysitting; laundry/dry cleaning. *In room:* A/C, TV, minibar, hair dryer.

Victoria Hotel *⋆* *Value* Set behind a graceful, bay-fronted facade, this hotel—one of the oldest in town—today operates as one of only two members of the Best Western chain in Bergen. Smaller and more personalized than many equivalently priced hotels in Bergen, and noted for relatively reasonable rates, it's cozy, staffed with concerned employees, and loaded with worthwhile, sometimes rather valuable, art—a result of almost 50 years of collecting on the part of the well-traveled owners. Guest rooms are clean and bright, outfitted with contemporary birch-veneer furniture and lots of contemporary art. Bathrooms are tiled and modern, each with shower but without bathtub.

Kong Oscarsgt 29, N-5017 Bergen. ℂ **800/528-1234** or 55-21-23-00. Fax 55-21-23-50. www.victoriahotel. no. 43 units. Mid-May to mid-Sept 1,490NOK ($198) double. Mid-Sept to mid-May Mon–Thurs 1,030NOK ($137) double, Fri–Sun 1,490NOK ($198) double. Rates include breakfast. AE, DC, MC, V. Parking 130NOK ($17). Bus: 2 or 4. **Amenities:** Restaurant (under separate ownership); bar; babysitting; laundry/dry cleaning. *In room:* A/C, TV, minibar, hair dryer.

Inexpensive

Hotel Park *⋆* This converted 1890 town house is in an attractive university area near Grieghall and Nygård Park. The rooms are traditionally furnished, often with antiques. Accommodations vary in size but all have good beds and adequate bathrooms equipped with shower-tub combinations. In the summer, a neighboring building (furnished in the same style) accommodates overflow guests. A delicious Norwegian breakfast is served in the dining room; later in the day, sandwiches, small hot dishes, and wine and beer are available there. In the summer, reserve well in advance. The Park is a 10-minute walk from the train and bus stations.

Harald Hårfagresgaten 35 and Allegaten 20, N-5007 Bergen. © **55-54-44-00.** Fax 55-54-44-44. www.park hotel.no. 33 units. 980NOK ($130) double. Rates include breakfast. AE, DC, MC, V. Parking 50NOK ($6.65). Bus: 11. **Amenities:** Lounge. In room: TV, hair dryer.

Steens Hotel (Value) Owned and operated by the same family since 1950, this stylish 1890 town house offers great accommodations at most-reasonable prices. The modern guest rooms are moderate in size and comfortable, and the bathrooms, though small, are beautifully maintained. The public rooms have plenty of atmosphere. The best rooms are in front and open onto a park. Within a short walk are the bus and railway stations and attractions in the center of town. All doubles have a private bathroom with a shower unit; a few singles are rented without bathroom for 620NOK ($82) per night. Coffee and light meals are served.

22 Parkveien, N-5007 Bergen. ©/fax **55-31-40-50.** 20 units, 16 with bathroom. 600NOK–920NOK ($80–$122) double. Extra bed 150NOK ($20). Rates include Norwegian breakfast. AE, MC, V. Bus: 1 or 5. Amenities: Lounge. In room: TV.

WHERE TO DINE
Expensive
Finnegaardstuene (Finds) NORWEGIAN/FRENCH The chefs of this popular restaurant have created magic in sleepy Bergen. The foundations of this building were laid around 1400, and today some of the woodwork dates from the 1700s. The four small-scale dining rooms create a cozy atmosphere. The menu is well thought out, with carefully prepared dishes. It revolves around Norwegian ingredients, especially fresh fish, and classical French methods of preparation. The menu might include lime-marinated turbot with caviar sauce; gratin of monkfish with sea scallops; filets of venison with juniper berry sauce; or breast of duck with lime and fig sauce. An appropriate and satisfying dessert is berries from the Norwegian tundra, especially lingonberries and cloudberries.

Rosenkrantzgate 6. © **55-55-03-00.** Reservations recommended. Main courses 285NOK–295NOK ($38–$39); fixed-price menu 635NOK ($84). AE, DC, MC, V. Mon–Sat 4:30–11pm. Closed 1 week at Easter, and Dec 22–Jan 8. Bus: 5 or 21.

To Kokker (¤) FRENCH/NORWEGIAN To Kokker ("Two Cooks") is a favorite with celebrities, including Britain's prince. Savvy local diners gravitate here for the chef's well-considered juxtaposition of flavors and textures. Menu items include such time-tested favorites as lobster soup; whitebait roe with chopped onions, sour cream, and fresh-baked bread; reindeer with lingonberry sauce; and filet of lamb with mustard sauce and pommes Provençal. The 1703 building is adjacent to the oldest piers and wharves in Bergen. The dining room, one floor above street level, has scarlet walls, old paintings, and a solid staff that works competently under pressure, albeit without a lot of flair.

Enhjørninggården. © **55-32-28-16.** Reservations required. Main courses 495NOK–695NOK ($66–$92). AE, DC, MC, V. Mon–Sat 5–10pm. Bus: 1, 5, or 9.

Inexpensive

Bryggeloftet and Stuene ⚓ NORWEGIAN   The Bryggeloftet and Stuene is the best-established restaurant along the harbor. At street level, the Stuene has low-beamed ceilings, carved banquettes, and 19th-century murals of old Bergen, along with dozens of clipper-ship models. For a more formal meal, head upstairs to the Bryggeloftet, with its high ceilings and wood paneling. Dinner in either section might include fried porbeagle (a form of whitefish) served with shrimp, mussels, and white-wine sauce; roast reindeer with cream sauce; or pepper steak with a salad. Several different preparations of salmon and herring are featured, along with roast pork with Norwegian sour cabbage. This is a quintessential Norwegian place—come here if you're seeking authentic flavors.

Bryggen 11. ⓒ **55-31-06-30.** Reservations recommended. Main courses 159NOK–275NOK ($21–$37); lunch smørbrød 85NOK–149NOK ($11–$20). AE, DC, MC, V. Mon–Sat 11am–11:30pm; Sun 1–11:30pm. Bus: 1, 5, or 9.

SEEING THE SIGHTS

In addition to the sights below, take a stroll around **Bryggen (the Quay)** ⚓⚓⚓. This row of Hanseatic timbered houses, rebuilt along the waterfront after the disastrous fire of 1702, is what remains of medieval Bergen. The northern half burned to the ground as recently as 1955. Bryggen is on UNESCO's World Heritage List as one of the world's most significant cultural and historical re-creations of a medieval settlement. It's a center for Arts and Crafts, where painters, weavers, and craftspeople have their workshops.

Det Hanseatiske Museum ⚓   In one of the best-preserved wooden buildings at Bryggen, this museum illustrates Bergen's commercial life on the wharf centuries ago. German merchants, representatives of the Hanseatic League centered in Lübeck, lived in these medieval houses built in long rows up from the harbor. The museum is furnished with authentic articles dating from 1704.

Finnegårdsgaten 1A, Bryggen. ⓒ **55-31-41-89.** May–Sept admission 40NOK ($5.30) adults; Oct–Apr admission 25NOK ($3.35) adults; free for children. June–Aug daily 9am–5pm; Sept–May daily 11am–2pm. Bus: 1, 5, or 9.

Mariakirke (St. Mary's Church) ⚓   The oldest building in Bergen (its exact date is unknown, but perhaps from the mid–12th c.) is this Romanesque church, one of the most beautiful in Norway. Its altar is the oldest ornament in the church, and there's a baroque pulpit, donated by Hanseatic merchants, with carved figures depicting everything from Chastity to Naked Truth. Church-music concerts are given several nights a week from May to August.

Dreggen. ⓒ **55-31-59-60.** Admission 10NOK ($1.35) adults, free for children; free to all Sept 10–May 17. May 18–Sept 9 Mon–Fri 11am–4pm; Sept 10–May 17 Tues–Fri noon–1:30pm. Bus: 5, 9, 20, 21, or 22.

Fløibanen   A short walk from the fish market is the station where the funicular heads up to Fløien, the most famous of Bergen's seven hills. At 320m (1,050 ft.), the view of the city, the neighboring hills, and the harbor is worth every øre.

Vetrlidsalm 23A. ⓒ **55-33-68-00.** Round-trip 60NOK ($8) adults, 25NOK ($3.35) children. May 25 to Aug Mon–Fri 7:30am–midnight, Sat 8am–midnight, Sun 9am–midnight; Sept to May 24 Mon–Thurs 8am–11pm, Fri–Sat 8am–11:30pm, Sun 9am–11pm. Bus: 6.

Gamle Bergen ⚓   At Elsesro and Sandviken is a collection of houses from the 18th and 19th centuries set in a park. Old Town is complete with streets, an open square, and narrow alleyways. Some of the interiors are exceptional, including a merchant's living room in the typical style of the 1870s—padded sofas, heavy curtains, potted plants—a perfect setting for Ibsen's *A Doll's House*.

Elsesro and Sandviken. (C) **55-39-43-00**. Admission 50NOK ($6.65) adults, 25NOK ($3.35) children and students. Houses, mid-May to Aug only, guided tours daily on the hour 10am–5pm. Park and restaurant, daily noon–6pm. Bus: 1 or 9 from the city center (every 10 min.).

Troldhaugen (Troll's Hill) This Victorian house, in beautiful rural surroundings at Hop, near Bergen, was the summer villa of composer Edvard Grieg. The house contains Grieg's own furniture, paintings, and mementos. His Steinway grand piano is frequently used at concerts given in the house during the annual Bergen festival, as well as at Troldhaugen's own summer concerts. Grieg and his wife, Nina, are buried in a cliff grotto on the estate.

Troldhaugveien 65, Hop. (C) **55-91-17-91**. www.troldhaugen.com. Admission 50NOK ($6.65) adults, free for children. Jan to Apr 20 Mon–Fri 10am–2pm; Apr 21 to Sept daily 9am–6pm; Oct–Nov Mon–Fri 10am–2pm, Sat–Sun 10am–4pm. Closed Dec. Bus: To Hop from the Bergen bus station (platforms 18–20), exit, turn right, walk about 180m (600 ft.), turn left at Hopsvegen, and follow signs. Hop is about 5km (3 miles) from Bergen.

ORGANIZED TOURS
For information about and tickets to tours, contact **Tourist Information, Bryggen** 7 ((C) **55-32-14-80**).

The most popular and most highly recommended tour of Bergen is the 3-hour city bus tour. It departs daily at 10am and covers the major attractions, including Troldhaugen and "Old Bergen." It operates from May to September and costs 250NOK ($33) for adults, 160NOK ($21) for children.

THE SHOPPING SCENE
Bargain hunters head to the **Torget (Marketplace).** Many local handicrafts from the western fjord district, including rugs and handmade tablecloths, are displayed. This is one of the few places in Norway where bargaining is welcomed. The market keeps no set hours, but is best visited between 8am and noon. Take bus nos. 1, 5, or 9. You'll find the widest selection of national handicrafts in and around **Bryggen Brukskunst,** the restored Old Town near the wharf, where many craftspeople have taken over old houses and ply ancient Norwegian trades. Crafts boutiques often display Bergen souvenirs, many based on designs 300 to 1,500 years old. For example, we purchased a reproduction of a Romanesque-style cruciform pilgrim's badge. Other attractive items are likely to include sheepskin-lined booties and exquisitely styled handwoven wool dresses. The leading outlet for glassware and ceramics, **Prydkunst-Hjertholm,** Olav Kyrres Gate 7 ((C) **55-31-70-27**), purchases much of its merchandise directly from the studios of Norwegian and other Scandinavian artisans who turn out quality goods not only in glass and ceramics, but also in pewter, brass, wood, and textiles.

BERGEN AFTER DARK
The modern **Grieghallen (Grieg Hall),** Lars Hillesgate 3A ((C) **55-21-61-50**), is Bergen's monumental showcase for music, drama, and a host of other cultural events. The **Bergen Symphony Orchestra,** founded in 1765, performs here from August to May on Thursday at 7:30pm and Saturday at 12:30pm.

Norway's oldest theater performs from September to June at **Den National Scene,** Engen 1 ((C) **55-54-97-10**). Its repertoire consists of classical Norwegian and international drama and contemporary plays, as well as visiting productions of opera and ballet in conjunction with the annual Bergen Festival. Performances are held from Monday to Saturday.

In summer, the **Bergen Folklore dancing troupe** (© 97-52-86-30) arranges a 1-hour folklore program at the Bryggens Museum on Tuesday and Thursday at 9pm. Tickets, which cost 100NOK ($13), are on sale at the tourist information center or at the door.

The most-frequented pub in the city center, **Kontoret Pub,** Ole Bulls Plass 8–10 (© 55-36-31-33), lies adjacent to the Hotel Norge next to the Dickens restaurant/pub. Drinkers can wander freely between the two places, since they're connected. In the Kontoret you can order the same food served at Dickens, though most people seem to come here to drink. The pub is open Sunday through Thursday from 4pm to 1am and Friday and Saturday from noon to 3am.

EXPLORING THE FJORDS

Norway's fjords can be explored from both Oslo and Bergen by ship and car or by a scenic train ride. Here are the details.

BY CAR FROM BERGEN

Bergen is the best departure point for trips to the fjords: To the south lies the famous **Hardangerfjord** and to the north the **Sognefjord** , cutting 180km (111 miles) inland. We've outlined a driving tour of the fjords, starting in Bergen and heading east on Route 7 to Ulvik, a distance of 150km (93 miles).

ULVIK Ulvik is that rarity: an unspoiled resort. It lies like a fist at the end of an arm of the Hardangerfjord that's surrounded in summer by misty peaks and fruit farms. The village's 1858 church is attractively decorated in the style of the region. It's open June through August, daily from 9am to 5pm, and presents concerts.

From Ulvik, you can explore the **Eidfjord** district, which is the northern tip of the Hardangerfjord, home to some 1,000 people and a paradise for hikers. Anglers are attracted to the area because of its mountain trout.

The district contains nearly one-quarter of **Hardangervidda National Park** , which is on Europe's largest high-mountain plateau. It's home to 20,000 wild reindeer. Well-marked hiking trails connect a series of 15 tourist huts.

Several canyons, including the renowned **Måbø Valley,** lead down from the plateau to the fjords. Here, you'll see the famous 170m (550-ft.) **Voringfoss** waterfall. The **Valurefoss** in **Hjømo Valley** has a free fall of almost 245m (800 ft.).

Part of the 1,000-year-old road across Norway, traversing the Måbø Valley, has been restored for hardy hikers.

En Route to Voss From Ulvik, take Highway 20 to Route 13. Follow Route 13 to Voss, 40km (25 miles) west of Ulvik and 100km (63 miles) east of Bergen.

VOSS Between the Sogne and Hardanger fjords, Voss is a famous year-round resort, also known for its folklore and as the birthplace of football hero Knute Rockne. Maybe the trolls don't strike fear into the hearts of farm children anymore, but they're still called out of hiding to give visitors a little fun.

Voss is a natural base for exploring the two largest fjords in Norway, the Sognefjord to the north and the Hardangerfjord to the south. In and around Voss are glaciers, mountains, fjords, waterfalls, orchards, rivers, and lakes.

A ride on the **Hangursbanen cable car** (© 56-51-12-12) offers panoramic views of Voss and the environs. The hardy can take the cable car up, then spend the rest of the afternoon strolling down the mountain. A round-trip ride costs 60NOK ($8) adults, 40NOK ($5.30) children 8 to 16, and free for children 7 and under. The cable-car entrance is on a hillside that's a 10-minute walk north of the town center. It's open in summer and winter, but is closed in May and from September to November.

Built in 1277, the **Vangskyrkje,** Vangsgata 3 (© **56-51-22-78**), with a timbered tower, contains a striking Renaissance pulpit, a stone altar and triptych, fine woodcarvings, and a painted ceiling. It's a 5-minute walk east of the railroad station. We recommend that you call in advance to reserve an English-speaking guide. Admission is 15NOK ($2); free for children 17 and under. The church is open only June through August, daily from 10am to 4pm.

Voss Folkemuseum, Mølster (© **56-51-15-11**), is a collection of authentically furnished houses that shows what early farm life was like. Lying just north of Voss on a hillside overlooking the town, the museum consists of more than a dozen farmhouses and other buildings, ranging in age from the 1500s to around 1870. Admission is 35NOK ($4.65) adults, free for children. It's open May and September daily from 10am to 5pm; from June to August daily from 10am to 7pm; and from October to April Monday through Saturday from 10am to 3pm and Sunday from noon to 3pm.

A little west of Voss in Finne, **Finnesloftet** (© **56-51-16-75**) is one of Norway's oldest timbered houses, dating from the mid–13th century. It's a 15-minute walk west of the railway station. Admission is 20NOK ($2.65) adults and 10NOK ($1.35) children. It's open Tuesday through Sunday from 11am to 4pm from June 15 to August 15.

BALESTRAND   Long known for its arts and crafts, Balestrand lies on the northern rim of the Sognefjord, at the junction of the Vetlefjord, the Esefjord, and the Fjaerlandsfjord.

Kaiser Wilhelm II, a frequent visitor to Balestrand, presented the district with two statues of old Norse heroes, King Bele and Fridtjof the Bold, which stand in the town center.

You can explore by setting out in nearly any direction, on scenic country lanes with little traffic, or a wide choice of marked trails and upland farm tracks. A touring map may be purchased at the **tourist office** in the town center (© **57-69-12-55** in summer; **57-69-16-17** in winter). There's good sea fishing, as well as lake and river trout fishing. Fishing tackle, rowboats, and bicycles can all be rented in the area.

En Route to Flåm   From Balestrand, follow Route 55 east along the Sognefjord, crossing the fjord via ferry at Dragsvik and by bridge at Sogndal. At Sogndal, drive east to Kaupanger, where you'll cross the Ardalsfjord by ferry, south to Revsnes. In Revsnes, pick up Route 11 heading southeast. Drive east until you connect with a secondary road heading southwest through Kvigno and Aurland. When you arrive in Aurland, take Route 601 southwest to the town of Flåm, 95km (60 miles) southeast of Balestrand and 165km (103 miles) east of Bergen.

FLÅM ⚘   Flåm (pronounced *Flawm*) lies on the Aurlandsfjord, a tip of the more famous Sognefjord. In the village you can visit the old church dating from 1667, with painted walls done in typical Norwegian country style.

Flåm is an excellent starting point for excursions by car or boat to other well-known centers on the Sognefjord, Europe's longest and deepest fjord. Worth exploring are two of the wildest and most beautiful fingers of the Sognefjord: Nærøyfjord and Aurlandfjord. Ask at the **tourist office,** near the rail station (© **57-63-21-06**), about a summer-only cruise from Flåm, when you can experience the dramatic scenery of both of these fjords. From Flåm by boat, you can disembark either in Gudvangen or Aurland and continue the tour by coach. Alternatively, you can return to Flåm by train.

There are also a number of easy walks in the Flåm district. The tourist office has a map detailing these walks.

BY SHIP/TOUR FROM BERGEN

There are several ways to visit Sognefjord, Norway's longest fjord, from Bergen. One way is to cross the fjord on an express steamer that travels from Bergen to **Gudvangen.** From Gudvangen, passengers go to Voss (see above), and from Voss a train runs back to Bergen. You can go by boat, bus, and then train for 630NOK ($84) round-trip. Details about this and other tours are available from **Bergen Visitor Information** in Bergen, Bryggen 7 (© **55-32-14-80**).

If you have more than a day to see the fjords in the environs of Bergen, you can take the grandest fjord cruise in the world, a **coastal steamer** going to the North Cape and beyond. The coastal steamers are elegantly appointed ships that cruise the western coast of Norway from Bergen to Kirkenes, carrying passengers and cargo to 34 ports along the Norwegian coast. Eleven ships in all make the journey year-round. The ships sail through Norway's more obscure fjords, providing panoramic scenery and numerous opportunities for adventure. Along the way, sightseeing excursions to the surrounding mountains and glaciers are offered, as well as sails on smaller vessels through some of the more obscure fjords.

The chief operator of these coastal cruises is the **Norwegian Coastal Voyage/ Bergen Line,** 405 Park Ave., New York, NY 10022 (© **800/323-7436** or 212/ 319-1300 in the U.S.; www.coastalvoyage.com). Tours may be booked heading north from Bergen, or south from Kirkenes. The 12-day northbound journey costs $981 to $1,340 per person double occupancy, including meals and taxes.

14

Portugal

by Herbert Bailey Livesey

Lisbon presides over a country that has recently enjoyed one of Europe's fastest-growing economies, much of it fueled by investments that have poured in since Portugal joined the European Union. About 260km (160 miles) south of Lisbon, the maritime region of the Algarve, often called the "garden of Portugal," is the southwesternmost part of Europe. Its coastline stretches 160km (100 miles) and is dotted with hundreds of beaches—the finest in the country.

1 Lisbon & Environs

Europe's smallest capital is no longer a backwater at the far edge of Iberia. Lisbon has blossomed into a cosmopolitan city. Sections of Avenida da Liberdade, the main street, evoke Paris in miniature. Some of the formerly clogged streets of the downtown Baixa district have been closed to traffic, and cobblestone pedestrian malls have been created. Sidewalk portrait painters offer to sketch your likeness, and vendors peddle jewelry and handcrafts ranging from embroidery to leatherwork. In the cooler months, smoke billows from charcoal braziers roasting chestnuts.

The world dropped in on this city of seven hills as it celebrated EXPO '98, marking the 500th anniversary of Vasco da Gama's journey to India. Although Portugal has since stubbed its toe on its way to greater prosperity, many of its attractions and facilities were left behind after the exhibition, including the Oceanarium, the largest aquarium in Europe, indoor stadia, convention centers, and a marina that can moor between 700 and 900 leisure craft.

Some 1.6 million people now call Lisbon home, and many Lisboetas, having drifted in from the distant corners of the former empire, don't even speak Portuguese. Consider an off-season visit, when the city is at its most glorious, before or after the hot and humid days of July and August. Lisbon isn't infested with visitors during spring and fall, and prices for lodgings are significantly lower than in summer.

ESSENTIALS

GETTING THERE   By Plane   Both foreign and domestic flights land at Lisbon's **Aeroporto de Lisboa** (© **21-841-3500** or 21-849-4323; www.ana-aeroportos.pt), located about 13km (8 miles) from the heart of the city. The yellow **Aero-Bus** makes 10 intermediate stops, including Praça dos Restauradores and Praça do Comercio, between the airport and the Cais do Sodre train station, every 20 minutes, from 7am to 9pm. The fare is 2.30€. Passengers line up for taxis in an orderly fashion on the sidewalk in front of the airport. The average fare to central Lisbon is 9€ to 15€, depending upon traffic and your final destination. Luggage is 1.70€ extra per piece.

For ticket sales and flight reservations, get in touch with the Lisbon personnel of TAP Air Portugal at Praça do Marquês de Pombal 3A (℅ **21-841-6990** for reservations).

By Train   Most international rail passengers from Madrid and Paris arrive at the **Estação Santa Apolonia,** the major terminal, by the Tejo River near the Alfama district. Two daily trains make the 10-hour run between Madrid and Lisbon. Rail lines from northern and eastern Portugal also arrive at this station. Other rail terminals are **Estação do Rossio,** for trains to Sintra, and the **Cais do Sodré,** with trains to Cascais and Estoril on the Costa do Sol. **Sul e Sueste,** a ferry ride from downtown, is the place to board trains to the Algarve. For **rail information** at any of the terminals, call ℅ **21-888-4025.**

Rail Europe (℅ **888/382-RAIL** in the U.S., and 800/361-RAIL; www. raileurope.com) offers a **Portuguese Railpass,** good for 4 days of first-class travel in a 15-day period within the country, for 105€. Travelers visiting both Spain and Portugal might prefer the **Iberic Railpass,** good for any 3 days in first class over a period of 2 months, for 205€.

By Bus   Buses from all over Portugal arrive at the **Rodoviaria da Estremadura,** Avenida Casal Ribeiro 18B (℅ **21-357-7715**), which lies near Praça Saldanha, about a 30-minute walk from the Praça dos Restauradores. Bus nos. 1, 21, and 32 will deliver you to the Rossio, and bus no. 1 goes on to the Cais do Sodré, if you're checked into a hotel at Estoril or Cascais. Every day, at least 10 buses leave for Lagos, a gateway to the Algarve, and 15 buses head north to Porto. Eight daily buses leave Lisbon for Coimbra, the university city in the north.

By Car   International motorists must arrive through Spain, the only nation connected to Portugal via road. Roads are moderately well maintained. Heading west from Madrid, the main road (N-620) from Tordesillas goes southwest by way of Salamanca and Ciudad Rodrigo to reach the Portuguese frontier at Fuentes de Onoro.

If you have a rented car, make sure that your insurance covers Portugal. Drive on the right side of the road; international signs and symbols are used. There are 15 border crossings, most of which are open daily from 7am to midnight.

VISITOR INFORMATION   The main tourist office in Lisbon is at the **Palácio da Foz,** Praça dos Restauradores, at the Baixa end of Avenida da Liberdade (℅ **21-346-3314;** www.portugal.org; Metro: Restauradores). It's open Monday through Saturday from 9am to 8pm, Sunday from 10am to 6pm. Attendants sell the **Lisboa Card,** an open sesame for visitors that bestows free admission to 26 museums and historic buildings, and free unrestricted access to all forms of public transport. The cards are valid for 24, 48, and 72 hours and cost 11€, 18€, and 23€, respectively. Cards for children are discounted by over 60%. When buying the card, keep in mind that most museums offer free admission on Sunday and are closed on Monday. A new **Welcome Center Lisboa** has opened on Praça Comercio at Loja 1 (℅ **21-031-2810**). They have currency exchange, brochures, and examples of native crafts. Find the office with the banners at the front of the arcade that read ASK ME LISBOA.

Websites   In addition to the tourist office's website, **www.portugalvirtual.pt** offers an extensive collection of links for exploring Portugal in depth. Other possibilities are **www.portugal.sunscale.com**, **www.portugal-info.net**, and **www. portugal-insite.pt**.

CITY LAYOUT   The best orientation to Lisbon is obtained by locating your-self in its waterside gateway, **Praça do Comércio (aka Black Horse Sq.),** bor-dering the River Tejo. A majestic square that regained its dignity when parking was banned, it's the site of the Stock Exchange and various government min-istries. One block west stands the late-19th-century City Hall, fronting Praça do Município.

Castelo São Jorge tops the hill up to the right, and the steep slopes below are crowded with the medieval quarter called the **Alfama.** As you walk north from Praça do Comércio through the grid of the **Baixa** shopping district, the high ground to the left contains the **Chiado** district and the **Bairro Alto,** a neigh-borhood almost as old as the Alfama.

Continuing north, you'll enter the bustling **Praça Dom Pedro IV,** known to all as the "Rossio." A long reclamation project was recently completed, and the square looks better than it has in living memory. The visual undulation of the sidewalks, set with irregular black and white cubes, has led to the appellation "the dizzy praça." Facing the Rossio is the Teatro Nacional Dona Maria II. A block to its left is the **Estação do Rossio,** whose exuberant Manueline architec-ture is worth seeing. Separating the Rossio from Avenida da Liberdade is **Praça dos Restauradores,** named in honor of the Restoration, when the Portuguese chose their own king and freed themselves from 60 years of Spanish rule. An obelisk marks the event.

Lisbon's main street, **Avenida da Liberdade,** dating from 1880 and once called the "antechamber of Lisbon," is a mile-long concourse with shade trees and promenades. Flanking it are branches of upmarket international clothing chains, headquarters for many major airlines, travel agents, coffeehouses with sidewalk tables, and several large hotels. At the top of the avenue is **Praça Marquês de Pombal,** with a statue erected in honor of Pombal, the 18th-century prime minister credited with Lisbon's reconstruction in the aftermath of the 1755 earthquake. Proceeding north, you'll enter **Parque Eduardo VII,** named in honor of Queen Victoria's son, who paid a state visit to Lisbon. In the park is the Estufa Fria, a greenhouse that's well worth a visit.

GETTING AROUND **Carris** (☎ 21-363-2044) operates the network of funiculars, trains, subways, and buses in Lisbon. They sell a **tourist pass**—*passe turistico*—good for 7 days of unlimited travel for 13€. Passes are sold in Carris booths, open from 8:30am to 6:30pm daily, and in most Metro stations and network train stations. You must show a passport to purchase one of these passes.

By Metro Metro (subway) stations are designated by large "M" signs. Trains run daily from 6:30am to 1am. A single ticket costs .60€ per ride. A 10-trip ticket, called a *cademeta,* costs 4.65€. The 1-day unlimited pass is 1.40€, and the 7-day unlimited pass is 4.80€. For more information, call ☎ **21-355-8457** or visit **www.metrolisboa.pt.** Single-ride, round-trip, and 10-day tickets can also be purchased at automatic vending machines in Metro stations.

By Bus & Tram These are among the cheapest public buses and trams in Europe. Electric trams *(electricos)* make the steep run up to the Bairro Alto and Alfama and out to Belém. You pay a flat fare of .90€ on a bus if you buy the ticket from the driver. The transportation system within the city limits is divided into zones ranging from 1 to 5, and your fare depends on how many zones you traverse. Buses and electricos run daily from 6am to 1am.

By Electric Train Lisbon is connected to all the towns and villages along the Portuguese Riviera by a smooth-running modern electric train system. You can board at the waterfront **Cais do Sodre** station in Lisbon and head up the coast all the way to Cascais. Only one class of seating is offered, and the rides are cheap and generally comfortable. Sintra can't be reached by the electric train. You must go to the **Estação do Rossio,** opening onto Praça Dom Pedro IV, where frequent connections can be made.

By Taxi Newer, beige Mercedes taxis have all but replaced the older green-and-black versions. If the green roof lights are on, the taxi is occupied. The initial charge at flag drop is 1.80€. Fares in the city average 4.50€, with an extra 20% supplement from 10pm to 6am. The driver is allowed by law to tack on another 50% if your luggage weighs more than 30 kilograms (66 lb.). Portuguese tip about 10%. Verify that the meter has indeed been activated the moment you step into a cab. To **radio a taxi,** call ☎ **21-815-5061** or 21-793-2756.

By Car Car-rental kiosks at the airport and in the city center include **Avis,** Avenida Praia da Vitoria 12C (☎ **21-351-4560**); **Hertz,** Qto. Frangelha Baixio (☎ **21-849-2722**); and **Budget,** rue Castillo Cas 167R (☎ **21-994-0443**). That said, be advised that driving in congested Lisbon is extremely difficult and potentially dangerous; the city has an alarmingly high accident rate, and parking is all but impossible. It's a good idea to rent a car only for excursions into the countryside.

Lisbon

ACCOMMODATIONS ■
As Janelas Verdes **2**
Avenida Palace **20**
Britânia **16**
Casa de São Mamede **5**
Dom Carlos **11**
Dom Pedro **6**
Dom Rodrigo **8**
Four Seasons
The Ritz Lisbon **9**
Ibis Lisboa-Saldanha **12**
Jorge V **7**
Lapa Palace **4**
Lisboa Plaza **18**
Lisboa Sheraton
& Towers **10**
Mundial **21**
Tivoli Lisboa **15**
Veneza **17**
York House **3**

ATTRACTIONS ●
Alfama **24**
Bairro Alto **19**
Belém **27**
Castelo São Jorge **25**
Monumento dos
Descobrimentos **31**
Mosteiro dos
Jerónimos **29**
Museu Antóniano **22**
Museu de Arte Popular **30**
Museu de Fundação
Calouste Gulbenkian **13**
Museu da Marinha **28**
Museu Nacional
de Arte Antiga **1**
Oceanario de Lisboa **14**
Sé Cathedral **23**
Torre de Belém **26**

797

FAST FACTS: **Lisbon**

American Express Amex is represented by Top Tours, Avenida Duque de Loule 108 (© **21-315-5872**; Metro: Restauradores). It's open Monday through Friday from 9:30am to 1pm and 2:30 to 6:30pm.

Business Hours Typically, **shops** are open Monday through Friday from 9am to 1pm and 3 to 7pm (some stay open through lunch) and Saturday from 9am to 1pm; some are also open Saturday afternoon. **Banks** are open Monday through Friday from 8:30am to 3pm; some offer a foreign-exchange service Monday through Saturday from 6 to 11pm.

ATMs (called *caíxas automáticos*) are widely available, including machines in the arrivals lobby of the airport terminal—look for the sign MULTIBANCO. You can get cash with major credit cards or with Cirrus or PLUS network debit cards.

Dentists/Doctors Contact **Clinica Medical Espanha,** Rua Dom Luis de Noroha 32 (© **21-796-7457**; Metro: Plaça Espanha), where some dentists speak English. Virtually every hotel maintains a list of doctors and dentists who can be called upon in emergencies.

Drugstores A central and well-stocked drugstore is **Farmácia Vall,** Avenida Visconde Valmor 60A (© **21-797-3043**; Metro: Saldanha). Pharmacies that are closed post a notice indicating the nearest one that's open.

Embassies/Consulates If you lose your passport or have some other pressing problem, you'll need to get in touch with the embassy of the **United States,** Avenida das Forcas Armadas (Sete Rios), 1600 Lisboa (© **21-727-3300**; Metro: Entre Campos). Hours are Monday through Friday from 8am to 12:30pm and 1:30 to 5pm. If you've lost a passport, the embassy can take photos for you and help you obtain the proof of citizenship needed to get a replacement. The embassy of **Canada** is at Avenida da Liberdade 144, 1269-121 Lisboa (© **21-316-4600**; Metro: Avenida); hours are Monday through Friday from 9:30am to 12:30pm and 1:30 to 5pm (in July and Aug, the embassy closes at 1pm on Fri). The embassy of the **United Kingdom,** Rua São Bernardo 33, 1249-082 Lisboa (© **21-392-4000**; Metro: Avenida), is open Monday through Friday from 9:30am to 12:30pm and 3 to 4:30pm. The British embassy also services citizens of **Australia** and **New Zealand.** The embassy of the **Republic of Ireland,** Rua de Imprensa à Estrêla 1, 1249-082 Lisboa (© **21-392-9440**; Metro: Rossio), is open Monday through Friday from 9:30am to noon and 2:30 to 4:30pm.

Emergencies For the **police** or an **ambulance** in Lisbon, call © **112.** In case of **fire,** call © **21-342-2222.**

Hospitals In case of a medical emergency, inquire at your hotel or call your embassy and ask the staff there to recommend an English-speaking physician. You can also try the **British Hospital,** Rua Saraiva de Carvalho 49 (© **21-395-5067**; bus: 7, 40, 49, or 60), where the telephone operator, staff, and doctors all speak English.

Post Office The general post office is on Praça dos Restauradores 58 (© **21-323-8700**; Metro: Restauradoes), open Monday through Friday from 8am to 10pm, and Saturday, Sunday, and holidays from 9am to 6pm.

Safety Portugal remains one of the safest countries in western Europe, but crime rose dramatically in the 1990s, sparked by the flood of homeless and penniless immigrants from the faraway countries of the former Portuguese empire. Lisbon is the most dangerous city, followed by the tourist-infested Algarve, where many hustlers prey on travelers. Pickpocketing remains the major crime against tourists; violent attacks are relatively rare. Take special care on crowded buses or trains, and leave your valuables at the hotel.

Taxes Portugal imposes a value-added tax (VAT) on most purchases made within its borders ranging from 8% to 30%. Known in Portugal as the **IVA,** the amount is almost always written into the bottom line of the bill for any purchase a foreign visitor makes. To get an IVA refund on purchases that qualify, present your passport to the salesperson and ask for the special stamped form. Present the form with your purchases at the booth marked for IVA tax refunds at the airport. You'll get your money refunded right at the booth.

Hotel and restaurant bills are taxed at 17.5%. Car rentals are subject to an additional 17.5% tax. Such deluxe goods as jewelry, furs, and expensive imported liquors include a 30% built-in tax.

Telephone The **country code** for Portugal is **351.** The **city code** for Lisbon is now **21;** use this code when calling from anywhere outside or inside Portugal—even within Lisbon itself.

You can make a **local call** in Lisbon in one of the many telephone booths. For most **long-distance calls,** particularly transatlantic calls, go to the central post office (see above). Give an assistant there the number you wish, and he or she will make the call, billing you at the end. Some phones are equipped to use calling cards, including American Express and Visa. You can also purchase phone cards at the post office; they can be used at any public phone in Portugal. Phone debit cards are used only in public phones in public places. These cards bear one of two different names: TLP or CrediFone. Both are sold at the cashier's desk of most hotels as well as at post offices.

To make an international call using your calling card, thereby bypassing many of the added-on charges imposed by your hotel, dial the appropriate access number to reach a North American operator or an English-language voice prompt. For **AT&T,** call (C) **05-017-1288;** for **MCI,** call (C) **05-017-1234;** for **Sprint,** call (C) **05-017-1877.**

Tipping Most service personnel expect a good tip. Hotels add a service charge (known as *serviço*), which is divided among the entire staff, but individual tipping is also expected. Tip .50€ to the bellhop; .50€ to 1€ to the porter hailing you a cab; and 1.50€ to the chambermaid. Tip cab drivers 15% to 20% of the total fare. Restaurants and nightclubs include a service charge and government taxes of 17.5%, which are distributed among the entire staff—not to mention the waiter's mistress and the owner's grandfather—so extra tipping is customary, about 5% in a moderately priced restaurant and 10% in a deluxe establishment.

WHERE TO STAY
IN THE CENTER
Very Expensive

Dom Pedro ⭐⭐   One of Lisbon's newest hotels, rated five stars by the Portuguese government and associated with some of the most glamorous hotels of the Algarve and Madeira, the Dom Pedro is set within the central Amoreiras district, across from one of the city's biggest shopping centers. The interior is as conservative and rich looking as the exterior is modernistic. Rooms are lavishly furnished, with video games, work desks, sitting areas, and double-glazed windows.

Avenida Engenheiro, Duarte Pacheco, 1070-109 Lisboa. ℂ **21-389-6600.** Fax 21-389-6601. www.dom pedro-hotels.com. 263 units. 145€–400€ double; from 290€ suite. AE, DC, MC, V. Free parking. Metro: Marqués de Pombal. **Amenities:** 2 restaurants; bar; access to nearby health club; concierge; business center; 24-hr. room service; same-day laundry/dry cleaning. *In room:* A/C, TV w/pay movies, minibar, hair dryer, safe.

Four Seasons The Ritz Lisbon ⭐⭐⭐   One of the most famous and legendary hotels in Lisbon, this place was built on the order of dictator Antonio Salazar in the late 1950s. In 1998, its management contract was taken over by the Four Seasons group, which immediately upgraded everything from the striking lobby to the supremely comfortable guest rooms. All but a handful of rooms have their own terraces, about half of them overlooking Edward VII Park. Among the electronic extras is high-speed Internet access. Bathrooms have double basins and robes. Service, especially among the concierge staff, is superb.

Rua Rodrigo Fonseca 88, 1200 Lisboa. ℂ **800/332-3442** in the U.S., or 21-383-2020. Fax 21-383-1783. www.fourseasons.com. 284 units. 340€–480€ double; from 650€ suite. AE, DC, MC, V. Free parking. Metro: Rotunda. Bus: 1, 2, 9, or 32. **Amenities:** 2 restaurants; bar; cafe; heated indoor pool; health club; concierge; car rental desk; business center; shopping arcade; salon; 24-hr. room service; babysitting; same-day laundry/dry cleaning; nonsmoking rooms. *In room:* A/C, TV w/pay movies, dataport, minibar, hair dryer, safe.

Lisboa Sheraton & Tower ⭐⭐   This skyscraper lies at a traffic-clogged intersection a bit removed from the center of town, a few blocks north of Praça Marquês de Pombal. Once inside, you may forget which city you're in, given the generically universal character of the Sheraton chain. Guest rooms don't match the grandeur of the public areas, but they're generally spacious, and each was renovated in the late 1990s. The most desirable are in the tower, opening onto views of the longest bridge in Europe.

Rua Latino Coelho 1, 1069 Lisboa. ℂ **800/325-3535** in the U.S., or 21-357-5757. Fax 21-314-2292. www. sheraton.com/lisboa. 381 units. 105€–215€ double; from 525€ suite. AE, DC, MC, V. Parking 12€. Bus: 1, 2, 9, or 32. **Amenities:** 2 restaurants; bar; heated outdoor pool; health club and spa; concierge; car rental desk; business center; shopping arcade; salon; 24-hr. room service; babysitting; same-day laundry/dry cleaning; nonsmoking rooms. *In room:* A/C, TV w/pay movies, minibar, hair dryer, safe.

Expensive

Avenida Palace ⭐   Built in 1892 and closed for years while undergoing a massive overhaul, the Avenida Palace is the grandest old-fashioned hotel in Lisbon, a true link to the past. The hotel's location, right at the Rossio, is convenient though quite noisy. Inside, however, you'll find a world etched in crystal and burnished woods. Still the grande dame of Lisbon hotels, it retains its polished Belle Epoque aura and elegance while offering the usual modern comforts. Rooms are soundproofed against the busy street and supplied with elegant, antique-style furnishings. Unfortunately, mattresses are pretty old, too.

Rua ler Dezembro 123, 1200 Lisboa. ℂ **21-346-0155.** Fax 21-342-2884. www.hotel-avenida-palace.pt. 96 units. 149€–197€ double; from 360€ suite. Rates include breakfast. AE, DC, MC, V. Free parking. Metro:

Restaurador. Tram: 35. **Amenities:** Bar; 24-hr. room service; same-day laundry/dry cleaning. *In room:* A/C, TV, minibar, hair dryer, safe.

Lisboa Plaza ⋒

This family-owned hotel, located in the heart of the city, is a charmer, with far more character than the bland Sofitel it faces. One of the commendable Heritage Lisboa lodging group that includes As Janelas Verdes and the Hotel Britânia (described below), it lavishes the visual delights of a country manor house on its public spaces—take a book to the inviting reading nook near the bar. Some meals are buffet-style, with a separate a-la-carte room. Guest rooms are comfortable and of good size, endearingly old-fashioned, with robes in the bathrooms. The TV has 40 channels; several broadcast in English. There's a computer in the lobby for guest use.

Travessa do Salitre 7, Avenida da Liberdade, 1269 Lisboa. ℭ **21-321-8218.** Fax 21-347-1630. www.heritage. pt. 106 units. 140€–198€ double; from 240€ suite. Children 12 and under stay free in parent's room. AE, DISC, MC, V. Parking nearby 13€. Metro: Avenida. Bus: 1, 2, 36, or 44. **Amenities:** Restaurant; bar; concierge; car rental desk; 24-hr. room service; babysitting; same-day laundry/dry cleaning; nonsmoking rooms. *In room:* A/C, TV, dataport, minibar, hair dryer, safe.

Tivoli Lisboa ⋒⋒

Contemporary in appearance and fittings, this central hotel includes, among its many amenities, the only hotel pool in downtown Lisbon. After a much-needed 1998 renovation, it sparkles again, and boasts extensive facilities. Best of all, its prices aren't extravagant, considering the amenities. The largest and best rooms face the front, many with views of the city, but those in the rear are quieter. Some are better appointed and more spacious than others. Facilities include access to the Tivoli Club, surrounded by a garden.

Avenida da Liberdade 185, 1298 Lisboa Codex. ℭ **21-319-8900.** Fax 21-319-8950. www.tivolihotels.com. 329 units. 149€–185€ double; from 290€ suite. AE, DC, MC, V. Parking 10€. Metro: Avenida. Bus: 1, 2, 9, or 32. **Amenities:** 2 restaurants; 3 bars (1 seasonal); outdoor pool; exercise room; concierge; car-rental desk; business center; shopping arcade; salon; 24-hr. room service; in-room massage; babysitting; same-day laundry/dry cleaning; nonsmoking rooms. *In room:* A/C, TV w/pay movies, minibar, hair dryer, safe.

Moderate

Britânia ⋒

In its own way, the Britânia is one of Lisbon's most traditional and refreshingly conservative hotels, designed in the Art Deco/Moderne style by Portuguese architect Cassiano Branco in 1944. On a quiet block just off Avenida da Liberdade, it shelters a distinguished clientele that returns repeatedly, and an old-fashioned, almost courtly, staff. The only meal served is a buffet breakfast, but the facilities of the much larger Hotel Lisboa Plaza (with which the Britânia is affiliated) lie just across the busy avenue.

Rua Rodrigues Sampaio 17, 1150 Lisboa. ℭ **21-315-5016.** Fax 21-315-5021. www.heritage.pt. 30 units. 140€–168€ double. Service and taxes included. AE, DC, MC, V. Metro: Avenida. Bus: 1, 2, 11, or 21. **Amenities:** Bar; concierge; 24-hr. room service; babysitting; same-day laundry/dry cleaning; nonsmoking rooms. *In room:* A/C, TV, minibar, dataport, hair dryer, safe.

Dom Carlos

Just off Praça Marquês de Pombal, the Dom Carlos faces a triangular square named for the partially blind 19th-century poet Camilo Castelo Branco. The curved facade is all glass, visually bringing the park's dark-green trees and garden beds of orange and red canna indoors. In a neighborhood of similar competitors, this is the best hotel of the lot, its rooms more spacious and accorded a higher level of maintenance.

Avenida Duque de Loulé 121, 1050 Lisboa. ℭ **21-351-2590.** Fax 21-352-0728. 76 units. 97€ double. Rates include buffet breakfast. AE, DC, MC, V. Metro: Marquês de Pombal. Bus: 7, 36, 44, or 45. **Amenities:** Restaurant; bar; 24-hr. room service; babysitting; laundry/dry cleaning. *In room:* A/C, TV, minibar, hair dryer.

Dom Rodrigo 🐦🐦   Most of the accommodations here are sizable two-room suites that can house families of three or four. There are two beds in one room and a full marble bathroom. The sitting area contains a convertible sofa and a dining table, and the complete kitchen comes with a stove, a sink, a fridge, and rudimentary utensils. Stated tariffs are nearly always negotiable (the corporate rate is about 95€ for a double). The quiet location, 2 blocks uphill from Praça Marquês de Pombal, is desirable. Fluent English is spoken at the front desk. The casual dining room serves light meals.

Rodrigo da Fonseca 44–50, 1200 Lisboa. ✆ **21-386-3800.** Fax 21-386-3000. htdrodrigo@mail.telepoc.pt. 57 units. 130€–150€ double. Rates include breakfast. AE, DC, MC, V. Free garage parking. Metro: Marquês de Pombal. **Amenities:** Cafe; lobby bar; unheated outdoor pool; limited room service; same-day laundry service/dry cleaning. *In room:* A/C, TV, hair dryer, safe.

Mundial 🐦🐦   The best business hotel in the downtown Rossio area took a giant step up in appeal with construction that nearly doubled its size. Its new wing looks out on a plaza filled with fountains and shopping booths, while the original structure and its good-size rooms have been repapered, repainted, and outfitted with fresh fabrics. Best of all is the rooftop restaurant, Varanda, with its views of the city and the illuminated castle above. The staff is starting to measure up to its surroundings. Rates have been kept relatively low in spite of the upgrade. The highest price below applies from April to June and from September to October, while in July and August, surprisingly, the prices are lower.

Dom Duarte 4, 1100 Lisboa. ✆ **21-886-4111.** Fax 21-887-9129. www.hotel-mundial.pt. 262 units. 78€–146€ double. Rates include breakfast. AE, DC, DISC, MC, V. Free garage parking. Metro: Rossio. Tram: 28. **Amenities:** 2 restaurants; 2 bars; concierge; 24-hr. room service; same-day laundry service/dry cleaning. *In room:* A/C, TV w/pay movies, minibar, hair dryer, safe.

Veneza   Opened as a hotel in 1990, the Veneza occupies one of the few remaining 19th-century mansions that once lined Avenida da Liberdade. Inside, a grand staircase leads to the three upper floors. The well-appointed midsize rooms are furnished in a soothing modern style, each with a firm mattress. The staff is uniformly pleasant. The hotel's position adjacent to the better-equipped Tivoli Lisboa (see above) ensures that its guests have access to all the facilities they might need. Rates below are for first nights, reduced by 20% for additional nights.

Avenida da Liberdade 189, 1250-141 Lisboa. ✆ **21-352-2618.** Fax 21-352-6678. www.3khoteis.com. 38 units. 119€–141€ double. Rates include continental breakfast. AE, DC, MC, V. Parking 9€. Metro: Avenida. **Amenities:** Bar; car-rental desk; same-day laundry/dry cleaning, nonsmoking rooms. *In room:* A/C, TV, minibar, hair dryer, safe.

Inexpensive

Ibis Lisboa-Saldanha   A unit of the monster European chain, Ibis, which owns hundreds of economical hotels, this relatively new mid-rise is on a busy but not unattractive street 3 blocks from the nearest Metro station and under 6.5km (4 miles) from the airport. Warmth isn't a hallmark—witness the curt demeanor of the overworked desk staff—but value is. The rooms are small and spare but certainly adequate for those who don't plan to do more than sleep there.

Casal Ribeiro 23, 1100 Lisboa. ✆ **21-319-1690.** Fax 21-319-1699. 116 units. 70€–74€ double. Rates include taxes. AE, DC, MC, V. Parking in garage 4€. Metro: Saldanha. **Amenities:** Cafe/bar; nonsmoking rooms. *In room:* A/C, TV.

Jorge V   A tidy little hotel with a 1960s design, Jorge V has a relatively quiet location (assuming the substantial construction out front is completed) near noisy Avenida da Liberdade. Its facade is constituted of rows of balconies, roomy enough for guests to have breakfast or afternoon drinks. A tiny elevator takes guests to a variety of aging rooms, which aren't generous in size but are comfortable enough; all have small shower-only bathrooms. There's an Internet console in the lobby.

Rua Mouzinho da Silveira 3, 1200 Lisboa. ℂ **21-356-2525.** Fax 21-315-0319. 49 units. 50€–77€ double; 95€ suite. Rates include continental breakfast. AE, DC, MC, V. Parking 7.50€. Metro: Avenida or Marquês de Pombal. **Amenities:** Cafe/bar; limited room service; laundry/dry cleaning, nonsmoking rooms. *In room:* A/C, TV, minibar, hair dryer, safe.

Miraparque ★★ This low-key contemporary hotel is worth every euro. Identified by its terra-cotta-hued exterior, it does indeed "look at the park" (the one named for Eduardo VII), as its name indicates. Management repaints the interior every year or so, and housekeeping standards are high. The rooms are spacious and uncluttered, with desks and an easy chair or two. The buffet breakfast is laid out in the full-service restaurant. A Metro stop is around the corner, and an ornate sports pavilion is across the street. English is spoken.

Sidónio Pais 12, 1050-214 Lisboa. ℂ **21-352-4286.** Fax 21-357-8920. www.miraparque.com. 102 units. 88€–96€ double. Rates include breakfast. AE, MC, V. Metro: Parque. **Amenities:** Restaurant; bar; concierge; car-rental desk; limited room service; babysitting; same-day laundry/dry cleaning. *In room:* A/C, TV, minibar, safe.

WEST OF THE CENTER
Very Expensive
As Janelas Verdes ★★ "Green Windows" is owned by the proprietors of the Lisboa Plaza (see above). It is an aristocratic 18th-century mansion, the former home of Portuguese novelist Eça de Queirós. Near the Museum of Ancient Art, the marvelously restored rooms of the original structure are furnished with handsome antiques, while rooms in the new wing compensate with abundant closet space and generous bathrooms. Breakfast is served as a buffet in the dining room, but it can also be brought on a tray to your room or to the rear walled-in terrace. View the River Tejo from the library.

Rua das Janelas Verdes 47, 1200 Lisboa. ℂ **21-396-8143.** Fax 21-396-8144. www.heritage.com. 17 units. 225€–245€ double. AE, DISC, MC, V. Parking 11€. Bus: 27, 40, 49, or 60. **Amenities:** Honor bar; concierge; 24-hr. room service; babysitting; same-day laundry/dry cleaning; nonsmoking rooms. *In room:* A/C, TV, dataport, minibar, hair dryer, safe.

Lapa Palace ★★★ Twenty years ago, the Ritz was the capital's premier hotel address. That was then. Now, the Lapa Palace rules. Its lush, meticulously manicured gardens and groves lie on a hill above the River Tejo, in a largely residential district west of the city center. All but about 20 of the opulently outfitted units are in a six-story modern wing; the rest are in the former mansion that is the core of the hotel. The public areas are impressively appointed with *azulejos*, multi-hued ceiling frescoes and patterned marble floors in striking geometric patterns. Free parking is available for 120 cars.

> **Tips** **Stateside Booking**
>
> You can make reservations for As Janelas Verdes and many other Lisbon hotels, as well as all the country's rural *pousadas* (inns), through **Marketing Ahead,** 381 Park Ave. S., Suite 718, New York, NY 10016 (ℂ **800/223-1356** or 212/686-9213; www.marketingahead.com).

Rua do Pau de Bandeira 4, 1249-021 Lisboa. © **21-394-9494.** Fax 21-395-0665. www.hotelapa.com. 127 units. 350€–525€ double; from 625€ suite. Rates include buffet breakfast. AE, DC, MC, V. Free parking. Bus: 13 or 27. **Amenities:** 2 restaurants; bar; heated outdoor and indoor pools; well-equipped health club and spa; concierge; business center; 24-hr. room service; same-day laundry/dry cleaning. *In room:* A/C, TV/VCR, dataport, minibar, hair dryer, safe.

Expensive

York House 🌟   York House blends the romance of the past with modern convenience. Originally a 17th-century convent, it's outside the center of traffic-filled Lisbon, down the street from the National Art Gallery. For its conversion to a hotel, it was furnished with notable good taste by a distinguished Lisbon designer. Guest rooms are of varying dimensions, given the uses to which they were first put, but most have antique beds and good mattresses. Linger over a coffee in the vine-draped courtyard or in the atmospheric adjacent bar. A garage is available. Book well in advance.

Rua das Janelas Verdes 32, 1200 Lisboa. © **21-396-2435.** Fax 21-397-2793. www.yorkhouselisboa.com. 34 units. 167€–190€ double. Parking 11€. AE, DC, MC, V. Bus: 27, 40, 49, 54, or 60. **Amenities:** Restaurant; bar; laundry service; nonsmoking rooms. *In room:* A/C, TV, hair dryer.

WHERE TO DINE
IN THE CENTER
Very Expensive

Gambrinus 🌟🌟 *(Overrated)* SEAFOOD   Long considered one of Lisbon's premier restaurants, Gambrinus is a favored choice for business negotiations and celebrations of sealed deals. A uniformed doorman greets the regulars, prosperous men in suits who populate the front bar and the two stereotypically masculine dining rooms. Patrons occupy leather chairs under the cathedral ceiling or select a table beside the fireplace. Laughing, drinking, and puffing cigars, they don't seem to notice that the food is remarkably uninspired for a restaurant of such high repute. The first clue is the plate of buttered toast—not rolls or bread—that arrives after your order. Next comes a mixed salad of school cafeteria ineptitude. Then fish with tartar sauce, boiled potatoes, and overcooked green beans. You could have had the same meal here during the Eisenhower administration. The captains and waiters are as gracious as the crush allows.

Rua das Portas de Santo Antão 25. © **21-342-1466.** Reservations required. Main courses 20€–32€. AE, MC, V. Daily noon–1:30am. Metro: Rossio.

Expensive

Clara 🌟 INTERNATIONAL   This emerald-tiled house atop a hill and opposite a large park contains an elegant restaurant with a garden terrace. Lunch outside amid the plants and fountain is a tempting option. At night, a table indoors beside the fireplace may be more appealing. Most evenings, a piano player provides background music. As in many of the city's top restaurants, dishes are rarely innovative, but are prepared with care. Also common are the often lethal prices for lobster and other shellfish—up to 80€ *and more* for lobster. For less damage to your credit rating, see if duck breast with fruit, poached fish of the day, or stuffed rabbit in red-wine sauce are available. Wines are mostly high-end Portuguese pressings.

Camp dos Mártires da Pátria 49. © **21-885-3053.** Reservations recommended. Main courses 17€–23€. AE, MC, V. Mon–Fri 12:30–3pm and 7:30pm–midnight.

Escorial INTERNATIONAL   Near Praça dos Restauradores, this place presents a menu of mostly Spanish and Portuguese dishes in a comfortable paneled dining room (it's time to re-think the avocado-and-burnt-orange color scheme, though). For an appetizer, you might consider oysters or the smoked duck *presunto*. Among the specialties are chargrilled lamb brochette, beef Stroganoff, and a partridge casserole. Escorial doesn't chart any new trails, but it has stood the test of time and remained an enduring favorite. Most dishes are under 20€; the costlier items, as always, are lobster and its cousins, which are priced by the kilo—70€ and up.

Rua das Portas de Santo Antão 47. © 21-346-4429. Reservations recommended. Main courses 16€–22€. AE, DC, MC, V. Daily 12:30pm–midnight. Metro: Rossio or Restauradores.

Moderate

Restaurant 33 PORTUGUESE/INTERNATIONAL   Burgundy shutters and dark beams—some real, some merely decorative—seek to convey the impression of a farmhouse or hunting lodge. The restaurant fills with business-people at lunch and with couples and friends at dinner, when a pianist performs. Fragrant soups fire the appetite, leading to such specialties as shredded duck tossed with rice or fish chunks mixed with rice baked in a crab shell. Steak is popular. Large portions, hearty stews, and flavorful ingredients characterize the food. Meals are served on the terrace in good weather. A glass of port in the small entry bar can cap a meal.

Rua Alexandre Herculano 33A. © 21-354-6079. Reservations recommended. Main courses 15€–21€. AE, DC, MC, V. Mon–Fri 12:30–3:30pm and 8–10pm; Sat 8–10pm. Metro: Rotunda. Bus: 6 or 9.

Solar dos Presuntos ☆☆ PORTUGUESE   A tank crammed with spiny lob-sters stands inside the door next to the service bar. The walls of both the ground floor and upstairs dining rooms are filled with photos and caricatures of domes-tic and international celebs. Many of the patrons have been regulars for years, and are greeted enthusiastically at the door. *Presunto* is a cured Iberian ham sim-ilar to Italian prosciutto, and a plate of thin slices comes as soon as you've ordered. A specialty is four lightly fried cod cakes with a side of soupy rice and beans. Most of the year, foreigners are barely in evidence, but some English is spoken by the hurried staff. Find the restaurant at the foot of the funicular east of the Avenida da Liberdad, the Elevador do Lavra.

Rua das Portas de Santo Antão 150. © 21-342-4253. Reservations suggested. Main courses 12€–19€. AE, MC, V. Mon–Sat noon–3pm and 7:30–10:30pm. Metro: Rossio or Restauradores.

Solmar PORTUGUESE   This is the biggest, gaudiest, loudest seafood empo-rium on this street of hip-to-hip restaurants, so it follows that it attracts more than its share of tourists. However, tourists are outnumbered by locals who know the freshest fish when they eat it. Solmar is two stories high, with an atrium, a wall-sized mosaic of marine life, a tank of lobsters in the middle, and display windows heaped with crustaceans. All that combines with a long bar along the left side, four tiled columns holding up the ceiling, and a design style that recalls the least adept conceits of the 1950s. Service is efficient and largely cheerless. Sea bass, boned and assembled at tableside, is superior to the same dish at Gambrinus (see above), and is served with lots more vegetables.

Rua das Portas de Santo Antão 106. © 21-342-3371. Main courses 14€–19€. AE, DC, MC, V. Daily 7am–11:30pm. Metro: Rossio or Restauradores.

Inexpensive

Bonjardim ⦅Value⦆ PORTUGUESE   Bonjardim caters to families and large groups of friends and co-workers, providing filling meals that fit almost any budget. The restaurant, one of the most popular in Lisbon, is just east of Avenida da Liberdade near the Praça dos Restauradores. The aroma of plump chickens roasting to a glistening brown on the charcoal spit is irresistible. An order of a house specialty, *frango no espeto* (supreme of chicken), with a side of fries, costs only 8.40€! There are other items on the card, but chicken is the reason to go. Try for a table on the quieter ground floor. Across the street is a smaller annex of the restaurant, also called Bonjardim.

Travessa de Santo Antão 10–12. Ⓒ **21-342-7424**. Main courses 6.75€–15€. AE, DC, MC, V. Daily noon–4pm and 7pm–12:30am. Metro: Restauradores.

Brilhante SEAFOOD/PORTUGUESE Lisboetas from every walk of life stop by this *cervejaria* for a stein of beer and a bowl of *mariscos* (seafood). Dine either at the bar or at marble tables. The front window is packed with an appetizing array of king crabs, oysters, lobsters, baby clams, shrimp, even goose barnacles. Prices change every day, depending on the market; you pay by the kilo or portion thereof. This is robust eating in an always-busy environment, where it can be a challenge to get a waiter's attention. There are outside tables in warm weather.

Rua das Portas de Santo Antão 105. Ⓒ **21-346-1407**. Main courses 12€–34€. AE, DC, MC, V. Daily 11am–midnight. Metro: Rossio. Bus: 1, 2, 36, 44, or 45.

Grill 20 ✿ *Value* PORTUGUESE Less than 2 blocks west of the top of Avenida da Liberdade, this effervescent newcomer is handy to several of the hotels recommended above. It's airy, bright, and contemporary, making it attractive to the younger professionals who work in the area. There's no need for an *entrada* (appetizer), as the price of each main course includes a visit to the salad bar. This is a grill—every item is meat, mostly beef or pork, in monster slabs or on skewers, all intensely flavorful and cooked precisely to order. The fries are good, as are the aromatic rice side dishes. You should be able to eat for under 15€, wine and tax included.

Braancamp 62. Ⓒ **21-385-8888**. Main courses 2.80€–11€. AE, DC, MC, V. Mon–Sat noon–4pm and 7–11pm. Metro: Marquês de Pombal.

Pastelaria Suíça PORTUGUESE Scores of *pastelarias* service the pronounced Portuguese sweet tooth, and many go well beyond tarts and cakes to soups, sandwiches, and even full meals. This always-busy cafe runs through an entire block, with tables on the east side of the Rossio and the west side of Praça da Figueira. It has been thoroughly refurbished, like the plazas on either side. It covers most bases, with pastry and ice cream counters, tearooms, and bars. Omelets and salads are available, as is a breakfast of juice, a croissant, bacon, eggs, and coffee for under 5€. At lunch, you might be asked to move inside from the sidewalk tables unless you've ordered a meal, not just a beverage.

Praça Dom Pedro IV 105. Ⓒ **21-321-4090**. Main courses 1.65€–9.50€. No credit cards. Daily 7am–10pm. Metro: Rossio.

Ribadoura SEAFOOD Midway along the major boulevard, at the corner of Rua do Salitre, this *cervejaria* (beer house) is typical of Lisbon's shellfish-and-beer joints. The decor is plain and simple, the better to focus on the featured seafood. The classic *bacalhau* (codfish) *à Bras* is a good choice; for a lighter bite, try the shrimp omelet. Most dishes are under 15€, an exception being the *mariscos à marinheira* (fish stew). Many diners follow fish with a meat dish, but be aware that those dishes accompanied by spicy-hot *piri-piri* sauce can be a gustatory challenge for anyone not accustomed to fiery seasonings. Lobster and other shellfish are priced by the kilo and can exceed 100€.

Avenida da Liberdade 155. ℂ 21-354-9411. Main courses 7.90€–13€. AE, DC, MC, V. Daily noon–1:30am. Metro: Avenida. Bus: 1, 2, 44, or 45.

IN CHIADO & BAIRRO ALTO
Expensive
Tavares ⍟ PORTUGUESE/CONTINENTAL   Lisbon's oldest restaurant is a nostalgic favorite, still serving competently prepared food with flawless service. While still one of the capital's more elegant settings, it shows a little wear, but then, it's stood at the same place since it was founded in 1784. Your meal may begin with *crepes de marisco*—crepes with shellfish. Among the main course selections are sole in champagne sauce, stuffed crab, and tournedos Grand Duc. Many Continental dishes are on the menu, including classic veal Viennoise. If the prices seem too rich, climb the stairs to the second floor for a self-service meal featuring entrees from 8€ to 9€.

Rua da Misericórdia 37. ℂ 21-342-1112. Reservations required. Main courses 19€–40€; fixed-price lunch or dinner 43€–53€. AE, DC, MC, V. Mon–Fri 12:30–3pm and 7:30–11pm; Sun 7:30–11pm. Closed Sat. Bus: 15.

Moderate
Bachus ⍟ INTERNATIONAL   Enter Bachus through a handsomely outfitted bar on the ground floor and be greeted by a maitre d' who is likely to address you in English before you open your mouth. He'll usher you upstairs to the dining rooms, which use Art Moderne touches in paintings and lamps to good effect. While the restaurant is only 20 years old, the building dates to the 17th century. Foreigners are in evidence, but the place isn't besieged by tourists. Oysters and clams are as fresh as the morning, to be followed, perhaps, by the mixed grill, chateaubriand with béarnaise, or beef Stroganoff. Preparation is fail-safe conservative, but no less satisfying for that.

Largo da Trindade 8–9. ℂ 21-342-2828. Reservations recommended. Main courses 13€–20€. AE, DC, MC, V. Sun and Tues–Fri noon–3pm and 7pm–midnight; Sat 7pm–midnight. Metro: Chiado. Bus: 58.

Brasserie de L'Entrecôte STEAK   A waiter brings you the wine list and asks how you would like your meat cooked. Wine is the last decision you make, for only one meal is served here. It proceeds as follows: a light green salad, bread and butter in a basket, and filet of beef in béarnaise sauce with *frites*. The dining room has a 5.4m (18-ft.) ceiling and a bar, and high stone archways lead up stairs to a chapel-like room in back. It all has an intended Parisian feel and a crowd to match, in suits or jeans, shaggy or close-cropped hair, but with less smoking and no dogs. Despite the restricted menu, the place is packed every night. There is a very modest dessert menu. Pick the cheesecake, more a slender tart than the towering versions of New York delis.

Rua do Alecrim 117–121. ℂ 21-347-3616. Reservations recommended. Fixed-price menu 14€. AE, MC, V. Daily 12:30–3pm and 8pm–midnight (closes at 11pm Sun). Tram: 28.

Conventual ⍟ PORTUGUESE   This is a favorite of in-the-know Lisbon executives, social insiders, and fashionistas. The ecclesiastical theme implied by the name is supported by fragments from choir stalls and religious sculptures, but there's nothing monastic about the food. The owner is the diminutive, grandmotherly lady who takes your order, and she developed many of the delectably flavored recipes, often derived from cuisines of the once far-flung empire. Among the choices are a silken coriander soup, curries, partridge stewed in port, duck in champagne sauce, grilled monkfish, and stewed clams in a sauce of red peppers, onions, and cream.

Praça das Flores 45. (✆ **21-390-9196.** Reservations required. Main courses 14€–27€. AE, DC, MC, V. Mon 7:30–11pm; Tues–Fri 12:30–3:30pm and 7:30–11pm; Sat 7:30–11pm. Metro: Avenida. Bus: 100.

Stravaganza ⚘ *Kids* PIZZA/ITALIAN   Attracting mostly under-30 customers, these bright, clean-lined dining rooms avoid the usual trattoria decorative clichés, and the wood-burning oven produces some of the best pizza in town. The thin-crusted (but not cracker-crisp) pies come in small and large sizes, and the kitchen fills orders past midnight, for takeout as well as for eating in. About half the pastas and some of the pizzas are vegetarian. If Stravaganza is full, the older **Mama Rosa,** no. 14 on the same block (✆ **21-346-5350**), is a capable but somewhat more expensive substitute.

Grémio Lusitano 24 (a short walk west of Rua de São Pedro Alcântara). (✆ **21-346-8868.** Pizzas and pastas 7€–21€; other main courses 12€–18€. MC, V. Mon–Sat noon–2am. Tram: 24.

Trindade ⚘ PORTUGUESE   Open since 1836, this cavernous *cervejaria* occupies the site of the 13th-century Convento dos Frades Tinos. The 1755 earthquake leveled that building, but several rooms with arched ceilings and fine blue-and-white tile murals recall its origins. Long hours make Trindade desirable when competitors are closed, especially on Sunday and at Saturday lunch. That means the hustling waiters don't have time to engage in friendly banter, let alone smile. The kitchen does a better job with seafood than with meat. Beware the pricier items, like spiny lobsters and huge tiger shrimp. Draft beer in foot-high glasses is served as often as wine. The high ceilings of the larger rooms in back help dissipate the clouds of tobacco smoke.

Rua Nova de Trindade 20C. (✆ **21-342-3506.** Main courses 6.95€–17€. AE, DC, MC, V. Daily 9am–2am. Metro: Rossio or Chiado. Bus: 15, 20, 51, or 100.

Inexpensive

A Brasileira SANDWICHES/PASTRIES   One of Lisbon's oldest coffeehouses, A Brasileira was once a gathering place of Lisbon literati. Patrons sit at small tables on chairs made of tooled leather, amid mirrored walls and marble pilasters. The restaurant here serves basic fare like omelets, steaks, and fish. Note that you'll pay more for sandwiches and pastries in the restaurant and at the outdoor tables than in the coffee bar.

Rua Garrett 120. (✆ **21-346-9541.** Sandwiches and pastries 1.45€–4.95€; meals in restaurant 7€–28€. AE, MC, V (restaurant only). Daily 7am–11pm. Metro: Rossio.

WEST OF THE CENTER
Expensive

Café Alcântara ⚘ INTERNATIONAL   You have to see this place: Cast-iron columns and beams hold up the 7.5m (25-ft.) ceiling, and a full-size replica of the Winged Victory looms over the zigzag bar. Fans turn lazily overhead. Half the cavernous space is given to the restaurant, the rest to the drinking trade. Because the place draws a hip young crowd, it isn't unusual for patrons to show up for dinner at midnight. Diners have a wide choice of uncomplicated fare in minimalist presentations, including cold lobster salad, steak tartare, and steamed skate. There used to be an attached disco, but that's been closed indefinitely. Friday and

Saturday evenings are big, so go another night to be assured of a table. You'll need a taxi coming and going in this bleak industrial district.

Rua Maria Luisa Holstein 15. © 21-363-7176. Reservations suggested on weekends. Main courses 14€–18€. AE, DC, MC, V. Kitchen daily 4pm–1am; bar daily 8pm–3am. Bus: 57.

Cipriani ✿✿ ITALIAN   The dignified dining room of the Lapa Palace hotel has views of one of the most lavish gardens in this exclusive neighborhood, and is a favorite with diplomats from the foreign embassies and consulates nearby. Tables are at good distances from each other, and service is close to unimprovable. A la carte items are available at lunch and dinner. In the fall, that means a special white truffle menu and such autumnal specials as stuffed pheasant. Start with one of the flawless pastas. The restaurant excels at pasta—it's managed by a famous Venetian restaurant family (the full name of the room is the unnecessarily confusing "Ristorante Hotel Cipriani"). The wine list isn't extensive, but the house choices are good and are available by the glass and half-bottle.

In the Lapa Palace, Rua do Pau de Bandeira 4. © 21-395-0005. Reservations recommended. Main courses 16€–32€. AE, DC, MC, V. Daily 12:30–3:30pm and 7:30–10:30pm. Tram: 25 or 28. Bus: 13 or 27.

Sua Excelência ✿✿ PORTUGUESE   Just a block up the hill from the National Art Gallery, the restaurant has an interior resembling a provincial drawing room. Some dishes are uncommon in Portugal, often hailing from outposts of the former empire, including Angolan chicken cooked in palm oil with vegetables. Specialties include spicy prawns *piri-piri*, and *lulas a moda da casa* (squid stewed in white wine, crème fraîche, and cognac). Other possibilities include smoked swordfish and clams cooked at least five ways. One unusual specialty is "little jacks," small fish eaten whole, served with a well-flavored "paste" made from 2-day-old bread.

Rua do Conde 34. © 21-390-3614. Reservations required. Main courses 12€–17€. AE, MC, V. Mon–Tues and Thurs–Fri 1–3pm; Thurs–Tues 8–10:30pm. Closed Sept. Tram: 25. Bus: 27 or 49.

ON THE WATERFRONT
Moderate

Espalha Brasas ✿ PORTUGUESE   A few blocks of two-story marine warehouses along the western waterfront—the Ribeirinha—have been converted into restaurants and clubs. This one is among the liveliest. The barbecue in the open kitchen turns out tempting plates such as grilled marlin and skewered turbot and shrimp (with salad and baked potato). While you can put together a standard dinner from the menu, this is mainly a grazing place. But even if you order only a side of fried squid, you'll still get the usual bread, flavored butters, a round of cheese, and four types of paté. The place is much in demand on weekends, and the walk-up reservation list can mean a wait of an hour or more. Many of the staff members speak English. *Note:* Take a taxi.

Doca de Santo Amaro, Armazém 12. © 21-396-9177. Reservations recommended on weekends. Main courses 7.50€–17€; *ementa turística* 16€. AE, MC, V. Mon–Sat 12:30pm–2am. Bus: 12, 20.

Jardim do Marisco ✿ PORTUGUESE/SEAFOOD   Another product of the ongoing gentrification of the waterfront, this sprawling emporium occupies a shedlike structure several blocks east of the Praça do Comércio. Glass walls afford unobstructed views of river traffic. The first room, on the left, is the *cervejaria* (beer hall), with a long, curving bar. It serves less expensive meals than the

Native Behavior

Machismo pertains in Portugal, as in most Latin countries, but it is of a gentler, often wistful variety. Over shots of cherry *ginginha,* a man is less likely to boast of his amorous accomplishments in the bedroom last night than of the prodigious amounts of food he ingested in the dining room. While he is proud of the work he does, he concedes that the true working-class heroes are fishermen, and deep inside he thinks that fishing is what a man *should* do. And, of course, in the Portuguese *tourada*—bullfight—not only does the animal leave the ring alive, but he is encouraged to charge repeatedly into a line of men with no weapons but their bravado.

A strain of nostalgia coupled with fatalism runs deep in Portuguese culture. There is a special word for it—*saudade*—which is, as always seems true of such words, not easily translated into English. It concerns a longing melancholy, for a place, a person, a spirit, even a practice now lost. Hardly unusual for a nation of seafarers and explorers and reluctant emigrants, who are gone from their homes and loves for years or forever, it is expressed in the musical art form called *fado* (see "The Quintessential Lisbon Experience: Fado," later in this chapter). Fado is a mournful wail about loss, and ordinary people, not just professional performers, are still known to break into the sobbing lament in clubs, at fiestas, and even on street corners.

---

glossy main dining room straight ahead. Before turning into the cafe section, take a moment to walk along the fish display counter bordering the open kitchen. A specialty is *feijoada da gambas*——not the inky-black Brazilian stew full of pig parts, but a comparatively light ragout of white beans and shrimp, served with a ball of rice in a copper pan. Have the staff call a taxi when you're ready to leave, because they're hard to come by out here.

Doca Jardim do Tabaco, Avenida Infante D. Henrique. ⓒ **21-882-4242.** Main courses 5.45€–13€. AE, MC, V. Mon–Sat noon–2am. Bus: 11, 13.

Porcão ⓐ BRAZILIAN Get ready for a dinner here by skipping lunch, because what you get is a *rodizio,* a carnivore's fantasy realized. If you've yet to experience the Brazilian extravaganza of a *rodizio,* come to this converted warehouse on the waterfront for the full over-the-top treatment. After you've been seated, cruise the center sushi/cheese/salad bar—with over 30 items—then check out the nearby self-serve counter, with enough soup, sausages, rice, and beans to tide you over until the main events. On a signal, waiters march out from the kitchen bearing steaming gifts of ribs, beef, chicken, lamb, pork, kidneys, and fish. Most are on skewers, and the guys wield huge knives with controlled abandon, slicing and pushing all you want onto your plate—cascades of meat that only stop when you cry uncle. (Save room for the trolley of roast suckling pig.) They give you a paper medallion saying "No, thanks" and "Yes, please," but that's just part of the ritual. There's music every night. *Note:* Take a taxi.

Rua Cintura do Porto de Lisboa, Cais de Santos, Docas. ⓒ **21-393-2090.** Reservations suggested. Fixed-price meal 22€. AE, DC, MC, V. Tues–Sun 12:30–4pm and 7:30pm–midnight. Tram: 25.

SEEING THE SIGHTS
SIGHTSEEING SUGGESTIONS FOR FIRST-TIME VISITORS

If You Have 1 Day This is just enough time to take a walking tour of the **Alfama,** Lisbon's most colorful district. Visit the 12th-century **Sé (Cathedral)** and take in a view of the city and the River Tejo from the **Santa Luzia Belvedere.** Climb up to the **Castelo São Jorge (St. George's Castle).** Later, take a taxi or tram to **Belém** to see the **Mosteiro dos Jerónimos (Jerónimos Monastery)** and the **Torre de Belém (Tower of Belém).** Back in Lisbon proper, end your day at a **fado cafe** in the **Bairro Alto.**

If You Have 2 Days Spend the morning of day 2 at the **Museu Calouste Gulbenkian,** one of Europe's artistic treasure troves. Have lunch at a *típico* restaurant in the Bairro Alto. In the afternoon see the **Fundção Ricardo Esprito Santo (Museum of Decorative Art)** and the **Museu Nacional de Arr Antlgu (National Museum of Ancient Art).** At the day's end, wander through **Parque Eduardo VII.** That night, explore the dance clubs and bars of the waterfront.

If You Have 3 Days On day 3, head for **Sintra,** the single most visited sight in the environs— Byron called it a "glorious Eden." Spend the day here, exploring the castle and other palaces in the area. Must-sees are the **Palácio Nacional de Sintra** and the **Palácio Nacional da Pena.** Return to Lisbon for dinner.

If You Have 4 or 5 Days On day 4, take an excursion from Lisbon (perhaps an organized tour) to visit the fishing village of **Nazaré** and the walled city of **Óbidos.** On your final day, slow your pace a bit with a morning at the beach at **Estoril** on Portugal's Costa do Sol. Then continue along the coast to **Cascais** for lunch. After lunch, wander around this old fishing village, which is now a major resort. Go to **Guincho,** 6km (4 miles) along the coast from Cascais, which is near the westernmost point on the European continent and has panoramic views.

NEIGHBORHOODS

The Alfama ☆☆ Ancient Lisbon lives on in this hillside district. A wall built by the Visigoths and incorporated into some of the houses is testimony to its past. The Alfama was the Saracen sector centuries before its conquest by the Christians. Some of the buildings were spared from the devastating 1755 earthquake, and the Alfama has retained much of its original aspect—narrow cobblestone streets, cages of warbling canaries hung outside windows, housewives dropping baskets on ropes from upper stories to take delivery of food, strings of garlic and pepper beside doorways of *típico* taverns, street markets, and flower-decked balconies.

One of the best views is from the belvedere of **Largo das Portas do Sol,** near the Museum of Decorative Art. It's a balcony opening onto the sea, overlooking the tiled-front houses that sweep down to the River Tejo. One of the older churches is **Santo Estevão (St. Stephen),** at Largo de Santo Estevão. It was first built in the 13th century; the present marble structure dates from the 18th. Also of medieval origin is the **Church of São Miguel (St. Michael),** at Largo de São Miguel, deep in the Alfama on a palm-shaded square. **Rua da Judiaria (Street**

of the Jews) is another reminder of the past. It was settled largely by Jewish refugees fleeing Spain's Inquisition.

Bairro Alto 𝕮   Like the Alfama, the Bairro Alto (Upper Quarter) preserves the characteristics of an older Lisbon. It was once called the heart of the city, probably for both its location and its inhabitants. Many of its buildings survived the 1755 earthquake. Today it's the home of the most notable fado cafes and many bars and restaurants, both humble and elevated, making it a center of nightlife. The quarter is also an intriguing place to visit during the day, when its narrow cobblestone streets and alleys, lined with aged buildings, can be appreciated in the warm light coming off the sea.

From the windows and balconies, laundry hangs out to dry, and beside the windows are cages containing canaries, parrots, parakeets, and other birds. In the morning, the street scene is made up of housewives emerging from their homes to shop, following the cries of the *varinas* (fishmongers) and other food vendors.

Belém 𝕮𝕮   At Belém, the most southwestern district of Lisbon, the River Tejo meets the sea. From here, the caravels that charted the unknown oceans were launched on their missions: Vasco da Gama to India, Ferdinand Magellan to circumnavigate the globe, and Bartolomeu Dias to round the Cape of Good Hope. From these explorations, wealth flowed into Belém, especially from the spice trade with the Far East. Belém emerged from the Restelo, the point of land from which the ships set sail across the so-called Sea of Darkness. In time, the royal family established a summer palace here. Wealthy Lisboetas began moving out of the city center and building town houses, establishing the character of the district. For many years Belém was a separate municipality, but it is now incorporated into Lisbon as a parish.

THE TOP ATTRACTIONS

Castelo São Jorge 𝕮𝕮𝕮   Believed to have predated the Romans, this fortress on a hilltop was used to guard the River Tejo and the settlement below. Beginning in the 5th century A.D., the site was a Visigothic fortification; it fell in the early 8th century to Arab invaders. Many of the walls still standing were erected during the centuries of Moorish domination. The Moors were in control until 1147, when Afonso Henríques, the country's first king, pushed them out and extended his kingdom south. Even before Lisbon was made the capital of the newly emerging nation, the site was used as a royal palace. For the finest view of the Tejo and the city, walk the esplanades and climb the ramparts of the old castle, named in commemoration of an Anglo-Portuguese pact dating from as early as 1371. On the grounds, you can stroll through a setting of olive, pine, and cork trees, graced by swans and rare white peacocks.

Rua da Costa do Castelo. © **21-887-7244.** Free admission. Apr–Sept daily 9am–9pm; Oct–Mar daily 9am–6pm. Tram: 12 or 28. Bus: 37.

Mosteiro dos Jerónimos (Jerónimos Monastery) 𝕮𝕮𝕮   In an expansive mood of celebration, Manuel I, the Fortunate, ordered this monastery built in 1502 to commemorate Vasco da Gama's voyage to India and to give thanks to the Virgin Mary for its success. Manueline, the style of architecture to which the king contributed his name, combines Flamboyant Gothic and Moorish influences with elements of the nascent Renaissance. The 1755 earthquake damaged the monastery, and extensive restoration, some of it ill-conceived, was carried out. The church interior is divided into a trio of naves, noted for their fragile-looking pillars. Some of the ceilings, like those in the monks' refectory, have ribbed barrel vaults. The "palm tree" in the sacristy is exceptional.

Praça do Império. ☎ **21-362-0034.** Church free. Cloisters 3€ adults, 1.20€ seniors and ages 15–25, free for children under 15. Tues–Sun 10am–5pm (until 6pm May–Sept). Tram: 15. Bus: 28, 43, 49, 51.

Museu de Fundação Calouste Gulbenkian ✵✵✵ Opened in 1969, this museum houses the collection of Armenian oil tycoon Calouste Gulbenkian— declared by one critic "one of the world's finest private art collections." It covers Egyptian, Greek, and Roman antiquities; remarkable Islamic art; and vases, prints, and lacquerwork from China and Japan. European works include medieval illuminated manuscripts and ivories, 15th- to 19th-century painting and sculpture, 18th-century French decorative works, French Impressionist painting, and Lalique jewelry and glassware. Notable are two Rembrandts, Rubens's *Portrait of Hélène Fourment,* and Renoir's *Portrait of Madame Claude Monet.*

Avenida de Berna 45. ☎ **21-795-0236.** Admission 3€ adults; free for seniors, students, and children. Free for everyone on Sun. Tues 4–6pm; Wed–Sun 10am–6pm. Metro: São Sebastião. Bus: 16, 18, 26, 31, 42, 46, 56.

Museu Nacional de Arte Antiga (National Museum of Ancient Art) ✵ This museum has a number of notable paintings, including the famous 15th-century polyptych from St. Vincent's monastery attributed to Nuno Gonçalves.

Outstanding works are Hieronymus Bosch's triptych *The Temptation of St. Anthony;* Hans Memling's *Mother and Child;* Albrecht Dürer's *St. Jerome;* and paintings by Velázquez, Zurbarán, Poussin, and Courbet. Paintings from the 15th through the 19th centuries trace the development of Portuguese art. The museum also exhibits a remarkable collection of gold- and silversmiths' work.

Rua das Janelas Verdes 9. ℭ 21-391-2800. Admission 3€ adults, 1.50€ seniors and students, free for children under 14. Tues 2–6pm; Wed–Sun 10am–6pm. Tram: 15, 18, or 25. Bus: 27, 40, 49, or 60.

Museu Nacional dos Coches (Coach Museum) 🐨🐨

This famous collection of hundreds of aristocratic coaches and sedan chairs is ensconced, appropriately, in a former royal riding school. Some of the carriages are as long as railroad cars, decorated in a mind-boggling, excessive manner, with lashings of gilt, swags of velvet, and swirls of carvings. The oldest dates from 1581; Elisabeth II of Great Britain used the most recent, from 1824, during her 1958 state visit.

Praça Alfonso de Albuquerque. ℭ 21-361-0850. Admission 3€ adults; 1.50€ seniors, teachers, students; free for children under 14; free for everyone Sun. Tues–Sun 10am–5:30pm. Closed holidays. Tram: 15. Bus: 14, 27, 28, 43, 49, or 51.

Oceanário de Lisboa 🐨🐨 *Kids*

This world-class aquarium remains the most enduring and impressive achievement of EXPO '98 (the EXPO site has been renamed the Parque das Nações). Described as the second-biggest aquarium in the world, exceeded in size only by a facility in Osaka, Japan, it's contained within a stone and glass building whose centerpiece is a 5-million-liter (1.3-million-gallon) holding tank. Its waters are divided into four distinct ecosystems replicating the Atlantic, Pacific, Indian, and Antarctic oceans. Each is supplemented with land portions on which birds, amphibians, and reptiles flourish. Look for otters in the Pacific, penguins in the Antarctic, Polynesian trees and flowers in the Indian, and puffins, terns, and seagulls in the Atlantic.

Parque das Nações. ℭ 21-891-7002. Admission 8.50€ adults, 4.50€ seniors and children 6–17. Daily 10am–6pm (until 7pm in summer). Metro: Oriente.

ELSEWHERE IN LISBON

Monumento dos Descobrimentos (Monument of the Discoveries)

Like the prow of a caravel from the Age of Discovery, this exploration memorial stands on the Tejo, looking as if it's ready to strike out across the Sea of Darkness. Memorable explorers, chiefly Vasco da Gama, are immortalized in stone along the ramps. At the point where the two ramps meet is a representation of Henry the Navigator, whose genius opened up new worlds. One of the stone figures is that of a kneeling Philippa of Lancaster, Henry's English mother; other figures symbolize Crusaders, navigators, monks, cartographers, and cosmographers. Beneath the heroic representations of figures crucial to the country's history, the monument contains a permanent exhibition on the role of the Portuguese in exploring the world, as well as a temporary exhibition related to the Portuguese experience.

Avenida Brasilia, Belém. ℭ 21-303-1950. Admission 2€ adults, free for children under 12. Tues–Sun 9:30am–6pm. Tram: 15. Bus: 28, 29, 43, or 51.

Museu Antóniano

St. Anthony of Padua, an itinerant Franciscan monk who became Portugal's patron saint, was born in 1195 in a house that once stood here. The original church was destroyed by the 1755 earthquake, and the present building was designed by Mateus Vicente in the 18th century. In the crypt, a guide points out the spot where the saint was allegedly born (he's buried in Padua, Italy). The devout come to this little church to light candles under his picture. He's known as a protector of young brides and also has a special connection with the children of Lisbon.

Largo de Santo António de Sé. (© 21-886-9145. Admission .95€ adults; free for seniors, students, and to all on Sun. Daily 7:30am–7:30pm. Metro: Rossio. Tram: 28. Bus: 37.

Museu da Marinha (Maritime Museum) ⚓ The pageant and the glory that characterized Portugal's domination of the high seas is evoked for posterity at the Maritime Museum. Appropriately, it's installed in the west wing of the Mosteiro dos Jerónimos, which was built in celebration of Vasco da Gama's voyage. These royal galleys re-create an age of opulence that never feared excess, as exemplified by dragons' heads dripping with gilt and sea monsters coiling with abandon. The museum contains hundreds of models, from 15th-century sailing ships to 20th-century warships. In a special room is a model of the queen's stateroom on the royal yacht of Carlos I, the Bragança king who was assassinated at Praça do Comércio in 1908.

Praça do Império. (© 21-362-0019. Admission 3€ adults, 1.50€ seniors and children 6–17, free for children under 6. Tues–Sun 10am–6pm (to 5pm off season). Tram: 15. Bus: 28, 43.

Museu de Arte Popular (Folk Art Museum) This is the most dramatic exhibition of the folk arts and customs of the Portuguese. The walls of the building were painted by contemporary artists, including Carlos Botelho, Eduardo Anahory, Estréla Faria, Manuel Lapa, Paulo Ferreira, and Tomás de Melo. The 1948 opening of the Folk Art Museum was the result of António Ferro's campaign for ethnic revival. The collections—including ceramics, furniture, wickerwork, clothes, farm implements, and paintings—are displayed in five rooms that correspond more or less to the provinces, each of which maintains its distinct personality.

Avenida Brasília. (© 21-301-1282. 1.80€ adults, free for children 12 and under. Tues–Sun 10am–12:30pm and 2–5pm. Closed holidays. Tram: 15. Bus: 27, 28, 29, 43, 49, or 51.

Sé (Cathedral) ⚓ Characterized by twin towers flanking its entrance, the Sé represents an architectural wedding of Romanesque and Gothic styles, with a facade resembling a medieval fortress. When Christian Crusaders, led by Portugal's first king, Afonso Henríques, captured the city early in the 12th century, the Sé became the first church in Lisbon. It was damaged in the earthquakes of 1344 and 1755. Inside the rough exterior are many treasures, including the font where St. Anthony of Padua is said to have been christened in 1195. The cloister, built in the 14th century by King Dinis, is of Gothic ogival construction, with garlands, a Romanesque wrought-iron grille, and tombs with inscription stones. In the sacristy and Treasury Museum, you'll find marbles, relics, valuable images, and ecclesiastical treasures from the 15th and 16th centuries.

Largo da Sé. (© 21-886-6752. Cathedral, free; cloister, .50€. Mon–Sat 10am–6pm. Tram: 28 (Graça). Bus: 37.

Torre de Belém The quadrangular Tower of Belém is a monument to Portugal's Age of Discovery. Erected between 1515 and 1520, the tower is Portugal's classic landmark. It stands near the spot where the caravels once set out to sea on their courageous exploratory voyages. Its architect, Francisco de Arruda, blended Gothic and Moorish elements in what became known as the Manueline style, using such details as twisting ropes carved in stone. The coat-of-arms of

Manuel I rests above the loggia, and balconies grace three sides. Along the balustrade of the loggias, stone crosses symbolize the Portuguese crusaders.

Avenida Brasilia, Belém. ℭ 21-362-0034. Admission 3€ adults, 1.20€ seniors and students, free for children under 15. Tues–Sun 10am–6pm (until 5pm Oct–Apr). Bus: 14, 28, 43, or 53.

ORGANIZED TOURS

BY TRAM Along its entire route, **tram 28** passes through Lisbon's most picturesque neighborhoods—the Bairro Alto, Alfama, and Graça. With its swoops and sudden swift turns, it is almost as much fun as an amusement park ride.

Since 1901, trams have negotiated the intimate alleys and tight corners of Lisbon's old quarters, and they're still going strong. The city's public transport company, **Carris** (ℭ **21-358-2334**), offers a 1½-hour tram tour of historic districts and monuments, with guides and interpreters aboard. The tour departs from Praça do Comércio four times daily in July and August, twice daily in June. Tickets (sold on board) are 15€ adults and 8€ ages 4 to 10; those 3 and under ride free.

Carris also offers two tours on **double-decker buses,** allowing passengers to get on and off at any of the 16 to 18 stops along the Tejo circuit from Baixa to Belém or the Oriente circuit from the center to the Parque das Nações. Tickets cost 13€ adults and 6.50€ children 4 to 10. They're good for a full day (hang onto your ticket), and you can buy them on board. The buses leave Praça do Comércio hourly from 11:30am to 5:30pm March through October; and at 11:30am, 1:30pm, and 3:30pm November through February. Private companies offering tours in Lisbon (and to such regional destinations as Sintra, Estoril, and Queluz) are **Gray Line** (ℭ **21-352-2594**), **Cityrama** (ℭ **21-319-1091**), and **Portugal Tours** (ℭ **21-352-2902**).

THE SHOPPING SCENE

Baixa, a grid of streets dating from the 18th-century restoration of central Lisbon, is a major shopping area between the Rossio and the River Tejo. **Rua do Ouro (Street of Gold), Rua da Prata,** and **Rua Augusta** are the principal streets. Another major upscale shopping artery is **Rua Garrett,** in Chiado, the district on the hill due west of Baixa. You used to be able to reach the area by the Elevador Santa Justa, but the bridge connection is closed indefinitely. A walk up steep Rua do Carmo is now an access, along with the series of escalators that rise from the Metro station at the west end of Rua Vitoria to Rua Garret.

At the **Feira da Ladra,** an open-air flea market, vendors peddle their wares on Tuesday and Saturday; haggling is expected. Portable stalls and dropcloth displays are lined up in Campo de Santa Clara behind the Igreja São Vicente. Take bus no. 12 from the Santa Apolónia station.

For many browsers, the desirable buys are *azulejos*—hand-painted glazed tiles—and pottery from all over Portugal. Ceramics from Barcelos, decorated with brightly colored roosters, are legendary, as is the ubiquitous blue-and-white pottery made in Coimbra. From Caldas da Rainha come yellow-and-green dishes in the shapes of vegetables, fruits, and animals. Vila Real is known for its black pottery, polychrome pieces come from Aceiro, and the red-clay pots from the Alentejo region are based on designs that go back to the Etruscans.

Founded in 1741 in the Chiado district, **Sant'Anna,** Rua do Alecrim 95–97 (ℭ **21-342-2537;** Metro: Estação do Cais do Sodré), is a leading ceramics center, famous for its hand-painted glazed tiles. The showroom is on Rua do Alecrim, but you can also visit the factory at Calçada da Boa Hora 96; make an appointment by calling ✆ **21-363-3117. Vista Alegre,** Largo do Chiado 18 (✆ **21-347-5481;** Metro: Chiado), turns out some of the finest porcelain dinner services in the country, along with objets d'art and limited-edition porcelain for collectors and a range of practical day-to-day tableware.

Another good buy in Portugal is gold. Gold is strictly regulated by the government, which requires jewelers to put a minimum of 19¼ karats in the jewelry they sell. Filigree jewelry, made of fine gold or silver wire, is an art that dates from ancient times. **W. A. Sarmento,** Rua Aurea 251 (✆ **21-347-0783;** Metro: Rossio or Chiado), is the most distinguished silver- and goldsmith in Portugal, specializing in lacy filigree jewelry, including charm bracelets. Well on its way to being a century old, the **Joalharia do Carmo,** Rua do Carmo 87B (✆ **21-342-4200;** Metro: Rossio), is an important shop for gold filigree work.

MORE SELECT SHOPS   In the same building as the Hotel Avenida Palace, **Casa Bordados da Madeira,** Rua 1 de Dezembro 137 (✆ **21-342-1447;** Metro: Restauradores), offers handmade embroideries from Madeira and Viana. If you wish to place an order, the staff will mail it to you. **Madeira House,** Rua Augusta 131–135 (✆ **21-342-6813;** Metro: Chiado), specializes in high-quality regional cottons, linens, and gift items.

Adelia Almeida has the finest collection of linens in Lisbon at **Lavandaria,** 11–13 Rua Augusto Rosa (✆ **21-887-5691;** tram: 12 or 28). Much of her stock comes from Guimarães in northern Portugal, where hand weavers still work at home. Other linens are copies of 18th-century designs, including tablecloths. Look for the green-and-yellow embroidery of mimosa flowers on many of the linens.

LISBON AFTER DARK

Consult the official biweekly guide, *Follow Me Lisboa,* available at most newsstands, for the latest entertainment listings (in English). A local newspaper, *Diário de Notícias,* also carries cultural listings, but in Portuguese. Few discount tickets are offered, but students get 50% off tickets purchased for the national theater. Also of interest is *Agenda Cultural,* an English- and Portuguese-language seasonal periodical that's often available without charge at cafes, at hotels, and at the Portuguese tourist office. In it, you'll find an abbreviated listing of musical, theatrical, and cultural choices available throughout the city.

THE PERFORMING ARTS

Teatro Nacional de São Carlos, Rua Serpa Pinto 9 (✆ **21-346-8408;** tram: 12), attracts opera and ballet aficionados to performances by top companies from around the world at this 18th-century theater. The season begins in mid-September and extends through July. The box office is open daily from 1 to 7pm. Tickets run from about 15€ to 75€, depending upon seat location and attraction.

A full menu of jazz, dance, light opera, and chamber concerts is presented at the **Centro Cultural de Belém,** Praça do Império (✆ **21-361-2400;** www.ccb. pt; tram: 15). Check locally to see what's happening when you're in town. Tickets are usually 6€ to 18€.

Originally built in the 1840s and restored after a disastrous fire in 1964, the **Teatro Nacional Doña Maria II,** Plaza Dom Piedro IV (Rossio; ✆ **21-325-0800;** Metro: Rossio), ranks along with the Teatro São Carlos as one of the most

Moments The Quintessential Lisbon Experience: Fado

Fado is Portugal's most vivid folkloric art form. No visit to Lisbon is complete without at least one experience in one of the taverns where this traditional music is heard. Fado is typically sung by women, called *fadistas,* accompanied by guitar and viola. The songs express romantic longing and melancholy—*saudade,* the Portuguese sense of nostalgia for the past.

Adega Machado, Rua do Norte 91 (© **21-322-4640**; bus: 58 or 100), is still one of Portugal's favored fado clubs. Alternating with the fadistas are folk dancers in costume whirling, clapping, and singing. Dinner is a la carte, and the cuisine is Portuguese, featuring regional dishes. Expect to spend at least about 50€ for a complete meal. The dinner hour starts at 8:30pm, the first show starts at 9:15pm, and doors don't close until 3am. Cover (including two drinks) is 15.50€. The club is open from Tuesday to Sunday.

Every night at **A Severa,** Rua das Gaveas 51 (© **21-346-4006**; bus: 20 or 24), male and female singers, alternating with folk dancers, perform. In a niche is a statue honoring the club's namesake, Maria Severa, the legendary 19th-century Gypsy fadista who made fado famous. The kitchen turns out regional dishes based on recipes from the north of Portugal. Expect to spend from at least 35€ per person for a meal with wine. Cover (including two drinks) is 18€ and the club is open Friday through Wednesday from 8pm to 3:30am.

Seemingly every fadista worth her shawl has sung at the old-time **Parreirinha da Alfama,** Beco do Espirito Santo 1 (© **21-886-8209**; bus: 39 or 46), just a minute's walk from the docks of the Alfama. It's fado only here, open daily from 8pm to 2am; music begins at 9:30pm. In the first part of the program, fadistas get all the popular songs out of the way, then settle into their more classic favorites. An average dinner goes for about 35€, although many visitors come here just for a drink. Cover, including a drink, is 10€.

important cultural venues in Lisbon. Despite being funded by the Ministry of Culture, it does not limit its repertoire to just Portuguese-language productions, although those are the most common. Tickets are about 20€. Students with a valid ID get a 50% discount.

From October to June, jazz and other concerts, plus recitals and occasional ballet shows, are performed at the **Museu de Fundação Calouste Gulbenkian,** Avenida de Berna 45 (© **21-782-3000;** Metro: Sebastião; bus: 16, 18, 26, 31, 42, 46, or 56). Inquire locally about what is happening at the time of your visit.

BARS

Bachus (p. 807), Largo da Trindade 9 (© **21-342-2828;** bus: 58 or 100), is both a restaurant and a convivial watering spot. Amid Oriental carpets, fine hardwoods, bronze statues, and intimate lighting, mingle with some of Lisbon's stylish people. The array of drinks is international, starting at 3€. Bachus is open daily from noon to midnight. There's no cover.

A longtime favorite of journalists, politicians, and actors, the once-innovative **Procópio Bar,** Alto de San Francisco 21A (ⓒ **21-385-28-51;** bus: 9), has become a tried-and-true staple. It might easily become your favorite bar—if you can find it. It lies just off Rua de João Penha, which itself is near the landmark Praça das Amoreiras. It's open Monday through Saturday from 6pm to 3am. Mixed drinks start at 4.25€, while a beer begins at 3€. There's no cover. It's open Monday through Friday from 6pm to 3am, Saturday from 9pm to 3am; closed August 1 to 15.

It would take an appraiser years to catalog the stuff filling the walls and ceilings of the **Pavilhão Chinês Bar,** Dom Pedro V 89 (ⓒ **21-342-4729;** tram: 28). An often-kitschy collection of toys, collectibles, and oddities packs several rooms. The main bar has a lovely marquetry top, a touch of class amid the rows of souvenir plates, armies of tin soldiers, bronze Cupids, cartoons of the Great War antagonists, gobs and gaggles of Victoriana, cases of Toby jugs, ceramics of Buddha, Hussars . . . and Popeye. Martini olives are skewered with hand-carved toothpicks. There are two billiard tables and another bar in a rear room. It's open Monday through Friday from 5pm to 2am, Saturday from 6pm to 2am.

Panorama Bar, Rua Latino Coelho 1 (ⓒ **21-357-5757;** Metro: Picos), occupies the top floor of the Hotel Lisboa Sheraton. The view sweeps across the old and new cities, the River Tejo, and the towns on the river's far bank. A polite uniformed staff serves you amid a decor of chiseled stone and stained glass. Mixed drinks cost 7€ to 10€. The bar is open daily from 6pm to 2am.

It's also a restaurant (p. 808), but many people come to the **Café Alcântara,** Rua Maria Luisa Holstein 15 (ⓒ **21-363-7176;** bus: 12 or 18), for its bar. Long and curvy, it has a full-size replica of the *Winged Victory of Samothrace* rearing above it. It's open nightly from 8pm to 3am; there's no cover.

PORT WINE TASTING   A bar devoted exclusively to the drinking and enjoyment of port in all its known types, **Solar do Vinho do Porto,** Rua de São Pedro de Alcântara 45 (ⓒ **21-347-5707;** bus: 58 or 100), is at the edge of the Bairro Alto. Owned by the Port Wine Institute, the facility displays many artifacts related to the industry. But the real reason for dropping in is its *lista de vinhos*—there are more than 200 wines from which to choose. Solar is across the street from the upper terminus of the Gloria funicular. It's open Monday through Saturday from 2pm to midnight. A glass of wine costs from as little as 1€ to as much as 45€ for a rare vintage.

LIVE-MUSIC CLUBS

Fusion jazz and mainstream are featured at the appropriately named **Hot Clube de Portugal,** Praça da Alegria 39 (ⓒ **21-346-7369;** Metro: Avenida), a smoky subterranean dive. This is one of the city's best jazz clubs, attracting a wide age group from 18 to 50. A beer costs 2.50€, and the cover is 2.50€ to 8€.

Havana, Doca de Santo Amaro, Armazem 5 (ⓒ **21-397-9893;** Metro: Alcântara), brings the Cuban music craze sweeping Europe to Lisbon. Decorated accordingly, it is both a bar and a restaurant. Of course it plays salsa, but it also plays pop and dance tunes. Palm trees and ceiling fans evoke the Havana of Hemingway days. Most of the patrons are in the 25-to-40 age range. The food is pretty good. Havana is open daily from noon to 2am (bar daily midnight–4am). There's no cover.

Salsa Latina, Gare Maritima de Alcântara, Docas (ⓒ **21-395-0550;** bus: 12 and 20), rocks with Latino rhythms, everything from its namesake salsa to the tango and mambo that evoke 1940s movies starring Carmen Miranda. Some nights the music is recorded; at other times the club vibrates to the sound of live acts. The cover for the bar is 8€ to 12€. The restaurant is open Tuesday through Saturday from 8 to 11:30pm, the bar the same days from 10:30pm to 6:30am.

THE PORTUGUESE RIVIERA: EXCURSIONS ALONG THE COSTA DO SOL

Lisbon's environs are most appealing, and at least 2 or 3 days should be budgeted to take them in. At minimum, your tour should incorporate the former fishing port of Cascais, the headlands at Guincho, and Lord Byron's "glorious Eden" of Sintra. If you have more time, add in the wonders of the pink rococo palace at Queluz or check out the casino or golf at Estoril.

The **Costa do Sol** 𝕗𝕗𝕗 is the string of beach resorts that forms the Portuguese Riviera, along the northern bank of the mouth of the Tejo, west of Lisbon. Many visitors choose to stay in seaside hotels in Estoril or Cascais, near enough to Lisbon to dart in and out of the capital to see the sights or visit the fado clubs. An inexpensive electric train leaving from the Cais do Sodré in Lisbon makes the trip frequently throughout the day and evening, ending its run in Cascais.

Do ride out on the train, even if you don't plan to stay there. Along the way, you'll pass pastel-washed houses with tile roofs and facades of antique blue-and-white *azulejos;* miles of modern apartment blocks; rows of pine, mimosa, and eucalyptus; and, in the background, green hills studded with villas, chalets, and housing developments. The "Sun Coast" is sometimes known as the Costa dos Reis, the "Coast of Kings," because of all the members of Europe's deposed royalty who settled here over the last 60 years—exiled kings, pretenders, marquesses from Italy, princesses from Russia, baronesses from Germany.

ESTORIL 𝕗   The first stop is 24km (15 miles) west of Lisbon. This once-chic resort has long basked in its reputation as a playground of monarchs. The **Parque Estoril,** in the town center, is a well-manicured piece of landscaping, a subtropical setting with plants and stands of palm swaying in the breeze. At night, when it's floodlit, you can go for a stroll. At the top of the park sits the **casino,** which offers not only gambling but international floor shows, dancing, and movies.

Across the railroad tracks is the **beach,** where fashionable men and women sun themselves on peppermint-striped canvas chairs along the Tamariz Esplanade. The atmosphere is cosmopolitan and the beach is sandy, unlike the pebbly strand found at Nice. If you don't want to swim in the polluted ocean, you can check in at an oceanfront pool for a plunge.

CASCAIS 𝕗   Just 6km (4 miles) west of Estoril and 30km (19 miles) west of Lisbon, Cascais has more of a Portuguese atmosphere than Estoril, even though it has been increasingly overbuilt. Apartment houses, new hotels, and some of the best restaurants along the Costa do Sol draw a never-ending stream of visitors every year.

Even so, commercial fishermen still set out in their boats each day and return to the beach with their catches. Auctions of their bounty, called *lotas,* take place on the main square, though a modern hotel has sprouted up in the background. In the small harbor, rainbow-colored fishing boats share space with pleasure craft owned by an international set that flocks to Cascais from early spring until autumn.

The most popular excursion outside Cascais is to the **Boca de Inferno (Mouth of Hell)** ⚔. Reached by heading out on the highway to Guincho, then turning left toward the sea, the Boca deserves its ferocious reputation. Thundering waves sweep in with such power that they long ago carved a wide hole in the cliffs. However, if you should arrive when the sea is calm, you'll certainly wonder why it's called the Mouth of Hell. This place can be a windswept roaring attraction if you don't stumble over too many souvenir hawkers.

The three sandy **beaches** at Cascais are almost as overcrowded as those at Estoril, but the waters here are said to be less polluted. Still, hotel pools remain the safer choice. Though there's a dangerous undertow, the best beach—at least from the standpoint of lying on the sand—is Praia do Guincho, around Cabo da Roca, right outside Cascais. The beach has dunes, and is relatively uncrowded and pollution-free. The Continental winds make it a favorite of surfers.

QUELUZ ⚔⚔   From the Estação Rossio in Lisbon, take the Sintra-line train 15km (9 miles) northwest to Queluz. Trains depart every 15 minutes (trip time: 30 min.). After leaving the train station in Queluz, take a left turn and follow the signs to the **Palácio de Queluz** ⚔, Largo do Palácio (© **21-435-0039**), a brilliant example of the rococo style in Portugal. Pedro III ordered its construction in 1747, and the work dragged on until 1787. What you see now isn't exactly what you would have seen in the 18th century. Queluz suffered a lot during the French invasions, and almost all of its belongings were transported to Brazil with the royal family. A 1934 fire destroyed a great deal of Queluz, but tasteful reconstruction has restored the lighthearted aura of the 18th century. Inside, you can wander through the queen's dressing room, lined with painted panels depicting a children's romp; the Don Quixote Chamber (Dom Pedro was born here and returned from Brazil to die in the same bed); the Music Room, complete with a French grand pianoforte and an 18th-century English harpsichord, and the mirrored Throne Room adorned with crystal chandeliers. The palace is open Wednesday through Monday (except holidays) from 10am to 5pm. Admission is 4€. It's always free for anyone under 12, and there's free general admission every Sunday morning.

SINTRA ⚔⚔⚔   Sintra, 29km (18 miles) northwest of Lisbon, is a 45-minute train ride from the Estação Rossio in Lisbon. Lord Byron called it a "glorious Eden," and so it remains. Visitors flock here not only to absorb the town's beauty and scenic setting but also to visit two major sights.

Opening onto the central town square, the **Palácio Nacional de Sintra** ⚔⚔, Largo da Rainha D. Amélia (© **21-923-0085**), was a royal palace until 1910. Much of it was constructed in the days of Manuel the Fortunate. The palace's two conical chimney towers are the most distinctive landmarks on the Sintra skyline. The Swan Room was a favorite of João I, one of the founding kings of the Aviz dynasty, father of Henry the Navigator, and husband of Philippa of Lancaster. The Room of the Sirens or Mermaids is one of the most elegant in the palace. In the Heraldic or Stag Room, coats-of-arms of aristocratic Portuguese families and hunting scenes are depicted. The palace is rich in paintings and Iberian and Flemish tapestries. But it's at its best when you wander into the tree- and plant-shaded patio and listen to the fountain. Admission is 4€ adults, half price for children 6 to 16, free for children under 6. The palace is open Thursday through Tuesday from 10am to 1pm and 2 to 5pm.

Towering over Sintra, the **Palácio Nacional da Pena** ✦✦, Estrada de Pena (© 21-923-0227), sits on a plateau about 450m (1,500 ft.) above sea level. At the top, the castle is a soaring agglomeration of towers, cupolas, and battlements. Crossing a drawbridge, you'll enter the palace proper, whose last royal occupant was Queen Amélia in 1910. Pena has remained much as Amélia left it, which is part of its fascination; it emerges as a rare record of European royal life in the halcyon days preceding World War I. Admission is 4€, free for children under 15. The palace is open October through May, Tuesday through Sunday from 10am to 5:30pm (last admittance at 5pm); June through September, Tuesday through Sunday from 10am to 6:30pm (last admittance 6pm).

2 The Algarve

The Algarve region, at the southwesternmost corner of Europe, is the nation's foremost resort destination. Its coast stretches 160km (100 miles)—all the way from Henry the Navigator's Cape St. Vincent to the border town of Vila Real de Santo António. The varied shore contains sluggish estuaries, sheltered lagoons, low-lying areas where the cluck of the marsh hen can be heard, long sandy spits, and promontories jutting into the whitecapped ocean. Called Al-Gharb by the Moors, the land south of the *serras* (hills) of Monchique and Caldeirão remains a spectacular anomaly that seems more like a transplanted section of North Africa. Inland, nudging the heavily developed shore, the countryside is heavily cultivated with groves of almonds, lemons, oranges, carobs, pomegranates, and figs.

Phoenicians, Greeks, Romans, Visigoths, Moors, and Christians all touched this land. A distinct Arabic flavor prevails in the region's fretwork chimneys, mosquelike cupolas, and whitewashed houses, and some Moorish and even Roman ruins remain. However, much of the historic flavor is gone forever, swallowed by the swarms of dreary high-rise apartment blocks surrounding most towns. Many former fishing villages, now summer resorts, dot the Algarvian coast: Carvoeiro, Albufeira, Olhão, Portimão. The Atlantic and nearby Mediterranean remain primary sources of life, as they always have been. The marketplaces in the villages sell mats made of *esparto* (a long, coarse grass), copperwork, pottery, and almond and fig sweets that are sometimes shaped like birds and fish.

Both Lagos and Faro make logical home bases, with ample lodging choices, railroad and air connections with Lisbon, and an easy driving range to all the likely destinations along the coast. From Lagos, the road 34km (21 miles) west to Sagres (N-125) generally has minor traffic, while a limited-access highway, the IP1, runs across two-thirds of the region to the Spanish border near Monte Gordo.

LAGOS ✦

Known to the Lusitanians and Romans as Locobriga and to the Moors as Zawaia, Lagos developed as a town dedicated to shipbuilding during the time of Henry the Navigator. Edged by the Costa do Ouro (Golden Coast), the Bay of Sagres at one point in its epic history was big enough to allow 407 warships to maneuver with ease. A port city that has traced its origins back to the Carthaginians, 3 centuries before the birth of Christ, Lagos was well known by the sailors of Admiral Nelson's fleet.

The principal reasons to go to Lagos are to enjoy the pleasures of the table and the beach. Even in winter, the almond blossoms match the whitecaps on the

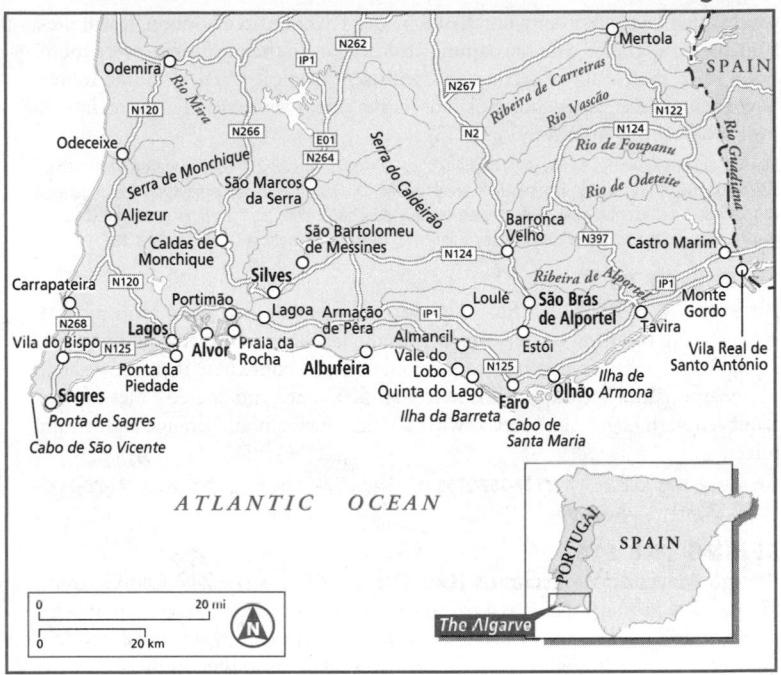

water and the climate is often warm enough for sunbathing. In town, a flea market sprawls through narrow streets, with vendors selling rattan baskets, earthenware pottery, fruits, vegetables, crude furniture, cutlery, knitted shawls, and leather boots.

Just down the coast, the rocky headland of the **Ponta da Piedade (Point of Piety)** ⚔ appears. This is arguably the most beautiful spot on the entire coast. Amid the colorful cliffs and secret grottoes carved by the waves are flamboyant examples of Manueline architecture.

ESSENTIALS
GETTING THERE By Ferry & Train From Lisbon's Praça do Comércio, take the ferry across the Tagus to Barreiro. The railroad station is only a short distance away, where the connection can be made with the Southern Line Railway on its run to Faro (𝒞 **21-206-4630** for information). Three trains per day depart from Lisbon (trip time: 6½ hr.). Tickets cost from 10€ one-way.

By Bus Eight **Rodoviária** buses (𝒞 **21-357-7715**) a day make the run between Lisbon and Lagos (trip time: 5 hr.) at a cost of 14€ one-way.

By Car Take N-120 south of Lisbon to Lagos.

VISITOR INFORMATION The **Lagos Tourist Office** is at Rua Vasco da Gama (𝒞 **28-276-3031**).

WHERE TO STAY
Tivoli Lagos ⚔ This is a 20th-century castle of Moorish and Portuguese design, with its own ramparts and moats. Standing at the eastern side of the old town, far removed from the beach, this first-class hotel is spread over a hilltop

overlooking Lagos. Recently purchased by the Tivoli chain of Lisbon, it will presumably be upgraded over the coming year or two. In the meantime, every room has a view, even if it's of a courtyard with semitropical greenery. Some rooms have ground-level patios, but most are on the upper six floors. The hotel has its own beach club a mile away.

Rua António Crisógono dos Santos, 8600 Lagos. © 28-279-0079. Fax 28-279-0345. www.tivolihotels.com. 324 units. 70€–149€ double. Rates include breakfast. AE, DC, MC, V. Free parking outside; 6€ in garage. **Amenities:** 2 restaurants; 2 bars; cafe; heated outdoor pool and indoor pool; 2 tennis courts; health club; game rooms; limited room service; same-day laundry/dry cleaning. *In room:* A/C, TV, hair dryer, safe.

WHERE TO DINE

Alpendre *☆* PORTUGUESE   Alpendre offers one of the most sophisticated menus along the Algarve, but considering the lackluster competition, that's not saying too much. Service tends to be slow, so don't come here if you're rushed. House specialties include shellfish rice, steak Diane, and sautéed filet of sole flambéed with cognac and served with a sauce of cream and orange and lemon juices.

Rua António Barbosa Viana 17. © **28-262-2705.** Reservations recommended. Main courses 7.60€–21€. AE, DC, MC, V. Daily noon–11pm.

SEEING THE SIGHTS

Antigo Mercado de Escravos (Old Customs House)   The Old Customs House, now in ruins, stands as a painful reminder of the age of exploration. The arcaded slave market, the only one of its kind in Europe, looks peaceful today, but under its four Romanesque arches captives taken from their homelands were sold to the highest bidders. The house opens onto a peaceful square dominated by a statue of Henry the Navigator.

Praça Infante Dom Henríques. No phone. Free admission. Open for viewing any time.

Igreja de Santo António (Church of St. Anthony) *☆*   Just off the waterfront sits this 18th-century church. Of special note are the rococo gilt carvings of the altar. They were damaged in the 1755 earthquake but subsequently restored. What you see represents the work of many artisans—at times, each apparently pursuing a different theme.

Rua General Alberto Silveira. © **28-276-2301.** Admission 1.65€. Tues–Sun 9:30am–12:30pm and 2–5pm.

Museu Municipal Dr. José Formosinho (Municipal Museum)   Replicas of the fret-cut chimneys of the Algarve are on view, along with three-dimensional cork carvings, 16th-century vestments, ceramics, 17th-century embroidery, ecclesiastical sculpture, a painting gallery, weapons, minerals, and a coin collection. In the archaeological wing are Neolithic artifacts, as well as Roman mosaics found at Boca do Rio near Budens, fragments of statuary and columns, and other remains of antiquity from excavations along the Algarve.

Rua General Alberto Silveira (connected to the Igreja de Santo António, above). © **28-276-2301.** Admission 1.65€. Tues–Sun 9:30am–12:30pm and 2–5pm. Closed holidays.

PLAYING GOLF

Parque da Floresta, Budens, Vale do Poco, 8650 Vila do Bispo (© **282-69-0054**), lies 16km (10 miles) west of Lagos, just inland from the fishing hamlet of Salema. Designed by Spanish architect Pepe Gancedo and built as the centerpiece of a complex of holiday villas, it offers sweeping views. Some shots must be driven over vineyards and others over ravines, creeks, and gardens. Critics of the course have cited its rough grading and rocky terrain. Greens fees are 49€ to 70€.

Some 4km (2½ miles) west of Lagos is the par-71 **Palmares** course (*C* **28-276-2961**), designed by Frank Pennink with many differences in altitude. Some fairways require driving a ball across railroad tracks, over small ravines, or around groves of palm, fig, and almond trees. The view from the 17th green is among the most dramatic of any golf course on the Algarve. Greens fees are 46€ to 75€, depending on the season.

SAGRES 🏖🏖: "THE END OF THE WORLD"

At the extreme southwestern corner of Europe—once called *o fim do mundo* (the end of the world)—Sagres is a rocky escarpment jutting into the Atlantic Ocean. It was from here that Henry the Navigator, the Infante of Sagres, launched Portugal and the rest of Europe on the seas of exploration. Here he established his school of navigation, where Magellan, Diaz, Cabral, and even Vasco da Gama apprenticed. Henry died in 1460, before the great discoveries of Columbus and Vasco da Gama, but the later explorers owed a lot to him. A virtual ascetic, he brought together the best navigators, cartographers, geographers, scholars, sailors, and builders, infused them with his rigorous devotion, and methodically set Portuguese caravels upon the Sea of Darkness.

ESSENTIALS

GETTING THERE   By Bus   Some 10 **Rodoviária** buses (*C* **28-276-2944**) per day head west from Lagos to Sagres (trip time: 1 hr.). A one-way ticket costs 2.50€.

By Car   From Lagos, drive west on N-125 to Vila do Bispo, then head south along N-268 to Sagres.

VISITOR INFORMATION   A rudimentary **tourist office** is at Rua Commandante Matoso (*C* **28-262-4873**); it observes unpredictable hours.

WHERE TO STAY

Da Baleeira   The name means "whaleboat" in Portuguese, and the hotel occupies the edge of a cliff above the fishing port. The largest hotel on this land projection, it offers rooms with balconies. The hotel has nearly doubled the number of its rooms in recent years; the older ones are quite small and some have linoleum floors. Bathrooms are also tiny, so check the proffered room before accepting. If you're in Sagres just for the day, you can still use the dining room. Cantilevered toward the sea, every seat has a view.

Sítio da Baleeira, Vila do Bispo, 8650 Sagres. *C* **28-262-4212**. Fax 28-262-4425. 121 units. 41€–139€ double. Rates include breakfast. AE, DC, MC, V. Free parking. **Amenities:** Restaurant; bar; limited room service; laundry/dry cleaning. *In room:* TV, safe.

Pousada do Infante 🏖   Built in 1960, this glistening white-painted government-owned inn is the best address in the area. Behind a long colonnade of arches is an extended stone terrace above the crashing surf. The public areas are generously proportioned, gleaming with marble and decorated with fine tapestries depicting the exploits of Henry the Navigator. On the second floor are midsize rooms with private balconies. Room nos. 1 to 12 are the most desirable. Every copper pot, candlestick, and chair is in its perfect place, and every corner is scrubbed clean—giving rise on occasion to the remarkable complaint that it is sterile in appearance. Nonsense. At the very least, stop by for a leisurely meal.

Ponta da Atalaia, 8650 Sagres. ⓒ **282-624-222.** Fax 28-262-4222. www.pousadas.pt. 39 units. 94€–148€ double; from 104€ suite. Rates include breakfast. AE, DC, MC, V. Free parking. **Amenities:** Restaurant; bar; outdoor pool; tennis court; limited room service; laundry service. *In room:* A/C, TV, minibar.

WHERE TO DINE

Fortaleza do Belixe PORTUGUESE/INTERNATIONAL   Set on a stretch of the coastal road between Sagres and southwestern Cabo de São Vicente, this establishment occupies the much-restored remnants of a medieval fortress built around the time of Henry the Navigator. The menu offerings are simple, straightforward, and flavorful, and include such items as *caldo verde* soup; fried or grilled squid; grilled swordfish; uncomplicated preparations of veal, pork, and beef; and whatever fresh fish was available that morning at the local market.

In addition to its restaurant, the establishment maintains a quartet of rooms, each with TV. With breakfast included, doubles cost 78€ to 89€.

Fortaleza do Belixe, Vila do Bispo, 8650 Sagres. ⓒ **28-262-4124.** Main courses 5.65€–21€; fixed-price menu 20€. AE, MC, V. Daily 1–3pm and 7:30–9:30pm. Closed Nov 20–Jan 20. From Sagres, drive west for 5km (3 miles) along the coastal road, following the signs to Cabo de São Vicente.

EXPLORING THE AREA

Both the Cabo de São Vicente and Sagres (especially from the terrace of the Pousada) offer unobstructed views of sunsets over the Atlantic. To the ancient world, the cape was the last explored point, although in time the Phoenicians pushed beyond it. Many mariners thought that when the sun sank beyond the cape, it plunged over the edge of the world, and thus to venture around the promontory was to face the demons of the unknown.

Today, at the reconstructed site of Henry's windswept fortress on Europe's land's end, is a huge stone compass dial, Venta de Rosa, that Henry is alleged to have used in the naval studies pursued at Sagres. Housed in the fortress is a small museum of minor interest that documents some of the area's history. Admission is 1.35€, and it's open Tuesday through Sunday from 10am to noon and 2 to 6pm. At a simple chapel, restored in 1960, sailors are said to have prayed for help before setting out into uncharted waters. The chapel is closed to the public.

The promontory of **Cabo de São Vicente** ✦✦ is 5km (3 miles) away. According to legend, the body of St. Vincent arrived mysteriously here on a boat guided by ravens, hence the name. Others claim that the body of the patron saint, murdered at Valencia, Spain, washed up on Lisbon's shore. A lighthouse, the second most powerful in Europe, beams light 100km (60 miles) across the ocean. It's generally open daily from 8am to noon and 2 to 9pm, but you must get permission from the gatekeeper to climb it. Here, seagulls glide on the air currents, and on the approach, a few goats graze on a hill where even the trees are bent from the gusty winds.

No buses connect the cape with Sagres. You must go by car.

OUTDOOR ACTIVITIES

BEACHES   Many beaches fringe the peninsula—some attracting nude bathers. **Mareta,** at the bottom of the road leading from the center of town toward the water, is not only the best, but the most popular. Rock formations can be seen jutting far out into the Atlantic. East of town is **Tonel,** also a good sandy beach. The beaches west of town, **Praia de Baleeira** and **Praia de Martinhal,** are better for windsurfing than for swimming.

EXPLORING   If you'd like to rent a **bike** to explore the cape, go to **Turinfo,** Praça da República in Sagres (② **28-262-0003**). The charge is 6€ per half day. Turinfo also offers **Jeep tours** of the natural preserve on the cape, including lunch, at a cost of 36€.

PRAIA DA ROCHA

En route to Praia da Rocha, off N-125 between Lagos and Portimão, 18km (11 miles) away, you'll find several good beaches and rocky coves, particularly at **Praia dos Três Irmãos** and **Alvor.** But the most popular seaside resort on the Algarve is the creamy yellow beach of Praia da Rocha. At the outbreak of World War II there were only two small hotels on the Red Coast, but nowadays Praia da Rocha is booming, as many have been enchanted by the spell cast by its shoreline and climate.

The area is named Praia da Rocha, the "Beach of the Rock," because of its sculptural rock formations. At the end of the mussel-encrusted cliff, where the Arcade flows into the sea, are the ruins of the **Fort of St. Catarina,** whose location offers many views of Ferragudo (the village adjacent to Portimão) and of the bay.

To reach Praia da Rocha from Portimão, you can catch a bus for the 2.5km (1½-mile) trip south. Service is frequent. Algarve buses aren't numbered but are marked by their final destination, such as PRAIA DA ROCHA.

WHERE TO STAY

Algarve Casino ℱ   Over 32 years old, with a decor that became retro simply because the owners didn't change anything except the TV sets (dig the quilted telephone alcoves next to the dining room), this relative old-timer nevertheless delivers on many levels. Its rooms are of substantial size, with the extra storage space expected by guests staying for a week or more, and many have balconies overlooking the water. The piano bar is a calming retreat before dinner in one of three restaurants, and the attached casino is a major attraction and offers floor shows and live lounge music. Outside is a long, wide beach of hard-packed sand suitable for jogging, gardens to stroll around, and two outdoor pools. Few conveniences are neglected here.

A. Tómas Cabreira, Praia da Rocha, 8500 Portimão. ② **28-241-5001.** Fax 28-241-5999. 208 units. 90€–222€ double; from 268€ suite. Rates include breakfast. AE, DC, MC, V. Free parking outside; garage available. **Amenities:** 3 restaurants; 3 bars; 2 outdoor pools; access to 8 nearby golf courses; 2 tennis courts; fitness room with sauna and massage; children's program (June–Sept); 24-hr. room service; babysitting; same-day laundry/dry cleaning; nonsmoking rooms. *In room:* A/C, TV, minibar, hair dryer, safe.

Bela Vista   An artfully rustic Mudéjar-style mansion built as a summer home by a wealthy 19th-century family, Bela Vista is set atop its own palisade, with access to a sandy cove where you can swim. The villa is ideal for those who respond to the architecture of the past and those who make a reservation way in advance. The entry hall has an Art Nouveau bronze torchier and a winding staircase. Rooms facing the sea, the former master bedrooms, are the most desirable, though all the rooms have character. Decorations vary from an inset tile shrine to the Virgin Mary to crystal sconces.

Avenida Tómas Cabreira, Praia da Rocha, 8500 Portimão. ② **28-245-0480.** Fax 28-241-5369. www@hotel belavista.net. 16 units. 50€–80€ double; from 97€ suite. Rates include breakfast. AE, DC, MC, V. Free parking. **Amenities:** Bar; limited room service; laundry service. *In room:* TV, minibar, hair dryer.

WHERE TO DINE

Titanic INTERNATIONAL   Complete with gilt and crystal, the air-conditioned Titanic, a couple of blocks from the beach, is the most elegant restaurant in town. From its open kitchen, it sends forth superior shellfish and flambé dishes. Dine well on fish of the day, pork filet with mushrooms, prawns *à la plancha,* and sole Algarve. Service is among the best at the resort.

Edifício Colúmbia, Rua Engenheiro Francisco Bivar. ℂ **28-242-2371.** Reservations recommended, especially in summer. Main courses 9.30€–23€. AE, DC, MC, V. Daily 7pm–midnight. Closed Nov 27–Dec 27.

PLAYING GOLF

Vale de Pinta (Pestana Golf), Praia do Carvoeiro (ℂ **28-234-0900**), are twin par-72 courses, sharing a clubhouse and staff. They're set amid a landscape of tawny rocks and arid hillocks, and they route their players through groves of twisted olive, almond, carob, and fig trees. Views from the fairways, designed in 1992 by Californian Ronald Fream, sweep over the low masses of the Monchique mountains, close to the beach resort of Carvoeiro. Experts cite the layouts of these two courses as some of the most varied sets of challenges in the competitive world of Portuguese golf. Clusters of bunkers, barrier walls, and abrupt changes in elevation make the course complicated. Greens fees are 45€ to 64€.

PRAIA DOS TRÊS IRMÃOS & ALVOR 🏖🏖

You can visit **Praia dos Três Irmãos (Beach of the Three Brothers)** for its beach, even if you prefer not to stay overnight. It's just a 5km (3-mile) drive southwest of Portimão, or you can reach it (or the tourist development at Alvor) by bus. Service is frequent throughout the day. At Praia dos Três Irmãos, you'll find 14km (9 miles) of golden sand, broken only by an occasional crag riddled with arched passages. Snorkelers and scuba divers have discovered this beach and enjoy exploring its undersea grottoes and shoreside cave.

Praia dos Três Irmãos's neighbor is the whitewashed fishing village of **Alvor,** where Portuguese and Moorish arts and traditions have mingled since the Arabs gave up their 500 years of occupation. Alvor was a favorite coastal haunt of João II. The summer hordes descend on the long strip of sandy beach here. It's not the best beach in the area, but at least you'll have ample space.

WHERE TO STAY

Le Meridien Penina 🏖🏖🏖   The first deluxe hotel on the Algarve between Portimão and Lagos continues to be a major sporting mecca. Most rooms contain picture windows and honeycomb balconies, with views of the golf course and pool or vistas of the Monchique hills. Standard rooms are spacious and contain good-size Portuguese provincial spool beds; the so-called attic rooms have the most charm, with French doors opening onto terraces. Facilities include three championship golf courses (one 18-hole and two 9-hole) and a private beach.

Penina, 8502 Portimão. ℂ **800/645-5687** in the U.S. and Canada, or 800/28-2502 in Europe. www.lemeridian-penina.com. 213 units. 137€–241€ double; from 294€ suite. Children 1–11 stay free in parent's room. Rates include breakfast. AE, DC, MC, V. Free parking. **Amenities:** 4 restaurants; 2 bars; outdoor pool; 3 golf courses; 5 tennis courts; health club with sauna; children's programs; game room; concierge; car-rental desk; salon; 24-hr. room service; massage; babysitting; same-day laundry/dry cleaning; nonsmoking rooms. *In room:* A/C, TV w/pay movies, minibar, hair dryer, safe.

Pestana Carlton Alvor 🏖🏖   On a landscaped hillcrest, this citadel of hedonism is so self-contained that you may never stray from the premises. Rooms are decorated in a classically modern style, and most contain oversize beds. Many have private balconies where guests can eat breakfast with a view of the Bay of Lagos. Avoid those in the rear with so-so views, small balconies, and Murphy beds. The bi-level main dining room boasts three glass walls so every guest has an ocean view. The beach is accessible by elevator. Horseback riding and water-skiing are just some of the offered activities.

Praia dos Três Irmãos, Alvor, 8500 Portimão. (C) 28-240-0900. Fax 28-240-0999. www.pestana.com. 198 units. 131€–241€ double; from 271€ suite. Rates include breakfast. AE, DC, MC, V. Free parking. Amenities: 3 restaurants; bar; outdoor pool; 7 tennis courts; access to nearby health club; sauna; bike rental; concierge; car-rental desk; salon; 24-hr. room service; massage; babysitting; same-day laundry/dry cleaning (Mon–Fri). In room: A/C, TV, minibar, hair dryer, safe.

WHERE TO DINE

O Búzio INTERNATIONAL   This restaurant stands at the end of a road that encircles a resort development dotted with exotic shrubbery. Lunch and dinner are served in separate locations. Your dinner might include fish soup, gazpacho, *carre de borrego Serra da Estrela* (gratinéed roast lamb with mustard), Italian pasta, or lamb kabobs with saffron-flavored rice. The wine cellar is extensive.

Aldeamento da Prainha, Praia dos Três Irmãos. (C) 28-240-1948. Reservations recommended. Main courses 7.60€–18€. AE, DC, MC, V. Daily 6–10:30pm. Closed Dec.

PLAYING GOLF

Penina, Apartado 146 ((C) 28-242-0200), lies 5km (3 miles) west of Portimão, farther west than many of the other great golf courses of the Algarve. Completed in 1966, it was one of the first courses built in the area. It is the acknowledged masterpiece of British designer Sir Henry Cotton. It occupies what was once a network of marshy rice paddies, on level terrain that critics said was unsuited for anything except wetlands. The solution involved planting groves of eucalyptus (350,000 trees in all), which grew quickly in the muddy soil, eventually drying it out enough to bulldoze dozens of water traps and a labyrinth of fairways and greens. The course wraps itself around a luxury hotel (Le Meridien Penina, reviewed above). Greens fees are 64€ to 96€.

ALBUFEIRA 🛪

This cliffside town, once a fishing village, is the St-Tropez of the Algarve. Sunshine, beaches, and the lazy days they inspire make it a haven for young people and artists, though local old-timers still regard the tourist invasion that began in the late 1960s with ambivalence. Some residents open the doors of their cottages to those seeking a place to stay. Travelers without the money often sleep in tents on the cliff or under the sky.

The big, bustling resort has the characteristics of a North African seaside community. Its streets are steep, and villas are staggered up and down the hillside. Albufeira rises above a sickle-shaped beach that shines in the sunlight. A rocky, grotto-filled bluff separates the strip used by the sunbathers from the working beach, where brightly painted fishing boats are drawn up on the sand. Beach access is through a passageway tunneled through the rock.

ESSENTIALS

GETTING THERE   By Train   Trains connect Albufeira with Faro (see below), which has good connections with Lisbon. The train station is 6km (4 miles) north of the center, but buses run back and forth to the resort every 30 minutes. The fare is .90€ one-way. Call (C) 28-980-1726 for information and schedules.

By Bus   Buses run between Albufeira and Faro every hour (trip time: 1 hr.) at a cost of 3€ one-way. Seven buses per day link Portimão with Albufeira (1 hr.) at a cost of 3.65€. Call ✆ **28-958-9755** for information and schedules.

By Car   From Portimão, take N-125 east; from Faro, take N-125 west.

VISITOR INFORMATION   The **Tourist Information Office** is on Rua 5 de Outubro (✆ **28-958-5279**).

WHERE TO STAY

Boavista ⍟   Set on a high ridge in a residential neighborhood, this hotel has been around for decades, but the massive renovation that the owners just completed brings it fully up-to-date. The TV sets, for example, have 57 channels, a quantity still rare in Europe. There is a lot of new furniture, and every wall has been sponge-painted in bright hues. Rooms overlooking the pool and the town, which tumbles down to the ocean, are the most desirable, and the most expensive, of course (the highest rates below apply only in July and Aug).

Rua Samora Barros 20, 8200 Albufeira. ✆ 28-931-0120. Fax 28-932-3908. 86 units. 70€–140€ double. AE, DC, MC, V. Limited free parking on street. **Amenities:** Restaurant; bar; outdoor pool; limited room service; babysitting; same-day laundry/dry cleaning. *In room:* A/C, TV, minibar; hair dryer and iron available at the front desk.

Montechoro ⍟⍟   The largest hotel in or around Albufeira, this four-star resort is set in the holiday-oriented suburb of Montechoro, about 1.6km (1 mile) northeast of the town center. Rooms are done in streamlined style, opening onto views of the sun-baked countryside. The only drawback is that the resort lacks a beach that's adjacent to its grounds, but management supplies frequent minivan shuttles to both Oura Beach, about 1.6km (1 mile) away, and the bar-packed center of Albufeira.

Rua Alexandre O'Neill (Apartado 928), 8200 Albufeira. ✆ 28-958-9423. Fax 28-958-9947. www. maisturismo.pt/hmontech. 362 units. 72€–131€ double; from 109€ suite. Rates include breakfast. AE, V. **Amenities:** 2 restaurants; bar; 2 pools (indoor and outdoor, both heated); 2 tennis courts lit for night play; fitness room; 24-hr. room service; same-day laundry/dry cleaning. *In room:* A/C, TV, hair dryer.

WHERE TO DINE

O Cabaz da Praia FRENCH/PORTUGUESE   This 3-decades-old "Beach Basket" sits on a colorful little square near the Church of São Sebastião, which is now a museum. Located in a former fishing cottage, the restaurant has an inviting ambience and good food. With its large sheltered terrace, it offers diners a view over the main Albufeira beach. Main courses, including favorites like seafood cassoulet, seafood salad, and monkfish with mango sauce, are served with fresh vegetables. The restaurant is renowned for its soufflés. If you're visiting in winter, call first, since they change their vacation dates frequently.

Praça Miguel Bombarda 7. ✆ 28-951-2137. Reservations recommended. Main courses 12€–25€. AE, MC, V. Fri–Wed noon–2:30pm and 7–10:30pm. Closed Jan 3–Feb 15.

VALE DO LOBO ⍟

Almancil, 13km (8 miles) west of Faro and 24km (15 miles) east along N-125 from Albufeira, is a small market town of little interest, yet it's a center for two of the most exclusive tourist developments along the Algarve: **Vale do Lobo,** 6km (4 miles) southeast of Almancil, and **Quinta do Lago,** 10km (6 miles) southeast of town. Both are golfers' paradises.

WHERE TO STAY

Le Meridien Dona Filipa 🌟🌟🌟   Dona Filipa is a deluxe golf hotel with impressive grounds embracing 180 hectares (450 acres) of rugged coastline. The exterior is somewhat uninspired, but greater care was brought to the interior, which features green-silk banquettes, marble fireplaces, Portuguese ceramic lamps, and old prints over baroque-style loveseats. The carefully furnished rooms have balconies. The property is adjacent to the Ria Formosa nature reserve, which contains the highly regarded São Lourenço golf course; greens fees for guests are 55€ to 60€.

Vale do Lobo, 8136 Almancil. © 28-939-4141. Fax 28-939-4288. www.lemeridien-donafilipa.com. 154 units. 237€–395€ double; 310€–875€ suite. Rates include breakfast. AE, DC, MC, V. Free parking. **Amenities:** 2 restaurants; 2 bars; heated outdoor pool; noted golf course; 3 tennis courts; watersports equipment; children's center; concierge; car-rental desk; salon; 24-hr. room service; babysitting; same-day laundry/dry cleaning. In room: A/C, TV w/pay movies, minibar, hair dryer, safe.

Quinta do Lago 🌟🌟🌟   This hotel is associated with the massive Quinta do Lago resort development, a sprawling, 800-hectare (2,000-acre) estate that incorporates private villas, golf courses, beaches, swimming pools, and a host of resort-oriented amenities. Rooms are generally spacious, with balconies that open onto views of the ocean and the Formosa estuary. Substantial renovations have been completed on the guest rooms, and attention has now turned to the health club and spa. The riding facilities and golf courses are among some of the best in all of Europe. At night, there's a disco.

Quinta do Lago, 8135 Almancil. © 28-935-0350. Fax 28-939-6293. www.quintadolagohotel.com. 141 units. 212€–430€ double; from 256€ suite. Rates include breakfast. AE, DC, MC, V. Free parking. **Amenities:** 2 restaurants; pool cafe; 2 bars; 2 pools (heated indoor and heated outdoor); golf course; 2 tennis courts lit for night play; spa; bike rental; children's programs (during school vacations); concierge; car-rental desk; business center; 24-hr. room service; babysitting; same-day laundry/dry cleaning. In room: A/C, TV/VCR, dataport, minibar, hair dryer, safe.

WHERE TO DINE

Casa Velha 🌟🌟 FRENCH   Casa Velha is the consensus choice as best restaurant in the area. It's not part of the Quinta do Lago development but overlooks the resort's lake from a century-old farmhouse. The menu is French, with a scattering of Portuguese and international dishes as well. Specialties include a roasted duck *en service* (the staff presents different parts of the bird throughout the meal, beginning with the thighs *confit* and ending with the breast). Other choices are carefully flavored sea bass, *délices* of sole, and lobster salad flavored with an infusion of vanilla.

Quinta do Lago. © 28-939-4983. Reservations recommended. Main courses 17€–29€; fixed-price dinner menu 47€. AE, MC, V. Mon–Sat 7:30–10:30pm. Closed Dec–Jan.

Ermitage 🌟 ITALIAN/SWISS/INTERNATIONAL   Surrounded by gardens and flowering vines, the 18th-century farmhouse housing this homey restaurant has fireplaces for winter and a dining terrace for warm days. This is serious food, with such starters as goose-liver terrine with blackberry sauce and shrimp, and spinach-stuffed ravioli surrounded with four other pastas and sauces. Main courses include grilled fish of the day with hollandaise and filet of monkfish with prawn-and-curry sauce.

Estrada Almancil-Vale de Lobo. © 28-939-4329. Reservations recommended. Main courses 18€–34€; fixed-price dinner 65€. AE, MC, V. Tues–Sat 7–10:30pm. Closed Dec–Jan and 10 days in June. From Almancil, drive 3km (2 miles) south, following the signs to Vale do Lobo.

PLAYING GOLF

Vale do Lobo, 8135 Almancil (© **28-939-3939**), has played an important role in establishing Portugal's image as a golfer's mecca. Its name, which means Valley of the Wolf, suggests some forlorn spot set amid bleak terrain, but this course is hardly that. Originally designed by British golfer Henry Cotton as three 9-hole courses, the courses have been reconfigured into the 18-hole Oceanfront Course and the 18-hole Royal Course. Some of the long shots along both of these courses require driving the ball over ravines, where variable winds make a straight shot difficult. Greens fees, depending on the day of the week, range from 50€ to 60€ for nine holes and 90€ to 110€ for 18 holes.

Since opening in 1991, **Vila Sol,** Alto do Semino (© **28-930-0505**), has been judged as having the best fairways and the boldest and most inventive contours of any course in the Algarve. Designed by English architect Donald Steel, it's part of a 145-hectare (362-acre) residential estate. Great care was taken in allowing the terrain's natural contours to determine the layout of the fairways and greens. Golfers especially praise the configuration of holes 6, 8, and 14, which collectively manage to funnel golf balls around and over ponds, creek beds, and pine groves in nerve-racking order. Par is 72, and greens fees for 18 holes are 75€ to 90€.

The most famous and sought-after of these three golf courses is the **Vilamoura Old Course,** sometimes called Vilamoura I (© **28-931-0341**), laid out in 1969 by noted English architect Frank Pennink. Its design, texture, and conception are the most English of south Portugal's golf courses. The course is invariably cited for its beauty, its lushness, and the maturity of its trees and shrubberies. Though some of its holes are almost annoyingly difficult (four of them are par-5s), the course is among the most consistently crowded on the Algarve. Par is 73, and greens fees are 64€ to 100€ for 18 holes.

Quinta do Lago resort (p. 831) also has superb facilities and is one of the most elegant "tourist estates" on the Algarve. This pine-covered beachfront property has been *the* retreat for everybody from movie stars to European presidents. The resort's 27 superb holes of golf are a potent lure.

Of the four golf courses that undulate across the massive Quinta do Lago development, the par-72 **São Lourenço** ✦✦ (© **28-939-6522**) is the most challenging and prestigious. Set amid the grassy wetlands of the Rio Formosa Nature Reserve, home to millions of waterfowl, its contours were crafted by American golf designers William (Rocky) Roquemore and Joe Lee. In 1997, *Golf World* magazine voted it the second-most-desirable course in continental Europe. Although the course lies within the confines of Quinta do Logo, it's closely associated with Le Meridien Dona Felipa Hotel in Vale do Lobo, 7km (4½ miles) to the west. Many long drives, especially those aimed at the 17th and 18th holes, soar over the waters of a saltwater lagoon. Greens fee for 18 holes is 140€, less than half that for guests of the Meridien hotel.

FARO ✦

Loved by the Romans and later by the Moors, Faro is the principal city of the Algarve. Since Afonso III drove out the Moors for the last time in 1266, Faro has been Portuguese. On its outskirts, an international jet airport brings in thousands of visitors every summer. The airport, currently being expanded, with new access roads, has done more than anything else to speed tourism not only to Faro but also to the entire Algarve.

ESSENTIALS
GETTING THERE **By Plane** Fly to Faro from Lisbon in 45 minutes. For **flight information,** call ℂ 28-980-0801. You can take bus nos. 14 or 16 to the railway station in Faro, where there are frequent connections to other towns along the coast. The bus operates daily from 7:10am to 9:45pm, leaving every 45 minutes. The one-way fare is .85€.

By Train Trains arrive in Faro from Lisbon six times a day (trip time: 4–7 hr.). The one-way fare is 10€. For rail information in Faro, call the **railway station** at Largo Estação (ℂ 28-980-1726). For information in Lisbon, dial ℂ 21-888-4025.

By Bus Buses arrive every hour from Lisbon (trip time: 4½ hr.). The **bus station** is on Avenida da República (ℂ 28-989-9760), adjacent to the railway station. A one-way ticket costs 12€.

By Car After leaving Vale do Lobo, continue east along N-125 directly into Faro.

VISITOR INFORMATION The **Tourist Office** is at Rua da Misericórdia 8–12 (ℂ 28-980-3604).

WHERE TO STAY
Eva ✦ The top choice within the city limits, this modern hotel dominates the harbor like a fortress, occupying an entire side of the yacht-clogged harbor. It was beginning to look worn and tired, but a recent rejuvenation has perked it up. There are direct sea views from most of the guest rooms, which are furnished in a restrained, even austere, style. The better rooms open onto the water and have large balconies.

Avenida da República, 8000 Faro. ℂ 28-931-0120. Fax 28-932-3903. 148 units. 88€–126€ double; from 129€ suite. Rates include breakfast. AE, DC, MC, V. Limited free parkinq on street. **Amenities:** 2 restaurants; 2 bars; outdoor pool; game room; salon; 24-hr. room service; babysitting; same-day laundry/dry cleaning. *In room:* A/C, TV, minibar, hair dryer.

WHERE TO DINE
Dois Irmãos *Value* PORTUGUESE Founded in 1925, this popular bistro obviously knows a thing or two about keeping its patrons happy. The menu is as modest as the no-nonsense atmosphere, with low prices for good choices of fresh fish and shellfish, simply prepared. Ignore the paper napkins and concentrate on the bowls of succulent seafood placed before you. Clams in savory sauce is a favorite, and sole is regularly featured—of course, everything depends on the catch of the day. Service is amiable, if none too swift.

Largo do Terreiro do Bispo 13–15. ℂ 28-982-3337. Reservations recommended. Main courses 6.75€–18€; fixed-price menu 9.90€. AE, MC, V. Daily 9:30am–11:30pm.

Griséus ✦ INTERNATIONAL/PORTUGUESE Even though Faro is the capital of the Algarve, it is a bit of a gastronomic wasteland. With one or two exceptions, it offers little more than some taverns with questionable sanitation. However, the Griséus, located on the ground level of the town's best hotel, provides an elegant setting for some satisfying dishes. Start with the smoked salmon, and most definitely try the *açorda de mariscos,* which is a kettle of mixed seafood with some enticing spicing. The chefs also prepare an excellent beef *à la pimienta* (with peppers).

Hotel Eva, Avenida da República 1. ℂ 28-280-3354. Reservations required. Main courses 9.65€–22€. AE, DC, MC, V. Daily 9am–11pm.

SEEING THE SIGHTS

The most bizarre attraction in Faro is the **Capela d'Ossos (Chapel of Bones)** ⊛, entered via a courtyard from the rear of the Igreja (Church) de Nossa Senhora do Monte do Carmo do Faro, on Largo do Carmo. Erected in the 19th century, this chapel is completely lined with human skulls and bones, an extraordinarily bizarre display. It's estimated that there are 1,245 skulls. The chapel is open Monday through Friday from 10am to 1pm and 2:30 to 5pm, Saturday from 10am to 1pm. Entrance is free to the church, but 1.35€ to the chapel.

Other religious monuments include the old Sé (cathedral), **Largo da Sé,** merging Gothic and Renaissance styles. A Muslim mosque once stood on this site but was razed for this church, a common practice in Iberia. Another church, the **Igreja de São Francisco,** Largo de São Francisco, has panels of glazed earthenware tiles in milk white and Dutch blue depicting the life of the patron saint. The church is open Monday through Friday from 10am to 5pm, Saturday from 10am to 1:30pm. Entrance to the church is 1.35€. Yes, they charge admission to the church, a rare practice in Portugal. Sunday Mass is conducted at 10am and 11am (no charge then, of course).

But most visitors don't come to Faro to look at churches. Rather, they take the harbor ferry to the wide white-sand beaches called the **Praia de Faro,** on an islet. The ride is available only in summer. The beach is also connected to the mainland by bridge, a distance of 6km (4 miles) from the town center. Once here, you can water-ski and fish or just rent a deck chair and umbrella and lounge in the sun.

DAY TRIPS FROM FARO

OLHÃO ⊛   Described as the living re-creation of a Georges Braque collage, Olhão is the famed cubist town of the Algarve, so long beloved by painters. In its heart, white blocks stacked one on the other, with flat red-tile roofs and exterior stairs on the stark walls, evoke the casbahs of Africa. But don't imagine too romantic a portrait. Some readers have found it disappointing—dirty, dusty, and too commercial.

If you do go here, try to attend the **fish market** near the waterfront when a *lota* (auction) is underway. Olhão is also known for its bullfights of the sea, in which fishermen wrestle with struggling tuna trapped in nets and headed for the smelly warehouses along the harbor.

For the best view, climb **Cabeça Hill,** its grottoes punctured with stalagmites and stalactites, or **St. Michael's Mount,** offering a panorama of the casbah-like Barreta. Finally, for a visit to what is one of the most idyllic beaches on the Algarve, take a 10-minute motorboat ride to the **Ilha de Armona,** a nautical mile away. Olhão is 10km (6½ miles) west of Faro and is reached by going east on N-125.

SÃO BRAS DE ALPORTEL   Traveling north from Faro for 20km (13 miles), you'll pass through groves of figs, almonds, and oranges, and through pine woods where resin collects in wooden cups on the tree trunks. At the end of the run is isolated São Bras de Alportel, one of the Algarve's most charming and least-known spots.

Far from the crowded beaches, it attracts those wanting pure air, peace, and quiet—a bucolic setting filled with flowers pushing through nutmeg-colored soil. Northeast of Loulé, this whitewashed, tile-roofed town rarely gets lively except on market days. Like its neighbor, Faro, it's noted for its perforated plaster chimneys.

Lying at the foot of the Serra do Caldeirão, the whole area has been called one vast garden.

A change of pace from seaside accommodations is offered at **Pousada de São Brás** 🅰️, Estrada de Lisboa, N2, 8150 São Brás de Alportel (ℭ **28-984-2305**). This government-owned inn, built in 1942, is a hilltop villa, with fret-cut limestone chimneys and a hawk's-eye view of the surrounding *serras*. Many visitors arrive just for lunch or dinner (daily 12:30–3pm and 7:30–10pm). The food is exemplary regional cuisine, and tasty indeed. Try the *galinha mourisca*—stewed chicken and meat over bread slices and topped with a poached egg sprinkled with cinnamon. Main courses are 9.75€ to 23€. The pousada, one of three in the admirable chain, also offers 22 well-furnished rooms, each with air-conditioning, TV, and minibar. Rates are 89€ to 169€ (double) a day with breakfast included. American Express, MasterCard, and Visa are accepted.

VILA REAL DE SANT ANTÓNIO/MONTE GORDO

Twenty years after the marquês de Pombal rebuilt Lisbon, which had been destroyed in the 1755 earthquake, he sent architects and builders to Vila Real de Santo António, where they re-established the frontier town on the bank opposite Spain. It took only 5 months. Pombal's motivation was jealousy of Spain. Much has changed, of course, though Praça de Pombal remains. An obelisk stands in the center of the square, which is paved with inlays of black-and-white tiles radiating like rays of the sun. Separated from its Iberian neighbor by the Guadiana River, a car ferry connects Vila Real de Santo António with Ayamonte, Spain.

Today, Vila Real is a mostly residential and industrial community that prides itself on its royal and antique associations as a border town. Adjacent to Vila Real is Monte Gordo, a town whose buildings mostly date from the 1920s and later. Set 3km (2 miles) to the east, it's the site of most of the region's tourist facilities and hotels, with easier access to the sandy beaches that attract tourists every summer from as far away as northern Europe.

ESSENTIALS
GETTING THERE   By Train   The rail terminal in Vila Real is bigger and more convenient than the one in Monte Gordo, which is the site of a railway stopping point but not a bona-fide station. In Vila Real, 11 trains per day arrive from Faro (trip time: 2½ hr.). Tickets are 2.75€ each way. Four direct trains arrive from Lagos (4½ hr.), at a cost of 4.20€ each way. For information and schedules, call ℭ **21-888-4025.**

By Bus   It's faster to take the bus from Faro to Vila Real. Five *espressos* per day arrive from Faro (trip time: 1 hr.). The cost is 3.65€. Call ℭ **28-989-9661** for information. Buses pull into Vila Real at the bus station on the Avenida da República.

By Car   From Faro, take N-125 85km (53 miles) east to reach the Spanish frontier.

VISITOR INFORMATION   The **tourist office** on Avenida Infante Henrique in Monte Gordo (ℭ **28-154-4495**) is open daily from 9:30am to 5:30pm.

WHERE TO STAY
In Vila Real
Hotel Apolo   Built in the mid-1980s, this hotel lies on the western edge of town as you enter from Monte Gordo or Faro. Near the beach and the river, it

attracts vacationers as well as travelers who don't want to cross the Spanish border at night. The hotel is a marginal but economical choice, with a spacious lobby, flooded with sunlight, leading into a large bar. Each of the simply furnished rooms has a balcony.

Avenida dos Bombeiros Portugueses, 8900 Vila Real de Santo António. © **28-151-2448.** Fax 28-151-2450. 42 units. 51€–66€ double. Rates include breakfast. AE, DC, MC, V. Free parking. **Amenities:** Bar; outdoor pool; bike rental; babysitting; laundry service. *In room:* A/C, TV, hair dryer.

In Monte Gordo

Alcázar   A free-form pool is situated on a terrace behind the walls that shelter this hotel from the wind and extend the warm-weather season into autumn. The interior is a vaguely Arabian-style series of repetitive arches and vaults of distressed concrete. Each rather austere guest room has its own patio. A new wing has added 16 double rooms and 8 suites with whirlpools. The basement disco is open in summer.

Rua de Ceuta 9, Monte Gordo, 8900 Vila Real de Santo António. © **28-151-0184.** Fax 28-151-2242. 119 units. 43€–101€ double. Rates include breakfast. AE, DC, MC, V. **Amenities:** Restaurant; cafe; 2 bars; outdoor pool; tennis court lit for night play; exercise room; limited room service; babysitting; laundry service. *In room:* A/C, TV, minibar, hair dryer, safe.

Navegadores *(Kids)*   Vacationing Portuguese and British families congregate under the dome covering the pool at this hotel. The public areas are clean and functional, and about three-fourths of the standardized rooms have balconies. The beach is a 5-minute walk away. There are dull boutiques in a corridor along the grounds.

Monte Gordo, 8900 Vila Real de Santo António. © **28-151-0864.** Fax 28-151-0879. 431 units. 59€–130€ double; from 82€ suite. Rates include breakfast. AE, DC, MC, V. Free parking. **Amenities:** Restaurant; bar; exercise room; same-day laundry/dry cleaning. *In room:* A/C, TV, minibar, hair dryer, safe.

Vasco da Gama   The owners of this property know what their guests like—lots of sunbathing and swimming. The hotel enjoys a favored position directly on a long, firm beach, with nearly an acre of flagstoned terrace. All of the spartan rooms are furnished conservatively, and glass doors open onto balconies.

Avenida Infante Dom Henrique, Monte Gordo, 8900 Vila Real de Santo António. © **28-931-0120.** Fax 28-932-3903. 170 units. 48€–107€ double; from 72€ suite. Rates include breakfast. AE, DC, MC, V. Free parking. **Amenities:** Restaurant; 2 bars; tennis court; limited room service; babysitting; same-day laundry/dry cleaning. *In room:* A/C, TV, hair dryer, safe.

WHERE TO DINE

Edmundo PORTUGUESE   Long known in the Algarve, this restaurant attracts Spaniards, who often visit just for the day. It overlooks the river and Spain across the water—try to get a sidewalk table. The people who run it are friendly and proud of their repertoire of local cuisine, especially fresh fish. You might begin with shrimp cocktail, followed by fried sole, crayfish, or sautéed red mullet. You can also order such land-based dishes as pepper steak and grilled pork chops. Meat items are priced under 12€; it's the lobster and other shellfish that fly past 30€.

Avenida da República 55. © **28-154-4689.** Reservations recommended. Main courses 7.65€–35€. AE, DC, MC, V. Mon–Sat 11:15am–3pm and 7–10pm; Sun 7–10pm.

EXPLORING VILA REAL

A long esplanade, **Avenida da República,** borders the river. Often, more Spanish than Portuguese is heard along the promenade, for this is a popular day trip for Spaniards looking for bargains. Gaily painted **horse-drawn carriages** take visitors sightseeing past the shipyards and the lighthouse.

A short drive north on the road to Mertola will bring you to the gray castle-fortress of **Castro Marim,** a legacy of the old border wars between Spain and Portugal. The ramparts and walls peer across the river at the former enemy. Afonso III, who expelled the Moors from this region, founded the original fortress, which was leveled by the 1755 earthquake. Inside the walls are the ruins of the **Church of São Tiago,** dedicated to St. James.

Directly southwest of Vila Real is the emerging resort of **Monte Gordo,** which has the greatest concentration of hotels in the eastern Algarve after Faro. Monte Gordo is the last in a long line of Algarvian resorts, located 3km (2 miles) southwest of the frontier town of Vila Real de Santo António at the mouth of the Guadiana River. Pine-studded lowlands back the resort's wide beach, one of the finest along the southern coast of Portugal. This was once a sleepy little fishing village. Now young men work in hotels instead of on the sea, fishing for tips instead of tuna. Monte Gordo has succumbed to high-rises, attracting Spaniards from across the border. It has many good hotels, and a number of Europeans use it as their place in the Algarvian sun.

15

Scotland

by Darwin Porter & Danforth Prince

Whether you go to Scotland to seek out your ancestral roots, explore ancient castles, drive the Malt Whisky Trail, or partake in the internationally acclaimed Edinburgh Festival, you'll find a country rich in history, legend, and romance. If it's the outdoors you love, Scotland offers great salmon fishing, peaceful walks in heather-covered Highland hills, and some of the best (and oldest) golf courses.

1 Edinburgh & Environs

Called one of Europe's fairest cities, the "Athens of the North," Edinburgh is the second-most-visited city in Britain after London. In contrast to industrialized bastions like Aberdeen and Glasgow, it's a white-collar city. Home of the Royal Mile, Princes Street, and the ever-growing Edinburgh Festival with its action-packed list of cultural events, Edinburgh is both hip and historic. John Knox, Mary Queen of Scots, Robert Louis Stevenson, Sir Arthur Conan Doyle, Alexander Graham Bell, Sir Walter Scott, Bonnie Prince Charlie, and Deacon Brodie are all part of the city's past; you can walk in their footsteps and explore sights associated with them.

ESSENTIALS

GETTING THERE   By Plane   Edinburgh is 632km (393 miles) north of London, about an hour's flying time. **Edinburgh Airport** (© **0131/333-1000** for flight info; www.edinburgh-airport.com) lies 10km (6 miles) west of the city's center. Flights from within the British Isles and Europe land here; most transatlantic flights go to Glasgow's airport. A double-decker Airlink bus makes the trip between the airport and the city center every 10 minutes, letting you off near Waverley Bridge, between Old Town and New Town; the one-way fare is £3.40 ($5.45). A taxi suitable for up to four passengers into the city costs £14 ($22) or more, depending on traffic.

By Train   Fast air-conditioned InterCity trains with restaurant and bar service link London with Edinburgh. Trains from London's King's Cross or Euston stations arrive in Edinburgh at **Waverley Station,** at the east end of Princes Street (© **08457/484950;** www.railtrack.co.uk). Trains depart London every hour or so (trip time: 4½-5 hr.). An overnight sleeper requires reservations. Taxis and buses are found right outside the station in Edinburgh.

By Bus   The least expensive way to go from London to Edinburgh is by bus, but it's an 8-hour journey. The fare is £27 ($43) one-way or £38 ($61) round-trip. National Express coaches depart from London's Victoria Coach Station, delivering you to Edinburgh's **St. Andrew Square Bus Station,** St. Andrew Square (© **0131/663-3233** in Edinburgh).

By Car Edinburgh lies 74km (46 miles) east of Glasgow and 169km (105 miles) north of Newcastle upon Tyne in England. There's no express motorway linking London and Edinburgh. The M 1 from London takes you part of the way north, but you'll have to come into Edinburgh along secondary roads: A-68 or A-7 from the southeast, A-1 from the east, or A-702 from the north. A-71 or A-8 comes in from the west, A-8 connecting with M-8 just west of Edinburgh. A-90 comes down from the north over the Forth Road Bridge.

VISITOR INFORMATION   Tourist Offices   The **Edinburgh & Scotland Information Centre,** 3 Princes St., above the Princes Mall shopping center (*©* **0131/473-3800**), can give you sightseeing information and can help with accommodations. The center sells bus tours, theater tickets, and souvenirs. It's open May, June, and September, Monday through Saturday from 9am to 7pm and Sunday from 10am to 7pm; July and August, Monday through Saturday from 9am to 8pm and Sunday from 10am to 8pm; October through April, Monday through Saturday from 9am to 6pm and Sunday from 10am to 6pm. There's also an **information and accommodation desk** at Edinburgh Airport (*©* **0131/473-3800**), which is open April through October daily from 6:30am to 10:30pm, and November through March daily from 7:30am to 9:30pm.

Websites   The official site of the Scottish Tourist Board (**www.holiday. scotland.net**) is an excellent source for events, lodging, getting around, and outdoor activities. However, the "Special Offers" section requires a lot of clicks for

Edinburgh

SCOTLAND

Edinburgh

ACCOMMODATIONS ■

Allison 3
Balmoral Hotel **23**
Bank Hotel **25**
The Bonham **8**
Caledonian Hotel **10**
Carlton Highland Hotel **24**
Channings Hotel **5**
The Edinburgh Residence **9**
Greenside Hotel **35**
Jarvis Ellersly Country House Hotel **12**
Nova Hotel **15**
Point Hotel **14**
Roxburghe Hotel **11**
7 Danube Street **6**
Sheraton Grand Hotel **13**
Thrums Private Hotel **28**
Walton Hotel **2**

✝ Church
ⓘ Information
— Railway

To Arthur's Seat →

little payoff. The Edinburgh and Lothians Tourist Board (**www.edinburgh.org**) discusses what's new, travel tips, and events and festivals for city, coast, and country; they include a page about what to do with kids, written *by* kids.

Scotland Holiday Net (**www.aboutscotland.co.uk**) combines information on dining, lodging, and sightseeing with personal accounts. Curious about Scotland's top 20 free attractions? Interested in restaurant reviews from other diners? Try **www.travelscotland.co.uk**. Listing locations and greens fees, **www.uk-golf guide.com** will help you find a course wherever you plan to be.

CITY LAYOUT   Edinburgh is divided into an **Old Town** and a **New Town.** Chances are, you'll find lodgings in New Town and visit Old Town for dining, drinking, shopping, or sightseeing.

New Town, with its world-famous **Princes Street,** came about in the 18th century in the "Golden Age" of Edinburgh. The first building went up in New Town in 1767, and by the end of the century, classical squares, streets, and town houses had been added. Princes Street runs straight for about a mile; it's known for its shopping and for its beauty, as it opens onto the **Princes Street Gardens** with stunning views of Old Town.

North of Princes Street, and running parallel to it, is the second great street of New Town, **George Street.** It begins at Charlotte Square and runs east to St. Andrew Square. Directly north of George Street is another impressive thoroughfare, **Queen Street,** opening onto Queen Street Gardens on its north side.

You'll also hear a lot about **Rose Street,** directly north of Princes Street. It has more pubs per square block than any other place in Scotland, and is also filled with shops and restaurants.

Everyone seems to have heard of the **Royal Mile,** the main thoroughfare of Old Town, beginning at Edinburgh Castle and running all the way to the Palace of Holyroodhouse. A famous street to the south of the castle (you have to descend to it) is **Grassmarket,** where convicted criminals were hanged on the dreaded gallows that once stood here.

GETTING AROUND   Walking is the best way to explore Edinburgh, particularly Old Town with its narrow lanes, wynds, and closes. Most attractions are along the Royal Mile, along Princes Street, or on one of the major streets of New Town.

By Bus   This will probably be your chief method of transport within the Scottish capital. The fare you pay depends on the distance you ride, based on a confusing system derived from "stages" that usually incorporate between two and five bus stops and a distance of about a half mile. The minimum fare depends on the distance you travel, based on what you tell the driver, who will determine the fare, sell you your ticket, and even make change. Minimum fare is 60p (95¢) for three stages or less, going up to a maximum of £1.70 ($2.70) for travel

---

Value Travel Passes

The **Edinburgh Freedom Ticket** allows 1 day of unlimited travel on city buses at a cost of £1.50 to £2.50 ($2.40–$4) adults and £1.80 ($2.90) children ages 5 to 15. For daily commuters or for die-hard Scottish enthusiasts, a **RideCard** season ticket allows unlimited travel on all buses for 1 week at £11 ($18) adults, £7 ($11) children; and for 4 weeks at £33 ($53) adults, £21 ($34) children. Travel must begin on Sunday.

between 44 or more stages. Children 5 to 15 pay a flat rate of 50p (80¢), regardless of how many stages they traverse, and children 4 and under ride free and must be accompanied by an adult. There's a family ticket for two adults and four children for £6 ($9.60) a day and another for £1.60 ($2.55), which operates from 6:30pm onward.

Travel passes and further information may be obtained in the city center at the **Waverley Bridge Transport Office,** Waverley Bridge (© **0131/554-4494;** bus: 3 or 31), open daily from 8:30am to 6:30pm; or at the Hanover Street office, which operates daily from 8:30am to 6:30pm. For information on timetables call © **0131/555-6363.**

By Taxi   Cabs can be hailed on the street or met at any of several taxi stands, each of which lie at prominent intersections throughout the city. Some of the more important of these are at Hanover Street, North St. Andrew Street, Waverley Station, Princes Street (at the Caledonian Hotel), Haymarket Station, Frederick Street, Castle Street, and Lauriston Place. Fares are prominently displayed in the front of each taxi. The meter begins ticking at £1.80 ($2.90). Regardless of the time of day, you'll be charged 20p (30¢) per 270m (900 ft.) of distance your cab covers. If you phone for a cab to come to a specified point, you'll pay a surcharge of 60p (95¢) at any time of the day or night. To call a taxi, try **City Cabs** (© **0131/228-1211**).

By Car   Car rentals are relatively expensive, and driving in Edinburgh is a tricky business. The city is a warren of one-way streets, with parking spots at a premium. However, a car is convenient, and sometimes a must, for touring the countryside. Most companies will accept your U.S. or Canadian driver's license, provided you have held it for more than a year and are over 21. At the Edinburgh airport, try **Avis** (© **0131/333-1866**), **Hertz** (© **0131/333-1019**), or **Europcar** (© **0131/333-2588**).

By Bicycle   You can rent bikes by the day or by the week from a number of outfits. Nevertheless, bicycling is not a good idea for most visitors because the city is constructed on a series of high ridges and terraces.

You may, however, want to rent a bike to explore the flatter countryside. Try **Central Cycle Hire,** 13 Lochrin Place (© **0131/228-6333;** bus: 10), off Home Street in Tollcross, near the Cameo Cinema. Depending on the type of bike, rates range from £10 to £18 ($16–$29) per day. A deposit of £50 to £100 ($80–$160) is imposed. The shop is open Monday through Saturday from 10am to 5:30pm; June through September it is also open Sunday from 9:30am to 6pm.

 FAST FACTS: Edinburgh

American Express   The office at 139 Princes St. (© **0131/225-7881;** bus: 3, 39, or 69), 5 blocks from Waverley Station, is open Monday through Wednesday and Friday from 9am to 5:30pm; Thursday from 9:30am to 5:30pm; Saturday from 9am to 4pm.

Business Hours   In Edinburgh, **banks** are usually open Monday through Wednesday from 9:30am to 3:45pm, and Thursday and Friday from 9:30am to 5 or 5:30pm. **Shops** are generally open Monday through

Wednesday and Saturday from 10am to 5:30 or 6pm; on Thursday stores are open until 8pm. **Offices,** in the main, are open Monday through Friday from 9am to 5pm.

Currency The basic unit of currency is the **pound sterling** (£), which is divided into 100 **pence** (p). The exchange rate at press time is £1 = $1.60. Note that though the United Kingdom is part of the EU, it does not plan to switch to the euro at this time.

Currency Exchange There's a **Bureau de Change** of the Clydesdale Bank at 20 Hanover St. (℃ **08457/826-302**).

Dentists/Doctors For a dental emergency, go to the **Edinburgh Dental Institute,** 39 Lauriston Place (℃ **0131/536-4900**; bus: 23 or 41), open Monday through Friday from 9am to 3pm. In a medical emergency, you can seek help from the **Edinburgh Royal Infirmary,** 1 Lauriston Place (℃ **0131/536-1000**; bus: 23 or 41). Medical attention is available 24 hours.

Drugstores There are no 24-hour drugstores ("chemists" or "pharmacies") in Edinburgh. The major drugstore is **Boots,** 48 Shandwick Place (℃ **0131/225-6757**; bus: 3 or 31), open Monday through Friday from 8am to 9pm, Saturday from 8am to 7pm, and Sunday from 10am to 4pm.

Embassies/Consulates The consulate of the **United States** is at 3 Regent Terrace (℃ **0131/556-8315**; bus: 26, 85, or 86), which is an extension of Princes Street beyond Nelson's Monument. All the other embassies are in London.

Emergencies Call ℃ **999** in an emergency to summon the police, an ambulance, or firefighters.

Hospital The best and most convenient is the **Edinburgh Royal Infirmary,** 1 Lauriston Place (℃ **0131/536-1000**; bus: 23, 41).

Internet Access You can check your e-mail or send messages at the **International Telecom Centre,** 52 High St. (℃ **0131/559-7114**; bus: 1 or 6), along the Royal Mile. The rate is £1 ($1.60) for 15 minutes. The center is open daily from 9am to 10pm.

Post Office The Edinburgh Branch **Post Office,** St. James's Centre (℃ **0845/722-3344**; bus: 23 or 41), is open Monday through Friday from 9am to 5:30pm and Saturday from 9am to noon.

Telephones The United Kingdom's **country code** is **44.** The city code for **Edinburgh** is **0131.** If you're calling from inside the United Kingdom but outside the city code area, dial the complete area code; if you're calling from outside the United Kingdom, drop the zero. If you're calling from inside the code area, dial just the seven-digit number.

Public phones cost 10p (15¢) for the first 3 minutes and accept coins of various denominations. You can also buy a phone card for use in special phones at post offices and newsstands. You can receive U.S. rates for collect or credit card calls by dialing toll-free **AT&T** (℃ **0800/890011**), **World Phone** (℃ **0800/890222**), or **Sprint** (℃ **0800/890877**).

Tipping In most restaurants, tax and service charge are included, so it's unnecessary to leave a tip. If a service charge hasn't been included in the bill, the standard tip is 10%. Taxi drivers also expect a 10% tip.

WHERE TO STAY
IN THE CENTER
Very Expensive
Balmoral Hotel ✮✮✮   This legendary establishment was opened in 1902 as the largest, grandest, and most impressive hotel in the north of Britain. Its soaring clock tower is a city landmark. Rooms are distinguished, conservative, and rather large, a graceful reminder of Edwardian sprawl with a contemporary twist. Many benefit from rounded or oversize windows and the many Victorian/Edwardian quirks that were originally designed as part of its charm.

Princes St., Edinburgh, Lothian EH2 2EQ. (C) **0131/556-2414.** Fax 0131/557-3747. www.roccofortehotels.com. 188 units. Apr–Oct £275 ($440) double; from £440 ($704) suite. Off season £210 ($336) double; from £440 ($704) suite. AE, DC, MC, V. Parking £15 ($24). Bus: 50. **Amenities:** Restaurant (see "Where to Dine," later); bar; pool; heath club; room service. *In room:* A/C, TV, minibar, hair dryer.

Caledonian Hilton Hotel ✮✮✮   "The Caley" is Edinburgh's most visible hotel, with commanding views over Edinburgh Castle and the Princes Street Gardens. The pastel-colored public areas are reminiscent of Edwardian splendor. Rooms are conservatively but individually styled, and are often exceptionally spacious. Fifth-floor rooms are the smallest. Although the accommodations are comparable to other first-class hotels in Edinburgh, the Caledonian lacks the leisure facilities of its major competitor, the Balmoral.

Princes St., Edinburgh EH1 2AB. (C) **0131/222-8888.** Fax 0131/222-8889. www.hilton.com. 249 units. From £235 ($376) double; from £360 ($576) suite. Children 15 and under stay free in parent's room. AE, DC, DISC, MC, V. Parking £7.50 ($12). Bus: 33. **Amenities:** 3 restaurants; 2 bars; pool; gym; room service; laundry/dry cleaning. *In room:* TV, minibar, coffeemaker, hair dryer, safe.

Expensive
The Bonham ✮✮   One of Edinburgh's newest and most stylish hotels occupies a trio of Regency town houses. Rooms are outfitted in an urban and very hip blend of old and new. The decor combines ancient vases, Art Nouveau objects, marble busts, contemporary art—an eclectic but tasteful mix. Each unit has a TV with a keyboard hooked up to a barrage of facilities on the Internet, the first setup of its kind in Scotland.

35 Drumsheugh Gardens, Edinburgh EH3 7RN. (C) **0131/623-6060.** Fax 0131/226-6080. www.thebonham.com. 48 units. £165–£295 ($264–$472) double; £255–£295 ($408–$472) suite. AE, MC, V. Bus: 41 or 42. **Amenities:** Restaurant; bar; 24-hr. room service; babysitting; laundry/dry cleaning. *In room:* TV, dataport, minibar, coffeemaker, hair dryer, iron.

Carlton Highland Hotel ✮✮   The Victorian turrets, Flemish gables, and severe gray stonework rise imposingly from a street corner on the Royal Mile, a few steps from Waverley Station. The former department store has been converted into a bright and airy milieu full of modern conveniences. Rooms have a kind of Scandinavian simplicity. Bathrooms tend to be small. To relax, enjoy the sounds of a pianist in the lounge area, or stop by the cafe, Central Perk, based on the same coffee bar as the one on the TV show *Friends*. Although the hotel doesn't have the style and grandeur of the Caledonian, it has more facilities.

19 N. Bridge, Edinburgh, Lothian EH1 1SD. (C) **0131/556-7277.** Fax 0131/556-2691. 197 units. £225 ($360) executive double. Rates include breakfast. Children 14 and under stay free in parent's room. AE, DC, MC, V. Parking £6 ($9.60). Bus: 55 and 80. **Amenities:** Restaurant; bar; pool; gym; aerobics studio; 2 squash courts; solarium; whirlpool. *In room:* TV, coffeemaker, hair dryer, trouser press.

Channings Hotel ✮✮   Five Edwardian terrace houses were combined to create this hotel 7 blocks north of Dean Village in a tranquil residential area. It maintains the atmosphere of a Scottish country house. Rooms are outfitted in a modern yet elegant style. Front units have views of a cobblestone street. Back units are quieter, and standard rooms are a bit cheaper but are much smaller. The most desirable rooms are labeled "Executive," and often have bay windows and wingback chairs.

S. Learmonth Gardens 15, Edinburgh EH4 1EZ. ℂ **0131/332-3232.** Fax 0131/332-9631. www.channings. co.uk. 46 units. £175–£240 ($280–$384) double; £235 ($376) suite. Rates include breakfast. Children 14 and under stay free in parent's room. AE, DC, MC, V. Bus: 41 or 42. **Amenities:** Restaurant; bar; room service; babysitting; laundry/dry cleaning. *In room:* TV, dataport, coffeemaker, hair dryer, trouser press.

The Edinburgh Residence ☆☆☆   If Robert Burns, who liked his luxuries, were checking into a hotel in Edinburgh today, he no doubt would be booked in here. It's one of the finest luxury hotels in Scotland, a series of elegant town-house suites installed in a trio of architecturally beautiful and sensitively restored Georgian buildings. As you enter, grand staircases and classic wood paneling greet you. A stay here is like finding lodging in an elegant town house from long ago, although with all the modern conveniences. This hotel is at the same level or better than its siblings, the Howard, Bonham, and Channings. Accommodations are the ultimate in local comfort. A trio of classic suites has private entrances. All units are spacious; even the smallest is the size of a tennis court.

7 Rothesay Terrace, Edinburgh EH3 7RY. ℂ **0131/226-3380.** Fax 0131/226-3381. . 29 units. £150–£265 ($240–$424) suite; £260–£395 ($416–$632) apt. AE, MC, V. Free parking. Bus: 19 or 37. Rates include continental breakfast. **Amenities:** Meals (room service only); honesty bar in the drawing room. *In room:* TV, minibar, hair dryer, iron/ironing board.

Roxburghe Hotel ☆   Originally a stately Robert Adam town house, the hotel stands on a tree-filled square a short walk from Princes Street. In 1999, it opened a new wing, more than doubling the original size of the hotel. The old wing maintains a traditional atmosphere with ornate ceilings and woodwork, antique furnishings, and tall, arched windows. The new wing offers government-rated four-star hotel comfort, completely contemporary styling, and up-to-date furnishings.

38 Charlotte Sq., Edinburgh EH2 4HG. ℂ **0131/225-3921.** Fax 0131/220-2518. www.macdonald hotels.co.uk. 197 units. £149–£195 ($238–$312) double; from £250 ($400) suite. Children 13 and under stay free in parent's room. AE, DC, MC, V. Parking £4.50 ($7.20). Bus: 100. **Amenities:** 2 restaurants; 2 bars; pool; gym; sauna; 24-hr. room service; babysitting; laundry/dry cleaning. *In room:* TV, minibar, coffeemaker, hair dryer, trouser press.

Sheraton Grand Hotel ☆☆   This elegant hotel, in a postmodern complex on a former railway siding a short walk from Princes Street, is the most appealing modern hotel in the capital. If you seek Victorian grandeur, make it the Caledonian. But if you'd like to be in the "new Edinburgh" (a financial center called The Exchange), then make it the Sheraton Grand. The hotel has more of international flavor than its rival, the Balmoral. Rooms may lack character but they are exceedingly comfortable. The best units are called "Castle View," and they are on the top three floors.

1 Festival Sq., Edinburgh, Lothian EH3 9SR. ℂ **888/625-5144** in the U.S. and Canada, or 0131/229-9131. Fax 0131/228-4510. www.sheraton.com. 278 units. June–Sept £240–£260 ($384–$416) double; from £350 ($560) suite. Off season, £220 ($352) double; £315 ($504) suite. Children 16 and under stay free in parent's room. AE, DC, MC, V. Bus: 4, 15, or 44. **Amenities:** 3 restaurants; 2 bars; pool; gym; room service; laundry/dry cleaning. *In room:* A/C, TV, dataport, minibar, coffeemaker, hair dryer.

Moderate

Bank Hotel *(Value)*   This modest hotel offers better value than many of its competitors in this congested neighborhood beside the Royal Mile. Until around 1990 it was a branch of the Royal Bank of Scotland, and the past is still evident in its bulky, no-nonsense design. Upstairs, high ceilings, simple furnishings, and king-size beds provide comfort in the clean guest rooms. Each comes with a shower-only bathroom.

Royal Mile at 1–3 S. Bridge St., Edinburgh EH1 1LL. © 0131/622-6800. Fax 0131/622-6822. www.festivalinns.co.uk. 9 units. £120 ($192) double. Rates include breakfast. AE, DC, MC, V. Nearby parking £6 ($9.60). Bus: 4, 15, 31, or 100. **Amenities:** Bar; laundry service. *In room:* TV, coffeemaker, hair dryer, trouser press.

Nova Hotel   The Nova, an 1875 Victorian, is on a quiet cul-de-sac a 10-minute ride from the center, with a view over Brunsfield Links in front and the Pentland Hills in back. It's within walking distance of the Royal Mile and Princes Street. You'll find its rooms large and well appointed, with shower-only bathrooms. On the ground floors, guests enjoy the lounge that also operates as a cocktail bar.

5 Brunsfield Crescent, Edinburgh FH10 4EZ. © 0131/447-6437. Fax 0131/452-8126. 13 units. £70–£140 ($112–$224) double; £90–£160 ($144–$256) family room for up to 6. AE, DC, MC, V. Parking on the street. Bus: 11, 15, 16, or 17. **Amenities:** 2 restaurants; 2 bars; lounge; room service; laundry/dry cleaning. *In room:* TV, minibar, coffeemaker, hair dryer, iron, safe.

Point Hotel   With one of the most dramatic contemporary interiors of any hotel in Edinburgh, this is a stylish place in the shadow of Edinburgh Castle. The decor has appeared in a book detailing the 50 premier hotel designs in the world, with a great emphasis on color and innovation, including a black stone floor at the front that's marked by "dusty footprints." In one area, red neon spots blue walls in different shades of brilliant light to create an optical fantasy. For a dramatic minimalist effect, a lone armchair and sofa will occupy 93 sq. m (1,000 sq. ft.) of space. Guest rooms are spacious and attractively furnished. Most of the guest rooms open onto views of the castle; however, those in the rear do not, so be duly warned. If you like stainless steel, laser projections, and chrome instead of Scottish antiques, this might be an address for you. Standard rooms are a bit small, the premium rooms more comfortable and spacious.

34 Bread St., Edinburgh EH3 9AF. © 0131/221-5555. Fax 0131/221-9929. www.point-hotel.co.uk. 136 units. Summer £105–£160 ($168–$256) double; £350 ($560) suite. Off season £68–£88 ($109–$141) double; £115 ($184) suite. Rates include English breakfast. AE, DC, MC, V. Bus: 4 or 31. **Amenities:** Restaurant; bar; room service; laundry/dry cleaning. *In room:* TV, hair dryer, iron.

Inexpensive

A-Haven   This semidetached 1862 Victorian house is a 15-minute walk or 5-minute bus ride north of the rail station. Rooms are of various sizes (the biggest on the 2nd floor). Some in back overlook the Firth of Forth, and those in the front open onto views of Arthur's Seat. Moira and Ronnie Murdock extend a Scottish welcome in this family-type place, and often advise guests about sightseeing.

180 Ferry Rd., Edinburgh EH6 4NS. © 0131/554-6559. Fax 0131/554-5252. www.a-haven.co.uk. 14 units. £30–£50 ($48–$80) double. Rates include breakfast. AE, MC, V. Free parking. Bus: 1, 7, 11, 14, or 14A. **Amenities:** Restaurant; bar. *In room:* TV, dataport, coffeemaker, hair dryer, iron, trouser press.

Greenside Hotel   This 1786 Georgian house is furnished with antiques to give it the right spirit. There are singles, doubles, twins, and three family rooms, all centrally heated and all with private bathrooms with showers. Rooms, refurbished in 1998, open onto views of a private garden or the Firth of Forth and are so large that 10 of them contain a double bed and two singles.

9 Royal Terrace, Edinburgh EH7 5AB. ⓒ/fax 0131/557-0022. www.townhousehotels.co.uk. 15 units. £45–£90 ($72–$144) double. Rates include breakfast. AE, DC, DISC, MC, V. Bus: 4, 15, or 44. **Amenities:** Restaurant; bar; lounge; babysitting. *In room:* TV, coffeemaker, hair dryer, iron.

7 Danube Street 🅡 This B&B is in Stockbridge, a quiet, stylish residential neighborhood a 10-minute walk north of the center. It's the 1825 home of Fiona Mitchell-Rose and her husband, Colin. The establishment is proud of its charmingly decorated rooms that reflect Fiona's experience as a decorator in London. Rooms look out onto the sloping garden. The most desirable has a four-poster bed and direct garden access. Bathrooms are shower-only. You're likely to meet your hosts and other guests in the formal dining room in the morning, where the lavish breakfast is inspired by Scotland's old-fashioned agrarian tradition.

7 Danube St., Edinburgh EH4 1NN. ⓒ 0131/332-2755. Fax 0131/343-3648. www.aboutedinburgh.com/danube.html. 5 units. £95–£110 ($152–$176) double. Rates include breakfast. MC, V. Free parking nearby. Bus: 28. **Amenities:** Breakfast room; laundry. *In room:* TV, coffeemaker, hair dryer, iron.

Walton Hotel 🅡 *Finds* A real discovery, this little hotel lies right in the heart of Edinburgh in a well-restored 200-year-old town house. A complete refurbishment and renovation have maintained the essential Georgian character and elegant features, but have revitalized and modernized the entire hotel. Guest rooms are midsize, cozy, comfortable, and tranquil. In the morning you're served a superior breakfast. The location is only a few minutes' walk to Princes Street.

79 Dundas St., Edinburgh EH3 6SD. ⓒ 0131/556-1137. Fax 0131/557-8367. . Summer £75 ($120) double. Off season £45 ($72) double. Rates include breakfast. MC, V. Bus: 23 or 27. **Amenities:** Breakfast lounge. *In room:* TV, beverage maker, hair dryer.

WEST OF THE CENTER

Jarvis Ellersly Country House Hotel 🅡 Standing in walled gardens, this three-story Edwardian country house offers the privacy of a home. It's in a dignified west-end residential section near the Murrayfield rugby grounds, about a 5-minute ride from the center, and is one of Edinburgh's best moderately priced hotels. The well-equipped rooms vary in size and are in either the main house or a less desirable annex. After recent refurbishments, the hotel is better than ever, and service is first class.

4 Ellersly Rd., Edinburgh EH12 6HZ. ⓒ 0131/337-6888. Fax 0131/313-2543. 57 units. £139 ($222) double; £154 ($246) suite. AE, DC, MC, V. Free parking. Take A-8 4km (2½ miles) west of the city center. Bus: 2, 2A, 21, 26, 31, 36, or 36A. **Amenities:** Restaurant; room service; laundry; wine cellar. *In room:* TV, hair dryer.

SOUTH OF THE CENTER

Thrums Private Hotel About a mile south of Princes Street, Thrums is a pair of connected antique buildings, one a two-story 1820 Georgian and the other a small inn from around 1900. The hotel contains recently refurbished high-ceilinged rooms with firm mattresses and contemporary furnishings (in the inn) or reproduction antique furnishings (in the Georgian). Each unit comes with a tidy midsize private bathroom with shower. The bistro-inspired Thrums restaurant serves set-price menus of British food, and there's also a bar and a peaceful garden.

14–15 Minto St., Edinburgh EH9 1RQ. ⓒ 0131/667-5545. Fax 0131/667-8707. 15 units. £70–£85 ($112–$136) double; £90–£120 ($144–$192) family room. Rates include breakfast. MC, V. Free parking. Bus: 3, 7, 8, 31, 81,or 87. **Amenities:** Restaurant; bar; laundry service. *In room:* TV, coffeemaker, hair dryer.

Native Behavior

The quickest way to brand yourself a tourist is to ask a kilt-wearing Scotsman what he wears underneath the kilt. A true Scotsman—and, of course, many a Scottish lass—already knows the answer to that one. A guard at Edinburgh Castle told us, "I must get asked that question at least 10 times a day."

It takes more than the swirl of tartan to make you blend in with the Scots. It also helps to perk up your ears at the skirl of pipes and to claim membership in a clan, the more ancient the better. If you're a big man, the ability to toss a giant caber (tree trunk) will get you a free round of brew at the local pub.

When talking with Scots, it helps if you express a firm belief in the existence of the Loch Ness monster and refer to her as "Nessie." If you really want to show your familiarity with the creature, call her "Beastie," as the locals do who actually live on the loch. To report an actual sighting will endear you even more to the Scots.

If you're invited to a Scottish home, you'll immediately be offered tea no matter what time of day. As a local told us, "It's always tea time in Scotland." In the Lowlands it's called "a fly cup"—that is, a quick cup between meals. In the Highlands, it's called "a wee strupach," which means the same thing.

And finally, on the subject of drink, it's wise to drink only Scottish whisky (spelled without the "e") and to express your loathing of such "hogwash" as American, Canadian, or Irish whiskey with an "e."

WHERE TO DINE
IN THE CENTER—NEW TOWN
Expensive

The Atrium *MODERN SCOTTISH/INTERNATIONAL* Since 1993, this is one of the most emulated restaurants in Edinburgh. The "deliberately moody" atmosphere is a fusion of Argentine hacienda and stylish Beverly Hills bistro. Flickering oil lamps create shadows on the dark walls while patrons enjoy dishes prepared by chef Alan Metheison. Our favorites include grilled salmon and roasted sea bass. Whether it's game or lamb from the Scottish Highlands, dishes have taste, style, and flair. The desserts are equally superb, especially the lemon tart with berry coulis and crème fraîche.

10 Cambridge St. (beneath Saltire Court). ℭ **0131/228-8882.** Reservations recommended. Main courses £10–£12 ($16–$19) lunch; £15–£19 ($23–$30) dinner. AE, DC, MC, V. Mon–Fri noon–2pm and 6:30–10pm; Sat 6:30–10pm. Closed 1 week at Christmas.

No. 1 Princes Street *SCOTTISH/CONTINENTAL* This intimate, crimson-colored enclave is the premier restaurant in the Balmoral Hotel. The walls are studded with Scottish memorabilia in formal yet sporting patterns. You can sample the likes of pan-seared Isle of Skye monkfish with saffron mussel broth; roulade of Dover sole with langoustine, oyster, and scallop garnish; or grilled filet of Scottish beef served with bourguignon sauce. For dessert you can have a variety of sorbets or British cheeses, or something more exotic such as mulled wine parfait with a cinnamon sauce. There's a separate vegetarian menu and a wide-ranging wine list with celestial tariffs.

In the Balmoral Hotel, 1 Princes St. © **0131/556-2414.** Reservations recommended. Main courses £20–£35 ($32–$56). Fixed-price dinners £43 ($68) 3 courses, £53 ($84) 6 courses. AE, DC, MC, V. Sun–Thurs 7–10pm; Fri–Sat 7–10:30pm.

Moderate

Café Saint-Honoré FRENCH/SCOTTISH   Between Frederick and Hanover Streets, this is a French-inspired bistro with a dinner format that's much more formal and expensive than its deliberately rapid lunchtime venue. An upbeat and usually enthusiastic staff serves a combination of Scottish and French cuisine that includes venison with juniper berries and wild mushrooms; local pheasant in wine and garlic sauce; and lamb kidneys with broad beans inspired by the cuisine of the region around Toulouse. Fish is very fresh.

34 NW Thistle St. Lane. © **0131/226-2211.** Reservations recommended. Main courses £7.50–£13 ($12–$20) lunch, £14–£17 ($22–$28) dinner; pre-theater fixed-price meal £14–£18 ($22–$29). AE, DC, MC, V. Mon–Fri noon–2:15pm and pre-theater meal 5–7pm; Mon–Sat 7–10 or 11pm. Bus: 3, 16, 17, 23, 27, or 31.

Duck's at Le Marché Noir ⭐ SCOTTISH/FRENCH   The cuisine here is more stylish and more tuned to the culinary sophistication of London than the cuisine at many other restaurants in Edinburgh. Set within a wood house whose outside and inside are decorated in dark green, it honors the traditions of Scotland with a handful of dishes. (An example is their baked haggis in phyllo pastry on a bed of turnip purée and red wine sauce.) More modern dishes include a boudin of chicken and foie gras served with wilted spinach and applesauce; seared salmon with leeks, asparagus, zucchini, and a pickled ginger and sesame salad; roasted rack of lamb with thyme juice and roasted vegetables; and grilled red snapper with wild rice and lime-marinated sweet-potato pickles.

2/4 Eyre Place. © **0131/558-1608.** Reservations recommended. Set-price lunch £15 ($24); dinner main courses £18–£22 ($28–$34). AE, DC, MC, V. Mon–Sat noon–2pm and 7–9:30pm. Bus: 23 or 27.

Haldanes Restaurant ⭐ SCOTTISH   Set in the cellar of the Albany Hotel building, within a pair of royal blue and gold-tinted dining rooms, Haldanes features the cuisine of George Kelso. During clement weather, the venue moves out to the building's verdant garden. Our recent party of Scottish friends dug into such delights as braised shank of Scottish lamb with Puy lentils; pan-fried breast of guinea fowl stuffed with a leek mousse; and baked filet of Scottish salmon topped with a chive crème fraîche. If you want to go truly local, order the Highland venison with black pudding and red beet root in a rosemary sauce.

39A Albany St. © **0131/556-8407.** Reservations recommended. Set-price lunch £11–£15 ($17–$24); dinner main courses £15–£22 ($24–$35). AE, DC, MC, V. Daily noon–1:30pm and 6–9:30pm. Bus: 15.

The Tower ⭐⭐ SEAFOOD/MODERN BRITISH   This is a hot dining ticket set at the top of the Museum of Scotland. The inventive kitchen will regale you with hearty portions of some of the finest steaks and roast beef, along with excellent and freshly caught seafood. Dig into an array of oysters or lobsters, or try a platter of mixed seafood. We still remember fondly the smoked haddock risotto with a poached egg and shavings of Parmesan cheese. Sea bass is perfectly seasoned and grilled, and there's even sushi on the menu. Scottish loin of lamb is given a modern twist with a side dish of minted couscous.

In the Museum of Scotland, Chambers St. © **0131/225-3003.** Reservations required. Main courses £10–£14 ($16–$22) lunch, £15–£25 ($24–$40) dinner. AE, DC, MC, V. Daily noon–11pm. Closed Dec 25–26. Bus: 3, 7, 21, 30, 31, 53, 69, or 80.

Inexpensive

Far Pavilions INDIAN/CONTINENTAL   Established in 1987, this Indian restaurant offers finely tuned service. Highly recommended is the house specialty, *murg masala*, concocted with tandoori chicken that falls off the bone thanks to slow cooking in a garlic-based butter sauce. Menu items include curry dishes influenced by British tastes, as well as authentic platters whose composition is faithful to their original Indian tradition. Most items are suitably pungent, and are concocted from lamb, seafood, vegetables, and beef. The staff is always able to combine them with the garnishes and side dishes to form a worthy Indian meal.

10 Craigleith Rd., Comely Bank. ✆ **0131/332-3362.** Reservations recommended. Main courses £8–£17 ($13–$27) lunch, £9–£15 ($14–$24) dinner. Lunch buffet £7 ($11) per person. AE, MC, V. Mon–Fri noon–2pm; Mon–Sat 5:30–11:30pm. Bus: 19, 39, 55, 81, or X91.

Henderson's Salad Table ✿ *Value* VEGETARIAN   This is a Shangri-la for health-food lovers. Hot dishes such as peppers stuffed with rice and pimiento are served on request, and a vegetarian twist on the national dish of Scotland, haggis, is usually available. Other well-prepared dishes filled with flavor include cheese and onion potato croquette, vegetable lasagna, and a broccoli and cheese crumble. The homemade desserts include a fresh fruit salad and a cake with double-whipped cream and chocolate sauce. The wine cellar offers 30 wines. Live music, ranging from classical to jazz to folk, is played every evening.

94 Hanover St. ✆ **0131/225-2131.** Main courses £3.95–£5 ($6.30–$8). Fixed-price meals £7.25 ($12) lunch, £11 ($18) dinner. AE, MC, V. Mon–Sat 8am–10:30pm. Bus: 23 or 27.

Valvona & Crolla INTERNATIONAL   In 1872, a recent arrival from Italy opened this restaurant, and it's still going strong. It shares space with a delicatessen and food emporium. A few steps down from the main shopping area, this cafe and lunch restaurant serves very fresh food at refreshingly low prices. Here, you can order three kinds of breakfast (continental, Scottish, or vegetarian) for a fixed price of £3.95 ($5.95); or you can order platters of pasta, mixed sausages, cold cuts, crostini, risottos, or omelets. Don't expect leisurely dining, as the place caters to office workers and shoppers who appreciate the informality, low prices, and freshness of the food.

19 Elm Row. ✆ **0131/556-6066.** Pizzas, pastas, or platters £3–£10 ($4.80–$16). AE, MC, V. Mon–Sat noon–3pm. Bus: 7, 10, 11, 12, or 14.

IN THE CENTER—OLD TOWN
Moderate

Dubh Prais SCOTTISH   Dubh Prais (Gaelic for "The Black Pot") conjures up an image of an old-fashioned Scottish recipe bubbling away in a stewpot above a fireplace. Menu items are time-tested and not at all experimental, but flavorful nonetheless. Examples include smoked salmon; ragout of wild mushrooms and Ayrshire bacon served with garlic sauce; saddle of venison with juniper sauce; and a supreme of salmon with grapefruit-flavored butter sauce.

123B High St., Royal Mile. ✆ **0131/557-5732.** Reservations recommended. Main courses £6.50 ($10) lunch; £13–£18 ($20–$28) dinner. AE, MC, V. Tues–Fri noon–2pm; Tues–Sat 6–10:30pm. Closed 2 weeks at Christmas and 1 week at Easter. Bus: 11.

Inexpensive

Baked Potato Shop *Value* VEGETARIAN/WHOLE FOOD   This is the least expensive restaurant in a very glamorous neighborhood, and it attracts mobs of office workers every day. Many carry their food away. Only free-range eggs, whole foods, and vegetarian cheeses are used. Vegan cakes are a specialty.

56 Cockburn St. ℂ 0131/225-7572. Reservations not accepted. Food items 75p–£3.20 ($1.20–$5.10). No credit cards. Daily 9am–9pm (to 10pm in summer). Bus: 5.

Pierre Victoire FRENCH   This was the original model for a series of franchises that have sprouted up in recent years in six other areas of Edinburgh. Many residents still prefer the original to the newer versions. It's an ideal, if chaotic, stopover if you're antiques shopping and climbing Victoria Street. It's also one of the most popular evening gathering places, as it keeps long hours. In a bistro setting with crowded tables, you can order grilled mussels in garlic with Pernod butter, salmon with ginger, or roast pheasant with cassis. Vegetarians will also find selections to suit your taste.

10–14 Victoria St. ℂ 0131/225-1721. Reservations recommended. Main courses £8.50–£13 ($14–$20); fixed-price lunches £7.90 ($13) and £9.95 ($16). MC, V. Daily noon–3pm and 6–7:30pm. Bus: 1, 23, 27, 42, 46, or 47.

SOUTH OF THE CENTER

Kelly's ℛ MODERN SCOTTISH/MODERN FRENCH   Catering to a crowd of barristers, artists, financiers, and employees of the nearby university, this stylish restaurant is a 20-minute walk south of the center in a residential neighborhood. The menu includes such dishes as *asado* (barbecue) of lamb in olive-and-herb crust with spicy couscous, roast breast of Barbary duck with black pepper and blueberries, and ravioli of lobster with asparagus. Dessert might be a caramelized lemon tart.

46 W. Richmond St. ℂ 0131/668-3847. Reservations recommended. Main courses £13–£15 ($21–$24). Fixed-price 3-course meal £12 ($19) lunch, £27 ($43) dinner. DC, MC, V. Mon–Sat noon–2pm and 6–10pm. Bus: 11, 12, or 14.

LEITH

In the northern regions of Edinburgh, Leith is the old port town, opening onto the Firth of Forth. Once it was a city in its own right until it was slowly absorbed into Edinburgh.

Expensive

Martin Wishart ℛℛℛ MODERN FRENCH   Several gourmet associations claim this is the "Scottish restaurant of the year." The chef/owner Martin Wishart takes it all in stride and continues to improve the quality of his cuisine in a fashionable part of the Leith docklands. With white walls and modern art, the decor is minimalist. The menu is short but sweet and ever changing. Many dishes are simply prepared, the natural flavors coming through. Others show a touch of elegance and fantasy, including partridge breast with black truffle and foie gras, and the lobster ravioli with a light shellfish cream. After you eat the glazed lemon tart with praline ice cream on which white raspberry coulis has been dribbled, the day is yours.

54 The Shore, Leith. ℂ 0131/553-3557. Reservations required. Main courses £16–£20 ($25–$32). Set-price lunch £14–£16 ($22–$25). MC, V. Tues–Fri noon–2pm; Tues–Sat 7–10pm. Bus: 7 or 10.

Moderate

Vintner's Room ℛ *Finds* FRENCH/SCOTTISH   Join locals and visitors down by the waterfront in Leith. Chances are they are heading to this restaurant. Near the entrance, beneath a venerable ceiling of oaken beams, a wine bar serves platters and drinks beside a large stone fireplace. Most diners, however, head for the small but elegant dining room, illuminated by flickering candles. Fresh ingredients are used in a vast array of specialties. You might begin with such appetizers as pear-and-watercress soup or pigeon-and-juniper terrine. The baked halibut with lobster bisque makes a tasty main course, as does the saddle of hare with brandy and grapes. Game delights are the thyme-flavored roast partridge with Marsala or the noisettes of venison with heather honey and red currants. Finish off with grilled apricots flavored with Amaretto and served with a basil-flavored ice.

The Vaults, 87 Giles St., Leith. ℂ 0131/554-6767. Reservations recommended. Table d'hôte lunch £12–£15 ($18–$24); dinner main courses £15–£32 ($24–$51). AE, MC, V. Mon–Sat noon–2pm and 7–10:30pm. Closed 2 weeks at Christmas. Bus: 7 or 10.

SEEING THE SIGHTS
SIGHTSEEING SUGGESTIONS FOR FIRST-TIME VISITORS

If You Have 1 Day Visit **Edinburgh Castle** as soon as it opens in the morning, then walk the **Royal Mile** to the Palace of **Holyroodhouse,** former abode of Mary, Queen of Scots. Look out over the city from the vantage point of **Arthur's Seat.** Stroll through **Princes Street Gardens,** capping your day with a walk along the major shopping thoroughfare, **Princes Street.**

If You Have 2 Days In the morning of your second day, head for Old Town again, but this time explore its narrow streets, wynds, and closes, and visit the **John Knox House,** the **High Kirk of St. Giles,** and the small museums. After lunch, climb the **Scott Monument** for a good view of Old Town and the Princes Street Gardens. Spend the rest of the afternoon exploring the **National Gallery of Scotland.**

If You Have 3 Days Spend day 3 getting acquainted with the major attractions of New Town, including the **National Museum of Scotland, National Portrait Gallery, Georgian House,** and **Royal Botanic Garden.**

If You Have 4 or 5 Days On the fourth day, take a trip west to **Stirling Castle** and see some of the dramatic scenery of the **Trossachs.** On the fifth day you'll feel like a native, so seek out some of the city's minor but interesting attractions, such as the **Camera Obscura,** the **Scotch Whisky Heritage Centre,** and **Dean Village.**

THE ROYAL MILE 𝕽𝕽
The Royal Mile (bus: 1, 6, 23, 27, 30, 34, 35, or 36) stretches from Edinburgh Castle all the way to the Palace of Holyroodhouse. Walking along it, you'll see some of the most interesting old structures in Edinburgh, with turrets, gables, and towering chimneys.

High Kirk of St. Giles   Built in 1120, a short walk downhill from Edinburgh Castle, this church is one of the most important architectural landmarks along the Royal Mile. It combines a dark and brooding stone exterior with surprisingly graceful and delicate flying buttresses. One of its outstanding features is its **Thistle Chapel,** housing beautiful stalls and notable heraldic stained-glass windows. Cathedral guides are available at all times to conduct tours.

High St. ℂ 0131/225-9442. Free admission; £1 ($1.60) donation suggested. Easter–Sept Mon–Fri 9am–7pm, Sat 9am–5pm, Sun 1–5pm; Oct–Easter Mon–Sat 9am–5pm, Sun 1–5pm. Sun services at 8am, 10am, 11:30am, 6pm, and 8pm. Weekday services: Mon–Sat at noon, Mon–Fri at 8am, Sat at 6pm.

Writers' Museum   This 1622 house takes its name, Lady Stair's House, from a former owner, Elizabeth, the dowager countess of Stair. Today it's a treasure trove of portraits, relics, and manuscripts relating to three of Scotland's greatest men of letters. The Robert Burns collection includes his writing desk, rare manuscripts, portraits, and many other items. Also on display are some of Sir Walter Scott's possessions, including his pipe, chess set, and original manuscripts. The museum holds one of the most significant Robert Louis Stevenson collections anywhere, including personal belongings, paintings, photographs, and early editions.

In Lady Stair's House, off Lawnmarket. © 0131/529-4901. Free admission. Mon–Sat 10am–5pm; Sun 2–5pm.

Museum of Childhood *Kids* The world's first museum devoted solely to the history of childhood stands just opposite John Knox's House. Contents of its four floors range from antique toys to games to exhibits on health, education, and costumes, plus video presentations and an activity area. Because of the youthful crowd it naturally attracts, it ranks as the noisiest museum in town.

42 High St. © 0131/529-4142. Free admission. Mon–Sat 10am–5pm; July–Aug, also Sun 2–5pm.

The Real Mary King's Close *Finds* Beneath the City Chambers on the Royal Mile lies Old Town's deepest secret, a warren of hidden streets where people lived and worked for centuries. Opening in 2003, this new attraction allows you to go back into the turbulent days of plague-ridden Edinburgh in the 17th century. Today's visitors can see a number of underground "closes," originally very narrow walkways with houses on either side, some dating back centuries. When the Royal Exchange (now the City Chambers) was constructed in 1753, the top floors of the buildings of the close were torn down, although the lower sections were used as the foundations of the new building, leaving a number of dark and mysterious passages intact. In April 2003, guided parties were allowed to visit these dwellings for the first time. Subtle lighting and audio effects add to the experience. You can visit everything from a gravedigger's family stricken with the plague to a grand 16th-century town house. The haunted Shrine Room is the best surviving 17th-century house in Scotland.

Writers' Court, off the Royal Mile. © 0870/243-0160. Admission £7 ($11) adults, £5 ($8) children, £21 ($34) family. Bus: 1 or 6.

John Knox's House Even if you're not interested in the reformer who founded the Scottish Presbyterian Church, you may want to visit his house, as it's characteristic of the "lands" that used to flank the Royal Mile. All of them are gone now, except Knox's house, with its timbered gallery. Inside, you'll see the tempera ceiling in the Oak Room, along with exhibitions of Knox memorabilia.

43–45 High St. © 0131/556-9579. Admission £2.25 ($3.60) adults, £1.75 ($2.80) seniors/students, 75p ($1.20) children. Mon–Sat 10am–4:30pm (July–Sept also Sun noon–5pm).

The People's Story If you continue walking downhill along Canongate toward Holyroodhouse, you'll see one of the handsomest buildings on the Royal Mile. Built in 1591, the **Canongate Tolbooth** was once the courthouse, prison, and center of municipal affairs for the burgh of Canongate. Now it contains a museum celebrating the social history of the inhabitants of Edinburgh from the late 18th century to the present, with lots of emphasis on the cultural displacements of the Industrial Revolution.

163 Canongate. © 0131/529-4057. Free admission. Mon–Sat 10am–5pm. Bus: 1.

Museum of Edinburgh Across from the Canongate Tolbooth is this fine example of a restored 16th-century mansion. Today it functions as Edinburgh's principal museum of local history. The interior contains faithfully crafted reproductions of rooms inspired by the city's traditional industries, including exhibits devoted to glassmaking, pottery, wool processing, and cabinetry, always with a focus on the stamina and struggles of the workers who labored within.

142 Canongate. ℂ 0131/529-4143. Free admission. Mon–Sat 10am–5pm; during the Edinburgh Festival, also Sun 2–5pm. Bus: 1.

Scotch Whisky Heritage Centre   This center is privately funded by a conglomeration of Scotland's biggest distillers. It highlights the economic effect of whisky on both Scotland and the world and illuminates the centuries-old traditions associated with whisky making, showing the science and art of distilling. There's a 7-minute audiovisual show and an electric car ride past 13 sets showing historic moments in the whisky industry. A tour entitling you to sample five whiskies and take away a miniature bottle is £12 ($18) per person.

354 Castlehill. ℂ 0131/220-0441. www.whisky-heritage.co.uk. Admission £7.50 ($12) adults, £5.50 ($8.80) seniors and students with ID, £3.95 ($6.30) ages 5 to 17, free for children 4 and under. Daily 10am–5pm.

HISTORIC SITES

Edinburgh Castle ★★   Although its early history is vague, it's believed that Edinburgh was built on the dead volcano, Castle Rock. It's known that in the 11th century Malcolm III (Canmore) and his Saxon queen, later venerated as St. Margaret, founded a castle on this same spot. The only fragment left of their original castle—in fact the oldest structure in Edinburgh—is **St. Margaret's Chapel.** Built in the Norman style, the oblong structure dates principally from the 12th century.

Inside the castle you can visit the **State Apartments,** particularly Queen Mary's bedroom, where Mary, Queen of Scots, gave birth to James VI of Scotland (later James I of England). The highlight is the Crown Chamber, which houses the Honours of Scotland (Scottish Crown Jewels), used at the coronation of James VI, along with the scepter and the sword of state of Scotland.

You can also view the Stone of Scone or "Stone of Destiny," on which Scottish kings had been crowned since time immemorial. Edward I of England carried the stone off to Westminster Abbey in 1296, where it rested under the British coronation chair. It was finally returned to its rightful home in Scotland in November 1996, where it was welcomed with much pomp and circumstance.

Castlehill. ℂ 0131/225-9846. Admission £8 ($13) adults, £6 ($9.60) seniors, £2 ($3.20) children 15 and under. Apr–Sept daily 9:30am–6pm; Oct–Mar daily 9:30am–5pm. Bus: 1 or 6.

Moments **For Mr. Hyde Fans**

Near Gladstone's Land is **Brodie's Close,** a stone-floored alleyway. You can wander into the alley for a view of old stone houses that'll make you think you've stepped into a scene from a BBC production of a Dickens novel. It was named in honor of the notorious Deacon Brodie, a respectable councilor by day and a thief by night (he was the inspiration for Robert Louis Stevenson's *The Strange Case of Dr. Jekyll and Mr. Hyde*, though Stevenson set his story in foggy London town, not in Edinburgh). Brodie was hanged in 1788, and the mechanism used for the hangman's scaffolding had previously been improved by Brodie himself—for use on others, of course. Across the street is the most famous pub along the Royal Mile: **Deacon Brodie's Tavern** (see later in this chapter).

Palace of Holyroodhouse 🍁🍁   This palace was built adjacent to an Augustinian abbey established by David I in the 12th century. The nave, now in ruins, remains today. James IV founded the palace nearby in the early part of the 16th century, but only the north tower is left. Much of what you see today was ordered built by Charles II.

The most dramatic incident in the history of Holyroodhouse occurred in the old wing when Mary, Queen of Scots, was in residence. Her Italian secretary, David Rizzio, was murdered (with 56 stab wounds) in the audience chamber by Mary's husband, Lord Darnley, and his accomplices. The palace suffered long periods of neglect, although it basked in glory at the ball thrown by Bonnie Prince Charlie in the mid–18th century. The present queen and Prince Philip live at Holyroodhouse whenever they visit Edinburgh. When they're not in residence, the palace is open to visitors.

Canongate, at the eastern end of the Royal Mile. © 0131/556-7371. www.royal.gov.uk/output/page559. asp. Admission £6.50 ($10) adults, £5 ($8) seniors, £3.30 ($5.30) children 15 and under, £17 ($26) family (2 adults and 2 children). Daily 9:30am–4:45pm. Closed 2 weeks in May and 3 weeks in late June and early July (dates vary). Bus: 24 or 35.

MORE ATTRACTIONS

Scott Monument 🍁   Completed in the mid–19th century, the Gothic-inspired Scott Monument is the most famous landmark of Edinburgh. Sir Walter Scott's heroes are carved as small figures in the monument, and you can climb to the top. You can also see the first-ever **floral clock,** which was constructed in 1904, in the West Princes Street Gardens.

In the East Princes St. Gardens. © 0131/529-4068. Admission £2.50 ($4). Mar–May and Oct, Mon–Sat 9am–6pm, Sun 10am–6pm; June–Sept, Mon–Sat 9am–8pm, Sun 10am–6pm; Nov–Feb, Mon–Sat 9am–4pm, Sun 10am–4pm. Bus: 1 or 6.

National Gallery of Scotland 🍁🍁🍁   This museum is located in the center of Princes Street Gardens. The gallery is rather small, but the collection was chosen with great care. The duke of Sutherland has lent the museum some paintings, including two Raphaels, Titian's two Diana canvases and his *Venus Rising from the Sea,* and the *Seven Sacraments,* a work of the great 17th-century Frenchman Nicolas Poussin. The Spanish masters are represented as well. You can also see excellent examples of English painting: Gainsborough's *The Hon. Mrs. Graham* and Constable's *Dedham Vale,* along with works by Turner, Reynolds, and Hogarth. Naturally, the work of Scottish painters is prominent, including Alexander Naysmith and Henry Raeburn, whose most famous work, *The Reverend Walker,* can be seen here.

2 The Mound. © 0131/624-6200. Free admission. Mon–Sat 10am–5pm; Sun noon–5pm (during the Edinburgh Festival, Mon–Sat 10am–6pm; Sun 11am–6pm). Bus: 3, 21, or 26.

Our Dynamic Earth 🍁 *Kids*   The Millennium Dome at Greenwich outside London may have been a bust, but the new millennium museum for Scotland is packing in the crowds. Not far from the Palace of Holyroodhouse, Our Dynamic Earth tells the story of Earth in all its diversity. You can push buttons to simulate earthquakes, meteor showers, and views of outer space. You can see replicas of the slimy green primordial soup where life began. Time capsules wind their way back through the eons, and a series of specialized aquariums re-create primordial life forms. That's not all; there is so much more, ranging from simulated terrains of polar ice caps to tropical rainforests with plenty of creepy-crawlies. All 11 galleries have stunning special effects.

Holyrood Rd. ⓒ **0131/550-7800**. www.dynamicearth.co.uk. Admission £8.45 ($14) adults; £6 ($10) students, £4.95 ($8) seniors and children ages 5–15; free for children under 5; £15–£26 ($24–$42) family. Apr–Oct daily 10am–6pm; Nov–Mar Wed–Sun 10am–5pm. Bus: 24 or 35.

Outlook Tower & Camera Obscura   The 1853 periscope is at the top of the Outlook Tower, from which you can view a panorama of the surrounding city. Trained guides point out the landmarks and talk about Edinburgh's fascinating history. In addition, there are several entertaining exhibits, all with an optical theme, and a well-stocked shop selling books, crafts, and compact discs.

Castlehill. ⓒ **0131/226-3709**. Admission £4.95 ($7.90) adults, £3.95 ($6.30) students, £3.15 ($5.05) seniors, £2.50 ($4) children, £15 ($23) family. Apr–June and Sept–Oct daily 9:30am–6pm; July–Aug daily 9:30am–7:30pm; Nov–Mar daily 10am–5pm. Bus: 1 or 6.

Royal Observatory Visitor Centre   On display here are the works of the Scottish National Observatory at home and abroad, featuring the finest images of astronomical objects, Scotland's largest telescope, and antique instruments. There's also a panoramic view of the city from the balcony. An exhibit, *The Universe,* uses photographs, videos, computers, and models to take you on a cosmic whirlwind tour from the beginning of time to the farthest depths of space in a couple of hours.

Blackford Hill. ⓒ **0131/668-8405**. Admission £3.50 ($5.60) adults; £2.50 ($4) students, seniors, and children 5–16; free for children 4 and under. Mon–Sat 10am–5pm; Sun noon–5pm. Bus: 40 or 41.

National Museum of Scotland (NMS) ✹✹✹   In 1998, two long-established museums, the Royal Museum of Scotland and the National Museum of Antiquities, were united into this single institution 2 blocks south of the Royal Mile. The museum showcases exhibits in the decorative arts, ethnography, natural history, geology, archaeology, technology, and science. Six modern galleries distill billions of years of Scottish history, a total of 12,000 items ranging from rocks found on the island of South Uist dating back 2.9 billion years to a Hillman Imp, one of the last 500 cars manufactured at the Linwood plant near Glasgow before it closed in 1981. One gallery is devoted to Scotland's role as an independent nation before it merged with the United Kingdom in 1707. Another gallery, devoted to industry and empire from 1707 to 1914, includes exhibits on shipbuilding, whisky distilling, the railways, and such textiles as the tartan and paisley.

Chambers St. ⓒ **0131/225-7534**. Free admission. Mon and Wed–Sat 10am–5pm; Tues 10am–8pm; Sun noon–5pm. Walk south from Waverley Station for 10 min. to reach Chambers St. Bus: 42, 23, 24, 29, 5, 3.

Scottish National Gallery of Modern Art ✹✹   Scotland's national collection of 20th-century art is set on 5.5 hectares (12 acres) of grounds, just a 15-minute walk from the west end of Princes Street. The collection is international in scope and high in quality despite its modest size. Major sculptures outside the building include pieces by Henry Moore and Barbara Hepworth. Inside, the collection ranges from a fauve Derain and cubist Braque and Picasso to recent works by Paolozzi. There's a strong representation of English and Scottish artists—William Turner, John Constable, Henry Raeburn, and David Wilkie, to name a few. Works by Matisse, Miró, Kirchner, Kokoschka, Ernst, Ben Nicholson, Nevelson, Balthus, Lichtenstein, Kitaj, and Hockney are also on view.

Belford Rd. ⓒ **0131/556-8921**. Free admission, except for some temporary exhibits. Mon–Sat 10am–5pm; Sun noon–5pm. Bus: 13, or take 18, 20, or 41 and ask the driver for the stop closest to the museum and then take the 5-min. walk up Queensferry Terrace and Belford Rd. to the gallery.

Britannia: The People's Yacht

In case the queen never invited you to sail aboard her 125m (412-ft.) yacht, there's still a chance to go aboard this world-famous vessel. Launched on April 16, 1953, the luxury yacht was decommissioned December 11, 1997. Today, the yacht—technically a Royal Navy ship— which has sailed more than a million miles, rests at anchor in the port of Leith, 3km (2 miles) from the center of Edinburgh. The gangplank is now lowered for the public, whereas it once was lowered for such world leaders as Mahatma Gandhi, Tony Blair, and Nelson Mandela.

British taxpayers spent £160 million maintaining the yacht throughout most of the 1990s. Even a major refit would have prolonged the vessel's life for only a few more years. Because of budgetary constraints, a decision was made to put it in dry dock. The public reaches the vessel by going through a visitor center designed by Sir Terence Conran. At its centerpiece is the yacht's 12m (41-ft.) tender floating in a pool.

Once on board, you're guided around all five decks by an audio tour. You can also visit the drawing room and the Royal Apartments, once occupied by the likes of not only the queen, but Prince Philip and princes William, Harry, Edward, and Andrew, as well as princesses Anne and Margaret. Even the engine room, the galleys, and the captain's cabin can be visited.

All tickets should be booked as far in advance as possible by calling ℂ **0131/555-5566.** The yacht is open daily except Christmas, with the first tour beginning at 10:30am, the last tour at 3:30pm. Lasting 90 to 120 minutes, each tour is self-guided with the use of a headset lent to participants. Adults pay £8 ($13), seniors £6 ($9.60), and ages 5 to 17 £4 ($6.40); those 4 and under visit free. A family ticket, good for two adults and up to two children, is £6 ($9.60). From Waverley Bridge, take either city bus (Lothian Transport) X50, the Guide Friday tour bus marked BRITANNIA, or bus 22, 34, or 35.

Dean Gallery ⭐ (Finds) Across from the Scottish National Gallery of Modern Art, Dean Gallery houses the Modern Art's extensive collections of Dada and Surrealism. For those of us who are fascinated by these art movements, there's nothing better in Scotland. All of our favorite artists—and maybe yours too— are here, from Max Ernst to Joan Miró and, of course, Salvador Dalí. The major exhibit here consists of a large part of the works of Sir Eduardo Paolozzi, a hip modern Scottish sculptor. The collection of prints, drawings, plaster maquettes (models), molds, and contents of his studio are housed in the gallery.

73 Belford Rd. ℂ **0131/624-6200.** Free admission except for special exhibitions (prices vary then). Mon–Sat 10am–5pm; Sun noon–5pm. Bus: See "Scottish National Gallery of Modern Art," above.

Scottish National Portrait Gallery Housed in a red stone Victorian Gothic building by Rowand Anderson, this portrait gallery gives you a chance to see what the famous people of Scottish history looked like. The portraits, several by Ramsay and Raeburn, include everybody from Mary, Queen of Scots, to Sean Connery, and from Flora Macdonald to Irvine Welsh.

Moments A Step Back in Time at Historic Dean Village

The village is one of the most photographed sights in the city. Set in a valley about 30m (100 ft.) below the level of the rest of Edinburgh, it's full of nostalgic charm. The settlement dates from the 12th century, and for many centuries it was a grain-milling center. The current residents worked hard to restore the old buildings—many of which were converted into flats and houses—and managed to maintain all of the original Brigadoonlike charm. A few minutes from the West End, it's located at the end of Bell's Brae, off Queensferry Street, on the Water of Leith. You can enjoy a celebrated view by looking downstream under the high arches of Dean Bridge, designed by Telford in 1833. The most scenic walk is along the water in the direction of St. Bernard's Well.

---

1 Queen St. (*C* 0131/624-6200. Free admission, except for some temporary exhibits. Mon–Sat 10am–5pm; Sun noon–5pm. Bus: 18, 20, or 41.

A GARDEN
Gardeners and nature lovers will be attracted to the **Royal Botanic Garden,** Inverleith Row (*C* **0131/552-7171**). Main areas of interest are the Exhibition Hall, Alpine House, Demonstration Garden, annual and herbaceous borders (summer only), copse, Woodland Garden, Wild Garden, Arboretum, Peat Garden, Rock Garden, Heath Garden, and pond. Admission is by voluntary donation. It's open April through August from 9:30am to 7pm, March and September from 9:30am to 6pm, February and October from 9:30am to 5pm, and November through January from 9:30am to 4pm.

ORGANIZED TOURS
If you want a quick introduction to the principal attractions in and around Edinburgh, consider one or more of the tours offered by **Lothian Region Transport,** 14 Queen St. (*C* **0131/555-6363;** www.lothianbuses.co.uk). You won't find a cheaper way to hit the highlights. You can see most of the major sights of Edinburgh, including the Royal Mile, the Palace of Holyroodhouse, Princes Street, and Edinburgh Castle, by double-decker motor coach for £7.50 ($12) adults, £6 ($9.60) seniors and students, and £2.50 ($4) children. This ticket is valid all day on any LRT Edinburgh Classic Tour bus, which allows passengers to get on and off at any of the 15 stops along its routes. The tours are given from April to late October; a curtailed winter program is also offered. Buses start from Waverley Bridge, near the Scott Monument, every day beginning at 9:15am; they depart every 15 minutes in summer and about every 30 minutes in winter, then embark on a circuit of Edinburgh that, if you remain on the bus without getting off, takes about 2 hours. Commentary is offered along the way.

Tickets for any of these tours can be bought at LRT offices at Waverley Bridge, or at 14 Queen St., or at the tourist information center in Waverley Market. Advance reservations are a good idea.

THE SHOPPING SCENE
The best buys are tartans and woolens, along with bone china and Scottish crystal. Princes Street, George Street, and the Royal Mile are the major shopping arteries. Here are a few suggestions.

Looking for a knitted memento? Moira-Anne Leask, owner of the **Shetland Connection,** 491 Lawnmarket (© **0131/225-3525;** bus: 1), promotes the skills of the Shetland knitter, and her shop is packed with sweaters, hats, and gloves in colorful Fair Isle designs. She also offers hand-knitted mohair, Aran, and Icelandic sweaters. Items range from fine-ply cobweb shawls to chunky ski sweaters handcrafted by skilled knitters in top-quality wool.

If you've ever suspected that you might be Scottish, **Tartan Gift Shops,** 54 High St. (© **0131/558-3187;** bus: 1), has a chart indicating the place of origin, in Scotland, of your family name. You'll then be faced with a bewildering array of hunt-and-dress tartans. The high-quality wool is sold by the yard as well as in the form of kilts for both men and women.

Clan Tartan Centre, 70–74 Bangor Rd., Leith (© **0131/553-5161;** bus: 7 or 10), is one of the leading tartan specialists in Edinburgh, regardless of which clan you claim as your own. If you want help in identifying a particular tartan, the staff at this shop will assist you. At the same location is the **James Pringle Woollen Mill** (© **0131/553-5161**), which produces a large variety of top-quality wool items, including a range of Scottish knitwear—cashmere sweaters, tartan and tweed ties, travel rugs, tweed hats, and tam-o'-shanters. In addition, the mill has the only Clan Tartan Centre in Scotland, where more than 2,500 sets and trade designs are accessible through their research facilities.

The two best department stores in Edinburgh are **Debenham's,** 109–112 Princes St. (© **0131/2251320;** bus: 3, 31, or 69), and **Jenners,** 48 Princes St. (© **0131/2252442;** bus: 3, 31, or 69). Both stock Scottish and international merchandise.

Another Scottish shopping venue worth checking out is **Old Town Weaving Company,** 555 Castlehill (© **0131/557-0256;** bus: 1), where you can converse with craftspeople and purchase their work. If you're interested in old-fashioned Scottish crafts, this is the place. Established in 1866, **Hamilton & Inches,** 87 George St. (© **0131/225-4898;** bus: 41 or 42), is a gold- and silversmith with both modern and antique designs. It has a stunning late-Georgian interior as well.

EDINBURGH AFTER DARK

For a thorough list of entertainment options during your stay, pick up a copy of *The List,* a biweekly entertainment paper available free at the Edinburgh & Scotland Information Centre.

FESTIVALS

The highlight of Edinburgh's year—some would say the only time the real Edinburgh emerges—comes in the last weeks of August during the **Edinburgh International Festival.** Since 1947, the festival has attracted artists and companies of the highest international standard in all fields of the arts, including music, opera, dance, theater, exhibition, poetry, and prose, and "Auld Reekie" takes on a cosmopolitan air.

During the festival, one of the most exciting spectacles is the Military Tattoo on the floodlit esplanade in front of Edinburgh Castle, high on its rock above the city. Vast audiences watch the precision marching of Scottish regiments and military units from all parts of the world, and of course the stirring skirl of the bagpipes and the swirl of the kilt.

Less predictable in quality but greater in quantity is the **Edinburgh Festival Fringe** (180 High St., Edinburgh EH1 1BW; © **0131/226-5257;** www.ed fringe.com), an opportunity for anybody—professional or nonprofessional, an individual, a group of friends, or a whole company of performers—to put on a show wherever they can find an empty stage or street corner. Late-night reviews, outrageous and irreverent contemporary drama, university theater presentations, maybe even a full-length opera—Edinburgh gives them all free rein. A **Film Festival, Jazz Festival, Television Festival,** and **Book Festival** (every 2nd year) overlap in August.

Ticket prices for the various festivals range from £5 ($8) up to about £50 ($80) per seat. (The Fringe festival's Fringe Sun, on the 2nd weekend of the festival, is a free open-air showcase for hundreds of festival acts.) Information can be obtained at **Edinburgh International Festival,** The Hub, Castle Hill, Edinburgh EH1 7ND (© **0131/473-2000;** fax 0131/473-2003; www.eif.co.uk). The office is open Monday through Friday from 9:30am to 5:30pm.

Other sources of event information include **Edinburgh Book Festival,** 137 Dundee St., Edinburgh EH11 1BG (© **0131/228-5444;** www.edbookfest.co. uk); **Edinburgh International Film Festival,** 88 Lothian Rd., Edinburgh EH3 9BZ (© **0131/228-4051;** www.edfilmfest.org.uk); and **Edinburgh Military Tattoo,** 32 Market St., Edinburgh EH1 1QB (© **0131/225-1188;** www. edintattoo.co.uk).

THEATER

Edinburgh has a lively theater scene. In 1994, the **Festival Theatre,** 13–29 Nicolson St. (© **0131/662-1112** for administration, 0131/529-6000 for tickets during non-festival times, or 0131/225-5756 for tickets during the festival; bus: 3, 31, or 33), opened in time for some aspects of the Edinburgh Festival. Set on the eastern edge of Edinburgh, near the old campus of the University of Edinburgh, it has since been called "Britain's de facto Dance House" because of its sprung floor, its enormous stage (the largest in Britain), and its suitability for opera presentations of all kinds. Tickets are £5.50 to £46 ($8.80–$73).

Another major theater is the **King's Theatre,** 2 Leven St. (© **0131/529-6000;** bus: 10 or 11), a Victorian venue offering a wide repertoire of classical entertainment, including ballet, opera, and West End productions. The **Netherbow Arts Centre,** 43 High St. (© **0131/556-9579;** bus: 1), has been called "informal," and productions here are often experimental and delightful—new Scottish theater at its best. Ask about lunchtime performances.

The resident company of **Royal Lyceum Theatre,** Grindlay Street (© **0131/248-4848;** bus: 11 or 15), also has an enviable reputation; its presentations range from the works of Shakespeare to works by new Scottish playwrights. The **Traverse Theatre,** Cambridge Street (© **0131/228-1404;** bus: 11 or 15), is one of the few theaters in Britain funded solely to present new plays by British writers and first translations into English of international works.

BALLET, OPERA & CLASSICAL MUSIC

The **Scottish Ballet** and the **Scottish Opera** perform at the **Playhouse Theatre,** 18–22 Greenside Place (© **0131/7839-4401;** bus: 7 or 14). With 3,100 seats, it's the town's largest theater. The **Scottish Chamber Orchestra** makes its home at the **Queen's Hall,** Clerk Street (© **0131/668-3456;** bus: 3, 33, or 31), also a major venue for the Edinburgh International Festival.

FOLK MUSIC & CEILIDHS

Folk music is presented in many clubs and pubs in Edinburgh, but these strolling players tend to be somewhat erratic in their appearances. Ceilidhs (pronounced

⌢ Moments A Wee Dram for Fans of Malt Whisky

It requires a bit of an effort to reach it (take bus nos. 10A, 16, or 17 from Princes Street to Leith), but for fans of malt whisky, the **Scotch Malt Whisky Society** has been called "The Top of the Whisky Pyramid" by distillery-industry magazines in Britain. It's on the second floor of a 16th-century warehouse at 87 Giles St., Leith (© **0131/554-3451**), and was originally designed to store Bordeaux and port wines from France and Portugal. All you can order are single-malt whiskies, served neat, usually in a dram (unless you want yours watered down with branch water) and selected from a staggering choice of whiskies from more than 100 distilleries throughout Scotland. Hours are Monday through Wednesday from 10am to 5:30pm, Thursday through Saturday from 10am to 11pm.

kay-lee) are large gatherings where traditional music and folk dancing are featured. It's best to read notices in pubs and talk to the tourist office to see where the ceilidh will be on the night of your visit.

Some hotels regularly feature traditional Scottish music in the evenings. You might check with the **George Hotel** at 19–21 George St. (© **0131/225-1251**; bus: 3, 31, or 33). "Jamie's Scottish Evening" is presented at the **King James Hotel** on Leith Street (© **0131/556-0111**; bus: 7 or 14), Tuesday through Sunday at 7pm; the four-course dinner with wine and show costs £41 ($66).

PUBS & BARS

Edinburgh's most famous pub, **Café Royal Circle Bar,** 17 W. Register St. (© **0131/556-1884**; bus: 3, 31, or 33), is a long-enduring favorite. Part of it is now occupied by the Oyster Bar of the Café Royal, but life in the Circle Bar continues at its old pace. The opulent trappings of the Victorian era are still to be seen. Go up to the serving counter, which stands like an island in a sea of drinkers, and place your order.

The **Abbotsford,** 3 Rose St. (© **0131/225-5276**; bus: 3, 31, or 33), is near the eastern end of Rose Street, a short walk from Princes Street. This pub has served stiff drinks and oceans of beer since it was founded in 1887. Inside, the gaslight era is alive and thriving, thanks to a careful preservation of the original dark paneling, long battered tables, and ornate plaster ceiling. The inventories of beer on tap change about once a week, supplementing a roster of single-malt Scotches. Platters of food, priced from £2.20 to £7 ($3.50–$11), are dispensed from the bar. Established in 1806, **Deacon Brodie's Tavern,** 435 Lawnmarket (© **0131/225-6531**; bus: 1), is the neighborhood pub along the Royal Mile. It perpetuates the memory of Deacon Brodie, good citizen by day, robber by night (see earlier in this chapter). The tavern and wine cellars contain a restaurant and lounge bar.

DAY TRIPS FROM EDINBURGH

LINLITHGOW   In this royal burgh, a county town in West Lothian, 29km (18 miles) west of Edinburgh, Mary, Queen of Scots, was born in 1542. Her birthplace, the roofless **Linlithgow Palace** (© **01506/842-896**), can still be explored today, even if it's but a shell of its former self. The queen's suite was in the north quarter but was rebuilt for the homecoming of James VI (James I of England) in 1620. The palace burned to the ground in 1746. The Great Hall is on the first floor, and a small display shows some of the more interesting architectural relics. The ruined palace is 1km (½ mile) from Linlithgow Station. Admission is £2.80 ($4.50) adults, £2 ($3.20) seniors, £1 ($1.60) children. Hours are Monday through Saturday from 9:30am to 4pm, Sunday from 2 to 4pm.

South of the palace stands the medieval kirk of **St. Michael's Parish Church** (℃ **01506/842188**), open only May through September from 10am to 4:30pm. Many a Scottish monarch has worshiped here since its consecration in 1242. Despite being ravaged by the disciples of John Knox and transformed into a stable by Cromwell, it's one of Scotland's best examples of a parish church.

In the midst of beautifully landscaped grounds, laid out along the lines of Versailles, sits **Hopetoun House** (℃ **0131/331-2451**), 16km (10 miles) from Edinburgh. This is Scotland's greatest Adam mansion, and a fine example of 18th-century architecture. The splendid reception rooms are filled with 18th-century furniture, paintings, statuary, and other artworks. From a rooftop platform you see a panoramic view of the Firth of Forth. You can take the nature trail, explore the deer parks, investigate the Stables Museum, or stroll through the formal gardens, all on the grounds. The house is 3km (2 miles) from the Forth Road Bridge near South Queensferry, off A-904. If you don't have a car, take a cab from the rail station in Linlithgow for about £7 to £9 ($11–$14). Admission is £5.30 ($8.50) adults, £4.70 ($7.50) seniors, £2.70 ($4.30) children, £15 ($24) family (up to six). Hours are from 10am to 5:30pm (last admission 4:30pm), daily May through September, Easter weekend, and weekends in October.

Getting There   From Edinburgh, direct **trains** (℃ **0345/484950**) run every 15 minutes during the day to Linlithgow (trip time: 20 min.). Round-trip fare is £6 ($9.60) adults, £3 ($4.80) children. **Buses** also leave from St. Andrew's Square in Edinburgh (℃ **01324/613-777** for schedules), every 20 minutes (trip time: 1 hr.). Round-trip fare is £4.50 ($7.20) adults, £2.30 ($3.70) children. **Motorists** can take A902 to Corstorphine, then A8 to M9, getting off at the signposted junction (no. 3) to Linlithgow.

NORTH BERWICK   This royal burgh, created in the 14th century, was once an important Scottish port. Located in East Lothian, 39km (24 miles) east of Edinburgh, it's today a holiday resort popular with the Scots. Visitors are drawn to its golf courses, beaches, and harbor life on the Firth of Forth. You can climb the rocky shoreline or enjoy the heated outdoor swimming pool in July and August.

At the **information center,** Quality Street (℃ **01620/892-197**), you can pick up information on boat trips to the offshore islands, including **Bass Rock,** a volcanic island that is a breeding ground for about 10,000 gannets (a type of seabird). Hours are Monday through Saturday from 9:15am to 4:45pm.

Some 3km (2 miles) east of North Berwick, and 40km (25 miles) east of Edinburgh on A-198, stand the ruins of the 14th-century diked and rose-colored **Tantallon Castle** (℃ **01620/892-727**). This was the ancient stronghold of the Douglases until their defeat by Cromwell's forces in 1650. Overlooking the Firth of Forth, the castle ruins are still formidable, with a square, five-story central tower and a dovecote, plus the shell of its east tower, a D-shaped structure with a wall from the central tower. The best way to get to the castle is by car; buses run every 2 hours from North Berwick. The castle can be visited April through September, Monday through Friday from 9:30am to 6:30pm, Sunday from 2 to 6:30pm; the rest of the year it's open Monday through Wednesday and Saturday from 9:30am to 4pm, Thursday from 9:30am to 4:30pm, and Sunday from 2 to 4:30pm. Admission is £2.80 ($4.50) adults, £2 ($3.20) seniors, and £1 ($1.60) children.

Getting There   Trains (© 0845/748-4950) leave from Edinburgh about every half hour for the 30-minute trip. The round-trip costs £7.60 ($12). **Buses** (© 0800/232-323) leave from Charlotte Square in Edinburgh at 33 minutes past the hour, daily from 8:03am to 5:33pm; the round-trip takes 1¼ hours and costs £4.50 ($7.20) adults, £2.25 ($3.60) children. **Motorists** follow A198 from Edinburgh to North Berwick (it's signposted all the way).

DIRLETON   This little town, a preservation village, vies for the title of "prettiest village in Scotland." The town plan, drafted in the early 16th century, is essentially unchanged today. Dirleton has two greens shaped like triangles, with a pub opposite Dirleton Castle, placed at right angles to a group of cottages.

A rose-tinted 13th-century castle with surrounding gardens, once the seat of the wealthy Anglo-Norman de Vaux family, **Dirleton Castle** (© 01620/850-330) looks like a fairy-tale fortification, with its towers, arched entries, and oak ramp. Ruins of the Great Hall and kitchen can be seen, as well as what's left of the lord's chamber where the de Vaux family lived. The 16th-century main gate has a hole through which boiling tar or water could be poured to discourage unwanted visitors. The castle's country garden and bowling green are still in use. Admission is £2.80 ($4.50) adults, £2 ($3.20) seniors, £1 ($1.60) children. You can tour the castle April through September, Monday through Saturday from 9:30am to 6pm, Sunday from 10am to 6pm; October through March, Monday through Saturday from 9:30am to 4pm, Sunday from 2 to 4pm.

Getting There   Dirleton is on the Edinburgh–North Berwick road (A-198), 8km (5 miles) west of North Berwick and 3km (2 miles) east of Edinburgh. **Buses** (© 0800/23-23-23) leave from the St. Andrew's Square station in Edinburgh at 10 past and 20 till the hour (trip time: 1 hr.). The last bus departs at 5:10pm. One-way fare is £1.60 ($2.55) adults, 85p ($1.35) children.

2 Tayside & Grampian

Tayside and Grampian, two history-rich sections in northeast Scotland, offer a vast array of sightseeing, even though they're relatively small areas. Tayside, for example, is about 137km (85 miles) east to west, and some 97km (60 miles) south to north. The two regions share the North Sea coast between the Firth of Tay in the south and the Firth of Moray farther north. The so-called Highland Line separating the Lowlands in the south from the Highlands in the north crosses both regions. The Grampians, the highest mountain range in Scotland, are to the west of this line.

Carved out of the old counties of Perth and Angus, **Tayside** is named for its major river, the 190km (119-mile) Tay. The region is easy to explore, and its tributaries and dozens of lochs and Highland streams are among the best salmon and trout waters in Europe. One of the loveliest regions of Scotland, Tayside is filled with heather-clad Highland hills, long blue lochs under tree-lined banks, and miles and miles of walking trails. Perth and Dundee are among the six leading cities of Scotland. Tayside provided the backdrop for many novels by Sir Walter Scott, including *The Fair Maid of Perth, Waverley,* and *The Abbot.* Its golf courses are world famous, ranging from the trio of 18-hole courses at Gleneagles to the open championship links at Carnoustie.

The **Grampian** region has Aberdeen, Scotland's third-largest city, and Braemar, site of the most famous of the Highland gatherings. The queen herself comes here to holiday at Balmoral Castle, her private residence, a tradition dating back to the days of Queen Victoria and her consort, Prince Albert. As you journey on the scenic roads of Scotland's northeast, you'll pass heather-covered moorland and peaty lochs, wood glens and salmon-filled rivers, granite-stone villages and ancient castles, and fishing harbors as well as North Sea beach resorts.

After exploring Edinburgh, you can tour Tayside and Grampian. Perth, 70km (44 miles) north of Edinburgh, makes the best "gateway" to the region.

PERTH ✿

From its majestic position on the Tay, the ancient city of Perth was the capital of Scotland until the middle of the 15th century. It's here that the Highlands meet the Lowlands. Perth itself has few historic buildings. The main attraction, Scone Place, lies on the outskirts.

ESSENTIALS

GETTING THERE   By Train   ScotRail (© 08457/484950; www.railtrack.co.uk) provides service between Edinburgh and Perth (trip time: 90 min.), with continuing service to Dundee. The trip to Perth costs £9.40 ($15) from Edinburgh.

By Bus   Edinburgh and Perth are connected by frequent bus service (trip time: 1½ hr.). The fare is £5 ($8). For more information and schedules, check with **CityLink** (© 0990/505050).

By Car   To reach Perth from Edinburgh, take A-90 northwest and cross the Forth Road Bridge, and continue north along M-90 (trip time: 1½ hr.).

VISITOR INFORMATION   The **tourist information center** is at Lower City Mills, West Mill St. (© 01738/450600). It's open April through June daily from 9am to 6pm; July through September daily from 9am to 7pm; October daily from 9:30am to 6:30pm; and November through March, Monday through Saturday from 10am to 5pm.

WHERE TO STAY

Dupplin Castle ⚜⚜   This modern, severely dignified mansion was built in 1968 by well-known architect Schomber Scott to replace the last of the three castles that had once risen proudly from the site. Surrounded by 14 hectares (30 acres) of forest and spectacular gardens (some of its specimens are 250 years old), the site is one of the most beautiful near Perth. Rooms are rented in a spirit of elegance and good manners. Views from many overlook the valley of the River Earn. Meals must be booked 24 hours in advance.

Near Aberdalgie, Perth PH2 0PY. © 01738/623224. Fax 01738/444140. www.dupplin.co.uk. 7 units. £60–£75 ($96–$120) double. Rates include breakfast. MC, V. From Perth, follow the main highway to Glasgow, turning left onto B-9112 toward Aberdalgie and Forteviot. **Amenities:** Dining room; golf; salmon fishing; pheasant or partridge shooting. *In room:* Coffeemaker, hair dryer.

Hunting Tower ⚜   This late-Victorian country house, about a 10-minute drive from the city center, is set in 1.5 hectares (3½ acres) of well-manicured gardens. A modern wing of rooms was added in 1998. Taste and concern went into the interior decoration. Rooms, which vary wildly in size, have their specific charms. Seven offer spa baths.

Crieff Rd., Perth PH1 3JT. © 01738/583771. Fax 01738/583777. www.huntingtowerhotel.co.uk. 34 units. £92 ($147) double; from £102 ($163) cottage suite. Rates include Scottish breakfast. AE, DC, MC, V. Drive 6km (3½ miles) west on A-85. **Amenities:** Restaurant; bar; room service; laundry. *In room:* TV, minibar, coffeemaker, hair dryer.

Parklands Hotel & Restaurant ⚜   Luxuriously overhauled, this country-house hotel lies in the middle of the city. The beautifully decorated rooms overlook the South Inch Park. All are spacious and well furnished. Light traditional fare is served in country-house style.

2 St. Leonard's Bank, Perth PH2 8EB. © 01738/622451. Fax 01738/622046. www.parkslandhotel.co.uk. 14 units. £73–£115 ($117–$184) double. Rates include breakfast. AE, DC, MC, V. **Amenities:** Restaurant; bar; room service; laundry/dry cleaning. *In room:* TV, coffeemaker, hair dryer.

WHERE TO DINE

Let's Eat ⚜ BRITISH/INTERNATIONAL   The most visually striking, and most appealing, restaurant in Perth occupies the premises of an 1822 theater and intersperses its tables amid its soaring white columns. There's a particularly cozy lounge, site of a log-burning iron stove and comfortable sofas, where you might want a drink or aperitif before your meal. Menu items might include a gratin of goat's cheese studded with roasted peppers; filet of roasted venison with port wine sauce; marinated tuna on a bed of couscous; or grilled brochettes of monkfish with king prawns, rice, and salad. Dessert might be a baked chocolate pudding or the honey, whiskey and oatmeal parfait with local strawberries and a tuile biscuit. Be careful not to confuse this restaurant with its less grand, less expensive sibling, Let's Eat Again.

77–79 Kinnoul St. ✆ **01738/643377**. Reservations recommended. Main courses £8.50–£13 ($14–$20) lunch, £13–£17 ($20–$26) dinner. AE, MC, V. Tues–Sat noon–2pm and 6:30–9:45pm.

Littlejohn's SPANISH   On one of Perth's busiest commercial streets, this restaurant has one large dining room with old-fashioned wood paneling, antique signs, and lots of Scottish charm. Despite the conservative nature of the setting, the food offerings are eclectic and include pizzas, pastas, Mexican tortillas, burgers, steaks, and an occasional lobster dish.

24 St. John's St. ✆ **01738/639888**. Main courses £10–£15 ($16–$24). No credit cards. Daily 11am–11pm.

SEEING THE SIGHTS

Kirk of St. John the Baptist   This is the main sightseeing attraction of "the fair city." It's believed that the original foundation is from Pictish times. The present choir dates from 1440 and the nave from 1490. In 1559 John Knox preached his famous sermon here attacking idolatry, which caused a turbulent wave of iconoclasm to sweep across the land. In its wake, religious artifacts, stained glass, and organs were destroyed all over Scotland. The church was restored as a World War I memorial in the mid-1920s.

31 St. John Place. ✆ **01738/622241**. Free admission. Mon–Fri 10am–noon and 2–4pm.

Branklyn Garden   Once the finest hectare (2 acres) of private garden in Scotland, the garden now belongs to the National Trust for Scotland. It has a superb collection of rhododendrons, alpine plants, and herbaceous and peat-garden plants from all over the world.

116 Dundee Rd. (A 85), in Branklyn. ✆ **01738/625535**. Admission £3.50 ($5.60) adults; £2.60 ($4.15) children, students, and seniors, £9.50 ($15) family. Mar Oct daily 10am 5pm; closed in winter.

A DAY TRIP TO SCONE

Old Scone, 3km (2 miles) from Perth on the River Tay, was the ancient capital of the Picts. On a lump of sandstone called the "Stone of Destiny," the early Scottish monarchs were enthroned. In 1296 Edward I, the "Hammer of the Scots," moved the stone to Westminster Abbey, and for hundreds of years it rested under the chair on which British monarchs were crowned. The Scots have always bitterly resented this theft, and at last it has been returned to Scotland, to find a permanent home in Edinburgh Castle, where it can be viewed by the public.

The seat of the earls of Mansfield and birthplace of David Douglas of fir-tree fame, **Scone Palace** 🏰🏰, along A-93 (✆ **01738/552300**), was largely rebuilt in 1802, incorporating the old palace of 1580. Inside is an impressive collection of French furniture, china, ivories, and 16th-century needlework, including bed hangings executed by Mary, Queen of Scots. A fine collection of rare conifers is found on the grounds in the Pinetum. Rhododendrons and azaleas grow profusely in the gardens and woodlands around the palace. To reach the palace, head northeast of Perth on A-93. The site is open Good Friday to mid-October only, daily from 9:30am to 5pm. Admission to both house and grounds is £6.35 ($10) adults, £5.50 ($8.80) seniors, and £3.75 ($6) children under 17. Admission to the grounds only is £3.25 ($5.20) adults and £1.80 ($2.90) children.

Where to Stay & Dine

The Murrayshall ★★★ This elegant country-house hotel is set in 120 hectares (300 acres) of parkland. It was completely refurbished in 1987 and reopened as one of the showpieces of Perthshire. Because of the excellence of its challenging courses, this hotel is frequented by golfers and their families. Rooms come in a wide range of styles and space. Suites and executive rooms have the best amenities and views. The less-desired standard rooms are also comfortable but lack the character of the others. *Note:* On a windy night in Scotland there is no better place to be than the well-stocked bar with its log fire.

New Scone, Perthshire PH2 7PH. © **01738/551171.** Fax 01738/552595. 27 units. £130–£140 ($208–$224) double; £160–£170 ($256–$272) suite; £150 ($240) lodge. Rates include Scottish breakfast. AE, DC, MC, V. Take A-94 2.5km (1½ miles) east of New Scone. **Amenities:** 2 restaurants; 2 bars; 2 golf courses; tennis courts; gym; room service; babysitting; laundry/dry cleaning. *In room:* TV, hair dryer.

GLENEAGLES

This famous golfing center and sports complex is on a moor between Strathearn and Strath Allan. Gleneagles has four **18-hole golf courses:** King's Course, the longest one; Queen's Course, next in length; Prince's Course, shortest of all; and Glendevon, the newest of the quartet, built in 1980. They're among the best in Scotland, and the sports complex is one of the best equipped in Europe.

ESSENTIALS

GETTING THERE   By Train   The 15-minute ride from Perth costs £3.90 ($6.25). The trip from Edinburgh takes 1 hour and 40 minutes and costs £8.40 ($13). For information call © **08457/484950** or visit www.railtrack.co.uk.

By Bus   The only service departs from Glasgow. The trip takes slightly more than an hour and costs £6 ($9.60). For information and schedules, call © **0870/608-2608.**

By Car   Gleneagles is on A-9, about halfway between Perth and Stirling, a short distance from the village of Auchterarder. It lies 88km (55 miles) from Edinburgh and 72km (45 miles) from Glasgow.

VISITOR INFORMATION   The year-round **tourist center** is at 90 High St., Auchterarder (© **01764/663450**). It's open November through March, Monday through Friday from 9:30am to 5pm, Saturday from 11am to 3pm; April through June, Monday through Saturday from 9:30am to 5:30pm, Sunday from 11am to 4pm; July and August, Monday through Saturday from 9am to 7pm, Sunday from 11am to 6pm; and September and October, Monday through Saturday from 9:30am to 5:30pm, Sunday from 11am to 4pm.

WHERE TO STAY & DINE

Gleneagles Hotel ★★★ Britain's greatest golf hotel stands on its own 390-hectare (830-acre) estate. When it was built in isolated grandeur in 1924, it was Scotland's only five-star hotel. It's a true resort and has tried to keep ahead of the times by offering spa treatments. Rooms vary greatly in size. The best and most spacious choices are in the 60- to 90-block series; these have recently been refurbished. The less desirable rooms, called courtyard units, are a bit small and equipped with shower-only bathrooms. As for cuisine, the golfers rarely complain, but no one dines here to collect recipes.

Auchterarder PH3 1NF. © **01764/662231.** Fax 01764/662134. www.gleneagles.com. 211 units. £255–£410 ($408–$656) double; from £595 ($952) suite. Rates include Scottish breakfast. AE, DC, MC, V. Free parking. Take A-9 2.4km (1½ miles) southwest of Auchterarder. **Amenities:** 3 restaurants; 2 bars; pool; health spa; hunting excursions; room service; babysitting laundry/dry cleaning. *In room:* TV, minibar, coffeemaker, hair dryer, iron, safe.

CRIEFF

From Perth, head west on A-85 for 29km (18 miles) to Crieff. At the edge of the Perthshire Highlands, with good fishing and golf, Crieff makes a pleasant stopover. This small burgh was the seat of the court of the earls of Strathearn until 1747, and the gallows in its marketplace was once used to execute Highland cattle rustlers.

You can take a "day trail" into **Strathearn,** the valley of the River Earn, the very center of Scotland. Here highland mountains meet gentle Lowland slopes, and moorland mingles with rich green pastures. North of Crieff, the road to Aberfeldy passes through the narrow pass of the **Sma' Glen,** a famous spot of beauty, with hills rising on either side to 600m (2,000 ft.).

ESSENTIALS

GETTING THERE By Train There's no direct service. The nearest rail stations are at Gleneagles, 14km (9 miles) away, and at Perth, 29km (18 miles) away. Call © **08457/484950** or visit www.railtrack.co.uk for information.

By Bus Once you arrive in Perth, you'll find regular connecting bus service hourly during the day. For information and schedules, call **Stagecoach** at © **01738/629339.** The bus service from Gleneagles is too poor to recommend.

By Taxi From Gleneagles, a taxi will cost £20 to £30 ($32–$48).

VISITOR INFORMATION The year-round **tourist information office** is in the Town Hall on High Street (© **01764/652578**). It's open November through March, Monday through Friday from 9:30am to 5pm, Saturday from 10am to 2pm; April through June, Monday through Saturday from 9:30am to 5:30pm, Sunday from 11am to 4pm; July and August, Monday through Saturday from 9am to 7pm, Sunday from 11am to 6pm; and September and October, Monday through Saturday from 9:30am to 5:30pm, Sunday from 11am to 4pm.

WHERE TO STAY & DINE

Murraypark Hotel This stone-fronted house lies in a residential neighborhood about a 10-minute walk from Crieff's center and close to a golf course. In 1993, a new wing was opened, enlarging the public areas and the number of well-furnished rooms. The property has been considerably upgraded. Rooms in this 19th-century former sea captain's house vary in size and shape, but most open onto views. Although rooms in the new wing are more comfortable, they're hardly as evocative and we prefer the older wing's traditional Victorian aura.

Connaught Terrace, Crieff PH7 3DJ. © **01764/653731.** Fax 01764/655311. www.murraypark.com. 19 units. £70 ($112) double or suite. Rates include Scottish breakfast. AE, MC, V. Free parking. **Amenities:** Dining room; bar; room service; babysitting. *In room:* TV, coffeemaker, hair dryer.

SEEING THE SIGHTS

Glenturret Distillery Ltd Scotland's oldest distillery, Glenturret was established in 1775 on the banks of the River Turret. Visitors can see the milling of malt, mashing, fermentation, distillation, and cask filling, followed by a free "wee dram" dispensed at the end of the tour. Guided tours take about 25 minutes and leave at frequent intervals—sometimes as often as every 10 minutes when there's a demand for it. The tour can be followed or preceded by a 20-minute video, *The Water of Life,* presented adjacent to a small museum devoted to the implements of the whisky trade.

Hwy. A-85, Glenturret. © **01764/656565.** Guided tours £3.50 ($5.60) adults, £3 ($4.80) seniors, £2.30 ($3.70) persons 12–17, £9 ($14) family, free for children 11 and under. Mar–Dec Mon–Sat 9:30am–6pm, Sun noon–6pm; Feb Mon–Fri 11:30am–4:30pm, Sun noon–4pm. Closed Jan and Dec 25–26. Take A-85 toward Comrie; 1.5km (¾ mile) from Crieff, turn right at the crossroads; the distillery is .5km (¼ mile) up the road.

Drummond Castle Gardens ☆   The gardens of Drummond Castle, first laid out in the early 17th century by John Drummond, second earl of Perth, are among the finest formal gardens in Europe. There's a panoramic view from the upper terrace, overlooking an example of an early Victorian parterre in the form of St. Andrew's Cross. The multifaceted sundial by John Mylne, master mason to Charles I, has been the centerpiece since 1630.

Muthill, Crieff. © **01764/681257.** Admission £3.50 ($5.60) adults, £2.50 ($4) seniors, £1.50 ($2.40) children. May–Oct daily 2–6pm; Easter weekend 2–6pm. Closed Nov–Apr. Take A-822 for 5km (3 miles) south of Crieff.

PLAYING GOLF

Crieff Golf Club (© **01764/652909**) has two courses—both with panoramic views and excellent facilities. The most challenging is the 18-hole Fern Tower, a par-71 course with three par-5 holes. The Dornock is a 64-par, 9-hole course with three par-3 holes. It's not quite as difficult as the Fern Tower, but a test nonetheless. Greens fees for the Fern Tower are £25 ($40) per round Monday through Friday, and £33 ($53) weekends. Greens fees for the Dornock are £9 ($14) for 9 holes and £14 ($22) for 18 holes. Carts cost £14 ($22) per round. April through October, the golf club is open from 8am to 11pm; November through March, it's open Friday from 9am to 7pm and Saturday and Sunday from 8am to 7:30pm.

ABERFELDY ☆

The "Birks o' Aberfeldy" are among the beauty spots made famous by the poet Robert Burns. Once a Pictish center, this small town makes a fine base for touring Perthshire's glens and lochs. Loch Tay lies 10km (6 miles) to the west; Glen Lyon, 24km (15 miles) west; and Kinloch Rannoch, 29km (18 miles) northwest. The town's shops offer good buys in tweeds and tartans, plus other items of Highland dress.

ESSENTIALS

GETTING THERE   By Train   There's no direct service into Aberfeldy. You can take a train to either Perth or Pitlochry, then continue the rest of the way by bus. Call © **08457/484950** or visit www.railtrack.co.uk for information.

By Bus   Connecting buses at either Perth or Pitlochry make the final journey to Aberfeldy. The private bus line **Stagecoach** (© **01738/629339**) handles much of the bus travel to the smaller towns and villages in the area.

By Car   From Crieff, take A-822 on a winding road north to Aberfeldy. The 48km (30-mile) drive from Perth takes 30 to 45 minutes.

VISITOR INFORMATION   The **tourist office** is at The Square (© **01887/820276**). Hours are July and August, daily from 9:30am to 5pm; April through June, September, and October, daily from 9am to 5:30pm; and October through March, Monday through Saturday from 9am to 5:30pm.

WHERE TO STAY & DINE

Farleyer House Hotel ✿   A tranquil oasis, this hotel of character stands on 33 hectares (70 acres) of grounds in the Tay Valley. Although restored and altered over the years, the building dates back to the 1500s. The staff entertains guests as if you are in a private home. The public areas are immaculate and beautifully furnished, and the guest rooms are well maintained and comfortable.

Hwy. B-846, Aberfeldy PH15 2JE. ✆ 01887/820332. Fax 01887/829430. www.farleyer.com. 19 units. £120–£140 ($192–$224) double; £120–£150 ($192–$240) family suite. Rates include breakfast. AE, DC, MC, V. Take B-846 3.2km (2 miles) west of Aberfeldy. **Amenities:** 2 restaurants; 2 bars; room service; babysitting; laundry/dry cleaning. *In room:* TV, coffeemaker.

PLAYING GOLF

Aberfeldy Golf Club, at Aberfeldy (✆ **01887/820535**), is a flatland course located on the banks of the River Tay. It's an 18-hole par 68 that is viewed as a "challenge" by the local pro. The River Tay comes into play on several holes, and if you're not careful, you'll be making trips back to the Pro Shop for more balls. Greens fees are £15 ($24) for 18 holes (£20/$32 on weekends), and pull-cart fees are £2 ($3.20) per round. April through October, the club is open daily from 8am to 11pm. During other months, call first to see if they're open: It depends on the weather.

DUNKELD ✿

A cathedral town, Dunkeld lies in a thickly wooded valley of the Tay River at the edge of the Perthshire Highlands. Once a major ecclesiastical center, it's one of the seats of ancient Scottish history and an important center of the Celtic church.

ESSENTIALS

GETTING THERE   By Train   Trains from Perth arrive every 2 hours and cost £5 ($8; trip time: 17–20 min.). Call ✆ **08457/484950** or visit www.railtrack.co.uk for information.

By Bus   Pitlochry-bound buses leaving from Perth make a stopover in Dunkeld, letting you off at the Dunkeld Car Park, which is at the train station (trip time: 50 min.). The cost is £3.10 ($4.95). Contact **Stagecoach** at ✆ **01738/629339.**

By Car   From Aberfeldy, take A-827 east until you reach the junction of A-9 heading south to Dunkeld.

VISITOR INFORMATION   A **tourist information office** is at The Cross (✆ **01350/727688**). It's open April through June, Monday through Saturday from 9:30am to 5:30pm and Sunday from 11am to 4pm; July 1 through September 8, Monday through Saturday from 9am to 7:30pm and Sunday from 11am to 7pm; September 9 through October 27, Monday through Saturday from 9:30am to 5:30pm and Sunday from 11am to 4pm; October 28 through December, Monday through Saturday from 9:30am to 1:30pm (closed Jan–Mar).

WHERE TO STAY & DINE

Hilton Dunkeld House ✿✿   The hotel, offering the quiet dignity of life in a Scottish country house, is ranked as one of the leading leisure and sports hotels in the area. On the banks of the Tay, the surrounding grounds—132 hectares (280 acres) in all—make for a parklike setting. The house is beautifully kept, and guest rooms come in a wide range of styles, space, and furnishings. In 1999, an annex was converted into an extra wing offering another nine rooms. Salmon and trout fishing are possible right on the grounds, as well as an array of other outdoor activities.

Dunkeld PH8 0HX. ⓒ **01350/727771.** Fax 01350/728924. www.hiltondunkeldhouse.co.uk. 97 units. £110–£149 ($176–$238) double; £180–£219 ($288–$350) suite. Rates include Scottish breakfast. AE, DC, MC, V. **Amenities:** Restaurant; 2 bars; pool; tennis courts; room service; babysitting; laundry/dry cleaning; fishing. *In room:* TV, minibar, coffeemaker, hair dryer.

Kinnaird 𝄞𝄞𝄞   On a 4,200-hectare (9,000-acre) private estate, this is a small hotel of great warmth, charm, and comfort. Built in 1770 as a hunting lodge, the house has been restored to its previous grandeur. All the beautifully fur-nished rooms have king-size beds, full private bathrooms, and views. Some rooms overlook the valley of the River Tay; others open onto gardens and wood-lands. There are eight cottages on the estate, two of which sleep eight and the others four.

Kinnaird, Kinnaird Estate, Dunkeld PH8 0LB. ⓒ **01796/482440.** Fax 01796/482289. www.kinnairdestate. com. 9 units and 8 estate cottages. £275–£345 ($440–$552) double; £440 ($704) suite; £375–£1,000 ($600–$1,600) estate cottage. Rates include dinner and Scottish breakfast. MC, V. Free parking. No children under 12 accepted in the main house. **Amenities:** Restaurant; bar; tennis courts; room service; babysitting; laundry/dry cleaning; fishing and hunting excursions. *In room:* TV, hair dryer.

SEEING THE SIGHTS

Founded in A.D. 815, the **Cathedral of Dunkeld** 𝄞 was converted from a church to a cathedral in 1127 by David I. It stands on Cathedral Street in a sce-nic setting along the River Tay. The cathedral was first restored in 1815, and traces of the 12th-century structure remain today. Admission is free, and the cathedral is open May through September, Monday through Saturday from 9:30am to 6:30pm, Sunday from 2 to 6:30pm; October through April, Monday through Saturday from 9:30am to 4pm.

The National Trust for Scotland has restored many of the old houses and shops around the marketplace and cathedral. The trust owns 20 houses on High Street and Cathedral Street as well. Many of these houses were constructed in the closing years of the 17th century after the rebuilding of the town following the Battle of Dunkeld. The trust runs the **Ell Shop,** The Cross (ⓒ **01350/727460**), which specializes in Scottish handcrafts. Easter weekend through December 24, it's open Monday through Saturday from 10am to 5:30pm.

Scottish Horse Museum, The Cross (no phone), has exhibits tracing the his-tory of the Scottish Horse Yeomanry, a cavalry force first raised in 1900. The museum is open Easter through September only, Saturday through Wednesday from 10am to noon and 1:50 to 5pm. Admission is 50p (80¢).

Shakespeare fans may want to seek out the oak and sycamore in front of the destroyed Birnam House, a mile to the south. This was believed to be a rem-nant of the **Birnam Wood** in *Macbeth;* you may recall, "Macbeth shall never vanquished be until great Birnam Wood to high Dunsinane Hill shall come against him."

The **Hermitage,** lying off A-9 about 3km (2 miles) west of Dunkeld, was called a "folly" when it was constructed in 1758 above the wooded gorge of the River Braan. Today it makes for one of the most scenic woodland walks in the area.

PLAYING GOLF

Dunkeld & Birnam, at Dunkeld (ⓒ **01350/727524**), is touted as the best in the area. The 18-hole course is not too long, but it can be quite difficult. It's edged in many areas with bracken, and many a golfer has had to take a drop instead of searching for the errant ball. There are sweeping views of the surrounding environs. Greens fees: Monday through Friday £18 ($29) for 18 holes; Saturday and Sunday £21 ($34) for 18 holes. There are no electric carts; pull-carts are available for £2 ($3.20) per round. Hours are daily from 7am to 11pm April through September. October through March, greens fees are reduced to £9 to £10 ($14–$16) and hours are daily from 8am to 4pm. There's no official dress code, although if the starter feels you are not dressed "appropriately," you will be asked to "smarten up" the next time you play the course.

DUNDEE & GLAMIS CASTLE 🏆🏆

This royal burgh and old seaport is an industrial city on the north shore of the Firth of Tay. When steamers took over the whaling industry from sailing vessels, Dundee became the leading home port for ships from the 1860s until World War I. Long known for its jute and flax operations, we think today of the Dundee fruitcakes, marmalades, and jams. This was also the home of the man who invented stick-on postage stamps, James Chalmers. Dundee has a raffish charm and serves well as a base for a trip to Glamis Castle.

Spanning the Firth of Tay is the **Tay Railway Bridge,** opened in 1888. Constructed over the tidal estuary, the bridge is some 3km (2 miles) long, one of the longest in Europe. There's also a road bridge 2km (1¼ miles) long, with four traffic lanes and a walkway in the center.

ESSENTIALS

GETTING THERE   By Train   ScotRail offers frequent service between Perth, Dundee, and Aberdeen. One-way fare from Perth to Dundee is £4.70 ($7.50), from Aberdeen £18 ($29). Call them at © **08457/484950** or visit www.railtrack.co.uk for information.

By Bus   CityLink buses offer frequent bus service from Edinburgh and Glasgow. Call © **0990/505050** for information.

By Car The fastest way to reach Dundee is to cut south back to Perth along A-9 and link up with A-972 going east.

VISITOR INFORMATION The **tourist information office** is at 21 Castle St. (© **01382/527-527**). Hours are April through September, Monday through Saturday from 9am to 6pm, Sunday from 10am to 4pm; October through March, Monday through Saturday from 9am to 5pm.

WHERE TO STAY

Hilton Dundee 🏆 This chain hotel helps rejuvenate the once-seedy waterfront of Dundee. Built in a severe modern style, the five-story block takes its name from a famous English tea, which most often accompanies marmalade and Dundee fruitcakes, the city's two most famous products. Some of the well-furnished rooms overlook the Firth, the river, or the Tay Bridge. Both the business and the leisure traveler will find solace here in rooms with bright floral upholstery and draperies, blond wood furnishings, and small bathrooms.

Earl Grey Place, Dundee DD1 4DE. © **01382/229271.** Fax 01382/200072. www.hilton.com. 129 units. £68–£145 ($109–$232) double; from £220 ($352) suite. AE, DC, MC, V. Free parking. Bus: 1A, 1B, or 20. **Amenities:** Restaurant; pool; health club; room service; babysitting; laundry/dry cleaning. *In room:* TV, coffeemaker, hair dryer, safe, trouser press.

Invercarse Hotel In landscaped gardens overlooking the River Tay, this privately owned hotel lies 5km (3 miles) west of the heart of Dundee. Many prefer it for its fresh air, tranquil location, and Victorian country-house aura. Well-maintained rooms come in a variety of sizes and open onto views across the Tay to the hills of the Kingdom of Fife.

371 Perth Rd., Dundee DD2 1PG. ✆ **01382/669231.** Fax 01382/644112. 44 units. £90 ($144) double; £100 ($160) suite. Rates include Scottish breakfast. AE, DC, MC, V. Free parking. **Amenities:** Restaurant; bar; room service; laundry/dry cleaning. *In room:* TV, coffeemaker, hair dryer.

WHERE TO DINE

Jahangir Tandoori INDIAN   Built around an indoor fishpond in a dining room draped with the soft folds of an embroidered tent, this is one of the most exotic restaurants in the region. Meals are prepared with fresh ingredients and cover the gamut of recipes from both north and south India. Some preparations are slow-cooked in clay pots (tandoori) and seasoned to the degree of spiciness you prefer. Both meat and meatless dishes are available.

1 Sessions St. (at the corner of Hawk Hill). ✆ **01382/202022.** Reservations recommended. Main courses £8–£15 ($13–$24). AE, MC, V. Daily 5pm–midnight.

SEEING THE SIGHTS

For a panoramic view of Dundee, the Tay bridges across to Fife, and mountains to the north, go to **Dundee Law,** a 175m (572-ft.) hill just north of the city. The hill is an ancient volcanic plug.

HM Frigate *Unicorn* ⚓ *Kids*   This 46-gun wooden ship of war commissioned in 1824 by the Royal Navy, now the oldest British-built ship afloat, has been restored and visitors can explore all four decks: the quarterdeck with 32-pound cannonades, the gun deck with its battery of 18-pound cannons and the captain's quarters, the berth deck with officers' cabins and crews' hammocks, and the orlop deck and hold. Displays portraying life in the sailing navy and the history of the *Unicorn* make this a rewarding visit.

Victoria Dock. ✆ **01382/200900.** Admission £3.50 ($5.60) adults, £2.50 ($4) seniors and children, £7.50–£9.50 ($12–$15) family ticket. Easter–Oct daily 10am–5pm; Nov–Easter Wed–Sun 10am–4pm. Bus: 6, 23, or 78.

Broughty Castle   This 15th-century estuary fort lies about 6km (4 miles) east of the city center on the seafront, at Broughty Ferry, a little fishing hamlet and once the terminus for ferries crossing the Firth of Tay before the bridges were built. Besieged by the English in the 16th century, and attacked by Cromwell's army under General Monk in the 17th century, it was eventually restored as part of Britain's coastal defenses in 1861. Its gun battery was dismantled in 1956, and it's now a museum with displays on local history, arms and armor, and Dundee's whaling story. The observation area at the top of the castle provides fine views of the Tay estuary and northeast Fife.

Castle Green, Broughty Ferry. ✆ **01382/436916.** Free admission. Apr–Sept Mon–Sat 10am–4pm, Sun 12:30–4pm; Oct–Mar Tues–Sat 10am–4pm, Sun 12:30–4pm. Bus: 75 or 76.

PLAYING GOLF

Caird Park, at Dundee (✆ **01382/438-871**), is an 18-hole, par-72 course that presents most golfers with an average challenge. The course is quite flat, but there are more than a few bunkers to navigate. There's also a restaurant and bar on the premises. Greens fees are £18 ($29) for 18 holes, or £26 ($42) for a day ticket. No carts of any sort are allowed on the course, and there's no particular dress code. The park is open April through October daily from 7am to 8pm.

A DAY TRIP TO GLAMIS

The little village of Glamis (pronounced without the "i") grew up around **Glamis Castle** ⊛⊛, Castle Office (℃ **01307/840393**). Next to Balmoral Castle, visitors to Scotland most want to see Glamis Castle for its link with the crown. For 6 centuries it has been connected to members of the British royal family. The Queen Mother was brought up here; and Princess Margaret was born here, becoming the first royal princess born in Scotland in 3 centuries. The present owner is the queen's great-nephew. The castle contains Duncan's Hall—the Victorians claimed this was where Macbeth murdered King Duncan, but in the play, the murder takes place at Macbeth's castle near Inverness. In fact, Shakespeare was erroneous, as well—he had Macbeth named Thane of Glamis, but Glamis wasn't made a thaneship (a sphere of influence in medieval Scotland) until years after the play takes place.

The present Glamis Castle dates from the early 15th century, but there are records of a castle having been in existence in the 11th century. Glamis Castle has been in the possession of the Lyon family since 1372, and it contains some fine plaster ceilings, furniture, and paintings.

The castle is open to the public, with access to the Royal Apartments and many other rooms, as well as the fine gardens, from the end of March to the end of October only, daily from 10:30am to 5:30pm. Admission to the castle and gardens is £6.70 ($11) adults, £3.50 ($5.60) children, £18 ($29) family. If you wish to visit the grounds only, the charge is £3.50 ($5.60) adults, £2.50 ($4) children. Buses run between Dundee and Glamis. The 35-minute ride costs £3.70 ($5.90) one-way. *Note:* Buses don't run on Sunday, and they don't stop in front of the castle, which lies 1.6km (1 mile) from the bus stop.

Where to Stay

Castleton House ⊛ *(Finds)*   This Victorian hotel is run with love and care by its owners, Anthony and Sheila Lilly. In cool weather you're greeted by welcoming coal fires in the public lounge. The youthful staff is the most considerate we've encountered in the area. Rooms of various sizes are furnished with reproductions of antiques.

Eassie by Glamis, Forfar, Tayside DD8 1SJ. ℃ 01307/840340. Fax 01307/840506. www.castletonglamis. co.uk. 6 units. £110 ($176) double. Children 10 and under stay free in parent's room. Rates include Scottish breakfast. MC, V. Drive 5km (3 miles) west of Glamis on A-94. **Amenities:** 2 restaurants; bar; room service; babysitting; laundry/dry cleaning. *In room:* TV, coffeemaker, hair dryer.

Where to Dine

Strathomore Arms CONTINENTAL/SCOTTISH   Try this place near the castle for one of the best lunches in the area. You might begin with freshly made soup of the day or the fresh prawns. Regularly featured dishes might include steak pie or venison. For something a little more exotic there's the Indian chicken breast, marinated in yogurt and spices; and for vegetarians, phyllo parcels stuffed with asparagus and cauliflower.

The Square Glamis. ℃ 01307/840248. Reservations recommended. Main courses £6.95–£16 ($11–$26). AE, MC, V. Daily noon–2pm and 5–9pm.

BRAEMAR

In the heart of some of Grampian's most beautiful scenery, Braemar is not only known for its own castle, but it makes a good center from which to explore Balmoral Castle (see "Ballater & Balmoral Castle," below). In this Highland village, set against a massive backdrop of hills covered with heather in summer, Clunie

Playing the World's Oldest Course

At **St. Andrew's,** 23km (14 miles) southeast of Dundee and 82km (51 miles) northeast of Edinburgh, the rules of golf in Britain and the world were codified and arbitrated. Golf was played for the first time in the 1400s, probably on the site of St. Andrew's Old Course, and enjoyed by Mary, Queen of Scots, there in 1567. All six of St. Andrew's golf courses are open to the public on a more-or-less democratic basis—ballots are polled 1 day in advance. To participate in the balloting, you first must be staying in St. Andrews for a minimum of 2 days, and you must be able to present a current handicap certificate issued by the governing golf body of your home country. If you meet those requirements, you can enter the ballot in person at the golf course, or by phone at *C* **01334/466666,** before 1:45pm on the day before the one on which you wish to play. At 2pm each day, the balloting is drawn, and the following day's players are announced at 4pm. Bear in mind that your wait to play will most likely be from 4 to 6 days; however, some lucky players get on the course the next day. Players who call the golf course several weeks in advance to make reservations can often circumvent the balloting system, depending on demand.

The **Old Course,** St. Andrews, Golf Place, St. Andrew's, Fife (*C* **01334/466666**), is a 6,000m (6,566-yd.) 18-hole course billed as "the Home of Golf." Greens fees are £90 ($144) per round from April to September or £42 to £60 ($67–$96) otherwise. A caddy will cost £35 ($56) plus tip. Golf clubs rent for £20 to £30 ($32–$48) per round. Electric carts are not allowed, and you can rent a cart only on afternoons from May to September for £3 ($4.80). The course is a par 72.

To reach St. Andrews from Edinburgh, travel along the A90 north to Dunfermline. From there, continue northeast along A910, which becomes A915 at Leven. From Leven, drive northeast on A915 directly to St. Andrews (trip time: 1 hr.).

Water joins the River Dee. The massive **Cairn Toul** towers over Braemar, reaching a height of 1,293m (4,241 ft.).

ESSENTIALS

GETTING THERE   By Train   Take the train to Aberdeen, then continue the rest of the way by bus. For information, call *C* **08457/484950** or visit www.railtrack.co.uk.

By Bus   Buses run daily from Aberdeen to Braemar at the rate of six per day (trip time: 2 hr.). One-way fare is £7.50 ($12). The bus and train stations in Aberdeen are next to each other on Guild Street (*C* **01224/212266** for information about schedules).

By Car   To reach Braemar from Dundee, return west toward Perth, then head north along A-93, following the signs into Braemar. The 113km (70-mile) drive will take 70 to 90 minutes.

VISITOR INFORMATION   The year-round **Braemar Tourist Office** is in The Mews, Mar Road (*C* **013397/42208**). In June, hours are daily from

9:30am to 6pm; July and August, daily from 9am to 7pm; and September, daily from 10am to 1pm and 2 to 6pm. In the off season, hours are Monday through Saturday from 10am to 1pm and 2 to 5pm, Sunday from noon to 5pm.

SPECIAL EVENTS The spectacular **Royal Highland Gathering** takes place annually in late August or early September in the Princess Royal and Duke of Fife Memorial Park. The queen herself often attends the gathering. These ancient games are thought to have been originated by King Malcolm Canmore, a chieftain who ruled much of Scotland at the time of the Norman conquest of England. He selected his hardiest warriors from all the clans for a "keen and fair contest."

Call the tourist office (see "Visitor Information," above) for more information. Braemar is overrun with visitors during the gathering—anyone thinking of attending would be wise to reserve accommodations anywhere within a 32km (20-mile) radius of Braemar no later than early April.

WHERE TO STAY & DINE

Braemar Lodge Hotel *(Kids)* This hotel, popular with skiers who frequent the nearby Glenshee slopes, is set on 1 hectare (2 acres) of grounds at the head of Glen Clunie. Units vary in shape and size, but each is comfortable and well equipped, containing a well-maintained bathroom with tub and shower. Rooms are bright and airy, with soothing color schemes. Two rooms are large enough for families. On cool evenings, you're greeted by log fires. The hotel is on the road to the Glenshee ski slopes near the cottage where Robert Louis Stevenson wrote *Treasure Island.* On the grounds, three log cabins have been recently built. Fully equipped with all modern conveniences, they can sleep up to six persons.

6 Glenshee Rd., Braemar AB35 5YQ. (*C*)/fax 013397/41627. 7 units. £70 ($112) double; £200–£500 ($320–$800) log cabin. Rates include Scottish breakfast. MC, V. Free parking. Closed Nov. **Amenities:** Restaurant; laundry/dry cleaning. *In room:* TV, hair dryer.

Invercauld Arms Thistle Hotel *(★)* This is the leading inn of the town, with superior amenities and greater comfort than Braemar Lodge. The oldest part of this old granite building dates from the 18th century. In cool weather there's a roaring log fire on the hearth. You can go hill walking and see deer, golden eagles, and other wildlife. Fishing and winter skiing are other pursuits in the nearby area. Rooms are comfortably furnished. Although they lack any style or glamour, they serve their purpose well, and come in a wide range of sizes. In the pub close by, you'll meet the "ghilles" and "stalkers" (hunting and fishing guides).

Braemar AB35 5YR. (*C*) **013397/41605.** Fax 013397/41428. www.peelhotel.com. 68 units. £109 ($174) double. Rates include Scottish breakfast. AE, DC, MC, V. Free parking. Bus: 201. **Amenities:** Restaurant; bar; room service; babysitting; laundry/dry cleaning. *In room:* TV, coffeemaker, hair dryer.

SEEING THE SIGHTS

If you're a Royal Family watcher, you might be able to spot members of the family, even the queen, at **Crathie Church,** 14km (9 miles) east of Braemar on A-93 ((*C*) **013397/42208**), where they attend Sunday services when in residence. Services are at 11:30am; otherwise, the church is open for viewing April through October, Monday through Saturday from 9:30am to 5:30pm and Sunday from 2 to 5:30pm.

Nature lovers may want to drive to the **Linn of Dee,** 10km (6 miles) west of Braemar, a narrow chasm on the River Dee, which is a local beauty spot. Other beauty spots include Glen Muick, Loch Muick, and Lochnagar. A **Scottish Wildlife Trust Visitor Centre,** reached by a minor road, is located in this Highland glen, off the South Deeside road. An access road joins B-976 at a point 26km (16 miles) east of Braemar. The tourist office (see above) will give you a map pinpointing these beauty spots.

Braemar Castle ☞   This romantic 17th-century castle is a fully furnished private residence with architectural grace, scenic charm, and historical interest. The castle has barrel-vaulted ceilings and an underground prison and is known for its remarkable star-shaped defensive curtain wall.

On the Aberdeen–Ballater–Perth Rd. (A-93). ℰ **013397/41219**. Admission £3 ($4.80) adults, £2.50 ($4) seniors and students, £1 ($1.60) ages 5–15, free for ages 4 and under. Mon after Easter to Oct, Sat–Thurs 10am–6pm. Closed Nov–Easter. Take A93 .5km (⅓ mile) northeast of Braemar.

PLAYING GOLF
Braemar Golf Course, at Braemar (ℰ **013397/41618**), is the highest golf course in the country. The green of the second hole is 380m (1,250 ft.) above sea level—this is the trickiest hole on the course. Pro golf commentator Peter Alliss has deemed it "the hardest par 4 in all of Scotland." Set on a plateau, the hole is bordered on the right by the River Clunie and lined on the left by rough. Greens fees are as follows: Monday through Friday £16 ($26) for 18 holes and £21 ($34) for a day ticket; Saturday and Sunday £19 ($30) for 18 holes and £24 ($38) for a day ticket. Pull-carts can be rented for £2 ($3.20) per day, and sets of clubs can be borrowed for £5 ($8) per day. The only dress code is "Be reasonable." The course is open daily from April to October only (call in advance, as hours can vary).

BALLATER & BALMORAL CASTLE ☞☞
Ballater is a vacation resort center on the Dee River, with the Grampian Mountains in the background. The town is still centered around its Station Square, where the Royal Family used to be photographed as they arrived to spend vacations. The railway is now closed.

ESSENTIALS
GETTING THERE   By Train   Go to Aberdeen and continue the rest of the way by connecting bus. For information, call ℰ **08457/484950** or visit www.railtrack.co.uk.

By Bus   Buses run hourly from Aberdeen to Ballater. The bus and train stations in Aberdeen are next to each other on Guild Street (ℰ **01224/212266** for information). Bus no. 201 from Braemar runs to Ballater (trip time: 1¼ hr.). The fare is £3 ($4.80).

By Car   From Braemar, go east along A-93.

VISITOR INFORMATION   The **tourist information office** is at Station Square (ℰ **013397/55306**). Hours are July and August, daily from 10am to 5pm; September, October, May, and June, Monday through Saturday from 10am to 6pm and Sunday from 1 to 5pm; November through April, Monday through Saturday from 10am to 5pm and Sunday from 1 to 5pm.

WHERE TO STAY
Hilton Craigendarroch Hotel ☞   This hotel, built in the Scottish baronial style, is set amid old trees on a 13-hectare (28-acre) estate. Modern comforts have been added, but the owners have tried to maintain a 19th-century aura. The public rooms include a regal oaken staircase and a large sitting room. The fair-size rooms open onto views of the village of Ballater and the River Dee. Each is furnished in individual style, with private bathrooms (showers only). Public

facilities are luxurious, especially the study with oak paneling, a log fire, and book-lined shelves.

Braemar Rd., Ballater AB35 5XA. © 013397/55858. Fax 013397/55447. www.hilton.com. 45 units. £169 ($270) double; £244 ($390) suite. Rates include Scottish breakfast. Half board £15 ($24) extra per person. AE, DC, MC, V. **Amenities:** 2 restaurants; bar; tennis courts; solarium; salon; 24-hr. room service; babysitting; laundry/dry cleaning. *In room:* TV, fridge, hair dryer, trouser press.

Monaltrie Hotel *(Kids* This 1835 hotel, the first in the region, was built of Aberdeen granite to accommodate the clients of a now-defunct spa. Today it bustles with a clientele who come for the live music in its pub and for the savory food served, the most unusual of which is a Thai cuisine. Each of the fair-size rooms has comfortable beds along with neatly maintained bathrooms with shower stalls. The hotel lies a 3-minute walk east of the center of town.

5 Bridge Sq., Ballater AB35 5QJ. © 013397/55417. Fax 013397/55180. www.monaltriehotel.co.uk. 24 units. £50–£80 ($80–$128) double. Rates include Scottish breakfast. AE, DC, MC, V. Free parking. **Amenities:** 2 restaurants; bar; children's play area. *In room:* TV, radio, coffeemaker, hair dryer.

WHERE TO DINE
Green Inn SCOTTISH   In the heart of town, what was once a temperance hotel is now one of the finest dining rooms in town, especially for traditional Scottish dishes. The chef places emphasis on local produce, including home-grown vegetables when available. In season, loin of venison is served with a bramble sauce, and you can always count on fresh salmon and the best of Angus beef. Three very simply furnished double rooms are rented here, all with private bathrooms (with showers) and TV. Half board costs £55 ($88) per person.

9 Victoria Rd., Ballater AB35 5QQ. ©/fax 013397/55701. Reservations required. Fixed-price menu £27 ($43) for 2 courses, £30 ($48) for 3 courses. AE, DC, MC, V. Mar–Oct daily 7–9pm; Nov–Feb Tues–Sat 7–9pm.

Oaks Restaurant BRITISH   The most glamorous restaurant in the region, the Oaks is in the century-old mansion that was originally built by the "marmalade kings" of Britain, the Keiller family. (The company's marmalade is still a household word throughout the United Kingdom.) This is the most upscale of the three restaurants in a resort complex that includes hotel rooms, timeshare villas, and access to a nearby golf course. To start, try the venison and duck terrine flavored with orange and brandy and served with a warm black conch vinaigrette. Other main courses are roast rack of lamb, breast of Grampian chicken, loin of venison, and filet of Aberdeen Angus beef.

In the Hilton Craigendarroch Hotel, Braemar Rd. © 013397/55858. Reservations strongly recommended. Fixed-price dinners £29 ($46) 4 courses, £25 ($40) 3 courses, £20 ($32) 2 courses. AE, DC, MC, V. Daily 7–10:30pm.

THE CASTLE
Balmoral Castle   "This dear paradise" is how Queen Victoria described Balmoral Castle, rebuilt in the Scottish baronial style by her "beloved" Albert and completed in 1855. Today Balmoral, 13km (8 miles) west of Ballater, is still a private residence of the British sovereign. Its principal feature is a 30m (100-ft.) tower. On the grounds are many memorials to the royal family. In addition to the gardens there are country walks, pony trekking, souvenir shops, and a refreshments room. Of the actual castle, only the ballroom is open to the public; it houses an exhibition of pictures, porcelain, and works of art.

Balmoral, Ballater. © 013397/42334. Admission £4.50 ($7.20) adults, £3.50 ($5.60) seniors, £1 ($1.60) children 5–16, free for ages 4 and under. Apr 1–July 31 Mon–Sat 10am–5pm. Crathie bus from Aberdeen to the Crathie station; Balmoral Castle is signposted from there (a short walk).

PLAYING GOLF

Ballater Golf Club, at Ballater (② **013397/55567**), is one of the more scenic courses in the area. Set in a bowl of mountains and situated on the banks of the River Dee, this is a 5,155m (5,638-yd.), par-67 course. Greens fees are as follows: Monday through Friday, £19 ($30) for 18 holes or £28 ($45) for a day ticket; Saturday and Sunday, £22 ($35) for 18 holes or £32 ($51) for a day ticket. There are no electric carts for hire; pull-carts rent for £2 ($3.20) per day. Dress should be smart but casual. The course is open daily April through September from 7:30am to sunset. October through March, hours are daily from 9am to sunset but only if the weather permits.

ABERDEEN ❀ & THE CASTLE COUNTRY ❀❀

The city of **Aberdeen,** Scotland's "third city," is bordered by fine sandy beaches (delightful if you're a polar bear) and is one of the largest fishing ports in the country. However, far more interesting to visitors with limited time is the array of 40 inhabited castles on the city's periphery, which has earned the area the title of "Castle Country." Since time is limited for most motorists, we've spotlighted only the most intriguing.

ESSENTIALS

GETTING THERE **By Train** **ScotRail** runs trains from Edinburgh to Aberdeen at the rate of nine per day Monday through Saturday and 10 per day on Sunday; a one-way ticket costs £6 ($9.60). For information, call ② **08457/ 484950** or visit www.railtrack.co.uk.

By Bus **Scottish CityLink** (② **01224/212-266**) arrives in Aberdeen from Edinburgh at the rate of at least one bus per hour during the day, at a cost of £10 to £13 ($16–$20) one-way.

WHERE TO STAY

Mannofield Hotel Built of silver granite around 1880, this hotel is a Victorian fantasy, with step gables, turrets, spires, bay windows, and a sweeping mahogany-and-teakwood staircase. Owners Bruce and Dorothy Cryle offer a warm Scottish welcome. The nicely sized rooms, refurbished in 1998, are equipped with well-maintained shower-only bathrooms.

447 Great Western Rd., Aberdeen AB10 6NL. ② **01224/315-888.** Fax 01224/208-971. 9 units. £32–£75 ($51–$120) double. Rates include Scottish breakfast. AE, DC, MC, V. Free parking. Bus: 18 or 24. **Amenities:** Restaurant; lounge area; room service; babysitting; laundry/dry cleaning. *In room:* TV, coffeemaker, hair dryer.

Marcliffe at Pitfodels ❀❀❀ It's the best in Aberdeen, dwarfing the competition. On Aberdeen's western edge, this traditional manor house was built around a courtyard and stands on 26 hectares (8 acres) of landscaped grounds. The spacious rooms are furnished in Chippendale and reproduction pieces. We like the big, mirrored closets and the green marble bathrooms. Many patrons prefer the ground-floor rooms that open onto patios, even though they're less expensive.

N. Deeside Rd., Aberdeen AB1 9YA. ② **01224/861-000.** Fax 01224/868-860. www.marcliffe.com. 42 units. £165–£185 ($264–$296) double. AE, DC, MC, V. Free parking. Drive about 1.6km (1 mile) off A90 at the Aberdeen ring road, A93. **Amenities:** 2 restaurants; lounge area; room service; laundry/dry cleaning. *In room:* TV, minibar, hair dryer, iron.

WHERE TO DINE

Elrond's Cafe Bar INTERNATIONAL White marble floors, a long oak-capped bar, evening candlelight, and a garden-inspired decor create the ambience.

No one will mind if you show up just for a drink, a pot of tea, a midday salad or snack, or a full-blown feast. Specialties are burgers, steaks, pastas, fresh fish, lemon chicken supreme, chicken Kiev, and vegetarian dishes. This isn't the world's greatest food, but it's popular nevertheless. Though it's in one of Aberdeen's well-known hotels, the restaurant has a separate entrance onto Union Terrace.

In the Caledonian Thistle Hotel, 10–14 Union Terrace. (𝒸 **01224/640-233**. Main courses £5.95–£13 ($9.50–$20); pot of tea with pastry £2 ($3.20). AE, DC, MC, V. Mon–Sat 10am–midnight; Sun 10am–11pm. Bus: 16 or 17.

Ferryhill House INTERNATIONAL In its own park and garden on Aberdeen's southern outskirts, Ferryhill House dates back 250 years. It was built by the region's most successful brick maker/quarry master. It has Georgian detailing, but recent refurbishment has removed many of the original panels and all the ceiling beams. The restaurant boasts one of the region's largest collections of single-malt whiskies—more than 140 brands. There's a fireplace for chilly afternoons and a beer garden for midsummer, as well as a conservatory. Food items include steak or vegetable tempura, chicken dishes like chicken fajita, fried haddock filet, pastas, and chili. Ferryhill House also rents nine standard rooms, with TVs and hair dryers. Breakfast included, the double rate is £79 ($126) from Sunday to Thursday and £50 ($80) Friday and Saturday.

Bon Accord St., Aberdeen AB11 6UA. (𝒸 **01224/590-867**. Fax 01224/586-947. Reservations recommended Sat–Sun. Main courses £6–£12 ($9.60–$19). AE, DC, MC, V. Noon–2:30pm and 6–9pm. Free parking. Bus: 16.

SEEING THE CASTLES

Castle Fraser 𝒻 One of the most impressive of the fortresslike castles of Mar, Castle Fraser stands in a 12-hectare (25-acre) parkland setting. The sixth laird, Michael Fraser, began the structure in 1575, and his son finished it in 1636. Its Great Hall is spectacular, and you can wander around the grounds, which include an 18th-century walled garden.

Sauchen, Inverurie. (𝒸 **01330/833463**. Admission £6 ($9.60) adults, £4.50 ($7.20) seniors, £1.30 ($2.10) children, free for ages 4 and under. Mar 25–June 28 and Sept 2–Oct 27 Fri–Tues noon–5pm; June 29–Sept 1 daily 10am–5pm. Head 5km (3 miles) south of Kemnay, 26km (16 miles) west of Aberdeen, off A944.

Kildrummy Castle 𝒻 This is the most extensive example of a 13th-century castle in Scotland. Once the ancient seat of the earls of Mar, you can still see the four round towers, the hall, and the chapel from the original structure. The great gatehouse and other remains date from the 16th century. The castle played a major role in Scottish history up to 1715, when it was dismantled.

Hwy. A-97, Kildrummy. (𝒸 **019755/71331**. Admission £2 ($3.20) adults, £1.50 ($2.40) seniors, 75p ($1.15) children. Easter–Sept daily 9:30am–6:30pm; Oct–Nov daily 9:30am–4pm. Closed Dec–Easter. Take A-97 for 56km (35 miles) west of Aberdeen; it's signposted off A-97, 16km (10 miles) west of Alford.

Fyvie Castle 𝒻 The National Trust for Scotland opened this castle to the public in 1986. The oldest part, dating from the 13th century, is the grandest existing example of Scottish baronial architecture. There are five towers, named after Fyvie's five families—the Prestons, Melddrums, Setons, Gordons, and Leiths—who lived here over 5 centuries. Originally built in a royal hunting forest, Fyvie means "deer hill" in Gaelic. The interior, created by the first Lord Leith of Fyvie, a steel magnate, reflects the opulence of the Edwardian era. His collections contain arms and armor, 16th-century tapestries, and important artworks by Raeburn, Gainsborough, and Romney. The castle is rich in ghosts, curses, and legends.

Turriff, on the Aberdeen–Banff road. ℂ **01651/891266.** Admission £7 ($11) adults, £5.25 ($8.40) seniors and children. Easter–June and Sept daily 1:30–5pm; July–Aug daily 10am–5pm; Oct Sat–Sun noon–5pm. Closed Nov–Mar. Take A947 for 37km (23 miles) northwest of Aberdeen.

Craigievar Castle 🏰 Structurally unchanged since its completion in 1626, Craigievar Castle is an exceptional tower house where Scottish baronial architecture reached its pinnacle of achievement. It has contemporary plaster ceilings in nearly all its rooms. The castle had been continuously lived in by the descendants of the builder, William Forbes, until it came under the care of the National Trust for Scotland in 1963. The family collection of furnishings is complete. Some 6km (3¾ miles) south of the castle, clearly signposted on a small road leading off A980, near Lumphanan, is **Macbeth's Cairn,** where the historical Macbeth is supposed to have fought his last battle. Built of timber in a rounded format known by historians as "motte and bailey," it's now nothing more than a steep-sided rounded hillock marked with a sign and a flag.

Hwy. A980, 10km (6 miles) south of Alford. ℂ **013398/83635.** Admission £8.50 ($14) adults, £6.40 ($10) seniors/children. Castle May–Sept daily 1:30–4:45pm. Grounds year-round daily 9:30am–sunset. Head west on A96 to Alford, then south on A980.

SPEYSIDE 🏰 & THE MALT WHISKY TRAIL 🏰

Much of the Speyside region covered in this section is in the Moray district, on the southern shore of the Moray Firth, a great inlet cutting into the northeastern coast of Scotland. The district stretches in a triangular shape south from the coast to the wild heart of the Cairngorm Mountains near Aviemore. It's a land steeped in history, as its many castles, battle sites, and ancient monuments testify. It's also a good place to fish and, of course, play golf. Golfers can purchase a 5-day ticket from tourist information centers that will allow you to play at more than 11 courses in the area.

One of the best of these courses is **Boat of Garten,** Speyside (ℂ **01479/831282**). Relatively difficult, the almost 5,500m (6,000-yd.) course is dotted with many bunkers and wooded areas. April through October, greens fees are £28 to £33 ($45–$53) Monday through Friday from 7:30am to 11pm. On Saturday, greens fees are £33 to £38 ($53–$61), from 10am to 4pm. In winter, call to see if the course is open. Greens fees are then reduced to £12 ($19). Pull-carts can be rented for £2 ($3.20) and electric carts are available for £5 ($8). Dress reasonably; blue jeans are not acceptable.

The valley of the second-largest river in Scotland, the Spey, lies north and south of Aviemore. It's a land of great natural beauty. The Spey is born in the Highlands above Loch Laggan, which lies 64km (40 miles) south of Inverness. Little more than a creek at its inception, it gains in force, fed by the many "burns" that drain water from the surrounding hills. One of Scotland's great rivers for salmon fishing, it runs between the towering Cairngorms on the east and the Monadhliath Mountains on the west. Its major center is Grantown-on-Spey.

The major tourist attraction in the area is the **Malt Whisky Trail,** 113km (70 miles) long, running through the glens of Speyside. Here distilleries, many of which can be visited, are known for their production of *uisge beatha* or "water of life." "Whisky" is its more familiar name.

Half the malt distilleries in the country lie along the River Spey and its tributaries. Here peat smoke and Highland water are used to turn out single-malt (unblended) whisky. There're five malt distilleries in the area: **Glenlivet, Glenfiddich, Glenfarclas, Strathisla,** and **Tamdhu.** Allow about an hour each to visit them.

The best way to reach Speyside from Aberdeen is to take A-96 northwest, signposted ELGIN. If you're traveling north on the A-9 road from Perth and Pitlochry, your first stop might be Dalwhinnie, which has the highest whisky distillery in the world at 575m (1,888 ft.). It's not in the Spey Valley but is at the northeastern end of Loch Ericht, with views of lochs and forests.

KEITH

Keith, 18km (11 miles) northwest of Huntly, grew up because of its strategic location, where the main road and rail routes between Inverness and Aberdeen cross the River Isla. It has an ancient history, but owes its present look to the "town planning" of the late 18th and early 19th centuries. Today it's a major stopover along the Malt Whisky Trail.

The oldest operating distillery in the Scottish Highlands, the **Strathisla Distillery,** on Seafield Avenue (© **01542/783044**), was established in 1786. Hours are February through mid-March, Monday through Friday from 9:30am to 4pm; mid-March through November 30, Monday through Saturday from 9:30am to 4pm and Sunday from 12:30 to 4pm; closed December and January. Admission is £4 ($6.40) adults, free for ages 8 to 18; children under 8 are not admitted. The admission fee includes a £2 ($3.20) voucher redeemable in the distillery shop against a 70-centiliter bottle of whisky. Be warned that tours of this distillery are self-guided.

Where to Stay

Grange House ⚗   This dignified-looking stone house dates from 1815 when it was the manse (home of a minister) for the nearby Church of Scotland, which is still the most prominent building in this tiny hamlet. Doreen Blanche, assisted by her husband Bill, rents two well-decorated and comfortable rooms within her private home. The venue is upscale, charming, and comfortable, with a calm enhanced by the 4 hectares (8 acres) of park and garden that surround this isolated place. Ask the owners to point out the late Victorian addition here, completed in 1898, that greatly enlarged the size of the original house. Smoking is not permitted inside.

Grange, near Keith AB55 6RY (©/fax **01542/870206.** 2 units, £60 ($96) double year-round. Rate includes breakfast. No credit cards. From Keith, drive 5km (3 miles) east of town, following the signs to Banff, into the hamlet of Grange. **Amenities:** Dining area; babysitting; laundry/dry cleaning. *In room:* Coffeemaker, hair dryer.

DUFFTOWN

James Duff, the fourth earl of Fife, founded this town in 1817. The four main streets of town converge at the battlemented **clock tower,** which is also the tourist information center. A center of the whisky-distilling industry, Dufftown is surrounded by seven malt distilleries. The family-owned **Glenfiddich Distillery** is on A-941, just north of Dufftown (© **01340/820373**). It's open Monday through Friday from 9:30am to 4:30pm; Easter through mid-October it's also open on Saturday from 9:30am to 4:30pm and on Sunday from noon to 4:30pm. Guides in kilts show visitors around the plant and explain the process of distilling. A film of the history of distilling is also shown. At the finish of the tour, you're given a dram of malt whisky to sample. The tour is free, but there's a souvenir shop where the owners hope you'll spend a few pounds.

Other sights include **Balvenie Castle,** along A-941 (© **01340/820121**), the ruins of a moated stronghold from the 14th century on the south side of the Glenfiddich Distillery. During her northern campaign against the earl of Huntly,

Mary, Queen of Scots, spent 2 nights here. It's open April through September, daily from 9:30am to 6:30pm. Admission is £1.50 ($2.40) adults, £1.10 ($1.75) seniors, and 50p (80¢) children under 16.

Mortlach Parish Church in Dufftown is one of the oldest places of Christian worship in the country. It's reputed to have been founded in 566 by St. Moluag. A Pictish cross stands in the graveyard. The present church was reconstructed in 1931 and incorporates portions of an older building.

Where to Dine

Taste of Speyside ✿ SCOTTISH   True to its name, this restaurant in the town center, just off the main square, avidly promotes a Speyside cuisine as well as malt whiskies. In the bar you can buy the product of each of Speyside's 46 distilleries. A platter including a slice of smoked salmon, smoked venison, smoked trout, paté flavored with malt whisky, locally made cheese (cow or goat), salads, and homemade oat cakes is offered at noon and at night. Nourishing soup is made fresh daily and is served with homemade bread. There's also a choice of meat pies, including venison with red wine and herbs, or rabbit. For dessert, try Scotch Mist, which contains fresh cream, malt whisky, and crumbled meringue.

10 Balvenie St. ✆ **01340/820860.** Reservations recommended in the evening. Main courses £11–£17 ($17–$27); Speyside platter £14 ($22) at lunch, £14 ($22) at dinner. AE, MC, V. Mon–Sat noon–9pm. Closed Nov–Feb.

GRANTOWN-ON-SPEY

This vacation resort, with its gray granite buildings, is 55km (34 miles) southeast of Inverness, in a wooded valley from which it commands views of the Cairngorm Mountains. It's a key center of winter sports in Scotland. Fishers are also attracted to this setting, because the Spey is renowned for its salmon. One of Scotland's many 18th-century planned towns, it was founded on a heather-covered moor in 1765 by Sir James Grant of Grant and became the seat of that ancient family. The town was famous in the 19th century as a Highland tourist center.

From a base here, you can explore the valleys of the Don and Dee, the Cairngorms, and Culloden Moor, scene of the historic battle in 1746, when Bonnie Prince Charlie and his army were defeated.

A year-round **tourist information office** is on High Street (✆ **01479/ 872773**). Hours are April through October, Monday through Saturday from 9am to 7pm and Sunday from 10am to 5pm; November through March, Monday through Friday from 9am to 5pm and Saturday from 10am to 5pm.

Where to Stay

Garth Hotel   The elegant, comfortable Garth stands on 2 hectares (4 acres) of ground beside the town square. Guests enjoy the use of a spacious upstairs lounge, whose high ceilings, wood-burning stove, and vine-covered veranda make it an attractive place for morning coffee or afternoon tea. The comfortable and handsomely furnished rooms have all the necessary amenities. Extensive and selective meals with a French slant favor "Taste of Scotland" dishes, with emphasis on fresh local produce.

The Square, Castle Rd., Grantown-on-Spey, Morayshire PH26 3HN. ✆ **01479/872836.** Fax 01479/872116. 18 units. £59–£69 ($94–$110) double. Rates include Scottish breakfast. MC, V. Free parking. **Amenities:** Restaurant; bar; room service; laundry/dry cleaning. *In room:* TV, coffeemaker, hair dryer.

Tulchan Lodge ✿✿   Built in 1906 to serve as the 10,800-hectare (23,000-acre) Tulchan Estate's fishing and shooting lodge, this is a place for both sports-oriented

Spotting Nessie

Sir Peter Scott's *Nessitera rhombopteryx* continues to elude her pursuers. "Nessie," as she's more familiarly known, has captured the imagination of the world, drawing thousands of visitors yearly to Loch Ness. The Loch Ness monster has been described as one of the world's greatest mysteries. Half a century ago, A82 was built alongside the western banks of the loch. Since that time, many more sightings have been recorded.

All types of high-tech underwater contraptions have searched for the Loch Ness monster, but no one can find her. Dr. Robert Rines and his associates at the Academy of Applied Science in Massachusetts maintain a year-round watch with sonar-triggered cameras and strobe lights suspended from a raft in Urquhart Bay.

The loch is 39km (24 miles) long, 1.6km (1 mile) wide, and some 230m (755 ft.) deep. Even if the monster doesn't put in an appearance, you can enjoy the loch seascape. In summer, you can take boat cruises across Loch Ness from both Fort Augustus and Inverness.

Buses from either Fort Augustus or Inverness traverse A82, taking you to Drumnadrochit. Call © **08705/808-080** for schedules and more information. The bucolic hamlet of Drumnadrochit lies a mile from Loch Ness at the entrance to Glen Urquhart. It's the nearest village to the part of the loch from which sightings of the monster have been reported most frequently.

From Grantown-on-Spey, take A938 west until you merge with northwest-bound E15/A9, which leads to Inverness, on the north tip of Loch Ness. From Inverness, travel on the A02 south, which runs the length of the western shoreline. The eastern shoreline can be traveled by following signposted rural roads from Inverness.

visitors and travelers who want to experience a place designed with the elegance required by Edward VII, who came here for sports. The lodge has panoramic views of the Spey Valley, and each room is different in size and furnishings. In the two elegant dining rooms, Scottish and international dishes are served, with only full-board residents accepted.

Advie, Grantown-on-Spey PH26 3PW. © **01807/510200.** Fax 01807/510234. www.tulchan.com. 13 units. £368–£525 ($589–$840) double. Rates include full board. MC, V. Closed Feb–Mar. Drive 14km (9 miles) northeast of Grantown on B-9102. **Amenities:** 2 dining areas; lounge; tennis court; room service; babysitting; laundry/dry cleaning; shooting. *In room:* Hair dryer.

Where to Dine

Craggan Mill BRITISH/ITALIAN   This licensed restaurant and lounge bar, a 10-minute walk south of the town center, is housed in a restored ruined granite mill whose water wheel is still visible. The owners offer British or Italian cuisine at attractive prices. Main courses might be breast of chicken with cream, or chicken cacciatore, followed by a dessert of rum-raisin ice cream or peach Melba. You've probably had better versions of all the dishes offered here, but what you get isn't bad. A good selection of Italian wines is offered.

Hwy. A-95 1km (³/₄ mile) south of Grantown-on-Spey. ℂ **01479/872288.** Reservations recommended. Main courses £4.25–£18 ($6.80–$29). MC, V. May–Sept daily 10am–midnight; Oct–Apr Tues–Sun 7–10pm. Closed the 1st 2 weeks of Nov.

GLENLIVET

As you leave Grantown-on-Spey and head east along A-95, drive to the junction with B-9008; drive south and you won't miss the **Glenlivet Distillery.** The location of the **Glenlivet Reception Centre** (ℂ **01542/783220**) is 16km (10 miles) north of the nearest town, Tomintoul. Near the River Livet, a Spey tributary, this distillery is one of the most famous in Scotland. It's open April through October, Monday through Saturday from 10am to 4pm and Sunday from 12:30 to 4pm. The £3 ($4.80) admission fee for visitors over 18 includes a £2 ($3.20) voucher against the purchase of a bottle of whisky.

Back on A-95, you can visit the **Glenfarclas Distillery** at Ballindalloch (ℂ **01807/500245**), one of the few malt whisky distilleries that's still independent of the giants. Founded in 1836, Glenfarclas is managed by the fifth generation of the Grant family. It's open year-round, Monday through Friday from 10am to 4pm; June through September, it's also open Saturday from 10am to 5pm. There's a small crafts shop, and each visitor is offered a dram of Glenfarclas Malt Whisky. The admission of £3.50 ($5.60) is for visitors over 18 and there's a discount of £7 ($11) on any purchase of £10 ($16) or more.

Where to Stay

Minmore House Hotel 🅰   Standing on 2 hectares (5 acres) of private grounds adjacent to the Glenlivet Distillery, this is an impressive country house. It was the home of the distillery owners before becoming a hotel. The drawing room opens onto views of the plush Ladder Hills. Well-furnished rooms have vital amenities, and the oak-paneled lounge bar has an open log fire on chilly nights.

Glenlivet, Ballindalloch AB37 9DB. ℂ **01807/590378.** Fax 01807/590472. www.minmorehousehotel.com. 10 units. £60 ($96) double year-round. Rates include breakfast, afternoon tea, and 4-course dinner. MC, V. Closed mid-Oct to mid-Apr. **Amenities:** Dining room; bar; pool. *In room:* Coffeemaker, hair dryer.

KINCRAIG

Kincraig enjoys a scenic spot at the northern end of Loch Insh, overlooking the Spey Valley to the west and the Cairngorm Mountains to the east. Near Kincraig, the most notable sight is the **Highland Wildlife Park** 🅰 (ℂ **01540/651270**), a natural area of parkland with a collection of wildlife, some of which is extinct elsewhere in Scotland. Herds of European bison, red deer, shaggy Highland cattle, wild horses, St. Kilda Soay sheep, and roe deer range the park. In enclosures are wolves, polecats, wildcats, beavers, badgers, and pine martens. Protected birds to see are golden eagles and several species of grouse—of special interest is the capercaillie (horse of the woods), a large Eurasian grouse native to Scotland's pine forests. There's a visitor center with a gift shop, cafe, and exhibition areas. Ample parking and a picnic site are also available.

You need a car to go through the park; walkers are discouraged and are picked up by park rangers. The park is open daily at 10am. April through October, the last entrance is at 4pm, except during July and August and November through March, when the last entrance is at 5pm. All people and vehicles are expected to vacate the park within 2 hours of the day's last admission. Admission to the park is £7.50 ($12) adults, £6 ($9.60) seniors, and £5 ($8) children. A family ticket costs £25 ($40).

KINGUSSIE

Your next stop along the Spey might be at the little summer vacation resort and winter ski center of Kingussie (it's pronounced King-*you*-see), just off A-9. It's the capital of Badenoch, a district known as "the drowned land" because the Spey can flood the valley when the snows of a severe winter melt in the spring.

Kingussie, 188km (117 miles) northwest of Edinburgh, 66km (41 miles) south of Inverness, and 18km (11 miles) southwest of Aviemore, practically adjoins Newtonmore (see below), directly northeast along A-86.

Highland Folk Museum ⚘, Duke Street (② **01540/661307**), is the first folk museum established in Scotland (1934), and its collections are based on the lives of the Highlanders. You'll see domestic, agricultural, and industrial items. Open-air exhibits are a turf kailyard (kitchen garden), a Lewis "black house," and old vehicles and carts. Traditional events such as spinning, music making, and handcraft fairs are held throughout the summer. Admission is £5 ($8) adults, £3 ($4.80) children and seniors, £15 ($24) family. Hours are April through October, Monday through Friday from 10:30am to 4pm, Saturday and Sunday from 1 to 4pm.

A summer-only **tourist center** is on King Street (② **01540/661297**). It's open only from May 22 to September 22, Monday through Saturday from 10am to 1pm and 2 to 6pm and Sunday from 10am to 1pm and 2 to 5pm.

Where to Stay

Homewood Lodge ⚘ *Kids*   One of the best B&Bs in the area, this small Highland house offers large, simply furnished rooms. In a garden and woodland setting, the house has a sitting room with an open fire. Good traditional local fare is served in the evening (reservations recommended). Summer barbecues are also offered. Children are welcome.

Newtonmore Rd., Kingussie PH21 1HD. ② **01540/661507**. www.homewood-lodge-kingussie.co.uk. 4 units. £40 ($64) double. Rates include Scottish breakfast. No credit cards. Free parking. **Amenities:** Dining area; laundry/dry cleaning. *In room:* TV, radio, coffeemaker, hair dryer.

Osprey Hotel   This 1895 Victorian structure, 275m (300 yd.) from the rail station, is a convenient place to stay, with comfortable although very plain rooms, all with hot and cold running water, central heating, electric blankets, and electric fires. The hotel has a residents' lounge and a TV lounge. The place is known for its pure, fresh, 100% homemade food. Prime Scottish meats are served; in summer, salmon and trout from local rivers are offered either fresh or peat-smoked.

Ruthven Rd. (at High St.), Kingussie PH21 1EN. ②/fax **01540/661510**. www.ospreyhotel.co.uk. 8 units. £25–£36 ($40–$58) per person double. Rates include breakfast. AE, DC, MC, V. Free parking. **Amenities:** Restaurant; bar; babysitting. *In room:* TV, coffeemaker, hair dryer.

Where to Dine

The Cross ⚘⚘ SCOTTISH   This chic restaurant comes as a surprise: In an out-of-the-way setting in a remote Highland village, it serves superlative meals that involve theater as much as fine food. The restaurant has an open-beam ceiling and French doors leading onto a terrace over the water's edge where alfresco dinners are served. Specialties might include venison Francatelli, wild pigeon with grapes, or Highland lamb with sorrel.

Nine rooms are rented in a new building. Each room is different in size and style—for example, two rooms have canopied beds, and another has a balcony overlooking the millpond. Doubles, including half board, cost from £190 ($304). Personal service and attention to detail go into the running of this place, operated by Ruth and Tony Hadley, and Ruth's cooking has put it on the gastronomic map of Scotland.

Tweed Mill Brae, off the Ardbroilach road, Kingussie PH21 1TC. ✆ **01540/661166.** Fax 01540/661080. Reservations recommended. Fixed-price 5-course dinner £40 ($63). MC, V. Wed–Mon 7–9pm. Closed Dec–Feb.

NEWTONMORE

This Highland resort in Speyside is a good center for the Grampian and Monadhliath mountains, and it offers excellent fishing, golf, pony trekking, and hill walking. A track from the village climbs past the Calder River to Loch Dubh and the massive 940m (3,087-ft.) **Carn Ban,** where eagles fly. **Castle Cluny,** ancient seat of the MacPherson chiefs, is 10km (6 miles) west of Newtonmore.

You may want to stop and have a look at **Clan MacPherson House & Museum,** Main Street (✆ **01540/673332**). Displayed are clan relics and memorials, including the Black Chanter and Green Banner, as well as a "charmed sword" and the broken fiddle of the freebooter, James MacPherson—a Scottish Robin Hood. Relics associated with Bonnie Prince Charlie are also here. An annual clan rally is held in August. Admission is free, but donations are accepted. It's open only from April to October: Monday through Saturday from 10am to 5pm, Sunday from 2:30 to 5pm.

Where to Stay

Pines Hotel   Built in 1903, this somber-looking house sits on a hill overlooking the Spey Valley, and lies just west of the hamlet's center. Your hosts are Colin and Pamela Walker, who charge the bargain price of £25 ($38) for a double if it's taken by one person. All rooms have pleasant views of the Highland countryside and each comes with a small but neat shower-only bathroom. The food is wholesome, straightforward Scottish cuisine, made from fresh ingredients such as salmon, lamb, venison, and Aberdeen Angus beef. Pamela is an expert on desserts and has a particular interest in creating treats for diabetics.

Station Rd., Newtonmore PH20 1AR. ✆ **01540/673271.** 5 units. £48–£50 ($77–$80) double. Rates include Scottish breakfast. MC, V. Free parking. Closed Dec 28–Jan 15. *In room:* TV, coffeemaker, hair dryer.

Spain

by Herbert Bailey Livesey

The history of Spain is palpable in its towns small and large, but this country of 40 million is no musty relic entombed in the past. Spain today is a vital, exhilarating place. Still a land of sun-washed beaches, terraced vineyards, tranquil hill towns, and dazzling Moorish palaces, it is also well into a remarkable cultural and economic renaissance.

That rebirth began with the death of Franco in 1975 and gathered speed with the nation's 1986 entry into the European Union. Contemporary art, literature, cinema, and fashion are the tools of fresh and original expression, and cafes and bars hum with animated discussion about politics, society, and Spain's newfound prosperity.

1 Madrid ★★★

Landlocked Madrid lies at the center of a high arid tableland called the Meseta, a location chosen due to political considerations. Rulers of the 16th century chose the site in an attempt to counter the forces of the frequently rebellious outer regions. The city is populated by citizens from virtually every region of Spain and, increasingly, by immigrants from Africa, Asia, and Latin America. As a result, in only a few years It has become one of the most multicultural cities in Europe, adding to its cosmopolitan gloss. Despite its position as the cultural beacon of the Spanish-speaking world, Madrid lacks features that for many bespeak Spain—beaches and castles, for two. There is a vast royal palace, though, and buildings that date back to the Golden Age (the 16th and 17th c.). Madrileños long ago learned how to make the most of their hometown: They take long strolls through the city's verdant parks and along its *paseos,* and pursue nightlife with a passion, dining at midnight, partying until dawn, and welcoming the new day with hot chocolate and deep-fried tubes of dough called *churros.*

Over the last decade or so, the city has revived its central gathering places, including Puerta del Sol, the Plaza de Oriente, and the Teatro Real opera house. Now the authorities have turned their efforts to lifting the medieval gloom from the side streets and smaller plazas. New paving stones have been laid, lighting has been installed, hundreds of trees have been planted, and larger pedestrian areas have been designated. The Prado Museum, one of the world's most prominent, has begun construction on a major annex that will allow for the display of artworks that languished in storage for a long time. Madrid has begun the 21st century at a full run.

ESSENTIALS

GETTING THERE By Plane Aeropuerto Madrid Barajas (© **91-305-8343;** www.aena.es/madrid-barajas), Madrid's international airport, is 14km (9 miles) east of the city center and has three terminals. Most international flights arrive at Terminal 1. Air-conditioned yellow airport buses take passengers from the arrivals terminal to the bus depot under Plaza de Colón, a central point in Madrid. You can also get off at stops along the way, provided that your baggage isn't stored in the hold. The fare is 2.50€. The buses leave every 10 to 15 minutes from 6am to 10pm, less often between 4:45am and 6am and between 10pm and 1:30am; there is no service from 1:30am to 4:45am. You can also take the Metro to the city center, but the station is at Terminal 3, the ride involves at least one train change, and the trip takes longer than the trip by airport bus.

If you go into town by taxi, expect to pay about 20€ plus surcharges for the trip to/from the airport and for baggage handling. Avoid unmetered limousines.

By Train Madrid has three major railway stations: **Atocha,** Avenida Ciudad de Barcelona (Metro: Atocha RENFE), for trains to and from Lisbon, Toledo, Andalucía, and Extremadura; **Chamartín,** in the northern suburbs at Augustín de Foxá (Metro: Chamartín), for trains to Barcelona, Asturias, Cantabria, Castilla y León, the Basque country, Aragón, Catalonia, Levante (Valencia), Murcia, and the French border; and **Estación Príncipe Pío** or Norte, Paseo del Rey 30 (Metro: Norte), for trains to northwest Spain (Salamanca and Galicia).

For information about connections from any of these stations, contact **RENFE,** the Spanish railway company (© **90-224-0202** daily 7am–11pm; www.renfe.es). For tickets, go to the principal office of RENFE, Alcalá 44 (Metro: Banco de España), open Monday through Friday from 9:30am to 8pm; or go to any of the three main stations listed above.

In the United States, **Rail Europe** sells a variety of **rail passes** valid for use throughout Europe or in one or more specific countries, including Spain. For details, call © **888-382-7245** or visit **www.raileurope.com.**

By Bus Madrid has at least eight major bus terminals, including the large **Estación Sur de Autobuses,** Calle Méndez Alvaro (© **91-468-42-00;** Metro: Alvaro). Most buses pass through or arrive at this station.

By Car The following are the major highways into Madrid, with driving distances to the city: Route NI from Irún, 507km (314 miles); NII from Barcelona, 626km (389 miles); NIII from Valencia, 349km (217 miles); NIV from Cádiz, 624km (388 miles); NV from Badajoz, 409km (254 miles); and NVI from Galicia, 602km (374 miles).

VISITOR INFORMATION The **regional government's tourist office** is on Calle Duque de Medinacel 2 (© **91-429-3177;** www.spaintour.es; Metro: Banco de España). It's open Monday through Saturday from 9am to 7pm and Sunday and holidays from 9am to 3pm. A more convenient **information office,** at **Plaza Mayor 3** (© **91-588-1636;** Metro: Sol), is open Monday to Saturday from 9am to 7pm. This office is primarily a distribution center for brochures and maps, although attendants can answer questions.

Websites The Tourist Office of Spain (**www.okspain.org**) can help you plan your trip with listings of lodging options, attractions, tour operators, and packages, plus handy tips on getting around. Very extensive information is provided by **www.red2000.com/spain** and **www.cyberspain.com**, which cover the basics on lodging and dining and much, much more. Madrid Man's Yankee Home Page (**www.madridman.com**) looks frivolous but hides a surprising amount of info, with nuts-and-bolts details that surpass most other sources.

CITY LAYOUT The **Gran Vía** cuts an angled path across the city, west to east, beginning at **Plaza de España,** with one of Europe's tallest skyscrapers, Edificio España. Great numbers of shops, hotels, restaurants, and cinemas are concentrated on this principal avenue. Gran Vía ends at Calle de Alcalá, and at this juncture lies **Plaza de la Cibeles,** with its fountain to Cybele, "the mother of the gods," and what has become known as "the cathedral of post offices." From Cibeles northward, the wide **Paseo de Recoletos** begins a short run to **Plaza de Colón.** From this latter square, the majestic **Paseo de la Castellana** begins, flanked by expensive shops, apartment buildings, luxury hotels, and foreign embassies. Parallel to the Paseo de la Castellana, **Calle de Serrano** is a prominent shopping street that forms the spine of the prosperous Salamanca neighborhood.

Heading south from Cibeles is **Paseo del Prado,** home to the eponymous **Museo del Prado,** as well as the **Jardín Botánica (Botanical Garden).** The paseo continues on to the Atocha Station. To the east of the Prado lies the **Parque del Retiro,** once reserved for royalty, with restaurants, nightclubs, a rose garden, and two lakes.

South of Gran Vía is the central **Puerta del Sol,** a half-moon-shaped plaza. All road distances in Spain are measured from here, and it is an important hub for buses and the Metro. Here, **Calle de Alcalá** begins and runs east for 4km (2½ miles).

A couple of blocks west is the **Plaza Mayor,** the heart of Old Madrid, and an attraction in itself with its mix of French and Georgian architecture. Pedestrians pass under the arches of the huge square onto the narrow streets of the old town, where some of the capital's most intriguing restaurants and *tabernas* are found.

GETTING AROUND The tourist office (see above) provides a street map that includes a schematic of the public transit system. The bus and expanding Metro networks are efficient and extensive, and taxis are abundant. Since traffic is nearly always heavy, though, plan to cover distances under 10 blocks by walking.

Madrid Metro

Parque de Santa María **4**

San Lorenzo

Barajas **8**

Mar de Cristal **8**

Aeropuerto

Campo de las Naciones

Pío XII

Canillas

Colombia

Esperanza

Concha Espina

Arturo Soria

Cruz del Rayo

Avda. de la Paz

5 Canillejas

Alfonso XIII

Prosperidad

TorreArias

Avda. de América

Cartagena

Parque de las Avenidas

Barrio de la Concepción

Suanzes

Diego de León

Ciudad Lineal

Núñez de Balboa

Ventas

Pueblo Nuevo

7 Las Musas

Lista

El Carmen

Quintana

Manuel Becerra

Ascao

2

García Noblejas

Simancas

San Blas

Velázquez

Goya

Príncipe de Vergara

O'Donnell

Ibiza

Sáinz de Baranda

Estrella

Vinateros

6

Artilleros

Pavones

Conde de Casal

Valdebernardo

Vicálvaro

San Cipriano

Menéndez Pelayo

Puerta de Arganda

Pacífico

Puente de Vallecas

Nueva Numancia

Portazgo

Buenos Aires

Rivas Urbanizaciones

Alto del Arenal

Miguel Hernández

Rivas Vaciamadrid

Sierra de Guadalupe

La Poveda

Villa de Vallecas

1

ZONA B1

ZONA B2

ZONA B3

9

Congosto

Arganda del Rey

893

By Metro (Subway) The Metro (© 91-552-5909; www.metromadrid.es) is convenient and easy to understand and use. The central converging point is under the Puerta del Sol. A single fare *(una sencilla)* is 1.10€. The Metro operates daily from 6am to 1:30am; avoid rush hours if possible. You can save money on the Metro by purchasing a 10-trip pass known as a *Metrobús*. It costs 5.20€, a substantial savings.

By Bus A bus network also services the city and suburbs, with routes clearly shown at each stop on a schematic diagram. Buses are fast and efficient because they travel along special lanes. Both red and yellow buses charge .95€. For 5.20€ you can purchase a 10-trip *Metrobús*. It's sold at **Empresa Municipal de Transportes (EMT)** kiosks in Plaza de Cibeles, Puerta del Sol, Plaza de Callao, and Atocha station. The offices are open Monday through Friday from 8am to 8:15pm.

The hop-off, hop-on **Madrid Vision Bus** lets you set your own pace and itinerary. A scheduled panoramic tour lasts a half hour, provided that you don't get off the bus. Otherwise, you can opt for an unlimited number of stops, getting on and off at your leisure.

By Taxi Cab fares have risen recently, and are no longer as reasonable as they were a few years ago. When you flag down a taxi, the meter should register 1.45€; for every kilometer thereafter, the fare increases by .65€ to .95€, depending upon the time and day of the week. A supplement is charged for trips to the rail station or the bullring, as well as on Sundays and holidays. The ride to Barajas Airport carries a 4€ surcharge, and there's a 2€ supplement for trips from the rail stations. It's customary to tip about 10% of the fare. To call a taxi, dial © 91-447-5180.

By Car Driving is nightmarish and potentially dangerous in very congested Madrid—it always feels like rush hour. It's not a good idea to maintain a rental car while staying in the city. It's nearly impossible to park, and rental cars are the frequent targets of thieves.

Should you want to rent a car to tour the environs, however, you'll have several choices. Save money before leaving for Spain by making arrangements with **Auto Europe** (© 800/223-5555), which brokers economical rates with established firms abroad, including some of the companies mentioned below. In addition to its office at Barajas Airport (© 91-393-7222), **Avis** has a main office downtown at Gran Vía 60 (© 91-547-2048). **Hertz,** too, has an office at Barajas Airport (© 91-393-7228), and another at Gran Vía 88 (© 91-345-1897). **Budget Rent-a-Car** maintains offices at Barajas Airport (© 91-393-7216) and at Alcántara 59 (© 91-402-1480).

Note: You'll need only your state or provincial driver's license to rent a car, but if you're in an accident or stopped on the road by police, a recent regulation stipulates you must produce an **International Drivers Permit.** These are available at AAA offices in the States for $10 to $15. Know, too, that stiff fines are collected when drivers are caught speaking on a hand-held cellphone while driving.

 FAST FACTS: Madrid

American Express For your mail or banking needs, you can go to the Amex office at the corner of Marqués de Cubas and Plaza de las Cortes 2, across the street from the Palace Hotel (© 91-572-0303; Metro: Sevilla).

It's open Monday through Friday from 9am to 5:30pm and Saturday from 9am to 2pm.

Consulates The consulate of the **United States,** Calle Serrano 75 (© **91-577-3400;** Metro: Núñez de Balboa), is open Monday through Friday from 9:30am to 12:30pm and 3 to 5pm. The consulate of **Canada,** Núñez de Balboa 35 (© **91-421-4300;** Metro: Velázquez), is open Monday through Friday from 9am to 12:30pm. The **United Kingdom** consulate, at Marqués de la Ensenada 16 (© **91-308-5244;** Metro: Colón), is open Monday through Friday from 8am to 2:30pm. The Republic of **Ireland** consulate, Paseo de La Castellana 46 (© **91-436-4093;** Metro: Serrano), is open Monday through Friday from 10am to 2pm. The consulate of **Australia,** at Plaza Descubridor Diego de Ordás 3 (© **91-441-9300;** Metro: Ríos Rosas), is open Monday through Thursday from 8:30am to 1:30pm and 2:30 to 4:45pm, Friday from 8:30am to 2pm. The **New Zealand** consulate, Plaza de la Lealtad 2 (© **91-523-0226;** Metro: Banco de España), is open Monday through Friday from 9am to 1:30pm and 2:30 to 5pm.

Currency The Spanish peseta gave way to the **euro** on March 1, 2002.

Dentist/Doctor For an English-speaking dentist or doctor, contact the U.S. embassy, Calle Serrano 75 (© **91-587-2200**), which maintains a list of dentists and doctors who have offered their services to Americans abroad. For dental services, consult also **Unidad Médica Anglo-Americana,** Conde de Arandá 1 (© **91-435-1823;** Metro: Retiro), near Plaza de Independencia. Office hours are Monday through Friday from 9am to 8pm, Saturday from 10am to 1pm; there's a 24-hour answering service. Also, hotel concierges *(conserjes)* usually have lists of available doctors and dentists.

Drugstores For a late-night pharmacy, dial © **098** or look in the daily newspaper under *"Farmacias de Guardia"* to learn what drugstores are open after 8pm. Another way to find an open pharmacy is to go to any pharmacy, even if it's closed—it will have posted a list of nearby pharmacies that are open late on that date.

Emergencies In an emergency, call © **080** to report a fire, © **091** to reach the **police,** or © **734-2554** to request an **ambulance.**

Hospitals/Clinics **Unidad Médica Anglo-Americana,** Conde de Arandá 1 (© **91-435-1823;** Metro: Retiro), isn't a hospital but a private outpatient clinic where someone is always available. It's open daily from 9am to 8pm. For a medical emergency, call © **734-2554** for an ambulance.

Post Office If you don't want to receive your mail at your hotel or the American Express office, direct it to *Lista de Correos* at the central post office in Madrid. To pick up mail, go to the window marked LISTA, where you'll be asked to show your passport. Madrid's central office is the **Palacio de Comunicaciones** at Plaza de Cibeles (© **902/197-197**).

Safety Leave valuables in a hotel safe or other secure place when going out. You may need your passport, however, as the police sometimes stop foreigners for identification checks. Carry only enough cash for the day's needs. Pickpockets and purse snatchers work major tourist sites, trains, restaurants, and ATM machines. Criminals often work in pairs, grabbing purses from pedestrians, cyclists, even cars. Several scams are meant to divert the victim's attention, such as spilling something on his or her clothing, or thrusting maps or newspapers into his or her face. Even "Do you know the time?" can be used to establish that you are a foreigner and distract you.

Taxes The internal sales tax (known in Spain as IVA) ranges between 7% and 33%, depending on the commodity being sold. Food, wine, and basic necessities are taxed at 7%; most goods and services (including car rentals) at 13%; luxury items (jewelry, all tobacco, imported liquors) at 33%; and hotels at 7%.

If you are not a European Union resident and make purchases in Spain worth more than 90€, you can get a tax refund. To get the refund, you must complete three copies of a form that the store will give you, detailing the nature of your purchase and its value. Citizens of non–EU countries show the purchase and the form to the Spanish Customs Office. The shop is then supposed to refund the amount due to you. Discuss in what currency your refund will arrive.

Telephone The country code for Spain is **34** and the city code for Madrid is **91**. All numbers in Spain are now nine digits, starting with the two- or three-digit city code. Telephone centers are called *locutorios*. The formerly state-owned **Telefónico** company still dominates the industry, although some smaller companies offer competing services. Many public phones accept only Telefónico phone cards, along with major credit cards; you may have to hunt around to find a telephone that accepts other phone cards.

Tipping Don't overtip. The government requires that hotels and restaurants include service charges in the bill—usually 15% of the total bill. That doesn't mean, however, that you should skip out of a place without dispensing some extra money. Add another 3% to 5%, depending on the quality of the service. Tip the hotel porter .60€ per bag, doorman .60€ for assisting with baggage, and hotel maid .85€ per day. Tip cab drivers 10% of the fare.

WHERE TO STAY
ALONG THE PASEO DE LA CASTELLANA
Very Expensive

Hesperia Madrid 🌟🌟🌟   Located in a northerly district that houses imposing office blocks and a multitude of competing hotels that also boast the government's five-star rating, the Hesperia handily holds its own, with sleek styling and smooth service. The hotel's signature restaurant, Santceloni, found itself at the pinnacle of the capital's gastronomic pyramid almost as soon as it opened its doors (so reserve well in advance). A less rarified but thoroughly competent dining room, La Manzana, is on the main floor. Guest rooms are of sufficient size, with exceedingly comfortable beds and such extras as fax machines, terry robes, and fresh flowers. While the hotel is distant from most of the major sights, it is closer to the airport than city-center hotels.

Paseo de la Castellana 57, 28046 Madrid. ℂ **91-210-8800.** Fax 91-210-8899. www.hoteles-hesperia.es. 171 units. 316€–409€ double; from 661€ suite. AE, DC, MC, V. Parking 25€. Metro: Gregorio Marañón. **Amenities:** 2 restaurants; bar; concierge; car-rental desk; business center; 24-hr. room service; babysitting; same-day laundry/dry cleaning. *In room:* A/C, TV w/pay movies, dataport, minibar, hair dryer.

Ritz Madrid 🏵🏵🏵   Despite recent challengers, this remains Madrid's most prestigious address, a bastion of glamour and an enduring relic of the Edwardian Age. Its grand public areas, with their soaring ceilings and graceful columns, were built in 1908 at the request of Alfonso XIII, who was embarrassed that his capital didn't have suitable accommodations for visiting royals. Rooms are spacious, elegantly furnished, and filled with fresh flowers. Each is equipped with a well-accessorized bathroom. The restaurant, which receives good reviews, has tables that spill onto a garden terrace in warm months.

Plaza de la Lealtad 5, 28014 Madrid. 📞 **800/225-5843** in the U.S. and Canada, or 91-521-2857. Fax 91-532-8776. www.ritz.es. 156 units. 260€–380€ double; from 80€ suite. AE, DC, MC, V. Parking 24€. Metro: Banco de España. **Amenities:** 2 restaurants; bar; health club with sauna; concierge; 24-hr. room service; babysitting; same-day laundry/dry cleaning. *In room:* A/C, TV, dataport, minibar, coffeemaker, hair dryer.

The Westin Palace 🏵🏵🏵   An ornate 1912 structure that captures the pre–World War I grand hotel style, the Palace faces the Prado and Neptune Fountain. When it first opened, it was the largest hotel in Europe. Everyone from Dalí to Picasso, from Sarah Bernhardt to Sophia Loren, has spent the night here. Nevertheless, the Westin Palace hasn't achieved the cachet of its sibling, the Ritz, across the Paseo de Castellana, perhaps because the Westin is so much larger. Rooms are traditional, with plenty of space, containing large marble bathrooms with all the amenities. Do have a drink under the great stained-glass dome at the back of the main floor.

Plaza de las Cortes 7, 28014 Madrid. 📞 **800/325-3535** in the U.S., 800/325-3589 in Canada, or 91-360-8000 in Spain. Fax 91-360-8100. www.westin.com. 417 units. 295€–425€ double; from 800€ suite. AE, DC, MC, V. Metro: Banco de España. **Amenities:** 2 restaurants; bar; well-equipped health club; concierge; 24-hr. room service; babysitting; same-day laundry/dry cleaning. *In room:* A/C, TV, dataport, minibar, hair dryer, safe.

Inexpensive
Mora 🏵 *Value*   Long one of Madrid's top budget choices, even with recent modest rate hikes, the Mora still has few equals. The spacious lobby with chandeliers sets the tone. The narrow but bright halls lead to adequately furnished rooms that come in a variety of configurations (many singles are small, with mere slivers of bathrooms, so inspect first). The helpful staff at the front desk speaks English. The adjacent restaurant, Bango (separate management), attracts a varied crowd for low-cost meals. The Prado is across the street and the Reina Sofía is a short walk away.

Paseo del Prado 32, 28014 Madrid. 📞 **91-420-1569.** Fax 91-420-0564. 62 units. 39€–69€ double. AE, DC, MC, V. Metro: Atocha. **Amenities:** Restaurant; bar. *In room:* A/C, TV, safe.

NEAR THE ROYAL PALACE
Moderate
Opera 🏵 *Finds*   A couple of blocks from the Royal Palace and opposite the opera house, this hotel offers first-rate comfort. You'll receive a warm welcome from the English-speaking staff. Rooms, some of which boast balconies, range in size from medium to surprisingly spacious. Each room is furnished with twin or double beds that feature quality mattresses. Some bathrooms have whirlpools. The Opera remains one of Madrid's relatively undiscovered boutique hotels.

Cuesta de Santo Domingo 2, 28013 Madrid. 📞 **91-541-2800.** Fax 91-541-6923. hotelopera@sinix.net. 79 units. 105€–114€ double. AE, DC, MC, V. Metro: Opera. **Amenities:** Restaurant; bar; limited room service; babysitting; laundry/dry cleaning service. *In room:* A/C, TV, minibar, hair dryer, safe.

Inexpensive
Campomanes 🏵 *Finds*   Up a quiet side street from the opera house is a row of attached houses that were scooped out and rebuilt to house this spiffy hotel.

Madrid

✝ Church
ⓘ Information
Ⓜ Metro
⊠ Post Office
---- Railway

Contemporary and minimalist, the colors here are black, white, and pearl gray. However, the surroundings are cozy, not chilly. There are two "mini-suites," which are really just large doubles. Singles are relatively large and offer full-size beds. At this moment, hardly anyone knows about this hotel, so get there before they do.

Campomanes 4 (near Arrieta), 28013 Madrid. © **91-548-8548.** Fax 91-559-1288. 30 units. 84€–108€ double. Rates include breakfast. AE, MC, V. Metro: Opera. **Amenities:** Bar; laundry/dry cleaning service. *In room:* A/C, TV, minibar, safe.

ON OR NEAR THE GRAN VIA
Expensive

Gaudí A majestic early-1900s building at the end of the Gran Vía was gutted to be transformed into this near-luxury hotel. Plaza Mayor and the Prado and Thyssen museums are within walking distance. A siesta-time retreat to these quiet teak-lined quarters is restorative. The weekend rates include an extensive breakfast buffet with hot and cold items, which otherwise costs 12€ during the week.

Gran Vía 9, 28013 Madrid. © **91-531-2222.** Fax 91-531-5469. www.hoteles-catalonia.es. 185 units. 118€–186€ double. AE, DC, MC, V. Metro: Gran Vía. **Amenities:** Restaurant; bar; exercise room with sauna/whirlpool; 24-hr. room service; same-day laundry/dry cleaning. *In room:* A/C, TV, dataport, minibar, hair dryer, safe.

Moderate

Best Western Hotel Arosa Following extensive renovations, the Arosa has gained the government's four-star rating. The broad side of this late-19th-century building occupies a block in the middle of the Gran Vía, but double-paned glass keeps the street noise out. Rooms vary significantly in size and layout, but with this many, if you're unhappy with the room you get, a better one is nearly always available. An airport shuttle van operates from 6:25am to 6:10pm. Discounts for seniors are available here.

Salud 21, 28013 Madrid. © **91-532-1600.** Fax 91-531-3127. www.bestwestern.com. 140 units. 120€–199€ double. AE, DC, MC, V. Metro: Gran Vía. **Amenities:** Restaurant; bar; limited room service; same-day laundry/dry cleaning. *In room:* A/C, TV, dataport, minibar, hair dryer, safe.

Best Western Hotel Carlos V *Value* Two years of major renovations were worth the wait—everything here is fresh, from the carpets to the drapes. Located in the pedestrian shopping district north of Puerta del Sol, and owned and operated by three generations of the same English-speaking family, the Carlos V is a bastion of good value. In addition to the expected comforts, each room has a compact bathroom, and some fifth-floor rooms have balconies with retractable awnings. A new bar and breakfast/snack area adjoins the tasteful lounge, and there's a computer so you can surf the Net and check e-mail for free. A shuttle van makes hourly runs to Barajas airport.

Maestro Vitoria 5, 28013 Madrid. © **91-531-4100.** Fax 91-531-3761. www.bestwestern.com/carlosv. 67 units. 99€–110€ double. Rates include breakfast. AE, DC, MC, V. Metro: Sol. **Amenities:** Limited room service; same-day laundry/dry cleaning. *In room:* A/C, TV, minibar, hair dryer, safe.

Liabeny This hotel, named after the original owner (pronounced, more or less, *Ya-bay-nee*) is on a busy plaza midway between the Gran Vía and the Puerta del Sol—the pedestrian shopping district containing the main branch of El Corte Inglés is down a short hill. The contemporary-styled rooms are newly redecorated. Personalized attention from the staff adds to the comfort of your stay. The hotel has its own secure garage. Prices jumped a bit after the latest renovations, but in its category, this hotel is still solid value.

Salud 3, 28013 Madrid. ☎ **91-531-9000.** Fax 91-532-7421. www.hotelliabeny.com. 222 units. 126€ double. AE, MC, V. Parking 9.05€. Metro: Puerta del Sol, Callao, or Gran Vía. **Amenities:** Restaurant; 2 bars; concierge; limited room service; babysitting; same-day laundry/dry cleaning. *In room:* A/C, TV, minibar, hair dryer, safe.

Inexpensive

Anaco   The guest rooms look better than the lobby, but a long-term, step-by-step cosmetic upgrading is nearing completion. To be sure, ask for a room on one of the first five floors—each has fresh paint, carpeting, and furniture—while the sixth is still being renovated. Off the lobby, the busy *cafetería* offers a *menú del día* for under 9€ and stays open daily from 7:30am to 2am.

Tres Cruces 3 (at Plaza del Carmen), 28013 Madrid. ☎ **91-522-4604.** Fax 91-531-6484. www.anacohotel. cvom. 40 units. 86€ double. AE, DC, MC, V. Metro: Gran Vía. **Amenities:** Restaurant; bar; laundry/dry cleaning service; nonsmoking rooms. *In room:* A/C, TV, hair dryer, safe.

AROUND PLAZA SANTA ANA & PLAZA MAYOR
Expensive

Catalonia Moratín ⚜   This new hotel follows the formula of the rapidly expanding Catalonia chain, which transforms neglected historic buildings into first-class, moderately expensive hotels that are attractive to both business and leisure travelers. In this case, an aristocratic 18th-century mansion was reclaimed. The great granite blocks in its entryway and a marvelous grand staircase are some of the majestic features. The cellar here was used as a bomb shelter during the Civil War and was said to be connected by tunnel to the Royal Palace. Heritage aside, the guest rooms are sizeable, many with foldout sleeping sofas and king-size beds. The Puerta del Sol and Plaza Mayor are both 5 minutes away.

Atocha 23, 28012 Madrid. ☎ **91-369-7171.** Fax 91-360-1231. www.hoteles-catalonia.es. 156 units. 161€ double. AE, DC, MC, V. Metro: Sol or Tirso de Molina. **Amenities:** Restaurant; bar; concierge; limited room service; same-day laundry/dry cleaning. *In room:* A/C, TV, dataport, minibar, hair dryer, safe.

Tryp Reina Victoria ⚜   Having just undergone a renovation and upgrading under the expansive Tryp chain, this hotel is less staid and more impressive than ever. Though it's in a congested and noisy neighborhood in the center of town, Reina Victoria opens onto a sloping plaza, rich in tradition as a meeting place of intellectuals during the 17th century. Rooms contain sound-resistant insulation and bathrooms with many amenities. This is a very popular hotel, so reserve well in advance.

Plaza de Santa Ana 14, 28012 Madrid. ☎ **91-531-4500.** Fax 91-522-0307. reinavictoria@trypnet.com. 201 units. 148€–169€ double. AE, DC, MC, V. Parking 11€. Metro: Tirso de Molina or Puerta del Sol. **Amenities:** Restaurant; bar; concierge; limited room service; babysitting; same-day laundry/dry cleaning. *In room:* A/C, TV, minibar, hair dryer, safe.

Inexpensive

Inglés   A large ship model in the front window alerts you to this popular little hotel. Enter the lobby, with its comfy sofas and armchairs, and you'll find that little has changed in recent years, including the room rates and the too-often dour gents at the front desk. Just beyond the TV lounge is the bar/cafetería where breakfast is served. Many rooms have sitting areas. Nearby Plaza Santa Ana and Calle de las Huertas are brimming with tapas and music bars. A parking garage has 25 spaces for guests.

Echegaray 8, 28014 Madrid. ☎ **91-429-6551.** Fax 91-420-2423. comercial@hotelingles.com. 51 units. 85€–96€ double. AE, DC, MC, V. Metro: Sol. **Amenities:** Restaurant; bar; exercise room; limited room service. *In room:* TV, safe.

Plaza Mayor 🍄   A crisp new hotel in the shell of a 19th-century church, this is a welcome addition to Madrid's often dreary budget lodgings. Despite its name, the brick-red building wedges into Plaza Santa Cruz, slightly east of Plaza Mayor. A new entrance has been carved out of the ground floor *taberna*. The bright, contemporary (though often oddly shaped) rooms are of sufficient size, with double-thick windows sealing off traffic noise; four have double beds. The corner rooms offer light and extra space. English is spoken.

Atocha 2, 28012 Madrid. ℂ **91-360-0606** or 91-360-0828. Fax 91-360-0610. www.h-plazamayor.com. 20 units. 70€–85€ double. Rates include breakfast. AE, MC, V. Metro: Sol. **Amenities:** Restaurant; bar. *In room:* A/C, TV, safe.

NEAR SALAMANCA
Very Expensive
Villa Magna 🍄🍄🍄   Villa Magna, one of Madrid's honored luxury hotels, is set behind a bank of pines and laurels bordering the Paseo de la Castellana. Expensive cars purr and growl in the driveway. The hotel surpassed the Westin Palace as soon as it opened, and is equaled in luxury, class, and exquisitely antic-ipatory service only by the Ritz. This contemporary palace offers plush, digni-fied rooms decorated in Louis XVI, English Regency, or Italian provincial styles. The hotel is known for its summer terraces set amid gardens.

Paseo de la Castellana 22, 28046 Madrid. ℂ **800/223-1234** in the U.S. and Canada, or 91-587-1234. Fax 91-431-2286. www.madrid.hyatt.com. 182 units. 365€–730€ double; from 1,090€ suite. AE, DC, MC, V. Parking 18€. Metro: Rubén Darío. **Amenities:** 2 restaurants; 2 bars; health club with sauna; concierge; car-rental desk; salon; 24-hr. room service; babysitting; same-day laundry/dry cleaning. *In room:* A/C, TV, dataport, minibar, coffeemaker, hair dryer, safe.

Expensive
Emperatriz 🍄   This hotel is just off the Paseo de Castellana, in the orbit of some of Madrid's most deluxe hotels and restaurants, but with relatively more reasonable rates than surrounding hotels. Guest rooms, once decked in gloomy earth tones, have been lightened up with both traditional and modern furniture. They're easier on the eye than the somewhat unimaginative public areas. Ask for a 7th-floor room, where you'll get a private terrace at no extra charge, and if you're going for all-out luxe, ask for a suite with a whirlpool and/or saunas.

López de Hoyos 4, 28006 Madrid. ℂ **91-563-80-88.** Fax 91-563-98-04. www.hotel-emperatriz.com. 158 units. 240€–252€ double; from 330€ suite. AE, DC, MC, V. Metro: Rubén Darío. **Amenities:** Restaurant; bar; concierge; salon; 24-hr. room service; in-room massage; babysitting; same-day laundry/dry cleaning. *In room:* A/C, TV, dataport, minibar, hair dryer, safe.

NEAR BARAJAS AIRPORT
Moderate
La Casa Grande 🍄🍄   Despite the small number of rooms (all on the 3rd floor with no elevator access), this hotel is conveniently located in a large gated complex near the airport, containing a tavern, a garage, wine *bodegas,* and a 16th-century main building that has served as royal farmhouse and Jesuit monastery. Rooms are small but sumptuously furnished. Meals are served in the regal dining room or on the star-lit terrace, where a singer-guitarist performs nightly in season. Check out the basement gallery's remarkable collection of Russian icons.

28850 Torrejón de Ardoz (19km/12 miles east of Madrid on the Carretera de Barcelona, a few min. from the airport). ℂ **91-675-3900.** Fax 91-675-0691. www.lacasagrande.es. 8 units. 96€–129€ double. Rates include breakfast and unlimited use of minibar. AE, MC, V. Closed Aug. **Amenities:** 2 restaurants; 2 bars; sauna; 24-hr. room service; same-day laundry/dry cleaning. *In room:* A/C, TV, fax, minibar, hair dryer, safe.

WHERE TO DINE
ON OR NEAR THE GRAN VIA
Moderate

La Barraca ✮ REGIONAL SPANISH   On a narrow side street parallel to the Gran Vía, this place has acquired its folkloric atmosphere of lace curtains, ceramic pitchers, and hanging plates over a span of 68 years. The kitchen excels in *arroces*—the rice dishes of southeastern Spain's Valencia, ranging from one dish flavored with squid ink to one that substitutes thin noodles for rice (*fideua marinera*). If it's your first Spanish rice dish, you might want to order the *paella mixta*, with bits of chicken, sausage, shrimp, mussels, pork, and squid. Expect some time to pass before being served—everything is prepared to order. A smooth liver paté with good bread is an inexpensive appetite-calmer as you await the main event.

Reina 29. ✆ 91-532-7154. Main courses 11€–21€. AE, DC, MC, V. Daily 1–4pm and 8:30pm–midnight. Metro: Gran Vía or Banco de España.

Suite INTERNATIONAL   Beginning life a couple of years ago as the "Mad Cafe Club," this hip restaurant/bar remains a popular haunt for the young and fashionable. There's a garden where patrons relax on hot summer nights and a disco that cranks up at midnight. About half of the starters are salads, which are a good choice, since main courses are comprised almost entirely of meat. The least expensive of the main dishes is duck breast with caramelized pears; the priciest is lobster in oyster sauce. Preparations are attractive, if decidedly minimalist, as is the case with the three small sea bass filets touched with trout-roe-flavored butter sauce and served with a few chunks of boiled potato scattered around one edge of the plate.

Virgin de los Peligros 4 (between Alcalá and Gran Vía). ✆ 91-532-6228. Reservations recommended. Main courses 11€–17€; menú del día 9.50€ (lunch only). AE, DC, MC, V. Mon–Wed 1–4pm and 9:30pm–3am; Thurs–Sat 1–4pm and 9:30pm–4am. Dinner served until 12:30am. Metro: Sevilla, Gran Vía.

NEAR THE PUERTA DEL SOL
Expensive

Lhardy SPANISH/INTERNATIONAL   A Madrileño legend since it opened in 1839, this restaurant's street level room contains what might be the most elegant snack bar in town. Cups of steaming consommé are self-dispensed from silver samovars into delicate porcelain cups, accompaniments to tasty tapas that run along the lines of creamy-centered croquettes. Early evening is the fashionable time for a stop here. Although it is a gathering place for some of the city's older literati and politicians, food in the formal restaurant upstairs is pricey and rarely better than mediocre; downstairs is the place to go, and is far less expensive.

Carrera de San Jerónimo 8 (east of Puerta del Sol). ✆ 91-521-3385. Reservations recommended in the upstairs dining room. Main courses 24€–48€. AE, DC, MC, V. Daily 1–3:30pm and 8:30–11:30pm. Closed Aug. Metro: Puerta del Sol or Sevilla.

Inexpensive

Cornucopia ✮✮ ECLECTIC   Here's a place that will alter your perception of Madrid: Walk down a passage, turn left at the tiny sign, and enter the foyer of a 19th-century house. The hostess, an American actress appearing on a Spanish soap opera, co-owns the restaurant with a Frenchman and a Spaniard. The two rooms, decorated in ocher and brick, with intricately patterned wood floors and amusing semi-abstract paintings, perfectly suit the international artistic (or at least bohemian) 30-ish crowd. The surroundings are enough for an entertaining

Tapa to Tapa to Tapa

No need to go hungry waiting around for the traditional Madrid dinner hour—10pm or later. Throughout the city you'll find bars—variously known as *mesónes, tascas,* and *tabernas*—that set out platters of tempting hot and cold appetizers known as *tapas:* mushrooms, salads, baby eels, shrimp, lobster, mussels, sausages, ham, and, in one establishment at least, bull testicles. Described below are some favorite tapas bars out of hundreds. *Tip:* You can often save money by eating at the bar rather than occupying a table.

La Trucha, Núñez de Arce 6 (© **91-532-0882**; Metro: Sol), serves trout as its signature dish. One version is *trucha a La Trucha*—the whole fish is split open, filled with chopped ham and garlic, then sautéed. Most tapas and larger dishes are cooked to order. This is a favorite stop on the tapas circuit, partly because the men behind the counter make new patrons feel like old friends. There's a larger but similar La Trucha at Manuel Fernández y González 3 (© **91-429-5833**; Metro: Sol).

Casa Mingo, Paseo de la Florida 2 (© **91-547-7918**; Metro: Norte), has been known for decades for its cider, both still and bubbly. The perfect accompanying tidbit is a piece of Asturian *cabrales* (goat cheese), but the roast chicken is the specialty of the house. Patrons share big tables under the vaulted ceiling of the dining room; in summer, the staff sets tables out on the sidewalk. Hemingway and the bullfighter Luís Miguel Dominguín used to frequent the casual **Cervecería Alemania,** Plaza de Santa Ana 6 (© **91-429-7033**; Metro: Alonso Martín or Tirso de Molina), which earned its name because of its long-ago German clients. Opening onto one of the liveliest plazas in Madrid, it clings to its early-1900s traditions. To accompany your *caña* (a short beer), try the fried sardines or a wedge of *tortilla,* a firm potato-and-egg omelet served at room temperature.

Unique in Madrid, the **Cervecería Santa Bárbara,** Plaza de Santa Bárbara 8 (© **91-319-04-49**; Metro: Alonzo Martínez; bus: 3, 7, or 21), is an outlet for a beer factory, and the management has spent a lot to make it modern and inviting. Globe lights and spinning ceiling fans hang above the black-and-white marble floor. You come here for beer, of course: *cerveza negra* (black beer) or *cerveza dorada* (golden beer). Brews are best accompanied by the very pricey shrimp, the lobster, or the ugly but tasty goose barnacles called *percebes.* It's open daily from 11:30am to midnight. Many Madrileños begin their nightly *tapeo* at **Toscana,** Manuel Fernandez y Gonzales 10 (© **91-429-6031**; Metro: Puerta del Sol or Sevilla). They sit on crude stools, under sausages, peppers, and sheaves of golden wheat hung from the dark beams, as a man behind the bar ladles out bowls of the nightly specials—kidneys in sherry sauce, perhaps, or veal stew.

evening, but happily, the food's pretty good, too. It starts with excellent crusty bread, followed perhaps by a thick disk of goat cheese on tomatoes and grilled vegetables, or skate wings with spinach tossed with raisins and toasted pine nuts.

Flora 1 (west of Plaza Descalzas). ℭ **91-547-6465.** Reservations advised for dinner. Main courses 11€–18€; *menú del día* 12€ lunch, 13€ dinner. AE, DC, MC, V. Tues–Sat 1:30–4pm and 9pm–midnight. Metro: Sol.

La Finca de Susana ⭐ *Value* MEDITERRANEAN   A concern for light, healthy eating is far from a priority in most Spanish restaurants. But maybe they'll think again after they see the business this newcomer is doing. It's housed in a space that looks like a former bank, with potted palms and a long wall of windows. You'll find a choice of five vegetable dishes and a similar number of low-calorie options. The manager even declares that the specialty of the house is grilled vegetables. That doesn't mean that all diners go the green and leafy route. There's plenty of fish, chicken, and pork on the menu, but prepared with less oil, fat, and salt than at most other restaurants. All classes of age, profession, and society show up, partly because they'd have to go out of their way to spend more than 12€ per person, with wine. Reservations aren't accepted.

Arlaban 4 (at Sevilla). ℭ **91-369-3557.** Main courses 2.60€–9€. MC, V. Daily 1–3:45pm and 8:30–11:45pm. Metro: Sevilla.

NEAR PLAZA SANTA ANA
Inexpensive

Casa Alberto CASTILIAN   One of the oldest *tascas* in the neighborhood, Casa Alberto is on the street level of the house where Miguel de Cervantes lived briefly in 1614. The restaurant contains an appealing mixture of bullfighting memorabilia, engravings, and reproductions of old master paintings. Tapas are continually replenished from platters on the bar top, but there's also a sit-down dining area in the back for more substantial meals. Specialties include fried squid, shellfish in green sauce, *chorizo* (sausage) in cider sauce, and several versions of baked or roasted lamb.

Huertas 18 (at Principe). ℭ **91-429-9356.** Reservations recommended. Main courses 12€–22€; fixed-price lunch 12€. AE, DC, MC, V. Tues–Sat 1–4pm; Tues–Sun 8:30pm–midnight. Metro: Antón Martín.

Champagnería Gala ⭐ *Value* SPANISH   The main room here is a glassed-over courtyard with real and artificial plants and a Venetian chandelier. It's filled with a frisky, well-heeled crowd that makes the low prices all the more remarkable. *Arroces* (rice dishes) are featured. Italian risottos have joined the paellas and *fideuàs* (a dish similar to paella, with thin noodles instead of rice) and come with a choice of ingredients, from cheese and oxtail to rabbit and fish. Included in the *menú* are do-it-yourself *pa amb tomaquet* (Catalan bread rubbed with garlic and tomato pulp and drizzled with oil), a seasonal salad, wine, aioli and *romesco* sauces, dessert, and coffee. Avoid the crowded Sunday afternoons or reserve the day before. Owner Esperanza Fernandez Aranda is the hostess, previously identifiable by her flaming-orange or Windex-blue hair. These days, who knows?

Moratín 22 (west of Paseo del Prado). ℭ **91-429-2562.** Paellas and risottos 13€–18€. *Menú del día* 13€. No credit cards. Daily 1:30–4:30pm and 9pm–2am. Metro: Atocha.

La Creazione ITALIAN   On one of Madrid's favorite restaurant streets, this trattoria satisfies several dining needs. The main room is a brick-lined pizzeria where diners gather over tablecloth- or glass-topped tables to assault pasta platters (gnocchi with sage-and-butter drizzle or five other sauces) and impressive pizzas. Both pastas and pizzas are made on the premises and prepared to order. Below the open kitchen is a more formal cellar, where dishes run to saltimbocca and sea bass with porcini, and prices become significantly higher. Appealing Italianate touches include espresso that comes with a plate of sweets and the offer of a *digestif* of *limoncello* or grappa. Most food is available *para llevar*—for takeout.

Ventura de la Vega 9 (near Carrera de San Jerónimo). ℂ **91-429-0387.** Main courses 10€–19€; pizzas and pastas 8€–9€; *menú turístico* 15€. AE, DC, MC, V. Tues–Sat 1:30–4:30pm and 9pm–12:30am; Sun 1:30–4:30pm. Metro: Sol.

NEAR THE ROYAL PALACE
Expensive/Moderate
Café de Oriente FRENCH/SPANISH   Bordering on one of Madrid's most historic and royal squares, the Oriente offers bistro informality in the main-floor cafe (inexpensive); grand dining (very expensive) in the 17th-century cellar called the Horno de Leña; and an adjoining tapas bar, La Botillería. Expect members of high-powered corporate groups downstairs, while the cafe is filled with a workaday crowd during the day and fashionable night owls in the evening. All patrons appreciate the generous array of tapas.

Plaza de Oriente 2. ℂ **91-541-3974.** Reservations recommended (restaurant only). In cafe and bar, tapas 5.20€–10€. In restaurant, main courses 15€–21€. AE, DC, MC, V. Cafe daily 8:30am–1:30am. Restaurant daily 1–4pm and 9pm–midnight. Metro: Opera.

Inexpensive
La Bola REGIONAL SPANISH   Easily spotted by its crimson exterior, La Bola has been on the scene since 1870. Hemingway and Ava Gardner were patrons, as attested to by photos above the carved wainscoting. Ask about the restaurant's history and you'll get a leaflet. The big menu item is *cocido madrileño,* the traditional Castilian Sunday boiled dinner: Several kinds of meat and vegetables are slow-cooked together for hours and the rich broth is then strained off and tiny noodles are dropped in as a first course. This course is followed by the vegetables (potatoes, chickpeas, cabbage) and the meats (usually chicken, *chorizo,* beef, and pork). Fish dishes are well suited to smaller appetites.

Bola 5 (2 blocks north of the Teatro Real). ℂ **91-547-6930.** Main courses 11€–20€; *menú del día* 16€. No credit cards. Mon–Sat 1:30–4pm and 9pm–12:30am; Sun 1:30–4pm. Metro: Santo Domingo.

NEAR RETIRO & SALAMANCA
Expensive
Alkalde BASQUE/INTERNATIONAL   Alkalde affects a humble, countrified mien, with a barn-like *típico* tavern upstairs and a maze of stone-sided cellars downstairs that are pleasantly cool in summer. You might begin with the cream-of-crabmeat soup, followed by *gambas a la plancha* (grilled shrimp), chicken cutlets, or *cigalas* (crayfish). Other recommended dishes are *mero en salsa verde* (sea bass in a green sauce), trout, stuffed peppers, and chicken steak. The only exception to the price range listed below are *angulas*—baby eels boiled in oil—for 65€!

Jorge Juan 10 (near Claudio Coello). ℂ **91-576-3359.** Reservations advised. Main courses 13€–29€; *menú del día* 36€. AE, DC, MC, V. Daily noon–midnight. Metro: Serrano. Bus: 8, 21, 29, or 53.

El Amparo ✶✶ BASQUE   This superior gastronomic enclave hides with four other restaurants behind a curtain of vines at the end of a mews. The multi-tiered space is defined by rough-hewn beams, and is illuminated by sunlight through the long skylight. The innovative offerings have included cod cheeks in a red pepper puree, and ravioli with crayfish. A battalion of correct, unobtrusive waiters bring two different *aperitivos* to stoke the appetite, then serve such main courses as cold marinated salmon with tomato sorbet, *lubina* (sea bass), bisque of shellfish with Armagnac, pigs' feet stuffed with morels, and platters of steamed fish of the day.

Callejón de Puígcerdá 8 (at the corner of Jorge Juan). ℂ **91-431-6456.** Reservations required. Main courses 23€–29€. AE, MC, V. Mon–Fri 1:30–3:30pm and 9–11:30pm; Sat 9:30–11:30pm. Closed the week before Easter and 1 week in Aug. Metro: Goya. Bus: 21 or 53.

Horcher 🍷🍷 GERMAN/INTERNATIONAL   Berlin was the first home of this legendary luxury restaurant, which opened in 1904. Prompted by a tip from a high-ranking officer that Germany was losing World War II, Herr Horcher moved his restaurant to neutral Madrid in 1943. Ever since, the restaurant has continued its grand European traditions, including service by knowledgeable careerist waiters and uniformed doormen. Among the tempting possibilities are shrimp tartare and a distinctive warm hake salad. The venison stew in green pepper with orange peel, and the crayfish with parsley and cucumber, are examples of the elegant fare, served with impeccable style. The kitchen does well with wild boar, veal, and sea bass, as well.

Alfonso XII 6 (near Valenzuela). © 91-532-3596. Reservations required. Jackets and ties required for men. Main courses 23€–30€. AE, DC, MC, V. Mon–Fri 1:30–4pm and 8:30pm–midnight; Sat 8:30pm–midnight. Metro: Retiro.

Viridiana 🍷 INTERNATIONAL   Long praised as one of Madrid's most notable restaurants, Viridiana is named after the 1961 Luís Buñuel film classic. As soon as patrons are settled, the captain launches into a lengthy recitation of the day's specials, from salads to desserts. Among these are contemporary takes on traditional recipes, often with Asian touches. Past examples have included tuna tartare, salads of exotic greens with smoked fish, steak filet with truffles, guinea fowl stuffed with herbs and wild mushrooms, baby squid with curry on a bed of lentils, and roast lamb in puff pastry with fresh basil. While rarely as brilliant as it was perceived to be 2 decades ago, the food here is never predictable—you'll find an exciting twist or two in every dish.

Juan de Mena 14 (west of Alfonso XII). © 91-523-4478. Reservations recommended. Main courses 25€–40€. AE, MC, V. Mon–Sat 1:30–4pm and 9pm–midnight. Closed Aug and 1 week at Easter. Metro: Retiro Banco de España.

Moderate

El Espejo 🍷 INTERNATIONAL   You'll find good-tasting food and one of the most perfectly crafted Art Nouveau interiors in Madrid at this restaurant. There's an attractive cafe/bar, a neo-Victorian glass pavilion out on the promenade, and outdoor tables and chairs nearby. A piano player often performs on warm nights. Menu items include grouper ragout with clams, steak tartare, guinea fowl with Armagnac, and duck with pineapple.

Paseo de Recoletos 31 (near Zurbarán). © 91-308-2347. Reservations required. *Menú del día* 12€ (lunch Mon–Fri at the pavilion), 22€ (dinner in the cafe). AE, DC, MC, V. Sun–Fri 1–4pm and 9pm–midnight; Sat 9pm–1am. Metro: Banco de España or Colón. Bus: 27.

La Gamella 🍷 FUSION   Illinois-born chef-owner Dick Stephens has been in Spain for over 30 years, and he has taken it upon himself to introduce Madrileños to the creative American cuisine that has developed over that period. At his latest venue, near the Puerta de Alcalá, the interior blooms with vibrant colors, as if Matisse had a hand in the decor. Grilled vegetables are a welcome starter. You can follow them with such delectables as *merluza* (hake) grilled or sautéed with balsamic vinegar, duck breast with sweet-and-sour sauce, or tangy Thai chicken. Homesick Yanks may prefer what has been called "the only edible hamburger in Madrid," for 11€. The lunch-only *menú* is a great way to experience this upscale cuisine and setting.

Alfonso XII 4 (at Valenzuela). © 91-532-4509. Reservations advised. Main courses 11€–24€; *menú especial mediodía* 18€. AE, DC, MC, V. Mon–Fri 1:30–4pm and 9pm–midnight; Sat 9pm–midnight. Closed 2 weeks around Easter and 2 weeks in Aug. Metro: Retiro. Bus: 19.

CHAMBERI
Very Expensive

Jockey ☆☆ INTERNATIONAL   On the scene for over 55 years, this was Madrid's premier restaurant during the Franco era. Still strong, it has slipped down the list of gastronomic meccas as more venturesome competitors have opened and flourished. At any rate, it's still a favorite of international celebrities and executives. The chef prides himself on coming up with new and creative dishes featuring ingredients that justify the steep prices, such as lobster ragout with fresh pasta showered with grated truffle. The cold melon soup with shrimp is soothing on a hot day, especially when followed by roasted pigeon from Talavera cooked in its own juice or monkfish en papillote with Mantua sauce. Dress up for your meal.

Amador de los Ríos 6. ℂ **91-319-2435.** Reservations required. Main courses 29€–36€. AE, DC, MC, V. Daily 1–3pm and 9pm–midnight. Closed Aug. Metro: Colón or Serrano.

NEAR PLAZA MAYOR
Moderate

Botín ☆ SPANISH   A visit to Botín is almost as obligatory as one to the Prado. Hemingway helped make this place famous when he had Jake Barnes invite Lady Brett here for dinner. They had the house specialty, roast suckling pig, washed down with Rioja. The restaurant's four floors and cellar have had since 1725 to accumulate the artifacts that fill their walls. You'll see an open kitchen with a charcoal hearth, hanging copper pots, an 18th-century tile oven for roasting suckling pig, and a big pot of regional soup whose aroma drifts across the room. Roast lamb is also good. Yes, it's packed with tourists, but don't let that stop you.

Cuchilleros 17 (off southwest corner of Plaza Mayor). ℂ **91-366-4217.** Reservations required. Main courses 6.90€–24€; *menú del día* 28€. AE, DC, MC, V. Daily 1–4pm and 8pm–midnight. Closed Christmas. Metro: Puerta del Sol or Tirso de Molina.

Julián de Tolosa ☆ STEAK   This is a Basque version of a steakhouse. The menu is simplicity itself and hasn't changed in over 20 years. Appetizers are fish soup, and hearts of lettuce or unadorned spears of fat white asparagus, mayo on the side. A nice lady comes to announce the night's possibilities, shifting easily into English if you look perplexed. There are two meats, two fish. Have the steak. You'll get a piece the size of a baby's fist. Just as you're feeling virtuous for not overindulging, the rest of the slab of meat that encircled the tender kernel of filet is delivered. With coffee, you get an icy cranberry-and-anise liqueur.

Cava Baja 18 (south of Plaza de Puerta Cerrada). ℂ **91-365-8210.** Reservations advised on weekends. Main courses 16€–24€. AE, DC, MC, V. Mon–Sat 1–4pm and 9pm–midnight; Sun 1–5pm. Metro: Sol.

CHAMARTIN
Very Expensive

Zalacaín ☆☆ INTERNATIONAL   Outstanding in food, decor, and service, Zalacaín occupies the apex of Madrid's gastronomical pyramid, although younger challengers are crowding it. When it opened in 1973, it introduced nouvelle cuisine to Madrid. The menu features dishes of French and Basque origin subjected to a great deal of experimentation. The chefs might offer a superb sole in a green sauce, but they also know the glory of grilled pigs' feet. Among other recommendable dishes are roast duck with peppers and cherries, crepes stuffed with smoked fish, and bouillabaisse. One quibble is the restaurant's inclination to stick with one set of menu items for too long, not justifiable at these prices. Men are expected to wear jackets and ties.

Alvarez de Baena 4 (north of María de Molina). ✆ **91-561-4840.** Reservations required. Main courses 29€–58€; *menu degustación* 82€. AE, DC, MC, V. Mon–Fri 1:30–4pm; Mon–Sat 9pm–midnight. Closed Holy Week and Aug. Metro: Rubén Darío.

Expensive

El Olivo ✿ MEDITERRANEAN   French-born chef-owner Jean Pierre Vandelle makes no bones about his enthusiasm for olive oil, exemplified by the live olive tree at the entrance. No matter what you order in the dining room, a cart of olive oils and vinegars will be wheeled over with an invitation to shake a few drops on whatever dish sits before you. Menus often include a medallion of marinated and grilled *rape* (monkfish) over a tangy compote of fresh tomatoes, quail in their reduced juices with a cube of foie gras on the side, or four preparations of cod—an always featured ingredient—arranged on a single platter and served with a spicy *pil-pil* sauce. With a selection of over 100 sherries at the bar (another of the chef's enthusiasms), you might try a dry *oloroso* as an aperitif.

General Gallegos 1 (near Padre Damián). ✆ **91-359-1535.** Reservations recommended. Main courses 18€–26€; *menú del día* 42€. AE, DC, MC, V. Tues–Sat 1–4pm and 9pm–midnight. Closed Aug 15–31 and 4 days around Easter. Metro: Plaza de Castilla.

SEEING THE SIGHTS

As the capital of Spain since the 16th century, Madrid is the repository of the lion's share of the national patrimony, gathered by monarchs and conquistadors and placed on display in over 50 museums. Between museums and palaces are the former private hunting grounds of kings, now transformed into vast public parks. Madrid has something to amuse and enlighten everyone.

SIGHTSEEING SUGGESTIONS FOR FIRST-TIME VISITORS

If You Have 1 Day Spend the morning at the **Prado,** one of the world's great art museums. It's best to arrive when it opens at 9am (remember, it's closed Mon). Have lunch and then visit the **Palacio Real (Royal Palace),** on the other side of the city. Have an early dinner near Plaza Mayor.

If You Have 2 Days On day 2 visit the **Thyssen-Bornemisza Museum** in the morning, stroll around Madrid's medieval area, and visit the **Museo Nacional Centro de Arte Reina Sofía** in the late afternoon or early evening (it closes at 9pm most nights). Here you can see Picasso's *Guernica* and other great art of the 20th century. Have dinner once again at one of the many restaurants off Plaza Mayor.

If You Have 3 Days On your third day take a trip to **Toledo,** where you can visit the cathedral, the Santa Cruz Museum, and the Alcázar. Return to Madrid in the evening.

If You Have 4 Days On day 4 take a 1-hour train ride to the **Monastery of San Lorenzo de El Escorial,** in the foothills of the Sierra de Guadarrama. Return to Madrid in the evening.

THE TOP SIGHTS

Museo del Prado ✿✿✿   With more than 20,000 paintings and other artworks, the Prado is one of the most important repositories of art in the world. The Prado has no equal when it comes to paintings from the Spanish school, so on your first visit, concentrate on the Spanish masters. You'll find a treasure trove of works by El Greco, the Crete-born artist who lived much of his life in Toledo. Look for *Las Meninas,* the museum's most famous painting, and other works by the incomparable Diego Velázquez. The Francisco de Goya collection includes the artist's unflattering portraits of his patron, Charles IV, and his family, as well as the *Clothed Maja* and the *Naked Maja* and pictures from his black period. Look also for paintings by Zurbarán and Murillo, and be sure to search out Flemish genius Hieronymus Bosch's best-known work, *The Garden of Earthly Delights*. After decades of searching for additional gallery space, a new annex is to open behind the main building in 2004.

Paseo del Prado s/n. (C) **91-330-2900**. http://museoprado.mcu.es. Admission to permanent collection 4.80€ adults, 3€ seniors/students, free for children under 12; to temporary exhibits 3€ adults, 1.50€ students, free for seniors and children under 12. Free to all on Sun. Tues–Sat 9am–7:30pm; Sun 9am–2pm. Metro: Atocha or Banco de España. Bus: 9, 10, 14, 19, 27, 34, 37, or 45.

Museo Thyssen-Bornemisza 🟊🟊🟊   The Thyssen-Bornemisza family's unrivaled private collection was amassed over a period of about 60 years. Baron von Thyssen is married to a Spaniard who desperately wanted to see the collection permanently reside in her native country. After extensive negotiation, Spain acquired the works for $350 million. The 18th-century Villahermosa Palace, adjacent to the Prado, was retrofitted to house the collection. You can trace the chronology of European and American painting from the 13th century through the 20th century by following the order of the rooms from the top down. The nucleus of the collection consists of 700 world-class paintings, including works by El Greco, Velázquez, Dürer, and Rembrandt, as well as art from the Impressionist period. Works from the American Abstract Expressionist movement and related movements are also featured

Paseo del Prado 8. (C) **91-369-0151**. www.museothyssen.org. Admission 4.80€ adults, 3€ seniors and students, free for children 12 and under; temporary exhibits extra. Tues–Sun 10am–7pm. Metro: Banco de España. Bus: 1, 2, 5, 9, 10, 14, 15, 20, 27, 34, 45, 51, 52, 53, 74, 146, or 150.

Museo Nacional Centro de Arte Reina Sofía 🟊   This 19th-century hospital was converted into a museum that serves as a repository of 20th-century art. Unfortunately, the collection remains sparse and unbalanced. To date, its successes have usually been temporary exhibits rather than highlights from its permanent collection. One triumph, however, was the wresting of Picasso's fabled *Guernica* 🟊🟊🟊 from the Prado, which had held it since its return from New York's Museum of Modern Art after Franco's death. The mural is now the museum's centerpiece. Largely second-rank works by Spanish artists like **Dalí, Miró, Gris,** and **Solana** supplement Picasso's masterwork. For the moment, the center's most interesting element (outside of *Guernica*) might be the former 18th-century hospital itself.

Santa Isabel 52 (at the corner of Atocha). (C) **91-467-5062**. http://museoreinasofia.mcu.es. Admission 3€ adults, 1.50€ students/children under 12. Free for everyone Sat after 2:30pm and Sun. Mon, Wed–Sat 10am–9pm; Sun 10am–2:30pm. Metro: Atocha. Bus: 6, 10, 14, 18, 19, 26, 27, 32, 34, 36, 37, 41, 45, 46, 55, 57, 59, 68, 86, or 119.

Palacio Real (Royal Palace) 🟊🟊   This opulent palace was begun in 1738 for Felipe V on the site of the Alcázar, which burned in 1734. The decor is a mix of baroque and neoclassical styles. Some of the palace's 2,800 rooms are open to the public, while others are still used for state business. The multilingual guided tour includes the reception room, the state apartments, the royal pharmacy, and the stunning state dining room. The rooms are filled with art treasures and antiques—salon after salon of monumental grandeur, with no apologies for the damask, mosaics, stucco, Tiepolo ceilings, gilt and bronze, chandeliers, and paintings. In the Armory, a collection of weaponry includes scaled-down suits of armor for the royal progeny.

Plaza de Oriente, Calle de Bailén 2. (② 91-547-5350. Admission 6.90€ adults, 3€ seniors/students/children 11 and under; additional fees for temporary exhibits. Mon–Sat 9am–6pm; Sun and holidays 9am–3pm; slightly shorter hours in winter. Metro: Opera. Bus: 3, 25, 39, or 148.

MORE ATTRACTIONS

Monasterio de las Descalzas Reales   In the heart of old Madrid, near the Puerta del Sol, this richly endowed royal convent was founded in the mid–16th century in the palace where Juana of Austria, Felipe II's sister, was born. She used it as a retreat and brought the Poor Clare nuns here. For many years, the convent sheltered only royal women. Typically, the daughters of aristocrats were sequestered here until they were old enough for arranged marriages. The girls didn't live a spartan existence, though, judging from the wealth of religious artwork that surrounded them, including tapestries, sculptures, and paintings by **Rubens, Brueghel the Elder,** and **Titian.** The main staircase features trompe-l'oeil paintings and frescoes, and you can view 16 of the 32 lavishly decorated chapels. Compulsory tours for groups of 25 or fewer are conducted in Spanish by guides who hasten visitors from canvas to tapestry to chapel. Try to slow their pace, for there's much to savor. There are frequent alterations to the visiting hours noted below.

Plaza de las Descalzas Reales. (② **91-454-8700.** Admission 4.80€ adults, 2.40€ seniors and children 11 and under. Mon–Sat 9:30am–5pm; Sun 9am–2pm. Bus: 1, 2, 5, 20, 46, 52, 53, 74, M1, M2, M3, or M5. From Plaza del Callao, off Gran Vía, walk down Postigo de San Martín to Plaza de las Descalzas Reales; the convent is on the left.

Museo Arqueológico Nacional 🏛🏛   Reopened after a couple of years of renovations, this underrated museum is in the same vast building as the National Library (which has a separate entrance on Paseo de Recoletos). It houses antiquities from prehistory to the Middle Ages. Most of the artifacts are related specifically to the development of the Iberian Peninsula, although there are some Egyptian and Greek objects. Most illuminating are the rooms devoted to the Iberian period, before Christ and the waves of sequential conquerors, and those rooms containing relics of the Visigoths, who left relatively little behind, rendering these objects of even greater interest. A particular treasure is the *Dama de Elche* 🏛🏛, a resplendent example of 4th-century B.C. Iberian sculpture, easily equal to the better-known works produced in Greece at the same time.

Serrano 13 (facing Calle Serrano). (② **91-577-7912.** Admission 2.50€ adults, free for seniors/students/children 11 and under. Free for everyone Sat after 2:30pm, and Sun. Tues–Sat 9:30am–8:30pm; Sun and holidays 9:30am–2:30pm. Metro: Serrano.

Museo Lázaro Galdiano   Madrid was the beneficiary of financier/author José Lázaro Galdiano's largesse, for when he died, he left the city his 30-room early-1900s mansion and a substantial private art collection. Every floor attests to Galdiano's devotion to art. There are paintings from Spain's Golden Age, including works by Spaniards El Greco, Zurbarán, Murillo, and Goya; works by Renaissance Italians Tiepolo and Leonardo da Vinci; and canvases by Englishmen Gainsborough and Constable. However, the museum is most admired for its comprehensive array of enamels, ivories, and works in gold and silver, much of it created during the Middle Ages.

Serrano 122. (② 91-561-6084. Admission 2€ adults, 1.50€ students, free for seniors/children under 12. Free for everyone Wed. Tues–Sun 10am–2pm. Closed holidays and Aug. Metro: Núñez de Balboa. Bus: 9, 16, 19, 51, or 89.

Real Academia de Bellas Artes de San Fernando (San Fernando Royal Fine Arts Academy) 🏛   An easy stroll from the Puerta del Sol, this museum is located in the restored and remodeled 17th-century baroque palace of Juan de Goyeneche. The collection—more than 1,500 paintings and 570 sculptures, ranging from the 16th century to the present—was started in 1752 during the reign of Fernando VI (1746–59). It emphasizes works by Spanish, Flemish, and Italian artists. Masterpieces by El Greco, Rubens, Velázquez, Zurbarán, Ribera, Cano, Coello, Murillo, and Sorolla are here. The Goya collection in itself is worth a visit. Goya was a member of the academy from 1780, and the museum houses two of his self-portraits, along with a full-size portrait of the actress La Tirana, and a portrait of the royal favorite Manuel Godoy. Goya's carnival scene, *Burial of the Sardine,* and eight more of his oils are also on view.

Alcalá 13. ⓒ 91-522-0046. Admission 2€ adults. Free Sat, Sun. Thurs–Fri 9am–7pm; Sat–Mon and holidays 9am–2pm. Metro: Sol or Sevilla. Bus: 3, 5, 15, 20, 51, 52, or M12.

PARKS & GARDENS

Casa de Campo (Metro: Lago or Batán), the former royal hunting grounds, is composed of miles of parkland west of the Royal Palace across the Manzanares River. You can see the gate through which the kings rode out of the palace grounds—either on horseback or in carriages—on their way to the park. Casa de Campo has a zoo, many trees, and a lake that's usually filled with rowers. You can have refreshments around the lake or go swimming in a municipally operated pool. The park can be visited daily from 8am to 9pm.

Parque del Retiro ⓐⓐ (Metro: Retiro), originally a playground for the Spanish monarchs and their guests, is now a park of over 120 hectares (260 acres). The huge palaces that once stood here were destroyed in the early 19th century, and only the former dance hall, Casón del Buen Retiro (housing some of the Prado's modern works), remains. The park has many fountains and statues, plus a large lake in front of an extravagant monument to Alfonso XII. Along the promenade beside the lake are rows of tarot card readers, puppeteers, musicians, and other street performers. There are also two exposition centers: the Velázquez and the Crystal palaces. In summer, the rose gardens are worth a visit. The park is open daily 24 hours, but it's safest, as most public parks are, during daylight hours.

Immediately south of the Prado Museum is the **Real Jardín Botánico (Royal Botanical Garden),** Plaza de Murillo 2 (ⓒ **91-420-3017;** Metro: Atocha; bus: 10, 14, 19, 32, or 45). Founded in the 18th century, the garden contains more than 100 species of trees and 3,000 types of plants. The park is open daily from 10am to 9pm; admission is 1.50€ for adults, .75€ for children, free for children 10 years old and under.

ORGANIZED TOURS

The best deals for organized bus tours of Madrid are the two companies whose buses follow set routes and allow you to hop off and reboard any of the subsequent buses at over a dozen museums, plazas, and other major stops. One of them is the distinctive **Madrid Vision Bus** (ⓒ **91-767-1743;** www.trapsa. com/mvision). Ticket in hand, you can get off and reboard as many times in a day as you want. Tickets for adults are 9.60€ for 1 day, 12€ for 2 days, with a 1.20€ supplement on weekends and holidays; you can purchase tickets on board the bus. Seniors and children 7 to 16 receive a 50% discount. The double-decker, open-top buses carry multilingual guides who provide commentary over earphones. Daily departures from the starting point, Gran Vía 32, are at intervals of 8 to 18 minutes, depending on the season. Convenient places to pick up the bus are at Plaza de España, Puerta del Sol, and Plaza de Colón. A similar hop-on, hop-off service is provided by **Sol Open Tours** (© 90-230-3903), using yellow double-decker buses with open tops. Ticket prices are the same as those for the Madrid Vision Bus. Buy tickets at the Puerta del Sol. The circuits start from Plaza de España at 20- to 30-minute intervals. Hours of operation for both companies vary from month to month and season to season.

Pullmantur, Plaza de Oriente 8 (© **91-556-1114;** Metro: Opera), offers full-day tours to Toledo, Avila, and Segovia. **Juliá Tours,** Gran Vía 68 (© **91-559-9605;** Metro: Gran Vía), runs similar trips.

THE SHOPPING SCENE
THE MAIN SHOPPING AREAS

The sheer diversity of Madrid's shops is staggering. One of the greatest concentrations of stores lies immediately north of **Puerta del Sol,** radiating out from Calle del Carmen, Calle Montera, and Calle Preciados.

Conceived, designed, and built in the 1910s and 1920s as a showcase for the city's best shops, hotels, and restaurants, the **Gran Vía** has since been eclipsed by other shopping districts, although fragments of its Art Nouveau and Art Deco glamour still survive. The book and music shops along here are among the best in the city, as are the outlets for fashion, shoes, jewelry, and handcrafts from all regions of Spain.

The **Salamanca** district is the quintessential upper-bourgeois neighborhood. Here, you'll find exclusive furniture, fur, fashion, and jewelry stores, plus rug and art galleries. The main shopping streets here are Serrano and Velázquez. This district lies northeast of the center of Madrid, a few blocks north of Retiro Park. Its most central Metro stops are Serrano and Veláquez.

SOME NOTEWORTHY SHOPS

Established in 1904 as the "first house of Spanish ceramics," **Antigua Casa Talavera,** Isabel La Católica 2 ((© **91-547-3417;** Metro: Callao), is an excellent source for hand-painted ceramics in the distinctive traditional designs of several regions of Spain. You have to ring the bell to be admitted to the shop. It's closed Saturday afternoon and Sunday. A intriguing little shop, **Mambrino,** Espoz y Mina 9 ((© **91-531-9695,** Metro: Sol), is a draw for gastronomes and serious cooks. Principal among its wares is saffron *(azafrán),* the world's costliest spice, which is critical to the success of paella. It also carries several kinds of powerfully flavored paprika *(pimentón)*—not the kind used as a coloring for deli salads—as well as sausages, cheese, honey, olive oil, and patés.

El Corte Inglés, Preciados 3 (© **91-379-8000;** Metro: Puerta del Sol), is the mother of all Spanish department stores, and this is the flagship store in Madrid.

(Tips Spain's Biggest Flea Market

Foremost among Madrid's flea markets is **El Rastro,** Plaza Cascorro and Ribera de Curtidores (Metro: La Latina; bus: 3 or 17), which occupies a roughly triangular area of streets and plazas that are a few minutes' walk south of Plaza Mayor. This market will delight anyone attracted to sometimes-intriguing kitsch. Goods are sold from open stalls arranged in front of stores selling antiques and paintings. Thieves are rampant here, so secure your purse and wallet, be alert, and proceed with caution. The market is open Saturday and Sunday only, from 9:30am to 1:30pm and (to a lesser extent) from 5 to 8pm.

The store sells Spanish handcrafts along with glamorous fashion articles, such as Pierre Balmain designs, often at lower prices than you'll find in most European capitals. Competition for El Corte Inglés has arrived just up the street in the form of **FNAC,** Preciados 28 (© **91-595-6100;** Metro: Sol), a chain of stores concentrating on photographic and audio equipment, video games, TVs, software, computers, and books. Predictably, El Corte Inglés has opened a mirror-image operation right next door. With a substantial stock of CDs in most musical genres, **Madrid Rock,** Gran Vía 25 (© **91-523-2652;** Metro: Gran Vía), also sells tickets to pop concerts. Near Madrid Rock is **La Casa del Libro,** Gran Vía 29 (© **91-521-2113;** Metro: Gran Vía), a large bookstore with a sizable English-language section.

Since 1846, **Loewe,** Gran Vía 8 (© **91-522-6815;** Metro: Gran Vía), has been Spain's most elegant leather store. Its designers keep abreast of changing tastes and styles, but the inventory retains a timeless chic. The store sells luggage, handbags, and jackets for men and women (in leather or suede). At **Casa de Diego,** Puerta del Sol 12 (© **91-522-6643;** Metro: Puerta del Sol), you'll find a wide inventory of fans, ranging from plain to fancy, from plastic to exotic hardwood, from cost-conscious to lavish.

MADRID AFTER DARK

From May through September, the municipal government sponsors a series of plays, concerts, and films, and the city has the atmosphere of a free arts festival. Pick up a copy of *Guía del Ocio* (available at most newsstands) for listings of these events. This guide also provides information about occasional discounts for commercial events, such as the concerts given in Madrid's parks. The guide is in Spanish, but it's not difficult to make out the times, locations, and prices for various events. Also check the program of the **Fundación Juan March,** Calle Castello 77 (© **91-435-4240;** Metro: Núñez de Balboa), which frequently stages free classical and chamber music concerts.

With some exceptions, flamenco in Madrid is geared primarily to tourists, and nightclubs are expensive. But since Madrid is a city of song and dance, you can often be entertained at very little cost—for the price of a glass of wine or beer, in fact—if you sit at a bar with live entertainment.

Tickets to dramatic and musical events usually range from 5€ to 120€, with discounts of up to 50% granted on certain days (usually Wed and early performances on Sun). In the event that your choice is sold out, you may be able to get tickets (with a reasonable markup) at **Localidades Galicia,** Plaza del Carmen 1 (© **91-531-2732;** Metro: Puerta del Sol). This agency, however, mainly sells tickets to bullfights and sports events. It's open Tuesday through Sunday from 9:30am to 1pm and 4:30 to 7pm. Telephone ticket sales are also provided by the following agencies: **Caja de Cataluña** (© **90-210-1212**), **Servi-Caixa** (© **90-233-2211**), and **Entradas.com** (© **90-222-1622**).

THE PERFORMING ARTS

Ballet Nacional de España (© **91-517-4686;** http://balletnacional.mcu.es) is devoted exclusively to dances created by Spanish choreographers. Its performances are always well attended. Also look for performances by choreographer Nacho Duato's **Compañía Nacional de Danza** (http://cndanza.mcu.es).

World-renowned flamenco sensation António Canales and his troupe, **Ballet Flamenco António Canales** (© **91-531-2732**), offer high-energy, spirited performances. Productions are centered around Canales's impassioned *Torero*—his interpretation of the physical and emotional struggles of a bullfighter.

CLASSICAL MUSIC

Madrid's opera company is the **Teatro de la Opera,** and its symphony orchestra is the outstanding **Orquesta Sinfónica de Madrid** (at Teatro Real, see below).

Reopened in 1997 after a massive $157-million renovation, the **Teatro Real,** Plaza Isabel II (© **90-224-4822;** Metro: Opera), is one of the world's finest stage and acoustic settings for opera. Its extensive state-of-the-art equipment affords elaborate stage designs and special effects. Today, the building is home to the Compañía del Teatro Real and the Teatro de la Opera, and is the major venue for classical music and opera. Tickets are 12€ to 102€.

Auditorio Nacional de Música, Príncipe de Vergara 146 (© **91-337-0100;** Metro: Cruz del Rayo), is the ultramodern home of both the **National Orchestra of Spain,** which pays particular attention to the music of Spanish composers, and the **National Chorus of Spain.** Just north of Madrid's Salamanca district, the concert hall ranks as a major addition to the classical music circuit in Europe. Tickets are 9€ to 60€.

FLAMENCO

One of the best-attended *tablaos* in town, **Café de Chinitas,** Torija 7 (© **91-559-5135;** Metro: Santo Domingo; bus: 1 or 2), features an array of performers whose acts change about once a month. It's open from Monday to Saturday, with dinner served from 9 to 11pm and the show lasting from 10:30pm to 3am. Reservations are recommended. Dinner and the show start at 62€, and the show and one drink cost 27€ after 12:15am.

Following an upswing in interest in flamenco after a period of decline in the 1980s, **Casa Patas,** Cañizares 10 (© **91-369-0496;** Metro: Tirso de Molina), is now one of the best places to see "true" flamenco, as opposed to the more tourist-oriented version. It's a bar/restaurant with a separate space in the rear reserved for performances. Shows are presented Thursday, Friday, and Saturday at midnight and during Madrid's major fiesta month of May. The club itself is open daily from 9pm to 5am. Admission depends on the performers, but is usually about 20€. Reservations are essential, but they're worth the cost and effort because this is modern flamenco at its best.

Although **La Soleá,** Cava Baja 34 (© **91-365-5264;** Metro: Tirso de Molina), has moved down the street to larger, slightly fancier quarters, the club observes the same musical format as before: one or two guitarists and two or three singers who try to outdo one another in performing the hoarse, plaintive *cante hondo* (deep song) far into the night. It's a very intimate experience. There is no cover, and on some nights they switch to jazz or blues. Closing days are unpredictable. Incidentally, kids seem to love this.

LIVE MUSIC

Off Plaza de Santa Ana, **Café Central,** Plaza del Angel 10 (© **91-369-4143;** Metro: Antón Martín), is *the* place for live jazz. Black bench seating, marble-topped tables, and glistening brass set the scene, and the place is usually packed with students, tourists, and Madrid's night beauties. Performances are usually at 10pm and midnight. While jazz is the main course, the cafe also hosts folkies, blues belters, and performers of related music. Calle de las Huertas runs through this plaza, so a visit to the cafe could be the start or the end of an extended pub-crawl. Café Central is open daily from 10am to 2 or 3am, with a cover that's usually about 8€ Monday, and up to 12€ the rest of the week.

Not far from the Central is **Café Jazz Populart,** Huertas 22 (℃ **91-429-8407;** Metro: Antón Martín), a showcase for American blues, Latin salsa, and Caribbean reggae as well as many varieties of jazz. The large space allows for a little elbowroom, and the atmosphere is laid-back. You can relax at the marble-topped bar or the tables ringing the stage. One sour note is the caricature of a blackface minstrel that the club uses as a logo. Admission is often free, but when a cover is charged, it's usually 2.40€ to 6€, invariably cheaper than at the better-known Café Central. It's open daily from 4pm to 2:30 or 3:30am, with shows at 11pm and 12:30am.

With dozens of small tables and a huge bar in its dark and smoky interior, **Clamores,** Albuquerque 14 (℃ **91-445-7938;** Metro: Bilbao), is the largest and one of the most popular jazz clubs in Madrid. It has thrived because of the noted American and Spanish jazz bands that appear here. Clamores is open daily from 6pm to 3am or so, but jazz is presented only from Tuesday to Saturday. From Tuesday to Thursday, performances are at 11pm and 1am; Saturday they're at 11:30pm and 1:30am. There are no live performances Sunday or Monday. Cover from Tuesday to Saturday is 4.80€ to 9.20€, depending on the act.

DANCE CLUBS

Madrid's most popular dance clubs operate with a selective entrance policy, so dress stylishly and try to look as young, gorgeous, celebrated, and/or rich as possible. Admission, usually including a drink, can exceed 12€, and even a Coke can cost over 6€. Clubs are usually open nightly until 5am or later, with nothing much happening before 2am, though it's easier to get past the unsmiling gents at the door if you arrive earlier in the evening. Some have a matinee, usually from 7 to 9 or 10pm, attended primarily by teenagers. After closing for an hour or two to clear out the youngsters, they re-open to older patrons.

Years ago, a palatial 1930s movie house was transformed into the popular disco **Joy Madrid,** Arenal 11 (℃ **91-366-3733;** Metro: Sol or Opera). The owners tore out the orchestra seats to make room for three bars and a dance floor, but kept the box seats and stage. Laser shows, videos, and energetic performers keep things moving. The best nights are Friday and Saturday, and because this place is well into its post-chic phase, it isn't difficult to get past the velvet ropes. There are even 20% discount coupons available around town. It's open Monday through Thursday from 11:30pm to 5am and Friday through Sunday until 6am. Cover is 9€ to 12€ and includes the first drink. "Matinees" (geared to teens) are held Friday and Saturday from 6:30 to 11pm.

Monster discos aren't new to Spain. **Kapital,** Atocha 125 (℃ **91-420-2906;** Metro: Atocha), has seven floors, with the main dance floor at street level, a terrace up top, and more bars and dance floors (with different kinds of music) in between. Laser shows, karaoke, a movie room, and what used to be called "go-go dancers" are added attractions. Throngs of kids show up for the "afternoon" dance session at 6pm, trying with all their might to look older than 14. They are ushered out at 11pm and grownups are allowed in after midnight. The club stays open until 6am; it's open Thursday through Sunday. The cover is from 6€ to 12€.

PUBS & BARS

Hemingway and his journalist buddies suffered the Civil War siege of Madrid at **Chicote,** Gran Vía 12 (℃ **91-532-6737;** Metro: Gran Vía). Photos on the walls to the left and right of the entrance document the patronage of Coop, Ty, Orson, and Ava. A superior martini is still available, and they've added breakfast and light meals. **Cock,** Reina 12 (℃ **91-532-2826;** Metro: Gran Vía), a dark, cavernous room on a narrow street parallel to Gran Vía, is another old-timer, where Madrid's artistic and showbiz elite routinely assault their livers. It was given renewed cachet by the presence of internationally known film director Pedro Almodóvar.

If you want to witness a supremely assured professional mixologist in action, head up the same street a few doors. **Del Diego,** Reina 12 (© **91-523-3106;** Metro: Gran Vía), is a stylish contemporary watering hole that attracts exactly the upmarket crowd it seeks, including government ministers and upper-echelon executives. The maestro twirling the swizzle sticks is the eponymous head man, never losing his composure as he shakes and stirs everything from pure martinis to Long Island iced teas and Madrid's drink of the moment, the *mojito* (rum, lime juice, and mint). He's put in 32 years at Chicote.

Pop in for at least a quick drink to admire the variety of pictorial ceramic tiles covering the walls of the five rooms of **Los Gabrieles,** Echegaray 17 (© **91-429-6261;** Metro: Sol or Sevilla), a century-old tavern. Live music, mostly flamenco, is presented Tuesday nights (no cover). Students and 20-something singles have given the 1890 tavern **Viva Madrid,** Manuel Fernández González 7 (© **91-429-3640;** Metro: Sol or Antón Martín), new life as a trendy meeting place. Both the facade and the interior are resplendent with intricately patterned tiles, and mythical creatures hold up carved ceilings. Light meals and tapas are served in the room behind the bar.

GAY & LESBIAN CLUBS & CAFES
The **Plaza Chueca** area, between Calles Hortaleza and Barquillo, until only a few years ago the center of Madrid's illicit drug market, has been transformed by ever-multiplying numbers of bars and restaurants catering to gay men, with a smaller number for lesbians. There are over two dozen gay- and lesbian-geared spots within a 2-block radius of the once forbidding plaza. Among these are **Café Figueroa,** Augusto Figueroa 17 (© **91-521-1673**), and **Café Aquarella,** Gravina 10 (© **91-522-2143**), where table-hopping is elevated to high art. Open daily from 4pm to midnight, their diverse clienteles include both gay men and lesbians.

DAY TRIPS FROM MADRID
TOLEDO ✿✿✿ Once the capital of Visigothic Spain, Toledo—70km (43 miles) southwest of Madrid—bristles with steeples and towers spread over an unlikely hill that's almost completely moated by the River Tajo. Toledo is undeniably a must-see, one of the most photogenic cities on the peninsula, its streets tilting and twisting past buildings representing over 1,500 years of construction. Here is history . . . deep, palpable, warming the stones. Those familiar with the painting of the city by El Greco, who lived most of his creative life here, will be struck by how closely his 16th-century canvas, *View of Toledo,* conforms to the present view, in overall impression if not in detail.

The streets are clogged all year with tour buses and their occupants and crammed with shops hung with Toledo cutlery, fake armor, Lladró figurines, and every kind of gaudy souvenir. If possible, stay overnight to get a less feverish picture of the city when it's briefly returned to its citizens.

Getting There   **RENFE trains** run frequently between Madrid and Toledo (© **90-224-0202;** www.renfe.es). Those departing Madrid's Atocha Station run daily from 7:05am to 8:40pm; those leaving Toledo for Madrid run daily from 6:30am to 8:55pm (trip time: approximately 1 hr. 15 min).

Bus transit between Madrid and Toledo is somewhat faster and more convenient than travel by train. Buses, operated by several companies, the largest of which include Continental and Galiano, depart from Madrid's **Estacíon Sur de Autobuses (South Bus Station),** Calle Méndez Alvaro (© **91-527-2961** for tickets and information). Buses depart at 30-minute intervals every day from 6:30am to 10pm.

Motorists exit Madrid via Cibeles (Paseo del Prado) and take N-401 south.

Visitor Information The **tourist office** is at Puerta de Bisagra (© **92-522-0843**), open Monday through Saturday from 9am to 7pm, and Sunday from 9am to 3pm.

Exploring Toledo Although ranked among the greatest of Gothic structures, the **Cathedral** ✲✲✲, Arcos de Palacio (© **92-522-2241**), actually reflects a variety of styles because of the more than 2½ centuries that passed during its construction, from 1226 to 1493. Among its art treasures, the *transparente* stands out—a wall of marble and florid baroque alabaster sculpture overlooked for years because of the cathedral's poor lighting. The sculptor Narciso Tomé cut a hole in the ceiling, much to the consternation of Toledans, and now light touches the high-rising angels, a *Last Supper* in alabaster, and a Virgin in ascension. The Treasure Room has a 225-kilogram (500-lb.) 15th-century gilded monstrance (receptacle of the Host)—allegedly made with gold brought back from the New World by Columbus—that's still carried through the streets of Toledo during the feast of Corpus Christi. Admission to the cathedral is free; admission to the Treasure Room is 3€. Both are open Monday through Saturday from 10:30am to 1:30pm and 3:30 to 7pm, and Sunday from 10:30am to 1:30pm and 4 to 7pm; there are shorter hours October through May.

The **Alcázar,** General Moscardó 4, near Plaza de Zocodover (© **92-522-3038**), at the eastern edge of the old city, dominates the Toledo skyline. It was damaged frequently over its centuries as a fortress and royal residence and leveled during a siege of the Spanish Civil War. The existing structure is essentially a replica but is built over the old cellars and foundations. Admission is 1.20€, and hours are daily from 9:30am to 2:30pm.

Queen Isabel had a hand in arranging the construction of the 16th-century building housing the **Museo Santa Cruz,** Cervantes 3 (© **92-522-1036**), with its impressive Plateresque facade. The paintings within are mostly from the 16th century and 17th century, with yet another by El Greco. Find the museum immediately east of Plaza de Zocodover. Admission is 1.20€. Hours are Monday from 10am to 6pm, Tuesday through Saturday from 10am to 6:30pm, and Sunday from 10am to 2pm.

SAN LORENZO DE EL ESCORIAL ✲✲ The second most important excursion from Madrid is a 48km (30-mile) trip to the Royal Monastery in the village of San Lorenzo de El Escorial. Felipe II commissioned Juan Bautista de Toledo and his assistant, Juan de Herrera, to build this gloomy Xanadu in the Sierra de Guadarrama, northwest of Madrid. Its purported intent was to commemorate an important victory over the French in Flanders, but the likely real reason was that the ascetic Felipe was unnerved by the stress of overseeing an empire bridging four continents and this retreat insulated him from the intrigues of the Madrid court. He ruled his troubled empire from the rooms here for the last 14 years of his life, and it was from here that he ordered his doomed "Invincible Armada" to set sail.

Getting There   More than two dozen **trains** depart daily from Madrid's Atocha and Chamartín stations (trip time: 60–80 min.). For schedules and information, contact **RENFE** (© **90-224-0202;** www.renfe.es).

Buses are preferable. They leave from Empresa Herranz, Isaac Peral 10, Moncloa (© **91-543-3645**), and make the trip in 55 minutes, dropping passengers closer to Felipe's royal retreat than the trains do.

Visitor Information   The **tourist office** at Floridablanca 10 in El Escorial can be reached at © **91-890-1554.**

Exploring the Monastery   The huge monastery/palace/mausoleum that is the **Real Monasterio de San Lorenzo de El Escorial** ✶✶✶, San Lorenzo de El Escorial 1 (© **91-890-5902**), is typically praised for its massive, brooding simplicity. That impression is allayed inside, as the wealth of sumptuous detail, the hundreds of rooms, and the 24km (15 miles) of corridors are revealed. An extraordinary library reflects the scholarly king's intellectual interests, with tens of thousands of volumes and rare manuscripts in many languages, representative of the three primary religions that had existed in Spain. Also in the building is a sizable church with a frescoed dome over 90m (300 ft.) high. The main altar is four stories high with gold sculptures and paintings framed in jasper. Beneath the basilica is a royal pantheon with sarcophagi containing the remains of most of Spain's monarchs since Carlos V. Galleries and royal apartments contain canvases by El Greco, Titian, Ribera, Tintoretto, Rubens, and Velázquez, among others. Throughout the building, you'll see copies of a gridlike symbol that echoes the layout of the palace itself. These symbols represent St. Lawrence, who was roasted alive on a grill by the Romans. From April to September, El Escorial is open Tuesday through Sunday and holidays from 10am to 6pm (to 5pm in winter). Admission and guided tours are 6.90€ adults; non-guided visits are 6€adults, 3€ seniors/students, and guided tours are .90€ adults and .60€ for seniors/students.

SEGOVIA ✶✶✶   Less commercial than Toledo, Segovia, 87km (54 miles) northwest of Madrid, typifies the glory of Old Castile. Wherever you look, you'll see reminders of a golden era—whether it's the spectacular Alcázar or the well-preserved Roman aqueduct. Segovia lies on the slope of the Guadarrama Mountains, where the Eresma and Clamores rivers converge. Isabel was proclaimed queen of Castile here in 1474.

Getting There   Fifteen **trains** leave Madrid's Chamartín and Atocha stations every day (trip time: 2 hr.). Segovia's station, **Paseo Obispo Quesada** (© **90-224-0202**), is a 20-minute walk from the town center. Bus no. 3 departs every quarter hour for the Plaza Mayor.

Buses are preferable to trains for price, convenience, and speed. Between Madrid and Segovia, the bus takes 75 to 90 minutes and the train 2 hours. The unmarked bus station in Madrid is on Paseo de Florida, opposite the Estación del Norte and next to the Hotel Florida del Norte. Up to 15 buses depart daily from Madrid. Buses drop passengers at the Estación Municipal de Autobuses at Paseo de Ezequile González 10 in Segovia. From the front of the terminal, turn left, cross the street, and walk down the largely pedestrian and arcaded Avenida Fernández Ladreda. You'll arrive in Plaza del Azoguejo, beneath the city's principal site, the Roman Aqueduct.

Motorists can take NVI northwest from Madrid. After about 98km (61 miles), exit north on Route 603. It's 55km (34 miles) from there to Segovia.

Visitor Information   The **tourist office** is at Plaza Mayor 10 (© **92-146-0334**), open daily from 10am to 2pm and 5 to 7pm.

Exploring Segovia   The town is quite walkable. Its narrow medieval streets suffer less from the ravages of mass tourism (except on weekends and holidays) than other destinations in Madrid's orbit and reveal much about what life must have been like here 500 years ago.

Located here is what might be the most recognizable structure in Spain—an intact **Acueducto Romano** 🟊🟊, Plaza de Azoguejo. A spectacular engineering feat even if it were contemplated today, the double-tiered Roman aqueduct cuts across the city to the snow-fed waters of the nearby mountains. Almost 730m (2,400 ft.) long and nearly 30m (95 ft.) at its highest point at the east end of town, it contains over 160 arches fashioned of stone cut so precisely that no mortar was needed in the construction. Probably completed in the 2nd century A.D. (although some sources date it as many as 3 centuries earlier), it has survived war and partial dismantling by the Moors. Amazingly, it carried water until only a few decades ago.

Constructed between 1515 and 1558, the **Catedral de Segovia** 🟊🟊, Plaza de la Catedral, Marqués del Arco (© **92-146-2205**), was the last Gothic cathedral built in Spain. Fronting the Plaza Mayor, it stands on the spot where Isabel I was proclaimed queen of Castile. It contains numerous treasures, such as a chapel created by the flamboyant Churriguera, elaborately carved choir stalls, and 16th- and 17th-century paintings. More interesting, if only for historical reasons, is the attached 15th-century **cloister** 🟊. After rebels razed the earlier cathedral, its cloister was moved here stone by stone and reassembled. The cloister now contains a small museum. To reach the cathedral, walk west along Calle de Cervantes, which becomes Calle Bravo. Admission to cathedral is free, but the cloister and museum cost 1.50€. June through September, hours are from 10am to 7pm daily (to 6pm for the rest of the year).

Continue west on Calle de Daolz, where the prow of the old town rears above the confluence of the Clamores and Eresma rivers. The **Alcázar,** Daolz s/n (© **92-146-0759**), a fortified castle almost as familiar a symbol of Castilla (Castile) as the aqueduct, occupies this dramatic location. Though it satisfies our "castles in Spain" fantasies, at least from the outside, note that it's essentially a late-19th-century replica of the medieval fortress that stood here before a devastating fire in 1868. Admission is 2.40€ adults and 1.65€ ages 8 to 14. April through September, it's open daily from 10am to 7pm (to 6pm the rest of the year).

2 Barcelona 🟊🟊🟊

Hard-charging Barcelona enjoys the most diversified and prosperous economy of any region in Spain. And culturally, it is as rich as any other area in the country. Its natives and longtime residents—the *modernista* architect Antoni Gaudí; artists Pablo Picasso, Salvador Dalí, and Joan Miró; opera stars Montserrat Caballé and José Carreras—have been instrumental in defining Catalan culture.

The years leading up to and following the successful 1992 Olympics were hugely stimulating for the city. Residual benefits from the games have included construction of impressive new hotels, top-notch sporting facilities, and new ring roads that have helped alleviate some crucial traffic problems; the refurbishment of an airport capable of funneling 18 million annual visitors into Catalunya; and the resurrection of the once dark and forbidding waterfront.

And Barcelona, despite its dearly protected Catalan cultural and linguistic identity, continues its proud role as Spain's literary and publishing headquarters.

With a reputation as the savviest business center in Spain, Barcelona boasts buildings by I. M. Pei, Arata Isozaki, Richard Meier, Norman Foster, Victorio Gregotti, and native son Ricardo Bofill. Miles of grimy industrial waterfronts have been renewed to become clean and sandy beaches. In fact, the entire city has been reoriented toward the Mediterranean. Flower stalls, birdcages, and decorative pavements along the grand pedestrian boulevard La Rambla have been rejuvenated, and a revitalized transportation network carries visitors past monuments that look better than when they were first erected.

Despite the city's burgeoning population and attendant urban social problems, people are flocking to trend-setting Barcelona. Nearly 40% of business and leisure visitors to Spain—over 50 million of them most years—spend part of their time in Catalunya.

ESSENTIALS

GETTING THERE   By Plane   The **Aeropuerto de Barcelona,** 08820 Prat de Llobregat (© **93-298-3838;** www.aena.es/barcelona), lies 12km (7½ miles) southwest of the city. For the time being, transatlantic passengers are obliged to change aircraft in Madrid before continuing on to Barcelona. A train runs at 30-minute intervals between the airport and Estació Sants, continuing to the more central Plaça de Catalunya daily from 6:13am to 11:40pm. The 24-minute trip costs 2.15€. **Aerobúses** run daily every 15 minutes from 6am to midnight. The fare is 3.15€. A taxi from the airport into central Barcelona will cost about 18€, including supplements.

By Train   Trains arriving and departing from the **Estació de Franca,** Avenida Marqués de l'Argentera, cover long distances in Spain as well as international routes. There are express night trains to and from Madrid, Paris, Milan, and Geneva. All the international routes served by the state-owned RENFE rail company use the Estació de Franca. For general information, contact **RENFE** (© **90-224-0202;** www.renfe.es). **Rail Europe** (© **888/382-7245;** www.raileurope.com) sells a variety of rail passes to people who make arrangements before leaving North America.

By Bus   Bus travel to Barcelona is cheaper than train travel and faster than all but the TALGOS (fast trains). The main bus terminal is the **Estació del Nord,** Ali-bei 80 (© **93-265-6508;** Metro: Arc de Triomf), near the Old Town. Some bus companies stop near the Estació Sants, which has a Metro station.

By Car   From France, the major access route is at the eastern end of the Pyrenees, with the choice of the express highway (E-15) or the more scenic coastal road. From France, it's possible to approach Barcelona via Toulouse. Cross the border into Spain at Puigcerdá (frontier stations are there), near the principality of Andorra. From here, take N-152 to Barcelona. From Madrid, take N-2 to Zaragoza, then A-2 to El Vendrell, followed by A-7 to Barcelona.

VISITOR INFORMATION   A conveniently located tourist office is the subterranean **Centre d'Informació,** Plaça de Catalunya, 17-S (© **93-304-3232;** Metro: Catalunya). It's open Monday through Friday from 9am to 8pm, Saturday from 10am to 8pm, and Sunday and holidays from 10am to 2pm.

Websites   A good place to start is **www.okspain.org**, where you can find up-to-date information and book hotels, restaurants, and tours. Additional sources are **www.barcelona-on-line.es**, **www.barcelonaturisme.com**, and

Barcelona

FRANCE

PORTUGAL

Barcelona ●

★ Madrid

SPAIN

↑ TIBIDABO ↑ **5**

Avinguda de Madrid

Carrer del Vallespir

Carrer de Berlin

Carrer de Numància

Carrer de la Infanta Carlota Joaquima

Carrer de Córsega

Carrer de Rosselló

Carrer de Sant Antoni

Carrer de Provença

Carrer de Sants de la Creu Coberta

Avinguda de Roma

Carretera de la Bordeta

Carrer de Tarragona

PARC JOAN MIRÓ

Carrer d'Entença

Carrer de Rocafort

Carrer de Calàbria

Carrer de Vilad...

Plaça de Espanya

Gran Vía de les Corts Catalanes

Carrer de Sant Fructuós

Av. de Marqués de Comillas **④**

Av. de la Reina Maria Cristina

Carrer de Sepúlve

Carrer de Floridablan...

Avinguda de Paral·lel

Carrer de Tamar

Carrer de Man...

Carrer d Parlamen...

Avinguda de l'Estadi

③

②

Avinguda de Miramar

PARC DE MONTJUÏC

PARC D'ATRACCIONS DE MONTJUÏC

①

Passeig de Josep Carn...

0 —— 1/4 mi
0 —— 0.25 km

Plaça de
Francesc Macia

8

9

(i) Information

Carrer de Buenos Aires

Travessara de Gràcia

Carrer de Londres

Gran Gràcia

Travessara de Gràcia

Carrer de Paris

Avinguda Diagonal

Av. de Sant Antoni Maria Claret

7

Carrer de la Industria

Carrer de Còrsega

EIXAMPLE (i)

Carrer de Provença

Carrer de Rosselló

11

Carrer Enric Granados

Carrer de Balmes

Rambla de Catalunya

Passeig de Gràcia

Carrer de Pau Claris

12

Avinguda Diagonal

Carrer de Roger de Flor

Plaça de la
Sagrada
Família **10**

13

Carrer de Mallorca

15

Carrer de València

16

14

Carrer d'Aragó

Carrer del Consell de Cent

Carrer de R. de l'Uria

Carrer del Bruc

Carrer de Girona

Carrer de Bailèn

Passeig de Sant Joan

Carrer de Nàpols

Carrer de Sicilia

Carrer del Comte d'Urgell

Carrer de Villarroel

Carrer de Casanova

Carrer de Muntaner

Carrer d'Aribau

Carrer de la Diputació

Gran Via de les Corts Catalanes

Plaça de la
Universitat

17

Plaça de
Tetuan

Ronda Universitat

19

18 Plaça
Catalunya

Plaça
Urquinaona

Carrer de Sardenya

Ronda de Sant Antoni

Carrer de Pelai

(i)

Av. del Portal de l'Angel

23

Carrer de Casp

Carrer d'Ausias Marc

Ronda de Sant Pere

Carrer d'Ali Bei

20

RAVAL

21

La Rambla

22

24

Via Laietana

Ronda Sant Pau

Ronda de Sant Antoni

Carrer de Hospital

Palau de la
Música Catalana

Carrer de Ribes

Carrer de la Marina

**BARRI
GÒTIC**

Passeig de
Lluis Companys

25 **26** **27**

28

Carrer de Sant Pau

Gran Teatre
del Liceu

C. de

Ferran

C. de la Princesa

Passeig de Pujades

Carrer Nou de la Rambla

29

Carrer del Comerç

LA RIBERA

30

Carrer de Wellington

**PARC DE LA
CIUTADELLA**

Avda. de les Drassanes

La Rambla

Carrer Ample

Passeig de Colom

Pg. Isabel II

34

31

Moll de la Fusta

Passeig de Picasso

Villa
Olímpica →

32

Avinguda d'Icaria

**PARC
ZOOLOGIC**

35 →

Plaça Portal
de la Pau

Moll d'Espanya

Port
Vell

33

BARCELONETA

Passeig Marítim

923

www.bcn-guide.com. See Madrid "Visitor Information," earlier in this chapter, for additional websites.

CITY LAYOUT **Plaça de Catalunya** is the city's heart, and the famous **La Rambla** and the grand boulevard **Paseo de Gracia** are its major arteries. La Rambla begins at Plaça Portal de la Pau, with its 50m (164-ft.) monument to Columbus and a panoramic view of the port, and runs north a little over a mile to Plaça de Catalunya, with its fountains and trees.

At the harbor end of La Rambla is the **Barri Xinés,** the "Chinese Quarter," which in the past was notorious as an area of prostitution and drugs. It is being cleaned up, but is still best viewed during the day. Off La Rambla is **Plaça Reial,** Barcelona's most harmoniously proportioned and increasingly gentrified square.

The major wide boulevards are **Avinguda Diagonal, Passeig de Colom,** and the elegant shopping street **Passeig de Gràcia (Paseo de Gracia).** A short walk from La Rambla will take you to **Passeig del Moll de la Fusta,** a waterfront promenade lined with bars and restaurants. To the east is the 18th-century fishermen's quarter, **La Barceloneta,** known for its seafood restaurants.

Barri Gòtic, the Gothic Quarter, lies east of La Rambla. It contains the city's oldest buildings, including the cathedral. North of Plaça de Catalunya, the **Eixample** unfolds. An area of wide boulevards, in contrast to the Gothic Quarter, it contains two major roads leading out of Barcelona, Avinguda Diagonal and Gran Vía de les Corts Catalánes (abbreviated as Gran Vía C.C.). Another area, **Gràcia,** once an independent village, lies north of the Eixample. **Montjuïc,** a brooding hill at the western end of the harbor, begins at Plaça d'Espanya, a traffic rotary. This was the setting for the 1992 Summer Olympic Games. The other mountain is **Tibidabo,** in the northwest, offering fine views of the city and the Mediterranean and boasting an amusement park.

GETTING AROUND

There are several types of **discount passes,** most of them good on both the Metro (subway) and buses. There is a 3-day pass for 14€ and a 5-day version for 18€. A 10-trip pass, costing 5.60€, can be shared by two or more people. Passes are available at most Metro stations, tourist offices, many newsstands and lottery shops, and the office of **Transports Metropolita de Barcelona (TMB;** ⓒ 93-318-7074 for information).

BY METRO (SUBWAY) Barcelona's Metro consists of five main lines, including two commuter railway lines that are integrated into the system, fanning out to the suburbs. A one-way fare is 1€, and the major station for all subway lines is Plaça de Catalunya.

BY BUS Some 50 bus lines traverse the city. The driver will issue a ticket when you board at the front. Most buses operate daily from 6:30am to 10pm, and some night buses go along the principal arteries from 10pm to 4am. Buses are color-coded—red ones cut through the city center during the day, and blue ones do the job at night. A one-way fare is 1€, the same as the Metro fare.

BY TAXI Taxis are black and yellow. When available, they display a sign reading LIBRE (Spanish) or LLIURE (Catalan) and/or an illuminated green roof light. The initial charge is 1.80€. Each additional kilometer costs .65€ from 6am to 10pm, .80€ from 10pm to 6am. For a taxi, call ⓒ **93-433-1020.**

BY CAR Driving is a headache in congested Barcelona, but a car is ideal for touring the environs. All three of the major U.S.-based car-rental firms are

Barcelona Metro

Mediterranean Sea

Legend:
- ● Metro Terminals
- ○ Metro Stations
- ⧉ Transfer Stations
- ┼┼┼ FGC Railway Lines
- ╌╌╌ FGC Funicular
- ╌╌╌ Funicular
- ▓▓▓ Telefèric
- ═══ Tramvia Blau
- ┼┼┼ RENFE train

represented in Barcelona, both at the airport and at downtown offices. Check with **Budget,** at Barcelona Airport 71 (© **93-298-3500**); **Avis,** at Rita Bonnat 5 (© **90-213-5531**); or **Hertz,** at Aragó 382 (© **93-270-0330**).

BY FUNICULAR & TELEFERIC   Two of Barcelona's high-altitude vantage points, Montjuïc and Tibidabo, accessible by funicular, are popular for panoramic views of the city. The departure point for Tibidabo lies on the northern outskirts of Barcelona's central core, on the Avinguda del Tibidabo. To reach the funicular's departure point, halfway up the hill, take a taxi (by far the easiest and least confusing way); a conventional bus (marked TIBIDABO); or, on weekends, the **Tramvía Blau** (blue streetcar), a trolley car that operates only on Saturday and Sunday, and which charges 2.70€. The core of the Tibidabo experience, however, is the funicular itself, which operates at 20- to 30-minute intervals every day from 7:15am to 9:45pm. A one-way ride costs 1.90€.

Tibidabo's counterpart is the peak of Montjuïc, a hump of hill at the southwest end of the harbor. Site of some of the sporting activities during the 1992 Olympic games, it can be reached by the Montjuïc funicular, whose point of origin is the Paral.lel Metro station. The funicular operates in summer daily from 11am to 8pm, and in winter only on Saturday, Sunday, and holidays from 10:45am to 2pm. It charges a one-way fare of 1.70€.

You can get off the funicular partway up Montjuïc to explore the attractions there (the Joan Miró museum is nearby), and it's fun to continue to the top of the hill on the *teleféric,* an aerial cable car. It arrives near the Castell de Montjuïc, a 17th-century fortress. Operating daily, summer from 11am to 10pm and winter from 10:45am to 8pm, the teleféric charges a one-way fare of 3.20€ and round-trip fare of 4.50€.

 FAST FACTS: Barcelona

American Express   The Amex office at Rosselló 261 (© **93-217-0070**; Metro: Diagonal), near the corner of Passeig de Gràcia, is open Monday through Friday from 9:30am to 6pm and Saturday from 10am to noon.

Consulates   The consulate of the **United States,** at Reina Elisenda 23 (© **93-280-2227**; Metro: Reina Elisenda), is open Monday through Friday from 9am to 12:30pm and 3 to 5pm. The consulate of **Canada,** Passeig de Gràcia 77 (© **93-215-0704**; Metro: Plaça Molina), is open Monday through Friday from 10am to noon. The consulate of the **United Kingdom,** Avinguda Diagonal 477 (© **93-366-6200**; Metro: Hospital Clínic), is open Monday through Friday from 9:30am to 1:30pm and 4 to 5pm. The consulate of **Australia** is at Gran Vía Carles III 98, 9th Floor (© **93-330-9496**; Metro: María Cristina), open Monday through Friday from 10am to noon.

Currency Exchange   Most banks will exchange currency Monday through Friday from 8:30am to 2pm and Saturday from 8:30am to 1pm. *Oficinas de cambio* (exchange offices) are located in the airport and at the central rail station. Avoid the small exchange offices found in tourist areas that claim to charge no commission: They don't have to, because their rates are so much in their favor. ATMs are widely available; most machines provide directions in English. *You'll need a 4-digit PIN,* so call your credit card company if you don't have one.

Dentists Call **Clinica Dental Beonadex,** Paseo Bona Nova 69, 3rd Floor (*(C)* **93-418-4433;** bus: 22), for an appointment. It's open Monday from 3 to 9pm and Tuesday through Friday from 8am to 3pm.

Drugstores After hours, various pharmacies take turns staying open at night. All pharmacies that are not open post the names and addresses of the pharmacies that are open all night in the area.

Emergencies In an emergency, *(C)* **112** is the central number for the municipal **police,** to report a **fire,** or to request an **ambulance.** To call the national **police,** the best choice if you are the victim of a crime, dial *(C)* **091.** To make a direct request for an **ambulance,** call *(C)* **061.**

Hospitals Barcelona has many hospitals and clinics, including **Hospital Clínic,** Casanova 143 (*(C)* **93-227-5400;** Metro: Hospital Clinic), and **Hospital de la Santa Creu i Sant Pau,** at the intersection of Carrer Cartagena and Carrer Sant Antoni Maria Claret (*(C)* **93-291-9000;** Metro: Hospital de Sant Pau).

Post Office The main post office is at Plaça d'Antoni López (*(C)* **93-219-7197;** Metro: Jaume I). It's open Monday through Friday from 8am to 9pm and Saturday from 9am to 1pm.

Safety Be particularly careful with cameras, purses, and wallets, all favorite targets of thieves and pickpockets in Barcelona—especially on La Rambla, in the Gothic Quarter, in the streets around the Picasso Museum, and in the parts of the old town near the waterfront. Avoid those sections at night or travel them by taxi. Muggings, increasingly violent, are reportedly on the upswing. New lighting on side streets is intended to alleviate the problem, but urban caution is still in order.

Telephone The country code for Spain is **34.** The city code for Barcelona is **93.** To make an **international call,** dial **07,** wait for the tone, and dial the country code, the area code, and the number. Note that an international call from a public phone booth requires stacks of coins. As an alternative, purchase a **phone card** from a tobacco shop *(estanco),* the post office, or other authorized dealer.

WHERE TO STAY
CIUTAT VELLA (OLD CITY)

Reservations at most of the following hotels can be made in the United States and Canada through **Marketing Ahead,** 381 Park Ave. S., Suite 718, New York, NY 10016 (*(C)* **800/223-1356** or 212/686-9213; www.marketingahead.com).

Very Expensive

Le Meridien Barcelona *(R)(R)(R)* This is the finest hotel in the old town, thanks in large part to a major refurbishment over the last 3 years. A fave with CEOs and celebs—Madonna stayed here—it's far superior in both amenities and comfort to any competitor in the old town. It's a genteel retreat in the middle of the area's action. Have a cocktail in the calming piano bar after a long day of sightseeing. Rooms are spacious and comfortable, with double-glazed windows, extra-large beds, and bathrooms with heated floors.

La Rambla 111, 08002 Barcelona. *(C)* **800/543-4300** In the U.S., or 93-318-6200. Fax 93-301-7776. www.lemeridien-barcelona.com. 212 units. 330€–395€ double; from 475€ suite. AE, DC, MC, V. Parking

12€. Metro: Liceu or Plaça de Catalunya. **Amenities:** Restaurant; bar; access to a nearby health club; concierge; car-rental desk; business center; 24-hr. room service; babysitting; same-day laundry/dry cleaning. *In room:* A/C, TV w/pay movies, dataport, minibar, hair dryer, safe.

Expensive

Colón 🏵🏵   This immensely popular hotel is blessed with one of the most dramatic locations in Barcelona, opposite the cathedral. Inside you'll find conservative and slightly old-fashioned public areas and a helpful staff. Rooms are filled with cushy furniture and (despite continuing renovations) an appealingly dowdy kind of charm. Though lacking views, those in back are quieter, especially when celebrations and rock concerts take place in front of the cathedral. Sixth-floor rooms have terraces overlooking the square, and are the most desirable and hardest to reserve. Some lower rooms are dark.

Av. de la Catedral 7, 08002 Barcelona. ℂ 800/845-0636 in the U.S., or 93-301-1404. Fax 93-317-2915. www.hotelcolon.es. 147 units. 220€–310€ double; from 340€ suite. AE, DC, MC, V. Metro: Catalunya or Jaume I. **Amenities:** Restaurant; bar; concierge; 24-hr. room service; babysitting; same-day laundry/dry cleaning. *In room:* A/C, TV, minibar, hair dryer, safe.

Moderate

Albinoni 🏵   Until recently, this was called the Allegro, and some confusion still remains, but it's worth the trouble of finding it. First, there is the beautiful building, a stately 1886 neoclassical mansion. Imagine the horse-drawn carriages wheeling into what is now the lobby, depositing their guests at the grand staircase, and continuing on to the stables beyond (there's a tented breakfast room back there now). Rooms are of decent dimensions, with 18 facing the courtyard and another 18 in front, over the street. All the street-side rooms have balconies, and they're the ones to request. Unusual for a center-city hotel, it rents bicycles (12€).

Av. Portal de l'Angel 17 (south of Plaça de Catalunya), 08002 Barcelona. ℂ **93-318-4141.** Fax 93-301-2631. www.hoteles-catalonia.es. 74 units. 114€–162€ double. AE, DC, MC, V. Metro: Catalunya. **Amenities:** Bar; bike rental; limited room service; same-day laundry/dry cleaning. *In room:* A/C, TV w/pay movies, minibar, hair dryer, safe.

Ducs de Bergara 🏵🏵   Here, guests can enjoy a striking 1898 mansion that underwent a recent expansion to triple the number of rooms. Some *modernista* (the Catalan version of Art Deco) details have been retained, including the magnificent carved wood and marble entry, although most everything else is sleekly contemporary. The halls were constructed to allow for relatively spacious rooms, many of which have separate seating and desk areas. The desk staff is multilingual.

Bergara 11 (off Plaça de Catalunya), 08002 Barcelona. ℂ **93-301-5151.** Fax 93-317-3442. www.hotel es-catalonia.es. 148 units. 138€–228€ double. AE, DC, MC, V. Metro: Universitat. **Amenities:** Restaurant; bar; small rooftop pool; business center; 24-hr. room service; same-day laundry/dry cleaning; nonsmoking rooms. *In room:* A/C, TV w/pay movies, minibar, hair dryer, safe.

Mesón Castilla   Established in 1952, this hotel occupies a former apartment building. Owned and operated by the vast Spanish hotel chain HUSA, the Castilla is clean, charming, and well maintained. Its nearest rival is the Regencia Colón, to which it is comparable in atmosphere. Rooms, which benefited from a renovation in 1997, are adequately comfortable—beds have ornate headboards—and some open onto large terraces.

Valldoncella 5, 08002 Barcelona. ℂ **93-318-2182.** Fax 93-412-4020. www.husa.es. 56 units. 118€–125€ double. V. Parking 20€. Metro: Plaça de la Universitat. **Amenities:** Concierge; same-day laundry/dry cleaning. *In room:* A/C, TV, minibar, hair dryer, safe.

Regencia Colón   This stately stone hotel is located behind its superior sibling, the more expensive Hotel Colón, which stands opposite the cathedral. The formal lobby is a bit dour, but the well-maintained rooms are comfortable and often spacious, albeit worn. Rooms are insulated against sound, and 40 of them have full-tub bathrooms (the remainder have showers only). The hotel used to be a relatively good value for this popular neighborhood, but prices have been raised too high of late.

Sagristans 13–17, 08002 Barcelona. © **93-318-9858.** Fax 93-317-2822. www.hotelregenciacolon.com. 55 units. 148€ double. AE, DC, MC, V. Metro: Jaume 1 or Urquinaona. **Amenities:** Restaurant; bar; concierge; babysitting; same-day laundry/dry cleaning. *In room:* A/C, TV, minibar, hair dryer, safe.

DIAGONAL
Very Expensive

Hilton Barcelona 🏨🏨🏨   This luxury property is part of a huge commercial complex. Its location is more useful to businesspeople than to tourists. Most rooms are of good size and substantially equipped. Rooms are filled with thick carpeting, rich wood furnishings (though Hilton-standardized), and some of the best combination bathrooms in the city, with all the extras, including video games and bathrobes. Some units are reserved exclusively for women.

Av. Diagonal 589–591, 08014 Barcelona. © **800/445-8667** in the U.S. and Canada, or 93-495-7777. Fax 93-495-7700. www.hilton.com. 287 units. 247€–395€ double; from 395€ suite. AE, DC, MC, V. Parking 20€. Metro: María Cristina. **Amenities:** 2 restaurants; bar; small exercise room; access to nearby health club; concierge; car-rental desk; business center; 24-hr. room service; in-room massage; same-day laundry/dry cleaning; nonsmoking rooms, executive floors. *In room:* A/C, TV w/pay movies, dataport, minibar, hair dryer, safe.

Moderate/Expensive

Derby/Gran Derby   These twin hotels are in a peaceful neighborhood about 2 blocks south of the busy intersection of Avinguda Diagonal and Avinguda Sarría, and the nightlife district around Plaça Francesc Macià. The Derby has 111 conventional rooms, and the Gran Derby (across the street) boasts 12 duplex suites among its 40 units, many of which have small balconies overlooking a flowered courtyard. Drinking and dining facilities are located in the Derby. Rooms and suites are outfitted with simple furniture in a variety of styles, and each is comfortable and quiet.

Loreto 21–25, and Loreto 28, 08029 Barcelona. © **93-322-3215.** Fax 93-410-0062. www.derbyhotels.es. 141 units. 156€–210€ double; from 235€ suite. AE, DC, MC, V. Parking 14€. Metro: Hospital Clínic. **Amenities:** 2 restaurants; bar; outdoor pool; concierge; limited room service; same-day laundry/dry cleaning. *In room:* A/C, TV, dataport, minibar, hair dryer, safe.

EIXAMPLE
Very Expensive

Claris 🏨🏨   An 1882 aristocratic residence was converted into one of only two officially designated *gran lujo* (grand luxury) hotels in the city center. The hotel opened in 1992, in time for the Olympics, and has a small pool and garden on its roof, as well as a gallery of Egyptian antiquities on its second floor. Rooms with clean-lined contemporary furnishings incorporate pieces of ancient Egyptian art, both real and copies, and all the high-end electronic accessories you could wish for.

Carrer de Pau Claris 150, 08009 Barcelona. © **800/888-4747** in the U.S., or 93-487-6262. Fax 93-215-7970. www.derbyhotels.es. 120 units. 257€–483€ double; 901€ suite. AE, MC, V. Parking 14€. Metro: Passeig de Gràcia. **Amenities:** 2 restaurants; bar; outdoor pool; exercise room; sauna; concierge; 24-hr. room service; in-room massage; babysitting; same-day laundry/dry cleaning. *In room:* A/C, TV, minibar, hair dryer, safe.

Ritz 🏨🏨🏨   Although it has competition now, this was the most prestigious hotel in Barcelona for decades. Built in 1919 in Belle Epoque style, its customer base has seen millionaires, celebrities, and bluebloods since its inception. After a period of perceptible decline and changes in ownership, it has returned to its former stature. The hotel's most jaw-dropping feature is the grand cream-and-gilt lobby, featuring marble floors and potted palms. Rooms are large, formal, and amply furnished, sometimes with Regency furniture; bathrooms are accented with mosaics and tubs inspired by those in ancient Rome. The concierges could give mastery classes to their less accomplished colleagues in the field.

Gran Vía de les Corts Catalanes 668, 08010 Barcelona. (℃ **93-318-5200** or 93-318-4837. Fax 93-318-0148. www.ritzbcn.com. 125 units. 380€–505€ double; from 475€ suite. AE, DC, MC, V. Parking 21€. Metro: Passeig de Gràcia. **Amenities:** Restaurant; bar; new health club; concierge; salon; 24-hr. room service; in-room massage; babysitting; same-day laundry/dry cleaning. *In room:* A/C, TV/VCR, high-speed Internet access, minibar, hair dryer, safe.

Expensive

Condes de Barcelona ⚘ This fine old mansion on a corner of Barcelona's most glamorous avenue was stripped to the walls in 1988, and a postmodern minimalist interior was installed. Business was so good after the Olympic Games that the hotel opened a 74-room annex on the opposite corner. The annex lacks the style of the original but has better rooms. Some of the rooms in the original building are showing wear, but all have soundproof windows. The handsome marble bathrooms are well equipped with such extras as makeup mirrors, and some have whirlpool baths. There's a nonsmoking floor.

Passeig de Gràcia 73–75, 08008 Barcelona. (℃ **93-467-4780.** Fax 93-467-4785. www.condesdebarcelona. com. 183 units. 213€–250€ double; from 410€ suite. AE, DC, MC, V. Parking 16€. Metro: Passeig de Gràcia. **Amenities:** Restaurant; bar; outdoor pool; fitness center; concierge; limited room service; same-day laundry/ dry cleaning. *In room:* A/C, TV, minibar, dataport, hair dryer, safe.

Moderate/Expensive

Majestic ⚘⚘ If they only asked, you assume, the Majestic would be elevated to the government's five-star rank in the blink of an eye. It has all the prerequisites, from the highly capable folks at the front desk and on the housekeeping staff to the excellent little fitness room (still infrequent in Spanish hotels) and the stunning Michelin-honored restaurant, Drolma (see "Where To Dine," below). Rooms are immaculate, spacious, and often centered around antique furniture pieces. Both public and private spaces are decorated with original artworks by two generations of Spanish modernists. And, if you have a laptop, you don't even have to plug it in—simply connect with the hotel's wireless Internet service.

Passeig de Gràcia 68, 08007 Barcelona. (℃ **93-488-1717.** Fax 93-488-1880. www.hotelmajestic.es. 273 units. 161€–230€ double; from 300€ suite. AE, DC, MC, V. Parking 19€. Metro: Passeig de Gràcia. **Amenities:** 2 restaurants; piano bar; outdoor rooftop pool; well-equipped fitness center with sauna, steam, and massage; concierge; business center; 24-hr. room service; same-day laundry/dry cleaning; nonsmoking rooms. *In room:* A/C, TV w/pay movies, minibar, dataport (and wireless Internet service), hair dryer, safe.

Astoria *Value* Another property from the growing Derby chain, the 1954 Astoria has a between-the-wars facade that makes it appear older than it is. The high ceilings, geometric designs, and brass-studded detailings in the gracious public areas hint of Moorish Andalucía. Rooms are soundproofed and feature the warmth of exposed cedar as well as elegant modern accessories.

París 203, 08036 Barcelona. (℃ **93-209-83-11.** Fax 93-202-30-08. www.derbyhotels.es. 117 units. 126€–173€ double. AE, DC, MC, V. Metro: Diagonal. **Amenities:** Cafe; bar; modest exercise room, sauna; concierge; limited room service; same-day laundry/dry cleaning. *In room:* A/C, TV, minibar, hair dryer, safe.

Inexpensive

Urquinaona ⋆ *(Finds)* Tucked into a narrow building off the plaza of the same name, this admirable little hostel-turned-hotel easily qualifies as a find. Located off the heavily used tourist trails, it's nonetheless handy to La Ribera and the Eixample district. A substantial but canny investment by the new owners graced the hotel with rooms boasting three-star furnishings and amenities (despite the low price). High standards of cleanliness are rigorously observed. Breakfast can be served in your room. English is spoken.

Ronda de Sant Pere 24, 08010 Barcelona. ⓒ **93-268-1336.** Fax 93-295-4137. www.barcelonahotel.com/ urquinaona. 16 units. 84€double. MC, V. Metro: Urquinaona. **Amenities:** Restaurant; laundry service. *In room:* A/C, TV, minibar, hair dryer, safe.

VILA OLIMPICA
Very Expensive

Arts ⋆⋆⋆ This deluxe hotel is the only lodging in Barcelona that gives the Ritz serious competition. In the opinion of many knowledgeable travelers, the Arts actually eclipses the Ritz. Managed by the Ritz-Carlton chain, it occupies part of a postmodern tower marked by a huge Frank Gehry sculpture of a fish above the terrace facing the sea. The location is about 2.5km (1½ miles) east of Barcelona's historic core, adjacent to the sea and the Olympic Port. The decor is contemporary and elegant, and both the public and private areas are filled with contemporary art. Views from the rooms sweep the skyline and the Mediterranean. Stay over during the weekend and you can save up to 50% on the rates listed below.

Marina 19–21, 08005 Barcelona. ⓒ **800/241-3333** in the U.S., or 93-221-1000. Fax 93-221-10-70. www.ritz carlton.com. 482 units. 320€–535€ double; from 430€ suite. AE, DC, MC, V. Parking 19€. Metro: Ciudadela– Vila Olímpica. **Amenities:** 4 restaurants; 2 bars; outdoor and indoor pools; health club and spa; concierge; business center; salon; 24-hr. room service; in-room massage; babysitting; same-day laundry/dry cleaning. *In room:* A/C, TV, minibar, hair dryer, safe.

WHERE TO DINE
CIUTAT VELLA (OLD CITY)
Expensive

Casa Leopoldo ⋆ SEAFOOD This surprisingly sophisticated restaurant in an intimidating Raval neighborhood has thrived since 1929. It offers some of the freshest seafood in town, and caters to a loyal clientele. Pictographic tiles and bullfighting paraphernalia constitute much of the traditional decor. There's a thriving tapas bar in front, plus two dining rooms, one slightly more formal than the other. Specialties include stuffed oxtail; roast *merluza* (hake) and *rape* (monkfish) with a *sofrito* of garlic and shrimp; and baby eels boiled in oil— a pricey delicacy. An enduring specialty is the enormous platter of fish and shellfish, prepared only for two. Take a taxi coming and going.

Sant Rafael 24 (near Carrer de la Riereta). ⓒ **93-441-3014.** Reservations advised. Main courses 10€–21€; menú del día 39€ dinner. AE, DC, MC, V. Tues–Sat 1:30–4pm and 9–11pm; Sun 1:30–4pm. Closed Aug and Holy Week. Metro: Liceu.

Hofman ⋆ CATALAN/INTERNATIONAL This restaurant is, in effect, a classroom of a demanding cooking school. The chefs, working under close professorial supervision, are all students. Don't take that to mean that the food is in any way amateurish. On the contrary, it is some of the most creative cuisine in Barcelona, full of twists and surprises. Trendy foams appear as garnish and fish is fashionably underdone. Menus change every 2 months, with frequent daily specials. Expect such items as foie gras wrapped in puff pastry, ragout of crayfish with green risotto, and steak braised in Rioja wine and served with a confit of shallots and a gratin of potatoes. Celebrities have discovered the place—Mel Gibson, John Travolta, and Kevin Costner among them.

Argenteria 74–78 (at Plaça de Santa María). ℂ **93-319-5889.** Reservations strongly advised. Main courses 14€–36€; *menú del día* 39€ lunch. AE, DC, MC, V. Mon–Fri 1:30–4pm and 9–11:30pm. Metro: Jaume I.

Moderate

Agut ★★ SPANISH   If it weren't for Agut's location in a dark corner of the Gothic Quarter, you might not be able to get in at all. As it is, be there when the doors open to have a chance at a table if you don't have reservations. The chefs give all their attention to delicately balancing ingredients and allowing every flavor to take its bow. Their precision shows up even in salads, such as young basil and arugula leaves with toasted pine nuts and croutons on a bed of diced tomatoes, draped with slivers of smoked fish. The beef is superb—look for *filetitos de buey con salsa trufa* (beef filets with truffle sauce) with *trumpetas de la muerte* (black mushrooms). Around since 1924, the restaurant occupies several rooms on two floors with wooden wainscoting, marble floors, and early-1900s paintings.

Gignàs 16 (a block south of the main post office). ℂ **93-315-1709.** Reservations strongly advised. Main courses 8.10€–16€. DC, MC, V. Tues–Sat 1:30–4pm and 8:30–11pm; Sun 9pm–midnight. Metro: Barceloneta.

Can Culleretes CATALAN   Founded in 1786 as a pastry shop, Barcelona's oldest restaurant is located in the Gothic quarter. The restaurant retains many original architectural features, with wooden beams overhead and a long bas-relief mural in wood depicting folkloric Catalunya. Every last dish on the menu is a Catalan standard, making this a good place to learn what the simple traditional form of this regional cuisine is all about. Just don't expect novelty. Rabbit with garlic mayo is typical, as is the sausage *butifarra* with beans. From October to January, game is featured, including *perdiz* (partridge).

Quintana 5 (between Fernando and Boquería). ℂ **93-317-6485.** Reservations suggested. Main courses 6€–16€, *menú del día* 14€ lunch. DC, V. Tues–Sun 1:30–4pm; Tues–Sat 9–11:30pm. Closed 3 weeks in July. Metro: Liceu. Bus: 14 or 59.

El Gran Café SPANISH   The tobacco-brown ceiling of this restaurant is high enough to accommodate 4.5m (15-ft.) windows and a dining balcony over the service bar. The building is 19th century, and the restaurant has been given a Belle Epoque appearance. A piano player adds to the mood in the evening, when the crowd has a polished look. Fish and game dominate the menu, but specific ingredients are changed frequently, a sign that the chef follows the market. The fast-moving staff doesn't waste a step bringing the chef's creations to the table.

Avinyo 9 (a block south of Carrer Ferrán). ℂ **93-318-7986.** Main courses up to 21€; *menú del día* 12€. AE, DC, MC, V. Mon–Sat 1–3pm and 8pm–12:30am. Metro: Liceu or Jaume I.

Estrella de Plata ★★ SPANISH   For tapas elevated well beyond the traditional norm, it is next to impossible to equal, let alone surpass, this tony tavern near the harbor. Everything is wonderfully fresh, and much of it is made to order. Dishes are either upgraded versions of common recipes—*ensaladilla rusa* or *gambas* with *aioli*—or utterly new creations, such as the cylinder of barely poached shredded cod laid over salmon, tomatoes, and onions; or the artichoke heart baked with a soft quail egg inside and dusted with caviar. There is no menu; instead the specialties that are not displayed on the bar are described by a waiter or waitress, some of whom speak English. There's only one dessert, a tiny square of chocolate served on a bit of toast with a sauce tinged with olive oil and cocoa powder. Service could be faster.

Plaça del Palau 13 (north of Passeig d'Isabel II). ℭ 93-268-0635. Tapas and *raciónes* 5€–8€. MC, V. Mon 8–11:30pm; Tues–Sat 1–4:30pm and 8–11:30pm. Closed last 2 weeks in Aug. Metro: Barceloneta.

Flo *Kids* FRENCH/CATALAN   The dining room is a sprawling, brightly lit, palm-filled replica of a Left Bank brasserie. Everyone is welcome, be they kids, tourists, execs, oldsters, or families visiting from the suburbs. The wait crew is adroit and unflappable, even when a child gets whiny. Menu items are equally divided between specialties from the bistro traditions of France and those of Catalonia. French-derived items include fresh foie gras and large platters of Alsatian *choucroute* (sauerkraut). Catalan specialties include *mariscado* (shellfish stew) and *rissoto de calamares en su tinta* (squid served in its own ink). Keep this place in mind for dinner after a concert at the nearby Palau de la Música, or for Sunday, when most restaurants are closed.

Jonqueras 10 (near Laietana). ℭ 93-319-3102. Main courses 13€–19€, *menú del día* 16€ or 21€. AE, DC, MC, V. Mon–Thurs 1–4pm and 8:30pm–midnight; Fri–Sun 1–4pm and 8:30pm–1am. Metro: Urquinaona.

Les Quinze Nits *Finds* MEDITERRANEAN   There's an a la carte menu, but most patrons choose the fixed-price deals here. A large front room overlooks an enclosed plaza, with tables out under the loggia most of the year. A smaller, quieter room in back suits couples who don't need to be seen. The earnest young staff swiftly brings fare like spinach-filled cannelloni under a blanket of melted cheese, and tender beef filet with shoestring potatoes. A *paella mixta* for two costs only 11€, and a half-carafe of one of the palatable house wines is only 1.95€.

Plaça Reial 6 (east of La Rambla). ℭ 93-317-3075. Main courses 5.65€–9.90€; *menú del día* 9€. AE, MC, V. Daily 1–3:30pm and 8:30–11:30pm. Metro: Liceu.

Los Caracoles *Overrated* CATALAN/SPANISH   Still one of the most famous restaurants in town, few guidebooks neglect to mention Los Caracoles. It's been around since 1835, it retains its ancient ambience, and it still serves the dishes it always did, but the competition has buried it. An outside grill always has a rank of glistening chickens rotating. Inside, roast suckling pig and lamb are on the menu, as are the namesake *caracoles* (snails). Other possibilities are the lobster paella or a fish stew called *bullabesa*. It remains a number-one tourist attraction—or is that tourist trap?

Escudellers 14 (east of La Rambla). ℭ 93-302-3185. Reservations suggested. Main courses 6.90€–25€. AE, DC, MC, V. Daily 1pm midnight. Metro: Drassanes.

Pitarra *Finds* SPANISH   Pitarra occupies the former home/watch shop of the prolific and much-honored 19th-century playwright/poet Frederic Soler Hubert (pseudonym: Pitarra). There are many antique clocks on display, some that hardly look like timepieces. Express interest in the surroundings, and Jaume, the partner who runs the front, may bring you a complimentary flute of Catalan cava, a sparkling wine (his brother Marc is the chef). The atmosphere is friendly, the service swift, and the food hearty. Look for game dishes in winter, like jugged wild boar in a sauce perfumed by bitter chocolate; or the most expensive item, woodcock with mushrooms.

Avinyó 56 (south of Carrer Ferrán). ℭ 93-301-1647. Main courses 7€–29€; *menú del día* 8€ (lunch only). MC, V. Mon–Sat 1–4pm and 8:30–11pm. Closed Aug. Metro: Liceu or Jaume I.

Taxidermista ℛ CATALAN/INTERNATIONAL   While it's named for the business of a previous tenant, you'll be the one stuffed. The creative kitchen provides worthy antidotes to usually vegetable-free Spanish meals. Ringing the couscous and lamb at the center of its plate, for example, are discreet portions of chickpeas, zucchini, carrots, and potatoes, with a small pitcher of broth and a spoonful of hot sauce on the side. A tasty little *aperitivo* (say, a pig's foot stuffed with duck confit) arrives with your drink order. The setting is an effective blend of 19th-century architecture and hand-hewn beams with post-industrial lighting.

Plaça Reial 8. ℭ **93-412-4536.** Main courses 7.20€–16€; *menu del día* 7.95€ lunch. AE, DC, MC, V. Dining room Tues–Sun 1:30–4pm and 8:30pm–12:30am; tapas bar Tues–Sun noon–1am. Metro: Liceu.

Inexpensive

Biocenter VEGETARIAN   This is Barcelona's largest and best-known vegetarian restaurant, a funky, counterculture sort of place on one of the better streets in Raval. Meals are served in two ground-floor dining rooms. Take a tray and plate and fill up first at the self-service soup and salad bar. A waiter or waitress brings your choice of four main courses, which typically include a pasta, a rice dish, a vegetable tart, and something else. After eating, you pay at the cash register on the honor system.

Pintor Fortuny 25 (west of La Rambla). ℭ **93-301-4583.** Main courses 2.50€–7.25€; *menú del día* 7.50€. No credit cards. Restaurant Mon–Sat 1–5pm. Bar Mon–Sat 9am–11pm. Metro: Plaça de Catalunya.

Irati TAPAS   One of the latest food crazes to take hold of the city is a subcategory of tapas that hail from the Basque Country—*País Vasco*—in the north-central part of the country. Up there, they pin piles of delectable toppings to thick slices of bread with toothpicks. The possibilities are endless, from sardines to sweet peppers to sausages, and on and on. You simply ask for a plate and go down the bar to select as many toppings as you wish from the trays and platters arrayed there. Order a *copa* of the fizzy Basque wine and the staff will pour it from above their heads into a glass held 3 feet below. To tote up your check, they count your toothpicks. (No fair throwing them away.)

Cardenal Casañas 17 (between La Rambla and Plaça de Pi). ℭ **93-302-3084.** Tapas 1€. No credit cards. Tues–Sat noon–midnight; Sun 6–11pm. Metro: Liceu.

ON & NEAR DIAGONAL
Very Expensive

Botafumiero ℛ SEAFOOD   Here is the traditional *tasca* taken to a higher plateau. No greasy grill, no debris-strewn floor, no jostling for space. Take a seat at a bar stool, with plenty of elbowroom, and a linen place mat and flatware are laid before you in a wink. And while the average corner tavern has two or three men flinging dishes around, this one has an entire squad in white coats and gold braid. And that's just the bar. Beyond it is a ramble of rooms with blond wood and potted greenery. Fish, clams, mussels, lobster, crayfish, and scallops are the pride of the kitchen, along with several varieties of crustaceans that you may never have seen before. The only problem? Some of the highest prices in town.

Gran de Gràcia 81 (north of Travessera de Gràcia). ℭ **93-218-4230.** Reservations recommended for dining rooms, not necessary for meals at the bar. Main courses 12€–60€. AE, DC, MC, V. Mon–Sat 1pm–1am; Sun 1–5pm. Metro: Fontana.

Drolma ℛℛ FRENCH/SPANISH   The setting here meets the high expectations fostered by the glowing reviews this trendsetter has garnered since the day it opened. The lamps are by Phillipe Starke, the china is Rosenthal, and the glasses are Baccarat. A squad of scrupulously trained male and female servers tends to your needs. They'll wheel over a trolley of wines and offer any of them as an aperitif. Following that, they bring not one but two *aperitivos*—Spanish for *amuse-bouche*—an airy little dumpling, maybe, or a shot glass of crabmeat in basil oil. That's only a hint of what's to come. There's the salad with four quail eggs and four chunks of grilled foie gras, the potato soup with mushrooms and slivered truffles, the glazed goat, the lamb—some dishes even come with second helpings. The restaurant has a faint aura of corporate calm, but the bravura display of skill and largesse is not soon forgotten by serious diners.

In the Hotel Majestic, Passeig de Gràcia 68. ✆ **93-496-7710**. Main courses 29€–43€. AE, DC, MC, V. Mon–Sat 1:30–4pm and 8:30–11:30pm. Closed Aug. Metro: Passeig de Gràcia.

Neichel ✿✿✿ MEDITERRANEAN   Years ago, Alsatian-born Jean Louis Neichel came to Barcelona and melded French techniques with Catalan ingredients to create a cuisine all his own. Manipulating an array of ingredients that border on perfection, he employs a palette that features olive oil and distilled natural juices instead of the butter and cream of his homeland. Neichel displays a wizardry that manages to produce both pretty plates and supernal marriages of flavor and texture. With his artistry at the stove and his obsession with every detail of service, this is a high-wire act that is a privilege to witness. Nothing stays on the menu for long, so there isn't much point in listing dishes. Just put yourself in his hands. The *menú degustación* is the way to go. Save room for the memorable cheese tray.

Beltran i Rózpide 1 (off av. de Pedralbes). ✆ **93-203-8408**. Reservations advised. Main courses 21€–39€; *menú degustación* 60€. AE, DC, MC, V. Tues–Sat 1:30–3:30pm and 8:30–11pm. Closed Aug and holidays. Metro: María Christina.

Expensive

La Dama ✿✿ CATALAN/INTERNATIONAL   Long possessed of a Michelin star, this stylish and adroitly managed place fully deserves the honor. A marvelously baroque elevator carries diners to the main floor of a splendid *modernista* building. Sinuously carved lines decorate the door panels, cornices, walls, and etched glass. Tables are set far enough apart for intimate conversation. If you arrive during the fall wild mushroom season, get a plate of the fungi, four or five kinds, sautéed lightly with garlic. Monkfish in an earthy sauce of thumb-sized squid and black olives is another winner. An extra selling point is that La Dama is open for lunch and dinner every day of the week, unlike most in this high-echelon category.

Av. Diagonal 423 (at Eric Granados). ✆ **93-202-0686**. Reservations required. Main courses 14€–24€; *menu degustación* 65€. AE, DC, MC, V. Daily 1–4pm and 8:30–11:30pm. Metro: Provença.

Tragaluz ✿ CREATIVE CATALAN   Down an alley connecting Rambla de Catalunya and Passeig de Gràcia, this intelligently conceived enterprise broke rules and caused a stir when it opened back in the late 1980s. The overall design was startlingly new at the time. Downstairs, you'll find a bar and what amounts to a high-style fast-food emporium called Tragarrapid; upstairs is a more ambitious dining room with two tiers under an expansive skylight. You're not likely to be disappointed whichever level you choose—the light, casual, inexpensive meals downstairs, or the inventive, leisurely repasts upstairs. Consider hake with tomato sauce, or grilled sardines on sweet pepper couscous. Or try a selection from the menu of low-calorie dishes.

Passatage de la Concepció 5 (off Passeig de Gràcia). ✆ **93-487-0621**. Reservations advised for main dining room. Main courses 13€–22€; *menu degustación* 50€. AE, DC, MC, V. Daily 1:30–4pm and 8:30pm–midnight (until 1am Thurs–Sat). Metro: Diagonal.

LA RIBERA & BARCELONETA
Moderate/Expensive

El Suquet de l'Almirall ⭐⭐ SEAFOOD   The boulevard bordering the old fishermen's quarter is lined with seafood restaurants, most raucous and gaudy, often with sidewalk barkers trying to snare pedestrians. This retreat is the classiest of the strip, with tables on the terrace, where you can peer through palm trees at the boats in the harbor. The dishes served at the row of seafood restaurants aren't all that different in basic recipe, but the execution here is superior to that of most of the immediate neighbors, resulting in lighter, less oily food. Representative is the creamy fish chowder laced with *romescu*, a tangy Catalan sauce. For a memorable repast, leap for the *menú ciego*, composed of seven tapas and a final paella-like rice dish. If you head in that direction, you'll encounter red peppers draped with anchovies, puffy cod fritters, baby squid on potato slices, and a small piece of grilled tuna scattered with pine nuts (chopsticks provided, for some reason).

Passeig Joan de Borbó 65. ℭ **93-221-6233**. Reservations advised weekends. Main courses 11€–19€; *menú ciego* 32€. DC, MC, V. Mon 8–11:30pm; Tues–Sat 1:30–4pm and 8:30–11:30pm. Closed holiday evenings. Metro: Barceloneta.

Set Portes CATALAN   In business since 1836, these "Seven Doors" open into a food emporium that is a lunchtime favorite for businesspeople (the Stock Exchange is across the way) and an evening favorite for the anyone who enjoys the peachy glow of the hanging lamps and the ministrations of the piano player. Known for its paellas, changed daily, there are also regional dishes that include grilled rabbit, fresh herring with onions and potatoes, a wide selection of super-fresh fish and oysters, and an herb-laden stew of black beans with pork. Portions are enormous. Note that the restaurant stays open straight through from 1pm to 1am, so visitors don't need to adhere to late Spanish dining hours.

Passeig d'Isabel II 14. ℭ **93-319-3033**. Reservations required. Main courses 8€–23€. AE, DC, MC, V. Daily 1pm–1am. Metro: Barceloneta.

Inexpensive

Cal Pep SPANISH   Long a local secret despite its proximity to the Picasso Museum (it's a short walk south from the museum), this fine little tapas bar is now drawing attention from visitors. There are 20 seats at the long marble bar and a tiny sit-down back room. While you'll probably get a seat if you arrive at 1:30pm during the week, expect a wait after 2pm and on weekends. (If it *is* full, there are two other cafes on the same square.) There's no menu—the manager will tell you what's available and use his lapel mike to relay your order to the kitchen when it gets busy. What comes forth from the kitchen doesn't stray far from the traditional repertoire, but it's so much better prepared. This is the way *pescados fritos* (fried fish), *almejas con jamón* (steamed clams with ham), and *pan con tomate* (Catalan tomato bread) rarely taste in less skilled hands. The bunch behind the bar joke and laugh with patrons and each other all the while.

Plaça de les Olles 8. ℭ **93-310-7961**. Reservations required for dining room. Main courses and tapas 6.10€–13€. AE, DC, MC, V. Mon 8-11:30pm; Tues–Sat 1:15–4pm and 8–11:30pm. Closed Aug. Metro: Jaume I.

SEEING THE SIGHTS

Spain's second-largest city is also its most cosmopolitan. Barcelona is more European and internationalist than Madrid. The city is filled with landmark buildings and important museums, including Antoni Gaudí's Sagrada Familia, Museu Picasso, the Gothic cathedral, and La Rambla, the famous tree-lined promenade cutting through the heart of the old city from Plaça de Catalunya to the harbor.

SIGHTSEEING SUGGESTIONS FOR FIRST-TIME VISITORS

If You Have 1 Day Spend the morning exploring the **Barri Gótic (Gothic Quarter).** In the afternoon visit the **Museu Picasso** in the Ribera quarter, which is filled with Renaissance mansions and is the site of the notable **Santa María del Mar church.** Return to the Plaça de Catalunya for a walk down **La Rambla.** To cap your day, take the funicular to the top of **Tibidabo** for a panoramic view of Barcelona and its harbor.

If You Have 2 Days On day 2, see Antoni Gaudí's unfinished masterpiece, **La Sagrada Família.** Have a seafood lunch in **Barceloneta** and, in the afternoon, stroll up La Rambla again. Explore **Montjuïc** and visit the **Museu d'Art de Catalunya** and the nearby **Poble Espanyol,** a village with replicas of regional architecture created for the 1929 World's Fair. End the day with a meal of paella at **Set Portes,** one of the oldest restaurants in the city.

If You Have 3 Days On day 3, take the train to the monastery of **Montserrat,** about 45 minutes outside of Barcelona, to see the venerated Black Virgin and the art museum, and to hear the famous 50-member boys' choir.

If You Have 4 or 5 Days On day 4, take a morning walk through the **Eixample** district, the planned urban expansion area from 1860. It has over 100 buildings in the *modernista* (Catalan Art Deco) style. Have lunch at one of the tapas bars along the Passeig de Gràcia. After lunch, visit La Pedrera, Gaudí's signature apartment house. On day 5, take another excursion from the city. If you're interested in history, visit the former Roman city of **Tarragona** to the south. If you want to unwind on a beach, head south to **Sitges.**

THE TOP ATTRACTIONS

Catedral de Barcelona (La Seu) ⋆⋆ Begun in the late 13th century and completed in the mid–15th century (except for the main facade, which dates from the late 19th), this Gothic cathedral attests to the splendor of medieval Barcelona. Its main points of interest are the central choir, the 14th-century alabaster crypt of Santa Eulàlia, and the *Cristo de Lepanto,* whose twisted torso allegedly dodged a bullet during the naval battle of the same name. Do see the adjoining **cloister** ⋆, with access down on the right from the front entrance. It encloses palm and magnolia trees, flowering medlars, a fountain erupting from a moss-covered rock, and a gaggle of live geese, said to be reminders of the Roman occupation (or of the Apostles or the virtuous St. Eulàlia, depending on the various convictions of writers and guides). On the steps at noon on Sunday, a band with ancient instruments plays the eerily haunting *sardana,* the music of the hallowed Catalan folk dance.

Plaça de la Seu. ℂ 93-315-3555. Cathedral and cloister, free; choir .90€; museum 1€. Cathedral daily 8am–1:30pm and 4–7:30pm; museum daily 10am–1pm. Metro: Jaume I. Bus: 16, 17, 19, 22, or 45.

Fundació Joan Miró ⋆⋆ A tribute to the Catalan lyrical surrealist Joan Miró, this contemporary museum (reminiscent of Bauhaus style) follows his work from 1914 to 1978 and includes many of his sculptures, paintings, and multimedia tapestries. Even the roof displays his whimsical sculptures as well as bestows impressive city vistas. Temporary exhibits of other contemporary artists are held on a regular basis. From the top of the Montjuïc funicular, turn left and walk down to the museum.

Parc de Montjuïc. (*C*) 93-443-9470. www.bcn.fjmiro.es. Admission to both permanent and temporary exhibitions 7.50€ adults, 3€ seniors/students; to permanent collection only, 4€ adults, 2€ seniors/students; free for ages 14 and under. July–Sept Tues–Wed and Fri–Sat 10am–8pm, Thurs 10am–9:30pm, Sun and holidays 10am–2:30pm; Oct–June Tues–Sat 10am–7pm, Sun and holidays 10am–2:30pm. Funicular: Montjuïc. Bus: 50 from Plaça de Espanya.

La Sagrada Família ★★ An ambitious work in progress, this *modernista* rendition of a cathedral will, when and if finished, be Europe's largest. Work began on the Church of the Holy Family in 1882, and while the Archbishop of Barcelona recently declared that it would be completed by 2020, this claim was met with skepticism. Architect Antoni Gaudí took over the project after 2 years and proposed a temple of immense proportions—the central dome is slated to be 160m (525 ft.) high. His vision, as seen in his other commissions around the city, amounts to a flamboyant surrealism with extensive stone carving, ceramics, and intricate ironwork. At the pinnacles of the completed towers are vivid mosaic sunbursts of gold and crimson, and much of the east facade appears to have melted under the blast of a giant blowtorch. Controversy swirls around the cathedral's completion: Gaudí died in 1926 after being run over by a tram and left no detailed plans. The style and direction of recent additions (especially the stunningly inept sculptures on the west facade) aren't to everyone's liking. As Robert Hughes has written, Gaudí "is not someone with whom one can collaborate posthumously."

Mallorca 401. (*C*) 93-455-0247. www.sagradafamilia.org. Admission 6€ adults, 4€ seniors/students, free for ages 9 and under. Elevator 1.50€; guided tours 4€. May–Sept daily 9am–8pm; Oct–Apr daily 9am–6pm. Metro: Sagrada Família. Bus: 19, 34, 43, 50, 51, or 54.

Museu Picasso ★★★ Barcelona's most popular single attraction, this museum reveals much about the artist whose long, prolific career extended well beyond Cubism. Most of the paintings, drawings, engravings, and ceramics relate to Picasso's early years, when he lived and studied in Barcelona and spent summers in Catalan hill towns. If you're expecting to see anything more than hints of his most famous later works, you might be disappointed. The galleries in the original three Renaissance mansions have been expanded into two more adjoining palaces.

Montcada 15–19. (*C*) 93-319-6310. www.museupicasso.bcn.es. Admission to permanent collection 5€ adults, 2.50€ seniors/students/ages 12–16; admission to temporary exhibitions 7.80€ extra for adults, 4.50€ extra seniors/students; free for under age 12 and for everyone 1st Sun of every month. Tues–Sat and holidays 10am–8pm; Sun 10am–3pm. Metro: Jaume I.

MORE ATTRACTIONS

Casa Battló ★★ As part of the 2002 citywide celebration of Gaudí, this, the architect's second most important commission on the Passeig de Gràcia, was opened to public visits for the first time. The opportunity to visit was greeted with such enthusiasm that the offers was extended through 2003. Unlike La Pedrera (below), Gaudí didn't design this building from the ground up. Instead, he transformed an existing structure with a facade of shimmering tiles and a free-form roofline that evokes the scaly back of a dragon. The interior is just as striking. Inquire ahead to be certain it is still open.

Passeig de Gràcia 43 (corner of Aragó). (*C*) 93-216-0306. Admission 10€. Mon–Sat 9am–2pm; Sun 9am–8pm. Metro: Passeig de Gràcia.

La Pedrera ★★ Formally the Casa Milà, the popular name of this apartment/office block means the "Stone Quarry." Antoni Gaudí didn't restrain himself here: the undulating exterior of carved stone gives the building the aspect of the lair of a mythical dragon, its balconies enclosed by freeform wrought iron. The top floor and an apartment are open to visitors. Don't miss the roof terrace, populated with highly sculptural chimneys and vents that might have been imagined by H. G. Wells.

Provença 261–265 (at the corner of Passeig de Gràcia). © **93-484-5995.** Admission to attic, terrace, and apt. 6€ adults, 3€ students. Daily 10am–8pm; guided tours to attic and terrace Mon–Fri at 6pm and Sat, Sun, and holidays at 11am; tours in English of the apt Mon–Fri at 4:30pm and Sat, Sun, and holidays at 10:30am. Metro: Diagonal.

L'Aquàrium ✺ *Kids* The crowning attraction of the entertainment pier jutting into the harbor, this carefully conceived aquarium is one of the largest in Europe. It exhibits over 8,000 marine creatures of 450 species in 21 tanks. A highlight is the Perspex tunnel that allows you to walk through a tank stocked with prowling sharks and gliding rays.

On the Moll d'Espanya, in the harbor. © **93-221-7474.** Admission 9€ adults, 6€ seniors/children 4–12. July–Aug daily 9:30am–11pm; June, Sept, and weekends 9:30am–9:30pm; Oct–May daily 9:30am–9pm. Metro: Drassanes or Barceloneta. Bus: 14, 17, 19, 36, 38, 39, 40, 45, 57, 59, 64, 91, or 157.

Monument à Colom (Columbus Monument) This waterfront landmark was erected in 1888 to commemorate Columbus's triumphant return after his first expedition to the New World. An 8m (25-ft.) bronze statue of the explorer surmounts the Victorian-era monument. Inside the iron column is a creaky elevator that ascends to a panoramic view.

Plaça Portal de la Pau. © **93-302-5224.** Admission 1.80€ adults, 1.20€ seniors/ages 4–12, free for ages 3 and under. June–Sept: daily 9am–8:30pm; Oct–Mar: Mon–Fri 10am–1:30pm and 3:30–6:30pm; Sat, Sun, and holidays 10am–6:30pm; Apr–May: Mon–Fri 10am–1pm and 3:30–7:30pm; Sat, Sun, and holidays 10am–7:30pm. Metro: Drassanes. Bus: 14, 36, 57, 59, or 64.

Poble Espanyol ✺ *Kids* This "village," executed for the 1929 World's Fair, houses examples of architectural styles found throughout Spain. After renovations and changes in operational philosophy, the once-stuffy open-air museum has become almost a village in its own right, with working artisans, dozens of crafts shops, restaurants, and assorted nightclubs and bars. Some visitors judge it a slightly kitschy theme park, but, in fact, the buildings are accurate full-size replicas of specific structures in the various regional styles of Spain. Nightclubs, discos, and restaurants take over in the evening; most stay open well into the early hours.

Marqués de Comillas, Montjuïc. © **93-325-7866.** Admission 7€ adults, 4.40€ seniors/students/children 7–14, free for ages 6 and under. Mon 9am–8pm; Tues–Thurs and Sun 9am–midnight; Fri–Sat 9am–4pm. Metro: Plaça de Espanya, then bus 61 or the free double-decker Poble Espanyol shuttle bus (on the half hour).

MORE MUSEUMS

Fundació Antoni Tàpies ✺ Housed in a *modernista* building designed by Lluís Domènech i Montaner and refurbished by his great-grandson in 1989, this museum continues the Barcelona tradition of honoring prominent native artists. Tàpies is thought by many to be the living heir to Miró and Picasso, and this exhibit space rotates examples of his work and that of younger Catalan artists. The tangle of tubing atop the building is a Tàpies sculpture that makes more sense when you realize it's called *Chair and Cloud*.

Aragó 255. © **93-487-0315.** Admission 4.50€ adults, 2.10€ seniors/students. Tues–Sun 10am–8pm. Metro: Passeig de Gràcia.

Museu Barbier-Mueller ✺ Dedicated by Queen Sofia in 1997, this collection contains 6,000 pieces of pre-Columbian sculpture. It contains religious, funerary, and ornamental objects of considerable variety, in stone and ceramics and, in some cases, jade. Richest are the exhibits relating to Mayan culture, with origins going back to 1000 B.C. Descriptions are in English.

Montcada 12–14. © 93-310-4516. Admission 3€ adult, 1.50€ seniors/students, free under age 16. Free to all 1st Sat of the month 3–6pm. Tues–Sat 10am–6pm; Sun and holidays 10am–3pm. Metro: Jaume I. Bus: 17, 39, 40, 45, or 51.

Museu Frederic Marés   This repository of medieval sculpture is located just behind the cathedral, with a pleasant shaded courtyard in front. Housed in an ancient palace that's impressive in its own right, it displays hundreds of polychrome ecclesiastical sculptures.

Plaça de Santa Iú 5–6. © 93-310-5800. Admission 3€ adults, 1.50€ students, free for children under 16. Free for all Wed 3–7pm and 1st Sun of month. Tues–Thurs 10am–5pm (until 7pm Wed); Fri–Sat 10am–7pm; Sun 10am–3pm. Metro: Jaume I. Bus: 17, 19, or 45.

Museu d'Historia de la Ciutat (Museum of the History of the City) ⭐ Housed in a 15th-century mansion that was moved here stone by stone from Carrer Mercaders, several blocks away, this museum features **excavations** ⭐ of Roman and Visigothic remains below ground. On the upper floors are jumbled assortments of sculptures, weapons, ceramics, household implements, and more—a sort of municipal attic.

Plaça del Rei. © 93-315-1111. Admission 3€ adult, 1.80€ seniors and ages 16–25, free under age 16. Free to all 1st Sat afternoon of the month. June–Sept Tues–Sat 10am–2pm and 4–8pm; Sun and holidays 10am–2pm (the rest of the year closes 2–4pm). Metro: Jaume I.

Museu Marítim (Maritime Museum) ⭐ Located in the Drassanes, the 14th-century Gothic royal shipyards, this museum's superb collection of maritime vessels and artifacts is distinguished by a full-size replica of Don Juan of Austria's galleon. The baroque flagship of the Spanish and Italian fleet defeated a naval force of the Ottoman Empire in the 1571 Battle of Lepanto. There are also humbler fishing boats, intricate ship models, and a map owned by Amerigo Vespucci.

Av. de les Drassanes. © 93-3301-1831. Admission 5.50€ adults, 2.70€ seniors and ages 8–15, free for ages 7 and under. Free for all 1st Sat each month 3–6pm. Daily 10am–7pm (to 6pm in winter). Metro: Drassanes. Bus: 14, 36, 57, or 59.

Museu Nacional d'Art de Catalunya ⭐ In this building—built for the 1929 World's Fair and redesigned inside by controversial Italian architect Gae Aulenti in the 1990s—is a collection of Catalan art from the Romanesque and Gothic periods as well as the 16th century to the 18th century, along with works by high-caliber non-Catalan artists like El Greco, Velázquez, Zurbarán, and Tintoretto. Pride of place goes to the sculptures and frescoes removed from the Romanesque churches strung across Catalunya's northern tier. The view of the city from the front steps is a bonus.

In the Palau Nacional, Parc de Montjuïc. © 93-622-0375. Admission to permanent collection 5.50€ adults, 3€ seniors/students; extra fee for special exhibits. Free for everyone 1st Thurs of the month. Tues–Sat 10am–7pm; Sun and holidays 10am–2:30pm. Metro: Espanya.

Museu d'Art Contemporàni ⭐ Much excitement attended the 1995 opening of this light-filled building by American architect Richard Meier. Standing in stark contrast to the 16th-century convent opposite and the surrounding tenements with laundry drying on their balconies, this museum has generated a renewal of the El Raval neighborhood. The permanent collection comprises

---

◆ Tips An Ancient Neighborhood to Explore

The **Barri Gótic** ✦✦ is Barcelona's old aristocratic quarter, parts of which
have survived from the Middle Ages, and fragments of which have lasted
from the Roman settlement here. To explore the Gothic Quarter's narrow
streets and squares, start walking up Carrer del Carme, east of La Rambla.
A nighttime stroll adds drama, but exercise caution. The buildings, for the
most part, are austere and sober, and the cathedral is the crowning
achievement. Roman ruins and the vestiges of 3rd-century walls add further interest. This area is packed full of details and attractions that are
easy to miss, so take your time.

---

about 1,300 paintings and sculptures from the late 1940s, including works by
many Catalan and Spanish artists and a few by non-Spaniards like Calder and
Dubuffet. To get here, walk 5 blocks west from the upper Rambla along Carrer
Bonsucces, which changes to Elisabets.

Plaça dels Angels 1. ✆ 93-412-0810. General admission 5.10€, 2.55€ on non-holiday Wed, 3.50€ for
temporary exhibits. Mon and Wed–Fri 11am–7:30pm; Sat 10am–8pm; Sun and holidays 10am–3pm. Metro:
Catalunya or Universitat.

Museu d'Art Modern Despite its name, this museum focuses somewhat nar-
rowly on the work of Catalan painters and sculptors during the *modernista*
period (1880–1930), along with examples of furniture and decorative arts by
craftspeople and designers of the time. Its importance has been markedly dimin-
ished by the Museu Nacional d'Art de Catalunya (see above), which has appro-
priated much of this museum's collection.

Plaça de les Armes, Parc de la Ciutadella. ✆ 93 319 5023. Admission 3C adults, 2.10C seniors/students,
free for children under 7. Free to all 1st Thurs of the month. Tues–Sat 10am–7pm; Sun and holidays
10am–2:30pm. Metro: Arc de Triomf.

PARKS & GARDENS

Parc Güell ✦, a fanciful park on the northern edge of Barcelona's inner core, is
much more than green space. Begun by Antoni Gaudí as an upper-crust real-
estate venture for his wealthy patron, Count Eusebi Güell, it was never completed. Only two houses were constructed, but Gaudí's whimsical creativity, seen
in soaring columns that impersonate trees and splendid winding benches of broken mosaics, is on abundant display. The city took over the property in 1926
and turned it into a public park. Don't miss the ceramic mosaic lizard at the
park's entrance stairway, the Hall of a Hundred Columns, and the panoramic
views from the plaza above.

The **Parc de la Ciutadella** ✦ occupies the former site of a detested 18th-
century citadel, some remnants of which remain. Here, you'll find the Museu
d'Art Modern, the Museu de Zoología, the Museu de Geología, the regional Parliament, the zoo, and an ornate fountain that's in small part the work of the
young Gaudí.

Another attraction, **Tibidabo** ✦, offers the best panoramic view of Barcelona.
A funicular takes you up 490m (1,600 ft.) to the summit. A retro amusement
park—with Ferris wheels and airplanes that spin over Barcelona—has been there
since the thirties. There's also a church in this carnival-like setting called Santa
Creu (Sacred Heart), plus bars and restaurants. Take the funicular uphill from
Plaça John Kennedy.

ORGANIZED TOURS

Take advantage of the bargain **Bus Turístic** ⚑. A single ticket permits unlimited travel on these buses, many of them open-topped double-deckers. Originating at Plaça de Catalunya, the red bus makes two circular sweeps. Highlights of the northern route are the Parc Güell, La Sagrada Família, the base of Tibidabo, and the Monestir de Pedralbes. The southern circuit makes stops on Montjuïc, at the Port Olímpic, and in the Barri Gòtic. Together, the buses make 24 stops, and you can get off and reboard as often as you please. The 6 to 10 buses in service run daily, about every 15 minutes in summer and every 30 minutes during the rest of the year, from 9am to 9:30pm. If you stay on the bus, without debarking, each tour takes about 3½ hours. An all-day ticket is 14€, and a ticket good for 2 consecutive days is 18€. Tickets for children ages 4 to 12 are 8€. You can buy tickets on the bus; they come with a guidebook in six languages, plus vouchers providing discounts on admission to attractions like the zoo and the Poble Espanyol. Multilingual guides/conductors announce stops and answer questions.

Children and adults enjoy **Las Golondrinas** (© **93-442-3106**), the 30-minute round-trip boat ride from the Portal de la Pau, near the Monument à Colom, to the lighthouse on the harbor breakwater and back. The mini-voyage offers close-up views of the maritime traffic and the skyline. While room has been made for pleasure craft, this is a working harbor, with tugs, cranes off-loading freighters, dry docks, and shipyards. The company also offers 2-hour cruises to the Olympic Port and back for 7.70€ adults, 5.40€ seniors and students, and 3.30€ children 4 to 10. Departures are at 11:30am, 1:15pm, and 4:30pm, with an extra dusk voyage at 6:15pm on Saturday, Sunday, and holidays.

THE SHOPPING SCENE

THE BEST SHOPPING STREETS

The main shopping street in Barcelona is **Passeig de Gràcia.** Stroll this street from the Avinguda Diagonal to the Plaça de Catalunya, and you'll pass some of Barcelona's most elegant boutiques.

In the **old quarter,** the principal shopping streets are La Rambla, Carrer del Pi, Carrer de la Palla, and Avinguda Portal de l'Angel. Moving north in the Eixample are Passeig de Catalunya, Passeig de Gràcia, and Rambla de Catalunya.

THE BEST BUYS

Adolfo Domínguez, Passeig de Gràcia 32 (© **93-487-4170**), "the Spanish Armani," offers suits in earth tones for both men and women that have a rather austere but very stylish look. One of the best showcases for Catalan fashion designers for women is **On Land,** Carrer Valencia 273 (© **93-215-5625**). For designer housewares and the best in Spanish contemporary furnishings, a good bet is **Vinçón,** Passeig de Gràcia 96 (© **93-215-6050**), housed in the former home of artist Ramón Casas.

In the city of Miró, Tàpies, and Picasso, art is a major business. There are dozens of galleries, especially in the Barri Gótic and around the Picasso Museum. In business since 1840, **Sala Parés,** Petritxol 5 (© **93-318-7020;** Metro: Plaça de Catalunya), displays paintings in a two-story amphitheater; exhibitions change about once a month. **Galeria Maeght,** Montcada 25 10 (© **93-310-4245;** Metro: Jaume I), occupies a mansion a few doors down from the Picasso Museum that's worth a visit for the architecture alone. Paintings, prints, and sculptures by Spanish and European artists are on view.

For antiques, drop by **El Bulevard des Antiquarius,** Passeig de Gràcia 55. This 70-unit complex, just off the city's most aristocratic avenues, has a huge collection of art and antiques assembled in a series of boutiques. Seekers after antiques should enjoy the open-air **Mercat Gòtic de Antigüedades** by the cathedral (Metro: Jaume I), held every Thursday from 9am to 8pm (except Aug), and more often during holiday periods.

El Corte Inglés is Spain's most prominent department store. Its main Barcelona emporium is at Plaça de Catalunya 14 (© **93-302-1212;** Metro: Catalunya), with a large new branch a block away on Portal de l'Angel and another at the top of La Rambla, in what was recently a Marks & Spencer outlet. It stays open through the siesta period and has a full-size supermarket in the basement and a pleasant cafeteria/restaurant on the ninth floor.

Seeking out small specialty shops is a particular treat. A number of shops offer authentic ceramics from various regions of the country that are known for their pottery. Two worthwhile stops are **La Caixa de Frang,** Carrer Freneria (no phone; Metro: Jaume I), behind the cathedral; and **Itaca,** Carrer Ferrán (© **93-301-3044;** Metro: Jaume I), near Plaça Sant Jaume.

Papier-mâché masks are featured at **Arlequí Màscares,** Princesa 7 (© **93-68-2752;** Metro: Jaume I), many in classical Venetian, kabuki, and Carnaval designs. They'll make one for you to order. Stop by on the way to the Picasso Museum. **La Manual Alpargatera,** Avinyo 7 (© **93-301-0172;** Metro: Jaume I), is the best shop for the handmade espadrilles seen on dancers of the *sardana.* It offers many styles and also sells hats and folk art.

Angel Jobal, Princesa 38 (no phone; Metro: Jaume I), offers a variety of teas and spices, along with especially good prices on thread saffron, the world's costliest spice. Find it a block past the turn for the Picasso Museum. **La Boquería,** Rambla 101, officially the Mercat de Sant Josep, is Spain's most extensive, most fascinating market, purveying glistening-fresh produce, meats, cheeses, fish, and every imaginable edible daily. An open market of artisan food items, including cheeses, honey, vinegars, patés, fruit preserves, and quince pastes, is held on **Plaça del Pi** (Metro: Liceu) on Friday, Saturday, and Sunday.

BARCELONA AFTER DARK

Barcelona's nightlife runs from the campy burlesque of El Molino to the bizarre opulence of the Palau de la Música Catalana. For the latest information on concerts and other musical events, call the **Amics de la Música de Barcelona** at © **93-302-6870,** Monday through Friday from 10am to 1pm and 3 to 8pm. For information on the **Ballet Contemporáneo de Barcelona,** call © **93-322-1037.**

For a comprehensive list of evening activities, pick up a copy of the weekly *Guía del Ocio* or the entertainment guide offered with the Thursday edition of *El País.*

THE PERFORMING ARTS

The **Gran Teatre del Liceu,** La Rambla 51–59 (© **93-485-9913;** www.liceu barcelona.com; Metro: Liceu), is the traditional home to opera and ballet. It suffered a devastating fire in 1994 but has reopened after extensive renovations. The result is glorious, especially considering that only the walls were left standing after the fire. The decision was made to replicate the neo-baroque interior, with lashings of gilt, intricate carvings, and swaths of brocade and velvet. Music lovers and ballet-goers will find more comfortable seats and better sightlines.

The theater presents 8 to 12 operatic productions every season and strives to make them accessible to a wide audience: Prices are as low as 9€ for operas and about 6€ for concerts, some ballets, and recitals. You can book tickets with credit cards from outside the country daily from 9am to 9pm Barcelona time at ℂ 34-93-417-0060. In Barcelona, call ℂ 90-233-2211 any time up to 3 hours before the performance you want to see.

A magnificent *modernista* concert hall, the **Palau de la Música Catalana,** Amadeu Vives 1 (ℂ **93-268-1000;** www.palaumusica.org; Metro: Urquinaona), is the work of Catalan architect Lluís Domènech i Montaner, a rival of Antoni Gaudí. Its distinctive facade is a tour de force of brick, mosaic, and glass. Inside, the interplay of ceramic mosaics, stained glass, and a central skylight build to the stunning crescendo of massive carvings framing the stage. Many of the seats have limited sightlines, but this hall is devoted to music, not opera and dance, and even the cheapest corners enjoy superb sound. The Palau is home to the Orquestra Simfònica de Barcelona, one of whose directors is American Lawrence Foster, and hosts a variety of classical and jazz concerts and recitals. Tickets generally cost 5€ to 75€; the box office is open daily from 10am to 9pm. There are tours of the theater daily, some in English; tickets cost 7€.

Symphonic and chamber music has a new home at **L'Auditori,** Lepant 150 (ℂ **93-247-9300;** www.auditori.com; Metro: Glories), with both large and small performance spaces. The Barcelona Symphony Orchestra, traveling groups, the Joven Orquestra de España (Young Orchestra of Spain), and string quartets all perform here. Tickets are 15€ to 40€, half price for students. You can buy them outside the country with a credit card 24 hours a day at ℂ **34-93-479-9920** or inside Spain at ℂ **90-210-1212.**

LIVE-MUSIC CLUBS

Enjoying great popularity of late, the subterranean **Jamboree,** Plaça Reial 17 (ℂ **93-301-7564;** Metro: Liceu), is on a raucously diverse plaza off the lower Rambla. After paying 6€ to 12€, which includes the first drink, you descend to a vaulted brick cellar filled with young to middle-aged natives and tourists. The early show, usually around 10pm, often features a soloist on piano or guitar, while the later set can be hip-hop, fusion jazz, reggae, or soul with a band. Arrive around 9:30pm and you'll probably get in free and might also catch the rehearsal.

A popular old-timer is the **Harlem Jazz Club,** Comtessa de Sobradiel 8 (ℂ **93-310-0755**), with live jazz nightly in all its permutations—flamenco fusion, Brazilian salsa, Afro-Caribbean, blues. Admission is free during the week, but costs 5€ on Friday, Saturday, and holidays.

A reliable venue for top-drawer jazz performers, **La Cova del Drac,** Vallmajor 33 (ℂ **93-200-7032;** Metro: Muntaner or La Bonanova), is in a less intimidating neighborhood than most, with many other fun spots on nearby blocks. There's dancing here too. It's open daily from 8pm to 3am, with a cover of between 6€ and 12€, including the first drink.

Flamenco is best seen in Seville or Madrid, but if you aren't getting to those cities on your trip, **El Tablao de Carmen,** Arcs 9 (ℂ **93-325-6895**), is the best place in Barcelona to see the passionate dance and music of Andalucía. Admission is 50€ for dinner and the first show or 27€ for the first show and a drink. Dinner begins at 9pm; the first show is at 10:30pm, the second at 1am. Closed Monday.

DANCE CLUBS

In the basement of a shopping center, **Bikini,** Deu i Mata 105 (© **93-322-0005;** Metro: Les Corts), covers the bases in a comprehensive entertainment compound that offers up multiple venues for dancing to music of every genre (including funk, rock, and oldies music). There's a separate room for salsa and a large area where fans applaud wildly for their favorite band of the minute. The club is open Tuesday through Thursday from 7pm to 4:30am, Friday and Saturday from 7pm to 6am. Cover is 9€ to 18€.

Up and Down, Numancia Diagonal 179 (© **93-205-5194;** Metro: María Cristina), attracts the elite of Barcelona, spanning a couple of generations. The mature black-tie, post-opera crowd heads for the upstairs section, leaving the downstairs to the thumping rock meant for their children. In business for many years, Up and Down continues to polish its reputation as the most cosmopolitan club in town. Technically, it is members only and you can be turned away at the door, so dress well and be nice to the doormen. The club is open Tuesday through Saturday from midnight to anytime between 5am and 6:30am, depending on business. Cover is 9€ to 16€, including your first drink.

Conjure up an abandoned county jail or a two-story parking garage in the South Bronx and you'll have **Otto Zutz,** Lincoln 15 (© **93-238-0722;** Metro: Plaça Molina). Go early to avoid the restrictive entrance policy. There are eight bars, there's dancing everywhere, and there's live rock on Wednesday night. The club is open Tuesday through Saturday from midnight to 4am or later, with a 15€ cover that includes a drink.

BARS & COCTELERIAS

Over in **Poble Nou,** near the Parc de la Ciutadella, the two skyscrapers marking the location of the former Olympic Port also point the way to the site of a frenetic bar scene. The artificial harbor that was the launch point for the Olympic sailing competition is now lined on three sides with over 200 bars and cafes that pound on till dawn. This is one of the safest nightlife districts.

Otherwise, you might start your evening at the **Bar Hivernacle,** Parc de la Ciutadella (© **932-95-4017;** Metro: Arco del Triunfo), a wine tavern that lures a young, hip crowd to a setting of towering palms in a 19th-century greenhouse, just inside the gates of the city's most centrally located park. A restaurant adjoins it. The bar is open Monday through Saturday from 10am to midnight and Sunday from 10am to 4pm.

Located in a *modernista* building, chummy **Velvet,** Balmes 161 (© **93-217-6714;** Metro: Diagonal), has a dance floor and two bars lined with buttocks-shaped stools. Don't miss the bathrooms. The music is mostly retro British and American rock, older than most of the patrons. It's open daily from 7pm to 5am, with no cover.

An exceptional retreat that eclipses all the rest for elegance and panache is the **Palau Dalmases,** Montcada 20 (© **93-310-0673;** Metro: Jaume I), a 16th-century mansion a few doors down from the Picasso Museum. The multiple archways and ancient stone walls are hung with large copies of florid baroque paintings, and candles are lit on the marble-topped tables. Vivaldi and Bach provide the stereo underscore for murmured confidences and romantic intimacies. It's open Tuesday through Friday from 8pm to 2am and Saturday from 6 to 10pm; opera singers perform Thursday at 11pm. On those nights, the cover (including a drink) is 18€. No food is served.

GAY & LESBIAN BARS

Gays have a number of beguiling bars and dance clubs to choose from, but lesbians have very few. For the latest on the scene, log on to **www.gaybarcelona. net**. It's in Spanish, but it's not too difficult to decipher. Ads and listings in such weekly guides as *Guía del Ocio* referring to *el ambiente* nearly always mean places with a mostly or totally gay clientele.

Santanassa, Aribau 27 (no phone; Metro: Universidad), is a staple on the gay nightlife circuit, boasting a bar and dance floor along with provocative art. The percentage of gay women in the clientele has greatly increased in recent years. It's open nightly from 11pm to 3am. Cover is 6€, including your first drink, only on Friday and Saturday nights.

Upfront about its orientation, the **Dietrich Gay Teatro Cafe,** Consell de Cent 255 (© 93-451-7707; Metro: Universitat or Urgüell), is one of the more long-lived music bars, with dancing and a long black bar leading into a lounge area where friends can chat.

DAY TRIPS FROM BARCELONA

SITGES ℛ   The most frequented resort of the Costa Dorada, Sitges is packed in summer, mostly with affluent young northern Europeans, many of them gay. For years, the resort, 40km (25 miles) south of Barcelona, was patronized largely by middle-class industrialists from Barcelona, but those rather staid days have gone. Sitges is as lively today as Benidorm and Torremolinos in the south, but it's nowhere near as tacky. By mid-October it goes into hibernation, but its scenic charms and museums may be motive enough for a winter visit. Things pick up with Carnaval in February, a riotously turbulent event with costumed revelers partying for days.

Long known as a city of culture, thanks in part to resident artist/playwright/Bohemian mystic Santiago Rusinyol, this was the birthplace of the 19th-century *modernista* movement. The town remained a scene of artistic encounters and demonstrations long after *modernisme,* the Catalan form of Art Nouveau, waned. Salvador Dalí and the poet Federico García Lorca were regular visitors.

Getting There   RENFE (© 90-224-0202; www.renfe.es) runs trains from Barcelona-Sants or Passeig de Gràcia to Sitges. From 5:45am to 10pm daily, there's a train at the rate of one every 10 to 15 minutes (trip time: 40 min.). A typical round-trip fare is 5€, with variations depending upon day of the week and other factors.

Sitges is a 45-minute drive from Barcelona along C-246, a coastal road. An express highway, A-7, opened in 1991. The coastal road is more scenic, but it can be extremely slow on summer weekends, as all of Barcelona heads for the beaches.

Visitor Information   The **tourist information office** is at Carrer Sínis Morera 1 (© 93-894-4251; www.sitgestur.com). It's open June through September 15, daily from 9am to 9pm; September 16 through May, Monday through Friday from 9am to 2pm and 4 to 6:30pm, and Saturday from 10am to 1pm.

Exploring Sitges   It's the **beaches** that attract most visitors. They have showers and changing facilities, and kiosks rent such items as motorboats and floating air cushions. Beaches on the eastern end and those inside the town center are the most peaceful, including **Aiguadoiç** and **Els Balomins. Playa San Sebastián, Fragata Beach,** and "**Beach of the Boats**" (under the church and next to the yacht club) are the area's family beaches. Most young people go to the **Playa de la Ribera,** in the west. The main gay beach is the **Playa del Mort.**

Beaches aside, Sitges has a couple of interesting museums. The **Museu Cau Ferrat,** Fonollar s/n (© **93-894-0364**), is the legacy of wealthy Catalan painter Santiago Rusinyol, a leading light of Belle Epoque Barcelona. His 19th-century house, fashioned of two 16th-century fishermen's homes, not only contains a collection of his works, but also several pieces by Picasso and El Greco, much ornate wrought iron (a Catalan specialty), folk art, and archaeological finds.

Next door is the **Museu Maricel de Mar,** Fonollar s/n (© **93-894-0364**), the legacy of Dr. Pérez Rosales, whose impressive accumulation of furniture, porcelain, and tapestries draws largely from the medieval, Renaissance, and baroque periods. Both museums are open Tuesday through Sunday from 9:30am to 2pm and 4 to 6pm. Admission to each is 3€.

MONTSERRAT ✦ The vast **Montserrat Monastery** complex, 51.5km (32 miles) northwest of Barcelona, contains a basilica with a venerated Black Virgin, an art museum, hotels, restaurants, and an excess of souvenir shops and food stalls. One of the most important pilgrimage spots in Spain, it's a good place to avoid on weekends.

Getting There   The least expensive transport from Barcelona is the train from Plaça de Espanya. It leaves five times daily for the Aeri de Montserrat station, where a funicular carries passengers up to the complex. Combination tickets that include round-trip Metro and train rides and unlimited funicular and cable car rides, as well as admission to the museum and lunch at the cafeteria, are sold at the site for 32€. For information contact **FGC** (© **93-205-1515;** www.fgc. catalunya.net).

Motorists can take N-2 southwest of Barcelona toward Tarragona, turning west at the junction with N-11. The signposts and exit to Montserrat will be on your right. From the main road, it's 14km (9 miles) to the monastery through dramatic scenery with eerie rock formations.

Visitor Information   The **tourist office** is at Plaça de la Creu (© **93-877-7777**), open daily from 10am to 6pm.

Exploring Montserrat   The monastery—a 19th-century structure that replaced a former monastery leveled by Napóleon's army in 1812—is 730m (2,400 ft.) up Montserrat. Its name, Montserrat, refers to the serrated peaks of the mountain, bulbous elongated formations that provided shelter for 11th-century Benedictine monks. One of the noted institutions of the monastery is the 50-voice **Boys' Choir** ✦, begun in the 13th century. The boys sing at 1 and 6:45pm. Their performances are thrilling to the faithful and curious alike and are the best reason for a visit. Admission is free.

Second on that list is the newly constituted subterranean **Museu de Montserrat** (© **93-877-7777**), near the entrance to the basilica. It brings together artworks that were once scattered around the complex, including gold and silver liturgical objects, archaeological artifacts from the Holy Land, and paintings from both the Renaissance and the 20th century. Numerous funiculars and paths lead to **hermitages** and **shrines** higher up the mountain.

Thousands travel here every year to see and touch the 12th-century statue of **La Moreneta (The Black Virgin),** the patron saint of Catalunya. To view the statue, enter the church through a side door to the right. The museum is open Monday through Friday from 9:30am to 6pm; Saturday and Sunday from 9:30am to 6:30pm. Admission is 3.60€ adults, 1.80€ children and students.

3 Andalucía & the Costa del Sol

Eight provinces constitute the region of Andalucía, which occupies the bottom of the Iberian Peninsula. In 711, a coalition of fierce North African desert tribes swept across the Straits of Gibraltar with a plan to move on to Paris in mere decades before they were stopped. It took over 700 years for generations of Catholic monarchs to push back the occupiers, culminating in the capture of the last Moorish stronghold by Queen Isabel and King Fernando in 1492.

Islamic Spain is still profoundly apparent in Andalucía, which contains some of the country's most celebrated architectural treasures: the Mezquita (mosque) in Córdoba, the Alhambra in Granada, and the great Gothic cathedral in Seville. This is also the land of the famed *pueblos blancos* ("white villages") and undulating olive groves that roll over tawny hillsides to the skirts of impressive mountain ranges. Give Andalucía a week and you'll still have only skimmed the surface of its many offerings.

Andalucía also embraces the Costa del Sol (Sun Coast), Spain's most noted and visited—inundated—strip of beach resorts. (Málaga, Marbella, and Torremolinos are covered here.) Go to the Costa del Sol for golf, tennis, watersports, after-dark partying, and relaxation, but save some days for the folklore, history, and architectural wonders of the major Andalucían cities.

The mild winter climate and almost-guaranteed sunshine in summer have made the Costa del Sol a year-round attraction. It begins at the western frontier harbor city of Algeciras and stretches east to the port city of Almería. Sandwiched between these points is a rugged coastline backed by the Sierra Nevada. The beaches are no better than poor-to-fair, it should be said, but there are sandy coves, whitewashed houses, olive and almond trees, phalanxes of new apartment houses, fishing boats, a couple of dozen world-class golf courses, souvenir stands, fast-food outlets catering to the tastes of every national group, and widely varied flora and fauna—both human and vegetable. From June to October the coast is mobbed, so make sure that you've nailed down a reservation.

SEVILLE 🏵🏵🏵

Seville is justly celebrated for its mythic romance and shimmering beauty. It is 550km (341 miles) southwest of Madrid and 217km (135 miles) northwest of Málaga. In spite of the sultry (many say oppressive) heat in summer and the city's undeniable problems, such as intractable unemployment and street crime, it remains one of the most beguiling of the Spanish cities. This is the city that gave life, real or imagined, to Don Juan, Carmen, and that wily barber, Figaro—aided by Mozart, Bizet, and Rossini. If there will be only one chance in a lifetime to see Spain, Seville must be an obligatory stop. Unlike most Spanish cities, it has fared well under most of its conquerors—the Romans, Arabs, and Christians—in part because its people chose to embrace them rather than fight them. When Cristóbal Colón—Christopher Columbus—docked here with news of his first voyage into the unknown, Spain entered its 16th-century Golden Age. For decades after, the treasure galleons from the New World emptied their cargos here. That heritage is evident in every street and *barrio* of the historic center.

ESSENTIALS

GETTING THERE   By Plane   Iberia flies several times a day from Madrid and Barcelona to the **Aeropuerto de Sevilla,** Calle Almirante Lobo (© **95-467-2981;** www.aena.es), 10km (6 miles) north of the center of Seville. A bus,

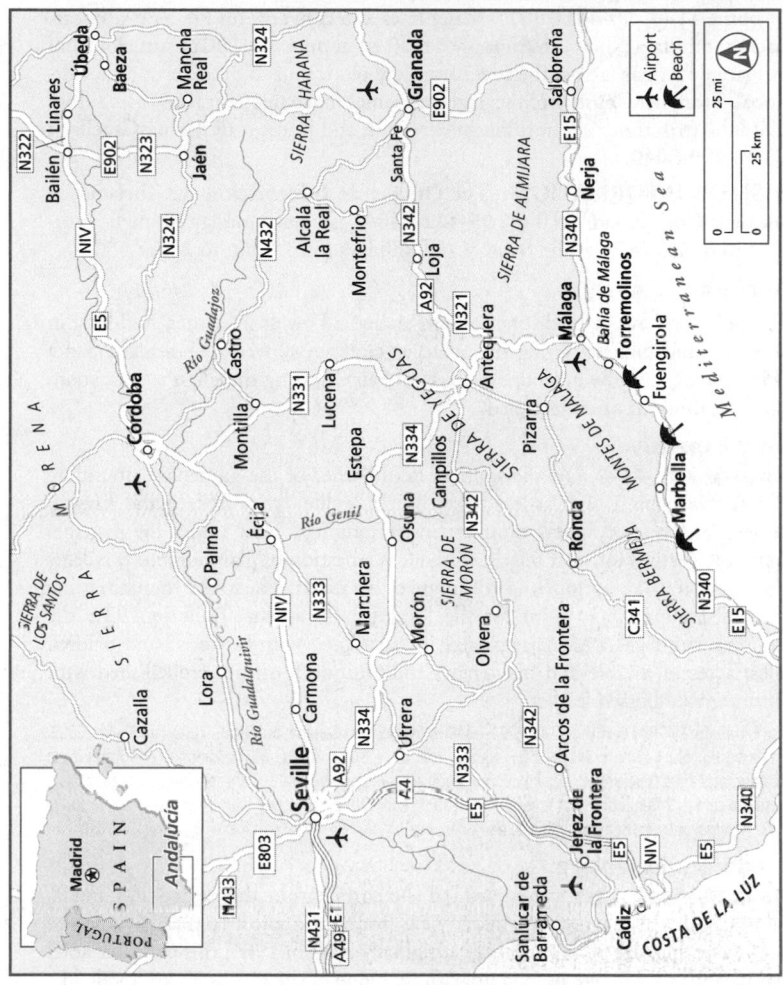

identified by the sign AE *(Aeropuerto),* runs at frequent intervals between the airport, the bus station, and points within the city center.

By Train   Train service into Sevilla is now centralized at the 10-year-old **Estación Santa Justa,** Avenida Kansas City (℗ **90-224-0202;** www.renfe.es for information and reservations). Buses C1 and C2 travel between the railway station and the town's bus station at Prado de San Sebastian. The high-speed AVE train between Madrid and Seville charges 53€ to 111€ each way, subject to frequent change and depending on class and the days and hours of travel (trip time: 2½ hr.). It makes 14 cross-country runs a day, with a stop in Córdoba. Between Seville and Córdoba, the AVE train takes 40 minutes, the *talgo* train 1½ hours, and conventional trains, which charge 6.80€ each way, about 2 hours, with many stops en route.

By Bus   Most buses arrive and depart from the city's largest **bus terminal,** on the southeast edge of the old city, at Prado dc San Sebastián, Calle José María

Osborne 11 (© 95-441-7111). Many lines also converge on Plaza de la Encarnación, on Plaza Nueva, in front of the cathedral on Avenida Constitución, and at Plaza de Armas (across the street from the old train station, Estación de Córdoba). From here, buses from several companies make frequent runs to and from Córdoba (trip time: 2½ hr.). For information and prices, call **Alsina Graells** at © 95-490-8040.

VISITOR INFORMATION　The **Oficina de Información del Turismo,** at Av. de la Constitución 21B (© 95-422-1404), is open Monday through Saturday from 9am to 7pm and Sunday and holidays from 10am to 2pm.

WHERE TO STAY

Seville hotels have three distinct pricing periods: Lowest in winter, middling in summer, and highest during the adjacent celebratory weeks of Semana Santa (Holy Week) and the Fería de Abril (April Fair). During these last events, room rates are doubled or even tripled.

Very Expensive

Alfonso XIII ⭐⭐⭐　At the southwestern corner of the gardens surrounding the Alcázar, this is a near-legendary hotel, Seville's *gran lujo* (grand luxury) address and one of Spain's most expensive lodgings. Now under the management of Westin Hotels, it reigns supreme as a bastion of glamour and privilege, the site of royal receptions and corporate celebrations. The lobby fountain is the cocktail-hour rallying point for the local Establishment. Built in 1929, the building simulates a Mudéjar palace, its halls lined with lustrous hand-painted tiles, acres of marble and mahogany, and antique furniture embellished with intricately embossed leather.

San Fernando 2, 41004 Sevilla. © 800/221-2340 in the U.S. and Canada, or 95-491-7000. Fax 95-491-7099. www.westin.com. 147units. 342€–360€ double; from 621€ suite. AE, DC, MC, V. Parking 18€. **Amenities:** Restaurant; 2 bars (1 seasonal); heated outdoor pool; access to nearby health club; concierge; car-rental desk; business center; 24-hr. room service; in-room massage; babysitting; same-day laundry/dry cleaning. *In room:* A/C, TV w/pay movies, dataport, minibar, hair dryer, safe

Moderate/Expensive

Doña María ⭐　Its location around the corner from the cathedral, Giralda, and the Alcázar creates a dramatic view from the rooftop terrace (where the postage-stamp-size pool is located). Originally built in 1969, this compact hotel has recently undergone needed upgrading. None of the rooms looks exactly like any other, but the decor favors elaborate headboards and some four-poster beds combined with provincial furniture and flowered patterns. Some rooms are rather small.

Don Remondo 19, 41004 Sevilla. © 95-422-4990. Fax 95-421-9546. www.hdmaria.com. 69 units. 96€–176€ double. AE, DC, MC, V. Parking 12€. **Amenities:** Restaurant; bar; unheated rooftop pool; concierge; limited room service; babysitting; same-day laundry/dry cleaning. *In room:* A/C, TV, minibar, hair dryer, safe.

Inglaterra ⭐　Opened in 1857 and updated countless times since, this respectable and rather staid hotel is on a central plaza within a 10-minute walk of the cathedral and the Barrio Santa Cruz. Rooms still have old-fashioned touches of Iberian gentility; the best are on the fifth floor. The dining room overlooks the plaza. A wheezing English taxi stands out front as the symbol of the hotel ("Inglaterra" means "England").

Plaza Nueva 7, 41001 Sevilla. © 95-422-4970. Fax 95-456-1336. www.hotelinglaterra.es. 116 units. 111€–168€ double. AE, DC, MC, V. Parking 9€. **Amenities:** Restaurant; bar; limited room service; babysitting; laundry/dry cleaning. *In room:* A/C, TV, minibar, hair dryer, safe.

Seville

ATTRACTIONS ●

Alcázar **11**
Barrio de Santa Cruz **8**
Catedral **5**
La Giralda **4**
Museo de Bellas Artes
  de Sevilla **1**
Parque María Luisa **13**

ACCOMMODATIONS ■

Alfonso XIII **12**
Amadeus **10**
Doña María **6**
Hosteria del Laurel **7**
Inglaterra **2**
Las Casas de la Judería **9**
Las Casas de los
  Mercaderes **3**

Las Casas de la Judería 𝒜𝒜   Long on charm, short on modernity, this is Old Seville with a vengeance. Expect neither voice mail nor Internet connections. The hotel is constituted of a connected row of noble 16th-century residences, and the exteriors, up a cobblestone lane from a discreet archway, hint at Seville's Moorish past, as do the interior patios and splashing fountains. Some suites have saunas and whirlpools. The genteel staff, many of whom speak English, provides alert but understated attention. A new restaurant has been added, and a piano is now played during the evenings in the lounge. Except during the holidays, you should be able to haggle reductions in the rates below.

Callejón de Dos Hermanas 7 (off Plaza Santa María la Blanca), 41004 Sevilla. ℭ **95-441-5150.** Fax 95-442-2170. www.casasypalacios.com. 57 units. 124€–346€ double; 175€–199€ suite. AE, DC, DISC, MC, V. **Amenities:** Restaurant; bar; 24-hr. room service; same-day laundry/dry cleaning. *In room:* A/C, TV, minibar, hair dryer, safe.

Las Casas de los Mercaderes 𝒜𝒜   Under the same ownership as Las Casas de la Judería (above) and demonstrating a similar sensibility, this recently converted mansion has a far better location than its older sibling. It's right in the middle of things, with many of the best shops and department stores within 2 or 3 blocks and every major sight within walking distance. The grand lobby leads to an 18th-century inner court with a stained-glass skylight. Rooms are larger than usual, with carpeting, a small desk, and an easy chair or two.

Alvarez Quintero 9–13 (1 block south of Plaza del Salvador), 41004 Sevilla. ℭ **95-422-5858.** Fax 95-422-9884. www.casasypalacios.com. 47 units. 123€–200€ double. AE, DC, MC, V. **Amenities:** Cafe/bar; 24-hr. room service; same-day laundry/dry cleaning. *In room:* A/C, TV, minibar (some rooms), hair dryer, safe.

Inexpensive

Amadeus 𝒜 *Finds*   Charm and economy rarely apply to the same place in Spain. Here's an exception—a delightful retreat at the quiet edge of this often raucous *barrio*. The reason for the hotel's name and for its popularity with musicians after only a few months of operation is that it's owned and operated by a family of music-lovers, both performers and enthusiasts. It was a private home and retains that feeling, in no small part due to the warm reception. Music is always present, on the stereo and the three pianos; visiting musicians can reserve one of the soundproofed rooms for practice. The hotel is fetchingly decorated with antiques and family pieces; some rooms have Jacuzzis.

Calle Farnesio 6 (1 block east of Calle Mateos Gago), 41004 Sevilla. ℭ **95-450-1443.** Fax 95-450-0019. www.hotelamadeussevilla.com. 14 units. 72€–120€ double. *In room:* A/C, TV, dataport, minibar, hair dryer, safe.

Hosteria del Laurel 𝒜𝒜   Touristy, yes; trashy, absolutely not. Sooner rather than later, every visitor comes upon this atmospheric restaurant in the Barrio's heart, with squat little tables beside the orange trees in the plaza. Most are unaware that there's also a spiffy little hotel behind the tavern. Rooms are immaculate and of decent size, although the marble floors amplify the noise of late-night comings and goings. Tapas in the bar go for under 4€ and *raciónes* up to 14€; main dishes in the charming dining room are 11€ to 21€.

Plaza de los Venerables 5, 41004 Sevilla. ℭ **95-422-0295.** Fax 95-421-0450. www.sol.com/host_laurel. 21 units. 57€–84€ double. AE, DC, MC, V. **Amenities:** Restaurant; bar; 24-hr. room service; laundry service. *In room:* A/C, TV, hair dryer.

WHERE TO DINE
Very Expensive

Egaña Oriza 𝒜 *Overrated* BASQUE/INTERNATIONAL   Seville's most honored restaurant occupies a mansion built for the 1929 Ibero-Americana Exposition. It is a large vaulted space, with fabric panels to regulate the sun through the skylight. The menu features game, which is rare in this region devoted to seafood. Service by the young staff is attentive, the meal proceeds smoothly, and the mood is serenity itself. The problem lies with a kitchen that isn't keeping up, and it's difficult to avoid the impression that its leaders are mired in the 1980s. Make no mistake: This is a capable restaurant, fine for an evening when food isn't to be the main event. But when dinner for two can slip past $200, it should be better.

San Fernando 41. ✆ **95-422-7254.** Reservations advised. Main courses 16€–27€. AE, DC, MC, V. Restaurant Mon–Fri 1:30–4pm and 9pm–midnight; Sat 9–11:30pm. Bar daily 9pm–midnight. Closed Aug.

Moderate/Expensive

Casa Robles ☆ REGIONAL   With a row of outdoor tables, a busy bar, and a formal upstairs dining room, this restaurant covers most bases, in a setting that retains touches of old-fashioned formality. While the menu remains somewhat conservative, some surprisingly creative dishes are peppered throughout, most of them full of flavor and well prepared. Among these are *lubina con naranjas* (sea bass with Sevillana oranges); a suprême of hake garnished with clams, shrimp, and strips of Serrano ham; and filet of beef layered with foie gras. From time to time, you might even find *ortiguillas*—sea anemones.

Calle Alvarez Quintero 58. ✆ **95-421-3150.** Reservations recommended. Main courses 9€–19€; fixed-price menu 33€. AE, DC, MC, V. Daily 1–4:30pm and 8:30pm–1am.

Enrique Becerra ☆ REGIONAL   Off Plaza Nueva near the cathedral, this restaurant has flourished since 1979 and just might provide one of your best meals in Seville. A popular tapas bar occupies the front, with a daily menu of over 25 possibilities, most of them notches above the usual renditions and only about 2€. The dining rooms upstairs and at the ground level are intimate settings made warmer by the friendly welcome. It's as good a place as any for your first taste of gazpacho and icy sangria. Specialties include roast lamb stuffed with spinach, honey, and pine nuts; rockfish cooked in Amontillado sherry; and oxtail braised in red wine. Many vegetarian dishes are also featured.

Gamazo 2. ✆ **95-421-3049.** Reservations recommended. Main courses 14€–17€. AE, DC, MC, V. Mon–Sat 1–4:30pm and 8pm–midnight.

La Albahaca BASQUE/SPANISH   On a corner of an attractive square in the Barrio de Santa Cruz, this elegant little manse dates from 1929 but looks much older. The high ceilings, many antiques and paintings, and extensive use of *azulejos* make it one of the most idyllic dining settings in Seville. In concert with the ministrations of the creative young Basque chef, this makes a most desirable place for a farewell dinner or an amorous proposal. The menu is adjusted seasonally, but look for such intriguing dishes as vegetables *escabeche* with oysters, or pork loin roasted with pear and vanilla sauce. The service is discreet. At the least, stop for a drink in the intimate snuggery.

Plaza de Santa Cruz 12. ✆ **95-422-0714.** Main courses 17€–21€; *menú del día* 27€. AE, DC, MC, V. Mon–Sat noon–4pm and 8pm–midnight.

EXPLORING SEVILLE

Alcázar ☆☆☆   This magnificent 14th-century Mudéjar palace was built by Pedro the Cruel after the re-conquest of the city from the Moors. From the Dolls' Court to the Maidens' Court through the domed Ambassadors' Room, it contains some of the finest work of Sevillian artisans, most of them descendants of the former occupants of the palace. In many ways, it evokes the Alhambra at Granada. Isabel and Fernando, who at one time lived in the Alcázar, welcomed

Moments Splendid Strolls

What was once a ghetto for Spanish Jews, who were forced out of Spain in the 15th century in the wake of the Inquisition, the **Barrio de Santa Cruz** 𝘳𝘳𝘳 today is Seville's most colorful district. Near the old walls of the Alcázar, winding medieval streets with names like *Vida* (Life) and *Muerte* (Death) open onto pocket plazas. Balconies with draping bougainvillea and potted geraniums jut out over this labyrinth, and through numerous wrought-iron gates, you can glimpse tile-lined patios filled with fountains and plants. To enter the Barrio Santa Cruz, turn right after leaving the Patio de Banderas exit of the Alcázar. Turn right again at Plaza de la Alianza and go down Calle Rodrigo Caro to Plaza de Doña Elvira. Use caution when strolling through the area, particularly at night.

About a 7-minute walk northeast of the cathedral on the northern edge of the Barrio de Santa Cruz is the **Casa de Pilatos** 𝘳, Plaza Pilatos 1 (℃ **954/225-298**). This 16th-century palace of the dukes of Medinaceli recaptures the splendors of the past, combining Gothic, Mudéjar, and Plateresque styles in its courtyards, fountains, and salons. Don't miss the two old carriages or the rooms filled with Greek and Roman statues. Admission to the museum upstairs is 5€; to the patios and gardens only, 2.50€. The museum and gardens are open daily from 9am to 7pm.

Parque María Luisa 𝘳𝘳, dedicated to María Luisa, sister of Isabel II, was once the grounds of the Palacio de San Telmo, Avenida de Roma. The former private royal park later became the site of the 1929 Ibero-Americana exposition, for which the vast Plaza de España was created. Running south along the Guadalquivir River, the park attracts those who want to take boat rides, walk along paths bordered by flowers, jog, or go bicycling. The most romantic way to traverse it is by rented horse and carriage, but this can be expensive, depending on your negotiation with the driver. Exercise caution while walking through this otherwise delightful park, as many muggings have been reported.

Columbus here on his return from America. On the top floor, the Oratory of the Catholic Monarchs has a fine altar in polychrome tiles made by Pisano in 1504.

Plaza del Triunfo. ℃ 95-450-2323. Entrance is north of the cathedral. Admission 5€. Free for seniors, students, and children under 13. Apr–Sept Tues–Sat 9:30am–7pm, Sun 9:30am–1:30pm; Oct–Mar Tues–Sat 9:30am–5pm, Sun 9:30am–1:30pm.

Catedral 𝘳𝘳𝘳 Alleged to be the largest Gothic building in the world, Seville's cathedral was designed by builders with a stated goal—that "those who come after us will take us for madmen." Construction began in the late 1400s and took centuries to complete. Built on the site of an ancient mosque, the cathedral claims to contain the remains of Columbus, with his tomb mounted on four statues. That claim is in doubt, but it's fairly certain his son Fernando is buried here. Works of art abound, most immediately evident in the side chapels, the 75 stained-glass windows, and the elaborate choir stalls, and also including paintings by Murillo, Goya, and Zubarán. On the north side you'll find the fresh citrus scents and chirping birds of the Patio of Orange Trees, a relic of the original mosque, as is the Giralda (below).

Plaza del Triunfo, Av. de la Constitución. © 95-421-4971. Admission including La Giralda 6€ adults, 1.50€ seniors/students, free for children under 13. Free for all Sun. Mon–Sat 11am–5pm; Sun 2:30–6pm.

La Giralda ★★★   Just as Big Ben symbolizes London, La Giralda evokes Seville. This square-sided, 98m (322-ft.) bell tower, next to the cathedral, is the city's most famous monument. It began as a minaret for the mosque, progressing from the austere stonework of the fundamentalist Almohad Dynasty to the decorative brick patterns and pointed arches of their less rigid successors, and culminating in the florid Renaissance-influenced upper floors added by the Catholic bishops. Determined visitors can take the 35 ramps inside up to a **viewing platform** ★★★ at the 70m (230-ft.) level. Make it to the top and you'll have an unsurpassed vista of the city.

Plaza del Triunfo. Entrance through the cathedral (admission is included with cathedral).

Museo de Bellas Artes de Sevilla ★★   A lovely old convent off Calle de Alfonso XII, this museum houses an important Spanish art collection. Some art experts claim that after the two leading art museums of Madrid, this is the most valuable and significant repository of art in Spain. A whole gallery is devoted to two paintings by El Greco, and works by Zurbarán are also exhibited; however, the devoutly religious paintings of the Seville-born Murillo outnumber all the others. An entire wing is given over to macabre paintings by the 17th-century artist Valdés-Leál. The top floor, which displays modern paintings, is less interesting.

Plaza del Museo 9. © 95-422-1829. Admission 1.50€ adults, free for students. Tues 3–8pm; Wed–Sat 9am–8pm; Sun 9am–2pm. Bus: 21, 24, 30, or 31.

SHOPPING

Close to Seville's town hall, **Ceramics Martian,** Sierpes 74 (© 95-421-3413), sells a wide array of painted tiles and ceramics, all made in or near Seville. Many pieces reproduce traditional patterns of Andalucía. Near the cathedral, **El Postigo,** Arfe s/n (© 95-456-0013), contains one of the biggest selections of Andalucían ceramics in town. Some of the pieces are much too big to fit into your suitcase; others—especially the hand-painted tiles and plates—make attractive souvenirs that can be packed in your luggage.

Casa Rubio, Sierpes 56 (© 95-422-6872), stocks a large collection of fans and castanets that range from the austere to the dramatic to some of the most florid and fanciful aids to coquetry available in Spain.

SEVILLE AFTER DARK

In the 1990s, Seville finally got its own opera house, **Teatro de la Maestranza,** Núñez de Balboa (© 95-422-65-73), which quickly became a premier venue for world-class operatic performances. Jazz, classical music, and the quintessentially Spanish *zarzuelas* (operettas) are also performed here. The opera house can't be visited except during performances. The box office is open daily from 11am to 2pm and 5 to 8pm. Tickets vary in cost depending on the performance.

Any other time, head for the Barrio de Santa Cruz to the flamboyant **El Tamboril,** Plaza de Santa Cruz 15 (no phone). In a room to the right of the eccentrically decorated bar, guitarists and singers assemble informally most nights, and patrons take to the dance floor to perform the *rumba* and *sevillanas,* a dance related to flamenco, as well as improvisations thereon. The doors open at 10pm and things start heating up by midnight. Get there well before midnight to have hope of a seat. There's no cover.

La Carbonería, Leviés 18 (© **95-421-4460**), is a curious place. The vestibule looks like the entry hall of a grand but decaying farmhouse in the mountains, with a fireplace to ward off winter chills. Beyond that is a space with tables on a raised platform, then a concrete floor with crude beams for seating beneath a corrugated plastic roof. There is music every night, year-round, with at least one guitarist, one singer, and one dancer, all working hard to make themselves heard above the hubbub of 200 or more people. Alert tourists have discovered it, but not the mass tours—yet. No cover, no minimum.

CORDOBA ✦✦✦

Ten centuries ago, Córdoba was one of the world's greatest cities. The capital of Muslim Spain, it was Europe's largest city (with a reported population of 900,000) and a prominent cultural and intellectual center. This seat of the Western Caliphate flourished, constructing public baths, mosques, a great library, and palaces. But greedy hordes descended on the city, sacking ancient buildings and carting off art treasures. Despite these assaults, Córdoba retains traces of its former glory—enough to rival Seville and Granada in attraction.

A visit to Andalucía can easily begin in Córdoba, 418km (260 miles) southwest of Madrid. The city lies astride NIV (E-5) connecting Madrid with Seville and is one of the few stops made by the high-speed AVE train, only 1¾ hours out of Madrid. Today, this provincial capital is known chiefly for its great mosque, but it is filled with other artistic and architectural riches, especially its domestic dwellings. The old Arab and Jewish quarters are famous for their narrow streets lined with whitewashed homes and flower-filled patios and balconies; it's perfectly acceptable to walk along gazing into the courtyards.

ESSENTIALS
GETTING THERE   By Train   Córdoba is a railway junction for routes to the rest of Andalucía and Spain. The main rail station is on the town's northern periphery, at Avenida de América 130, near the corner of Avenida de Cervantes. For information about services in Córdoba, contact **RENFE** (© **95-740-0202;** www.renfe.es). There are about 22 *talgo* and AVE trains daily between Córdoba and Madrid (trip time: 1½-2 hr.). Other trains *(tranvías)* take 5 to 8 hours for the same trip. There are also 25 trains from Seville every day (45 min. by AVE).

By Bus   Several different bus companies maintain separate terminals. The town's most important bus terminal is at Calle Torrito 10, 1 block south of Avenida Medina Azahara 29 (© **95-740-4040**), on the western outskirts of town (just west of the gardens beside Paseo de la Victoria). There are at least 10 buses per day to Seville (trip time: 2 hr.).

VISITOR INFORMATION   Córdoba's **tourist information office** is at Calle Torrijos 10 (© **95-747-1235;** www.andalucia.org). It's open Monday through Saturday from 9:30am to 7pm and Sunday from 10am to 2pm.

WHERE TO STAY
Very Expensive
El Conquistador ✦   Benefiting from one of the most evocative locations in Córdoba, this hotel lies just across a narrow street from one side of the Mezquita. It opened in 1986 within the renovated premises of a connected pair of 19th-century villas. The marble-and-granite lobby opens onto an interior

courtyard filled with seasonal flowers, a pair of splashing fountains, and a symmetrical stone arcade. The quality, size, and comfort of the rooms have earned the hotel four stars in the government rating system.

Magistral González Francés 15, 14003 Córdoba. © **95-748-1102.** Fax 95-747-4677. 103 units. 113€–186€ double; from 180€ suite. AE, DC, MC, V. Garage parking 13€. Bus: 12. **Amenities:** Cafe; bar; sauna; car-rental desk; 24-hr. room service; babysitting; same-day laundry/dry cleaning. *In room:* A/C, TV, minibar, hair dryer, safe.

Expensive

Parador de la Arruzafa 🏵️   About 4km (2½ miles) outside of town, in the suburb of El Brillante, this hotel from around 1960 (named after an Arab word meaning "palm grove") offers the conveniences and facilities of a resort hotel at reasonable rates. Built atop the foundations of a former caliphate palace, with panoramic views, the spacious rooms within have been furnished with fine darkwood pieces; some have balconies.

Avenida de la Arruzafa 33, 14012 Córdoba. © **95-727-5900.** Fax 95-728-0409. www.parador.es. 96 units. 115€–141€ double; from 183€ suite. AE, DC, MC, V. Free parking. **Amenities:** Restaurant; bar; heated outdoor pool; tennis court; limited room service; babysitting; same-day laundry/dry cleaning. *In room:* A/C, TV, dataport, minibar, hair dryer, safe.

Inexpensive

González   Located in the Judería, within easy walking distance of the Mezquita, this is among the more impressive of the city's inexpensive hotels. The converted 16th-century mansion is decorated in Andalucian style, with a dining courtyard. Rooms are plain and functional. Readers have praised the staff's attitude.

Manríquez 3, 14003 Córdoba. © **95-747-9819.** Fax 95-748-6187. 17 units. 68€–102€ double. Rates include breakfast. MC, V. Parking 9€. **Amenities:** Restaurant; bar; same-day laundry/dry cleaning. *In room:* A/C, TV, hair dryer.

Mezquita *(Finds*   The owners have incorporated ancient columns, arches, and genuinely old paintings for a downright grand effect. Many of the guest rooms carry through with that theme. Opposite the east entrance to the Mezquita, the intriguing parts of the Judería are a mere stroll away. Prices go up during Holy Week and the Feria de Abril.

Plaza Santa Catalina 1, 14003 Córdoba. (© **95-747-5585.** Fax 95-747-6219. 21 units. 39€–65€ double. AE, DC, MC, V. **Amenities:** Laundry service. *In room:* A/C, TV, hair dryer, safe.

WHERE TO DINE
Moderate

El Caballo Rojo 🏵️ SPANISH   Córdoba's best-known restaurant is up an alley opposite the Mezquita's Puerta del Perdón. Hugely popular with both locals and tourists, the place has the noise level you'd expect, but the skilled waiters cope smoothly with all the demands. As soon as you order, they bring a dish of fritters and pour a complimentary aperitif. There are three floors, and enough room to get away from smokers if you wish. In addition to regional dishes, the chef offers centuries-old Sephardic and Mozarabic recipes, an example of the latter being monkfish with pine nuts, currants, carrots, and cream. *Rabo de toro* (oxtail stew) is among the favorites on the long menu.

Cardinal Herrero 28, Plaza de la Hoguera. © **95-747-5375.** Reservations required. Main courses 9€–27€; *menú degustación* 31€. AE, DC, MC, V. Daily 1–4:30pm and 8pm–midnight. Bus: 12.

La Almudaina 🏵️ SPANISH/FRENCH   Fronting the river in the former Judería—the Jewish Quarter—La Almudaina is widely regarded as the city's top restaurant. That's a reach, in truth, but it's an attractive place, with dining in the central courtyard, with its stained-glass roof, or in one of the lace-curtained salons to the side. In cool weather, braziers under the table warm your feet. Specialties include salmon crepes, *merluza* (hake) with baby clams and shrimp, and spring lamb and pork loin in wine sauce. Meats are the best options, because fish is too often cooked to mushiness.

Plaza de los Santos Mártires 1. ℭ **95-747-4342.** Reservations required. Main courses 12€–18€; *menu degustatión* 31€. AE, DC, MC, V. Mon–Sat noon–4pm and 8:30pm–midnight; Sun noon–5pm. Closed Sun mid-June to Aug. Bus: 12.

EXPLORING CORDOBA

Alcázar de los Reyes Cristianos 🎖 Commissioned in 1328 by Alfonso XI (the "Just"), the Alcázar de los Reyes Cristianos (Fortress of the Christian Kings) is a fine example of military architecture. Fernando and Isabel governed Castile from this fortress on the river as they prepared their assault on Granada, the last Moorish stronghold in Spain. Columbus journeyed here to fill Isabel's ears with his plans for exploration. Two blocks southwest of the mosque, this quadrangular building is notable for mighty walls and a trio of towers: the Tower of the Lions, the Tower of Allegiance, and the Tower of the River. The Tower of the Lions contains intricately decorated ogival ceilings that are the most notable example of Gothic architecture in Andalucía. The beautiful gardens (illuminated May–Sept Tues–Sat 10pm–1am) and the Moorish bathrooms are celebrated attractions. The Patio Morisco is a lovely spot, its pavement decorated with the arms of León and Castile.

Amador de los Ríos. ℭ **95-742-0151.** Admission 3€ adults, 1.50€ children. May–Sept Tues–Sat 10am–2pm and 6–8pm, Sun 10am–3pm; Oct–Apr Tues–Sat 9:30am–3pm and 4:30–6:30pm, Sun 9:30am–3pm. Bus: 3 or 12.

Mezquita-Catedral 🎖🎖🎖 Dating from the 8th century, this mosque was the crowning Muslim architectural achievement in the West, rivaled only by the architecture at Mecca. Córdoba's mosque boasts a fantastic labyrinth of red-and-white-striped pillars, over 850 of them, topped with double arches, some of them with scalloped edges. They are made from marble, onyx, granite, limestone, even wood. Of different heights and thickness, many were scavenged from Roman, Carthaginian, and Visigothic sites. They support a flat roof covering almost 3 hectares (8 acres).

Dropped into this graceful space is a Gothic-baroque cathedral that the bishops of the Church Triumphant ordered built after the re-conquest of the city. While it squats awkwardly in the middle of the mosque, it would be impressive in its own right if it stood alone, somewhere else. The mosque's most interesting feature is the *mihrab,* a domed shrine lined with golden, glittering mosaics. The *mihrab* once housed a *Koran.* After exploring the interior, stroll through the Courtyard of the Orange Trees with its beautiful fountain.

Calle Cardenal Herrero. ℭ **95-747-0512.** Admission 6.50€ adults and students 14 and up, 3.25€ children 10–13, free for children 9 and under. May–Sept daily 10am–7pm; Oct–Apr daily 10am–6pm. Bus: 3 or 12.

Museo de Bellas Artes Housed in an old hospital, the Fine Arts Museum contains medieval Andalucian paintings, examples of Spanish baroque art, and works by many of Spain's important 19th- and 20th-century painters, including Goya. The museum is east of the Mezquita, about a block south of the Church of St. Francis (San Francisco).

Plaza del Potro 1. ℭ **95-747-3345.** Admission 1.60€, free for children under 12. June 15–Sept 15, Tues 3–8pm, Wed–Sat 9am–8pm, Sun 9am–3pm (shorter hours during the rest of the year). Bus: 3 or 4.

Museo Municipal de Arte Taurino   Memorabilia of great bullfights are housed in this museum, a 16th-century building in the Jewish Quarter, inaugurated in 1983. Its galleries honor Córdoba's great bullfighters in their "suits of light," with pictures, trophies, posters, and the mounted heads of memorable bulls. You'll see Manolete in repose and the blood-smeared uniform of El Cordobés—both of these famous matadors came from Córdoba.

Plaza de las Bulas (also called Plaza Maimónides). ℭ 95-720-1056. Admission 2.70€, free for children under 18 and to all on Tues. May–Sept Tues–Sat 10am–2pm and 5:30–7:30pm, Sun 9:30am–2:30pm; Oct–Apr Mon–Sat 10am–2pm and 4:30–6:30pm, Sun 9:30am–2:30pm. Bus: 3 or 12.

THE SHOPPING SCENE

The largest and most comprehensive association of craftspeople in Córdoba is **Arte Zoco,** Júdios s/n (no phone). Opened in the Jewish quarter as a business cooperative in the mid-1980s, it assembles the creative output of about a half dozen artisans, whose media include leather, wood, silver, crystal, terra cotta, and iron. Some of the artisans maintain on-premises studios, which you can visit to check out the techniques and tools they use to pursue their crafts. The center is open Monday through Friday from 9:30am to 7pm and Saturday and Sunday from 9:30am to 2pm. The workshops and studios of the various artisans open and close according to the whims of their occupants, but are usually open Monday through Friday from 10am to 2pm and 5:30 to 8pm.

At **Meryan,** Calleja de las Flores 2 (ℭ **95-747-5902**), artisans make leather objects in a 250-year-old building. Most items must be custom ordered, but there are some ready-made pieces for sale, including cigarette boxes, jewel cases, attaché cases, book and folio covers, and ottoman covers. Meryan is open Monday through Friday from 9am to 8pm and Saturday from 9am to 2pm.

GRANADA 🎭🎭

Granada, 122km (76 miles) northeast of Málaga, is 670m (2,200 ft.) above sea level. Named for the symbol of the city, the pomegranate (*granada* in Spanish), its oldest districts sprawl over two adjacent hills, the Alhambra and the Albaycín, and are crossed by two rivers, the Genil and the Darro. The **Cuesta de Gómerez** is one of the most important streets in Granada, climbing uphill from Plaza Nueva, the center of the modern city, to the Alhambra, Spain's greatest tourist attraction. The last stronghold of Moorish Spain, the Alhambra didn't fall to the Catholic monarchs Isabel and Fernando until 1492—quite a year. The complex stands above the city in the foothills of the snowcapped Sierra Nevada range. It is saturated with romance and heritage. Author/diplomat Washington Irving lived in a former royal apartment on the grounds before he wrote his *Tales of the Alhambra.*

ESSENTIALS

GETTING THERE   By Plane   Iberia flies to Granada's small airport once or twice daily from both Barcelona and Madrid. Granada's airport (ℭ **95-824-5223**) is 16km (10 miles) west of the city center. Airline ticketing problems and information are more easily handled at the **Iberia ticketing office** in the city center, at Plaza Isabel la Católica 2 (ℭ **95-822-7592**). A shuttle bus makes runs several times a day between the airport and the city center, at hours that are timed to coincide with the arrivals and departures of flights. The buses meander through the city center before heading out to the airport, but the most convenient and central place to catch one is on the Gran Vía de Colón, immediately in front of the city's cathedral. It costs 3.40€ each way.

By Train   Two trains daily connect Granada with Madrid's Atocha Station (trip time: 6–8 hr.), and there are four trains daily between Seville and Granada (3 hr.). Granada's railway station is on Calle Dr. Jaime García Royo (© **90-224-0202;** www.renfe.es), at the end of Avenida Andaluces.

By Bus   Most buses pull into the station on the fringe of Granada at Carretera de Jaen s/n, the extension of Avenida de Madrid. **Alsina Graells** (© **95-818-5010**) is the most useful company here, offering eight buses per day to Córdoba (3 hr.), 12 per day from Jaen (1½ hr.), nine per day from Madrid (5 hr.), 15 per day from Málaga (2 hr.), and nine per day from Sevilla (3 hr.).

VISITOR INFORMATION   The **tourist information office** is at Plaza de Mariana Pineda 10 (© **95-822-1022**), open Monday through Saturday from 9am to 7pm and Sunday from 10am to 2pm.

WHERE TO STAY

Alhambra Palace 🕰🕰   Renovations in recent years have swept away the cobwebs of creeping dowdiness, and this old favorite, built in 1910, now fully deserves its four-star government rating. Guests enjoy fine views of the city from here, and it's only about 270m (900 ft.) from the entrance to the Alhambra itself. Inside and out, the design borrows Moorish elements, with swaths of ceramic tiles, brass braziers, horseshoe arches, and the crenellated roof brow of an Arab fortress. Rooms with balconies are the most desirable.

Peña Partida 2-4, 18009 Granada. © 95-822-1468. Fax 95-822-6404. www.h-alhambrapalace.es. 121 units. 157€ double; from 231€ suite. AE, DC, MC, V. Parking 12€. **Amenities:** Restaurant; bar; concierge; 24-hr. room service; in-room massage; babysitting; same-day laundry service. *In room:* A/C, TV w/pay movies, dataport, minibar, hair dryer, safe.

Palacio de Santa Inés 🕰🕰 *(Finds)*   Every new visitor to Spain looks for lodgings that are both charming and economical. That combination is rare, but it's found here, in double portions. This 16th-century mansion has only been a hotel for a few years. The owners have retained as much as they could of the building's handsome features, including grand salons with paneled Mudéjar ceilings, and a three-story inner court with wooden balustrades around the balconies, featuring fragments of ancient frescoes with classical themes. Mattresses are new, beds have fanciful headboards, and furnishings are traditional. Some rooms have clear views of the Alhambra. The suites have small kitchens. The hotel faces an enclosed square a couple of blocks from Plaza Nueva. You'll not want to miss this lodging—book well in advance.

Cuesta de Santa Inés 9, 18010 Granada. © 95-822-2362. Fax 95-822-2465. www.palaciosantaines.com. 13 units (including 4 suites). 100€ double; from 225€ suite. AE, MC, V. **Amenities:** Cafe/bar; 24-hr. room service; same-day laundry/dry cleaning. *In room:* A/C, TV, minibar, hair dryer, safe.

Parador de San Francisco 🕰🕰🕰   The most famous hotel of Spain's "Parador" lodging chain (a distinguished chain of Spanish government-owned hotels, normally set in notable historical buildings) is housed in a 15th-century structure with a modern annex, set within the grounds of the Alhambra. A decidedly Andalucian ambience informs the decor, which is respectful of the rich history of its surroundings. Part of the building is a former convent founded by the Catholic monarchs immediately after they conquered the city in 1492. They were interred in one of its enclosed courts until the cathedral was built downtown. From the hotel's terrace, outside the dining room, there are views of Alhambra gardens and Albayzín hill. Rooms are generally spacious and comfortable, if not extravagant. The hotel cannot begin to meet demand, though, and reservations must be made months in advance. (In the confusing manner of the Parador chain, this is also known as the "Parador de Granada.")

Alhambra, 18009 Granada. ✆ **800/343-0020** in the U.S., or 95-822-14-40. Fax 95-822-2264. www.parador.es. 212€ double. AE, DC, MC, V. Free parking. Bus: 13. **Amenities:** Restaurant; bar; limited room service; same-day laundry/dry cleaning. *In room:* A/C, TV, minibar, hair dryer, safe.

WHERE TO DINE

Cunini SEAFOOD   The bar in front is always active, with scores of tapas selections. Over the course of an evening, many patrons drift into the small dining room in back, painted canary yellow so it won't seem claustrophobic. Meals often begin with soup, such as *sopa Sevillana* (with ham, shrimp, and whitefish), but the fried sweet peppers tossed with onions are a good alternative. They come with nearly perfect, almost hot bread. The deep fry of small fish called a *fritura Cunini* is a worthy example of the famous Andalucian dish. Seafood—*zarzuela* (fish stew), smoked salmon, grilled shrimp—is what to have, but chosen with care, given the ever escalating prices of shellfish. Regulars get suggestions about what's good tonight. Strangers don't. Plaza de la Pescadería is just below the cathedral.

Plaza de la Pescadería 14. ✆ **95-825-0777**. Reservations recommended. Main courses 7.50€–25€ (not counting lobster). AE, DC, MC, V. Tues–Sun noon–4pm and 8pm–midnight.

Pilar del Toro ✿ SPANISH   You'll find this former home of nobility partially hidden up a flight of stairs near the north end of the Plaza Nueva. You enter an atmospheric bar, cross into a large inner patio with an array of cushioned wicker chairs arranged around a bubbling fountain, and finally climb the stairs to one of the four dining rooms. Start with the *pimientos de piquillo*—small triangular sweet peppers stuffed with a cod brandade—a classic of the Basque kitchen. The veal *solomillo* (tenderloin) is butter-tender, served with a mustard and mushroom sauce.

Hospital de Santa Ana 12. ✆ **95-822-3847**. Main courses 8.45€–15€. MC, V. Daily 1:30–4pm and 8:30–11pm.

Sevilla REGIONAL SPANISH   Attracting a mixed crowd of all ages, the Sevilla was the favorite restaurant of such hometown boys as García Lorca and Manuel de Falla—it's been around for over 70 years. Out front is one of the city's best tapas bars, and you can easily put together lunch or dinner there. For a more formal meal, there's a different take on standard rice dishes, including one with broad beans, green asparagus, and ham. For a main course, the "shepherd's style" lamb with pine nuts and raisins is a winner. You can dine in any of four attractively decorated rooms, or out on the terrace.

Oficios 12. ✆ **95-822-1223**. Reservations recommended. Main courses 7.50€–17€. AE, DC, MC, V. Mon–Sat 1–4pm and 8–11pm; Sun 1–4pm.

EXPLORING GRANADA

Alhambra ✿✿✿   A fortress-palace of grand ambition, built over centuries for the governing caliphs during the long Moorish occupation, the Alhambra was a royal city surrounded by walls. The heart of the Alhambra, the **Palacios Nazaríes (Nasrid Palaces),** is a series of three connected palaces. Here, sultans and emirs conducted state business, concocted conspiracies, raised their families, and were entertained by their harems.

The first structure you'll enter is the **Casa Real,** built between 1335 and 1410. Signs direct visitors through rooms with reliefs of Arabic script and floral motifs carved in the plaster walls. This pathway leads into one of the Alhambra's most-photographed spaces, the **Patio de Comares (Court of the Myrtles),** a long, flat band of water bordered by rows of sculptured myrtle. At one end is the splendid **Salón de Embajadores (Hall of the Ambassadors),** one of the palace's loveliest rooms, with a high vaulted ceiling of carved cedar and walls of lustrous tiles and carved script. Exiting, you soon arrive in the **Patio de los Leones (Court of Lions),** named after its highly stylized fountain, a basin resting on the haunches of 12 stylized stone lions standing in a circle.

This was the heart of the palace, the most private section. Opening onto the court are the Hall of the Two Sisters, where the "favorite" of the moment was kept, and the Gossip Room, a factory of intrigue. In the dancing room in the Hall of Kings, entertainment was provided nightly to amuse the sultan's party. You can see the room where Washington Irving lived (in the chambers of Carlos V).

Carlos V may have been horrified when he saw the cathedral placed in the middle of the great mosque at Córdoba, but he's responsible for his own architectural meddling here, building a ponderous Renaissance palace in the middle of the Alhambra. Today, it houses the **Museo de la Bellas Artes en la Alhambra** (© 95-822-4883), a site devoted to painting and sculpture from the 16th to the 19th centuries; and the **Museo de la Alhambra** (© 95-822-6279), which focuses on the region's breathtaking traditions of Hispanic-Muslim art and architecture. Both museums are open Monday through Saturday from 9am to 2pm.

Note: With over two million visitors a year, crowds can be overwhelming. Management's experiments in crowd control lead to frequent changes in policy, so the details outlined here cannot be considered definitive. Though you can visit the vast grounds at almost any time, visits to the Nasrid Palaces are timed. To be safe, arrange for tickets in advance. Branches of the Banco de Bilbao de Vizcaya across the country sell tickets, and an online reservation service is provided at http://w3.grupobbva.com/ALHAMBRA/alhambra/home.html. It is also possible to purchase tickets at www.alhambratickets.com. Hotel concierges in Granada can also arrange for tickets. Or show up at the gate to the Alhambra by 7:30am on the day you wish to visit. The tickets stipulate the half-hour period during which you will be admitted, in the morning, afternoon, or evening.

Palacio de Carlos V. © 95-822-8359. Comprehensive ticket, including Alhambra and Generalife (below), 7€ adults, 5€ seniors/students, free under age 8. Mar–Oct daily 8:30am–8pm, floodlit visits Tues–Sat 10–11:30pm; Nov–Feb daily 8:30am–6pm, floodlit visits Fri–Sat 8–9:30pm.

Generalife ⚘ The sultans used to spend their summers in this palace (pronounced, roughly, hay-nay-rahl-*ee*-fay) with their wives, consorts, and extended families. Built in the 13th century to overlook the Alhambra, the Generalife's glory is in its gardens and courtyards. Don't expect an Alhambra in miniature: There are no major buildings—the Generalife is a place of fragrances and fountains, a retreat even from the splendors of the Alhambra.

Alhambra, Cerro de Sol. © 91-374-5420. For tickets and hours, see the Alhambra above.

Catedral & Capilla Real ⚘ This Renaissance-baroque cathedral, with its spectacular altar, is one of the country's architectural highlights, acclaimed for its beautiful facade and gold-and-white decor. It was begun in 1521 and completed in 1714. Behind the cathedral (entered separately) is the Flamboyant Gothic **Capilla Real (Royal Chapel)** where the remains of Isabel and Fernando lie. It was their wish to be buried in recaptured Granada, not their home regions of Castile or Aragón. The coffins are remarkably tiny—a reminder of how short they must have been. Accenting the tombs is a wrought-iron grill masterpiece.

In much larger tombs are the remains of their daughter, Joanna the Mad, and her husband, Philip the Handsome. The Capilla Real abuts the cathedral's eastern edge.

Plaza de la Lonja, Gran Vía de Colón 5. © **95-822-2959.** Admission to cathedral 2.50€. Mon–Sat 10:45am–1:30pm and 4–7pm; Sun and holidays 4–7pm.

ALBAYZIN ⊛

This old Arab quarter (also spelled "Albaicín") occupies one of the two main hills of Granada, but it doesn't belong to the city of 19th-century buildings and wide boulevards beneath it. The district once flourished as the residential section of the Moors, even after the city's reconquest, but it fell into decline when the Christians eventually drove the Moors out. A labyrinth of steep, crooked streets, it escaped the fate of much of Granada, which was torn down in the name of progress. Fortunately, it has been preserved, as have its plazas, whitewashed houses, villas, and the decaying remnants of the old city gate. Here and there, you can catch a glimpse of a private patio filled with fountains and plants—these are home to a traditional and graceful way of life that flourishes today. To reach the Albayzín from downtown, take bus no. 7 to Calle de Pagés. Alternatively, hop aboard any of the red-and-white shuttle buses marked ALBAYZIN that make runs at 15-minute intervals from the Plaza Nueva. The buses operate daily from 7am to 11pm; the fare is .85€.

THE GYPSY CAVES OF SACROMONTE

Next to Albayzín are the Gypsy caves of Sacromonte. They are tawdry tourist traps, and wouldn't even be mentioned here if so many visitors didn't get conned into going, despite warnings. A few of the caves serve as troglodyte nightclubs. Strung with colored lights and furnished with stubby little tables and chairs, they function as flamenco *tablaos*. They aren't remotely romantic. With few exceptions, the performances of the singers, guitarists, and dancers are execrable. Patrons are hounded to buy vile sherry, shoddy trinkets, and cassettes, and to tip everyone in sight. You will be encouraged by leaflets scattered around the city and in every hotel lobby to join a "Granada By Night" tour. My heartfelt advice: *Don't!*

THE SHOPPING SCENE

The **Alcaicería,** once the Moorish silk market, is next to the cathedral in the lower city. The narrow streets of this rebuilt village of shops are filled with vendors selling the arts and crafts of the province. The Alcaicería offers you one of Spain's most diverse assortments of tiles, castanets, and wire figures of Don Quixote chasing windmills. The jewelry found here compares favorably with the finest Toledan work. For the window-shopper in particular, it makes a pleasant stroll.

MALAGA

Málaga is a bustling commercial and residential center whose economy doesn't depend exclusively on tourism. Its chief attraction is the mild off-season climate—summer can be sticky. Málaga's most famous native son is Pablo Picasso, born in 1881 at Plaza de la Merced, in the center of the city.

ESSENTIALS

GETTING THERE   Iberia (© **800/772-4642** in the U.S.) has flights every 2 hours into Málaga from Madrid. There are at least five trains a day from Madrid (trip time: 4½ hr.). For rail information in Málaga, contact **RENFE**

(© **90-224-0202;** www.renfe.es). Buses from all over Spain arrive at the terminal on Paseo de los Tilos, behind the RENFE office. Málaga is linked by bus to all the major cities of Spain. Call © **95-235-0061** in Málaga for **bus information** or log on to www.andalucia.com/travel/bus.

VISITOR INFORMATION The **tourist information office** at Pasaje de Chinitas 4 (© **95-221-3445**) is open Monday through Friday from 9am to 7pm and Saturday and Sunday from 9am to 2pm. Keeping longer hours is **Municipal,** Av. Cervantes 1 (© **95-260-4410**), open Monday through Friday from 8:15am to 2:45pm and 4:30 to 7pm, Saturday from 9:30am to 1:30pm.

WHERE TO STAY

Parador de Málaga-Gibralfaro 🐾   Originally established in 1948 and renovated in the 1990s, this member of the Parador chain is immediately adjacent to the foundations of a medieval castle. The lodging occupies the steep hill that dominates the city center, providing a vista that takes in the harbor, the bullring, mountains, and beaches. Rooms have sitting areas and wide glass doors opening onto terraces with garden furniture. They're tastefully decorated with modern furnishings and reproductions of Spanish antiques.

Monte Gibralfaro, 29016 Málaga. © **95-222-1902.** Fax 95-222-1904. www.parador.es. 38 units. 116€ double. AE, DC, MC, V. Free parking. **Amenities:** Restaurant; bar; rooftop outdoor pool; concierge; limited room service; laundry service. *In room:* A/C, TV, minibar, hair dryer, safe.

WHERE TO DINE

Café de Paris 🐾   FRENCH/SPANISH   Málaga's best restaurant is in La Malagueta, the district surrounding the Plaza de Toros (bullring). Much of the menu is French cuisine adapted to the Spanish palate, but classic Spanish recipes are also featured. Try crepes gratinées (filled with *angulas*—baby eels) or *lubina* or *dorada al sal*—fish baked in a hard crust of salt and cracked open at table; the fish proves to be exceptionally moist and not at all salty. Beef Stroganoff is made here, but with *rabo de toro*—oxtail. Other specialties include artichokes stuffed with foie gras and a version of hake wrapped around pulverized shellfish and served with a tomato sauce.

Vélez Málaga 8. © **95-222-5043.** Reservations required. Main courses 12€–23€. *Menú del día* 30€, *menu degustación* 50€. AE, DC, MC, V. Mon 8:30pm–midnight; Tues–Sat 1–4pm and 8:30pm–midnight. Closed Holy Week and last 2 weeks of July. Bus: 13.

EXPLORING MALAGA

The remains of the Moorish **Alcazaba** 🐾, Plaza de la Aduana, Alcazabilla (© **95-221-6005;** bus: 4, 18, 19, or 24), are within easy distance of the city center, off Paseo del Parque (plenty of signs point the way up the hill). The fortress was erected in the 10th or 11th century, though there have been later additions and reconstructions. Fernando and Isabel stayed here when they reconquered the city. The Alcazaba has extensive gardens and houses a small archaeological museum, with artifacts from cultures ranging from Greek to Phoenician to Carthaginian. Admission is free.

The 16th-century Renaissance **cathedral,** Plaza Obispo (© **95-221-5917;** bus: 14, 18, 19, or 24), in Málaga's center, was built on the site of a great mosque. It suffered damage during the Civil War, but it remains vast and impressive, reflecting changing styles of interior architecture. Its most notable attributes are its richly ornamented choir stalls by Ortiz, Mena, and Michael. Admission is 1.50€. It's open daily from 10am to 12:45pm and 4 to 6:30pm; closed holidays.

MARBELLA

Though packed with tourists, ranking just behind Torremolinos in numbers of visitors, Marbella is still the most exclusive resort along the Costa del Sol—with such bastions of posh as the Hotel Puente Romano. Despite the hordes, Marbella persists as a large, busy, but still mostly pleasant town at the foot of the Sierra Blanca, 80km (50 miles) east of Gibraltar and 76km (47 miles) east of Algeciras, or 600km (373 miles) south of Madrid.

Traces of the recent and distant past are found in Marbella's palatial town hall, its medieval ruins, and fragments of its Moorish walls. The most attractive area is the **old quarter,** with its narrow cobblestone streets and clustered houses, centering around Plaza de los Naranjos, which is planted with palms, trumpeteer vines, and orange trees. Seek out the Plaza de la Iglesia and the streets around it, with a church on one side and a rampart of an old fortress on the other.

The biggest attractions in Marbella are **El Fuerte** and **La Fontanilla,** the two main beaches. There are other, more secluded beaches, but you'll need your own transportation to get to them.

ESSENTIALS

GETTING THERE   At least 18 buses run between Málaga and Marbella daily. Four buses come in from Madrid and another three come from Barcelona.

VISITOR INFORMATION   The **tourist office,** on Glorieta de la Fontanilla (© **95-277-1442;** www.pgb.es/marbella), is open April through October, Monday through Friday from 9:30am to 9pm and Saturday from 10am to 2pm. Another tourist office is on Plaza Naranjos (© **95-282-3550**), keeping the same hours.

WHERE TO STAY

El Castillo   This small 1960s hostel is at the foot of the castle in the narrow streets of the old town. The spartan rooms are scrubbed clean and look out onto a small, covered courtyard. No meals are served, but many cafes, suitable for breakfast, are nearby.

Plaza San Bernabé 2, 29600 Marbella. © **95-277-1739.** 26 units. 26€–32€ double. MC, V. *In room:* No phone.

El Fuerte ♠   This is the largest and most recommendable hotel in the center of Marbella. An underground tunnel leads beneath an all-pedestrian, traffic-free promenade to the sands of the beach. Built in 1957, it was last renovated in 1994. It caters to a sedate clientele of conservative northern Europeans. There's a palm-fringed pool across the street from a sheltered lagoon and a wide-open beach. The hotel offers a handful of terraces, some shaded by flowering arbors.

Av. del Fuerte, 29600 Marbella. © **800/448-8355** in the U.S., or 95-286-1500. Fax 95-282-4411. www.fuerte hoteles.com. 263 units. 114€–208€ double; from 220€ suite. AE, DC, MC, V. Parking 5.30€. **Amenities:** Restaurant; cafe; covered pool; heated outdoor pool; golf nearby; outdoor tennis courts lit for night play; fitness room; salon; nonsmoking rooms. *In room:* A/C, TV, minibar, hair dryer, safe.

Marbella Club ♠♠♠   The first luxury hotel on the coast, this exclusive enclave was established in 1954 and has been renovated and refreshed many times since to keep up with newer competitors. It sprawls over a generously landscaped property that slopes from a roadside reception area down to the beach, incorporating small clusters of garden pavilions, bungalows, and small-scale annexes. Elegantly furnished rooms have private balconies or terraces. Golf can be arranged nearby, and tennis courts are within a 2-minute walk.

Bulevard Príncipe Alfonso von Hohenlohe, 29600 Marbella. © **800/448-8355** in the U.S., or 95-282-2211. Fax 95-282-9884. www.marbellaclub.com. 129 units. 313€–550€ double; from 455€ suite. AE, DC, MC, V. Free parking. **Amenities:** Restaurant; bar; 3 pools; health club and spa; bike rental; concierge; business center; 24-hr. room service; babysitting; same-day laundry/dry cleaning. *In room:* A/C, TV, minibar, hair dryer, safe.

Puente Romano 🏨🏨🏨 This hotel began life as a condo annex of the older Marbella Club, down the road, but it soon surpassed its sibling in luxe and panache. There is no finer resort on the Costa. Like many of its fellows, the exterior style is mock Andalucian *pueblo*. The clustered buildings enclose luxuriant gardens, with a brook, spanned at one point by the Roman bridge that inspired the hotel's name. The always-stylish international clientele is afforded a beach club, twice-daily maid service, and reassuring security patrols. Service excels: Order breakfast as you step into the shower and it arrives before you've reached for the towel.

Carretera de Cádiz, Km 177.5, 29600 Marbella. © **95-282-0900.** Fax 95-277-5766. www.puenteromano. com. 235 units. 232€–301€ double; from 357€ suite. AE, DC, MC, V. Limited free parking. **Amenities:** 3 restaurants; bar; 2 large heated outdoor pools; golf nearby; 7 lighted tennis courts; state-of-the-art health club; watersports equipment; concierge; car-rental desk; secretarial services; 24-hr. room service; in-room massage; babysitting; same-day laundry/dry cleaning. *In room:* A/C, TV, minibar, hair dryer, safe.

WHERE TO DINE

Altamirano SPANISH Take the trouble to seek out this fine little tapas bar on a quiet square in the old town, up a narrow lane from Avenida de Nabeul. Conventional meals aren't the point. Put together a selection from the long list of traditional dishes available as *tapas* (small), *media raciones* (medium), and *raciones* (full plate). Beware the choices that list only their weight in grams—they're costly. *Almejas*—baby clams in garlicky wine sauce—are good starters. *Gambas pil-pil*—spicy shrimp—are another, and, if you're acclimated to calamari back home, discover a similar texture but new flavor in the *navajas*—grilled razor clams. It's smoky inside, so grab one of the tables outside if you're not a smoker.

Plaza Altamirano 3. No phone. Tapas and *raciones* 4.50€–9.25€. MC, V. Thurs–Tues 1–4pm and 7:30pm–midnight.

Cipriano SPANISH Puerto Banús, a satellite of Marbella centered on a large marina, has become a small city in the last 20 years. At the harbor, yachts have Mercedes in attendance to take their owners to dinner. This is one of their destinations, a crisply corporate enclave in a glass office building. With its burnished wood paneling, marble floors, and platoon of uniformed waiters, you'll not want to show up in shorts and T-shirts. Otherwise, everyone, even single diners, is made to feel special. Service is polished, balanced between warmth and professionalism, a pleasure to experience. Fish is your best bet, especially the classic *dorada a la sal,* sea bass baked in a hard salt shell. There are two main rooms and a terrace that seats over 200 diners.

Avenida Playas del Duque. © **95-281-1077.** Reservations suggested. Main courses 15€–23€; *menú degustación* 55€. AE, DC, MC, V. Daily 1:30–4pm and 8–11pm. Closed mid-Jan to mid-Feb.

El Balcón de la Virgen SPANISH Set in the historic core of old Marbella, this restaurant is named after a 200-year-old statue of the Virgin that adorns a wall niche. The ancient house is all but hidden under a blanket of flowering vines. You'll find it within a short walk of the Plaza de los Naranjos. Regardless of when you arrive, it's likely to be well patronized. The interior is as picturesque as anything, with amphorae and antique farm tools hanging on the white plaster walls. The menu is mostly Andalucian, which means lots of seafood, such as the mixed grill of three shrimp, three cuttlefish, and three fish filets. The food is unremarkable but prices are fair, the service attentive, and the setting entrancing. Note that it is open only for dinner.

Remedios 2. ✆ **95-277-6092.** Reservations recommended. Main courses 7€–16€. AE, MC, V. Daily 7pm–midnight. Closed Tues Nov–May.

La Hacienda ✿ MEDITERRANEAN   La Hacienda, 13km (8 miles) east of Marbella, has long enjoyed a reputation for serving some of the best food along the Costa del Sol. In cooler months, dine in the rustic tavern before an open fireplace; in fair weather, meals are served on a patio. The chef may offer foie gras with leeks, Serrano ham with green gazpacho, and saddle of hare with mushrooms and juniper, but the menu changes frequently. The expert kitchen knows how to heighten the flavors of the fresh ingredients, and the food presentation is stylish. Several items—guinea fowl, roast lamb, wild duck—are for two persons. Although the food is admirable, the service is sometimes lacking.

Urbanización Hacienda Las Chapas, Carretera de Cádiz, Km 193. ✆ **95-283-1267.** Reservations recommended. Main courses 15€–28€; *menu degustación* 44€. AE, DC, MC, V. Summer daily 8:30–11:30pm. Winter Wed–Sun 1–3:30pm and 8:30–11:30pm. Closed Nov 15–Dec 15.

MARBELLA AFTER DARK

Near Puerto Banús, **Casino Nueva Andalucía Marbella,** Urbanización Nueva Andalucía (✆ **95-281-4000**), is on the lobby level of the Andalucía Plaza Hotel. It stands in an upscale development surrounded by foreign-owned condos and lush golf courses, 7km (4½ miles) from Marbella's center beside the road leading to Cádiz. Gambling includes individual games such as French and American roulette, blackjack, punto y banco, craps, and chemin de fer. Entrance to the casino is 5€ and you'll have to present a valid passport. You can dine in the Casino Restaurant before or after gambling. The casino is open daily from 6pm to 4 or 5am. La Caseta Bar offers flamenco shows at 11pm on Friday and Saturday. Cover is free but drinks cost 11€ and up.

TORREMOLINOS

This is the most famous—which isn't to say the finest—Mediterranean beach resort in Spain. It's a gathering place for international visitors, a stew of northern Europeans and North and South Americans. The once tranquil fishing village of Torremolinos has been engulfed in concrete-walled resort hotels. Some travelers relax here after whirlwind tours of Spain—the living is easy, the people are in a party mood, and there are no historic monuments to visit. Torremolinos is often a cacophonous refuge for people with nothing more elevated in mind than an all-over tan by Sunday. The sands along the beachfront tend to be gritty and grayish. The best beaches are **El Bajondillo** and **La Carihuela,** the latter bordering an old fishing village. All beaches here are public, but don't expect changing facilities. Many women go topless on the beaches.

ESSENTIALS

GETTING THERE   Torremolinos is served by the nearby Málaga airport, 14km (9 miles) west. There are frequent rail departures from the terminal at Málaga; for information, contact **RENFE** (✆ **90-224-0202;** www.renfe.es). Buses run frequently between Málaga and Torremolinos; for information, call ✆ **95-235-0061.**

VISITOR INFORMATION   The **tourist information office** is at Plaza de las Comunidades Autonomas (✆ **95-221-3445**). It's open daily from 8am to 3pm (Mon–Fri 9:30am–2:30pm in winter).

WHERE TO STAY

Meliá Costa del Sol   Admittedly nothing memorable, this massive chain hotel provides most everything expected of it. The beach is just across the street and the attached Centro de Talasoterapia purveys that non-tiring, non-dietary route to robust health so dear to Europeans—water therapy. The facility offers massages, a mud bath, a whirlpool, a sauna, a pool, and a Turkish bath. Forgive the management the stunningly unattractive sand-colored stucco exterior—it's better inside.

Paseo Marítimo 19, 29620 Torremolinos. ℭ **95-238-6677.** Fax 95-238-6417. www.solmelia.com. 535 units. 107€–135€ double; from 164€ suite. AE, MC, V. **Amenities:** 2 restaurants; 2 bars; outdoor pool; health club and spa; concierge; car-rental desk; babysitting; same-day laundry/dry cleaning, nonsmoking rooms. *In room:* A/C, TV, hair dryer, safe.

Parador de Málaga Golf 🏌   Also known as the Parador de Torremolinos and other variations thereof, this resort hotel was created by the Spanish government. The hacienda-style hotel is flanked by a golf course on one side and the Mediterranean on another. It's 3km (2 miles) from the airport, 10km (6½ miles) from Málaga, and 4km (2½ miles) from Torremolinos. Rooms have balconies with a view of the golfing greens, the circular pool, or the water; some are equipped with Jacuzzis. Long tiled corridors lead to the air-conditioned public areas and graciously furnished lounges.

Carretera de Málaga, Torremolinos, 29080 Apartado 324, Málaga. ℭ **95-238-1255.** Fax 95-238-8963. www.parador.es. 60 units. 107€ double. AE, DC, MC, V. Free parking. **Amenities:** Restaurant; bar; outdoor pool; golf course; tennis court; limited room service; babysitting; same-day laundry/dry cleaning. *In room:* A/C, TV, minibar, hair dryer, safe.

Sol Elite Aloha Puerto   Heralded as one of the most modern hotels along the Costa del Sol when it was built in 1972, this now-aging hotel stands on the seashore in the residential suburb of El Saltillo, on the southwestern edge of Torremolinos. Away from the noise of the town center, it offers spacious rooms, all facing the sea, the Benalmádena marina, or the beach. There's live entertainment most nights in a vast lounge with row after row of tub chairs. Drinks are generously poured and cost under 5€. During the day, you can take part in activities like darts, shuffleboard, archery, and Spanish classes.

Salvador Allende 45, 29620 Torremolinos. ℭ **800/336-3542** in the U.S., or 95-238-7066. Fax 95-238-5701. 430 units. 78€–195€ double. AE, DC, MC, V. **Amenities:** 2 restaurants; 4 bars; heated indoor and outdoor pools; tennis court; concierge; car-rental desk; limited room service; same-day laundry/dry cleaning. *In room:* A/C, TV, minibar, hair dryer, safe.

Sol Elite Don Pablo 🏌   Despite its undistinguished exterior, this is one of the most desirable resort hotels in Torremolinos, a minute from the beach and surrounded by its own garden and playground. The surprise is the glamorous interior, which borrows heavily from Moorish palaces and medieval castles. Splashing fountains are found in the arched-tile arcades, and niches with life-size stone statues of nude figures line the grand staircase. The comfortably furnished rooms have sea-view terraces and private bathrooms. Live entertainment is staged inside and out most days and nights, with dancing to a live band as well as a separate disco. A variety of activities, including group games and fitness classes, are offered.

Paseo Marítimo, s/n, 29620 Torremolinos. ℭ **95-238-3888.** Fax 95-238-3783. 443 units. 76€–142€ double. Free parking. AE, DC, MC, V. **Amenities:** Restaurant; bar; indoor pool with whirlpool; large circular outdoor pool; golf nearby; tennis court; children's program; limited room service; babysitting; same-day laundry/dry cleaning. *In room:* A/C, TV, minibar, hair dryer.

WHERE TO DINE

Antonio ✦ SPANISH   Facing the quiet west end of La Carihuela beach, across a paved promenade, the glass sides of this large room open wide in summer to accept the sea breezes. On the face, the menu looks indistinguishable from those of hundreds of others along the coast; but the execution and presentation here are decidedly superior to most. The *lenguado al champan,* for one, is a large filet of sole in a champagne sauce scattered with red peppercorns and mushroom bits—simple, pretty, tasty. While meat dishes are available, go for the seafood—that's the Mediterranean out there.

Plaza del Remo 6. ⓒ **95-205-0735.** Reservations suggested. Main courses 7.90€–28€. AE, DC, MC, V. Daily noon–midnight. Closed Nov.

Casa Juan SEAFOOD   Nautical decor, such as boat models and brass-bordered windows, not to mention a lavish display of lobsters and company near the door, make clear the objectives of this restaurant. That in mind, you have some difficult choices to make. *Gazpachuelo,* a warm, creamy chowder crowded with fish and vegetables, is a splendid way to begin. Then, perhaps, the *fritura mixta*—lightly fried fish, squid, and other creatures—or *paella,* or *zarzuela,* a tomato-based fish stew. The restaurant is in a modern building in the old-fashioned satellite hamlet of La Carihuela, west of Torremolinos center. Whenever it gets busy (which is frequently), the staff is inclined to impatience. There are outdoor tables.

Calle Mar 14, La Carihuela. (ⓒ **95-237-3512.** Reservations recommended. Main courses 7.60€–42€. AE, DC, MC, V. Tues–Sun 1–4:30pm and 7pm–midnight. Closed Dec.

El Gato Viudo SPANISH   Simple and amiable, this old-fashioned tavern with sidewalk seating occupies the street level and cellar of a building off Calle San Miguel. The menu lists platters of grilled fish, marinated hake, roasted pork and veal, calamari with spicy tomato sauce, grilled shrimp, and *zarzuela,* a Catalan fish stew similar to bouillabaisse.

La Nogalera 8. ⓒ **95-238-51-29.** Main courses 7.40€–18€. AE, DC, MC, V. Nov–Apr Thurs–Tues 1–3pm and 6–11:30pm. May–Oct daily 1–4pm and 6–11:30pm.

TORREMOLINOS AFTER DARK

One of the major casinos along the Costa del Sol, **Casino Torrequebrada,** Carretera de Cádiz 220, Benalmádena Costa (ⓒ **95-244-6000**), is on the lobby level of the Hotel Torrequebrada. The Torrequebrada combines a nightclub/cabaret, a restaurant, and an array of tables devoted to blackjack, chemin de fer, punto y banco, and two kinds of roulette. The nightclub presents a flamenco show from Tuesday to Saturday at 10:30pm. Many visitors prefer to just attend the show, paying 5€, including the first drink. Dinner is served from Wednesday to Saturday at 9pm and costs 42€, which includes admission to the show. The casino is especially lively in midsummer. The casino, its facilities, and its gaming tables are open daily from 9pm to 4am. The entrance fee to the gaming rooms is 5€. You need a passport to enter.

Sweden

by Darwin Porter & Danforth Prince

Although it was founded 7 centuries ago, Stockholm didn't become Sweden's capital until the mid–17th century. Today it's the capital of a modern welfare state with a strong focus on leisure activities and access to nature only a few minutes away.

1 Stockholm & Environs

Stockholm is built on 14 islands in Lake Mälaren, marking the beginning of an archipelago of 24,000 islands, skerries, and islets that stretches all the way to the Baltic Sea. It's a city of bridges and islands, towers and steeples, cobblestone squares and broad boulevards, Renaissance splendor and steel-and-glass skyscrapers. The medieval walls of Gamla Stan (Old Town) no longer stand, but the winding streets have been preserved. You can even go fishing in downtown waterways, thanks to a long-ago decree from Queen Christina.

Once an ethnically homogeneous society, Stockholm has experienced a vast wave of immigration in the past several years. More than 10% of Sweden's residents are immigrants or children of immigrant parents, with most coming from other Scandinavian countries. Because of Sweden's strong stance on human rights, the country has also become a major destination for political and social refugees from Africa, the Middle East, and the former Yugoslavia as well.

An important aspect of Stockholm today is a growing interest in cultural activities. Over the past quarter of a century, attendance at live concerts has grown, book sales are up, and more and more people are visiting museums.

ESSENTIALS

GETTING THERE **By Plane** You'll arrive at **Stockholm Arlanda Airport** (© **08/797-61-00;** www.lfv.se), about 46km (28 miles) north of Stockholm on the E-4 highway. **SAS** (© **800/221-2350**) is the most common carrier. A **bus** (© **08/600-10-00**) outside the terminal building goes to the City Terminal, Klarabergsviadukten, in the city center every 10 to 15 minutes (trip time: 35 min.), for 80SEK ($8.50). A taxi to or from the airport is expensive, costing 400SEK to 500SEK ($42–$53) or more. *Travelers beware:* Smaller taxi companies may charge up to 650SEK ($69) for the same ride. Be sure to ask in advance what the price is to your destination. For the name of a reputable company, see "Getting Around," below.

By Train The first high-speed train between Stockholm and Oslo has reduced travel time to 4 hours and 50 minutes between these two once remotely linked Scandinavian capitals. Depending on the day, there are two to three trains daily in each direction. This high-speed train now competes directly with air travel. Trains arrive at Stockholm's **Centralstationen (Central Station)** on Vasagatan, in the city center (© **07/717-575-75** in Sweden, or 08/696-75-09 from

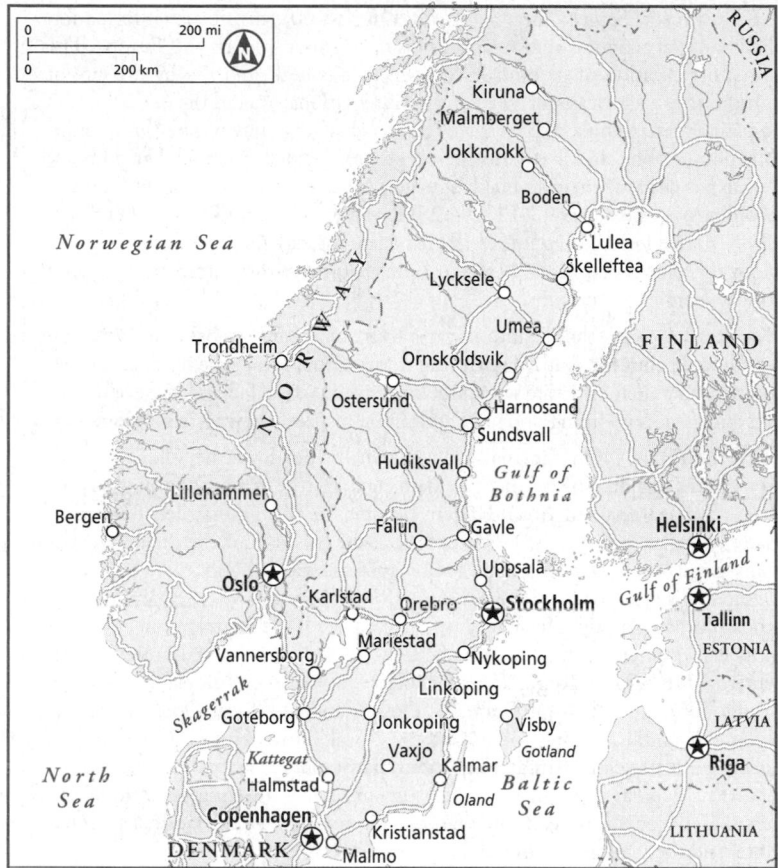

Sweden

abroad). There you can make connections to Stockholm's subway, the T-bana. Follow the TUNNELBANA sign.

By Bus Buses arrive at the **Centralstationen** on Vasagatan, and from here you can catch the T-bana (subway) to your Stockholm destination. For information in the Stockholm area, call ✆ **08/440-85-70.** Ticket office hours are Monday through Friday and Sunday from 9am to 6pm; Saturday from 9am to 4pm.

By Car Getting into Stockholm by car is relatively easy because the major national expressway from the south, E-4, joins with the national express highway, E-3, coming in from the west and leads right into the heart of the city. Stay on the highway until you see the turnoff for Central Stockholm or Centrum.

VISITOR INFORMATION Tourist Offices The **Tourist Centre** is at Sweden House, Hamngatan 27, off Kungsträdgården (Box 7542), S-103 93 Stockholm (✆ **08/789-24-00** or 08/789-24-90). It's open from June to August, Monday through Friday from 9am to 7pm, Saturday and Sunday from 9am to 5pm; from September to May, Monday through Friday from 9am to 6pm, Saturday and Sunday from 10am to 3pm. Maps and other free materials are available.

Kulturhuset, Sergels Torg 3 (© **08/508-314-00**), distributes information about cultural activities and organizations throughout Sweden and Europe. The largest organization of its kind in Sweden, it was built in 1974 by the city of Stockholm as a showcase for Swedish and international art and theater. There are no permanent exhibits; display spaces hold a changing array of paintings, sculpture, photographs, and live performance groups. Inside are a snack bar, a library (which has newspapers in several languages), a reading room, and a collection of recordings. Admission is 40SEK ($4.25) for adults, 20SEK ($2.10) for children 12 to 18, free for children under 12. It's open Tuesday through Thursday from 11am to 7pm, Friday from 11am to 6pm, Saturday from 11am to 4pm, and Sunday from noon to 4pm.

Websites   Go to the Scandinavian Tourism Board website at **www.go scandinavia.com** for maps, sightseeing information, ferry schedules, and other advice. Other useful sites are **www.stockholmtown.com**, for updated events listings and advice on dining, lodging, and museums, and **www.visit-sweden.com**.

CITY LAYOUT   On the island of Norrmalm north of the Old Town are Stockholm's major streets, such as **Kungsgatan** (the main shopping street), **Birger Jarlsgatan,** and **Strandvägen** (leading to the Djurgården—home of many of the city's top sights). **Stureplan,** at the junction of the major avenues Kungsgatan and Birger Jarlsgatan, is the city's commercial hub.

About 4 blocks west of the Stureplan rises **Hötorget City,** a landmark of modern urban planning. Its main traffic-free artery is the **Sergelgatan,** a 3-block shoppers' promenade that eventually leads to the modern sculptures in the center of the **Sergels Torg.** About 9 blocks south of the Stureplan, at **Gustav Adolfs Torg,** are the Royal Dramatic Theater and the Royal Opera House. A block east of the flaming torches of the Royal Opera House is the verdant north–south stretch of **Kungsträdgården,** part avenue, part public park, which serves as a popular gathering place for students and as a resting perch for shoppers. Three blocks southeast, on a famous promontory, lie the landmark Grand Hotel and the National Museum.

Kungsholmen, King's Island, is across a narrow canal from the rest of the city, a short walk west of the Central Station. It's visited chiefly by those wanting to tour Stockholm's elegant Stadshuset (City Hall). South of the island where **Gamla Stan (Old Town)** is located and separated from it by a narrow but much-navigated stretch of water, is **Södermalm,** the southern district of Stockholm. Quieter than its northern counterpart, it's an important residential area with a distinctive flavor of its own.

To the east of Gamla Stan, on a large and forested island completely surrounded by the complicated waterways of Stockholm, is **Djurgården (Deer Park).** The rustically unpopulated summer pleasure ground of Stockholm, it's the site of many of the city's most popular attractions: the open-air museums of Skansen, the *Vasa* man-of-war, Gröna Lund's Tivoli, the Waldemarsudde estate of the "painting prince" Eugen, and the Nordic Museum.

GETTING AROUND   Walking is the best way to get to know the city. In any case, you have to explore Gamla Stan on foot, as cars are banned from most of the streets. Djurgården and Skeppsholmen are other popular haunts for strolling.

By Public Transportation   You can travel throughout Stockholm county by bus, local train, subway (T-bana), and tram, going from Singö in the north to Nynäshamn in the south. The routes are divided into zones, and one ticket is valid for all types of public transportation in the same zone within 1 hour of being stamped.

Regular Fares   The basic fare for public transportation (subway, tram, streetcar, or bus) is 20SEK ($2.10). Purchase a ticket for a tram or streetcar at the tollbooth on the subway platform. On buses you pay the driver. To travel in most of Stockholm, all the way to the borders of the inner city, requires two tickets. The maximum ride, to the outermost suburbs, requires five tickets. You can transfer free (or double back and return to your starting point) within 1 hour of your departure. Day passes can be purchased at the SL Center.

Special Discount Tickets   Your best transportation bet is a **tourist season ticket**. A 1-day card costs 80SEK ($8.50) and is valid for 24 hours of unlimited travel by T-bana (subway), bus, and commuter train within Stockholm. It also includes passage on the ferry to Djurgården. Most visitors will probably prefer the 3-day card for 150SEK ($16), valid for 72 hours in Stockholm and the adjacent county. The 3-day card is also valid for admission to the Skansen museum, the Kaknäs tower, and Gröna Lunds Tivoli. A card for a child 8 to 17 costs 50SEK to 90SEK ($5.30–$9.55); kids under 8 travel free with an adult. Tickets are available at tourist information offices, in subway stations, and from most news vendors. Call © **08/689-10-00** for more information.

You can also opt for the **Stockholm Card;** see the box above for full details.

By T-bana (Subway)   Subway entrances are marked with a blue T on a white background. Tickets are bought on the platform. For information about schedules, routes, and fares, phone © **08/600-10-00.**

By Bus   Where the subway line ends, the bus begins. If the subway doesn't reach an area, a bus will. Many visitors ride the bus to Djurgården (although you can walk), where the T-bana doesn't go. If you're staying long enough to warrant it, you can buy the *SL Stockholmskartan* booklet (80SEK/$8.50) at the Tourist Centre at Sweden House, Hamngatan 27, off Kungsträdgården (© **08/789-24-95**), for a list of bus routes.

By Ferry   Ferries from Skeppsbron on Gamla Stan (near the bridge to Söder-malm) can take you to Djurgården if you don't want to walk or go by bus. They leave every 20 minutes Monday through Saturday, and about every 15 minutes on Sunday, from 9am to 6pm. The fare is 20SEK ($2.10) for adults, 15SEK ($1.60) for seniors and children 7 to 12. Free for children under 7.

By Taxi   Taxis in Stockholm are the most expensive in the world. The meter starts at 32SEK ($3.40), and a short ride can easily cost 80SEK ($8.50). You can hail those that display the sign LEDIG, or you can request one by phone. **Taxi Stockholm** (© 08/15-00-00 or 08/15-04-00) is a large, reputable company.

By Car   In general, you can park in marked spaces Monday through Friday from 8am to 6pm, but these spaces are hard to come by. Consider leaving your car in a parking garage—there are several in the city center and on the outskirts—and using public transportation. Parking exceptions or rules for specific areas are indicated on signs in the area. At Djurgården, parking is always prohibited, and from April to mid-September, it's closed to traffic Friday through Sunday.

   Avis (© 08/797-99-70) and **Hertz** (© 08/797-99-00) maintain offices at Arlanda Airport. Hertz's downtown office is at Vasagatan 26 (© 08/24-07-20); Avis's downtown office is at Vasagatan 10B (© 08/20-20-60). Rentals at both organizations are usually cheaper if you reserve them by phone before leaving North America.

By Bicycle   The best place to go cycling is on Djurgården. You can rent bicy-cles from **Skepp o Hoj,** Djurgårdsbron (© 08/660-57-57), for about 150SEK ($16) a day. A valid credit-card number is held as a deposit on any bicycle rental. The shop is open May through August, daily from 9am to 9pm.

 FAST FACTS: **Stockholm**

American Express   For local 24-hour customer service call © 08/429-56-00.

Currency   You'll pay your way in Sweden with Swedish krone (singular, krona), or crowns, which is universally abbreviated SEK. These are divided into 100 øre. The exchange rate used throughout this chapter was US$1 = 9SEK (or 1SEK = 10.6¢). At press time, £1 = 14SEK (or 1SEK = 7.2 pence). Note that although Sweden is a member of the EU, it opted not to adopt the euro as its national currency on January 1, 2002.

Dentists   In an emergency, go to **Sct. Eriks Hospital,** Fleminggatan 22 (© 08/545-51-20), open daily from 8am to 5pm.

Doctors   For 24-hour emergency medical care, check with **Medical Care Information** (© 08/672-10-00). There's also a private clinic, **City Akuten,** Apelberg Sq. 481, 4th Floor (© 08/412-29-61).

Drugstores   One 24-hour pharmacy is **C. W. Scheele,** Klarabergsgatan 64 (© 08/454-81-00; T-bana: Centralen).

Embassies/Consulates   The embassy of the **United States** is at Strandvägen 101, S-115 89 Stockholm (© 08/783-53-00; T-bana: Östermalmstorg); the embassy of the **United Kingdom** (© 08/671-30-00) is at Skarpügatan 6–8 (mailing address: P.O. Box 27819, S-115 93 Stockholm); the embassy of **Canada** is at Tegelbacken 4, S-103 23 Stockholm (© 08/453-30-00; T-bana: Centralen); the embassy of **Ireland** (© 08/661-80-05; T-bana:

Östermalmstorg) is at Östermalmsgatan 97 (mailing address: P.O. Box 10326, S-100 55 Stockholm); the embassy of **Australia** (© **08/613-29-00**; T-bana: Hötorget) is at Sergels Torg 12 (mailing address: P.O. Box 7003, S-103 86 Stockholm); and the embassy of **South Africa** is at Linnég 76, S-115 00 Stockholm (© **08/24-39-50**; T-bana: Östermalmstorg). **New Zealand** doesn't maintain an embassy in Sweden. Inquiries should be made through the embassy of New Zealand in The Hague (© **070/346-93-24**). Call for hours.

Emergencies Call © **112** for the police, ambulance service, or the fire department.

Internet One of the most central places for receiving e-mail or checking messages is **Café Nine,** Odengatan 44 (© **08/673-67-97**; info@ninestudios. com; T-Bana: Odenplan). It charges only 1SEK (10¢) per minute, and is open Monday through Friday from 10am to 1am and Saturday and Sunday from 11am to 1am.

Post Office The main post office is at Vasagatan 28–34 (© **08/781-20-00**), open Monday through Friday from 8am to 6pm and Saturday from 9am to 1pm. Mail can be sent c/o general delivery as follows: Post Restante, c/o Postens Huyudkontor (Main Post Office), Vasagatan 28–34, S-104 30 Stockholm, Sweden.

Taxes Sweden imposes a "value-added tax," called *moms,* on most goods and services. Visitors from North America can beat the tax, however, by shopping in stores with the yellow-and-blue tax-free shopping sign. There are more than 15,000 of these stores in Sweden. To get a refund, your total purchase must cost a minimum of 200SEK ($21). Tax refunds range from 14% to 18%, depending on the amount purchased. *Moms* begins at 10% on food items, but is 25% for most goods and services. The tax is part of the purchase price, but you can get a tax-refund voucher before you leave the store. When you leave Sweden, take the voucher to a tax-free customs desk at the airport or train station you're leaving from. They will give you your *moms* refund (minus a small service charge) before you wing off to your next non-Swedish destination. Two requirements: You cannot use your purchase in Sweden (it should be sealed in its original packaging), and it must be taken out of the country within 1 month after purchase. For more information, call **Global Refunds** at © **0410/486-06.**

Telephone The **country code** for Sweden is **46.** The **city code** for Stockholm is **8;** use this code when you're calling from outside Sweden. If you're within Sweden but not in Stockholm, use **08.** If you're calling within Stockholm, simply leave off the code and dial the regular phone number.

Instructions in English are posted in **public phone boxes,** which can be found on street corners. Very few phones in Sweden are coin operated; most require the purchase of a phone card (called a **Telekort**). You can obtain phone cards at most newspaper stands and tobacco shops.

You can make international calls from the **TeleCenter Office** on the Central Station's ground floor (© **08/789-24-56**), open daily from 8am to 9pm, except major holidays. Long-distance rates are posted. To make a collect or calling-card call, dial one of the following access numbers to reach an American operator or an English-language voice prompt: **AT&T,** © **800/CALL-ATT;** or MCI, © **800/888-8000.**

For directory listings or other information for Stockholm or other parts of Sweden only, dial ℂ **118118**; for other parts of Europe, dial ℂ **118119**.

Tipping Hotels include a 15% service charge in your bill. Restaurants, depending on their class, add 13% to 15% to your tab. Taxi drivers are entitled to 8% of the fare, and cloakroom attendants usually get 6SEK (65¢).

WHERE TO STAY

By the standards of many U.S. and Canadian cities, hotels in Stockholm are very expensive. If the prices make you want to cancel your trip, read on. Dozens of hotels offer reduced rates on weekends all year and daily from around mid-June to mid-August. For further information, inquire at a travel agency or the tourist office (see "Visitor Information," above). In the summer, it's best to make reservations in advance just to be on the safe side.

Most medium-priced hotels are in Norrmalm, north of the Old Town, and many of the least expensive lodgings are near the Central Station. There are comparably priced inexpensive accommodations within 10 to 20 minutes of the city, easily reached by subway, streetcar, or bus. We'll suggest a few hotels in the Old Town, but they're limited and more expensive.

Note: In most cases a service charge ranging from 10% to 15% is added to the bill, plus the inevitable 21% *moms* (value-added tax). Unless otherwise indicated, all our recommended accommodations come with a private bathroom.

IN THE CITY CENTER
Very Expensive

Grand Hotel ⋇⋇⋇   Opposite the Royal Palace, this hotel—a bastion of elite hospitality since 1874—is the finest in Sweden. The most recent restoration was in 1996, but its old-world style has always been maintained. Guest rooms come in all shapes and sizes, all elegantly appointed with traditional styling. Some feature an air-cooling system. The bathrooms are decorated with Italian marble and tiles and have heated floors and shower-tub combinations. The priciest rooms overlook the water. The hotel's ballroom is an exact copy of Louis XIV's Hall of Mirrors at Versailles.

Södra Blasieholmshamnen 8, S-103 27 Stockholm. ℂ **800/223-5652** in the U.S. and Canada, or 08/679-35-00. Fax 08/611-86-86. www.grandhotel.se. 320 units. 3,295SEK–4,095SEK ($349–$434) double; from 7,995SEK ($847) suite. Rates include breakfast. AE, DC, MC, V. Parking 350SEK ($37). T-bana: Kungsträdgården. Bus: 46, 55, 62, or 76. **Amenities:** 2 restaurants; bar; fitness center; sauna; room service; laundry/dry cleaning. *In room:* TV, minibar, hair dryer, safe.

Expensive

Berns Hotel ⋇⋇   During its 19th-century heyday, this was the most elegant hotel in Sweden, with an ornate Gilded Age interior that was the setting for many a legendary rendezvous. In 1989, following years of neglect, it was rebuilt in the original style, and the restaurant facilities were upgraded. Although the dining and drinking areas are usually crowded with club kids and bar patrons, the guest rooms are soundproof and comfortably isolated from the activities downstairs. Each room has a bathroom sheathed in Italian marble; the bathrooms are small but have neatly maintained shower units. Some units are reserved for nonsmokers, and others are accessible to those in wheelchairs. The Red Room is the setting and namesake of Strindberg's novel *Röda Rummet*.

Näckströmsgatan 8, S-111 47 Stockholm. ℂ 08/566-322-00. Fax 08/566-322-01. www.berns.se. 65 units. 2,750SEK–3,900SEK ($292–$413) double; 4,600SEK–6,300SEK ($488–$668) suite. Rates include breakfast. AE, DC, MC, V. Parking 300SEK ($32). T-bana: Östermalmstorg. **Amenities:** Restaurant; bar; sauna; room service; babysitting; laundry/dry cleaning. *In room:* TV, minibar, hair dryer.

Lydmar Hotel ℛ   Opposite the garden of the King's Library, in what looks like an office building, the Lydmar opened in 1930 (as the Eden Terrace). The guest rooms are cozy and traditionally furnished, and come in many shapes and sizes. Although the rooms aren't large, they are exceptionally well maintained. The bathrooms are well appointed and contain shower-tub combinations. The hotel has a large dining room and a rooftop terrace where guests can enjoy drinks in the summer. In recent years, the Matsalen restaurant has become ever-so-chic.

Sturegatan 10, S-114 36 Stockholm. ℂ 08/566-113-00. Fax 08/566-113-01. www.lydmar.se. 62 units. 2,250SEK–4,950SEK ($239–$525) double; 7,500SEK ($795) junior suite. Rates include buffet breakfast. AE, DC, MC, V. Parking 300SEK ($32). T-bana: Östermalmstorg. Bus: 41, 46, 56, or 91. **Amenities:** 2 restaurants; bar; room service; babysitting; laundry/dry cleaning. *In room:* TV, minibar, hair dryer.

Nordic Hotel ℛℛ *Finds*   There's nothing in Scandinavia quite like Stockholm's newest major hotel. It's sort of a split personality—its astrological sign is definitely Gemini. You're given a choice of a room of "watery calm" in the 367-room Nordic Sea or "post-minimalist luminescence" in the 175-room Nordic Light. Lying on either side of a new square, Vasaplan, the hotel stands adjacent to the express rail link with the airport, or the central rail station. Each hotel has its own individual design. Nordic Sea, of course, turns to the ocean for its inspiration and features a 530-liter (2,400-gal.) aquarium. Nordic Light is filled with sun-shaped projections that guarantee a bright light even in the darkest winter days. Surprisingly for a hotel, the lobby emits sounds and lighting effects when it senses the presence of a guest. The suggestive light patterns projecting from the walls re-create the ever-changing patterns of the lights of the north. This hotel is not just about gimmicks, however—it offers real comfort. Nordic Light guest rooms have the best sound insulation in town. Wood, steel, and glass create both clublike and maritime auras in Nordic Sea rooms.

4-7 Vasaplan. ℂ 800/337-4685 in the U.S., or 08/50-56-30-00, Fax: 08/50-56-30-60. www.nordichotels.se. 367 units in Nordic Sea, 175 units in Nordic Light. 2,400SEK–3,600SEK ($254–$382) double in Nordic Sea; 2,900SEK–3,600SEK ($307–$382) double in Nordic Light. June 20–Aug 17, and during selected Fri–Sun nights throughout the winter, rates are reduced to 1,190SEK–1,990SEK ($126–$211) double in Nordic Sea, and 1,390SEK–1,990SEK ($147–$211) double in Nordic Light. AE, DC, MC, V. T-bana: Centralen. **Amenities:** Restaurant; bar; mini-gym; spa treatments; sauna; steam bath; room service; laundry/dry cleaning. *In room:* TV, minibar, coffeemaker, iron/ironing board, safe.

Scandic Hotel Sergel Plaza ℛℛ   This hotel opened in 1984 at the entrance to Drottninggatan, the main shopping street. Designed as living quarters for parliament members, improvements have made it one of the city's leading hotels. The elegant decor includes 18th-century artwork and antiques. The beautifully decorated guest rooms are done in modern but traditional style. The average-size tiled bathrooms have shower-tub combinations. Maintenance is first rate. There are some accommodations for nonsmokers and wheelchair users. A special executive floor offers enhanced luxuries and several electronic extras, such as dataports.

Brunkebergstorg 9, S-103 27 Stockholm. ℂ 800/THE-OMNI in the U.S., or 08/517-263-00. Fax 08/517-263-11. www.scandic-hotels.se. 418 units. 1,250SEK–2,280SEK ($133–$242) double; from 7,000SEK ($742) suite. Rates include breakfast. AE, DC, MC, V. Parking 210SEK ($22). T-bana: Centralen. Bus: 47, 52, or 69. **Amenities:** Restaurant; bar; room service; laundry/dry cleaning. *In room:* TV, minibar, hair dryer.

Stockholm

ATTRACTIONS ●

Drottningholm Palace & Theater **6**
Historiska Museet **18**
Kaknästornet **20**
Kungliga Slottet & Museum **12**
Millesgården **17**
Moderna Museet **1**
Nationalmuseum **25**

Nordiska Museet **21**
Prins Eugens Waldemarsudde **24**
Rådhuset **4**
Riddarholm Church **9**
Royal Warship *Vasa* **22**
Skansen **23**
Stadshuset **5**

Tips **Native Behavior**

Although not as common as it once was, partaking in a Swedish smörgåsbord is the most typical of Swedish culinary delights. Some restaurants and hotels stage this lavish banquet. The secret of it is to go gracefully to the groaning table overburdened with heaping platters of food and not overload your plate. You can always return for more of the *gravad lax* (thinly sliced salmon cured in dill) or Swedish Ping-Pong-shaped meatballs.

And when you've had too much smörgåsbord or other Swedish food delicacies, and joined in too many toasts fueled by the lethal aquavit, you can also always do as the Swedes do and retire to the nearest sauna bath to revitalize yourself for yet more revelry in the evening to come.

Moderate

Elite Hotel Stockholm Plaza Built on a triangular lot that might remind some visitors of New York's Flatiron Building, this first-class hotel is a well-run and inviting choice in the city center. From the time of its construction in 1903 until its renovation in 1984, the building had many uses—a run-down rooming house, private apartments, and offices. The light, fresh guest rooms have firm beds and tiled bathrooms with shower-tub combinations.

Birger Jarlsgatan 29, S-103 95 Stockholm. ℂ **08/566-220-00.** Fax 08/566-220-20. www.elite.se. 151 units. 1,290SEK–2,190SEK ($137–$232) double; 2,690SEK–4,045SEK ($285–$429) suite. Rates include breakfast. AE, DC, MC, V. Parking 260SEK ($28). T-bana: Hötorget or Östermalmstorg. **Amenities:** Restaurant; bar; dance club; sauna; room service; laundry/dry cleaning. *In room:* TV, minibar, hair dryer.

Esplanade Hotel This informal hotel, next to the more expensive Diplomat, attracts representatives from the nearby embassies and others who like its comfortable charm and traditional atmosphere. Constructed in 1910, it became a family-style hotel in 1954. Many of the rooms, furnished in old-fashioned style, have minibars. Single rooms are minuscule. Most doubles have double-glazed windows, extra-long beds, and well-kept, decent-size tile bathrooms with shower-tub combinations. Four rooms have a water view, and the English lounge features a balcony with a view of Djurgården. Only breakfast is served.

Strandvägen 7A, S-114 56 Stockholm. ℂ **08/663-07-40.** Fax 08/662-59-92. www.hotelesplanade.se. 34 units. Mon–Thurs 2,295SEK ($243) double; Fri–Sun 1,795SEK ($190) double. Rates include breakfast. AE, DC, MC, V. Parking 250SEK ($27). T-bana: Östermalmstorg. Bus: 47 or 69. **Amenities:** Lounge; sauna; laundry/dry cleaning. *In room:* TV, minibar.

Inexpensive

Hotell Örnsköld The five-story building that contains this hotel was built in 1910, and today the nearby Royal Dramatic Theater uses most of it for prop storage and staff housing. The hotel is situated on the second floor. High-ceilinged rooms have simple, contemporary furnishings, and more expensive units are big enough to hold extra beds if necessary. All units contain well-kept bathrooms with shower units.

Nybrogatan 6, S-114 34 Stockholm. ℂ **08/667-02-85.** Fax 08/667-69-91. 27 units. 1,275SEK–1,975SEK ($135–$209) double. Rates include breakfast. AE, MC, V. Parking 250SEK ($27) in nearby public garage. T-bana: Östermalmstorg. **Amenities:** Lounge; laundry/dry cleaning. *In room:* TV, minibar, hair dryer.

Hotel Tegnérlunden ⚡ *Kids*   In a 19th-century building at the edge of a city park, this hotel has a few public rooms, a lobby, and a bar. The best feature is the tasteful, functionally furnished rooms, many suitable for families. They're blissfully quiet, especially those opening onto the rear. The rooms vary in size and shape, and those we inspected were well maintained. The hotel offers comfort but not a lot of style. The bathrooms equipped with shower units are small but beautifully kept.

Tegnérlunden 8, S-113 59 Stockholm. ⓒ **08/545-455-50.** Fax 08/545-455-51. www.hoteltegnerlunden.se. 103 units. 990SEK–1,560SEK ($105–$165) double; 1,895SEK ($201) junior suite. Rates include breakfast. AE, DC, MC, V. Parking 150SEK ($16) in nearby garage. Bus: 47, 53, or 69. **Amenities:** Bar; sauna; laundry/dry cleaning. *In room:* TV, hair dryer.

IN GAMLA STAN (OLD TOWN)
Expensive
Lady Hamilton Hotel ⚡ *Finds*   This hotel, consisting of three connected buildings, stands on a quiet street surrounded by antiques shops and restaurants—a very desirable location indeed. Dozens of antiques are scattered among the well-furnished guest rooms. Most rooms have beamed ceilings. The beds (queen or double) are of high quality. Bathrooms are tiled but vary in size from spacious to cramped. All have heated towel racks, heated floors, and shower-tub combinations. Top-floor rooms have skylights and memorable views over the Old Town. Some rooms for nonsmokers are available. You'll get a sense of the 1470 origins of this hotel when you use the luxurious sauna, which encompasses the stone-rimmed well that formerly supplied the building's water. The ornate staircase wraps around a large model of a clipper ship suspended from the ceiling.

Storkyrkobrinken 5, S-111 28 Stockholm. ⓒ **08/506-401-00.** Fax 08/506-401-10. www.lady-hamilton.se. 34 units, some with shower only. 1,690SEK–2,390SEK ($179–$253) double. Rates include breakfast. AE, DC, MC, V. Parking: 295SEK ($31). T-bana: Gamla Stan. Bus: 48. **Amenities:** Restaurant; bar; sauna; room service; babysitting; laundry/dry cleaning. *In room:* TV, minibar, hair dryer.

Victory Hotel ⚡⚡   A small but stylish hotel, the Victory offers warm, inviting rooms, each named after a prominent sea captain. They sport a pleasing combination of exposed wood, antiques, and 19th-century memorabilia. Many rooms are smoke-free, and the beds are comfortable, with firm mattresses. The average-size bathrooms are tiled and have heated floors and shower units. Only the suites have tubs. The hotel rests on the foundations of a 1382 fortified tower. In the 1700s the building's owners buried a massive silver treasure under the basement floor—you can see it in the Stockholm City Museum. From the stairs you'll see one of Sweden's largest collections of 18th-century nautical needlepoint, much of it created by the sailors during their long voyages.

Lilla Nygatan 3–5, S-111 28 Stockholm. ⓒ **08/506-400-00.** Fax 08/506-400-10. www.victory-hotel.se. 48 units, some with shower only. 1,790SEK–2,490SEK ($190–$264) double; 2,690SEK–3,890SEK ($285–$412) suite. Rates include breakfast. AE, DC, MC, V. T-bana: Gamla Stan. Bus: 48. **Amenities:** Restaurant; bar; pool; sauna; room service; babysitting; laundry/dry cleaning. *In room:* TV, minibar, hair dryer, safe.

Moderate
Mälardrottningen ⚡ *Finds*   During its heyday, this was the most famous motor yacht in the world, the subject of gossip columns everywhere, thanks to the complicated friendships that developed among the passengers and, in some cases, the crew. Built in 1924 by millionaire C. K. G. Billings, it was the largest (72m/240 ft.) motor yacht in the world, and was later acquired by the Woolworth heiress, Barbara Hutton. The below-deck space originally contained only seven suites. The yacht was converted into a hotel in the early 1980s, and was

permanently moored beside a satellite island of Stockholm's Old Town. The cabins are now cramped and somewhat claustrophobic. Most have bunk-style twin beds. All units have neatly kept bathrooms with shower-tub combinations. Considering the hotel's conversation-piece status, and its location close to everything in the Old Town, it might be worth an overnight stay.

Riddarholmen, S-111 28 Stockholm. ℂ **08/545-187-80.** Fax 08/24-36-76. www.malardrottningen.se. 60 units. Mon–Thurs 1,100SEK–2,100SEK ($117–$223) double; Fri–Sun 980SEK–1,300SEK ($104–$138) double. Rates include breakfast. AE, DC, MC, V. Parking 17SEK ($1.80) per hour. T-bana: Gamla Stan. **Amenities:** Restaurant; bar; sauna; laundry/dry cleaning. *In room:* TV, hair dryer.

ON LÅNGHOLMEN

Långholmen Hotel   Beginning in 1724, on the little island of Långholmen, this structure was a state penitentiary for women charged with "loose living." The last prisoner was released in 1972 and today it's a newly restored and reasonably priced accommodation which, in addition to comfortable but small rooms, also houses a museum of Sweden's prison history and one of the best restaurants in the country. Instead of a prison induction area, you get the hotel's reception area and a 24-hour snack bar. Accommodations were carved from some 200 cells, creating cramped but serviceable rooms equipped with small showers and toilets.

Ten of the guest rooms are suitable for persons with disabilities, and 91 are reserved for nonsmokers. This is one of the best hotels in Stockholm for the single visitor on a budget, as 89 rooms are rented only to solo travelers. Just 13 rooms are large enough to accommodate two persons.

Kronohåktet, S-102 72 Stockholm. ℂ **08/668-05-00.** Fax 08/720-85-75. www.langholmen.com. 102 units. Sun–Thurs 1,395SEK ($175) double, 995SEK–1,155SEK ($125–$145) single; Fri–Sat 1,095SEK ($138) double, 695SEK–855SEK ($88–$108) single. Extra bed 210SEK ($22) per person. Rates include breakfast. AE, MC, V. T-bana: Hornstul. Bus: 4, 40, or 66. **Amenities:** Restaurant; bar; laundry/dry cleaning. *In room:* TV, hair dryer.

WHERE TO DINE
IN THE CITY CENTER
Very Expensive

Operakällaren ☆☆☆ FRENCH/SWEDISH   Opposite the Royal Palace, this is the most famous and unashamedly luxurious restaurant in Sweden. Its elegant decor and style are reminiscent of a royal court banquet. The service and house specialties are impeccable. Many come here for the elaborate fixed-price menus; others prefer the classic Swedish dishes or the modern French ones. A house specialty that's worth the trip is the platter of northern delicacies, with everything from smoked eel to smoked reindeer, along with Swedish red caviar. Salmon and game, including grouse from the northern forests, are prepared in various ways. There's a cigar room, too.

Operahuset, Kungsträdgården. ℂ **08/676-58-00.** Reservations required. Main courses 370SEK–420SEK ($39–$45); 3-course fixed-price menu 520SEK ($55); 4-course fixed-price menu 880SEK ($93); 7-course *menu dégustation* 1,450SEK ($154). AE, DC, MC, V. Daily 5–10pm. Closed July. T-bana: Kungsträdgården.

Paul & Norbert ☆☆☆ CONTINENTAL   In a patrician residence dating from 1873, adjacent to the Hotell Diplomat, this is the finest and most innovative restaurant in Stockholm. Seating only 30 people, it has vaguely Art Deco decor, beamed ceilings, and dark paneling. Owners Paul Beck and Norbert Lang worked in many top European restaurants before opening this establishment. To start, they prepare a tantalizing terrine of scallops in saffron sauce. The foie gras is the finest in town. Perfectly prepared main dishes include sautéed medallion of fjord salmon, scallops, and scampi in lobster sauce; crisp breast of duck with caramelized orange sauce; and juniper-stuffed noisettes of reindeer immersed in caraway sauce with portobello mushrooms.

Strandvägen 9. ⓒ **08/663-81-83**. Reservations required. Main courses 250SEK–310SEK ($27–$33); 9-course *grand menu de frivolité* 1,300SEK ($138). AE, DC, MC, V. Mid-Aug to June Tues–Fri noon–3pm, Mon–Sat 6–10pm. July to mid-Aug Mon–Sat 6–10pm. Closed Dec 24–Jan 6. T-bana: Östermalmstorg.

Expensive

Franska Matsalen (French Dining Room) ⚲⚲ FRENCH Widely acclaimed as one of the greatest restaurants in Stockholm, this elegant establishment is on the street level of the city's finest hotel. The dining room is appointed with polished mahogany, ormolu, and gilt accents under an ornate plaster ceiling. Tables on the enclosed veranda overlook the Royal Palace and the Old Town. Begin with a cannelloni of foie gras with cèpes, or perhaps mousseline of scallops with sevruga caviar. Main dishes include seared sweetbreads served with artichokes, *langoustines* (prawns) and frogs' legs with broad beans, and veal tartare with caviar. Fresh Swedish salmon is also featured. The chefs—highly trained professionals working with the finest ingredients—have pleased some of Europe's more demanding palates.

In the Grand Hotel, Södra Blasieholmshamnen 8. ⓒ **08/679-35-84**. Reservations required. Main courses 225SEK–465SEK ($24–$49); 7-course fixed-price menu 925SEK–1,300SEK ($98–$138). AE, DC, MC, V. Mon–Fri 6–11pm. T-bana: Kungsträdgården. Bus: 46, 55, 62, or 76.

Wedholms Fisk ⚲⚲⚲ SWEDISH/FRENCH This is one of the classic—and one of the best—restaurants in Stockholm. It has no curtains in the windows and no carpets, but the display of modern paintings by Swedish artists is riveting. You might begin with marinated herring with garlic and bleak roe, or tartare of salmon with salmon roe. The chef has reason to be proud of such dishes as perch poached with clams and saffron sauce, prawns marinated in herbs and served with Dijon hollandaise, and grilled filet of sole with Beaujolais sauce. The cuisine is both innovative and traditional—for example, chèvre mousse accompanies simple tomato salad. On the other hand, the menu features grandmother's favorite: cream-stewed potatoes.

Nybrokajen 17 ⓒ **08/611-78-74**. Reservations required. Main courses 110SEK–225SEK ($12–$24) lunch, 265SEK–525SEK ($28–$56) dinner. AE, DC, MC, V. Mon–Sat 5–11pm. Closed July. T-bana: Östermalmstorg.

Moderate

Bakfickan ⚲ *Finds* SWEDISH Tucked away behind the Operakällaren, the "Back Pocket" is a chic place to eat for a moderate price. It shares a kitchen with its glamorous neighbor Operakällaren (see above), but its prices are more bearable. Main dishes are likely to include salmon in several varieties, including boiled with hollandaise and salmon roe. You might also try beef Rydberg (thinly sliced tenderloin). In season you can order reindeer and elk. In the summer, nothing's finer than the rich ice cream with a sauce of Arctic cloudberries. Many patrons prefer to eat at the horseshoe-shaped bar.

Jakobs Torg 12. ⓒ **08/676-58-09**. Reservations not accepted. Main courses 92SEK–189SEK ($9.75–$20). AE, DC, MC, V. Aug–June Mon–Sat noon–11:30pm. T-bana: Kungsträdgården.

Eriks Bakfica *Value* SWEDISH Although other restaurants in Stockholm bear the name Eriks, this one is relatively inexpensive and offers particularly good value. Established in 1979, it features a handful of Swedish dishes from the tradition of *husmanskost* (wholesome home cooking). A favorite opener is toast Skagen, with shrimp, dill-flavored mayonnaise, spices, and bleak roe. There's also a daily choice of herring appetizers. Try the tantalizing "archipelago stew," a ragout of fish prepared with tomatoes and served with garlic mayonnaise. Marinated salmon is served with hollandaise sauce. You might also try Eriks cheeseburger with the special secret sauce, but you have to ask for it—the secret specialty is not on the menu.

Fredrikshovsgatan 4. ℂ **08/660-15-99.** Reservations recommended. Main courses 145SEK–298SEK ($15–$32). AE, DC, MC, V. Mon–Fri 11:30am–11pm; Sat 5–11pm; Sun 5–10pm. Bus: 47.

KB Restaurant SWEDISH/CONTINENTAL   A traditional artists' rendezvous in the center of town, KB Restaurant features good Swedish food as well as Continental dishes. Fish dishes are especially recommended. You might begin with salmon trout roe and Russian caviar, followed by boiled turbot or lamb roast with stuffed zucchini in thyme-flavored bouillon. Dishes usually come with aromatic, freshly baked sourdough bread. Desserts include sorbets with fresh fruits and berries, and a heavenly lime soufflé with orange-blossom honey. There's also a relaxed and informal bar.

Smålandsgatan 7. ℂ **08/679-60-32.** Reservations recommended. Main courses 210SEK–300SEK ($22–$32). Fixed-price meals 270SEK–335SEK ($29–$36) lunch; 375SEK–470SEK ($40–$50) dinner. AE, DC, MC, V. Mon–Fri 11:30am–11:30pm; Sat 5–11:30pm. Closed June 23–Aug 7. T-bana: Östermalmstorg.

Lisa Elmquist ✵ *Kids* SEAFOOD   Under the soaring roof, amid the food stalls of Stockholm's produce market (the Östermalms Saluhall), you'll find this likable cafe and oyster bar. Because of its good, affordable food, this is the most popular choice for Stockholm families visiting the market. It's owned by one of the city's largest fish distributors, so its menu varies with the catch. Some patrons come here for shrimp with bread and butter for 90SEK to 115SEK ($9.55–$12). Typical dishes include fish soup, salmon cutlets, and sautéed filet of lemon sole. It's not the most refined cuisine in town—it's an authentic "taste of Sweden," done exceedingly well. The establishment looks like a pleasant bistro under the tent at a country fair.

Östermalms Saluhall, Nybrogatan 31. ℂ **08/553-404-10.** Reservations recommended. Main courses 86SEK–336SEK ($9.10–$36). AE, DC, MC, V. Mon–Thurs 10am–6pm; Fri 10am–6:30pm; Sat 10am–4pm. T-bana: Östermalmstorg.

Prinsens SWEDISH   A 2-minute walk from Stureplan, this artists' haunt has become increasingly popular with foreign visitors. It has been serving people since 1897. Seating is on two levels, and in summer some tables are outside. The fresh, flavorful cuisine is basically Swedish food prepared in a conservative French style. It includes such traditional Swedish dishes as veal patty with homemade lingonberry preserves, sautéed fjord salmon, and roulades of beef. For dessert, try the homemade vanilla ice cream. Later in the evening, the restaurant becomes something of a drinking club.

Mäster Samuelsgatan 4. ℂ **08/611-13-31.** Reservations recommended. Main courses 124SEK–269SEK ($13–$29). AE, DC, MC, V. Mon–Fri 11:30am–10:30pm; Sat 1–10:30pm; Sun 5–9:30pm. T-bana: Östermalmstorg.

IN GAMLA STAN (OLD TOWN)
Very Expensive
Pontus in the Green House ✵✵ FRENCH/SWEDISH/ASIAN   Set within a building whose foundations date back to the 16th century, this well-orchestrated and elegant restaurant attracts some of the most powerful figures in Stockholm. Your dining experience will begin with a drink or aperitif in the ground-floor bar and cocktail lounge, where a staff member will explain the menu. You'll then be ushered upstairs to a gold-and-green dining room with high arched windows and an undeniable sense of respect for the presentation of

food. Chef Pontus Frithiof was inspired by two of the grand Francophile chefs of England, Marco Pierre White and Gordon Ramsay. Their influence is seen in dishes that include tender veal tongue with Jerusalem artichokes; steamed turbot with horseradish, prawns, and brown butter; and citrus-glazed *Challonais* duck breast served with foie gras, shiitake mushrooms, spring onions, and teriyaki sauce. In our view, the herring with vinegar-and-onion marmalade is the Old Town's tastiest. It's worth the trek across town to sample the creamy Roquefort made from the first milk produced by nursing cows. After tasting this cheese, you'll never go back—except with regret—to that store-bought stuff again.

Österlånggatan 17. © 08/23-85-00. Reservations recommended. Main courses 350SEK–450SEK ($37–$48); 8-course fixed-price menu 985SEK ($104). AE, DC, MC, V. Mon–Fri 11:30am–3pm and 6–11pm; Sat noon–4pm and 5:30–11pm. T-bana: Gamla Stan.

Expensive

Den Gyldene Freden *ℱ* SWEDISH "Golden Peace" is said to be Stockholm's oldest tavern. The restaurant opened in 1722 in a structure built the year before. The Swedish Academy owns the building, and members frequent the place every Thursday night. The cozy dining rooms are named for Swedish historical figures who were patrons. Today it's popular with artists, lawyers, and poets. You get good traditional Swedish cooking, especially fresh Baltic fish and game from the forests. Herring is a favorite appetizer. More imaginative appetizers include a creamy artichoke soup, Jerusalem artichokes with a dollop of caviar, and an especially intriguing consommé of oxtail with tiny ravioli stuffed with quail breast. Notable main courses are fried breast of wild duck in Calvados sauce, and roast of reindeer in juniper-berry sauce. A particular delight is homemade duck sausage with three kinds of mushrooms in black pepper sauce. Want something different for dessert? How about warm rose hip soup with vanilla ice cream? Of course, if you order that, you'd be denying yourself the "symphony" of lingonberries or the longtime favorite, Stockholm's best chocolate cake.

Österlånggatan 51. © 08/24-97-60. Reservations recommended. Main courses 98SEK–395SEK ($10–$42). AE, DC, MC, V. Mon–Fri 6–11pm; Sat 1–11pm. T-bana: Gamla Stan.

Inexpensive

Cattelin Restaurant *(Value* SWEDISH This restaurant on a historic street opened in 1897 and continues to serve fish and meat in a boisterous, convivial setting. Don't expect genteel service—the clattering of china can sometimes be almost deafening, but few of the regular patrons seem to mind. First-rate menu choices include various preparations of beef, salmon, trout, veal, and chicken, which frequently make up the daily specials often preferred by lunch patrons. This restaurant has survived wars, disasters, and changing food tastes, so it must be doing something right. It remains a sentimental favorite—and not just for the memories. In a city where people have been known to faint when presented with their dining tabs, it has always been a good, reasonably priced choice. The fixed-price lunch is served only Monday through Friday from 11am to 2pm.

Storkyrkobrinken 9. © 08/20-18-18. Reservations recommended. Main courses 95SEK–200SEK ($10–$21); *dagens* (daily) menu 72SEK ($7.65). AE, DC, MC, V. Mon–Fri 11am–10pm; Sat–Sun noon–10pm. T-bana: Gamla Stan.

ON DJURGÅRDEN

Ulla Winbladh *ℱ* SWEDISH Since it opened in 1994, this restaurant has enjoyed an explosion of publicity, which has impressed even the most jaded of Stockholm's restaurant aficionados. It's in a white stone structure, built as part of Stockholm's International Exposition of 1897. There's a large dining room decorated with works by Swedish artists, and a summer-only outdoor terrace laced with flowering plants. The menu focuses on conservative Swedish cuisine, all impeccably prepared. (Patrons who agree with this assessment include members of the Swedish royal family and a bevy of well-known TV, theater, and art-world personalities.) In 1996 the king presented a medal to chef Emel Ahalen for his proficiency in preparing Swedish cuisine. Menu choices include tender steak with artichokes, and a perfectly prepared rack of Swedish lamb flavored with bacon. Fish selections might be platters of herring (marinated and fried), whitefish, or pikeperch in white-wine sauce; divine turbot with saffron sauce; the inevitable salmon with dill sauce; and others that vary with the season.

Rosendalsvägen 8. © 08/663-05-71. Reservations required. Main courses 95SEK–270SEK ($10–$29). AE, DC, MC, V. Mon 11:30am–10pm; Tues–Fri 11:30am–11pm; Sat 1–11pm; Sun 1–10pm. Bus: 47.

EXPLORING STOCKHOLM

Everything from the *Vasa* Ship Museum to the changing of the guard at the Royal Palace to the Gröna Tivoli amusement park will keep you intrigued. Even just window-shopping for well-designed Swedish crafts can be a great way to spend an afternoon.

SIGHTSEEING SUGGESTIONS FOR FIRST-TIME VISITORS

If You Have 1 Day Take a ferry to Djurgården to visit the **Royal Warship Vasa,** Stockholm's most famous attraction, and to explore the open-air **Skansen** folk museum. In the afternoon, walk through **Gamla Stan (Old Town)** and have dinner at one of its restaurants.

If You Have 2 Days On day 2, get up early and visit the **Kaknästornet** TV tower for a panoramic view of Stockholm, its many islands, and the archipelago. Go to the **Nordic Museum** for insight into 5 centuries of life in Sweden. After lunch, visit the **Millesgården** of Lidingü, the sculpture garden and former home of Carl Milles.

If You Have 3 Days Spend your third morning walking through the center of Stockholm and doing some shopping. At noon (1pm on Sun), return to Gamla Stan to see the **changing of the guard at the Royal Palace.** View this French-inspired building that has been the residence of Swedish kings for more than 700 years. In the afternoon, see the attractions at the **National Museum.**

If You Have 4 or 5 Days On day 4, take one of the many tours of the **Stockholm archipelago.** Return to Stockholm and spend the evening at the **Gröna Tivoli** amusement park on Djurgården. On your last day, visit **Drottningholm Palace** and its 18th-century theater. In the afternoon, explore the university town of **Uppsala,** north of Stockholm, easily reached by public transportation.

THE TOP ATTRACTIONS
At Djurgården

Royal Warship Vasa 𝄐𝄐𝄐 This 17th-century man-of-war is the number-one attraction in Scandinavia—and for good reason. Housed in a museum specially constructed for it at Djurgården near Skansen, the *Vasa* is the world's oldest identified and complete ship. In 1628, on its maiden voyage and in front of thousands of horrified onlookers, the ship capsized and sank to the bottom of Stockholm harbor. When it was salvaged in 1961, more than 4,000 coins,

> **_Moments_ The Changing of the Royal Guard**
>
> It may not have the pomp of a similar show in London, but the **Changing of the Royal Guard** in Stockholm at least provides a photo op. In summer you can watch the parade of the military guard daily. In winter it takes place on Wednesday and Sunday; on the other days there's no parade, but you can see the changing of the guard. For information on the time of the march, ask at the Tourist Centre in Sweden House. The changing of the guard takes place at noon Monday through Saturday and at 1pm on Sunday in front of the Royal Palace.

carpenters' tools, and other items of archaeological interest were found on board. Best of all, 97% of the ship's 700 original sculptures were retrieved. Carefully restored and preserved, they're back aboard the ship, which looks stunning now that it once again carries grotesque faces, lion masks, fish-shaped bodies, and other carvings, some with their original paint and gilt.

Galärvarvsvägen, Djurgården. © **08/519-548-00**. Admission 70SEK ($7.40) adults, 40SEK ($4.25) seniors and students, 10SEK ($1.05) children 7–15, free for children under 7. June 10–Aug 20 daily 9:30am–7pm; Aug 21–June 9 Wed 10am–8pm, Thurs–Tues 10am–5pm. Closed Jan 1, May 1, Dec 23–25. Bus: 44, 47, or 69. Ferry from Slussen year-round, from Nybroplan in summer only.

Skansen 𝕬𝕬𝕬 Often called "Old Sweden in a Nutshell," this 35-hectare (75-acre) open-air museum, near Gröna Lund's Tivoli, contains more than 150 dwellings, most from the 18th and 19th centuries. Exhibits range from a windmill to a manor house to a complete town quarter. Browsers can explore the old workshops and see where the early book publishers, silversmiths, and pharmacists plied their trade. Handcrafts (glass blowing, for example) are demonstrated here, along with peasant crafts like weaving and churning. Folk dancing and open-air symphonic concerts are also featured.

Djurgården 49–51. © **08/442-80-00**. Depending on time of day, day of the week, and season, admission is 30SEK–60SEK ($3.20–$6.35) adults, 20SEK–30SEK ($2.10–$3.20) children 6–15, free for children 5 and under. Historic buildings, May–Aug daily 10am–8pm; Sept–Apr daily 10am–5pm. Bus: 47 from central Stockholm. Ferry from Slussen.

Nordiska Museet 𝕬𝕬 This museum houses an impressive collection of implements, costumes, and furnishings of Swedish life from the 1500s to the present. The highlights are the period costumes ranging from matching garters and ties for men to purple flowerpot hats from the 1890s. In the basement is an extensive exhibit of the tools of the Swedish fishing trade, plus relics from nomadic Lapps.

Djurgårdsvägen 6–16, Djurgården. © **08/519-560-00**. Admission 60SEK ($6.35) adults, 50SEK ($5.30) seniors, 30SEK ($3.20) students, 20SEK ($2.10) children 7–12, free for children under 7. Daily 10am–5pm. Bus: 44, 47, or 69.

Prins Eugens Waldemarsudde 𝕬𝕬 This once-royal residence is today an art gallery and a memorial to one of the most famous royal artists in recent history, Prince Eugen (1865–1947). The youngest of King Oscar II's four children, he is credited with making innovative contributions to the techniques of Swedish landscape paintings, specializing in depictions of his favorite regions in central Sweden. Among his most visible works are the murals on the inner walls of the Stadshuset.

Prins Eugens Väg 6. (© **08/545-837-00.** Admission 70SEK ($7.40) adults, 50SEK ($5.30) seniors and students, free for children under 17. June–Aug Tues and Thurs 11am–8pm, Wed and Fri–Sun 11am–5pm; Sept–May Tues–Sun 11am–4pm. Bus: 47 to the end of the line.

On Gamla Stan & Neighboring Islands

Kungliga Slottet (Royal Palace) & Museum 🕉🕉   Severely dignified, even cold looking on the outside, this palace has a lavish interior designed in the Italian baroque style. Kungliga Slottet is one of the few official residences of a European monarch that's open to the public. Although the Swedish king and queen prefer to live at Drottningholm, this massive 608-room showcase, built between 1691 and 1754, remains their official address. The most popular rooms are the **State Apartments** 🕉🕉; look for at least three magnificent baroque ceiling frescoes and fine tapestries. In the building's cellar is the **Stattkammaren (Treasury)** 🕉🕉, the repository for Sweden's crown jewels. Most intriguing to any student of war and warfare is the **Royal Armoury,** whose entrance is on the castle's rear side, at Slottsbacken 3. Gustavas III's collection of sculpture from the days of the Roman Empire can be viewed in the **Antikmuseum (Museum of Antiquities).**

Kungliga Husgerådskammaren. (© **08/402-61-30** for Royal Apartments & Treasury, 08/402-61-34 for the Skattkammaren, 08/10-24-88 for Royal Armory, 08/402-61-30 for Museum of Antiquities. Royal Apartments, 70SEK ($7.40) adults, 50SEK ($5.30) students, free for children under 7; Royal Armory, 65SEK ($6.90) adults, 50SEK ($5.30) seniors and students, 20SEK ($2.10) children, free for children under 7; Museum of Antiquities, 70SEK ($7.40) adults, 35SEK ($3.70) seniors and students, free for children under 7; Treasury, 70SEK ($7.40) adults, 60SEK ($6.35) seniors and students, free for children under 7. Combination ticket to all parts of palace 120SEK ($13) adults, 60SEK ($6.35) students and children. Apartments and Treasury, Sept–June Tues–Sun noon–3pm; July–Aug daily 10am–4pm; closed during government receptions. Royal Armory, Sept–Apr Tues–Sun 11am–4pm; May–Aug daily 11am–4pm. Museum of Antiquities, May–Aug daily 10am–4pm. T-bana: Gamla Stan. Bus: 43, 46, 59, or 76.

Riddarholm Church 🕉   The second-oldest church in Stockholm is on the tiny island of Riddarholmen, next to Gamla Stan. It was founded in the 13th century as a Franciscan monastery. Almost all the royal heads of state are entombed here, except for Christina, who is buried in Rome. There are three principal royal chapels, including one, the Bernadotte wing, that belongs to the present ruling family.

Riddarholmen. (© **08/402-61-30.** Admission 20SEK ($2.10) adults, 10SEK ($1.05) students and children. May–Aug daily 10am–4pm; Sept Sat–Sun noon–3pm. Closed Oct–Apr. T-bana: Gamla Stan.

In the City Center

Historiska Museet (Museum of National Antiquities) 🕉🕉   If you're interested in Swedish history, especially the Viking era, here you'll find the nation's finest repository of relics left by those legendary conquerors who once terrorized Europe. Many relics have been unearthed from ancient burial sites. The collection of artifacts ranges from prehistoric to medieval times, including Viking stone inscriptions and 10th-century coins, silver and gold jewelry, large ornate charms, elaborate bracelet designs found nowhere else in the world, and a unique neck collar from Färjestaden.

Narvavägen 13–17. (© **08/519-556-00.** Admission 60SEK ($6.35) adults, 50SEK ($5.30) seniors and students, 35SEK ($3.70) children 7–15, free for children under 7, 140SEK ($15) family. Apr–Sept Tues–Sun 11am–5pm; Oct–Mar Tues–Wed and Fri–Sun 11am–5pm, Thurs 11am–8pm. T-bana: Karlaplan or Östermalmstorg. Bus: 44, 47, or 54.

Nationalmuseum (National Museum of Art) 🕉🕉   At the tip of a peninsula, a short walk from the Royal Opera House and the Grand Hotel, is Sweden's state treasure house of paintings and sculpture, one of the oldest museums in the world. The first floor is devoted to applied arts (silverware, handcrafts, porcelain, furnishings), but first-time visitors may want to head directly to the second floor to the painting collection with works by Rembrandt and Rubens, Lucas Cranach's most amusing *Venus and Cupid,* and a rare collection of mid-16th-century Russian icons. The most important room in the gallery has one whole wall devoted to Rembrandt, and features his *Portrait of an Old Man, Portrait of an Old Woman,* and *Kitchen Maid.*

Södra Blasieholmshamnen. © 08/519-543-00. Admission 75SEK ($7.95) adults, 60SEK ($6.35) seniors and students, free for children under 16. Tues and Thurs 11am–8pm; Wed and Fri–Sun 11am–5pm. T-bana: Kungsträdgården. Bus: 46, 62, 65, or 76.

Moderna Museet (Museum of Modern Art) 🎯 This museum focuses on contemporary works by Swedish and international artists, including kinetic sculptures. Highlights are a small but good collection of Cubist art by Picasso, Braque, and Léger; Matisse's *Apollo* decoupage; the famous *Enigma of William Tell* by Salvador Dalí; and works by Brancusi, Max Ernst, Giacometti, and Arp, among others.

Klaravergsviadukten 61. © 08/519-552-00. Free admission. Tues–Thurs 10am–8pm; Fri–Sun 10am–6pm. T-bana: Kungsträdgården. Bus: 65.

Stadshuset (Stockholm City Hall) 🎯🎯 Built in what is called the "National Romantic Style," the Stockholm City Hall, on the island of Kungsholmen, is one of Europe's finest examples of modern architecture. Designed by Ragnar Ostberg, the redbrick structure is dominated by a lofty square tower, topped by three gilt crowns and the national coat-of-arms. The Nobel Prize banquet is held annually in the Blue Hall. About 18 million pieces of gold and colored mosaics made of special glass cover the walls, and the southern gallery contains murals by Prince Eugen, the painter prince.

Hantverksgatan 1. © 08/508-290-59. Admission 50SEK ($5.30) adults, free for children under 12. Tower additional 15SEK ($1.60). May–Sept daily 10am–4pm. City Hall tours (subject to change), June–Sept daily at 10am, 11am, noon, and 2pm; Oct–Apr daily at 10am and noon. T-bana: Centralen or Rådhuset. Bus: 3 or 62.

JUST OUTSIDE STOCKHOLM

Drottningholm Palace and Theater 🎯🎯🎯 Conceived as the centerpiece of Sweden's royal court, this regal complex of stately buildings sits on an island in Lake Mälaren. Dubbed the "Versailles of Sweden," Drottningholm (Queen's Island) lies about 11km (7 miles) west of Stockholm. The palace, loaded with courtly art and furnishings, sits amid fountains and parks, and still functions as one of the royal family's official residences.

On the grounds is one of the most perfectly preserved 18th-century theaters in the world, **Drottningholm Court Theater** (© 08/759-04-06). Between June and August, 30 performances are staged. Devoted almost exclusively to 18th-century opera, it seats only 450 for one of the most unusual entertainment experiences in Sweden. Many performances sell out far in advance to season-ticket holders. The theater can be visited only as part of a guided tour, which focuses on the original sets and stage mechanisms.

For tickets to the evening performances, which cost 165SEK to 600SEK ($17–$64), call © **08/660-82-25.**

Ekerö, Drottningholm. © 08/402-62-80. Palace, 60SEK ($6.35) adults, 30SEK ($3.20) students and persons under 26; theater, guided tour 60SEK ($6.35) adults, 30SEK ($3.20) students and persons 7–26, free for children under 7. Palace, Oct–Apr Sat–Sun noon–3:30pm; May–Aug daily 10am–4:30pm; Sept daily noon–3:30pm. Theater, guided tours in English, May daily 12:30, 1:30, 2:30, 3:30, and 4:15pm; June–Aug daily 11:30am, 12:30, 1:30, 2:30, 3:30, and 4:15pm; Sept daily 1:30, 2:30, and 3:30pm. T-bana: Brommaplan, then bus no. 301 or 323 to Drottningholm. Ferry from the dock near City Hall.

Millesgården 🎯🎯 On the island of Lidingö, northeast of Stockholm, is Carl Milles's former villa and sculpture garden beside the sea, now a museum. Many of his best-known works are displayed here (some are copies), as are works of other artists. Milles (1875–1955), who relied heavily on mythological themes, was Sweden's most famous sculptor.

Carl Milles Väg 2, Lidingö. (✆ **08/446-75-90.** Admission 75SEK ($7.95) adults, 60SEK ($6.35) seniors and students, 20SEK ($2.10) children 7–16, free for children under 7. May–Sept daily 10am–5pm; Oct–Apr Tues–Sun noon–4pm. T-bana: Ropsten, then bus to Torsviks Torg or train to Norsvik.

ORGANIZED TOURS

CITY TOURS   The quickest and most convenient way to see the highlights of Stockholm is to take one of the bus tours that leave from Karl XII Torg, near the Kungsträdgården.

Stockholm Sightseeing, Skeppsbron 22 (✆ **08/587-140-20**), offers a variety of tours, mostly in the summer. The 3-hour "Royal Stockholm" tour visits the Royal Palace or the Treasury and the *Vasa* Museum, with daily departures from mid-April to mid-October from Gustav Adolfs Torg, by the Royal Opera House. The tour costs 280SEK ($30). The quickest, cheapest tour—but also the most superficial—is the 1-hour "City Tour," for 170SEK ($18). It leaves daily year-round from Gustav Adolfs Torg. "Under the Bridges" takes 2 hours and goes through two locks and two bodies of water. Departures are from Stromkajen (near the Grand Hotel), daily from mid-April to mid-September. The cost is 190SEK ($20). The 1-hour "Sightseeing Anno 1935" explores the Stockholm harbor in an open-topped wooden boat, with a captain in period uniform. The tour costs 110SEK ($12). Daily departures, from early July to mid-August, are from the statue of Gustavus III by the Royal Palace.

THE SHOPPING SCENE

A whopping 25% goods tax makes shopping in Sweden expensive, and you can get most items at home for less money. On the positive side, Swedish stores usually stock items of the highest quality. Swedish glass is world famous. The wooden items are outstanding, and many people love the functional furniture in blond pine or birch. Other items to look for include children's playsuits, silver necklaces, reindeer gloves, hand-woven neckties and skirts, sweaters and mittens in Nordic patterns, clogs, and colorful handicrafts from the provinces. The most famous souvenir is the Dala horse from Dalarna.

For full details on **tax rebates** on local goods, go to the "Fast Facts" section, earlier in this chapter.

For the best shopping and window-shopping, stroll along the streets of **Gamla Stan** (especially **Västerlånggatan**), filled with boutiques, art galleries, and jewelry stores. Attractive shops and galleries can also be found along the **Hornsgats-Puckeln** (the Hornsgatan-Hunchback, a reference to the shape of the street), on **Södermalm.** Other good browsing streets are **Hamngatan, Birger Jarlsgatan, Biblioteksgatan,** and **Kungsgatan,** all in **Norrmalm.**

In the center of Stockholm, the largest department store in Sweden is **Åhlesns City,** Klarabergsgatan 50 (✆ **08/676-60-00;** T-bana: T-Centralen), with a gift shop, a restaurant, and a famous food department. Also seek out the fine collection of home textiles and Orrefors and Kosta crystal ware. **Nordiska Kompanient (NK),** Hamngatan 18–20 (✆ **08/762-80-00;** T-bana: Kungsträdgården), is another high-quality department store. Most of the big names in Swedish glass are displayed at NK. Swedish handcrafted items are in the basement.

At **Loppmarknaden i Skärholmen (Skärholmen Shopping Center),** Skärholmen (✆ **08/710-00-60;** T-bana: 13 or 23 to Skärholmen), the biggest flea market in northern Europe, you might find *anything.* Try to go on Saturday or Sunday (the earlier the better) when the market is at its peak. Weekend admission is 10SEK (95¢), but weekdays are free. The location is 10km (6 miles) southwest of the center.

STOCKHOLM AFTER DARK

Pick up a copy of *Stockholm This Week,* distributed at the Tourist Centre in the Sweden House (see "Visitor Information," earlier in this chapter), to see what's on.

THE PERFORMING ARTS

All the major opera, theater, and concert seasons begin in autumn, except for special summer festival performances. Fortunately, most of the major opera and theatrical performances are funded by the state, which keeps the ticket price reasonable.

Founded by Gustavus III in 1766, the **Drottningholm Court Theater** (© 08/ 660-82-25; T-bana: Brommaplan, then bus no. 301 or 323; boat from the City Hall in Stockholm), Drottningholm, is on an island in Lake Mälaren, 11km (7 miles) from Stockholm. It stages operas and ballets with full 18th-century regalia, period costumes, and wigs. Its machinery and 30 or more complete theater sets are intact and in use. The theater, a short walk from the royal residence, seats only 450, which makes it difficult to get tickets. Eighteenth-century music performed on antique instruments is a perennial favorite. The season is from May to September. Most performances begin at 7:30pm and last 2½ to 4 hours. You can order tickets in advance by phone with an American Express card. Tickets cost 150SEK to 550SEK ($16–$58).

Filharmonikerna I Konserthuset (Concert Hall), Hötorget 8 (© 08/10-21-10; T-bana: Hötorget), home of the **Stockholm Philharmonic Orchestra,** is the principal place to hear classical music in Sweden. (The Nobel Prizes are also awarded here.) Box office hours are Monday through Friday from noon to 6pm, Saturday from 11am to 3pm. Tickets are 120SEK to 400SEK ($13–$42).

Founded in 1773 by Gustavus III (who was later assassinated here at a masked ball), the **Operahauset (Royal Opera House),** Gustav Adolfs Torg (© 08/24-82-40; T-bana: Kungsträdgården), is the home of the Royal Swedish Opera and the Royal Swedish Ballet. The building dates from 1898. Performances are usually Monday through Saturday at 7:30pm (closed mid-June to Aug). The box office is open Monday through Friday from noon to 6pm (until 7:30pm on performance nights), Saturday from noon to 3pm;© 08/24-82-40. Tickets cost from 100SEK to 400SEK ($11–$42); ask about the 10% to 30% senior and student discounts.

NIGHTCLUBS

Café Opera, Operahuset, Kungsträdgården (© 08/676-58-07; T-bana: Kungsträdgården)—Swedish beaux arts at its best—functions as a brasserie-style restaurant during dinner hours and one of the most popular nightclubs in Stockholm late at night. Near the entrance of the cafe is a stairway leading to one of the Opera House's most beautiful corners, the clublike Operabaren (Opera Bar). Café Opera is open daily from 5pm to 3am. There's no cover before 11pm, 100SEK ($11) after.

Göta Källare, in the Medborgplatsen subway station, Södermalm (© 08/642-08-28; T-bana: Medborgplatsen), is the largest and most successful supper-club-style dance hall in Stockholm. Large, echoing, and paneled with lots of wood in a *faux-Español* style, it has a large terrace that surrounds an enormous tree, and a restaurant. Expect a crowd of people ages 45 and older, and music from a live orchestra. The place is open every night from 8:30pm. Cover is 80SEK ($8.50) after 11pm only.

ROCK & JAZZ CLUBS

Some of Sweden's and the world's best-known jazz musicians regularly play **Fasching,** Kungsgatan 63 (✆ **08/21-62-67;** T-bana: T-Centralen). It's so small, you'll almost feel like you're in the band. Weekend late nights are for dancing, and after midnight on Friday there's salsa; Saturday late hours are dedicated to soul. Hours can be irregular, so it's best to call in advance, but the club is usually open nightly from 7pm to at least 1am. Cover is 100SEK to 250SEK ($11–$24).

The Swedish branch of **Hard Rock Cafe,** Sveavägen 75 (✆ **08/545-494-00;** T-bana: Rådmansgaten), is fun and gregarious. Club sandwiches, hamburgers, T-bone steaks, and barbecued spareribs are available. It's open in summer, Sunday through Thursday from 11am to midnight and Friday and Saturday from 11am to 1am. There's no cover.

Pub Engelen/Nightclub Kolingen, Kornhamnstorg 59B ✆ **08/20-10-92;** T-bana: Gamla Stan), share a single address. The restaurant, which serves some of the best steaks in town, is open Sunday through Thursday from 5 to 11:30pm, Friday and Saturday from 5pm to 1:30am. Prices for platters of bar food run 80SEK to 200SEK ($8.50–$21). Live performances, usually soul, funk, and rock by Swedish groups, take over the pub daily from 8:30pm to midnight. The pub is open Tuesday through Thursday from 4pm to 1am, Friday and Saturday from 4pm to 3am, Sunday from 5pm to 3am. Beer begins at 34SEK ($3.60), and items on the bar menu cost 30SEK to 70SEK ($3.20–$7.40). The Nightclub Kolingen is a dance club nightly from 10pm to about 3am. It charges the same food and drink prices as the pub, and you must be at least 23 to enter. Cover runs from 40SEK to 60SEK ($4.25–$6.35) after 8pm.

BARS

One of the most talked-about bars in Stockholm, **Tiger Bar/Avec Bar,** 18 Kungsgatan (✆ **08/24-47-00;** T-bana: Östermalmstorg), attracts a bevy of supermodels and TV actors. The street-level Tiger Bar has black leather upholstery and an atmosphere of postmodern cool. The clean, modern decor of the basement-level Avec Bar draws an equally chic crowd. On both levels, everybody's favorite drink seems to be the Russian-inspired *caprinoshka,* concocted from vodka and limes. You might hear anything from recorded dance hits (Fri and Sat at midnight) to live salsa and merengue (every Wed 9pm–5am). The place is open Thursday from 7pm to 3am, Friday and Saturday from 7pm to 4am. Incidentally, no one will object if you light up a cigar. Cover is 60SEK ($6.35) Wednesday, 70SEK ($7.40) Thursday, and 125SEK ($13) Friday and Saturday.

The **Cadier Bar,** Södra Blasieholmshamnen 8 (✆ **08/679-35-00;** T-bana: Kungsträdgården), is one of the most sophisticated places in Stockholm. From the bar, which is situated in the Grand Hotel—one of the most famous hotels in Europe—you'll have a view of the harbor and the Royal Palace. Light meals— open-faced sandwiches and smoked salmon—are served all day in the extension overlooking the waterfront. Drinks run 96SEK to 120SEK ($10–$13); imported beer is 45SEK ($4.75). The bar is named for the hotel's builder. It's open Monday through Saturday from noon to 2am, Sunday from noon to 12:30am; a piano player performs Wednesday through Saturday from 9:30pm to 1:30am.

Looking for a nonconfrontational bar peopled with regular guys who happen to be gay? Consider a round or two at **Sidetrack,** Wollmar Yxkullsgatan 7 (✆ **08/ 641-16-88;** T-bana: Mariatorget). Small, and committed to shunning trendiness, it's named after the founder's favorite gay bar in Chicago. It's open every night from

6pm to 1am. Tuesday here seems to be a gay Stockholm institution. Other nights are fine, too—Sidetrack is something like a Swedish version of a bar and lounge at the local bowling alley, where everyone happens to be into same-sex encounters.

DAY TRIPS FROM STOCKHOLM

SKOKLOSTER CASTLE *☆☆*   Skokloster, S-746 96 Skokloster (© **018/38-60-77**), is a splendid 17th-century castle and one of the most interesting baroque museums in Europe. It's next to Lake Mälaren, 64km (40 miles) west of Stockholm and 40km (31 miles) south of Uppsala. Original interiors aside, the castle is noted for its rich collections of paintings, furniture, applied art, tapestries, arms, and books. Admission is 65SEK ($6.90) adults, 50SEK ($5.30) seniors, and 20SEK ($2.10) students and children. Guided tours are conducted from May to August daily every hour from 11am to 4pm. In September the guided tours are given from Monday to Friday at 1pm; Saturday and Sunday at 1, 2, and 3pm. The site is closed from October to April.

Skokloster Motor Museum (© **018/38-61-06**), on the palace grounds, contains the largest collection of vintage automobiles and motorcycles in the country. One of the most notable cars is a 1905 8-horsepower De Dion Bouton. Unlike the castle, the museum is open year-round. It costs 40SEK ($4.25) adults, 10SEK ($1.05) children 7 to 14, free for children under 7. It's open from May to September, daily from noon to 4pm; from October to April, Saturday and Sunday from 11am to 5pm.

Getting There   From Stockholm take a **train** to the hamlet of Bålsta, which lies 19km (12 miles) from the castle. At the village train station, you can either take **bus** no. 894 directly to Skokloster, or call for a **taxi** from a direct telephone line that's prominently positioned just outside the railway station.

UPPSALA *☆☆*   The major university city of Sweden, Uppsala, 68km (42 miles) northwest of Stockholm, is the most popular destination for day-trippers from Stockholm, and for good reason. Uppsala not only has a great university, but also a celebrated 15th-century cathedral. Even in the time of the Vikings, this was a religious center, the scene of animal and human sacrifices in honor of the old Norse gods. And it was once the center of royalty as well; Queen Christina occasionally held court here. The church is still the seat of the Swedish archbishop, and the first Swedish university was founded here in 1477.

Getting There   The **train** from Stockholm's Central Station takes about 45 minutes. Trains leave about every hour during peak daylight hours. Some visitors spend the day in Uppsala and return to Stockholm on the commuter train in the late afternoon. Eurailpass holders ride free. **Boats** between Uppsala and Skokloster depart Uppsala Tuesday through Sunday at 11:45am, returning to Uppsala at 5:30pm. Round-trip passage costs 120SEK ($13). For details, check with the tourist office in any of the towns.

Visitor Information   The **Tourist Information Office** is at Fyris Torg 8 (© **018/27-48-00**), open Monday through Friday from 10am to 6pm and Saturday from 10am to 3pm.

Exploring Uppsala   At the end of Drottninggatan is the **Carolina Rediviva (University Library)** *☆* (© **018/471-39-00;** bus: 6, 7, or 22), with its more than five million volumes and 40,000 manuscripts, among them many rare works from the Middle Ages. But the manuscript that really draws visitors is the *Codex Argenteus* (Silver Bible), translated into the old Gothic language in the middle of the 3rd century and copied in about A.D. 525. It's the only book extant in the old Gothic script. Also worth seeing is *Carta Marina,* the earliest map (1539), a fairly accurate map of Sweden and its neighboring countries. Admission is 20SEK ($2.10), free for children under 12. The library's exhibition room is open Monday through Friday from 9am to 8pm.

Linnaeus Garden & Museum, Svartbäcksgatan 27 (© **018/10-94-90** for the museum, or 018/10-94-90 for the garden; walk straight from the rail station to Kungsgatan, and proceed for about 10 min. to Svartbäcksgatan), is the former home of Swedish botanist Carl von Linné, also known as Carolus Linnaeus, who developed a classification system for the world's plants and flowers. This museum is on the spot where he restored Uppsala University's botanical garden, which resembles a miniature baroque garden. His detailed sketches and descriptions of the garden have been faithfully followed. Admission to the museum is 25SEK ($2.65) adults, free for children. A donation is suggested for admission to the gardens. The museum is open from June to August, Tuesday through Sunday from noon to 4pm; closed from September to May. The gardens are open from May to August daily from 9am to 9pm and September daily from 9am to 7pm; closed October through April.

The largest cathedral in Scandinavia at nearly 120m (400 ft.) tall, the twin-spired Gothic **Uppsala Domkyrka** ☆, Domkyrkoplan 5 (© **018/18-72-01;** bus: 1 or 2), was founded in the 13th century. It was severely damaged in 1702 in a disastrous fire that swept over Uppsala, then was restored near the turn of the last century. Among the regal figures buried in the crypt is Gustavus Vasa. The remains of St. Erik, patron saint of Sweden, are entombed in a silver shrine. Botanist Linnaeus and philosopher-theologian Emanuel Swedenborg are also buried here. A small museum displays ecclesiastical relics of Uppsala. Admission to the cathedral is free; museum admission is 30SEK ($3.20) adults, 15SEK ($1.60) seniors and students, and 10SEK ($1.05) children 7 to 15, free for children under 7. The cathedral is open daily from 8am to 6pm. The museum is open April through August, daily from 10am to 5pm; September through March, Tuesday through Saturday from 11am to 3pm, Sunday from 12:30 to 3pm.

GRIPSHOLM CASTLE ☆☆   On an island in Lake Mälaren, Gripsholm Castle (Gripsholm Slottsfervaltning), P.O. Box 14, 64721 Mariefred (© **0159/ 101-94**)—the fortress built by Gustavus Vasa in the late 1530s—is one of the best-preserved castles in Sweden. It lies near Mariefred, an idyllic small town known for its vintage narrow-gauge railroad.

Even though Gripsholm was last occupied by royalty (Charles XV) in 1864, it's still a royal castle. Its outstanding features include a large collection of portrait paintings depicting obscure branches of the Swedish monarchy, its brooding architecture, and its 18th-century theater built for the amusement of the 18th-century actor-king Gustavus III. It's open from May to August, daily from 10am to 4pm; in September, Tuesday through Sunday from 10am to 3pm; and from October to April, Saturday and Sunday from noon to 3pm. Admission is 60SEK ($6.35) adults, 30SEK ($3.20) children 7 to 15, free for ages 6 and under.

Getting There   Gripsholm Castle is 68km (42 miles) southwest of Stockholm. By **car,** follow E20 south; you can drive directly to the castle parking lot. The Eskilstuna **bus** runs to the center of Mariefred, as do the boats. **Boats** leave from mid-May to September at 10am from Klara Mälarstrand Pier. The castle is a 10-minute walk from the center of Mariefred.

18

Switzerland

by Darwin Porter & Danforth Prince

Switzerland evokes images of towering peaks, mountain lakes, lofty pastures, and alpine villages, but it also offers a rich cultural life in cities such as sophisticated Geneva and perfectly preserved medieval Bern.

1 Geneva ★★★

Geneva is in the Rhône Valley at the southwestern corner of Lake Geneva (Lac Léman in French), between the Jura Mountains and the Alps. It's the capital of the canton of Geneva, the second-smallest canton in the Swiss confederation.

Switzerland's second-largest city is truly cosmopolitan. The setting is idyllic, on one of the biggest alpine lakes and within view of the glorious pinnacle of Mont Blanc. Filled with parks and promenades, the city becomes a virtual garden in summer. It's also one of the world's healthiest cities because the prevailing north wind blows away any pollution.

The yachts bobbing in the harbor and the Rolls-Royces cruising the promenades testify that Geneva is home to some of the richest people in the world. Its state religion is said to be banking—half of Switzerland's banks are located here.

Geneva has long held a position as a center of enlightenment and humane tolerance. Over the years it has offered a refuge to such controversial figures as Voltaire, Lenin, and native son Jean-Jacques Rousseau. Geneva also hosted religious reformers Knox and Calvin, and provided a safe haven for many artists. Today the headquarters of the International Red Cross and the World Health Organization are here, and they attract many other international organizations.

ESSENTIALS

GETTING THERE **By Plane** Geneva International Airport (© 022/717-71-11; www.gva.ch), though busy, is compact and easily negotiated. **Swiss International Airlines** (© 877/359-7947 in the U.S.; www.swiss.com) has the most frequent flights from North America.

To get into the center of Geneva, there's a train station linked to the air terminal with trains leaving about every 8 to 20 minutes from 5:39am to 11:36pm (trip time: 7 min.); the one-way fare is 8.40SF ($5.90) first class and 5SF ($3.50) second class. A taxi into town costs 30SF ($21) and up, or you can take bus no. 10 for 2.50SF ($1.75).

By Train Geneva's busiest, most central, and most visible CFF (Chemins de Fer Fédéraux) rail station is **Gare Cornavin** (sometimes referred to as Genève-Cornavin), place Cornavin (© 0900/300-300). Don't confuse it with **Gare Genève-Cointrin,** near the airport, which handles some of the spillover from its larger sibling.

By Car From Lausanne, head southwest on N1 to the very "end of southwestern Switzerland."

Switzerland

By Lake Steamer From late May to late September there are frequent daily arrivals by Swiss lake steamer from Montreaux, Vevey, and Lausanne (you can use your Eurailpass). If you're staying in the Left Bank (Old Town), get off at the Jardin Anglais stop in Geneva; Mont Blanc and Pâquis are the Right Bank stops. For more information, call ℂ **022/312-52-23.**

VISITOR INFORMATION Tourist Office The **Office du Tourisme de Genève,** 3 rue du Mont-Blanc (ℂ **022/909-70-00;** www.geneve-tourisme.ch), is at Gare Cornavin. The staff provides information and can arrange hotel reservations (in Geneva and throughout Switzerland) and excursion bookings, and can refer you to car-rental agencies. The office is open July through August, Monday from 10am to 6pm, Tuesday through Sunday from 9am to 6pm.

Websites After visiting the Geneva tourist office website noted above, check the following. Not so much a destination in itself as a good launching pad to other websites, **www.switzerland.com** can point the way to museums, hotels, restaurants, and other attractions. Although awkwardly designed, **www.myswitzerland. com** does have useful travel advice on hotels and travel packages and throws in current snow reports.

CITY LAYOUT Geneva is divided by **Lac Léman (Lake Geneva)** and the **Rhône River** into two sections: the Right Bank and Left Bank. You may rent an audio-guided tour in English from the tourist office (see above) for 10SF ($7). This tour covers more than two dozen highlights in Old Town and comes with a cassette player and map. It lasts approximately 1½ hours. A 50SF ($35) deposit is required.

Rive Gauche (Left Bank) This compact and colorful area is the oldest section. Here you'll find Old Town, some major shopping streets, the famous Flower Clock, the university, and several important museums. **Grand' Rue** is Old Town's well-preserved main street, flanked by many houses from the 15th and 18th centuries. The street winds uphill from the ponts de l'Ile; at place Bel-Air it becomes rue de la Cité, then Grand' Rue, and finally rue Hôtel-de-Ville.

Eventually it reaches **place du Bourg-de-Four**—one of Geneva's most historic squares (Rousseau was born in no. 40).

South of this street is **promenade des Bastions,** a greenbelt area with a monument to the Reformation; it overlooks the Arve River. Directly to the west, in the northern corner of promenade des Bastions, is **place Neuve,** Geneva's finest square. From place Neuve, you can take **rue de la Corraterie,** once surrounded by the city wall, to the Rhône and the **ponts de l'Ile.** On this bridge is the Tour de l'Ile, what's left of the 13th-century bishop's castle.

On the shore of Lake Geneva is the **Jardin Anglais (English Garden)** with its Flower Clock, and farther out are the **Parc La Grange** and **Parc des Eaux-Vives.**

Rive Droite (Right Bank)   You can cross to the other side of the Rhône on any of several bridges, including **pont du Mont-Blanc, pont de la Machine, pont des Bergues,** and **ponts de l'Ile.** The Right Bank is home to **Gare Cornavin** (the train station), the major international organizations, and several attractive parks. **Place St-Gervais** is in the St-Gervais district; since the 18th century this has been an area for jewelers and watchmakers. Along the northern shore of Lake Geneva is **quai du Président-Wilson,** named for the U.S. president who helped found the League of Nations.

The Right Bank is surrounded by parks, from the tree-shaded promenades along the Rhône to the **Parc de la Perle du Lac, Parc Barton,** and **Parc Mon-Repos** on the outskirts.

GETTING AROUND   By Public Transportation   For the most part, all of Geneva's bus and tram lines begin at place Cornavin, in front of the rail station—running roughly from 5:30am to midnight daily. From here, you can take bus F or 8 to the Palais des Nations. Tickets for Zone 10, the urban area, are sold from automatic vending machines at each stop, operated by coins or magnetic cards (free cards are available from Geneva public transport agencies). Tickets for other zones, including Geneva's suburbs and France, are sold by drivers on the corresponding buses.

Four **basic tickets** are provided: free transfers for 1 hour in Zone 10, with as many changes as you wish on any vehicle, for 2.20SF ($1.55); a trip limited to three stops, valid for half an hour, allowing a return trip, at 1.50SF ($1.05); unlimited transportation for 1½ hours in all zones of the Geneva network, at 5SF ($3.50); and a ride for 1 hour in Zone 10 for children 6 to 12 as well as seniors (women over 62 and men over 65), at 1.50SF ($1.05). Children 5 and under ride free.

You can buy **multiuse tickets** and **daily cards** from agents whose addresses are listed on posts at the various stops. A wide range of these is available, and often you can adapt the system to your needs. For example, a daily ticket for unlimited transportation in Zone 10 is 6SF ($4.20) for as many trips and changes as you need; it's valid from the time you stamp it up to the termination of the day's service, around midnight. There's also a daily ticket at 12SF ($8.40) that includes transportation not only in Zone 10, but in Zones 21, 31, and 41, taking in practically the whole network of greater Geneva. Many worthy attractions and restaurants are in the suburbs.

These tickets and many other kinds, including combined bus/cable-car tickets to climb to the top of Mont Salève, are available from the Geneva public-transport systems agencies or from official dealers. For customer service and more information, call ✆ 022/308-34-34.

Geneva

SWITZERLAND
★ Bern
• Geneva

ATTRACTIONS ●

Baur Collections **25**
Cathédrale St-Pierre **22**
Flower Clock **18**
Jardin Anglais **19**
Jardin Botanique **4**
Jet d'Eau **17**
Maison Travel **21**
Musée Ariana **2**
Musée d'Art et d'Histoire **24**
Musée International de la
   Croix-Rouge et du
   Croissant-Rouge **1**
Palais des Nations **3**

ACCOMMODATIONS ■

Bel-Espérance **23**
Edelweiss Manotel **13**
Hôtel Beau-Rivage **15**
Hôtel Central **10**
Hôtel de la Cloche **16**
Hôtel des Bergues **12**
Hôtel du Midi **11**
Hôtel International & Terminus **5**
Hôtel Moderne **7**
Hôtel St-Gervais **8**
Hôtel Tiffany **9**
Hôtel Touring-Balance **20**
Le Richemond **14**
Strasbourg-Geneva **6**

✝ Church
ⓘ Information
✉ Post Office
— Railway

Lac Léman

quai de Cologny

rampe de Cologny

place de Traînant

PARC DES EAUX-VIVES

PARC LA GRANGE

quai Wilson

16

rue des Pâquis

15
14
13

quai du Mont-Blanc

Jet d'Eau

17

rte de Frontenex

av. William-Favre

rue des Eaux-Vives

rue des Montchoisy

Vollandes

rue du 31- de Décembre

Mont-Blanc

12
11

quai des Bergues

pont du Mont-Blanc

LES EAUX-VIVES

quai Gustave-Ador

pont de la Machine

pont des Bergues

quai Général-

JARDIN ANGLAIS

18 **19**

Guisan

av. Pictet-de-Rochemont

rte de Chêne

av. Th. Weber

place du Rhône

rue du Rhône

rue du Rhône

20

rue de Rive

rond-point de Rive

rue Pierre-Fatio

bd. Helvétique

place des Eaux-Vives

rue de la Terrassière

place Bel-Air

rue de la Croix-d'Or

10

rue de la Rôtisserie Madeleine

Vieux-Collège

23

rue Ferdinand-Hodler

rte de Malagnou

VIEILLE VILLE (Old Town)

21 **22**

Grand-Rue

rue Hôtel-de-Ville

place du Bourg-de-Four

rue Charles-Galland

24

bd. des Tranchées

MALAGNOU

place Neuve

rue de la Croix-Rouge

rue Général-Dufour

PROMENADE DES BASTIONS

rue de Candolle

rue St-Léger

bd. J.-

Dalcroze

rue St-Victor

bd. Helvétique

25

rue des Contamines

rte de Florissant

av. Krieg

Chemin Rieu

rond-point de Plainpalais

PLAINE DE PLAINPALAIS

bd. des Philosophes

rue de Carouge

place Claparède

rue de l'Athénée

PARC BERTRAND

av. Peschier

av. Louis-Aubert

PLAINPALAIS

bd. du Pont-d'Arve

bd. de la Cluse

av. de Champel

By Taxi   Cab fares start at 6.50SF ($4.55), plus 2.70SF to 3.30SF ($1.90–$2.30) for each kilometer in the city. No tipping is required. For a taxi, call ℭ **022/331-41-33** or 022/320-20-20.

By Car   Driving isn't recommended—parking is too difficult and the many one-way streets make navigation complicated. However, should you wish to rent a car and tour Lake Geneva, you'll find many rental companies at the airport or in the city center. Major offices include **Avis,** 44 rue de Lausanne (ℭ **022/731-90-00,** or 022/929-03-30 at the airport); **Budget,** 36 rue de Zurich (ℭ **022/900-24-00**); **Hertz,** 60 rue de Berne (ℭ **022/731-12-00,** or 022/798-22-02 at the airport); and **Europcar** (ℭ **022/909-69-90,** or 022/798-11-10 at the airport).

By Bicycle or Motor Scooter   Touring the city by bicycle isn't practical because of the steep cobblestone streets and general congestion. However, you might want to rent a bike to visit the nearby countryside. The major rental outlet is at the *bagages* desk at **Gare Cornavin** (ℭ **051/225-14-80**), where city bikes are 26SF ($18) per day and mountain bikes 35SF ($25) per day.

If you're interested in renting a motorbike, try **Horizon Motos,** 51 rue de Lausanne (ℭ **022/732-29-90**), where rentals begin at 76SF ($53) per day.

 FAST FACTS: **Geneva**

American Express   The office at 7 rue du Mont-Blanc (ℭ 022/731-76-00; bus: 1) is open Monday through Friday from 8:30am to 6pm and Saturday from 9am to noon.

Business Hours   Most **banks** are open Monday through Friday from 8:30am to 4:30pm (to 5:30pm on Wed). Most **offices** are open Monday through Friday from 8am to noon and 2 to 6pm, though this can vary. It's always best to call first.

Consulates   If you lose your passport or have other business with your home government, go to your nation's consulate: **United States,** 7 rue Versonnex (ℭ 022/840-51-60; tram to Gare Genè-Cointrin [airport]); **Australia,** 56–58 rue Moillebeau (ℭ 022/79-991-00; bus: 3); **Canada,** 1 chemin du Pré-de-la-Bichette (ℭ 022/919-92-00; bus: 5, 8, or 18); **New Zealand,** 28A chemin du Petit-Saconnex (ℭ 022/929-03-50; bus: 3); the **United Kingdom,** 37–39 rue de Vermont (ℭ 022/918-24-00; bus: 3); or **South Africa,** 65 rue de Rhône (ℭ 022/849-54-54; bus: 2, 9, or 22). Call for hours.

Currency   Unlike most of the other nations of western Europe, Switzerland is not part of the euro zone. The country has opted to retain its allegiance to its national currency, the **Swiss franc (SF),** which is composed of 100 centimes. At press time, the rate of exchange for the dollar vs. the Swiss franc, and the rate used throughout this chapter, is $1 = 1.40SF. Stated differently, 1SF = approximately 70 US cents. Since the euro and the US dollar are trading more or less at par, the same exchange rates, more or less, apply to the euro vs. the Swiss franc. Also at press time, the approximate rate of exchange for the British pound is as follows: 1£ = 2.64SF, or1SF = approximately 38 pence.

Currency Exchange   The exchange at **Gare Cornavin,** 10 place Cornavin (ℭ 022/375-33-60; tram to Gare Cornavin), is open Monday through

Friday from 8:30am to 4:30pm. For other financial transactions, the **Société de Banque Suisse (Swiss Bank Corporation)** is at 2 rue de la Confédération (℅ **022/375-75-75**; bus: 12).

Dentists/Doctors English-speaking dentists are available at one of the *cliniques dentaires* at 5 rue Malombré (℅ **022/346-64-44**; tram: 12), Monday through Friday from 8am to 7pm and Saturday and Sunday from 9am to 5pm. In a medical emergency, call ℅ **022/322-20-20**; or arrange an appointment with an English-speaking doctor at the **Hôpital Cantonal**, 24 rue Micheli-du-Crest (℅ **022/372-33-11**; tram: 12).

Drugstores One of the world's biggest drugstores, **Pharmacie Principale,** Confédération-Centre, rue de la Confédération (℅ **022/318-66-60**; bus: 12), offers everything from medicine to clothing, perfumes, optical equipment, cameras, and photo supplies. It's open Monday through Friday from 9am to 7pm and Saturday from 9am to 6pm.

Emergencies In an emergency, dial ℅ **117** for the police, ℅ **144** for an ambulance, and ℅ **118** to report a fire.

Hospitals You can go to the **Hôpital Cantonal**, 24 rue Micheli-du-Crest (℅ **022/372-33-11**).

Internet Access You can check your e-mail at **Charly's Multi-Media Check Point Bittar Charles,** 7 rue de Fribourg, near Gare Cornavin. An Internet connection costs 55SF per hour. It's open Monday through Friday from 9am to midnight and Saturday and Sunday from 2 to 10pm.

Post Office The city's main post office, **Bureau de Poste Montbrillant,** rue de Gares (℅ **022/739-21-11**; tram to Gare Cornavin), offers a full range of telephone, telegraph, and mail-related services Monday through Friday from 7:30am to 10pm, Saturday from 8am to 8pm, and Sunday from noon to 8pm. There's a branch, which offers less extensive services, at **Gare Cornavin,** 16 rue de Gares (℅ **022/739-23-58**), open Monday through Friday from 6am to 10:45pm, Saturday from 6am to 8pm, and Sunday from noon to 8pm.

Safety Crimes of violence, such as muggings, are rare in Switzerland. It is generally safe to walk the streets of cities day and night. The most common crime reported by visitors is a picked pocket.

Taxes No taxes are added to purchases in Switzerland. Swiss merchants pay tax to the government, and the percentage is included in the price marked on any object.

Telephones/Telex/Fax The **country code** for Switzerland is **41**. The **city code** for Geneva is **22**; use this code when you're calling from outside Switzerland. If you're within Switzerland but not in Geneva, use **022**. If you're calling within Geneva, simply leave off the code and dial the regular phone number.

There's a big, 24-hour **long-distance phone center** at the main train station, Gare Cornavin, place Cornavin. It's much cheaper to make your calls here than at your hotel—some Geneva hotels add a 40% surcharge to long-distance calls. Telegrams and faxes can be sent at the post office at 16 rue des Gares (℅ **022/739-21-21**), 2 blocks from the train station. For **AT&T Direct,** call ℅ **0-800-89-0011**; for **Sprint,** call ℅ **800/877-4646**; for **World Phone,** call ℅ **800/444-4141**.

Tipping A 15% service charge is automatically included in all hotel and restaurant bills, although some people leave an additional tip for exceptional service. For taxis, a tip is usually included in the fare; look for the notice posted in the cab.

WHERE TO STAY
ON THE RIGHT BANK
Very Expensive

Hôtel Beau-Rivage 🏨🏨🏨 This landmark 1865 hotel receives our highest recommendation for its traditional Victorian charm and impeccable service. However, you pay dearly for them. The "romantic" rooms are bigger than the "classical." Double-glazed windows cut down on street noise. Each unit has a roomy bathroom, with robes and a tub/shower combo. Units in front open onto views of the Right Bank. Its deluxe restaurant, Le Chat-Botté, is recommended below.

13 quai du Mont-Blanc, CH-1201 Genève. © **022/716-66-66.** Fax 022/716-60-60. www.beau-rivage.ch. 97 units. 475SF–860SF ($333–$602) double; 1,080SF–8,100SF ($756–$5670) suite. AE, DC, MC, V. Parking 35SF ($25). Bus: 1. **Amenities:** 2 restaurants; piano bar; 24-hr. room service; babysitting; laundry. *In room:* A/C, TV, minibar, hair dryer.

Hôtel des Bergues 🏨🏨🏨 Even more dazzling than the Beau-Rivage, this is one of the world's grand hotels, the choice of any visiting monarch. It's grandly memorable from its central position at the edge of the Rhône. The staff is the most hospitable in Geneva. Rooms have Directoire and Louis-Philippe furnishings. Those ranked superior on the Bel Etage floor are the finest choices, although lake view rooms are more expensive. Bathrooms have tub/shower combos, phones, and full-length mirrors.

33 quai des Bergues, CH-1211 Genève. © **022/908-70-00.** Fax 022/908-70-90. www.hoteldesbergues.com. 123 units. 670SF–990SF ($469–$693) double; from 1,190SF ($833) suite. AE, DC, MC, V. Parking 35SF ($25) per night. Bus: 7. **Amenities:** 2 restaurants; bar; 24-hr. room service; laundry. *In room:* A/C, TV, minibar, hair dryer, safe.

Le Richemond 🏨🏨🏨 This regal palace is Geneva's greatest hotel and counts some of the world's most prominent people among its guests. Erected in 1875, the neoclassical building is near the lake. Nearly half of the units are suites. A large number are renovated every year but even those between rehabs look as good as new. This is true Grand Hotel living, with luxurious beds and spacious bathrooms with tub/shower combos. Gentilhomme is among the finest dining rooms in Geneva, and Le Jardin is the city's most fashionable cafe.

Jardin Brunswick, CH-1211 Genève. © **022/715-70-00.** Fax 022/715-70-01. www.richemond.ch. 100 units. 790SF–890SF ($553–$623) double; from 1,400SF ($980) suite. AE, DC, MC, V. Parking 55SF ($39). Bus: 1. **Amenities:** Restaurant; cafe; piano bar; health club; 24-hr. room service; laundry; nonsmoking rooms. *In room:* A/C, TV, minibar, hair dryer.

Moderate

Hôtel du Midi On a tree-lined square near the center of Geneva, this hotel resembles an apartment building. Midsize rooms, though not spectacular, are well maintained and comfortable, with double-glazed windows to keep out traffic noise. Bathrooms are a bit cramped but have adequate shelf space and warming racks for towels.

4 place Chevelu, CH-1211 Genève. ⓒ 022/544-1500. Fax 022/731-00-20. www.hotel-du-midi.ch. 90 units. 240SF–360SF ($168–$252) double. AE, DC, MC, V. Parking 20SF ($14). Bus: 7. **Amenities:** Restaurant; bar; room service; laundry. *In room:* A/C, TV, minibar, hair dryer, safe.

Hôtel Moderne   This hotel is near the rail station and the lake. Public areas are modern. Rooms, with soundproof windows, are modern, clean, and sunny, though predictably furnished and a bit sterile. You'll probably wish the bathrooms had more room to spread out your stuff. The nearest parking is at the Cornavin rail station's underground garage.

1 rue de Berne, CH-1211 Genève. ⓒ 022/732-81-00. Fax 022/738-26-58. www.hotelmoderne.ch. 55 units. 190SF–200SF ($133–$140) double. Rates include buffet breakfast. AE, DC, MC, V. Bus: 10. **Amenities:** Breakfast room; restaurant (under separate management); room service; babysitting; laundry; nonsmoking rooms. *In room:* TV.

Strasbourg-Geneva   It may have been constructed at the beginning of this past century, but 1999 renovations mean it's up to date and better than ever. For decades it has offered a safe haven for those arriving at the Geneva train station. The most spacious rooms tend to be those on the lower floors. The compact bathrooms are minimally equipped, each with a shower unit.

10 rue J.-J.-Pradier, CH-1201 Genève. ⓒ Best Western, 800/528-1234 in the U.S., or 022/906-58-00. Fax 022/738-42-08. www.strasbourg-geneva.ch. 53 units. 220SF–250SF ($154–$175) double; 260SF–500SF ($182–$350) suite. Rates include continental breakfast. AE, DC, MC, V. Bus: 1, 2, 3, 4, 8, 12, 13, or 44. **Amenities:** Breakfast room; lounge. *In room:* TV, minibar, hair dryer, iron, safe.

Inexpensive

Bel-Espérance ⭐ *Value*   This is an accommodation oddity, and a bit of a discovery. Once it was known as a *foyer pour dames* or boardinghouse for women. Right near the Old Town's place du Bourg-de-Four, it's owned by the Salvation Army, but don't fear that this is a rawboned joint. This little hotel of charm and grace has a panoramic terrace and bright midsize rooms; bathrooms have showers. It's also a choice for families, as some rooms are large enough for four beds. Try to get one with a balcony with a view of the Cathedrale St-Pierre.

1 rue de la Vallée, CH-1204 Geneva. ⓒ 022/818-3737. Fax 022/818-3773. www.hotel-bel-esperance.ch. 40 units. 130SF–170SF ($91–$119) double; 150SF–180SF ($105–$126) triple. Rates include breakfast. AE, MC, V. Bus: 0. Tram: 12. **Amenities:** Breakfast room. *In room:* TV.

Hôtel de la Cloche *Value*   This small hotel, one of Geneva's best deals, occupies the second floor of a 19th-century apartment building on a narrow street behind the Noga Hilton. It's unpretentious despite a glamorous location. Rooms are spacious, well cared for, and designed with an eye to old-fashioned comfort. Some have views over a quiet inner courtyard and others open onto views over the lake. Private bathrooms have rather cramped shower stalls; corridor bathrooms are well maintained, and there's rarely a wait.

6 rue de la Cloche, CH-1211 Genève. ⓒ 022/732-94-81. Fax 022/738-16-12. www.smpage.ch/cloche. 8 units, 5 with bathroom. 95SF ($67) double without bathroom, 120SF ($84) double with bathroom; 105SF ($74) triple without bathroom; 145SF ($102) quad without bathroom. Rates include breakfast. AE, MC, V. Bus: 1. **Amenities:** Breakfast room; lounge.

Hôtel International & Terminus   This hotel lies across from the main entrance of Geneva's railway station and has been run by three generations of the Cottier family. Built around 1900, it was radically upgraded in 2000, with pairs of smaller rooms reconfigured into larger units. Don't expect grand style; the allure of this place is its exceedingly good value. Bathrooms seem to have been added as an afterthought in areas not designed for them, and are a bit cramped, each with a shower stall.

20 rue des Alpes, CH-1201 Genève. © **022/732-80-95.** Fax 022/732-18-43. 53 units. 150SF–180SF ($105–$126) double. Rates include continental breakfast. AE, DC, MC, V. Bus: 6, 10, or 33. **Amenities:** Restaurant and bar. *In room:* TV, minibar.

Hôtel St-Gervais *Value* This good-value hotel lies in an old-fashioned, vaguely nondescript building within Geneva's medieval core, a 3-minute walk from Gare Cornavin. The old inn has the kind of quirky idiosyncrasies that appeal to architects and historic renovators. If you don't mind the lack of a bathroom, you'll find the midsize guest rooms tidily kept, tastefully furnished, and most comfortable. Most rooms have a sink, but the hall bathrooms are frequently tidied for the next guest's use.

20 rue des Corps-Saints, CH1201 Genève. ©/fax **022/732-45-72.** 26 units, 2 with bathroom. 78SF ($55) double without bathroom; 98SF–105SF ($69–$74) double with bathroom. AE, MC, V. Tram: 1, 3, 4, 5, or 6. **Amenities:** Pub; lounge; laundry. *In room:* No phone.

ON THE LEFT BANK
Moderate

Edelweiss Manotel *Finds* This is the most artfully folkloric hotel in Geneva, evoking the kind of cozy alpine decor that most Swiss people associate with isolated hamlets in the country's mountains. Although it was built in a seven-story boxy-looking design in 1967 and renovated in 1999, the interior—including each guest room—showcases the meticulous craftsmanship of another era. That's thanks to carefully finished pinewood paneling and country-baroque accessories that show off *gemutlich* Switzerland at its most charming. The hotel's social centerpiece is its restaurant.

2 place de la Navigation, CH-1201 Genève. © **022/544-51-51.** Fax 022/544-51-99. www.manotel.com. 42 units. 250SF ($175) double; 285SF ($200) triple. Rates include breakfast. AE, DC, MC, V. Bus: 1. **Amenities:** Restaurant; bar; concierge; massage; babysitting; laundry/dry cleaning. *In room:* A/C, TV, minibar, safe.

Hotel Tiffany *Value* This little charmer of a Belle Epoque boutique hotel lies on a Left Bank street 3 blocks south of the river and about a 12-minute stroll from the center and the lake. Although it can hardly match the style and glamour of the lakeside palaces, it is attractive in its modest way. In its category, it offers some of the most reasonable prices in Geneva. Rooms are midsize with lots of extras, including soundproofing and spacious bathrooms with tub/shower combos. We like the rooms in the "attic," with their beams, rooftop vistas, and sloping walls.

1 rue des Marbriers, CH-1204 Genève. © **022/708-1616.** Fax 022/708-1617. www.hotel-tiffany.ch. 46 units. 300SF–320SF ($210–$224) double; from 470SF ($329) suite. Buffet breakfast included. AE, DC, MC, V. Bus: 1 or 4. **Amenities:** Restaurant; English bar. *In room:* A/C, TV, minibar, hair dryer, safe.

Hôtel Touring-Balance Previously two hotels across the street from each other, the Touring-Balance is in the heart of the Left Bank's shopping district. A major renovation in 1999 transformed the lobby with a theme like that of an Italian garden, complete with *jardinières* and potted plants. Rooms in both sections are comparable in style and amenities. Upper floors are more modern than the traditional lower floors. Some units are air-conditioned. Bathrooms are compact, neat, and well kept.

13 place Longemalle, CH-1204 Genève. © **022/818-62-62.** Fax 022/818-62-61. 60 units. 270SF ($189) double; 270SF–380SF ($189–$266) suite. Rates include buffet breakfast. AE, DC, MC, V. Bus: 6, 8, or 9. **Amenities:** Restaurant; coffee shop; laundry. *In room:* TV, minibar.

Inexpensive

Hotel Central *Value* This Left Bank bargain has been completely rejuvenated. Since its reopening, it's been a success as word of its good value has spread to budget-minded travelers. On a shopping street, it has a warm and inviting Bali-inspired decor. The location is at the foot of the Old Town and only a 3-minute walk to the lake. The Gansted family is on hand to welcome you, and each of their rooms is personalized, containing comfortable beds and small but neat bathrooms with shower stalls. A few rooms have bunk beds suitable for families or friends traveling together. Some rooms are very large with two separate bathrooms.

2 rue de la Rôtisserie, CH-1204 Genève. ✆ 022/818-8100. Fax 022/818-8101. www.hotelcentral.ch. 30 units. 75SF–160SF ($53–$112) double; 200SF ($140) junior suite; 80SF ($56) per person bunk bed. Rates include breakfast. AE, DC, MC, V. Tram: 12. **Amenities:** Lounge. *In room:* TV.

WHERE TO DINE
ON THE RIGHT BANK
Very Expensive
Le Chat-Botté 🔒🔒🔒 FRENCH "Puss in Boots" is in one of Geneva's grandest hotels. It's a close race between this deluxe dining room and the Hilton's Le Cygne (see below) as to which serves the best cuisine in Geneva. We'd give the honors to Le Chat Botté for French dishes, with Le Cygne winning for fresh seafood. In nice weather you can dine on the flower-decked terrace, overlooking the Jet d'Eau. The cuisine, though inspired by French classics, is definitely contemporary. The large selection includes filets of red mullet vinaigrette, a divine lobster salad with eggplant "caviar," and breast of chicken stuffed with vegetables. Highly recommended is delicate perch filet from Lake Geneva, sautéed until it's golden and sometimes served with fava beans. In the autumn, gourmets flock here for the roast saddle of roebuck, prepared only for two or more diners.

In the Hôtel Beau-Rivage, 13 quai du Mont-Blanc. ✆ 022/716-69-20. Reservations required. Main courses 45SF–55SF ($32–$39). Fixed-price menus (Mon–Fri only) 60SF–145SF ($42–$102) lunch, 115SF–145SF ($81–$102) dinner. AE, DC, MC, V. Daily noon–2pm and 7–10pm. Bus: 6 or 33.

Le Cygne 🔒🔒🔒 FRENCH This swank restaurant overlooks the harbor with the famous Jet d'Eau and, in the distance, the Alps. A refined cuisine is offered, with impeccable service. The menu may present such stellar choices as terrine of blackened chicken in crayfish- and anise-flavored aspic. Also worthy of an award are the smoked filet of sea bass with truffle-flavored vinaigrette and the roasted lamb with coriander and tomatoes stuffed with moussaka. Five elaborate carts make one of the most spectacular arrays of desserts in Switzerland.

In the Noga Hilton International, 19 quai du Mont-Blanc. ✆ 022/908-90-85. Reservations required. Main courses 52SF–98SF ($36–$69). Fixed-price meal 61SF–81SF ($43–$57) lunch; 109SF–159SF ($76–$111) dinner. AE, DC, MC, V. Daily noon–2pm and 7–10:30pm. Closed 1 week in Jan, 11 days at Easter, and Aug 11–Sept 1. Bus: 1.

Le Neptune 🔒🔒🔒 SEAFOOD This place is hot on the heels of Le Cygne for the title of Geneva's finest seafood restaurant. The decor is intimate, intensely floral, and graced with an enormous fresco displaying an inside view of Neptune's kingdom. Though the menu changes, you're likely to be offered such dishes as herbed vichyssoise with hazelnut oil and a dollop of foie gras; a perfect cassolette of oysters seasoned with algae-flavored butter sauce; or a memorable Atlantic sea bass roasted in a salt crust with thyme. If you're not in the mood for fish, try rack of Scottish lamb in puff pastry with spices or partridge roasted en casserole with autumn herbs.

In the Hôtel du Rhône, 1 quai Turrettini. ✆ 022/909-00-06. Reservations required. Main courses 45SF–65SF ($32–$46). Fixed-price meal 68SF ($48) lunch; 68SF–130SF ($48–$91) dinner. AE, DC, MC, V. Mon–Fri noon–2pm and 7:30–10pm. Bus: 6, 8, 10, or 15.

Moderate

Chez Jacky ⚘ SWISS   This French provincial bistro is a delightful place for dining, attracting everyone from staid grandmothers to young skiers en route to Verbier. It's the domain of Jacky Gruber, an exceptional chef from Valais. You might begin with Chinese cabbage and mussels and continue with filet of turbot roasted with thyme or beautifully prepared pink duck on spinach with onion confit. Be prepared to wait for each course, as everything is prepared to order.

9–11 rue Necker. ✆ 022/732-86-80. Reservations recommended. Main courses 42SF–45SF ($29–$32); 3-course business lunch 45SF ($32). AE, DC, MC, V. Mon–Fri 11am–3pm and 6:30–11pm. Closed 1st week of Jan and 3 weeks in Aug. Bus: 5, 10, or 44.

Jeck's Place ⚘ PAN-ASIAN   Near the Cornavin rail station, this delightful place is like taking a culinary trip to southeast Asia, with stopovers in such places as China, Malaysia, Thailand, and India. The cuisine of Asian specialties provides temptation with every order. We often make a meal of the appetizers alone, including homemade steamed dumplings stuffed with a blend of pork and vegetables flavored with coriander. The house specialty, and our favorite dish, is Jeck's chicken in green curry. Another exotic treat is a delicate whiting spread with spicy lemon grass sauce and grilled on banana leaves.

14 rue de Neuchâtel. ✆ 022/731-3303. Reservations recommended. Main courses 18SF–32SF ($13–$22). Special lunch platter 13SF ($9.10). AE, DC, MC, V. Mon–Fri 11:30am–2pm and 6:30–10pm. Bus: 4, 5, or 9.

La Mère Royaume ⚘ FRENCH   Opened around the turn of the 20th century, this is one of the oldest restaurants in town. It's named after a heroine who in 1602 poured boiling stew over a Savoyard soldier's head and cracked his skull with the kettle. With an antecedent like that, you'd expect some of the heartiest fare in Geneva, but instead the kitchen offers perfectly cooked French specialties such as *omble chevalier,* a delicate Lake Geneva whitefish known as "the world's most divine trout." Less expensive meals are served in the brasserie.

9 rue des Corps-Saints. ✆ 022/732-70-08. Reservations required. Brasserie, main courses 18SF–35SF ($13–$25); fixed-price menu 44SF–50SF ($31–$35). Restaurant, main courses 30SF–50SF ($21–$35); fixed-price menus 50SF–98SF ($35–$69). AE, DC, MC, V. Mon–Fri noon–2pm and 7–10:30pm; Sat 7–10:30pm. Bus: 4, 6, or 7.

Le Boeuf Rouge ⚘ LYONNAISE   This brasserie serves Geneva's best cookery in the style of Lyons, the gastronomic capital of France. As such, you'll find authentic versions of such dishes as Lyonnais sausage with scalloped potatoes; chateaubriand in red wine sauce; blood sausage; and quenelles of pikeperch, any of which might be preceded by a delectable version of onion soup or green salad with croutons and bacon. The decor is appealingly kitschy, complete with lots of Art Nouveau posters and late-19th-century ceramics. The staff here is brusque but kindly.

17 rue Alfred-Vincent (at the corner of rue Paquis). ✆ 022/732-75-37. Reservations recommended. Main courses 18SF–50SF ($13–$35). Set-price meals 37SF ($26) lunch; 47SF–52SF ($33–$36) dinner. AE, DC, MC, V. Mon–Fri noon–2pm and 7–10:30pm. Bus: 1.

Les Armures ⚘ (Kids) SWISS/INTERNATIONAL   In spite of the government-rated five-star elegance of the hotel that contains this restaurant, this is surprisingly unpretentious and affordable. Dining is possible on three different floors. The lower you go, the more animated the scene becomes. This stone building is located on a cobblestone street across from a medieval arsenal in one of the most colorful neighborhoods of the Old Town. The building was constructed in the 16th century, and this place has thrived as one of the most atmospheric restaurants since its founding in 1957. The three different fondues offered are the best in Geneva. Many Swiss children make an entire meal out of *rösti* or Swiss-style hash browns. Other specialties include raclette and several pizza and pasta dishes, plus our favorite dishes here, duck liver terrine followed by seared scallops Provençal. The winter-only sauerkraut garni is also a savory meal—made with several types of sausage and pork. The staff still remembers the day in January 1994 when Bill Clinton dropped in to sample the sauerkraut during a break in political negotiations. Pastas and hamburgers round out the menu, which should make any child's palate happy.

Hôtel Les Armures, 1 rue des Puits-St-Pierre. ℂ 022/310-34-42. Main courses 25SF–45SF ($18–$32); fixed-price menu 50SF ($35). AE, DC, MC, V. Mon–Fri noon–3pm and 6–11:30pm; Sat–Sun noon–11:30pm. Bus: 3 or 5.

ON THE LEFT BANK
Expensive

Le Béarn 🏵🏵🏵 FRENCH This is the only deluxe restaurant on the Left Bank that matches the previously recommended three-star choices on the Right Bank. Jean-Paul Goddard and his excellent staff have created the best restaurant in Geneva's business center. With only 10 tables, everything is on a small scale, and the service is personal. The chef prepares dishes that appeal to the Rothschild palates, including such spectacular delights as tender morels stuffed with fresh asparagus tips. One of the world's most expensive birds, roasted Scottish thrush, might rest on your platter, or our all-time favorite concoction here, a platter called "three terrines of autumn" (rabbit, partridge, and thrush).

4 quai de la Poste. ℂ 022/321-00-28. Reservations required. Main courses 40SF–60SF ($28–$42). Fixed-price meals 55SF–60SF ($39–$42) lunch; 125SF–190SF ($88–$133) dinner. AE, DC, MC, V. Mon–Fri noon–2pm; Mon–Sat 7:30–10pm. Closed mid-July to mid-Aug and Sat June–Sept. Bus: 2, 10, or 22.

Moderate

Au Pied de Cochon LYONNAISE/SWISS Come here for hearty Lyonnaise fare if you don't mind smoke and noise. A lot of young people are attracted to this place, as well as lawyers from the Palais de Justice across the way, artists, and local workers. The cooking is like grandma's—provided she came from Lyon. Naturally, the namesake *pieds de cochon* (pigs' feet) is included on the menu, along with *petit salé* (lamb), tripe, and some of the best grilled andouillettes (sausages made of chitterlings) in Geneva.

4 place du Bourg-de-Four. ℂ 022/310-47-97. Reservations recommended. Main courses 33SF–42SF ($23–$29). AE, DC, MC, V. Daily 7:30am–2:30pm and 6:30–10pm (closed Sun June–Aug). Bus: 2 or 22. Tram: 12.

Brasserie de l'Hôtel de Ville SWISS This is one of the most deliberately archaic-looking restaurants in Geneva, with a reputation that goes back to 1764 and a clientele who prefer that its old-fashioned decor and menu items absolutely not change. The menu is stylish and fashionable, offering such time-tested Swiss dishes as fondue, *tafelspitz* (boiled beef), Wiener schnitzel, glazed ham with béarnaise sauce, and, best of all, filets of perch and fera from the nearby lake.

19 Grand Rue. ℂ 022/311-70-30. Reservations recommended. Main courses 33SF–48SF ($23–$34); set-price menus 57SF–104SF ($40–$73). AE, DC, MC, V. Daily 11:30am–11:30pm. Bus: 17.

Brasserie Lipp SWISS/FRENCH This bustling place is named after the famous Parisian brasserie, and when you enter (especially at lunch), you'll think you've been transported to France. The impossibly long menu contains a sampling of the repertoire of bistro dishes, but, like its namesake, the Geneva Lipp specializes in several versions of charcuterie. You can also order three kinds of pot-au-feu and such classics as Toulousian cassoulet with *confit de canard* (duckling), available in autumn and winter. The fresh oysters are among the best in the city, and tables are placed outside in summer.

Confédération-Centre, 8 rue de la Confédération. © **022/311-10-11.** Reservations recommended. Main courses 18SF–46SF ($13–$32). AE, DC, MC, V. Daily 11:45am–1am. Bus: 12.

La Coupole SWISS/FRENCH/ITALIAN This is a true brasserie, and far more elegant than its Parisian namesake. The place is most popular at noon, especially with shoppers and office workers. The menu is limited but well selected; the *cuisine du marché* (cooking based on market-fresh ingredients) is some of the finest in this part of town. Chefs search the market in the early morning for the freshest and best ingredients.

116 rue du Rhône. © **022/787-50-10.** Main courses 24SF–39SF ($17–$27); fixed-price menus 42SF–48SF ($29–$34). AE, DC, MC, V. Mon–Sat 11:30am–2:30pm and 7:30pm–12:30am. Bus: 2, 9, or 22. Tram: 12.

La Favola TUSCAN/ITALIAN This is the best Italian dining spot in Geneva, and its most devoted habitués go even further, hailing it as the best restaurant in Geneva. The menu is small and short but choice, varying with the availability of ingredients and the season. Look for such well-crafted dishes as carpaccio of beef; *vitello tonnato* (paper-thin veal with a tuna sauce); lobster salad; potato salad with cèpe mushrooms; and a highly pleasing ravioli made with either eggplant or mushrooms.

15 rue Jean-Calvin. © **022/311-74-37.** Reservations required. Main courses 40SF–55SF ($28–$39). AE, MC, V. Mon–Fri noon–2pm and 7:15–10pm. Closed 1 week at Christmas, 2 weeks July–Aug. Tram: 12.

L'Aïoli PROVENÇAL This popular neighborhood restaurant stands opposite Le Corbusier's Maison de Verre. Something of a local secret, it offers personalized service and the finest Provençal cooking in town. We recommend frogs' legs Provençal, simmered in a savory tomato, onion, and garlic sauce; and also lamb *gigot,* in which the meat is infused with fresh herbs and garlic and baked to a tender perfection. The chefs also prepare a delectable lamb stew called *gardiane camarguaise.*

6 rue Adrien-Lachenal. © **022/736-79-71.** Reservations not necessary. Main courses 20SF–35SF ($14–$25); *menu dégustation* 73SF ($51). AE, DC, MC, V. Mon–Fri 11am–2:30pm and 7–10:30pm. Closed Aug. Bus: 1 or 6. Tram: 12.

Le Lyrique SWISS This is the best place for a pre-theater dinner, with both a formal restaurant and a brasserie. The brasserie, which has a terrace, is open all day but serves hot meals only during the hours mentioned below. When there's a performance at the nearby Grand Théâtre de Genève on Saturday or Sunday, the restaurant is also open. You can try such carefully prepared dishes as filet of sea wolf with grapefruit segments, a roulade of rabbit with pasta maison, and tagliatelle with scampi. In the brasserie, menu items include chicken suprême with ravioli and leeks, and an *assiette Lyrique,* a meal in itself that combines four vegetarian and fish dishes—tartare of salmon, tartare of vegetables, terrine of vegetables, and eggplant "caviar."

12 bd. du Théâtre. © **022/328-00-95.** Reservations recommended. Restaurant, main courses 25SF–45SF ($18–$32); fixed-price menus 50SF–62SF ($35–$43). Brasserie, main courses 39SF–50SF ($27–$35); fixed-price menus (lunch or dinner) 39SF–50SF ($27–$35). AE, MC, V. Mon–Fri noon–2pm and 6:30–10pm. Bus: 2 or 22.

Nô Sushi *(Value* JAPANESE Popular, hip, and mobbed every day at lunchtime, this is the only automated sushi bar in Switzerland and, as such, adds an eccentric and trend-conscious flair to a neighborhood that's better known for its relative conservatism. You'll pluck everything except the miso soup, which is carried to your seat by a waitress, directly from the moving conveyer belt. Hot foods remain hot thanks to a candle flickering beneath. Sushi (with rice) and sashimi (without rice) choices include mullet, calamari, octopus, salmon, and tuna. There's also teriyaki dishes, tempura, and a medley of rice and noodle dishes, any combinations of which make a full meal.

Confédération Centre, 8 rue de la Confédération. ✆ **022/810-39-73**. Reservations not necessary. Sushi, sashimi, rolls, and small platters 5SF–10SF ($3.50–$7). AE, MC, V. Mon–Thurs 11:30am–midnight; Fri–Sat 11:30am–1am. Closed Sun. Bus: 12.

Inexpensive

Pizzeria da Paolo *Value* ITALIAN/PIZZA   Bustling, convivial, and completely unpretentious, this simple pizzeria offers a cozy, wood-sheathed setting from a position very close to the Jet d'Eau. More than 20 kinds of pizza are offered—the house specialty is a Pizza Paolo, made from fresh spinach and cheese. But if pizzas aren't your thing, there's a full complement of chicken parmigiana; stuffed and roasted turkey; fresh salads; ham dishes; and fresh fish. Don't expect glamour or too much cosseting from the overworked staff—instead, you'll get a dose of reality, everyday grittiness, good value, and some filling and very tasty Italian food.

3 rue du Lac. ✆ **022/736-3049**. Reservations recommended. Pizza 14SF–22SF ($9.80–$15). Main platters 20SF–48SF ($14–$34). AE, DC, MC, V. Daily 11:45am–2pm and 6:45–11pm. Tram 12.

Taverne de la Madeleine SWISS/FRENCH   This very good restaurant is set against the old city wall beside the Eglise de la Madeleine. The brusquely efficient staff caters to a lunchtime business crowd, and the place is operated by a philanthropic organization that forbids the consumption of alcohol (alcohol-free beer is available). You can order a variety of well-prepared dishes or specials like four types of pasta, vegetarian sandwiches, and a big plate of *osso buco* (braised veal shank) with *pommes frites* (French-fried potatoes). The kitchen prides itself on its filet of lake perch meunière style (in butter sauce) or Vevey style with exotic mushrooms. Most dishes are at the lower end of the price scale.

20 rue Toutes-Ames. ✆ **022/310-60-70**. Reservations recommended. Main courses 15SF–27SF ($11–$19); *plat du jour* 15SF ($11). MC, V. Sept–June Mon–Fri 11:30am–2:30pm, Sat 9am–4:30pm; July–Aug Tues–Sat 7:30am–9pm. Bus: 2. Tram: 12.

SEEING THE SIGHTS

You can see most of Geneva on foot, which is the best way to familiarize yourself with the city.

THE TOP ATTRACTIONS

In addition to the sights below, Geneva's top attractions are the **Jet d'Eau,** the famous fountain that has virtually become the city's symbol; the **Flower Clock,** in the Jardin Anglais; and the **Old Town,** the oldest part of the city.

Baur Collections ✦   The collections, housed in a 19th-century mansion with a garden, constitute a private exhibit of artworks from 7th- to 20th-century China and 17th- to 20th-century Japan. The choice ceramics here are from the Tang Dynasty (618–908). On display are jade, ceramics, lacquer, ivories, and delicate sword fittings.

8 rue Munier-Romilly. ✆ **022/346-17-29**. Admission 5SF ($3.50) adults, free for children. Tues–Sun 2–6pm. Bus: 1 or 8.

Cathédrale St-Pierre ✦   The old town, **Vieille Ville,** on the Left Bank, is dominated by the cathedral, built in the 12th and 13th centuries and partially reconstructed in the 15th century. In 1536, the people of Geneva gathered in

---

Moments **Exploring Geneva's Parks & Gardens**

If you walk along the quays, heading north as if to Lausanne, you'll come to some of the lushest parks in Geneva. **Parc Mon-Repos** is off avenue de France and **La Perle du Lac** lies off rue de Lausanne. Directly to the right is the **Jardin Botanique (Botanical Garden)**, opened in 1902. It has an alpine garden, a little zoo, greenhouses, and exhibitions. You can visit it free daily, October through March from 9:30am to 5pm and April through September from 8am to 7:30pm. From Cornavin Station, take bus no. 4.

Back at the lakeside, you can take a boat to the other bank, getting off at quai Gustave-Ador. From here you can explore two more lakeside parks—**Parc la Grange,** which has the most extravagant rose garden in Switzerland (especially in June), and, next to it, **Parc des Eaux-Vives.**

When you leave the Botanical Garden on the Left Bank, you can head west, along avenue de la Paix, about a mile north from pont du Mont-Blanc, to the Palais des Nations in **Parc de l'Ariana.**

---

the cloister of St-Pierre's and voted to make the cathedral Protestant. The church has a modern organ with 6,000 pipes. The northern tower was reconstructed at the end of the 19th century. If you don't mind the 145 steps, you can climb to the top of the north tower for a panoramic view.

To enter the St-Pierre archaeological site, called **Site Archéologique de St-Pierre,** go through the entrance in the Cour St-Pierre, at the right corner of the cathedral steps. The underground passage extends under the present cathedral and the High Gothic (early-15th-c.) **Chapelle des Macchabées,** which adjoins the church's southwestern corner. Excavations have revealed baptisteries, a crypt, the foundations of several cathedrals, the bishop's palace, 4th-century mosaics, sculptures, and geological strata.

Cour St-Pierre. © 022/311-75-75. Admission 5SF ($3.50), 3SF ($2.10) seniors and students. Cathedral, tower, and excavations open June–Sept daily 9am–7pm; Oct–May Mon–Sat 10am–noon and 2–5pm, Sun 11:30am–12:30pm and 1:30–5pm. Bus: 3, 5, or 17.

Maison Tavel 𝄐 Built in 1303 and partially reconstructed after a fire in 1334, this is the city's oldest house and one of its newest museums. The museum exhibits historical collections from Geneva dating from the Middle Ages to the mid–19th century. The Magnin relief in the attic is outstanding, as is the copper-and-zinc model of 1850s Geneva. Objects of daily use are displayed in the old living quarters.

6 rue du Puits-St-Pierre. © 022/418-37-00. Free admission. Tues–Sun 10am–5pm. Bus: 3, 5 or 17.

Musée Ariana 𝄐𝄐 This is one of the top porcelain, glass, and pottery museums of Europe. To the west of the Palais des Nations, this Italian Renaissance building was constructed by Gustave Revilliod, the 19th-century Genevese patron who began the collection. Here you'll see Sèvres, Delft faience, and Meissen porcelain, as well as pieces from Japan and China. It's also the headquarters of the International Academy of Ceramics.

10 av. de la Paix. © 022/418-54-50. Free admission, but 4.50SF ($2.50) for special exhibits. Wed–Mon 10am–5pm. Bus: 8 or F.

Fun Fact **The Red Cross Flag**

When Henry Dunant founded the Red Cross in Geneva in 1863, he needed a recognizable symbol to suggest neutrality. The Swiss flag (a white cross on a red field), with the colors reversed, ended up providing the perfect symbol for one of the world's greatest humanitarian movements.

Musée d'Art et d'Histoire (Museum of Art and History) 🏛️🏛️ Geneva's most important museum is between boulevard Jacques-Dalcroze and boulevard Helvétique. It virtually presents the story of civilization from prehistoric times up to the present. Displays include prehistoric relics, Greek vases, medieval stained glass, 12th-century armor, Swiss timepieces, and Flemish and Italian paintings. The Etruscan pottery and medieval furniture are quite impressive. A 1444 altarpiece by Konrad Witz depicts the "miraculous" draught of fishes. Many galleries also contain works by such artists as Rodin, Renoir, Le Corbusier, Picasso, Chagall, Corot, Monet, and Pissarro.

2 rue Charles-Galland. ℂ 022/418-26-00. Free admission; 4.50SF ($2.50) temporary exhibitions. Tues–Sun 10am–5pm. Bus: 2, 3, 5, 7, 12, or 16.

Musée International de la Croix Rouge et du Croissant-Rouge (International Red Cross and Red Crescent Museum) 🏛️ Here you can experience the legendary past of the Red Cross in the city where it started; it's across from the visitors' entrance to the European headquarters of the United Nations. The dramatic story from 1863 to the present is revealed through displays of rare documents and photographs, films, multiscreen slide shows, and cycloramas. You're taken from the battlefields of Europe to the plains of Africa to see the Red Cross in action.

17 av. de la Paix. ℂ 022/748-95-11. Admission 10SF ($7) adults; 5SF ($3.50) seniors, students, and children Wed–Mon 10am–5pm. Bus: 8, F, V, or Z.

Palais des Nations 🏛️ Surrounded by ancient trees and modern monuments, these buildings comprise the second-largest complex in Europe after Versailles. Until 1936, the League of Nations met at the Palais Wilson, when the League's headquarters were transferred to the Palais des Nations. The international organization continued minor activities through the war years until it was dissolved in 1946, just as the newly created United Nations met in San Francisco. Today the Palais des Nations is the headquarters of the United Nations in Europe, with a modern wing added in 1973.

Inside are a **philatelic museum** and the **League of Nations Museum,** though the building itself is the most interesting attraction. Daily tours leave from the visitors' entrance at 14 av. de la Paix, opposite the Red Cross building. For information, contact the **Visitors' Service,** United Nations Office, 14 av. de la Paix (ℂ 022/907-45-60).

Parc de l'Ariana, 14 av. de la Paix. ℂ 022/907-48-96. Admission 8.50SF ($5.95) adults, 6.50SF ($4.55) students, 4SF ($2.80) children under 6. June–Aug daily 9am–6pm; Sept–Oct daily 10am–noon and 2–5pm; Nov–May Mon–Fri 10am–noon and 2–4pm. Bus: 2, 5, 8, 18, F, or V.

ORGANIZED TOURS

A 2-hour city tour is operated daily by **Key Tours S.A.,** 7 rue des Alpes, square du Mont-Blanc (ℂ 022/731-41-40). The tour starts from the Gare Routière, the bus station at place Dorcière, near the Key Tours office. November through

March, a tour is offered only once a day at 2pm; the rest of the year, two tours leave daily, at 10am and 2pm. A bus will drive you through the city to see the monuments, landmarks, and lake promenades. In the Old Town, you can take a walk down to the Bastions Park to the Reformation Wall. After an English-language tour through the International Center—where you'll be shown the headquarters of the International Red Cross—the bus returns to its starting place. Adults pay 39SF ($27), children 4 to 12 accompanied by an adult pay 19SF ($13), and children 3 and under go free.

THE SHOPPING SCENE

As you might suspect, watches, knives, cheese, and chocolate are among Geneva's best buys. Check prices carefully; many Swiss watches are currently cheaper in the United States than in Switzerland. Swiss army knives are still a good deal, and as for chocolate, well, it's incomparable and just not the same when you buy it in another country.

Geneva's Left Bank shopping area is along the exclusive **rue du Rhône** and adjacent streets. Here you'll find shop after shop of designer fashions and expensive watches. Along the winding streets of the **Old City** you can explore antiques stores and galleries. For Swiss army knives and watches, stroll along the pedestrians-only **rue du Mont-Blanc** on the Right Bank. You'll find an endless assortment of watches, knives, and other souvenirs, all priced similarly.

Colorful **outdoor markets,** overflowing with flowers and fruit, take place several times a week at places Rive, Coutance, Carouge, and others. A **flea market** is held every Wednesday and Saturday on the Plaine de Plainpalais; markets for books offer wares on place de la Madeleine on most days during summer.

SELECT SHOPS   Virtually all the inventory at **Antiquorum,** 2 rue du Mont-Blanc (✆ **022/909-28-50;** bus: 1), consists of antique jewelry and antique watches—a sure attraction for a city that derives so much of its income from selling timepieces. The array includes some of the world's most historically important watches.

The aroma of chocolate from the **Confiserie Rohr,** 3 place du Molard (✆ **022/311-63-03;** bus: 9, 10, or 12), practically pulls you in off the street. You'll find chocolate-covered truffles, "gold" bars with hazelnuts, and *poubelles au chocolat* (chocolate "garbage pails"). There's another branch at 42 rue du Rhône (✆ **022/311-68-76;** bus: 2, 9, or 22).

Opposite pont du Mont-Blanc, the chrome-and-crystal **Bucherer,** 45 rue du Rhône (✆ **022/319-62-66;** bus: 2, 9, or 22), sells expensive watches and diamonds. The store offers such name brands as Rolex, Piaget, Baume & Mercier, Tissot, Rado, and Swatch. The third floor is filled with relatively inexpensive watches, cuckoo clocks, music boxes, embroideries, souvenirs, porcelain pillboxes, and other gift items.

GENEVA AFTER DARK

For a preview of events at the time of your visit, pick up a copy of the monthly "List of Events" issued by the tourist office.

THE PERFORMING ARTS

Modeled on Paris's Opéra Garnier, the **Grand Théâtre de Genève,** place Neuve (✆ **022/418-31-30;** bus: 12), was opened in 1879, and is often included in lists of the world's 10 best opera houses. It burned down in 1951 and was subsequently rebuilt in the same style, except for the modern auditorium. From

September to July, it presents operas, ballets, recitals, and chamber music concerts. Tickets are 25SF to 148SF ($18–$104) for opera, 20SF to 150SF ($14–$105) or more for ballet.

The 1,866-seat **Victoria Hall,** 14 rue du Général-Dufour, is home to the celebrated **Orchestre de la Suisse Romande** (© **022/328-81-21;** bus: 12). Tickets are 16SF to 100SF ($11–$70).

BARS

Sheathed in mahogany, brass, and dark-green upholstery, the fashionable **Bar des Bergues,** in the Hôtel des Bergues, 33 quai des Bergues (© **022/908-70-00;** bus: 7), is decorated with a series of late-19th-century menus from the Cercle des Arts et des Lettres. Though most people come just for a drink or two, the place also serves lunches and platters from the hotel's top-notch kitchen. Ask the bartender for the list of daily specials. Beginning in the early evening, there's an international array of pianists.

Though this is technically the aperitif bar for the elegant Restaurant Le Gentilhomme, many visitors consider **Le Jardin,** in the Hôtel Richemond, Jardin Brunswick (© **022/715-77-20;** bus: 1 or 9), an attractive and stylish option in its own right. It attracts a chic crowd, ranging from U.S.-based beneficiaries of corporate mergers to Zurich bankers to glamorous women in $50,000 furs.

DAY TRIPS FROM GENEVA

MONT SALÈVE ⚅ The limestone ridge of Mont Salève (House Mountain) is 6km (4 miles) south of Geneva in France, so you'll need your passport. Its peak is at 1,200m (4,000 ft.). If you have a car, you can take a road that goes up the mountain; it's also popular with rock climbers. Bus no. 8 will take you to Veyrier, on the French border, where there's a passport and Customs control. A 6-minute cable-car ride will carry you to a height of 1,140m (3,750 ft.) on Mont Salève. From the top you'll have a panoramic sweep of the Valley of the Arve, with Geneva and Mont Blanc in the background.

MONT BLANC & CHAMONIX ⚅⚅⚅ We highly recommend a Mont Blanc excursion; an all-day trip to Chamonix, France, by bus; and a cable-car ride to the 3,850m (12,610 ft.) summit of the Aiguille du Midi. **Key Tours** (details below) leaves Geneva daily at 8am and returns at 6pm. Buses depart from Gare Routière, and you must take your passport.

Other climbs on this tour are to Vallée Blanche by télécabin, an extension of the Aiguille du Midi climb, from April to October; to Mer de Glâce via electric rack railway to the edge of the glacier, from where you may descend to the ice grotto (the climb isn't available in winter); and to Le Brevent, an ascent by cable car to a rocky belvedere at 2,400m (7,900 ft.), facing the Mont Blanc range.

An English-speaking guide will accompany your bus tour. Key Tours S.A., 7 rue des Alpes (place du Mont-Blanc), Case Postale 1745, CH-1211 Genève (© **022/731-41-40**), requires a minimum of eight people per trip. Tours begin at 85SF ($60) adults and 48SF ($34) children.

LAKE GENEVA CRUISES ⚅⚅⚅ Two companies offer cruises on Lac Léman. The smaller one, **Mouettes Genevoises Navigation,** 8 quai du Mont-Blanc (© **022/732-29-44**), specializes in small-scale boats carrying only about 100 passengers. Each features some kind of guided (pre-recorded) commentary, in French and English. An easy promenade that surveys the landscapes and bird life along the uppermost regions of the Rhône draining the lake is the company's

"Tour du Rhône" (Rhône River Tour). The trip originates at a point adjacent to Geneva's ponts de l'Ile and travels downstream for about 15km (9 miles) to the Barrage de Verbois (Verbois Dam) and back. April through October, departures are daily at 2:15pm and Wednesday, Thursday, Saturday, and Sunday at 10am. It costs 22SF ($15) adults and 15SF ($11) children 4 to 12; free for children under 4. The same company also offers 1¼-hour tours (four times a day) and 2-hour tours (twice a day) out onto the lake. The longer tour includes a pre-recorded commentary on the celebrity residences and ecology of the lake. It's 12SF ($8.40) for the shorter tour and 20SF ($14) for the longer tour; no stops are made en route.

Bateaux de la Mouette's largest competitor, **CGN (Compagnie General de Navigation),** quai du Mont-Blanc (© **0-848-811848** or 022/311-25-21; www.cgn.ch), offers roughly equivalent tours, May through September, that last an hour and depart four to six times a day from the company's piers along the quai du Mont-Blanc. Known as "Les Belles Rives Genevoises," they charge 13SF ($9.10) adults and 6SF ($4.20) children 6 to 16 (free for children under 6). Tours include pre-recorded commentaries and are about as long in duration as many short-term visitors to the city really want.

2 Bern & the Berner Oberland

Dating from the 12th century, Bern is one of the loveliest and oldest cities in Europe. Since much of its medieval architecture has remained untouched, the United Nations declared it a world landmark in 1983. As the capital of Switzerland, it's also a city of diplomats and the site of many international organizations and meetings.

Bern is a convenient center for exploring the lakes and peaks of the Berner Oberland—a vast recreation area only minutes from the capital, sprawling between the Reuss River and Lake Geneva. It's an important center for winter sports, one of the best-equipped areas for downhill skiers, and a challenging place for hikers and mountain climbers. The 4,158m (13,642-ft.) Jungfrau and the 4,274m (14,022-ft.) Finsteraarhorn are the highest alpine peaks. The canton of Bern, encompassing most of the area, is Switzerland's second largest, and contains 260 sq. km (100 sq. miles) of glaciers.

The best center for exploring the Berner Oberland is Interlaken, a popular summer resort. Summer and winter playgrounds are Gstaad, Grindelwald, Kandersteg, and Mürren. You can ski in the mountains in winter, and surf, sail, and water-ski on Lake Thun in summer.

BERN

The modern mingles harmoniously with the old in this charming city. Contemporary buildings are designed to discreetly blend in with the historic environment. Bern stands on a thumb of land that's bordered on three sides by the Aare River, and several bridges connect the old city with the newer sections.

Market days in Bern are Tuesday and Saturday, when people from the outlying areas come to town to sell their produce and wares. If you're fortunate enough to arrive on the fourth Monday of November, you'll witness the centuries-old Zwiebelmarkt (Onion Market), the city's last big event before the onset of winter, as residents traditionally stock up on onions in anticipation of the first snows.

Bern

ATTRACTIONS ●
Bärengraben (Bear Pits) **13**
Cathedral of St. Vincent **8**
Kunstmuseum **2**
Parliament **6**
Zutglogeturm **9**

ACCOMMODATIONS ■
Belle Epoque **12**
Bellevue Palace **7**
Goldener Schlüssel **10**
Hotel Ambassador **5**
Hotel Schweizerhof **4**
Innere Enge **1**
Jardin **11**
Savoy Hotel **3**

✝ Church
ⓘ Information
— Railway

ESSENTIALS
GETTING THERE By Plane The **Bern-Belp Airport** (© 031/960-21-11) is 10km (6 miles) south of the city in Belpmoos. International flights arrive from Geneva, Zurich, and Lugano, but transatlantic jets are not able to land here. Fortunately, it's a short hop to Bern from the international airports in Zurich and Geneva.

Taxis are about 50SF ($35) to the city center, so it's better to take the shuttle bus that runs between the airport and the Bahnhof (train station), costing 14SF ($9.80) one-way. Departures coincide with the arrival and departure of flights.

By Train Bern has direct connections to France, Italy, Germany, and the Benelux countries, even Scandinavia and Spain. The superfast TGV train connects Paris with Bern (trip time: 4½ hr.). Bern also lies on major Swiss rail links, particularly those connecting Geneva and Zurich (90 min.).

The **Bahnhof,** on Bahnhofplatz, is in the center of town near all the major hotels. If your luggage is light, you can walk to your hotel; otherwise, take one of the taxis waiting outside the station. For **information** about tickets and train schedules for the Swiss Federal Railways, call © **0900/300-300.**

VISITOR INFORMATION Tourist Office The **Bern Tourist Office,** in the Bahnhof, on Bahnhofplatz (© **031/328-12-12;** www.berntourism.ch), is open June through September, daily from 9am to 8:30pm; October through May, Monday through Saturday from 9am to 6:30pm and Sunday from 10am to 5pm. If you need help finding a hotel room, the tourist office can make a reservation for you. There is also a branch of the tourist office at the Bear Pits that is only open in summer (same phone).

Websites Besides the Bern Tourist Office website noted above, check this guide under Geneva "Visitor Information" for other Swiss websites. Get the low-down on skiing the high country at **www.goski.com/switz.htm.** This website will help you find a resort, tell you the best time to go, and keep you posted about conditions.

GETTING AROUND By Bus & Tram The public transportation system, the **Bern Mobil,** is a reliable 77km (48-mile) network of buses and trams. Before you board, purchase a ticket from the self-service automatic machines at each stop (conductors don't sell tickets). If you're caught traveling without one, you'll be fined 60SF ($42). A short-range ticket (six stations) costs 1.70SF ($1.20). A regular ticket, valid for 45 minutes one-way only, is 2.60SF ($1.80).

By Taxi You can catch a taxi at the public cab stands, or you can call a dispatcher. Try **Nova Taxi** at © **031/301-11-11.** The meter registers at 6.50SF ($4.55) when you get in, then goes up to 3.10SF ($2.15) per kilometer. After 8pm and until 6am daily, the per-kilometer rate rises to 3.50SF ($2.45).

Value One-day Tickets

To save time, and possibly money, you can purchase a **1-day ticket** for 6.50SF ($4.55), entitling you to unlimited travel on the Bern Mobil network. Just get the ticket stamped at the automatic machine before you begin your first trip. One-day tickets are available at the ticket offices at Bubenbergplatz 5 and in the underpass of the Bahnhof, as well as at other outlets in the city.

By Car   Don't try to drive in the city; use your car for exploring the environs. Car-rental companies in Bern include **Hertz,** Casinoplatz at Kochergasse 1 (© **031/318-21-60;** www.hertz.ch); and **Avis,** Wabernstrasse 41 (© **031/378-15-15;** www.avis.ch).

By Bicycle   The Altstadt is compressed into such a small area that it's better to cover it on foot rather than on a bike. Bicycles aren't allowed on the many pedestrians-only streets anyway. However, in Greater Bern and its environs there are 400km (248 miles) of cycling paths. These are marked on a special cycling map available at the tourist office (see above). Bicycle lanes are indicated by yellow on parts of the road network. The point of departure for most official cycling routes is Bundesplatz (Parliament Square). Special red signs will guide you through a wide variety of landscapes. For 28SF ($20) per day, you can rent a bicycle at the SBB Railway Station, Bahnhofplatz (© **0900/300-300**). Call the day before for a reservation.

WHERE TO STAY
Very Expensive
Bellevue Palace 𝄢𝄢𝄢   All the grand allure of the Belle Époque era lives on here in a hotel that respects tradition but is also completely modernized. This government-rated five-star hotel stands next to the Bundeshaus, the seat of the Swiss government, and is by far the most lavish hotel in town, although we prefer the antique charms of Hotel Schweizerhof (see below). Built in 1913 and restored in 2003, the gray-stone building has carved Corinthian columns and ornate details, and one of its public salons is covered in stained glass. The opulent bedrooms are spacious and luxuriously furnished, many opening onto views of the Jungfrau and the Bernese Alps. The market-fresh cuisine is among the most sophisticated in Bern, and the Bellevue Bar is a gathering place of bon viveurs, journalists, and politicians.

Kochergasse 3–5, 3001 Bern. © 031/320-45-45. Fax 031/311-47-43. www.Bellevue-palace.ch. 130 units. 460SF–540SF ($322–$378) double; from 650SF ($455) suite. AE, DC, MC, V. Tram: 9. **Amenities:** 2 restaurants; bar; room service; babysitting; laundry/dry cleaning. *In room:* TV, minibar, hair dryer, safe.

Hotel Schweizerhof 𝄢𝄢𝄢   Built in 1859, this central hotel, owned by the prestigious Richmond Heritage Group, is popular with diplomats and remains the grandest hotel in the Swiss capital. It contains many antiques and some of the best decorative art in Bern. Some rooms are quite contemporary, others more antique; some are air-conditioned. The bathrooms are luxurious.

Bahnhofplatz 11, CH-3001 Bern. © 031/326-80-80. Fax 031/326-80-90. www.schweizerhof-bern.ch. 84 units. 416SF–465SF ($291–$326) double; from 525SF ($368) suite. AE, DC, MC, V. Parking 28SF ($20). Tram: 3, 9, or 12. **Amenities:** 2 restaurants; formal bar; room service; babysitting; laundry/dry cleaning. *In room:* A/C, TV, minibar, hair dryer, safe.

Expensive
Belle Epoque 𝄢𝄢   Though not as swanky as the Schweizerhof, this renovated medieval home in Bern's historic core is a delight. One of the highlights is a bar outfitted like an art and antiques gallery, lined with late-19th- and early-20th-century oil paintings and filled with Jugendstil (German Art Nouveau) furnishings and comfortable settees. Many bathrooms have both tubs and showers. A tiny restaurant is used mainly for breakfast, although it's often possible to order light meals at other times. There's a charming bar dedicated to Toulouse-Lautrec.

Gerechtigkeitsgasse 18, CH-3001 Bern. © 031/311-43-36. Fax 031/311-39-36. www.belle-epoque.ch. 17 units. 320SF ($224) double; 420SF ($294) suite. AE, DC, MC, V. Bus: 12. **Amenities:** Restaurant; bar; babysitting; laundry/dry cleaning; nonsmoking rooms. *In room:* TV, minibar, hair dryer.

Innere Enge ⭐ *(Finds)* When you tire of impersonal bandboxes, head for this small, choice hotel just outside the city center. The light, spacious, and airy rooms have style and character, with traditional (if not antique) beds and roomy bathrooms, sometimes with a tub/shower combo. Many have a view of the Bernese Alps.

Engestrasse 54, CH-3012 Bern. (𝐶) 031/309-61-11. Fax 301/309-61-12. www.ghotels.ch. 26 units. 290SF–320SF ($203–$224) double. Rates include continental breakfast. AE, DC, MC, V. Free parking. Bus: 21 from the rail station. **Amenities:** Restaurant; bar; room service; babysitting; laundry/dry cleaning. *In room:* TV, minibar, hair dryer.

Moderate

Hotel Ambassador This nine-story hotel in a neighborhood of older houses with red-tile roofs is not far from the train station and easily reached by tram. Rooms tend to be smallish and furnished impersonally, but they're well maintained, each with a tidy bathroom containing a shower stall. Many have a view of the Bundeshaus.

Seftigenstrasse 99, CH-3007 Bern. (𝐶) 031/371-41-11. Fax 031/371-41-17. www.fhotels.ch. 97 units. 210SF ($147) double. AE, DC, MC, V. Free parking. Tram: 9. **Amenities:** 2 restaurants; lounge; 24-hr. indoor pool; sauna; solarium; room service; laundry/dry cleaning. *In room:* TV, minibar, hair dryer, safe.

Savoy Hotel *(Value)* Close to the main rail depot and the commercial center, this is a traditional Bern hotel of some charm and grace, achieving a four-star rating from the government. This place is more welcoming than many straitlaced Bern hotels; you're even given a free welcome drink. Rooms are fairly standardized and plain but have recently been renovated and are quite comfortable, with mostly tub/shower combo bathrooms (15 with shower only). Soundproof windows keep the noise outside, and there is also individually adjustable ventilation.

Neuengasse 26, CH-3011 Bern. (𝐶) 031/311-44-05. Fax 031/312-19-78. www.ehi.com/travel/ehi/switzerl/berne-hotels-savoy-hotel.htm. 56 units. 230SF–290SF ($161–$203) double; 275SF–335SF ($193–$235) junior suite. AE, DC, MC, V. **Amenities:** Cafe-bar; room service; laundry/dry cleaning. *In room:* TV, minibar, hair dryer.

Inexpensive

Goldener Schlüssel In the heart of Altstadt, opening onto Rathausgasse, this little inn dates from the 13th century, when it was used as a stable. Rooms are beautifully maintained, and they're comfortably furnished but a little shopworn. The bathrooms are extremely small. There's more atmosphere here than luxury. As it's fairly busy on the street outside, ask for a rear room if you want less noise. If you're a bargain hunter, request a room without a bathroom—the hallway plumbing is adequate.

Rathausgasse 72, CH-3011 Bern. (𝐶) 031/311-02-16. Fax 031/311-56-88. www.goldener-schluessel.ch. 29 units, 21 with bathroom. 125SF ($88) double without bathroom, 155SF ($109) double with bathroom; 170SF ($119) triple without bathroom, 205SF ($144) triple with bathroom. Rates include continental breakfast. AE, MC, V. Garage nearby 28SF ($20) per day. Bus: 12. Tram: 9. **Amenities:** Restaurant (see "Where to Dine," below); beer tavern; room service. *In room:* TV.

Jardin Set above the Old Town, this is a good choice for those who want a clean, well-maintained room at a decent price for the night, but can do without a lot of frills. In 1985, this building just north of the city center was converted from a restaurant and apartment building into a modern and warmly appealing hotel. Rooms are larger than virtually any others in their price range. The hotel is run by identical twins Andy and Daniel Balz, whose similarities may confuse you; one or the other is almost always available to help guests. Joggers and nature lovers appreciate the verdant areas across the street; they're part of the land surrounding Bern's largest military academy.

Militarstrasse 38, CH-3014 Bern. ℂ 031/333-01-17. Fax 031/333-09-43. www.hoteljardin.ch. 19 units. 145SF ($102) double; 205SF ($144) triple. Rates include breakfast. AE, DC, MC, V. Free parking. Tram: 9 to Breitenrainplatz. **Amenities:** Restaurant (see "Where to Dine," below); lounge; laundry/dry cleaning. *In room:* TV.

WHERE TO DINE
Expensive
Della Casa ✸ CONTINENTAL   From under an arcade, you enter a low-ceilinged paneled room that's often crowded with chattering diners. For those eager to follow the latest political trends and opinions, an inner room has all the day's newspapers—indeed, the place has been called Switzerland's "unofficial Parliament headquarters." Upstairs is a quieter, somewhat more formal dining room. The menu features Continental and Italian dishes. Two of our favorites are the ravioli maison and the fried zucchini; a justifiably popular meat specialty is filet mignon à la bordelaise with Creole rice. More typical, however, is the calf's heart with onions, tomatoes, and potatoes with an herbed vinaigrette.

Schauplatzgasse 16. ℂ **031/311-21-42.** Reservations recommended. Main courses 22SF–38SF ($15–$27). Mon–Fri 11am–2pm and 6–9.30pm; Sat 9:30am–3pm. Upstairs level closed in July. Tram: 3, 5, or 9.

Jack's Brasserie (Stadt Restaurant) ✸ FRENCH/CONTINENTAL   Although this restaurant is the less formal eatery within the Schweizerhof, it's perfectly acceptable as the site for an important meal or even a celebratory dinner. Nostalgically outfitted in a style that evokes a Lyonnais bistro, it bustles in a way that's chic, convivial, and matter-of-fact, all at the same time. The best dishes on the menu include the kind of Wiener schnitzels that hang over the sides of the plate, succulent versions of sole meunière and sea bass, veal head vinaigrette for real regional flavor, tender pepper steaks, and smaller platters piled high with salads, risottos, and succulent pastas.

In the Hotel Schweizerhof, Bahnhofplatz 11. ℂ **031/327-67-20.** Reservations recommended. Main courses 29SF–65SF ($20–$46); set-price menu 110SF ($77). AE, DC, MC, V. Daily 6am–11:30pm. Limited menu daily 1:45–6:15pm. Tram: 3, 9, or 12.

Räblus ✸ FRENCH/SWISS REGIONAL   A popular haunt, this 2-century-old restaurant lies near the landmark Clock Tower. It has a ground-floor bar where you can stop for an aperitif before proceeding up to the dining room. The kitchen prepares French cuisine with a definite Swiss/German influence. Try our favorites: saffron-flavored sole, a splendid potpourri of seafood flavored with Pernod, or citrus-flavored veal.

Zeughausgasse 3. ℂ **031/311-59-08.** Reservations required. Main courses 22SF–39SF ($15–$27); 3-course fixed-price menus 32SF–57SF ($22–$40). AE, DC, MC, V. Tues–Wed 6pm–1:30am; Thurs 6pm–2:30am; Fri–Sat 6pm–3:30am. Tram: 3 or 9.

Moderate
Goldener Schlüssel ✸ SWISS   You'll relish both the food and the bustling atmosphere at this very Swiss restaurant. Serving wholesome food in ample portions, the restaurant is on the street level of a budget-priced hotel of the same name. Specialties include a well-flavored *mignon d'agneau au poivre vert* (tenderloin of lamb with green-pepper sauce and corn croquettes), *schweinbratwurst mit zwiebelsauce* (butter-fried sausage with onion sauce), and rösti.

Rathausgasse 72. ℂ **031/311-02-16.** Reservations recommended. Main courses 25SF–35SF ($18–$25); fixed-price lunch 18SF–22SF ($13–$15). AE, MC, V. Sun–Thurs 7am–midnight; Fri–Sat 7am–12:30am. Bus: 12. Tram: 9.

Restaurant Harmonie ✿ SWISS/BERNESE   Located at the corner of Münstergasse a few blocks from Parliament, this Art Nouveau local favorite evokes 1890s Paris with its grimy overlay. It has been in the hands of the Gyger family since 1915. Service is efficient, and tables are spaced far enough apart to allow a feeling of privacy. There are two dining rooms and a handful of sidewalk tables set beneath ivy-clad trellises. You get the same regional specialties that Grandmother Gyger might have served between the wars: pork sausage with rösti, tripe with tomatoes, and cheese fondues. In the unlikely event that you're not ravenously hungry, the simple platter of cooked ham might be consumed with pickles, pickled onions, and sliced bread.

Hotelgasse 3. 🕻 **031/313-11-41.** Reservations recommended. Main courses 20SF–46SF ($14–$32). MC, V. Mon–Fri 8am–11:30pm. Closed mid-July to mid-Aug. Tram: 9.

Inexpensive

Ratskeller SWISS   There is no more typical Bernese restaurant than this local favorite, serving ample portions of good, rib-sticking food. Specialties include rack of lamb à la diable for two, an omelet soufflé aux fruits, veal kidneys Robert, and côte de beau in butter sauce. Your best bet is the *egli* (tiny filet of perch) with white sauce on a bed of spinach. Prized by gourmets, this tiny fish is native to the lakes around Bern. Most dishes are priced at the lower end of the scale.

Gerechtigkeitsgasse 81. 🕻 **031/311-17-71.** Reservations recommended. Main courses 20SF–51SF ($14–$36). AE, DC, MC, V. Daily 11:30am–2pm and 6–11pm. Tram: 9.

SEEING THE SIGHTS

Zutgloggeturm (Clock Tower) ✿, on Kramgasse, was built in the 12th century and restored in the 16th. Four minutes before every hour, crowds gather for the world's oldest (since 1530) and biggest horological puppet show: Mechanical bears, jesters, and emperors put on an animated performance. The tower marked the west gate of Bern until 1250.

   Bärengraben (Bear Pits) ✿, on the opposite side of the river, is a deep moon-shaped den where bears, Bern's mascots, have been kept since 1480. According to legend, when the duke of Zähringen established the town in 1191, he sent his hunters into the encircling woods, which were full of wild game. The duke promised to name the city after the first animal slain, which was a Bär (bear). Since then the town has been known as Bärn or Bern. Today, the bears are beloved, pampered, and fed by residents and visitors (carrots are most appreciated). The **Nydegg Bridge (Nydeggbrücke)** was built over one of the gorges of the Aare River; its central stone arch has a span of 55m (180 ft.) and affords a sweeping view of the city from its center. Below the Bear Pits, you can visit the **Rosengarten (Rose Gardens),** from which there's a much-photographed view of the medieval sector and the river.

Cathedral of St. Vincent ✿   The Münster is one of Switzerland's newer Gothic churches; although dating from 1421, the belfry was completed only in 1893. The most exceptional feature of this three-aisle pillared basilica is the tympanum over the main portal, depicting the Last Judgment with more than 200 figures, some painted. Mammoth 15th-century stained-glass windows line the chancel. The 1523 choir stalls brought the Renaissance to Bern. In the Matter Chapel is a remarkable stained-glass window, the *Dance of Death,* created in the last year of World War I, but based on a much older design. The 90m (300-ft.) belfry offers a panoramic sweep, though you must climb 270 steps to get to the viewing platform. Outside the basilica on Münsterplatz is the 1545 Moses Fountain.

> ### *Moments* Taking a Cable-Train to Mont Gurten
>
> The most panoramic attraction in the immediate vicinity is the **belvedere atop Mont Gurten** 👣👣, where there's also a children's fairyland and a walking area. The belvedere is connected to Bern by the Gurtenbahn cable-train, one of the fastest in all Europe. The train departs from a station beside the Monbijoustrasse, about 2.5km (1½ miles) from Bern's center. Round-trip passage on the cable-train is 9SF ($6.30). The train operates year-round, daily from 7:30am to sunset. For details, contact **Gurtenbahn Bern,** Eigerplatz 3 (© **031/961-23-23**). To reach the departure platform, take tram no. 9 to the Gurtenbahn station for 2.50SF ($1.75) each way. If you're driving, follow the road signs to Thun. There's a parking lot in the hamlet of Wabern, a short walk from the cable-train station.

Münsterplatz. © **031/312-04-62.** Cathedral, free; viewing platform, 3SF ($2.10) adults, 1SF (70¢) children. Easter Sun to Oct Tues–Sat 10am–5pm, Sun 11:30am–5pm; off season Tues–Fri 10am–noon and 2–4pm, Sat 10am–noon and 2–5pm, Sun 11:30am–2pm. Viewing platform closes ½ hr. before cathedral. Bus: 12.

Kunstmuseum (Fine Arts Museum) 👣👣 The world's largest collection of Swiss-born Paul Klee's works is the star attraction here. The Klee collection includes 40 oils and 2,000 drawings, gouaches, and watercolors. Other works emphasize the 19th and 20th centuries. The important 20th-century collection has works by Kandinsky, Modigliani, Matisse, Soutine, and Picasso, and by the Surrealist and Constructivist schools as well as contemporary Swiss artists. There's also a collection of Italian 14th-century primitives, notably Fra Angelico's *Virgin and Child,* and Swiss primitives, including the *Masters of the Carnation.*

Hodlerstrasse 12. © **031/328-09-44.** Permanent collection, 7SF ($4.90) adults, 5SF ($3.50) seniors; special exhibit, 8SF–18SF ($5.60–$13) extra. Tues 10am–9pm; Wed–Sun 10am–5pm. Bus: 20.

ORGANIZED TOURS

Highly recommended is the 2-hour **bus tour** leaving from the tourist office at the Bahnhof, at Bahnhofplatz. An English-speaking guide will take you through the city's residential quarters, past museums, and down to the Aare River, which flows below the houses of Parliament. You'll see the Rose Gardens and the Late Gothic cathedral and stroll under the arcades to the Clock Tower. After visiting the Bear Pits, you'll be led through medieval streets and back to the railroad station. Tours are offered from April to October daily at 2pm; from November to March, Saturday only at 2pm. The cost is 25SF ($18) adults, and 13SF ($8.75) children 6 to 16; free for children under 6.

The tourist office also conducts 9-minute **walking tours** of Bern from June to September. Tours leave daily at 11am from the tourist office. The cost is 14SF ($9.80) adults and 7SF ($4.90) children 6 to 16; free for children under 6.

BERN AFTER DARK

This Week in Bern, distributed free by the tourist office, has a list of cultural events.

PERFORMING ARTS The **Bern Symphony Orchestra,** one of Switzerland's finest, is directed by the widely acclaimed Russian-born Dmitrij Kitajenko; famous guest conductors also frequently appear. Performances are usually at the concert facilities in the **Bern Casino,** Herrengasse 25 (© **031/311-42-42**) for tickets.

Major opera and ballet performances are usually staged in the century-old **Stadttheater,** Kornhausplatz 20 (© **031/329-51-51**). Plays and dance programs are presented in the **Theater am Käfigturm,** Spitalgasse 4 (© **031/311-61-00**). Plays are usually in German and, to a lesser degree, French. Contemporary German-language, usually very experimental theater, is featured in the **Klein-theater,** Kramgasse 6 (© **031/320-26-26**).

WINE CELLARS & TRADITIONAL MUSIC **Klötzlikeller,** 62 Gerechtig-keitsgasse (© **031/311-74-56**), the oldest wine tavern in Bern, is near the Gerechtigkeitsbrunnen (Fountain of Justice), the first fountain you see on your walk from the Bear Pits to the Clock Tower. Watch for the lantern outside an angled cellar door. The tavern, dating from 1635, is owned by the city and leased to an independent operator (by tradition, an unmarried woman). Some 20 wines are sold by the glass, with prices ranging from 4SF to 6SF ($2.80– $4.20). The traditional kitchen serves various dinner plates from 22SF to 50SF ($15–$35) that reflect regional specialties and prices. The bar is open Tuesday through Saturday from 4pm to 12:30am.

Kornhaus Keller, Kornhausplatz 18 (© **031/327-72-70**), a former grain warehouse in the Altstadt, is the city's best-known wine cellar. The symmetrical stone building, with an arcade on the ground floor, seats 462 diners in a baronial atmosphere; musical acts are often performed in the evening. Main courses—go for the classic, a plate of smoked meats and sauerkraut—are 20SF to 60SF ($14–$42); the tagesteller (a meal itself) costs 20SF ($14), but is served only at lunch. Food is served daily from 11:30am to 1:45pm and 6 to 9:45pm, but guests usually linger over their drinks till around midnight.

A JAZZ CLUB The Louis Armstrong Bar, site of **Marians' Jazzroom** in the Innere Enge Hotel, Engerstrasse 54 (© **031/309-61-11**), has its own entrance separate from the hotel's. Unique in Bern, it's a setting for not only food and drink, but the finest traditional jazz performed live by top artists from around the world. It's open Tuesday through Thursday from 7 to 11pm, Friday and Sat-urday from 7:30pm to 2:30am. On Saturday, there is a Concert Apéro from 4 to 6:30pm. Cover is usually 25SF ($18), depending on the act. The club is closed from June 6 to September 6.

GAY BARS **Samurai Club,** Aarbergergasse 35 (© **031/311-88-03**), draws many people who work in the local embassies, Bern locals, and young men from the Bernese Oberland in for a night on the town. Women are also welcome. The club is open Sunday through Thursday from 8pm to 2:30am, Friday and Satur-day from 8pm to 3:30am. **Bar aux Petits Fours,** Kramgasse 67 (© **031/312-73-74**), is a contender for the title of best gay bar in Bern, attracting a multilingual, attractive, and international group of gay people, mostly men. There's no dance floor and no restaurant, but what you get is a low-key bar, filled with regular clients, where a newcomer with a bit of effort can usually break the glacial freeze of Swiss reserve. The bar is open daily from 5pm to 12:30am.

CASINO ACTION The only place in town to gamble is **Grand Casino Kur-saal Bern,** Kornhausstrasse 3 (© **031/339-5555**), open Sunday through Thurs-day from 11:30am to 2am and Friday and Saturday from 11:30am to 4am, to non-Swiss people 18 or over. You must present a passport to enter. Entrance to the casino costs 10SF ($7) per person, including your first drink. Gambling laws in Switzerland have now changed. Each casino determines maximum betting limits; the Bern limit is set at 3,000SF ($2,100). On-site are two restaurants.

THE BERNER OBERLAND

The Berner Oberland is Valhalla for walkers, hikers, and skiers. Here nature's scenery satisfies both the most ambitious adventurer and the slowest stroller. It's one of the world's best-equipped regions for winter sports, and walking trails branch out from almost every junction. Most of these are paved and signposted, with distances and estimated walking times given. Most tourist offices, including those at Interlaken (see below), will provide guidance and suggested itineraries.

EXPLORING THE AREA BY TRAIN & BICYCLE   If you're not driving, you'll find that public transport is quite adequate for exploring the area. You can buy a **transportation pass** for the Bernese Oberland from the **Swiss Rail System** (℡ 051/220-1111). The train ticket is valid for 7 days, and costs 180SF ($126) in second class and 220SF ($154) in first class. Another Swiss Rail pass, valid for 15 days, costs 220SF ($154) in second class and 265SF ($186) in first class. With the 7-day pass, you'll travel free for 3 days and pay a reduced fare for the final 4. With a 15-day pass, you'll travel free for 5 days and pay reduced fares for the rest of the time. Children travel at half price. The pass is valid on most railroads; on all mountain trains, cable cars, chairlifts, and steamers on Lakes Thun and Brienz; and on most postal-bus lines in the area. The ticket also qualifies you for a 25% reduction on the Kleine Scheidegg–Eigergletscher–Jungfraujoch railway, the Mürren–Schilthorn aerial cable line, and the bus to Grosse Scheidegg and Bussalp. You must purchase your pass at least 1 week before you arrive. For information, call ℡ **212/757-5944** in New York City, **310/640-8900** in Los Angeles, or **877/794-8037** in Chicago.

Cycling tours through the Berner Oberland often begin at Interlaken. Hundreds of miles of cycling paths cover the area. Separate from the network of hiking paths, the bicycle routes are signposted and marked on rental maps distributed at bike rental agencies. Some 13 rail stations in the Berner Oberland offer bike rental services, and rates are reasonable. For example, families can rent four bikes (two for adults, two for children 15 and under) for an all-inclusive price of 37SF ($26) per day or 250SF ($175) per week. Individual rentals cost 27SF ($19) per day or 180SF ($126) per week. You must make reservations at least the evening before your tour at any of the rail stations providing the service. Call ℡ **033/828-73-19** or 033/826-47-50 for reservations.

INTERLAKEN 🏵🏵🏵

Interlaken is the Berner Oberland's tourist capital. Cableways and cog railways designed for steeply inclined hills and mountains connect it with most of the region's villages. A dazzling sight is the snowy heights of the Jungfrau, which rises a short distance to the south.

The "town between the lakes" (Thun and Brienz) has been a holiday resort for more than 300 years. Though it was once a summer resort, it has developed into a year-round playground. Interlaken charges low-season prices in January and February, when smaller resorts at higher altitudes charge their highest rates. The most expensive time to visit is midsummer, when high-altitude ski resorts often charge their lowest rates.

ESSENTIALS

GETTING THERE   By Train   There are several trains daily between Zurich and Interlaken (trip time: 2 hr.) and between Bern and Interlaken (40 min.). Frequent train service also connects Geneva and Interlaken (2½ hr.). Though the town has two rail stations, about 3km (2 miles) apart, **Interlaken East** and

The Berner Oberland

Interlaken West, most of the city center lies near or around Interlaken West. Call 🕾 **033/826-47-50** for schedules and fares.

By Car To reach Interlaken from Bern, drive south on N6 to Spiez, then continue west on N8 to Interlaken.

VISITOR INFORMATION The **Tourism Organization Interlaken** is at Höheweg 37 (🕾 **033/826-53-00;** www.interlakentourism.ch), in the Hotel Metropole, and will provide itineraries for hikers. It's open July and August, Monday through Friday from 8am to noon and 1:30 to 6:30pm, Saturday from 8am to 5pm, and Sunday from 10am to noon and 4 to 6pm; the rest of the year, hours are Monday through Friday from 8am to noon and 1:30 to 6pm, Saturday from 9am to noon.

WHERE TO STAY

Hotel Beau-Site A short walk from the Interlaken West train station, this hotel is surrounded by spacious gardens with parasol-shaded card tables and chaise longues in summer, and provides a pleasant, relaxing oasis. Rooms are modern; some open onto mountain views. Rooms on upper floors are a bit small and often rented as singles. The spotless bathrooms are a bit small, too.

Seestrasee 16, CH-3800 Interlaken. 🕾 **033/826-75-75.** Fax 033/826-75-85. www.beausite.ch. 50 units, 43 with bathroom (showers only). 115SF ($81) double without bathroom, 170SF–250SF ($119–$175) double with bathroom. Rates include buffet breakfast. AE, DC, MC, V. Free parking outside. Closed Oct 15–Dec 15. **Amenities:** 2 restaurants; bar; room service; laundry. *In room:* TV, minibar (most units).

Hotel Bellevue In a central spot opening directly onto the Aare, this hotel retains something of its original 1789 design as a mock fortified castle and is surrounded by an English-style garden. The modernized rooms, in a variety of shapes and sizes, often have balconies with a view of the river and the distant mountains. All contain a mixture of modern and traditional furniture. Bathrooms are compact, often with a tub and shower. Breakfast and dinner are served in the formal dining room, and guests relax in a nicely furnished salon facing the garden and a view of the Alps.

Marktgasse 59, CH-3800 Interlaken. ⓒ 033/822-44-31. Fax 033/822-92-50. www.bellevue-interlaken.ch. 38 units. 150SF–220SF ($105–$154) double. Half-price reduction for children up to 12 sharing parent's room. Rates include buffet breakfast. AE, DC, MC, V. Free parking. **Amenities:** Room service; laundry. *In room:* TV.

Hotel de la Paix This family-run hotel is a block from the Interlaken West train station. You'll recognize it by its ornate roofline, which is gabled and tiled like a house in a Brothers Grimm fairy tale. Gillian and Georges Etterli offer a pleasant, relaxed atmosphere. Rooms are simply but comfortably furnished. Those downstairs are quite spacious. Bathrooms are small.

Bernastrasse 24, CH-3800 Interlaken. ⓒ 033/822-70-44. Fax 033/822-87-28. www.interlkentourism.ch. 22 units. 120SF–150SF ($84–$105) double. Rates include buffet breakfast. AE, DC, MC, V. Free parking. Closed mid-Oct to mid-Mar. **Amenities:** Restaurant; room service; laundry. *In room:* TV.

Swiss Inn *Value* This is a small-scale Edwardian-era inn with a sense of economy. Mrs. Vreny Müller Lohner offers conventional doubles that are simply decorated and a bit sparc. Bathrooms are very small and have shower stalls. There are also some self-contained apartments with kitchens that receive cleanup service only once a week. Guests have access to a lounge, a sitting area with a fireplace, a laundry, and, within the garden, a barbecue grill.

Général-Guisan-Strasse 23, CH-3800 Interlaken. ⓒ 033/822-36-26. Fax 033/823-23-03. www.swiss-inn. com. 10 units. 100SF–170SF ($70–$119) double; 130SF–210SF ($91–$147) apt for 2, 220SF–240SF ($154–$160) apt for 4. AE, MC, V. Free parking. **Amenities:** Breakfast room; lounge; room service; laundry/dry cleaning. *In room:* TV.

Victoria-Jungfrau Grand Hotel & Spa *🏨🏨* Opened in 1865, this grand resort is one of Switzerland's best, and has lost none of its luster over the years. Were Mark Twain—who stayed here in 1878—to return today, he would surely sing his praises as he did during his stay here. In richly ornate Victorian styling, it sits in the town center at the foot of rigidly symmetrical gardens. The hotel boasts one of the best-trained staffs in the country. Deluxe rooms open onto views of the Jungfrau. Nearly all are spacious. Bathrooms have tub/shower combos.

Höheweg 41, CH-3800 Interlaken. ⓒ 800/223-6800 in the U.S., or 033/828-28-28. Fax 033/828-28-80. www. victoria-jungfrau.ch. 216 units. Summer 590SF–660SF ($413–$462) double. Winter 440SF–520SF ($308–$364) double. Year-round from 750SF ($525) junior suite; from 1,250SF ($875) suite. Half board 100SF ($70) per person extra. AE, DC, MC, V. Parking free outside, 20SF ($14) in garage. **Amenities:** 2 restaurants; 2 bars; indoor and outdoor pools; 7 tennis courts; sauna; solarium; whirlpools; steam baths; one of Switzerland's best spas. *In room:* TV, minibar, hair dryer, iron.

WHERE TO DINE

Gasthof Hirschen *Value* SWISS This hotel restaurant offers some of the best and most reasonably priced meals in town, and the menu is varied, with most dishes at the lower prices on the menu. The potato soup with mountain cheese is the finest we've ever tasted. Another appetizer is salmon-filled ravioli. For a main dish, try such standard but well-prepared fare as sautéed calves' liver, filet of beef bordelaise, broiled trout, or the resort's best chateaubriand. Many of the items it features are homegrown, including Bio-Angus beef, veal, cheese, and fresh vegetables and herbs.

Hauptstrasse 11, Matten. © **033/822-15-45.** Reservations recommended. Main courses 20SF–60SF ($14–$42). AE, DC, MC, V. Wed 6:30–9:30pm; Thurs–Mon 11:30am–2pm and 6:30–9:30pm.

Il Bellini 𝄞 ITALIAN   This is the finest Italian restaurant in the area, with food that evokes some of the best trattorie south of the border. An assortment of antipasti from the buffet or a homemade minestrone is followed by such main courses as beefsteak Florentine, saltimbocca (veal with ham), or chicken breast grilled with tomatoes and mozzarella. The fish selections are limited but well chosen, and can be grilled on request.

In the Hotel Metropole, Höheweg 37. © **033/828-66-66.** Reservations recommended Fri–Sun. Main courses 25SF–50SF ($18–$35); pastas 14SF–30SF ($9.80–$21). AE, DC, MC, V. Daily noon–2pm and 6:30–10pm.

Schuh SWISS/CONTINENTAL   This attractive restaurant and tearoom in the center of town offers a sunny terrace with a view of the Jungfrau. The calves' liver is excellent, perfectly grilled and seasoned, and their daily soups are pure homemade goodness. Salads rely on market-fresh ingredients, and the desserts often incorporate locally grown berries and fruits. Their pastries are justifiably acclaimed as the finest in the area. A pianist provides music.

Höheweg 56. © **033/822-94-41.** Main courses 21SF–55SF ($15–$39); set-price menu 37SF–43SF ($26–$30). AE, DC, MC, V. Tues–Sun 8am–11pm. Closed Oct 25–Dec 9.

EXPLORING INTERLAKEN

What you do in Interlaken is walk. You can walk at random, as there are panoramic views in virtually all directions, or, if you'd like some guidance, go to the tourist office for a copy of "What to Do in Interlaken"; it maps out walks of all levels of difficulty.

The **Höheweg** 𝄞𝄞 covers 16 hectares (35 acres) in the middle of town, between the west and east train stations. Once the property of Augustinian monks, it was acquired in the mid–19th century by Interlaken's hotel keepers, who turned it into a park. As you stroll along **Höhenpromenade,** admire the famous view of the Jungfrau. Another beautiful sight is the **Flower Clock** at the Kursaal (casino), and you'll also see *fiacres* (horse-drawn cabs). The promenade is lined with hotels, cafes, and gardens.

Cross the Aare River to **Unterseen,** built in 1280 by Berthold von Eschenbach. Here you can visit the **parish church,** with its Late Gothic tower from 1471. This is one of the most photographed sights in the Berner Oberland. The Mönch mountain appears on the left of the tower, the Jungfrau on the right.

Back in Interlaken, visit the **Touristik-Museum der Jungfrau-Region,** am Stadthausplatz, Obere Gasse 26 (© **033/822-98-39**), the country's first regional museum of tourism, showing the development of tourism over the past 2 centuries. It's open May through mid-October, Tuesday through Sunday from 2 to 5pm. Admission is 5SF ($3.50), or 3SF ($2.10) with a visitor's card. Children 12 and under pay 2SF ($1.40).

For a sightseeing fiacre ride, go to the Westbahnhof. The half-hour round-trip is 35SF ($25) for one or two, plus 10SF ($7) for each extra person; children 7 to 16 are charged half fare, and those 6 and under ride free.

Other attractions include animal parks, afternoon concerts, and the luscious pastries sold in cafes. During summer, you can sit in covered grandstands and watch Schiller's version of the William Tell story. Steamers carry passengers across Lakes Brienz and Thun.

Moments Glaciers in the Sky: A Trip to Jungfraujoch

A trip to **Jungfraujoch** ⭑⭑⭑, at 3,454m (11,333 ft.), can be the high-light of your visit. Since the 1860s it's been the highest rail station in Europe. It's also one of the most expensive: A round-trip tour is 174SF ($122) first class or 162SF ($113) second. However, families can fill out a Family Card form, available at the rail station; it allows children 16 and under to ride free. There are departures from Interlaken's **Bahn-hof Interlaken Ost (East Railway Station)** every hour in winter, and every half hour in summer, but for true aficionados of the experience, the area is at its panoramic best if you depart at 8:05am and return to Bahnhof Interlaken Ost at 4pm. You'll get to see the mountain when it is most dazzlingly lit, and will have enough time for a leisurely lunch. To check times, contact the sales office of **Jungfrau Bahnen (Jungfrau Railways),** Höheweg 37 (© **033/828-71-11;** www.jungfraubahn.ch).

Once at the Jungfraujoch terminus, you may feel a little giddy until you get used to the air. You'll find much to do in this eerie world high up, Jungfrau. But take it slowly—your metabolism will be affected and you may tire quickly.

Within a 5-minute, well-marked walk from the Jungfraujoch railway terminus is an elevator that leads to the famed **Eispalast (Ice Palace)** ⭑. Here you'll be walking within what's called "eternal ice"—caverns hewn out of the slowest-moving section of the glacier. Cut 20m (65 ft.) below the glacier's surface, they were begun in 1934 by a Swiss guide and sub-sequently enlarged and embellished with additional sculptures. The cost of entrance to the Ice Palace is included in the price of a railway ticket to the Jungfraujoch. Hours of the Ice Palace coincide with the arrival of the first and the departure of the last train.

After returning to the station, you can take the **Sphinx Tunnel** to another elevator. This one takes you up 108m (356 ft.) to an observa-tion deck called the **Sphinx Terraces,** overlooking the saddle between the Mönch and Jungfrau peaks. You can also see the **Aletsch Glacier,** a 23km (14-mile) river of ice—the longest in Europe. The snow melts into Lake Geneva and eventually flows into the Mediterranean.

MÜRREN ⭑⭑

At 1,650m (5,414 ft.) above the Lauterbrunnen Valley, Mürren is the highest permanently inhabited village in the Berner Oberland. It's an exciting excursion from Interlaken in summer and a major ski resort in winter. Downhill skiing was developed and the slalom invented here in the 1920s, and Mürren is also the birthplace of modern alpine racing.

ESSENTIALS
GETTING THERE   By Train   Trains from Interlaken to Mürren's train station require a change of equipment in both Lauterbrunen and Grutschalp. The com-bined trip takes an hour from Interlaken, and the round-trip fare is 19SF ($13).

By Bus & Car   A regular postal-bus service departs once an hour from Lauter-brunnen to the hamlet of Stechelberg, the last town along the Lauterbrunnen

Valley road, the end of the line for cars and buses, and the departure point for a cable car which runs uphill to Mürren. The cable car that continues from Stechelberg on to Mürren departs at 30-minute intervals, costs 29SF ($20) round-trip, and takes about 10 minutes each way.

VISITOR INFORMATION The **Mürren Tourist Information Bureau** is at the Sportzentrum (© **033/856-86-86**), and is open from November to April, Monday through Friday from 9am to noon and 1 to 6:30pm. From May to October, it's open Monday, Wednesday, and Friday from 9am to noon and 2 to 7:30pm, Thursday from 9am to noon and 2 to 8pm, Saturday from 2 to 7pm, and Sunday from 1 to 5:30pm.

WHERE TO STAY

Hotel Alpenruh   In the most congested, yet still charming, section of the village, the Alpenruh offers a plusher interior than its chalet-style facade implies. The old building was upgraded to three-star status without sacrificing any of its small-scale charm. Rooms have pine paneling and a mix of antique and contemporary furniture; most have a view of the Jungfrau. The tidy bathrooms are small, compact, and efficiently organized, each with a shower stall.

CH-3825 Mürren. © **033/856-88-00**. Fax 033/856-88-88. www.muerren.ch/alpenruh. 26 units. 200SF–250SF ($140–$175) double. 50% discount for children 12 and under sharing parent's room. Half board 35SF ($25) per person. Rates include breakfast. AE, DC, MC, V. **Amenities:** Restaurant; bar; private sauna. *In room:* TV, minibar.

Hotel Blumental   Centrally located and redecorated and remodeled, this is a small chalet-type hotel, with stone masonry and wood-paneled public areas. Run by the von Allmen family, it offers a cozy atmosphere inspired by the nearby mountains. Several rooms have private balconies, and the small bathrooms have shower stalls.

CH-3825 Mürren. © **033/855-18-26**. Fax 033/855-36-86. www.muerren.ch/blumental. 16 units. 150SF–190SF ($105–$133) double. Half board 25SF ($18) per person. Rates include buffet breakfast. AE, DC, V. **Amenities:** Restaurant; bar; room service; laundry/dry cleaning. *In room:* TV, hair dryer.

Hotel Eiger ⭐   Founded in the 1920s and last renovated in 1994, this chalet is the longest-established hotel in Mürren. The public areas are warmly decorated, and many of the windows have panoramic views. Rooms are small, cozy, comfortable, and decorated in a typical alpine style. The hotel, managed by Annelis Sähli-von Allmen and family, lies across the street from the terminus of the cable car from Lauterbrunne.

CH-3825 Mürren. © **033/856-54-54**. Fax 033/856-54-56. www.muerren.ch./eiger. 44 units. Summer 260SF–360SF ($182–$252) double; 480SF–520SF ($336–$364) suite. Winter 280SF–400SF ($196–$280) double; 440SF–620SF ($308–$434) suite. Rates include breakfast. AE, DC, MC, V. Closed Easter to mid-June and mid-Sept to Dec 19. **Amenities:** Restaurant (see below); popular après-ski bar; room service; laundry. *In room:* TV, hair dryer.

WHERE TO DINE

Eigerstübli ⭐ SWISS   Here you'll find Mürren's best food, served in a festive ambience. The cuisine includes fondue as well as an international range of hearty specialties well suited to the alpine heights and chill. Try, for example, roast lamb shoulder with lentils, roast breast of duck with orange sauce, or—our favorite—poached filet of trout with a sauce flavored with alpine herbs. All main dishes may be ordered with rösti.

In the Hotel Eiger. © **033/856-54-54**. Reservations recommended. Main courses 23SF–54SF ($16–$38). AE, DC, MC, V. Daily 10:30am–2pm and 6–9pm. Closed Easter to mid-June and mid-Sept to mid-Dec.

HITTING THE SLOPES & OTHER ACTIVE ENDEAVORS

There are 48km (30 miles) of prepared ski runs, including 16 downhills; the longest run measures 12km (7½ miles). For cross-country skiers there's a 12km (7½-mile) track in the Lauterbrunnen Valley, 10 minutes by railway from Mürren.

The alpine **Sportzentrum (Sports Center; ℂ 033/856-86-86)**, in the middle of Mürren, is one of the finest in the Berner Oberland. The modern building has an indoor pool, a lounge, a snack bar, an outdoor skating rink, a tourist information office, and a children's playroom and library. There are facilities for playing squash, outdoor tennis, and curling. Hotel owners subsidize the operation, tacking the charges onto your hotel bill. Supplemental charges include 16SF to 22SF ($11–$15) per hour for tennis or per 45-minute session for squash, and 16SF to 22SF ($11–$15) per hour for use of the sauna. The facility is usually open year-round Monday through Friday from 9am to noon and 2 to 6pm; from Christmas to April and from July to mid-September, it's also open on Saturday from 1 to 6:30pm and Sunday from 1 to 5:30pm. Check locally, as these times can vary.

NEARBY EXCURSIONS

The famous **Mürren-Allmendhubel Cableway** leaves from the northwestern edge of Mürren. From the high destination, there's a panoramic view of the Lauterbrunnen Valley as far as Wengen and Kleine Scheidegg, and from mid-June to late August, the alpine meadows are covered with wildflowers. A hill walk in this region might be a highlight of your trip. The cable car operates daily from 9am to 5pm. However, there are annual closings for maintenance in May and November. It costs 14SF ($9.80) per person round-trip. For information call ℂ **033/823-14-44.**

The most popular excursion from Mürren is a cable-car ride to the **Schilthorn** ☆☆☆, famous for its 360° view. The panorama extends from the Jura to the Black Forest and includes the Eiger, Mönch, and Jungfrau. The Schilthorn is also called "Piz Gloria" after the James Bond film *On Her Majesty's Secret Service,* partly filmed at this dramatic location. Today Piz Gloria is the name of the revolving restaurant here, and the summit is the start of the world's longest downhill ski race. The cable car to Schilthorn leaves every 30 minutes. A round-trip ticket is 64SF ($45), and the journey to the top takes 20 minutes. For details, call ℂ **033/823-14-44.**

WENGEN ☆☆☆

The Mönch, Jungfrau, and Eiger loom above this sunny resort, built on a sheltered terrace high above the Lauterbrunnen Valley, at about 1,270m (4,160 ft.). Wengen (pronounced *Ven*-ghen) is one of the more chic and better-equipped ski and mountain resorts in the Berner Oberland. It has 30 hotels in all price categories, as well as 500 apartments and chalets for rent.

In the 1830s, the International Lauberhorn Ski Race was established here. At that time, Wengen was a farm community, but the Brits popularized the resort after World War I. Parts of the area retain their rural charm, but the main street is filled with cafes, shops, and restaurants. No cars are allowed in Wengen, but the streets still bustle with service vehicles and electric luggage carts.

ESSENTIALS

GETTING THERE   By Train   Take the train (frequent service) from Interlaken East to Lauterbrunnen. For information, call ℂ **0900/300-300.** From here, the journey to Wengen is by cog railway, a 15-minute trip. A one-way fare is 12SF ($8.70).

By Car Unlike Mürren, Wengen, 26km (16 miles) south of Interlaken, can be reached by car—at least for part of the trip. From Interlaken, head south in the direction of Wilderswil, following the minor signposted road to Lauterbrunnen, where there are garages or open-air spaces for parking. After that, it's cog railway the rest of the way to Wengen.

VISITOR INFORMATION The **Wengen Tourist Information Office** (© 033/855-14-14; www.wengen-muerren.ch), in the center of the resort, is open Monday through Friday from 8am to noon and 2 to 6pm, Saturday from 8:30 to 11:30am only.

WHERE TO STAY

Hotel Eden You'll feel comfortable and at home in this economy oasis that stands among guesthouses and private chalets above the commercial center of town. Kerstin Bucher directs a cooperative staff. There's a small TV lounge and a tiny Jägerstübli, where guests mix with locals over Swiss wine and specialties. Although the rooms are a bit spartan, the beds are comfortable. Only a few units have private bathrooms, and these are quite small without much room for your stuff.

CH-3823 Wengen. © 033/855-16-34. Fax 033/855-39-50. 30 units, 6 with bathroom. Summer 150SF ($105) double without bathroom, 165SF ($116) double with bathroom. Winter 170SF ($119) double without bathroom, 190SF ($133) double with bathroom. Half board 30SF ($21) per person. Rates include breakfast. AE, DC, MC, V. Closed Nov to Dec 20. **Amenities:** Restaurant; beer tavern. *In room:* No phone.

Hotel Eiger Rustic timbers cover the walls and ceilings of this attractive hotel behind the cog-railway station. Karl Fuchs and his family offer spacious, attractive rooms with balconies. A modern dining room has views of the Jungfrau massif and the Lauterbrunnen Valley. Rooms have cozy, alpine styling, but bathrooms are small and cramped, each with a shower stall. In the lobby is an inviting sitting area with a fireplace.

CH-3823 Wengen. © 800/528-1234 in the U.S. and Canada, or 033/856-05-05. Fax 033/855-10-30. www. eiger-wengen.ch. 33 units. Summer 200SF–246SF ($140–$172) double. Winter 278SF–302SF ($195–$211) double. Suite for 2, 286SF–330SF ($200–$231). Half board 25SF ($18) per person. Rates include breakfast. AE, DC, MC, V. Closed mid-Apr to June 1 and Nov to Dec. 10. **Amenities:** Restaurant; bar; laundry/dry cleaning. *In room:* TV.

WHERE TO DINE

Hotel Hirschen Restaurant SWISS An alpine flavor permeates this tranquil retreat at the foot of the slopes. The rear dining room is decorated with hunting trophies, pewter, and wine racks. Johannes Abplanalp and his family offer a dinner special called Galgenspiess—filet of beef, veal, and pork flambéed at your table. Other dishes include filet of breaded pork; rump steak Café de Paris; and fondue Bacchus (in white-wine sauce), bourguignon (hot oil), or chinoise (hot bouillon). A hearty lunch is *winzerrösti,* consisting of country ham, cheese, and a fried egg with homemade rösti.

In the Hotel Hirschen. © 033/855-15-44. Reservations recommended. Main courses 23SF–48SF ($16–$33); set-price menu 23SF–69SF ($16–$48). DC, MC, V. Mon–Fri 5–11pm; Sat–Sun 11:30am–2:30pm and 5–11pm (closed Wed in summer and Tues in winter). Closed mid-Apr to May and Nov to Dec 15.

EXPLORING THE AREA

The ski area around Wengen is highly developed, with both straight and serpentine trails carved into the sides of such sloping geological formations as Männlichen, Kleine Scheidegg, Lauberhorn, and Eigergletscher. A triumph of alpine engineering, the town and its region contain three mountain railways, two aerial cableways, one gondola, five chairlifts, nine ski lifts, and three practice lifts. You'll also find a branch of the Swiss Ski School, more than 12km (7 miles) of trails for cross-country skiing, an indoor and outdoor skating rink, a curling hall, an indoor pool, and a day nursery.

In summer, the district attracts hill climbers from all over Europe. Hiking trails are well maintained and carefully marked, with dozens of unusual detours to hidden lakes and panoramas.

NEARBY ATTRACTIONS
In winter, skiers take the cableway to **Männlichen** ✿, at 2,236m (7,335 ft.), which opens onto a panoramic vista of the treacherous Eiger. From here, there's no direct run back to Wengen; however, skiers can enjoy an uninterrupted ski trail stretching 7km (4½ miles) to Grindelwald.

There are many sights you can visit up and down the Lauterbrunnen Valley from either Wengen or Grindelwald. **Trümmelbach Falls** ✿✿✿ plunges in five powerful cascades through a gorge. An elevator built through the rock leads to a series of galleries; the last stop is at a wall where the upper fall descends (bring a raincoat). You can visit the falls daily May through June and September through October from 9am to 5pm; July through August daily from 8:30am to 6pm. Admission is 10SF ($7) adults, 4SF ($2.80) children 6 to 16, free for children under 6. It takes about 45 minutes to reach the falls on foot. For information, call ☎ **033/855-32-32**. The postal bus from Lauterbrunnen departs once an hour and stops at Trümmelbach Falls; fares are 1.30SF ($.90) adults, .60SF (40¢) children.

You might also want to visit the base of the **Staubbach Waterfall** ✿✿, which plunges nearly 300m (1,000 ft.) in a sheer drop over a rock wall in the valley above Lauterbrunnen. Lord Byron compared this waterfall to the "tail of the pale horse ridden by Death in the Apocalypse."

GRINDELWALD ✿✿✿
The "glacier village" of Grindelwald, both a summer and a winter resort, is set against a backdrop of the Wetterhorn and the towering north face of the Eiger. Grindelwald is surrounded with folkloric hamlets, swift streams, and as much alpine beauty as you're likely to find anywhere in Switzerland. It's also easier to reach from Interlaken than either Wengen or Mürren. Though at first the hiking options and cable car networks might seem baffling, the tourist office can provide helpful maps.

ESSENTIALS
GETTING THERE **By Train** The **Berner Oberland Railway (BOB)** leaves from the Interlaken East station (trip time: 35 min.). Call ☎ **0900/300-300** for information.

VISITOR INFORMATION Grindelwald's **tourist office**, Sportszentrum, Hauptstrasse, CH-3818 Grindelwald (☎ **033/854-12-12**; www.grindelwald. ch), is open from mid-June to late September Monday through Friday from 8am to 7pm, Saturday from 8am to 5pm, and Sunday from 9 to 11am and 3 to 5pm. Otherwise, hours are Monday through Friday from 8am to noon and 2 to 6pm, Saturday from 8am to noon, and Sunday from 9am to noon and 2 to 6pm.

WHERE TO STAY
Grand Hotel Regina ✿✿ Across from the Grindelwald train station, this turn-of-the-19th-century hotel is part rustic, part urban slick. The facade of the oldest part has an imposing set of turrets with red-tile roofs. Antiques blend with

modern furnishings into a harmonious whole, and the beds are exceedingly comfortable. Bathrooms are well maintained, with tub/shower combo.

CH-3818 Grindelwald. © **800/223-6800** in the U.S., or 033/854-86-00. Fax 033/854-86-88. www.grandregina. ch. 98 units. 430SF–540SF ($301–$378) double; from 640SF ($448) junior suite. AE, DC, MC, V. Parking free outside, 18SF ($13) in garage. Closed mid-Oct to Dec 18. **Amenities:** Restaurant; disco; indoor and outdoor pools; 2 tennis courts; sauna; solarium; salon; room service; massage; laundry. *In room:* TV, minibar, hair dryer, robe.

Hotel Hirschen *Value* In the three-star Hirschen, the Bleuer family offers one of the resort's best values. Rooms are a bit small but each is cozy, warm, and a great place to retreat to on a cold winter's night. Bathrooms are tiny but tidy, each with a shower stall.

CH-3818 Grindelwald. © **033/854-84-84.** Fax 033/854-84-80. www.hirschen-grindelwald.ch. 27 units. 150SF–260SF ($105–$182) double. Half board 30SF ($21) per person. Rates include continental breakfast. AE, DC, MC. Free parking outside; 10SF ($7) garage. Closed Nov to Dec 7. **Amenities:** Restaurant; bowling alley. *In room:* TV.

WHERE TO DINE

Il Mercato ITALIAN/SWISS The dining room's centerpiece is a large window with a sweeping view over the mountains; during warm weather, tables are set on the terrace. Menu items include virtually everything Italian, with an emphasis on cold-weather dishes from the Val d'Aosta (northern Italy's milk and cheese district). Especially good are the risottos, simmered rice dishes that come in infinite varieties. The chefs also specialize in grilled meats and homemade salads. Their pizzas are the best in town. Daily pastas are featured, each with a succulent sauce.

In the Hotel Spinne. © **033/854-88-88.** Reservations recommended. Main courses 15SF–25SF ($11–$18). AE, DC, MC, V. Daily 6:30–11pm. Closed Nov to mid-Dec.

Restaurant Français ⭐ INTERNATIONAL Special buffets are featured at Grindelwald's best restaurant. After you study the ever-changing menu to the soothing sounds of a live pianist, you may decide on an appetizer of game terrine, Grindelwald air-dried meat, or thinly sliced lamb carpaccio. On recent visits, the best dishes have included poached turbot filet on zucchini, a superb peppercorn-coated lamb entrecôte, and breast of guinea fowl with red wine and prunes.

In the Hotel Belvedere. © **033/854-54-54.** Reservations recommended. Main courses 30SF–48SF ($21–$34); set-price menu 54SF–66SF ($38–$46). AE, DC, MC, V. Daily 6:45–9pm.

SEEING THE GLACIERS

Adjacent to the base of the **Untere Gletscher (Lower Grindelwald Glacier)** ⭐⭐ is a sheltered observation gallery offering a look at the rock-strewn ravine formed by the glacier and its annual snowmelt. The half-mile gallery stretches past deeply striated rocks, which include formations of colored marble worn smooth by the glacier's erosion. Don't expect a view of the glacier from this point, as you'll have go to a higher altitude, at least in summer, to see the actual ice. The gallery is easy to reach on foot or by car from the center of Grindelwald. Yellow-sided buses labeled GLETSCHERSCHLUCHT depart from a point in front of Grindelwald's rail station at least four times a day, year-round, for the lower glacier and points beyond. Passage to the lower glacier costs 11SF ($7.85) each way, but since the distance from the center of Grindelwald is about 4km (2½ miles), in nice weather many hardy souls opt to trek across well-marked hiking trails.

A more exotic destination farther afield is the **Blue Ice Grotto** ⭐, whose frozen mass is part of the **Obere Gletscher (Upper Grindelwald Glacier).** Popular with hill climbers, it's a 3-hour hike (which includes navigating up an 890-step alpine staircase) or a 15-minute bus ride from the Lower Grindelwald Glacier. The upper and lower glaciers are separated by rocky cliffs and flow in different valleys. At midday, the 45m (150-ft.) thick ice walls of the grotto take on an eerie blue tinge. Local guides assure you that though the grotto—and the glacier containing it—are moving slowly downhill, you're perfectly safe. The grotto is open daily, mid-June through October from 9am to 6pm. If you don't want to make the uphill trek on foot from Grindelwald, a yellow-sided bus marked GROSSE SCHEIDEGG departs at approximately 1-hour intervals, year-round, during daylight hours. Round-trip fares from Grindelwald to the Obere Gletscher and its grotto cost 11SF ($7.85). *Note:* Once you get off the bus, you still have to climb 900 steps to reach the grotto.

HIKING & MOUNTAIN CLIMBING

Grindelwald and environs offer dozens of challenging paths and mountain trails that are well marked and maintained. Outdoor adventures range from an exhilarating ramble across the gentle incline of an alpine valley to a dangerous trek with ropes and pitons along the north face of Mount Eiger. The choice depends on your inclination, degree of experience, and mountaineering skills. Maps showing the paths, trails, and their various elevations are available at the town's tourist office.

From Grindelwald, you can reach the high-altitude plateau known as **First Mountain** *★★* at 2,168m (7,113 ft.) after a 30-minute ride on a six-passenger gondola ("bubble car"). The round-trip transport is 46SF ($32). You can stop at such intermediate stations as Bort and Grindel (a site that some locals refer to as Scheckfeld) on your way to **First Mountain terminal and sun terrace.** From First, where there are dining facilities, you'll have many hiking possibilities into the neighboring Bussalp or Grosse Scheidegg area. Also, from First, an hour's brisk hike will take you to the still high-altitude waters of **Bachalpsee (Lake Bachalp).** Buses depart from Grindelwald from both Bussalp and Grosse Scheidegg if you opt not to walk all the way back.

Faulhorn *★★★*, at 2,681m (8,796 ft.), is a historic vantage point with a panorama of untouched alpine beauty. Near the summit is the **Faulhorn Hotel** (*☎* **033/853-27-13**), which has been here for more than 150 years. Faulhorn is a 7-hour hike from Grindelwald. For a shorter climb, take either the bus to Bussalp, the cable car to First, or the train to Schynige Platte. From any of these intermediate points, climbers can continue their treks on to Faulhorn. Hikes from Bussalp take 2¾ hours; from First, 2½ hours; and from Schynige Platte, 4 hours.

Grosse Scheidegg *★*, at 1,961m (6,434 ft.), is a famous pass between the Grindelwald and Rosenlaui valleys. You can hike here in 3 hours from Grindelwald or can take a 40-minute bus ride from Grindelwald to Grosse Scheidegg and begin hill walking at a point that's far from the village traffic and crowds. Round-trip bus passage from Grindelwald to Grosse Scheidegg is 34SF ($24).

KANDERSTEG *★*

Between Grindelwald and Gstaad, Kandersteg is a popular resort at one of the southern points of the Berner Oberland. It's a tranquil and lovely mountain village with rust- and orange-colored rooftops and green Swiss meadows. The summer and winter resort is spread over 4km (2½ miles), so nothing is crowded. The village itself is at the foot of the 3,660m (12,000-ft.) Blumlisalp chain and provides access to six remote alpine hamlets.

Kandersteg developed as a resting point on the road to the Gemmi Pass, which long ago linked the Valais with the Berner Oberland. The village still has many old farmhouses and a tiny church from the 16th century.

ESSENTIALS
GETTING THERE   By Train   Kandersteg is at the northern terminus of the 14km (9-mile) Lotschberg Tunnel, which, ever since the beginning of World War I, has linked Bern with the Rhône Valley. The railroad that runs through the tunnel can transport cars. Trains leave every 30 minutes; no reservations are necessary. The resort is also served by the Bern–Lotschberg–Simplon railway. Call ☏ **0900/300-300** for information. The station is in the center of town.

By Car   Kandersteg is 43km (27 miles) southwest of Interlaken. Take N8 east to where the Kandersteg road then heads south into the mountains. The journey from Spiez to Kandersteg along a well-built road takes only 20 minutes.

VISITOR INFORMATION   The **Kandersteg Tourist Office,** Hauptstrasse CH-3718 Kandersteg (☏ **033/675-80-80;** www.kandersteg.ch), is open Monday through Friday from 8am to noon and 2 to 6pm.

WHERE TO STAY & DINE
Hotel Adler   An open fire crackling in the foyer sets the tone at this cozy inn, a wood-sided chalet on the main street near the town center. The fourth-generation owner, Andreas Fetzer, and his Finnish-born wife, Eija, offer comfortable pinewood-paneled rooms, some with Jacuzzis. Almost all open onto private balconies. The small, neat bathrooms are inviting and have adequate shelf space and shower stalls. The Adler-Bar is a popular après-ski hangout.

CH-3718 Kandersteg. ☏ **033/675-80-10.** Fax 033/675-80-11. www.chalethotels.ch. 24 units. Feb–Mar and July–Sept 180SF–210SF ($126–$147) double. Off season, 170SF ($119) double. Rates include breakfast. Half board 30SF ($21). AE, DC, MC, V. Free parking. Closed Nov 22–Dec 26. **Amenities:** Restaurant; brasserie; bar. *In room:* TV, minibar.

OUTDOOR ACTIVITIES
Around Kandersteg is an extensive network of level footpaths and strategically located benches; these paths are open year-round. In summer, qualified riders in proper clothes can rent horses at the local riding school. In winter, the resort attracts cross-country skiers and downhill novices (top-speed skiers go elsewhere). It has a cable car, two chairlifts, and four ski tows; the National Nordic Ski Center offers a ski-jumping station. The 2.5km (1½-mile) cross-country ski trail is floodlit in the evening. Other facilities include indoor and outdoor ice rinks.

EXCURSIONS NEARBY
The most popular excursion from Kandersteg is to **Oeschinensee (Lake Oeschinen)** ✰✰✰, high above the village. The lake is surrounded by the snow-covered peaks of the Blumlisalp, towering 1,830m (6,000 ft.) above the extremely clear water. You can walk to it from the Victoria Hotel, or you can take a chairlift, costing 19SF ($13), to the Oeschinen station and walk down from that point. If you opt to walk, allow about 1½ hours, or 2 hours if you'd like to stroll. Many visitors who take the chairlift decide to hike back to Kandersteg. Be aware, however, of the steep downhill grade.

Another popular excursion is to **Klus Gorge** ✰✰. Park your car at the cable station's lower platform at Stock and walk 3km (2 miles) to the gorge, which was formed by the abrasive action of the Kander River. The rushing water creates a romantic, even primeval, setting. There's a tunnel over the gorge, but in winter, the access route is dangerous and icebound.

GSTAAD 𝕬𝕬

Against a backdrop of glaciers and mountain lakes, Gstaad is a haven for the rich and famous. Built at the junction of four quiet valleys near the southern tip of the Berner Oberland, Gstaad was once only a place to change horses on the grueling trip by carriage through the Berner Oberland. As the rail lines developed, it grew into a resort for the wealthy who flocked to the Palace Hotel, which promised the ultimate in luxury.

The town retains much of its late-19th-century charm. Some first-time visitors, however, say that the resort is a bore if you can't afford to stay at the Gstaad Palace or mingle with the stars in their private chalets. Yet the town has many moderately priced hotels, taverns, and guesthouses, with an allure of their own.

ESSENTIALS

GETTING THERE   By Train   About a dozen trains come into Gstaad every day from Interlaken (trip time: 30 min.) and Montreux (1⅓ hr.). Call 🅒 **0900/ 300-300** for information.

By Car   From Spiez, follow Route 11 southwest to Gstaad.

VISITOR INFORMATION   The **Gstaad-Saanenland Tourist Association,** CH-3780 Gstaad (🅒 **033/748-81-81;** www.gstaad.ch), can help you find hotels, restaurants, and attractions if the signposts don't point you in the right direction. It's open Monday through Friday from 8am to noon and 1:30 to 6pm, and Saturday from 9am to noon only.

WHERE TO STAY

Hostellerie Alpenrose 𝕬𝕬𝕬   For those who like the charm of a small inn, this is the preferred choice, the only Relais & Châteaux listing within 50km (30 miles). Its owner, Michel von Siebenthal, is a memorable host, setting the fashionable tone of the chalet, which is famous for its cuisine. The pine paneled public areas are exquisitely decorated with rustic furnishings. Rooms are tastefully appointed and have mountain views, and bathrooms have showers, but no tubs. Although the original house has more character, accommodations in the contemporary annex are more spacious and luxurious—some are fireplace suites, quite romantic on a wintry night.

Hauptstrasse, CH-3778 Schönried Gstaad. 🅒 **033/744-67-67.** Fax 033/744-67-12. www.relaischateaux.ch. 19 units. Summer 380SF–460SF ($266–$322) double. Winter 480SF–710SF ($336–$497) double. Half board 45SF ($32) per person extra. AE, DC, MC, V. Free parking. Closed Nov to Dec 10. **Amenities:** Restaurant; bar; sauna; whirlpool; solarium. In room: TV, minibar.

Hotel Olden 𝕬   This is a low-key and gracefully unpretentious hotel, a sort of Victorian country inn set amid a sometimes chillingly glamorous landscape. The facade is painted with regional floral designs and pithy bits of folk wisdom. The folkloric alpine-style rooms are very cozy. The small bathrooms don't have a lot of extras, but maintenance is spotless, and each comes with a shower stall. Rooms in the chalet wing are generally roomier and more up to date.

Hauptstrasse, CH-3780 Gstaad. 🅒 **033/744-34-44.** Fax 033/744-61-64. 15 units. 500SF ($350) double. Rates include continental breakfast. AE, DC, MC, V. Free parking. Closed Nov to Dec 5 and late Apr to late May. **Amenities:** Restaurant (see "Where to Dine," below); bar; summer terrace; room service; laundry. In room: TV, minibar.

Palace Hotel Gstaad 𝕬𝕬𝕬   This landmark hotel is on a wooded hill overlooking the center of Gstaad. It's one of the most sought-after luxury hideaways in the world, attracting corporation heads, film stars, jet-setters, and the titled. The nerve center of this chic citadel is an elegantly paneled main salon, with an eternal flame burning in the baronial stone fireplace. Rooms (some large enough for Elizabeth Taylor and all her husbands) are country deluxe with regional artifacts, cheerful print wallpaper, and rustic pine furnishings. Bathrooms are exceedingly luxurious with tub/shower combos.

CH-3780 Gstaad. ℂ **800/223-6800** in the U.S., or 033/748-50-50. www.palace.ch. 124 units. Summer 490SF–800SF ($343–$560) double; from 1,720SF ($1204) suite. Winter 790SF–1,200SF ($553–$840) double; from 1,950SF ($1,365) suite. Rates include breakfast. Half board 85SF ($60) per person extra. AE, DC, MC, V. Parking free outside, 20SF ($14) in garage. Closed end of Mar to mid-June and Nov to Dec 16. **Amenities:** 4 restaurants; piano bar; night club; indoor and outdoor pools; 4 tennis courts; health club; steam room; 2 saunas. *In room:* TV, minibar, hair dryer, robes.

WHERE TO DINE

Olden Restaurant 🍴 MEDITERRANEAN/SWISS   Although there are grander restaurants in Gstaad, and dining rooms serving a more haute cuisine, the Olden remains our most satisfying choice year after year after countless visits. The service is formal and refined, the food as good as, or better than, anything in the area. The always tempting menu might include smoked salmon, fresh goose-liver terrine, shrimp bisque with green peppercorns, house-style tagliatelle, raclette, Scottish lamb, or a truly memorable sea bass with olives, potatoes, tomatoes, and onions.

In the Hotel Olden, Hauptstrasse. ℂ **033/744-34-44.** Reservations recommended. Main courses 28SF–75SF ($20–$53). AE, DC, MC, V. Tues–Sun noon–2:30pm and 6:30–10:30pm. Closed mid-Apr to mid-May and Nov.

Restaurant Chesery 🍴🍴🍴 FRENCH/SWISS   One of Switzerland's 10 best restaurants perches at an elevation of 1,100m (3,600 ft.). Natural stone floors and polished pine walls pair naturally with a menu that changes daily but is always based on the freshest of ingredients—grouse from Scotland, Charolais beef from France, truffles from Umbria. Taste the salt-crusted sea bass with wild rice or chicken Houban (a special breed from France), each a sensation. In the basement bar, Casino, a piano player entertains nightly; the bar is open from 6pm to around 3am.

Lauenenstrasse. ℂ **033/744-24-51.** Reservations required. Main courses 46SF–80SF ($32–$56). Set-price meals 64SF–78SF ($45–$55) lunch; 139SF–159SF ($97–$111) dinner. AE, DC, MC, V. Tues–Sun 11:30am– 2:30pm and 7pm–midnight. Closed mid-Oct to mid-Dec and in winter (Tues–Fri) for lunch. Closed after Easter to June 10.

SKIING & HIKING

The resort is rich in **sports facilities.** Many skiers stay in Gstaad and go to one of the nearby ski resorts in the daytime. Cable cars take passengers to altitudes of 1,500m and 3,000m (5,000 ft. and 10,000 ft.)—at the higher altitude there's skiing even in summer. Other facilities include tennis courts, heated indoor and outdoor pools, and some 320km (200 miles) of hiking trails. Many of these scenic trails are possible to walk or hike year-round (the tourist office will advise). The Gstaad International Tennis Tournament, held the second week in July, is the most important tennis event in Switzerland.

Skiers setting off from Gstaad have access to 70 lifts, mountain railroads, and gondolas. The altitude of Gstaad's highest skiable mountain is 2,000m (6,550 ft.), with a vertical drop of 1,084m (3,555 ft.). Most beginner and intermediate runs are east of the village in **Eggli,** a sunny, south-facing ski area that's reached by cable car.

Wispellan-Sanetch is good for afternoon skiing, and has lots of runs down to the village. At the summit is the Glacier des Diablerets, at 3,000m (9,900 ft.). **Wasserngrat,** prized by skilled skiers for its powder skiing on steep slopes, is reached from the south side of the resort.

Appendix

A Metric Conversions

LIQUID VOLUME

To convert	Multiply by
U.S. gallons to liters	3.8
Liters to U.S. gallons	.26
U.S. gallons to imperial gallons	.83
Imperial gallons to U.S. gallons	1.20
Imperial gallons to liters	4.55

1 liter = .26 gallons   1 gallon = 3.8 liters

DISTANCE

To convert	Multiply by
Inches to centimeters	2.54
Centimeters to inches	.39
Feet to meters	.30
Meters to feet	3.28
Yards to meters	.91
Meters to yards	1.09
Miles to kilometers	1.61
Kilometers to miles	.62

1 mile = 1.6km   1 kilometer = .62 mile   1 foot = .90m   1 meter = 3.3 ft.

WEIGHT

To convert	Multiply by
Ounces to grams	28.35
Grams to ounces	.35
Pounds to kilograms	.45
Kilograms to pounds	2.20

1 ounce = 28 grams   1 gram = .04 ounces
1 pound = 4,555 kilograms   1 kilogram = 2.2 pounds

TEMPERATURE

To **convert °F to °C,** subtract 32 and multiply by $\frac{5}{9}$ (.555).
To **convert °C to °F,** multiply by 1.8 and add 32.
32°F = 0°C

B Clothing Size Conversions

WOMEN'S CLOTHING

American	6	8	10	12	14	16
Continental	36	38	40	42	44	46
British	8	10	12	14	16	18

WOMEN'S SHOES

American	5	6	7	8	9	10
Continental	36	37	38	39	40	41
British	4	5	6	7	8	9

CHILDREN'S CLOTHING

American	3	4	5	6	6X
Continental	98	104	110	116	122
British	18	20	22	24	26

CHILDREN'S SHOES

American	8	9	10	11	12	13	1	2	3
Continental	24	25	27	28	29	30	32	33	34
British	7	8	9	10	11	12	13	1	2

MEN'S SUITS

American	34	36	38	40	42	44	46	48
Continental	44	46	48	50	52	54	56	58
British	34	36	38	40	42	44	46	48

MEN'S SHIRTS

American	14½	15	15½	16	16½	17	17½	18
Continental	37	38	39	41	42	43	44	45
British	14½	15	15½	16	16½	17	17½	18

MEN'S SHOES

American	7	8	9	10	11	12	13
Continental	39½	41	42	43	44½	46	47
British	6	7	8	9	10	11	12

Index

Frommer's Portable Guides
Complete Guides for the Short-Term Traveler

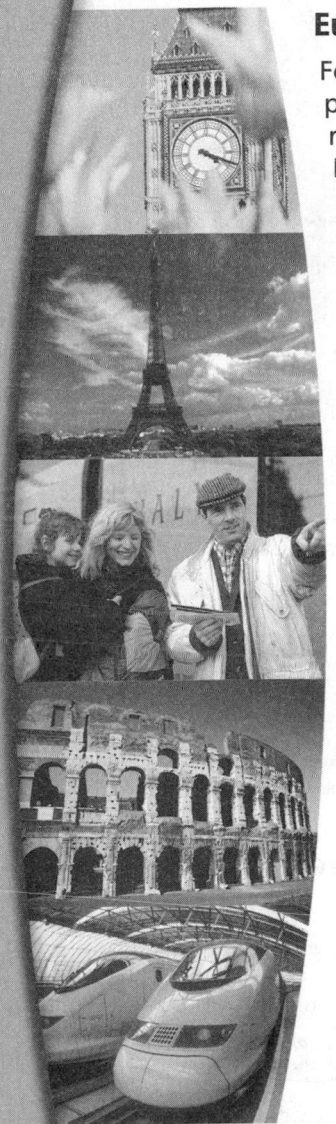

eat Trips Like Great Days Begin with a Plan

klinCovey and Frommer's Bring You *Frommer's Favorite Places®* Planner

The planning experts at FranklinCovey have teamed up with the travel experts at Frommer's. The result is a full-year travel-themed planner filled with rich images and travel tips covering fifty-two of Frommer's Favorite Places.

- Each week will make you an expert about an intriguing corner of the world
- New facts and tips every day
- Beautiful, full-color photos of some of the most beautiful places on earth
- Proven planning tools from FranklinCovey for keeping track of tasks, appointments, notes, address/phone numbers, and more

Save 15%

when you purchase Frommer's Favorite Places travel-themed planner and a binder.

Order today before your next big trip.

www.franklincovey.com/frommers
Enter promo code 12252 at checkout for discount. Offer expires June 1, 2005.

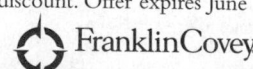

FranklinCovey

Frommer's is a trademark of Arthur Frommer.

FROMMER'S® COMPLETE TRAVEL GUIDES

Alaska
Alaska Cruises & Ports of Call
Amsterdam
Argentina & Chile
Arizona
Atlanta
Australia
Austria
Bahamas
Barcelona, Madrid & Seville
Beijing
Belgium, Holland & Luxembourg
Bermuda
Boston
Brazil
British Columbia & the Canadian
   Rockies
Brussels & Bruges
Budapest & the Best of Hungary
California
Canada
Cancún, Cozumel & the Yucatán
Cape Cod, Nantucket & Martha's
   Vineyard
Caribbean
Caribbean Cruises & Ports of Call
Caribbean Ports of Call
Carolinas & Georgia
Chicago
China
Colorado
Costa Rica
Cuba
Denmark
Denver, Boulder & Colorado Springs
England
Europe
European Cruises & Ports of Call

Florida
France
Germany
Great Britain
Greece
Greek Islands
Hawaii
Hong Kong
Honolulu, Waikiki & Oahu
Ireland
Israel
Italy
Jamaica
Japan
Las Vegas
London
Los Angeles
Maryland & Delaware
Maui
Mexico
Montana & Wyoming
Montréal & Québec City
Munich & the Bavarian Alps
Nashville & Memphis
New England
New Mexico
New Orleans
New York City
New Zealand
Northern Italy
Norway
Nova Scotia, New Brunswick &
   Prince Edward Island
Oregon
Paris
Peru
Philadelphia & the Amish Country
Portugal

Prague & the Best of the Czech
   Republic
Provence & the Riviera
Puerto Rico
Rome
San Antonio & Austin
San Diego
San Francisco
Santa Fe, Taos & Albuquerque
Scandinavia
Scotland
Seattle & Portland
Shanghai
Sicily
Singapore & Malaysia
South Africa
South America
South Florida
South Pacific
Southeast Asia
Spain
Sweden
Switzerland
Texas
Thailand
Tokyo
Toronto
Tuscany & Umbria
USA
Utah
Vancouver & Victoria
Vermont, New Hampshire & Maine
Vienna & the Danube Valley
Virgin Islands
Virginia
Walt Disney World® & Orlando
Washington, D.C.
Washington State

FROMMER'S® DOLLAR-A-DAY GUIDES

Australia from $50 a Day
California from $70 a Day
England from $75 a Day
Europe from $70 a Day
Florida from $70 a Day
Hawaii from $80 a Day

Ireland from $60 a Day
Italy from $70 a Day
London from $85 a Day
New York from $90 a Day
Paris from $80 a Day

San Francisco from $70 a Day
Washington, D.C. from $80 a Day
Portable London from $85 a Day
Portable New York City from $90
   a Day

FROMMER'S® PORTABLE GUIDES

Acapulco, Ixtapa & Zihuatanejo
Amsterdam
Aruba
Australia's Great Barrier Reef
Bahamas
Berlin
Big Island of Hawaii
Boston
California Wine Country
Cancún
Cayman Islands
Charleston
Chicago
Disneyland®
Dublin
Florence

Frankfurt
Hong Kong
Houston
Las Vegas
Las Vegas for Non-Gamblers
London
Los Angeles
Los Cabos & Baja
Maine Coast
Maui
Miami
Nantucket & Martha's Vineyard
New Orleans
New York City
Paris
Phoenix & Scottsdale

Portland
Puerto Rico
Puerto Vallarta, Manzanillo &
   Guadalajara
Rio de Janeiro
San Diego
San Francisco
Savannah
Seattle
Sydney
Tampa & St. Petersburg
Vancouver
Venice
Virgin Islands
Washington, D.C.

FROMMER'S® NATIONAL PARK GUIDES

Banff & Jasper
Family Vacations in the National
   Parks

Grand Canyon
National Parks of the American West
Rocky Mountain

Yellowstone & Grand Teton
Yosemite & Sequoia/Kings Canyon
Zion & Bryce Canyon

Booked aisle seat.

Reserved room with a view.

With a queen – no, make that a king-size bed.

With Travelocity, you can book your flights and hotels together, so you can get even better deals than if you booked them separately. You'll save time and money without compromising the quality of your trip. Choose your airline seat, search for alternate airports, pick your hotel room type, even choose the neighborhood you'd like to stay in.

Travelocity

Visit **www.travelocity.com** or call **1-888-TRAVELOCITY**

Fly.
Sleep.
Save.

Now you can book your flights and
hotels together, so you can get even better deals
than if you booked them separately.

Travelocity
Visit www.travelocity.com
or call 1-888-TRAVELOCITY